15e

Small Business Management

Launching & Growing Entrepreneurial Ventures

Justin G. Longenecker

Baylor University

J. William Petty

Baylor University

Leslie E. Palich

Baylor University

Carlos W. Moore

Baylor University

SOUTH-WESTERN
CENGAGE Learning™

Australia • Brazil • Japan • Korea • Mexico • Singapore • Spain • United Kingdom • United States

SOUTH-WESTERN
CENGAGE Learning™

**Small Business Management: Launching &
Growing Entrepreneurial Ventures,
Fifteenth Edition**
Justin G. Longenecker, J. William Petty,
Leslie E. Palich, Carlos W. Moore

VP/Editorial Director:
  Jack W. Calhoun

Editor-in-Chief:
  Melissa Acuna

Senior Acquisitions Editor:
  Michele Rhoades

Senior Developmental Editor:
  Susanna C. Smart

Senior Editorial Assistant:
  Ruth Belanger

Marketing Manager:
  Nathan Anderson

Senior Marketing Communications Manager:
  Jim Overly

Marketing Coordinator:
  Suellen Ruttkay

Content Project Manager:
  Jacquelyn K Featherly

Media Editor:
  Rob Ellington

Senior Manufacturing Coordinator:
  Sandee Milewski

Production House/Compositor:
  S4Carlisle Publishing Services

Senior Art Director:
  Tippy McIntosh

Cover and Internal Designer:
  Ke Design, Mason, OH

Cover Image:
  ©Ke Design, Mason OH;
  ©Graeters, Cincinnati, OH

For product information and technology assistance, contact us at
Cengage Learning Customer & Sales Support, 1-800-354-9706

For permission to use material from this text or product,
submit all requests online at **www.cengage.com/permissions**

Further permissions questions can be e-mailed to
permissionrequest@cengage.com

Library of Congress Control Number: 2009932376

Student Edition ISBN 13: 978-0-324-82784-2
Student Edition ISBN 10: 0-324-82784-9
SE Package ISBN 13: 978-0-324-82783-5
SE Package ISBN 10: 0-324-82783-0
Instructor's Edition ISBN 13: 978-0-538-73711-1
Instructor's Edition ISBN 10: 0-538-73711-5

South-Western Cengage Learning
5191 Natorp Boulevard
Mason, OH 45040
USA

Cengage Learning products are represented in Canada by Nelson Education, Ltd.

For your course and learning solutions, visit **www.cengage.com**

Purchase any of our products at your local college store or at our preferred online store
www.ichapters.com

Printed in the United States of America
1 2 3 4 5 6 7 13 12 11 10 09

Justin G. Longenecker
Professor Emeritus of Management
Hankamer School of Business
Baylor University
May 4, 1917 – September 14, 2005

Carlos W. Moore
Edwin Streetman Professor of Marketing
Hankamer School of Business
Baylor University
February 3, 1943 – May 27, 2007

It is with deep sadness that we inform you of the deaths of our two co-authors and dear friends. We cannot put into words the loss we feel. Their deaths cannot be measured by their absence in revising this book. They were not only our colleagues, but also our confidants and mentors. They were tremendous role models for us and for literally thousands of individuals who knew and loved them. In this book, we encourage you to consider the legacy you will leave at the end of your entrepreneurial journey. Justin and Carlos left a legacy that few can ever dream of leaving. They will be missed for many years to come.

In working with Justin and Carlos for over a decade, we have developed a shared vision about the book. So, while the specific responsibilities have changed for this edition, the dream of helping others become entrepreneurs lives on. Be assured that we will continue to build on the great legacy of this textbook. Justin and Carlos would be disappointed with anything less, and we are not about to let them down.

brief contents

contents

©iStock

Part 3
Developing the New Venture Business Plan

Chapter 6   The Business Plan: Visualizing the Dream

Chapter 7   The Marketing Plan

Chapter 8   The Human Resources Plan: Managers, Owners, Allies, and Directors

Chapter 9   The Location Plan

Chapter 10 Understanding a Firm's Financial Statements   258

Chapter 11 Forecasting Financial Requirements   286

Chapter 12 A Firm's Sources of Financing   309

Chapter 13 Planning for the Harvest   338

Part 4

Focusing on the Customer: Marketing Growth Strategies 361

Chapter 14 Building Customer Relationships 362

Chapter 15 Product and Supply Chain Management 389

Chapter 16 Pricing and Credit Decisions 418

Chapter 23 Managing Risk in the Small Business 601

Cases 623

Welcome to the 15th edition of *Small Business Management: Launching and Growing Entrepreneurial Ventures* by Longenecker, *et.al*! Textbooks rarely survive in the marketplace for more than five or six editions—much less 15—but *Small Business Management* has proven to be one of those outliers. This edition of the book represents more than four decades of writing about small business. Furthermore, it is a book that students frequently choose to hold onto rather than selling it back to a bookstore at the end of a semester. As one student explained, "It is one of the few books from my college days that I have kept for future reference."

Why has Longenecker's *Small Business Management* not only survived, but been a market-leader for so long? We believe there are two reasons: *passion* and *commitment*—which are key success factors for any entrepreneurial venture. Our teaching, research, and consulting as related to small businesses are not something we do as an afterthought. Neither is it merely an academic exercise. It is our passion! We believe what we are doing makes a difference in others' lives. As a consequence, we have always been committed to giving you our very best. Over all these years, there has been one absolute constant—we have measured our success by the effectiveness of our presentation to you, the reader. And though you may not have selected this textbook yourself, we consider you to be our customer nonetheless. We make every effort to be sensitive to our readers' learning needs. In fact, we have taken your point of view into consideration when writing each chapter and have gone to great lengths to make the material informative, as well as easy to understand and interesting to read.

In writing *Small Business Management*, we celebrate the initiative of small business owners everywhere. They are our heroes! And among them is the Graeter's family, whose business is featured on the cover of the book. Graeter's Ice Cream is a family-owned and managed business now into the fourth generation. The firm has an outstanding reputation, which has led to its huge market share in super premium ice creams in the Ohio region.

Headquartered in Cincinnati, Ohio, Louis Graeter founded Graeter's Ice Cream in 1870. But the family credits his wife, Regina, for laying the foundation for what the company is today. She ran the company until her death in 1955 when her two sons (Wilmer and Paul) took charge. Wilmer bought out his brother and eventually passed the business on to his three sons. The fourth generation became owners in 2003—with Rich Graeter as CEO.

Rich and his cousins, Bob and Chip, have found it necessary to implement more professional management practices than their forebears. But they want all employees, family and otherwise, to feel "part of the tribe." The goal of the Graeter family is for their business to retain its historical culture of being "the little company that people adore." We can't think of a more fitting purpose for such an enterprise.

Small Business Management is a tribute to all the Graeter's of the world and to the entrepreneurs who want to build something of meaning. But, our being a small part of these individuals' dreams and endeavors, either directly or indirectly, has added so much to our lives. Writing *Small Business Management* continues to be a blessing for us. We hope reading it helps move you toward your entrepreneurial aspirations.

Follow Your Dreams

Entrepreneurs need to dream BIG dreams—to see opportunities where others only see chaos. Did you know that Benjamin Franklin was admonished to stop experimenting with electricity? It's true! Trying to improve on the reliable and perfectly functional oil lamp was considered an absurd waste of time! And even Thomas Edison, a shrewd entrepreneur in his own right, tried to discourage his friend Henry Ford from working on his daring idea of building a motorcar. Convinced the idea was worthless, Edison advised Ford to give up this wild fancy and work for him instead. Ford, however, remained steadfast and tirelessly pursued his dream. Progress was slow. Although his first attempt produced a vehicle without a reverse gear, Ford knew he could make it happen—and, of course, he did. People like Franklin and Ford dreamed big dreams and dared to do great things, and now we all benefit from their achievements. Can you imagine a world without electric lights and automobiles? The contributions of these two entrepreneurs have been immeasurable!

This book lays out, in a step-by-step fashion, the knowledge and insights needed to lead and manage a small business. At the same time, it focuses on a much broader concern—the pursuit of entrepreneurial dreams. Entrepreneurs build businesses to fulfill dreams—for themselves, for their families, for their employees, and for their communities. When we write about small companies, therefore, we are writing about individuals whose business lives have had an impact on a wide range of people.

The aim of the 15th edition of *Small Business Management* is to provide instruction and guidance that will greatly improve your odds for success as you take your own entrepreneurial journey. It is our hope that what we present in this book—and in the tools and ancillaries that accompany it—will support the varied goals of those seeking independent business careers, either directly or indirectly, through the wise counsel of the instructor who has selected this book.

There has never been a more exciting time to be an entrepreneur—even though we are in a recession at the time we are revising the book. The truth is that many vibrant, high-potential new ventures are launched during recessions, and there is no reason that yours cannot be one of them! We are seeing tremendous change these days, to be sure, but change opens the door to opportunity for those with the courage to pursue it. If you are committed strongly enough to your dream, in one creative way or another you will overcome all of the obstacles that lie ahead. New ventures can create tremendous personal value both for entrepreneurs and the investors who back them with time and money. New ventures can also protect and improve quality of life by creating jobs and providing new products and services to those who value them. On all of these fronts, you can make a difference.

Our best wishes to you for a challenging and successful learning experience!

What's New?

A central purpose of this revision of *Small Business Management* is to present current, relevant content in unique and interesting ways. When we started writing, we found many innovative ideas, trends, companies, and people to write about.

With an abundance of real-world examples to keep both first-time readers and readers of earlier editions totally engaged, this edition of *Small Business Management* offers plenty that's new, beginning with the area where many potential entrepreneurs struggle the most—accounting and finance.

- Understanding and using financial information is often challenging for small business owners and students alike. Some of our readers are uncomfortable with the topic or even feel intimidated by it. However, given its importance in managing a business, the topic would be ignored only at your own peril. Accordingly, we have always tried to pay particularly close attention to the matter, striving to make it very understandable, even intuitive. In previous editions, we carefully presented what we believe an entrepreneur should know about the financial position of a business. But in this latest edition, we have truly gone "back to the basics."

- In presenting financial statements, we begin with the assumption that the reader has little, if any, background knowledge related to financial statements. To accomplish this objective, we have split what had been one chapter on financials into two chapters, making it more of a building-block process. In the first (Chapter 10), we begin with a short story about three young sisters who start and run a very simple business—a lemonade stand. Many of the key concepts are illustrated through this story, avoiding the complexities of the "real world" that tend to confuse readers. We then build on the lemonade stand story to bring more realism into the presentation. But we continue to present this material piece-by-piece. Then, in the second (Chapter 11), we shift from understanding historical financial statements to learning the basics on how to forecast a company's financial statements. To make certain that the material is reader friendly, we classroom tested the materials with students in a small business management course, and it was extremely well received.

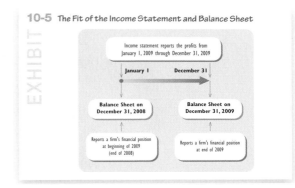

10-5 The Fit of the Income Statement and Balance Sheet

- If we have accomplished our goal, this new material should help create a level playing field for the "non-accounting" student. In fact, Bill Petty, the co-author who wrote these chapters, is prepared to make you an offer. If you carefully study these two chapters and conclude that they fail to live up to his claims, he will send you $10. There is only one catch: You have to provide him with a reference to instructional materials where you believe it is done better. Just call him directly (254-710-2260) or e-mail him (bill_petty@baylor.edu).

- In our work over the years, we have come to know many entrepreneurs, whom we believe represent the best of what small business is about. We wanted you to have the benefit of their life experiences, so we formed a group consisting of entrepreneurs who are the kind of individuals you would want to go to when you need advice and counsel. We call them our "Go-To Team." We will draw on their experience to complement what we present in the chapters. Their comments will appear in the "HOW I SEE IT" boxes throughout the book.

- There are numerous updated "Living the Dream" features in each chapter that capture entrepreneurs in action as they face the challenges of small business and entrepreneurship. To add depth to these features and ensure accuracy, the authors had personal conversations or correspondence with a number of the entrepreneurs profiled.

- In addition, eleven new text cases update the case selection at the end of the text. Cases include Nau, W. S. Darley and Co, Firewire Surfboards, CitiStorage, and many others. These up-to-date cases provide opportunities for students to apply chapter concepts to realistic entrepreneurial situations.

- Cases that have appeared in the text in the fourteenth edition, but were replaced in this edition, are now available on the Longenecker book website (www.cengage.com/management/longenecker). This new feature is provided so that if an instructor has a "favorite" case that he or she would like to continue to use, it is easily accessible.

- Student exercises for the *Small Business and Entrepreneurship Resource Center* (SBERC) are included at the end of each chapter. These exercises direct students to articles and company information on various entrepreneurial ventures, and ask them to discuss how the chapter topics apply to each situation. Companies covered include Dyson, Bear Naked Granola, Blue Nile, iSoldIt, LLC, and many others.

- A business plan for Atayne, LLC is provided in its entirety to illustrate what one "winning plan" at the Babson College Business Plan Competition contains. Of course, there is no *one right plan*, but it does let us visualize what a good plan looks like.

- Beginning in fall 2009, we will host two Web-based seminars *(Webinars)* each semester for instructors to offer instructional insights and share ideas. We are excited that technology has progressed to the point that we can easily communicate with each other with nothing more than a phone line and Internet access. Watch for an announcement about the webinars on the Longenecker website in the fall of 2009.

- We will be developing a link on the Longenecker Web site where we can share course syllabi. It is always good to draw on each other's work. Excellent ideas deserve such a forum.

- *Go Venture* is an exciting business simulation allowing you to experience virtually the challenges and satisfactions of small business management. As you take on the role of an entrepreneur, you are faced with a myriad of decisions that must be made—from what type of business you will launch, to what your measures of success will be, to how to keep control of inventory. Learn more at www.goventure.net, or ask your sales representative about packaging options with this text.

Achieving Your Best

Small Business Management is organized to help students and future entrepreneurs achieve success in whatever field they choose. The wide spectrum of content, applications, cases, graphics, stories, and other details offered in *Small Business Management* has assisted many small business entrepreneurs in making their dreams come true. With a focus on learning, our features emphasize hands-on activities that capture student interest and guarantee practical knowledge, including the following:

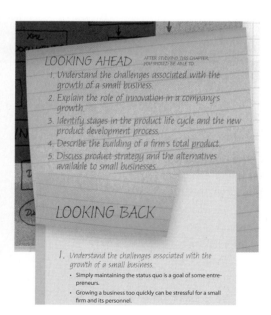

- **Unique Spotlight Features.** The chapter-opening "In the Spotlight" features profile an amazing collection of business owners, whose unique insights into how to start, run, and grow a business will help readers identify and explore the full range of issues facing today's business owners. More than half of the spotlights are video-enriched, because nothing helps students master the lessons of small business and entrepreneurship as much as seeing them put into practice.

- **Unique Support for Building a Business Plan.** The material in Part 3, "Developing the New Venture Business Plan," is integral to learning how to develop workable plans. Closely aligned with the approaches to planning that we present in the textbook, additional business plan templates can be found in ***Small Business Management Online*** (www.cengage.com/login) by registering the access code that accompanies this text.

- **Integrated Learning System.** Our integrated learning system uses each chapter's learning objectives to give structure and coherence to the text content, study aids, and instructor's ancillaries, all of which are keyed to these objectives. The numbered objectives are introduced in the "Looking Ahead" section, and each is concisely addressed in the "Looking Back" section at the end of each chapter.

The integrated learning system also simplifies lecture and test preparation. The lecture notes in the *Instructor's Manual* are grouped by learning objective and identify the PowerPoint slides that relate to each objective. Questions in the *Test Bank* are grouped by objective as well. A correlation table at the beginning of each *Test Bank* chapter permits selection of questions that cover all objectives or that emphasize objectives considered most important.

- **You Make the Call.** "You Make the Call" incidents at the end of each chapter are very popular with both students and instructors because they present realistic business situations that require examining key operating decisions. By having students take on the role of a small business owner, these exercises give them a leg up in addressing the concerns of small businesses.

- **Living the Dream.** Practical examples from the world of small business and entrepreneurship carry both instructional and inspirational value. "Living the Dream" boxes appear at critical junctures throughout the chapters, refueling and refreshing chapter concepts with documented experiences of practicing entrepreneurs.

- **Video Cases.** The video-enriched cases available with the 14th edition of *Small Business Management* are once again available with this edition. The cases draw on the resources of the popular PBS television series "Small Business School," and bring together high-interest video segments and in-text case material. Case instruction augmented by video filmed on location in diverse businesses such as Mo's Chowder, Joseph's Lite Cookies, and other entrepreneurial businesses makes studying effective small business management all the more interesting.

Updated and Enhanced Supplements

All resources and ancillaries that accompany *Small Business Management*, 15th edition, have been created to support a variety of teaching methods, learning styles, and classroom situations.

- **Instructor's Manual.** Lecture notes in the ***Instructor's Manual*** are grouped by learning objective and tied to PowerPoint slides that relate to each objective. The manual also contains sources of audio/video and other instructional materials, answers to the "Discussion Questions," comments on "You Make the Call" situations, and teaching notes for the cases. This edition's Instructor's Manual has been revised by Janice Gates of Western Illinois University. It is available on the text Web site at http://www.cengage.com/management/longenecker and on the Instructor's IRCD.

- **Test Bank.** The test bank has also been revised by J. David Allen, of Baylor University. Questions in the ***Test Bank*** are grouped by learning objectives and includes true/false, multiple-choice, and discussion questions. A correlation table at the beginning of each Test Bank chapter helps instructors select questions that cover all objectives or that emphasize objectives most important to the instructor's specific course. The test bank in Word is available on the text Web site at http://www.cengage.com/management/ Longenecker and on the Instructor's IRCD.

- **ExamView® Testing Software.** ExamView contains all of the questions in the printed test bank. This program is an easy-to-use test creation software compatible with Microsoft Windows. Instructors can add or edit questions, instructions, and answers. Questions may be selected by previewing them on screen, selecting them randomly, or selecting them by number. Instructors can also create quizzes online whether over the Internet, a local area network (LAN), or a wide area network (WAN).

- **PowerPoint® for Instructors.** A complete PowerPoint package is available to aid in lecture presentation. Computer-driven projection makes it easy to use these colorful images to add emphasis and interest to lectures. The PowerPoint slides, prepared by Charlie Cook of the University of West Alabama, are available on both the Instructor's Resource CD-ROM and on the password protected Instructor's Web site.

- **Instructor's Resource CD-ROM.** Instructors can get quick access to all of these ancillaries from the easy-to-use *Instructor's Resource CD-ROM* that lets the user electronically review, edit, and copy what's needed. The CD contains the Instructor's Manual, Test Bank in Microsoft Word and in ExamView, PowerPoint slides, and business plan templates.

- **"Small Business School" Videos.** Available in DVD format, selections from this popular television series on PBS stations let you in on some very big ideas at work in a variety of innovative small businesses. Some of the small businesses covered include Joseph's Lite Cookies, Rodgers Chevrolet, Nicole Miller, e-Harmony, and Modern Postcard, among many others. Use these videos to bring the real world into your classroom and let your students learn from the experts.

- **Small Business and Entrepreneurship Resource Center**
  The Small Business and Entrepreneurship Resource Center (*SBERC*) from Gale, a part of Cengage Learning and a leader in e-research for libraries and schools, is an optional package that gives your students access to 900,000 published full text articles directly related to small business management that are easily searchable by business topic, business type, and commonly asked how-to questions. This powerful resource also includes access to hundreds of sample business plans and legal forms necessary to start a new venture in every state. Powered by InfoTrac, the how-to section provides direct access to the most popular topics and questions students have about starting and running a small business.

- **Small Business Management Online (www.cengage .com/login).** SBM Online provides your students with a robust array of learning tools to enrich their course experience. Access to this pincode protected student Web site is packaged free with every new text and includes access to the Small Business School videos, Business Plan Templates, exercises to accompany the optional Small Business and Entrepreneurship Resource Center, and helpful Interactive Quizzes and e-lectures.

- **WebTutor™ on Blackboard or WebCT** This dynamic technology tool complements *Small Business Management* by providing interactive reinforcement that helps you fully grasp key concepts. WebTutor's online teaching and learning environment brings together content management, assessment, communication, and collaboration capabilities quizzes, tutorials, and other opportunities for interactive instruction that makes the world of small business come alive.

Optional Course Add-Ons

BizPlan Builder® Express: A Guide to Creating a Business Plan with BizPlan Builder
By JIAN and KAPRON

Now you can learn how to use the award-winning, best-selling professional software BizPlan Builder 8.1 to create your business plan.

This workbook/CD-ROM package provides all the essentials for creating winning business plans, from the latest BizPlanBuilder software to step-by-step instructions for preparing each section of a plan. Ready-to-customize samples, advice, a detailed marketing analysis with links to demographic and marketing tools, and helpful financial tools make it easy to create a solid plan. Hands-on exercises and activities throughout the workbook ensure you fully understand how to maximize BizPlanBuilder's dynamic tools.

Bundle your text with *BizPlanBuilder® Express* for a package that places you well ahead on your path to business success.

Contact your South-Western Cengage representative or visit http://www.cengage.com/management/JIAN for more information.

Special Thanks and Acknowledgments

There are numerous individuals to whom we owe a debt of gratitude for their assistance in making this project a reality. In particular, we thank our friends at South-Western Cengage; we really do count on them! We are especially indebted to Michele Rhoades, Susan Smart, Jacquelyn K Featherly, and word master Jeanne Yost. Without them, this book would only exist in our heads! They are masters of coordination and motivation, keeping us on track and moving forward—which is no easy task and their sending six pints of Graeter's Ice Cream to one of the co-authors who had been in the hospital got him back to work quicker, not to mention their thoughtfulness.

We thank, too, many others who worked on various aspects of the package: our designer, Tippy McIntosh, our marketing group consisting of Nate Anderson, Jim Overly, and Clint Kernen, and technology manager, Rob Ellington. We also offer our thanks to Elizabeth Vaughn and Peggy Davies, whose excellent word-processing skills made our burden much easier to bear, and to Mary Abrahams for reading chapters and catching our many errant keystrokes.

We owe a great debt of gratitude to Frank Hoy who helped us revise and improve four of the chapters in the text and made *countless* great suggestions on all of the other chapters—all while moving from his position at the University of Texas at El Paso to his new academic home at Worcester Polytechnic Institute in Massachusetts. Working with him was like having a valuable co-author, bringing expert and extraordinary insight to our work on the book. We cannot express adequately how much we value his participation and appreciate his friendship.

We also want to offer words of appreciation and acknowledgement to Wes Bailey who was a contributing author for the risk management chapter. Mr. Bailey is president of Bailey Insurance and Risk Management, Inc. (Waco, TX) and is well recognized as a leader in the industry. His serving as the author for this chapter insures readers that they are receiving timely and relevant information for managing risk in a small business. And we thank Bradley Norris, a colleague and lecturer for us here at Baylor, for his suggestions regarding the operations chapter.

A talented team of writers contributed an outstanding set of ancillary materials. Special thanks go to J. David Allen of Baylor University for his preparation of the Test Bank, and to Janice Gates of Western Illinois University for her revision of the Instructor's Manual. We offer our thanks as well to Charlie Cook, of the University of West Alabama, who created the PowerPoint images. And finally we offer a special word of appreciation for the understanding and patient support of our wives—Donna and Dianna—during this process.

For their helpful suggestions and thoughtful comments, which helped to shape this edition, we are grateful to the following reviewers and to many others who, for reasons of privacy, chose to remain anonymous:

Dr. Jeffrey Alstete
Iona College

David Ambrosini
Cabrillo College

Chandler Atkins
Adirondack Community College

Lee Baldwin
University of Mary Hardin-Baylor

Francis B. Ballard
Florida Community College

Hilton Barrett
Elizabeth City State University

Bill Bauer
Carroll College—Waukesha Wisconsin

Verona K. Beguin
Black Hills State University

Narendra C. Bhandari
Pace University, New York

Greg Bier
Stephens College

Karen Bishop
University of Louisville

Ross Blankenship
State Fair Community College

John Boos
Ohio Wesleyan University

Marvin Borgelt
University of Mary Hardin-Baylor

Steven Bradley
Austin Community College

Don B. Bradley III
University of Central Arkansas

Margaret Britt
Eastern Nazarene College

Mark Brosthoff
Indiana University

Penelope Stohn Brouwer
Mount Ida College

Rochelle R. Brunson
Alvin Community College

Kevin Chen
County College of Morris

Felipe Chia
Harrisburg Area Community College

Mike Cicero
Highline Community College

Edward G. Cole
St. Mary's University

Michael D. Cook
Hocking College

Roy A. Cook
Fort Lewis College

George R. Corbett
St. Thomas Aquinas College

Karen Cranford
Catawba College

George W. Crawford
Clayton College & State University

Bruce Davis
Weber State University

Terri Davis
Howard College

Bill Demory
Central Arizona College

Michael Deneen
Baker College

Sharon Dexler
Southeast Community College

Warren Dorau
Nicolet College

Max E. Douglas
Indiana State University

Bonnie Ann Dowd
Palomar College

Michael Drafke
College of Dupage

Franklin J. Elliot
Dine College

Franceen Fallett
Ventura College

R. Brian Fink
Danville Area Community College

Dennette Foy
Edison College

David W. Frantz
Purdue University

Janice S. Gates
Western Illinois University

Armand Gilinsky, Jr.
Sonoma State University

Darryl Goodman
Trident Technical College

William Grace
Missouri Valley College

William W. Graff
Maharishi University of Management

Mark Hagenbuch
University of North Carolina, Greensboro

James R. Hindman
Northeastern University

Betty Hoge
Limestone College

Eddie Hufft
Alcorn St University

Sherrie Human
Xavier University

Ralph Jagodka
Mt. San Antonio College

Larry K. Johansen
Park University

Michael Judge
Hudson Valley Community College

Mary Beth Klinger
College of Southern Maryland

Charles W. Kulmann
Columbia College of Missouri

Rosemary Lafragola
University of Texas at El Paso

William Laing
Anderson College

Ann Langlois
Palm Beach Atlantic University

Rob K. Larson
Mayville State University

David E. Laurel
South Texas Community College

Les Ledger
Central Texas College

Michael G. Levas
Carroll College

Richard M. Lewis
Lansing Community College

Thomas W. Lloyd
Westmoreland County Community College

Elaine Madden
Anne Arundel Community College

Kristina Mazurak
Albertson College

James J. Mazza
Middlesex Community College

Lisa McConnell
Oklahoma State University

Angela Mitchell
Wilmington College

Frank Mitchell
Limestone College

Douglas Moesel
University of Missouri-Columbia

Michael K. Mulford
Des Moines Area Community College

Bernice M. Murphy
University of Maine at Machias

Eugene Muscat
University of San Francisco

John J. Nader
Grand Valley State University

Charles "Randy" Nichols
Sullivan University

Robert D. Nixon
University of Louisville

Marcella M. Norwood
University of Houston

Donalus A. Okhomina, Sr.
Jackson State University

Rosa L. Okpara
Albany State University

Timothy O'Leary
Mount Wachusett Community College

Pamela Onedeck
University of Pittsburgh at Greensburg

Claire Phillips
North Harris College

Dean Pielstick
Northern Arizona University

Mark S. Poulos
St. Edward's University

Julia Truitt Poynter
Transylvania University

Fred Pragasam
University of North Florida

Mary Ellen Rosetti
Hudson Valley Community College

Jaclyn Rundle
Central College

John K. Sands
Western Washington University

Craig Sarine
Lee University

Duane Schecter
Muskegon Community College

Matthew Semadeni
Texas A&M University

Marjorie Shaprio
Myers University

Sherry L. Shuler
American River College

Cindy Simerly
Lakeland Community College

James Sisk
Gaston College

Victoria L. Sitter
Milligan College

Bernard Skown
Stevens Institute of Technology

Kristin L.H. Slyter
Valley City State University

William E. Smith
Ferris State University

Bill Snider
Cuesta College

Roger Stanford
Chippewa Valley Technical College

Phil Stetz
Stephen F Austin State University

Peter L. Stone
Spartanburg Technical College

James Swenson
Minnesota State University Moorhead

Ruth Tarver
West Hills Community College

Darrell Thompson
Mountain View College

Melodie M. Toby
Kean University

Charles N. Toftoy
George Washington University

Charles Torti
Schreiner University

Gerald R. Turner
Limestone College

Barry L. Van Hook
Arizona State University

Brian Wahl
North Shore Community College

Mike Wakefield
University of Southern California

Charles F. Warren
Salem State College

Janet Wayne
Baker College

Nat B. White, Jr.
South Piedmont Community College

Jim Whitlock
Brenau University

Ira Wilsker
Lamar Institute of Technology

To the Instructor

As a final word of appreciation, we express our sincere thanks to the many instructors who use our text in both academic and professional settings. Based on years of teaching and listening to other teachers and students, *Small Business Management* has been designed to meet the needs of its readers. And we continue to listen and make changes in the text. Please write or call us to offer suggestions to help us make the book even better for future readers. Our contact information is Bill Petty (254-710-2260, bill_petty@baylor.edu) or Les Palich (254-710-6194, les_palich@baylor.edu). We would love to hear from you.

JUSTIN G. LONGENECKER Justin G. Longenecker's authorship of Small Business *Management* began with the first edition of this book. He authored a number of books and numerous articles in such journals as *Journal of Small Business Management, Academy of Management Review, Business Horizons*, and *Journal of Business Ethics*. He was active in several professional organizations and served as president of the International Council for Small Business. Dr. Longenecker grew up in a family business. After attending Central Christian College of Kansas for two years, he went on to earn his B.A. in political science from Seattle Pacific University, his M.B.A. from Ohio State University, and his Ph.D. from the University of Washington. He taught at Baylor University, where he was Emeritus Chavanne Professor of Christian Ethics in Business until his death in 2005.

J. WILLIAM PETTY J. William Petty is Professor of Finance and the W. W. Caruth Chairholder in Entrepreneurship at Baylor University and the Executive Director of the Baylor Angel Network. He holds a Ph.D. and an M.B.A. from The University of Texas at Austin and a B.S. from Abilene Christian University. He has taught at Virginia Tech University and Texas Tech University and served as dean of the business school at Abilene Christian University. He taught entrepreneurship and small business courses in China, the Ukraine, Kazakhstan, Indonesia, Thailand, and Russia. He has been designated a Master Teacher at Baylor and was named the National Entrepreneurship Teacher of the Year in 2008 by the Acton Foundation for Excellence in Entrepreneurship. His research interests include acquisitions of privately held companies, shareholder value-based management, the financing of small and entrepreneurial firms, angel financing, and exit strategies for privately held firms. He has served as co-editor for the *Journal of Financial Research* and as editor of the *Journal of Entrepreneurial and Small Business Finance*. He has published articles in a number of finance journals and is the co-author of two leading corporate finance textbooks—*Financial Management* and *Foundations of Finance*. He is a co-author of *Value-Based Management in an Era of Corporate Social Responsibility* (Oxford University Press, 2010). Dr. Petty has worked as a consultant for oil and gas firms and consumer product companies. He also served as a subject matter expert on a best-practices study by the American Productivity and Quality Center on the topic of shareholder value-based management. He was a member of a research team sponsored by the Australian Department of Industry to study the feasibility of establishing a public equity market for small and medium-sized enterprises in Australia. Finally, he serves as the audit chair for a publicly traded energy firm.

LESLIE E. PALICH Leslie E. Palich is Associate Professor of Management and Entrepreneurship and the Ben H. Williams Professor of Entrepreneurship at Baylor University, where he teaches courses in small business management, international entrepreneurship, strategic management, and international management to undergraduate and graduate students in the Hankamer School of Business. He is also Associate Director of the Entrepreneurship Studies program at Baylor. He holds a Ph.D. and an M.B.A. from Arizona State University and a B.A. from Manhattan Christian College. His research has been published in the Academy of Management Review, Strategic Management Journal, Entrepreneurship Theory & Practice, Journal of Business Venturing, Journal of International Business Studies, Journal of Management, Journal of Organizational Behavior, Journal of Small Business Management, and several other periodicals. He has taught entrepreneurship and strategic management in a number of overseas settings, including Cuba, France, the Netherlands, the United Kingdom, and the Dominican Republic. His interest in entrepreneurial opportunity and small business management dates back to his grade school years, when he set up a produce sales business to experiment with small business ownership. That early experience became a springboard for a number of other enterprises. Since that time, he has owned and operated domestic ventures in agribusiness, automobile sales, real estate development, and educational services, as well as an international import business.

CARLOS W. MOORE Carlos W. Moore was the Edwin W. Streetman Professor of Marketing at Baylor University, where he was an instructor for more than 35 years. He was honored as a Distinguished Professor by the Hankamer School of Business, where he taught both graduate and undergraduate courses in Marketing Research and Consumer Behavior. Dr. Moore authored articles in such journals as *Journal of Small Business Management, Journal of Business Ethics, Organizational Dynamics, Accounting Horizons*, and *Journal of Accountancy*. His authorship of this textbook began with its sixth edition. Dr. Moore received an associate arts degree from Navarro Junior College in Corsicana, Texas, where he was later named Ex-Student of the Year. He earned a B.B.A. degree from The University of Texas at Austin with a major in accounting, an M.B.A. from Baylor University, and a Ph.D. from Texas A&M University. Besides fulfilling his academic commitments, Dr. Moore served as co-owner of a small ranch and a partner in a small business consulting firm until his death in 2007.

PART 1

Entrepreneurship:
A World of Opportunity

©iStockphoto.com/Zhang Maud

## chapter 1

The Entrepreneurial Life

In the SPOTLIGHT
Bridgecreek
http://www.bridgecreek.com

When Frank Jao left Communist Vietnam with his wife and headed for Camp Pendleton, California, it was not the first time he had struck out on his own. In fact, Jao had left home when he was 11 years old. Although still in school, he supported himself by working six hours a day delivering papers, and after two short years, the newspaper distributor assigned Jao the distribution routes for the entire city of Da Nang. He had six employees by the time he was 13 years old.

The lessons Jao learned from his family, his newspaper business, and his independent life in Vietnam provided the drive and persistence that helped him develop Bridgecreek, a unique Vietnamese cultural center in southern California. What started as a single-building shopping center is now a commercial campus of 3,500 Vietnamese-owned businesses and home to the largest Vietnamese population outside of Vietnam. A simple mall has become a city in its own right and was given the name "Little Saigon" by the governor of California. (You may already be familiar with Little Saigon: Its gates were featured in the movie *The Fast and the Furious*.)

The drivers of Frank Jao's success are similar to those driving millions of entrepreneurs across the country: the desire to be independent, to create, and to prosper. Watch this video spotlight to see how the persistence and resourcefulness of one entrepreneur can fuel the success and vitality of an entire community.

Source: Video material provided by Hattie Bryant, Producer of Small Business School, the series on PBS Stations, Worldnet, and the Web at http://www.smallbusinessschool.org.

© Nik Wheelly Corbis

LOOKING AHEAD

AFTER STUDYING THIS CHAPTER, YOU SHOULD BE ABLE TO...

1. Distinguish between an entrepreneur and a small business owner.
2. Explain the characteristics of entrepreneurial opportunities and give examples of successful businesses started by entrepreneurs.
3. Describe some motivators or rewards of entrepreneurial careers.
4. Identify the various types of entrepreneurs and entrepreneurial ventures.
5. Identify five potential competitive advantages of small entrepreneurial companies as compared to large firms.
6. Discuss factors related to readiness for entrepreneurship and getting started in an entrepreneurial career.
7. Explain the concept of an entrepreneurial legacy and the challenges involved in crafting a worthy legacy.

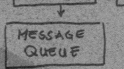

Since you are reading this book, you most likely have a serious interest in starting and operating your own business; or you may already be planning to own your own business someday, if not now. If so, you will be joining countless others on the entrepreneurial journey.

A major theme—if not *the* major theme—of the past 60 years in business is the rise of entrepreneurship, not only in the United States, but around the globe. One study estimates that a half-billion people worldwide are trying to create a new business every year.[1] Within the United States, it is estimated that 12 million people are involved in some form of an entrepreneurial venture, and that perhaps as many as half of all adults will be engaged in self-employment at some point during their work career.[2] The Small Business Administration notes the contribution of such businesses to the U.S. economy, reporting that small firms:[3]

- Comprise 99.7 percent of all firms with employees.
- Employ more than 50 percent of all employees working in the private sector.
- Account for 45 percent of private payrolls.
- Generated 60 to 80 percent of all net new jobs over the past decade.
- Create more than half of the country's gross domestic product.
- Hire 40 percent of high-tech employees, such as scientists, engineers, and programmers.
- Represent 97.3 percent of all exporters.

Don McLoughlin, vice president of marketing for the employment agency ADP, further highlighted the contribution of small business to the U.S. economy from 2002 through 2007, as follows:

> Small businesses have added positively to the economy every month since 2002. If you add those numbers up, that's 4.5 million new jobs—more than twice the number of jobs contributed by larger businesses. Small business really is the engine of job growth.[4]

But by the end of 2008, a financial crisis was looming, not only in the United States, but around the world. Both large and small companies alike were starting to feel the strain from an impending major recession. While larger firms were beginning to cut costs, most smaller companies did not have such an option—it is hard to cut back when you are already resource constrained. Also, according to the Federal Reserve Board, 90 percent of the banks had tightened lending standards for small companies, which severely limited their ability to grow.[5] The cost-cutting strategies of many large firms involve downsizing and layoffs, and this loss of jobs in the big companies often results in many individuals striking out on their own, some of them out of necessity. Thus, in tough economic times, the entrepreneurship option becomes all the more important to the economy, though small businesses still must face the challenges of economic recession.

The growth of small businesses and recognition of their worth to the economy is also reflected in the "entrepreneurial fever" sweeping throughout the nation's community colleges, universities, and career schools, as students take classes to learn how to launch, finance, and run their own companies. Universities across the United States are adding entire programs to teach entrepreneurship, and many more offer at least one or two classes—and still cannot handle all the student demand. John Fernandes, president and CEO of the Association to Advance Collegiate Schools of Business International (the organization that accredits business schools around the world), puts it this way, "Entrepreneurship will continue to grow and mature into a distinct management discipline. Elements of entrepreneurship will emerge as essential to any business education."[6] In other words, in today's world your business courses, whatever your particular specialty or major, had best include the study of entrepreneurship. Business students, along with engineers, teachers, artists, pharmacists, lawyers, nurses, and many others, are hearing the call to own their own businesses. To say the least, you are living in a world of entrepreneurial opportunities!

You are about to embark on a course of study that will prove invaluable if you elect to pursue a career in entrepreneurship or small business—or even if you don't. An entrepreneurial career can provide an exciting life and substantial personal rewards, while also contributing to the welfare of society. As a general rule, when you talk to entrepreneurs about what they are doing and what their plans are for the future, you can feel their excitement and anticipation.

Taking a small business or entrepreneurship class is not likely to turn a student who lacks basic business intuition into an opportunity-spotting, money-making genius. Yet there is considerable evidence suggesting that such classes can facilitate the learning curve for those who have the "right stuff." These classes teach many of the basic skills required, such as determining if a business idea is a good opportunity, acquiring needed resources, writing a business plan, marketing the product or service, and learning how to impose structure and deadlines on dreams that you might never achieve otherwise.

Megan Wettach is just one example among thousands. During high school, Megan opened a store to sell prom dresses in her hometown of Mount Pleasant, Iowa. After taking an entrepreneurship class at the University of Iowa, she began designing her own gowns and secured a $150,000 line of credit with a bank in Cedar Rapids. She then signed a contract with an apparel maker in China and negotiated a deal to sell her dresses. "My professors opened my eyes to the idea that I can be bigger than a little dress store in Iowa," Wettach says. "I can be a global force in fashion."[7] Who can blame her for shooting for the stars?

To get an idea of the unlimited potential of entrepreneurial ventures, think of the achievements of entrepreneurs such as Sergey Brin and Larry Page, the founders of Google. If success is having your firm's name become a verb in languages around the world, then these two individuals can without question claim that Google has clearly been a phenomenal success. Though few of us can relate to Brin and Page's level of success, their experience teaches us that we will never know what is possible until we try.

Having worked for over three decades both with entrepreneurs and students who aspire to own businesses, we have designed this book to prepare you for the life of an entrepreneur. We also will be drawing on the extensive experience of eight entrepreneurs who have studied the principles in this book and offer their advice and counsel on important issues. So, you are in for an exciting adventure!

Entrepreneurship and Small Business

Thus far, we have discussed entrepreneurship and small business opportunities in a very general way. However, it is important to note that, despite many similarities, the terms *entrepreneur* and *small business manager* are not synonymous. Some entrepreneurial endeavors, for example, begin as small businesses but quickly grow into large businesses. They may still be entrepreneurial. We need, then, to clarify the meanings of these terms.

1.Distinguish between an entrepreneur and a small business owner.

Who Are the Entrepreneurs?

Entrepreneurs are frequently thought to be individuals who discover market needs and launch new firms to meet those needs. They are risk takers who provide an impetus for change, innovation, and progress in economic life. (In contrast, salaried employees receive some specified compensation and do not assume ownership risks.)

For our purposes, we will not limit the term *entrepreneur* only to business founders; instead, we will include second-generation firm owners, franchisees, and owner-managers who have bought existing firms. While we will most often focus on business in the book, our thinking also includes individuals in not-for-profit organizations who think and act entrepreneurially.

1-1 The Independent Entrepreneur

B.C.

BY JOHNNY HART

Source: © Johnny Hart/Creators Syndicate Inc.

So for us, an *entrepreneur* is a person who relentlessly focuses on an opportunity, either in a new or existing enterprise, to create value, while assuming both the risk and reward for his or her effort.

What Is Small Business?

What does it mean to talk about "small business"? A neighborhood restaurant or bakery is clearly a small business, and Toyota is obviously not. But among small businesses, there is great diversity in size.

There have been many efforts to define the term *small business,* using such criteria as number of employees, sales volume, and value of assets. There is no generally accepted or universally agreed-on definition. Size standards are basically arbitrary, adopted to serve a particular purpose. For example, legislators sometimes exclude firms with fewer than 10 or 15 employees from certain regulations, so as to avoid imposing a financial burden on the owner of a very small business. However, for our purposes, primary attention will be given to businesses that meet the following criteria:

1. Compared to the biggest firms in the industry, the business is small; in most instances, the number of employees in the business is fewer than 100.

2. Except for its marketing function, the business's operations are geographically localized.

3. Financing for the business is provided by no more than a few individuals.

4. The business may begin with a single individual, but if the owner chooses to do so, it has the potential to become more than a "one-person show."

Obviously, some small companies fail to meet all of these standards. For example, a small executive search firm—a firm that helps corporate clients recruit managers from other organizations—may operate in many sections of the country and thereby fail to meet the second criterion. Nevertheless, the discussion of management concepts in this book is aimed primarily at the type of firm that fits the general pattern outlined by these criteria.

Thus, small businesses include tiny one-person firms—the kind you may decide to start. They also include small firms that have up to 100 employees. In most cases, however, they are drastically different in their structure and operations from the huge corporations that are generally featured in the business media.

entrepreneur
A person who is relentlessly focused on an opportunity, either in a new or existing business, to create value both for the customer and the owner. The entrepreneur assumes both the risk and reward for his or her effort.

small business
A business that is small compared to large companies in an industry, is geographically localized, is financed by only a few individuals, and has a small management team.

Entrepreneurial Opportunities

2. Explain the characteristics of entrepreneurial opportunities and give examples of successful businesses started by entrepreneurs.

entrepreneurial opportunity
An economically attractive and timely opportunity that creates value for interested buyers or end users.

bootstrapping
Doing more with less in terms of resources invested in a business, and where possible controlling the resources without owning them.

Entrepreneurial opportunities exist for those who can produce enough products or services desired by customers to make the enterprise economically attractive. It involves a product or service that is so attractive to customers that they are willing to pay their hard-earned money for it. In other words, an entrepreneur must find a way to create value for customers.

In short, an *entrepreneurial opportunity* is an *economically attractive* and *timely* opportunity that creates value for prospective customers and the firm's owners alike, which involves much more than merely having a good business idea. It is important to note that a given opportunity will not be equally attractive to everyone. Because of differences in experiences and perspectives, one person may see an opportunity where others do not. But, in any case, a true opportunity exists only for the entrepreneur who has the passion, persistence, and experience required to succeed.

To capture an entrepreneurial opportunity requires critical resources: (1) people, such as suppliers, customers, accountants, lawyers, and board members; (2) assets, such as inventories, equipment, and buildings; and (3) the needed capital to finance the venture.

An entrepreneur needs to be creative and resourceful in gaining control of these resources. As an entrepreneur, you can control some resources without having to own them. This is called *bootstrapping,* and represents one of the primary ways entrepreneurs gain access to resources that are critical to starting and running a business without having the money to buy them.

Let's look at three successful entrepreneurial ventures started by some present-day entrepreneurs.

Three Success Stories

TABLE OCCASIONS (EL PASO, TX)[8] From the perspective of Cecilia "Chia" Stewart, the mother of two small children and an entrepreneur in her own right, "moms" are constantly performing juggling acts when managing all their responsibilities. She observes, "The creative

© Tony Florez

side of life often has to take a backseat to all the daily responsibilities, including carpooling, soccer games, piano lessons, tennis lessons and the like." However, Chia, along with two friends, Stacey Hunt and Claudia Narvaez, decided that in spite of all the juggling they did, there were still enough hours in the day to launch a new business.

In 2006, the dynamic trio pooled their talents and put their determination to the test by entering the El Paso Pro Musica Tablescapes competition. The concept behind the event is to decorate tables with fabulous themes, all to benefit a nonprofit music organization. They decided that if their table was noticed, they would launch their business and, if not, at least their creative side would be given a great workout. Their entry, "An Enchanted Garden Baby Shower," was awarded a first-place prize and marked the beginning of their business, Table Occasions.

When Table Occasions opened its doors, its founders were averaging only one event a weekend. Now, they are juggling more than just their toddlers' schedules. They organize up to ten events each week, working with party planners, wedding consultants, floral designers, and others to come up with the perfect colors and schemes for any soiree, from intimate dinner parties to lavish events with 700 guests. "The most rewarding part of this business," Stewart observes, "is the opportunity to work one-on-one with clients and guide them with respect to their visions."

Stewart maintains that the most basic element of planning the table setting is the linen made in the borderland. "The fabrics are literally like works of art and provide the excitement, inspiration and passion for our designs," Stewart explains. "There is nothing but happiness for us when we see the joy in the eyes of our customers when their dream table comes to life." For Narvaez, it is about bringing it all together, from the perfect chair to the right wine goblet to the ideal vase filled with flowers that complements the design perfectly. "We are passionate about the creative aspects of our business, along with our desire to please our customers," Narvaez exclaims.

Stewart, Hunt, and Narvaez remain humbled by their newfound success and are grateful for the support that comes from their families. When they are in "creative mode," patient husbands and grandmothers have helped the trio work around school and play time. "We had a dream and worked hard to make it come to life," Stewart says. "We hope our story inspires others to dedicate their skills to spend every day doing what they love to do."

LIFE IS GOOD (BOSTON, MA)[9]

Most of us have seen Jake, but may not have known his name. Jake is the inspiration-cum-mascot of Life Is Good, a 206-employee wholesaler and retailer founded in 1994 by brothers Bert and John Jacobs. Based in Boston, the company markets everything from apparel to dog dishes to furniture, but its chief product is optimism. Jake appears on much of the brand's merchandise engaged in a variety of outdoor pursuits: running or skiing or golfing or simply reclining in an Adirondack chair. Beneath this depiction of good clean fun appear the words "Life Is Good," or some equally rosy assertion.

© Aimee Corrigan

From the roof deck of their $8 million, 10,000-square-foot design center and flagship store on Boston's Newbury Street, the Jacobs can see the site of their original business. Sixteen years earlier they sold $10 T-shirts, featuring their own artwork (not Jake—he came later), from a card table on the opposite corner of the street.

That first business, called Jacobs Gallery, had other Boston area locations as well, all of them similarly temporary. The brothers also sold shirts door-to-door at college dorms up and down the East Coast for five years, living in their van and sleeping on piles of merchandise.

From these humble beginnings, Life Is Good has grown to an $80 million business with 5,000 distributors operating in 14 countries. The company, which has been profitable every year since 1997, offers more than 900 items in 14 categories. Its products are used by virtually everyone, from toddlers to grandparents. "We don't miss any demographics but we miss one psychographic—people who can't see the positive side of things," explains John.

The broad acceptance of this brand—achieved with virtually no advertising—may stem from the different ways people interpret it. For many, it is a claim of the simple pleasures that enrich their lives. But "Life Is Good" has also become something of an anthem for survivors—the founders receive thousands of letters from people whose lives are seriously troubled, because they are sick or have lost a loved one, for example.

The Jacobs brothers are aware of the allure of their story. They print it everywhere—on tags attached to their products, on cards dropped into shopping bags, on their website, and even on some of their T-shirts. "I think it's interesting how many customers know the story about them traveling around selling shirts," says Carol Wilkes, co-owner of Highland Hiker, an outdoor gear store in Cashiers, North Carolina, that carries Life Is Good products. "You hear people telling it to each other. Someone might be in the store looking at things on the Life Is Good table and another customer says to them, 'Do you know about these guys? They started out of a little van.'"

In attitude and actions, John and Bert are Jake made flesh. They are ardent in their leisure pursuits, which include basketball, hiking, kayaking, and ultimate Frisbee. "What you see in the brand is how they live their everyday life," says Teague Hatfield, owner of FootZone of Bend, an Oregon running gear store that has sold Life Is Good products for a decade. "They do a wonderful job practicing what they preach," says REI's Jewell. "They are a real inspiration to our team."

The Jacobs brothers, of course, are well aware that they embody the thing that makes them money. It's an enviable situation. Laboring under the onus of happiness, they must keep their hours sane, their workloads manageable, and their vacations uncanceled—for the good of the business. "Like [the jazz musician] Charlie Parker said," remarks John, "If you don't live it, it won't come out your horn."

© Sara Remington

THE FRUITGUYS (SAN FRANCISCO, CA)[10] Chris Mittelstaedt was just a child at the controls of a Cessna aircraft when he got his first lesson in business. An entrepreneur and a pilot, Mittelstaedt's father taught him the importance of keeping an eye out for early indications of trouble. That lesson took on special meaning when the dotcom bust severely damaged his regional fruit delivery business, leaving The FruitGuys with about $50,000 of bad debt—after customers went belly up—and Mittelstaedt with $100,000 of personal debt. "We were growing so fast at the time, and I wasn't paying attention to my dashboard or thinking macroeconomically," admits Mittelstaedt. He recovered by restructuring his business to include a tighter credit policy, more variable costs, and national expansion.

The dotcom crash wasn't Mittelstaedt's first brush with adversity. Since the beginning, necessity has forced him to deal with problems. In 1998, Mittelstaedt was earning $9.50 an hour at a temp job when he learned his wife was pregnant. With no time to waste, he launched his business. By starting his 18-hour days at midnight, lugging heavy crates of produce, and making the deliveries personally, his business slowly came to fruition.

A decade later, The FruitGuys has grown into a full-scale operation that delivers fresh, high-quality produce to more than 3,000 businesses nationwide. But at the pit of the company is a proactive effort to promote wellness in the community—whether it's by helping clients establish athletic clubs at the office, reaching out to low-income communities, or working with farmers to maintain sustainable businesses.

Mittelstaedt believes that the secret to his success is thinking about all the options and never giving up. It literally required feats of herculean effort from a physical standpoint—getting up at midnight, sleeping five hours a day, lifting 50-pound boxes over and over again all day long, making deliveries, going in and out of trucks, doing sales on the phone, and managing the books.

According to Mittelstaedt, "If you believe in what you're doing, don't give up, even when people are saying it's not going to work. There are lots of examples in history of people who were amazing entrepreneurs, visionaries—people who believed in something and continued to go for it. Persevere and understand that it truly is a marathon. I'm always skeptical of get-rich-quick stuff. If you believe in it, root down and go for it."

But Mittelstaedt also cautions that, "I still don't know that we've made it, to be honest. I think that's actually one of the secrets to my success. I'm not going to believe that we've made it, and I'm going to keep pushing. I have a healthy dose of worst-case-scenario thinking, and that actually helps me be successful. Things are going to fall apart, so how do I avoid it, how do I grow fast, and how do I bring out great things and avoid the pitfalls when I'm doing it?"

In the previous three examples, we have described very different people who stepped out on their own to capture opportunities—three young women who have a passion for transforming the ordinary into the extraordinary, two brothers who want to share a message that "life is good," and a solo entrepreneur who is determined to overcome adversity to be successful and contribute to the community. Perhaps you will be able to see a glimmer of your own entrepreneurial hopes and dreams in their experiences.

So You Want to Be an Entrepreneur

3. Describe some motivators or rewards of entrepreneurial careers.

Don't let anyone deceive you: Being an entrepreneur is extremely challenging. As one entrepreneur said, "You get sand kicked in your face all the time, and worse. It takes undying love and passion to keep going. If your mind is wandering to something else you'd rather do, go do that." There will be times when you will be discouraged, maybe even terrified. Some days you will wish you had opted for the "security" of a regular job in an established company, or at least the perception of security. So why do people choose an entrepreneurial career?

For one thing, owning a business can run in a family, even for those who may not continue to work in the family company. Someone in your childhood—a parent or older sibling or close family friend—may have served as an inspirational role model. Researchers at Case Western Reserve University's Weatherhead School of Management found a strong connection between entrepreneurship and genetics. Also, the U.S. Census Bureau reports that half of all small business owners who were raised in a small business family worked in the family business before founding their own ventures.[11] In other words, it may just be in your genes.

What other factors might cause you to consider running your own business? Clearly, different individuals have varied reasons and motivations for wanting to own their own business, and we discuss some of these reasons in the following sections. Any attempt to identify all of the various attractions would at best be incomplete, but Exhibit 1-2 summarizes some of the reasons frequently cited by individuals for becoming entrepreneurs. We will discuss each in turn.

LIVING THE DREAM:

entrepreneurial experiences

The Entrepreneurial Gene

Most small business owners would be thrilled if their children wanted to follow in their footsteps. Javier Centeno did just that working for his parents, Manuel and Mirna, when he was growing up. He helped them by doing small tasks, such as making photocopies and stuffing envelopes, at their thriving printing business in El Salvador. "When I was 12, I started going to my dad's meetings," Javier says. "I always thought I would end up taking it over with my sisters when my parents decided to retire." But when his family immigrated to the United States in 1998 to escape civil war in El Salvador, Centeno watched his parents go from successful business owners to factory workers in Milwaukee.

"It was hard to see my parents work for someone else when I had always seen them working for themselves," says Javier, who co-owns Spanglish Diseño, a multicultural branding and design firm in Milwaukee, with three partners. "But from day one, they were determined to start new businesses here in the United States. My parents are not the kind of people who give up."

Last year, Centeno's father opened Centeno Home Improvement Solutions, and his mother began Paso a Pasito Family Child Care, a licensed child-care center she runs out of their home. "We have always been entrepreneurs, and this is a country of opportunities, so we knew we could make it happen eventually," Manuel says. "You have to have determination to make your dreams come true. You can have the desire, but if you don't have the determination, things are not going to happen."

Seeing his parents' determination helped Javier decide to leave his secure job as a Web designer and venture out on his own. "They always taught me to be dedicated and prepared," he says. "They said that a business takes a lot of effort, that things don't always happen as expected, and that you need to be prepared for any obstacle. They're proof of that. They were willing to do whatever it took to become business owners again—and they succeeded."

Source: Lena Basha, "The Entrepreneurial Gene," *MyBusiness*, December/January 2007, www.mybusinessmag.com/fullstory.php3?sid=1490.

© Spanglish Republik

Making Meaning

We first suggest a primary reason for becoming an entrepreneur and owning your own business: to make the world a better place. John Doerr, one of the most famous venture capitalists of all time, inspired the phrase *make meaning*, suggesting that the most impactful and sustainable businesses ever started are built on such a foundation.[12] Your first goal should be to create a product or service that makes the world a better place. Your company should be about something more significant than yourself. Then, when the days get long or you become discouraged, you will have a sense that what you are trying to do is significant and well worth the effort.

Erin McKenna is a great example of this philosophy. Some 12 million Americans suffer from food allergies, according to the Food Allergy & Anaphylaxis Network, and many of

EXHIBIT 1-2 Entrepreneurial Incentives

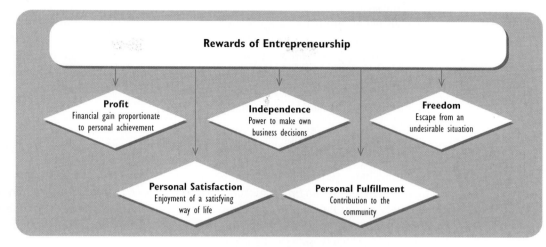

them choose a vegetarian or vegan diet to deal with the problem. Sales of vegetarian foods hit $1.2 billion in 2006. McKenna grew up in San Diego, the 10th of 12 children in her family. A few years ago, she was found to have wheat allergies. Unable to find a vegan bakery that could satisfy her sweet tooth, she decided to start her own, on the lower east side of Manhattan. Her business, BabyCakes NYC, sells gluten-free cupcakes, brownies, cookies, and pastries, made with ingredients such as coconut oil and bean flour and topped with agave-nectar frosting. *New York* named BabyCakes' cupcake the city's best in 2006, and she has been featured on Martha Stewart's television show.[13] As a result of her success, McKenna is making money while making a difference.

While we believe one of the most important reasons for becoming an entrepreneur is to "make meaning," there are a number of others that make becoming an entrepreneur tremendously attractive, as discussed next.

Develop Financial Wealth

Though we stress the importance of making meaning, there is nothing wrong with making money. As a general rule, when businesses are profitable, everyone benefits. Jobs are created, taxes are paid, and charities receive donations. Furthermore, like any other job or career, starting a business is a way to earn money and make ends meet. Of course, some entrepreneurs earn *lots* of money. In *The Millionaire Next Door*, Thomas Stanley and William Danko conclude that self-employed people are four times more likely to be millionaires than are those who work for others.[14]

How much money should an entrepreneur expect to get in return for starting and running a business? Making a profit is certainly necessary for a firm's survival. Many entrepreneurs work night and day (literally, in some cases) just to generate enough profits to survive; others receive a modest income for their time and investment. From an economic perspective, however, the financial return of a business should compensate its owner not only for his or her investment of personal time (in the form of a salary equivalent), but also for any personal money invested in the business (in the form of cash distributed to the owner and the increased value of the business) and for the risk he or she is taking. That is, entrepreneurs should seek a financial return that will compensate them for the time and money they invest and also reward them for the risks and initiative they take in starting and operating their own businesses.

A significant number of entrepreneurs are, no doubt, highly motivated by the prospect of making money. They have heard the stories about people who launched dotcom companies and quickly became multimillionaires. While some entrepreneurs do become rich quickly, the majority do not. Therefore, a more reasonable goal would be to "get rich slowly." Wealth will most likely come, provided the business is economically viable and the owner has the patience and determination to make it happen.

Be Your Own Boss

Many people have a strong desire to make their own decisions, take risks, and reap the rewards. Being one's own boss can be an attractive ideal. For these individuals, freedom to operate independently is important. This is evidenced by the results of one survey of small business owners, in which 38 percent of those who had left jobs at other companies said that their main reason for leaving was that they wanted to be their own boss.

The smallest businesses (i.e., part-time businesses and one-person firms), of which there are millions in the United States, probably offer the greatest flexibility to entrepreneurs. They can do things their own way, reap their own profits, and set their own schedules.

Of course, independence does not guarantee an easy life. Most entrepreneurs work very hard and for long hours. They must remember that the customer is, ultimately, the boss. But they do have the satisfaction of making their own decisions within the constraints required to build a successful business.

Escape a Bad Situation

People sometimes use entrepreneurship as an escape hatch, to free themselves from an undesirable situation. Some may wish to leave an unpleasant job situation, while others may seek change out of necessity. As noted, other individuals become entrepreneurs after being laid off by an employer. Unemployed personnel with experience in professional, managerial, technical, and even relatively unskilled positions often contemplate the possibility of venturing out on their own. Those who have entered business ownership as a result of financial hardship or other severe negative conditions have been described as *reluctant entrepreneurs*.[15]

reluctant entrepreneur
A person who becomes an entrepreneur as a result of some severe hardship.

Individuals may also flee the bureaucratic environment of a corporation that seems stifling or oppressive to them. In a survey of 721 office workers, 42 percent had considered quitting their jobs over bureaucratic hassles.[16] Entrepreneurship often provides an attractive alternative for individuals fleeing from such undesirable situations (sometimes called *refugees*).

refugee
A person who becomes an entrepreneur to escape an undesirable situation.

Karyn Couvillion, co-founder of Reeboot Strategy in Austin, Texas, is an example of a corporate refugee, someone who decided to leave a bad situation:

> Three hundred and fifty e-mails a day in my inbox. BlackBerry, cell phone, and laptop constantly in tow. Check my Outlook calendar and see that I'm double- or triple-booked in meetings every hour, plus a 7 a.m. global conference call. Being told by management that we cannot hire additional head count because of a hiring freeze, despite the hefty increase in responsibilities for my team. That was me a year ago. The red tape, politics, ridiculous expectations, and meager resources made it nearly impossible to do my job as an advertising and brand manager for a large tech company.[17]
>
> So I quit. So did my husband, who worked in a top advertising agency. We decided that life was too short and we had had enough. What was our worst-case scenario if we quit? Having to sell our home and look for jobs elsewhere? Better than losing our marriage and our sanity.

My husband started consulting immediately. I wanted to spend some time with my ill father. The marketing consulting business my husband started took off, and because of our similar backgrounds and experience, it was a natural fit for us to work together.

Ten months after quitting, we have more business than we can handle. My husband named the business Reeboot Strategy because in explaining our rationale for quitting our big corporate jobs he would say: "We needed to hit Control + Alt + Delete on our lives and start over."

When my father died, I was there by his side.

Enjoy Satisfying Work

Entrepreneurs frequently speak of the satisfaction they experience from running their own businesses; some even refer to their work as fun. Rick Davis, founder and CEO of Davaco, a Dallas-based company, says, "There is nothing else I would rather do. I love the challenges, working with others to see our dreams come true, and making a difference in the community. It is fun."[18]

Most small business owners report satisfaction in their careers. In a poll conducted by the National Federation of Independent Business, small employers rated the level of their personal satisfaction on average as an 8 on a scale of 1 (extremely dissatisfied) to 10 (extremely satisfied). A majority (51 percent) also indicated that they spend most of their time doing what they like to do best.[19]

The reward, then, may derive from a pleasurable activity associated with the particular product or service they provide, from enjoyable associations, from respect in the community, or from some other aspect of the business. The personal satisfaction many entrepreneurs receive from their enterprises is much more important than money—maybe even more than independence.

Finding Fulfillment

Some people are drawn to entrepreneurship as a way to make a positive contribution to their communities. They want not only personal satisfaction, as discussed earlier, but even more, fulfillment through giving back.

In most cases, this desire is one element in a mix of motivations. In some endeavors, however, it is a particularly strong force that drives the thinking of the entrepreneur. One survey found that 91 percent of small business owners give back to their communities each year through volunteering, in-kind contributions, and/or direct cash donations, totaling to some $40 billion.[20]

In a large corporation with operations spread out across the country—or even around the world—it can be difficult to pinpoint the communities served. But this is not the case for most small businesses, especially those that are an integral part of a community and its culture. Take, for example, The Title Place in Joplin, Missouri. The company opened its doors in 1903 to support the development of southwest Missouri at the turn of the century, and that's something that owner Nancy Good still views as a key mission for her firm:

> "The community is the lifeblood of why we are in business," says Good, whose business now has five offices across the region. "It is the community that supports business by opening doors to new customers. It would not be fair for our company only to take; it is our responsibility to give back, too."[21]

Small business owners don't—and shouldn't—expect anything in return for their community stewardship. But, as Gary Deaton points out, "To say there's not a benefit would be naive. Everything you do in life has a positive or a negative effect. So the more things you do for the right reasons, the more positive results you'll see."[22]

The Many Varieties of Entrepreneurship

Entrepreneurship is marked by diversity—that is, there is great variety both in the people and in the firms that are *entrepreneurial*. As a potential entrepreneur, you can be encouraged by this diversity; you do not need to fit some narrow stereotype. Let's consider some of the variety we observe in the entrepreneurial world.

4. Identify the various types of entrepreneurs and entrepreneurial ventures.

founder
An entrepreneur who brings a new firm into existence.

Founder Entrepreneurs versus Other Business Owners and Franchisees

As noted earlier, "pure" entrepreneurs are *founders,* such as inventors, who initiate businesses that bring new or improved products or services to market. They may also be artisans who develop skills upon which they can start their own firms. Or they may be enterprising individuals, often with marketing backgrounds, who draw on the ideas of others to launch new ventures. Whether acting as individuals or as part of a group, founders bring companies into existence by surveying the market, raising funds, and assembling the necessary resources. The process of starting an entirely new business is discussed in detail in Chapter 3.

At some point after a new firm is established, it may be purchased or taken over by a second-generation family member or another entrepreneur who was managing the company. These "second-stage" entrepreneurs do not necessarily differ greatly from founding entrepreneurs in the way they manage their businesses. Sometimes, these well-established small firms grow rapidly, and their orientation will be more akin to that of a founder than to that of a manager. Nevertheless, it is helpful to distinguish between entrepreneurs who start or substantially change companies (the "movers and shakers") and those who direct the continuing operations of established businesses.

franchisee
An entrepreneur whose power is limited by a contractual relationship with a franchising organization.

Franchisees comprise yet another category of entrepreneurs. *Franchisees* differ from other business owners in the degree of their independence. Because of the guidance and constraints provided by contractual arrangements with franchising organizations, franchisees function as limited entrepreneurs. Chapter 4 presents more information about franchisees.

High-Potential Ventures versus Attractive Small Firms and Microbusinesses

high-potential venture (gazelle)
A small firm that has great prospects for growth.

Small businesses differ drastically in their growth potential. The few businesses that have phenomenal prospects for growth are called *high-potential ventures,* or *gazelles.* Even within this group, there is variation in styles of operation and approaches to growth. Some are high-tech startups—the kind that have made Silicon Valley in California famous. The success stories often feature a technology wizard with a bright idea, backed by venture capitalists eager to finance the next Microsoft. When such companies prosper, they usually grow at blinding speed and make their founders wealthy by being sold or by issuing shares of stock to public investors.

attractive small firm
A small firm that provides substantial profits to its owner.

In contrast to such high-potential ventures, *attractive small firms* offer substantial financial rewards for their owners. Income from these entrepreneurial ventures may easily be in the millions or even tens of millions. They represent a major segment of small businesses—solid, healthy firms that can provide rewarding careers.

microbusiness
A small firm that provides minimal profits to its owner.

lifestyle business
A microbusiness that permits the owner to follow a desired pattern of living.

The least profitable types of businesses—including many service companies, such as dry cleaners, beauty shops, and appliance repair shops—provide modest returns to their owners. These are called *microbusinesses,* and their distinguishing feature is their limited ability to generate significant profits. Entrepreneurs who devote personal effort to such ventures receive a profit that does little more than compensate them for their time. Many companies of this type are also called *lifestyle businesses* because they permit an owner to follow a desired pattern of living, even though they provide only modest financial returns. Such enterprises usually do not attract investors.

Artisan versus Opportunistic Entrepreneurs

Because of their varied backgrounds, entrepreneurs display differences in the degrees of professionalism and the styles of management they bring to their businesses. The ways in which they analyze problems and approach decision making may differ radically.

Norman R. Smith has suggested two basic entrepreneurial patterns: artisan (or craftsman) entrepreneurs and opportunistic entrepreneurs.[23] *Artisan entrepreneurs* normally have technical job experience, but may lack good communication skills and managerial training. An artisan entrepreneur's approach to business decision making is often characterized by the following features:

- They are paternalistic—they guide their businesses much as they might guide their own families.
- They are reluctant to delegate authority.
- They use few (usually only one or two) capital sources to create their firms.
- They define marketing strategy in terms of the traditional components of price, quality, and company reputation.
- Their sales efforts are primarily personal.
- Their time orientation is short, with little planning for future growth or change.

artisan entrepreneur A person with primarily technical skills and little business knowledge who starts a business.

A mechanic who starts an independent garage, a beautician who operates a beauty shop, or a painter who opens a studio are examples of artisan entrepreneurs.

In contrast to the artisan entrepreneur, an *opportunistic entrepreneur* is one who has supplemented his or her technical education with the study of such nontechnical subjects as economics, law, or history. Opportunistic entrepreneurs generally avoid paternalism, delegate authority as necessary for growth, employ various marketing strategies and types of sales efforts, obtain original financing from more than two sources, and plan for future growth. An example of an opportunistic entrepreneur is a small building contractor and developer who adopts a relatively sophisticated approach to management, including detailed accounting and budgeting, precise bidding, and systematic marketing research.

opportunistic entrepreneur A person with both sophisticated managerial skills and technical knowledge who starts a business.

Smith's description of entrepreneurial styles illustrates two extremes: At one end is a craftsperson in an entrepreneurial position, and at the other end is a well-educated and experienced manager. The former "flies by the seat of the pants," and the latter uses systematic management procedures and something resembling a "scientific" approach. In practice, of course, the distribution of entrepreneurial styles is less polarized than that suggested by Smith's model, with entrepreneurs scattered along a continuum of managerial sophistication. This book is intended to help you move toward the opportunistic end of the continuum and away from the artisan end.

Women Entrepreneurs

Although entrepreneurship and business have historically been male dominated for decades, the scene has changed. More women are now starting new businesses than are men! Women are majority owners of 10.1 million firms, which is 40 percent of all U.S. companies. They employ 13 million people and generate nearly $2 trillion in annual sales. Exhibit 1-3 presents the dramatic change that occurred in a mere two years, from 2006 to 2008.

In 2008, the largest number of these women-owned firms was in retailing and the service sector; however, wholesalers generated the largest amount of revenues, over $400 billion. An increasing number of women are starting firms in nontraditional industries. In fact, some of the fastest-growing companies in construction, manufacturing, and computer services are now owned by women.

Female business owners obviously face problems common to all entrepreneurs. However, they must also contend with difficulties related to gender. For instance, a lack of access to credit

EXHIBIT

	2006	2008	Percentage Increase
Number of firms	7.7 million	10.1 million	31%
Sales	$1.1 trillion	$2 trillion	82%
Number of employees	7.2 million	13 million	81%
Percentage of all U.S. firms	30%	40%	33%

Source: Center for Women's Business Research, http://www.cfwbr.org/national/index.php, accessed January 31, 2007; and "New Numbers Show Women-Owned Firms Comprise Forty Percent of All Firms," Center for Women's Business Research, September 11, 2008, pp. 2 and 3, http://www.womensbusinessresearch.org, accessed September 30, 2008.

has been a common problem for women who enter business. This is a troublesome area for most small business owners, but women often carry the added burden of discrimination. Another barrier for some women is the limited opportunity they find for forming business relationships with others in similar positions. It takes time and effort to gain full acceptance and to develop informal relationships with others in local, male-dominated business and professional groups. And for women with families, the unending juggling act mentioned by Chia Stewart earlier in the chapter is more likely to be a challenge. But in the opinion of Leslie O'Connor, owner of Search Wizards Inc. in Atlanta, Georgia, this can actually be an advantage:

LIVING THE DREAM:

entrepreneurial experiences

Stand Your Ground

Heidi Smith Price might speak in a soft voice, but she's definitely loud enough to be heard. In fact, at only 29 years old, she has established a notable presence in a male-dominated industry. "You hardly see any women in the construction industry, much less the industrial industry," says Smith Price, who has grown her heavy industrial contractor business, Spartan Constructors LLC, from a mere $100,000 in revenue in 2003 to a projected $150 million in 2008, landing her securely at the top of this year's list of the 50 fastest-growing women-led companies.

In 2004, Smith Price bought majority partnership in the Sugar Hill, Georgia-based business and was up for the challenges that it presented, namely, earning respect from her peers. "You just have to stand your ground and not let other people walk all over you," says Smith Price, who has focused instead on the opportunities that she knew lay beneath the surface. She immediately certified her company as a Women's Business Enterprise and was thereby able to open up her business to major contracting opportunities. This simple decision has allowed her to enjoy substantial growth over the past four years—at a rate faster than even she thought possible.

And while many might find the turf unfamiliar, it's been Smith Price's stomping ground ever since she was a young girl learning the ins and outs of her father's construction company. That experience as his executive assistant prepared Smith Price well for her role today, which requires that she wear many hats to get the job done. This level of competency, coupled with high standards for quality control and attention to safety, has won over major clients such as Georgia Power and Southern Co.

Source: Sara Wilson, "Leading Ladies," *Entrepreneur Magazine*, November 2008, p. 64.

Be a great juggler. As a woman in business, you will always have lots of balls in the air, including the activities of running your business and being strategic in your decisions to grow your business. In many cases, [you also have] the role of being a wife, a mother, a daughter and a sister. The same traits that make us great in all of these roles are the ones that you will rely on to excel in business.[24]

Entrepreneurial Teams

Our discussion thus far has focused on entrepreneurs who function as individuals, each with his or her own firm, which is frequently the case. However, entrepreneurial teams are becoming increasingly common, particularly in ventures of any substantial size. An *entrepreneurial team* consists of two or more individuals who combine their efforts to function in the capacity of entrepreneurs. In this way, the talents, skills, and resources of two or more entrepreneurs can be concentrated on one endeavor. This very important form of entrepreneurship is discussed at greater length in Chapter 8.

entrepreneurial team
Two or more people who work together as entrepreneurs on one endeavor.

The Competitive Edge of Entrepreneurs

As emphasized at the outset of this chapter, small entrepreneurial businesses are a robust part of the total economy. For this to happen, small companies must compete effectively with firms of all sizes, including large, publicly owned companies.

5. Identify five potential competitive advantages of small entrepreneurial companies as compared to large firms.

How is it that small and entrepreneurial firms can hold their own and often gain an edge over successful, more powerful businesses? The answer lies in the ability of new and smaller firms to exploit opportunities. If a business can make its product or service "cheaper, faster, and better," then it can be competitive. Small companies—if well managed—have just as much ability as larger firms to develop strategies that offer a competitive advantage.

In this section, we will take a look at some ways in which new firms can gain a competitive advantage. In Chapter 3, we'll elaborate on strategies for exploiting these potential advantages and capturing the business opportunities they make possible.

Customer Focus

Business opportunities exist for those who can produce products and services desired by customers. Small companies are particularly adept at competing when they commit to a strong customer focus. Good customer service can be provided by a business of any size; however, in many instances, small businesses have a greater potential than larger firms do to achieve this goal. If properly managed, small entrepreneurial companies have the advantage of being able to serve customers directly and effectively, without struggling through layers of bureaucracy or breaking corporate policies that tend to stifle employee initiative. In many cases, customers are personally acquainted with the entrepreneur and other key people in the small business.

Not all small enterprises manage to excel in customer service, but many realize their potential for doing so. Having a smaller number of customers and a close relationship with them makes customer service a powerful tool for entrepreneurial businesses. For further discussion of this subject, see Chapter 14.

Quality Performance

There is no reason that a small business needs to take a back seat when it comes to achieving quality in operations. We talk to owners of small businesses frequently who not only have operations equal in quality to larger firms, but in fact surpass the quality performance of the giants.

Perhaps no finer examples can be found of quality performance than MFI International owned by Cecilia Levine in El Paso, Texas, and J&S Construction owned by Jack and Johnny Stites in Cookville, Tennessee. These two businesses, one a manufacturer and the other a general contractor, do not take second place to anyone when it comes to quality performance. When you visit their companies, you can feel their commitment to quality. It is a part of their DNA. In fact, they can insist on high levels of quality without experiencing the frustration of a large-company CEO who may have to push a quality philosophy through many layers of bureaucracy.

In short, quality is mostly independent of firm size, but if there is an advantage, it most often goes to the smaller business—a surprise to most people. So as a small business owner, you do not and should not have to accept anything less than the highest-quality performance. An uncompromising commitment to quality will move you a long way down the road toward having a competitive advantage relative to other firms in your industry.

Integrity and Responsibility

In order to maintain a strong competitive advantage, it is essential that you add to good customer service and excellent product quality a solid reputation for honesty and dependability. In fact, the quickest way to lose a competitive advantage is to act without regard for others, or worse, to act dishonestly. We all respond positively to evidence of integrity because we all have, at times, been taken advantage of when buying a product or service. Experience has taught us that advertising claims are sometimes not accurate, that the fine print in contracts often runs counter to our best interests, and that businesses sometimes fail to stand behind their work.

Jeffry Timmons[25] and Stephen Spinelli, nationally recognized entrepreneurship researchers at Babson College, conducted a study of 128 presidents/founders who were attending a management program at Harvard Business School. The participants were asked to identify the most critical concepts, skills, and know-how for success at their companies. Interestingly, 72 percent of the respondents stated that the single most important factor in long-term success was high ethical standards.[26]

Consistently operating with integrity can set a small business apart as being trustworthy at a time when stories of corporate greed and corruption abound. Above all else, the core values of the entrepreneur, as reflected in what that individual says and how he or she acts, determine the culture within a business. Chapter 2 discusses the critical importance of integrity and its role in entrepreneurship.

Innovation and Globalization

How the world is changing! When Bill Clinton was elected president in 1992, hardly anyone—with the exception of a small number of people in the government and academia—had e-mail. In his book *The World Is Flat*, Thomas Friedman describes the convergence of ten forces that have "flattened" the world.[27] Friedman's contention that the world is flat means that anything can now be done from anywhere in the world. Individuals, not governments or large corporations, are driving the globalization that we are experiencing all around us, Friedman says. Innovation, both in products or services and in ways to be more competitive, is within the reach of the small business in ways that were not thought possible a few years ago.

New product innovation often comes from the world of small business. Most of the radical inventions of the last century, such as the computer and the pacemaker, came from small companies, not large ones. And this will not change.

Research departments of big businesses tend to emphasize the improvement of existing products. Creative ideas may be sidetracked because they are not related to existing product lines or because they are unusual. But preoccupation with an existing product can obscure the value of a new idea. Scott Anthony, co-author of *Seeing What's Next*, says, "The thing that's so tricky is that everything an established company is trained to do—watch your markets carefully, listen to your best customers, innovate to meet their needs—oftentimes causes them to miss some of these disruptive transformation trends."[28]

The notion that entrepreneurs are good at developing others' ideas is described by Amar Bhide, a noted business researcher at Columbia University, when he discusses the role of entrepreneurs in innovation. He advises us not to equate innovation with technological breakthroughs and scientists in white coats, because few small businesses can afford the luxury of spending large amounts of money on research and development (R&D). Instead, he contends they are more capable in taking inventions or innovations developed elsewhere and putting them into use, which requires marketing, sales, and organization.[29] In Bhide's opinion, these latter activities are just as much innovation as creating something in a science lab. The mere fact that a small business is not "high tech" should not mean that it is not innovative. It may be just the opposite.

The bureaucracy within larger firms can also cause the delay or even the death of new ideas. Most large companies insist on a lengthy process for approving new ideas. That often is not the case at smaller companies. As observed by Luda Kopeikina, president of the Equinox Corporation (a firm that advises companies on innovation processes), "Entrepreneurs excel at creating new ideas, and that's a big advantage. Very rarely do you see large companies good at innovation, creating ideas and ramping them up. That, by its nature, creates opportunity for small companies."[30]

Globalization, encouraged by both access to technology and international offshoring, has also helped smaller firms compete. The Internet has helped to level the global playing field, allowing small companies to connect with individuals anywhere in the world in the blink of an eye. Sophisticated computer software, once accessible only to large businesses, is now available at prices small companies can afford. The liability of "smallness" is fading.

Offshoring is a recent phenomenon that has allowed small companies to be competitive. In a *Business Week* cover story on outsourcing, Pete Engardio, Michael Arndt, and Dean Foust observe, "Creative new companies can exploit the possibilities of offshoring even faster than established players." The authors hold up Crimson Consulting Group as a good example of this. The firm, with only 14 full-time employees, provides global market research on everything from routers to software. It farms out research to 5,000 independent experts all around the world. Crimson's CEO, Gleen Gow, comments, "This allows a small firm like us to compete with [giant consulting firms like] McKinsey and Bain on a very global basis with very low costs."[31]

Special Niche

Almost all small businesses try to shield themselves from competition by targeting a specific group of customers who have an identifiable but very narrow range of product or service interests, or what is called a *niche market*. The niche might consist of a uniquely specialized product or service, or it might be a focus on serving a particular geographical area.

niche market
A market segment identified by an identifiable but narrow range of product or service interests.

By finding a special niche, a small business may avoid intense competition from large corporations. In Chapter 3, much more will be said about the use of niche markets by small businesses as a way to capture a competitive edge.

The bottom line: Smaller firms have no reason to despair about not being competitive in an innovative world. They often lead in developing new and different products and services, they are frequently an equal beneficiary of new technologies with large companies, and they are uniquely positioned to capture niche markets.

Getting Started

S tarting any type of business career is exciting. Launching one's own business, however, can be far more demanding because of the risk and great potential of such a venture. Let's think for a moment about some special concerns of individuals who are ready to get their feet wet in the exciting waters of entrepreneurship.

Age and Entrepreneurial Opportunity

One practical question is, what is the right age to become an entrepreneur? As you might guess, there is no correct answer to this question. The driving factor is not so much age as it is a matter of knowledge and experience. As a general rule, you will need to know and understand the industry you plan to enter, as well as the finances and operations of the business you hope to launch. For example, Jody Hall worked for Starbucks for 12 years before starting Vérité Coffee in 2003. During her time at Starbucks, she had the opportunity to observe Howard Schultz, Starbucks' founder. Hall worked her way up to the position of Starbucks' head of promotions and events for new stores, and she explained, "I learned a lot about the coffeehouse experience through Schultz and his vision."[32]

Most prospective entrepreneurs must also accumulate at least some of the financial resources needed to launch a business. Sometimes they have the impression that startups are financed with bank loans and money provided by venture capitalists. As we will learn later, nothing could be further from the truth. New ventures are financed mostly with a founder's personal savings. This may then be followed by money from friends and family, based largely on personal relationship and not on the merits of the venture. Thus, having enough time to accumulate startup money is an important factor in determining when you will be able to start a new business.

Though the timing will vary according to individual circumstances, conventional wisdom suggests that the ideal age to start a business is between the late 20s and the early 40s, when there is a balance between preparatory experiences on the one hand and family obligations on the other. Research conducted by Paul Reynolds shows that the highest percentage of new ventures are launched by entrepreneurs in the 25 to 35-year age group.[33] As Tyler Self, co-founder of Vision Research Organization, observes, "It's about the tradeoff between confidence usually characterized by youth and wisdom based on experience."[34]

Given both the conventional wisdom and the research findings, the demographic group called the Generation Xers, those born between 1965 and 1980, would be in their prime for starting and growing new businesses. And according to Tamer Erikso, in an article appearing in *Business Week*, they are doing just that. Erikso contends that this age group is pursuing entrepreneurial opportunities more than ever. In her words:

> Xers want jobs that offer a variety of career paths and allow them to gain fresh, marketable skills, build a strong network of contacts, and put money in the bank. . . . Xers aspire to run their own entrepreneurial ventures.[35]

But conventional wisdom goes only so far. There are plenty who are younger and older who aspire just as strongly to own their own businesses, such as Generation Y, the Millennials or twenty-somethings. As a group, Millennials are usually portrayed as impatient, spoiled, and self-centered, but they are actually creating a new breed of entrepreneurs. Almost 80 million strong, they will make up the largest, the most educated, and the most diverse generation in American history, which in turn suggests that no one has a better understanding of this group than those who belong to it. As entrepreneurs, they have been described as follows:[36]

- They have no fear of technology. Many of them cannot even recall life before the Internet.
- They are idealistic and optimistic, which in turn influences their perceptions about business.

- They are far more collaborative than their predecessors. The idea of being a solo entrepreneur holds little attraction to them. Instead, they start businesses with partners, if not entire teams.

- They frequently build elements of community into their businesses. For example, Matt Mullenweg's wildly successful software company, Automattic, began as an open-source project to create better blogging software. A teen at the time and with no experience in software development, Mullenweg recruited volunteer coders who built, tested, and refined what has become WordPress—one of the most popular blogging platforms—all for no pay.

- Finally, they may start companies in dorm rooms while simultaneously studying entrepreneurship in the classroom. A number of colleges and universities have created funds to provide money to students for developing their ideas.

"One thing that differentiates the young founders is who they can connect with early on," says David Cohen, executive director of TechStars, a Boulder, Colorado, incubator that works with Millennial company founders. "People are starting companies at young ages. They fail fast, learn a lot, and keep going."[37]

At the other end of the age spectrum, we find an increasing number of 50- and 60-year-olds walking away from successful careers in big businesses when they become excited by the prospects of entrepreneurship and doing something on their own. Retirees who opt to start new careers as entrepreneurs often view retirement as an opportunity to pursue interests they never before had time for. More than the money, their new businesses offer them a chance to work on something they really want and love to do.

For instance, after a 30-year career as a magazine editor, Richard Busch decided to quit his job to pursue his passion for pottery. In his early 50s, Busch had started asking himself what his life would be when his magazine career ended and what it was that he really wanted to do in the years to come. Describing that stage in his life, Busch says, "The more I thought about it, the more I felt like I'd really like to be a potter. I set a timetable, which had me retire early, in my mid-late 50s. Then, as luck would have it, they offered me an [early retirement], at age 56." As a result, Glenfiddich Farm Pottery was born.[38]

So what is the ideal age to get into the game? It's when your passion, experience, and determination collide with an entrepreneurial opportunity.

Characteristics of Successful Entrepreneurs

What kinds of people become successful entrepreneurs? Clearly, no well-defined entrepreneurial profile exists; individual entrepreneurs differ greatly from each other. Knowing this should encourage you if you wish to start your own business: You do not need to fit some prescribed stereotype.

Some qualities, however, are common among entrepreneurs and probably contribute to their success. One of these characteristics is a strong commitment to or passion for the business. It is an attitude that results in tenacity in the face of difficulty and a willingness to work hard. Entrepreneurs do not give up easily.

Such individuals are typically confident of their ability to meet the challenges confronting them. This factor of self-confidence was described by psychologist J. B. Rotter as an *internal locus of control*—a feeling that success depends on one's own efforts.[39] In contrast, an *external locus of control* reflects an attitude of dependence on luck or fate for success.

Entrepreneurs are also portrayed as risk takers. Certainly, they do assume risk. By investing their own money, they assume financial risk. If they leave secure jobs, they risk their careers. Starting and running a business can place stress on the family. After all, when someone with a family starts and runs a business, the whole family is affected, which must be considered. Even though entrepreneurs assume risk, they are usually what we might term moderate risk takers—accepting risks over which they have some control. Also, it is interesting to see entrepreneurs who are so focused on the opportunity that they do not even think they are taking a risk.

internal locus of control
A belief that one's success depends on one's own efforts.

external locus of control
A belief that one's life is controlled more by luck or fate than by one's own efforts.

Timmons and Spinelli have summarized research on entrepreneurial characteristics. The entrepreneurs they describe as having and exhibiting "desirable and acquirable attitudes and behaviors" fall under the following six descriptions:[40]

1. *Commitment and determination* – tenacious, decisive, and persistent in problem solving.
2. *Leadership* – self-starters and team builders and focus on honesty in their business relationships.
3. *Opportunity obsession* – aware of market and customer needs.
4. *Tolerance of risk, ambiguity, and uncertainty* – risk takers, risk minimizers, and uncertainty tolerators.
5. *Creativity, self-reliance, and adaptability* – open-minded, flexible, uncomfortable with the status quo, and quick learners.
6. *Motivation to excel* – goal oriented and aware of personal strengths and weaknesses.

Looking at the other side of the coin, there are some attitudes and behaviors that should be avoided at all cost. An almost certain way to fail as an entrepreneur, and many have done so, is to do the following:

1. Overestimate what you can do
2. Lack an understanding of the market
3. Hire mediocre people
4. Fail to be a team player
5. Be a domineering manager
6. Not share ownership in the business in an equitable way

For the most part, this list describes a leader without humility. Contrary to popular belief, humility is a quality that serves leaders well. Scott Cook is the founder and CEO of Intuit, a computer software company that helps millions of consumers and businesses manage their financing, with products such as Quicken, QuickBooks, TurboTax, QuickBase, and Payroll. In his words, humility is an essential trait for any entrepreneur:

> The future belongs to humble leaders. Humble to let your people lead and be led by them. Humble to make the customer your boss. Humble to listen and listen intently. Humble to know that almost all of the best ideas come from others. Humble to admit you were wrong, and tell your team.[41]

The Importance of Mentors

Although there are many different types of entrepreneurs, most have one thing in common— they have found mentors along the way.

mentor
A knowledgeable person who can offer guidance from their experience in a given field.

As you begin and continue on the entrepreneurial journey, you can make no better decision than to find mentors who can show you the way. *Mentors* are individuals to whom you can go for advice and counsel—people who are pulling for you, wanting you to succeed, and supporting your efforts. They are people who can teach you what to do and how to do it and, most important, encourage you on those days when you want to throw in the towel. These "coaches" can show you how to avoid mistakes and be there to give you the benefit of their years of experience.

Although we strongly emphasize the importance of having good mentors, only you can develop these vital relationships. We can, however, provide you with insights from individuals who have traveled the road you hope to take. We have created what we call a "Go-To Team," whose experience-based knowledge will be showcased in the "How I See It" feature, which you will find throughout this textbook. You will be reading not only our perspective as co-authors of this text, but also that of a number of successful entrepreneurs. The members of the "Go-To Team" are introduced in the chapter appendix.

How I see it: Rick Davis on Mentoring

At different points in the book, our *Go-To Team* will share how mentors have played a role in their lives, especially relating to their entrepreneurial aspirations. Here, Rick Davis, founder and CEO of Davaco, Inc., explains how influential and important a mentor's guidance, help, and encouragement can be.

My number-one mentor and the person who has had the biggest influence on my professional career was my father, Charles "Skip" Davis. While both my father and my mother served as role models in many areas throughout my life, it was my father who nurtured my entrepreneurial spirit. He led by example through his own professional accomplishments and supported me—financially, emotionally, and spiritually.

Like my father, I served as a fireman, and, like him, I chose to take advantage of my "off-days" to venture into other business opportunities. He delved into plumbing and eventually started his own insurance company, while my interest was in real estate and construction.

Like many young men with an entrepreneurial spirit, I had a vision, but I didn't have the capital to make it all happen. Without my dad to co-sign my first $4,500 loan, I could not have financed my first HUD renovation project. In effect, his signature launched my career. Later, as I set my sights on multi-family apartment complexes, my dad was there to co-sign for me again. Obviously, this was a significant investment that could have resulted in financial ruin. Fortunately, that particular project turned a profit for both of us. His ongoing guidance and leadership throughout that project, as well as his support, demonstrated incredible faith in my abilities. This blend of risk taking, hard work, and trust ultimately gave me the confidence I needed to be successful.

My dad taught me values and skills that make for both an entrepreneur and a great person; do what you say you are going to do, never settle for anything less than the best, and learn from your mistakes and your triumphs.

Success in Business and Success in Life

So far, we have discussed entrepreneurship and small business from a number of angles. As you contemplate such a direction yourself, we now urge you to broaden your perspective. As aptly expressed by author and very seasoned entrepreneur Norm Brodsky,

7. Explain the concept of an entrepreneurial legacy and the challenges involved in crafting a worthy legacy.

Building a successful business is not an end in itself. It is a means to an end. It is a way to create a better life for you and those whom you love, however you—and they—may define it. You need to do the life plan first and then keep revisiting it, to make sure it's up to date and your business plan is helping you achieve it. That habit, I can assure you, will prove to be the most important of them all.[42]

When an entrepreneur makes that final exit from the entrepreneurial stage, his or her business achievements become history. Reflecting on their lives and businesses at that point in their journeys, many entrepreneurs have come face to face with questions such as: Was it a good trip?

What kind of meaning does it hold for me now? Can I feel good about it? What are my disappointments? How did I make a difference? Such questions lead entrepreneurs to reassess their values, priorities, and commitments. By anticipating these questions well in advance, an entrepreneur can identify his or her most basic concerns early in the journey. Without reflection, the entrepreneurial journey and its ending are much more likely to prove disappointing.

Beginning with the End in Mind

The criteria by which one evaluates entrepreneurship must be personal. Stephen R. Covey in *The Seven Habits of Highly Successful People* suggests that the most effective way "to begin with the end in mind" is to develop a personal mission statement or philosophy or creed.[43] Though individuals will have different mission statements because their goals and values will vary, widely shared values will underlie many of their judgments.

An entrepreneur builds a business, a life, and a legacy day by day, starting with the initial launch and proceeding through the months and years of operation that follow. A person exiting an entrepreneurial venture has completed the business part of his or her legacy—it must be constructed during the life of the enterprise itself.

EVALUATING ACCOMPLISHMENTS To achieve a positive outcome for the venture, entrepreneurial performance requires establishing criteria for assessment of progress. Obviously, no single criterion can be applied. For example, a person who measures everything by the dollar sign would determine the degree of an entrepreneur's success by the size of his or her bank account. However, we believe that most entrepreneurs will eventually think about achievements in terms of personal values and goals, rather than textbook criteria, popular culture, or financial rules of thumb. In all likelihood, a number of basic considerations will be relevant to the entrepreneur's sense of satisfaction.

Winning the Wrong Game

In the search for success, it is easy for entrepreneurs to get caught up in an activity trap, working harder and harder to keep up with the busy pace of life. Ultimately, such entrepreneurs may find their business accomplishments overshadowed by the neglect or sacrifice of something more important to them. It's possible to score points in the wrong game or win battles in the wrong war.

This type of entrepreneurial error produces a disappointing legacy, a sense that one's professional achievements are to some extent inadequate. Consider what happens, for example, when the legitimate goal of earning money becomes a consuming passion. The CEO of a former Inc. 500 company has critiqued the entrepreneurial experience in this way:

> I believe that when our companies fail to satisfy our fundamental need to contribute to the community and instead exist predominantly to fill a bank account, then we lose our souls. Life is short. No one's gravestone reads, "He made a lot of money." Making a difference in your own life, your employees' lives, and your customers' lives is the real payoff.[44]

Ed Bonneau revolutionized the distribution of sunglasses in the United States and eventually dominated that market with his highly successful business. Then, Bonneau sold the business and walked away from it all. From a business standpoint, his was a huge entrepreneurial success story. However, in a comment on how he'd like to be remembered, Bonneau downplayed his financial wealth:

> I would hope that they knew something else besides that I once ran the biggest sunglass company in the world. That's not the number one thing that I'd want to be known for. It's okay, but I'd much rather have that final assessment made by my kids and have them say, "He was a terrific dad." I never wanted to sacrifice my family or my church for my business.[45]

And Bonneau's advice to younger entrepreneurs follows a similar theme:

> Take God and your family with you when you go into business, and keep that balance in your life. Because when you get to be 60 years old and you look back over your life, if all you have is the biggest sunglass company in the world and a pot full of money in the bank . . . it won't be enough. Your life is going to be hollow, and you can't go back and redo it.[46]

Entrepreneurs typically work very long hours, especially in the beginning, and sometimes their obsession with work and the business can become extreme. Based on interviews with repeat entrepreneurs, Ilan Mochari summarized their reports of early mistakes: "If they had it to do all over again, most of the group would have spent more time away from their first companies, hanging with the family, schmoozing up other CEOs, and pondering the long-term picture."[47]

An excessive focus on money or work, then, can twist the entrepreneurial process. The outcome appears less satisfying and less rewarding when the time for exit arrives.

Crafting a Worthy Legacy

In anticipating this time of looking back, one should think in terms of a legacy. A legacy consists of those things passed on or left behind. In a narrow sense, it describes material possessions bequeathed to one's heirs. In a broader sense, it refers to everything that one leaves behind—material items, good or bad family relationships, and a record of integrity or greed, a history of exploitation or contribution. An *entrepreneurial legacy* includes both tangible items and intangible qualities passed on not only to heirs but also to the broader society. One can appreciate, then, the seriousness with which the entrepreneur needs to consider the kind of legacy he or she is building.

In entrepreneurial terms, what constitutes a worthy legacy? One aspect is the nature of the endeavor itself. A business that operates within the law, provides jobs, and serves the public provides a good foundation for a satisfying entrepreneurial experience. A business that peddles pornography on the Internet might make a lot of money for its owner, but most people would dismiss it as an unworthy enterprise because of its harmful effects.

Bernard Rapaport, a highly successful, principled, and generous entrepreneur, has stressed the importance of the means one takes to achieve a given end. "Whatever it is you want to achieve," he said, "how you achieve it is more important than if you achieve it." At 93 years of age, reflecting on life and legacy, he said, "What do I want to do? I want to save the world."[48]

Such idealism can guide an entrepreneur into many endeavors that are useful to our economic system. In fact, some entrepreneurial ventures are specifically designed to meet the particular needs of society. J. O. Stewart, a successful entrepreneur, has in his later years launched a firm whose primary objective is to provide good, low-cost housing to families who cannot otherwise afford it. His motivation for this venture is personal concern for the needs of low-income families.

For most entrepreneurs looking back on their careers, fulfillment requires that their businesses have been constructive or positive in their impact—at the least, their effect should have been benign, causing no harm to the social order. In most cases, entrepreneurial businesses make positive contributions by providing jobs and services. A few add the additional contribution of addressing special needs in society.

Thus, an entrepreneur needs to keep the end in mind while making the innumerable operating decisions throughout the process. By selecting the proper values and wisely balancing their application, an entrepreneur can make a satisfying exit, leaving a positive and substantial legacy to heirs, employees, the community, and the broader society.

entrepreneurial legacy
Material assets and intangible qualities passed on to both heirs and society.

Where to from Here

An airplane pilot not only controls the plane during takeoff but also flies it and lands it. Similarly, entrepreneurs not only launch firms but also "fly" them; that is, they manage their firm's subsequent operation. In this book, you will find a discussion of the entire entrepreneurial process. It begins in the remainder of Part 1 (Chapter 2) with a discussion of the fundamental values of the entrepreneur. This discussion is followed in Parts 2 and 3, which look at a firm's basic strategy, the various types of entrepreneurial ventures, and the initial planning that is required for business startups. Parts 4 through 6 deal with the marketing and management of a growing business, including its human resources, operations, and finances.

LOOKING BACK

1. Distinguish between an entrepreneur and a small business owner.

- Entrepreneurs are individuals who discover market needs and launch new firms to meet those needs.
- Owner-managers who buy out founders of existing firms, franchisees, and second-generation operators of family firms may also be considered entrepreneurs.
- Definitions of *small business* are arbitrary, but this book focuses on firms that are significantly smaller compared to the industry that have mostly localized operations and are financed by a small number of individuals.

2. Explain the characteristics of entrepreneurial opportunities and give examples of successful businesses started by entrepreneurs.

- Entrepreneurial opportunities exist for those who can produce enough products or services desired by customers to make the enterprise economically attractive.
- An entrepreneurial opportunity is an economically attractive and timely opportunity that creates value for prospective customers as well as the firm's owners.
- Exciting entrepreneurial opportunities exist for those who recognize them. However, a true opportunity exists only for those who have the interest, resources, and capabilities required to succeed.
- Resources for an entrepreneurial opportunity include (1) people such as suppliers, customers, accountants, lawyers, and board members, (2) assets, such as inventories equipment and buildings, and (3) the needed capital to finance the venture.

- Table Occasions, Life Is Good, and The FruitGuys are examples of highly successful businesses started by entrepreneurs.

3. Describe some motivators or rewards of entrepreneurial careers.

- One of the primary reasons for becoming an entrepreneur is to make the world a better place (make meaning).
- Important secondary attractions to entrepreneurship are profit, independence, freedom (escaping from a bad situation), personal satisfaction, and personal fulfillment (contributing to one's community).

4. Identify the various types of entrepreneurs and entrepreneurial ventures.

- Founders of firms are "pure" entrepreneurs, but those who acquire established businesses and franchisees may also be considered entrepreneurs.
- A few entrepreneurs start high-potential ventures (gazelles); other entrepreneurs operate attractive small firms and microbusinesses (lifestyle businesses).
- Based on their backgrounds and management styles, entrepreneurs may be characterized as artisan entrepreneurs or opportunistic entrepreneurs.
- The number of women entrepreneurs is growing rapidly, and they are entering many nontraditional fields.
- Entrepreneurial teams consist of two or more individuals who combine their efforts to function as entrepreneurs.

5. Identify five potential competitive advantages of small entrepreneurial companies as compared to large firms.

- Customer focus: entrepreneurial managers have an opportunity to know their customers well and to focus on meeting their needs.
- Quality performance: by emphasizing quality in products and services, small firms can build a competitive advantage.
- Integrity and responsibility: independent business owners can build an internal culture based on integrity and responsibility in relationships both inside and outside the firm; such a culture helps strengthen the firm's position in a competitive environment.
- Innovation and globalization: many small firms and individual operators have demonstrated a superior talent for finding innovative products and developing better ways of doing business in the global marketplace.
- Special niche: small firms that find a special niche of some type can gain an advantage in the marketplace.

6. Discuss factors related to readiness for entrepreneurship and getting started in an entrepreneurial career.

- The period between the late 20s and early 40s appears to be when a person's education (knowledge), work experience, family situation, and financial resources are most likely to enable him or her to become an entrepreneur.

- Many of the Millennial group, or Generation Y, are proving to be effective entrepreneurs, in spite of their young age.
- There is no well-defined entrepreneurial profile, but many entrepreneurs have such helpful characteristics as a passion for their business, strong self-confidence, and a willingness to assume moderate risks.
- Successful entrepreneurs are also thought to possess leadership skills, a strong focus on opportunities, creativity and adaptability, and motivation to excel.
- Entrepreneurs can make no better decision than to develop relationships with mentors who can provide advice and counsel.

7. Explain the concept of an entrepreneurial legacy and the challenges involved in crafting a worthy legacy.

- An entrepreneur's legacy includes not only money and material possessions but also nonmaterial things such as personal relationships and values.
- Part of the legacy is the contribution of the business to the community.
- A worthy legacy includes a good balance of values and principles important to the entrepreneur. Errors in choosing or applying goals and values can create a defective legacy.
- Building a legacy is an ongoing process that begins at the launch of the firm and continues throughout its operating life.

Key Terms

entrepreneur p. 5

small business p. 5

entrepreneurial opportunity p. 6

bootstrapping p. 6

reluctant entrepreneur p. 12

refugee p. 12

founder p. 14

franchisee p. 14

high-potential venture (gazelle) p. 14

attractive small firm p. 14

microbusiness p. 14

lifestyle business p. 14

artisan entrepreneur p. 15

opportunistic entrepreneur p. 15

entrepreneurial team p. 17

niche market p. 19

internal locus of control p. 21

external locus of control p. 21

mentor p. 22

entrepreneurial legacy p. 25

Discussion Questions

1. The outstanding success stories discussed at the beginning of the chapter are exceptions to the rule. What, then, is their significance in illustrating entrepreneurial opportunity? Are these stories misleading?

2. What is meant by the term *entrepreneur*?

3. Consider an entrepreneur you know personally. What was the most significant reason for his or her deciding to follow an independent business career? If you don't already know the reason, discuss it with that person.

4. The motivators/rewards of profit, independence, and personal satisfaction are three reasons individuals enter entrepreneurial careers. What problems might be anticipated if an entrepreneur were to become obsessed with one of these rewards—for example, if she or he had an excessive desire to accumulate

wealth, operate independently, or achieve a particular lifestyle?

5. Distinguish between an artisan entrepreneur and an opportunistic entrepreneur.

6. What is the advantage of using an entrepreneurial team?

7. Explain how customer focus and innovation can be special strengths of small businesses.

8. Why is the period from the late 20s to the early 40s considered to be the best time in life to become an entrepreneur?

9. Explain the concept of an entrepreneurial legacy.

10. Explain the following statement: "One can climb the ladder to success only to discover it is leaning against the wrong wall."

You Make the Call

SITUATION 1

In the following statement, a business owner attempts to explain and justify his preference for slow growth in his business.

I limit my growth pace and make every effort to service my present customers in the manner they deserve. I have some peer pressure to do otherwise by following the advice of experts—that is, to take on partners and debt to facilitate rapid growth in sales and market share. When tempted by such thoughts, I think about what I might gain. Perhaps I could make more money, but I would also expect a lot more problems. Also, I think it might interfere somewhat with my family relationships, which are very important to me.

Question 1 Should this venture be regarded as entrepreneurial? Is the owner a true entrepreneur?

Question 2 Do you agree with the philosophy expressed here? Is the owner really doing what is best for his family?

Question 3 What kinds of problems is this owner trying to avoid?

SITUATION 2

Nineteen-year-old Kiersten Berger, now in her second year at a local community college, has begun to think about starting her own business. She has taken piano lessons since she was seven years old and is regarded as a very good pianist. The thought has occurred to her that she could establish a piano studio and offer lessons to children, young people, and even adults. The prospect sounds more attractive than looking for a salaried job when she graduates in a few months.

Question 1 If Kiersten Berger opens a piano studio, will she be an entrepreneur?

Question 2 Which type of reward(s) will be greatest in this venture?

Question 3 Even though she is an artisan, she will need to make decisions of a business nature. What decisions or evaluations may be especially difficult for her?

SITUATION 3

Dover Sporting Goods Store occupies an unimpressive retail location in a small city in northern Illinois. Started in 1935, it is now operated by Duane Dover—a third-generation member of the founding family. He works long hours trying to earn a reasonable profit in the old downtown area.

Dover's immediate concern is an announcement that Walmart is considering opening a store at the southern edge of town. As Dover reacts to this announcement, he is overwhelmed by a sense of injustice. Why should a family business that has served the community honestly and well for 60 years have to fend off a large corporation that would take big profits out of the community and give very little in return? Surely, he reasons, the law must offer some kind of protection against big business predators of this kind. Dover also wonders whether small stores such as his have ever been successful in competing against business giants like Walmart.

Question 1 Is Dover's feeling of unfairness justified? Is his business entitled to some type of legal protection against moves of this type?

Question 2 How should Dover plan to compete against Walmart, if and when this becomes necessary?

Experiential Exercises

1. Analyze your own education and experience as qualifications for entrepreneurship. Identify your greatest strengths and weaknesses.

2. Explain your own interest in each type of entrepreneurial reward. Point out which type of incentive is most significant for you personally and explain why.

3. Interview someone who has started a business, being sure to ask for information regarding the entrepreneur's background and age at the time the business was started. In your report of the interview, indicate whether the entrepreneur was in any sense a refugee, and show how the timing of her or his startup relates to the ideal time for startup explained in this chapter.

4. Interview a woman entrepreneur about what problems, if any, she has encountered in her business because she is a woman.

Small Business & Entrepreneurship Resource Center

The Small Business and Entrepreneurship Resource Center offers complete small business management resources through a comprehensive database that covers all major areas of starting, operating, and maintaining a business from financing, management, marketing, accounting, taxes, and more. Use the access code that came with your new book to access the site and perform the exercises in each chapter.

Sherwood T. "Woody" Phifer, who builds handcrafted guitars, exemplifies the artisan entrepreneur. His business success rests on his extraordinary skill in building outstanding electric and acoustic guitars. As a child, if he wanted a toy that he could not afford or find, he would simply make his own. His childhood helped to prepare him for his career.

Describe how his ability to create, along with his fascination to take things apart and build them, have helped him to differentiate his business from large guitar competitors, such as Fender and Gibson.

Sources: Guitar man: his instruments have resounding curves. (Career At A Glance). Sonia Alleyne. *Black Enterprise* 33, 9 (April 2003): p. 64.

Case 1

NAU (P. 623)
Several business associates in the clothing industry start a new clothing company, knowing that the world did not need just another clothing business. Thus, they develop a business model that is unique, combining profits and social responsibility.

ALTERNATIVE CASES FOR CHAPTER 1
Case 9, Le Travel Store, p. 641
Case 15, Country Supply, p. 656

Following are descriptions of the entrepreneurs whose advice on starting and running a small business will appear in this feature throughout the text. Their perspectives are based on years of experience. Pay attention to them!

SARA BLAKELY
- Started SPANX, a leader in the shapewear revolution, with $5,000 in savings and had grown the company to $150 million in retail sales in 2006
- Launched The Sara Blakely Foundation, which is dedicated to supporting and empowering women around the world
- Launched ASSETS by Sara Blakely, a brand exclusive to Target
- Named Ernst & Young's Southeast Regional Entrepreneur of the Year
- Named Georgia's Woman of the Year

RICK DAVIS
- Formed his first company, Rick Davis Properties, at the age of 25
- Instrumental in startup of First Interstate National Bank in Dallas, Texas
- Founder and CEO of Davaco, Inc., the nation's number-one turn-key retail service provider and technology leader, with double-digit average annual growth
- Inducted into the 2006 Retail Construction Hall of Fame
- Finalist for the Ernst & Young Entrepreneur of the Year award in 2000 and 2006
- Member of the Salvation Army's Dallas/Fort Worth Metroplex Advisory Board

DENNY FULK
- President of Fulk Equipment Company, Inc., a provider of storage and distribution systems to multinational companies
- Managing partner for Hunters Row Properties, an industrial park real estate project
- Began second career as Director of Business Strategies for Keyway Associates in 2000, focusing on sharing principles of the free enterprise system and modeling ethical business leadership for Asian businesspersons
- Chairman of the Board of Trustees at Milligan College
- Only American trustee of the Springdale College Charitable Trust for Educational and Training Development in Birmingham, England

CECILIA LEVINE
- President of MFI International Mfg., LLC, a provider of manufacturing, warehousing, distribution, and consulting services, with locations in Mexico and the United States

- Member of the President's Export Council
- Founder, director, and president of the US/Mexico Strategic Alliance
- Founding member of the Midland, Texas, Hispanic Chamber of Commerce
- Small Business Association's 2007 Exporter of the Year
- USHCC Regional and National Hispanic Business Woman of the Year

SCOTT J. SALMANS
- Business development officer and events producer for the Greater Waco Chamber of Commerce
- President of WRS Group Ltd., the largest provider of supplemental teaching aids for health educators, operating under the brand names of HealthEdco, Childbirth Graphics, and Special/Health Impressions. Additional rapid growth as contract manufacturer for companies such as Gel Pro and Shadow Cast MBA 2003 University of Missouri Kansas City Vision and Strategy planning and implementation for nonprofit organizations
- Founder of SJS Family Enterprises, an umbrella entity for real estate and other small business ventures
- Chairman of the capital campaign for the New Life Children's Home in Guatemala
- Member of Baylor Development Council

JOHN (JOHNNY) STITES, II
- CEO of J&S Construction Company, Inc., a small, family-owned company
- Recognized by the Tennessee Center for Performance Excellence for his strategic approach to building a business and focus on risk reduction in the construction industry
- Trustee for the College of Business at Tennessee Technological University
- Trustee for Abilene Christian University
- Member of the President's Advisory Council of American Buildings Company
- State board member of the Associated General Contractors of Tennessee

WINSTON WOLFE
- Worked for seven years at Great Southern Corporation, selling and marketing its line of sunglasses
- Founder of Olympic Optical, a provider of industrial safety sunglasses to the shooting sports industry
- Licensed the names Remington, Smith & Wesson, and Zebco
- Owner-manager of Sherwood, a 500-acre rural property near Memphis
- Serving on the board of the Orpheum Theatre

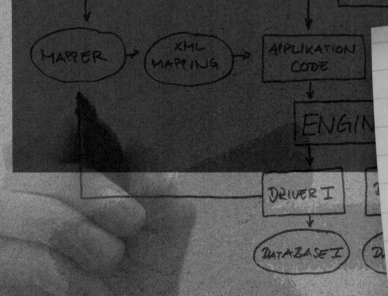

2

Entrepreneurial Integrity and Ethics

A Gateway to Small Business Opportunity

In the VIDEO SPOTLIGHT
Joseph's Lite Cookies
http://www.josephslitecookies.com

When growing a company to annual revenues of $100 million and hundreds of employees, a founder is sure to face any number of ethical dilemmas. In today's world, staying true to your convictions and acting with integrity seem to present a significant number of challenges. For Joseph Semprevivo, however, honesty and integrity have been key elements in building a successful company. Not only is Semprevivo committed to being socially responsible regarding the quality of the cookies his company sells, he is also committed to his employees, his customers, and his community.

When he was 12 years old, Semprevivo, a diabetic, developed a sugar-free ice cream that he sold in his parents' restaurant and in 197 grocery stores throughout New Mexico. Three years later, he asked his parents to develop a recipe for a sugar-free cookie. Joseph's Lite Cookies was born out of his desire to share that sugar-free treat with other diabetics, and this eagerness to share has shaped his company's culture.

Interdependence, reliability, and honesty characterize working relationships at the company, which has grown to have annual sales topping $100 million, dozens of products (not just cookies), and a presence in over 37 countries and 125,000 stores worldwide. Watch this video spotlight to see how integrity can create a strong foundation for growth.

Source: Video material provided by Hattie Bryant, Producer of Small Business School, the series on PBS Stations, Worldnet, and the Web at http://www.smallbusinessschool.org.

LOOKING AHEAD
AFTER STUDYING THIS CHAPTER, YOU SHOULD BE ABLE TO...

1. Define integrity and understand its importance to small businesses.

2. Explain how integrity applies to various stakeholder groups, including owners, customers, employees, the community, and the government.

3. Identify challenges to integrity that arise in small businesses and explain the benefits of integrity to small firms.

4. Explain the impact of the Internet and globalization on the integrity of small businesses.

5. Describe practical approaches for building a business with integrity.

6. Describe social entrepreneurship and the costs and opportunities of environmentalism for small businesses.

Tune in to "The Apprentice," and you get an all-too-common view of business. Every week, all of the wannabe moguls try to impress Donald Trump by preening, cajoling, and conniving. In this world, toughness is the measure of every CEO, and the boss glories in firing people and squeezing every penny out of suppliers.[1]

It may provide interesting television drama, but "The Apprentice" definitely depicts business as blood sport in prime time, and certainly doesn't focus much on ethics and integrity. In fact, when you consider the way business is presented in the media and entertainment in general, the picture often is not a pretty one (think major film productions such as *Wall Street, Erin Brockovich*, or even *Fun with Dick and Jane*).

Of course, these unflattering impressions of business are sometimes deserved. Decision makers occasionally respond to pressure to perform by compromising their principles, which explains why reports of corporate scandals continue to surface in the news. Corporations are run by people, after all, and it is reasonable to assume that some will give in to temptation as they make decisions for their companies. However, being aware of human frailties doesn't ease the shock of discovering that yet another corporation that enjoyed the public's trust has been seriously compromised. In this chapter, we discuss the personal integrity of the entrepreneur, which is the foundation of ethical behavior in small business, and provide insights that lead to the honorable management of enterprises.

Integrity and Entrepreneurship

S tories in the news media concerning insider trading, fraud, and bribery usually involve large corporations. However, in the less-publicized day-to-day activities of small businesses, decision makers regularly face ethical dilemmas and temptations to compromise principles for the sake of business or personal advantage. This strikes at the heart of integrity.

1. Define integrity and understand its importance to small businesses.

What Is Integrity?

The seeds of corporate misdeeds are sown when individuals compromise their personal *integrity*—that is, they do not behave in a way that is consistent with the noble values, beliefs, and principles they claim to hold. According to Karl Eller—the highly successful entrepreneur who turned the business of outdoor advertising into the revenue powerhouse that it is today—a person has integrity if his or her character remains whole, despite the pressure and circumstances of the worst of situations. In his words,

integrity
An uncompromising adherence to the lofty values, beliefs, and principles that an individual claims to hold.

> [A person of integrity] doesn't fold in a crunch; doesn't lie, cheat, flatter; doesn't fake credentials or keep two sets of books. He doesn't blame others for his mistakes or steal credit for their work. She never goes back on a deal: her handshake matches the tightest contract drawn up by the fanciest law firm in town.[2]

Some acts, such as cheating on taxes, clearly violate this standard, while others are less obvious but just as inappropriate. For example, one entrepreneur who owned a flooring sales business often sold sheets of linoleum at first-quality prices, even though they were graded as "seconds" by the factory. To hide his deception, he developed an ink roller that changed the factory stamp from "SECONDS" to read "SECONDS TO NONE!" Those who caught the inaccuracy probably figured it was a typo and gave it no more thought, but unsuspecting customers were paying for first-quality flooring, only to receive imperfect goods. By any measure, this shady business practice reveals a lack of integrity on the part of the entrepreneur.

As discussed in Chapter 1, a successful entrepreneur seeks financially rewarding opportunities while creating value, first and foremost, for prospective customers and the firm's owners.

This perspective makes clear that relationships are critical and integrity is essential to success. Financial gain is important, but it cannot be the only goal of interest. In fact, "doing anything for money" can quickly lead to distortions in business behavior. For example, one company ordered several thousand dollars worth of goods from its suppliers just as it was filing for bankruptcy, knowing that it would probably not have to pay for the merchandise because of legal protection. To act with integrity, an individual must consider the welfare of others.

Fortunately, many small business owners strive to achieve the highest standards of honesty, fairness, and respect in their business relationships. Although unethical practices receive extensive attention in the news, most entrepreneurs and other business leaders are people of principle whose integrity regulates their quest for profits.

How I see it: Scott Salmans on Doing the Right Thing

It's said that your people are your most valuable assets, but how should you deal with them when they become more of a liability than an asset to your company through no fault of their own? A successful business associate of mine found himself confronted with a difficult situation that, in turn, taught me the right way to handle a similar situation a few years later.

My friend was looking to replace himself as CEO with a high-caliber individual, as he considered taking a back seat and eventually retiring. He worked hard to find the best person for the job. After months of searching and evaluation, he chose a top-notch performer to take the role. Only a few months after he took the job, the highly paid executive developed a degenerative health condition that made it impossible for him to do the work my friend had hired him to do. In spite of the unfulfilled purpose, my friend paid the CEO for years and kept him on in an alternative capacity as long as it was physically possible.

A few years later, a key employee of mine developed a debilitating illness that was devastating to a new line of business we were creating at the time. The timing was critical and cost our company a great deal of money, but our team rallied, and the product was eventually completed and launched. Then came the ethical question, "How long do you keep this person on as a significant economic drain on the company?" I recalled my friend's situation, and it emboldened my decision to do the "right thing," at least for our situation. The employee remains a part of our team to this day, and we hope to see success with the product line and this individual for years to come.

Integrity and the Interests of Major Stakeholders

It is probably evident by now that the notion of integrity is closely tied to *ethical issues*, which involve questions of right and wrong. Such questions go far beyond what is legal or illegal; entrepreneurs often must make decisions regarding what is honest, fair, and respectful.

In order to pinpoint the types of ethical issues that are most troublesome for small companies, small business owners nationwide were asked the following question: "What is the most

2. Explain how integrity applies to various stakeholder groups, including owners, customers, employees, the community, and the government.

difficult ethical issue that you have faced in your work?" As might be expected, the question yielded a wide variety of responses, which have been grouped into the categories shown in Exhibit 2-1.

These responses provide a general idea of the issues that challenge the integrity of small business owners. As you can see in the exhibit, the issues mentioned most often are related to customers and competitors. However, the second most common category is concerned with the way a company treats its employees, including decisions about layoffs, workplace discrimination, and fairness in promotions. The fact that this set of issues received almost as many responses as the first should not be surprising, given the challenges of the current business environment. In fact, this category was near the bottom of the list when entrepreneurs responded to the same survey six years earlier.[3] Times are changing.

The third category is related to the obligations of employees to their employers, focusing on the actions of personnel that may not align with the best interests of their companies. In fourth place are management processes and relationships. Management relationship issues can be especially disturbing because they reflect the moral fiber or culture of the firm, including weaknesses in managerial actions and commitments.

The results of this survey reveal that entrepreneurs must consider the interests of a number of groups when making decisions—owners (or stockholders), customers, employees, the community, and the government. The individuals in these groups are sometimes referred to as stakeholders, indicating that they have a stake in the operation of the business. In essence, *stakeholders* are those who either can affect the performance of the company or are affected by it.

Because the interests of various stakeholder groups are different, they sometimes conflict; thus, decisions can be very difficult to make. And because there may not be one completely right or wrong position to take, managing the process can be extremely complicated.

One executive observed that running a business is sometimes like juggling (see Exhibit 2-2). In his words, "I am given four balls to balance: the customers', the employees', the community's, and the stockholders', by which I mean profit. It's never made clear to me how I am to keep them all going, but I know for certain that there is one that I'd better not drop, and that's profit."[4]

As if the job were not already difficult enough, we must add one more ball to the mix—government. Wandering beyond the limits of the law can quickly land a company in hot water, and there is no more certain way to compromise its integrity and its reputation. However, the concerns of all of these groups are fundamental to the management of the business. If neglected, any one group can use its influence to negatively affect the performance of the company.

Promoting the Owners' Interests

Nobel Prize–winning economist Milton Friedman outlined the responsibilities of businesses to society in very focused terms: "There is only one social responsibility of business—to use its resources and engage in activities designed to increase its profits so long as it stays within the rules of the game, which is to say, engages in open and free competition without deception or fraud."[5]

Friedman argued that businesses should be expected simply to earn profits honestly; any other use of the firm's resources is justified only if it enhances the firm's value. Though we believe there is adequate room for entrepreneurs to adopt a broader view of their social responsibilities, it is undeniable that owners have a clear and legitimate right to benefit from the financial performance of the company.

Many businesses, even small ones, have more than one owner. When this is the case, high standards of integrity require an honest attempt to promote the interests of all the owners, which include a commitment to financial performance and protection of the firm's reputation. But this does not always happen, which Jeff Dennis learned the hard way. In 1989, he and three co-founders started a financial investment company called Ashton-Royce Capital Corporation. When the venture started to take off, two of the partners decided to "check out" and spend a good part of their time in California in semiretirement. This left the two remaining co-founders

2-1 Difficult Ethical Issues Facing Small Firms

ETHICAL ISSUES	NUMBER OF RESPONDENTS	SAMPLE RESPONSES
Relationships with customers, clients, and competitors (relationships with outside parties in the marketplace)	111	"Avoiding conflicts of interest when representing clients in the same field" "Putting old parts in a new device and selling it as new" "Lying to customers about test results"
Human resource decisions (decisions relating to employment and promotion)	106	"Whether to lay off workers who [are] surplus to our needs and would have a problem finding work or to deeply cut executive pay and perks" "Sexual harassment" "Attempting to rate employees based on performance and not on personality"
Employee obligations to employer (employee responsibilities and actions that in some way conflict with the best interests of the employer)	90	"Receiving kickbacks by awarding over-priced contracts or taking gratuities to give a subcontractor the contract" "Theft of corporate assets" "Getting people to do a full day's work"
Management processes and relationships (superior–subordinate relationships)	63	"Reporting to an unethical person" "Having to back up the owner/CEO's lies about business capability in order to win over an account and then lie more to complete the job" "Being asked by my superiors to do something that I know is not good for the company or its employees"
Governmental obligations and relationships (compliance with governmental requirements and reporting to government agencies)	40	"Having to deal with so-called anti-discrimination laws which in fact force me to discriminate" "Bending state regulations" "Employing people who may not be legal [citizens] to work"
Relationships with suppliers (practices and deceptions that tend to defraud suppliers)	25	"Vendors want a second chance to bid if their bid is out of line" "Software copyright issues" "The ordering of supplies when cash flows are low and bankruptcy may be coming"
Environmental and social responsibilities (business obligations to the environment and society)	20	"Whether to pay to have chemicals disposed of or just throw them in a dumpster" "Environmental safety versus cost to prevent accidents" "Environmental aspects of manufacturing"

Source: Leslie E. Palich, Justin G. Longenecker, Carlos W. Moore, and J. William Petty, "Integrity and Small Business: A Framework and Empirical Analysis," proceedings of the forty-ninth World Conference of the International Council for Small Business, Johannesburg, South Africa, June 2004.

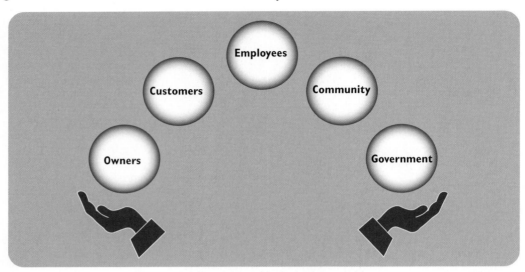

with more of the day-to-day work of the business and a growing resentment about the unfairness of the situation. In time, the conflict led to the dissolution of what had been a very profitable business.[6] Though entrepreneurs should be able to make their own decisions about personal matters, they have an obligation to make choices that protect the financial investment that others have in the company.

In many small businesses, a number of people own a small part of the enterprise but have no direct involvement in its operation. When this is the case, questions concerning proper conduct can show up in a number of areas. For example, entrepreneurs sometimes face ethical issues when reporting financial information. They must decide the extent to which they will be honest and candid. Because a firm has considerable discretion in reporting performance results, financial reports can sometimes be misleading without technically being illegal. But providing misleading financial information could easily persuade owners to make poor decisions regarding their investment in the company. The same could also be said for some who do not have ownership, outsiders such as bankers and suppliers who depend on a firm's financial reports to be accurate. It is always best to err on the side of honest disclosures that do not tend to mislead; doing so protects the reputation of the firm.

Caring about Customers

What do you call a business without customers? *Bankrupt!* Customers are obviously one of the most important stakeholder groups that a company must please. The fact that they are central to the purpose of any business has implications for integrity. Entrepreneurs who take customers seriously and care about them as individuals are apt to have more of them. And those they have are likely to return often because of that attitude.

Marc Katz sets an example as an entrepreneur with an appropriate view of customers. After joining with a partner to buy a building in which many other restaurants had failed, Katz began offering the first complete and authentic deli menu in Austin, Texas. Katz Deli thrives because customers love the high-quality food, and Marc and his staff love the customers. Katz treats his guests as valued friends and family, making people feel as if they were visiting his home. His driving motivation is not profit, though the deli is an undeniable success. Rather, it is out of concern for his customers that he is driven to provide a quality dining experience, marked by a genuine attitude of service.[7]

Katz Deli illustrates how a business can capitalize on integrity by treating customers with care and building strong relationships with them. But entrepreneurs are often tempted to take advantage of customers by being less than honest with them. When making marketing decisions, a business owner can be confronted with many ethical questions. For example, advertising content must sell the product or service but also tell "the truth, the whole truth, and nothing but the truth." Salespeople must walk a fine line between persuasion and deception. In some businesses, a salesperson might obtain contracts more easily by offering improper inducements to buyers or by joining with competitors to rig bids. This is clearly illegal, and eventually may result in damage to the company's reputation, which will affect relationships with existing and potential customers.

At its core, the formula for business success is actually quite simple: When a company delivers an excellent product with excellent service, customer satisfaction and healthy sales are almost certain to follow. Mike Jacobs, owner of two Wetzel's Pretzels franchises in California, believes his success in the marketplace has come from building employee teams that make things happen. With virtually no turnover since launching his businesses, Jacobs has communicated to his employees how important they are and how their performance impacts the business. In fact, their service orientation generates well over $1.1 million in annual sales.[8] This suggests that a company's response to its customers will often be determined by its employees.

Valuing Employees

A firm's level of integrity is also expressed by the value it places on employees. Through management decisions, an owner affects employees' personal and family lives. Issues of fairness, honesty, and impartiality are inherent in decisions and practices regarding hiring, promotions, salary increases, dismissals, layoffs, and work assignments. Employees are also concerned about privacy, safety, and health issues, and these should not be ignored.

In communicating with employees, an owner may be truthful and fair, vague and misleading, or totally dishonest. Some entrepreneurs treat outsiders with great courtesy but display demeaning behavior or attitudes toward subordinates, whom they regard as mere pawns in the game of business. Showing proper appreciation for subordinates as human beings and as valuable members of the team is an essential ingredient of managerial integrity. It is also wise, since employees are a firm's most important resource.

The enormous value of thoughtful treatment of employees is evident at companies like PAETEC, a communications solutions provider located outside Rochester, New York. Founded in 1998, the venture's revenue growth has been nothing short of extraordinary—at times averaging more than 250 percent per year. How could PAETEC go from startup to major player in such a short time? These results can be credited largely to a corporate culture that sincerely values its employees: "Everything at PAETEC revolves around respect for the employee. The word *customer* may be a little more prominent in the mission statement, but PAETEC puts employees first—and then watches them voluntarily put customers before themselves."[9] By doing things like treating one another as equals (regardless of position), faithfully recognizing achievement, emphasizing open communication between departments and between individuals, and honoring family life, PAETEC has shown what can be achieved when companies place employees first.

Small businesses do not always show the level of concern for employees that PAETEC expresses. And, unfortunately, lapses in integrity can sometimes be passed down from superiors to subordinates. Employees of small firms can face pressure from various sources to act in ways that conflict with their own sense of what is right and wrong. For example, a salesperson may feel pushed to compromise personal ethical standards in order to make a sale. Or an office employee may feel forced by her or his boss to act unethically, perhaps by destroying documents or misrepresenting sales data. Such situations are guaranteed to produce an organizational culture that fails to promote integrity.

LIVING THE DREAM:

entrepreneurship & integrity

Integrity Is Serious Business

Steelcase, Inc. has been around for nearly a century. It was launched in 1912 as The Metal Office Furniture Company and received its first patent two years later to build a metal wastebasket. That may not seem like much, but it was a very important innovation at a time when wastebaskets made of straw were a major office fire hazard.

Steelcase is always looking out for its customers and others who may be affected by its dealings. According to the company's website, "Steelcase was founded by people with a strong commitment to integrity and doing the right thing for their customers, employees, business partners, associates and neighbors," a foundation that has sustained the company and its reputation for nearly a century.

Surely Jim Hackett, the CEO of Steelcase, had no idea that he would one day have to "walk through fire" (so to speak) to save his customers from it, but a commitment to integrity will sometimes call for serious sacrifices. The problem surfaced when Steelcase decided to get into the business of selling walls for office buildings. The company developed panels that could be used for waist-high office cubicles or be stacked to form floor-to-ceiling walls. The product was an instant hit with building managers because it offered great flexibility, but there was a problem: The fire standards for full-length walls were more demanding

than those for cubicle panels. Because of the product's success, many wanted to ignore the oversight—including some very satisfied customers—and there were a number of justifications for doing exactly that (some of them quite persuasive), but Hackett knew in his gut that the "unyielding integrity" to which he had called Steelcase would hold him to a higher standard. He decided to recall the defective panels from dealers and replace them with an improved, more fire-retardant product. The costs were heavy—a $40 million expense to Steelcase and lost annual performance bonuses for Hackett and all of his executive team.

Did they do the right thing? Was the commitment to integrity worth the cost? Would anyone benefit from their sacrifices? These questions were answered on September 11, 2001. After the terrorist attacks destroyed a part of the Pentagon building, authorities determined that some of the walls installed in that part of the complex were from Steelcase—and fortunately they were made of panels with the added fire-retardant materials. Hackett recalls that "it was determined, with all the jet fuel and fire, if the new fire-retardant material was not there, the fire would have spread [and caused] a far more disastrous outcome." There is no telling how much pain and human suffering were avoided because of Hackett's dogged commitment to high standards of integrity.

Though it has been many years since Steelcase was truly a small company, its supporting principles have been a part of the formula for success right from the beginning. Living with integrity can be costly, but the payoff can sometimes be a life-and-death matter.

Sources: "About Steelcase," http://www.steelcase.com/na/about_steelcase_ourcompany.aspx?f=10036, accessed September 16, 2008; Noel M. Tichy and Warren G. Bennis, "Making the Tough Call: Greater Leaders Recognize When Their Values Are on the Line," *Inc. Magazine* (November 2007), Vol. 29, No. 11, pp. 36, 38.

Photos Courtesy of Steelcase, Inc.

Fortunately, most employees of small firms do not face such expectations, as was discovered by a research team at Baylor University.[10] In a nationwide survey of individuals holding managerial and professional positions in small firms, nearly three-fourths of the respondents (72.3 percent) reported an absence of pressure to compromise personal standards. This is encouraging, but the study also revealed that more than one-fourth of the respondents experienced either slight (24.1 percent) or extreme pressure (3.6 percent) to give in, which leaves room for improvement. The ideal is to develop a business environment in which the best ethical practices are consistently and uniformly encouraged, where employees feel completely free to do what they know is right.

Sometimes the offense runs in the opposite direction. That is, employees may engage in unethical behavior at their employer's expense. They may fail in their ethical obligation to do "an honest day's work." Loafing on the job, working too slowly, and taking unjustified sick leave are all examples of such failure. Though it creates serious disruption in a company, some employees actually *fabricate* crises at work only to solve them in order to reap praise for their amazing problem-solving skills, a phenomenon called "Munchausen at Work" because of obvious parallels to a particularly disturbing psychological disorder with a similar name.[11] Others have feigned injuries and drawn fraudulent workers' compensation checks, thereby inflating their employer's insurance costs.

According to FBI statistics, employees who steal supplies, merchandise, tools, or equipment from work may cost employers as much as $150 billion dollars each year,[12] a figure that does not even include losses from embezzlement (that is, when an employee steals *money* from the firm). These problems are serious, with some experts estimating that one-third of all new businesses fail because of employee theft of one kind or another.[13]

Social Responsibility and Small Business

To most people, an ethical business is one that not only treats customers and employees honestly but also acts as a good citizen in its community. These broader obligations of citizenship are called *social responsibilities.*

social responsibilities
A company's ethical obligations to the community

Some regard social responsibility as a price of freedom to operate independently in a free economy. They believe that the public has certain social expectations regarding business behavior, not all of which are required by law. Accordingly, they regard some socially responsible expenditures as proper, even when they are costly.

To varying degrees, companies have increasingly accepted responsibility to the communities where they do business. Their contribution starts with creating jobs and adding to local tax revenues, but many entrepreneurs feel a duty to give back even more to the community in return for the local support they enjoy—and they usually benefit from increased goodwill as a result. It is important to recognize that opinions differ as to the extent to which businesses are obligated to engage in socially desirable activities, and the response of small businesses to those obligations also varies. Some emphasize environmentalism, minority contracting, or regional economic development, while others focus their attention on volunteerism, philanthropy, or day care for employees' dependents. Still others give only minimal attention to peripheral social issues.

EXAMPLES OF CITIZENSHIP IN THE COMMUNITY Contributions to the community can take many different forms. Marc Benioff founded Salesforce.com in 1999 to offer online customer relationship management services, and his company has been very successful. A good part of that success may be due to a strong commitment to community support. In his book *Compassionate Capitalism,* Benioff argues that corporate philanthropy, done well, allows employees to find fulfillment in their workplace. But he also takes a deep interest in community needs. For example, he advocates the "1/1/1 Model," whereby 1 percent of Salesforce.com's profits, 1 percent of its equity, and 1 percent of employee hours are given back to the communities the company serves. In his book, he describes similar projects at several other firms, highlighting the practical advantages of and returns from such programs.[14]

In 1998, David Shapiro and Andrew Sherman started Fluid, an original music, sound design, and visual effects studio located in New York City. Today, the company has more than 20 employees, a growing list of very high-profile clients, and more than $6 million in annual revenues, but the company also does a great deal of pro bono work—that is, free service to the community. Many small businesses encourage their employees to make a difference in the community by donating their time to worthwhile causes, but companies like Fluid want more than just good PR from employee contributions of time and talent—they want maximum impact, which happens best when specific job skills are put to use.

This trend toward "skills-based volunteering" is growing rapidly; in fact, recent research shows that around 40 percent of volunteers look for opportunities to put their specific skill sets to use. The bottom line for Fluid: Nonprofit organizations receive services for free that they would otherwise not be able to afford, and the company's employees give back to their community by doing what they love to do. Now they are all making beautiful music together.[15]

Entrepreneurs should think carefully about their community commitments, because building a business on the foundation of "doing good" may add to a small company's financial burden. However, this is often more than offset by increased loyalty among customers and employees who buy into the mission, which leads to improved productivity and morale. It can also help to set a company apart from competitors that offer similar products or services but make no charitable contributions. Perhaps most important, this commitment is often rewarded by customers in two ways—repeat sales and a willingness to pay a little more for what they get. These are strong incentives for a company to give serious consideration to its dedication to the community.[16]

VARYING VIEWS ON SOCIAL RESPONSIBILITY
How do small business owners compare with big business CEOs in their view of social responsibility? The evidence is limited, but research suggests that entrepreneurs who head small, growth-oriented companies may be more narrowly focused on profits and, therefore less socially sensitive than CEOs of large corporations. Because simple survival may be the most pressing priority, many small-growth firms see social responsibility as a luxury they simply cannot afford. And in defense of small firm owners, we note that they usually spend their own money rather than corporate funds—it is easier to be generous when spending someone else's money. Small business philanthropy often takes place anyway, but in the form of personal contributions by business owners.

Entrepreneurs must reconcile their social obligations with the need to earn profits. Earning a profit is absolutely essential. Without profits, a firm will not be in a position to recognize its social responsibilities for very long. But meeting the expectations of society can be expensive. For example, small firms must sometimes purchase new equipment or make costly changes in operations in order to protect the environment, and auto repair shops incur additional costs when they dispose of hazardous waste, such as used oil and filters. It is evident that acting in the public interest often requires spending money, which reduces profits. There are limits to what particular businesses can afford.

Fortunately, many types of socially responsible actions can be consistent with a firm's long-term profit objective.[17] Some degree of goodwill is earned by such behavior. A firm that consistently fulfills its social obligations makes itself a desirable member of the community and may attract customers because of that image. Conversely, a firm that refuses its social responsibilities may find itself the target of restrictive legislation or local protests and discover that its customers and employees lack loyalty to the business.

Research conducted by Cone, Inc., a Boston-based strategic marketing firm, revealed that eight out of ten Americans claim corporate support of causes earns their trust in that firm.

Eighty-six percent of respondents said they would be very or somewhat likely to switch brands based on corporate citizenship commitments. Carol Cone, CEO of the research firm, concludes, "It's clear from our research that the public wants to know . . . what a company is doing in the community—good and bad."[18] Small businesses seem to be responding to this message. A recent National Federation of Independent Business study found that 91 percent of small businesses made contributions to their communities, through volunteering, in-kind contributions, and/or direct cash donations. The same study reported 74 percent of all small business owners volunteered for community and charitable activities, and the average commitment was just over 12 hours per month (which translates to 18 working days per year).[19] Overall, the evidence on performance impact is far from certain, but it suggests that commitment to the community may very well be good for business.

Governmental Laws and Regulations

Government at all levels serves a purpose, though there is room to debate whether it has too much power or too little. It intervenes directly in the economy when it establishes laws to ensure healthy competition. But its reach extends into other business matters as well—workplace safety, equal employment opportunities, fair pay, clean air, and safe products, to name a few. Entrepreneurs must comply with government laws and regulations if they are to maintain integrity, and avoid spending time behind bars.

One glaring example of unethical behavior by small firm management is fraudulent reporting of income and expenses for income tax purposes. This conduct includes *skimming*—that is, concealing some income—as well as improperly claiming personal expenses as business expenses. We do not mean to imply that all or even most small companies engage in such practices. However, tax evasion does occur within these firms, and the practice is widespread enough to be recognized as a general problem.

Tax avoidance can be flagrant and very intentional, but entrepreneurs often come up short on their tax commitments because of casual accounting systems, single-minded focus on their product or service, or both. One student entrepreneur confesses that he had a close brush with the law because he and his friends were creating clothing in his dorm room and selling it on his campus, but the company did not legally exist and he was not keeping track of sales and expenses because he didn't take seriously the obligations and advantages of keeping good records. He explains what he was thinking:

> At that time I refused to accept the responsibilities of accounting and the work it would take to follow through to make things sound. It's amazing how when things are going well, it is much easier to ignore the little formalities and nagging issues. It's almost as if you believe that as small as you are, you are above the legalities, requirements, and responsibilities of starting a business. I found myself with my ambition to be an entrepreneur outweighing my commitment to actually following through with the state and federal requirements.[20]

Eventually, the "tax man" came calling. This young entrepreneur learned from his close encounter with the IRS that accurate record keeping and legal formalities are necessary to ethical practice and, just as important, to peace of mind.

When the topic of tax avoidance comes up, most people think of income taxes, but employee payroll tax—local, state, and federal obligations such as Social Security, Medicare, and unemployment—must also be withheld. These often present the biggest tax burden on small businesses because they are owed regardless of whether the company makes a profit or not. And because tax authorities like the IRS do not always push hard enough to collect these taxes, small businesses can easily fall behind and eventually get into trouble.[21] Regardless of the circumstances, an entrepreneur must meet all tax obligations to preserve his or her integrity.

LIVING THE DREAM:

entrepreneurship & integrity

Not-So-Sweet Surrender

Toscanini's is an ice cream shop in Cambridge, Massachusetts, that is known for offering flavors so appealing that the *New York Times* declared it "the world's best ice cream." Co-owner Gus Rancatore launched the business in 1981 to serve up high-quality ice cream with superior customer service. The formula was immediately successful, and Toscanini's quickly built quite a following in the neighborhood. Soon national publications took notice and gave the shop rave reviews, prompting customers and friends to urge Rancatore to add new locations. After resisting the suggestion for years, he finally decided to open a second shop in 1987. Unfortunately, he had to close it down after more than a decade of less-than-impressive results. Seeing new possibilities, though, Rancatore soon got the expansion bug again and opened yet another shop; then, his ice cream mini-empire grew even more when he took over a coffeehouse called Someday Café and started selling pints of ice cream through grocery stores in New England.

Rancatore and his management system were soon overwhelmed, and the company started to slide into financial trouble. That led to problems with the government.

> The bottom line is that, in the day-to-day craziness of running a business that was in danger of going off the rails, I missed tax payments—both employment taxes and my state meals tax. When it came to paying the state on time or making payroll and paying the milkman, I felt I had to worry about taxes second.

This went on for some time—but it could not go on forever. Eventually he owed the government a crippling $177,000. Rancatore had to contract with a payroll service to keep his business from falling further behind on its tax obligations, and Massachusetts state officials worked with him on a repayment plan, but the interest and penalties compounded rapidly so the debt continued to spiral out of control. Rancatore's sister, Mimi, joined the company in 2006 to help resolve its problems. Together, they closed everything but the original shop, but they still owed the state $167,000 and had no way to pay that down.

This state of limbo dragged on for some time, but on the morning of January 17, 2008, state authorities showed up at Toscanini's, padlocked the door, and put a bright orange "seized" sticker on the window. With no money to pay back taxes owed, the situation looked hopeless—but it wasn't. The very next day, Rancatore launched an online campaign, pleading with his loyal customers to make contributions to a PayPal account that would be used as a down payment on his debt to the state. The plan worked! The site took in more than $25,000 in one week, enough to persuade the state to unchain the doors and let Toscanini's reopen. Rancatore expresses gratitude for his customers' generosity, and adds, "We certainly pay our taxes absolutely religiously on time, every month." It appears this is one mistake that is not likely to be repeated.

Sources: Jenn Abelson, "Shop Is Set to Lick Its Tax Problem," *The Boston Globe*, January 26, 2008; Matt Dunning, "Toscanini's Scoops $23k from Ice Cream Fans to Pay Tax Debt," January 21, 2008, http://www.wickedlocal.com/cambridge/archive/x1295940537, accessed September 9, 2008; Evelyn Ratigan, "The Ice Cream Man Cometh Back: Toscanini's Owner Learned some 'Friendly' Hard Lessons," July 17, 2008, http://www.wickedlocal.com/cambridge/archive/x379990667/The-ice-cream-man-cometh-back-Toscaninis-owner-learned-some-friendly-hard-lessons, accessed September 10, 2008; Gus Rancatore, "Local Hero or Tax Cheat?" *Inc. Magazine* (April 2008), Vol. 30, No. 4, pp. 107–111.

© Mikki Ansin

How I see it: John Stites on an Ethical Dilemma

A recent ethical dilemma I had to face involved a lot of money. I believe most every ethical dilemma is somehow wrapped up in how we value money and what priority it takes in our lives.

I was told by my accountant that I could save over $65,000 in franchise and excise taxes properly due to the state. He assured me it was definitely owed, and if I didn't pay the tax and the government discovered it, they would surely pursue me for the taxes and the penalties resulting from the failure to pay. However, he suggested I could put the return in my desk drawer, because it was very unlikely the state would ever know about the tax being due, since the company was new and the state would have no record of tax being due on a new company.

I had used this man for many years as my accountant, and he was very aware of our mission statement and values. I did not believe that losing my integrity in the eyes of this man was worth the money I would be saving. The realization of the good I could do with the money did not escape my mind, but I resolved I could not bless anyone with money that I had stolen from someone else, even if it was the government. After all, a gift that cost me nothing, because I stole it from someone else, is not my gift at all. My decision was made even harder knowing how poorly the government spends its money.

Finally, my faith demanded that I "do the right thing." Incidentally, shortly after paying the taxes due, I rented a 32,200-square-foot building for 10 years for $115,500 annually. I had been trying to rent that building for over two years.

The Challenges and Benefits of Acting with Integrity

Small companies sometimes face unique challenges to maintaining integrity, but the benefits of integrity are real and can offer small businesses a distinct advantage in the marketplace. However, small companies are often vulnerable because of their size and their desire to succeed. We'll discuss how the payoff from integrity can make a small business, and how lack of it can break one.

3. Identify challenges to integrity that arise in small businesses and explain the benefits of integrity to small firms.

The Vulnerability of Small Companies

Walking the straight and narrow may be more difficult and costly on Main Street than it is on Wall Street. That is, small, privately held firms that are not part of the corporate world epitomized by Wall Street may face greater pressures than large businesses do to act unethically. Indeed, because small firms usually do not have the deep pockets and superior resources of their larger competitors, entrepreneurs may find it easier to rationalize, say, inappropriate gift giving or bribery as a way of offsetting what seem to be unfair limitations in order to establish a level playing field. And isn't a "little white lie" justified when the life and future of the company are at risk? It's easy to cave in to the pressure when your back is against the wall.

When small business owners create false impressions to make their companies look good, are they being dishonest or simply resourceful? While there is nothing wrong with setting up an 800 number or establishing a Web presence to gain scale advantages to compete better against larger competitors, pretending to be something he or she is not is less than forthright and can lead a small business owner into what is, at best, a gray area. When one entrepreneur launched his own fund-raising business in South Carolina, he had only a few local projects to work on. Profits were slim, but that didn't stop him from telling everyone that business was great. To add to the charade, he set up an 800 number and launched a website to create an image of greater scale.[22] And when another small business owner was just starting a trucking company in Michigan, she sometimes used the phone in "creative ways" to shade customer impressions about the business. For example, "she pretended to transfer customers to different lines and used phony voices to make the company seem bigger."[23] The drive and ingenuity of these entrepreneurs is certainly impressive, but their behavior raises questions about ethical standards. Such moves may save companies, but how would customers feel if they knew they were being manipulated?

The temptation for small business owners to compromise ethical standards as they strive to earn profits is suggested in the results of a study of entrepreneurial ethics conducted by researchers from Baylor University.[24] In this study, small business owners' views about various ethical issues were compared with responses of managers who did not own their own businesses. Participants were presented with 16 scenarios, each describing a business decision with ethical overtones, and were asked to rate the degree to which they found each action compatible with their personal ethical views.

For the most part, all participants expressed a moral stance; they condemned decisions that were ethically questionable as well as those that were clearly illegal. But in five situations, the entrepreneurs appeared significantly less disapproving of questionable conduct than the other respondents,[25] and three of these involved opportunity for financial gain by cutting corners or underreporting income. Obviously, a special temptation exists for entrepreneurs who are strongly driven to earn profits.

Evidence shows, then, that most entrepreneurs exercise great integrity, but some are particularly vulnerable with regard to ethical issues that directly affect profits. While business pressures do not justify unethical behavior, they help explain the context in which such decisions are made. Decision making about ethical issues often calls for difficult choices on the part of the entrepreneur.

The Integrity Edge

The price of integrity is high, but the potential payoff is incalculable. For example, it is impossible to compute the value of a clear conscience. The entrepreneur who makes honorable decisions, even when it comes to the smallest of details, can take satisfaction in knowing that he or she did what was right, even if things do not turn out as planned.

But integrity yields other important benefits as well. In his book *Integrity Is All You've Got,* Karl Eller observes that through his long career as a successful entrepreneur, he has seen one constant: the crucial role of integrity to achievement in business. As he puts it, "Those who have [integrity] usually succeed; those who don't have it usually fail."[26] Eller suggests that integrity lubricates the important traits of an entrepreneur so that they work harmoniously together, which can give a company an enormous advantage over competitors. Entrepreneurs with integrity are aware of the importance of the bottom line, but this is not their singular focus; nonetheless, extraordinary financial performance often follows their efforts.

In a study of 207 American firms, John Kotter and James Heskett, professors at the Harvard Business School, found that the more a company focuses on the needs of shareholders alone, the lower its performance. Kotter and Heskett concluded that firms perform better when their cultures emphasize the interests of *all* stakeholders—customers, employees, stockholders, and the community. Over the 11-year period of the study, those companies that looked beyond the income statement "increased revenues by an average of 682 percent versus 166 percent for those companies that didn't, expanded their work forces by 282 percent versus 36 percent, grew their stock prices by 901 percent versus 74 percent, and improved their net incomes by 756 percent versus 1 percent."[27] While these results are impressive, they do not *guarantee* that doing the right thing will lead to positive results for a company. However, these findings suggest that exhibiting integrity in business does not rule out financial success—in fact, doing the right thing may actually boost the company's performance.

Perhaps the greatest benefit of integrity in business is the *trust* it generates. Trust results only when the stated values of a company and its behavior in the marketplace match. When a small business owner looks to the needs of others and follows through on her or his promises, stakeholders notice. Customers buy more of what a firm sells when they realize that the company is doing its best to make sure that its products are of high quality and its customer service is excellent. Employees are much more likely to "go the extra mile" for a small company when it is clear that they are more than simply replaceable parts in an impersonal machine.

And members of the community also respond positively to business integrity. When they are convinced that a firm is living up to its commitments to protect the environment and pay its fair share of taxes, their support can keep the company going even if it falls on hard times. It all comes down to trust. If they conclude that the business is simply taking advantage of them, then all bets are off. There is no substitute for trust, and there is little hope for trust without integrity.

Integrity in an Expanding Economy

For the entrepreneur with integrity, decisions are often complicated by developments in the world economy. Businesses that operate across national boundaries must consider the ethical standards that exist in other cultures, which often differ from those of their own country. And firms using the Internet face a host of ethical issues that have arisen in the online marketplace. As small firms move toward international commerce and harness the power of the Internet to launch and sustain their enterprises, these issues become all the more important.

4. Explain the impact of the Internet and globalization on the integrity of small businesses.

Integrity and the Internet

It is not surprising that issues of honesty, deception, and fraud have affected Internet-based businesses, just as they have traditional commerce. It simply follows from the fact that those who buy and sell on the Internet are the same people who participate in all other arenas of the marketplace. One quickly encounters questions of right and wrong in business relationships in every venue.

An issue of great concern to Internet users is personal privacy. Businesses and consumers often disagree about how private the identity of visitors to websites should be. For example, businesses can use cookies to collect data on patterns of usage related to a particular Internet address. In this way, a business may create a detailed profile of customers, which it may then sell to other parties for profit. Internet businesses—and even many of their customers—see the collection of personal information as helpful. A bookseller might, for example, welcome a customer back by name and tell him or her about a special book similar to those the customer ordered previously. To address customer concerns, a number of firms have developed privacy policies—they either will not share personal data or will not share it if the customer requests privacy.

The extent to which an employer may monitor an employee's Internet activity is also hotly debated. Many workers believe it is inappropriate for employers to monitor their e-mail, a practice they consider to be snooping and an invasion of privacy. Employers, on the other hand, are concerned that employees may be wasting company time dealing with personal e-mail, shopping online, and surfing the Internet. And it appears there is reason for concern. *Inc. Magazine* reviewed research indicating that accessing the Internet at work for personal reasons is escalating rapidly.

American workers spent the equivalent of 2.3 million years' worth of 40-hour work-weeks reading nonwork-related blogs while at work, according to a study by *Advertising Age* magazine. And that's just blogs. Millions more work years were spent shopping online, checking eBay listings, cruising social networks, looking for vacation deals, Googling old flames, and, of course, ogling porn. [This research indicates that] employers spend nearly $760 billion a year paying employees to goof off on the Web.[28]

While the author concluded that this Internet activity is not all bad (for example, an employee who spends time on the Internet can spot emerging trends and bring that insight to his or her work), it still hinders productivity in the workplace, and that makes it a concern for the employer. According to a study of employers conducted by the American Management Association and the ePolicy Institute, more than 75 percent of all businesses monitor employee Web use, 65 percent use software to block access to inappropriate websites, and 36 percent track what employees pull up on their screens and type on their keyboards.[29]

Widespread use of the Internet has also focused attention on the issue of *intellectual property*. Traditionally, protection has been granted to original intellectual creations—whether inventions, literary works, or artistic products such as music—in the form of patents and copyrights. The law allows originators of such intellectual property to require compensation for its use. However, the Internet has made it easy for millions of users to copy intellectual property free of charge.

Protection of intellectual property is a political as well as an ethical issue. Recent congressional hearings, lawsuits, and proposed legislation suggest that additions or changes to current laws are likely, and international enforcement continues to be a major problem. As Internet use continues to grow and practices such as online selling and file sharing are made easier, it is safe to assume that property rights will become more difficult to protect. Therefore, content providers and other intellectual property owners will have to take increasingly stronger measures to guard what is legally theirs.

The problem of intellectual property rights violations was highlighted in 2008 when accusations were leveled against eBay Inc., claiming that the online auction powerhouse was materially responsible for the rise in the sale of counterfeit goods (that is, unauthorized copies of a legitimate product). The *Economist* provides an idea of how widespread the problem has become:

> A few years ago sellers on eBay were mostly private individuals flogging second-hand goods. But now eBay is increasingly used by professional retailers selling new items. Many of them sell fakes. [The French company] LVMH claims that out of 300,000 products labelled Dior and 150,000 Louis Vuitton handbags offered on eBay in the second quarter of 2006, fully 90% were fake.[30]

Despite its aggressive fight against counterfeiting, the problem continues to dog the Internet icon. In fact, eBay has already lost lawsuits in Europe to luxury goods makers, though the online company's legal efforts have been more successful in the United States.[31] Regardless of eBay's legal liabilities, it is clear that the sale of counterfeit goods, though increasing, is a violation of the law and a breach of integrity. The practice cannot be defended.

International Issues of Integrity

Every country faces questionable business behavior within its borders, but some must deal with very serious forms of illegal business activity. For example, Italian police recently raided a Chinese-owned counterfeiting factory in the Tuscan town of Prato and confiscated more than 650,000 fake Gucci and Louis Vuitton handbags and accessories. Many such factories are setting up shop in Tuscany to be close to European consumers and to be able to add a "Made in Italy" label to their goods.[32] Other rogue businesses—some located in the United States—routinely exploit the weak and vulnerable in ways that stray far from ethical practice. Along these lines, some companies exploit labor in countries with weak labor laws in order to procure products at low costs. Though practices of this kind may be tolerated (even encouraged) by local governments, labor activists and human rights organizations have condemned them, and they are increasingly targeted by law enforcement authorities.

In operating abroad, U.S. businesspeople often encounter ethical issues that are clouded by cultural differences. So what are entrepreneurs to do? Frequently, they simply apply U.S. standards to the situation. In some cases, however, this approach has been criticized for resulting in *ethical imperialism,* an arrogant attempt to impose American perspectives on other societies. Some guidance is provided by restrictions specified in the Foreign Corrupt Practices Act, which makes it illegal for U.S. businesses to use bribery in their dealings anywhere in the world. (Some allowance is made for small "grease payments," which are those offered to speed up a legitimate process.) Regardless of local practices, American firms must comply with these laws even though "gray areas" exist in which there are no obvious answers.

ethical imperialism
The belief that the ethical standards of one's own country can be applied universally.

Another viewpoint is embodied in the saying "When in Rome, do as the Romans do." This philosophy, sometimes called *ethical relativism,* is troublesome, because it implies that anything goes if the local culture accepts it. To define its ethical landscape and work out its position on difficult issues, a small business must consider the nuances of its particular international environment. Training is also needed to ensure that each employee understands the firm's commitment to integrity, and consulting an attorney with appropriate expertise is highly recommended.

ethical relativism
The belief that ethical standards are subject to local interpretation.

Also, bear in mind that one-time practices may set a pattern for future behavior. Some business owners have observed that offering a bribe to make a business deal possible often creates expectations for more of the same in the future. Owners who refuse to pay these "fees" say that they may have to deal with frustrating inconveniences in the short-term (for example, shipped products being held up by customs), but it is likely to discourage such demands in the future. This is one of the ways in which integrity in business may offer unanticipated rewards.

Building a Business with Integrity

The goal of an entrepreneur with integrity is to have a business that operates honorably in all areas, which sets the entrepreneur on the path toward crafting a worthy legacy, as discussed in Chapter 1. This goal is not reached automatically, however. To build a business with integrity, management must provide the leadership, culture, and instruction that support ethical perspectives and appropriate behavior.

5. Describe practical approaches for building a business with integrity.

The Foundations of Integrity

The business practices that a firm's leaders or employees view as right or wrong reflect their *underlying values.* An individual's beliefs affect what that person does on the job and how she or he acts toward customers and others. Talk is cheap (that is, *anyone* can *sound* ethical), but actual behavior provides the best clues to a person's true underlying system of basic values. Behavior may reflect the level of a person's commitment to honesty, respect, truthfulness, and so forth—in other words, to integrity in all of its dimensions. Such values are often organized into the business enterprise's mission statement, as discussed in Chapter 1.

underlying values
Unarticulated ethical beliefs that provide a foundation for ethical behavior in a firm.

Values that serve as a foundation for integrity in business are based on personal views of the role of humankind in the universe and, naturally, are part of basic philosophical and/or religious convictions.[33] In the United States, Judeo-Christian ideals have traditionally served as the general body of beliefs underlying business behavior, although there are plenty of examples of honorable behavior based on principles derived from other religions. Since religious and/or philosophical principles are reflected in the business practices of firms of all sizes, a leader's personal commitment to certain basic values is an important determinant of a small firm's commitment to business integrity.

Entrepreneurs who are deeply committed to underlying standards of integrity operate their businesses in ways that reflect their personal values and ideals. One business that places the entrepreneur's personal values above dollars is Ukrop's Super Markets, a Richmond,

Virginia–based grocery chain that does not sell alcohol, closes every Sunday, and donates 10 percent of its profits to charity. Several times, *Fortune* magazine has named Ukrop's in its list of the 100 best companies to work for. And customers are happy with the company's policies, such as having staff carry and load groceries and refusing to take tips for this service.[34]

Steadfast devotion to integrity can lead to many other positive outcomes, as well. For example, a long-time observer of high-tech startups commented on the significance of an entrepreneur's personal standards to investment decisions:

> I can tell you, even with the smallest high-technology companies, the product had to be good, the market had to be good, the people had to be good. But the one thing that was checked out most extensively by venture capitalists was the integrity of the management team. And if integrity wasn't there, it didn't matter how good the product was, how good the market was—they weren't funded.[35]

It seems apparent that a deep commitment to basic values affects behavior in the marketplace and gives rise to business practices that are widely appreciated and admired. Without a strong commitment to integrity on the part of small business leadership, ethical standards can easily be compromised.

Leading with Integrity

In a small organization, the influence of a leader is more pronounced than it is in a large corporation, where leadership can become diffused. This fact is recognized by J. C. Huizenga, who in 1995 started a public school management company called Heritage Academies, which was ranked as one of the fastest-growing U.S. companies by *Inc. Magazine*:

> The executive of a small company must often face moral challenges more directly, because he or she has more direct contact with customers, suppliers, and employees than an executive in a large corporation who may have a management team to deliberate with. The consequences of his or her choices often affect the business more significantly because of the size of the issue relative to the size of the company.[36]

The opportunity for establishing high standards of integrity is more apparent in small firms than in large ones. For example, an entrepreneur who believes strongly in honesty and truthfulness can insist that those principles be followed throughout the organization. In effect, the founder or head of a small business can say, "My personal integrity is on the line, and I want you to do it this way." Such statements are easily understood. And a leader becomes even more effective when he or she backs up such statements with appropriate behavior. In fact, a leader's behavior has much greater influence on employees than his or her stated philosophy does. Everyone is watching how he or she behaves, and this conduct establishes the culture of the company—what is allowed or encouraged and what is prohibited.

In summary, the personal integrity of the founder or owner is the key to a firm's ethical performance. The dominant role of this one person (or the leadership team) gives him or her (or the team) a powerful voice in shaping the ethical performance of the small company, for good or for ill. Think about it: Employees owe their position to the founder or owner, so that person wields profound influence deriving from his or her unique position in the organization.

A Supportive Organizational Culture

Integrity in a business requires a supportive organizational culture. Ideally, every manager and employee should instinctively resolve every ethical issue by simply doing what is right. An ethical culture requires an environment in which employees at every level are confident that the firm is fully committed to honorable conduct. To a considerable degree, strong leadership helps build this understanding. As a small business grows, however, personal interactions between the owner and employees occur less often, creating a need to articulate and reinforce principles of integrity in ways that supplement the personal example of the entrepreneur. A good place to start is to establish an ethics policy for the company.

In their highly influential book *The Power of Ethical Management,* Kenneth Blanchard and Norman Vincent Peale offer insights to guide the development of an ethics policy. They suggest that the policy be based on the following five fundamental principles:[37]

- **Purpose.** The vision for the company and your core values will guide business conduct.
- **Pride.** When employees take pride in their work and their company, they are much more likely to be ethical in their dealings.
- **Patience.** If you push too hard for short-term results, sooner or later acting unethically will seem to be the only way to achieve the outcomes you seek.
- **Persistence.** Stand by your word, which is the foundation of trust. If you are not committed to an ethical framework, your integrity is at risk, as is the reputation of the company.
- **Perspective.** Stopping from time to time to reflect on where your business is going, why it is going that way, and how you plan to get there will allow you to be more confident that you are on the right track now and will continue to be in the future.

To define ethical behavior in the company more specifically, the owner-manager of a small firm should formulate a *code of ethics* (sometimes called a *code of values*) similar to that of most large corporations. Exhibit 2-3 offers an example of such a code. A survey of MBA students employed by small- and medium-size companies revealed that codes of ethics shape and improve conduct in their organizations in a number of ways: by defining behavioral expectations, by communicating that those expectations apply to employees at all levels in the business, by helping employees convey the company's standards of conduct to suppliers and customers, by serving as a tool for handling peer pressure, and by providing a formal channel for communicating with superiors without fear of reprisal.[38] In other words, a code of ethics identifies conduct that is ethical and appropriate, but it is also a practical tool that can encourage and protect ethical behavior.

A well-written code expresses the principles to be followed by employees of the firm and gives examples of these principles in action. A code of ethics might, for example, prohibit acceptance of gifts or favors from suppliers but point out standard business courtesies, such as a lunch or a couple of movie tickets, that might be accepted without violating the policy.[39] If a code of ethics is to be effective, employees must be aware of its nature and convinced of its importance. At the very least, each employee should read and sign it. As a company grows larger, employees will need training to ensure that the code is well understood and taken seriously.

Entrepreneurs further reinforce ethical culture in the business when they hire and promote ethical people, recognize and correct behavior that is unethical, and lead by example in business dealings, while encouraging all employees to do the same. With training and consistent management, a firm can then develop the level of understanding employees need to act in the spirit of the code in situations not covered by specific rules. However, a code of ethics will be effective only to the degree that the entrepreneur's behavior is consistent with his or her own stated principles. Some business owners are surprised by how readily employees spot hypocrisy, and these double standards quickly dull the ethical sensibilities of the organization.

code of ethics
Official standards of employee behavior formulated by a firm.

Better Business Bureaus

Sometimes the business conduct of small companies is shaped by external forces. Because unethical operations reflect adversely on honest members of the business community, privately owned companies in many cities have joined together to form Better Business Bureaus. The purpose of such organizations is to promote ethical conduct on the part of all businesses in a region.

A Better Business Bureau (BBB) encourages ethical practices by (1) providing consumers with free information to help them make informed decisions when dealing with a company, (2) creating an incentive for businesses to adhere to proper business practices and earnestly address customer complaints, and (3) resolving questions or disputes concerning purchases

EXHIBIT

CODE OF VALUES

We believe . . .

. . . in superior service to our customers, to our community, and to each other as members of The Dwyer Group family.

. . . in counting our blessings every day in every way.

. . . success is the result of clear, cooperative, positive thinking.

. . . that loyalty adds meaning to our lives.

. . . management should seek out and recognize what people are doing right, and treat every associate with respect.

. . . challenges should be used as learning experiences.

. . . our Creator put us on this earth to succeed. We will accept our daily successes humbly, knowing that a higher power is guiding us.

. . . in the untapped potential of every human being. Every person we help achieve their potential fulfills our mission.

. . . we must re-earn our positions every day in every way.

. . . in building our country through the free enterprise system. We demonstrate this belief by continually attracting strong people in The Dwyer Group.

We live our Code of Values by . . .

INTEGRITY

. . . making only agreements we are willing, able and intend to keep.

. . . communicating any potentially broken agreements at the first appropriate opportunity to all parties concerned.

. . . looking to the system for correction and proposing all possible solutions if something is not working.

. . . operating in a responsible manner: "above the line."

. . . communicating honestly and with purpose.

. . . asking clarifying questions if we disagree or do not understand.

. . . never saying anything about anyone that we would not say to him or her.

RESPECT

. . . treating others as we would like to be treated.

. . . listening with the intent to understand what is being said and acknowledging that what is said is important to the speaker.

. . . responding in a timely fashion.

. . . speaking calmly, and respectfully, without profanity or sarcasm.

. . . acknowledging everyone as right from their own perspective.

CUSTOMER FOCUS

. . . continuously striving to maximize internal and external customer loyalty.

. . . making our best effort to understand and appreciate the customer's needs in every situation.

HAVING FUN IN THE PROCESS!

Source: Reprinted with permission of The Dwyer Group, Waco, Texas.

through mediation or arbitration. As a result, unethical business practices often decline in a community served by a Better Business Bureau.

Though the BBB reports relevant information to law enforcement agencies, it is not a government entity, and it cannot collect money or impose penalties on companies that engage in unethical business practices. However, a BBB can provide information on a company's operating track record, which will affect the firm's reputation and, in turn, its success in the marketplace. This creates an incentive for companies to adopt fair and proper business practices and address customer complaints appropriately in order to avoid losing business.

An Ethical Decision-Making Process

Ethical decision making often is not a very clear-cut process. In fact, even after much thought and soul searching, the appropriate course of action still may not be apparent in some business situations. The Ethics Resource Center in Washington, D.C., offers a decision-making process that may help with challenging dilemmas. We have adapted this simple six-step decision-making process here to help small business owners see the issues more clearly and make better, ethical decisions.[40]

STEP 1: DEFINE THE PROBLEM How you define the problem is important because this will guide where you look for solutions. For example, in the case of a student who is consistently late for class, is the problem that he is not managing his time well, he is coming from a classroom that is on the other side of a very large campus, or the professor in the prior class consistently lets him out late? If the student is careless with his time, a penalty for tardiness may correct the problem; however, penalizing the student will not solve the problem if his tardiness is actually the result of one of the other two causes. Looking for the root of the problem is the best place to start in your search for a solution to a challenging ethical problem, whether it is a customer who is slow to settle his accounts or an overseas client who wants to give you a "tip" to overlook a questionable practice.

STEP 2: IDENTIFY ALTERNATIVE SOLUTIONS TO THE PROBLEM It's tempting to go with an "obvious" solution or the one that has been used in the past, but often this is not the best answer—even if it is ethical. Be open-minded and consider creative alternatives. Often an innovative solution is available that is consistent with your personal ethics, protects the interests of other affected parties, and offers superior outcomes. Seeking advice from trusted friends and advisors who have faced similar situations can spur your thinking and lead to options that you might otherwise overlook.

STEP 3: EVALUATE THE IDENTIFIED ALTERNATIVES Rotary Club International, a worldwide organization of business and professional leaders, has set a high standard for business conduct. It calls on its members to ask the following four questions when they prepare to make a decision about the things they think, say, or do:[41]

1. Is it the TRUTH?
2. Is it FAIR to all concerned?
3. Will it build GOODWILL and BETTER FRIENDSHIPS?
4. Will it be BENEFICIAL to all concerned?

Taking a similar approach, you might ask yourself, "How would I feel if my decision were reported in the daily newspaper?" Or, the question can be even more personal: "How well could I explain this decision to my mother or children?" The answer could help to steer you away from unethical behavior.

Perhaps the most widely recommended principle for ethical behavior is simply to follow the Golden Rule: "Treat others as you would want to be treated." This simple rule is embraced, in one form or another, by most of the world's religions and philosophies,[42] and its influence is very far reaching. For example, the philosopher Immanuel Kant presented the so-called categorical imperative, a sophisticated way of asking, "How would it be if everyone decided to do what you intend to do?"[43] Raising questions like these can be a very practical way for an entrepreneur to evaluate ethical decisions and guard her or his integrity.

No matter what approach you take, evaluating alternatives requires time and patience. And to make the exercise even more challenging, personal perceptions and biases are likely to cloud the way you see solutions. Therefore, it is important to separate what you *think* is the case from what you *know* to be true. It often helps to write down your thoughts about alternatives so that you can keep track of your concerns as well as important facts and details. You might list the ethical pros and cons of each alternative or identify the impact of each option on every person or company that will be affected. Another possibility is to rank all potential options based on their overall merits and then narrow the list to the two or three best solutions so that you can consider these further. This will allow you to organize your thoughts and make a better selection.

STEP 4: MAKE THE DECISION   The next step is to choose the "best" ethical response, based on your evaluation of all possible alternatives. On the surface, this sounds easy enough, but unfortunately no single option will completely solve the problem in most cases; in fact, you may not even be able to identify an obvious winner. No matter how you go about making the decision, keep your vision and core values firmly in mind—this is essential to making solid decisions that do not compromise your ethical standards.

STEP 5: IMPLEMENT THE DECISION   This may seem like a "no-brainer," but entrepreneurs sometimes put off responding to ethical challenges because the solution is not apparent or because any response will be bad news for someone involved. But putting off the decision may allow a small problem to grow into a major crisis. Even if the decision is not pressing, delaying your response will cause you to spend more time thinking about the dilemma when other important matters deserve your attention.

STEP 6: EVALUATE THE DECISION   The goal of making a decision is to resolve an ethical dilemma. So, how has your response panned out? Has the situation improved, gotten worse, or stayed about the same? Has the solution created ethical issues of its own? Has information come to light indicating that your decision was not the most ethical course of action? Everyone makes mistakes. You may very well need to reopen the matter to make things right. But remember, if your decision was based on the best of intentions and information available at the time, you can wade back into the waters of ethical turmoil with a clear conscience, and there is no substitute for that.

Social Entrepreneurship: A Fast-Emerging Trend

The social issues affecting businesses are numerous and diverse. Businesses are expected—at different times and by various groups—to help solve social problems related to education, crime, poverty, and the environment. In fact, these expectations—yet another aspect of integrity—are converging into a form of venturing called *social entrepreneurship,* which is rapidly gaining momentum. Though the term has been defined in different ways, Harvard researchers suggest that *social entrepreneurship* refers to "entrepreneurial activity with an embedded social purpose."[44] In other words, a social entrepreneur is one who comes up with innovative solutions to society's most pressing needs, problems, and opportunities.

Becoming a social entrepreneur usually does not mean that one is no longer concerned with making money—financial gain is just one of an expanded set of goals. In fact, the outcomes of interest are sometimes referred to as the "triple bottom line" because they focus on people, profits, and the planet. Profits are essential because, as you already know, no enterprise can exist for long without them. But social entrepreneurs believe ventures should also address the needs of people and the environment. To get a feel for the wide range of enterprises that fall under the social entrepreneurship umbrella, consider the following cases:

- Alicia Polak moved to South Africa and started Khayelitsha Cookie Co. to create jobs in the poor townships outside Capetown. Two years after launch, the company was providing employment for ten women and was poised to export cookies and brownies to the United States.[45]

6. Describe social entrepreneurship and the costs and opportunities of environmentalism for small businesses.

social entrepreneurship
Entrepreneurial activity whose goal is to find innovative solutions to social needs, problems, and opportunities.

- Windows of Opportunity is a for-profit business that has already replaced energy-wasting, lead-painted windows in inner-city homes, protecting children from lead poisoning and saving families more than $350,000 in energy costs.[46]

- For years, Bart Weetjens has been training rats in the African nation of Tanzania to sniff out the deadly unexploded land mines that litter the countryside in so many war-torn nations. It turns out that rats are better than dogs for this work—lighter, cheaper to keep, and less prone to tropical diseases—and they clear areas so that children can run and play without fear of stepping on a mine. "They save human lives," says Weetjens, who actually calls the rodents "heroes."[47]

These entrepreneurs clearly do not fit the money-obsessed stereotype that some associate with business owners. They are hoping to do more than make a profit, but they are doing well financially, too.

The Burden of Environmentalism

The triple-bottom-line formula specifically mentions the planet. In recent decades, deterioration of the environment has become a matter of widespread concern. Today, *environmentalism,* the effort to protect and preserve the environment, directly affects most businesses. Releasing industrial waste into streams, contaminants into the air, and noise into neighborhoods is no longer acceptable.

environmentalism
The effort to protect and preserve the environment.

The interests of small business owners and environmentalists are not necessarily—or uniformly—in conflict. Some business leaders, including many in small companies, have consistently worked and acted for the cause of conservation. For example, many small firms have modernized their equipment and changed their procedures to reduce air and water pollution. Others have taken steps to landscape and otherwise improve the appearance of plant facilities. Some small businesses have actually been in a position to benefit from the growing emphasis on the environment. For example, firms whose products do not harm the environment are generally preferred by customers over competitors whose products pollute. And some small companies actually build their business on planet-saving services. Small auto repair shops, for example, service pollution-control devices on automobiles.

Other small firms, however, are adversely affected by new laws passed to protect the environment. Businesses such as fast lube and oil change centers, medical waste disposal operations, self-service car washes, and asbestos removal services have been especially hard hit by expanding environmental regulations. The costs can be punishing. In fact, many companies in these industries and others have closed because of the financial burden of environmental controls. Small companies that enjoy favorable market conditions can often pass higher environmental costs on to their customers, but these can easily sink a small, marginal firm with obsolete equipment and limited resources to upgrade.

Regardless of the financial impact, it is critical to follow the environmental regulations that apply to your business; to ignore this responsibility is to violate the law. The authors of *Greening Your Business: A Primer for Smaller Companies* caution small businesses to comply with regulations at all levels—federal, state, and local—but their overall message is actually very upbeat: "There are dozens of ways companies of all sizes can reduce their environmental footprints, save money, earn consumer trust and stakeholder confidence, comply with government regulations, be ready to snag new market opportunities, and boost efficiency and productivity."[48]

Win-win solutions are possible. Compliance may actually lead to additional benefits, such as a reduction in governmental paperwork for companies that can show they are in line with regulations. And assistance is available. The Small Business Administration is prepared to lead you through the sometimes choppy waters of environmental law, and the U.S. Environmental Protection Agency (EPA) offers the Small Business Gateway, an Internet portal that will connect you to information, technical assistance, and solutions to challenges related to the environment. For example, the EPA provides online access to a guide called *Managing Your Hazardous Waste: A Guide for Small Businesses,* which makes compliance much easier to manage.[49] Taking advantage of resources such as these can help you avoid the potentially terrible consequences of noncompliance.

When the BigBelly Solar Compactor can is filled with trash, a solar-powered motor kicks on and compresses it. This one, in Boston, cuts trash collection trips, reduces the number of garbage trucks, and decreases the amount of diesel fuel burned each year.

The Potential of Environmentalism

Although it adds to the cost of doing business for some small companies, environmental concern opens up great opportunities for others. In fact, many startups have come to life precisely because of "the greening of business" and the potential this has created.

Recent reports indicate that investor dollars have started to flow into ventures based on technologies that are labeled "green," "clean," "sustainable," or "environmental."[50] Many of these businesses are focused on sophisticated technologies that run well beyond the reach of the typical small business. However, some opportunities in this category are accessible to small companies and startups.

James Poss founded Seahorse Power Company in 2003 to develop, manufacture, and sell innovative energy-efficient products. The company's flagship product is the BigBelly Solar Compactor, which is a trash can like no other. Boxy and green, this innovative product looks more like a mailbox with no legs than a garbage can. But what a difference! When the can is filled with refuse, a solar-powered motor kicks on and compresses the trash to one-eighth of its original size. This cuts trash collection trips by up to 80 percent, reducing the number of garbage trucks on the road, cutting down on traffic congestion, and decreasing the estimated 1 billion gallons of diesel fuel that the trucks burn each year. The formula makes sense and to date, more than 1,500 Big Bellies have been sold across the United States and in 15 other countries. Planned innovations will only make the value proposition more attractive—these include a wireless notification system (to signal workers when the bin needs to be emptied) and a larger commercial-scale compactor.[51] This is one recent startup that may cash in big on rising fuel costs.

For some, the ultimate goal is to save the planet, but more companies are likely to join the environmental movement because it actually generates value for shareholders. According to Stuart L. Hart, a professor of strategy at the University of North Carolina, the movement will provide huge opportunities for companies with "moxie" and creativity, as long as they can execute the plan.[52] This sounds like prime territory for small entrepreneurial companies, given their flexibility and innovative thinking. Entrepreneurs may be able to do well *and* do good—guarding the environment and their integrity at the same time.

LOOKING BACK

1. Define integrity and understand its importance to small businesses.

- Integrity is an uncompromising adherence to the lofty values, beliefs, and principles that an individual claims to hold.
- "Doing anything for money" can quickly lead to distortions in business behavior.
- Many small business owners strive to achieve the highest standards of honesty, fairness, and respect in their business relationships.

2. Explain how integrity applies to various stakeholder groups, including owners, customers, employees, the community, and the government.

- Closely tied to integrity are ethical issues, which go beyond what is legal or illegal to include more general questions of right and wrong.
- The most troublesome ethical issues for small businesses involve relationships with customers and competitors, human resource decisions, and employees' obligations to their employers.
- When they make business decisions, entrepreneurs must consider the interests of all stakeholder groups, in particular those of owners, customers, employees, the community, and the government.
- A company's owners have a clear and legitimate right to benefit from the financial performance of the business.
- Those companies who take customers seriously and serve them well are likely to have more of them.
- Research shows that about one-fourth of the employees in small businesses experience some degree of pressure to act unethically in their jobs.
- Most people consider an ethical small business to be one that acts as a good citizen in its community.
- Entrepreneurs must obey governmental laws and follow applicable regulations if they want to maintain their integrity and avoid jail time.

3. Identify challenges to integrity that arise in small businesses and explain the benefits of integrity to small firms.

- The limited resources of small firms make them especially vulnerable to allowing or engaging in unethical practices.
- Research suggests that most entrepreneurs exercise great integrity, but some are likely to cut ethical corners when it comes to issues that directly affect profits.

- Exhibiting integrity in business may actually boost a firm's performance.
- One of the greatest benefits of integrity is the trust it generates.

4. Explain the impact of the Internet and globalization on the integrity of small businesses.

- Use of the Internet has highlighted ethical issues such as invasion of privacy and threats to intellectual property rights.
- Cultural differences complicate decision making for small firms operating in the global marketplace.

5. Describe practical approaches for building a business with integrity.

- The underlying values of business leaders and the behavioral examples of those leaders are powerful forces that affect ethical performance.
- An organizational culture that supports integrity is key to achieving appropriate behavior among a firm's employees.
- Small firms should develop codes of ethics to provide guidance for their employees.
- Many small companies join Better Business Bureaus to promote ethical conduct throughout the business community.
- Following an ethical decision-making process can help entrepreneurs protect their integrity and that of their business.

6. Describe social entrepreneurship and the costs and opportunities of environmentalism for small businesses.

- Social entrepreneurship (entrepreneurship with an embedded social purpose) is a fast-emerging trend.
- Many small businesses help protect the environment, and some contribute positively by providing environmental services.
- Some small firms, such as fast lube and oil change centers, are adversely affected by costly environmental regulations.
- Small companies are sometimes launched precisely to take advantage of opportunities created by environmental concerns.
- Creating environmentally friendly products requires creativity and flexibility, areas in which small businesses tend to excel.

Key Terms

integrity p. 32

ethical issues p. 33

stakeholders p. 34

social responsibilities p. 39

intellectual property p. 46

ethical imperialism p. 47

ethical relativism p. 47

underlying values p. 47

code of ethics p. 49

social entrepreneurship p. 52

environmentalism p. 53

Discussion Questions

1. The owner of a small business felt an obligation to pay $15,000 to a subcontractor, even though, because of an oversight, the subcontractor had never submitted a bill. Can willingness to pay under these circumstances be reconciled with the profit goal of a business in a free enterprise system?

2. Give an example of an unethical business practice that you have personally encountered.

3. Based on your experience as an employee, customer, or observer of a particular small business, how would you rate its ethical performance? On what evidence or clues do you base your opinion?

4. Give some examples of the practical application of a firm's basic commitment to supporting the family life of its employees.

5. What is skimming? How do you think owners of small firms might attempt to rationalize such a practice?

6. What are some of the advantages of conducting business with integrity? Some people say they have no responsibility beyond maximizing the value of the firm in financial terms. Can this position be defended? If so, how?

7. Explain the connection between underlying values and integrity in business behavior.

8. Why might small business CEOs focus more attention on profit and less on social goals than large business CEOs do?

9. Give some examples of expenditures required on the part of small business firms to protect the environment.

10. Should all firms use biodegradable packaging? Would your answer be the same if you knew that using such packaging added 15 percent to the company's cost of producing a product?

You Make the Call

SITUATION 1

Sally started her consulting business a year ago and has been doing very well. About a month ago, she decided she needed to hire someone to help her since she was getting busier and busier. After interviewing several candidates, she decided to hire the best one of the group, Mary. She called Mary on Monday to tell her she had gotten the job. They both agreed that she would start the following Monday and that Mary could come in and fill out all the hiring paperwork at that time.

On Tuesday of the same week, a friend of Sally's called her to say that she had found the perfect person for Sally. Sally explained that she had already hired someone, but the friend insisted. "Just meet this girl. Who knows, maybe you might want to hire her in the future!"

Rather reluctantly, Sally consented. "Alright, if she can come in tomorrow, I'll meet with her, but that's all."

"Oh, I'm so glad. I just know you're going to like her!" Sally's friend exclaimed.

And Sally did like her. She liked her a lot. Sally had met with Julie on Wednesday morning. She was everything that Sally had been looking for and more. In terms of experience, Julie far surpassed any of the candidates Sally had previously interviewed, including Mary. On top of that, she was willing to bring in clients of her own which would only increase business. All in all, Sally knew this was a win-win situation. But what about Mary? She had already given her word to Mary that she could start work on Monday.

Question 1 What decision on Sally's part would contribute most to the success of her business?

Question 2 What ethical reasoning would support hiring Mary?

Question 3 What ethical reasoning would support hiring Julie?

Source: http://www.sba.gov/smallbusinessplanner/manage/lead/SERV_BETHICS.html, accessed September 21, 2008.

SITUATION 2

Software piracy is a serious problem in Ukraine. While the latest version of Microsoft's Windows normally sells for around $100 when purchased through a legitimate vendor, the same package can be picked up on the black market in Kiev for around $2, and it is usually bundled with additional software as a bonus! Brad, a project manager working in the Ukrainian office of an American consulting services firm, ponders the question of whether or not to buy 325 copies of pirated software through a local source for $1.85 per copy, versus purchasing these through an authorized vendor. The cost saving from this one decision would be nearly $32,000, and Brad knows that annual bonuses are tied to any cost savings.

To complicate matters further, Brad's office is up against strong rivals in the same market, and they usually purchase pirated software to control costs. The competition is so fierce and margins are so thin that Brad's company is thinking about pulling out of the market. Having to pay full price for legitimate software might be "the straw that breaks the camel's back"—that is, it might be all it takes to convince management in the United States to close the office down. The move to Ukraine was hard on Brad's wife and their twin daughters. After 14 months of settling in, they are finally getting comfortable with their new life in Kiev. Brad really doesn't want to move them again, at least not now. And furthermore, it is well known that social standards in Ukraine do not emphasize proprietary property rights anyway. Microsoft is so big that one lost order would hardly be noticed, and Microsoft won't even get the order if the company decides to close the Kiev office down.

Question 1 Is the project manager acting with integrity if he purchases unauthorized copies of the software on the black market?

Question 2 What might be the long-term effects of deciding to buy the pirated software? Of insisting on buying only legitimate copies of the software?

Question 3 What are the important questions to ask in a situation like this? Follow the ethical decision-making process outlined in the chapter. Does it work in this scenario?

Question 4 What course of action do you recommend? Why?

SITUATION 3

WizeGuyz Media, a small marketing firm, ordered key chains for a client named Bob Whitaker. The key chains were imprinted with three initials related to the theme of an advertising campaign created specifically for Whitaker's automobile sales business. The client approved the artwork but then, upon delivery, noticed there was no period after the last letter. Whitaker asked for a price adjustment, and the owner of WizeGuyz's responded by asking what he considered to be a reasonable discount. Whitaker still wanted the key chains but proposed that WizeGuyz pay $3,000 of the bill, which was 65 percent of the total cost.

Question 1 Is this a customer relations problem or an ethics problem?

Question 2 Is Whitaker's request reasonable?

Question 3 Should WizeGuyz accept the proposed settlement?

Experiential Exercises

1. Examine a recent business periodical, and report briefly on some lapse in integrity that is in the news. Could this type of problem occur in a small business? Explain.

2. Employees sometimes take sick leave when they are merely tired, and students sometimes miss class for the same reason. Separate into groups of four or five, and prepare a statement on the nature of the ethical issue (if any) in these practices.

3. Visit or telephone the nearest Better Business Bureau office to research the types of inappropriate business practices it has uncovered in the community and the ways in which it is attempting to support practices that reflect integrity. Report briefly on your findings.

4. Interview an entrepreneur or a small business manager to learn how environmental concerns affect her or his firm.

Small Business & Entrepreneurship Resource Center

The Small Business and Entrepreneurship Resource Center offers complete small business management resources through a comprehensive database that covers all major areas of starting, operating, and maintaining a business from financing, management, marketing, accounting, taxes, and more. Use the access code that came with your new book to access the site and perform the exercises in each chapter.

1. Craig Hall, the author of *The Responsible Entrepreneur*, encourages small business owners to practice what he calls "responsible entrepreneurship". His company

donates 5 percent of its income to charity, and any employee can take off up to 40 hours a year to work with charitable organizations. He believes that being responsible is vital to business success. Describe what is meant by the term "responsible entrepreneur" and the ways in which you feel that entrepreneurs can make a difference.

2. One executive observed that running a business is sometimes like juggling. In his words, "I am given four balls to balance: the customer's, the employees', the community's, and the stockholders', by which I mean profit. It's never made clear to me how I am to keep them all going, but I know for certain that there is one that I'd better not drop, and that's profit."

Hall Office Park has been built by Hall Financial Group in an effort to redefine the typical office environment and promote corporate responsibility toward employees. After reading the above articles, describe what Hall Office Park offers and how you feel it contributes to social responsibility.

Sources: Entrepreneurs make a difference. (Interview). (Craig Hall)(Interview). *Journal of Property Management* 67, 3 (May 2002): p. 72 (2). Entrepreneurs make a difference. (Interview).(Craig Hall)(Interview).
Redefining the office. (The Buzz).(Hall Office Park amenities)(Brief Article). *Buildings* 96, 1 (Jan 2002): p. 6(1). Redefining the office. (The Buzz). (Hall Office Park amenities)(Brief Article).
Pocket of Prosperity.(Far North Dallas seen as next big area of development), Perez, Christine. *National Real Estate Investor* 44, 11 (Nov 1, 2002): Gale. Higher Education. 9 June 2009.

Video Case 2

JOSEPH'S LITE COOKIES (P. 626)

This case explores some of the ways in which an entrepreneur can build a business on a foundation of honesty and integrity as expressed by a strong commitment to employees, customers, and the community.

ALTERNATIVE CASES FOR CHAPTER 2

PART 2
Starting from Scratch or Joining an Existing Business

Yuri Arcurs/Shutterstock.com

chapters

## chapter 3

Getting Started

Courtesy of Gena Stanisic for Hanover Community Bank

Entertainer Steve Martin points out in one of his comedy routines that it takes some business savvy to launch a new venture, beginning with the task of choosing a name for the enterprise. As Martin jokes, "You have to have a command of the English language . . . because nobody's gonna put their money in 'Fred's Bank.' Hi, I'm Fred [and] I have a bank." You may think it takes much more than coming up with an appropriate name to start a bank, and that is true, but going into the banking business may not be as impossible as you think. In fact, over the last five years, the U.S. government approved the creation of a total of 738 new banks—none of them named "Fred's Bank," incidentally.

Economic turmoil has a way of getting the entrepreneurial juices flowing, and when the economy spiraled its way into a serious downturn in 2008, many entrepreneurs focused their attention on the new business opportunities that began to open up. Some recognized the great promise of banking. For example, after years of mergers and a shrinking number of independent savings and lending institutions on Long Island, New York, entrepreneurs launched three new banks in two years, and at least three more are planned. One of the startups is Hanover Community Bank, which opened its first branch on December 10, 2008. "It's a great time to open," says James Jacovatos, the startup's CEO. "A lot of the existing operations might be pulling back on their lending. There's a great opportunity now to do the lending you want to do."

But isn't the banking sector in the tank? Yes, it is, and that is exactly the kind of opening Hanover was looking for. Despite the weak economy, one banking entrepreneur has concluded that this is arguably "the most opportune time to launch a commercial bank in our nation's history," precisely because existing banks are in such trouble. Compared to its established rivals, Hanover may not have a huge customer base or name recognition, but it has one very important advantage: It does not have to worry about a lending portfolio that is weighted down by distressed loans to defaulting borrowers. The basic economics of the startup situation are sound.

But there's more to it than that. Starting a new bank requires money (on average, $15 to

LOOKING AHEAD

AFTER STUDYING THIS CHAPTER YOU SHOULD BE ABLE TO . . .

1. Distinguish among the different types and sources of startup ideas and identify the most common sources of startup ideas.

2. Use innovative thinking to generate ideas for high-potential startups.

3. Describe external and internal analyses that might shape the selection of venture opportunities.

4. Explain broad-based strategy options and focus strategies.

5. Assess the feasibility of a startup idea before writing a business plan.

$20 million in initial investment), experienced management, and an acceptable risk profile—without these, the federal government will not guarantee customers' deposits. It also requires a sound plan, or strategy. Most new banks are emphasizing customer service (which has long been neglected by the big players) and a focus on the needs of small and medium-sized businesses. Others are catering to ethnic groups. For example, Hanover raised more than half of its money from nearby Asian and Indian communities. These are all indicators of opportunity, and the new kids on the lending block plan to make the most of them.

You may not see yourself as a potential banking entrepreneur, but you can learn a lot about starting a successful business—regardless of its type—by taking note of the moves of Hanover and its peers. You can also take comfort in knowing that these new lenders are focusing specifically on the needs of small businesses like the one you will launch. Their financial support may be exactly what your enterprise needs.

Sources: Jon Hilsenrath and S. Mitra Kalita, "It's a Great Time to Start a Bank," *Wall Street Journal* (March 17, 2009), http://online.wsj.com/article/SB123724564069748443.html, accessed March 19, 2009; Claude Solnik, "2008 Was a Good Year to Start a Bank," *Long Island Business News*, December 1, 2008, http://libn.com/blog/2008/12/01/it%E2%80%99s-been-a-good-year-for-community-banks, accessed March 19, 2009; Susan Harrigan, "Some Find LI Still Ripe for New Banks," *Newsday.com*, http://www.snl.com/snlitn/scans/051807somefnewday.pdf, accessed March 20, 2009.

As an Internet expert and author of a book on the power of tech-enabled social interaction, Clay Shirky has concluded that he knows a lot of things in life merely as a result of his experiences. For example, he knows that music comes from stores, that customers have to try on pants before they buy them, that people read newspapers to catch up on the latest in the world of politics, and that tourists arrange their trips by visiting a travel agent. But then he points out the obvious: "In the last 15 years or so, I have had to unlearn every one of [these] things and a million others."[1] To say it another way, entrepreneurs keep coming up with innovative ways of doing things, and the new businesses they create from these concepts change the way we live. But to get the ball rolling, someone must recognize high-potential startup ideas that others have overlooked. Identifying imaginative new products or services that may lead to promising business ventures is so central to the entrepreneurial process that it has its own name: *opportunity recognition*.

Business opportunities are like air—they are always around, even though you may not realize it. What sets entrepreneurs apart from everyone else is their ability to see the potential that others overlook and then take the bold steps necessary to get businesses up and running. How do they do it? Most entrepreneurs have uncommon observational skills and the motivation to act on what they see. In some cases, the identification of a new business opportunity may be the result of an active search for possibilities or insights derived from personal experience or work background. In other cases, the search for opportunities may be a less deliberate and more automatic process.[2] Economist Israel Kirzner proposed that entrepreneurs have a unique capability, which he called *entrepreneurial alertness*. According to this view, entrepreneurs are not actually the source of innovative ideas; rather, they are simply "alert to the opportunities that exist *already* and are waiting to be noticed."[3] When these opportunities are aligned with an entrepreneur's knowledge and aspirations, they are even more likely to be spotted.

A discussion of the finer points of entrepreneurial alertness is beyond the scope of this book,[4] but it is important to understand that thinking about the world around you and being aware of conditions that might lead to new business opportunities can really pay off.[5] Try it and see if new possibilities become apparent to you. Over the next week or so, instead of just passing through life, take note of trends, changes, or situations that might support a new business. You will probably be surprised at how many potential opportunities you can identify. If you continue this rather deliberate search, over time you may find it becomes a habit.[6]

Perhaps you already have a business idea in mind that you would like to pursue. With good planning and the right strategy, you may soon be well on your way to success as an entrepreneur. On the

opportunity recognition
Identification of potential new products or services that may lead to promising businesses.

entrepreneurial alertness
Readiness to act on existing, but unnoticed, business opportunities.

other hand, you may have a passionate desire to start your own company but are not sure you have come up with the right business idea to get you there. Or maybe you have an *idea* in mind but are not sure if it is a good *business opportunity*. No matter which group you fall into, this chapter will help to get you started on the right foot, with the right idea and the right strategy.

In Part 1 of this book (Chapters 1 and 2), we discussed the mind-set and lifestyle of the entrepreneur and the importance of integrity in the enterprise. Now, in Part 2, we focus on topics to help individual entrepreneurs decide what kind of venture would be best for them.

startups
New business ventures started "from scratch."

In this chapter, we describe opportunity recognition and strategy setting for *startups*— businesses that did not exist before entrepreneurs created them. The chapters that follow will go beyond a discussion of new ventures "started from scratch" and consider business opportunities that already exist, including purchasing a franchise or buying an existing business (Chapter 4) or joining a family business (Chapter 5).

Coming Up with Startup Ideas

1. Distinguish among the different types and sources of startup ideas and identify the most common sources of startup ideas.

Several motivations may lead you to consider starting an enterprise from scratch rather than pursuing other alternatives, such as buying a franchise or an existing business or joining a family business. For example, you may have a personal desire to develop the commercial market for a recently invented or newly developed product or service, or you may be hoping to tap into unique resources that are available to you—an ideal location, new equipment technologies, a powerful network of connections, and so forth. Some entrepreneurs get "startup fever" because they want the challenge of succeeding (or failing) on their own, or they hope to avoid undesirable features of existing companies, such as unpleasant work cultures or smothering legal commitments. There are almost as many reasons as there are aspiring entrepreneurs!

So how do you get started? It all begins with a promising business idea. But new venture concepts are not all equal, and they can come from many different sources. By recognizing the nature and origin of startup ideas, an entrepreneur can broaden the range of new ideas available for his or her consideration.

Types of Startup Ideas

Exhibit 3-1 shows the three basic types of ideas that develop into startups: ideas to enter new markets, ideas based on new technologies, and ideas that offer new benefits.

EXHIBIT 3-1 Types of Ideas That Develop into Startups

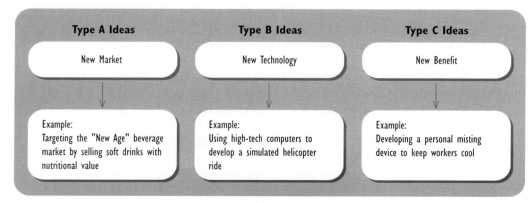

Type A Ideas	Type B Ideas	Type C Ideas
New Market	New Technology	New Benefit
Example: Targeting the "New Age" beverage market by selling soft drinks with nutritional value	Example: Using high-tech computers to develop a simulated helicopter ride	Example: Developing a personal misting device to keep workers cool

© R. Alcorn/Cengage

Getting started is the toughest part. I always tell aspiring entrepreneurs who have a business idea to keep their idea to themselves in the beginning. I didn't tell anyone my idea for footless panty-hose, not even friends or family. Every-one knew I was working on an invention, but they didn't know what it was until I had already invested a year of my time.

This is important because so many people stop dead in their tracks because someone, out of love, brings up 50 things for them to worry about. The minute you put your idea out there, you're forced to justify it. A year after working on my prototype for SPANX footless pantyhose, I told everyone my idea and was met with a lot of questions and skepticism. People asked, "Is that really such a good idea? The big guys will just knock you off." If I hadn't already invested a year, I might not have started SPANX.

Many startups develop from what we will call *Type A ideas*—those concerned with providing customers with a product or service that does not exist in a particular market but that exists somewhere else. Randall Rothenberg, an author and the director of intellectual capital at consulting powerhouse Booz Allen Hamilton, says that this type of startup idea may have the greatest potential: "There's ample evidence that some of the biggest businesses are built by taking existing ideas and applying them in a new context."[7]

Many small businesses are built on this platform. Filmmaker Christian D'Andrea was making a documentary on Special Forces when he saw a soldier chomping down a U.S. military–issued energy bar that was developed specifically to provide the extra boost those in uniform need on the battlefield. D'Andrea recognized an opportunity to take the product, which civilians couldn't buy, to a whole new market. He and his brother, Mark, signed a deal giving them license to tap the science behind the product, and they used it to create the Hoorah! Bar, a pick-me-up snack that today sells in thousands of stores and online outlets. Business is good, and growing; in fact, their Los Angeles–based startup, D'Andrea Brothers LLC, recently expanded its product line to include an energy drink based on the same formulation. With sales continuing to climb, it is clear that tapping "military intelligence" to take an existing product to the civilian market can yield impressive results.[8]

Some startups are based on *Type B ideas*, which involve new or relatively new technology. This type of business can be high risk because there is usually no model of success to follow, but it can also have tremendous potential. Rick Alden created such a venture when he recognized that those who wear headphones (himself included) often find it difficult to answer incoming calls on their cell phones. He knew that developing headphones that would work with both music devices and cell phones would be a relatively simple technological feat, and it would solve a hassle for cell phone users worldwide. So, after coming up with such a device, he launched a business in 2002 to take this and other audio products to customers around the globe. His instincts were right on

Type A ideas
Startup ideas centered around providing customers with an existing product not available in their market.

Type B ideas
Startup ideas, involving new technology, centered around providing customers with a new product.

Type C ideas
Startup ideas centered around providing customers with an improved product.

target. The company, called Skullcandy Inc., has been so successful that it now has 38 employees and will soon reach $100 million in annual sales![9]

Type C ideas—those based on offering customers benefits from new and improved products or ways of performing old functions—probably account for the largest number of startups. In fact, most new ventures, especially in the service industry, are founded on "me, too" strategies, but they usually set themselves apart through features such as superior service or lower prices. Laurie Johnson's effort to redefine the common crutch fits into the Type C category. As founder of LemonAid Crutches, Johnson found a way to take some of the sting out of having to be on crutches after an injury. Her designer props were born of experience. While Johnson was recovering from a broken leg sustained in a small-plane crash that took the lives of her husband and two-year-old son, her sister tried to cheer her up some by spray painting her crutches and trimming the handles in fabric. Her response? "I sat there thinking, 'Oh my gosh, this is so silly, but they make me feel better!'" Determined to turn life's lemons into lemonade (hence the name of the company), Johnson decided to run with the concept and help other crutch users feel better, too. In mid-2005, she launched her venture to sell a variety of fashionably functional crutches, with prices ranging from $140 to $175 a pair.[10] Sales took off, and Johnson's startup is now on a solid footing.

Common Sources of Startup Ideas

At this point, you may be saying, "I want to start a new business but still haven't come up with a startup idea that sounds like a good investment opportunity." There are a number of sources you can turn to for inspiration. And if one source fails to lead you to the idea of your dreams, keep looking. The spark for innovative ideas can come from many different places.

Several studies have identified sources of ideas for small business startups. Exhibit 3-2 shows the results of one such study by the National Federation of Independent Business (NFIB), which found that prior work experience accounted for 45 percent of new ideas. This finding is consistent

EXHIBIT 3-2 Common Sources of Startup Ideas

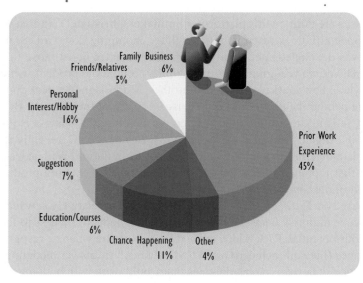

Source: Data developed and provided by the National Federation of Independent Business and sponsored by the American Express Travel Related Services Company, Inc.

with another national study of entrepreneurs, the Panel Study of Entrepreneurial Dynamics (PSED). The PSED data also show that entrepreneurs most often consider work experience in a particular industry or market to be the source of their startup ideas.[11] However, there are other important sources. As confirmed in the exhibit, the NFIB study found that personal interests and hobbies represented 16 percent of the total, and chance happenings accounted for 11 percent. Ideas for a startup can come from anywhere, but in this part of the chapter we will focus on four possible sources: personal experience, hobbies, accidental discovery, and change-based sources.

PERSONAL EXPERIENCE One of the primary sources of startup ideas is personal experience. Often knowledge gleaned from a present or former job allows a person to see possibilities for modifying an existing product, improving a service, becoming a supplier that meets an employer's needs better than current vendors, or duplicating a business concept in a different location. Or personal contacts may open up conversations with suppliers who are interested in working with you or customers who have needs that are not currently being met. Startup concepts may even come to mind as a result of trying personal circumstances or misfortunes, especially when the entrepreneur is able to use work experience or technical skills to address the challenge at hand. Regardless of the situation, these insights may lead you to an opportunity with tremendous potential.

How much does a typical, lightweight cotton T-shirt cut down the sun's rays before they reach your skin? Melissa Marks Papock found that the answer to that question is, *not much*. She was diagnosed with skin cancer at age 26, which led her to conclude that her clothing was not protecting her skin from sun damage. After overcoming cancer, she decided to focus her skills as a fashion industry veteran on helping others beat the disease too. In 2005, she started a company called Cabana Life to offer a line of sun-protective clothing that uses a patented technology to block 98 percent of the sun's UV rays. The concept seems to be catching on, with sales in 2007 reaching the $700,000 mark within only two years from startup. Reflecting on her progress, Papock concludes that facing challenges in life can actually help prime the pump of entrepreneurial success. "Using your own experience can make you more passionate about your business and help you convey more sincerity to customers," she says. "You discover the need when you're faced with a situation."[12]

HOBBIES AND PERSONAL INTERESTS Sometimes hobbies grow beyond being leisure activities to become businesses. For instance, people who love skiing might start a ski equipment rental operation as a way to make income from an activity that they enjoy, and those who love books might explore concepts that lead to new bookstores. Hobbies and personal interests can add surprising energy to the startup process, which was certainly the case for 39-year-old Alex Shogren. The number of extreme sports has grown exponentially over the past decade, and Shogren is bound and determined to ride that wave. His sport of choice is kiteboarding—which uses a large kite to propel a person across land, snow, or water on a kiteboard (similar to a surfboard) or other platform—and he has found a way to make it pay handsomely. "Originally, I looked at starting a kite company to write off my travel expenses," says Shogren. "But when I researched the industry, I realized there was a huge opportunity." And his instincts were right on the money. In 2003 he started a company in Delray Beach, Florida, called Best Kiteboarding, and in less than five years its sales reached $1 million. The venture definitely feeds off of the passion of Shogren and his associates. Its Website emphasizes that the company is staffed and run by "kiteboarders . . . who live, breathe, and dream kiteboarding," enthusiasts who would proudly declare, "This is my dream job."[13]

ACCIDENTAL DISCOVERY Another source of new startup ideas—accidental discovery—involves something called *serendipity*, a gift for making desirable discoveries by accident. Awareness obviously plays a role here, but anyone may stumble across a useful idea in the course of day-to-day living. This is exactly what happened to Tia Wou. It all started when she attended a friend's wedding in Bolivia, where she fell in love with the rich fabrics she saw in the marketplace. After returning to her work in the fashion industry, it occurred to Wou that she could use the materials she'd seen in Bolivia to make handbags with the Japanese designs she had in mind for sale in America. From that inspiration, Wou launched Tote Le Monde in 1994,

serendipity
A gift for making desirable discoveries by accident.

EXHIBIT 3-3

Change-Based Sources of Entrepreneurial Opportunities

Change Factor	Definition	Illustration
Industry or Enterprise Factors		
The unexpected	Unanticipated events lead to either enterprise success or failure.	Pet pharmaceuticals have been very successful, with more than 30% of dogs and cats now taking medication.
The incongruous	That which is expected is out of line with what will work.	Low-fat ice cream was developed for those trying to lose weight.
Process needs	Current technology is insufficient to address an emerging challenge.	General Motors creates an electric car called the Volt to deal with rising energy costs.
Structural change	Changes in technologies, markets, etc., alter industry dynamics.	The use of digital cinema technology has led to the widespread showing of 3-D movies.
External Factors		
Demographics	Shifts in population size, age structure, ethnicity, and income distribution impact product demand.	The rapid growth of the Hispanic market in the U.S. has spawned a flood of Spanish-language newspapers.
Changes in perception	Perceptual variations determine product demand.	Perceived security threats have led to the development of gated communities.
New knowledge	Learning opens the door to new product opportunities with commercial potential.	Breakthroughs in solar power technologies have fueled the growth of "green" residential developments.

a New York City-based handbag manufacturer. Today, the entrepreneurial spirit of the business is alive and well, as is Tote le Monde's original mission: "To create innovation where function finds form."[14] Wou's experience just goes to show that you can come up with promising business ideas when you're not even looking for them.

KEEPING AN EYE ON CHANGE   Change is one of the most important sources of ideas for entrepreneurs. Whereas large firms often prefer the status quo—why fix it if it's not broken?—entrepreneurs are much more likely to recognize change as an opportunity and to have the creativity and flexibility to adjust to it. Business guru Peter Drucker believed entrepreneurs should consider seven sources of opportunity as they prepare to launch or grow their enterprises.[15] These change-based sources of opportunity are outlined in Exhibit 3-3.

According to Drucker, "Innovation is the specific instrument of entrepreneurship." He further described it as "the act that endows resources with a new capacity to create wealth."[16] In other words, entrepreneurship harnesses the power of creativity to provide innovative products and services. Since change inspires innovation, recognizing shifts in the factors described in Exhibit 3-3 can expand the range of entrepreneurial opportunities.

OTHER IDEA LEADS   If analyzing emerging changes does not reveal the specific entrepreneurial opportunity that is right for you, other sources of leads are available. The following have been useful to many entrepreneurs:

- Tapping personal contacts with potential customers and suppliers, professors, patent attorneys, former or current employees or co-workers, venture capitalists, and chambers of commerce
- Visiting trade shows, production facilities, universities, and research institutes

- Observing trends related to material limitations and energy shortages, emerging technologies, recreation, fads, pollution problems, personal security, and social movements
- Reading trade publications, bankruptcy announcements, Commerce Department publications, and business classifieds

Inc. Magazine Entrepreneur, MyBusiness, and other periodicals are excellent sources of startup ideas, because they provide articles on the creativity of entrepreneurs and various business opportunities. Visiting the library and even looking through the Yellow Pages in other cities can spark creative thoughts as well. Traveling to other states to visit entrepreneurs in your field of interest can also be extremely helpful. Of course, the Internet provides an unlimited supply of information regarding the startup process and even specific opportunities. For example, *Entrepreneur* magazine (http://www.entrepreneur.com) offers online tools such as the Business Idea Center, which profiles around 1,000 business ideas that can be browsed by category, interest, profession, startup costs, and other criteria.

Using Innovative Thinking to Generate Business Ideas

A creative person can find useful ideas in many different places. It is important to commit to a lifestyle of creative thinking so that everyday thoughts can work in your favor.[17] Although the following suggestions are designed to help guide your search for that one great idea for a startup, they can also help keep an existing business fresh, alive, and moving forward.

2. Use innovative thinking to generate ideas for high-potential startups.

1. *When it comes to ideas, borrow heavily from existing products and services or other industries.* "Good artists borrow; great artists steal," said Pablo Picasso or T.S. Eliot or Salvador Dali—no one seems to know for sure. This principle launched Apple Computer on the road to greatness when one of its co-founders, Steve Jobs, identified technologies that Xerox had developed but was not using. It can work for you, too, within the limits of the law and ethical conduct. Explore ideas and practices that you come across, and think deeply about how you might put them to work in launching a startup or accelerating the growth of an existing business. Research shows that this is a powerful starting place for innovation.

2. *Combine two businesses into one to create a market opening.* Aimie's Dinner and Movie is just what you might guess: a restaurant and movie theater in one. This revolutionary concept is exceptionally practical for patrons. How many times have you rushed through dinner to get to the theater, only to find that the movie you wanted to see was already sold out? That won't happen at this Glens Falls, New York, startup. After a leisurely dinner, when the lights begin to dim, you need only to sit back in cushioned comfort and enjoy the show.[18] The restaurant business is often ruthless, and the theater industry is even more competitive, but bringing the two together puts Aimie's in a unique position.

   At some point, it may make sense to start (or buy) more than one business without merging their operations, a strategy known as *diversification.* To see how this can work to your advantage, consider the outdoor lighting company that Derek Norwood and his father have owned for more than a decade. Their Chicago business did pretty well over the years, but severe weather typically hit their winter revenues hard. To solve the problem, Norwood launched a new company that offers holiday lighting supplies. Now his outdoor illumination customers can buy holiday lights from him as well, and this cross-selling opportunity has helped boost the bottom line. Becoming too diversified can sometimes cause an entrepreneur to lose focus, and the performance edge that goes with it, but spreading out sometimes can be very helpful.[19]

3. *Begin with a problem in mind.* Bankable business ideas usually address problems that people have. Think about a significant problem, dissect it, chart it out on a sheet of paper, roll it over and over in your mind, and consider possible solutions. Sometimes amazing business ideas will come quickly to mind.

 For example, Sergio Stiberman wanted to end his car lease early, but he found it would cost him as much as his remaining payments to terminate the agreement. This is not what he had in mind, but unfortunately there were no alternatives. "I realized there was a need from a consumer standpoint, and there was no one in the market doing it," he says. After studying the problem, he decided to launch LeaseTrader.com, a website that brings lease buyers and sellers together quickly and conveniently. The service is now very popular, with more than 1,000 listings nationwide (each costing $39.95 to $189.95, depending on the package) and projected sales of $8 million.[20] Stiberman solved his original problem, and now he is cashing in on his own solution.

4. *Recognize a hot trend and ride the wave. Fads* can lead to serious, though sometimes short-lived, money-making opportunities (for example, google the Pet Rocks or Big Mouth Billy Bass phenomena), but *trends* provide a much stronger foundation for businesses because they are connected to a larger change in society. Even more powerful is the product or service that builds on three or four trends as they come together. For example, one entrepreneurship expert observed that the iPod's outrageous success right from the start was the result of multiple merging trends: the desire for increased mobility, instant gratification, and customization, all melded together with the natural pull toward fashion.[21]

 But what if the wave has already crashed on the shore? Look for countertrends— every trend has one. For example, even as wireless technologies extend the reach of communication, people pay more to travel to destinations beyond the reach of their BlackBerries. Interesting, isn't it? To identify a countertrend, you should make it a habit to ask those who resist a trend (such as the coffee drinker who refuses to go to Starbucks) what products or services would appeal to them and then see what possibilities come to mind.[22] Try to set aside your preconceived notions of what "ought to be" and get into the minds of those who resist the flow. If you use the trend as your starting point, you will know better where to look for the countertrend, and that's where you can get ahead of the game.

5. *Study an existing product or service and explore ways to improve its function.* Products or services that work can be improved so that they work even better. TissueKups is a tissue dispenser shaped so that it fits perfectly in a car cup holder. Lorraine Santoli came up with the seed of the idea in her car after struggling with a tissue box that kept sliding away from her. She knew there had to be a solution, and there was. The company was launched online in 2003 and reached sales of around $3 million within two years.[23] The simplicity of the product may be its best feature.

6. *Think of possibilities that would streamline a customer's activities.* Many people are busy, so they look to firms that can bear some of the burdens of life for them. That's what keeps businesses like dry cleaners and grocery delivery services going. Take some time to ponder the day-to-day experiences of people in the market segment you would like to serve. What activities would they gladly off-load onto a startup that could make life more manageable for them?

7. *Consider ways to adapt a product or service to meet customer needs in a different way.* Darren Hitz realized that bachelor parties could be about more than just serious drinking and exotic dancers. That's when he came up with the idea to launch Adventure Bachelor Party, a company that brings thrills to bachelor parties by taking guys on packaged experiences such as whitewater rafting trips. The startup has only been around since 2004, but Hitz already offers a wide variety of options, from

cattle herding in Texas to fishing off the California coast to bungee jumping over the Columbia River. He also provides trips for bachelorette parties, weekend adventures, corporate events, and retreats for church groups. Business is good and the company continues to expand, but just as important, Hitz is having a good time doing what he does. In Hitz's words, "I enjoy being able to provide a service where everyone has a great time and is happy."[24]

8. *Imagine how the market for a product or service could be expanded.* Friends of Nir Barak know that he is a physician and nutrition expert, but he can now add "entrepreneur" to his resume. While searching for a drug that would regulate a certain part of the brain chemistry that causes weight gain, he found Betahistine. Used since the 1940s, the drug has been prescribed to treat vertigo (a spinning sensation caused by an imbalance in the inner ear) and is known to be safe, but it was pulled from the U.S. market in 1970 because it was ineffective in treating the condition. Though it may not cure vertigo, the drug happens to alter the brain's chemistry in the very way Barak was hoping to discover. He immediately recognized that this could lead to an obesity-busting bonanza, and his company, Obecure, is pushing to reintroduce the drug to the market.[25]

9. *Study a product or service to see if you can make it "green."* In recent years, a great surge of effort and investment has been flowing toward businesses that focus on protecting the environment. Just pick up an issue of any business publication and see for yourself! The debate continues on environmental topics, such as global climate change and the need to protect certain endangered species, but the rapid rise in *market demand* for environment-preserving products and services is undeniable. To tap into this trend, Jon Grobe, David Morgan, and Ken Scheer launched Calsaway Pool Services, Inc. This Tempe, Arizona, startup offers an innovative filtration device that strips trouble-making minerals and other substances from pool water, allowing owners to reuse the same water for up to 12 years. Demand is strong: The company filtered more than seven million gallons of water in 2007, and annual sales are approaching $350,000.[26] Fifteen years ago this business would not have gotten off the ground, but rising environmental concerns has changed all that, and demand in the future is certain to increase. These days, it can pay to think "green."

10. *Keep an eye on new technologies.* New technologies often open up potential for startups, but only those who take note of the possibilities can reap the rewards. Read widely, talk to industry experts, consult government offices that promote new technologies, go to a nearby research university and drop by its technology transfer office or visit with faculty who work at the cutting edge of their fields—there are so many sources of insight! Regardless of where you look, be sure to research innovations that have commercial value, particularly for new ventures.

 That's what Chris Savarese did. He found a way to use new tracking technology (the kind used in the security tags that stores attach to apparel items) to locate golf balls hacked off into the rough and high brush. The radio frequency identification (RFID) technology can detect golf balls from as far away as 100 feet. Savarese's San Ramon, California–based company, Radar Corporation, now packages a dozen radio-tagged balls with a locator to find them for $199.99, and the market really likes his innovation. His business has been growing as much as 30 percent a year.[27] New technology was clearly the key that got the ball rolling for Savarese.

These options represent only a few of the many possibilities, but if you follow some of the suggestions provided here, you just might hit pay dirt with your own new venture. We encourage you to seek and size up new venture ideas *in whatever circumstances you find yourself.* Then, by considering a number of internal and external factors, you should be able to bring together the pieces of the opportunity puzzle.

LIVING THE DREAM:

putting technology to work

The U.S. Military Gives Fly Fishermen a Fighting Chance

Fly fisherman are always searching for better products to improve their odds of snagging waterborne prey. Until recently, they preferred to use poles made of bamboo because their light touch made it easier to maneuver that tiny little fly so precisely that an angler can practically drop it into a fish's mouth. However, bamboo is incredibly time-consuming to work with, so rod manufacturers tried other materials, including fiberglass and graphite. Early graphite rods were much better than fiberglass because they were lighter, stronger, and thinner, making them more aerodynamic, durable, and sensitive.

But serious anglers didn't want the product development to stop there, and one outdoor supplier—Manchester, Vermont–based Orvis—is always looking for ways to turn its customers into happy campers. The company adopts the latest technology to give purchasers what they want, but its most recent efforts have

definitely gone where no rod maker has gone before. Using a highly classified unidirectional carbon fiber technology (the kind used to make Predator drones and spy satellites for the U.S. military), Orvis developers were able to create a rod that the company calls the Helios. It is the world's lightest fly rod—less than half the weight of bamboo. At 2.1 ounces and with a hefty $750 price tag, never have serious anglers paid so much for so little, but those who make the purchase are happy as a trout floating in the shadows beneath a "No Fishing" sign.

The U.S. military may seem like an exceedingly odd source for fishing gear technologies, so how did Orvis get its hands on the highly classified concoction? The company won't name names, but it seems that "guys who had been developing military systems" found themselves out of a job after government contracts on some major aerospace projects expired, and Orvis was able to hire some of them and put their knowledge to good use. Orvis itself is not a startup, and it is not particularly small; however, when it comes to cutting-edge fly rod technologies, the company provides an example of how to harness breakthroughs that can steer other enterprises toward similar results, regardless of age or size. The story of the Helios should inspire startups and other small companies to keep in mind that interesting and useful technologies that could lead to excellent new business possibilities can come from just about anywhere. It obviously pays to keep your eyes, ears— and payrolls—open.

© iStockphoto.com/Ben Blankenburg

Sources: "Graphite Rod Making History," http://www.orvis.com/intro.asp?dir_id=758&subject=1124, accessed October 24, 2008; William Snyder, "Agent Angler: Military Secrets Help Produce the Ultimate Synthetic Fishing Rod," *Wired*, Vol. 16, No. 6 (June 2008), p. 72.

http://www.orvis.com

Using Internal and External Analyses to Identify Business Ideas

3. Describe external and internal analyses that might shape the selection of venture opportunities.

In his book *Making Sense of Strategy*, Tony Manning points out two general approaches that can help to identify business ideas: inside-out and outside-in.[28] In other words, entrepreneurs can evaluate their own capabilities and then consider new products or services they might be able to offer to the market (inside-out), or they can first look for needs in the marketplace and then determine how to use their own resources and capabilities to pursue those opportunities (outside-in).[29] It is important to understand the finer points of the two methods because they can reveal business ideas that may otherwise be overlooked.

Outside-In Analysis

According to research, entrepreneurs are more successful when they study context in order to identify business ideas and determine which are most likely to lead to success.[30] This outside-in analysis should consider the general environment, or big picture, and the industry setting in which the venture might do business. It should also factor in the competitive environment that is likely to have an impact. The *general environment* is made up of very broad factors that influence most businesses in a society. In comparison, the *industry environment* is defined more narrowly as the factors that directly impact a given firm and all of its competitors. Even more specifically, the *competitive environment* focuses on the strength, position, and likely moves and counter-moves of competitors in an industry.

THE GENERAL ENVIRONMENT   The general environment profiles a number of important trends, as shown in Exhibit 3-4. *Economic trends* include changes in the rate of inflation, interest rates, and even currency exchange rates, all of which promote or discourage business growth. *Sociocultural trends* refer to societal currents that may affect consumer demand, opening up new markets and forcing others into decline. *Political/legal trends* that are of interest here include changes in tax law and government regulation (perhaps safety rules) that may pose a threat to existing companies or devastate an inventive business concept. *Global trends* reflect international developments that create new opportunities to expand markets, outsource, and invest abroad. As people and markets around the world become increasingly connected, the impact of the global segment on small business opportunities will increase.

Technological trends are perhaps most important to small businesses, since developments that grow out of these spawn—or wipe out—many new ventures. For example, one new

general environment
The broad environment, encompassing factors that influence most businesses in a society.

industry environment
The combined forces that directly impact a given firm and its competitors.

competitive environment
The environment that focuses on the strength, position, and likely moves and counter-moves of competitors in an industry.

3-4   Trends in the General Environment

EXHIBIT

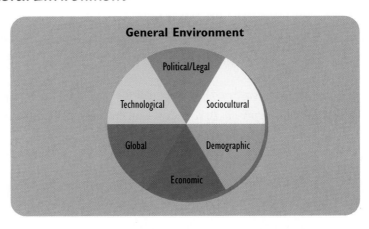

General Environment

Political/Legal · Sociocultural · Demographic · Economic · Global · Technological

technology that is making life interesting for many entrepreneurs is satellite-based cameras and the aerial imaging services they provide. At one time considered the stuff of military intelligence gathering and James Bond–like spy thrillers, the ready (and free!) availability of this technology through services like Google Earth and Windows Live Local is changing the opportunity landscape for anyone with the vision to use it. For example, Jay Saber, founder of RoofAds in Woodside, California, noticed a surge of interest in his rooftop advertising business when companies realized that a logo or message painted on the top of their buildings could be seen by anyone with a computer and an Internet connection, not just the occasional helicopter passenger.[31]

But it's not just advertising that notices the impact—this new technology promises to revolutionize a host of other industries as well. For example, real estate marketing is feeling the heat from Zillow.com, a website that allows a user to type in the address of a house and pull up a satellite photo of it, along with its price and a host of other details related to that home and its neighborhood.[32] And Keith Harper of Chattanooga, Tennessee, has used Google Earth to locate homes with large lawns that his landscaping business could mow, or those with large concrete patios that might be interested in his pressure-washing services. Pool maintenance firms are using it to identify homes with pools whose owners may need help with upkeep.[33] And this is just the beginning. As the technology develops further, the business landscape will again be reshaped and the rules will change.

Demographic trends also play an important role in shaping opportunities for startups; they include population size, age structure, ethnic mix, and wage distribution. Many entrepreneurs, for example, are looking at aging baby boomers (the 78 million Americans born between 1946 and 1964) and seeing dollar signs. Given their $2 trillion in annual spending power and self-indulgence, the focus on this segment may really pay off. And there is no limit to the products and services that can be targeted to this age group. Cell phones with larger keys that can easily be seen in dim lighting, health clubs that cater to those with more gray hair and less revealing apparel, and magazines that focus on health issues in the retirement years are all business ideas that have emerged with this demographic trend in mind.

Some people believe that evaluation of the general environment is appropriate only for large firms that have a corporate staff to manage the process, but small businesses can also benefit from such analysis. For example, entrepreneurs have taken note of the reality that many people struggle with their weight; in fact, government statistics show that the problem is big and getting bigger. Today, more than 60 million Americans qualify as obese, up from 23 million in 1980, and projections indicate that this number will rise another 28 million by 2013.[34] Entrepreneurs have realized that a multitude of business opportunities can be launched based on this trend toward obesity, from weight-loss services to products that help obese people live more comfortably with their condition. Among the many businesses that have been launched as a result of reading the trend are startups offering airline seatbelt extenders, plus-size fashion items, and oversized furniture. In other words, entrepreneurs have already proven that it can pay handsomely to look very carefully at trends in the general environment.

THE INDUSTRY ENVIRONMENT   An entrepreneur will be even more directly affected by the startup's industry than by the general environment. In his classic book *Competitive Advantage,* Michael Porter lists five factors that determine the nature and degree of competition in an industry:[35]

- *New competitors.* How easy is it for new competitors to enter the industry?
- *Substitute products/services.* Can customers turn to other products or services to replace those that the industry offers?
- *Rivalry.* How intense is the rivalry among existing competitors in the industry?
- *Suppliers.* Are industry suppliers so powerful that they will demand high prices for inputs, thereby increasing the company's costs and reducing its profits?
- *Buyers.* Are industry customers so powerful that they will force companies to charge low prices, thereby reducing profits?

Exhibit 3-5 shows these five factors as weights that offset the potential attractiveness and profitability of a target industry. It illustrates how profits in an industry tend to be inversely related to the strength of these factors—that is, strong factors yield weak profits, whereas weak factors yield strong profits.

Entrepreneurs who understand industry influences can better identify high-potential start-up opportunities—situations where, say, rivalry is weak and neither buyers nor suppliers have enough power to drive hard bargains on price. But these insights can also help entrepreneurs to anticipate threats they are likely to encounter and to begin thinking about ways to defend their startups from any downside risk. If entrepreneurs recognize and understand these forces, they can position their ventures in a way that makes the most of what the industry offers. In other words, analyzing Porter's five industry factors will provide a good overview of the broad sweep of the industry environment.

THE COMPETITIVE ENVIRONMENT Within any given industry, it is important to determine the strength, position, and likely responses of rival businesses to newcomers. In fact, experts insist such analyses are a critical input for the assessment of any business idea. William A. Sahlman of Harvard University contends that every aspiring entrepreneur should answer several questions about the competitors he or she is likely to encounter in the marketplace:[36]

- Who would be the new venture's current competitors?
- What unique resources do they control?
- What are their strengths and weaknesses?
- How will they respond to the new venture's decision to enter the industry?

3-5 Major Factors Offsetting Market Attractiveness

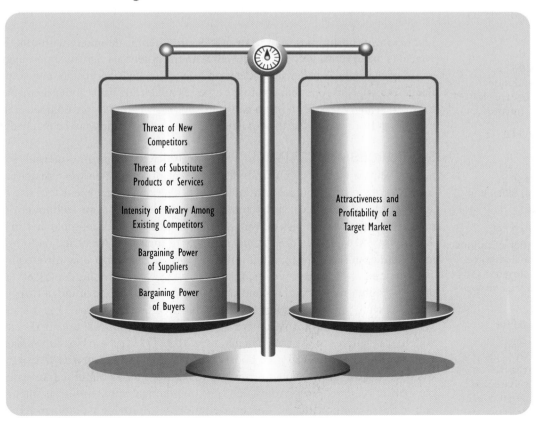

Threat of New Competitors

Threat of Substitute Products or Services

Intensity of Rivalry Among Existing Competitors

Bargaining Power of Suppliers

Bargaining Power of Buyers

Attractiveness and Profitability of a Target Market

- How can the new venture respond?
- Who else might see and exploit the same opportunity?
- Are there ways to co-opt potential or actual competitors by forming alliances?

This analysis helps an entrepreneur to evaluate the nature and extent of existing competition and to fine-tune future plans. It can also help to identify high-potential business opportunities based on the competitive situation.

Awareness of the competition has paid off in a big way for three German brothers in their 30s—Alexander, Oliver, and Mark Samwer. They have been accused of copying great ideas, and that is a fair assessment, but their fast-follower tactics have worked time and again. In January of 1999, at a time when eBay was still focused mostly on the U.S. market, the Samwer brothers started a clone of the company (Alando.de) in Germany. Five months later, eBay came calling and bought the knockoff venture for $50 million. Then came StudVZ, a two-year-old European Facebook-like venture that was sold to a publishing company in 2007 for $100 million. And their winning streak continues. What is the secret to the Samwers' success? Know your competitors, stay one step ahead of them, and create unique value by adapting a business idea to local culture and practices.[37] With a little luck and excellent timing, amazing results may just follow.

Strategy expert Gary Hamel recommends that entrepreneurs take one more step when analyzing the competition—identify the thinking that shapes rivals' behavior.[38] To illustrate, most companies assume that poor consumers in less developed countries around the world do not appreciate high-end consumer products, and could not afford them if they did. This view of the consumer can be unnecessarily limiting. The shampoo market in India, for example, is actually as large as that in the United States. And entrepreneurial luxury hair care product makers have penetrated nearly 90 percent of the market in India, many by selling shampoo in a single-use sachet that nearly anyone can afford. This shows how relaxing an old assumption can make a new business opportunity possible—and very profitable, as it turns out.[39]

Inside-Out Analysis

Identifying opportunities in the external environment is definitely worth the effort, but business concepts make sense only if they fit well with the potentials that an entrepreneur can bring to the world of business. Furthermore, the search for a startup opportunity can actually *begin* with an inside-out analysis, one that catalogues the resources and capabilities available to the startup (or those that can reasonably be obtained or created) as well as its core competencies. These can form a platform from which the fruit of new business opportunities can be reached and harvested.

RESOURCES AND CAPABILITIES   In order to assess the internal potentials of a business, it helps if the entrepreneur understands the difference between resources and capabilities. *Resources* refers to those available inputs that an entrepreneur can use to start a business and can include cash for investment, knowledge of important technologies, access to equipment, and capable business partners. Companies have both tangible and intangible resources. *Tangible resources* are visible and easy to measure. An office building, computer equipment, and cash reserves are all tangible resources. These are very different from *intangible resources*, which are invisible and difficult to assess. Intangible assets include intellectual property rights such as patents and copyrights, an established brand, a firm's reputation, and an entrepreneur's personal network of contacts and relationships.

Though the terms are often used interchangeably, *resources* are not the same as *capabilities*. Whereas resources are singular in nature, *capabilities* are best viewed as the integration of various resources in a way that boosts a firm's *competitive advantage,* a benefit that exists when a firm has a product or service that is seen by its target market as better than those of competitors. Like a keyboard, which is of no practical value until it is integrated into a system of computer components, resources are unlikely to provide a platform for competitive advantage until they are bundled into some useful configuration.

Margin glossary

resources
The basic inputs that a firm uses to conduct its business.

tangible resources
Those organizational resources that are visible and easy to measure.

intangible resources
Those organizational resources that are invisible and difficult to assess.

capabilities
The integration of various organizational resources that are deployed together to the firm's advantage.

competitive advantage
A benefit that exists when a firm has a product or service that is seen by its target market as better than those of competitors.

CORE COMPETENCIES   Once entrepreneurs have an accurate view of their resources and capabilities, they may be able to identify core competencies that can be created. *Core competencies* are those capabilities that distinguish a company competitively and reflect its personality. To illustrate how this works, consider Starbucks, which is known for its wide selection of gourmet coffees. But that is not its only edge in the marketplace. In fact, many of its competitors—large and small—also provide high-quality coffee products. So why has the company been so successful? Most observers believe that it is the premium product, combined with the special "Starbucks experience," that has allowed the coffee icon to grow from a single store in the mid-1980s to more than 16,000 retail locations around the world today.[40]

Though the success of Starbucks is undeniable, the franchise has not eliminated its competition. So, how do small firms compete in a Starbucks-saturated market? By focusing on the unique core competencies they offer consumers. Many small shops thrive in this environment by providing free refills, paying meticulous attention to product quality, emphasizing connections with the local community, or taking other steps to showcase their own unique character and individuality (something a large chain like Starbucks cannot afford to do). In other words, they establish core competencies by using resources and capabilities in unique ways that reflect the "personality" of their own enterprises. Though the words are different, the tune is still the same: Entrepreneurs who can identify core competencies and apply them effectively are in the best position to launch ventures that will achieve a competitive advantage and superior performance.

Integrating Internal and External Analyses

A solid foundation for competitive advantage requires a reasonable match between the strengths and weaknesses of a business and opportunities and threats present in its relevant environments. This integration is best revealed through a *SWOT analysis* (standing for Strengths, Weaknesses, Opportunities, Threats), which provides a simple overview of a venture's strategic situation. Exhibit 3-6 lists a number of factors that can be classified by this framework; however, these are merely representative of the countless possibilities that may exist.

core competencies
Those capabilities that provide a firm with a competitive edge and reflect its personality.

SWOT analysis
A type of assessment that provides a concise overview of a firm's strategic situation.

3-6   *Examples of SWOT Factors*

		POSITIVE FACTORS	**NEGATIVE FACTORS**
Inside the Company		*Strengths*	*Weaknesses*
		• Important core competencies	• Inadequate financial resources
		• Financial strengths	• Poorly planned strategy
		• Innovative capacity	• Lack of management skills or experience
		• Skilled or experienced management	• Inadequate innovation capacity
		• Well-planned strategy	• Negative reputation in the marketplace
		• Effective entry wedge	• Inadequate facilities
		• A strong network of personal contacts	• Distribution problems
		• Positive reputation in the marketplace	• Limited marketing skills
		• Proprietary technology	• Production inefficiencies
Outside the Company		*Opportunities*	*Threats*
		• An untapped market potential	• New competitors
		• New product or geographic market	• Rising demands of buyers or suppliers
		• Favorable shift in industry dynamics	• Sales shifting to substitute products
		• High potential for market growth	• Increased government regulation
		• Emerging technologies	• Adverse shifts in the business cycle
		• Changes allowing overseas expansion	• Slowed market growth
		• Favorable government deregulation	• Changing customer preferences
		• Increasing market fragmentation	• Adverse demographic shifts

In practice, a SWOT analysis provides a snapshot view of current conditions. Outside-in and inside-out approaches come together in the SWOT analysis to help identify potential business opportunities that match the entrepreneur and his or her planned venture. However, because a SWOT analysis focuses on the present rather than considering future opportunities, at this point the entrepreneur should ask a few additional questions:

- Will the targeted opportunity lead to other opportunities in the future?
- Will the opportunity help to build skills that can open the door to new opportunities in the future?
- Will pursuit of the opportunity be likely to lead to competitive response by potential rivals?

Obviously, the most promising opportunities are those that lead to others (which may offer value and profitability over the long run), promote the development of additional skills that equip the venture to pursue new prospects, and yet do not provoke competitors to strike back.

While still a student at Northeastern University, 25-year-old Neil Wadhawan met Raj Raheja, 32, and in 2002 they partnered to launch Heartwood Studios, a company that produces 3-D images and animations for architects and designers. "We knew our [product] was a necessary tool," says Wadhawan. "Being able to visualize something before it's built is powerful." It wasn't long, however, before the co-founders recognized that their 3-D animations could be important to more than just architects, so they began to investigate other industries where their technologies and skills could be adapted for use. They soon found clients in the defense and aerospace industries. And more recently, they have been moving into the sports world by providing stadium animations for teams like the Dallas Cowboys and New Jersey Nets. Wadhawan and Raheja will tell you that branching out requires careful study and modification, but Heartwood Studies has profited nicely from its expansion, with annual sales exceeding $2 million. And the future looks even brighter! "There's a need in every [industry] for 3-D," says Wadhawan. "Our biggest challenge . . . will be deciding what *not* to do."[41]

Like most successful entrepreneurs, Wadhawan and Raheja discovered areas of business opportunity that tap into emerging potentials in the environment, but they moved in the direction of those that matched their personal capabilities and the strengths of their current businesses. As shown in Exhibit 3-7, this is what we call the entrepreneur's "opportunity sweet spot."

When potentials in the external environment (revealed through analysis of the general, industry, and competitive environments) fit with the unique capabilities and core competencies

3-7 The Entrepreneur's Opportunity "Sweet Spot"

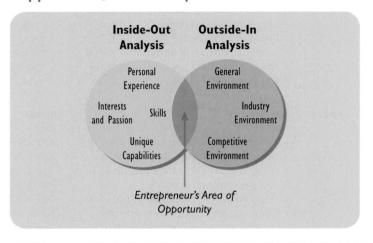

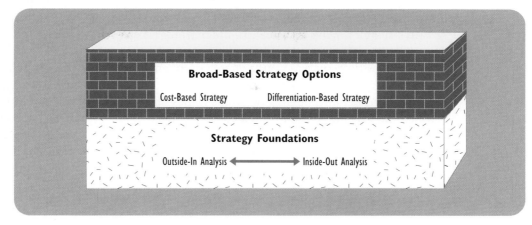

Broad-Based Strategy Options

Cost-Based Strategy   Differentiation-Based Strategy

Strategy Foundations

Outside-In Analysis ◄─────► Inside-Out Analysis

of the entrepreneur (highlighted by internal assessment), and threats outside the startup or weaknesses within it are manageable, the odds of success are greatly improved. Therefore, we encourage you to be observant and systematic in your search for opportunities and to think carefully about how these opportunities fit your background and skills, as well as your interests and passions. If you do so, you are much more likely to enjoy the adventure. Not a bad payoff!

Clearly, conducting outside-in and inside-out analyses and integrating the results can help build a solid foundation for competitive advantage. With that foundation, the entrepreneur can begin to create a strategy for achieving superior financial performance (see Exhibit 3-8), and it is to that subject that we turn next.

Selecting Strategies That Capture Opportunities

A *strategy* is, in essence, a set of actions that coordinate the resources and commitments of a business to boost its performance. Strategy selections should be guided by the firm's situation, rather than by past choices, the latest industry fad, or whatever "feels" right at the moment. Choosing a strategy that makes sense for a particular entrepreneur and his or her startup is a critical early step toward superior performance. But keeping an eye on strategy options—both broad-based and focus strategies—can also guide established companies toward success.

4. Explain broad-based strategy options and focus strategies.

strategy
A plan of action that coordinates the resources and commitments of an organization to achieve superior performance.

Broad-Based Strategy Options

Firms competing in the same industry can adopt very different strategies. Broadly speaking, companies can choose to build their strategies around an emphasis on either low cost or differentiation as they consider how to position themselves relative to their competitors.

COST-BASED STRATEGY A *cost-based strategy* requires a firm to be the lowest-cost producer within the market. The sources of cost advantages are varied, ranging from low-cost labor to efficiency in operations. Many people assume that cost-based strategies will not work for small companies, and often this is true.[42] However, cost-advantage factors

cost-based strategy
A plan of action that requires a firm to be the lowest-cost producer within its market.

are so numerous and diverse that, in some cases, small businesses may be able to use them with great success, especially if they do not spark a price war with established competitors who have deeper pockets and a great dislike for any company that steals away their customers. Of course, the great downside of this strategy is that it attracts customers who always search for the best deal. In other words, it can be a challenge to develop customer loyalty with this strategy.

Spirit Airlines provides an example of an entrepreneurial company that has relentlessly followed a cost-based strategy from its founding. In fact, it is now billed as an "ultra-low-cost carrier." The venture operates 28 Airbus planes (the youngest fleet in the Americas) and serves mostly Eastern and Midwestern cities in the United States with flights to many Caribbean and Latin American destinations—but this is no ordinary airline. Cost is always front and center in the firm's strategy deliberations. The company describes the heart and soul of its approach on its website.

> [Spirit Airlines] liberates customers from being forced into paying for services they do not desire or use. When customers are seeking the best value in travel, they can choose a low fare at spiritair.com and select the services and options appropriate for their travel needs. Spirit's ultra low cost model, driven from numerous efficiencies, new aircraft, advanced technology and dedicated staff, allows the airline to take this approach, offering savings to millions of customers. . . .[43]

Achieving its ambitious goals has required some bold moves. For example, Spirit charges passengers extra to check on luggage, change reservations, and even to use pillows and blankets. To make the bargain-basement fare model work (charging as little as $8 each way for some flights), the company has had to be innovative in its search for alternative revenues, which has included placing ads in airplane cabins and on flight attendants' uniforms. The company's revenue-stretching strategies don't always fly well with some passengers, but it certainly presents an interesting example of a creative, cost-based strategy.[44]

differentiation-based strategy
A plan of action designed to provide a product or service with unique attributes that are valued by consumers.

DIFFERENTIATION-BASED STRATEGY The second general option for building a competitive advantage is creating a *differentiation-based strategy*, an approach that emphasizes the uniqueness of a firm's product or service (in terms of some feature other than cost). A firm that can create and sustain an attractive differentiation strategy is likely to be a successful performer in the marketplace. For the strategy to be effective, the consumer must be convinced of the uniqueness and value of the product or service, whether real or perceived. A wide variety of operational and marketing tactics, ranging from design to promotion, can lead to product or service differentiation.

After spending many years in the music industry, Brian Landau and Pete Rosenblum were bothered that hit songs didn't always generate the music sales they deserved. So in 2003 they launched New York City based Radio Tag, a full-service marketing agency. Right from the start, differentiation was the foundation of their strategy, and at the core of that strategy was a rich promotional concept that has become the signature feature of the company. You see, most radio stations let the DJs do all the talking, but Radio Tag has changed all of that by allowing artists to introduce their own work via recording. With this approach, for example, Madonna can describe her emotional connection to a song, or members of the alternative metal band Breaking Benjamin can explain how their latest album came together. "That was really the whole point," says Rosenblum. "Put an artist on the radio and let people become more familiar with who the artist is, what the song is, and how they can buy it." It is clearly a different approach, and a successful one. Radio stations benefit from the free promotional content, artists are able to promote their creative works using their own voices, and the company has profited nicely, with nearly $5 million in sales at the close of 2008—just the kind of outcome you would expect for a business with a well-designed and competently executed differentiation strategy. It has certainly set Radio Tag apart from its competitors.[45]

Focus Strategies

If one firm controlled the only known water supply in the world, its sales volume would be huge. Such a business would not be concerned about differences in personal preferences regarding taste, appearance, or temperature. It would consider its customers to be one market. As long as the water product was wet, it would satisfy everyone. However, if someone else discovered a second water supply, the first company's view of the market would change. The first business might discover that sales were drying up and take measures to modify its strategy. The level of rivalry would likely rise as competitors struggled for position in the same industry space.

If the potential for water sales were enormous, small businesses would eventually become interested in entering the market. However, given their limited resources and lack of experience, small companies would be more likely to succeed if they avoided head-to-head competition with industry giants and sought a protected market segment instead. In other words, they could be competitive if they implemented a *focus strategy* by adapting their efforts to concentrate on the needs of a very limited portion of the market. To get started, these businesses might focus their resources on a fragment of the market that was small enough to escape the interest of major players (for example, filtered water delivered to individual homes) or perhaps take a completely new approach to permit access without immediate competitive response (perhaps by filling market gaps resulting from supply shortages).

focus strategy
A plan of action that isolates an enterprise from competitors and other market forces by targeting a restricted market segment.

Focus strategies represent a strategic approach in which entrepreneurs try to shield themselves from market forces by targeting a specific group of customers who have an identifiable but very narrow range of product or service interests (often called a *market niche*). By focusing on a specialized market, some small businesses develop unique expertise that leads to higher levels of value and service for customers, which is great for business. In fact, this advantage prompted marketing superstar Philip Kotler to declare, "There are riches in niches."[46]

The two broad options discussed earlier—a cost-based strategy and a differentiation-based strategy—can also be used when focusing on a niche market. Although few entrepreneurs adopt a cost-based focus strategy, it does happen. For example, outlets with names like The Watermarket Store, Drinking Water Depot, and H2O2Go have opened over the years, using an efficient purification system to offer high-quality, good-tasting drinking water to price-sensitive customers at a fraction of the price charged by competitors. These small businesses are following a cost-based focus strategy.

Contrast this approach with the differentiation-based focus strategy that Mark Sikes adopted for his small business, Personalized Bottled Water. Sikes may be in the business of selling bottled water, but his startup grew out of his knowledge of what goes on the outside of a bottle rather than what goes in it. He was traveling around the country selling stick-on labels to manufacturers for his successful label-brokering company when it dawned on him that he could go in a completely different direction with his enterprise. Why not sell bottled water featuring custom labels for corporate clients and anyone who wants to celebrate a special occasion? Sikes explains the thrust of his business on the company's website:

> I decided to enter the market . . . with one simple goal in mind, to offer great tasting bottled water to small businesses and schools with their own personalized label. From that single thought, our business has grown into several areas, and we now supply businesses, both big and small, as well as [providing] a single case of water for an individual or a special event.[47]

Sikes launched Personalized Bottled Water in 1997, operating out of a warehouse in Little Rock, Arkansas. This friendly and energetic man in his 30s hustled his product around the state and soon found interested customers—schools (especially during football season), funeral homes, hotels, and brides and grooms. By 2005, the company was very profitable, with around $350,000 in annual sales, but Sikes has even higher hopes for the future of the business.[48] The focus, however, remains the same: *personalization*. Without this emphasis, his enterprise would be dead in the water, so to speak. There is no way that Sikes would be able to compete head to head with the likes of bottling giants Coca-Cola Company (Dasani), Dr Pepper Snapple Group (Deja Blue), and PepsiCo (Aquafina), but flexibility and customization—foundations for differentiation—give Personalized Bottled Water a fighting chance.

Thus, entrepreneurs must select and implement a focus strategy that will allow them to target a niche market within a sizeable industry, thereby avoiding direct competition with larger competitors. This can be accomplished in a number of ways, as discussed in the next section.

FOCUS STRATEGY SELECTION AND IMPLEMENTATION

strategic decision
A decision regarding the direction a firm will take in relating to its customers and competitors.

By selecting a particular focus strategy, an entrepreneur decides on the basic direction of the business. Such a choice affects the very nature of the business and is thus referred to as a *strategic decision*. A firm's overall strategy is formulated, therefore, as its leader decides how the firm will relate to its environment—particularly to the customers and competitors in that environment. This can require the entrepreneur to manage a delicate balancing act, one that keeps the venture out of the crosshairs of industry heavyweights and yet offers enough market promise to provide the startup with a reasonable shot at getting off the ground.

Selection of a very specialized market is, of course, not the only possible strategy for a small firm. But focus strategies are very popular because they allow a small firm to operate in the gap that exists between larger competitors. If a small firm chooses to compete head to head with other companies, particularly large corporations, it must be prepared to distinguish itself in some way—for example, by attention to detail, highly personal service, or speed of service—in order to make itself a viable competitor.

Focus strategies can be implemented in any of the following ways:

- Restricting focus to a single subset of customers
- Emphasizing a single product or service
- Limiting the market to a single geographical region
- Concentrating on superiority of the product or service

To illustrate these strategies, consider how the following entrepreneurs—Dale Fox, Leslie Vander Baan, and Trey Cobb—each implemented a different focus strategy related to the same general product—automobiles.

It sounds humdrum to say that Dale Fox's company, Spin Automotive Group, is a car rental business, but his Venice, California, venture is anything but dull. His "rolling stock" consists of only classic, one-of-a-kind automobiles in museum-quality condition, such as a blue Space Age–looking 1962 Cadillac Eldorado convertible, or a stylish 1961 Alpha Romeo Giulietta sports car that wears its "Italian design" as prominently as its flashy and flawless red exterior, or a 1962 V8-powered Ford Cobra finished in blue with white racing stripes that is "loud, fast, and unapologetically rugged." A one-day rental of any of the company's cars will set you back $499, but renters can also choose to purchase the cars if they wish (with posted prices running from $28,000 to $69,000).[49] There was no way Spin could have gone head to head with mainstream car rental agencies, but Fox has his carefully considered niche pretty much all to himself, which is extremely good for business. The company generated $5 million in revenue in its first full year of operation.[50]

Thirty-year-old Leslie Vander Baan's start in the car business was inspired by her personal experience while trying to sell a car on her own. She was left waiting at a bowling alley while a potential buyer took her car in for a mechanical inspection. As she sat there thinking, she realized that both parties had their own anxieties about the deal. "[T]hey were spooked about my title because I had just moved and it was out of state," Vander Baan recalls. "I was concerned that the money I was taking wasn't going to be legit—that it wouldn't deposit and clear." It was at that point that she realized that there had to be a better way for buyer and seller to complete such transactions, and she was right. The solution was a unique used-car

LIVING THE DREAM:

entrepreneurial challenges

A Niche Market That Is Out of This World

Segmenting a market is a top-down approach that breaks a market into smaller and more manageable sub-markets; in contrast, niche marketing is more of a bottom-up perspective that identifies the needs of a small group of customers and then gradually builds a larger customer base from there. Eric Anderson, the 34-year-old CEO of Space Adventures, Ltd., is definitely following the latter path—he is building his company's strategy around a clearly identified market niche. His enterprise is in the business of "space tourism," and at the moment it has the market all to itself.

Founded in 1998, the company's website declares that "Space Adventures, Ltd., is the world's premier private space exploration company and the only company currently providing opportunities for actual private spaceflight and space tourism today." With around 20 employees, the Vienna, Virginia–based firm is focused like a laser beam on a very narrow market niche: *extremely* rich private citizens. The price of a package is absolutely stratospheric; so far, space tourists have paid between $30 million and $40 million each for a round-trip journey to the International Space Station aboard a Russian Soyuz space vehicle. A few "extras" can be included, so why not splurge and add

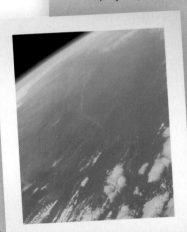

© Space Adventures

a spacewalk to that earth-escaping excursion? It would set you back only another $15 million.

Since April of 2001, Space Adventures has worked out the details for six outer-space travel clients, the latest being Richard Garriott, the son of NASA astronaut Owen Garriott. As the first American to follow a parent into space, the younger Garriott announced that his mission to the International Space Station "fulfilled a lifelong dream to experience spaceflight as [his] father did 35 years ago." With the company completing so few trips to date, Garriott's journey was only slightly more historic than it is unique, and that, by and large, explains the astronomically high price (which is also indicative of a well-planned focus strategy, by the way). But remember, a good niche plan may start with a focus on the needs of a small customer group, but it often includes a vision to build on that foundation to reach a larger customer base over time. Space Adventures is already headed in that direction. Anderson is working to develop new technologies that will allow his company "to achieve more reliable, affordable and safer access to the infinite resources of space," with the hope that he will still be the one selling tickets when the prices fall to within reach of ordinary folks.

Sources: "About Us," http://www.spaceadventures.com/index.cfm?fuse action=about_us.welcome, accessed November 5, 2008; Barbara De Lollis, "He's over the Moon About Space as a Tourist Mecca," *USA Today*, October 8, 2007, pp. 1B–2B; Press Release, "Garriott Makes History as 1st Second-Generation Astronaut," October 23, 2008, http://www.space adventures.com/index.cfm?fuseaction=news.viewnews&newsid=662, accessed November 5, 2008.

http://www.spaceadventures.com

dealership called Auto Consignment, a business that Vander Baan and her husband started in 2003 to help people sell their cars with less hassle and for more than the trade-in value. The company's "nearly a dozen" employees handle test drives, complete necessary paperwork, offer financing, and deal with other auto-sales frustrations. The business now sells cars off its $1.5 million property on auto row in Charlotte, North Carolina, and generates around $5 million a year in consignment sales.[51]

Trey Cobb's fascination with the automobile industry doesn't involve car rentals or sales—he is all about parts. As a huge fan of Subarus, he found that he could not get the high-performance parts he wanted to modify his Impreza 2.5RS, so he decided to make his own. That humble start in 1999 expanded into a sizeable business that today offers 40 to 50 aftermarket parts for cars built by five Asian automakers (including Subaru, of course). With only $10,000 in startup capital, Cobb launched his venture, COBB Tuning, out of his father's tire shop in Texas, but he later moved the business to Salt Lake City, Utah, in 2002 to take advantage of weather that is ideal for product testing.[52] Today the company's 35 employees keep sales revved up to an impressive $6 million per year, driven largely by the 33-year-old founder's resolute focus on a well-defined market niche: "tech-savvy enthusiasts with strong brand allegiances."[53]

But Cobb's niche concept is only one of many possibilities. Together, Spin Automotive Group, Auto Consignment, and COBB Tuning prove that very different focus strategies can be implemented within the same industry and that all of these strategies can be profitable. However, overspecialization and competition can threaten to erode the profits of such strategies, as we discuss next.

DRAWBACKS OF FOCUS STRATEGIES One small business analyst expresses a word of caution about selecting a niche market:

> Warning! A firm can be so specialized that it may not have enough customers to be viable. Do not plan to open a pen repair shop, a shoelace boutique, or a restaurant based on the concept of toast (although one based on breakfast cereal has apparently been founded).[54]

In addition to the dangers of becoming too specialized, firms that adopt a focus strategy tread a narrow line between maintaining a protected market and attracting competition. If their ventures are profitable, entrepreneurs must be prepared to face competition. In his classic book *Competitive Advantage,* Michael Porter cautions that a segmented market can erode under any of the following four conditions:[55]

1. The focus strategy is imitated.
2. The target segment becomes structurally unattractive because the structure erodes or because demand simply disappears.
3. The target segment's differences from other segments narrow.
4. New firms subsegment the industry.

The experience of Minnetonka, a small firm widely recognized as the first to introduce liquid hand soap, provides an example of how a focus strategy can be imitated. The huge success of its brand, Softsoap, quickly attracted the attention of several giants in the industry, including Procter & Gamble. Minnetonka's competitive advantage was soon washed away. Some analysts believe this happened because the company focused too much on the advantages of liquid soap in general and not enough on the particular benefits of Softsoap.

It should be clear that focus strategies do not guarantee a sustainable advantage. Small firms can boost their success, however, by developing and extending their competitive strengths. Good strategic planning can help point the way through these challenging situations, as well as determine the feasibility of success.

Is Your Startup Idea Feasible?

Coming up with a business idea you are excited about is the first step toward an adventure into entrepreneurship. Next, performing an outside-in analysis will show you the big picture, providing an overview of the general environment, the industry, and the competition. And an inside-out analysis will help you match your personal strengths and capabilities to the external environment. If a SWOT analysis reveals a fit between the strengths and weaknesses of your planned venture and the opportunities and threats in its external environment, this may offer evidence that your business idea deserves an even closer look. Finally, you can use the framework provided in this chapter to consider a strategic direction for the venture—low cost or differentiation—and to learn how to identify and maintain a market niche, as well as a focus strategy, that might work for your startup.

5. Assess the feasibility of a startup idea before writing a business plan.

These are all important steps on the road to launching your own business, but don't stop there. We will show you in later chapters how to create a business plan that will spell out the details of your planned enterprise and its startup considerations. But it is very important that you take an intermediate step first, one that tells you how *feasible* your business idea may be. A *feasibility analysis* is a preliminary assessment of a business idea that gauges whether or not the venture envisioned is likely to succeed. Of course, it may also indicate that the concept has merit, but only if it is adapted in some important way.

But you really want to get started, right? If so, you may be tempted to skip directly to the business plan. This can be a serious mistake. Many entrepreneurs have ideas about new products or services that seem like winners, but those who become infatuated with an idea sometimes underestimate the challenging factors they may face—such as trying to tap a target market that is hard to access, or overestimating its size. Aspiring small business owners may also misjudge the power of competitors to close out new rivals or to imitate an innovative approach and make it their own. In other cases, an entrepreneur may not be able to build the organization required to capture the business opportunity he or she has in mind. Such mistakes are the cause of the lion's share of startup failures.

Developing a solid feasibility analysis before jumping ahead to the business plan can help ensure that the planned venture will not be doomed by a *fatal flaw*—that is, a circumstance or development that, in and of itself, could render a new business unsuccessful. John Osher, serial innovator and entrepreneur, estimates that nine out of ten entrepreneurs fail because their business concept is deficient. In his words, "They want to be in business so much that they often don't do the work they need to do ahead of time, so everything they do is doomed. They can be very talented, do everything else right, and fail because they have ideas that are flawed."[56] It is important to look deeply and honestly for potential weaknesses in your own startup ideas. No matter how awesome the business concept may seem to be, moving forward is pointless if it uses a manufacturing process that is patent protected, requires startup capital that cannot be raised, ignores market limitations, or is unsound in some other way.

John W. Mullins is a serial entrepreneur and a professor at the prestigious London Business School. He is also author of *The New Business Road Test*, a book that underscores the importance of identifying the fatal flaws of a business idea before it is too late:

> If [entrepreneurs] can find the fatal flaw before they write their business plan or before it engulfs their new business, they can deal with it in many ways. They can modify their ideas—shaping the opportunity to better fit the hotly competitive world in which it seeks to bear fruit. If the flaw they find appears to be a fatal one, they can even abandon the idea before it's too late—before launch, in some cases, or soon enough thereafter to avoid wasting months or years in pursuit of a dream that simply won't fly.

feasibility analysis
A preliminary assessment of a business idea that gauges whether or not the venture envisioned is likely to succeed.

fatal flaw
A circumstance or development that alone could render a new business unsuccessful.

3-9 A Feasibility Analysis Framework

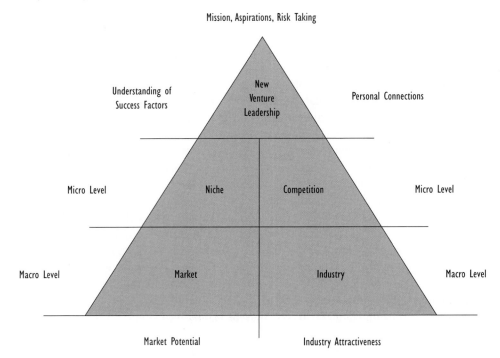

Mission, Aspirations, Risk Taking

New Venture Leadership

Understanding of Success Factors

Personal Connections

Micro Level   Niche   Competition   Micro Level

Macro Level   Market   Industry   Macro Level

Market Potential   Industry Attractiveness

Source: Adapted from John W. Mullins, *The New Business Road Test: What Entrepreneurs and Executives Should Do* Before *Writing a Business Plan* (London: Financial Times Prentice Hall, 2006).

Better yet, if, after [questioning] and probing, testing and especially experimenting for answers, the signs remain positive, they embrace their opportunity with renewed passion and conviction, armed with a new-found confidence that the evidence—not just their intuition—confirms their [insight]. Their idea really is an opportunity worth pursuing. Business plan, here we come![57]

Deciding to complete a feasibility analysis before proceeding to the business plan stage can save a lot of time, money, and heartache. Or, as Mullins points out, it may reaffirm the power of a business idea and strengthen your resolve to move forward, providing a reserve of energy and commitment that will come in handy when the going gets tough—and it definitely *will* get tough as the venture unfolds.

Keep in mind that success in entrepreneurship is generally the result of three elements that come together in such a way that the new enterprise gets the thrust it needs to launch and the sustained power to keep it going. These three elements are a market with potential, an attractive industry, and a capable individual or team with the skills and capabilities to pull it all together (see Exhibit 3-9). We will discuss each of these in the following sections.

Market Potential

It is important to make clear the distinction between a market and an industry, as the two are very different. A market consists of *buyers*, current or potential customers who are interested in purchasing a particular class of products or services to satisfy wants or needs—and they must also have the ability to pay for them. An industry, on the other hand, is composed of *sellers* who compete with one another by offering identical or similar products or services for sale to the same general group of buyers.

When assessing the pool of potential buyers that a business might serve, it is important to think of that market on two levels—the broad macro-market and the fragments or niches (micro-markets) that can be identified within the broader market. Entrepreneurs with limited business aspirations may find attractive niche opportunities acceptable. However, Mullins points out that "it is also important to know which way the tides are flowing."[58] That is, a desirable niche today is likely to lose its luster over time if the broad market from which it is derived is trending toward the negative. The health of the macro-market can definitely be a useful predictor of the future potential of the micro-markets located within it.

An entrepreneur with lofty ambitions and visions of "mogul status" down the road may be satisfied with an attractive niche, but only if it can serve as a point of entry into a macro-market with prospects for fast growth and ample long-term potential. The attractiveness of that niche is limited if the fundamental features of the macro-market that support it are not promising. In any case, assessments of the market should be completed on both levels, and each of these will be driven by a very different set of questions (see Appendix 3A, pp. 91–92).

As part of a feasibility analysis, an evaluation of the general environment (described on pp. 71–72.) will help you identify a potential-laden trend that can support promising startup ideas, one of which you will likely select for more thorough consideration. This will set the frame for your macro-market analysis, establishing the boundaries for the research you will need to conduct regarding the number of customers targeted and their overall purchasing power and habits.

The micro-market assessment, however, goes in a very different direction. Your startup idea will most likely be tied to a market niche that seems to offer acceptable prospects for growth and, perhaps more important, a path to market entry that is more protected from existing competition. (These dynamics are explained in some detail in the Focus Strategies section on pp. 79–82.) Your evaluation of the micro-market should clarify the unique value your startup idea would offer customers, but it should also provide estimates of the size of the niche, its rate of growth, and its long-run prospects.

Industry Attractiveness

As is the case with markets, industries should be considered from both a "big-picture" and a more focused point of view. A macro-level analysis assesses the overall attractiveness of the industry in which the startup will be established, perhaps summarized best by Michael Porter's model of industry forces (see pp. 72–73). This general view of the industry will be further shaped by answers to the associated questions presented in the appendix to this chapter. Ultimately, these insights will tell you whether the industry provides conditions that would be favorable for the startup you hope to pursue. The more favorable the forces, the more attractive the industry—but keep in mind that a single unfavorable force can be enough to tip the balance toward unattractiveness, so it is important to consider these forces with great care. Knowing about adverse conditions in advance can certainly show the entrepreneur how to make adjustments to compensate, or it may suggest that it is time to pull the plug on that particular enterprise concept. Either way, the feasibility analysis will have served its purpose by highlighting problems in that particular industry setting.

A micro-level industry assessment is focused less on whether industry conditions overall are suitable to launching a new business and more on the probability of a startup's success over the long run. This requires the aspiring entrepreneur to think carefully about the proposed venture itself to determine whether the advantage it has going for it can be protected from competitive pressures once rivals realize that they have a new challenger. This will be determined mostly by the startup's potential to generate sales and the strength of protective barriers that will shield it from competitors' efforts to replicate its strengths, which would erode the advantages that made the startup possible in the first place. The appendix to this chapter lists a number of questions that can guide this part of the feasibility analysis.

New Venture Leadership

Finally, a new business will only be as strong as its leader, so it is important to assess whether the entrepreneur, or entrepreneurial team, is up to the task. Mullins suggests that three dimensions of capability are important here: (1) the fit of the venture with its leader's mission, aspirations, and level of comfort with the risk involved, (2) the leader's grasp of factors that are critical to the success of the enterprise and his or her ability to execute on these, and (3) the leader's connection to suppliers, customers, investors, and others who will be essential to making the venture work. The questions in the appendix to this chapter will direct this part of the assessment.

Completing a feasibility analysis takes a lot of time and effort, but it serves the very important purpose of identifying flaws in a business concept that may be fatal to the proposed startup. As Yogi Berra, the former major leaguer and king of malapropisms (confused sayings), once said, "When you come to a fork in the road, take it." Berra's adage offers little insight to baseball or the startup decision. Feasibility analysis, on the other hand, will indicate when your proposed new venture has come to a fork in the road because it is faced with a serious weakness of one kind or another—but it can also give you some idea of where to go from there. If well executed, a feasibility analysis *will* reveal flaws—every business concept has them. But many of these flaws can be corrected, in which case a course adjustment may take care of the problem. On the other hand, the analysis might expose major flaws that cannot be addressed or corrected. If it does, you would be wise to abandon the concept and shift your energies to a more attractive alternative. Regardless of the final outcome, completing a feasibility analysis will let you know what needs to be done before you commit time, money, and energy to completing a full-scale business plan.

Looking Forward

This chapter has been all about launching new ventures. But you may not be interested in starting a business from scratch. This may leave you asking, "Is there room left in the entrepreneurial game for me?" Absolutely! Chapters 4 and 5 will provide a closer look at franchise and buyout opportunities and help you figure out whether you might want to join a family-owned business. These are all forms of entrepreneurship.

If, on the other hand, you really want to try a startup, and the feasibility analysis suggests that "all systems are go," then it is time to start thinking about a business plan. Chapters 6 through Chapter 12 will show you how to flesh out the specifics of your business concept, from start to finish. After communicating the importance of the business plan and providing a model to get you started (Chapter 6), the rest of Part 3 will help you plan for marketing (Chapter 7), organizing (Chapter 8), locating (Chapter 9), and financing (Chapters 10 and 11) your new venture. Looking down the road a bit, Chapter 12 even shows you how to plan for your eventual exit from that venture. It's time to continue the journey!

LOOKING BACK

1. **Distinguish among the different types and sources of startup ideas and identify the most common sources of startup ideas.**

   - Entrepreneurs decide to start businesses from scratch for many different reasons.
   - Type A startup ideas are concerned with products or services that exist but are not present in all markets.
   - Type B ideas involve new or relatively new technology.
   - Type C ideas are based on new and improved ways of performing old functions.
   - Research shows that entrepreneurs claim prior work experience is the leading source of inspiration for startup ideas.
   - Personal experience leads many aspiring entrepreneurs to the startup decision.
   - Some entrepreneurs start their new ventures based on their hobbies and personal interests, which can add passion and energy to the enterprise.
   - Accidental discoveries may also spur startup efforts.
   - Change often inspires innovation, which can expand the range of possible entrepreneurial opportunities.

2. **Use innovative thinking to generate ideas for high-potential startups.**

   - A commitment to creative thinking can generate many ideas for new businesses.
   - Business ideas can also be spurred by borrowing ideas from existing products and services or other industries, combining businesses to create a market opening, focusing on a problem, and responding to a trend.
   - Other ideas for new businesses can come from improving an existing product or service, making customers' lives easier, meeting customer needs in a new way, expanding the market for a product or service, making a product or service "green," and tapping into new technologies.

3. **Describe external and internal analyses that might shape the selection of venture opportunities.**

   - Outside-in analysis considers the external environment, including the general, industry, and competitive environments.
   - Major trends in the general environment are economic, sociocultural, political/legal, global, technological, and demographic in nature.
   - The major forces that determine the level of competition within the industry environment are the threat of new competitors, the threat of substitute products or services, the intensity of rivalry among existing competitors, the bargaining power of suppliers, and the bargaining power of buyers.
   - Opportunities arise for small businesses that are alert to changes or openings in the general, industry, and competitive environments.
   - Inside-out analysis helps the entrepreneur to understand the internal potentials of the business.
   - Tangible resources are visible and easy to measure, whereas intangible resources are invisible and difficult to quantify.
   - Capabilities represent the integration of several resources in a way that boosts the firm's competitive advantage.
   - Core competencies are those resources and capabilities that can be leveraged to enable a firm to do something that its competitors cannot do.
   - A SWOT analysis provides an overview of a firm's strengths and weaknesses, as well as opportunities for and threats to the organization.
   - The entrepreneur's "opportunity sweet spot" is found at the point of overlap of emerging potentials in the external environment and the unique strengths and capabilities of the entrepreneur and his or her venture.

4. **Explain broad-based strategy options and focus strategies.**

   - A competitive advantage can be created using broad-based strategy options—cost-based or differentiation-based strategies.
   - A cost-based strategy requires the firm to become the lowest-cost producer within the market.
   - Product or service differentiation is frequently used as a means of achieving superior performance.
   - Focusing on a specific market niche is a strategy that small firms often use successfully.
   - A focus strategy may involve restricting focus to a single subset of customers, emphasizing a single product or service, limiting the market to a single geographical region, or concentrating on product/service superiority.
   - Entrepreneurs can exploit very different market niches that derive from the same general industry.
   - The basic direction of the business is chosen when the entrepreneur makes a strategic decision and selects a particular focus strategy.
   - The benefits of a focus strategy can diminish when the firm becomes too specialized, the strategy is imitated, the target segment becomes unattractive or demand dwindles, the segment loses its uniqueness, or new firms subsegment the industry.

5. **Assess the feasibility of a startup idea before writing a business plan.**

- A feasibility analysis should be conducted before moving on to the business plan to identify potentially fatal flaws prior to making the decision to invest the substantial time, energy, and other resources required to put together a full-scale plan.
- A market consists of all buyers of a product or service; an industry is made up of all sellers who compete for the same market.
- A feasibility analysis should assess the potential of a market on two levels—the broad macro-market and the micro-market—because the long-run potential of a market niche is determined largely by the outlook for the overall market.

- The industry should be assessed for its overall attractiveness (potential for profits) and the specific context of direct competition that can greatly impact a startup's prospects for success.
- Entrepreneurs are likely to be successful in a startup situation to the degree that the planned venture fits with their mission, aspirations, and risk tolerance.
- Successful entrepreneurs also must understand and be able to manage the factors that are critical to the operation of the enterprise, and they must be connected to suppliers, customers, investors, and others whose involvement is crucial to the future performance of the planned venture.

Key Terms

opportunity recognition, p.61
entrepreneurial alertness, p.61
startups, p.62
Type A ideas, p.63
Type B ideas, p.63
Type C ideas, p.64
serendipity, p.65
general environment, p.71

industry environment, p.71
competitive environment, p.71
resources, p.74
tangible resources, p.74
intangible resources, p.74
capabilities, p.74
competitive advantage, p.74
core competencies, p.75

SWOT analysis, p.75
strategy, p.77
cost-based strategy, p.77
differentiation-based strategy, p.78
focus strategy, p.79
strategic decision, p.80
feasibility analysis, p.83
fatal flaw, p.83

Discussion Questions

1. Why might an entrepreneur prefer to launch an entirely new venture rather than buy an existing firm?

2. What are the three basic types of startup ideas? What are the most common sources of inspiration for startup ideas?

3. List the six general trends of the general environment. Give a hypothetical example of a way in which each trend might affect a small business.

4. What are the primary factors shaping competition in an industry, according to Porter's model? In your opinion, which of these factors will have the greatest impact on industry prices and profits?

5. How are capabilities related to tangible and intangible resources? How are these related to core competencies?

6. What is a SWOT analysis? How can a SWOT analysis help the entrepreneur match opportunities in the external environment with organizational capabilities?

7. What are the two basic strategy options for creating a competitive advantage?

8. Explain what is meant by the term *focus strategy*.

9. What are the advantages and disadvantages of a focus strategy? What must an entrepreneur know and do to maintain the potential of a focus strategy?

10. Name and describe the major features of a feasibility analysis. Why is feasibility analysis important?

You Make The Call

SITUATION 1
Jonathan Lugar, 17, had just finished helping his mom with a garage sale when it occurred to him that he might create a business to do for others what he had done for her and make

a little money that he could save for college. The idea was to offer a service that could take all of the headaches out of running a garage sale. Lugar would handle all advertising and sale setup, and his experience with other garage sales in the area would allow him to coach sellers on pricing so that items would actually be purchased. Lugar figured he could charge $200 per job for sales that bring in $400 or less, but he and the seller would split sales above $400 on a 50-50 basis. Lugar believes the greatest value added from his services would be from his pricing insights, since most people rarely have a garage sale and thus have little idea how much to ask for things. Pricing wisely should make his customers happy since they could maximize their sales and minimize the risk that they would be left with the very items they were trying to get rid of. In fact, Lugar planned to keep track of how much things sold for to fine-tune his pricing advice. He estimates that his startup costs would be minimal and would come mostly in the form of the use of a truck (which he already owned) and some fuel.

Question 1 How would you classify Lugar's startup idea? Is it a Type A, Type B, or Type C idea?

Question 2 What was the source of Lugar's startup idea?

Question 3 Would you recommend that he give this startup concept a try? Explain your reasoning.

SITUATION 2

Amy Wright is the owner of Fit Wright Shoes, a manufacturer of footwear located in Alice, Texas. Her company has pledged that all customers will have a lifetime replacement guarantee on all footwear bought from the company. This guarantee applies to the entire shoe, even though another company makes parts of the product.

Question 1 Do you think a lifetime guarantee is too generous for this kind of product? Why or why not?

Question 2 What impact will this policy have on the company's quality standards? Be specific.

Question 3 What alternative customer service policies would you suggest?

SITUATION 3

One day, after picking up a cup of coffee, Jay Sorenson promptly dropped it in his lap because the paper cup was simply too hot to hold. From that unpleasant experience, he concluded that there had to be a better way to serve a steaming "cup of joe." He was right. His lap-scorching encounter inspired him to create a product called the Java Jacket, which is a patented insulating sleeve that slides over a paper cup to make any hot beverage comfortable to hold. But coming up with the product was the easy part; getting started in business was a bit more challenging because startup resources were meager. In fact, the company had to use the Sorenson house as its headquarters in the early days. But sales began to pour in after Jay and his wife, Colleen, attended a coffee trade show in Seattle, and the business has grown impressively since then. In fact, the family-run business has already sold more than one billion sleeves to a wide range of customers, from small independent espresso stands to some of the biggest coffee chains in the world. You could say that business is really . . . well . . . percolating.

Source: "Java Jacket," http://www.javajacket.com, accessed November 20, 2008.

Question 1 Will the market for Sorenson's product continue to grow in the years ahead?

Question 2 Given the company's success, what sources of competition should he expect?

Question 3 What steps would you recommend that Sorenson take to protect his company from the onslaught of competition that is likely to come?

Experiential Exercises

1. Select a product that is manufactured by a small business and look for the likely drivers of its attributes in the dynamics of the general and/or industry environments.

2. Examine a recent issue of a business publication and describe the type of target market strategy you believe the newspaper or magazine uses.

3. Visit a local small retailer and ask the manager to describe the firm's customer service policies. Do you think these policies are consistent with the company's primary strategy? Be prepared to present a case defending your conclusions.

4. Working in small groups, write a brief but specific description of the best target market for a new product that is familiar to most of the class. Designate a member of each group to read the group's market profile to the class.

5. Interview the owner of a local small business about the venture's performance outcomes. Find out what results were achieved, and then systematically explore how those performance outcomes have been reinvested in the business. For example, if the venture has generated considerable customer loyalty, examine how that commitment has been leveraged for future results.

6. On the website of a small business, identify the factors in the external (general, industry, and competitive) environment and the internal (organizational) environment around which the business seems to have been built. Does it appear to you that the firm is more sensitive to internal or external factors? Given your knowledge of the firm's business, is that good or bad?

7. The Electric Transportation Company sells electrically powered bicycles, like the ETC Express. Review the information found at http://store.nycewheels.com/etc.html. Using the terminology introduced in this chapter, identify the specific type of strategy the Electric Transportation Company is using as it expands its business.

The *Small Business and Entrepreneurship Resource Center* offers complete small business management resources through a comprehensive database that covers all major areas of starting, operating, and maintaining a business from financing, management, marketing, accounting, taxes, and more. Use the access code that came with your new book to access the site and perform the exercises in each chapter.

1. Type C ideas, those based on offering customers benefits from new and improved ways of performing old functions, probably account for the largest number of startups. Also, the number one source for start up ideas is personal experience, either at work or at home. Insights gained can lead to opportunities with tremendous potential. Sergio Stiberman wanted to end his car lease early, but he found it would cost him as much as his remaining payments to terminate the agreement. This is not what he had in mind, but unfortunately there were no alternatives. Describe the process of how Sergio moved forward based on this experience as the source of his startup idea.

2. Entrepreneurial ideas can come at what may be considered the most inopportune time—when you are dreaming. Focus on that last word—dreaming—because that was exactly, and literally, the source of the idea for Monster.com. It's been more than a decade now, but when company founder Jeff Taylor awoke at 4:30 one morning after an interesting dream, he had a feeling he was on to something. Getting the idea is one thing, but pursuing it is another. Describe Jeff Taylor's attitude toward entrepreneurship and new ideas.

Source: "Drop That Lease." *Kiplinger Business Forecasts* 2007. (June 28, 2007): NA. *Small Business Resource Center.* Gale. Higher Education. 8 June 2009, http://find.galegroup.com/sbrc/start.do?prodId=SBRC. A165885951.

Source: WILLIAMS, GEOFF. "Toot Your Own Horn. (Brief Article)." *Entrepreneur* 29. 1 (Jan 2001): 308. *Small Business Resource Center.* Gale. Higher Education. 8 June 2009 <http://find.galegroup.com/sbrc/start.do?prodId=SBRC>.Gale Document Number: A69238285

Video Case 3

FIREWIRE SURFBOARDS (P. 628)
This case describes the experiences of entrepreneurs who started an innovative surfboard manufacturing business and are shifting its strategy to extend the company's competitive reach.

ALTERNATIVE CASES FOR CHAPTER 3:

APPENDIX: Questions for Feasibility Analysis

MACRO-MARKET

- Define your entrepreneurial aspirations. Do you want to start a business with the potential to become a huge corporation or a small "lifestyle" enterprise that will never expand beyond a narrow niche market? (It is important to answer this first question to determine the importance of the questions that follow to your particular startup.)
- How large is the broad market you hope to serve? How have you measured its size?
- How fast has it grown over the past one to five years?
- How quickly do you expect it to grow over the next five to ten years?
- What economic, demographic, sociocultural, technological, political-legal, or global trends can you identify that will shape your market? What effect—positive or negative—will these trends have on your business?

MICRO-MARKET

- What specific customer need or benefit will your proposed product or service address?
- Define precisely the customer group you plan to serve. Do you have detailed, accurate, and current information about who the customers are, where they live or do business, and how they live their lives?
- What benefits will customers get from your product or service that they cannot get from those offered by competitors?
- What evidence do you have that customers will buy what you hope to sell?
- What evidence suggests that the market niche you have targeted is likely to grow, and at a reasonable rate?
- What other market niches or segments could also benefit from the product or service that you propose to sell, or one that is similar to it?

MACRO-INDUSTRY

- What industry do you plan to compete in? Provide a specific definition of it.
- Is it difficult or easy for new businesses to enter that industry?
- Do suppliers to that industry have the bargaining power to set terms and conditions, or do buyers have the bargaining power?
- How difficult will it be for substitute products or services to take away your market?
- Is rivalry in the industry best described as intense or contained?
- Considering all of Porter's five forces, is the industry attractive or unattractive?
- If profitability in the industry overall is low, is there good reason to conclude that your startup will outperform this standard? (If not, it's time to move on.)

MICRO-INDUSTRY

- Is your intellectual property—patents, trade secrets, copyrights—protected so that other companies will not be able to duplicate or imitate your business?
- Will the startup face significant legal liability? If so, is adequate and affordable insurance available to cover that liability?
- Can your venture develop and employ extraordinary organizational resources or capabilities that others would find difficult to duplicate or imitate? What evidence do you have to support your conclusion?
- Can you show that your startup will not run out of cash quickly? Your conclusion should be based on your answers to the following questions:
  - Will your sales revenue be adequate relative to the projected financial investment and profit margins (after figuring in all relevant costs)?
  - How much will it cost to acquire and retain customers?
  - How long will it take to attract customers?
  - How much cash must be tied up in working capital (in inventory, for example), and for how long?
  - How long will it take customers to pay?
  - How long can payments to others (such as suppliers) be delayed?

NEW VENTURE LEADERSHIP
Mission, Aspirations, and Risk Propensity

- What is your entrepreneurial mission? To serve a particular market niche? To change a particular industry? To market a particular product or service?
- What is the essence of your entrepreneurial vision? To work for yourself? To start a substantive business that will always be limited in size, with very few employees? To build something really big? To change the world in some important way?
- What kinds of risks are you willing, or unwilling, to take? Will you risk a secure salary and the lifestyle that goes along with your current job? (If so, for how long?) Will you put your own money at risk? (If so, how much?) Will you risk your home or time with your family or loved ones? (Do those you love accept the risks you intend to take?)

Managing Success Factors

- Identify two to five factors that are critical to success in your selected industry. How do you know that you have identified these factors correctly?
- Can you demonstrate that you, or your team, can execute on each and every one of the critical factors you have identified?

- Have you identified critical factors that you, or your team, cannot manage? If so, what can you do to address these shortcomings?

Personal Connections
- Whom do you (or your team) know in the companies that are likely to be suppliers to your proposed business, to competitors in your industry, and to companies in other industries that offer products or services that may be substitutes for yours? Write down names, titles, and contact information.

- Whom do you (or your team) know in the companies that are likely to be distributors of and target customers for your product or service, immediately and in the future? Write down names, titles, and contact information.

- Whom do you (or your team) know in the companies that are likely to be competitors or to offer substitute products or services? Write down names, titles, and contact information.

Source: Adapted from John W. Mullins, *The New Business Road Test: What Entrepreneurs and Executives Should Do* Before *Writing a Business Plan* (London: Financial Times Prentice Hall, 2006), pp. 49, 75, 101, 127, 145, 170, 187.

Franchising and Buyouts

In the SPOTLIGHT
Country Place Living:
Doing Well While Doing Good
http://www.countryplaceliving.com

When she got the lunch invitation from Jack West, Cynthia Gartman was curious. Jack had been a client, but Cynthia's firm had completed its assignment. A couple of months earlier, Cynthia, a consultant with the iFranchise Group, had helped Jack's team at Country Place Living (a chain of assisted-living residences located in rural communities in the Midwest) look into franchising as a growth strategy. Cynthia felt the company had potential, but wasn't sure that management and the board of directors were enthusiastic about the changes franchising would bring to Country Place Living.

"How would you like to run my company?" was Jack's opening statement, as they sat down to lunch. Cynthia and her husband had actually been drafting a business plan to launch their own information technology and consulting business. But Cynthia had learned a lot about Country Place Living from having completed the feasibility study for its expansion. She knew that Jack was something of a habitual entrepreneur who had built and sold a number of businesses—he had even been a franchisee for KFC. And Jack had been in the assisted-living business for 30 years. After conducting her own due diligence, Cynthia found that Jack looked at businesses as more than ways to make money. He had developed a good business model, one that helped people.

After talking through the options with her husband, Cynthia agreed to become president and chief operating officer of Country Place Living. She came to that position with franchise-related experience in the real estate, tiling, pipe and valve fitting, and hotel industries. Working with Jack, she moved the corporate headquarters from Kansas to Texas and began structuring the organization to grow as a franchisor. Based on her initial calculations, Cynthia proposed expanding to 400 locations within five years, but the economic recession that started in 2008 caused them to scale back those plans.

Cynthia discovered that while she possessed great expertise in franchising, she had a lot to learn about assisted living. She decided to first engage in personal education, leading her to become licensed in 16 states as an assisted-living director. Cynthia also recognized that she needed to devote her time to operating the business, so she hired consultants to rewrite the operations and training manuals to be suitable for franchisees. In addition, she contracted out the development of the website.

Entrepreneurship shows up in lots of ways. Chapter 3 examined how entrepreneurs take their ideas, develop them into opportunities, and pursue their entrepreneurial dreams by starting a business from scratch. But entrepreneurs also buy existing businesses. Many times they see opportunities that the seller overlooked and take the acquired company to new heights. Sometimes they decide the best way to start is with a partner, a franchisor who has experienced the trials and errors of starting a business and can now make life easier for the franchisee. This chapter considers franchises and buyouts—startup options involving existing businesses.

What Is Franchising?

1. Define franchising and identify franchise options.

franchising
A marketing system involving a legal agreement, whereby the franchisee conducts business according to terms specified by the franchisor.

franchisor
The party in a franchise contract that specifies the methods to be followed and the terms to be met by the other party.

franchisee
An entrepreneur whose power is limited by a contractual relationship with a franchisor.

The franchise model has been around for a long time in various forms. Some say the first franchisor was the Roman Catholic Church, when the pope authorized parish priests to collect tithes and remit a portion to the Vatican while retaining the remainder for parish maintenance.[1] Others mark the beginning of franchising at the time that the king of England licensed public houses to serve travelers.[2] Theft and mistreatment of citizens on the roadways had become epidemic, requiring government intervention to assure that licensed pubs would charge honest prices for the products and services that they provided.

The Singer Sewing Machine company is credited with being the first franchisor in the United States.[3] In 1850, the company began contracting with local retailers to give them exclusive rights to sell Singer sewing machines. There are some historians, however, who contend that Benjamin Franklin was actually the first U.S. franchisor.[4] They cite the arrangement he made with a printer in South Carolina to reproduce the *Poor Richard's Almanac* columns that Franklin was producing in Philadelphia. (As an interesting side note, the widow of the South Carolina printer eventually took over her late husband's business, making her the first female franchisee in North America.)

The term *franchising* was derived from a French word meaning "freedom" or "exemption from duties." In business, *franchising* describes a unique type of business option that offers entrepreneurs the possibility of reducing the overall risk associated with buying an independent business or starting a company from scratch. The franchise arrangement allows new business owners to benefit from the accumulated business experience of all members of the franchise system.

What defines this method of doing business? According to the International Franchise Association,

Franchising is a method of distributing products or services. At least two levels of people are involved in the franchise system:

1. The *franchisor,* who lends his trademark or trade name and a business system, and

2. The *franchisee,* who pays a royalty and often an initial fee for the right to do business under the franchisor's name and system. Technically, the contract binding the two parties is the "franchise," but that term is often used to mean the actual business that the franchisee operates.[5]

choosing franchising

According to their website, "Floyd's 99 shops are genuine, hip places where most anyone will feel comfortable and know from their first visit that we care about the quality of service we provide. Old fashioned? Kinda, but for us it's why so many of our customers return time after time; it's what we stand for." The founders of Floyd's 99 like to think of their barbershops as hip places for getting haircuts at reasonable prices while having fun.

Brothers Paul, Rob, and Bill O'Brien opened the first Floyd's in 2001 in Denver, Colorado. Overcoming early adversity and discovering how loyal their customers were caused the brothers to decide to expand, and they chose franchising as their strategy. Jay Palmer of Fort Collins, Colorado, became a Floyd's 99 franchisee in 2007, three years after the company began franchising.

In 2008, Jay reported sales of over $1,000,000 at his two locations and wanted to add a third. The national economy was in a recession by then, and Jay could not get any banks to lend him the money he needed, not even with SBA guarantees. Eventually, he accepted $150,000 from a personal investor, a customer who liked his experience getting a shave and haircut at Floyd's 99. He saw that the employees enjoyed their jobs and performed them well. As Jay explains, it came down to "seeing a stream of people coming in and out the door, knowing our customers and our employees are happy, and realizing this is a good business."

Jay likes how Floyd's 99 combines old school service with new school appeal. Adhering to the themes of the franchisor, Jay's shops focus on traditional haircuts, styling, color services, and specialty barbering. They provide stations for customers to surf the Internet or jam to the music being played. The way Jay sees it, "Floyd's 99 Barbershop is rockin' your world in Ft. Collins!"

Sources: http://www.floydsbarbershop.com, accessed January 25, 2009; Sara Wilson, "How Are Franchisees Dealing?" *Entrepreneur*, Vol. 37, No. 1 (January 2009), p. 88.

© Floyd's 99 Holdings, LLC

Franchising Options

If you are considering entering into a legal agreement with a franchisor, you will want to learn all you can about that firm and its leaders. Why did they decide on the franchise model? What is their business philosophy? Do you want them as your business partners?

The potential value of any franchising arrangement is defined by the rights contained in a legal agreement known as the *franchise contract*; the rights it conveys are called the *franchise.* The extent and importance of these rights may be quite varied. When the main benefit the franchisee receives is the privilege of using a widely recognized product name, the arrangement between the franchisor (supplier) and the franchisee (buyer) is called *product and trade name franchising.* Chevrolet automobile dealers, Coca-Cola soft drink bottlers, and ExxonMobil service stations are examples of companies engaged in this type of franchising.

Alternatively, entrepreneurs who receive an entire marketing and management system are participating in a broader type of arrangement referred to as *business format franchising.* Fast-food outlets (such as Subway), hotels and motels (such as Marriott), and business services

franchise contract
The legal agreement between franchisor and franchisee.

franchise
The privileges conveyed in a franchise contract.

product and trade name franchising
A franchise agreement granting the right to use a widely recognized product or name.

(such as Liberty Tax Service) typically engage in this type of franchising. Although most people's stereotype of business format franchising is the fast-food restaurant, companies in over 75 industries make use of that particular franchise structure.

A *master licensee* is a firm or individual having a continuing contractual relationship with a franchisor to sell its franchises. This independent company or businessperson is a type of middleman or sales agent responsible for finding new franchisees within a specified territory. Master franchisees may even provide support services such as training and warehousing, which are more traditionally provided by the franchisor. Franchisors often expand internationally through agreements with master franchisees. Also gaining widespread usage is *multiple-unit ownership,* in which a single franchisee owns more than one unit of the franchised business. Some of these franchisees are *area developers*—individuals or firms that obtain the legal right to open several outlets in a given area.

Piggyback franchising refers to the operation of a retail franchise within the physical facilities of a host store. An example of piggyback franchising occurs when McDonald's operates a restaurant within a Walmart store. *Multi-brand franchising* involves operating several franchise organizations within a single corporate structure. The Dwyer Group is a pioneer in this form of franchising with six brands: Rainbow International, Mr. Appliance Corp., Mr. Rooter, Aire Serv, Mr. Electric, and Glass Doctor. *Co-branding* involves bringing two franchise brands together under one roof. A&W and KFC found that co-locating their brands worked so well in one outlet that they agreed to combine the brands in over 300 locations.

The Impact of Franchising

Periodically, the International Franchise Association (IFA) sponsors studies of the impact of franchising on the American economy. The IFA promotes itself as "the world's premier association dedicated to protecting, enhancing, and promoting franchising."[6] Founded in 1960, the IFA

EXHIBIT 4-1 Economic Impact of Franchising

Economic Activity in Franchised Businesses

There were 909,253 businesses in franchise systems in the United States in 2005, accounting for 3.3 percent of all U.S. business establishments. These businesses directly provided

- 11.0 million jobs,
- an annual payroll of $278.6 billion, and
- output worth $880.9 billion.

Their economic activity accounted for

- 8.1 percent of all private-sector jobs,
- 5.3 percent of all private-sector payrolls, and
- 4.4 percent of all private-sector output.

Economic Activity Because of Franchised Businesses

The economic significance of franchising is greater than indicated by the activity in franchised businesses alone, for it stimulates still more activity and supports the growth of many nonfranchised businesses. If we include economic results from both inside and outside of franchising, franchised businesses in the United States were the source of

- 21.0 million jobs, or 15.3 percent of private-sector jobs,
- $660.9 billion of payroll, or 12.5 percent of private-sector payrolls, and
- $2.31 trillion of output, or 11.4 percent of private-sector output.

Source: PriceWaterhouseCoopers, The Economic Impact of Franchised Businesses, Volume II (Washington, DC: International Franchise Association, 2008).

has more than 1,100 franchisors, 8,000 franchisees, and 400 suppliers as members. The impact studies report economic activity in franchised businesses—in terms of number of establishments, jobs, payroll, and output—and from the purchasing of goods and services by franchise businesses and the expenditures of franchise owners and employees in their communities.

The most recent impact results were published in 2008 and were based on 2005 data from government documents (see Exhibit 4-1). The analysis showed that franchised businesses actually provided more jobs than entire industries, including durable goods manufacturing, financial services, construction, nondurable goods manufacturing, and information (software and print publishing, motion pictures and videos, radio and television broadcasting, and telecommunications carriers and resellers).

The Pros and Cons of Franchising

In a way, we are all "experts" in franchising. You have been making purchases in franchise outlets since you were a child. If you have work experience, your first job may have been with a franchised business. We see their advertisements everywhere. Yet, how much do we really know about an opportunity until we have studied it? "Look before you leap" is an old adage that should be heeded by entrepreneurs considering franchising. Entrepreneurs should not let their enthusiasm blind them to the realities of franchising, both good and bad. Weighing the purchase of a franchise against alternative paths to starting a business is an important task, which deserves careful consideration. Exhibit 4-2 lists some of the major advantages you can gain through franchising.

2. Understand the pros and cons of franchising and the structure of the industry.

The Pros

Buying a franchise can be attractive for a variety of reasons. The greatest advantage is the probability of success. Franchisors offer a business model with a proven track record. A reputable franchisor has been through the trials and errors that an entrepreneur might face when starting a business from scratch. Franchisors report that finding qualified franchisees is among their biggest problems; as a result, one explanation for the low failure rate is how selective many franchisors are when granting franchises. Even potential franchisees who qualify financially can still be rejected.

There are other reasons why a franchise opportunity is appealing. Attractive franchises have names that are well known to prospective customers. They provide detailed operating manuals for franchisees to follow, so the hard work of blazing the trail has already been done. And they also support their franchisees by providing training, reducing purchasing costs, designing promotional campaigns, and assisting in obtaining capital. Naturally, different franchises vary in the depth of support they provide for each of these forms of assistance.

EXHIBIT 4-2 Advantages of the Franchise Model

- Reduced risk of failure
- Going into business for yourself, but not by yourself
- Use of a valuable trade name and trademark
- Access to a proven business system
- Management training provided by the franchisor
- Immediate economies of scale
- A way for an existing business to diversify

TRADE NAMES AND TRADEMARKS   When you open your own business, it can take a long time and a lot of money to get your name established and customers in your door or to your website. When you become a franchisee, however, you expect the franchisor to have laid the groundwork. An entrepreneur who enters into a franchising agreement acquires the right to use the franchisor's nationally advertised trademark or brand name, and this serves to identify the local enterprise with a widely recognized product or service. Ideally, customers who might have done business with another franchisee and been satisfied will be comfortable going to your new business. Doctor's Associates Inc., the company that owns Subway Restaurants, reports that over half of their new franchisees purchase their stores from retiring owners, demonstrating the value they attach to the brand.[7]

Success for many businesses results from their intellectual property. We usually think of patents when we see that term, but a trademarked name can be just as valuable if it has become part of common public use. Think "Big Mac®," "Oh Thank Heaven for 7-Eleven®," "Trust the Midas Touch®," and many others. Doctor's Associates Inc. has registered 15 different trademarks.[8] Trademarks and trade names make your business instantly identifiable to prospective customers and clients and can bring them right through your door.

OPERATIONS MANUAL   In addition to a proven line of business and readily identifiable products or services, franchisors offer well-developed and thoroughly tested methods of marketing and management. As a former franchisee, Jack West, whom we met at the start of this chapter, knew the importance of an operations manual and realized that he needed a franchise expert to refine the business practices of his centers so that franchisees could follow the steps necessary to be successful. As a result, he sought the experience and abilities that Cynthia Gartman could bring to Country Place Living. The manuals and procedures supplied to franchisees enable them to function more efficiently from the start. Reputable firms that grow through franchising begin with company-owned stores in which they develop their fundamental business model, leading to a tried-and-true method of operating the business. They document the procedures that work, compile them in an operations manual, and provide the manual to franchisees. Guidelines in the manual explain to franchisees and managers the specific steps required to operate the enterprise profitably.

An operations manual may be the single most valuable tool provided to a franchisee. Following the path laid out in the book helps the owner to avoid mistakes that often occur with a startup business, such as employing unqualified personnel, investing in the wrong equipment or inventory, or failing to control costs. The franchisee should use the manual to channel his or her energy toward the most productive activities leading to survival and profitability. And the franchisee should expect to be held accountable for following the manual. One of the most critical aspects of franchising is that customers find the same products, services, and methods of conducting business from one outlet to another. If one franchise is allowed to operate at a substandard level, it could easily destroy customers' confidence in the entire chain.

MANAGEMENT SUPPORT   The training received from franchisors is invaluable to many small entrepreneurs because it compensates for weaknesses in their managerial skills. Training by the franchisor often begins with an initial period of a few days or a few weeks at a central training school or another established location and then continues at a franchise site. McDonald's is widely recognized for its off-site franchisee training at Hamburger University. More and more franchisors are providing their training programs online.

The nature of both the product and the business affect the amount and type of training needed by the franchisee. In most cases, training constitutes an important advantage of the franchising system, as it permits individuals who have had little training or education in the industry to start and succeed in businesses of their own.

Joining a franchise network makes you part of a larger organization, which provides significant economies of scale. One critical benefit of these economies is efficiency in the purchasing function. A franchise network can buy in larger quantities than an individual business, lowering per unit costs for the franchisees. Additionally, centralized purchasing activities reduce operating expenses for the various outlets.

Franchisees are often required to contribute to marketing expenses above and beyond the royalties they pay on sales. These expenses are pooled for the benefit of the entire network. The franchisor is then able to invest in more sophisticated marketing research, in higher quality advertising campaigns, and more extensive media outlets than franchisees could do independently. This ability leads to wider and deeper acceptance of the brands and trade names and benefits each franchisee.

Some franchisors provide financial support to prospective and existing franchisees, assistance that can come in many forms. Companies such as GNC and Wingstop have formed alliances with banks to create preferred lending programs for franchisees. The International Franchise Association (IFA) encourages franchisors to recruit minorities and veterans as franchisees by offering financial incentives. In order for a franchisor to be listed in the IFA's VetFran Directory, the company must agree to provide initial fee discounts, special financing terms, or other incentives. Companies listed in the directory range alphabetically from AAMCO Transmissions to ZIPS Dry Cleaners.[9] Burger King and Yum! Brands (KFC, Taco Bell, Pizza Hut, etc.) have programs to fund franchisees to obtain valuations of their businesses so that they can restructure their financing.[10] Ace Hardware is an example of a company that offers financial assistance and other forms of management support for franchisees (see Exhibit 4-3).

EXHIBIT 4-3 Ace Hardware's Support for Co-Op Members

Our startup assistance includes help with:

- Financing programs for qualified individuals
- Finding the right location
- Set-up and design, including store planning, visual merchandising, pricing strategy development, office set-up, and product selection

Ace's comprehensive training covers strategies for:

- Effective store management
- Managing each revenue center
- Purchasing and inventory
- Implementing superior customer service
- Financial management and back-office procedures
- Hiring, training, and managing employees
- Effective marketing techniques

Our on-site support includes:

- Hands-on, on-site support at your grand opening
- Visits from our experienced retail support staff
- In-store tools for continual improvement, such as customer surveys, customer comment card programs, and mystery shopper programs

Marketing and advertising support includes:

- Grand opening planning, assistance, and awareness programs
- Local store marketing programs, such as newspaper ad slicks, direct marketing materials, and regional radio and television opportunities
- Comprehensive and effective national advertising
- Public relations strategies and materials
- Community involvement programs and local charity tie-ins
- Ace Rewards—our one-to-one consumer loyalty program
- System-wide website with store directory and e-commerce functions

Source: Adapted from http://www.myace.com/index.cfm?fa+training, accessed January 18, 2009. Reprinted by permission of Ace Hardware Corp.

The U.S. Small Business Administration (SBA) has introduced the Franchise Registry (http://www.franchiseregistry.com), which greatly expedites loan processing for small business franchisees. The Registry "enables lenders and SBA local offices to verify a franchise system's lending eligibility through the Internet. This reduces red tape, time, and cost for all concerned."[11] Being listed on this registry means that the SBA has deemed acceptable the control provisions on the franchisee found in that franchise agreement. This allows loan applications for registered franchises to be reviewed and processed more quickly.

Although many franchising systems have developed excellent training programs, be aware that this is by no means universal. Some unscrupulous promoters falsely promise extensive training and then leave the entrepreneur to run his or her own business with little or no guidance. This is where "doing your homework" before committing to a franchise can really pay off.

The Cons

The founders of the International Franchise Association were disturbed by dishonest and unethical acts of some companies that were growing through franchising and damaging the reputation of the entire industry; they also sought to preempt government regulation of franchising. Firms joining the IFA are required to adhere to a code of ethics, the foundational values of which are "trust, truth, and honesty." The code requires IFA members to engage in mutual respect and reward, as well as open and frequent communication. The IFA also demands adherence to the law and offers a conflict resolution service for franchisors and franchisees. To this day, however, some companies engage in practices that trouble regulators, legislators, and the business community at large. Some concerns that government officials have regarding franchising are listed in Exhibit 4-4.

FINANCIAL ISSUES Major concerns have arisen regarding the true costs of becoming and remaining a franchisee. New franchisees of some franchise organizations have felt misled about their earnings opportunities. They have reported being told that they could expect high returns on their investments, only to discover that few, if any, franchisees achieved those results. Current and former franchisees of Quiznos, for example, sued the firm in Illinois, Pennsylvania, and Wisconsin for luring "franchisees into the system by misrepresenting contract terms and

EXHIBIT

4-4 Government Concerns about Franchising

1. Misleading or exaggerated earnings claims by franchisors
2. Opportunity behavior by which the franchisor becomes a competitive threat to franchisees
3. Restrictions on franchisees who desire to liquidate their holdings in favor of alternative investment opportunities
4. Conflicts of interest, such as when a franchisor forces franchisees to be captive outlets for other suppliers owned by the franchisor
5. Churning: terminating a successful franchise operation in order to resell it and gain additional franchise fees
6. Encroachment: locating a new outlet or point of distribution too close to an existing franchisee, causing a material loss of sales
7. Imposing noncompete clauses on franchisees
8. One-sided contracts devised by franchisors
9. The imposition of new restrictions as a requirement of contract renewal
10. Franchisor intimidation of franchisees who attempt to form franchisee associations, seek alternative sources for products, or make other efforts to create a more level playing field

financial projections."[12] These cases may be resolved in Quiznos's favor, but they demonstrate a problem many franchisees claim to experience.

Other criticisms of franchisors by franchisees that have come to the attention of government agencies include refusing to permit franchisees to sell their businesses in order to invest their money elsewhere and forcing franchisees to purchase products and services from subsidiaries or business associates, resulting in higher than market prices. The term *churning* refers to actions by franchisors to void the contracts of franchisees in order to sell the franchise to someone else and collect an additional fee.

COMPETITIVE ISSUES   Franchisees have also reported that their franchisors have actually competed directly against them on occasion. This can occur when the franchisor opens a corporate-owned store within proximity of the franchisee's location or sells products via mail or over the Internet. A variation on this complaint is referred to as *encroachment*. A franchisor is said to encroach on a franchisee's territory when the franchisor sells another franchise location within the market area of an existing franchisee. For example, Dunkin' Donuts was sued by franchisees in Detroit, Michigan, for attempting to sell new franchise units in the Detroit market while refusing to allow current franchisees to expand.[13]

Another complaint stems from special clauses inserted into some franchise agreements. A number of franchisors impose noncompete clauses on their franchisees. From the franchisors' perspective, this makes perfect sense—after training and sharing secrets and strategies with a franchisee, they do not want the franchisee to sever the relationship and become a competitor. From the franchisees' perspective, however, this is restraint of trade, especially if they find the franchisor to be nonresponsive to their needs or if they project that they can make more money on their own. It is only natural to think that the next business you start would evolve from your current experience. Yet the franchisor may keep you from applying those experiential skills by claiming that your new enterprise competes with the franchisor's business.

MANAGEMENT ISSUES   The final set of issues focuses on the freedom of the franchisee to run his or her own business. As a franchisee, you are not a truly independent business owner. You have a contractual arrangement with the franchisor that stipulates various conditions, and that contract may specify the products you carry, the services you offer, your hours of operation, and other aspects of how you run your company. The contract was drafted by, and most likely favors, the franchisor. Many prospective franchisees fail to recognize that many franchisors are willing to negotiate some portions of the contract. In any case, you should always have an attorney review the contract before you sign. Some of the most common restrictions that franchise contracts impose on franchisees fall into the following categories:

- Limiting sales territories
- Requiring site approval for the retail outlet and imposing requirements regarding outlet appearance
- Limiting goods and services offered for sale
- Limiting advertising and hours of operation

A frequently heard complaint from franchisees is that when their contract expires, they are required to accept new and often costly provisions. Franchisees suspect this is an effort to extract more revenues and/or concessions from them or to force them out in order to sell the franchise to someone else or to take it over as a company store. A franchisor may have another explanation. During the years the contract was in force, the franchisor may have gained experience in working with multiple franchisees and may have found ways to improve the system that were incorporated into more recent franchise contracts. Additionally, some franchisors discover that long-time franchisees have not maintained their facilities or have failed to adapt to new marketing and operating procedures. From the franchisor's point of view, these franchisees need to improve their businesses so that they will not harm the entire network.

The Costs of Being a Franchisee

If you choose to become a franchisee, you pay for the privilege. You are buying a proven model, and the franchisor will charge you for the benefits being offered. Generally speaking, higher costs characterize the better known and more successful franchises. Franchise costs have several components, all of which need to be recognized and considered.

1. *Initial franchise fee.* The total cost of a franchise begins with an initial franchise fee, which may range from several hundred to many thousands of dollars. EagleRider Motorcycle Rentals charges a $30,000 initial fee but gives prospective franchisees the option of paying $750 per month, financed for 48 months.

2. *Investment costs.* Significant costs may be involved in renting or building an outlet and stocking it with inventory and equipment. Certain insurance premiums, legal fees, and other startup expenses must also be paid, and it is often recommended that funds be available to cover personal expenses and emergencies for at least six months. On its website, Ace Hardware presents estimated startup costs, but it also indicates the immediate benefits that a franchisee can expect to receive (see Exhibit 4-5). FAST-FIX, a jewelry repair chain, estimates the total initial investment to be between $130,000 and $270,000. An applicant to become a Baskin-Robbins franchisee must provide evidence of a personal net worth of at least $300,000.

3. *Royalty payments.* A royalty is a fee charged to the franchisee by the franchisor. It is calculated as a percentage of the gross income that the franchisee receives from customers for selling the franchised products and services. Phillips Seafood charges a 5 percent royalty. For Maui PlayCare, a new concept that provides hourly or full day care for small children, the royalty fee is 7 percent.

4. *Advertising costs.* Many franchisors require that franchisees contribute to an advertising fund to promote the franchise. These fees are generally 1 to 2 percent of sales, sometimes even more. Country Place Living calls these "marketing costs" and lists them between 1 and 2 percent.

EXHIBIT 4-5 An Estimate of Investment Costs and Benefits by Ace Hardware

The following is a brief summary of the initial investment. At Ace, we don't charge you royalty and franchise fees.

Membership Application	$5,000
Initial Ownership Stock Investment	$5,000
Liquid Capital	$250,000
Loan	$390,000–$740,000 (depending on store size)
Total Investment*	$650,000– $1,000,000

Total investment will vary based on store size. Items included in this figure are store fixtures, inventory, office equipment, computer system, decor, signage and operating capital. These costs do not include such things as land and building costs or leasehold improvements.

Incentive Benefits

Qualified individuals will receive our exclusive incentive package of up to $255,000 that can assist in your store's opening.

Our incentive package helps prepare you for ownership and can drive down the total investment for a business by nearly 20 percent. Additionally, an enhanced incentives package is available when you decide to open additional stores.

Source: http://www.myace.com/index.cfm?fa=investment, accessed August 6, 2009. Reprinted by permission of Ace Hardware Corp.

If entrepreneurs could generate the same level of sales by setting up an independent business, they would save the franchise fee and some of the other costs. However, if the franchisor provides the benefits previously described, the money that franchisees pay for their relationship with the franchisor may prove to be a very good investment.

Evaluating Franchise Opportunities

3. Describe the process for evaluating a franchise opportunity.

After making a decision to pursue a franchising opportunity, the prospective franchisee must identify a franchise candidate and investigate it completely. As we discuss the investigation process, we will use examples involving Country Place Living, the assisted-living facility franchisor introduced at the start of the chapter, and Valpak, a cooperative direct mail advertiser.

Selecting a Franchise

With the growth of franchising over the years, the task of selecting an appropriate franchise has become easier. Personal observation frequently sparks interest, or awareness may begin with exposure to an advertisement in a newspaper or magazine or on the Internet. The headlines of these advertisements usually highlight the financial and personal rewards sought by the entrepreneur. *Inc. Magazine, Entrepreneur,* and the *Wall Street Journal* are only three examples of the many publications that not only print stories about franchising, but also include the advertisements of franchisors.

Investigating the Potential Franchise

The nature of the commitment required in franchising justifies careful investigation of the situation. The investment is substantial, and the business relationship generally continues over many years.

The evaluation process is a two-way effort. The franchisor wishes to investigate the franchisee, and the franchisee obviously wishes to evaluate the franchisor and the type of opportunity being offered. Time is required for this kind of analysis. You should be skeptical of a franchisor who pressures you to sign a contract without time for proper investigation. Some of the factors to consider in assessing different franchise opportunities are listed in Exhibit 4-6. The first factor on the list warns against entering into an agreement with a company that primarily distributes its goods and services through corporate-owned stores. You should ask yourself whether this company will provide as much attention and the same support services to its franchisees as it does to the outlets that it owns. You also want to be associated with an organization that is well established and has enjoyed success in the marketplace. And you need to speak with current and past franchisees. What was their working relationship with the franchisor? Would they do it all over again?

There are many sources of information about franchisors to help you in your evaluation, including state and federal agencies. Since most states require registration of franchises, a prospective franchisee should not overlook state offices as a source of assistance. The Federal Trade Commission has produced various helpful reports and documents regarding franchising, including *Buying a Franchise: A Consumer Guide.* (These are available at http://www.ftc .gov/bcp/menus/business/franchise/shtm.) Also, a comprehensive listing of franchisors can be found in the *Franchise Opportunities Guide,* which is published by the International Franchise Association. Exhibit 4-7 displays two of those listings.

Business publications are also excellent sources of franchisor ratings. *Fortune, Entrepreneur,* and the *Wall Street Journal,* to name a few, can be found in most libraries, and all have websites with archives. The *Entrepreneur* magazine website contains a profile of the top-20

4-6 Evaluating Franchise Opportunities

1. Is the franchisor dedicated to a franchise system as its primary mechanism of product and service distribution?
2. Does the franchisor produce and market quality goods and services for which there is an established market demand?
3. Does the franchisor enjoy a favorable reputation and broad acceptance in the industry?
4. Will the franchisor offer an established, well-designed marketing and business plan and provide substantial and complete training to franchisees?
5. Does the franchisor have good relations with its franchisees, and do the franchisees have a strong franchisee organization that has negotiating leverage with the franchisor?
6. Does the franchisor have a history of attractive earnings by its franchisees?

4-7 Profiles from the Franchise Opportunities Guide (2009)

Country Place®
LIVING

Business Established:	2003	Offering Financial Assistance
Franchising Since:	2007	Special Incentives
		VetFran Participant
		MinorityFran Participant
Franchised Units:	8	VetFran Incentive

Serving our country is one of life's highest callings. If you are an honorably discharged veteran, you will qualify for our veteran's program, which entitles you to a reduction of $7,500 in the initial franchise fee and other benefits.

Company Owned Units:	8
Start-up Cost:	$150,000 to $400,000
Total Investment:	$600,000 to $2,300,000

Country Place Living has a respected reputation as a leader in the assisted living industry. We own, develop, and franchise quality senior living residences in rural and suburban areas. Our residences are welcoming, well-designed, and focus on the specific needs of older adults. We stress individual care and comfort, and are staffed to provide whatever level of assistance is necessary for our residents. Each residence is constructed to exacting standards for quality, and our modern and elegant interiors are designed to help seniors feel independent, secure, and dignified.

Country Place Living offers assisted living and group home residences where seniors truly feel at home and maintain their dignity. We specialize in small group residences consisting of either 18 apartments (Country Place Senior Living) or 8 bedrooms (Country Place Home Plus.) Country Place Senior Living is designed for active seniors, while Country Place Home Plus is created especially for those seniors who may need additional specialized care. All of our brands promote social interaction and a more intimate environment, while at the same time preserving the privacy and dignity of seniors.

TRAINING

We provide each franchisee with a comprehensive training program to get their Country Place Living residence off to a successful start. In addition to full operations manuals, cookbooks, and training tools, we offer in-depth franchisee, director, and nurse training, which is held with corporate staff and prepares the franchisee, director, and nurse with proven operational, marketing techniques and standards of care that help ensure your residence continues to thrive. In addition to our onsite training, we provide numerous ongoing educational opportunities.

EXHIBIT

QUALIFICATIONS

A Country Place Living owner is altruistic by nature and profit-minded by design. The best franchisee will have strong business or financial acumen while at the same time be caring, helpful, and enthusiastic. Honesty and integrity as well as willingness to collaborate, work hard, and be accountable is what Country Place Living franchising is all about. We require that each franchise owner use the utmost care to maintain a warm and welcoming residence where seniors can continue successful lives built on well-being and self-reliance and families can be secure in the knowledge that their loved ones are in an active and nurturing community.

Valpak®

A Valpak® franchise gives you more than you expect

Business Established:	1968
Franchising Since:	1988
Franchised Units:	203
Company-Owned Units:	9
Start-up Cost:	$75,000 to $150,000
Total Investment:	$60,200 to 104,800

Offering Financial Assistance
Member SBA

Special Incentives
VetFran Participant
MinorityFran Participant
Home-Based Franchise

VetFran Incentive
20% off on the franchise and training fee as well as territory acquisition fees

AboutValpak®

Almost 40 years ago, our founder pioneered the concept of large-scale local cooperative direct mail advertising. Today we're still the leader. We help local, regional, and national businesses prepare offers and messages and send them to a receptive audience with above-average income and spending habits. A *Valpak®* franchise has the opportunity to control its own destiny; enjoys a strong, positive public image; and is effective in helping local businesses achieve their marketing objectives.

A *Valpak®* franchise is a full-time, hands-on opportunity to share in the growth of a proven business. You will be supported by Team One—a team that focuses on developing first-year franchises—along with marketing and creative services, a website and a research department. Online services, monthly updates and news items, and a quarterly magazine are just a few of the other resources available to you. As a franchise owner, you and your sales staff will contact local business owners, offering them our proven direct mail advertising products, including *Valpak.com®*, our online source for savings and giveaways. *Valpak®* provides a full range of direct mail marketing services, including ad concept, graphic design, and top-quality printing and distribution services. The company's outstanding customer service begins with the *Valpak®* sales force, which has been named one of the nation's top sales forces by *Sales & Marketing Management* magazine. *Valpak®* is committed to franchising; over 95% of our offices are owned by franchisees. Our success depends on your success.

The Valpak® Opportunity

High income potential

- $52.7 billion industry is expected to grow to $67.2 billion by 2011.
- The sustained growth rate of *Valpak®* is more than double the industry average in recent years.
- You don't need to reinvent the wheel! Our successful franchisees have been refining this program for many years.
- Share in passive profits from over $150 million in national and intermarket sales garnered outside your franchise territory.
- Unlike most franchise opportunities, *Valpak®* is not a royalty-based system. This means you keep a larger share of the profits generated by five different revenue streams—local sales, intermarket sales, national sales, Solo Values®, and *Valpak.com®*.

continued

EXHIBIT

High visibility and recognition

- We pioneered the industry 40 years ago and continue to be the leader.
- *Valpak*® is twice as large as its next two competitors combined; supported by nearly $10 million worth of national media exposure annually—the #1 brand by far.
- We mail approximately 500 million envelopes a year containing more than 20 billion local, regional, and national offers to nearly 44 million households.
- Nearly 9 out of 10 adults receiving the *Valpak*® envelope open and look through it. (Source: Consumer Communications Inc., March 2004)

Simple business model

- *Valpak*® helps businesses grow by attracting new customers with repeated, high-quality direct mail offers.
- *Valpak*® is ideal for the sales-minded professional. Our successful franchisees and sales representatives build relationships by offering proven advertising and marketing solutions.
- Proprietary software and technology tools help you focus on the unique opportunities of running a *Valpak*® office.

Training

- More than 300 hours of training are available per year!
- Multiple regional and national conventions are held each year for owners and sales representatives.

Support

- Team One—a group of dedicated professionals provides close supervision and assistance to help insure smooth startup.
- The *Valpak*® Network is supported annually by a corporate advertising budget of more than $10 million.
- Monthly national promotions tie in with major entertainment names—recent mailings have included Warner Bros., CBS, TNT, NASCAR, Sony, 20th Century Fox, and Paramount.
- The *Valpak*® family of franchisees, along with home office support, provide the help and guidance necessary to grow your business effectively.

What is the initial investment?

- Initial franchise fees—$17,500
- Territory costs are based on size of market as little as $25,000
- Opening inventory—none
- Great Start Up program to help you get started fast
- Location—may be home-based or operate from office
- Net worth requirement—minimum of $150,000
- Liquidity requirement—minimum of $75,000
- Offered by prospectus only

Source: http://www.franchise.org, accessed January 24, 2009.

fastest-growing franchises in 2009 (see Exhibit 4-8). The rankings are based on the number of franchise units added in 2008.

In recent years, franchise consultants have appeared in the marketplace to assist individuals seeking franchise opportunities. Some consulting firms, such as Francorp, present seminars on choosing the right franchise. Of course, the prospective franchisee needs to be careful to select a reputable consultant. And since franchise consultants are not necessarily attorneys, an experienced franchise attorney should evaluate all legal documents.

THE FRANCHISOR AS A SOURCE OF INFORMATION   Obviously, the franchisor being evaluated is a primary source of information. However, information provided by a franchisor must be viewed in light of its purpose—to promote the franchise.

One way to obtain information about franchisors is to review their websites. For most franchisors, the website will be directed toward customers, presenting information about products, services, store locations, and so on. The websites should also direct you to information for prospective franchisees. If you enter your contact information, you can expect to receive

LIVING THE DREAM:

knowing Jack

Some entrepreneurs have found multi-unit franchising to be the road to wealth creation, and you do not have to start out wealthy to travel that road. Anil Yadav is the largest Jack in the Box franchisee in the United States, or in the world, for that matter. But his first step on the road to multi-unit franchising was just a part-time job to earn money for his college education.

Yadav was 17 years old when his family immigrated to America from India. He became a fry cook at a California Jack in the Box in 1984 to help pay tuition while working on his engineering degree. Eighteen months later, he was promoted to management. Within five years, Yadav was able to purchase his first restaurant, and by 2008, he owned and operated 78 Jack in the Box stores and 16 Denny's restaurants.

Yadav claims that one of his smartest moves was actually a mistake. In 2004, he owned 9 restaurants. An opportunity came along to purchase 25 more. The stretch was overwhelming, but when he bought them, it turned out to be a successful growth strategy. He also reported that his biggest mistake has been to trust people too quickly and too much. Trust is important is business relationships, but it can sometimes have negative consequences when people do not deserve that trust.

Successful entrepreneurs achieve their success through determination and hard work, but the work does not stop just because you acquire more wealth than you expected. Even as Jack in the Box's largest franchisee, Yadav explains that he stays close to his restaurants, making frequent visits and showing his employees that he is willing to be hands-on. A typical work week for Yadav might include 9- to 12-hour days.

To Yadav, the earnings are nice, but providing entrepreneurial and advancement opportunities for others is also important. He was able to help the person who first promoted him to later obtain his own franchise. He takes pride in promoting from within and in being large enough to give others responsibilities as area managers. According to Yadav, "Making a dollar is easy, but to maintain a dollar you have to work twice as hard."

Photo Courtesy of JIB Management

Source: John Carroll, "This Operator 'Knows Jack,'" *Multi-Unit Franchisee*, Issue IV (2008), pp. 12–14; http://www.jackinthebox.com, accessed January 25, 2009.

brochures and marketing materials that contain such information as startup costs and franchisees' testimonials.

If you express further interest in a franchise by completing the application form and the franchisor has tentatively qualified you as a potential franchisee, a meeting is usually arranged to discuss the disclosure document. A *disclosure document* is a detailed statement of such information as the franchisor's finances, experience, size, and involvement in litigation. The document must inform potential franchisees of any restrictions, costs, and provisions for renewal or cancellation of the franchise. Important considerations related to this document are examined more fully later in this chapter.

EXISTING AND PREVIOUS FRANCHISEES AS SOURCES OF INFORMATION There may be no better source of franchise facts than existing franchisees. Sometimes, however, the distant location of other franchisees precludes a visit to their place of business. In that case, a simple

disclosure document
A detailed statement provided to a prospective franchisee, containing such information as the franchisor's finances, experience, size, and involvement in litigation.

EXHIBIT 4-8 Entrepreneur's 2009 Top 20 Fastest-Growing Franchises

Franchise	Start-up Costs (2008)
1. Jan-Pro Franchising Int'l. Inc. Commercial cleaning	$3,300–54,300
2. Subway Submarine sandwiches & salads	$78, 600–238,300
3. Instant Tax Service Retail tax preparation & electronic filing	$39,000–89,000
4. Stratus Building Solutions Commercial cleaning	$3,500–57,800
5. Snap Fitness Inc. 24-hour fitness center	$71,100–241,900
6. Dunkin' Donuts Coffee, doughnuts, baked goods	Varies
7. Jazzercise Inc. Dance/exercise classes	$2,980–38,400
8. Bonus Building Care Commercial cleaning	$8,800–14,700
9. Anytime Fitness Fitness center	$30,000–292,600
10. Vanguard Cleaning Systems Commercial cleaning	$8,200–38,100
11. Jani-King Commercial cleaning	$11,300–34,100+
12. Domino's Pizza LLC Pizza, breadsticks, buffalo wings	$119,950–461,700
13.* Choice Hotels Int'l. Hotels, inns, suites, resorts	$2,500,000–15,300,000
14.* McDonald's Hamburgers, chicken, salads	$950,200–1,800,000
15. Liberty Tax Service Income-tax preparation	$53,800–66,900
16. Long John Silver's Restaurants Inc. Fish & chicken	$879,500–1,300,000
17. ExpressTax Tax preparation & electronic filing	$15,400–40,100
18. System4 Commercial cleaning	$5,500–37,800
19. Anago Cleaning Systems Commercial cleaning	$8,500–1,200,000
20. Massage Envy Therapeutic massage services	$291,900–469,800

*Tie

Source: http://www.entrepreneur.com, accessed January 24, 2009.

telephone call can elicit the owner's viewpoint. If possible, also talk with franchisees who have left the business; they can offer valuable insights into their decision to give up the franchise.

Becoming a Franchisor

We do not want to end the discussion of franchising without considering how you might choose this method to grow your independent business, just as Jack West of Country Place Living did.

After a few years of running your own business, you may conclude that you want to expand and that franchising is a reasonable option for you. It is not unusual for successful businesses to be approached by individuals who ask to become franchisees. Before entering into such an agreement, address the following considerations.

THE BUSINESS MODEL   Is your business replicable? In other words, do you have a model of doing business that someone else could adopt and use successfully in another location? A franchisee purchases an operating system as well as a product or service and a brand name. Is your system efficient, and can it be clearly explained so that others can apply it?

FINANCIAL CONSIDERATIONS   How will you finance the growth of the company? Many entrepreneurs think that franchising is a novel mechanism for financing their growing enterprises. They come up with a concept, collect franchise fees, and use those revenues to expand their operations. But franchising is not cost-free for the franchisor. There are legal documents to prepare, an operations manual to write, personnel to hire, and other tasks to be completed. Who will recruit and select franchisees? Who will orient and train them and their managers? Who will monitor their performance to ensure that they conform to contract requirements? Responsible franchisors often find that establishing a franchise costs more than the fee covers and that they only become profitable as a result of the royalties they eventually collect from successful franchisees.

REQUIRED ASSISTANCE   What expert assistance will you need to become a franchisor? Successful entrepreneurs learn quickly that they must choose the right experts, individuals who are qualified to provide the necessary help. If you decide to franchise your business, you should have an attorney with knowledge of and experience with the franchise method. As mentioned previously, there are many consultants who specialize in franchising and can assist with drafting operations manuals, preparing disclosure documents, assisting with franchisee selection, and many other aspects of the process. A good starting place for any prospective franchisor is joining the International Franchise Association and gathering information about reputable consultants.

THE OPERATIONS MANUAL   What will go into your operations manual? Many companies that have grown successfully through franchising brought in consultants who specialized in making the business operating model more efficient and easier to replicate prior to writing the manual. You should be able to present an operations manual to your franchisees that spells out what steps to take in daily activities to ensure customer satisfaction while controlling expenses. The operations manual should offer detailed instructions that help the franchisee avoid pitfalls and increase sales. It needs to be written from the perspective of the franchisee, who will not know the business as well as the franchisor. It is usually wise to hire a professional technical writer to put the manual together so that it communicates the process effectively.

GOVERNMENT REGULATIONS   Are you willing to satisfy the government's disclosure requirements? The Federal Trade Commission issued an amended *Franchise Rule* in May 2008. This rule prescribes that the franchisor must disclose certain information to prospective franchisees. Some business owners may decide that they would rather not disclose information such as prior bankruptcies, the business experience of the principals, or litigation in which the firm is involved. In such cases, franchising may not be the appropriate method to use for growth.

Franchise Rule
A rule that prescribes that the franchisor must disclose certain information to prospective franchisees.

ADDING LONG-TERM VALUE   Can you add value for your franchisees year after year? There are many good and successful business models. Those models may provide the right steps for another entrepreneur to follow in order to avoid trials and errors in the startup process. But does the originating business offer value to prospective franchisees year in and year out? A franchise agreement is in effect for a long time, typically between 10 and 15 years. What benefits will the franchisees derive from the franchisor each year? Will new products or services be introduced?

Will improved marketing strategies be implemented? Will additional, updated training be offered to franchisees and their managers? Why will franchisees want to continue to make royalty payments once they have been up and running and have learned the operating procedures? If the business model does not add value for the franchisees each year, franchising is not the right method for growing your company.

Legal Issues in Franchising

THE FRANCHISE CONTRACT The basic features of the relationship between the franchisor and the franchisee are embodied in the franchise contract. This contract is typically a complex document, running to many pages. Because of its importance as the legal basis for the franchised business, the franchise contract should never be signed by the franchisee without legal counsel. In fact, reputable franchisors insist that the franchisee have legal counsel before signing the agreement. An attorney may anticipate trouble spots and note any objectionable features of the contract.

In addition to consulting an attorney, a prospective franchisee should use as many other sources of help as would be practical. In particular, he or she should discuss the franchise contract with a banker, going over it in as much detail as possible. The prospective franchisee should also obtain the services of a professional accounting firm to examine the franchisor's statements of projected sales, operating expenses, and net income. An accountant can help evaluate the quality of these estimates and identify projections that may be overstated.

One of the most important features of the franchise contract is the provision relating to termination and transfer of the franchise. Some franchisors have been accused of devising agreements that permit arbitrary cancellation of the franchise relationship. Of course, it is reasonable for the franchisor to have legal protection in the event that a franchisee fails to obtain an appropriate level of operation or does not maintain satisfactory quality standards. However, the prospective franchisee should be wary of contract provisions that contain overly strict cancellation policies. Similarly, the rights of the franchisee to sell the business to a third party should be clearly spelled out. A franchisor who can restrict the sale of the business to a third party could potentially take back ownership of the business at an unfair price. The right of a franchisee to renew the contract after the business has been built up to a successful operating level should also be clearly stated in the contract.

FRANCHISE DISCLOSURE REQUIREMENTS The offer and sale of a franchise are regulated by both state and federal laws. At the federal level, the minimum disclosure standards are specified by Rule 436 of the Federal Trade Commission (FTC). The original rule, formally entitled "Disclosure Requirements and Prohibitions Concerning Franchising and Business Opportunity Ventures," went into effect in October of 1979. A guide to the rule can be found on the Federal Trade Commission's website at http://www.ftc.gov/bcp/edu/pubs/business/franchise/bus70.pdf. Addresses of the state offices that enforce franchise disclosure laws can be found at http://www.ftc.gov/bcp/franchise/netdiscl.htm.

Franchise Disclosure Document (FDD)
A document that provides the accepted format for satisfying the franchise disclosure requirements of the FTC.

A document called the *Franchise Disclosure Document (FDD)* provides the accepted format for satisfying the franchise disclosure requirements of the FTC. In May, 2008, the FDD replaced the Uniform Franchise Offering Circular (UFOC) as the legal document satisfying the FTC Franchise Rule. The UFOC had been created by the North American Securities Administrators Association (NASAA) to meet both state and federal government requirements.

The FDD must include information on a variety of items, including investment requirements and conditions that would affect renewal, termination, or sale of the franchise. Most franchise experts recommend that a franchisee's attorney and accountant review the document.

To this point we have been focusing on franchising opportunities. However, another option for making your dream a reality is buying an existing business. You can be just as entrepreneurial buying an existing enterprise as creating one from scratch. You may see an opportunity to turn around a company in trouble. Perhaps you have the skills needed to make a good business excellent. The existing firm may be the platform on which to build your dream. In the next section, we discuss some of the issues facing the individual who chooses this alternative.

Buying an Existing Business

4. List four reasons for buying an existing business and describe the process of evaluating a business.

For would-be entrepreneurs, one alternative to starting from scratch or buying a franchise is to buy an established business. The decision to purchase an existing business should be made only after careful consideration of the advantages and disadvantages of this option.

Reasons for Buying an Existing Business

The reasons for buying an existing business can be condensed into the following four general categories:

1. To reduce some of the uncertainties and unknowns that must be faced in starting a business from the ground up
2. To acquire a business with ongoing operations and established relationships with customers and suppliers
3. To obtain an established business at a price below what it would cost to start a new business or to buy a franchise
4. To begin a business more quickly than by starting from scratch

Let's examine each of these reasons in more detail.

REDUCTION OF UNCERTAINTIES   A successful business has already demonstrated its ability to attract customers, manage costs, and make a profit. Although future operations may be different, the firm's past record shows what it can do under actual market conditions. For example, just the fact that the location must be satisfactory eliminates one major uncertainty. Although traffic counts are useful in assessing the value of a potential location, the acid test comes when a business opens its doors at that location. This test has already been met in the case of an existing firm. The results are available in the form of sales and profit data. Noncompete agreements are needed, however, to discourage the seller from starting a new company that will compete directly with the one he or she is selling.

ACQUISITION OF ONGOING OPERATIONS AND RELATIONSHIPS   The buyer of an existing business typically acquires its personnel, inventories, physical facilities, established banking connections, and ongoing relationships with trade suppliers and customers. Fundamentally, you are acquiring the goodwill that the prior owner created. Extensive time and effort would be required to build these elements from scratch. Of course, the advantage derived from buying an established firm's assets depends on the nature of the assets. For example, a firm's skilled, experienced employees constitute a valuable asset only if they will continue to work for the new owner. The physical facilities must not be obsolete, and the firm's relationships with banks, suppliers, and customers must be healthy. In any case, new agreements will probably have to be negotiated with current vendors and leaseholders.

The late Ken Hendricks, who was CEO of ABC Supply and *Inc. Magazine's* Entrepreneur of the Year for 2006, was said to "buy businesses more often than most people buy toothpaste." He summarized his success in five rules:

1. *Make the call.* You must phone the prospect; don't delegate that to someone else.
2. *Find the why.* What is the *real* reason the current owner wants to sell?
3. *Gather the team.* Put together a solid fact-finding team of individuals who will run the company if their research leads to a buying decision.
4. *Look in back.* Do not just talk to management. Employees will tell you what may be wrong and what can make things better.

5. *Draw the dream.* After you take control of the company, share your vision with all employees; raise their horizons.[14]

A BARGAIN PRICE   If the seller is more eager to sell than the buyer is to buy, an existing business may be available at what seems to be a low price. Whether it is actually a good buy, however, must be determined by the prospective new owner. Several factors could make a "bargain price" anything but a bargain. For example, the business may be losing money, the neighborhood location may be deteriorating, or the seller may intend to open a competing business nearby. On the other hand, if research indicates that the business indeed is a bargain, purchasing it is likely to turn out to be a wise investment.

A QUICK START   Most entrepreneurs are eager to "get going" in their new business and may not be comfortable waiting the months and years sometimes required to launch a business from scratch. Buying an existing business may be an excellent way to begin operations much more quickly.

Finding a Business to Buy

Sometimes, in the course of day-to-day living and working, a would-be buyer comes across an opportunity to buy an existing business. For example, a sales representative for a manufacturer or a wholesaler may be offered an opportunity to buy a customer's retail business. In other cases, the prospective buyer needs to search for a business to buy.

Sources of leads about businesses available for purchase include suppliers, distributors, trade associations, and even bankers. Realtors—particularly those who specialize in the sale of business firms and business properties—can also provide leads. In addition, there are specialized brokers, called *matchmakers,* who handle all the arrangements for closing a buyout. A large number of matchmakers, such as Certified Business Brokers (http://www.certifiedbb.com) in Houston, Texas, deal with mergers and acquisitions of small and mid-sized companies in the United States. Entrepreneurs need to be wary of potential conflicts of interest with matchmakers, however. For example, if matchmakers are paid only if a buy–sell transaction occurs, they may be tempted to do whatever it takes to close the deal, even if doing so is detrimental to the buyer.

matchmakers
Specialized brokers that bring together buyers and sellers of businesses.

Investigating and Evaluating Available Businesses

Regardless of the source of the lead, a business opportunity requires careful evaluation—what some call *due diligence.* As a preliminary step, the buyer needs to acquire background information about the business, some of which can be obtained through personal observation or discussion with the seller. Talking with other informed parties, such as suppliers, bankers, employees, and customers of the business, is also important. The AlwaysOn Network offers a list of 31 items under the heading of due diligence, reproduced in Exhibit 4-9. This list may appear extensive and intimidating, but the purchase of a business is a serious investment and should be investigated thoroughly. If a seller cannot supply the documents on this list, you may want to back away. Some items will not exist, of course, for every business. Not every company finds itself in litigation. Sole proprietorships will not have shareholder statements. Nevertheless, you should be exhaustive in your effort to uncover the relevant information that could influence the selling price or whether even entering into the sale. If not, you may find yourself "on the hook" for unanticipated expenses that show up later.

due diligence
The exercise of reasonable care in the evaluation of a business opportunity.

RELYING ON PROFESSIONALS   Although some aspects of due diligence require personal checking, a buyer can also seek the help of outside experts. The two most valuable sources of outside assistance are accountants and lawyers. It is also wise to seek out others who have acquired a business, in order to learn from their experience. Their perspective will be different from that of a consultant, and it will bring some balance to the counsel received.

The time and money spent on securing professional help in investigating a business can pay big dividends, especially when the buyer is inexperienced. However, the final consequences

EXHIBIT

1. Term Sheets, Corporate Summary Fact Sheet
2. Business Plan
3. Marketing Plan
4. Key Personnel Resumes
5. Financial Planning, Cash Flow Model, Analysis Reports, Glossary
6. Financial Statements
7. Profit and Loss Statements
8. Balance Sheets, Intercompany Transfers
9. Accounts Receivable/Accounts Payable Aging Summaries
10. Tax Returns
11. Asset Ledger
12. Client List and Actual Sales
13. Shareholder Statements
14. Credit and Security Agreements
15. Book of Meeting Minutes
16. Summary of Litigation
17. Non-Competition, Non-Solicitation, or Non-Disclosure Agreements
18. Filings with agencies (U.S. and foreign) having jurisdiction over business operations
19. Customer and Vendor Contracts
20. License or Royalty Agreements
21. Promissory Notes, Bonds or Debentures
22. Options or Rights for Capital Stock or Company Assets
23. Partnership, Joint Venture, Marketing, or Similar Agreements
24. Material Contracts and Agreements
25. Cost-Sharing Agreements, Intercompany Transfers (Company Affiliates)
26. Contracts or Other Documents Affecting the Business Assets
27. Development or Technology Agreements and Documents Relating to Business Assets
28. Corporate Policies (Insurance, Operational, Health, Safety, HR)
29. Summary of Pending or Proposed Assessments or Tax Liens
30. Listing of Sales and Use Tax Returns (All Affected Jurisdictions)
31. Implementation Plan

Source: http://alwayson.goingon.com, accessed on January 24, 2009.

of a business purchase, good and bad, are borne by the buyer, and thus the prospective buyer should never leave the final decision to the experts. For one thing, it is a mistake to assume that professionals' help is either unbiased or infallible, particularly when their fees may be greater if the business is acquired. Prospective buyers should seek advice and counsel, but they must make the final decision themselves, as it is too important to entrust to someone else.

FINDING OUT WHY THE BUSINESS IS FOR SALE   The seller's *real* reasons for selling may or may not be the *stated* ones. When a business is for sale, always question the owner's reasons for selling. There is a real possibility that the firm is not doing well or that underlying problems exist that will affect its future performance. The buyer must be wary, therefore, of taking the seller's explanations at face value. Here are some of the most common reasons that owners offer their businesses for sale:

- Old age or illness
- Desire to relocate to a different part of the country
- Decision to accept a position with another company
- Unprofitability of the business
- Loss of an exclusive sales franchise
- Maturing of the industry and lack of growth potential

LIVING THE DREAM:

entrepreneurial challenges

Do Your Homework

Rick Detkowski was not planning to buy a business when Kim Beattie walked into his office. Through his real estate company, Detkowski owned eight buildings in an industrial park in Clarkston, Michigan, where Beattie's business was located. Beattie wanted to shut down his company, Moon Valley Rustic Furniture, and wanted Detkowski to buy the buildings that housed Moon Valley. On an impulse,

©Moon Valley Rustic Furniture

Detkowski proposed, "Tell you what. If you sell me the company operations, too, then I'll buy the properties."

In retrospect, Detkowski admits, "I might have been a little rash." But Moon Valley had built a solid reputation since its founding in 1928. Moon Valley specialized in cedar furniture designs that fit well with log houses, for which there had been increasing demand in recent years. After talking with dealers, Detkowski saw the potential for an expanded product line and other innovations. To bring operations under control, Detkowski brought in his son, Rick Jr. Rick Jr. had actually worked at Moon Valley before taking jobs managing production and logistics teams at major manufacturing companies. Rick Jr. found many areas in which costs could be reduced.

The Detkowskis arranged for bank loans to finance the purchase then increased both the production and the marketing budgets. One of the new product lines is called The Nicholas Collection and consists of indoor and outdoor children's furniture. Nicholas is the name of Rick Jr.'s son. It looks as though the Detkowskis plan to stay in the furniture business awhile.

Source: Alex Salkever, "The Furniture Company Wanted to Sell Him Its Buildings and Close Down," www.inc.com/magazine, accessed March 5, 2009. http://www.moonvalleyrusticfurniture.com

A prospective buyer cannot be certain that the seller-owner will be honest in presenting all the facts about the business, especially concerning financial matters. Too frequently, sellers have "cooked the books" or taken unreported cash out of the business. The only way for the buyer to avoid an unpleasant surprise later is to do his or her best to determine whether the seller is an ethical person. The following story highlights the importance of investigating the honesty of people selling a business:

> An employee at a private equity firm (a company that buys or invests in other companies) was responsible for expansion into Eastern Europe. He discovered an opportunity to invest in a manufacturing company that had been formerly owned by the government and recently privatized. The chief executive officer of this company was likable and highly competent. However, as the negotiations carried on for months, it was discovered that the CEO had been convicted of embezzling money from his former employer and had ties to organized crime. In light of this discovery, negotiations with the CEO were terminated immediately.[15]

The important lesson in this story is that background checks on key personnel are essential when conducting due diligence.[16]

EXAMINING THE FINANCIAL DATA The first stage in evaluating the financial health of a firm is to review the financial statements and tax returns for the past five years or for as many years as they are available. (*If these statements are not available, think twice before buying the business.*) This first stage helps determine whether the buyer and the seller are in the same ballpark. If so, the parties move on to valuing the firm.

To determine the history of the business and the direction in which it is moving, the buyer must examine financial data pertaining to the company's operation. If financial statements are available for the past five years, the buyer can use these to get some idea of trends for the business. As an ethical matter, the prospective buyer is obligated to show the financial statements to others—such as a potential lender or legal advisor—on a need-to-know basis. To do otherwise is a violation of trust and confidentiality.

The buyer should recognize that financial statements can be misleading and may require normalizing to yield a realistic picture of the business. For example, business owners sometimes understate business income in an effort to minimize their taxes. On the other hand, expenses for such entries as employee training and advertising may be reduced to abnormally low levels in an effort to make the income look good in the hope of selling the business.

Other financial entries that may need adjustment include personal expenses and wage or salary payments. For example, costs related to personal use of business vehicles frequently appear as a business expense, and family members may receive excessive compensation or none at all. All entries must be examined to ensure that they relate to the business and are appropriate.

The buyer should also scrutinize the seller's balance sheet to see whether asset book values are realistic. Property often appreciates in value after it is recorded on the books. In contrast, physical facilities, inventory, and receivables may decline in value, so their actual worth is less than their accounting book value. Although these changes in value are generally not reflected in the accountant's records, they should be considered by the prospective buyer.

Valuing the Business

Once the initial investigation and evaluation have been completed, the buyer must arrive at a fair value for the firm. Valuing a business is not easy or exact, even in the best of circumstances. Despite the fact that buyers prefer audited financial statements, many firms operate without them. In valuing such firms, the buyer will have to rely on federal tax returns and state sales tax statements. It may also be helpful to scrutinize supplier invoices and customer receipts, as well as the company's bank statements.

Although numerous techniques are used for valuing a company, they are typically derivations of three basic approaches: (1) asset-based valuation, (2) market-comparable valuation, and (3) cash flow–based valuation. These techniques are examined in detail in Appendix 4B.

Nonquantitative Factors in Valuing a Business

When applying the quantitative techniques discussed in Appendix B, you should consider a number of factors to evaluate an existing business:

- **Competition.** The prospective buyer should look into the extent, intensity, and location of competing businesses. In particular, the buyer should check to see whether the business in question is gaining or losing in its race with rivals. Additionally, new competitors in the local marketplace (e.g., Walmart) may dramatically change an existing firm's likelihood of success. Past performance is no guarantee of future performance.

- **Market.** The ability of the market to support all competing business units, including the one to be purchased, should be determined. This requires marketing research, study of census data, and personal, on-the-spot observation at each competitor's place of business.

- **Future community development.** Examples of future developments in the community that could have an indirect impact on a business include a change in zoning ordinances already enacted but not yet in effect, a change from a two-way traffic flow to a one-way traffic flow, and the widening of a road or construction of an overpass.

- **Legal commitments.** Legal commitments may include contingent liabilities, unsettled lawsuits, delinquent tax payments, missed payrolls, overdue rent or installment payments, and mortgages of record on any of the real property acquired.
- **Union contracts.** The prospective buyer should determine what type of labor agreement, if any, is in force, as well as the quality of the firm's employee relations. Private conversations with key employees and rank-and-file workers can be helpful in determining their job satisfaction and the company's likelihood of success.
- **Buildings.** The quality of the buildings housing the business should be checked, with particular attention paid to any fire hazards. In addition, the buyer should determine whether there are any restrictions on access to the buildings.
- **Product prices.** The prospective owner should compare the prices of the seller's products with those listed in manufacturers' or wholesalers' catalogs and also with the prices of competing products in the locality. This is necessary to ensure full and fair pricing of goods whose sales are reported on the seller's financial statements.

Negotiating and Closing the Deal

The purchase price of a business is determined by negotiation between buyer and seller. Although the calculated value may not be the price eventually paid for the business, it gives the buyer an estimated value to use when negotiating price. Typically, the buyer tries to purchase the firm for something less than the full estimated value; of course, the seller tries to get more than that value.

In some cases, the buyer may have the option of purchasing the assets only, rather than the business as a whole. When a business is purchased as a total entity, the buyer takes control of the assets but also assumes any outstanding debt, including any hidden or unknown liabilities. Even if the financial records are audited, such debts may not surface. If the buyer instead purchases only the assets, then the seller is responsible for settling any outstanding debts previously incurred. An indemnification clause in the sales contract may serve a similar function, protecting the buyer from liability for unreported debt.

An important part of the negotiation process is the terms of purchase. In many cases, the buyer is unable to pay the full price in cash and must seek extended terms. At this point, a lender may enter the picture and alter the purchase price. If a bank is providing a loan for buying the business, the bank may require assets of the company to serve as collateral for the loan. The bank must perform its own due diligence and estimate a value for the assets, and that value may be at a different level than the buyer and seller have agreed upon. Remember, bankers represent their depositors and cannot just accept a number because the buyer and seller are happy with it.

At the same time, the seller may be concerned about taxes on the profit from the sale. Terms may become more attractive to the buyer and the seller as the amount of the down payment is reduced and/or the length of the repayment period is extended. Like a purchase of real estate, the purchase of a business is closed at a specific time, and a title company or an attorney usually handles the closing. Preferably, the closing will occur under the direction of an independent third party. If the seller's attorney is the closing agent, the buyer should exercise great caution—*a buyer should never go through a closing without the aid of an experienced attorney who represents only the buyer.*

A number of important documents are completed during the closing. These include a bill of sale, certifications as to taxing and other government regulations, and agreements pertaining to future payments and related guarantees to the seller. The buyer should apply for new federal and state tax identification numbers to avoid being held responsible for past obligations associated with the old numbers. If you want a happy ending from the purchase and a clear path to your future, do not take short cuts at this stage. Meeting all legal and regulatory requirements secures your investment and your ability to successfully manage the business.

Starting a business, becoming a franchisee, or buying an existing business are all paths to your entrepreneurial dream. Each takes careful research and planning in its own way. As is so often the case in life, it is then up to you to invest your time, effort, and resources to achieve your goals.

LOOKING BACK

1. Define franchising and identify franchise options.

- Franchising is a method of distributing products or services involving two primary parties, a franchisor and a franchisee.
- The potential value of any franchising arrangement is determined by the rights contained in the franchise contract.
- In product and trade name franchising, the main benefit the franchisee receives is the privilege of using a widely recognized product name.
- In business format franchising, entrepreneurs receive an entire marketing and management system.
- A master licensee is a firm or individual having a continuing contractual relationship with a franchisor to sell its franchises.
- Multiple-unit ownership, in which a single franchisee owns more than one unit of a franchised business, is becoming widely used.
- Some single franchisees are area developers, individuals, or firms that obtain the legal right to open several outlets in a given area.
- Piggyback franchising is the operation of a retail franchise within the physical facilities of a host store. Multi-brand franchising involves operating several franchise organizations within a single corporate structure. Co-branding brings two or more franchise brands together within a single enterprise.
- Franchising has a significant impact on the economies of the United States and other nations, as measured by employment and output.

2. Understand the pros and cons of franchising and the structure of the industry.

- The primary advantage of franchising is its high rate of success.
- Other advantages of franchising include the value of trade names and trademarks, the franchisor's operations manual, and management support.
- Disadvantages of franchising include financial, competitive, and management issues.
- Costs associated with franchises go beyond just fees and royalties.

3. Describe the process for evaluating a franchise opportunity.

- The substantial investment required by most franchisors justifies careful investigation by a potential franchisee.

- Independent third parties such as state and federal government agencies, the International Franchise Association, and business publications can be valuable sources of franchise information.
- The most logical source of the greatest amount of information about a franchise is the franchisor.
- Existing and previous franchisees are also good sources of information for evaluating a franchise.
- Before becoming a franchisor, consider the efficiency of your business model, how you will finance the growth, what expert assistance you will need, what will go into your operations manual, government disclosure requirements, and your ability to add long-term value for franchisees.
- A franchise contract is a complex document and should be evaluated by a franchise attorney.
- An important feature of the franchise contract is the provision relating to termination and transfer of the franchise.
- Franchise disclosure requirements are specified by FTC Rule 436.
- The Franchise Disclosure Document (FDD) provides the accepted format for satisfying the franchise disclosure requirements of the FTC.

4. List four reasons for buying an existing business and describe the process of evaluating a business.

- Buying an existing firm can reduce uncertainties.
- In acquiring an existing firm, the entrepreneur can take advantage of the firm's ongoing operations and established relationships.
- An existing business may be available at a bargain price.
- Another reason for buying an existing business is that an entrepreneur may be in a hurry to start an enterprise.
- Investigating a business requires due diligence.
- A buyer should seek the help of outside experts, the two most valuable sources of outside assistance being accountants and lawyers.
- The buyer needs to investigate why the seller is offering the business for sale.
- The financial data related to the business should always be examined.
- Nonquantitative information about the business for sale should also be used in determining its value.

Key Terms

Discussion Questions

1. What makes franchising different from other forms of business? Be specific.

2. What is the difference between product and trade name franchising and business format franchising? Which one accounts for the majority of franchising activity?

3. Identify and describe the parties in the franchising system.

4. Discuss the advantages and limitations of franchising from the viewpoints of both the potential franchisee and the potential franchisor.

5. Should franchise information provided by a franchisor be discounted? Why or why not?

6. Do you believe that the Franchise Disclosure Document is useful for franchise evaluation? Defend your position.

7. Evaluate loss of control as a disadvantage of franchising from the franchisor's perspective.

8. What are possible reasons for buying an existing company versus starting a new business from scratch?

9. What are some common reasons that owners offer their businesses for sale? Which of these reasons might a buyer consider to be negative?

10. What are some of the nonquantitative factors in valuing a business?

You Make the Call

SITUATION 1

Danny Bone understands due diligence. He spent months investigating franchise options, focusing specifically on Elevation Burger. Elevation Burger uses the slogan "Ingredients Matter," emphasizing its "organically raised, grass-fed, free-range cows and fresh-cut french fries cooked in heart-healthy olive oil." The company had been in business three years when it started franchising in 2008. Danny's brother Dennis brought franchising experience to the company from his days managing their parents Dunkin' Donuts franchise. Danny and Dennis began their franchise agreement with Elevation Burger in the spring of 2008, intending to open their Austin, Texas, location by the end of that year.

What Danny hadn't counted on was the recession. Financing suddenly tightened, and forecasts for restaurant sales were especially negative. Nevertheless, Danny and Dennis remained confident and were convinced that they understood how to run a cost-efficient operation. The brothers were committed to opening three restaurants in the Austin area.

Source: "Optimistic Franchisees Undeterred by Downer Economy," *Franchise Times*, Vol. 15, No. 1 (January, 2009), p. 15; http://elevationburger.com, accessed January 25, 2009; http://www.franchisewire.com, accessed January 25, 2009.

Question 1 Should the Bone brothers have anticipated an economic downturn as part of their due diligence investigation?

Question 2 What steps would you take to attract people to your franchised restaurant when they are trying to save money?

Question 3 What can the Elevation Burger franchisor do to help franchisees during a recession?

SITUATION 2

Heather and Gentry Spell were in business as ticket brokers for 10 years, selling seats at sports and entertainment events in the Sacramento, California, region. One of their customers, Roni Deutch, was a tax attorney. Deutch had decided to build on her successful law practice by franchising tax centers for the preparation of tax returns. Heather, Gentry, and his sister, Lakota Verberne, jumped at the chance to join this new venture.

Heather had no experience with franchising, but knew and respected Deutch. Deutch negotiated an agreement that allowed Heather to continue to run the ticket brokerage out of the tax center. After a year in the business, Heather extended her involvement with the Roni Deutch Tax Center by agreeing to become an area developer. In that role, Heather will not only open an additional office of her own, but she will also be responsible for selling 50 franchise units in the Las Vegas area over the next five years. According to Heather, "The sky's the limit."

Source: Kerry Pipes, "Tickets to Taxes," *Multi-Unit Franchisee*, Issue III (2008), pp. 24–25; http://www.ronideutch.com, accessed January 25, 2009; http://www.rdtcfranchise.com, accessed January 25, 2009.

Question 1 If Heather Spell had come to you for advice when considering franchising with a brand new franchisor, what would you have told her?

Question 2 If you were the franchisor, what would your attitude be about Heather continuing to run her ticket business along with the franchise? Do you think that will be a distraction from time she should be devoting to the tax business?

SITUATION 3

Dave Garrett of Evansville, Indiana, wants to buy a business. He sold his minority interest in the construction company where he worked and left his job. He and a partner are concentrating full time on finding a company to buy. They are targeting manufacturing concerns with sales of $1 million to $8 million, businesses with strong cash flow and with management teams that want to remain with the company. They are working through business brokers and searching online, and they have offered a $10,000 finder's fee to anyone who gives them a lead that results in a purchase. So far, they have bid on two companies, but did not buy either one.

Question 1 Do you think Garrett's experience is normal for someone looking for a business to buy? Can you think of other sources of information about companies that might be for sale that would fit his criteria?

Question 2 For what reasons might someone bid on a business but not be successful in buying it?

Experiential Exercises

1. Interview a local owner-manager of a franchise. What was the process by which the owner obtained the franchise? Would she or he do it all over again?

2. Find an advertisement for the sale of a franchise in a magazine or newspaper. Research the franchise, and report back to the class on how the advertisement describes the franchise.

3. Is there a franchise operating on your campus? Interview the official who is responsible for that contract. Why did the school decide to have the outlet on the campus? Who is the franchisee?

4. Consult the Yellow Pages of your local telephone directory for the name of a business broker. Interview the broker and report to the class on how she or he values businesses.

Small Business & Entrepreneurship Resource Center

The Small Business and Entrepreneurship Resource Center offers complete small business management resources through a comprehensive database that covers all major areas of starting, operating, and maintaining a business from financing, management, marketing, accounting, taxes, and more. Use the access code that came with your new book to access the site and perform the exercises in each chapter.

1. McDonald's is well-known for its hamburgers worldwide, and is a popular choice for potential franchisees that do not want to fail in business. Of course, McDonald's likes reducing its odds of failure, too. The most successful quick-service restaurant chain in the world doesn't let just anybody buy a McDonald's restaurant and open for business. Their secret weapon to success isn't the Big Mac's secret sauce. It lies in the training that the company provides to every single franchise owner. McDonald's is McDonald's because of Hamburger University. Describe how Hamburger University works and why you feel it is such an effective training source.

2. Financing is often a major concern for those wanting to start a business, and with a franchise, there is no exception. The SBA has created the Franchise registry to help potential franchisees gain quick access to financing. Describe how the program works and the potential benefits to potential franchisees.

Sources: Behind the arches: our writer takes a sneak peek into the training grounds of McDonald's franchisees: hamburger university. (HAMBURGER U)(Company Profile). Geoff Williams. *Entrepreneur* 34, 1 (Jan 2006): p. 104.
Behind the arches: our writer takes a sneak peek into the training grounds of McDonald's franchisees: hamburger university. (HAMBURGER U)(Company Profile).

"The Franchise Registry." Small Business Resource Center. Thomson Gale. Thomson Higher Ed., 23 Aug. 2007. The Franchise Registry http://www.franchiseregistry.com

Video Case 4

MO'S CHOWDER (P. 630)

This case describes the experience of one entrepreneur who bought and transformed a simple family-owned diner into a successful, growing culinary destination.

chapter 5

The Family Business

In the SPOTLIGHT
Graeter's Ice Cream
www.graeters.com

For over a century, Graeter's Ice Cream has been the pride of Cincinnati, Ohio. Founded in 1870 by Louis C. Graeter, the company truly took shape under the leadership of his widow, Regina Berger Graeter, according to her great-grandson and Graeter's current CEO, Richard Graeter II. After Louis was killed in a street-car accident in 1917, Regina expanded the business from a single store to shops across Cincinnati and in other Ohio locations by the time of her death in 1955. The business passed to Regina's two sons, Wilmer and Paul, and then to Wilmer's four children: Lou, Dick, Jon, and Kathy. Today, the business is in the hands of Dick's son, Richard, and Lou's sons, Bob and Chip.

Because so few businesses survive to the fourth generation, it may appear that each transition of Graeter's was smooth and well planned. The current owners of Graeter's are open about the fact that their succession to leadership was not so smooth. Debates, disputes, distress, and negotiations characterized the most recent change of management and ownership. Calling on a business psychologist, the cousins worked diligently on communication, organizational structure, and strategic planning. Today, Bob, Chip, and Richard do not just accept each other as partners, but actually have a level of trust and comfort in each other that they might not share if they were not related.

Graeter's is moving forward with product distribution through major retail chains, rather than increasing its own stores. Richard sees the challenge now as avoiding domination by any one distributor. His goal, along with that of his cousins, is to be "the little business that people adore."

Sources: http://www.graeters.com, accessed February 14, 2009; Lisa Biank Fasig, "No Sugarcoating," *Business Courier*, February 6, 2004; and Richard Graeter, personal interview, February 6, 2009.

LOOKING AHEAD

AFTER STUDYING THIS CHAPTER, YOU SHOULD BE ABLE TO . . .

1. Define the terms family and family business.
2. Explain the forces that can keep a family business moving forward.
3. Describe the complex roles and relationships involved in a family business.
4. Identify management practices that enable a family business to function effectively.
5. Describe the process of managerial succession in a family business.

When you are in trouble, whom do you call for help? When you achieve success, whom do you want to tell? For most of us, the answer is family. The car goes into a ditch, and we need dad or mom. If we receive an award at school or work, it is all the more special when our parents or children see it happen. So, when we start our own business, whom do we count on to encourage and support us? Family.

It is well documented that a majority of businesses in most free-market countries fit some definition of family ownership and control. Even when examining large corporations, we find a sizeable percentage to be controlled by a single family. Although the stereotypical entrepreneur may not intentionally start a family enterprise, he or she often relies on family members to obtain the resources necessary for the startup and to pitch in when a problem arises. Family members are often the first people to lend you money or make an investment in your company, or to step in if you get sick or if an essential employee suddenly quits. Many times, it is that family member who knows and accepts your strengths and weaknesses and who is willing to work long hours, often at no pay, who helps to start the new venture.

But family members are not always cordial, cooperative, and compatible. Family members know which buttons to push to make you mad, to make you feel guilty, to embarrass you. Such actions have caused the downfall of many a family enterprise, large and small. In this chapter, we investigate how family and business interact, what makes them strong, and what can destroy them. From extensive research into family firms, we introduce strategies that have helped family businesses succeed.

What Is a Family Business?

1. Define the terms family and family business.

The family firm predates recorded history. Relatives, often in extended family tribal groups, hunted together, farmed together, governed together, and engaged in other similar activities to sustain and improved their lives. As economies developed and formalized, families created enterprises that passed knowledge and skills from one generation to another. Entrepreneurs generated and conserved wealth that led to the establishment of dynasties that survived war and pestilence. There are families in many countries whose enterprises have survived for centuries.

Perhaps the first question to be answered should be, What is a family? Definitions of *family* vary in different parts of the world. They may include the classic "nuclear" family, restricted to parents and children, or an entire community of extended relatives.

In this book, the word *family* refers to a group of people bound by a shared history and a commitment to share a future together, while supporting the development and well-being of individual members.[1] This definition acknowledges that there can be considerable differences in the compositions of families. Among other things, they can vary according to blood relationships, generational representation, and legal status.

Graeter's Ice Cream has what is labeled *cousin consortium* running the company in the fourth generation, but still with some advisory input from the third generation. Rich, Bob, and Chip maintain separate households, of course, but their bonds are strong, with the fifth generation well on its way to learning about family traditions and the family's vision for the future.

family
A group of people bound by a shared history and a commitment to share a future together, while supporting the development and well-being of individual members.

Why Should Anyone Care about Families in Business?

Family-owned and controlled firms are among the world's largest and oldest enterprises. According to *Family Business* magazine, Houshi Onsen, a spa and inn located a few hours from Tokyo that was founded in 718, took the title of oldest family business in 2006. This followed the demise of Osaka temple-builder Kongo Gumi Company, founded in 578, after struggling for more than a decade to deal with overextension and recession in its primary business.[2] For several years, Arkansas-based Walmart Stores, Inc., has been ranked as the world's largest family-owned company.[3]

Within the United States, family businesses are estimated to represent 80 to 90 percent of all enterprises and to account for 60 percent of total employment, 78 percent of all new jobs, and 65 percent of wages paid. Over 30 percent of Standard & Poor's 500 Index firms have been identified as family businesses.[4] This level of family enterprise activity is not unusual in the global economy. In most countries, family firms dominate, often as the largest enterprises within national economies.

Thus, you should care about families in business. If you start your own business, family members are likely to be involved. Perhaps you will join a firm owned by one or more of your relatives. Even if it is not your family's business, you may be employed in a business that is family-owned and controlled.

Family and Business Overlap

Any family business is composed of both a family and a business. Although the family and the business are separate institutions—each with its own members, goals, and values—they overlap in the family firm. For many people, these two overlapping institutions represent the most important areas of their lives.

Families and businesses exist for fundamentally different reasons. The family's primary function is the care and nurturing of family members, while the business is concerned with the production and distribution of goods and/or services. The family's goals include the personal development of each member (sometimes with scant concern for limitations in abilities) and the creation of equal opportunities and rewards for each member; the business's goal is to create value for the customer and wealth for the firm's owners.

Individuals involved, directly or indirectly, in a family business have interests and perspectives that differ according to their particular situations. The model in Exhibit 5-1 shows the ways in which individuals may be involved—as members of the family, employees of the business, individuals with a vested interest in the business, and various combinations of these—and the configuration of roles can affect the way they think about the enterprise. For example, a family member who works in the firm but has no personal or ownership interest (segment a) might favor more generous employment and advancement opportunities for family members than, say, a family member who owns part of the business but works elsewhere (segment b) or an employee with neither family nor ownership interest (segment c).

family business
An organization in which *either* the individuals who established or acquired the firm, *or* their descendants, significantly influence the strategic decisions and life course of the firm.

With Exhibit 5-1 in mind, we can define a *family business* as an organization in which *either* the individuals who established or acquired the firm, *or* their descendants, significantly influence the strategic decisions and life course of the firm.[5] The family influence might be exerted through management and/or ownership of the firm.[6]

Competing interests can complicate the management process, creating tension and sometimes leading to conflict. Relationships among family members in a business are more sensitive than relationships among unrelated employees. For example, disciplining an employee who consistently arrives late is much more problematic if he or she is also a family member. Or, consider a performance review session between a parent-boss and a child-subordinate. Even with nonfamily employees, performance reviews are potential minefields. The existence of a family relationship adds emotional overtones that vastly complicate the review process. As successful entrepreneur and author Lowell J. Spirer observes, no one wants his or her tombstone to read "Here lies a parent or spouse who fired his own flesh and blood without just cause."[7]

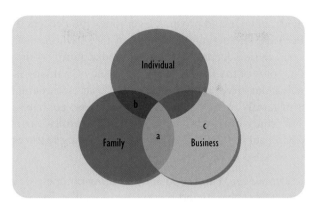

Source: Adapted from Tim Barnett and Franz W. Kellermanns, "Are We Family and Are We Treated as Family? Nonfamily Employees' Perceptions of Justice in the Family Firm," *Entrepreneurship Theory and Practice*, Vol. 30, No. 6 (November 2006), pp. 837–854.

Advantages of a Family Business

Problems with family firms can easily blind people to the unique advantages that come with participating in a family business. The benefits associated with family involvement should be recognized and discussed when recruiting both relatives and nonfamily members to work in the family firm.

One primary benefit derives from the strength of family relationships. Family members have a unique motivation because the firm is a family firm. Business success is also family success. Studies have shown that family CEOs possess greater internal motivation than do nonfamily CEOs and have less need to receive additional incentives through compensation.[8] Also, other family members are drawn to the business because of family ties, and they tend to stick with the business through thick and thin. A downturn in business fortunes might cause nonfamily employees to seek greener employment pastures elsewhere, but a son or daughter may be reluctant to leave. The family name, its welfare, and possibly its fortune are at stake. In addition, a person's reputation in the family and in the business community may hinge on whether she or he can continue the business that Mom or Grandfather built.

Family members may also sacrifice income to keep a business going. Rather than draw large salaries or high dividends, they are likely to permit resources to remain in the business in order to meet current needs. Many families have postponed the purchase of a new car or new furniture long enough to let a business get started or to get through a period of financial stress, thereby greatly increasing the company's chances of survival.

Businesses that are family owned often highlight this feature in their promotional materials to set themselves apart from competitors. On the SC Johnson Company website, for example, you will find the firm name consistently represented as "SC Johnson: A Family Company."[9] This is a "high-touch" message, one that resonates with customers who don't want to be treated as "just another number"; as a result, the theme is especially effective for companies that offer highly customized products or very personal services, such as investment planning, chiropractic care, funeral services, and fine dining. Such promotional efforts attempt to convey the fact that family-owned firms have a strong commitment to the business, high ethical standards, and a personal commitment to serving their customers and the local community.

And such messages are not only for customers. Family businesses can convey a sense of tradition and achievement to relatives considering joining the firm and to nonfamily employees who have become part of an epic saga. After all, any company that has achieved generational succession has undoubtedly overcome countless challenges and threats. True heroism emerges as firms are launched, survive, and prosper. Everyone who accepts a position with the business should learn the heritage and accomplishments of those who created and grew the company. They should be proud to be accepted into the extended family—or, proud to become, as Rich Graeter expresses it, "part of the tribe." The Walt Disney Company is especially astute in keeping the story of its founder alive, even more than 40 years following his death.

Other features of family involvement in a firm can also contribute to superior business performance. From their study of resource management in family businesses, business professors David Sirmon and Michael Hitt have identified the following features of these firms as offering unique advantages (see also Exhibit 5-2):[10]

1. *Firm-specific knowledge.* Family businesses often compete using firm-specific knowledge that is best shared and further developed by individuals who care deeply about the business and who trust one another. These companies are in a unique position to pass this knowledge along from generation to generation, sharpening the edge of that advantage over time.

2. *Shared social networks.* Family members bring valuable social capital to the business when they share their networks with younger members of the family and thus help to ensure the firm's future performance.

3. *A focus on the long run.* Most family managers tend to take a long-range perspective of the business, in part because they view it as an asset that must be maintained for the sake of future generations.

4. *Preservation of the firm's reputation.* Because they have a stake in preserving the family's reputation, members of the family are likely to maintain high standards when it comes to honesty in business dealings, such as offering quality and value to the consumer.

5. *Reduced cost of control.* Because key employees in a family business are related and trust one another, the firm can spend less on systems designed to reduce theft and to monitor employees' work habits.

EXHIBIT

5-2 **Advantages of a Family Business**

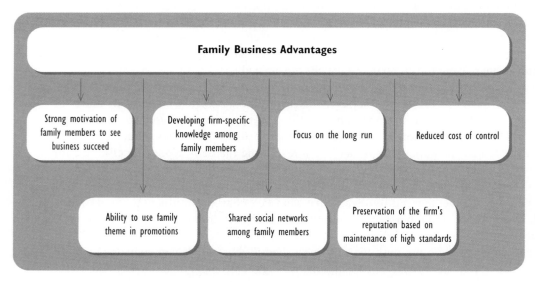

Disadvantages of a Family Business

Even before a venture is created, conflict may arise between family members. Often the spouse, parents, in-laws, or others will accuse a budding entrepreneur of putting the family at risk in launching the business. When this happens between married couples, the eventual result is often the failure of either the business or the marriage. From the perspective of the opposing family members, their position may appear quite reasonable. The entrepreneur may be gambling with retirement savings, the children's college funds, or the home mortgage. Consequences can be severe.

As the business grows, inherent differences in family and business values and commitments emerge:

- A family is a unit that balances relationships; a business must deal with differences in competence and merit.
- The family seeks to perpetuate traditions, while the business must innovate to prosper.
- A family is characterized by unity and cooperation, but a business grows through diversity and competition.
- Families tend to be stable, while businesses, especially those competing in the global economy, often face instability.
- For families, loyalty usually trumps opportunity, but businesses are regularly challenged by opportunities that arise for both the company and its employees.

Many publicly traded companies have policies against nepotism, the hiring of family members. The assumption is that employees and executives may show favoritism toward their relatives, regardless of competence or performance. Nepotism is a characteristic of the family firm. Unfortunately, many such businesses do, in fact, provide employment to relatives regardless of their qualifications and may keep them on the payroll even after their poor performance has become obvious to everyone. Not only is the effectiveness of the company diminished, but these practices also demoralize competent employees.

The fact that so many family firms are able to survive generational transitions demonstrates that the disadvantages can be overcome. Later in this chapter, we will introduce some of the strategies families have used to help their businesses succeed.

Family Business Momentum

2. Explain the forces that can keep a family business moving forward

organizational culture
Patterns of behaviors and beliefs that characterize a particular firm.

Like other organizations, family businesses develop particular ways of doing things and certain priorities that are unique to each firm. These special patterns of behaviors and beliefs comprise the firm's *organizational culture.* As new employees and family members enter the business, they pick up these unique viewpoints and ways of operating, which create staying power for the company.

The culture of the family firm deserves special attention because it can serve as either an advantage or a disadvantage. Organizational culture can be a strategic resource that promotes learning, risk taking, and innovation. In fact, family business expert John L. Ward has conducted research that suggests family businesses have an advantage precisely because of their cultures, which tend to emphasize important values like mutual respect, integrity, the wise use of resources, personal responsibility, and "fun" (enthusiasm, adventure, celebration, etc.) in the family business experience.[11]

Family Tree

Cloid H. Smith
Founder

Howard C. Smith

Chesley C. Smith

Carlton P. Smith

Wrede H. Smith

Garrett K. Smith

Photo courtesy of JOLLY TIME Pop Corn

The Founder's Imprint on the Family Business Culture

Research indicates that founders leave a deep impression on the family businesses they launch.[12] And the distinctive values that motivate and guide an entrepreneur in the founding of a company may help to create a competitive advantage for the new business. Business founders are often innovators who may cater to customer needs in a special way and emphasize customer service as a guiding principle for the company. The new firm may go far beyond normal industry practices in making sure customers are satisfied, even if it means working overtime or making deliveries on a weekend or at odd hours. Those who work in such an enterprise quickly learn that customers must always be handled with special care.

In a family business, the founder's core values may become part of both the business culture and the family code—that is, "the things we believe as a family." Garry Smith is president of American Pop Corn Company, makers of Jolly Time Pop Corn, in Sioux City, Iowa. He joined this now fourth-generation company at the age of 17, sweeping out corn cribs; he became a full-time employee at age 31. Smith reports learning two things from his father: "By example, I learned the importance of hard work and the value of treating employees with respect. It wasn't any one thing he said; I observed him managing people for 25 years." And from his mother, he learned "kindness. That's a 50-year observation."[13]

Of course, there is always a darker possibility—that of a founder's *negative* imprint on the organizational culture. Successful business founders may develop an unhealthy narcissism, or exaggerated sense of self-importance. Such individuals occasionally develop a craving for attention, a fixation with success and public recognition, and a lack of empathy for others. Unfortunately, these attitudes can harm the business by creating a general feeling of superiority and a sense of complacency. While contributions of founders deserve proper acknowledgment, any negative legacy must be avoided.

The Commitment of Family Members

The culture of a particular firm includes numerous distinctive beliefs and behaviors, which help to keep the business moving forward according to the vision of the founder. But sooner or later, the reins of leadership will have to be turned over to a new generation. The continuity of the business will depend, in large part, on next-generation family members and their level of commitment to the business. Recent research suggests that family members coming into a business do so for a variety of reasons, and these reasons shape the strength and nature of their commitment to the company.

The competing interests model pictured earlier in Exhibit 5-1 on page 123 is often used to summarize the complexities of dealing with the family firm's interactive components: the business, the family, and the individual. The model is usually applied to founders, who often have to balance their obvious interest in the business, their personal aspirations, and the needs of the family. However, next-generation family members who choose to pursue a career in the business must deal with some of these same challenges, and their commitment to the company will likely determine the value of their contribution to the business, the financial benefits they bring to the family, and their personal satisfaction with work-related roles.

To explore the connection between commitment and family business involvement, two family business experts from Canada studied the research on family enterprises. They found the following four bases of commitment among successors in family businesses: emotional attachment, a sense of obligation, cost considerations, and personal need.[14] In all cases, the outcome was the same—members of the family were persuaded to join the business—but the reasons for joining were very different.

EMOTIONAL ATTACHMENT (DESIRE-BASED COMMITMENT) When family members join a firm based on a deep-seated, gut-level attraction to the business, it is usually because they believe in and accept the purpose of the enterprise. Typically, their personal identity is closely tied to the business, and they believe they have the ability to contribute something to it. In short, these individuals join the company because they genuinely *want to*. This was clearly the situation for Tim, a young next-generation family member:

> We have an item that we manufacture from scratch, we warehouse it, we wholesale it, and we retail it. I see the business from every angle and I'm involved in it from every angle. It's kind of neat to be able to do that. . . . I love being a part of the family business.

OBLIGATION-BASED COMMITMENT *Obligation-based commitment* is what drives individuals who feel that they really *ought to* pursue a career in the family business. Often, the goal is to do what the parent-founder wants, even if that career path is not what the family member had in mind. In many cases, guilt is the primary motivator, as was the case with Polly, who "answered the call" to join the family business:

> [My father] said that the most important thing right now for you as a Stillman is to be visible here because your sister is out. . . . We need another family member here. And so with that kind of plea I had no choice in my mind. I couldn't let the family down. So I dropped everything I was doing and . . . went the next day and started working.

obligation-based commitment
Commitment that results from a sense of duty or expectation.

COST-BASED COMMITMENT If a family member concludes that there is too much to lose by turning away from a career opportunity within the family business, then his or her decision to join is based on a calculation, not a sense of obligation or emotional identification. Often, this *have to* response is motivated by the perception that the opportunity for gain is too great to pass up or that the value of the business will fall if somebody doesn't step in to take care of it. In other words, joining the business may be the best way to benefit from what the family firm has to offer or to protect the investment value of what is likely to be inherited in the future. Rob recognized this when he looked more closely at a business that his wife's family owned:

> At that point we really didn't know what [my wife's] involvement was from a shareholder's standpoint. And what we found out was she was heavily involved to the point where it dwarfed what we were doing personally and all of a sudden it did change our perspective. . . . It sort of changed our outlook on [the business] . . . and that is when we decided we cannot pass this up.

NEED-BASED COMMITMENT When family members join the business because of self-doubt or a concern that they might not be able to reach significant career success on their own, their commitment to the family enterprise is based on perceived necessity. That is, they *need to* join the business because they lack options for career success outside of it. This reasoning is common among young heirs who leapfrog over nonfamily employees into coveted positions, the demands of which exceed their knowledge and experience. They often feel guilty for their privileged status and are left to wonder if they have what it takes to succeed on their own. Ted

need-based commitment
Commitment based on an individual's self-doubt and belief that he or she lacks career options outside the current business.

was 33 years old when he was tapped to run his family's 900-employee business. His self-doubt rings loudly in his reflections:

> I always am a little bit concerned about whether I would have been able to have succeeded and achieved outside of the family's environment. . . . That's always something that I think most people in family businesses think about. Whether they believe they would have been as successful outside.

Why Should Anyone Care about Commitment?

desire-based commitment Commitment based on a belief in the purpose of a business and a desire to contribute to it.

unity Oneness of mind, feeling, and action, as among a number of persons.

cost-based commitment Commitment based on the belief that the opportunity for gain from joining a business is too great to pass up.

Research shows that any form of commitment is better than no commitment at all; however, next-generation family members motivated by *desire-based commitment* are most likely to pursue long-term careers with the family business. Their deep-seated connection with the enterprise and its alignment with their career interests make for a successful match. And since knowledge and insight passed down from one generation to the next is an advantage that is unique to family businesses, keeping family members in the enterprise can pay off in many ways.[15]

However, commitment is about more than just staying with the company—it also affects what a person does while he or she is on the job. Exhibit 5-3 illustrates the forms of commitment and their implications for family businesses. These various pressures for commitment should be reflected in a sense of *unity* among family members. For instance, family members with higher levels of desire- and obligation-based commitments to the business are more likely to support efforts to promote change, which are common in small businesses and very important to their performance and survival. *Cost-based commitment* may motivate a person to go "beyond the call of duty" to protect or extend his or her financial interests in the company. Obligation-based commitment, however, provides no such motivation, as family members may see their participation in the company as a requirement. Those with a deep-seated sense of identity with the enterprise (desire-based commitment) are the most likely to work hard, because of their passion for the business. Family members who are committed to the business

5-3 Commitment to the Family Business

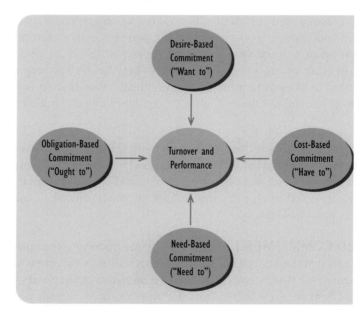

Source: Based on Pramodita Sharma and P. Gregory Irving, "Four Bases of Family Business Successor Commitment: Antecedents and Consequences," *Entrepreneurship Theory and Practice*, Vol. 29, No. 1 (January 2005), pp. 13–33.

mostly out of personal need, however, are often in a perpetual state of self-doubt and lack the confidence to excel; this problem is compounded if they are promoted only because of their last name and honestly lack the capabilities to do the job.

MassMutual Financial Group, in conjunction with Kennesaw State University and the Family Firm Institute, conducts periodic surveys of family business owners. The 2007 survey summarized responses related to family unity as follows:[16]

1. Family unity and cohesion were found to be critical to family business success, especially when family members identified unity as an important goal. In particular, 87 percent of respondents said family members share the same values. Agreement on values, attitudes, and beliefs indicates family unity and cohesion.

2. Considering business matters such as strategy, ownership, and management, 82.9 percent of the owners said that they were completely or very unified as an ownership group.

3. Unity of the ownership group is significantly associated with family commitment to the business in each generation, predictions of sales growth, and demonstrations of past growth. It is important to note that the greater the family unity, the more the firms had grown in the previous three years and the more they expected to grow in the future.

4. Family unity affects other stakeholders as well. Unified families reported they were more likely to share their values with customers and employees, with 85 percent sharing to a large extent with both groups.

In summary, the researchers concluded that the overlap between individual and organizational values may result in increased levels of employee loyalty, commitment, and organizational citizenship behavior.

Family Roles and Relationships

The overlapping of two institutions—a family and a business—adds complexity to management. "Family business," says the wife of one family business owner, "is an oxymoron. The hope of building something for your kids and passing on traditions is usually thwarted by dynamics within the family."[17] This dim view of the family enterprise is not shared by everyone; however, significant conflicts can result when family roles and business interests collide. Anticipating these challenges and planning for them can really pay off. This section examines a few of the many possible family roles and relationships that contribute to this managerial complexity.

3. Describe the complex roles and relationships involved in a family business.

Mom or Dad, the Founder

A common figure in family businesses is the founding entrepreneur who plans to pass it on to a son or a daughter. The business and the family have typically both grown since the company was organized. Entrepreneurs who have children typically think in terms of passing the business on to the next generation. Parental concerns associated with this process include the following:

- Does my child possess the temperament and ability necessary for business leadership?
- How can I, the founder, motivate my child to take an interest in the business?
- What type of education and experience will be most helpful in preparing my child for leadership?

- What timetable should I follow in employing and promoting my child?
- How can I avoid favoritism in managing and developing my child for a leadership role?
- Is sibling rivalry likely to be a problem, and can it be avoided?
- How can I prevent the business relationship from damaging or destroying the parent–child relationship?

Of all the relationships in a family business, the parent–child relationship has been recognized for generations as the most troublesome. In recent years, the problems inherent in this relationship have been addressed by counselors, seminars, and books too numerous to count. In spite of all this attention, however, the parent–child relationship continues to perplex many families involved in family businesses.

Co-Preneurs

Some family businesses are owned and managed by husband–wife teams. Such couples are popularly known as *co-preneurs*. Their roles vary depending on their backgrounds and expertise. In some cases, the husband serves as general manager and the wife runs the office. In others, the wife functions as operations manager and the husband keeps the books. Whatever the arrangement, both individuals are integral parts of the business.

One potential advantage of the husband–wife team is the opportunity to work with someone you really trust and to share more of your lives together. For some couples, however, the benefits can be overshadowed by problems related to the business. Differences of opinion about business matters can carry over into family life. And the energy of both parties may be so spent by working long hours in a struggling company that little zest remains for a strong family life. There is a recent trend of couples starting web-based businesses, often from home. In some of these cases, the co-preneurs have found there can be too much togetherness, in which case they establish rules for time apart.[18]

Many couples have had to set boundaries and develop routines to cope with the demands of everyday life (like raising children) and still have sufficient time for the business. For example, the objective of former pro football player Nate Wayne and his wife, Tamiko, was to open a business that would be both lucrative and family friendly so that their three children, ages 4, 8, and 13, would enjoy spending time with mom and dad at work. Tamiko convinced Nate that they should invest in a Cold Stone Creamery ice cream franchise. The Waynes set rules from the beginning, separating their business and personal accounts. To stay on track, they meet regularly with a business attorney, certified public accountant, and financial advisor. The Waynes are careful to give both their children and their marriage attention. Tamiko goes into Cold Stone early, while Nate sends their children off to school, after which he manages a trucking business they launched. They reserve weekends and most evenings for family time.[19]

Sons and Daughters

Should sons and daughters be groomed for the family business, or should they pursue careers of their own choosing? In the entrepreneurial family, the natural tendency is to think in terms of a family business career and to push a child, either openly or subtly, in that direction. Little thought may be given to the underlying issues, including the child's talent, aptitude, and temperament. The child may be "a chip off the old block" in many ways but may also be an individual with unique abilities and aspirations. He or she may prefer music or medicine to the world of business and may fit the business mold very poorly. It is also possible that the abilities of the son or daughter may simply be insufficient for a leadership role. Or, a child's talents may be underestimated by parents merely because there has been little opportunity for the child to develop or demonstrate those talents.

Another issue is personal freedom. Today's society values the right of the individual to choose his or her own career and way of life. If this value is embraced by a son or daughter, that child must be granted the freedom to select a career of his or her own choosing. Still, a strong argument can be made for an early introduction to the family firm, perhaps an entry-level part-time or summer job that exposes a teenaged child to what the parents face every day. Owners must remember, however, that their children are still children and may not have the maturity to cope with the responsibilities of employment. And nonfamily managers in the company should not be placed in the awkward position of reprimanding the boss's daughter or son, who refuses to follow procedures.[20]

Sue Birley, professor of entrepreneurship and director of the Entrepreneurship Centre at Imperial College in London, surveyed 412 children of business owner-managers to see if they planned to enter the family business in the future. Eighty percent of those who were not already working in the business did not intend to join it. And of those who intended to enter the business at some point, 70 percent planned to work somewhere else first.[21]

A son or daughter may feel a need to go outside the family business, for a time at least, to prove that he or she can make it without help from the family. To build self-esteem, he or she may wish to operate independently of the family. Entering the family business immediately after graduation from high school or college may seem stifling, as the child continues to "feel like a little kid with Dad telling me what to do."

In other cases, it is the parents who lay down the rules. Dan and Bubba Cathy established a policy that members of the third generation would be required to gain at least two years of experience outside of Chick-fil-A before they could apply for employment in the family firm. Most consultants to family businesses agree with this practice. Obtaining external work experience has two key benefits. First, it builds confidence for the family member that he or she can succeed without the family safety net. Second, nonfamily employees of the company will have more respect for a junior family member who has proven herself or himself in another setting.

Sibling Cooperation, Sibling Rivalry

In families with a number of children, two or more may become involved in the family business. This depends, of course, on the interests of the individual children. In some cases, parents feel fortunate if even one child elects to stay with the family firm. Nevertheless, it is not unusual for siblings to take positions within the company. Even those who do not work in the business may be more than casual observers on the sidelines because of their stake as heirs or partial owners.

At best, siblings work as a smoothly functioning team, each contributing services according to his or her respective abilities. Just as families can experience excellent cooperation and unity in their relationships with one another, some family businesses benefit from effective collaboration among brothers and sisters.

However, just as there are sometimes squabbles within a family, there can also be sibling rivalry within a family business. Business issues tend to generate competition, and this affects family, as well as nonfamily, members. Siblings, for example, may disagree about business policy or about their respective roles in the business. And, in some cases, the conflicts can spiral seriously out of control.[22]

Family Business publishes a column entitled "Ask the Experts." In the magazine's Autumn 2007 issue, a fourth-generation business owner wrote in with the following request:

> Since our father's death, my brother's ego has gone through the roof. He also has a problem keeping employees. I am treated as his employee, and he demands an explanation from me for every move I make, even though I am the president of the holding company. . . . Can you give me some advice?[23]

The advice of the experts included using a facilitator or a board of directors, improving the strategy and structure of the firm, and increasing communication. Imagine how much better this situation might have been if the writer's father had had the foresight to engage in these activities before his death.

family and community values

Developing Ventures and Contributing to Communities

According to its website,

Wente Vineyards is California's oldest family owned and continuously operated winery. Founded in 1883 by C. H. Wente, the winery is now managed by the fourth and fifth generations of the Wente family. The winery farms nearly 3,000 acres of estate vineyards in the Livermore Valley, San Francisco Bay, and Arroyo Seco, Monterey appellations, two premier Central Coast winegrowing regions.

This business did not survive over a century by standing still. Management by each generation of owners has been characterized by innovation—new product development and introductions, cutting-edge technology, advanced concerns for soil care, and expansion into related business ventures. And each generation has had to contend with changing social, cultural, and legal environments. Prohibition was an early test. At one time,

a change in state tax codes almost taxed them out of business, leading the family to consider relocating. Actions by competitors made Napa Valley and Sonoma Valley tourist destinations, bypassing Livermore Valley, the home base of Wente Vineyards. Through all this, the family and the business have not just survived, but prospered.

Critical to the success of this business has been the cultivation of family members, preparing those who enter the business through education and experience. Wente family members intentionally do things together. The different generations were not pressured to join the company, but from childhood they were expected to help out with farm work and entertaining customers. They were taught that the family as a whole depended on each member. And the attitude of caring was expected to be extended to the larger community.

The Wente family recognized that their survival was dependent on the economic health of Livermore Valley. While they were in the process of creating internal ventures such as a golf course, a restaurant, and an events management business, all to attract tourists, they also supported the startup of other wineries in the region. Today, visitors find dozens of tasting rooms along country roads in the Livermore Valley. Observers credit the Wente family's dedication to agriculture and wine to be a causal factor in the region's economic health.

Sources: Deanne Stone, "Social Entrepreneurship," *Family Business*, Vol. 19, No. 2 (Spring 2008), pp. 54–57; http://www.wentevineyards.com/winery/ourwinery.asp, accessed September 20, 2008; http://eastbay.bizjournals.com/eastbay/stories/2008/09/01/story1.html?b=1220241600%5E1692538, accessed September 28, 2008.

© iStockphoto.com/Ralph Oechsle

Another sibling dilemma has been labeled the predator/parasite conflict. Family members working in the firm are sometimes seen by their relatives as predators—extracting money from the business that the outsiders believe is rightfully theirs. From the inside, the family members external to the firm are, in turn, parasites. They have ownership rights, receive dividends, or make other claims on the business without contributing to its success. Many enterprises have formalized structures such as family business councils (described later in the chapter) to overcome these perceptions.

In-Laws In and Out of the Business

Marriage can bring significant actors into the family business drama. Some in-laws become directly involved by accepting positions in the family firm. Rivalry and conflict may develop, however, if family members disagree about how rewards for performance should compare for an in-law and a son or daughter.

For a time, effective collaboration may be achieved by assigning family members to different branches or roles within the company. But competition for leadership positions eventually will force decisions that distinguish among children and in-laws employed in the business. Being fair and maintaining family loyalty become more difficult as the number of family employees increases.

In-laws who are on the sidelines are also participants with an important stake in the business, and their influence on the business and the family can be considerable. They are keenly interested in family business issues that impact their spouses, but, unfortunately, their perspective is typically distorted because they often hear only half of the story when it comes to work-related situations. One highly regarded family business consultant put it this way:

> How many times do brothers and sisters in business together go rushing home or make a phone call home and say, "Dear, I just wanted to let you know that we are so lucky to be in partnership with my brother." Or, "We wouldn't be anywhere near as successful as we are without my sister's leadership skills." I don't think that conversation happens very often.[24]

When family frustrations come up at work, spouses tend to hear all about it at home, often just before the couple goes to bed. The family member vents, then feels better, and goes to sleep. The spouse, on the other hand, is just hearing about the situation and spends the rest of the night worried, angry, or both. Then, when the two siblings sort everything out at the office the next morning and get back to the challenging, satisfying work at hand, neither even thinks about phoning the spouse to let him or her know that the problem was just a silly little matter and that everything is fine. Spouses tend to hear only one side of the story—the bad side—and it shades their view of the business. So, the criticism they receive for having a bad attitude about the family and its enterprise is often undeserved.[25]

When in-laws are employed in the family business, a different set of dynamics can emerge. In some cases, the relationships can get very complicated. In 2000, Michael Kalinsky cofounded Empyrean Management Group, a recruiting and staffing company. His father-in-law, Bruce Kenworthy, offered to bankroll the startup with $100,000 of his own money... but only if his son, David, could be vice president and a minority shareholder. Kalinsky agreed to the terms, accepted the money, and launched the company. A few years later, however, he discovered that David was neglecting a critical client and had openly criticized Kalinsky and his leadership in front of employees. After thinking about the potential for family fallout, he decided to fire David, which led to a whole new set of problems. After a difficult legal battle, Kalinsky was forced to buy out Bruce's and David's shares of ownership in the company and to pay back the $100,000 he owed Bruce. Empyrean continues to operate, but Kalinsky and David have not spoken since the settlement. David has since opened his own business and wooed away Empyrean's biggest (by far) client. Bruce Kenworthy has concluded that Kalinsky and David will never speak to each other again. "[That] is sad for me," he laments. "It would have been nice if the family and the business had been able to stay together."[26]

The Entrepreneur's Spouse

One of the most critical roles in the family business is that of the entrepreneur's spouse. Traditionally, this role has been fulfilled by the male entrepreneur's wife and the mother of his children. However, many husbands have now assumed the role of entrepreneur's spouse.

In order for the spouse to play a supporting role in the entrepreneur's career, there must be effective communication between the spouse and the entrepreneur. The spouse needs to hear what's going on in the business; otherwise, she or he may begin to feel detached and respond by competing with the business for attention. The spouse can offer understanding and act as a sounding board for the entrepreneur only if the couple communicates on matters of obvious importance to them, both as individuals and as a family.

As a parent, the spouse helps prepare the children for possible careers in the family business. Researchers have found that one of the most frequent and stressful roles performed by the spouse is to serve as a mediator in business relationships between the entrepreneur and the children. One wife's comments to her husband, John, and son Terry illustrate the nature of this function:

- "John, don't you think that Terry may have worked long enough as a stockperson in the warehouse?"
- "Terry, your father is going to be very disappointed if you don't come back to the business after your graduation."
- "John, do you really think it is fair to move Stanley into that new office? After all, Terry is older and has been working a year longer."
- "Terry, what did you say to your father today that upset him?"

Ideally, the entrepreneur and his or her spouse form a team committed to the success of both the family and the family business. Such teamwork does not occur automatically—it requires a collaborative effort by both parties to the marriage.

The Need for Good Management in the Family Firm

"It used to be that there were professional businesses and there were family businesses," according to John L. Ward, but this is certainly less true today.[27] Facing global competition and rapidly changing markets, family businesses have to look carefully at family members who want a leadership position in the enterprise and determine whether they are up to the task. The complex relationships in family firms require the oversight of competent and professional management, whether from inside or outside the family. Significant deviations, for family reasons, from what would be considered good management practices only serve to weaken the firm. Compromising in this way runs counter to the interests of both the firm and the family.

4. Identify management practices that enable a family business to function effectively.

Family business experts and practitioners have proposed a number of "best practices" for family enterprises. Each family and each family business is different, so what is actually "best" will depend on the individual situation. Nonetheless, these best practices have helped many family businesses design effective management systems:

- Promote learning to stimulate new thinking and fresh strategic insights.
- Solicit ample input from outsiders to keep things in perspective.
- Establish channels for constructive communication and use them often.
- Build a culture that accepts continuous change.
- Promote family members only according to their skill levels.
- Attract and retain excellent nonfamily managers.
- Ensure fair compensation for all employees, including those outside the family.
- Establish a solid leadership succession plan.
- Exploit the unique advantages of family ownership.

The family firm is a business—a competitive business. Observing these and other practices of good management will help the business thrive and permit the family to function as a family. Disregarding them will pose a threat to the business and strain family relationships.

Nonfamily Employees in a Family Firm

Those employees who are not family members are still affected by family considerations. In some cases, their opportunities for promotion are lessened by the presence of family members who may have the inside track. Few parents will promote an outsider over a competent daughter or son who is being groomed for future leadership, and this is understandable. But this limits the potential for advancement of nonfamily employees, which may lead them to become frustrated, to feel cheated, or to leave the firm.

Consider the case of a young business executive who worked for a family business that operated a chain of restaurants. When hired, he had negotiated a contract that gave him a specified percentage of the business based on performance. Under this arrangement, he was doing extremely well financially—until the owner called on him to say "I am here to buy you out." When the young man asked why, the owner replied, "You are doing too well, and your last name is not the same as mine!"

Those outside the family may also be caught in the crossfire between family members who are competing with each other. It is difficult for outsiders to maintain strict neutrality in family feuds. If a nonfamily executive is perceived as siding with one of those involved in the feud, he or she may lose the support of other family members. Hardworking employees often feel that they deserve hazard pay for working in a firm plagued by family conflict.

The extent of limitations on nonfamily employees depends on the number of family members active in the business and the number of managerial or professional positions in the business to which nonfamily employees might aspire. It also depends on the extent to which the owner demands competence in management and maintains an atmosphere of fairness in supervision. To avoid future problems, the owner should make clear, when hiring nonfamily employees, the extent of opportunities available to them and identify the positions, if any, that are reserved for family members.

Reasons why the leader of a family-owned enterprise might decide to bring in a nonfamily member as an executive with the firm include the following:

- To bridge the gap between generations
- To set new directions for the firm
- To deal with change
- To provide new skills and expertise

In such cases, the owner should look for certain traits, including maturity, facilitation skills, mentoring skills, emotional sensitivity, trustworthiness, and the ability to understand and share the values of the family.

Family business owners need to plan carefully when bringing in an executive from outside. They should ensure that the position's responsibilities are commensurate with the nonfamily member's experience and have mechanisms for open communication. The nonfamily executive must also be involved in strategic planning and decision making.[28]

Family Retreats

Although consultants to family businesses recommend establishing mechanisms and protocols early in the life of a company to address the relationship between the family and the firm, such actions usually take place after the business matures and has created wealth. One of the first steps in formalizing processes for building a healthy family-to-business relationship is to hold a retreat. A *family retreat* is a meeting of family members (often including in-laws), usually held away from company premises, to discuss family business matters. In most cases, the atmosphere is informal to encourage family members to communicate freely and discuss their concerns about the business in an environment that does not feel adversarial. The retreat is not so much an *event* as it is the *beginning of a process* of connecting family members. It presents

family retreat
A gathering of family members, usually at a remote location, to discuss family business matters.

an opportunity to celebrate the founders and their sacrifices, as well as highlight the legacy they wanted to pass down to future generations of the family.

The prospect of sitting down together to discuss family business matters may seem threatening to some family members. As a result, some families avoid extensive communication, fearing it will stir up trouble. They assume that making decisions quietly or secretly will preserve harmony. Unfortunately, this approach often glosses over serious differences that become increasingly troublesome. Family retreats are designed to open lines of communication and to bring about understanding and agreement on family business issues.

Initiating discussion can be difficult, so it is standard for family leaders to invite an outside expert or facilitator to coordinate early sessions. The facilitator can help develop an agenda and establish ground rules for discussion. While chairing early sessions, the moderator can establish a positive tone that emphasizes family achievements and encourages rational consideration of sensitive issues. If family members can develop an atmosphere of neutrality, however, they may be able to chair the sessions without using an outsider.

To ensure the success of a family business retreat, Steven White, CEO of a family business consulting firm, suggests that these guidelines be followed:[29]

1. *Set a time and place.* The retreat should be held at a convenient time and in a central location so that everyone can be involved.

2. *Distribute an agenda prior to meeting.* An agenda helps participants organize their thoughts about the issues that are to be discussed.

3. *Plan a schedule in advance.* Details for sessions should be planned ahead of the retreat. Sufficient blocks of time should be provided to deal with important matters and room left in the schedule for refreshment breaks. It's a good idea to set aside one evening for the family to get together and do something fun as a group.

4. *Give everyone a chance to participate.* In sessions, family members should be honest, and they should not interrupt one another. The conversation may be allowed to wander a bit, if this is therapeutic, but the focus should stay on the business.

5. *Keep it professional.* The conversation may become emotional when sensitive topics are discussed, but it should never be allowed to become personal or to spiral out of control. Everyone should leave the retreat feeling good about what was accomplished.

But the talk at family retreats is not always about business. After a retreat, families often speak of the joy of sharing family values and stories of past family experiences. Thus, retreats can strengthen the family as well as the company.

Family Councils

family council
An organized group of family members who gather periodically to discuss family-related business issues.

A family retreat could pave the way for creation of a *family council,* in which family members meet to discuss values, policies, and direction for the future. A family council functions as the organizational and strategic planning arm of a family. It provides a forum for the ongoing process of listening to the ideas of all members and discovering what they believe in and want from the business. A family council formalizes the participation of the family in the business to a greater extent than does the family retreat. It can also be a focal point for planning the future of individual family members, the family as a whole, and the business, as well as how each relates to the others.

A council should be a formal organization that provides governance for the family in their relationship with the business. Council members are normally elected by the extended adult family members. The representatives hold regular meetings, keep minutes, and make suggestions to the firm's board of directors. During the first several meetings, an acceptable mission statement is usually generated, as well as a family creed.

Family businesses that have such councils find them useful for developing family harmony. The meetings are often fun and informative and may include speakers who discuss items of interest. Time is often set aside for sharing achievements, milestones, and family history. The younger generation is encouraged to participate because much of the process is designed to increase their understanding of family traditions and business interests and to prepare them for working effectively in the business.

Family Business Constitutions

Family councils also may be charged with the responsibility of writing a *family business constitution,* which is a statement of principles intended to guide a family firm through times of crisis and change, including the succession process. While this is not a legally binding document, it nonetheless helps to preserve the intentions of the founder and ensure that the business survives periods of change largely intact. When a transfer between generations occurs and there is no guiding document, issues such as ownership, performance, and compensation can become flash points for conflict.[30]

When Randall Clifford's father died in 1994, the ownership and control of Ventura Transfer Company, the oldest trucking company in California, were suddenly called into question. Clifford's stepmother sued him and his three brothers for an interest in the business. Then, to make matters worse, the four Clifford brothers began to struggle among themselves for control of the company. After a drawn-out legal battle, the sons decided to enlist the help of a consultant to draft a family business constitution. The resulting document helped the family sort out many of the issues that had plagued the transition process.

Family business constitutions are sometimes synonymous with *family protocols,* but the latter are usually more comprehensive and include such topics as

- ownership agreements (e.g., inheritance plans or buy–sell compacts),
- governance and personnel policies,
- policies and procedures for the use of resources by family members,
- conflicts of interest and noncompetition agreements, and
- codes of conduct.[31]

A family business constitution cannot foresee every eventuality, but that is not a problem since it is a "living, breathing document" that can be amended as needed.[32] The important point is that this document can smooth any transitions, including a change in leadership, which is the subject of the next section.

family business constitution
A statement of principles intended to guide a family firm through times of crisis and change.

family protocol
An extension of the constitution incorporating additional agreements.

The Process of Leadership Succession

The task of preparing family members for careers and, ultimately, leadership within the business is difficult and sometimes frustrating. Professional and managerial requirements tend to become intertwined with family feelings and interests, so the transfer of leadership can quickly run into trouble. And to make the succession process even more challenging, nobody wants to talk about it, for a variety of reasons.

5. Describe the process of managerial succession in a family business.

> The spouse doesn't want to talk about succession because he or she has to face changes at home. The patriarch or the matriarch doesn't want to talk about succession because what are they going to do after retirement? . . . The next generation doesn't want to bring it up. It's inappropriate and painful; it brings on all sorts of very difficult feelings.[33]

Because everyone is so uncomfortable with the subject, plans for succession often are not well developed or at least are poorly communicated. It is not unusual to hear family business owners begin to discuss eventualities with the phrase "If I die. . . ." It is not a question of "if," but of "when." Yet it is hard for the entrepreneurial owner to think of not being around and in charge. And the succeeding generation finds it hard to confront mom and dad with the prospect of death. The successor may feel that she or he is appearing to be mercenary. Certainly, even grown children do not want to contemplate the death of a parent.

At a major family business conference at Northwestern University in Chicago, potential leadership successors were asked if they knew the rules and plans for succession at their family firm, and 60 percent said they did not.[34] In other words, a majority of those who one day may be stepping into the primary role of responsibility for the family business are not really certain they are solidly on that track. This could lead to some very uncomfortable times ahead if things do not turn out as expected, and the health and prosperity of both the family business and the business family could hang in the balance.

Available Family Talent

A stream can rise no higher than its source, and the family firm can be no more brilliant than its leader. The business is dependent, therefore, on the quality of existing leadership talent. If the available talent is not sufficient, the owner must bring in outside leadership or supplement family talent to avoid a decline in the business under the leadership of second- or third-generation family members.

The question of competency is both a critical and a delicate issue. With experience, individuals can improve their abilities; younger family members should not be judged too harshly early on. Furthermore, potential successors may be held back by the reluctance of a parent-owner to delegate responsibility to them.

In some cases, a younger family member's skills may actually help to rescue the company, especially when the business becomes mired in the past and fails to keep up with changing

Photo courtesy of C. F. Martin & Co., Inc.

technology and emerging markets. In 1986, Chris Martin stepped in as the sixth-generation CEO of C. F. Martin & Co., Inc., a guitar maker. Interviewed in 2008, he recalled that when he joined the firm, it "was barely breaking even." The company had overexpanded through ill-advised acquisitions and was making and selling only 3,000 guitars a year, down from 20,000 in the late 1970s. Concentrating on the core business and on employee empowerment and teamwork, Chris increased production to 85,000 guitars in 2007. He proudly reported paying out $15 million to employees in profit sharing during his tenure as CEO.[35]

In any case, a family firm need not accept the existing level of family talent as an unchangeable given. Instead, the business may offer various types of development programs to teach younger family members and thereby improve their skills. Some businesses include mentoring as a part of such programs. As discussed in Chapter 1, mentoring is the process by which a more experienced person guides and supports the work, progress, and professional relationships of a new or less-experienced employee. In the family business, a

V. Declaration of Succession
IV. Formal Start in the Business
III. Proof of Competence
II. Education and Personal Development
I. Pre-Business Involvement

Source: Adapted from Johan Lambrecht, "Multigenerational Transition in Family Businesses: A New Explanatory Model," *Family Business Review*, Vol. 18, No. 4 (2005), pp. 267–282.

mentor and protégé have the opportunity to navigate and explore family as well as business-related roles and responsibilities.[36]

Perhaps the fairest and most practical approach is to recognize the right of family members to prove themselves. A period of development and testing may occur either in the family business or, preferably, in another organization. If children show themselves to be capable, they earn the right to increased leadership responsibility. If potential successors are found, through a process of fair assessment, to have inadequate leadership abilities, preservation of the family business and the welfare of family members demand that they be passed over for promotion. The appointment of competent outsiders to these jobs, if necessary, increases the value of the firm for all family members who have an ownership interest in it.

Stages in the Process of Succession

Sons or daughters do not typically assume leadership of a family firm at a particular moment in time. Instead, a long, drawn-out process of preparation and transition is customary—a process that extends over years and often decades. The succession process in family businesses has been described in terms of stages, or "stepping stones," that lead, in time, to the transfer of leadership to the next generation.[37] Exhibit 5-4 outlines this process as a series of *stages in succession.*

stages in succession
Phases in the process of transferring leadership of family business from parent to child.

PRE-BUSINESS STAGE In Stage I, a potential successor becomes acquainted with the business as a part of growing up. The young child accompanies a parent to the office, store, or warehouse or plays with equipment related to the business. This early stage does not entail any formal planning to prepare the child for entering the business. It simply forms a foundation for the more deliberate stages of the process that occur in later years. In the latter phases of this stage, the child is introduced to people associated with the firm and, in time, begins to work part-time in various functional areas to get a feel for the business.

EDUCATION AND PERSONAL DEVELOPMENT STAGE Stage II usually begins when the potential successor goes off to study at a college or university, which is often viewed from the family's perspective as a time to "grow up" in an environment that facilitates intellectual growth, personal maturity, and network development. This stage provides an opportunity to chart one's own course, but with an eye on the family business and its needs. For example, a business owner who sells pollution control equipment may convince his son or daughter to major in environmental science. Of course, the emphasis placed on a formal education varies with the business. In some cases, the family may not feel that formal studies are necessary; in other cases, earning a diploma is a pre-condition for a career in the business.

PROOF OF COMPETENCE STAGE One of the difficulties future successors are likely to face when joining a family business is the perception that they are not up to the task, that they have their position only because they are family. Thinking back to his early days with the company owned by his family, Austin Ramirez recalls, "I had the same name as my dad, [so] I was always concerned that there was this presumption that I was not competent unless proved otherwise."[38] No doubt, that thought crossed the minds of some employees, too, underscoring the importance of this stage. One way to establish competence is for a son or daughter to prove he or she can do the job somewhere else first. Often, mom or dad will push a potential successor to take a position in another company before returning to the family firm, hoping that the independent achievements of the son or daughter will speak for themselves and establish his or her credibility.

FORMAL START IN THE BUSINESS STAGE Stage IV starts when a son or daughter begins working at the family business full-time, starting on a low wrung of the corporate ladder. It is common practice for family members to start out by working in various departments in the firm to prove themselves, to win the confidence of employees, and to learn about the business from all perspectives. Handling potential successors wisely involves giving them reasonable freedom to "try their wings," learn from their own mistakes, and gravitate toward business functions that play to their personal strengths and natural capabilities. At this point, succession is not a sure bet, but it is a likely scenario.

DECLARATION OF SUCCESSION STAGE In Stage V, the son or daughter is named president or general manager of the business and presumably exercises overall direction, although a parent usually is still in the background. The successor has not necessarily mastered the complexities of the role, and the predecessor may be reluctant to give up decision making completely, but all the pieces are now in place. At this stage, it is important to establish a written plan so that there is no doubt about the soon-to-be predecessor's wishes, which could otherwise be questioned in the event of an untimely death or resignation. Establishing the plan in writing will help to minimize political positioning by others who aspire to take the lead, wrangling that can be emotionally explosive and counterproductive to the work of the firm.

Reluctant Parents and Ambitious Children

When the founder of a business is preparing her or his child to take over the firm, the founder's attachment to the business must not be underestimated. Not only is a father, for example, tied to the firm financially—it is probably his primary, if not his only, major investment—but he is also tied to it emotionally. The business is his "baby," and he is understandably reluctant to entrust its future to one whom he sees as immature and unproven. Unfortunately, parents often tend to see their sons and daughters through the lens of their childhood years, even decades after their adolescence.

The child may be ambitious, well educated, and insightful regarding the business. His or her tendency to push ahead—to try something new—often conflicts with the father's caution. As a result, the child may see the father as excessively conservative, stubborn, and unwilling to change.

At the root of many such difficulties is a lack of understanding between parent and child. They work together without a map showing where they are going. Children in the business may have expectations about progress that, in the founder's thinking, are totally unrealistic. The successor can easily become hypersensitive to such problems and deal with them in ways that harm the parent–child relationship and actually hinder the progress of the business. But the situation is far from hopeless. In many cases, these problems can be avoided or defused if communication channels are open and all parties come to a clear understanding of the development process and how it is to unfold.

Transfer of Ownership

A final and often complex step in the traditional succession process in the family firm is the *transfer of ownership*. Questions of inheritance affect not only the leadership successor but also other family members having no involvement in the business. In distributing their estate, parent-owners typically wish to treat all their children fairly, both those involved in the business and those on the outside.

One of the most difficult decisions is determining the future ownership of the business. If there are several children, should they all receive equal shares? On the surface, this seems to be the fairest approach. However, such an arrangement may play havoc with the future functioning of the business. Suppose each of five children receives a 20-percent ownership share, even though only one of them is active in the business. The child active in the business—the leadership successor—becomes a minority stockholder completely at the mercy of relatives on the outside.

A parent might attempt to resolve such a dilemma by changing the ownership structure of the firm. Those children active in the firm's management, for example, might be given common (voting) stock and others given preferred (nonvoting) stock.

Tax considerations are relevant, and they tend to favor gradual transfer of ownership to all heirs. As noted, however, transfer of equal ownership shares to all heirs may be inconsistent with the future successful operation of the business. Tax advantages should not be allowed to blind one to possible adverse effects on management.

Ideally, the founder has been able to arrange his or her personal holdings to create wealth outside the business as well as within it. In that case, he or she may bequeath gifts of similar value to all heirs while allowing business control to remain with the child or children active in the business. Planning and discussing the transfer of ownership is not easy, but it is strongly recommended. Over a period of time, the owner must reflect seriously on family talents and interests as they relate to the future of the firm. The plan for transfer of ownership can then be firmed up and modified as necessary when it is discussed with the children or other potential heirs. In discussing exit strategies in Chapter 12, we explain a variety of possible financial arrangements for the transfer of ownership.

In this chapter, we have tried to make one message very clear to prospective business owners—families and businesses are interrelated. Trying to separate them would be like trying to unscramble eggs. The better you understand that going in, the more successful you can be in both areas of your life.

LOOKING BACK

1. What is a family business, and why are family businesses important?

- The word *family* refers to a group of people bound by a shared history and a commitment to share a future together while supporting the development and well-being of individual members.

- A *family business* is an organizational entity in which either the individuals who established or acquired the firm or their descendants significantly influence the strategic decisions and life course of the firm—leading to the success or failure of the business.

- Most businesses in the United States and other countries with private enterprise economies are family-owned and controlled.

- A family business comprises the individual, the family, and the organization, yet each maintains its independent identity.

- The advantages of a family business include the strong commitment of family members to the success of the firm, the ability to use a family theme in advertising, the development of firm-specific knowledge, the sharing of social networks among family members, a focus on long-term goals, an emphasis on the firm's reputation, and reduced cost of control.
- Disadvantages of a family business include conflicts over risk taking (especially with money), conflicts over values, and conflicts over performance competence.

2. Explain the forces that can keep a family business moving forward.

- The organizational culture of a family business is composed of the patterns of behaviors and beliefs that emerge from the interaction of family and business.
- The founder often leaves a deep imprint on the culture of a family firm.
- The long-term survival of the business is dependent on the commitment of family members. They may be committed to the family business for different reasons (emotional attachment, sense of obligation, calculated costs, and personal needs), and these reasons will likely determine the nature and strength of that commitment.
- Because commitments among individuals can vary, family unity becomes an important factor in moving the business forward.

3. Describe the complex roles and relationships involved in a family business.

- Couples known as co-preneurs join in business together, which can strengthen or weaken their marriage.
- A primary and sensitive relationship is that between founder and son or daughter.
- Siblings and other relatives may similarly strengthen or weaken their working and personal relationships through a family business.
- In-laws play a crucial role in the family business, either as direct participants or as sideline observers.

- The role of the founder's spouse is especially important, as he or she often serves as a mediator in family disputes and helps prepare the children for possible careers in the family business.

4. Identify management practices that enable a family business to function effectively.

- Good management practices are as important as good family relationships in the successful functioning of a family business.
- Following best practices can help family firms design effective management systems.
- Motivation of nonfamily employees can be enhanced by open communication and fairness.
- Family retreats bring all family members together to discuss business and family matters.
- Family councils provide a formal framework for the family's ongoing discussion of family and business issues.
- Family business constitutions can guide a company through times of crisis or change.

5. Describe the process of managerial succession in a family business.

- Discussing and planning the transfer of leadership is sometimes difficult.
- The quality of leadership talent available in the family determines the extent to which outside managers are needed.
- Succession is a long-term process starting early in the successor's life.
- The succession process begins with the pre-business stage and includes introductions to people associated with the company and part-time jobs in the firm. Later stages involve education and personal development, proof of competence, a formal start in the business, and a declaration of succession.
- Tension often arises between the founder and the potential successor as the latter gains experience.
- Transfer of ownership involves issues of fairness, taxes, and managerial control.

Key Terms

family, p. 121
family business, p. 122
organizational culture, p. 125
obligation-based commitment, p. 127
need-based commitment, p. 127

emotional attachment (desire-based commitment), p. 128
unity, p. 128
cost-based commitment, p. 128
co-preneurs, p. 130
family retreat, p. 135

family council, p. 136
family business constitution, p. 137
family protocols, p. 137
stages in succession, p. 139
transfer of ownership, p. 141

Discussion Questions

1. Explain what makes a business a family business. What is the difference between a family business and any other type of business?

2. Suppose that you, as the founder of a business, have a sales manager position open. You realize that sales may suffer somewhat if you promote your son from sales representative to sales manager. However, you would like to see your son make some progress and earn a higher salary to support his wife and young daughter. How would you go about making this decision? Would you promote your son?

3. What advantages result from family involvement in a business? What are some disadvantages?

4. What are the bases of commitment to the family firm? What is the difference between commitment and unity?

5. With a college-level business degree in hand, you are headed for a job in the family business. As a result of your education, you have become aware of some outdated business practices in the family firm. In spite of them, the business is showing a good return on investment. Should you "rock the boat"? How should you proceed in updating what you see as obsolete approaches?

6. Describe a founder–son or founder–daughter relationship in a family business with which you are familiar. What strengths or weaknesses are evident in that business relationship?

7. Should a son or daughter feel an obligation to carry on a family business? What might happen if that prospective successor chooses not to join the firm?

8. Assume that you are an ambitious, nonfamily manager in a family firm and that one of your peers is the son or daughter of the founder. What, if anything, would keep you interested in pursuing a career with this company?

9. Identify and describe the stages outlined in the model of succession shown in Exhibit 5-4.

10. In making decisions about transferring ownership of a family business from one generation to another, how much emphasis should be placed on estate tax laws and other concerns that go beyond the family? Why?

You Make the Call

SITUATION 1

As a single mother of three teenagers, Jessica began her career as an interior designer. She put in long hours, but never ignored her children. As they came of age and left home for college and careers, a new man came into Jessica's life. Charley was a sales executive with a large electronics firm and had children from his prior marriage. Jessica and Charley married, and Charley joined her company, eventually becoming co-owner. By that time, Jessica had built a solid presence for her firm in her hometown. Coming out of a large corporation, Charley had bigger ideas for the business. They made a great team, with Jessica concentrating on design and Charley on sales and expansion.

At various times, other family members joined, and then left, the business. Jessica's sister worked in the family business for awhile, as did Charley's daughter. The one family member who joined and stayed was Jessica's second son, Lou. Lou was the classic computer nerd. He held the title of operations manager for the company, overseeing the work orders and delivery. He spent most of his time, however, working on the company's website and eventually started accepting contracts to do websites for other firms.

Lou's freelancing increasingly distracted him from his responsibilities to his mother's business. Orders were mishandled, deliveries were late, customers were irate. Behind the scenes, Jessica and Charley's other employees were grumbling. They wanted to know why Lou was drawing the salary of an executive, when all his time was spent on his own projects. And they wondered if this was the person who would eventually own the business.

Jessica and Charley did not have their eyes closed. They knew what Lou was doing and had spoken directly with him regarding their concerns. Lou's response was always that he was doing his job and did not see any reason for them to complain. He acknowledged his outside contracts, but said that he worked on those in his spare time. On one occasion, after a particularly heated conversation, Charley went to the restroom to wash up. He recognized Lou's sandals on the person sitting in a stall and could hear that person tapping away on a laptop.

Question 1 What do you think the employees of this family business will do if Lou's behavior continues as it has been?
Question 2 What advice would you offer to Jessica and Charley for handling Lou?

SITUATION 2

Morris was turning 80 and feeling great. Forty years earlier, he had founded a trucking and storage company and grown it into one of the industry's largest in his region. And he was proud that his two sons had chosen to make their careers with the family business. Tony, Morris's son from his first marriage, served as marketing manager, and Steven, his son with his current wife, was chief operating officer. Morris held the titles of CEO and Chairman of the Board.

Morris was especially happy at how well the boys got along. There had never been a sign of jealousy between them. Both had carved out their specialties in the business and cooperated beautifully. They made important contributions to the growth of the firm. They also showed respect to Morris and his wife, Irma, in the business and at home. It was not unusual for Tony and Steven to bring their respective families to their parents' house for Sunday dinner.

It was dawning on Morris that he was not going to live forever and that he had to make some disposition of his ownership of the business. Irma had been pressuring him for some time to back away and consider retirement. Although Morris had confidence in both boys, he faced a dilemma in management and ownership succession. He had applauded the accomplishments of his sons, but had come to the conclusion that Steven was the best one to take charge of the firm. But how could he make such a decision when his older son was a solid and competent executive in the company?

One night, Morris sat down with Irma and told her his decision. He was going to remain permanently in the CEO position. When he died, his sons would learn in the will that Steven was to be designated his successor. Irma gasped in response, stood up, and walked out of the room.

Question 1 If you learned your father's wishes for your position and ownership share in the family business at the reading of the will, how do you think you would react?

Question 2 Does Irma have a role to play in this? What would you recommend that she do at this point?

SITUATION 3

Brothers Sebastian and Alfonso grew up competing for their parents' attention. Everyone was surprised when they decided to go into business with each other. Alfonso was the reserved one. An engineer, he had developed the product that was the basis of their venture. Sebastian was outgoing, a born salesman. He was CEO of the company, while Alfonso worked in the laboratory, overseeing research and development. The business took off, but building it into a national competitor required that all profits be invested in product development and market expansion. After a few years, Sebastian wanted to know where his share of the profits were. He knew sales were growing exponentially. What was his brother doing with his money? One day, the brothers' dad called and offered to come in and run the business. He would make sure that everyone got their fair share.

Question 1 What would you recommend to Sebastian at this point?

Question 2 What would you recommend to Alfonso at this point?

Experiential Exercises

1. Interview someone in your community who has grown up in a family business about the ways she or he has been trained or educated, both formally and informally, for entry into the business. Prepare a brief report, relating your findings to the stages of succession shown in Exhibit 5-4.

2. Interview a college student who has grown up in a family business about parental attitudes toward his or her possible entry into the business. Submit a one-page report describing the extent of pressure on the student to enter the family business and the direct or indirect ways in which family expectations have been communicated.

3. Identify a family business and prepare a brief report on its history, including its founding, family involvement, and any leadership changes that have occurred.

4. Read and report on a biography or autobiography about a family in business or on a nonfictional book about a family business.

Small Business & Entrepreneurship Resource Center

The Small Business and Entrepreneurship Resource Center offers complete small business management resources through a comprehensive database that covers all major areas of starting, operating, and maintaining a business from financing, management, marketing, accounting, taxes, and more. Use the access code that came with your new book to access the site and perform the exercises in each chapter.

It is a well known fact that founders leave a deep impression on the family businesses they launch. Such is the case with Chick-fil-A, founded by Truett Cathy. This founder is raising eyebrows, not because of corporate missteps, but for adhering to old-fashioned values and principles. In his book, EatMorChikin: Inspire More People, Cathy tells of the secrets of his success. Describe the recipe for Chick-fil-A success.

Source: New on the shelf: franchisor's vision serves up recipe for success: put people ahead of profits. *Franchising World* 34, 8 (Nov–Dec 2002): p. 48.

"Chick-fil-A founder S. Truett Cathy was named winner of the 2008 William E. Simon Prize for Philanthropic Leadership by the Philanthropy Roundtable. (Awards & Honors)(Brief article)." *Franchising World* 41, 1 (Jan 2009): 126(1). Small Business Resource Center. Gale. Higher Education. 9 June 2009. http://find.galegroup.com/sbrc/start

Case 5

W.S. DARLEY & CO. (P. 632)

On the firm's website, the leaders of W.S. Darley & Co. proudly declare, "We remain a family owned and operated business committed to customer service and our employees." The current CEO, Bill Darley, was seven years old when his father, company founder W. S. Darley, died. Bill's mother might have sold the business then; instead, she selected a nonfamily member to manage the company until Bill was ready to take charge. In 1960, the year he turned 31, Bill Darley accepted responsibility for the family business.

W.S. Darley & Co. provides products and services for firefighting and emergency services. The company was founded in 1908 and sold its first fire truck in the 1920s for $690. Today, the company offers thousands of products on a global basis. In recent years, it has sold systems, pumps, and truck bodies and engaged in design services for customers in Australia, Brazil, Indonesia, Saudi Arabia, New Zealand, and many other countries. Most recently, it began investing heavily in the development of water purification and conservation products.

PART 3
Developing the New Venture Business Plan

chapters

The Business Plan

Visualizing the Dream

In the SPOTLIGHT
Stella & Dot
http://stelladot.com

An entrepreneur's first presentation of a business plan to investors can be a lesson in humility. That's what Jessica Herrin learned as a business school student who was trying to start an online wedding registry during the dot-com boom.

Her lack of experience in the wedding industry almost ended her plans for the startup before she began. Herrin's intent was to sell products directly to consumers and also through retailers. But, of course, retailers are not interested in supporting their competitors. Herrin was able to obtain financing only when she revised her business plan and used a retailer-only distribution system.

Herrin's experience is not uncommon. Such errors in business plans can doom a business with investors. But Herrin learned her lesson well.

In 2004, Herrin was able to quickly raise the $350,000 that her business, Stella & Dot, needed to get off the ground. This time, the 34-year-old Burlingame, California, entrepreneur went to a retailer to learn about the custom jewelry industry before she even began to solicit investors.

Stella & Dot currently has $1.2 million in sales and 10 employees. Clearly, a good business plan can make all the difference.

Source: Mark Henricks, "Build a Better Business Plan," February 2007, *http://www.entrepreneur.com/ startingabusiness/businessplans/article174002.html*, accessed January 6, 2009.

LOOKING AHEAD

AFTER STUDYING THIS CHAPTER, YOU SHOULD BE ABLE TO...

1. Explain the purpose and objectives of business plans.
2. Give the rationale for writing (or not writing) a business plan when starting a new venture.
3. Describe the preferred content and format for a business plan.
4. Offer practical advice on writing a business plan.
5. Explain what investors look for in a business plan.
6. Identify available sources of assistance in preparing a business plan.
7. Maintain the proper perspective when writing a business plan.

You're excited about an idea for a new business. But when you mention it to a friend who's also a business owner, she says, "You'll need to prepare a business plan." While the business idea sounds great, sitting down and writing some cold, formal document is not exactly your idea of fun, and you wonder if it is really necessary. After all, you know an entrepreneur who started and successfully grew a company based on an idea developed on the back of a napkin over dinner at a local restaurant. And isn't it true that the founders of such notable companies as Microsoft, Dell Computers, *Rolling Stone* magazine, and Calvin Klein all started their businesses without business plans?

An Overview of the Business Plan

To answer the question of whether or not you should write a business plan, you'll need to first understand its purpose and objectives. We'll help you examine the considerations in making a decision about whether to write a business plan for your venture. Then we'll look at the two basic forms a plan might take.

1. Explain the purpose and objectives of business plans.

The Purpose of a Business Plan

There is no one correct formula for a business plan. After all, no single plan will work in all situations. But, in general, a *business plan* is a document that outlines the basic idea underlying a business and describes related startup considerations. A business plan is an entrepreneur's game plan; it crystallizes the dreams and hopes that motivate an entrepreneur to take the startup plunge. The business plan should lay out your basic idea for the venture and include descriptions of where you are now, where you want to go, and how you intend to get there.

business plan
A document that presents the basic idea for the venture and includes descriptions of where you are now, where you want to go, and how you intend to get there.

David Gumpert, who for years headed up the MIT Enterprise Forum,[1] offers a concise and practical definition of a business plan, focusing on how it should lead to action: "It's a document that convincingly demonstrates that your business can sell enough of its product or service to make a satisfactory profit and to be attractive to potential backers."[2] For Gumpert, the business plan is essentially a selling document used to convince key individuals, both inside and outside the firm, that the venture has real potential. Equally important, it is an opportunity to convince yourself, the entrepreneur, that what appears to be a good idea is also a good investment opportunity, both financially and in terms of your personal goals.

The issue of your personal aspirations deserves careful thought: *If the business does not align with your personal goals, you are not likely to succeed and you certainly will not enjoy the journey.* So be sure to think about where you want to go in life and the personal costs of starting a business before becoming immersed in that special business opportunity.

For the entrepreneur starting a new venture, a business plan has three basic objectives:

1. To identify the nature and the context of the business opportunity—that is, why does such an opportunity exist?

2. To outline the approach the entrepreneur plans to use to exploit the opportunity

3. To recognize factors that will determine whether the venture will be successful

Stated differently, a business plan is used to provide a statement of goals and strategies to be used by company *insiders* and to aid in the development of relationships with *outsiders* (investors and others) who could help the company achieve its goals. Exhibit 6-1 provides an overview of those who might have an interest in a business plan for a proposed venture. The first group consists of the internal users of the plan: the entrepreneur and the new firm's management and employees. The second group consists of outsiders who are critical to the firm's success: its prospective customers, suppliers, lenders, and investors.

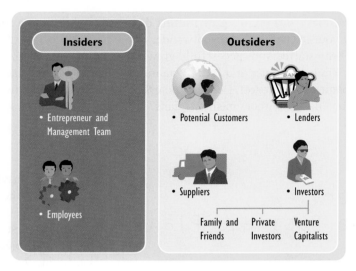

Do You Really Need a Business Plan?

2. Give the rationale for writing (or not writing) a business plan when starting a new venture.

The justification often used for *not* writing a business plan goes something like this: "Companies that start up based on business plans are no more successful than those that do not." It is true that studies attempting to measure the success of entrepreneurs with business plans against the success of those without them have produced mixed results. Some findings suggest a relationship; others find none.[3]

Given what we know about Apple, Calvin Klein, and other businesses started without business plans, having such a plan is clearly not a prerequisite for success. *This simply tells us that the business plan is not the business.* It may well be that some entrepreneurs spend untold hours writing a 60-page business plan with another 50 pages of appendixes but never follow the plan. In such cases, we can say confidently that writing the plan was a waste of time. What matters is not writing a plan, but implementing it. If the plan is not going to lead to action, don't bother to write it. Only if you *execute* the business plan does it have a reasonable chance of making a difference. Thomas Stemberg, the founder of Staples, who later became a venture capitalist, says it well:

> In my experience, entrepreneurs often confuse envisioning what a business will be with laying the foundation for what it could be. So they dream big dreams and construct detailed business plans, which is fine. But it's nowhere near as important as putting in place as early as humanly possible the people and systems that will carry them through their journey, no matter what unexpected directions changing markets or technology force them to take.
>
> To me, business plans are interesting chiefly as indications of how an entrepreneur thinks. Here at Highland Capital Partners, the venture capital firm I'm part of now, we spend most of our time talking about what really matters: management and markets. If you have the right management team and an exciting market, the rest will take care of itself.[4]

An entrepreneur must also find the right balance between planning and becoming operational. No matter how well your plan has been thought out, unexpected events will happen. One of the key attributes of a successful entrepreneur is adaptability, regardless of what the business plan says to do. So, if you have to choose between planning and action, go for action.

Vinay Gupta of Ann Arbor, Michigan, spent six months attending conferences, meeting with consultants, and writing a 60-page business plan before launching an outsourcing consulting firm for mid-sized businesses in 2004. But soon after he started the business, it became clear that far fewer mid-sized firms actually sought outsourcing help than his research had suggested.

So he scrapped his original idea and developed outsourcing-management software geared toward companies with annual revenues of more than $1 million. While the planning helped Gupta learn about the industry, it hadn't pointed out the fundamental flaw in his original idea.[5]

The benefits of a business plan also depend on the individual circumstances surrounding the startup. Consider the following:

- For some startups, the environment is too turbulent for extensive planning to be beneficial. Entrepreneurs in new fields may find that there is not enough information to allow them to write a comprehensive plan. And, as already noted, an entrepreneur's ability to adapt may be more important than a careful plan for the future. Having an excessively detailed plan can even be a problem if investors become so focused on "the plan" that they insist that the entrepreneur follow it "to the letter."

- Planning may also pose a problem when the timing of the opportunity is a critical factor. In some cases, becoming operational as quickly as possible may have to take priority over in-depth planning, but be careful not to use timing as an easy excuse not to write a business plan.

- A business may be so constrained by a shortage of capital that planning is not an option. In his study of *Inc. Magazine,* 500 companies (firms identified by *Inc. Magazine* as the fastest-growing firms in the United States), Amar Bhide concluded that a lack of planning may make sense for some companies: "Capital-constrained entrepreneurs cannot afford to do much prior analysis and research. The limited profit potential and high uncertainty of the opportunity they usually pursue also make the benefits low compared to the costs." [6]

Writing a business plan offers no guarantee of success, but most entrepreneurs need the discipline that comes with the process. The path of an enterprise started without adequate preparation tends to be haphazard. In the words of Thomas Carlyle, the Scottish mathematician and writer, "Nothing is more terrible than activity without insight." This is particularly true for a complex process like initiating a new business.

Although planning is a mental process, it should go beyond the realm of speculation. Thinking about a proposed new business must be more thorough for rough ideas to come together. A written plan helps to ensure the necessary systematic and complete coverage of factors important in starting a new business. Frank Moyes, a successful entrepreneur who for many years has taught courses on business planning at the University of Colorado, offers the following observations:

Perhaps the most important reason to write a business plan is that it requires you to engage in a rigorous, thoughtful and often painful process that is essential before you start a venture. It requires you to answer hard questions about your venture. Why is there a need for your product/service? Who is your target market? How is your product/service different than your competitor's? What is your competitive advantage? How profitable is the business and what are the cash flows? How should you fund the business?[7]

So the business plan becomes a model that helps the entrepreneur and the management team focus on important issues and activities for the new venture. Furthermore, it helps the entrepreneur communicate his or her vision to current and prospective employees of the firm. After all, entrepreneurs who are building good companies seldom, if ever, work alone.

The business plan also matters to outsiders. Although typically thought to be the primary risk takers in a startup, the entrepreneur and the management team are by no means the only risk takers. To make the company successful, the entrepreneur must convince outsiders—prospective customers, suppliers, lenders, and investors—to become linked with the firm. Why should they do business with your startup, rather than with an established firm? They need evidence that you will be around in the future. As Amar Bhide explains, "Some entrepreneurs may have an innate capability to outperform their rivals, acquire managerial skills, and thus build a flourishing business. But it is difficult for customers (and others) to identify founders with these innate capabilities." [8]

By enhancing the venture's credibility, the business plan serves as an effective selling tool with prospective customers and suppliers, as well as investors. For example, a well-prepared business plan can be helpful in gaining a supplier's trust and securing favorable credit terms. Likewise, a plan can improve sales prospects by convincing prospective customers that the new firm is likely to be around for a long time to service a product or to continue as a source of supply.

Finally, the entrepreneur may face the task of raising money to supplement personal savings. This requires an effective presentation to bankers, individual investors, or, in some cases, venture capitalists. Approach almost any investor for money today and the first thing she or he will ask is, "Where is your business plan?"

As discussed earlier, a business plan is not a prerequisite for entrepreneurial success. A plan may not be needed in certain situations, especially if you want only to build a very small company and have no plans for significant growth. But we encourage you to dream and hope for more. Ewing Marion Kauffman, who founded Marion Labs with $5,000 and later sold it for $6 billion, once said, "You should not choose to build a common company. It's your right to be uncommon if you can. You seek opportunity to compete, to take calculated risks, to dream, to build; yes, even to fail and succeed."[9] And Peter Drucker wrote, "Even if you are starting your business on a kitchen table, you must have a vision of becoming a world leader in your field, or you will probably never be successful."[10]

Granted, you may have no interest in building a company that is a world leader in its field, but neither should you dream too small.

How Much Planning?

For most entrepreneurs, the issue is not *whether* to prepare a business plan but *how* to engage in effective planning, given the situation. As we have already observed, different situations lead to different needs and, thus, to different levels of planning.

The issue, then, goes beyond answering the question "Do I plan?" It is more about deciding how much to plan. In starting a business, an entrepreneur has to make some tradeoffs, as preparing a plan requires time and money, two resources that are always in short supply. At the extremes, an entrepreneur has two basic choices when it comes to writing a business plan: the mini-plan or the comprehensive plan.[11]

mini-plan
A short form of a business plan that presents only the most important issues and projections for the business.

THE MINI-PLAN   As noted earlier, extensive planning may be of limited value when there is a great amount of uncertainty in the environment or when timing is a critical factor in capturing an opportunity. A *mini-plan* is a short form of a business plan, presenting only the most important issues and projections for the business. Focusing heavily on market issues, such as pricing, competition, and distribution channels, the mini-plan provides little in the way of supporting information.

This type of plan will often be adequate for seeking outside financing from banks, especially if it includes past and projected financial results. In fact, it is so rare for an entrepreneur to provide any form of a plan when requesting a loan that a brief mini-plan will probably make a favorable impression on a banker. Furthermore, a mini-plan may be helpful in trying to gauge investor interest, to determine whether writing a full-length plan would be worth the time and effort.

comprehensive plan
A full business plan that provides an in-depth analysis of the critical factors that will determine a firm's success or failure, along with all the underlying assumptions.

THE COMPREHENSIVE PLAN   When entrepreneurs and investors speak of a business plan, they are usually referring to a *comprehensive plan*, a full business plan that provides an in-depth analysis of the critical factors that will determine a firm's success or failure, along with all the underlying assumptions. Such a plan is beneficial when, for example, you are describing a new opportunity (startup), facing significant change in the business or the external environment (changing demographics, new legislation, developing industry trends), or explaining a complex business situation. In the remainder of this chapter and in those that follow, we will be discussing the comprehensive business plan.

Preparing a Business Plan

So you have decided to write a business plan. Like writing a term paper or report, getting started is usually the hardest part. Recall that, in Chapter 3, we emphasized the importance of first conducting a feasibility analysis and only then writing a business plan if your idea "passes muster," to use military speak. Three elements must be evident from the feasibility analysis before you move on to the business plan: strong market potential, an attractive industry, and the right individual or team to execute the plan. Often, entrepreneurs rush past these issues, wanting to "get going." Being oriented to action is a positive trait for an entrepreneur, but not at the expense of doing the basic homework. Never forget the need for balance. One entrepreneur told us, "It's not that hard. To meet the basic requirements, you have to have a large and growing market, an unfair competitive advantage, and a team of people who can capture the advantage."[12] So before you write a business plan, begin with a feasibility analysis to see if the basics are present.

Once the feasibility analysis is completed, it's time to begin the process of writing a business plan. For this, two issues are of primary concern: the content and format of the plan and the effectiveness of the written presentation.

The Content and Format of a Business Plan

When considering the content of a business plan, continue to think first and foremost about the opportunity, as identified by your feasibility analysis. Strategies and financial plans will follow naturally if the opportunity is a good one. In the evaluation of an opportunity, give thorough consideration to the following basic factors (presented graphically in Exhibit 6-2):

3. Describe the preferred content and format for a business plan.

1. The *opportunity* should reflect the potential and attractiveness of the market and industry.

2. *Critical resources* include not just money, but also human assets (suppliers, accountants, lawyers, investors, etc.) and hard assets (accounts receivable, inventories, etc.). An entrepreneur should think of ways to minimize the resources necessary for startup, a practice known as bootstrapping.

3. The *entrepreneurial team* must possess integrity and breadth and depth of experience.

6-2 A Business Plan Identifies the Key Factors for Success

EXHIBIT

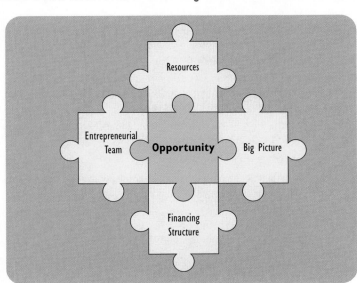

4. The financing structure—how a firm is financed (debt versus equity) and how the ownership percentage is shared by the founders and investors—will have a significant impact on an entrepreneur's incentive to work hard. The goal is to find a win-win deal.

5. The *context* (or external factors) of an opportunity includes the regulatory environment, interest rates, demographic trends, inflation, and other factors that inevitably change but cannot be controlled by the entrepreneur.

Thus, the business plan will need to demonstrate that the entrepreneur has pulled together the right opportunity, the right resources, the right people, the right financing structure, and the right context. Admittedly, there will always be uncertainties and ambiguities; the unanticipated is bound to happen. But by making decisions about these key factors, you can be sure that you are dealing with the important issues, and this will help you in determining the appropriate content to include in the plan.

There is no single format to be followed in writing a business plan. A plan for a retail store, restaurant, or wholesaling business will, by necessity, be somewhat different in terms of topics, order of presentation, and what is emphasized. However, investors want to see a format that is familiar to them. Thus, you do not want to write a business plan that is fundamentally different from what they are accustomed to seeing. Deviating significantly from this format would be a mistake.

Exhibit 6-3 summarizes the major sections common to most business plans, providing a bird's-eye view of what's usually included. A brief overview of each of these

6-3 Abbreviated Business Plan Outline

EXHIBIT

Section Heading	Information Provided
Cover Page	Company name, logo, tagline, contact information, copy number, date prepared, and disclaimer (if needed)
Table of Contents	Listing of the key sections of the business plan
Executive Summary	One to three-page overview of the significant points, intended to motivate the reader to continue reading
Industry, Target Customer, and Competitor Analysis	Key characteristics of the industry, including the different segments, and the niche where you plan to compete
Company Description	Company objectives, the nature of the business, its primary product or service, its current status (startup, buyout, or expansion) and history (if applicable), and the legal form of organization
Product/Service Plan	Justification for why people will buy the product or service, based on its unique features
Marketing Plan	Marketing strategy, including the methods of identifying and attracting customers, selling approach, type of sales force, distribution channels, types of sales promotions and advertising, and credit and pricing policies
Operations and Development Plan	Operating or manufacturing methods, operating facilities (location, space, and equipment), quality-control methods, procedures to control inventory and operations, sources of supply, and purchasing procedures
Management Team	Description of the management team, outside investors and/or directors, and plans for recruiting and training employees
Critical Risks	Any known inherent risks in the venture
Offering	How much capital the entrepreneur needs and how the money will be used (section used to attract investors)
Financial Plan	Contemplated sources of financing; any historical financial statements, if available; pro forma financial statements for three to five years, including income statements, balance sheets, cash flow statements, and cash budgets
Appendix of Supporting Documents	Various supplementary materials and attachments to expand the reader's understanding of the plan

sections follows;[13] Chapters 7 through 13 take an in-depth look at each section of the business plan.

COVER PAGE   The cover page should contain the following information:
- Company name, address, phone number, fax number, and website
- Tagline and company logo
- Name of contact person (preferably the president) with mailing address, phone number, fax number, and e-mail address
- Date on which the business plan was prepared
- If the plan is being given to investors, a disclaimer that the plan is being provided on a confidential basis to qualified investors only and is not to be reproduced without permission
- Number of the copy (to help keep track of how many copies have been given out)

TABLE OF CONTENTS   The table of contents provides a sequential listing of the sections of the plan, with page numbers. This allows the reader to spot-read the plan (a common practice) rather than reading it from front to back. Exhibit 6-4 presents the table of contents for the business plan for Atayne, LLC. (While the table of contents for Atayne's business plan does not follow exactly the format presented in Exhibit 6-3, note that it has much of the same content and follows a similar order.)

EXECUTIVE SUMMARY   The *executive summary* is often thought to be the most important section of the business plan. If you don't catch the readers' attention in the executive summary, most likely they will not continue reading. At the very outset, it must convey a clear and concise picture of the proposed venture and, at the same time, create a sense of excitement regarding its prospects. This means that it must be written—and, if necessary, rewritten—to achieve clarity and create interest. Even though the executive summary comes at the beginning of the business plan, it provides an overview of the whole plan and should be written last. In no more than three (preferably two) pages, the executive summary should include the following subsections:
- A description of the opportunity
- An explanation of the business concept

executive summary
A section of the business plan that conveys a clear and concise overall picture of the proposed venture.

6-4   Table of Contents for Business Plan of Atayne, LLC

EXHIBIT

- An industry overview
- The target market
- The competitive advantage you hope to achieve in the market
- The economics of the opportunity
- The management team
- The amount and purpose of the money being requested (the "offering") if you are seeking financing

Depending on the situation and the preference of the entrepreneur, the executive summary may be in the form of a synopsis or a narrative.

SYNOPSIS   The synopsis is the more straightforward of the two summary formats. A synopsis briefly covers all aspects of the business plan, giving each topic relatively equal treatment. It relates, in abbreviated fashion, the conclusions of each section of the completed business plan. Although it is easy to prepare, the synopsis can be rather dry reading for the prospective investor.

NARRATIVE   Because the narrative tells a story, it can convey greater excitement than the synopsis. However, composing an effective narrative requires a gifted writer who can communicate the necessary information and generate enthusiasm without crossing the line into hyperbole. A narrative is more appropriate for businesses that are breaking new ground, with a new product, a new market, or new operational techniques. It is also a better format for ventures that have one dominant advantage, such as holding an important patent or being run by a well-known entrepreneur. Finally, the narrative works well for companies with interesting or impressive backgrounds or histories.[14]

Atayne again provides us with an example, as Exhibit 6-5 shows the executive summary for the business.

INDUSTRY, TARGET CUSTOMER, AND COMPETITOR ANALYSIS   The primary purpose of this section is to present the opportunity and demonstrate why there is a significant market to be served. You should describe the broader industry in which you will be competing, including industry size, growth rate, fundamental trends, and major players. You should next identify the different segments of the industry and finally describe in detail the niche in which you plan to participate. It is tempting to begin describing your own company at this point. Instead, you should provide the context of the opportunity and demonstrate that a market segment is being underserved. There will be an opportunity later to introduce your product and/ or service.

Next, describe your target customers in terms of demographics and psychological variables, such as their values, their attitudes, and even their fears. The more clearly you can identify your customer, the more likely it is that you will provide a product/service that is actually in demand. Finally, knowing what the customer looks like and wants serves as the basis for understanding who your competitors are. Analyze competitors in terms of product or service attributes that they are or are not providing.

COMPANY DESCRIPTION   This section gives a brief description of the firm. If the business is already in existence, its history is included. The company description informs the reader of the type of business being proposed, the firm's objectives, where the firm is located, and whether it will serve a local or international market. In many cases, legal issues—especially those concerning the firm's form of organization—are addressed in this section of the plan. (Legal issues regarding the form of organization are discussed at

Atayne, LLC has a simple vision: inspire positive environmental and social change through the power of sports and active lifestyles.
We deliver a powerful message for fellow members of the eco-active community: you do not have to sacrifice your environmental and social values for performance.

Management Team
Jeremy Litchfield
Chief Pacesetter/President

Rebecca Darr
VP/International Development

Lara Dittoe
VP/Product Development

Michael Hall
VP/Community Development

Parker Karnan
VP/Strategy & Development

Kathleen Lendvay
VP/Operations

Board of Advisors
Charlie Jones
President and Founder
Brand Intersection Group

Brad Nierenberg
President/CEO
RedPeg Marketing

James F. Kenefick
Chairman and Co-founder
BetterWorld Telecom

Ray and Cathy Pugsley
Brendan and Margie Shapiro
Potomac River Running Stores

Legal Representation
Gordon Kushner & Dennis Lambert

Financing Plan
Round I - $350k (Dec 2008, $135k raised to date)

Round II - $650k (June 2009)

Round III -$2MM (Jan 2010)

Business and Company Overview

Atayne is a newly launched company established in May 2007 to fill a void in the sporting goods market: performance and lifestyle apparel, footwear, accessories, and equipment that are sensitive on the environment and safe for the people that make and use them. Atayne employs a fundamentally different approach than the traditional industry model in developing its line of products: guided by Cradle-to-Cradle™ design philosophy, Atayne uses "trash" (worn garments, factory scraps, plastic bottles, etc.) as the primary input materials for its products.

The Product Line

Atayne will fulfill the needs of the eco-active community as they pursue their athletic and life goals. Atayne's initial product offerings, performance and lifestyle apparel, are being developed from cutting edge recycled textiles and materials. Current materials include recycled polyester, Cocona (activated carbon derived from coconut shells), and Chitosan (derived from snow crab shells). Atayne will continually evolve its fabric and material composition with advancements in the sustainable textile industry.

The primary benefits of the line are technical performance, environmental sensitivity, and human safety. From a performance standpoint, recycled polyester provides the moisture management properties of virgin polyester, while the embedded, activated carbon particles from Cocona enhance moisture transfer, provide odor control, and offer SPF 50 UV protection.

On the environmental side, Atayne's products have a dramatically lower environmental impact than the industry norm. By using recycled polyester, production energy savings are estimated at over 75% as well as reductions in CO_2 emissions of over 70% when compared to virgin polyester manufacturing processes. Additionally, in its first six years, Atayne will avert the use of over 270,000 gallons of petroleum, the equivalent of removing 650+ cars from the road, and prevent nearly 540,000 pounds of waste from entering landfills—doing its part to help address climate change and pollution.

From a human safety standpoint, Atayne is designing products following a strict restricted substance list that will prevent the use of commonly used yet harmful materials and chemicals such as PVC, phthalates, heavy metals, antimony, and Azo dyes. Many of these are known carcinogens and contaminate ground water during production and laundering. Additionally, there are concerns about the absorption of these chemicals into the body of wearers, especially when their pores are wide open during exercise.

Atayne launched sales in late August 2008, with a product line that included a men's and a women's performance top. In 2009, Atayne will introduce an expanded line that includes performance and active lifestyle tops, bottoms, layering pieces, and outer wear, establishing the groundwork for a full line of apparel, footwear, accessories, and equipment. All products will be priced on par with or at a premium to other high-quality performance brands like Under Armour, Nike, Adidas, Brooks, and New Balance.

Continued

EXHIBIT

The Market

The opportunity for a sustainable performance sporting goods brand is readily apparent due to the convergence of two significant market-driven trends: the green movement and the increasing number of people aspiring to live more active lifestyles. Driving the convergence of these trends is a group of consumers who are ambitious and achievement-oriented, and strive for high performance in everything they do—from their career and athletic pursuits to their commitment to environmental and social causes.

This group of consumers, which Atayne calls the Game Changers, demand high quality products that are aligned with their values—compromises are rarely tolerated. However, the current market offerings of performance and lifestyle apparel, footwear, and accessories are forcing them to compromise, choosing between their environmental and social values and product performance. This market gap represents a highly profitable business opportunity. Based upon average Game Changer spending of US$90.13 per year on active apparel and the current base of 13.7MM[1] Game Changers, the estimated US market potential is over US$1.2bn. Conservatively, growth of the market over the next 5 years is expected to follow a similar pattern as traditional performance products, outperforming that of the sports apparel industry by a factor of two, if not more.

Revenue Model

Initially sales will come through four primary channels: direct web sales, direct event sales, wholesale through specialty retailers, and custom performance tops sales. Revenues will grow

Table 1: Six-Year Financial Summary

(all dollars in MM USD)	2008	2009	2010	2011	2012	2013
Units Sold (thousands)	.82	8.6	17.9	61.9	156.9	330.8
Revenues	$0.03	$0.30	$0.60	$2.24	$5.49	$11.13
Gross Margin	43%	57%	60%	64%	66%	67%
EBIT	($0.08)	($0.36)	($0.87)	($0.21)	$1.35	$3.68
Cum. Cash Flow	$0.06	$0.47	$1.43	$0.94	$1.30	$2.93

from over US$30k in 2008 to over US$11.1MM by 2013. In the first year of operation it is expected that 99% of sales will be direct to consumer (website and events). Wholesale revenues will start to gain traction in 2010 growing to approximately 30% of total sales by 2013, with the remaining 70% of sales to come from events, web, and custom sales. Gross margins will level off around 65% by 2013, a figure that is higher than the industry average due to Atayne's primarily direct sales model.

---

[1] The 13.7MM Game Changer figure was obtained from Simmons Market Research Bureau's National Consumer Survey.

---

length in Chapter 8.) In writing this section, the entrepreneur should answer the following questions:

- When and where is the business to be started?
- What is the history of the company?
- What are the firm's objectives?
- What changes have been made in structure and/or ownership?
- In what stage of development is the firm—for example, seed stage or full product line?
- What has been achieved to date?
- What is the firm's distinctive competence?
- What are the basic nature and activity of the business?
- What is its primary product or service?
- What customers will be served?
- What is the firm's form of organization—sole proprietorship, partnership, limited liability company, corporation, or some other form?

- What are the current and projected economic states of the industry?
- Does the firm intend to sell to another company or an investment group, does it plan to be a publicly traded company, or do the owners want to transfer ownership to the next generation of the family?

PRODUCT/SERVICE PLAN   The *product/service plan* describes the products and/or service to be offered to the firm's customers. Now is the time to make a convincing presentation of your company's competitive advantage. Based on your earlier description of the industry and its major players, explain how your product/service fills a gap in the market or how your product/service is "better, cheaper, and/or faster" than what is currently available. In the case of a physical product, try to provide a working model or prototype. Investors will naturally show the greatest interest in products that have been developed, tested, and found to be functional. Any innovative features should be identified and any patent protections explained. (Chapter 15 discusses this topic more fully.) Also, your growth strategy for the product/service should be explained in this section, as growth is a primary determinant of a firm's value. If relevant, describe secondary target markets the firm will pursue.

product/service plan
A section of the business plan that describes the product and/or service to be provided and explains its merits.

MARKETING PLAN   The *marketing plan* describes how the firm will reach and service customers within a given market. In other words, how will you entice customers to make the change to your product/service and to continue using it? This section should present the marketing strategy, including the methods of identifying and attracting customers; pricing strategies, selling approach, type of sales force, distribution channels; types of sales promotions and advertising; and credit and pricing policies. Based on the foregoing strategies, sales forecasts will need to be developed. Finally, in terms of servicing the customer, this section should describe any warranties, as well as planned product updates. (Chapter 7 provides in-depth coverage of the marketing plan.)

marketing plan
A section of the business plan that describes the user benefits of the product or service and the type of market that exists.

OPERATIONS AND DEVELOPMENT PLAN   The *operations and development plan* offers information on how the product will be produced and/or the service provided. Here, you will explain how the operations will contribute to the firm's competitive advantage—that is, how operations will create value for the customer. This section discusses such items as location and facilities, including how much space the business will need and what type of equipment it will require. In today's age, it is important to describe the choice between in-house production and outsourcing in order to minimize costs. Remember, however, that you should never plan to outsource a part of operations that contributes to your competitive advantage. (These aspects of the operations and development plan are discussed at length in Chapter 9 and 21.) The operating plan should also explain the firm's proposed approach to assuring quality, controlling inventory, and using subcontractors for obtaining raw materials. (See Chapter 21 for further discussion of these issues.)

operations and development plan
A section of the business plan that offers information on how a product will be produced or a service provided, including descriptions of the new firm's facilities, labor, raw materials, and processing requirements.

MANAGEMENT TEAM   Prospective investors look for well-managed companies. Of all the factors they consider, the quality of the *management team* is paramount; it may even be more important than the nature of the product/service. Investors frequently say that they would rather have an "A" management team and a "B" product or service than a "B" team and an "A" product. Unfortunately, an entrepreneur's ability to conceive an idea for a new venture is no guarantee of her or his managerial ability. The management team section, therefore, must detail the proposed firm's organizational structure and the backgrounds of those who will fill its key positions.

management team
A section of the business plan that describes a new firm's organizational structure and the backgrounds of its key players.

Ideally, a well-balanced management team—one that includes financial and marketing expertise as well as production experience and innovative talent—is in place. Managerial experience in related enterprises and in other startup situations is particularly valuable in the eyes of many prospective investors. (The factors involved in preparing the management team section are discussed in greater detail in Chapter 8.)

CRITICAL RISKS   The business plan is intended to tell a story of success, but there are always risks associated with starting a new venture. Thus, the plan would be incomplete if it did

critical risks
A section of the business plan that identifies the potential risks that may be encountered by an investor.

not identify the risks inherent in the venture. The *critical risks* section identifies the potential pitfalls that may be encountered by an investor. Common risks include a lack of market acceptance (customers don't buy the product as anticipated), competitor retaliation, longer time and higher expenses than expected to start and grow the business, inadequate financing, and government regulations.

offering
A section of the business plan that indicates to an investor how much money is needed and when, and how the money will be used.

OFFERING   If the entrepreneur is seeking capital from investors, an *offering* should be included in the plan to indicate clearly how much money is needed and when. It is helpful to convey this information in a *sources and uses table* that indicates the type of financing being requested (debt or equity) and how the funds will be used. For example, for a firm needing $500,000, including any money borrowed and the founder's investment, the sources and uses table for the first year might appear as follows:

Sources:

Bank debt	$100,000
Equity:	
New investors	300,000
Founders	100,000
Total sources	$500,000

Uses:

Product development	$125,000
Personnel costs	75,000
Working capital:	
Cash	20,000
Accounts receivable	100,000
Inventory	80,000
Machinery	100,000
Total uses	$500,000

If equity is being requested, the entrepreneur will need to decide how much ownership of the business she or he is willing to give up—not an easy task in most cases. Typically, the amount of money being raised should carry the firm for 12 to 18 months—enough time to reach some milestones. Then, if all goes well, it will be easier and less costly to raise more money later. (These issues will be discussed in greater detail in Chapters 11 and 12.)

financial plan
A section of the business plan that projects the company's financial position based on well-substantiated assumptions and explains how the figures have been determined.

FINANCIAL PLAN   The *financial plan* presents financial forecasts in the form of pro forma statements. In the words of Paul Gompers, a Harvard professor,

> One of the major benefits of creating a business plan is that it forces entrepreneurs to confront their company's finances squarely. That's because a business plan isn't complete until entrepreneurs can demonstrate that all the wonderful plans concerning strategy, markets, products, and sales will actually come together to create a business that will be self-sustaining over the short term and profitable over the long term.[15]

And as Rudy Garza, a venture capitalist in Austin, Texas, explains, "The financial plan helps me understand the entrepreneur's thought process about the opportunity."[16]

pro forma statements
Projections of a company's financial statements for up to five years, including balance sheets, income statements, and statements of cash flows, as well as cash budgets.

Pro forma statements, which are projections of the company's financial statements, are presented for up to five years. The forecasts ideally include balance sheets, income statements, and statements of cash flows on an annual basis for three to five years, as well as cash budgets on a monthly basis for the first year and on a quarterly basis for the second and third years. It is vital that the financial projections be supported by well-substantiated assumptions and explanations of how the figures have been determined.

While all the financial statements are important, statements of cash flows deserve special attention, because a business can be profitable but fail if it does not produce positive cash flows. A well-written statement of cash flows identifies the sources of cash—how much will be generated from operations and how much will be raised from investors. It also shows how much money will be devoted to investments in such areas as inventories and equipment. The statement of cash flows should clearly indicate how much cash is needed from prospective investors and for what purpose. (The preparation of pro forma statements and the process of raising needed capital are discussed in Chapters 11 and 12. Chapter 13 presents ways that an investor—and the entrepreneur—can cash out, or exit, the business investment.)

APPENDIX OF SUPPORTING DOCUMENTS The appendix should contain various supplementary materials and attachments to expand the reader's understanding of the plan. These supporting documents include any items referenced in the text of the business plan, such as the résumés of the key investors and owners/managers; photographs of products, facilities, and buildings; professional references; marketing research studies; pertinent published research; and signed contracts of sale.

The fact that it appears at the end of the plan does not mean that the appendix is of secondary importance. First, the reader needs to understand the assumptions underlying the premises set forth in the plan. Also, nothing is more important to a prospective investor than the qualifications of the management team. Thus, the presentation of the management team's résumés is no small matter, so each one should be carefully prepared.

Each chapter in this section (Part 3) of the book, with the exception of Chapter 10, ends with a special set of exercises to walk you through the process of writing a business plan. These exercise sets consist of questions to be thoughtfully considered and answered. They are entitled "The Business Plan: Laying the Foundation," because they deal with issues that are important to starting a new venture and provide guidelines for preparing the different sections of a business plan.

Making an Effective Written Presentation

When it comes to making an effective presentation, we should emphasize again that the quality of a business plan ultimately depends on the quality of the underlying business opportunity. We repeat, *the plan is not the business.* A poorly conceived new venture idea cannot be rescued by a good presentation. But, on the other hand, a good concept may be destroyed by a presentation that fails to communicate effectively.

Entrepreneurs tend to fall prey to a number of mistakes when preparing a business plan. It is critically important that you avoid these mistakes if you want readers to give your business plan serious consideration. Below are recommendations that will help you avoid some of the common mistakes.[17]

INSIST ON CONFIDENTIALITY Prominently indicate that all information in the plan is proprietary and confidential. Number every copy of the plan, and account for each outstanding copy by requiring all recipients of the plan to acknowledge receipt in writing. When a startup is based on proprietary technology, be cautious about divulging certain information—the details of a technological design, for example, or the highly sensitive specifics of a marketing strategy—even to a prospective investor. But, while you should be cautious about releasing proprietary information, entrepreneurs at times become overly anxious about someone stealing their idea and using it. Certainly, it does happen on rare occasions, and you want to protect yourself, *but do not become fixated on the notion that someone may take your idea and beat you to the market with it.* Remember, the plan is not the key to your success; your execution is the key! If someone can "out-execute" you, then you may not be the right person to start the business. Besides, being paranoid about someone stealing your idea is usually a turnoff for investors and can discourage you from moving forward with your enterprise.

USE GOOD GRAMMAR Nothing turns off a reader faster than a poorly written business plan. Find a good editor, and then review and revise, revise, revise.

4. Offer practical advice on writing a business plan.

LIMIT THE PRESENTATION TO A REASONABLE LENGTH   The goal is not to write a *long* business plan, but to write a *good* business plan. People who read business plans appreciate brevity and view it as an indication of your ability to identify and describe in an organized way the important factors that will determine the success of your business. In all sections of your plan, especially the executive summary, get to the point quickly.

GO FOR AN ATTRACTIVE, PROFESSIONAL APPEARANCE   To add interest and aid readers' comprehension, make liberal but effective use of visual aids, such as graphs, exhibits, and tabular summaries. The plan should be in a three-ring loose-leaf binder to facilitate future revisions, as opposed to being bound like a book and printed on shiny paper with flashy images and graphs.

PROVIDE SOLID EVIDENCE FOR ANY CLAIMS   Too often, entrepreneurs make broad statements without good, solid data to support them. Factual support must be supplied for any claims or assurances made. When promising to provide superior service or explaining the attractiveness of the market, for example, include strong supporting evidence. In short, the plan must be believable.

DESCRIBE THE PRODUCT IN LAY TERMS   Present your product/service in simple, understandable terms, and avoid the temptation to use too much industry jargon. Answer the question "Why would anyone want to buy our product or service?"

EMPHASIZE THE QUALIFICATIONS OF THE MANAGEMENT TEAM   Typically, investors look first at the management team, searching for relevant experience, and only after that will they assess the product/service. Without the right people in management, investors seldom will have any interest.

ANALYZE THE MARKET THOROUGHLY   Everyone has competitors. Saying, "We have no competition," is almost certain to make readers skeptical. You must show in your plan where your business will fit in the market and what your competitors' strengths and weaknesses are. If possible, include estimates of their market shares and profit levels.

INCLUDE FINANCIAL STATEMENTS THAT ARE NEITHER OVERLY DETAILED NOR INCOMPLETE   Entrepreneurs tend to err either by providing incomplete financial statements or by including page after page of monotonous financial data. They also fall prey to being overly optimistic, even to the point of wishful thinking, which gives investors the impression that they have no idea what it takes to run a company. In terms of completeness, you should provide an exhaustive list of the assumptions that underlie the financial information. Most importantly, make sure that the numbers make sense.

DON'T HIDE WEAKNESSES—IDENTIFY POTENTIAL FATAL FLAWS   One difficult aspect of writing a business plan is effectively dealing with problems or weaknesses—and every business has them. An entrepreneur, wanting to make a good impression, may become so infatuated with an opportunity that he or she cannot see potential fatal flaws.

For instance, an entrepreneur might fail to ask, "What is the possible impact of new technology, e-commerce, or changes in consumer demand on the proposed venture?" And ignoring or glossing over a negative issue when trying to raise financing for the venture can prove damaging, even fatal. If there are weaknesses in the plan, the investors will find them. At that point, an investor's question will be "What else haven't you told me?" The best way to properly handle weaknesses is to be open and straightforward and to have an action plan that effectively addresses the problem. To put it another way, *integrity matters*.

The guidelines just listed are designed to help you avoid elements that are unacceptable to frequent readers of business plans. If you ignore these recommendations, the plan will detract from the opportunity itself, and you may lose the chance to capture a good opportunity. Ideally, you should have experienced entrepreneurs critique the business concept and the effectiveness of the business plan presentation. They know the minefields to avoid.

Presenting the Business Plan to Investors

5. Explain what investors look for in a business plan.

Many small firms do not seek outside capital, except in the form of small loans. But where there is a substantial need for outside capital, both investors and lenders use the business plan to understand the new venture, the type of product or service it will offer, the nature of the market, and the qualifications of the entrepreneur and the management team. In today's world, a sophisticated investor will rarely consider investing in a new business before he or she has reviewed a properly prepared business plan.

The significance of the business plan in dealing with investors is aptly expressed by Mark Stevens, an advisor to small businesses:

> If you are inclined to view the business plan as just another piece of useless paperwork, it's time for an attitude change. When you are starting out, investors will justifiably want to know a lot about you and your qualifications for running a business and will want to see a step-by-step plan for how you intend to make it a success.[18]

If you are preparing a business plan in order to seek outside capital, you must understand the investor's basic perspective and see the world as the investor sees it—that is, you must think as the investor thinks. However, most entrepreneurs perceive a new venture very differently than an investor does. The entrepreneur characteristically focuses on the positive potential of the startup—what will happen if everything goes right. The prospective investor, on the other hand, plays the role of the skeptic, thinking more about what could go wrong.

Contrary to what many entrepreneurs think, it is not about who is right and who is wrong; both perspectives have merit when evaluating a venture opportunity. As Jeffrey Bussgang, who has been both an entrepreneur and a venture capitalist, advises, "You should think like [an investor] and act like an entrepreneur."[19] In this way, you bring to the analysis both the energy of the entrepreneur and the discipline of the investor.

At the most basic level, prospective investors have a single goal: to maximize potential return on an investment through cash flows that will be received, while minimizing the risk they are taking. Even investors in startups who are thought to be risk takers want to minimize their exposure to risk. Like any informed investor, they look for ways to shift risk to others, usually to the entrepreneur.

Given the fundamentally different perspectives of the investor and the entrepreneur, the important question becomes "How do I write a business plan that will capture a prospective investor's interest?" There is no easy answer, but two facts are relevant: Investors have a short attention span, and certain features attract investors, while others repel them.

The Investor's Short Attention Span

Kenneth Blanchard, Don Hotson, and Ethan Willis wrote a great book about being a "one-minute entrepreneur," an entrepreneur who practices principles that can be applied quickly and produce great results.[20] Investors in startups and early-stage companies are, in a sense, one-minute investors. Because they receive so many business plans, they cannot possibly read them all in any detailed fashion. Tim Smith, a former officer of the Capital Southwest Corporation, a Dallas-based venture capital firm, observed, "We receive some 300 or more plans per year but invest in only three or four firms in any given year. Thus, we simply do not have the luxury of analyzing each opportunity thoroughly."[21]

At the annual Rice University business plan competition in Houston, Texas, competing teams from different universities have only 15 minutes to present their business venture. In the 2009 competition, the total prize money was $800,000, with the first-place winner receiving $350,000. Not bad for a 15-minute presentation! Of course, there is more involved than just the presentation, but the point is that you should be able to present your concept concisely and effectively.

An example of an investor's short attention span was witnessed by one of the authors when he delivered an entrepreneur's business plan to a prospective investor with whom he had a personal relationship. The plan was well written, clearly identifying a need. While the investor was courteous and listened carefully, he made a decision not to consider the opportunity in a matter of five minutes. A quick read of the executive summary did not spark his interest, and the discussion quickly changed to other matters. We may be overstating the case when we refer to investors in startups and early-stage firms as one-minute investors, but even five minutes is not much time to work with.

Business Plan Features That Attract or Repel Investors

In order to raise capital from outside investors, the business plan must speak the investors' language. The entrepreneur must know what is important and what is not important to investors and how to present the business idea or concept in a way that is meaningful to them. Otherwise, the entrepreneur will immediately lose credibility—and a potential source of financing.

For one thing, investors are more *market-oriented* than *product-oriented,* realizing that most patented inventions never earn a dime for the inventors. The essence of the entrepreneurial process is to identify new products or services that meet an identifiable customer need. Thus, it is essential for the entrepreneur to appreciate investors' concerns about the target customers' response to a new product or service.

Like any readers of a business plan, investors require that the plan be credible. On several occasions, the authors have had the opportunity to watch entrepreneurs present business plans to prospective investors. More than once, an entrepreneur has presented financial projections that were extremely optimistic, being beyond believable. The opportunity would still have been attractive with more conservative projections. But instead of adjusting the forecasts to make them more credible to the investors, the entrepreneur continued to argue that the numbers were already "conservative." It's no surprise that investors declined to invest in these deals.

Bill Sahlman at the Harvard Business School has seen a lot of business plans in his time and has heard most of the "lines" used by entrepreneurs when presenting to investors. With tongue only a little in cheek, Sahlman tells how investors interpret an entrepreneur's language in his "Glossary of Business Plan Terms" (see Exhibit 6-6). In writing and when presenting a business plan, you may want to keep in mind how skeptical your audience is likely to be. As Sahlman illustrates, a presentation that is not believable to investors is a deal killer.

Investors are quickly disillusioned by plans that contain page after page of detailed computer-generated financial projections, suggesting—intentionally or unintentionally—that the entrepreneur can predict with great accuracy what will happen. The experienced investor knows this isn't the case.

Finally, it should be understood that the business plan is not a legal document for actually raising needed capital. When it comes time to solicit investment, a *prospectus,* or *offering memorandum,*

prospectus (offering memorandum)
A document that contains all the information necessary to satisfy federal and state requirements for warning potential investors about the possible risks of the investment.

LIVING THE DREAM:

entrepreneurial experiences

College Students Write Business Plans, Too

A large number of colleges are now offering business plan competitions to prepare young aspiring entrepreneurs for starting businesses and to provide some seed capital to get them started. Here are the stories of three students who competed in these events:

Alex Farkas and Greg Rosborough, both 24 years old, and Stephen Tanenbaum, 25, won $20,000 in a business plan competition, combined with an additional $80,000 contributed from friends and family. The money helped them launch their business plan idea, Ugallery.com. The University of Arizona graduates attended three competitions during their senior year, including one in Canada. "I think we succeeded in the business plan competitions because our business model was very realistic," says Tanenbaum.

The business plan developed by 26-year-old Dee Murthy and 27-year-old Andres Izquieta also won an award. But [along with] thousands of dollars in prize money from the University of Southern California, which hosted the competition, Five Four Clothing had something else working in its favor: the right place and the right timing. Los Angeles proved to be the ideal location for the business partners to launch their hip urban men's line of apparel. Murthy says his friends started wearing Five Four to local clubs, and soon they were in talks with hot boutiques like Fred Segal.

For 28-year-old entrepreneur Rodrigo Veloso, winning the Latin American division of the Moot Corp Competition while a graduate student in Sao Paulo, Brazil, provided him with the contacts he needed to introduce Brazilian coconut water to the U.S. As the first-place winner, Veloso was invited to attend the global competition at the University of Texas at Austin. Though he didn't win, Veloso gained valuable business contacts and met his now-wife, Emilie Fritz….Veloso relied on his new-found connections when he moved to Los Angeles to turn his plan into a business. Upon his arrival, Veloso met with investors who introduced him to other investors. He combined the seed money from one investor and contributions from friends and family with his own savings to create O.N.E. World Enterprises.

Source: Adapted from Kristin Edelhauser, "College Business Plans That Made the Grade," *Entrepreneur*, http://www.entrepreneur.com/startingabusiness/businessplans/article182608.html, accessed November 2008.

must be prepared. This document contains all the information necessary to satisfy federal and state requirements for warning potential investors about the possible risks of the investment. But because the prospectus alone is not an effective marketing document with which to sell a concept, an entrepreneur must first use the business plan to create interest in the startup. He or she should then follow up with a formal offering memorandum to those investors who seem genuinely interested.

Resources for Business Plan Preparation

When writing a business plan, it is important to know what works and what does not work. There are many books, websites, and computer software packages that you can use to guide you step by step through the preparation of a business plan.[22] (A listing of some of these materials appears at the end of this chapter.) Such

6. Identify available sources of assistance in preparing a business plan.

EXHIBIT

What They Say . . .	. . . and What They Really Mean
We conservatively project . . .	We read a book that said we had to be a $50 million company in five years, and we reverse-engineered the numbers.
We took our best guess and divided by 2.	We accidentally divided by 0.5.
We project a 10% margin.	We did not modify any of the assumptions in the business plan template that we downloaded from the Internet.
The project is 98% complete.	To complete the remaining 2% will take as long as it took to create the initial 98% but will cost twice as much.
Our business model is proven . . .	If you take the evidence from the past week for the best of our 50 locations and extrapolate it for all the others.
We have a six-month lead.	We tried not to find out how many other people have a six-month lead.
We only need a 10% market share.	So do the other 50 entrants getting funded.
Customers are clamoring for our product.	We have not yet asked them to pay for it. Also, all of our current customers are relatives.
We are the low-cost producer.	We have not produced anything yet, but we are confident that we will be able to.
We have no competition.	Only IBM, Microsoft, Netscape, and Sun have announced plans to enter the business.
Our management team has a great deal of experience . . .	Consuming the product or service.
A select group of investors is considering the plan.	We mailed a copy of the plan to everyone in Pratt's Guide.
We seek a value-added investor.	We are looking for a passive, dumb-as-rocks investor.
If you invest on our terms, you will earn a 68% rate of return.	If everything that could ever conceivably go right does go right, you might get your money back.

Source: William A. Sahlman, "How to Write a Great Business Plan," *Harvard Business Review*, July–August 1997, p. 106.

resources can be invaluable. In general, however, you should resist the temptation to adapt an existing business plan for your own use. Changing the numbers and some of the verbiage of another firm's business plan is simply not effective.

Computer-Aided Business Planning

The use of a computer greatly facilitates preparation of a business plan. Its word-processing capabilities, for example, can speed up the writing of the narrative sections of the report. Computer spreadsheets are likewise helpful for preparing the financial statements needed in the plan.

A number of business plan software packages have been designed to help an entrepreneur think through the important issues in starting a new company and organize his or her thoughts to create an effective presentation. However, these software packages are not capable of producing a unique plan and thus may limit an entrepreneur's creativity and flexibility. Just plain old common sense is also required when using business plan software. One of the authors recently received a business plan that was almost 80 pages in length. When questioned about the excessive length, the entrepreneur responded, "By the time I answered all the questions in the software package, that's the length that resulted."

Remember, there is no simple procedure for writing a business plan—no "formula for success"—despite what software advertisements may claim. If you recognize their limitations, however, you can use business plan software packages to facilitate the process.

Professional Assistance in Business Planning

As previously discussed, company founders are most notably doers—and evidence suggests that they had better be, if the venture is to be successful. But most entrepreneurs lack the breadth of experience and know-how, as well as the inclination, needed for planning.

An entrepreneur who is not able to answer tough questions about the business may need a business planning advisor—someone accustomed to working with small companies, startups, and owners who lack financial management experience. Such advisors include accountants, marketing specialists, attorneys (preferably with an entrepreneurial mindset), incubator organizations, small business development corporations (SBDCs), and regional and local economic development offices.

An investment banker or financial intermediary can draw up a business plan as part of a firm's overall fundraising efforts. Also, a well-chosen advisor will have contacts you lack and may even help you reformulate your business plan entirely.[23] However, using a business planning advisor will cost you; consultants frequently charge an hourly fee as well as a contingency percentage based on the amount raised.

The Small Business Administration (SBA) and the Service Corps of Retired Executives (SCORE) can also be helpful. Both organizations have programs to introduce business owners to volunteer experts who will advise them. SCORE, in particular, is a source for all types of business advice, such as how to write a business plan, investigating market potential, and managing cash flow. SCORE counselors work out of local chapters throughout the United States and can be found by contacting the national office.

Another source of assistance is the FastTrac Entrepreneurial Training Program sponsored by the Kauffman Center for Entrepreneurial Leadership in Kansas City, Missouri. Located in universities, chambers of commerce, and SBDCs across the country, the FastTrac program teaches the basics of product development, concept recognition, financing strategies, and marketing research, while helping entrepreneurs create a written business plan in small, well-organized increments.

You definitely have options when it comes to seeking out business plan assistance. However, if you choose to hire a consultant, the following suggestions may help you avoid some costly mistakes when hiring a consultant:[24]

1. *Get referrals.* Ask colleagues, acquaintances and professionals such as bankers, accountants, and lawyers for the names of business plan consultants they recommend. A good referral goes a long way to easing any concerns you may have. Few consultants advertise anyway, so referrals may be your only option.

2. *Look for a fit.* Find a consultant who is an expert in helping businesses like yours. Ideally, the consultant should have lots of experience with companies of similar size and age in related industries. Avoid general business experts or those who lack experience in your particular field.

3. *Check references.* Get the names of at least three clients the consultant has helped to write business plans. Call the former clients and ask about the consultant's performance. Was the consultant's final fee in line with the original estimate? Was the plan completed on time? Did it serve the intended purpose?

4. *Get it in writing.* Have a legal contract outlining the consultant's services. It should state in detail the fee, when it will be paid, and under what circumstances. And make sure you get a detailed written description of what the consultant must do to earn the fee. Whether it's an hourly rate or a flat fee isn't as important as each party knowing exactly what's expected of them.

Keep in mind that securing help in business plan preparation does not relieve the entrepreneur of the responsibility of being the primary planner. Her or his ideas remain essential to producing a plan that is realistic and believable.

Keeping the Right Perspective

7. Maintain the proper perspective when writing a business plan.

To summarize, we contend that the business plan has an important place in starting and growing a business. As suggested in the chapter, writing an effective plan is important both for internal purposes and for telling the firm's story to outsiders who can contribute to the firm's success. But good judgment should be used in deciding if and how much to plan, given your unique circumstances. No single answer can be applied to all situations. Furthermore, it is important to avoid the misconception, held by far too many aspiring entrepreneurs, that a good business plan will ensure success. The business plan, no matter how beneficial, is not the business. Building a good business involves much more than just planning. A good business plan leads to a successful company only when it is effectively executed by the entrepreneur and the management team.

Writing a business plan should be thought of as an ongoing process and not as the means to an end. In fact, when it comes to writing a plan, the process is just as important as the final outcome, which some entrepreneurs have difficulty accepting, given their orientation to "bottom line" results. But this point deserves to be repeated: *Writing a business plan is primarily an ongoing process and only secondarily the means to an outcome. The process is just as important as—if not more so than—the finished product.*

While your plan will represent your vision and goals for the firm, it will rarely reflect what actually happens. With a startup, too many unexpected events can affect the final outcome. Thus, a business plan is in large part an opportunity for an entrepreneur and management team to think about the potential key drivers of a venture's success or failure. Anticipating different scenarios and the ensuing consequences can significantly enhance an entrepreneur's adaptability—an essential quality for an entrepreneur, when so much is uncertain.

Now that you are aware of the role of the business plan in a new venture, you are ready for Chapters 7 through 13, which will closely examine each of the plan's components.

How I see it: Winston Wolfe on Staying Focused

If someone asked me what I felt is the single most important personality trait for an entrepreneur, I would say it's the ability to stay focused.

First of all, you must stay focused on the goals you have for your company. Don't lose sight of the vision you have in your business plan. Keep in mind that you can't be everything to everybody. If you try, you'll likely end up being nothing to everybody.

I have always been amazed at how easy it is for the original focus of a meeting to go astray. If you are meeting with three or four of your key employees, keep the focus of the discussion going in the proper direction. Solve the problem, and don't get distracted. And, in the process, you'll teach your employees the value of staying focused.

Being intense and focused will not only help you solve problems—it will make you a more effective leader.

1. Explain the purpose and objectives of business plans.

- A business plan is a document that sets out the basic idea underlying a business and describes related startup considerations. It should describe where the entrepreneur is presently, indicate where she or he wants to go, and outline how she or he proposes to get there.

- A business plan has three basic objectives: (1) to identify the nature and the context of a business opportunity, (2) to present the approach the entrepreneur plans to take to exploit the opportunity, and (3) to recognize factors that will determine whether the venture will be successful.

2. Give the rationale for writing (or not writing) a business plan when starting a new venture.

- Studies attempting to test whether entrepreneurs who have business plans do better than those who don't have produced mixed results. Some findings suggest a relationship; others do not.

- What ultimately matters is not writing a plan, but implementing it. The goal is to execute the plan.

- An entrepreneur must find the right balance between planning and becoming operational.

- The benefits of a business plan depend on the individual circumstances surrounding a startup.

- Most entrepreneurs need the discipline that comes with writing a business plan. A written plan helps to ensure systematic, complete coverage of the important factors to be considered in starting a new business.

- A business plan helps an entrepreneur communicate his or her vision to current and prospective employees of the firm.

- By enhancing the firm's credibility, a business plan serves as an effective selling tool with prospective customers and suppliers, as well as investors.

- A mini-plan is a short form of a business plan that presents only the most important issues and projections for the business.

- A comprehensive plan is beneficial when you are, for example, describing a new opportunity (startup), facing significant change in the business or the external environment (changing demographics, new legislation, developing industry trends), or explaining a complex business situation.

3. Describe the preferred content and format for a business plan.

- The opportunity, the resources, the entrepreneurial team, the financing structure, and the context of an opportunity are all interdependent factors that should be given consideration when thinking about the content of a business plan.

- Key sections of a business plan are the (1) cover page, (2) table of contents, (3) executive summary, (4) industry, target customer, and competitor analysis, (5) company description, (6) product/service plan, (7) marketing plan, (8) operations and development plan, (9) management team, (10) critical risks, (11) offering, (12) financial plan, and (13) appendix of supporting documents.

4. Offer practical advice on writing a business plan.

- Insist on confidentiality.
- Use good grammar.
- Keep the presentation to a reasonable length.
- Go for an attractive, professional appearance.
- Provide solid evidence for any claims.
- Describe the product in lay terms.
- Emphasize the quality of the management team.
- Analyze the market thoroughly.
- Include financial statements that are neither overly detailed nor incomplete.
- Don't hide weaknesses; try to identify potential fatal flaws.

5. Explain what investors look for in a business plan.

- When writing the business plan, remember that (1) investors have a short attention span and (2) certain features appeal to investors, while others are distinctly unappealing.

- In seeking financing, an entrepreneur must first use the business plan to create interest in the startup and then follow up with a formal offering memorandum to solicit investment from those investors who seem genuinely interested.

6. Identify available sources of assistance in preparing a business plan.

- A variety of books, websites, and computer software packages are available to assist in the preparation of a business plan.

- Professionals with planning expertise, such as attorneys, accountants, and marketing specialists, can provide useful suggestions and assistance in the preparation of a business plan.

- The Small Business Administration (SBA), the Service Corps of Retired Executives (SCORE), and the FastTrac Entrepreneurial Training Program can also be helpful.

7. Maintain the proper perspective when writing a business plan.

- Despite the potential benefits of a well-drafted plan, good judgment should be used in deciding how much to plan in view of the specific circumstances.

- The business plan, no matter how beneficial, is not the business. A good business plan leads to a successful company only when it is effectively executed by the entrepreneur and the management team.

- A business plan can be viewed as an opportunity for the entrepreneur and the management team to think about the potential key drivers of a venture's success or failure.

Key Terms

business plan, p. 149

mini-plan, p. 152

comprehensive plan, p. 152

executive summary, p. 155

product/service plan, p. 159

marketing plan, p. 159

operations and development plan, p. 159

management team, p. 159

critical risks, p. 160

offering, p. 160

financial plan, p. 160

pro forma statements, p. 160

prospectus (offering memorandum), p. 164

Discussion Questions

1. Describe what entrepreneurs mean when they talk about a business plan.

2. When should you write a business plan? When might it not be necessary or even advisable to write a plan?

3. Explain the two types of business plans. In what situation(s) would you use each type of plan?

4. Why is the executive summary so important?

5. How might an entrepreneur's perspective differ from that of an investor in terms of the business plan?

6. Describe the major sections to be included in a business plan.

7. If the income statement of a financial plan shows that the business will be profitable, why is there a need for a statement of cash flows?

8. Describe common mistakes that entrepreneurs make in writing a business plan.

9. Discuss whether a sophisticated investor would really make a decision based on a five-minute review of a business plan.

10. Investors are said to be more market-oriented than product-oriented. What does this mean? What is the logic behind this orientation?

You Make the Call

SITUATION 1

You want to start an online clothing store and need information about the size of the market for the marketing section of your business plan. From a Google search, you found that Americans spent $18.3 billion online for apparel, accessories, and footwear in 2008 and that the forecast for their spending on these items in 2009 is $22.1 billion. You have also researched publicly traded apparel companies, like Gap, to discover trends in online sales for these firms.

Question 1 Why is your research thus far inadequate for what you need to know?

Question 2 Do you think it will be difficult to find all the information you need?

Question 3 What else might you do to find the information you need?

SITUATION 2

A young journalist is contemplating launching a new magazine that will feature wildlife, plant life, and nature around the world. The prospective entrepreneur intends for each issue to contain several feature articles—about the dangers and benefits of forest fires, the features of Rocky Mountain National Park, wild flowers found at high altitudes, and the danger of acid rain, for example. The magazine will make extensive use of color photographs, and its articles will be technically accurate and interestingly written. Unlike *National Geographic*, the proposed publication will avoid articles dealing with the general culture and confine itself to topics closely related to the natural world. Suppose you are a prospective investor examining a business plan prepared by this journalist.

Question 1 What are the most urgent questions you would want the marketing plan to answer?

Question 2 What details would you look for in the management plan?

Question 3 Do you think this entrepreneur would need to raise closer to $1 million or $10 million in startup capital? Why?

Question 4 At first glance, would you consider the opportunity potentially attractive? Why or why not?

SITUATION 3

John Martin and John Rose decided to start a new business to manufacture noncarbonated soft drinks. They believed that their location in East Texas, close to high-quality water, would give them a competitive edge. Although Martin and Rose had never worked together, Martin had 17 years of experience in the soft drink industry. Rose had recently sold his firm and had funds to help finance the venture; however, the partners needed to raise additional money from outside investors. Both men were excited about the opportunity and spent almost 18 months developing their business plan. The first paragraph of their executive summary reflected their excitement:

> The "New Age" beverage market is the result of a spectacular boom in demand for drinks with nutritional value from environmentally safe ingredients and waters that come from deep, clear springs free of chemicals and pollutants. Argon Beverage Corporation will produce and market a full line of sparkling fruit drinks, flavored waters, and sports drinks that are of the highest quality and purity. These drinks have the same delicious taste appeal as soft drinks while using the most healthful fruit juices, natural sugars, and the purest spring water, the hallmark of the "New Age" drink market.

With the help of a well-developed plan, the two men were successful in raising the necessary capital to begin their business. They leased facilities and started production. However, after almost two years, the plan's goals were not being met. There were cost overruns, and profits were not nearly up to expectations.

Question 1 What problems might have contributed to the firm's poor performance?

Question 2 Although several problems were encountered in implementing the business plan, the primary reason for the low profits turned out to be embezzlement. Martin was diverting company resources for personal use, even using some of the construction materials purchased by the company to build his own house. What could Rose have done to avoid this situation? What are his options after the fact?

Experiential Exercises

1. Appendix A provides the complete business plan for Atayne, LLC. Based on your reading of this chapter, write a one-page report on what you like about the plan and what you do not like.

2. A former chef wants to start a business to supply temporary kitchen help (such as chefs, sauce cooks, bakers, and meat cutters) to restaurants in need of staff during busy periods. Prepare a one-page report explaining which section or sections of the business plan would be most crucial to this new business and why.

3. Suppose that you wish to start a tutoring service for college students in elementary accounting courses. List the benefits you would realize from preparing a written business plan.

4. Interview a person who has started a business within the past five years. Prepare a report describing the extent to which the entrepreneur engaged in preliminary planning and his or her views about the value of business plans.

Small Business & Entrepreneurship Resource Center

The Small Business and Entrepreneurship Resource Center offers complete small business management resources through a comprehensive database that covers all major areas of starting, operating, and maintaining a business from financing, management, marketing, accounting, taxes, and more. Use the access code that came with your new book to access the site and perform the exercises in each chapter.

The Small Business Development Center (SBDC) is a federally and locally funded small business assistance program that offers advisory services at no charge.

They can offer business planning assistance as the firm is developing and growing. A recent study has found that entrepreneurs who used SBDC services and then later started their businesses had higher than average rates of survival. Discuss the types of services that are offered by the SBDC, and how their counseling services are different than consulting services.

Sources: Chrisman, J.J. and E. McMullan, "A Preliminary Assessment of Outsider Assistance as a Knowledge Resource: The Longer-Term Impact of New Venture Counseling," *Entrepreneurship: Theory and Practice* 24, 3 (Spring 2000): p. 37.

Lesonsky, Rieva, "The long road: enlightening travels find SBDC funding reaching new lows, generous big guys and inspiring entrepreneurs (EDITOR'S NOTE)," *Entrepreneur* 33, 11 (Nov 2005): 10(1).

Case 6

BENJAPON'S RAISING CAPITAL FOR A THAI RESTAURANT. (P. 634)

Benjapon Jivasantikarn is planning to start Benjapon's, a Thai restaurant, after graduating from Babson College. In recent years, Asian fast casual restaurant players have begun to emerge in various regions in the U.S. This is Jivasantikarn's story of joining this emerging market. To do so she'll need to raise the needed capital and prepare a business plan.

ALTERNATIVE CASES FOR CHAPTER 6

Case 7, eHarmony, p. 636

The Business Plan: Laying the Foundation

Part 3 (Chapters 6 through 13) deals with issues that are important in starting a new venture. This chapter presented an overview of the business plan and its preparation. Chapters 7 through 13 focus on major segments of the business plan, such as the marketing plan, the organizational and development plan, the location plan, the financial plan, and the exit plan. After you have carefully studied these chapters, you will have the knowledge you need to prepare a business plan.

Since applying what you study facilitates learning, we have included, at the end of each chapter in Part 3 (except for Chapter 10), a list of important questions that need to be addressed in preparing a particular segment of a business plan. In this chapter, we also include lists of books, websites, and software packages useful for preparing business plans.

Company Description Questions

Now that you have learned the main concepts of business plan preparation, you can begin the process of creating a business plan by writing a general company description. In thinking about the key issues in starting a new business, respond to the following questions:

1. When and where is the business to start?
2. What is the history of the company?
3. What are the company's objectives?
4. What changes have been made in structure and/or ownership?
5. In what stage of development is the company?
6. What has been achieved to date?
7. What is the company's distinctive competence?
8. What are the basic nature and activity of the business?
9. What is its primary product or service?
10. What customers will be served?
11. What is the company's form of organization?
12. What are the current and projected economic states of the industry?
13. Does the company intend to become a publicly traded company or an acquisition candidate, or do the owners want to transfer ownership to the next generation of the family?

Books on Preparing Business Plans

Abrams, Rhonda M. M., *Successful Business Plan: Secrets and Strategies* (Atlanta, GA: Rhonda, Inc., 2003).

Bangs, David H., *Business Plans Made Easy,* 3rd ed. (*Entrepreneur Made Easy* Series, 2005).

Bangs, David H., *The Business Planning Guide: Creating a Winning Plan for Success,* 9th ed. (New York: Kaplan Professional Company, 2002).

Burke, Franklin, Jill E. Kapron, and JIAN Tools for Sale, Inc., *BizPlanBuilder Express: A Guide to Creating a Business Plan with BizPlanBuilder,* 2nd ed. (Mason, OH: South-Western, 2007).

Bygrave, William D., and Andrew Zacharakis (eds.), *The Portable MBA in Entrepreneurship,* 3rd ed. (New York: John Wiley & Sons, 2003).

Deloitte & Touche, LLP, *Writing an Effective Business Plan* (New York: Author, 2003).

Gumpert, David E., *How to Really Create a Successful Business Plan,* 4th ed. (Needham, MA: Lauson Publishing, 2003).

Kawasaki, Guy, *The Art of the Start: The Time-Tested, Battle-Hardened Guide for Anyone Starting Anything* (New York: Portfolio, 2004).

King, Jan B., *Business Plans to Game Plans: A Practical System for Turning Strategies into Action,* rev. ed. (Hoboken, NJ: John Wiley & Sons, 2004).

Mancuso, Joseph R., *How to Write a Winning Business Plan* (New York: Simon & Schuster, 2006).

Patsula, Peter J., and William Nowik (eds.), *Successful Business Planning in 30 Days: A Step-by-Step Guide for Writing a Business Plan and Starting Your Own Business,* 2nd ed. (Singapore: Patsula Media, 2002).

Peterson, Steven D., and Peter E. Jaret, *Business Plans Kit for Dummies* (Indianapolis, IN: For Dummies, 2005).

Pinson, Linda, *Anatomy of a Business Plan: A Step-by-Step Guide to Building a Business and Securing Your Company's Future* (Chicago: Enterprise/Dearborn, 2004.)

Rich, Stanley R., and David E. Gumpert, *Business Plans That Win $$$: Lessons from the MIT Enterprise Forum* (New York: HarperCollins, 1987).

Rogoff, Edward, *Bankable Business Plans* (Mason, OH: South-Western, 2003).

Sutton, Garrett, and Robert T. Kiyosaki, *The ABC's of Writing Winning Business Plans: How to Prepare a Business Plan That Others Will Want to Read—and Invest In* (New York: Rich Dad's Advisors, 2005).

Tiffany, Paul, and Steven Peterson, *Business Plans for Dummies,* 2nd ed. (Indianapolis, IN: For Dummies, 2004).

Timmons, Jeffrey A., Andrew Zacharakis, and Stephen Spinelli, *Business Plans That Work* (New York: McGraw-Hill, 2004).

Tooch, David, *Building a Business Plan,* 2nd ed. (Upper Saddle River, NJ: Prentice Hall, 2004).

Articles on Preparing Business Plans

Bygrave, W. D., J. E. Lange, and T. Evans, "Do Business Plan Competitions Produce Winning Businesses?" *Frontiers of Entrepreneurship Research*, 2004, p. 275.

Chrisman, J. J., E. McMullan, and J. Hall, "The Influence of Guided Preparation on Long-Term Performance of New Ventures," *Journal of Business Venturing*, Vol. 20 (2005), pp. 769–791.

Delmar, Frederic and Scott Shane, "Does Business Planning Facilitate the Development of New Ventures?" *Strategic Management Journal*, Vol. 24, No. 12 (2003), pp. 1165–1185.

Gartner, W. B., and J. Liao, "Cents and Sensemaking in Pre-Venture Business Planning: Evidence from the Panel Study of Entrepreneurial Dynamics," *Frontiers of Entrepreneurship Research*, 2005, p. 298.

Guber, M., "Uncovering the Value of Planning in New Venture Creation: A Process and Contingency Perspective," *Journal of Business Venturing*, Vol. 22 (2007), pp. 782–807.

Honig, B., and T. Karlsson, "Institutional Forces and the Written Business Plan," *Journal of Management*, Vol. 30, No. 1 (2004), pp. 29–48.

Hormozi, Amir M., et al., "Business Plans for New or Small Businesses: Paving the Way to Success," *Management Decision,* Vol. 40, Nos. 7 and 8 (2002), pp. 755–763.

Karlsson, Thomas, Benson Honig, and Wilfrid Laurrier, "Business Planning Practices in New Ventures: An Institutional Perspective," paper presented at the Babson Conference, April 2007.

Lange, Julian E., et al., "Pre-Startup Formal Business Plans and Post-Startup Performance: A Study of 116 Ventures," *Venture Capital Journal*, Vol. 9, No. 4 (2007), pp. 237–256.

Liao, J., and W. B. Gartner, "The Effects of Pre-Venture Plan Timing and Perceived Environmental Uncertainty on the Persistence of Emerging Firms," *Small Business Economics*, Vol. 27 (2006), pp. 23–40.

Mason, C., and M. Stark, "What Do Investors Look for in a Business Plan?: A Comparison of the Investment Criteria of Bankers, Venture Capitalists, and Business Angels," *International Small Business Journal*, Vol. 22, No. 3 (2004), pp. 227–248.

Melloan, J., "*Inc.*'s 5000 Fastest Growing Privately Owned Companies," *Inc.*, August 2007.

Perry, Stephen C., "The Relationship Between Written Business Plans and the Failure of Small Business in the U.S.," *Journal of Small Business Management*, Vol. 39, No. 2 (2001), pp. 201–208.

Rich, Stanley R., and David E. Gumpert, "How to Write a Winning Business Plan," *Harvard Business Review,* Vol. 63, No. 3 (May–June 1985), pp. 156–166.

Sahlman, William A., "How to Write a Great Business Plan," *Harvard Business Review,* Vol. 75, No. 4 (July-August 1997), pp. 114–121.

Schilit, W. K., "How to Write a Winning Business Plan," *Business Horizons,* Vol. 30, No. 5 (1987), pp. 13–22.

Shane, Scott, and Frederick Delmar, "Planning for the Market: Business Planning Before Marketing and the Continuation of Organizing Efforts," *Journal of Business Venturing,* Vol. 19 (2004), pp. 767–785.

Online Resources for Preparing Business Plans

BPlans.com, Inc., *BPlans.com: The Business Planning Experts,* http://www.bplans.com. Designed for self-preparers by PaloAlto Software; provides advice, sample plans, and links to many consultants.

Business Confidant, Inc., *Business Confidant: Your Business Planning Specialist,* http://businessconfidant.com. Provides strategic thinking, technical writing, and financial analytical skills needed to produce professional, investor-ready business plans.

Business PlanWare, *Business Plan Software,* http://www.planware.org. Features financial projection and cash flow forecasting software, business plan freeware, white papers, and other tools and resources; based in Ireland.

Business Tools and Advice, *BusinessWeek,* http://allbusiness.businessweek.com/3473091-1.html#2976247. Provides guidelines and examples for writing business plans.

Dow Jones & Company, *Startup Journal: The Wall Street Journal Center for Entrepreneurs,* http://www.startupjournal.com. Features a mini-plan business assumptions test, sample business plans, and calculators for startup costs and cash flow, as well as articles on starting a business.

Entrepreneur.com., *Entrepreneur.com: Solutions for Growing Businesses,* http://www.entrepreneur.com. Has a site search engine through which you can find articles and tips by entering keywords such as *business plan writing.*

Good-to-Go Business Plans Inc., *Good-to-Go Business Plans: Plans for Every Business,* http://www.goodtogobusinessplans.com. Provides a range of services, including business-specific templates in pre-drafted language and other tools and forms.

One Economy Corporation, *Entrepreneur's Center,* http://www.thebeehive.org. Serves as a clearinghouse for weblinks to business-planning articles.

Small Business Administration, *Small Business Administration: Your Small Business Resource,* http://www.sba.gov. The federal government's online business planning and finance resource center classroom and library.

SmartOnline, http://smallbusiness.smartonline.com. Builds a business plan around simple questions posed to the user one by one, with explanations and examples; uses a wizard-driven approach; also integrates forms for incorporation and loan applications from the Small Business Administration.

The Small Business Administration funds programs designed to help entrepreneurs. One of these programs, the Service Corps of Retired Executives (SCORE), has a gallery of detailed downloadable templates for business plans and financial statements on its website (http://www.score.org), under "business toolbox."

Bank websites are another source for business-planning tools and advice. For example, Bank of America has a downloadable outline and business-planning guide at http://www.bankofamerica.com/smallbusiness/resourcecenter/index.cfm?template=rc_startingyourbusiness&context=rc_businessplan.

Software for Preparing Business Plans

JIAN, Inc., *BizPlan*Builder *2007,* http://www.jian.com. A suite of business planning software and other business tools.

PaloAlto Software, *Business Plan Pro 2008,* http://www.paloalto.com. Business plan–creating software featuring over 400 sample business plans.

Smart Online, Inc., *Smart Business Plan Deluxe,* http://www.smartonline.com. Software suite that features the "Smart Wizard," which guides users through the creation of a tailored business plan; includes a "Financial Advisor," which helps to find ways to fund businesses.

7
The Marketing Plan

In the SPOTLIGHT
Spira
http://spirafootwear.com

Why would any startup want to compete in the footwear industry, especially when its focus is on running shoes? The largest firm in the entire industry is Nike, a dominant player that could easily squash a new entrant. Nevertheless, husband-and-wife team Andy Krafsur and Holly Fields thought they had something special that would make their venture a success. Krafsur is chief executive officer and Fields is vice president of marketing and public relations for Spira Footwear, Inc. The basis for the company is the patented WaveSpring® technology, which provides cushioning for both heel and forefoot. Studies indicate significant improvements in both comfort and energy return.

But given the well-known brand names and design features of its competitors, how could Spira find a market niche? As marketing vice president, Fields had to examine Spira's strengths and weaknesses relative to the competition. Despite Spira's advanced technology, Krafsur and Fields understood that customers buy benefits, not features. And they knew they did not have the resources to go head to head with the billion-dollar corporations already established in the marketplace.

Although they had devised a budget to prepare advertising materials and engage in promotional activities such as participating in trade shows, in the beginning they put a lot of

emphasis on public relations. For example, the governing body for track and field in the United States, USA Track & Field, has a rule prohibiting the use of technologies that give a runner an unfair advantage. A spring is considered to be just such a technology. Knowing the company's product would be prohibited under that rule, Fields designed a "Banned in Boston" campaign, offering a $1-million-dollar prize to any athlete who won the Boston Marathon wearing Spira running shoes. The media picked up on the story, mentioning the Spira name and products in both print and broadcast stories during and after the race in 2007. The exposure exceeded any corporate advertising that the small business could have afforded. Creative efforts like this one stretch limited marketing budgets.

Sources: http://spirafootwear.com, accessed July 16, 2009; http://www.usatf.org, accessed July 16, 2009; and http://industries.hoovers.com, accessed July 16, 2009.

LOOKING AHEAD AFTER STUDYING THIS CHAPTER, YOU SHOULD BE ABLE TO

1. Describe small business marketing.
2. Identify the components of a formal marketing plan.
3. Discuss the nature of the marketing research process.
4. Define market segmentation and its related strategies.
5. Explain the different methods of forecasting sales.

Entrepreneurs tend to be doers, not planners. And they are often passionate about their product or service. They can talk about its features all day—it's the biggest; it weighs less; it's made of the best materials. Entrepreneurs tend to ignore the fact that customers buy a product or service because they get a benefit from it. Customers ask, How does this item solve my problem? make me a better person? keep me safe? Entrepreneurs need to put themselves in the shoes of their customers and figure out why customers buy what they do—they need a marketing plan.

In Chapter 6, we discussed the importance of a business plan for both the entrepreneur and potential investors. In this chapter, we look at the nature of marketing and the marketing plan. Then, in Chapters 8 through 13, we'll consider the other major components of a business plan. Although our presentation in this chapter does not cover the specific elements of all plans, the features we discuss are important components of any well-written plan.

It is appropriate first to answer a few basic questions about marketing:

- How can marketing be defined for a small business?
- What are the components of an effective marketing philosophy?
- What does a consumer orientation imply about the business?

small business marketing
Business activities that direct the creation, development, and delivery of a bundle of satisfaction from the creator to the targeted user and that satisfy the targeted user.

What Is Small Business Marketing?

Marketing means different things to different people. Some entrepreneurs view marketing as simply selling a product or service. Others see marketing as those activities directing the flow of goods and services from producer to consumer or user. In reality, small business marketing is much broader. It consists of many activities, some of which occur even before a product is produced and made ready for distribution and sale. People thinking about starting businesses should do their homework to make sure a market exists for what they plan to sell *before* they ever launch their companies.

1. Describe small business marketing.

We begin with a comprehensive definition of small business marketing in order to convey its true scope to entrepreneurs. *Small business marketing* consists of those business activities that direct the creation, development, and delivery of a *bundle of satisfaction* from the creator to the targeted user and that satisfy the targeted user. Notice how this definition emphasizes the concept of a bundle of satisfaction—the benefits customers will gain from the core product and/or service. It may be helpful to view a product/service as having three levels: core product/service, actual product/service, and augmented product/service (see Exhibit 7-1). The *core product/service* is the fundamental benefit or solution sought by customers. The *actual product/service* is the basic physical product/service that delivers those benefits. The *augmented product/service* is the basic product/service plus any extra or unsolicited benefits to the consumer that may prompt a purchase. In the case of shoes, for example, the core product is basic protection for the feet; the actual product is the shoe itself. The augmented product might be increased running speed, greater comfort, or less wear and tear on feet and legs.

Ultimately, a business provides satisfaction to its customers, not merely the tangible product or intangible service that is the focus of the exchange. Consider the case of ARAMARK. This company rents houseboats to visitors at Lake Powell in Arizona. Making the houseboats available to tourists at this resort location is its core product. By surveying their customers after the visits, ARAMARK executives discovered people visited once, but did not return. The customers reported that staying on the houseboats was hard work and stressful. They found it difficult to obtain groceries and to maneuver the boats. In other words, the bundle of satisfaction the firm needed to provide included more than the houseboat as a

core product/ service
The fundamental benefit or solution sought by customers.

actual product/ service
The basic physical product/service that delivers those benefits.

augmented product/service
The basic product/ service plus any extra or unsolicited benefits to the consumer that may prompt a purchase.

7-1 The Three Levels of a Product/Service

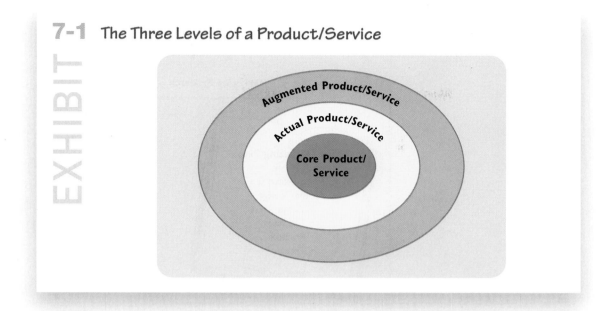

place to stay. This led to the introduction of new services designed to meet customers' needs. These services included grocery-buying assistance, on-board chefs, and training or assistance with steering and anchoring the boats. Immediately after implementing the changes, ARAMARK recorded a 50-percent drop in complaints and a 12-percent increase in repeat business.[1]

Marketing Philosophies Make a Difference

Just as an individual's personal philosophy influences the strategy he or she uses to achieve personal goals, a firm's marketing philosophy determines how its marketing activities are developed, reflected in the marketing plan, and used to achieve business goals. Three different marketing perspectives that guide most small businesses are the production-oriented, sales-oriented, and consumer-oriented philosophies.

A *production-oriented philosophy* emphasizes the product as the single most important part of the business. The firm concentrates resources on developing the product or service in the most efficient manner, even if promotion, distribution, and other marketing activities are slighted. On the other hand, a *sales-oriented philosophy* deemphasizes production efficiencies and customer preferences in favor of a focus on "pushing product." Achieving sales goals becomes the firm's highest priority. In contrast, a firm adopting a *consumer-oriented philosophy* believes that everything, including production and sales, centers on the consumer and his or her needs. The result: All marketing efforts begin and end with the consumer.

A Consumer Orientation—The Right Choice

Over the years, both large and small businesses have gradually shifted their marketing emphasis from production to sales and, more recently, to consumers. Adhering to this marketing concept is essential to marketing success. The marketing concept is a two-stage process that underlies all marketing efforts: identifying customer needs and satisfying those needs. This simple formula is easy to understand but difficult to implement, given the competitive nature of most markets. Still, for a company to be successful, it is essential that a product and/or service meet a real need in the marketplace. *We strongly recommend that all new businesses begin with a consumer orientation, as this philosophy is most consistent with long-term success.* Remember, customer satisfaction is not a means to achieving a goal—it *is* the goal!

7-2 The Marketing Plan and Supporting Marketing Activities

Marketing Research

The Marketing Plan
- Market Analysis
- The Competition
- Marketing Strategy
  - Product/Service
  - Distribution
  - Promotion
  - Pricing

Market Segmentation

Sales Forecasting

Why have some small firms failed to adopt a consumer orientation when the benefits seem so obvious? The answer lies in three key factors. First, the state of competition always affects a firm's marketing orientation. If there is little or no competition and if demand exceeds supply, a firm is tempted to emphasize production. This is usually a short-term situation, however, and so the approach often leads to disaster in due time.

Second, an entrepreneur may have strong production skills but be weak in marketing ability. Naturally, such owners will concentrate on production considerations.

Third, some entrepreneurs are simply too focused on the present. They expect the firm's marketing efforts to reap immediate dividends and, consequently, favor a sales-oriented philosophy. However, putting too much emphasis on selling merchandise often creates customer dissatisfaction, especially if high-pressure selling is used with little regard for customers' needs.

Both production- and sales-oriented philosophies may generate short-run success. However, a consumer orientation not only recognizes production efficiency goals and professional selling but also adds concern for customer satisfaction. In effect, a firm that adopts a consumer orientation incorporates the best of each marketing philosophy.

Once a small firm makes a commitment to a customer orientation, it is ready to develop a marketing strategy to support this goal. Marketing activities include taking the steps necessary to locate and describe potential customers—a process called *market analysis*. Marketing activities also encompass product/service, pricing, promotion, and distribution, which combine to form the *marketing mix*. Marketing research, market segmentation, and sales forecasting are additional key activities underlying market analysis and the development of a marketing mix.

Exhibit 7-2 depicts the major components of the marketing plan and the marketing activities required to generate the information needed for the plan—marketing research, market segmentation, and sales forecasting. In the remainder of the chapter, we will take a more in-depth look at these plan components and marketing activities.

market analysis
The process of locating and describing potential customers.

marketing mix
The combination of product, pricing, promotion, and distribution activities.

The Formal Marketing Plan

2. Identify the components of a formal marketing plan.

After the entrepreneur completes a feasibility study (discussed in Chapter 3) and determines the venture idea to be a viable opportunity, he or she is ready to prepare the formal marketing plan. Each business venture is different; therefore, each marketing plan is unique. An entrepreneur should avoid developing a cloned version of a plan created by someone else, even the one suggested by the authors of this textbook. But certain subjects—market analysis, the competition, and marketing strategy—*must be* covered.

This chapter contains excerpts from actual marketing plans as examples of what might be included in certain sections. The following discussion is not intended to be complete or comprehensive. In fact, more detailed treatment of marketing activities and strategies for both new and established small businesses is provided in Part 4, in Chapters 14 through 18. Much of this later material will also be helpful for writing the actual marketing plan.

Market Analysis

In the market analysis section of the marketing plan, the entrepreneur describes the target market. This description of potential customers is commonly called a *customer profile*. Marketing research information, compiled from both secondary and primary data, can be used to construct this profile. A detailed discussion of the major benefits to customers provided by the new product or service should also be included in this section of the plan. Obviously, these benefits must be reasonable and consistent with statements in the product/service section of the plan.

customer profile
A description of potential customers in a target market.

The following excerpt from the market needs section of the marketing plan of Calico Computer Consulting, a home-based business offering technical help for small ventures and home office businesses, uses research by industry experts to outline benefits the company would offer to prospective customers.

> Experts in the consulting industry have identified three different opportunities that exist for computer consultants:
>
> 1. Temporary Technical Aid
>   Short-term assignments finding solutions for businesses—this is noted as the largest market
> 2. Specific Skill—the largest area is software specialty
>   System setup & purchasing guidance
>   Systems reengineering/optimization
>   Network administration
>   Training
>   Repair
>   Database/application development
>   Data storage
>   Disaster recovery
>   Security/data protection
>   Telecommunications
> 3. Bail-out (Troubleshooting)
>
> According to *Entrepreneur* magazine, private home computer users are NOT a viable market for computer consultants.[2]

If an entrepreneur envisions several target markets, each segment must have a corresponding customer profile. Likewise, different target markets may call for an equal number of related marketing strategies. Typically, however, a new venture will initially concentrate on a select few target markets—or even just one. Think for a moment just how expensive it would be to try to market to all possible customers: You might be spending money in geographic areas where none of your customers live or work, trying to reach people with a broad range of reading, listening, and viewing habits instead of on the television shows, websites, radio stations, and magazines that most of your customers access. Attempting to reach all potential customers would be way too costly for a small business.

Another major component of market analysis is the actual sales forecast. It is usually desirable to include three sales forecasts covering the "most likely," "best-case," and "worst-case" scenarios. These alternatives provide investors and the entrepreneur with different numbers on which to base their decisions.

As we point out later in this chapter, forecasting sales for a new venture is extremely difficult. While it will be necessary to make assumptions during forecasting, they should be minimized. The forecasting method should be described and backed up by data wherever feasible.

The Competition

Frequently, entrepreneurs ignore the reality of competition for their new ventures, believing that the marketplace contains no close substitutes or that their success will not attract other entrepreneurs. This is simply not realistic.

Existing competitors should be studied carefully, and their key management personnel profiled. A brief discussion of competitors' overall strengths and weaknesses should be a part of the competition section of the plan. Also, related products currently being marketed or tested by competitors should be noted. The entrepreneur should also assess the likelihood that any of these firms will enter the targeted market. Performing a SWOT analysis at this point is always a good idea. (As we discussed in Chapter 3, SWOT stands for Strengths, Weaknesses, Opportunities, and Threats.) It is important that your company have a clear understanding of what it does well (strengths), what it doesn't do so well (weaknesses), available market opportunities, and threats from competitors as well as from changes in the company's operating environment (social, technological, economic, political, and other environmental variables).

Consider the following excerpt from the competition section of a marketing plan for Borrow My Tools, a startup home improvement tool-rental business:

A to Z Rentals

A large, comprehensive rental company. Selection, not service, is key here.

Pros: Rents a wide range of tools and equipment including wood tools, machining tools, catering supplies, even pianos.
Cons: The staff is not able to provide support for products.

The Tool Shed

A tool leasing company that leases a wide range of tools. The primary customers are contractors.

Pros: Wide selection of high-end tools, a lot of leasing options.
Cons: Tool experts need only apply; this company does not hold the hands of beginners.[3]

If you were the owner of Borrow My Tools, would these descriptions give you information about your strengths and weaknesses relative to those of competitors? Would you know how to compete with A-Z Rentals and The Tool Shed?

Many competitors can be monitored by visiting their websites. Todd Stoner, owner of Waco, Texas–based Disciplined Investors, an investment advisement firm, uses several search engines to keep tabs on his competition. "I am always curious to see what other investment firms in and around Waco are up to," Stoner says. "I can see which firms are growing and what types of products and services they offer."[4]

Marketing Strategy

A well-prepared market analysis and a discussion of the competition are important to the formal marketing plan. But the information on marketing strategy forms the most detailed section of the marketing plan and, in many respects, is subject to the closest scrutiny from potential investors. Such a strategy plots the course of the marketing actions that will make or break the entrepreneur's vision. It's one thing to know that a large target market exists for a product or service. It's another to be able to explain why customers will buy that product or service from you!

In the process of analyzing sales, Spira Footwear, Inc., discovered that its customer profile was a 35- to 55-year-old female with above average income who purchased walking shoes. But the research also indicated that the Spira brand appealed to buyers because of its image as a running shoe, regardless of the actual product purchased. As a result, the owners chose to focus their marketing plan on running shoes. The following excerpt describes a small portion of Spira's marketing strategy:

> From a brand building perspective, the Company has focused its efforts on the running market. This is a very difficult market to penetrate, but the Company believes the long-term brand-building potential of the category is limitless. If the Company can achieve credibility in the highly competitive and technically oriented running market, it will act as a catalyst as the Company shifts into other categories of footwear. This strategy was employed by Nike, which built its brand in the 1970s around its running shoe.[5]

The marketing mix of the "4 P's" highlights the areas that a company's marketing strategy should address: (1) *product* decisions that will transform the basic product or service idea into a bundle of satisfaction, (2) distribution (*place*) activities regarding the delivery of the product to customers, (3) *pricing* decisions that will set an acceptable exchange value on the total product or service, and (4) *promotion* activities that will communicate the necessary information to target markets.

Obviously, the nature of a new venture has a direct bearing on the emphasis given to each of these areas. For example, a service business will not have the same distribution problems as a product business, and the promotional challenges facing a new retail store will be quite different from those faced by a new manufacturer. Despite these differences, we can offer a generalized format for presenting marketing strategy in a business plan.

THE PRODUCT AND/OR SERVICE SECTION   The product and/or service section of the marketing plan includes the name of the product and/or service and the name of the business and why they were selected. Any legal protection that has been obtained for the names should be described. It is also important to explain the logic behind the name selection. An entrepreneur's family name, if used for certain products or services, can sometimes make a positive contribution to sales. Think about how cleverly the J.M. Smucker Company has used the slogan "With a name like Smucker's, it has to be good."® In other situations, a descriptive name that suggests a benefit of the product may be more desirable. In the How I See It feature, Holly Fields explains that the name "Spira" was chosen to help customers remember the benefits of the spring technology. A good name is simple, memorable, and descriptive of the benefit provided by the product or service. We will look at this in more depth in Chapters 14 and 15. Whatever the logic behind the choice of names, the selection should be defended and the names registered with the appropriate agencies to provide protection.

Sometimes, names selected for a business or a product or service may be challenged many years later, particularly if they haven't been registered. Basic Sports Apparel (BSA), a company owning the rights to the name "Spiral," accused Spira Footwear, Inc., of violating its trademark by infringing on its brand name. Although BSA was demanding $10,000,000, shortly before the trial date it reached a settlement with Spira that granted BSA a license to use the Spira trademark for apparel manufacture. The owners of BSA determined that the growing market awareness of the Spira name could be leveraged into an entire line of clothing.

Other components of the total product, such as the packaging, should be presented via drawings. Sometimes, it may be desirable to use professional packaging consultants to develop these drawings. Customer service plans such as warranties and repair policies also need to be discussed in this section. These elements of the marketing strategy should be tied directly to customer satisfaction. (Chapter 14 further examines the importance of creating and maintaining good customer relationships.)

Another legal issue many small business owners face relates to unique features of their products or services. These special features may not merely be why people buy from you; they may also justify why someone might invest in your company or lend you money. For this reason, Spira established patents on its footwear features; the company wanted to differentiate its products from those of other footwear manufacturers and to prevent rivals from stealing that competitive advantage.

Rather than patenting their products or technologies, some enterprises prefer to maintain trade secrets. We all have heard the stories of the secret CocaCola formula and of KFC's mysterious 11 herbs and spices. These features fall under the term *intellectual property*. Many companies build their marketing strategies around their intellectual property, promoting the idea that only they offer a particular benefit to customers.

intellectual property
Original intellectual creations, including inventions, literary creations, and works of art, that are protected by patents or copyrights.

THE DISTRIBUTION SECTION

Quite often, new ventures will use established intermediaries to handle the distribution of their product. This strategy reduces the investment necessary for start up and helps the new company get its products to customers faster. How those intermediaries will be persuaded to carry the new product should be explained in the distribution section of the marketing plan. Any intention the new business may have of licensing its product or service should also be covered in this section.

Some new retail ventures require fixed locations; others need mobile stores. The layouts and configurations of retail outlets should be explained in this section of the marketing plan. Of course, Internet-based firms must have their distribution methods designed and tested before they ever begin marketing, and many questions should be addressed. For example, will the

How I see it: Holly Fields on Choosing a Name and Designing a Website

We wanted a name for our company that was catchy, easy to remember. We went through an exercise with an agency. We started brainstorming, maybe 300 names. Some names were absolutely crazy, some literal, some imaginative. We did searches on a short list of names. So many were already trademarked. The moment an agency person mentioned "Spira," I knew that was it. It reminded me of spiral, aspire, inspiration. All those things came through. And it's Latin for coil. Our spring is WaveSpring technology, not a coil, but it's coil-shaped. There were so many things you could do with that name. We used an existing font, but stylized it, creating our own. We got as detailed as the dot on the "i," compressed down a little bit to show the movement of the spring.

We started with a marketing plan. It's critical when talking with potential investors. The website is a huge focus of my marketing plan. It has evolved to be the most important component. We have always had the website. We learned it is the easiest way to reach those customers who come looking for your product. You really need to have a dynamic website. The focus for 2008–2009 was my website. I redid the whole thing. I think it was a very important move, to keep up with selling direct to the customer, and with the customer being able to find us. The first thing most people do when they want to know about a product is look it up on the website. They look up a keyword. We've worked hard on our keywords so that people will know who we are and find us easily. It's been an interesting journey, learning all this.

customer get the product by regular mail or by express delivery? Will the service be provided from home or the office or from the location of a licensed representative? How long will it take between order placement and actual delivery?

When a new firm's method of product delivery is exporting, the distribution section must discuss the relevant laws and regulations governing that activity. Knowledge of exchange rates between currencies and distribution options must be reflected in the material discussed in this section. (Distribution concepts are explained in greater detail in Chapter 15, and exporting is discussed in Chapter 18.)

THE PRICING SECTION   At a minimum, the price of a product or service must cover the cost of bringing it to customers. Therefore, the pricing section must include a schedule of both production and marketing costs. Break-even computations should be included for alternative prices. (Naturally, forecasting methods used for analysis in this section should be consistent with those used in preparing the market analysis section.) However, setting a price based exclusively on break-even analysis is not advisable, as it ignores other aspects of pricing. If the entrepreneur has found a truly unique niche, he or she may be able to charge a premium price—at least in the short run.

Competitors should be studied to learn what they are charging. To break into a market, an entrepreneur will usually have to price a new product or service within a reasonable range of the competition. Many new business owners think their best strategy is to under-price the competition in order to gain market acceptance and boost sales. It is important to keep in mind, however, that existing competitors probably have more resources than you do. If they consider your business to be a threat and engage you in a price war, they can probably outlast you. In addition, do you really want your customers to come to you only because you sell a cheaper product or service? That's no way to build loyalty; you will lose those customers to the next company that prices lower than you do. (Chapter 16 examines break-even analysis and pricing strategy in more depth.)

THE PROMOTION SECTION   The promotion section of the marketing plan should describe the entrepreneur's approach to creating customer awareness of the product and/or service and explain why customers will be motivated to buy. Among the many promotional options available to the entrepreneur are personal selling (that is, direct person-to-person selling) and advertising. Holly Fields and Andy Krafsur of Spira Footwear demonstrated how public relations can also be an effective marketing strategy.

If personal selling is appropriate, the section should outline how many salespeople will be employed and how they will be compensated. The proposed system for training the sales force should also be mentioned. If advertising is to be used, a list of the specific media to be employed should be included and advertising themes should be described. Often, it is advisable to seek the services of a small advertising agency when developing a marketing strategy. In this case, the name and credentials of the agency should be provided. A brief mention of successful campaigns supervised by the agency can add to the appeal of this section of the marketing plan. (Personal selling and advertising are discussed more extensively in Chapter 17.)

Marketing Research for the New Venture

3. *Discuss the nature of the marketing research process.*

A marketing plan can be based on intuition alone, or intuition can be supplemented by sound market information. *In every case, it is advisable to write the marketing plan only after collecting and evaluating marketing research data.* A marketing plan based on research will undoubtedly be stronger than a plan without such a foundation.

The Nature of Marketing Research

Marketing research may be defined as the gathering, processing, interpreting, and reporting of marketing information. It is all about finding out what you want to know. A small business typically conducts less marketing research than does a big business, partly because of the expense involved but also because the entrepreneur often does not understand the basic research process. Therefore, our discussion of marketing research focuses on the more widely used and practical techniques that entrepreneurs can employ as they analyze potential target markets and make preparations to develop their marketing plans.

Although a small business can conduct marketing research without the assistance of an expert, the cost of hiring such help is often money well spent, as the expert's advice may help increase revenues or cut costs. Marketing researchers are trained, experienced professionals, and prices for their research services typically reflect this. For example, focus groups run from $3,000 to $10,000 each, and a telephone survey may range anywhere from $5,000 to $25,000 or more, depending on the number of interviews and the length of the questionnaire. However, companies such as SurveyMonkey (http://www.surveymonkey.com) are now reducing overall research costs by taking advantage of the Internet to offer Web-based surveys and online focus groups.

LIVING THE DREAM:

entrepreneurial experiences

Market Driven Restoration

www.guayaki.com

Alex Pryor and David Karr co-founded Guayakí Sustainable Rainforest Products, Inc., with the idea of pioneering an innovative business model. According to their website, they are engaging in market-driven restoration by "linking consumer purchases of healthy yerba mate products in North America with indigenous communities engaged in sustainable agriculture and reforestation projects in Argentina, Paraguay, and Brazil. Each person [who] drinks two servings per day of Guayakí Yerba Mate helps protect approximately one acre of rainforest every year." Yerba mate is a tea containing an abundance of vitamins, minerals, and antioxidants. Customers may drink mate because they love the beverage, but the Guayakí team wants them

© Guayakí

to know that they are also contributing to community development and conservation by paying a fair trade price for a rainforest-grown product.

Although Pryor and Karr describe themselves as having been "captivated" by the beverage from the moment they first tried it, they found convincing the public to purchase it was not easy. Who would their customer be? How were they going to reach that customer? They knew they could not pick a traditional marketing strategy for introducing a brand new product. They chose to hit the road, introducing mate at festivals, sporting events, and natural food stores. According to Karr, "People would come back 15 minutes later saying, 'What is this stuff? How come I feel so good?'" Even though their products are now carried in thousands of stores in the United States and Canada, Pryor and Karr still have employees traveling cross-country in a biodiesel van, offering an ever-increasing audience their first taste of Guayakí yerba mate.

Sources: Sara Wilson, "Tea for Two" *Entrepreneur*, September 2007, p. 83; and http://www.guayaki.com, accessed February 22, 2009.

Before committing to research, an entrepreneur should always estimate the projected costs of marketing research and compare them with the benefits expected. Such analysis is never exact, but it will help the entrepreneur to decide what research should be conducted.

Steps in the Marketing Research Process

The typical steps in the marketing research process are (1) identifying the informational need, (2) searching for secondary data, (3) collecting primary data, and (4) interpreting the data gathered.

STEP ONE: IDENTIFYING THE INFORMATIONAL NEED

The first step in marketing research is to identify and define the informational need. Although this step seems almost too obvious to mention, the fact is that entrepreneurs sometimes commission surveys without pinpointing the specific information needed. Obviously, a broad statement such as "Our need is to know if the venture will be successful" will do little to guide the research process, but even a more specific goal can easily miss the mark. For example, an entrepreneur thinking about a location for a restaurant may decide to conduct a survey to ascertain customers' menu preferences and reasons for eating out when, in fact, what he or she needs to know most is how often residents of the target area eat out and how far they are willing to drive to eat in a restaurant.

Once a venture's informational needs have been defined correctly, research can be designed to concentrate on those specific needs. Later in this chapter, you will see a survey questionnaire developed for the owner of a therapeutic spa who wanted to assess customer satisfaction and identify growth opportunities for her business.

STEP TWO: SEARCHING FOR SECONDARY DATA

Information that has already been compiled is known as *secondary data*. Generally, collecting secondary data is much less expensive than gathering new, or primary, data. Therefore, after defining their informational needs, entrepreneurs should exhaust available sources of secondary data before going further into the research process. It may be possible to base much of the marketing plan for the new venture solely on secondary data. A massive amount of information is available in libraries throughout the United States and on the Internet. The libraries of higher education institutions can be especially valuable. Not only do they have or have access to numerous databases containing business-related information, but they also have librarians with the skills necessary to guide you through those databases.

As you already know, the Internet is a rich source of secondary data. Information that once took days and even weeks to obtain is now often only a mouse-click away. Software programs and hundreds of websites (many offering free information) can help an entrepreneur research customers for her or his product and/or service. Don't make the mistake, however, of thinking that the Internet is the *only* source of secondary data or even the most reliable source. Like all repositories of information, it is most helpful when used in tandem with other sources. And one must be very careful to verify the accuracy of all secondary data gathered from the Internet and other sources.

A particularly helpful source of secondary data for the small firm is the Small Business Administration, or SBA (http://www.sba.gov). This agency publishes extensive bibliographies on many topics, including marketing research.

Unfortunately, the use of secondary data has several drawbacks. One is that the data may be outdated. Another is that the units of measure in the secondary data may not fit the current problem. For example, a firm's market might consist of individuals with incomes between $20,000 and $25,000, while secondary data may report only the number of individuals with incomes between $15,000 and $50,000.

Finally, the question of credibility is always present. Some sources of secondary data are less trustworthy than others. Mere publication of data does not in itself make the data valid and reliable. It is advisable to compare several different sources to see whether they are reporting

secondary data
Market information that has been previously compiled.

similar data. Professional research specialists can also help assess the credibility of secondary sources.

STEP THREE: COLLECTING PRIMARY DATA
If the secondary data are insufficient, a search for new information, or *primary data*, is the next step. Observational methods and questioning methods are two techniques used in accumulating primary data. Observational methods avoid interpersonal contact between respondents and the researcher, while questioning methods involve some type of interaction with respondents.

primary data
New market information that is gathered by the firm conducting the research.

OBSERVATIONAL METHODS Observation is probably the oldest form of research in existence; indeed, learning by observing is quite common. It is hardly surprising that observation can provide useful information for small businesses. A simple but effective form of observation research is mystery shopping. Mystery shoppers gather observational data about a store (yours or a competitor's) by looking at how items are displayed, in-store advertising, and other features of the store. Mystery shopping can also be used to test employee product knowledge, sales techniques, and more. The results of such activities are used to make important changes in store design and merchandising as well as to reward good employees.[6]

Douglas Canning and John Alves launched Dirtbag Clothing, a manufacturer of alternative streetwear, when they were senior film majors at San Francisco State University. They wanted to learn more about their competitors, so they, like many college students, turned to the Internet. Along with observing the designs of the websites and the keywords used, Canning and Alves obtained the names and e-mail addresses of buyers of different apparel lines. They e-mailed the buyers and received responses from approximately half of those contacted, which led to establishing accounts with 20 firms. The entrepreneurs also gathered information by attending several major industry trade shows and checking out competitors' booths. Not only have Canning and Alves gained a lot of good ideas from observing their competitors, but they also spent far less money in their marketing efforts than others in their industry.[7]

As shown by the owners of Dirtbag Clothing, observational methods can be inexpensive. Furthermore, they avoid the potential bias that can result from a respondent's contact with an interviewer during questioning. Observation—for example, counting customers going into a store—can be conducted by a person or by mechanical devices, such as hidden video cameras. The cost of mechanical observation devices is rapidly declining, bringing them within the budget of many small businesses.

QUESTIONING METHODS Surveys and experimentation are both questioning methods that involve contact with respondents. Surveys can be conducted by mail, telephone, the Web, or personal interview. Mail surveys are often used when target respondents are widely dispersed; however, they usually yield low response rates—only a small percentage of the surveys sent out are typically returned. Telephone surveys and personal interview surveys achieve higher response rates. But personal interviews are very expensive, and individuals are often reluctant to grant such interviews if they think a sales pitch is coming. Some marketing researchers, such as i.think inc., offer firms a new way to survey customers—through an online questionnaire. Although some websites claim that online surveys have better response rates than do paper surveys, Internet surveying is still relatively new and data on response rates are questionable.

A questionnaire is the basic instrument guiding the researcher who is administering the survey and the respondent who is taking it. A questionnaire should be developed carefully and pre-tested before it is used in the market. Here are several considerations to keep in mind when designing and testing a questionnaire:

- Ask questions that relate to the issue under consideration. An interesting question may not be relevant. A good test of relevance is to assume an answer to each question and then ask yourself how you would use that information.
- Select the form of question that is most appropriate for the subject and the conditions of the survey. Open-ended and multiple-choice questions are two popular forms.

- Carefully consider the order of the questions. Asking questions in the wrong sequence can produce biased answers to later questions.

- Ask the more sensitive questions near the end of the questionnaire. Age and income, for example, are usually sensitive topics.

- Carefully select the words in each question. They should be as simple, clear, and objective as possible.

- Pre-test the questionnaire by administering it to a small sample of respondents who are representative of the group to be surveyed.

Exhibit 7-3 shows a questionnaire developed for Changes Therapeutic, an alternative medicine spa in El Paso, Texas. This survey illustrates how the considerations above can be incorporated into a questionnaire. Note the use of both multiple-choice and open-ended questions. As it turned out, the answers to the open-ended questions were particularly useful to this firm.

STEP FOUR: INTERPRETING THE DATA GATHERED   After the necessary data have been gathered, they must be transformed into usable information. Without interpretation, large quantities of data are only isolated facts. Methods of summarizing and simplifying information for users include tables, charts, and other graphics. Descriptive statistics (for example, the average response) are most helpful during this step in the research procedure. Inexpensive personal computer software, such as Excel, is now available to perform statistical calculations and generate report-quality graphics.

It is important to remember that *formal* marketing research is not always necessary. The entrepreneur's first decision should be whether to conduct primary research at all. It may be best not to conduct formal research in the following situations:[8]

1. Your company doesn't have the resources to conduct the research properly or to implement any findings generated from the proposed research.

2. The opportunity for a new business or product introduction has passed. If you've been beaten to the punch, it may be wise to wait and see how the early entrant to the market fares.

3. A decision to move forward has already been made. There's no need to spend good money on a decision that has already been made.

4. You can't decide what information is needed. If you don't know where you are going, any road will take you there.

5. The needed information already exists (that is, secondary information is available).

6. The cost of conducting the research outweighs the potential benefits.

Isabella Trebond suggests several ways entrepreneurs can do their own research with very little money. First, read everything you can—newspaper and magazine articles, as well as any information that can be acquired from industry trade associations. Usually, membership in a trade association gives you access, for a nominal fee, to research that the association conducts in your business sector. Second, you will be amazed at the specific information and sources that can be located on the Web. Existing research should always be reviewed—it's quick, cheap, and easy to access. Third, check out your competition. This can involve a search of their websites as well as a drive-by and/or walk-through of their businesses. Finally, you can always enlist students from local colleges to help stretch your limited research budget.[9]

As important as marketing research is, it should never be allowed to suppress entrepreneurial enthusiasm or be used as a substitute for a hands-on feel for the target market. It should be viewed as a supplement to, not a replacement for, intuitive judgment and cautious experimentation in launching new products and services. Ultimately, the marketing plan should reflect the entrepreneur's belief about the best marketing strategy for her or his firm.

EXHIBIT

7-3 Small Business Survey Questionnaire

Changes Therapeutic of El Paso

Customer Satisfaction Survey

Gender:						
○	○					
M	F					

Age range:						
○	○	○	○	○	○	
4–15	16–25	26–35	36-45	46–55	56–over	

Annual Income range:						
○	○	○	○	○		
Less than $20,000	$20,001–$25,000	$25,001–$35,000	$35,0001–$45,000	More than $45,000		

In what part of the city do you live?						
○	○	○	○			
West	East	North East	Central			

For how long have you been using Change's services?						
○	○	○	○			
Days	Weeks	Months	Years			

How often do you visit Changes Therapeutic of El Paso?						
○	○	○	○			
Daily	Weekly	Monthly	Annually			

What services of Changes Therapeutic of El Paso do you normally use?						
○	○	○	○	○	○	○
Massage	Facials	Synergie cellulite treatments	Reiki	Waxing	Paraffin Treatments	Aromatherapy

Which of the following services would you like to see in Changes?						
○	○	○	○	○		
Yoga	Karate	Acupuncture	Self-care workshops	None		

How did you hear about Changes Therapeutic of El Paso?						
○	○	○	○	○		
Friend	Yellow Pages	Internet	Doctor	Other		

What is your knowledge of the following?	None	Little	Fair	Very Much
1) Massage therapy:	○	○	○	○
2) Yoga:	○	○	○	○
3) Acupuncture:	○	○	○	○
4) Facial:	○	○	○	○
5) Synergie (massage helps to reduce cellulite):	○	○	○	○

EXHIBIT

How often do you	Not at all	Once a week	Once a month	Twice a month	Other
1) Receive a massage service?	○	○	○	○	○
2) Practice yoga?	○	○	○	○	○
3) Get acupuncture services?	○	○	○	○	○
4) Get facial services?	○	○	○	○	○
5) Get Synergie services?	○	○	○	○	○

If you have tried any of the services mentioned above, where did you receive those services? (Specify business name, home, etc. ....)

_____

_____

Would you like to attend a workshop where you can learn more about these services?

○	○	
No	Yes (if time permits)	If no, why?_____

In which of the services are you most interested? (please select one or more)

○	○	○	○	○	○
Therapeutic Massage	Yoga	Acupuncture	Facials	Synergie	None

Would you prefer a spa that offers all of these services?

○	○	○
No	Yes	Maybe

How far are you willing to travel to such a spa?

○	○	○	○	○	
0–10 miles	11–20 miles	21–30 miles	31–40 miles	41–50 miles	

Understanding Potential Target Markets

4. Define market segmentation and its related strategies.

To prepare the market analysis section of the marketing plan, an entrepreneur needs a proper understanding of the term *market*, which means different things to different people. It may refer to a physical location where buying and selling take place ("They went to the market"), or it may be used to describe selling efforts ("We must market this product aggressively"). Still another meaning is the one we emphasize in this chapter: A *market* is a group of customers or potential customers who have purchasing power and unsatisfied needs. Note carefully the three ingredients in this definition of a market:

market
A group of customers or potential customers who have purchasing power and unsatisfied needs.

1. A market must have buying units, or *customers*. These units may be individuals or business entities. Thus, a market is more than a geographic area; it must contain potential customers.

2. Customers in a market must have *purchasing power*. Assessing the level of purchasing power in a potential market is very important. Customers who have unsatisfied needs but who lack money and/or credit do not constitute a viable market because they have nothing to offer in exchange for a product or service. In such a situation, no transactions can occur.

3. A market must contain buying units with *unsatisfied needs.* Consumers, for instance, will not buy unless they are motivated to do so—and motivation can occur only when a customer recognizes his or her unsatisfied needs. It would be extremely difficult, for example, to sell luxury urban apartments to desert nomads!

In light of our definition of a market, determining market potential is the process of locating and investigating buying units that have both purchasing power and needs that can be satisfied with the product or service that is being offered.

Market Segmentation and Its Variables

In Chapter 3, cost- and differentiation-based strategies were described as they apply to marketplaces that are relatively homogeneous, or uniform, in nature. As discussed, these strategies can also be used to focus on a market niche within an industry. In his book *Competitive Advantage*, Michael Porter refers to this type of competitive strategy—in which cost- and differentiation-based advantages are achieved within narrow market segments—as a *focus strategy.*[10]

A focus strategy depends on market segmentation and becomes a consideration in competitive markets. Formally defined, *market segmentation* is the process of dividing the total market for a product or service into groups with similar needs, such that each group is likely to respond favorably to a specific marketing strategy. Think about what used to be called "sneakers." They were comfortable canvas and rubber shoes worn primarily by students and athletes, distinguished only by whether they were low-top or high-top styles. Consider how many market segments for this type of shoe exist today: running, walking, basketball, tennis, hiking and outdoor, and many others, all of which have their own subcategories.

In order to divide the total market into appropriate segments, an entrepreneur must consider *segmentation variables*, which are parameters that identify the particular dimensions that distinguish one form of market behavior from another. Two broad sets of segmentation variables that represent major dimensions of a market are benefit variables and demographic variables.

BENEFIT VARIABLES   The definition of a market highlights the unsatisfied needs of customers. *Benefit variables* are related to customer needs since they are used to identify segments of a market based on the benefits sought by customers. For example, senior citizens might patronize a health club to get cardiovascular exercise. The draw for young men might be bodybuilding, while young girls may attend gymnastics classes there. A single health club may offer services that are used for different reasons and in different ways by different market segments.

DEMOGRAPHIC VARIABLES   Benefit variables alone are insufficient for market analysis; it is impossible to implement forecasting and marketing strategy without defining the market further. Therefore, small businesses commonly use demographic variables as part of market segmentation. Recall the definition of a market—customers with purchasing power and unsatisfied needs. *Demographic variables* refer to certain characteristics that describe customers and their purchasing power. Typical demographic variables are age, marital status, gender, occupation, and income.

Marketing Strategies Based on Segmentation Considerations

There are several types of strategies based on market segmentation efforts. The three types discussed here are the unsegmented approach, the multisegment approach, and the single-segment approach. Few companies engage in all three approaches simultaneously. These strategies can best be understood by using an example, so we return to Changes Therapeutic Practices.

THE UNSEGMENTED STRATEGY   When a business defines the total market as its target, it is following an *unsegmented strategy* (also known as *mass marketing*). This strategy

---

market segmentation
The division of a market into several smaller groups with similar needs.

segmentation variables
The parameters used to distinguish one form of market behavior from another.

benefit variables
Specific characteristics that distinguish market segments according to the benefits sought by customers.

demographic variables
Specific characteristics that describe customers and their purchasing power.

unsegmented strategy (mass marketing)
A strategy that defines the total market as the target market.

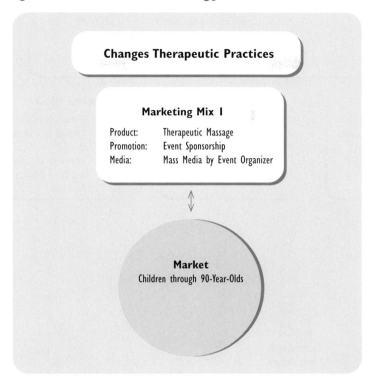

7-4 An Unsegmented Market Strategy

EXHIBIT

Changes Therapeutic Practices

Marketing Mix I

Product: Therapeutic Massage
Promotion: Event Sponsorship
Media: Mass Media by Event Organizer

Market
Children through 90-Year-Olds

---

can sometimes be successful, but it assumes that all customers desire the same basic benefit from the product or service. This may hold true for water but certainly does not hold true for shoes, which satisfy numerous needs through a wide range of styles, prices, colors, and sizes. With an unsegmented strategy, a firm develops a single marketing mix—one combination of product, price, promotion, and distribution. Its competitive advantage must be derived from either a cost- or a differentiation-based advantage. The unsegmented strategy of the Changes Therapeutic spa is shown in Exhibit 7-4. The company's initial service was therapeutic massages. Tanya Finney, founder of Changes Therapeutic, discovered that virtually anyone was a prospect for a therapeutic massage—she drew customers from 8- to 90-year-olds. One promotional tactic that worked in reaching this broad customer base was sponsoring races for charitable causes, including breast cancer, heart disease, arthritis, and many others.

multisegment strategy
A strategy that recognizes different preferences of individual market segments and develops a unique marketing mix for each.

THE MULTISEGMENT STRATEGY With a view of the market that recognizes individual segments with different preferences, a firm is in a better position to tailor marketing mixes to various segments. If a firm determines that two or more market segments have the potential to be profitable and then develops a unique marketing mix for each segment, it is following a *multisegment strategy*.

Although Tanya Finney initially chose to adopt an unsegmented approach for Changes Therapeutic, over time she discovered that she did indeed have multiple market segments: athletes, autistic children, executives, people with arthritis, women age 35 to 55, and more. Following the multisegment approach, the company developed competitive advantages with multiple marketing mixes, based on differences in pricing, promotion, distribution, or the product itself, as shown in Exhibit 7-5. For stressed executives and office workers, Finney designed a chair massage, offered in offices and schools at $1 per minute. She reached these customers through health fairs and advertisements in school administration offices.

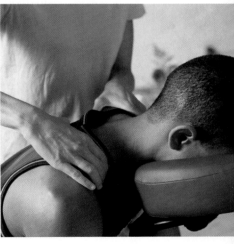

Duncan Smith/Photodisc/Getty Images

7-5 A Multisegment Market Strategy

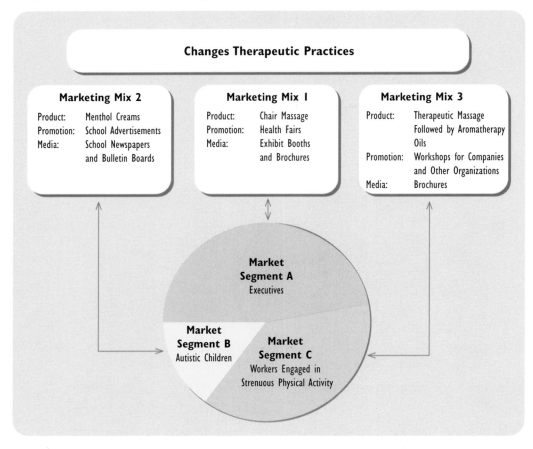

Changes Therapeutic Practices

Marketing Mix 2

Product:	Menthol Creams
Promotion:	School Advertisements
Media:	School Newspapers and Bulletin Boards

Marketing Mix 1

Product:	Chair Massage
Promotion:	Health Fairs
Media:	Exhibit Booths and Brochures

Marketing Mix 3

Product:	Therapeutic Massage Followed by Aromatherapy Oils
Promotion:	Workshops for Companies and Other Organizations
Media:	Brochures

Market Segment A
Executives

Market Segment B
Autistic Children

Market Segment C
Workers Engaged in Strenuous Physical Activity

For autistic children, Finney developed scented menthol and lavender creams that are especially appealing to children diagnosed as autistic. (And other oils have been found to be attractive to other market segments.) A third market segment comprises people who spend much of their workday on their feet—military personnel, law enforcement officers, retail workers, etc. Finney found that this segment often has to be educated about the nature of therapeutic massages. She typically begins with chair massages, attending to neck and shoulder. In this way, the client becomes acclimated to the service and discovers the benefits of the massage for health and stress reduction. This experience leads them to purchase other products and services. Many small businesses in their early stages are resistant to using the multisegment strategy because of the risk of spreading their limited resources too thinly among several marketing efforts.

THE SINGLE-SEGMENT STRATEGY When a firm recognizes that several distinct market segments exist but chooses to concentrate on reaching only one segment, it is following a *single-segment strategy*. The segment selected is the one that promises to offer the greatest profitability. Once again, a competitive advantage is achieved through a cost- or differentiation-based strategy. Changes Therapeutic decided to pursue a single-segment approach and selected the teenager market segment (see Exhibit 7-6). In this case, the firm specifically targeted young people with acne problems. Its products and services have been introduced to that market segment by way of school and health fairs.

The single-segment approach is probably the wisest strategy for small businesses to use during initial marketing efforts. It allows a small firm to specialize and make better use of its limited resources. Then, once its reputation has been established, the firm will find it easier to enter new markets.

single-segment strategy
A strategy that recognizes the existence of several distinct market segments but focuses on only the most profitable segment.

7-6 A Single-Segment Market Strategy

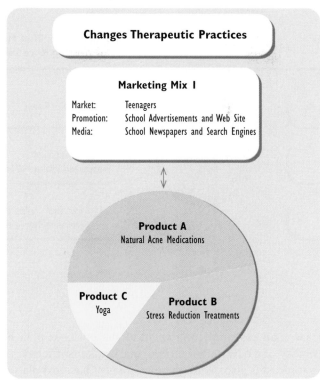

Changes Therapeutic Practices

Marketing Mix I

Market:	Teenagers
Promotion:	School Advertisements and Web Site
Media:	School Newspapers and Search Engines

Product A
Natural Acne Medications

Product C
Yoga

Product B
Stress Reduction Treatments

Estimating Market Potential

A small business can be successful only if sufficient market demand exists for its product or service. The sales forecast is the typical indicator of market adequacy, so it is particularly important to complete this assessment prior to writing the marketing plan. An entrepreneur who enters the marketplace without a forecast is much like an enthusiastic swimmer who leaves the diving board without checking the depth of the water—and the results can be nearly as painful! Many types of information from numerous sources are required to gauge market potential. This section discusses these information needs as it examines the forecasting process.

5. Explain the different methods of forecasting sales.

The Sales Forecast

Formally defined, a *sales forecast* is an estimate of how much of a product or service can be sold within a given market in a defined time period. The forecast can be stated in terms of dollars and/or units.

Because a sales forecast revolves around a specific target market, that market should be defined as precisely as possible. The market description forms the forecasting boundary. If the market for desks is described as "all offices," the sales forecast will be extremely large. A more precise definition, such as "government agencies seeking solid wood desks priced between $800 and $1200," will result in a smaller but possibly more useful forecast.

One sales forecast may cover a period of time that is a year or less, while another may extend over several years. Both short-term and long-term forecasts are needed for a well-constructed business plan.

sales forecast
A prediction of how much of a product or service will be purchased within a market during a specified time period.

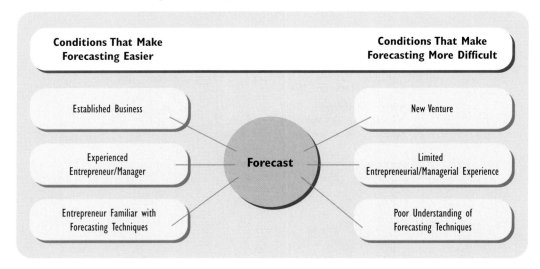

A sales forecast is an essential component of the business plan because it is critical to assessing the feasibility of a new venture. If the market is insufficient, the business is destined for failure. A sales forecast is also useful in other areas of business planning. Production schedules, inventory policies, and personnel decisions all start with a sales forecast. Obviously, a forecast can never be perfect, and entrepreneurs should remember that a forecast can be wrong in either direction—underestimating potential sales or overestimating potential sales.

Limitations to Forecasting

For a number of practical reasons, forecasting is used less frequently by small firms than by large firms. First, for any new business, forecasting circumstances are unique. Entrepreneurial inexperience, coupled with a new idea, represents the most difficult forecasting situation, as illustrated in Exhibit 7-7. An ongoing business that requires only an updated forecast for its existing product is in the most favorable forecasting position.

Second, a small business manager may be unfamiliar with methods of quantitative analysis. Not all forecasting must be quantitatively oriented—qualitative forecasting is often helpful and may be sufficient—but quantitative methods have repeatedly proven their value in forecasting.

Third, the typical small business entrepreneur and his or her team know little about the forecasting process. To overcome this deficiency, the owners of some small firms attempt to keep in touch with industry trends through contacts with appropriate trade associations. The professional members of a trade association are frequently better qualified to engage in sales forecasting. Most libraries have a copy of *National Trade and Professional Associations of the United States,* which lists these groups. Entrepreneurs can also obtain current information about business trends by regularly reading trade publications and magazines focused on small business ownership, such as *Entrepreneur* and *Inc. Magazine.* Government publications, such as the *Federal Reserve Bulletin, Survey of Current Business,* and *Monthly Labor Review,* may also be of general interest. Subscribing to professional forecasting services is another way to obtain forecasts of general business conditions or specific forecasts for given industries.

Despite the difficulties, a small business entrepreneur should not neglect the forecasting task. Instead, she or he should remember how important the sales outlook in the business plan is to obtaining financing. The statement "We can sell as many as we can produce" does not satisfy the information requirements of potential investors.

The Forecasting Process

Estimating market demand with a sales forecast is a multistep process. Typically, the sales forecast is a composite of several individual forecasts, so the process involves merging these individual forecasts properly.

The forecasting process can be characterized by two important dimensions: the point at which the process is started and the nature of the predicting variable. Depending on the starting point, the process may be designated as a *breakdown process* or a *buildup process.* The nature of the predicting variable determines whether the forecasting is direct or indirect.

THE STARTING POINT In the *breakdown process*, sometimes called the *chain-ratio method*, the forecaster begins with a variable that has a very large scope and systematically works down to the sales forecast. This method is frequently used for consumer products forecasting. The initial variable might be a population figure for the target market. Through the use of percentages, an appropriate link is built to generate the sales forecast. For example, consider a market segment identified by Spira Footwear. Although Spira primarily promotes its running shoes, the company's best-selling products are in the walking shoe category. And the owners have observed that the largest number of purchasers are women in the 35- to 65-year-old age bracket who are from households that earn above the median income in their localities. The United States Census Bureau compiles statistics on various population segments by, for example, gender, age, geographic location, and household income. Additional data on customer segments may be obtained through state and local government agencies; chambers of commerce; trade associations; private enterprise sources, such as *Sales & Marketing Management* magazine's *Survey of Buying Power;* and direct information gathering, such as Changes Therapeutic's survey shown in Exhibit 7-3.

In contrast to the breakdown process, the *buildup process* calls for identifying all potential buyers in a target market's submarkets and then adding up the estimated demand. For example, a local dry-cleaning firm forecasting demand for cleaning high school letter jackets might estimate its market share within each area school as 20 percent. Then, by determining the number of high school students obtaining a letter jacket at each school—perhaps from school yearbooks—an analyst could estimate the total demand.

The buildup process is especially helpful for industrial goods forecasting. To estimate potential, forecasters often use data from the Census of Manufacturers by the U.S. Department of Commerce. The information can be broken down according to the North American Industry Classification System (NAICS), which classifies businesses by type of industry. Once the code for a group of potential industrial customers has been identified, the forecaster can obtain information on the number of establishments and their geographic location, number of employees, and annual sales. A sales forecast can be constructed by summing this information for several relevant codes.

THE PREDICTING VARIABLE In *direct forecasting*, which is the simplest form of forecasting, sales is the forecasted variable. Many times, however, sales cannot be predicted directly and other variables must be used. *Indirect forecasting* takes place when surrogate variables are used to project the sales forecast. For example, if a firm lacks information about industry sales of baby cribs but has data on births, the strong correlation between the two variables allows planners to use the figures for births to help forecast industry sales for baby cribs.

For a new business, there are few things as important as identifying your market—nothing happens until someone buys something from your company. And if you plan to grow your business, understanding your market is essential. In this chapter, we introduced you to the steps necessary for putting together a marketing plan. The plan will be a living document for you as you manage your business. Every day, you will learn more about your market and how you can meet customer needs. And the marketing plan has an impact on many other areas of your business. In later chapters, you will see that your marketing strategy affects how many people you employ and what skills they need, the volume and selection of your inventory, the production processes you use, and many other business functions.

breakdown process (chain-ratio method)
A forecasting method that begins with a larger-scope variable and works down to the sales forecast.

buildup process
A forecasting method in which all potential buyers in the various submarkets are identified and then the estimated demand is added up.

direct forecasting
A forecasting method in which sales is the estimated variable.

indirect forecasting
A forecasting method in which variables related to sales are used to project future sales.

LOOKING BACK

1. Describe small business marketing.

- The product and/or service as a bundle of satisfaction has three levels: (1) core product/service, (2) actual product/service, and (3) augmented product/service.
- Three distinct marketing philosophies are the production-, sales-, and consumer-oriented philosophies.
- A small business should adopt a consumer orientation to marketing, as that philosophy is most consistent with long-term success.
- Small business marketing consists of numerous activities, including market analysis and determining the marketing mix.

2. Identify the components of a formal marketing plan.

- The formal marketing plan should include sections on market analysis, the competition, and marketing strategy.
- The market analysis should include a customer profile.
- A SWOT analysis is helpful in assessing the competition.
- The "4 P's" of marketing strategy that should be discussed in the marketing plan are (1) product decisions affecting the total product and/or service, (2) distribution (place) activities, (3) pricing decisions, and (4) promotion activities.

3. Discuss the nature of the marketing research process.

- Marketing research involves the gathering, processing, interpreting, and reporting of marketing information.
- The cost of marketing research should be evaluated against its benefits.
- The steps in the marketing research process are identifying the informational need, searching for secondary data, collecting primary data, and interpreting the data gathered.

4. Define market segmentation and its related strategies.

- A focus strategy relies on market segmentation, which is the process of dividing the total market for a product and/or service into groups with similar needs, such that each group is likely to respond favorably to a specific marketing strategy.
- Broad segmentation variables that represent major dimensions of a market are benefit variables and demographic variables.
- Three types of market segmentation strategies are (1) the unsegmented approach, (2) the multisegment approach, and (3) the single-segment approach.
- The unsegmented strategy—when a business defines the total market as its target—is also known as mass marketing.
- A firm that determines that two or more market segments have the potential to be profitable and then develops a unique marketing mix for each segment is following a multisegment strategy.
- A firm that follows a single-segment strategy recognizes that several distinct market segments exist but chooses to concentrate on reaching only one segment.

5. Explain the different methods of forecasting sales.

- A sales forecast is an estimation of how much of a product or service will be purchased within a market during a defined time period.
- The forecasting process may be either a breakdown or a buildup process and may be either direct or indirect, depending on the predicting variable.

Key Terms

small business marketing p. 176
core product/service p. 176
actual product/service p. 176
augmented product/service p. 176
market analysis p. 178
marketing mix p. 178
customer profile p. 179
intellectual property p. 182
marketing research p. 184

secondary data p. 185
primary data p. 186
market p. 189
market segmentation p. 190
segmentation variables p. 190
benefit variables p. 190
demographic variables p. 190
unsegmented strategy (mass marketing) p. 190

multisegment strategy p. 191
single-segment strategy p. 192
sales forecast p. 193
breakdown process (chain-ratio method) p. 195
buildup process p. 195
direct forecasting p. 195
indirect forecasting p. 195

Discussion Questions

1. What is the scope of small business marketing? What do you think the differences might be if you were a manager in a large corporation?

2. How do the three marketing philosophies differ? Select a product and discuss marketing tactics that could be used to implement each philosophy.

3. What are the obstacles to adopting a consumer orientation in a small firm?

4. Briefly describe each of the components of a formal marketing plan.

5. What are the steps in the marketing research process? Which step do you feel would be the hardest for you to take? Why?

6. What are the major considerations in designing a questionnaire?

7. Briefly explain the three components of the definition of a market, as presented in this chapter.

8. What types of variables are used for market segmentation? Would a small firm use the same variables as a large business? Why or why not?

9. Explain the difference between a multisegment strategy and a single-segment strategy. Which one is more likely to be appealing to a small firm? Why?

10. Explain why forecasting is used more widely by large firms than by small ones.

You Make the Call

SITUATION 1

Tina and George Showalter opened the Blonde Bear Bed & Breakfast in Kenai, Alaska, in 2005. According to Tina, "Our first summer, we did great with word-of-mouth advertising, and then we got involved in the Internet, and it has pretty much exploded from there." In this town with a population of under 10,000, 50 businesses signed up with MerchantCircle.com, a local business listing service. The site provides business descriptions, reviews, blogs, coupons, maps, and links among the companies. The cross-promotional and networking benefits have proven valuable to the businesses on the site.

Sources: Amanda C. Kooser, "Go Local," *Entrepreneur*, March 2007, pp. 72–75; and http://www.merchantcircle.com, accessed March 14, 2009.

Question 1 What businesses do you think would benefit most from being on a local website in your hometown?

Question 2 How do businesses that provide such local Web services differ from newspapers and Yellow Pages?

SITUATION 2

Should infomercials be part of your marketing plan? The Sharper Image began marketing with infomercials in 2000, when they ran a two-minute spot for the Razor Scooter 10 to 50 times per day. According to company founder Richard Thalheimer, The Sharper Image sold just enough scooters over the phone to break even on the ads. What made it worthwhile was the effect on in-store sales. Those jumped tenfold.

Thalheimer developed some guidelines for infomercials:

- Margins for products advertised should be at least 50 percent.
- You have to cover the costs of airtime.
- Longer infomercials are more costly, but the costs are worth it for complex products.

- If you are breaking even or better, expand to more channels and time slots.
- When sales flatten, stop.

Flattening sales at The Sharper Image eventually led to Thalheimer's departure. His newest company, RichardSolo.com, relies on Internet sales rather than infomercials.

Sources: Richard Thalheimer, "Ask Richard Thalheimer," *Inc. Magazine*, March 2007; and http://richardsolo.com, accessed March 14, 2009.

Question 1 Do you think that infomercials might work better for certain market segments than others? If so, describe those segments.

Question 2 Do you watch infomercials? If so, did you ever purchase a product as a result? If not, why not?

SITUATION 3

In June 2007, *Entrepreneur* magazine published an article telling companies they should be targeting unmarried adults as a market. More specifically, its recommendation was to focus on single women. According to the United States Census Bureau, more than half of adult women in the United States are single or separated. Creative marketers might think about the needs of single women with regard to financing or insuring home purchases or purchasing home improvement items. Many older single women would likely have the resources to purchase luxury items.

Source: Nichole L. Torres, "The Power of One," *Entrepreneur*, June 2007, p. 28; and http://factfinder.census.gov, accessed March 14, 2009.

Question 1 What products and services can you think of that might appeal to single women who are your age? What products or services might be directed toward a market segment of financially independent single women who are retired?

Question 2 What promotion strategies would you choose to reach single women in order to sell home improvement products?

Experiential Exercises

1. View the website of a local small business. Interview the owner of that business about how the website fits into his or her overall marketing plan.

2. Assume you are planning to market a new breath mint. Write a detailed customer profile, and explain how you would develop the sales forecast for this product.

3. Interview someone from a small business assistance organization (e.g., Small Business Development Center, Service Corps of Retired Executives, chamber of commerce, etc.). Does she or he help clients or members with marketing research? What does she or he consider to be the best sources of market information?

Small Business & Entrepreneurship Resource Center

The Small Business and Entrepreneurship Resource Center offers complete small business management resources through a comprehensive database that covers all major areas of starting, operating, and maintaining a business from financing, management, marketing, accounting, taxes, and more. Use the access code that came with your new book to access the site and perform the exercises in each chapter.

1. A business must supply satisfaction to its customers if it is to thrive in today's markets. Mark Vadon started a company called, Blue Nile, that sells diamonds and jewelry on-line. Describe how Blue Nile is differentiated from other diamond sellers.

Sources: Beyond their years: these entrepreneurs have it all: brains, business savvy and millions of dollars. Find out what you can learn from the best and the brightest America has to offer. Amanda C. Kooser, April Y. Pennington, Karen E. Spaeder, and Nichole L. Torres. *Entrepreneur* 31,11 (Nov 2003): p74(10).

"A boy's best friend; Internet jewellers.(Blue Nile)." *The Economist (US)* 386, 8572 (March 22, 2008): 76US.

Video Case 7

eHARMONY (P. 636)

This case illustrates the use of a marketing plan, from conception to implementation, in the development and ultimate success of one of the most highly recognized online dating services.

ALTERNATIVE CASES FOR CHAPTER 7:

Case 14, Rodgers Chevrolet, p. 654

 ## The Business Plan: Laying the Foundation

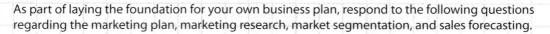

As part of laying the foundation for your own business plan, respond to the following questions regarding the marketing plan, marketing research, market segmentation, and sales forecasting.

Marketing Plan Questions

1. Who is your competition?
2. Have you conducted a SWOT analysis?
3. What is the customer profile for your product and/or service?
4. How will you identify prospective customers?
5. What geographic area will you serve?
6. What are the distinguishing characteristics of your product and/or service?
7. What steps have already been taken to develop your product and/or service?
8. What do you plan to name your product and/or service?

9. Will there be a warranty?

10. How will you set the price for your product and/or service?

11. What type of distribution plan will you use?

12. Will you export to other countries?

13. What type of selling effort will you use?

14. What special selling skills will be required?

15. What types of advertising and sales promotion will you use?

16. Can you use public relations and publicity to promote your company and product/service?

Marketing Research Questions

1. What types of research should be conducted to collect the information you need?

2. How much will this research cost?

3. What sources of secondary data will address your informational needs?

4. What sources of relevant data are available in your local library?

5. What sources of outside professional assistance would you consider using to help with marketing research?

6. Is there information available on the Internet that might be helpful?

7. What research questions do you need answers to?

Market Segmentation Questions

1. Will you focus on a limited market within the industry?

2. What segmentation variables will you use to define your target market?

3. If you determine that several distinct market segments exist, will you concentrate on just one segment?

Forecasting Questions

1. How do you plan to forecast sales for your product and/or service?

2. What sources of forecasting assistance have you consulted?

3. What sales forecasting techniques are most appropriate to your needs?

4. What is the sales forecast for your product and/or service?

5. How reliable is your sales forecast?

chapter 8

The Human Resources Plan

Managers, Owners, Allies, and Directors

In the VIDEO SPOTLIGHT
Biosite, Inc.
http://www.biosite.com

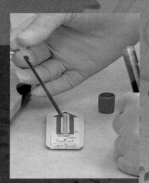

Small Business School, the series on PBS Stations, Worldnet, and the Web at http://www.smallbusinessschool.org. Printed with permission of Hattie Bryant, producer.

Few entrepreneurs imagine going public when they initially structure their business. Most small businesses start out as simple proprietorships, with a single owner (the founder). For the three founders of Biosite, Inc., however, things were a bit different. The company they worked for had been acquired, and the new owner, pharmaceutical giant Eli Lilly, was not interested in letting Kim Blickenstaff, Dr. Ken Buechler, and Dr. Gunars Valkirs set up their own internal company to develop unique medical testing technologies. So these three scientists decided to start their own company.

From the start, the success of Biosite has hinged on the overlapping strengths of its founders, the commitment they have to one another, their recognition that the structure of the business should be formalized, and their ability to bring all these elements to bear on the development of extremely innovative medical technologies. The result has been a highly creative biotechnology company, built on a strong business foundation.

How a company is structured can significantly affect the business activities of the founders. Before going public, the three founders of Biosite were creative, nimble, and focused on science. Once they changed the company structure by recreating it as a public corporation, however, almost half of their time was immediately relegated to investor relations. Watch this video spotlight to see how a strong team can propel great ideas, even when the structure of the business changes.

Video material provided by Hattie Bryant, Producer of Small Business School, the series on PBS Stations, Worldnet, and the Web at http://www.smallbusinessschool.org.

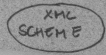

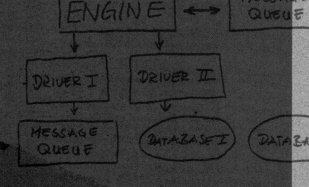

LOOKING AHEAD
AFTER STUDYING THIS CHAPTER, YOU SHOULD BE ABLE TO...

1. Describe the characteristics and value of a strong management team.

2. Explain the common legal forms of organization used by small businesses.

3. Identify factors to consider in choosing among the primary legal forms of organization.

4. Describe the unique features and restrictions of five specialized organizational forms.

5. Explain the nature of strategic alliances and their uses in small businesses.

6. Describe the effective use of boards of directors and advisory councils.

What image comes to mind when you hear the word *entrepreneur?* You may see a person with powerful ideas, an inspiring personality, and dogged determination. Perhaps Michael Dell, Bill Gates, and Henry Ford, all of whom launched fabulously successful enterprises. These "can do" individuals turned creative business ideas into high-potential startups—and the rest, as they say, is history. Lone-wolf entrepreneurs accept the challenge to build something truly great, which makes for fascinating stories, but is that how it usually happens?

One small business writer has expressed doubt about the storyline: "There is no question that small companies are almost always driven, at least at the outset, by the passion of a single risk-taking individual. But the myth of the solo flier, however romantic, obscures something crucial: Business success depends on collaboration."[1] In many cases, collaboration begins almost from the start, when two or more individuals come together as a team to launch a new enterprise.

To be sure, there are still plenty of solo entrepreneurs starting new businesses,[2] but evidence is mounting to show that team-founded ventures tend to outperform ventures with a single founder.[3] This suggests that, in most cases, it is very helpful for an entrepreneur to identify and attract a strong management team. A business plan that provides for strong leadership is appealing to both potential investors and prospective managerial personnel. Clearly, the management team can have a profound impact on the performance of the venture, and founders have much greater control over this factor than they do over others, including market conditions and competitor reactions.[4]

Whether potential investors and prospective managerial personnel have the opportunity also to become partial owners of the company depends on the ownership structure selected by the entrepreneur—that is, the legal form of organization. The direction of the business will be strongly affected by whether the entrepreneur chooses to go with a sole proprietorship, a partnership, a corporation, or one of various other forms. We discuss legal forms of organization in greater depth later in this chapter.

And a new business rarely has the financial resources to incorporate into the organization all of the leadership and managerial personnel it could use. One way to deal with this limitation is to build alliances with other companies; another is to take advantage of the expertise of outside directors. Evidence shows that strategic alliances are becoming increasingly important to small businesses, as are active, objective boards of directors.

Wise decisions regarding the management team, the form of organization, strategic alliances, and the board of directors can greatly enhance the performance of a company. On the other hand, even *brilliant* ideas can be doomed if an enterprise is not connected to the human resources it needs or fails to use them effectively. The tired old slogan "Our People Make the Difference" can be true, but only if those people are carefully selected, well organized, and effectively led.

Building a Management Team

If a firm is extremely small, the founder will probably be the key manager and perhaps the only manager. In most firms, however, others share leadership roles with the owner or owners, which creates opportunities to leverage their combined networks and resources for the good of the company. In general, the *management team* consists of individuals with supervisory responsibilities, as well as nonsupervisory personnel who play key roles in the business.[5] For example, members of a management team might include a financial manager who supervises a small office staff and another person who directs the marketing effort.

1. Describe the characteristics and value of a strong management team.

management team
Managers and other key persons who give a company its general direction.

If you should find that you don't have your "dream team" in place, understand that the team arrangement does not have to be permanent. Though it can be difficult to do, sometimes you have to respectfully and appropriately let individuals go when they cannot or will not effectively support the business; new members can be added to the team as the need arises.[6]

Strong management can make the best of a good business idea by securing the resources needed to make it work. Of course, even a highly competent management team cannot rescue a firm that is based on a weak business concept or that lacks adequate resources. But the importance of strong management to startups is evident in the attitudes of prospective investors, who consider the quality of a new venture's management to be one of the most important factors in decisions to invest or take a pass. In other words, they know that enterprises typically perform poorly if they are guided by weak or incapable managers.

As indicated earlier, a management team often can bring greater strength to a venture than an individual entrepreneur can. One reason for this is that a team can provide a diversity of talent to meet various managerial needs, which can be especially helpful to startups built on new technologies that must manage a broad range of factors. In addition, a team can provide greater assurance of continuity, since the departure of one member of a team is less devastating to a business than the departure of a sole entrepreneur.

The competence required in a management team depends on the type of business and the nature of its operations.[7] For example, a software development firm and a restaurant call for very different types of business experience. Whatever the business, a small firm needs managers with an appropriate combination of educational background and experience. In evaluating the qualifications of an applicant for a key position, an entrepreneur needs to know whether she or he has experience in a related type of business, as a manager or as an entrepreneur.

In many cases, startup owners stack the management team with family and friends, rather than seeking balanced expertise. This has a definite upside. The owner knows these people well and trusts them, they often work for less compensation (despite the elevated risk of joining a new venture), and they are more likely to make personal sacrifices to keep the business alive. The downside is that the team can quickly become very homogeneous, lack overall competence, lean toward feelings of entitlement, and carry the baggage of family dysfunction into the enterprise. All of these factors—the negative and the positive—should be taken into consideration when hiring family and friends.

Achieving Balance

Not all members of a management team need competence in all areas—the key is balance. If one member has expertise in finance, another should have an adequate marketing background. And the venture will need someone who can supervise employees effectively.[8] This diversity in perspectives and work styles is what enables the completion of complex tasks, but it can also lead to serious conflict, which can squeeze all the energy and enthusiasm out of a venture.[9]

Even when entrepreneurs recognize the need for team members with varying expertise, they frequently seek to replicate their own personalities and management styles. Interpersonal compatibility and cooperation among team members are necessary for effective collaboration, and cohesive teams tend to perform better.[10] However, experience suggests that a functionally diverse and balanced team will be more likely to cover all the bases, giving the company a competitive edge.

A management team, then, should comprise both competent insiders and outside specialists. For example, a small firm will benefit by developing working relationships with a commercial bank, a law firm, and an accounting firm. (A number of outside sources of managerial assistance are identified and discussed in Chapter 19.) The role of an active board of directors in providing counsel and guidance to the management team is discussed later in this chapter.

LIVING THE DREAM:

entrepreneurial challenges

Friends in Fashion
www.bonobos.com

Andy Dunn, 29, and Brian Spaly, 31, are trouser-making entrepreneurs and cofounders of Bonobos, Inc., a New York–based startup that produces innovative pants for men.

These two close friends bring their own unique skills and insights to the business. The venture's website identifies three things that Dunn loves about Bonobos:

> A cult of passionate consumers. The potential to create sustainable business model innovation in a stagnant industry. And an opportunity to build a company in a market that Andy knows well—one where he himself is the target customer. Andy is a self-described "wannabe" fashionable guy who doesn't enjoy shopping or have a talent for it. What's authentic about Bonobos for Andy is not in the design of Bonobos [pants], but in their consumption. Andy [is] building a company for consumers like himself . . . guys who want awesome pants, but not enough to go shopping for them at a store.

Dunn is CEO of the company and certainly has a mind for the business model behind it, but Bonobos actually got its start from Spaly, whose designer instincts told him that the only way he would find pants that fit him correctly would be to make them himself. And that's exactly what he did. In 2005, Spaly borrowed a girlfriend's sewing machine and went to work, "learning to sew the seat of my pants by the seat of my pants," he quips. From personal experimentation, Spaly "designed the trademark Bonobos pattern to solve his own trouser woes: a curved waist band to better accommodate a real guy's body, a slight bootcut to flatter the figure, and less fabric in the thighs so they weren't so baggy and boxy."

The results of this foray into fashion were very impressive. Spaly made some samples, and then he pulled off a limited production run so that others could give his innovation a try. Ninety percent of the guys who slipped into a pair of his unique trousers wanted to buy them, often placing orders for more. From that early experience, Bonobos was born; Spaly teamed up with Dunn to launch the company online in 2007.

Dunn and Spaly know a thing or two about the world of business. They each have MBAs from Stanford University's Graduate School of Business and have worked with high-profile corporations, like the global business and strategy consulting giant Bain & Company. Their venture, however, represents a healthy mix of both men's unique and complementary skills and personalities, which appears to be a recipe for success. In its first month, the startup sold $12,000 worth of trousers; today, the company is grossing $160,000 a month, with orders coming from as far away as New Zealand and Dubai. The competition is fierce, though, so the entrepreneurial team will have to work fast if it is to make a "material difference" in its already-crowded market space.

Sources: Dylan Machan, "By the Seat of Their Pants," *Smart Money*, November 2008, p. 56; Justin Petruccelli, "A Perfect Pair," Entrepreneur, July 24, 2008, http://www.entrepreneur.com/startingabusiness/successstories/article195864.html accessed December 12, 2008; and http://www.bonobos.com, accessed December 8, 2008.

© Bonobos

Expanding Social Networks

Sometimes it's not *what* you know but *who* you know that matters. Not only can the management team help the venture obtain investment and technology resources, but it can also (perhaps most important) connect the enterprise with a social network that provides access to a wide range of resources beyond the reach of individual team members. A *social network* is the web of relationships that a person has with other people, including roommates or other acquaintances from college, former employees and business associates, contacts through community organizations like the Rotary Club, and friends from church or synagogue. But it doesn't end there. A friend from college may not have what you need, but she may know someone who does. It is often said that business is all about relationships, a principle that is certainly not lost on successful entrepreneurs. And the power of social networks is expanded tremendously as well-connected people are added to the management team.

What does an entrepreneur need from his or her network? That all depends on the situation. Howard Aldrich and Nancy Carter, two highly regarded experts on building management teams and social networks, have found that nearly half of those who are starting businesses use their networks to access information or get advice. About one-fourth use their networks to gain introductions to other people, while a much smaller percentage use connections to obtain money, business services, physical facilities and equipment, help with personal needs, and other forms of assistance.[11] Clearly, a healthy system of personal relationships can help a small business access the resources it needs to get established and grow.

Beyond providing access to resources, social networks can be especially helpful in communicating legitimacy and jump-starting sales. New ventures and small businesses often find it difficult to "get the business ball rolling" because potential customers simply don't know them well enough. Reputable firms may hesitate to do business with a company that doesn't have a demonstrated track record for reliable delivery or quality products or services. But acquiring one or more high-profile customers may persuade others to give a relatively unknown company a shot at their business, too. For an entrepreneur, having a healthy social network and a management team with helpful connections can be critical in establishing a solid reputation.

Some small business owners are tapping into the expanding universe of social-networking tools to attract customers, connect with peers, and share advice about common problems. In fact, Forrester Research found that in 2008 more than one-fifth of the small companies it surveyed were adopting some kind of social-networking technology in that year alone.[12] Here are a few of the more popular choices:

- *LinkedIn.com:* Allows users to record contact details of people they know and trust in business; excellent for recruiting professionals
- *MySpace.com:* Offers an interactive, user-submitted network of friends, featuring personal profiles, blogs, groups, photos, etc.; useful in marketing to Gen Y customers (those born in the 1980s and 1990s)
- *Twitter.com:* Enables people to send brief updates, or micro-blogs, to those signed up to receive them via computer or cell phone; powerful tool for sending out information and doing publicity and mobile marketing
- *Yelp.com:* Permits users to rate and comment on local businesses; good for getting feedback from customers; cheaper than surveys
- *Facebook.com:* Lets users join networks organized by city, workplace, school, or region; superb for connecting with business contacts you seldom see and for observing how people interact in social networks

The number of social-networking tools continues to expand rapidly, and keeping up with all of them is a challenge. However, these alternatives can help you make connections easier, faster, and more conveniently—but only if you use them.

Regardless of how you pull it together, an active and robust network is necessary for building *social capital,* which we define as the advantage created by an individual's connections within a network of social relationships. But this advantage doesn't develop overnight or by accident. It takes years to build social capital, and the building blocks are well known—being reliable as a friend, being fair in your dealings, being true to your word.

The principle of reciprocation can be extremely helpful in adding to whatever social capital you already have. In his popular book on influence, Robert Cialdini defines *reciprocation* as a subtle but powerful obligation, deeply embedded in every society, to repay in kind what another person has done for us or provided to us.[13] In general, people naturally feel that they should return favors. You can easily prime the pump of social capital by being the first to lend a hand and then watch those you assist come to your rescue when you run up against a challenge and ask for help. You don't have to fake it; just slow down a bit, and take a genuine interest in the needs of your friends and acquaintances. And helping others doesn't have to be costly; in today's information economy, passing along an important bit of information or insight is easy and free—but it can be as good as gold! So, think ahead, and reach out to help where you can. Your social capital is sure to increase, binding friends and acquaintances to you and providing a solid foundation for building a business.

social capital
The advantage created by an individual's connections in a social network.

reciprocation
A powerful social rule based on an obligation to repay in kind what another has done for or provided to us.

Specifying Structure

Once members of the management team have been selected, an entrepreneur must design an internal management structure that defines relationships among all members of the organization. Relationships among the various positions—such as advertising manager, marketing director, financial officer, and human resource manager—should be determined to avoid overlapping responsibilities that invite conflict.

The management plan should be drawn up in a way that provides for business growth. Any unfilled positions should be specified, and job descriptions should spell out the duties of and necessary qualifications for such positions. Methods for selecting key employees should be explained. Compensation arrangements, including bonuses or other incentive plans for key organization members, should be carefully considered and specified in the plan.

Choosing a Legal Form of Organization

In launching a new business, an entrepreneur must choose a legal form of organization, which will determine who the actual owners of the business are. The most basic options are the sole proprietorship, partnership, and C corporation. More specialized forms of organization exist, but many small businesses find one of these common forms suitable for their needs. After outlining the primary options, we look first at some criteria for choosing among them and then introduce five specialized forms that offer their own unique features and advantages. Exhibit 8-1 shows some of the various forms of organization.

2. Explain the common legal forms of organization used by small businesses.

The Sole Proprietorship Option

A *sole proprietorship,* the most basic business form, is a company owned by one person. An individual proprietor has title to all business assets and is subject to the claims of creditors. He or she receives all of the firm's profits but must also assume all losses, bear all risks, and pay all debts. Although this form certainly is not right for everyone, forming a sole proprietorship

sole proprietorship
A business owned by one person, who bears unlimited liability for the enterprise.

EXHIBIT 8-1

Forms of Legal Organization for Small Businesses

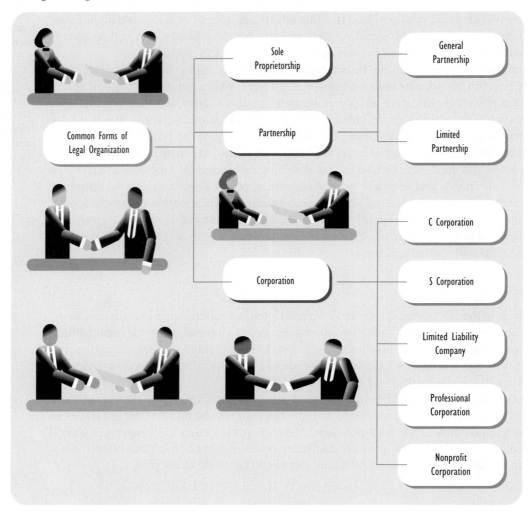

is nonetheless the simplest and cheapest way to start operation. Most states do not even require such companies to have a business license. Because of the ease of startup, the vast majority of small businesses (69 percent)[14] adopt this legal structure (see Exhibit 8-2).

In a sole proprietorship, an owner is free from interference by partners, shareholders, and directors. However, a sole proprietorship lacks some of the advantages of other legal forms. For example, there are no limits on the owner's personal liability—that is, the owner of the business has *unlimited liability,* and thus his or her personal assets can be taken by business creditors if the enterprise fails. For this reason, the sole proprietorship form is usually the practical choice only for very small businesses. In addition, sole proprietors are not employees of the business and cannot receive the advantage of many tax-free fringe benefits, such as insurance and hospitalization plans, which are often provided by corporations for their employees.

The death of the owner terminates the legal existence of a sole proprietorship. Thus, the possibility of the owner's death may cloud relationships between a business and its creditors and employees. It is important that the owner have a will, because the assets of the business minus its liabilities will belong to her or his heirs. In a will, a sole proprietor can give an executor the power to run the business for the heirs until they can take it over or it can be sold.

Another contingency that must be provided for is the possible incapacity of the sole proprietor. For example, if she or he were badly hurt in an accident and hospitalized for an extended

unlimited liability
Liability on the part of an owner that extends beyond the owner's investment in the business.

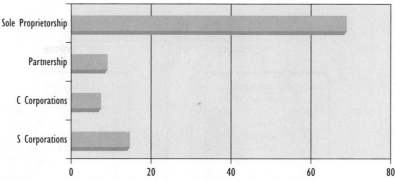

Sources: Table 1A, Internal Revenue Service, http://www.irs.gov/pub/irs-soi/d6187.pdf, accessed December 5, 2008; and Table 1, Internal Revenue Service, http://www.irs.gov/pub/irs-soi/d6292.pdf, accessed January 13, 2009.

period, the business could be ruined. A sole proprietor can guard against this contingency by giving a competent person legal power of attorney to carry on in such circumstances.

In some cases, circumstances argue against selecting the sole proprietorship option. If the nature of a business involves exposure to legal liability—for example, the manufacture of a potentially hazardous product or the operation of a child-care facility—a legal form that provides greater protection against personal liability is likely to be a better choice. For most companies, however, various forms of insurance are available to deal with the risks of a sole proprietorship, as well as those related to partnerships.[16]

The Partnership Option

A *partnership* is a legal entity formed by two or more co-owners to operate a business for profit. Because of a partnership's voluntary nature, owners can set it up quickly, avoiding many of the legal requirements involved in creating a corporation. A partnership pools the managerial talents and capital of those joining together as business partners. As in a sole proprietorship, however, the owners share unlimited liability.

partnership
A legal entity formed by two or more co-owners to carry on a business for profit.

QUALIFICATIONS OF PARTNERS   Any person capable of contracting may legally become a business partner. Individuals may become partners without contributing capital or having a claim to assets at the time of dissolution; such persons are partners only in regard to management and profits. The formation of a partnership involves consideration not only of legal issues but also of personal and managerial factors. A strong partnership requires partners who are honest, healthy, capable, and compatible.

Operating a business as a partnership has benefits, but it is also fraught with potential problems. Most experts discourage the use of partnerships as a way to run a business, even though there are good and bad qualities associated with this form of organization (see Exhibit 8-3). The benefits of partnerships include the ability to share the workload as well as the emotional and financial burdens of the enterprise and to buy management talent that might otherwise break the budget. And it should not be overlooked that partners can add companionship to life in a small business.

However, many believe the personal conflicts common in partnerships more than offset the benefits, and partners often fall short of one another's expectations. Of course, decision making is more complicated in partnerships because leadership is shared, and owners must also share their equity position in the business, which naturally dilutes the control of each partner. While some of the difficulties of partnerships are financial in nature, most are relational—for example, coping with a partner's dishonesty or dealing with differing priorities. Partnerships

EXHIBIT

8-3 The Advantages and Disadvantages of Partnerships

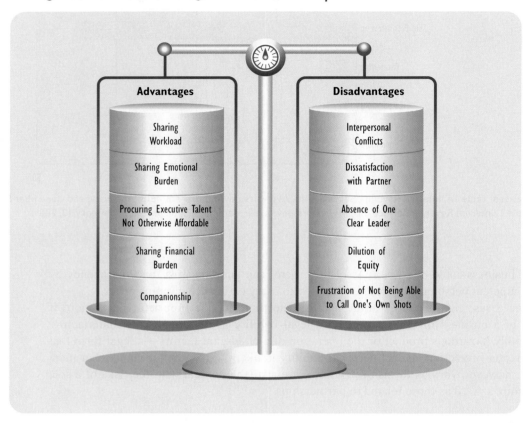

Advantages	Disadvantages
Sharing Workload	Interpersonal Conflicts
Sharing Emotional Burden	Dissatisfaction with Partner
Procuring Executive Talent Not Otherwise Affordable	Absence of One Clear Leader
Sharing Financial Burden	Dilution of Equity
Companionship	Frustration of Not Being Able to Call One's Own Shots

clearly have both disturbing and redeeming qualities, so the issue is not black and white. The important point is that *a partnership should be formed only if it appears to be the best option when all features of the enterprise are taken into consideration.*

Many entrepreneurs have learned about partnerships the hard way—from "the school of hard knocks." Based on the experiences of those who have seen firsthand the extraordinary ups and debilitating downs of partnerships, the following suggestions may help entrepreneurs make the most of this form of organization.

- *Choose your partner carefully.* Partnerships are like marriages—they work best when you pick the right partner. Many sources are available to help you find that "perfect someone," including trade magazines, client contacts, professional associations, even online matching services like BusinessPartners.com. But identifying a promising partner is just a start; you also need to be sure that your goals, values, and work habits are compatible and that your skills are complementary before committing to the deal. Above all, team up with a person you can trust, since the actions of your partner can legally bind you, even if a decision is made without your knowledge or consent.[17]

- *Be open, but cautious, about partnerships with friends.* If trust is critical to the success of a partnership, then wouldn't it be best to look first to friends as potential partners? Not necessarily. Valued relationships can take a quick turn for the worse when a business deal gets rocky, and a Dr. Jekyl friend can sometimes transform into a Mr. Hyde business associate when money enters the picture. And remember, the stakes are high: A minor business deal can quickly ruin a very important friendship.

- *Test-drive the relationship, if possible.* Of course, the best way to determine if you can work well with another person is to actually give the partnership a try before finalizing the deal. Karen Cheney, co-author of the book *How to Start a Successful Home Business,* recommends trying more limited forms of business collaboration before jumping in with both feet. For example, you could share a booth at a trade show and observe the behavior, style, and work habits of the person you hope to team up with. This allows you to assess his or her strengths and weaknesses before committing to a long-term relationship.[18]

- *Create a combined vision for the business.* It's important that partners be on the same page when it comes to forming the business concept they hope to develop together. This takes time, patience, and a lot of conversation. Hal Scogin, owner of a multimedia design business in Olympia, Washington, had hopes of creating a company with two partners, but it soon became obvious that they did not see the business in the same way. Scogin thought the venture was a multimedia design company, but his partners considered it to be a technology company. Needless to say, the partnership did not last long.[19] Some of the specific matters you should discuss before joining forces include the expectations of all partners (contributions of time, money, expertise, etc.), planned division of work, anticipated vacation time, and the sharing of profits and losses.

- *Prepare for the worst.* Keep in mind that more than half of all partnerships fail. That is why most experts recommend having an exit strategy for the partnership from the beginning. What looks like a good business arrangement at the outset can quickly fall apart when market conditions shift, a partner becomes involved in another business venture, or personal circumstances change. For example, the birth of a child, a sudden divorce, or the unexpected death of a spouse can alter everything. If it becomes necessary, exiting a partnership is far more difficult when plans for such an unfortunate outcome were not considered early on.

Failure to take concerns like these into account can derail efforts to build an effective working relationship or doom an otherwise workable partnership to an unnecessary or painful demise.

RIGHTS AND DUTIES OF PARTNERS An oral partnership agreement is legal and binding, but memory is always less than perfect. In his book *Legal Guide for Starting and Running a Small Business,* author and practicing business attorney Fred Steingold strongly recommends that partners sign a written *partnership agreement* to avoid problems later on.[20] This document, which explicitly spells out the partners' rights and duties, should be drawn up before the venture is launched. Though the partners may choose to have an attorney draft the agreement in order to ensure that all important features are included, many other sources of assistance (such as online resources) also are available to guide you through this process. For example, a Google search on "partnership agreements" will pull up hundreds of helpful resources.

Unless the articles of the partnership agreement specify otherwise, a partner is generally recognized as having certain implicit rights. For example, partners share profits or losses equally, unless they have agreed to a different ratio. But these rights are also balanced against serious liabilities. In a general partnership, each party bears *joint and several liability,* which means that a business decision by one partner binds all other partners, even if they were not consulted in advance, didn't approve the agreement or contract in question, or didn't even know about it![21] And as with a sole proprietorship, the unlimited personal liability of the partners can be terrifying. The assets of the business are at risk, of course, but so are the personal assets of the partners, including their homes, cars, and bank accounts. Good faith, together with reasonable care in the exercise of managerial duties, is required of all partners in the business.

Unfortunately, complications can arise even if partners have been careful to match their expectations at the start of the partnership and the arrangement has been formalized through a partnership agreement. When problems emerge and trust begins to break down, partners should move quickly to try to resolve the underlying issues. If they cannot do so, they should

partnership agreement
A document that states explicitly the rights and duties of partners.

joint and several liability
The liability of each partner resulting from any one partner's ability to legally bind the other partners.

consider hiring a business mediator. Working with a business mediator can be expensive, but the dissolution of the partnership is likely to be far more costly.

TERMINATION OF A PARTNERSHIP   Death, incapacity, or withdrawal of a partner ends a partnership and requires liquidation or reorganization of the business. Liquidation often results in substantial losses to all partners, but it may be legally necessary, because a partnership represents a close personal relationship of the parties that cannot be maintained against the desire of any one of them.

When one partner dies, loss due to liquidation may be avoided if the partnership agreement stipulates that surviving partners can continue the business after buying the decedent's interest. This option can be facilitated by having each partner carry life insurance that names the other partners as beneficiaries.

Partnerships sometimes have immediate concerns to address when a partner decides to leave the business, especially if the departure was unexpected. Aaron Keller, Brian Aducci, and a third partner started a marketing and design firm in Minneapolis called Capsule. Eighteen months later, when their partner decided to leave the business and start a competing company (taking several employees and clients with him), Keller and Aducci knew they would have to move quickly to avoid serious losses. Lea A. Strickland, small business expert and author of *Out of the Cubicle and Into Business,* analyzed their situation and offered the following emergency prescription: First, cut off the departing partner's access to bank accounts, physical facilities, and company assets to avoid loss or damage to equipment critical to the business. Then quickly assess that partner's role in the enterprise and take steps to fill his shoes, to get the business back to normal as soon as possible. Once these very pressing matters are under control, sort out any legal issues that remain, such as abiding by any exit agreements that may have been signed. With time, and a lot of hard work, Keller and Aducci were able to regain their footing, but the experience helped them to understand just how fragile a partnership can be—and how important it is to have a rapid response plan when things go wrong.[22]

The C Corporation Option

corporation
A business organization that exists as a legal entity and provides limited liability to its owners.

In 1819, Chief Justice John Marshall of the United States Supreme Court defined a *corporation* as "an artificial being, invisible, intangible, and existing only in contemplation of the law." With these words, the Supreme Court recognized the corporation as a *legal entity,* meaning that it can file suit and be sued, hold and sell property, and engage in business operations that are stipulated in the corporate charter. In other words, a corporation is a separate entity from the individuals who own it, which means that the corporation, *not* its owners, is liable for the debts of the business. The implications of this arrangement for risk taking and business formation are profound and far-reaching, prompting one highly influential business executive to declare the creation of the modern corporation to have been the single greatest innovation over the last several hundred years, at least where wealth creation is concerned.[23] The ordinary corporation—often called a *C corporation* to distinguish it from more specialized forms—is discussed in this section.

legal entity
A business organization that is recognized by the law as having a separate legal existence.

C corporation
An ordinary corporation, taxed by the federal government as a separate legal entity.

corporate charter
A document that establishes a corporation's existence.

THE CORPORATE CHARTER   To form a corporation, one or more persons must apply to the secretary of state (at the state level) for permission to incorporate. After completing preliminary steps, including payment of an incorporation fee, the written application (which should be prepared by an attorney) is approved by the secretary of state and becomes the *corporate charter.* This document—sometimes called *articles of incorporation* or *certificate of incorporation*—shows that the corporation exists.

A corporation's charter should be brief, in accord with state law, and broad in its statement of the firm's powers. Details should be left to the *corporate bylaws,* which outline the basic rules for ongoing formalities and decisions of corporate life, including the size of the board of directors, the duties and responsibilities of directors and officers, the scheduling of regular meetings of the directors and shareholders, the means of calling for a special meeting

LIVING THE DREAM:

entrepreneurial challenges

The Pain Potential of Partnerships

In the fairytale of entrepreneurship, your partners work as hard and as diligently as you. They watch your back as you build armies of skilled employees, take strategic market positions, and share the triumphs of vanquished competition and exceeded milestones.

During the early years of my partnership, I imagined my partner sharing important family moments—whether that meant beaming at each other's children at graduation or leaning on each other in times of personal loss and need. It hardly mattered. My belief was I had formed a team to tackle the coming journey.

As a seasoned entrepreneur of fifteen years who had never had a business partner, I imagined the new venture as more of a brotherhood. We would combine our Rolodexes, our life experiences, and be twice as prepared for any eventuality. We had different styles, of course, and very different strengths, which would bring differing and invaluable perspectives to each new business problem. We were roughly the same age and both had new families with young children.

Although I didn't know him well, his family was well-known and respected, and his educational credentials were solid. Our fledgling company was growing in triple

© Capsule US

digits and cash was pouring in. By all appearances, we were well-positioned for a happy ending to the story.

Like any good "B" movie, after the build up just detailed, you know the train wreck is eminent. Yet as a participant, I never saw it coming. There was one moment a year into the venture when I took a cryptic e-mail, which had raised my suspicion, to my lawyer. Together we puzzled over it until, with great feigned wisdom, he responded, "If you can't trust your partners, who can you trust?" Who indeed? The opportunity to discover a big problem was missed and we pressed ahead.

When the problem was finally discovered, two and a half years after our founding, I was completely unprepared. The headlines of this story are gory and embarrassing; more than $1 million lost from the company, balance sheet inventory securing bank debt revealed to lack title (it had never been paid for), one-third of the company employees (mostly located overseas) involved in some way in this, as well as two of our three joint-venture factories.

We had outstanding contracts for personal residences of household names in the entertainment industry and suddenly had neither the cash, staff, nor production facilities to fulfill them. To make matters worse, consistent with our industry, we had taken 50 percent deposits on these multi-million dollar contracts and had spent the money to procure materials; the money was now gone.

Meanwhile, my now ex-partner had liquidated all his U.S. assets and moved them overseas and he contacted my customers and offered to finish their contracts for lower prices. With no sizeable assets to recover, huge legal bills burning limited capital and a disinterested judiciary, it became painfully obvious that I was unlikely to find satisfaction.

Source: Richard Rhodes, "Partnership Problems and Loss," February 1, 2007, http://www.entrepreneurship.org/Resources/Detail/Default.aspx?id=11126, accessed December 4, 2008.

of these groups, procedures for exercising voting rights, and restrictions on the transfer of corporate stock.

RIGHTS AND STATUS OF STOCKHOLDERS

stock certificate
A document specifying the number of shares owned by a stockholder.

pre-emptive right
The right of stockholders to buy new shares of stock before they are offered to the public.

Ownership in a corporation is evidenced by *stock certificates,* each of which stipulates the number of shares owned by a stockholder. An ownership interest does not confer a legal right to act for the firm or to share in its management. It does, however, provide the stockholder with the right to receive dividends in proportion to stockholdings, but only when the dividends are properly declared by the firm. Ownership of stock typically carries a *pre-emptive right,* or the right to buy new shares, in proportion to the number of shares already owned, before new stock is offered for public sale.

The legal status of stockholders is fundamental, of course, but it may be overemphasized. In many small corporations, the owners typically serve both as directors and as managing officers. The person who owns most or all of the stock can control a business as effectively as if it were a sole proprietorship. Thus, this form of organization can work well for individual- and family-owned businesses, where maintaining control of the firm is important.

LIMITED LIABILITY OF STOCKHOLDERS

For most stockholders, their limited liability is a major advantage of the corporate form of organization. Their financial liability is restricted to the amount of money they invest in the business. Creditors cannot require them to sell personal assets to pay the corporation's debts. However, small corporations are often in a somewhat shaky financial condition during their early years of operation. As a result, a bank that makes a loan to a small firm may insist that the owners assume personal liability for the firm's debts by signing the promissory notes not only as representatives of the firm but personally as well. If the corporation is unable to repay the loan, the banker can then look to the owners' personal assets to recover the amount of the loan. In this case, the corporate advantage of limited liability is lost.

Why would owners agree to personally guarantee a firm's debt? Simply put, they may have no choice if they want the money. Most bankers are unwilling to loan money to an entrepreneur who is not prepared to put his or her own personal assets at risk.

DEATH OR WITHDRAWAL OF STOCKHOLDERS

Unlike a partnership interest, ownership in a corporation is readily transferable. Exchange of shares of stock is sufficient to transfer an ownership interest to a different individual.

Stock of large corporations is exchanged continually without noticeable effect on the operation of the business. For a small firm, however, a change of owners, though legally similar, can involve numerous complications. For example, finding a buyer for the stock of a small company may prove difficult. Also, a minority stockholder in a small firm is vulnerable. If two of three equal shareholders in a small business sold their stock to an outsider, the remaining shareholder would then be at the mercy of that outsider.

The death of a majority stockholder can have unfortunate repercussions in a small firm. An heir, the executor, or a purchaser of the stock might well insist on direct control, with possible adverse effects for other stockholders. To prevent problems of this nature, legal arrangements should be made at the outset to provide for management continuity by surviving stockholders and fair treatment of a stockholder's heirs. As in the case of a partnership, taking out life insurance ahead of time can ensure the ability to buy out a deceased stockholder's interest.

MAINTAINING CORPORATE STATUS

Establishing a corporation is one thing; keeping that status is another. Certain steps must be taken if the corporation is to retain its standing as a separate entity. For example, the corporation must hold annual meetings of both the shareholders and the board of directors, keep minutes to document the major decisions of shareholders and directors, maintain bank accounts that are separate from owners' bank accounts, and file a separate income tax return for the business.

Criteria for Choosing an Organizational Form

3. Identify factors to consider in choosing among the primary legal forms of organization.

Choosing a legal form for a new business deserves careful attention because of the various, sometimes conflicting features of each organizational option. Depending on the particular circumstances of a specific business, the tax advantages of one form, for example, may offset the limited-liability advantages of another form. Some tradeoffs may be necessary. Ideally, an experienced attorney should be consulted for guidance in selecting the most appropriate form of organization.

Some entrepreneurship experts insist that the two most basic forms of business—sole proprietorship and partnership—should *never* be adopted. While these forms clearly have drawbacks, they are workable. As illustrated in Exhibit 8-2, the IRS projected that 69 percent of all new businesses in 2009 would be formed as sole proprietorships, 9 percent would be set up as partnerships, 7 percent would be established as C corporations, and 15 percent would be formed as S corporations.[24] (The S corporation represented in Exhibit 8-2 is discussed as a special form of organization later in the chapter.)

Exhibit 8-4 summarizes the main considerations in selecting one of the three primary forms of ownership. A brief description of each factor follows.

INITIAL ORGANIZATIONAL REQUIREMENTS AND COSTS Organizational requirements and costs rise as the formality of the organization increases. That is, a sole proprietorship is typically less complex and less expensive to form than a partnership, and a partnership is less complex and less expensive to form than a corporation. In view of the relatively modest costs, however, this consideration is of minimal importance in the long run.

LIABILITY OF OWNERS As discussed earlier, a sole proprietorship and a partnership have the built-in disadvantage of unlimited liability for the owners. With these forms of organization, there is no distinction between the firm's assets and the owners' personal assets. In contrast, setting up a corporation limits the owners' liability to their investment in the business. Liability risks are among the most important factors to consider when selecting an organizational form.

Choosing a form of organization merely for the sake of simplicity can sometimes cost an entrepreneur dearly—and more than just money! Against the advice of his attorney, Max Baer decided to operate his production studio in Memphis, Tennessee, as a sole proprietorship, to make startup easier. Things were going well until he was sued by a former employee. That's when the folly of Baer's decision became evident. The litigation went on for nearly a year. During that agonizing period, Baer was tormented by the possibility of losing all of his personal assets, including his house, his boat, and his savings account. Fortunately, the suit was settled for a modest sum, but Baer learned his lesson. He decided to convert his business to a corporation and enjoy the peace of mind that comes with limited liability.[25]

Two final cautions are in order regarding liability and organizational forms. First, incorporation will not protect a firm's owners from liability if it is used to perpetuate a fraud, skirt a law, or commit some wrongful act. In such cases, the courts may decide that there is no legal separation between the owners and the corporate entity, a concept known as *piercing the corporate veil*. Protection from financial liability may be jeopardized if, for example, the company is bankrupt but its owners knowingly take on debt, the board of directors does not meet as required by law or observe other corporate formalities, or business and personal accounts are not kept separate and company funds are used to pay an owner's personal expenses. Legal action is taken most often against smaller, privately held business entities and "sham corporations" that are set up with the specific goal of deceiving others.[26]

piercing the corporate veil A situation in which the courts conclude that incorporation has been used to perpetuate a fraud, skirt a law, or commit some wrongful act, and thus remove liability protections from the corporate entity.

EXHIBIT

Form of Organization	Initial Organizational Requirements and Costs	Liability of Owners	Continuity of Business
Sole proprietorship	Minimum requirements; generally no registration or filing fee	Unlimited liability	Dissolved upon proprietor's death
General partnership	Minimum requirements; generally no registration or filing fee; written partnership agreement not legally required but strongly suggested	Unlimited liability	Unless partnership agreement specifies differently, dissolved upon withdrawal or death of partner
C corporation	Most expensive and greatest requirements; filing fees; compliance with state regulations for corporations	Liability limited to investment in company	Continuity of business unaffected by shareholder withdrawal or death
Form of organization preferred	Proprietorship or partnership	C corporation	C corporation

Of course, some forms of organization, such as the sole proprietorship, offer no shield against liability in the first place, which is one of the reasons that choosing a form carefully is so important.

Second, no form of organization can protect entrepreneurs from *all* forms of liability. For example, if an owner causes a traffic accident and is taken to court and declared personally liable for damages or injuries, he or she will have to pay the judgment, even if it means selling personal assets to satisfy the ruling. If, on the other hand, an employee caused the accident while on company business, the assets of the business will be at risk, but the personal assets of the owner(s) will be shielded from liability—*but only if the business is organized as a corporation or limited liability company*. This protection does not extend to the owners of a sole proprietorship or a partnership, whose personal assets would also be at risk.

As previously discussed, most banks and many suppliers will require small business owners to sign a personal guarantee before loaning money or extending credit to them, regardless of the form of organization. The entrepreneurs will have to pay off these obligations if their businesses are unable to, even if doing so requires the use of personal assets. This is the lender's way of trying to ensure that debts are repaid, but it illustrates one of the practical limitations of selection of an organizational form when it comes to liability protection.[27]

CONTINUITY OF BUSINESS   A sole proprietorship is immediately dissolved on the owner's death. Likewise, a partnership is terminated on the death or withdrawal of a partner, unless the partnership agreement states otherwise. A corporation, on the other hand, offers continuity. The status of an individual investor does not affect the corporation's existence.

TRANSFERABILITY OF OWNERSHIP   Ownership is transferred most easily in the corporation. The ability to transfer ownership, however, is not necessarily good or bad—it all depends on the owners' preferences. In some businesses, owners may want the option of evaluating any prospective new investors; under other circumstances, unrestricted transferability may be preferred.

MANAGEMENT CONTROL   A sole proprietor has absolute control of the firm. Control within a partnership is normally based on the majority vote, so it follows that an increase in the

Transferability of Ownership	Management Control	Attractiveness for Raising Capital	Income Taxes
May transfer ownership of company name and assets	Absolute management freedom	Limited to proprietor's personal capital	Income from the business is taxed as personal income to the proprietor
Requires the consent of all partners	Majority vote of partners required for control	Limited to partners' ability and desire to contribute capital	Income from the business is taxed as personal income to the partners
Easily transferred by transferring shares of stock	Shareholders have final control, but usually board of directors controls company policies	Usually the most attractive form for raising capital	The C corporation is taxed on its income and the stockholder is taxed if and when dividends are received
Depends on the circumstances	Depends on the circumstances	C corporation	Depends on the circumstances

number of partners reduces each partner's voice in management. Within a corporation, control has two dimensions: (1) the formal control vested in the stockholders who own the majority of the voting common shares and (2) the functional control exercised by the corporate officers in conducting daily operations. In a small corporation, these two forms of control usually rest with the same individuals.

ATTRACTIVENESS FOR RAISING CAPITAL

A corporation has a distinct advantage when raising new equity capital, due to the ease of transferring ownership through the sale of common shares and the flexibility in distributing the shares. In contrast, the unlimited liability of a sole proprietorship and a partnership discourages new investors.

INCOME TAXES

Income taxes frequently have a major effect on an owner's selection of a form of organization. To understand the federal income tax system, you must consider the following twofold question: Who is responsible for paying taxes, and how is tax liability determined? The three major forms of organization are taxed in different ways.

SOLE PROPRIETORSHIP Self-employed individuals who operate a business as a sole proprietorship report income from the business on their individual federal income tax returns. They are then taxed at the rates set by law for individuals.

PARTNERSHIP A partnership reports the income it earns to the Internal Revenue Service, but the partnership itself does not pay any taxes. The income is allocated to the partners according to their agreement. The partners each report their own shares of the partnership's income on their personal tax returns and pay any taxes owed.

C CORPORATION The C corporation, as a separate legal entity, reports its income and pays any taxes related to these profits. The owners (stockholders) of the corporation must report on their personal tax returns any amounts paid to them by the corporation in the form of dividends. (They must also report capital gains or losses, but only at the time they sell their stock in the company.) Keep in mind that dividends are, in essence, taxed twice—first as part of the corporation's earnings and then as part of the owners' personal income. However, taxes on most dividends have recently been reduced to 5 percent for taxpayers in the 10- and 15-percent tax brackets and to 15 percent for taxpayers in higher tax brackets.

To learn more about the specifics of tax matters relevant to the various forms of organization outlined in this chapter, visit the IRS's small business webpage at http://www.irs.gov/ businesses/small/index.html. It's easy to navigate and provides hundreds of pages of useful information with just a few clicks of a mouse. You'll find links to tax information on the different organizational forms, insights related to important small business topics, and answers to industry-specific questions, as well as forms and publications that will help with tax planning and preparation.

Specialized Forms of Organization

The majority of new and small businesses use one of the three major organizational forms just described—the sole proprietorship, partnership, or C corporation. However, other specialized types of organization are also used by small firms. Five of these alternatives merit further consideration: the limited partnership, the S corporation, the limited liability company, the professional corporation, and the nonprofit corporation.

4. Describe the unique features and restrictions of five specialized organizational forms.

limited partnership
A partnership with at least one general partner and one or more limited partners.

general partner
A partner in a limited partnership who has unlimited personal liability.

limited partner
A partner in a limited partnership who is not active in its management and has limited personal liability.

S corporation (Subchapter S corporation)
A type of corporation that offers limited liability to its owners but is taxed by the federal government as a partnership.

THE LIMITED PARTNERSHIP The *limited partnership* is a special form of partnership involving at least one general partner and one or more limited partners. The *general partner* remains personally liable for the debts of the business, but *limited partners* have limited personal liability as long as they do not take an active role in the management of the partnership. In other words, limited partners risk only the capital they invest in the business. An individual with substantial personal wealth can, therefore, invest money in a limited partnership without exposing his or her personal assets to liability claims that might arise through activities of the business. If a limited partner becomes active in management, however, his or her limited liability is lost. To form a limited partnership, partners must file a certificate of limited partnership with the proper state office, as state law governs this form of organization.

THE S CORPORATION The designation *S corporation,* or *Subchapter S corporation,* is derived from Subchapter S of the Internal Revenue Code, which permits a business to retain the limited-liability feature of a C corporation while being taxed as a partnership. To obtain S corporation status, a corporation must meet certain requirements, including the following:

- No more than 100 stockholders are allowed.[28]
- All stockholders must be individuals or certain qualifying estates and trusts.[29]
- Only one class of stock can be outstanding.
- Fiscally, the corporation must operate on a calendar-year basis.
- Nonresident alien stockholders are not permitted.

A restriction preventing S corporations from owning other corporations, including C corporations, has recently been removed, resulting in tax advantages for some small firms. Whereas in the past different businesses had to be legally separate, individual subsidiaries now may consolidate under one S corporation and submit one tax return.[30] However, combining two businesses under one legal entity can create problems. For example, liability is shared, so if one business gets sued or is bogged down in debt, the other will be exposed to that legal or financial risk. And combined businesses are more difficult to market and sell because potential buyers find it hard to distinguish between the two and determine their individual values.[31]

An S corporation does not pay corporate income taxes and instead passes taxable income or losses on to the stockholders. This allows stockholders to receive dividends from the corporation without double taxation on the firm's profit (once through a corporate tax and again through a personal tax on received dividends). A competent tax attorney should be consulted before selecting S status, as tax law changes have considerable effect on the S corporation arrangement.

THE LIMITED LIABILITY COMPANY

The *limited liability company* is a relatively new form of organization. It has grown in popularity because it offers the simplicity of a sole proprietorship and the liability protection of a corporation. A limited liability company can have an unlimited number of owners (even a single owner), and these may include non-U.S. citizens. This form differs from the C corporation in that it avoids double taxation. Limited liability companies are not taxed on corporate income but simply pass that income on to their owners, who pay taxes on it as part of their personal income.

The major advantage of the limited liability company over the partnership form is the liability protection it affords. While general partners are exposed to personal liability, owners in a limited liability company are, as the name implies, protected with respect to their personal assets.

According to many attorneys, the limited liability company is usually the best choice for new businesses. It has the same ability as the S corporation to pass taxable income on to shareholders, and compared to an S corporation, the limited liability company is easier to set up, is more flexible, and offers some significant tax advantages.[32] But a limited liability company isn't always the best way to go. For example, under the following conditions, it would be better to use a C corporation:

- *You want to provide extensive fringe benefits to owners or employees.* The C corporation can deduct these benefits, and they are not treated as taxable income to the employees.

- *You want to offer stock options to employees.* Since limited liability companies do not have stock, they cannot offer such incentives.

- *You hope to go public or sell out at some time in the future.* A C corporation can go public or sell out to another corporation in a tax-free, stock-for-stock exchange.

- *You plan to convert to a C corporation eventually.* You cannot change from a pass-through entity like a limited liability company without paying additional taxes.

THE PROFESSIONAL CORPORATION

Have you noticed the initials PC or PA as part of the corporate name on the letterhead or signage of your doctor, dentist, or attorney? These letters indicate that the practice is set up as a *professional corporation* in order to offer professional services. Though its meaning varies from state to state, the term *professional* usually applies to those individuals whose professions require that they obtain a license before they can practice, including doctors, chiropractors, lawyers, accountants, engineers, architects, and other highly trained individuals. But unlike other liability-shielding organizational forms, the professional corporation does not protect a practitioner from her or his own negligence or malpractice; rather, it shields one owner from the liability of other owners in the practice. In some states, a different business structure called a limited liability partnership can serve the same purpose and may have additional advantages. Obviously, the professional corporation applies to a fairly narrow range of enterprises, but it is usually the best option for businesses that fall into that category. In fact, many state laws require this form of organization before a practice can operate.

THE NONPROFIT CORPORATION

For some ventures, the most practical form of organization is the *nonprofit corporation.* Most elect to become 501(c)(3) organizations, which are created to serve civic, educational, charitable, or religious purposes. To qualify for 501(c)(3) status, the money-raising concern, fund, or foundation must be a corporation; the IRS will not grant this option to an individual or partnership. In the application process, the officers need to

organizational
test
Verification of whether a
nonprofit organization is
staying true to its stated
purpose.

submit articles of organization that spell out and limit the range of activities of the enterprise—for a tax exemption to be granted, the organization must pass the *organizational test* ("IRS-speak" for verification that the organization is staying true to the articles filed). A nonprofit corporation must establish a board of directors or trustees to oversee its operations, and if it should dissolve, it is required to transfer its assets to another nonprofit corporation.

Though social entrepreneurs certainly do not have to charter their enterprises as nonprofit corporations, they often choose this option. Matthew Gutschick and Ben Whiting, both 2006 graduates of Wake Forest University, started a social enterprise called MagicMouth Theatre, to teach theater and magic to young people and offer opportunities for them to perform. As Gutschick recalls, when they selected a business structure, the two "decided to go nonprofit because it gave us a larger measure of credibility and authenticity."[33] In other words, choosing to structure an organization as a nonprofit corporation can be a way to reinforce the message and work of the organization.

Forming Strategic Alliances

5. Explain the
nature of strategic
alliances and
their uses in
small businesses.

*strategic
alliance*
An organizational
relationship that
links two or more
independent business
entities in a common
endeavor.

A *strategic alliance* is an organizational relationship that links two or more independent business entities in some common endeavor. Without affecting the independent legal status of the participating business partners, it provides a way for companies to improve their individual effectiveness by sharing certain resources. And these alliances can take many forms, from informal information exchanges to formal equity or contract-based relationships and everything in between. According to a recent study by the National Federation of Independent Business, some types of alliances that are most popular with small businesses include licensing contracts, working with long-term outside contractors, entering production agreements, and distribution-focused deals (see Exhibit 8-5).[34]

Strategic alliances are more important to small businesses today than ever before, and an increasing number of entrepreneurs are finding creative ways to use these cooperative strategies to their advantage. In fact, statistics show that nearly two-thirds of small businesses use alliances, and three-fourths of these companies report having positive experiences with them.[35] Given the escalating pace of competition and the rising cost of developing essential capabilities, alliances provide a way for small companies to access another firm's world-class resources so that they can be more competitive. Since a competitive advantage often goes to the entrepreneur who is quick to exploit it, many small business owners see strategic alliances as an essential part of their plan for growth. Cooperative strategies represent one way to keep up with the accelerating pace of change in today's business environment. (See Chapter 18 for a discussion of strategic alliances as a strategy option for global enterprises.)

Strategic Alliances with Large Companies

Large corporations create strategic alliances not only with other large corporations but also with small businesses. Typically, these alliances are formed to join the complementary skills and expertise of the partnered firms, in order to promote the competitive edge of both (or all) parties. For example, large manufacturers sometimes team up with innovative small manufacturers in product development efforts, and giant retailers form alliances with smaller suppliers to work hand in hand to achieve specific quality requirements and meet demanding delivery schedules.

Combining the speed, flexibility, and creative energy of a small business with the industry experience, production capabilities, and market reach of a large corporation can be a winning strategy. In 1998, Katherine Kent started The Solar Store in Tucson, Arizona, to retrofit existing

Most Popular Small Business Alliances by Type

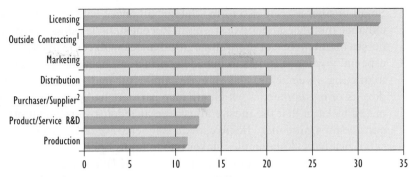

¹These alliances include only relationships that are long-term in nature.

²These alliances include agreements relating to programs, such as just-in-time supply or total quality management that are relatively long-term in nature.

Source: William J. Dennis, Jr. (ed.), "Strategic Alliances," *National Small Business Poll*, Vol. 4, No. 4 (Washington, DC: NFIB Research Foundation, 2004), pp. 1–8.

homes with solar power systems. The focus of her business changed six years later, however, when she struck a deal with residential construction heavyweight Pulte Homes. Pulte was scheduled to start a new subdivision that would eventually have 1,500 new homes with solar heating and electricity, but it needed a supplier to demonstrate how to install and operate the energy-saving equipment. Enter The Solar Store. Kent's company "gave Pulte's people a crash course in solar power," and "Pulte showed The Solar Store how to outfit entire subdivisions from the ground up and how to save time in the assembly process." Furthermore, the arrangement gave The Solar Store tremendous purchasing power and allowed it to start buying directly from manufacturers, which shaved the tiny partner's materials costs by a very helpful 7 percent in the first year alone.[36]

Alliances with large firms can give a tremendous boost to performance, but some small businesses discover that bigger isn't always better. The advantages created by joining forces with large firms must be weighed against the risk of being squeezed financially or of running into smothering bureaucratic complications. One small company, for example, jumped at the chance to form an alliance with a major multinational firm in the same industry. Everything seemed to be running smoothly until the small enterprise learned that a simple invoice discrepancy was holding up a $1.2 million payment that it desperately needed to meet future expansion commitments. Part of the problem may have been that the money seemed like small change to the multinational—it didn't see the urgency of the matter, and it certainly wasn't going to pay on a disputed invoice. But the cash was critical to its small partner. The two companies reached a stalemate, the alliance failed, and the small business was never able to recover $300,000 of the money that it was owed.

This true story reveals how small venture alliances with prestigious partners can be a double-edged sword. Such affiliations may offer a substantial boost to status and market access, but the parties' strategic priorities may not mesh and a major corporation can wield enormous power over a small, struggling enterprise. Some large firms have a track record of misbehavior as partners, and you need to know this *before* entering an alliance with them. The guidelines outlined in Chapter 4, regarding the evaluation of a franchisor (see pages 103–110), can be helpful when deciding whether to take on a particular venture partner. For example, it would be wise to investigate whether the corporation has been a good, ethical partner for other small companies. Knowing this in advance will help you to make an informed and profitable decision.

Strategic Alliances with Small Companies

Small businesses can also form strategic alliances with other firms similar in size in ways that enhance mutual competitive strength. Recent statistics suggest that about half of all small businesses maintain one or more strategic alliances with companies that are smaller or equal in size, especially when it comes to outside contractors, licensing partners, import/export operations, marketing agreements, and shared manufacturing.[37] When *Inc. Magazine* researchers asked dozens of entrepreneurs which alliance partners had performed best for them, they were surprised to learn that the most enthusiastic anecdotes were about other small companies. These partnerships were more flexible, dedicated, creative, and understanding of the specific needs of small business. Apparently, it takes one to know one!

The Center for Systems Management (CSM), a small Vienna, Virginia–based consulting and training company, found that it was in over its head when it accepted a contract from NASA to develop coursework that would help with problems in the space shuttle program. CSM had been given just 45 days to produce a slick video for an internal marketing campaign. This was a huge opportunity, one that could boost the small company's image and generate business in a whole new category of work, but a botched job would probably damage its relationship with NASA for good. Rather than attempting to go it alone, CSM contracted the job out to Technovative Marketing, a seven-person business in Peapack, New Jersey. Within a few days, Harriet Donnelly, Technovative's president, was on the job, and she personally worked on the video and stayed with the project, even attending all meetings with NASA as if she were the chief marketing officer of CSM. As far as Donnelly was concerned, she was part of the CSM team. In the end, the video project was a huge success. CSM was hired to do more internal marketing campaign work for NASA as a result—and, of course, Donnelly was asked to help.[38]

Strategic alliances hold great promise for small entrepreneurial businesses. By combining resources with carefully selected partners, small firms can increase their competitive strength and reach goals that would otherwise be too costly or too difficult for them to accomplish on their own.

In 2000 TOPICS Entertainment focused all its energy on publishing. Sales continued to grow as new titles were released and new categories were conquered. Due to this strong growth, expanded relationships with major retailers, and its outstanding balance sheet, the company has attracted many important partners and brands.

Setting Up and Maintaining Successful Strategic Alliances

Although an appropriate strategic alliance may be essential to business growth, finding a suitable partner can be challenging. Some small business owners have given up in frustration after months—even years—of trying to establish such connections. But persistent entrepreneurs are always finding ways to bridge the gap.

Launched by Greg James in 1990, TOPICS Entertainment is a publisher of education, language-learning, and entertainment multimedia products based in Renton, Washington. TOPICS's software can be found on the shelves of major retailers such as Best Buy and Costco, but James is always looking for possible new paths for growth. A few years back, he recognized a clear market opportunity, one that would require a coordinated business effort with small educational video production houses that had similar offerings but too little market power to get the big retailers to distribute for them. His plan was simple: bundle products from four children's DVD makers into boxed sets and use TOPICS's connections to get them on the shelves of major retailers under a new label called Little Steps. The strategy was a huge success, and today licensing and bundling partnerships with other small companies generate 80 percent of TOPICS's total revenue. Business has been so good that James estimates his sales may soon top $100 million.[39]

An alliance strategy, such as the one used by TOPICS Entertainment, can be powerful for growing companies—it spreads the risk of entering new markets and helps small players with unattractive balance sheets appear stable to the end buyer. It can also provide a fast track to reaching the critical mass required for pre-sale and post-sale support. To make alliances work for everyone involved, James recommends that entrepreneurs select partners with a "division of labor" mentality that allows all parties to focus their efforts on what they do best. Identifying intersections between product lines and expertise opens up the potential for cross-selling that creates growth opportunities for everyone involved. But working closely with other companies can introduce significant hazards. Because partners are in a unique position to learn about your strategy and customer base, they can become competitors overnight. Therefore, it is crucial to select partners with care and to structure contracts to ensure growth, including an "easy out" clause if the alliance does not work out for some reason.[40]

For help in making essential linkages, especially with large corporations, many entrepreneurs consult *strategic alliance matchmakers*. These brokers provide two basic services. First, they maintain a wealth of contacts with decision makers at corporations that have the resources small companies need to fill in the gaps in their operations. Second, they help entrepreneurs fine-tune their alliance proposals to ensure that corporate insiders take them seriously.

The problem is that large corporations like Microsoft, Hewlett-Packard, and 3M receive countless partnership requests each month, so only those with a compelling business plan have a chance of getting a second look. And this is completely understandable: A large firm needs to know why it should be willing to invest its resources before even contemplating a partnership. But this does not mean that powerful corporations are slow to consider alliances with small companies. Microsoft's IP Ventures division, for example, is set up specifically to license intellectual property that the firm cannot or does not want to use, but potential licensees must be able to present a compelling case before Microsoft will sign on.[41]

Strategic alliances often are not easy to set up, and they can be difficult to maintain. Although many small businesses report that they are happy with the results of their strategic alliances,[42] a number of alliances run into trouble and, in time, fail. Fortunately, when setting up alliances, entrepreneurs can take the following steps to improve their chances of success:

- *Establish a healthy network of contacts.* These people can lead you to still other contacts, and eventually to the one you need. Industry analysts, executive recruiters, public relations agencies, business reporters, and even the government can provide important leads.

- *Identify and contact individuals within a firm who are likely to return your call.* "Dialing high" (calling contacts at the vice presidential level or higher) works in small or medium-size firms, but in large firms you may need to call managers or other mid-level employees to get a response.

- *Do your homework, and you will win points just for being prepared.* You should be able to clearly outline the partner's potential financial benefits from the alliance. If possible, show that your firm can deliver value to the alliance across several fronts.

- *Learn to speak and understand the "language" of your partner.* You will not pick up on subtle messages in conversations with partners unless you know how they communicate, and this can eventually make or break the alliance.

- *Make sure any alliance offer is clearly a win–win opportunity.* It's easy to push for terms that are good for your own business and forget that only those agreements that benefit all participating parties will endure.

- *Continue to monitor the progress of the alliance to ensure that goals and expectations are being met, and make changes as they become necessary.*

The goal is to form strategic alliances that are beneficial to all partners and to manage these alliances effectively. In their book *Everyone Is a Customer,* Jeffrey Shuman, Janice Twombly, and David Rottenberg point out that a key to successful strategic alliances is understanding the true nature of the relationship: "Relationships are advertised as being between companies, whereas in reality relationships are built between people. And that's a very important distinction."[43]

Making the Most of a Board of Directors

board of directors
The governing body of a corporation, elected by the stockholders.

In entrepreneurial firms, the *board of directors* tends to be small (usually five or fewer members) and serves as the governing body for corporate activity. In concept, the stockholders elect the board, which in turn chooses the firm's officers, who manage the enterprise. The directors also set or approve management policies, consider reports on operating results from the officers, and declare any dividends.

All too often, the majority stockholder in a small corporation (usually the entrepreneur) appoints a board of directors only to fulfill a legal requirement (since corporations are required by law to have a board of directors) or as mere window dressing for investors. Such owners make little or no use of directors in managing their companies. In fact, the entrepreneur may actively resist the efforts of these directors to provide managerial assistance. When appointing a board of directors, such an entrepreneur tends to select personal friends, relatives, or businesspersons who are too busy to analyze the firm's circumstances and are not inclined to argue. Entrepreneurs who take a more constructive approach find an active board to be both practical and beneficial, especially when the members are informed, skeptical, and independent.

Making use of boards of directors is becoming increasingly attractive for a number of reasons. The growing complexity of small businesses, arising in part from globalization and technological developments, makes the expertise of well-chosen directors especially valuable. In a family business, outsiders can play a unique role in helping evaluate family talent and mediate differences among family members.

Contributions of Directors

Small businesses stand to gain significantly from a strong board of directors, especially when its members help the entrepreneur look beyond the next few months to make important, long-term strategic decisions. In other words, good directors will be able to help entrepreneurs keep their eyes on the big picture, to help them step back and see the forest for the trees.

A well-selected board of directors can also bring supplementary knowledge and broad experience to enterprise management. By virtue of their backgrounds, directors can fill gaps in the knowledge of a management team and monitor its actions. The board should meet regularly to provide maximum assistance to the chief executive. In board meetings, ideas should be debated, strategies determined, and the pros and cons of policies explored. In this way, the chief executive is informed by the unique perspectives of all the board members. Their combined knowledge makes possible more intelligent decisions on issues crucial to the firm.

By utilizing the experience of a board of directors, the chief executive of a small corporation is in no way giving up active control of its operations. Instead, by consulting with and seeking the advice of the board's members, he or she is simply drawing on a larger pool of business knowledge. A group will typically make better decisions than will a single individual working in isolation.

An active board of directors serves management in several important ways: by reviewing major policy decisions, by advising on external business conditions and on proper reaction to the business cycle, by providing informal advice from time to time on specific problems that arise, and by offering access to important personal contacts. With a strong board, a small firm may gain greater credibility with the public, as well as with business and financial communities.

Selection of Directors

Many resources are available to an entrepreneur who is attempting to assemble a cooperative and experienced group of directors. The firm's attorney, banker, accountant, local management consultants, and other business executives might all be considered as potential directors, but such individuals lack the independence needed to critically review an entrepreneur's plans. Also, the owner is already paying for their expertise. For this reason, the owner needs to consider the value of an outside board, one with members whose income does not depend on the firm. The National Association of Corporate Directors surveyed the directors of nearly 100 boards of entrepreneurial firms and found that, on average, 28 percent were independent outside directors. This number is increasing—which is good—but the study also reports that private company boards tend to have only half as many independent members as their public counterparts.[44]

Objectivity is a particularly valuable contribution of outside directors. They can look at issues more dispassionately than can insiders who are involved in daily decision making. Outside directors, for example, are freer to evaluate and to question a firm's ethical standards. Some operating executives, without the scrutiny of outside directors, may rationalize unethical or illegal behavior as being in the best interest of the company.

In a family business, an outside board can help mediate and resolve issues related to leadership succession, in addition to providing more general direction. As outsiders, they bring to the business a measure of detachment from potentially explosive emotional differences.

Working with outside board members is not always easy, but the tough decisions the board may advise an entrepreneur to make can provide the subtle (or not-so-gentle) pressure required to move the business forward. For example, they may keep bringing the conversation back to issues that are easy to avoid, such as the need to build long-term relationships with important individuals in the banking community or the value of converting intentions for the company's future into a formal business plan that can be studied, debated, perfected, and used as a tool to attract crucial resources to the enterprise. Entrepreneurs often spend as much as 20 percent of their time on board-related activities, but the time commitment is worth the cost if the directors are doing their jobs well.

The nature and needs of a business will help determine the qualifications required in its directors. For example, a firm that faces a marketing problem may benefit greatly from the counsel of a board member with a marketing background. Business prominence in the community is not essential, although it may help give the company credibility and enable it to attract other well-qualified directors. Having a "fat" Rolodex can only be helpful, as directors with influential business contacts can contribute greatly to the company's performance.

After deciding on the qualifications to look for, a business owner must seek suitable candidates as board members. Effective directors are honest and accountable, offer valuable insights based on business experience, and enhance the company's credibility with its stakeholders (especially customers and suppliers). Suggestions for such candidates may be obtained from the firm's accountant, attorney, banker, and other associates in the business community. Owners or managers of other, noncompeting small companies, as well as second- and third-level executives in large companies, are often willing to accept such positions. Before offering candidates positions on the board, however, a business owner would be wise to do some discreet background checking.

Compensation of Directors

The compensation paid to board members varies greatly, and some small firms pay no fees at all. If compensation is provided, it is usually offered in the form of an annual retainer, board meeting fees, and pay for committee work. (Directors may serve on committees that evaluate executive compensation, nominate new board members, and oversee the work of the company's auditors.) One study found that entrepreneurial firms pay, on average, over $12,500 in total annual compensation for directors of private companies and almost $26,000 for public firm directors.[45] Some small businesses also offer each board member a small percentage of the company's stock or profits (typically one-half of 1 percent) for her or his participation,[46] but keep in mind that some directors may serve for free because of their interest in seeing a new or small business prosper.

The relatively modest compensation offered for the services of well-qualified directors suggests that financial compensation is not their primary motivation for serving on a board. Reasonable compensation is appropriate, however, if directors are making important contributions to the firm's operations. (Remember, you usually get what you pay for.)

An Alternative: An Advisory Council

advisory council
A group that functions like a board of directors but acts only in an advisory capacity.

In recent years, increased attention has been directed to the legal responsibilities of directors. Because outside directors may be held responsible for illegal company actions, even though they are not directly involved in wrongdoing, some individuals are reluctant to accept directorships. Thus, some small companies use an *advisory council* as an alternative to a board of directors. Qualified outsiders are asked to serve on a council as advisors to the company. This group then functions in much the same way as a board of directors does, except that its actions are only advisory in nature.

The legal liability of members of an advisory council is not completely clear. However, limiting their compensation and power is thought to lighten, if not eliminate, the personal liability of members. Since its role is advisory in nature, the council also may pose less of a threat to the owner and possibly work more cooperatively than a conventional board.

Without a doubt, a well-selected board of directors or advisory board can do a great deal for a small company, but bear in mind that this is only one part of an effective organizational plan. The success of any business depends on the quality of its people, who must also be well organized and skillfully led. That's why having a balanced management team, selecting an organizational form that makes sense for the enterprise and its circumstances, and joining advantageous strategic alliances are all so important. This chapter has touched on each of these topics to help you think through key factors involved in a solid organizational plan that will give your business a good running start and help to ensure its long-term success.

LOOKING BACK

1. **Describe the characteristics and value of a strong management team.**

   - A strong management team nurtures a good business idea and helps provide the necessary resources to make it succeed.
   - The skills of management team members should complement each other, forming an optimal combination of education and experience.
   - A small firm can enhance its management by drawing on the expertise of outside specialists.
   - Building social capital through networking and goodwill is extremely helpful in developing a small business.
   - An entrepreneur should create a management structure that defines relationships among all members of the organization.

2. **Explain the common legal forms of organization used by small businesses.**

   - The most basic legal forms of organization used by small businesses are the sole proprietorship, partnership, and C corporation.
   - In a sole proprietorship, the owner receives all profits and bears all losses. The principal disadvantage of this form is the owner's unlimited liability.
   - In a partnership, which should be established on the basis of a written partnership agreement, success depends on the partners' ability to build an effective working relationship.
   - C corporations are particularly attractive because of their limited-liability feature. The fact that ownership is easily transferable makes them well suited for combining the capital of numerous owners.

3. **Identify factors to consider in choosing among the primary legal forms of organization.**

   - Currently, 69 percent of all new businesses are organized as sole proprietorships, 9 percent are set up as partnerships, and 7 percent are established as C corporations.
   - The key factors in the choice among different legal forms of organization are initial organizational requirements and costs, liability of the owners, continuity of the business, transferability of ownership, management control, attractiveness for raising capital, and income tax considerations.
   - Self-employed individuals who operate businesses as sole proprietorships report income from the businesses on their individual tax returns.
   - A partnership reports the income it earns to the Internal Revenue Service, but the partnership itself does not pay income taxes. The income is allocated to the owners according to their partnership agreement.
   - A C corporation reports its income and pays any taxes due on this corporate income. Individual stockholders must also pay personal income taxes on dividends paid to them by a corporation.

4. **Describe the unique features and restrictions of five specialized organizational forms.**

   - In a limited partnership, general partners have unlimited liability, while limited partners have only limited liability as long as they are not active in the firm's management.
   - S corporations, also called Subchapter S corporations, enjoy a special tax status that permits them to avoid the corporate tax but requires individual stockholders to pay personal taxes on their proportionate shares of the business profits.
   - In limited liability companies, individual owners have the advantage of limited liability but pay only personal income taxes on the firm's earnings.
   - Professional corporations are set up for those who offer professional services (usually those that require a license), to protect them from the liability of other owners in the practice.
   - Some enterprises (especially those with a social focus) benefit from greater credibility and authenticity when they organize as a nonprofit corporation, such as a 501(c)(3) organization.

5. **Explain the nature of strategic alliances and their uses in small businesses.**

   - Strategic alliances allow business firms to combine their resources without compromising their independent legal status.
   - Strategic alliances may be formed by two or more independent businesses to achieve some common purpose. For example, a large corporation and a small business or two or more small businesses may collaborate on a joint project.
   - Strategic alliance matchmakers can help small businesses find suitable alliance partners.
   - Entrepreneurs can improve their chances of creating and maintaining a successful alliance by establishing productive connections, identifying the best person to contact, being prepared to confirm the long-term benefits of the alliance, learning to speak the partner's "language," ensuring a win-win arrangement, and monitoring the progress of the alliance.

6. *Describe the effective use of boards of directors and advisory councils.*

- Boards of directors can assist small corporations by offering counsel and assistance to their chief executives.

- To be most effective, a board of directors should include properly qualified, independent outsiders.
- One alternative to an active board of directors is an advisory council, whose members are not personally liable for the company's actions.

Key Terms

management team p. 201
social network p. 204
social capital p. 205
reciprocation p. 205
sole proprietorship p. 205
unlimited liability p. 206
partnership p. 207
partnership agreement p. 209
joint and several liability p. 209

corporation p. 210
legal entity p. 210
C corporation p. 210
corporate charter p. 210
stock certificate p. 212
pre-emptive right p. 212
piercing the corporate veil p. 213
limited partnership p. 216
general partner p. 216

limited partner p. 216
S corporation (Subchapter S corporation) p. 216
limited liability company p. 217
professional corporation p. 217
nonprofit corporation p. 217
organizational test p. 218
strategic alliance p. 218
board of directors p. 222
advisory council p. 224

Discussion Questions

1. Why would investors tend to favor a new business led by a management team over one headed by a lone entrepreneur? Is this preference justified?

2. Discuss the merits of the three major legal forms of organization.

3. Does the concept of limited liability apply to a sole proprietorship? Why or why not?

4. Suppose a partnership is set up and operated without a formal partnership agreement. What problems might arise? Explain.

5. Evaluate the three major forms of organization in terms of management control by the owner and sharing of the firm's profits.

6. What is an S corporation, and what are its principal advantages?

7. Why are strategic alliances helpful to many small businesses? What steps can an entrepreneur take to create strategic alliances and to prevent their failure?

8. How might a board of directors be of value to management in a small corporation? What qualifications are essential for a director? Is ownership of stock in the firm a prerequisite for being a director?

9. What may account for the failure of most small companies to use boards of directors as more than "rubber stamps"? What impact is this likely to have on the business?

10. How do advisory councils differ from boards of directors? Which would you recommend to a small company owner? Why?

You Make the Call

SITUATION 1

Ted Green and Mark Stroder became close friends as 16-year-olds when both worked part-time for Green's dad in his automotive parts store. After high school, Green went to college, while Stroder joined the National Guard Reserve and devoted his weekends to auto racing. Green continued his association with the automotive parts store by buying and managing two of his father's stores.

In 2007, Green conceived the idea of starting a new business that would rebuild automobile starters, and he asked Stroder to be his partner in the venture. Originally, Stroder was somewhat concerned about working with Green because their personalities are so different. Green has been described as outgoing and enthusiastic, while Stroder is reserved and skeptical. However, Stroder is now out of work, and so he has agreed to the offer. They will set up a small shop behind one of Green's automotive parts stores. Stroder will do all the work; Green will supply the cash. The company will be called Startover Automotive Services, which seems appropriate, given the nature of the business.

Question 1 How relevant are the individual personalities to the success of this entrepreneurial team? Do you think Green and Stroder have a chance to survive their "partnership"? Why or why not?

Question 2 Do you consider it an advantage or a disadvantage that the members of this team are the same age?

Question 3 On balance, is it good or bad that the company will be started by two men who are very close friends? What are the potential benefits and drawbacks of mixing business and friendship in this case?

SITUATION 2

Matthew Freeman started a business in 2003 to provide corporate training in project management. He initially organized his business as a sole proprietorship. Until 2009, he did most of his work on a contract basis for Corporation Education Services (CES). Under the terms of his contract, Freeman was responsible for teaching 3- to 5-day courses to corporate clients—primarily *Fortune* 1000 companies. He was compensated according to a negotiated daily rate, and expenses incurred during a course (hotels, meals, transportation, etc.) were reimbursed by CES. Although some expenses were not reimbursed by CES (such as those for computers and office supplies), Freeman's costs usually amounted to less than 1 percent of his revenues.

In 2009, Freeman increasingly found himself working directly with corporate clients rather than contracting with CES. Over the years, he had considered incorporating but had assumed the costs and inconveniences of this option would outweigh the benefits. However, some of his new clients said that they would prefer to contract with a corporation rather than with an individual. And Freeman sometimes wondered about potential liability problems. On the one hand, he didn't have the same liability issues as some other businesses—he worked out of his home, clients never visited his home office, all courses were conducted in hotels or corporate facilities, and his business involved only services. But he wasn't sure what would happen if a client

were dissatisfied with the content and outcomes of his instruction. Finally, he wondered whether there would be tax advantages to incorporating.

Question 1 What are the advantages and disadvantages of running the business as a sole proprietorship? As a corporation?

Question 2 If Freeman decided to incorporate his business, which types of corporations could he form? Which type would you recommend? Why?

SITUATION 3

Julie Patton is cofounder and president of PM Meals, a food-services business that prepares and sells boxed meals and convenience snacks to hotels, convention operators, corporate clients, and community event planners. Patton makes most of the business decisions related to the company and is in charge of generating new accounts, but the firm's cofounder, Angela Marks, has culinary training and oversees the meal-preparation side of the operation. The food they offer represents relatively simple fare, but it is flavorful and attractively presented, exceeding by far what most clients would expect from a boxed meal provider.

The company has entered a growth phase, which has attracted the attention of an angel investor. PM Meals could certainly use the money to support its growing business, but the investment would come with major strings attached. For example, even though the company has been performing nicely without a board of directors, the investor insists that it form one and that he be given a seat on the new board. In his words, "If I am going to put up money for the business, I want to be able to influence how my money is being used."

Patton and Marks are concerned that forming a board and including at least one outside investor (the angel) will undermine their control and paralyze the business. As they weigh alternatives, they are leaning toward forming a three-person board and accepting the new investment—but they are far from certain as to what they should do.

Question 1 Would you accept the investment and the conditions that go along with it, or refuse it and go a different direction?

Question 2 Can one outside member on a board of three make any real difference in the way the board operates?

Question 3 If you were the owners, whom would you include on the board?

Question 4 If Patton and Marks decide to form a board of directors, what will determine its usefulness or effectiveness? Do you predict that it will be helpful? Why or why not?

Experiential Exercises

1. Prepare a one-page résumé of your personal qualifications to launch a software instruction business at your college or university. Then write a critique that might be prepared by an investor, evaluating your strengths and weaknesses, as shown on the résumé. Identify in the critique any gaps or weaknesses you have that could be covered by forming a management team to start the business.

2. Interview an attorney whose clients include small businesses. Inquire about the legal considerations involved in choosing the form of organization for a new business. Report your findings to the class.

3. Interview the partners of a local business. Inquire about the factors they considered when drawing up their partnership agreement. Report your findings to the class.

4. Discuss with a corporate director, attorney, banker, or business owner the contributions of directors to small firms. Prepare a brief report on your findings. If you discover a particularly well-informed individual, suggest that person to your instructor as a possible guest speaker.

Small Business & Entrepreneurship Resource Center

The Small Business and Entrepreneurship Resource Center offers complete small business management resources through a comprehensive database that covers all major areas of starting, operating, and maintaining a business from financing, management, marketing, accounting, taxes, and more. Use the access code that came with your new book to access the site and perform the exercises in each chapter.

1. Small businesses often think that they must invent new innovative products or services in order to start successfully. Large companies often partner with entrepreneurs to make such products and services available. A good example is Microsoft, which has an Intellectual Property (IP) Ventures division. Describe how large corporations benefit by making intellectual property available for licensing. Also describe how entrepreneurs benefit as well.

2. One of the stated advantages of the corporate business form is the concept of limited liability. Limited liability refers to the fact that stockholders personal assets can not be taken by business creditors if the business fails. Describe the concept of limited liability

for corporate business owners. Also discuss if and how the veil of limited liability can be overcome when trying to collect debts from a corporate debtor.

3. Alliances provide an important mechanism for accessing new resources, which can enhance firm performance. The greater emphasis a firm puts on resource combination activities—combining new resources with existing resources—the more it realizes the potential value of the alliance. Strategic alliances are more important to small businesses today than ever before, and an increasing number of entrepreneurs are finding creative ways to use these cooperative strategies to their advantage. In fact, statistics show that nearly two-thirds of small businesses use alliances, and three-fourths of these companies report having positive experiences with them. Describe some research that has been done on alliances.

Sources: License to thrive: how you can profit from big companies' tech ideas. (Brief Article). Hericks, Mark. *Entrepreneur* 33, 10 (Oct 2005): p. 22(1).

Behind the mask: when the corporation doesn't protect its owner. (Brief Article). Jane Bahls Easter. *Entrepreneur* 34, 3 (March 2006): p. 80(1).

Wiklund, Johan, and Dean A. Shepherd. "The effectiveness of alliances and acquisitions: The role of resource combination activities. (Report)." *Entrepreneurship: Theory and Practice* 33, 1 (Jan 2009): 193(20).

Case 8

D'ARTAGNAN (P. 638)

This case highlights some of the common problems that surface when entrepreneurs work together to start and manage a small business.

ALTERNATIVE CASES FOR CHAPTER 8:

Case 5, W.S. Darley & Co., p. 632
Case 6, Benjapon's, p. 634

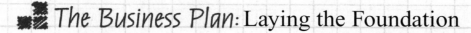

The Business Plan: Laying the Foundation

As part of laying the foundation to prepare your own business plan, respond to the following questions regarding your management team, legal form of organization, strategic alliances, and board of directors.

1. Who are the members of your management team? What skills, education, and experience do they bring to the team?

2. What other key managers do you plan to recruit?

3. Do you plan to use consultants? If so, describe their qualifications.

4. What are your plans for future employee recruitment?

5. What will be the compensation and benefit plans for managers and other employees?

6. What style of management will be used? What will be the decision-making process in the company? What mechanisms are in place for effective communication between managers and employees? If possible, present a simple organization chart.

7. How will personnel be motivated? How will creativity be encouraged? How will commitment and loyalty be developed?

8. What employee retention and training programs will be adopted? Who will be responsible for job descriptions and employee evaluations?

9. Who will have an ownership interest in the business?

10. Will the business function as a sole proprietorship, partnership, or corporation? If a corporation, will it be a C corporation, an S corporation, a limited liability company, a professional corporation, or a nonprofit corporation?

11. What are the liability implications of this form of organization?

12. What are the tax advantages and disadvantages of this form of organization?

13. If a corporation, where will the corporation be chartered and when will it be incorporated?

14. What attorney or legal firm has been selected to represent the firm? What type of relationship exists with the company's attorney or law firm?

15. What legal issues are presently or potentially significant?

16. What licenses and/or permits may be required?

17. What strategic alliances are already in place, and what others do you plan to establish in the future? Describe the forms and nature of these alliances. What are the responsibilities of and benefits to the parties involved? What are the exit strategies?

18. Who are the directors of the company? What are their qualifications? How will they be compensated?

chapter 9

The Location Plan

Troy Ylitalo and his wife, Sarah Schaller Linn, realized that work responsibilities were crowding something far more important out of their schedules—time with one another. As they began to explore their options, they realized that starting an eBay business could lead to more flexible job commitments *and* allow them to work together. Little did they know where that simple notion would take them.

While Troy was trying to peddle a stack of old magazines on eBay, he noticed that some of these simply would not sell, and yet a single ad from one magazine was purchased for a hefty price. Could it be that "vintage advertising" offered just the opening the couple was looking for? After researching the category on eBay, Troy and Sarah soon realized that this was something they had to try. So, in September of 2004, they launched

Period Papers, an online venture that specializes in the sale of "vintage advertising art, authentic antique prints, and collectible paper ephemera [like greeting cards, posters, and other printed items that were not really created to be saved]." In the years since then, business has really taken off. The company currently offers more than 100,000 print art items that were produced from the early 1800s to the late 1900s.

Troy and Sarah are now spending more time together than ever before, as they work side by side in the business, which also employs several additional workers. "EBay has been pivotal in launching our business," the couple says. The boundless market that can be reached on the Internet in general, and through eBay more specifically, is obviously an important part of the formula.

Another powerful advantage of starting a business online is the flexibility it provides. Troy and Sarah recently decided to move their home to Wisconsin and expand the business into a 2,000-square-foot facility there. "The beauty of an eBay business is you can do it anywhere," observes Troy, "with no interruption in business. We're moving closer to family, and the new facility will

LOOKING AHEAD
AFTER STUDYING THIS CHAPTER YOU SHOULD BE ABLE TO...

1. Describe the five key factors in locating a brick-and-mortar startup.

2. Discuss the challenges of designing and equipping a physical facility.

3. Understand both the attraction and the challenges of creating a home-based startup.

4. Understand the potential benefits of locating a startup on the Internet.

You have probably heard people say that the three most important factors in determining the value of a property are *location, location, location.* This may seem like an overstatement, but it's true. And just as location influences the value of a residential property, it can also determine the fate of a business.

Can you think of a single McDonald's that is no longer serving up Big Macs at the same location? More than likely, the answer is no. Few of the franchisor's restaurants ever close because of its remarkable ability to identify excellent locations—with the perfect combination of kids, interstates, and suburbs—and to snap them up before anyone else can. In fact, some businesses select their own locations based on McDonald's choice of sites.

According to Eric Schlosser, author of *Fast Food Nation*, McDonald's has perfected the art of site selection. Schlosser provides an interesting history of the company's methods—from the early days when Ray Kroc (who bought the company in 1961) used private planes and helicopters to find cheap land along highways and roads that one day would run through suburbs to today's infinitely more sophisticated computerized methods. By Schlosser's account,

> In the 1980s, the chain became one of the world's leading purchasers of satellite photography, using it to predict [urban] sprawl from outer space. McDonald's later developed a computer software program called Quintillion that automated its site selection process, combing satellite imagery with detailed maps, demographic information, [computer-aided] drawings, and sales information from existing stores.... [T]he software developed by McDonald's permits businessmen to spy on their customers with the same equipment once used to fight the cold war.[1]

But Quintillion is old news now, and McDonald's has moved on to even more advanced systems. Why did McDonald's choose to take this very expensive path? Because choosing a high-potential location is one of the most critical factors in the formula for success in business!

The entrepreneur who decides to purchase an existing business or a franchise usually receives considerable location guidance from members of the acquired firm or the franchisor. However, small business owners who choose to start a venture from scratch will quickly find that the location decision is very time consuming. Regardless of how the selection is made, all location intentions should be described in the business plan. This chapter will provide guidance for that challenge.

Locating the Brick-and-Mortar Startup

In many cases, the choice of a location is a one-time decision. However, an entrepreneur may later consider relocating the business to reduce operating costs or gain other advantages. For example, Mitchell Greif, CEO of Coast Converters, relocated his plastic bag manufacturing plant to Las Vegas, Nevada, because of the high taxes and pricey real estate in his hometown of Los Angeles.[2] Also, as a business grows, it is sometimes desirable to expand operations to other

1. Describe the five key factors in locating a brick-and-mortar startup.

9-1 Location Options for the Startup

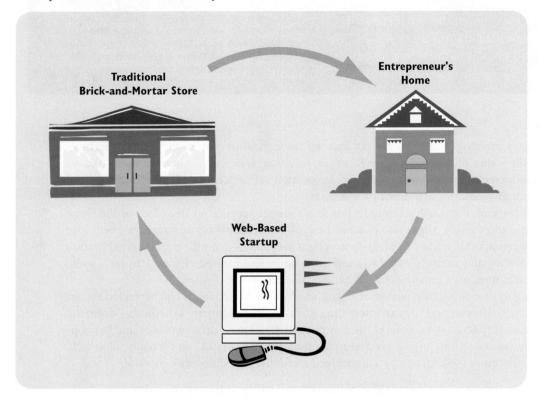

locations in order to be closer to customers.[3] Perhaps the single biggest reason why companies have been relocating in recent years is to improve their access to critical employee talent, which can be difficult to find.[4]

In this chapter, we discuss three primary options for the initial location decision—a traditional physical building, the entrepreneur's home, and a website on the Internet. Although we recognize that the Internet can be an integral part of operations for both a traditional and a home-based business, we treat e-commerce ventures in a separate category because of the Internet's significance as a sole sales outlet for these small businesses. Exhibit 9-1 depicts the three location options.

The Importance of the Location Decision

brick-and-mortar
store
The traditional physical store from which businesses have historically operated.

The importance of the initial decision as to where to locate a traditional physical building—a *brick-and-mortar store*—is underscored by both the high cost of such a store and the hassle of pulling up stakes and moving an established business. Also, if the site is particularly poor, the business may never become successful, even with adequate financing and superior managerial ability. The importance of location is so clearly recognized by national chains that they spend hundreds of thousands of dollars investigating sites before establishing new stores.

The choice of a good location is much more vital to some businesses than to others. For example, the site chosen for a clothing store can make or break the business because it must be convenient for customers. The physical location of a painting contractor's office, on the other hand, is of less importance, since customers do not need frequent access to the facility. But even painting contractors may suffer if their business site is poorly chosen. For example, some communities are more willing or able than others to invest resources to keep property in good condition, thereby providing greater opportunities for painting jobs.

EXHIBIT

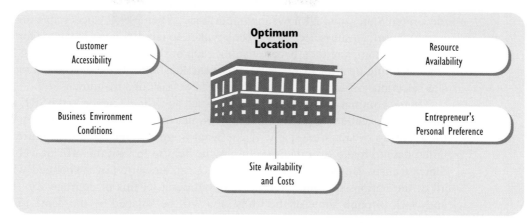

Key Factors in Selecting a Good Location

Five key factors, shown in Exhibit 9-2, guide the location selection process: customer accessibility, business environment conditions, availability of resources, the entrepreneur's personal preference, and site availability and costs. Other factors relevant to the location decision include the following:[5]

- *Neighbor mix:* Who's next door?
- *Security and safety:* How safe is the neighborhood?
- *Services:* Does the city provide trash pickup, for example?
- *Past tenants' fate:* What happened to previous businesses in that location?
- *Location's life-cycle stage:* Is the area developing, stagnant, or in decline?

For a particular business and its unique situation, one factor may carry more weight than others. However, each of the five key factors should always have some influence on the final location decision.

CUSTOMER ACCESSIBILITY   Customer accessibility is generally an important consideration in selecting a location. Retail outlets and service firms are typical examples of businesses that must be located so as to make access convenient for target customers. Rarely will customers be willing to travel long distances on a repeat basis just to shop. That's why Glenn Campbell and Scott Molander decided to sell hats in high-traffic areas. Each store, located in a shopping mall or airport, offers a vast assortment of officially licensed baseball-style hats. The first store was opened in 1995, and in five years the company, Hat World Corporation, had grown to 157 stores. By 2003, it had purchased several competitors, and in 2008, it reported operating more than 800 stores in 46 states.[6]

Many products, such as snack foods and gasoline, are convenience goods, which require a retail location close to target customers; otherwise, consumers will substitute competitive brands when a need arises. Services such as tire repair and hair styling also require a location readily accessible to customers.

Choosing the best location for a retail store used to be a hit-or-miss proposition. The recent emergence of site-selection software has removed much of the guesswork from finding a good place to set up shop, and the popularity of these packages among small business owners has taken off as the software has become more sophisticated and user-friendly. Site-selection programs can give users access to demographic information such as age, income, and race for specific neighborhoods, as well as details about other businesses located nearby, climate conditions, traffic flow, and much more.

Incorporated in 1936, Carvel Ice Cream was the very first franchisor of ice-cream shops in the United States, and it knows the importance of being easily accessible to customers. Carvel hired MapInfo, a site-selection software maker, to identify good locations for Carvel Ice Cream shops. The company then began visiting each of the 127 sites identified by MapInfo with the hope of lining up franchisees for most of the locations. The franchisor understood that using site-selection software was less likely to lead to "risk of a meltdown."[7]

Many commercial service providers (such as Urban Science and ESRI, Inc.) can help you identify an excellent site for your business, but their services are typically far too expensive for a startup or small company. If you want to go it alone but still capture the power of detailed data to make your decision, it may be helpful to visit the official website of the United States Census Bureau (www.census.gov). Users are often overwhelmed when they first see all of the options presented on this site, but don't let this discourage you. If you are patient and work through some of the links, you will be amazed by the depth of helpful information you can uncover. We also suggest that you visit the website of *Site Selection* magazine (www.siteselection.com), which offers a "suite of online tools . . . [to help] you research locations and demographics," including a link to "Fast, Free Location Assistance." This Internet site also offers a wealth of practical information to those with a little patience and the willingness to sift through it.

Ready access to customers is important in many situations, but it is absolutely critical for many businesses. It is vital, for example, in industries in which the cost of shipping the finished product is high relative to the product's value. Products such as packaged ice and soft drinks, for example, must be produced near consuming markets because of the excessive transportation costs involved.

Convenient access for customers is one reason many small businesses have successfully established a strong presence on the Internet. With a suitable computer connection, customers can access a small company's home page from anywhere in the world. (Locating a startup on the Internet is discussed later in this chapter.)

BUSINESS ENVIRONMENT CONDITIONS   A startup business is affected in a number of ways by the environment in which it operates. Environmental conditions can hinder or promote success. Weather is one important environmental feature that influences the location decision, as well as the demand for many products such as air conditioners and outdoor swimming pools. Such factors are particularly important to entrepreneurs like Trey Cobb, the owner of COBB Tuning, the high-performance car parts maker you learned about in Chapter 3. In 2002, Cobb took the bold step of moving his entire company from Texas to a custom-built facility in Utah. This particular move was all about climate—in this case, improving product-testing conditions. Cobb recognized the advantages of locating the company in an area that provided access to the varied geographic and weather conditions that would be necessary to fully test the car parts that his company manufactures. According to his analysis, Salt Lake City was just the place for that.[8]

Competition, legal requirements, and tax structure are a few of the other critical environmental factors. Entrepreneurs seek profits; therefore, all factors affecting the financial picture are of great concern. State and local governments can help or hinder a new business by forgiving or levying taxes. State corporate income tax rates vary considerably across the United States, with only a few states having no such tax. One of those with a very generous tax policy is Wyoming,[9] whose website proudly states, "The state of Wyoming does not levy a personal or corporate income tax . . . . Further, there is no legislative plan to implement any of these types of taxes."[10] This is certainly an attractive feature to consider.

Tax relief for the business is important, but don't forget to factor in the impact of a state's personal income tax rates, which will affect the pay your employees ultimately receive for their labor. These taxes will determine how far wage dollars will go and, in turn, the benefit and

LIVING THE DREAM:

entrepreneurial challenges

There's Something Fishy about This Location

Husband-and-wife team George Sanders and Linda Nelson are world-class scuba divers and owners of a salt-water diving center called Bonneville Seabase. Their training facility draws divers and snorkelers from as far away as Australia and Thailand, despite the fact that it is situated in the middle of the Utah desert, 900 miles from the nearest ocean and 4,250 feet above sea level. Sometimes selecting a geographic location for a business takes a little vision and a lot of imagination.

"We call it an interactive aquarium," says Sanders of their artificial diving center. "The sharks won't bite unless you pull their tails." But you are sure to see more than just sharks in this oceanic oasis. Divers make the long journey to Bonneville Seabase to see tropical species from around the world concentrated in an underwater setting that can be fully explored in a few short hours. The facility has been hailed as "a pioneer in a movement to create artificial environments where

© Linda Nelson

divers can swim with big fish that are increasingly rare in the wild." In fact, the idea is catching on, and resorts, casinos, and public aquariums are starting to explore the possibility of setting up their own Seabase-like facilities.

Coming up with the concept for the business was truly a team project. Nelson studied geothermal maps and knew that subsurface saltwater springs were present at the potential new location—and Sanders owned a construction company with the equipment needed to excavate the property. While others mocked their efforts, the couple created a watery wonderland from what was once a garbage-covered stretch of wasteland. Startup costs ran about $100,000, but the business now generates $300,000 in annual sales.

And customers are thrilled. For $15 a day, they can explore three pools open for diving, including a 62-foot-deep hole called the Abyss, and see a variety of tropical fish and, yes, even sharks.

Sources: Stephen Regenold, "Sea Hunt in the Desert," nytimes.com, November 28, 2008, http://travel.nytimes.com/2008/11/28/travel/escapes/28scuba.html?scp=1&sq=sea%20hunt%20in%20the%20desert&st=cse, accessed December 23, 2008; Sara Wilson, "More than a Mirage," *Entrepreneur*, Vol. 35, No. 7 (July 2007), p. 110; and "Bonneville Seabase," http://www.seabase.net, accessed December 22, 2008.

http://www.seabase.net

---

satisfaction your workers receive from the business.[11] And there are other important elements in the equation, such as the overall cost of living, which is driven by the price of residential real estate, food, energy, and other necessities of life. A lower *cost* of living can mean a higher *standard* of living for employees. It's possible to do cost-of-living research yourself: Consult websites like money.cnn.com and salary.com, or contact local economic development agencies and request data on this and other factors, which they will provide free of charge.[12]

Many states offer location incentives. One popular strategy is to establish *enterprise zones*, which are created to attract jobs to economically deprived areas. Sponsored by local city and county governments, these zones lure businesses by offering regulatory and tax relief. In exchange for locating or expanding in these areas, eligible business firms receive total exemption, for 3 to 5 years, from the property taxes normally assessed on a new plant and equipment. To give you an idea of how widespread enterprise zones are becoming, Oregon had 59 such zones as of December 2008.[13]

enterprise zones
State-designated areas that are established to bring jobs to economically deprived regions through regulatory and tax incentives.

Enterprise zones are not a cure-all. Locating a business or facility in one of these areas will not solve problems such as those created by poor management, and it certainly will not make up for an ill-conceived business idea. However, enterprise zones can be used as a catalyst to help jump-start a small firm.

While most efforts of state and city governments are designed to support startups, many cities have regulations that restrict new business operations under certain circumstances. For example, cities have zoning ordinances that may limit the operations of home-based businesses. Limitations typically relate to factors such as traffic and parking, signage, nonrelated employees working in a home, the use of a home more as a business than as a residence, the sale of retail goods to the public, and the storage of hazardous materials and work-related equipment.[14]

AVAILABILITY OF RESOURCES   The availability of resources needed to operate a business should also be considered when selecting a location. Raw materials, labor supply, and transportation are some of the factors that have a bearing on location. The proximity of important sources of raw materials and a suitable labor supply are particularly critical considerations in the location of most manufacturing businesses.

ACCESS TO RAW MATERIALS   If raw materials required by a company's operations are not readily available in all areas, then regions in which these materials abound will offer significant location advantages. This is especially true for businesses that are dependent on bulky or heavy raw materials that lose much of their size or weight in the manufacturing process. A sawmill is an example of a business that must stay close to its raw materials in order to operate economically.

SUITABILITY OF THE LABOR SUPPLY   A manufacturer's labor requirements depend on the nature of its production process. Labor-intensive operations need to be located near workers with appropriate skills and reasonable wage requirements. A history of acceptable levels of labor productivity and peaceful relations with employers are also important factors. Companies that depend on semiskilled or unskilled workers usually locate in an area with surplus labor, while other firms may need to be close to a pool of highly skilled labor. If the required talent is unavailable, relocation may be necessary, even it if means moving to another state. According to Tim Nitti, a location expert with a major site-selection firm, "Probably the single biggest emerging reason why anyone is moving companies . . . is access to talent."[15]

AVAILABILITY OF TRANSPORTATION   Access to good transportation is important to almost all firms. For example, good highways and bus systems provide customers with convenient access to retail stores, which encourages sales. For small manufacturers, quality transportation is especially vital. They must carefully evaluate all trucking routes, considering the costs of both transporting supplies to the manufacturing location and shipping the finished product to customers. It is critical that they know whether these costs will allow their product to be competitively priced.

PERSONAL PREFERENCE OF THE ENTREPRENEUR   As a practical matter, many entrepreneurs tend to focus primarily on their personal preference and convenience when locating a business. Statistics hint at this, showing that nearly half of all entrepreneurs (47 percent) live no more than a five-minute drive from their venture's location.[16] And, despite a world of alternatives, small business owners often choose to stay in their home community; in fact, the thought of locating elsewhere never even enters their minds. Just because an individual has always lived in a particular town, however, does not automatically make the town a satisfactory business location.

On the other hand, locating a business in one's home community sometimes makes perfect sense. In fact, doing so may offer certain unique advantages that cannot be found elsewhere. From a personal point of view, the entrepreneur generally appreciates and feels comfortable with the atmosphere of the home community, whether it is a small town or a large city. As a practical business matter, the entrepreneur may find it easier to establish credit. Hometown bankers who know an entrepreneur's personal background and reputation can be more confident in their support of a startup, and having personal connections in the local business community can lead to invaluable business advice. If local residents are potential customers, the prospective entrepreneur probably has a better idea of their tastes and preferences than would an outsider. And friends and relatives may be the entrepreneur's first customers and gladly spread positive reports about the products or services they buy. Though such decisions are usually based on emotion, there are clearly some potential upside benefits of locating a startup close to home.

James Dyson smiles when he talks about his neon-colored, warhead-shaped, English-made vacuum cleaners. His bagless upright vacuum cleaner is the result of 15 years of innovation and failed prototypes, which led Dyson to a technology of spinning air in a plastic cone to achieve superior cleaning action. But from the start, Dyson decided to locate the company's manufacturing facilities in his home community of Malmesbury, England. For years, his firm was the town's largest employer. "I live here, this is my home, and it is the home of everybody here at Dyson," he said. "We love being here; we're a big employer and, I hope, a big contributor to the community." You can feel the emotional connection in his comments. Nevertheless, in 2002 Dyson moved production of his upright vacuum to Asia, where labor costs are much lower. The move resulted in a loss of 800 jobs in a town with only 4,500 residents—painful, to be sure—but that is not the end of the story. The move helped double the firm's business and allowed it to employ almost as many employees in Malmesbury as it had prior to the move. And wages are higher, because the jobs remaining at home are primarily in research and development.[17] Even after having to make agonizing changes to keep up with trends, Dyson's roots remain firmly planted in his hometown.

AP Images

The personal preferences that drive the location decision are as varied as the entrepreneurs who make it. Sometimes entrepreneurs choose a location offering unique lifestyle advantages. Artist Lolly Shera has set up her studio in a 156-square-foot treehouse behind her home in Fall City, Washington, where she draws and paints most afternoons. "When it's blowing hard, this structure moves, and it feels like a boat that's moored," says Shera, of her leafy workplace. "It groans and creaks. It's like being in a live animal. There's a soul in it that, if you're open to it, you can feel."[18] It's easy to see how an artist would draw inspiration from such an unusual "high-rise" location, but it does have its limitations. Convenient parking and customer access, for example, would not exactly be a "plus" for this choice of locations.

Personal preference is important, but it should not be allowed to take priority over obvious location weaknesses that are almost certain to limit or even doom the success of the enterprise. The location decision must take all relevant factors into consideration.

SITE AVAILABILITY AND COSTS
Once an entrepreneur has settled on a certain area of the country, a specific site must still be chosen. The availability of potential sites and the costs associated with obtaining them must be investigated.

SITE AVAILABILITY
After evaluating a site for his new business, one entrepreneur is said to have exclaimed, "It must be a good site—I know of four businesses that have been there in the last two years!" Fortunately, such a misguided approach to site evaluation is not typical of entrepreneurs, many of whom recognize the value of seeking professional assistance in determining site availability and appropriateness, based on the needs of the business. Local realtors can serve as a good source of insight.

If an entrepreneur's top choices are unavailable, other options must be considered. One alternative is to share facilities with other enterprises. In recent years, business incubators have sprung up in all areas of the country. A *business incubator* is a facility that rents space to new businesses or to people wishing to start businesses. Incubators are often located in repurposed buildings, such as abandoned warehouses or schools. They serve fledgling

business incubator
A facility that provides shared space, services, and management assistance to new businesses.

businesses by making space available, offering management advice, and providing other forms of assistance (including clerical support), all of which help lower operating costs. An incubator tenant can be fully operational the day after moving in, without buying phones, renting a copier, or hiring office employees.

Since its start in an incubator at the University of Alabama at Birmingham, MedMined, Inc., has been in the business of saving lives as well as saving money for hospitals and insurance companies. Using data mining and artificial intelligence models to identify the sources of infections, it helps hospitals reduce hospital-acquired infections in patients, which saves lives. MedMined's sales grew from $5,000 in 2000 to $1.2 million in 2003 (the year it "graduated" from the incubator) and $3.3 million in 2004. That was over 600-percent growth in five years! The incubator contributed to this growth by developing a training program for MedMined's sales force and coaching the company's team on how to create an effective fund-raising presentation that led to $2 million in initial venture capital funding in 2001. According to MedMined founder Stephen Brossette, being an incubator client provided the stamp of approval the company needed to woo clients.[19] Building from its start in the incubator, the company did so well that it caught the eye of Cardinal Health, a global healthcare products and technologies provider, which acquired MedMined in 2006. The positive experience of MedMined highlights the valuable role an incubator can play in the life of a young company.

The purpose of business incubators is to see new businesses hatch, grow, and leave the incubator, so the situation is temporary *by design*. But it appears that businesses are increasingly looking for a permanent shared-office arrangement. As an indication of the trend, Regus Group PLC, a leading provider of shared office space, reported in 2008 that inquiries for its services were way up, and that in the previous year alone the company had opened 100 new office centers in the United States, Canada, and Latin America.[20] Michael Einhorn, founder of a medical supplies sales venture called Dealmed, Inc., was operating out of the basement of his in-laws' home when he concluded that he would be able to greatly expand his company if he had more professional-looking facilities. He moved his business into a shared office location, and sales soared from just under $1 million to nearly $6 million *in just one year*! He now has access to fully furnished offices, attractive meeting spaces, support staff, and an impressive address—without making a large cash outlay or signing a long-term lease.[21]

SITE COSTS Ultimately, the site selection process must depend on evaluation of all relevant costs. Unfortunately, an entrepreneur is frequently unable to afford the "best" site. The costs involved in building on a new site may be prohibitive, or the purchase price of an existing structure may exceed the entrepreneur's budget.

Assuming that suitable building space is available, the entrepreneur must decide whether to lease or buy. Although more small business owners choose to purchase their buildings,[22] the advantages of leasing often outweigh the benefits of owning. Leasing certainly offers two important advantages:

1. A large cash outlay is avoided. This is important for a new small firm, which typically lacks adequate financial resources.

2. Risk is reduced by avoiding substantial investment and by postponing commitments for space until the success of the business is assured and the nature of building requirements is better known.

When entering into a lease agreement, the entrepreneur should check the landlord's insurance policies to be sure there is proper coverage for various types of risks. If not, the lessee should seek coverage under his or her own policy. And it is important to have the terms of the lease agreement reviewed by an attorney. Sometimes, an attorney can arrange for special clauses to be added to a lease, such as an escape clause that allows the lessee to exit the agreement under certain conditions. And an attorney can also ensure that an entrepreneur will not be unduly exposed to liability for damages caused by the gross negligence of others. Consider the experience of one firm that wished to rent 300 square feet of storage space in a large complex of offices and shops. On the sixth page of the landlord's standard lease, the firm's lawyer found language that could have made the firm responsible for the entire 30,000-square-foot complex if it burned down, regardless of blame! Competent legal counsel may not be cheap, but the service it provides can certainly save an entrepreneur a lot of money and heartache.

Designing and Equipping the Physical Facilities

2. Discuss the challenges of designing and equipping a physical facility.

A well-written location plan should describe the physical space in which the business will be housed and include an explanation of any equipment needs. Although the plan may call for a new building or an existing structure, ordinarily a new business occupies an existing building, with minor or major remodeling.

Challenges in Designing the Physical Facilities

When specifying building requirements, the entrepreneur must avoid committing to a space that is too large or too luxurious for the company's needs. At the same time, the space should not be so small or limited that operations are hindered or become inefficient. Buildings do not produce profits directly; they merely house the operations and personnel that do so. Therefore, the ideal building will be practical, not extravagant.

The general suitability of a building for a given type of business operation depends on the functional requirements of the enterprise. For example, a restaurant should ideally be on one level; a manufacturer's production processes that are interlinked should be in the same building and located near one another. Other important factors to consider include the age and condition of the building, potential fire hazards, the quality of heating and air conditioning systems, the adequacy of lighting and restroom facilities, and appropriate entrances and exits. Obviously, these factors are weighted differently for a factory operation than for a wholesale or retail operation. But in every case, the comfort, convenience, and safety of the business's employees and customers should be taken into consideration.

Challenges in Equipping the Physical Facilities

The final step in arranging for physical facilities is the purchase or lease of equipment and tools. The *Wall Street Journal* reported that, overwhelmingly, owners of small businesses would rather own their equipment than lease it (see Exhibit 9-3). The majority believe that, in the long run, it is cheaper to buy than to lease. Having the flexibility to use the equipment as they wish and to keep it until it is no longer needed are also important reasons why small business owners prefer to own rather than lease.[23] Still, the leasing option has advocates as well. So what is a small business owner to do? To make an informed decision on this, use an equipment lease-versus-buy calculator. (A number of these can be found online with a simple Internet search.) It's also a good idea to check with an accountant to be sure that any tax consequences of your decision to lease or buy are considered.

The types of equipment and tools required obviously depend on the nature of the business. Even within the three areas discussed here—manufacturing, retailing, and office equipment— there is great variation in the need for tools and equipment.

MANUFACTURING EQUIPMENT Machines used in a factory may be either general purpose or special purpose. *General-purpose equipment* requires a minimal investment and is easily adapted to various types of operations. Small machine shops and cabinet shops, for example, use this type of equipment, which includes lathes, drill presses, milling machines, and table saws. In

general-purpose equipment
Machines that serve many functions in the production process.

9-3 Small Business Owners Choose Buying over Leasing

EXHIBIT

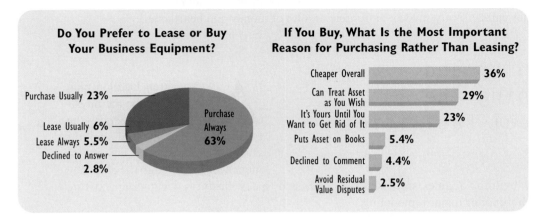

Do You Prefer to Lease or Buy Your Business Equipment?

Purchase Usually **23%**
Lease Usually **6%**
Lease Always **5.5%**
Declined to Answer **2.8%**
Purchase Always **63%**

If You Buy, What Is the Most Important Reason for Purchasing Rather Than Leasing?

Cheaper Overall — **36%**
Can Treat Asset as You Wish — **29%**
It's Yours Until You Want to Get Rid of It — **23%**
Puts Asset on Books — **5.4%**
Declined to Comment — **4.4%**
Avoid Residual Value Disputes — **2.5%**

Source: Richard Breeden, "Small Businesses Favor Buying over Leasing," *Wall Street Journal*, February 24, 2004, p. B11. Copyright 2004 by Dow Jones & Company, Inc. Reproduced with permission of Dow Jones & Company, Inc. in the format Textbook via Copyright Clearance Center.

each case, jigs, fixtures, and other tooling items set up on the basic machinery can be changed so that two or more shop operations can be accomplished using the same piece of equipment. General-purpose equipment offers flexibility, which is most important to industries in which products are so new that the technology is not yet well developed or there are frequent design changes.

special-purpose equipment
Machines designed to serve specialized functions in the production process.

Special-purpose equipment is more limited in its application and can reduce costs when the technology is fully established and operating at capacity is more or less ensured by high sales volume. Bottling machines and manufacturing robots are examples of special-purpose equipment used in factories. A small firm can use special-purpose equipment economically only if it makes a standardized product on a fairly large scale. Upgrading special-purpose machines with specialized tooling can result in greater output per machine-hour of operation, which will reduce the labor cost per unit of product even further. However, the initial cost of such equipment is much higher, and it has little or no resale value because it is restricted to a narrow range of possible applications.

RETAILING EQUIPMENT Small retailers need merchandise display racks or counters, storage racks, shelving, mirrors, seats for customers, customer pushcarts, cash registers, and other items to facilitate selling. Such equipment may be costly, but it is usually less expensive than that necessary for a factory operation.

If a store is intended to serve a high-income market, its fixtures should signal this by displaying the elegance and style expected by such customers. For example, polished mahogany showcases with bronze fittings can help to create an upscale setting. Indirect lighting, thick rugs, and oversized easy chairs also communicate luxury to clients. In contrast, a store that caters to lower-income customers should concentrate on simplicity. Luxurious fixtures and plush seating suggest an atmosphere that is inconsistent with low prices, and they also add to the cost of the operation, which makes it more difficult to keep prices low.

OFFICE EQUIPMENT Every business office needs furniture, storage cabinets, and other such items. Major manufacturers of office furniture, such as Steelcase, Herman Miller, and Haworth, can certainly provide the necessary desks, chairs, and cabinetry, but so can scores of smaller vendors. Check out local sources of used office furniture, which may have items for sale that are still very presentable but a lot less expensive. And always make your decisions with the future in mind. If you select furnishings that are simple, free-standing, and detachable, then, when your business takes off, you can easily move them all to a larger facility.

Perhaps an even more challenging task is selecting office equipment—computers, fax machines, copiers, printers, and telephone systems—that reflect the latest technological advances applicable to a particular business. Careful selection of these items can help a business operate efficiently.

The location plan should list the major pieces of equipment needed to outfit a business office. By identifying major equipment needs in this part of the business plan, the small business owner can ensure that the financial section of the plan includes funds for their purchase.

Business Image

All new ventures, whether they are retailers, wholesalers, manufacturers, or service businesses, should be concerned with projecting the most appropriate image to customers and the public at large. The look and "feel" of the workplace should create an impression that says something about the quality of a firm's product or service and about the way the business is operated in general. For a small firm, and especially a startup, it is important to use the physical facilities to convey the image of a stable, professional company. Potential customers are likely to avoid doing business with a company that has every appearance of a fly-by-night operation.

Factors as basic as color and interior design should be considered. Even before the first customer shows up, companies sometimes find that their financial backers are unwilling to hand over investment dollars until an office or retail store is perceived as attractive and inviting. It is not unusual for a small company to go through a process similar to that of a California-based chain of sandwich shops, which had to choose between suggested color/design options:

> First came a palette inspired by images of a sun-drenched picnic at the beach. The second riffed on farmers' markets, with their warm yellow light, woody stations wagons, and baskets full of colorful vegetables.[24]

The farmers' market theme was eventually chosen because "it evokes intimacy, freshness, and quality in a casual environment."[25] This design choice may have been obvious, but only to the trained eye. And that is exactly the point. If the image aspect of the facilities equation is beyond your expertise and insight, consult with someone who can help you to make decisions that work.

Image is the engine of sales, so carefully consider how to mold your space to create a distinct and appropriate impression, yet still provide plenty of space, allow easy traffic flow, pass building inspections, and more—all in keeping with your budget and business goals. The way your facilities, customers, and employees come together is critical to the success of your new business.

Locating the Startup in the Entrepreneur's Home

3. Understand both the attraction and the challenges of creating a home-based startup.

Rather than lease or buy a commercial site, many entrepreneurs choose instead to use their basement, garage, or spare room for their operations, creating a *home-based business*. In the past, a home location for a business was almost always considered second-rate. But times have changed. Despite the limitations and potential for image problems, home-based entrepreneurs no longer feel embarrassed about their location. In fact, recent research has shown that home-based businesses may actually enjoy an advantage over other companies when it comes to certain dimensions of financial performance (for example, achieving a first sale).[26] The home office, once viewed as a passing phase on the path to growth for many businesses, has become a viable permanent option for some. Today, many entrepreneurs have no plans to ever move their operations out of the home.

home-based business
A business that maintains its primary facility in the residence of its owner.

EXHIBIT 9-4 Some Common Reasons for Starting a Home-Based Business

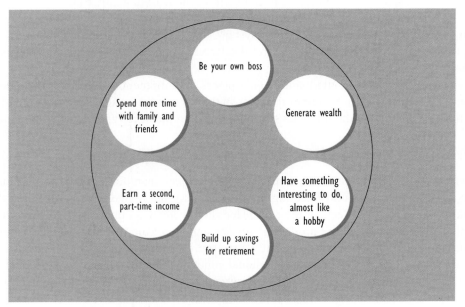

Be your own boss

Spend more time with family and friends

Generate wealth

Earn a second, part-time income

Have something interesting to do, almost like a hobby

Build up savings for retirement

Source: Adapted from "Potential Reasons for Starting a Home Based Business," http://www.perfectsystem.co.uk, accessed January 13, 2009.

The Attraction of Home-Based Businesses

Why do many entrepreneurs find operating a business at home so attractive? Motivations vary (see Exhibit 9-4), but the main attractions of a home-based business relate to financial and family lifestyle considerations.

FINANCIAL CONSIDERATIONS Like most business ventures, a home-based business has an important goal—earning money—and locating at home helps increase profits by reducing costs. For example, a freelance writer of magazine articles may need only a computer, a few office supplies, and an Internet connection to launch a business from home. Nearly all writers own a computer, so the true startup costs for such a business may be only a few hundred dollars.

With the ups and downs of the advertising industry, Donavan Andrews and Stephen Smyk thought it would be best to start their fledgling advertising agency in their home. "We . . . built the business slowly and were conservative until we got to the point where we had excess capital," says Andrews. This conservative approach worked well; Andrews and Smyk moved into office space in a professional building only four months after they started the business.[27]

Rose Anne Raphael's motivation for starting a home-based business was to receive full compensation for her work. Her boyfriend noticed that her employer was billing clients more than seven times as much as Raphael was earning. "I was getting paid $17 an hour and the company was billing clients at $125 an hour for my work . . . . That's when I thought I had the opportunity to become self-employed," says Raphael. It wasn't long before she decided to strike out on her own, running a public-relations firm out of her one-bedroom apartment in Berkeley, California.[28]

FAMILY LIFESTYLE CONSIDERATIONS Many young entrepreneurs remain in a family business because of close family ties. Similarly, entrepreneurs who locate business operations in the home are frequently motivated by the desire to spend more time with family members. Consider the following examples.

Joyce Thomas owns Chino Hills, California–based Medical Reimbursement Specialists (MRS), a Medicare-compliance company. MRS started out handling electronic claims for local physicians. After two years, Thomas decided to use her experience to train other women to process claims from their homes. She helped start 500 affiliate businesses across the country and won contracts with hospitals nationwide. Thomas explains that she really likes being her own boss: "I can set my own hours and decide if I want to do something or not." She initially went into the business so that she could work from home and take care of her three children. Despite having to travel about two weeks each month to give seminars, she appreciates being at home the rest of the time. "I do the Little League thing, keep up with my two boys . . . . I'm also a grandmother, so I do a little of that role when I'm home," she adds. Thomas states that she couldn't do what she does without the help of her husband: "It has to be a partnership." Her mother, too, plays an important role; she calls Thomas every night when she's on the road and even travels with her on occasion.[29]

Marisa Shipman, owner of Shipman Associates, Inc., the manufacturer of The Balm line of cosmetics, launched her business from her home in 2001. "I love working from home," says Shipman. Her home, however, has had to change several times to accommodate her growing business with sales of over $2 million. Shipman Associates is a true family affair; despite being spread across the country, her family helps run the business. Her dad, who is in Greenwich, Connecticut, and a sister in Philadelphia both work out of their homes to help grow the business. Shipman thinks that a home is a great place to start a business: "If you have something you think could work, do it on a small scale and see."[30]

The Challenges of Home-Based Businesses

Just as most businesses located at commercial sites have their problems, home-based businesses face special challenges attributable to their location. We briefly examine two of these challenges—business image and legal considerations. Another major challenge—family and business conflicts—was discussed in Chapter 5.

BUSINESS IMAGE   Maintaining an image of professionalism when working at home is a major challenge for home-based entrepreneurs. Allowing young children to answer the telephone, for example, may undermine a professional image. Likewise, a baby crying or a dog barking in the background during a phone call can be distracting to a client.

If clients or salespeople visit the home-based business, it is critical that a professional office area be maintained. Space limitations sometimes make this difficult. For example, when you own a home-based business, house guests can create a real problem. Unless you want Aunt Zerelda wandering into a client meeting in her bathrobe or your nephew Jimmie playing his electric guitar during a work call, ground rules need to be set for house guests. These rules should be clearly spelled out in advance of the visit to avoid any major disruptions to your business.

LEGAL CONSIDERATIONS   Local laws can sometimes pose serious problems for home-based businesses. *Zoning ordinances,* for example, regulate the types of enterprises permitted to operate within certain areas, and some cities outlaw any type of home-based business within city limits.

Many zoning laws, dating as far back as the 1930s, have never been updated. The intent of such laws is to protect a neighborhood's residential quality by forbidding commercial signs and preventing parking problems. The neighborhood you live in may have a homeowners' association that can limit your ability to run a home-based business (see Exhibit 9-5). Some entrepreneurs first become aware of these zoning laws when neighbors initiate zoning enforcement actions. Consider "good neighbor" Lauren Januz of Libertyville Township, Illinois.

> One of Januz's neighbors was running a landscaping and tree-service business out of his home. He erected a large fence to obscure the view of his heavy equipment which was fine with the subdivision's other residents, but he had 10 to 15 workers parking their cars on the street every day. "This is an area of $300,000 homes, and a lot of the cars were really wrecks," explains Januz. Although several neighbors approached the

zoning ordinances
Local laws regulating land use.

© Scott Adams/Dist. by United Feature Syndicate, Inc.

offending property owner, he made no attempt to correct the problem, and a complaint was finally filed with the Lake County Building and Zoning Department. He ended up selling the property and relocating the business.[31]

There are also tax issues related to a home-based business. For example, a separate space must be clearly devoted to the activities of the business if an entrepreneur is to claim a tax deduction. A knowledgeable accountant can help explain these tax regulations.

And don't forget the insurance considerations that may affect a home-based business. A homeowner's policy is not likely to cover an entrepreneur's business activities, liabilities, and equipment. Therefore, he or she should always consult an insurance agent about policy limitations to avoid unpleasant surprises down the road.

Technology and Home-Based Businesses

Advances in business-application technology have facilitated the rapid growth of home-based businesses. Personal computers, wireless communication devices, voice mail, text messaging, and e-mail are among the tools that help the home-based business compete effectively with commercial-site businesses. Such technology makes it possible to operate many types of businesses from almost any location.

One important technological tool available to home-based businesses is the Internet. Millions of small firms—many of them based at home—are using websites to sell products and services. Virtually every product sold in traditional retail outlets is now also available online. In the next section, we examine the potential of the Internet as a place to host a new business.

Locating the Startup on the Internet

4. Understand the potential benefits of locating a startup on the Internet.

We live in an ever-changing digital economy that is fueled by the tremendous growth of the Web. Access to the Internet continues to transform the way we live and the way business is conducted. It is important for aspiring entrepreneurs to learn as much as they can about cyberspace because online business opportunities continue to expand.

How does the Internet support e-commerce? What benefits does e-commerce offer a startup? What business models reflect an e-commerce strategy? These are the primary questions we address in this section of the chapter. We hope that our discussion will help you understand both the opportunities and the limitations associated with today's digital economy. Additional e-commerce topics are discussed in other chapters.

What Is E-Commerce?

What does the term *e-commerce* really describe? *E-commerce* refers to electronic commerce, or the paperless exchange of business information via the Internet. It is an alternative means of conducting business transactions that traditionally have been carried out by telephone, by mail, or face to face in a brick-and-mortar store. Following the crash of Web-based enterprises about a decade ago, Internet businesses have definitely caught a second wind, and they are now growing in new ways and faster than ever!

In a way, the Internet is like the telephone—it is simply a tool that parties use to communicate with each other. Each of these technologies has transformed the way people interact and how they conduct business. But the comparison ends there. The Internet is a communication medium unlike any previously available to companies. Locating on the Web can fundamentally reshape the way small firms conduct business. Far more than a simple alternative to the brick-and-mortar store, the Internet can significantly boost a small company's financial performance.[32]

E-commerce
The paperless exchange of business information via the Internet.

Benefits of E-Commerce to Startups

Electronic commerce can benefit a startup in many ways. It certainly allows a new venture to compete with bigger businesses on a more level playing field. Because of their limited resources, small firms often cannot reach beyond local markets. When confined to the brick-and-mortar world, small firms typically can serve only a restricted region. But the Internet blurs geographic boundaries. E-commerce allows any business access to customers almost anywhere.

The Internet is proving to be a great equalizer, giving small firms a presence comparable to that of marketplace giants. For example, in the large field of perfume and beauty products heavyweights, a young Southern California–based player, Beauty Encounter (formerly called Perfume Bay), is taking on all challengers—and thriving. The business is an extension of three physical stores that were started by a Vietnamese couple who emigrated to the United States in 1980. Their daughter, Jacquelyn Tran, recognized the limitations of such operations and decided to carve out her own space in the global marketplace by establishing an online presence in 1999. Now, with nearly $20 million in annual sales, and growing, BeautyEncounter .com is proving that the Internet allows small companies to play in the big leagues, and the sky seems to be the limit. In fact, Tran recently launched a direct-mail catalogue and expanded into a larger warehouse facility with a retail showroom.[33] Going online can be the key that unlocks the door of opportunity for small firms, regardless of their industry.

An e-commerce operation can help the startup with early cash flow problems by compressing the sales cycle—that is, reducing the time between receiving an order and converting the sale to cash. E-commerce systems can be designed to generate an order, authorize a credit card purchase, and contact a supplier and shipper in a matter of a few minutes, all without human assistance. The shorter cycle translates into quicker payments from customers and improved cash flows to the business.

E-commerce also enables small firms to build on one of their greatest strengths—customer relationships. The Internet has brought new life and technology to bear on the old-fashioned notion of customer service. *Electronic Customer Relationship Marketing (eCRM)* is an electronically based system that helps a company handle its customer relationships more effectively. At the heart of eCRM is a customer-centric data warehouse. A typical eCRM system allows an e-commerce firm to integrate data from websites, call centers, sales force reports, and other customer contact points, with the goal of building customer loyalty. In addition to the benefits from e-commerce already mentioned, there are countless others; space does not allow us to discuss them all here.

Most often, an entrepreneur who chooses not to engage in e-commerce has concluded that this option is not important to his or her business,[34] but there are also a number of specific deterrents. For example, e-commerce has significant limitations that should be considered when deciding whether to locate a business online and how to operate it. These limitations fall into two categories: technical limitations and non-technical limitations. *Technical limitations* include the cost of developing and maintaining a website, insufficient telecommunications bandwidth, constantly changing software, and the need to integrate digital and non-digital sales and production information. The small business owner should also take into account customer access limitations with regard to dial-up, cable, wireless, and other connectivity options, as well as the fact that some potential customers still do not have any convenient access to the Internet. *Non-technical limitations* include factors such as customer concerns about their privacy, the security of your Internet operations, customers' inability to touch or try on products, and the challenges of dealing with global cultures and languages.[35]

Electronic Customer Relationship Marketing (eCRM)
An electronically based system that emphasizes customer relationships.

E-Commerce Business Models

business model
A group of shared characteristics, behaviors, and goals that a firm follows in a particular business situation.

One of the fundamental features of an online operation is the business model upon which it is built. The term *business model* describes a group of shared characteristics, behaviors, and goals that a firm follows in a particular business situation. More simply, a business model is the

EXHIBIT

operational design that allows an enterprise to sustain itself. Online companies differ in their decisions concerning which customers to serve, how best to become profitable, and what to include on their websites. Exhibit 9-6 shows some possible alternatives for business models. None of these models can currently be considered dominant, and some more complex Internet operations cannot be described by any single model. In reality, the world of e-commerce contains endless combinations of business models. As you consider a direction for your small business and its online aspirations, keep in mind that a poorly devised business model is often the primary cause of an online company's failure.

TYPE OF CUSTOMERS SERVED Marketing frameworks classify traditional brick-and-mortar firms as manufacturers, wholesalers, or retailers, depending on the customers they serve. In a similar way, e-commerce businesses also are commonly distinguished according to customer focus. There are three major categories of e-commerce business models: business-to-business (B2B), business-to-consumer (B2C), and auction sites. In this section, we examine some strategies used by e-commerce firms within these three categories.

BUSINESS-TO-BUSINESS MODELS   The dollar amounts generated by firms using a *business-to-business (B2B) model* (selling to business customers) are significantly greater than those for firms with a business-to-consumer (B2C) model (selling to final consumers). Because B2B success stories generally receive less publicity than B2C ventures do, the potential of B2B opportunities is often overlooked. Aspiring entrepreneurs should be sure to consider the B2B model.

business-to-business (B2B) model
A business model based on selling to business customers electronically.

B2B operations "come in all shapes and sizes," but the most popular form of this strategy emphasizes sales transactions. By using online capabilities, a B2B firm can achieve greater efficiency in its buying and selling activities. International Business Machines (IBM) is a good example of this. By dealing directly with its business clients online, it is able to build its computer systems and related products to meet the specific needs of its customers. IBM relies heavily on the Internet to deliver its business solutions, but it also has an extensive sales force and consulting services to deliver value to its many customers worldwide.

One unique form of B2B trade online is related to work outsourcing, which helps to connect freelancers and other specialists with companies that need their services. One market research firm estimates that close to 100 online marketplaces for work outsourcing already exist, and the market continues to grow rapidly, with sales increasing around 20 percent each year.[36] Some of the better known sites include Elance.com, RentACoder.com, oDesk.com, Guru.com, and Sologig.com, which allow you to "hire, manage, and pay remote contractors as if they were in your office."[37] Now, the market for talent (worldwide!) is as close as your computer keyboard.

While work-outsourcing marketplaces help freelancers to reach the customers they need to build their businesses, they can also help entrepreneurs locate the support services necessary to improve their own operations. Danielle Godefroy, co-founder of Princeton, New Jersey–based Lingolook Publishing, first used Elance.com to connect with a software developer in Colorado, who contracted to make the language-pronunciation flashcards that the company now offers to travelers for use on their iPhones. Godefroy had to pay the iPhone applications developer $5,000 for his services, but now the company has a product that sells on iTunes and is competitive with offerings from much larger companies, like Lonely Planet Publications. Elance.com has helped Godefroy with a dozen other projects, and she has learned many valuable lessons along the way—that it pays to be specific about project details and to keep the lines of communication open, for example. But the benefits have been considerable. "We have been able to [out]source all these developments at a very competitive cost," she says, "with no overhead, and extremely fast."[38] These advantages can very easily translate to sales growth and an improved bottom line.

business-to-consumer (B2C) model
A business model based on selling to final customers electronically.

BUSINESS-TO-CONSUMER MODELS In contrast to the B2B model, a *business-to-consumer (B2C) model* focuses on final consumers as customers. In the traditional retail setting, customers typically go to a business location (a brick-and-mortar store) with the intent of shopping or making a purchase. Alternatively, customers might purchase goods or services via telephone or by mail order, using a printed catalog. The B2C model introduces another alternative for consumers, one with which you are probably quite familiar—buying online.

Amazon.com represents the classic B2C firm, which is directly focused on individual final consumers. B2C ventures sell a wide variety of products, with offerings ranging from clothing to pet items, computer software, toys, and groceries. The B2C model offers three main advantages over brick-and-mortar retailing: convenient use, immediate transactions, and round-the-clock access to products and services, which is sometimes referred to as *24/7 e-tailing*.

24/7 e-tailing
Electronic retailing providing round-the-clock access to products and services.

And opening up an online business has never been easier, thanks to the online "storefront" option and support services offered by online giants like Amazon, Yahoo!, and eBay. Some companies do business only through such a storefront; others establish an independent website as well and sell through both. Benson Altman is the founder, CEO, and president of Kosher.com, an enterprise that sells food items "adher[ing] to the strictest rabbinical supervision guidelines" and nonfood products that appeal to Jewish customers. The focus is on helping buyers find what they need at good prices, with quality service that keeps them coming back for more. However, the company also offers its goods through Amazon.com, which makes it possible for Altman to sell more than 20,000 kosher products, from canned fish to cosmetics, from all over the world. Customers can readily find what they are looking for through Amazon's search feature, which allows the niche retailer's products to be located and purchased with ease. Kosher.com handles the shipment of products to customers, but Amazon takes care of everything else, including customer support and billing.

There is also a downside to all of this, of course. It cost Altman about $25,000 to integrate operations with the online giant, and the expansion required him to hire four additional employees just to keep up with the increase in orders. Beyond that, Kosher.com has to pay Amazon a commission on each sale, which can add up quickly. Then there are also inventory worries. Still, Altman predicts that the alliance will boost his revenues by 10 to 20 percent (on $2 million in annual sales), and it certainly presents an opportunity to reach a much broader market.[39]

B2C e-commerce businesses certainly face unique challenges (payment security risks, customers who refuse to purchase a product without first seeing it or trying it on, etc.), but they also enjoy the advantages of flexibility. For example, they are able to change merchandise mixes and prices quickly, and they can easily modify the appearance of their "store" (their website). Traditional merchants located in brick-and-mortar stores would find such changes to be very costly and time-consuming, making it nearly impossible for them to keep up with fast-moving markets.

In some cases, market conditions or opportunities persuade wholesalers in a B2B operation to bypass the middleman and take their product or service directly to the final consumer, which is sometimes referred to as *disintermediation.* Eli Mechlovitz and his family had been selling glass and tile as a wholesaler in New York for more than two decades, but slowing sales forced Mechlovitz to reconsider the company's strategy. In September of 2007, he decided to launch a new website, GlassTileStore.com, to sell custom tiles and mosaics directly to consumers looking for deals on the Internet. The strategic adjustment is paying off. The company can sell products at much lower prices (sometimes as much as 50 percent below their cost in retail stores), and sales through the website now exceed those typical during the best of months before beginning online operations. Mechlovitz plans to keep the wholesale side of the business running as well.[40] That's the power of the online option—it offers market reach and flexibility that would not otherwise be available.

As B2C e-commerce models continue to develop and evolve, new alternatives will emerge, which is bound to catch some competitors off guard. Even some very large competitors find it difficult to keep up with the online game. For example, Google's creative service offerings have forced Microsoft to reconsider how it prices its software, and Blockbuster is trying to adjust its video rental model to deal with the competition created by Netflix. Major moves in the marketplace are sure to come, but an alert entrepreneur will monitor these changes to be able to respond quickly to potential risks and identify emerging opportunities.

AUCTION SITE MODELS   A growing number of entrepreneurs sell their wares over the Internet without either a website or a storefront, by means of e-commerce that is based on the auction site model. Internet *auction sites* are Web-based businesses that allow businesses and individuals to list products available for sale to potential bidders. Revenues to the auction site are most often derived from listing fees and commissions on sales.

Online auctions have become one of the most celebrated success stories on the Internet. And, as you might have guessed, eBay, founded in 1995 by computer programmer Pierre Omidyar, is the 900-pound gorilla of auction sites. "I got it on eBay" is quickly becoming part of our collective vocabulary. You can buy or sell nearly anything on eBay—and it's incredibly easy. EBay consultants abound; for a fee, they will coach you on how to be a successful seller. Or you can attend eBay University, in person or via online tutorials, to learn the ins and outs of operating an eBay business. To show you how easy it is to get started, Exhibit 9-7 provides a simple six-step procedure for selling items on eBay.

disinter-mediation
A situation where a wholesaler in a B2B operation chooses to bypass the "middleman" and sell its product or service directly to the final consumer.

auction sites
Web-based businesses offering participants the ability to list products for consumer bidding.

EXHIBIT 9-7   Selling Your Item on eBay

Step 1: Register as an eBay member, which is free of charge.

Step 2: Sign up to accept electronic payments, which is required.

Step 3: Research your items and rules of play; eBay provides information for both.

Step 4: Create a listing for the item to be offered for sale.

Step 5: Check your listing to see how bidding is going.

Step 6: Wrap up your sale with the buyer.

Source: Adapted from http://pages.ebay.com/help/sell/sell-getstarted.html, accessed January 5, 2009.

As easy as it is to sell a few items on eBay, it is a very different matter to actually make money as an ongoing business on the site. As in the more conventional forms of retailing, a well-thought-out business plan is helpful in turning your business idea (or hobby) into a money-making proposition. Here are a few statistics about eBay that will show you what an amazing phenomenon it has become:[41]

- Approximately $1,839 worth of goods are sold on eBay *every second*.
- eBay has approximately 85.7 million active users around the world.
- At any given time, 112.3 million items are listed on eBay.
- More than 7 million new items are listed every day.
- eBay has more than 50,000 categories of merchandise.
- The most expensive item sold to date on eBay was a private business jet (for $4.9 million).

As mentioned earlier, eBay generates most of its revenue through listing fees and commissions. To continue its rapid growth, eBay is expanding its services and entering new markets across the globe through new sites, acquisitions, and co-ventures. Overall, eBay does business in more than 39 countries, and PayPal, eBay's global payments platform, has 165 million total accounts. No longer the only show in town, however, eBay now faces competition from the likes of Amazon and smaller competitors such as Overstock.com. Exhibit 9-8 provides a list of the top 10 auction sites. How many of these have you visited?

In 2006, eBay took the bold step of opening eBay Express, a site dedicated to selling new merchandise at set prices. This site allowed eBay to target consumers who were looking for bargains and didn't like the auction format.[42] More recently, however, eBay Express has been phased out. The company's website explains the reasoning behind this move:

> We've integrated many of the great features from eBay Express onto eBay.com. In addition, we've made some big improvements to areas of eBay such as search, checkout, and seller standards. Now that the two sites are so similar, we have made the decision to retire eBay Express and concentrate all our inventory and buyer traffic in a single site: eBay.com.[43]

It appears that eBay will maintain the auction format that made it so popular, but the company is also taking steps to expand the eBay Stores side of its business, which gives sellers access to millions of shoppers worldwide. An entrepreneur can launch an eBay Store in just three easy steps (see the firm's website for details), and 75 percent of eBay sellers report that opening an eBay Store increased their sales. This option makes sellers successful by providing powerful tools to help them build, manage, promote, and track their eBay presence. Plus, eBay Stores sellers can create a listing for just $0.03 for each 30-day period, regardless of quantity listed.[44]

EXHIBIT 9-8 Top 10 Online Auction Sites

1. eBay
2. uBid
3. Bidz.com
4. Overstock.com
5. Amazon
6. OnlineAuction.com
7. WeBidz Auctions
8. Auction-Warehouse
9. ePier
10. It's Gotta Go

Source: http://www.auctions.nettop20.com, accessed January 5, 2009.

NATURE OF ONLINE PRESENCE   A second broad way of categorizing e-commerce models relates to the firm's intended level of online presence. The role of a website can range from merely offering content and information to enabling complex business transactions.

CONTENT-BASED MODEL   In a *content-based model* of e-commerce, a website provides access but not the ability to buy or sell products and services. During the early days of e-commerce, the content-based model was the option of choice. Companies like America Online (AOL) got their start using this approach. Originally, revenue for AOL came from fees paid by users for the privilege of connecting and gaining access to its content. Today, content models still operate, but these are found mostly in countries where Internet usage by small firms is less developed.

INFORMATION-BASED MODEL   The *information-based model* is a slight variation of the content-based alternative. A website built on this model contains information about the business, its products, and other related matters but doesn't charge for its use. It is typically just a complement to an existing brick-and-mortar store. Many small businesses use this model for their online operations. Your dentist or plumber may have a website that simply describes the services offered but probably will require a phone call to set up an appointment. These sites often feature a "Contact Us" link that will take the user to a separate webpage displaying the company's address and phone number and sometimes offers "click-through" access that allows the user to get in touch with the business via e-mail.

TRANSACTION-BASED MODEL   In a *transaction-based model* of e-commerce, a website is set up to provide a mechanism for buying or selling products or services. The transaction-based model could be considered the center of the e-commerce universe. This model calls for websites to be online stores where visitors go to shop, click, and buy.

Many Internet ventures sell a single product or service. For example, Huber and Jane Wilkinson market their reading comprehension program, IdeaChain, through their MindPrime, Inc., website. Similarly, Phil and Stephanie Rockell sell hillbilly teeth pacifiers only online. (For a good laugh, see the product for yourself by visiting their website at http://www.billybobteeth.com.) Other ventures are direct extensions of a brick-and-mortar store, creating what is sometimes called a bricks-and-clicks or a clicks-and-mortar strategy. For example, if you were interested in purchasing a new computer printer, you might research options on Office Depot's website and then choose either to buy your selection online or to drive to the neighborhood Office Depot store and pick up the printer there. Although Office Depot is a large corporation with millions of customers, small businesses can follow the same general model with excellent results.

EMERGING MODELS   The Internet world is known for how fast it moves, and entrepreneurial minds are constantly finding new ways to cash in on its potential. For example, blogging, or Web logging, creates an online venue to chronicle users' thoughts. Bloggers produce online journals to trade comments with friends and other readers. Small firms have found blogs easy to use and thus an attractive platform from which to promote a sale on an overstocked item or to give an employee special recognition. But drawing Web traffic to a blog can also generate substantial income from advertising, and a growing array of services and tools are making it easier than ever for bloggers to add this feature to their site.

The vast majority of bloggers earn only around $10 to $20 a month through advertising, but the amount earned is dependent on such factors as how much traffic the site generates, the trustworthiness of the content offered, and how relevant the ads are to those who visit. A popular blog can bring in more income than you might imagine. Rhett Butler started an environmental conservation blog because of his intense interest in the subject, but he quit his job as a production manager in 2003 when he realized just how much money could be generated through blogging. "The rainforest has always been my passion," says Butler, "but I never expected to make a living off of it." Butler recently reported that he makes between $15,000 and $18,000 a month

---

content-based model
A business model in which the website provides access but not the ability to buy or sell products and services.

information-based model
A business model in which the website provides information about a business, its products, and other related matters but doesn't charge for its use.

transaction-based model
A business model in which the website provides a mechanism for buying or selling products or services.

in ad revenue from the 1.3 million unique visitors drawn to his website each month.[45] And he is just getting warmed up!

Others have taken a different approach to making money from the blogging trend. Adam Weinroth used his winter break from the University of Texas in 2001 to build his initial version of the Easyjournal website, designed to attract novice bloggers. Weinroth built his site on a shoestring budget of less than $10,000, but Easyjournal now has over 125,000 registered members and offers both a free account and a paid account with additional features. These features include a public comment board and journal templates, as well as other services. The site also brings in revenue from advertising. Easyjournal was acquired in 2005 by Pluck, a company focused on social media software solutions, but Weinroth has remained with the company as director of product marketing.[46]

Internet-Based Businesses and the Part-Time Startup Advantage

When an entrepreneur launches a new company, many times she or he has to wrestle with whether to give up an existing job and jump full-time into the startup or hold on to the job while getting a part-time business going on the side. There are advantages and drawbacks to each approach, of course, but research shows most entrepreneurs prefer to launch a part-time enterprise and keep the income flowing until they can afford to make a complete transition to the new business. It's also less risky; if the new venture fails, the aspiring entrepreneur's income will not be interrupted. Though many kinds of businesses can be started on a part-time basis, a growing number of small business owners are finding that the flexibility and low cost of launching an online business make this a very attractive option.

Brian Eddy and Chad Ronnebaum chose the part-time startup path when they started their own new venture back in 1999. Both in their mid-20s at the time, these long-time friends decided to keep their successful careers *and* launch Q3 Innovations, a product design, development, and distribution company that creates personal safety and monitoring devices. In line with their niche strategy, they came up with some unique and very interesting products to sell. Their AlcoHAWK® Series is a line of handheld breath alcohol screeners for personal or professional use. The pen-sized thermometers of the ThermoHAWK™ Series feature patent-pending technology that allows a user to determine the surface temperature of almost any object without actually touching it. And the UV HAWK™ measures the intensity of ultraviolet light, making it easier to know when your skin has had enough exposure to the sun. Most recently, the company has added a series of radar/laser detectors called RadarHAWK™ to its stable of products.[47]

As with most startups, launching Q3 Innovations was a very satisfying, but grueling, experience. Eddy figures that he and Ronnebaum were booking 90- to 100-hour work weeks during the company's six-year startup phase (only about half of those at their regular jobs), so the part-time business wasn't always so part-time. They always knew what they were doing for the weekend, and the task took up most of their evenings, too. However, Q3 Innovations grew so much that Eddy decided to leave his legal practice to become the company's full-time CEO, and Ronnebaum made the transition from his career as a pharmacist to become the full-time president of the startup a few years later.[48] With 15 employees and annual sales of just over $1 million, the company is now on a very sound footing, but the part-time strategy that the founders followed took much of the risk out of making the transition to life as entrepreneurs. And the decision to use the Internet as a business platform played a significant part in making their Q3 Innovations dream a reality.[49]

Clearly, the location decision is complicated, but it is extremely important to get it right. If your business needs a physical facility, can you find a location that is convenient to customers, offers a supportive business climate, and provides access to necessary resources? As the owner of the business, would you be happy to show up to work at that location, day after day and year after year? When you think of the costs involved, does the location make sense?

Perhaps you are short on startup funding, which is leading you to think about starting your business at home. A home-based business is certainly cheaper to launch, but it can be challenging to operate. Some entrepreneurs have a difficult time keeping their involvement in the business separate from their life as a parent or spouse, and it can be difficult to operate a business out of your house and still abide by the zoning and legal requirements of your community or to maintain an image for your enterprise that attracts customers. These considerations can make the location decision much more complicated.

Perhaps you've decided to locate your business on the Internet to avoid the image risks and the high costs of starting up in a physical facility. Many other small business owners are making the same decision, but there are still a number of questions that have to be answered—for example, what kind of customer will you serve, what sort of business model will you adopt, and what will you need to get started? Are you going to keep your present job and try to start your new venture on the side, or do you plan to jump into the startup with both feet?

There are many questions to be answered, but there are also many sources of information to help you decide what will work best for your planned venture. Don't get impatient—just take your time, do your research, and make a wise choice. A world of endless business opportunities awaits you. So what's holding you back?

LOOKING BACK

1. Describe the five key factors in locating a brick-and-mortar startup.

- Customer accessibility is a key factor in the location decision of retail and service businesses.
- Climate, competition, legal requirements, and the tax structure are types of environmental factors affecting the location decision.
- Availability of resources such as raw materials, a labor supply, and transportation can be important to location decisions.
- Though it can interfere with sound decision making, the entrepreneur's personal preference is a practical consideration in selecting a location.
- An appropriate site must be available and priced within the entrepreneur's budget.

2. Discuss the challenges of designing and equipping a physical facility.

- The ideal building is practical, not extravagant.
- The general suitability of a building depends on the functional requirements of the business.
- The comfort, convenience, and safety of the business's employees and customers must not be overlooked.

- Most small manufacturing firms must use general-purpose equipment, but some can use special-purpose equipment for specialized operations.
- Small retailers must have merchandise display racks and counters, mirrors, and other equipment that facilitates selling.
- Display counters and other retailing equipment should create an atmosphere appropriate for customers in the retailer's target market.
- Entrepreneurs must select office equipment that reflects the latest advances in technology applicable to a particular business.

3. Understand both the attraction and the challenges of creating a home-based startup.

- Home-based businesses are started both to make money and to accommodate family lifestyle considerations.
- Operating a business at home can pose challenges, particularly in the areas of business image and legal considerations.
- Technology, especially the Web, has helped entrepreneurs start home-based businesses.

4. *Understand the potential benefits of locating a startup on the Internet.*

- E-commerce offers small firms the opportunity to compete with bigger companies on a more level playing field.
- Internet operations can help small firms with cash flow problems by compressing the sales cycle.
- E-commerce enables small firms to build stronger customer relationships.
- Business-to-business (B2B) companies generate far more sales than ventures following alternative models.
- The three main advantages of online business-to-consumer (B2C) firms are convenient use, immediate transactions, and continuous access to products and services, often referred to as 24/7 e-tailing.

- Internet auction sites, like eBay, have become very popular, and they can help even the smallest of businesses access a worldwide market with great convenience.
- The role of a website can range from merely offering content and information to permitting the buying and selling of products and services online.
- Emerging models of e-commerce include blogging, which can be used to generate significant amounts of advertising revenue for the entrepreneur-blogger.
- Internet-based businesses can be started on a part-time basis, which reduces the personal risk of the entrepreneur if the venture should fail.

Key Terms

brick-and-mortar store p. 232
enterprise zones p. 235
business incubator p. 237
general-purpose equipment p. 239
special-purpose equipment p. 240
home-based business p. 241
zoning ordinances p. 243
e-commerce p. 245

Electronic Customer Relationship Marketing (eCRM) p. 246
business model p. 246
business-to-business (B2B) model p. 247
business-to-consumer (B2C) model p. 248
24/7 e-tailing p. 248

disintermediation p. 249
auction sites p. 249
content-based model p. 251
information-based model p. 251
transaction-based model p. 251

Discussion Questions

1. What are the key attributes of a good business location? Which of these would probably be most important for a retail location? Why?

2. What is the special appeal of an enterprise zone to an entrepreneur seeking the best site for his or her business?

3. Which resource factors might be most vital to a new manufacturing venture that produces residential home furniture? Why?

4. Is the hometown of the business owner likely to be a good location? Is it logical for an owner to allow personal preferences to influence a decision about business location? Explain your answers.

5. What is the difference between general-purpose equipment and special-purpose equipment? What are the advantages and disadvantages of each?

6. Under what conditions would it be most appropriate for a new firm to buy rather than lease a building for the business?

7. What factors should an entrepreneur evaluate when considering a home-based business? Be specific.

8. Discuss how zoning and tax laws might impact the decision to start a home-based business.

9. Discuss the two different ways of categorizing business models used for e-commerce.

10. Contrast B2B and B2C businesses. Identify some of the reasons final consumers give for *not* shopping online.

SITUATION 1

Entrepreneurs Joe Stengard and his wife, Jackie Piel, had a decision to make. Located just outside of Saint Louis, their five-year-old company, S&P Crafts, was growing rapidly. But with only 4,000 square feet of production area, they were in desperate need of more space to make their custom-ordered craft kits.

A move always involves a certain measure of risk, so the couple was hesitant to transfer the company's operations. However, an economic development organization in Warren County, Missouri, offered attractive incentives in the form of tax breaks and financial assistance if they would move to a new facility in the rural town of Hopewell. Initial research indicated that a local workforce was readily available and had skills appropriate to the operation, so Stengard and Piel decided to move.

Since the change of address, company sales have tripled. And the new facility has grown from 10,000 square feet to 40,000 square feet in just two short years.

Question 1 How important was the location decision for these two entrepreneurs? Why?

Question 2 What types of permits and zoning ordinances did Stengard and Piel need to consider before deciding to relocate?

Question 3 How could Stengard and Piel use the Internet to expand the business of S&P Crafts?

SITUATION 2

Is it possible to build a $1.2-million business in a town with only 650 residents? Duane Ruh did just that. Ruh co-founded and is now sole owner of Little Log Company, which manufactures log birdhouses and feeders in Sargent, Nebraska. Ruh believes it is all about treating your employees right. His 32 employees enjoy flexible schedules and ample personal time.

Ruh's love for his employees and loyalty to the town of Sargent (where he employs 5 percent of the population) has paid off. Clients include 65 U.S. colleges, John Deere, and *National Geographic* magazine. Failure isn't an option for Ruh and his employees. Ruh says, "I think if you really love something, you can't fail at it."

Source: Michelle Prather, "Talk of the Town," http://www.entrepreneur.com/magazine.entrepreneur/2003/february/58828.html, accessed June 12, 2007.

Question 1 What impact, if any, do you think Internet-based competitors have had on Ruh's business?

Question 2 In what ways could he use e-commerce to grow his business?

Question 3 How much presence on the Web, if any, do you think Ruh should consider?

Question 4 What do you think will happen to this firm if it ignores the Internet?

SITUATION 3

Entrepreneur Karen Moore wants to start a catering and decorating business to bring in money to help support her two young children. Moore is a single parent; she works in the banking industry but has always had the desire to start a business. She enjoys decorating for friends' parties and is frequently told, "You should do this professionally. You have such good taste, and you are so nice to people."

Moore has decided to take this advice but is unsure whether she should locate in a commercial site or in her home, which is in rural central Texas. She is leaning toward locating at home because she wants more time with her children. However, she is concerned that the home-based location is too far away from the city, where most of her potential customers live.

Initially, her services would include planning wedding receptions and other special events, designing flower arrangements, decorating the sites, and even cooking and serving meals.

Question 1 What do you see as potential problems with locating Moore's new business at home?

Question 2 What do you see as the major benefits for Moore of a home-based business?

Question 3 How could Moore use technology to help her operate a home-based business?

Experiential Exercises

1. Search for articles in business periodicals that provide rankings of states or cities as business locations. Report on your findings.

2. Identify and evaluate a local site that is now vacant because of a business closure. Point out the strengths and weaknesses of that location for the former business, and comment on the part location may have played in the closure.

3. Interview a small business owner concerning the strengths and weaknesses of his or her business's location. Prepare a brief report summarizing your findings.

4. Talk to the owner of a local small business that you believe might benefit from e-commerce. Prepare a report on the e-commerce strategy being pursued or the reasons this particular business is not involved in e-commerce.

5. Contact the Chamber of Commerce office in your local area and ask what e-commerce assistance it provides to small firms. Report on your findings.

Small Business & Entrepreneurship Resource Center

The *Small Business and Entrepreneurship Resource Center* offers complete small business management resources through a comprehensive database that covers all major areas of starting, operating, and maintaining a business from financing, management, marketing, accounting, taxes, and more. Use the access code that came with your new book to access the site and perform the exercises in each chapter.

1. Small businesses are increasingly using the Internet as one of their location choices when starting their business. Chapter 9 introduced eBay as a viable option for entrepreneurs to establish a web presence. Most entrepreneurs think of eBay as an Internet auction site that is best used to sell used items from around the house or other relatively low priced goods. What about selling automobiles on eBay? Describe the challenges to selling automobiles over the Internet, and how eBay has successfully met them. If you were to sell new automobiles over the Internet, what could you do to help improve your reputation and sales?

2. James Dyson started his own vacuum cleaner manufacturing business in his hometown. He enjoyed growth in the business, but hit obstacles as the concept of globalization became a reality. As the text mentions, he moved his factory to Malaysia and was able to cut manufacturing costs by two-thirds. Discuss how this location decision (in this era of globalization) has impacted his hometown, both positively and negatively.

Sources: Will They Buy Vehicles Online?. Ward's Dealer Business 41.6 (June 1, 2007) p. 8: pNA. Suck it and see. (Suck it and see). *The Economist* (US) 382.8514 (Feb 3, 2007): p. 8 US.

Video Case 9

LE TRAVEL STORE (P. 641)

This case study illustrates the importance of location to a business and demonstrates how desired growth, along with the maturing of the business, can alter the optimal location, requiring relocation for continued desired growth.

ALTERNATIVE CASES FOR CHAPTER 9

Case 15, Country Supply, p. 656

Case 17, Glidden Point Oyster Company, A.G.A. Correa & Son, Hardy Boat Cruises, Maine Gold, p. 660

Case 18, Smarter.com, p. 662

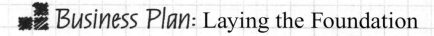

Business Plan: Laying the Foundation

As part of laying the foundation for preparing your own business plan, respond to the following questions regarding location.

Brick-and-Mortar Startup Location Questions

1. How important are your personal reasons for choosing a location?
2. What business environment factors will influence your location decision?
3. What resources are most critical to your location decision?
4. How important is customer accessibility to your location decision?
5. What special resources do you need?
6. How will the formal site evaluation be conducted?
7. What laws and tax policies of state and local governments need to be considered?
8. What is the cost of the proposed site?
9. Is an enterprise zone available in the area where you want to locate?

Physical Facility Questions

1. What are the major considerations in choosing between a new and an existing building?
2. What is the possibility of leasing a building or equipment?
3. How feasible is it to locate in a business incubator?
4. What is the major objective of your building design?
5. What types of equipment do you need for your business?

Home-Based Startup Location Questions

1. Will a home-based business be a possibility for you?
2. For the venture you are planning, what would be the advantages and disadvantages of locating the business in your home?
3. Have you given consideration to family lifestyle issues?
4. Will your home project the appropriate image for the business?
5. What zoning ordinances, if any, regulate the type of home-based business you want to start?

Internet Startup Questions

1. What type of customers will be served by the Internet startup?
2. What technical limitations (such as the cost of developing a website or constantly changing software needs) might hinder the company you plan to launch?
3. How will you deal with non-technical issues (privacy concerns, website security, dealing with global languages and cultures, etc.) that may limit the success of your online business?
4. Do you plan to open a storefront hosted by Amazon, eBay, or one of the other online giants, or would an independent website be better suited to the needs of your business?
5. What will be the nature of the online presence you hope to establish—content-based, information-based, transaction-based, or some other form?
6. Will you start the business on a part-time basis, or do you plan to be involved full-time?

Understanding a Firm's Financial Statements

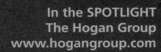

In the SPOTLIGHT
The Hogan Group
www.hogangroup.com

As an entrepreneur, you cannot afford to acquire a customer at any price. You must decide if the customer is worth the effort based on the profitability of the account. Mike Hogan tells his experience of trying to keep a customer, regardless of the profits generated—and the lesson he learned.

"It wasn't a joyful moment for anyone" That's how Mike Hogan describes his team's spirits when his Omaha, Neb.–based company, The Hogan Group, decided to walk away from a client that represented almost 25 percent of its annual revenue.

"We had done business with them for more than 10 years," says Hogan, whose business provides IT consultants to large companies to help with enterprise information needs. "And some years, we did almost $1 million in business with them."

But in 2002, The Hogan Group was frozen out of its longtime client's plans when the client signed an exclusive deal with an offshore firm, sending all its IT business to a company in India. "The only stuff we were allowed to compete for was providing consultants their India firm couldn't find," Hogan says.

Undeterred by the major setback, Hogan's employees poured their energy into locating the hard-to-find consultants—always hopeful the client would notice their hard work and return to The Hogan Group when the deal with the India firm didn't work out. "We kept thinking that somehow we had to change their minds," Hogan says. But when they submitted 200 qualified applicants within 12 months and not a single one was hired, Hogan knew they couldn't afford to keep trying.

"We spent a tremendous amount of sales and management time trying to keep this account alive and getting nowhere," he says. "We had four recruiters who spent 40 percent of their time trying to turn the tide in our favor, and we never got paid a cent. At some point you have to step back and say, 'This isn't going to work.'"

Cutting ties is unnerving, but in Hogan's case, it freed his employees to focus on new business—something they hadn't

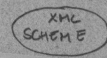

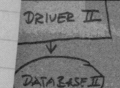

LOOKING AHEAD

AFTER STUDYING THIS CHAPTER, YOU SHOULD BE ABLE TO...

1. Describe the purpose and content of an income statement.
2. Explain the purpose and content of a balance sheet.
3. Explain how viewing the income statement and balance sheets together gives a more complete picture of a firm's financial position.
4. Use the income statement and balance sheets to compute a company's cash flows.
5. Analyze the financial statements using ratios to see more clearly how decisions are affecting a firm's financial performance.

Entrepreneurs do not start companies so that they can learn accounting—that's for certain. In fact, for many students—and aspiring entrepreneurs—accounting is not their favorite subject. But, if you have or plan to start a business, you had better learn some accounting—sooner rather than later. Norm Brodsky, a serial entrepreneur and noted columnist for *Inc. Magazine*, puts it plainly:

> When I started out, I thought that CEOs ran businesses with the help of their top executives. What I didn't realize is that a business is a living entity with needs of its own, and unless the leaders pay attention to those needs, the business will fail. So how do you know what those needs are? There's only one way: by looking at the numbers and understanding the relationships between them. They will tell you how good your sales are, whether you can afford to hire a new salesperson or office manager, how much cash you will need to deal with new business coming in, how your market is changing, and on and on. You can't afford to wait until your accountant tells you these things. Nor do you have to become an accountant. You do have to know enough accounting, however,

How I see it: Johnny Stites on Knowing Your Numbers

When you start and run your own business, it no longer matters whether you were a marketing, management, finance, or any other specific major. As an entrepreneur, you have to know how a business operates, which requires more than having knowledge in a specific academic field.

So whatever your major, you had best know the basics of accounting and finance. You do not need to be an accountant, but you had better be able to read and understand financial statements. Sure, you can hire an accountant, but if you do not understand what the numbers are telling you, you are in big trouble.

The construction industry is one of the riskiest industries you can enter, second only to the restaurant industry. For years, we would bid a job based on our best understanding of the costs that would be incurred. Then we would have to wait until the completion of the job to see if we made or lost money—not exactly an ideal situation to be in. Today, we have the ability to know how we are doing in terms of profits and costs on a daily basis. Not having accurate and timely accounting information would be deadly. We simply could not exist in such a competitive industry, and certainly not profitably, without understanding where we are financially.

to figure out which numbers are most important in your particular business, and then you should develop the habit of watching them like a hawk.[1]

In other words, some things can be learned about a business without understanding accounting, but other things can only be known by understanding the accounting numbers. Also, most of us cannot learn accounting by simply reading about accounting; we have to be engaged with it. We are reminded of the ancient saying "What I hear, I forget. What I see, I remember. What I do, I understand."

In this chapter, you will learn how to construct an *income statement*, a *balance sheet,* and a *cash flow statement.* Equally important, you will learn some basics of interpreting what these *financial statements* tell you about your business. Then, in Chapter 11, you will learn how to forecast a company's financial requirements, a key part of a business plan.

Before we begin a systematic study of financial statements, we will lay a foundation by telling a story about two young sisters who started their own small business, a lemonade stand.

financial statements (accounting statements)
Reports of a firm's financial performance and resources, including an income statement, a balance sheet, and a cash flow statement.

The Lemonade Girls

Ashley and Cameron Bates, ages 11 and 9, wanted to buy a Wii game system, one game, and an extra remote, which they estimated would cost $360. Their parents said they would pay most of the cost, but that the two girls would need to contribute $100 to the purchase price.

To earn money, the girls decided to operate a lemonade stand for two Saturdays in a nearby park frequented by walkers and runners. To start the business, they each invested $5 from their savings. Their mom, Krista, liked the girls' idea and said she would loan them any additional money they would need with two conditions: (1) The girls would have to repay her in two weeks, and (2) she would keep the books for the girls' business and expect them to learn

what the numbers meant. Krista thought this would provide the girls a valuable opportunity to learn about business.

Setting Up the Business

A balance sheet, Krista explained to the girls, is a picture of a firm's assets and its sources of financing at a point in time, when the financing comes from owners putting money into the business or from borrowing money. For instance, the girls' beginning $10 in cash represented their only asset and since it was their own money as the owners, it was also their equity in the business. She then wrote out a simple balance sheet:

Assets		Loans (debt) and owners' equity	
Cash	$10	Ashley & Cameron's equity	$10
Total assets	$10	Total loans & equity	$10

After thinking about what they would need in supplies to operate the lemonade stand, the girls requested a $40 loan from their mom. After the loan was made, the new balance sheet appeared as follows:

Assets		Loans (debt) and owners' equity	
Cash	$50	Loan from Mom	$40
Total assets	$50	Ashley & Cameron's equity	10
		Total loans & equity	$50

In preparing for their opening day, the girls bought $40 of "premium pink lemonade mix" and paper cups. Their mom explained that the lemonade mix and cups constituted their *inventory* of supplies. After paying for the inventory, the resulting balance sheet was as follows, where cash decreased and inventory increased by $40:

Assets		Loans (debt) and owners' equity	
Cash	$10	Loan from Mom	$40
Inventory	40	Ashley & Cameron's equity	10
Total assets	$50	Total loans & equity	$50

Opening Day

Being astute young businesswomen, Ashley and Cameron were aware that not all passers-by carried cash. So the girls created a signup sheet where customers could record their contact information for payment later in the week. The girls chose a prime location for their lemonade stand and prepared to serve some very fine ice-cold pink lemonade. By the end of the day, they had sold 60 cups at $1 each −30 cups that were bought on "credit" and 30 with cash. Since the lemonade only cost the girls 25 cents a cup, they made 75 cents per cup in profits, for a total of $45 in profit. Krista told the girls that an income statement reports the results of a firm's operations over a period of time—in this case, for a day. So the income statement for their first Saturday of selling looked like this:

Sales (60 cups × $1 per cup sales price)	$60
Cost of lemonade sold (60 cups × $0.25 cost per cup)	(15)
Profits	$45

Their balance sheet at the end of the day was as follows:

Assets		Loans (debt) and owners' equity	
Cash	$40	Loan from Mom	$40
Accounts receivable	30	Ashley & Cameron's equity	55
Inventory	25	Total loans & equity	$95
Total assets	$95		

This time, cash increased by $30, from $10 to $40, even though they had sold $60 of lemonade. The remaining $30 was still owed by their credit customers; the girls hoped to collect this money during the coming week. This asset, they learned, was called "accounts receivable" in business jargon. Also, there was a $15 decline in inventory, the result of the lemonade sold. Finally, the girls' equity increased by $45, the amount of the day's profits.

When Cameron looked at the income statement and balance sheet, she questioned why cash had only increased $30, even though profits were $45 for the day. Why were they not the same? Krista told her she was about to learn an important lesson: *To compute a company's cash flows requires you to look both at the income statement and at the changes in the balance sheet.* For one thing, they did not collect $30 of their sales, which resulted in $30 of accounts receivable, instead of cash. Second, the $15 cost of goods sold was not a cash outflow, since the inventory that was sold had already been purchased previously. In other words, they "sold" $15 of inventory and received the cash. Thus, to reconcile their profits with the change in cash requires the following calculation:

Profits		$45
Increase in accounts receivable	($30)	
Decrease in inventory	15	
Net increase in assets		$(15)
Change in cash		$30

Collecting Accounts Receivable

Not wanting to let their accounts receivable go uncollected too long, the girls hired their little sister, Erin, for $5 to make calls during the week on their credit customers. To their delight, by Friday night Erin (accompanied by a few of her friends) had collected all the money owed. With the money collected, cash increased $30 with a corresponding $30 decrease in accounts receivable. As a result, the balance sheet appeared as follows:

Assets		**Loans (debt) and owners' equity**	
Cash	$70	Loan from Mom	$40
Accounts receivable	0	Ashley & Cameron's equity	55
Inventory	25	Total loans & equity	$95
Total assets	$95		

Strategic Planning for the Following Saturday

Anticipating the next weekend, Ashley and Cameron decided to relocate their operation to Town Lake, an area in their town with a high volume of joggers and walkers. In addition, the girls decided to hire two friends, agreeing to pay each $10 a day, which allowed them to expand their business operations to three stands. However, since Town Lake is not in their local neighborhood, they decided not to sell on credit, choosing to do business on a cash-only basis.

The Second Saturday of Business

Ashley and Cameron arrived at Town Lake with their two friends early Saturday morning, and soon found themselves surrounded by customers. By mid-afternoon, they had sold 100 cups of lemonade, depleting all of their inventory! After paying their two friends $10 dollars each and Erin $5 for her collection work, the girls were delighted to learn that they had made $50 in profits—their income statement looked like this:

Sales	$100
Cost of lemonade	(25)
Salaries	(25)
Profits	$ 50

The balance sheet at the end of the day appeared as follows:

Assets		Loans (debt) and owners' equity	
Cash	$145	Loan from Mom	$ 40
Accounts receivable	0	Ashley & Cameron's equity	105
Inventory	0	Total loans & equity	$145
Total assets	$145		

Now cash assets had increased $75 as a result of the $100 in cash sales less the $25 paid to Erin and the girls' two friends. Inventory was now zero, and the girls' equity once again increased by the day's profits, in this case $50.

The sisters had accomplished their goal! They had enough to pay for their portion of the Wii, repay the $40 loan to their mom, and still had $5 to split. When they went to bed that night, they discussed the possibility of starting a summer business. The entrepreneurial flame had been lit, and they had big dreams for their next venture.

The hypothetical story of Ashley and Cameron and their lemonade stand allows us to think about accounting statements in a simplified and uncomplicated way. If you understand—really understand—the Lemonade Girls' financial results, you are ready to move on to the next step. This will not make you an accountant, but will give you the skill needed to manage a small business by the numbers. Our starting point is the income statement.

The Income Statement

An *income statement*, or *profit and loss statement*, indicates the amount of profits generated by a firm over a given time period, usually monthly, quarterly, or yearly. In its most basic form, the income statement may be represented by the following equation:

$$\text{Sales (revenue)} - \text{Expenses} = \text{Profits (income)}$$

(In this text, we primarily use the term *profits*, instead of *earnings* or *income*, but all three terms can be used interchangeably. That is, *net profits* is the same thing as *net income*.)

A more complete overview of an income statement is presented in Exhibit 10-1. As shown in the exhibit, you begin with sales (e.g., the number of lemonade drinks sold times the sales price per cup). You then subtract the *cost of goods sold* (e.g., the cost per cup of lemonade times the number of cups sold) to compute the firm's *gross profit*. Next, *operating expenses,* consisting of marketing and selling expenses, general and administrative expenses, and depreciation expense (e.g., Ashley and Cameron paying their friends and Erin to work for them) are deducted to determine *operating profits.* As shown in the exhibit, operating profits reflects only the decisions the owner has made relating to sales, cost of goods sold, and operating expenses. How the firm is financed, debt versus equity, has no effect on operating profits.

From the firm's operating profits, we deduct any *interest expense* incurred from borrowing money (debt) to find *profits before taxes,* or *taxable profits*—a company's taxable income. A firm's income taxes are calculated by multiplying profits before taxes by the applicable tax rate. For instance, if a firm has profits before taxes of $100,000 and its tax rate is 28 percent, then it will owe $28,000 in taxes ($0.28 \times \$100,000 = \$28,000$).

The number that results when taxes are subtracted from profits before taxes is the *net profits,* which represents profits that may be reinvested in the firm or distributed to the owners—provided, of course, the cash is available to do so. As you will come to understand,

1. Describe the purpose and content of an income statement.

income statement (profit and loss statement)
A financial report showing the profit or loss from a firm's operations over a given period of time.

cost of goods sold
The cost of producing or acquiring goods or services to be sold by a firm.

gross profit
Sales less the cost of goods sold.

operating expenses
Costs related to marketing and selling a firm's product or service, general and administrative expenses, and depreciation.

EXHIBIT

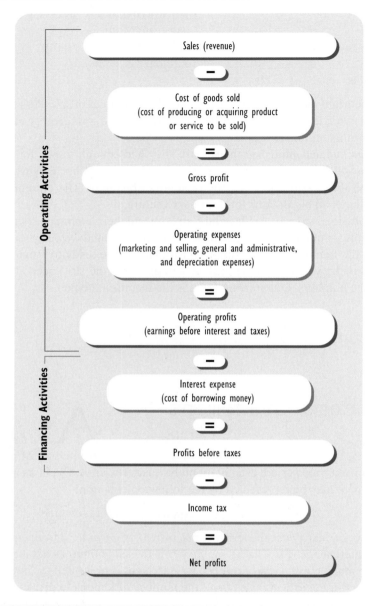

Operating Activities

Sales (revenue)

−

Cost of goods sold
(cost of producing or acquiring product
or service to be sold)

=

Gross profit

−

Operating expenses
(marketing and selling, general and administrative,
and depreciation expenses)

=

Operating profits
(earnings before interest and taxes)

Financing Activities

−

Interest expense
(cost of borrowing money)

=

Profits before taxes

−

Income tax

=

Net profits

operating profits
Earnings or profits after operating expenses but before interest and taxes are paid.

interest expense
The cost of borrowed money.

profits before taxes (taxable profits)
Earnings after operating expenses and interest expenses but before taxes.

net profits
Income that may be distributed to the owners or reinvested in the company.

depreciation expense
The cost of a firm's building and equipment, allocated over their useful life.

positive net profits in an income statement does not necessarily mean that a firm has generated positive cash flows.

Exhibit 10-2 shows the 2009 income statement for Gilbert & Associates Leasing, Inc., an equipment leasing company owned by Kristy Gilbert. The company had sales of $850,000 for the 12-month period ending December 31, 2009. The cost of goods sold was $550,000, resulting in a gross profit of $300,000. The company had $200,000 in operating expenses, which included marketing expenses, general and administrative expenses, and depreciation expense. (*Depreciation expense* is the cost of a firm's equipment and building allocated over their useful life. For example, if a business paid $10,000 for a piece of equipment with a four-year life expectancy, the depreciation expense each year would be $2,500, or $10,000 ÷ 4 years.) After total operating expenses were subtracted, the company's operating profits amounted to $100,000. To this point, we have calculated profits based only on expenses related to the firm's operations.

10-2 Income Statement for Gilbert & Associates Leasing, Inc., for the Year Ending December 31, 2009

Sales		$850,000
Cost of goods sold		550,000
Gross profits		$300,000
Operating expenses:		
Marketing expenses	$90,000	
General and administrative expenses	80,000	
Depreciation	30,000	
Total operating expenses		$200,000
Operating profits		$100,000
Interest expense		20,000
Profits before tax		$ 80,000
Income tax (25%)		20,000
Net profits		$ 60,000
Net profits		$ 60,000
Dividends paid		15,000
Change in retained earnings		$ 45,000

Gilbert & Associates' interest expense of $20,000 (the expense it incurred from borrowing money) is then deducted from operating profits to arrive at the company's profits before taxes of $80,000. Given a 25 percent tax rate, the company paid $20,000 in income taxes ($80,000 × 0.25), leaving net profits of $60,000.

The net profits of $60,000 are the profits that the business earned for its owners after paying all expenses—cost of goods sold, operating expenses, interest expense, and income taxes.

Now the owners have to decide what to do with these profits. They either can pay themselves a dividend or retain the earnings in the business to help finance the firm's growth, or some combination of the two.

So what did the Gilbert & Associates' stockholders do with their profits? As shown at the bottom of Exhibit 10-2, $15,000 of dividends was paid to the owners; the remaining $45,000 ($60,000 net profits less $15,000 in dividends) was retained by the firm—an amount you will see later in the balance sheet. *Also, dividends paid to a firm's owners, unlike interest expense, are not considered an expense in the income statement.* Instead, they are viewed as a return of principal to the owners.

In summary, the income statement answers the question "How profitable is the business?" In providing the answer, the income statement reports financial information related to five broad areas of business activity:

1. Sales (revenue)
2. Cost of producing or acquiring the goods or services sold by the company
3. Operating expenses
4. Interest expense
5. Tax payments

Being able to measure profits, as explained above, isn't enough; you must also consider how your decisions affect your company's profits. Philip Campbell, a CPA, a consultant, and the author of *Never Run Out of Cash: The 10 Cash Flow Rules You Can't Afford to Ignore,* offers this advice:

If you ask a business owner whether he runs his company to make money, the answer will always be "Yes." The reality is, he doesn't. . . . More often than not, you hear words like "brand," "market share," or "shelf space." When you hear those words, you can be sure that you've just found an opportunity to make some money.

Why? Because those words always are used to justify unprofitable decisions. They are big red flags that you are not making decisions based on a common-sense approach to profitability. When you hear those words, ask yourself this simple question, "Are we making this decision based on profitability or for some other (possibly hidden) reason?"[2]

Let's Check for Understanding

Understanding the Income Statement
Take a few minutes to see if you can answer these two questions:

1. What is the difference between gross profits, operating profits, profits before taxes, and net profits?
2. Construct an income statement, using the following information. What are the firm's gross profits, operating profits, and net profits? Which expense is a *noncash* expense?

Interest expense	$ 10,000
Cost of goods sold	160,000
Marketing expenses	70,000
Administrative expenses	50,000
Sales	400,000
Stock dividends	5,000
Income tax	20,000
Depreciation expense	20,000

(Answers to these two questions are provided on page 269.)

The Balance Sheet

2. Explain the purpose and content of a balance sheet.

While an income statement reports the results of business operations over a period of time, a *balance sheet* provides a snapshot of a business's financial position at a *specific point in time*. Thus, a balance sheet captures the cumulative effects of all earlier financial decisions up to a specific date. At a given point in time, the balance sheet shows the assets a firm owns, the liabilities (or debt) outstanding or owed, and the amount the owners have invested in the business (ownership equity). In its simplest form, a balance sheet follows this formula:

$$\text{Total assets} = \text{Debt} + \text{Ownership equity}$$

In other words, for every dollar of assets, there must be a dollar of financing in the form of debt or owners' equity.

Exhibit 10-3 illustrates the elements in the balance sheet of a typical firm. Each of the three main components of the balance sheet—assets, debt, and ownership equity—is discussed in the following sections.

balance sheet
A financial report showing a firm's assets, liabilities, and ownership equity at a specific point in time.

EXHIBIT

10-3 The Balance Sheet: An Overview

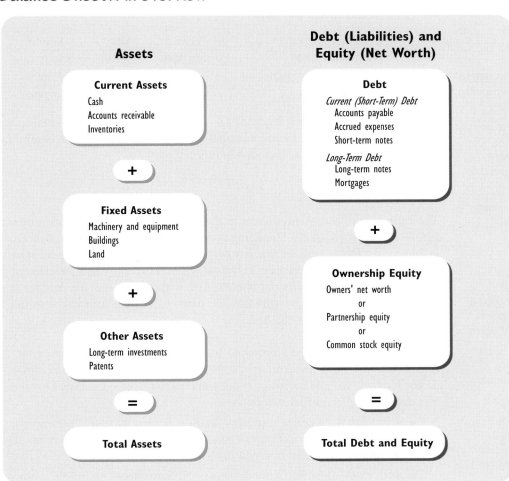

Assets

A company's assets, shown on the left side of Exhibit 10-3, fall into three categories: (1) current assets, (2) fixed assets, and (3) other assets. *Current assets* include those assets that are relatively liquid—that is, assets that can be converted into cash relatively quickly. Current assets primarily include cash, accounts receivable, and inventory.

- Every firm must have *cash* for current business operations.
- When a firm sells its products or services, customers may pay in cash or be given credit terms, such as being allowed 30 days to pay for purchases. The amount of money that customers owe a company is called *accounts receivable*.
- *Inventory* is the raw materials and products held by a firm for eventual sale.

Fixed assets are the more permanent assets in a business. They typically include equipment, buildings, and land. Some businesses are more capital-intensive than others—for example, a motel is more capital-intensive than a gift store—and, therefore, it will have a greater amount invested in fixed assets.

Most fixed assets are also *depreciable assets*; that is, their value declines, or depreciates, over time. For instance, a truck that was purchased for $20,000 may be depreciated over four years. The depreciation expense shown in the income statement for each year would be $5,000 ($20,000 ÷ 4 years = $5,000). When the firm buys the truck, the original cost of $20,000 is shown on the balance sheet as a *gross fixed asset*. Each year, the cumulative depreciation expense, or what is called *accumulated depreciation*, is subtracted from the original cost to yield the *net fixed asset*. For this example, the balance sheet at the end of each year would appear as follows:

	Year 1	Year 2	Year 3	Year 4
Gross fixed asset	$20,000	$20,000	$20,000	$20,000
Accumulated depreciation	5,000	10,000	15,000	20,000
Net fixed asset	$15,000	$10,000	$ 5,000	$ 0

The third category, *other assets*, includes such assets as patents, copyrights, and goodwill. For a startup company, organizational costs—costs incurred in organizing and promoting the business—may also be included in this category.

Debt and Equity

The right side of the balance sheet in Exhibit 10-3, showing debt and equity, indicates how a firm is financing its assets. Financing comes from two main sources: debt (liabilities) and ownership equity. Debt is money that has been borrowed and must be repaid at some predetermined date. Ownership equity, on the other hand, represents the owners' investment in the company—money they have personally put into the firm without any specific date for repayment. Owners recover their investment by withdrawing money from the firm in the form of dividends or by selling their ownership in the firm.

DEBT *Debt* is financing provided by a creditor. As shown in Exhibit 10-3, it is divided into (1) current, or short-term, debt and (2) long-term debt. *Current debt,* or *short-term liabilities,* include borrowed money that must be repaid within 12 months. Sources of current debt may be classified as follows:

- *Accounts payable* represent credit extended by suppliers to a firm when it purchases inventory. The purchasing firm usually is given 30 or 60 days to pay for the inventory. This form of credit is also called **trade credit**.
- *Accrued expenses* are expenses that have been incurred but not yet paid. For example, employees may have performed work for which they will not be paid until

---

Sidebar glossary (left margin):

current assets
Assets that can be converted into cash within a company's operating cycle.

accounts receivable
The amount of credit extended to customers that is currently outstanding.

inventory
A firm's raw materials and products held in anticipation of eventual sale.

fixed assets
Relatively permanent assets intended for use in the business, such as plant and equipment.

depreciable assets
Assets whose value declines, or depreciates, over time.

gross fixed assets
Original cost of depreciable assets before any depreciation expense has been taken.

accumulated depreciation
Total depreciation expense taken over the assets' life.

net fixed assets
Gross fixed assets less accumulated depreciation.

other assets
Assets other than current assets and fixed assets, such as patents, copyrights, and goodwill.

debt
Business financing provided by creditors.

current debt (short-term liabilities)
Borrowed money that must be repaid within 12 months.

How Did You Do?

Understanding the Income Statement

On page 266, you were asked two questions. Your answers should be similar to those provided below.

1. What is the difference between gross profits, operating profits, profits before taxes, and net profits?

    To understand a firm's profits, think about the process. For instance, a retailer buys merchandise from a wholesaler. The merchandise is then placed on display shelves in the store, where sales personnel, a bookkeeper, and a maintenance person work. The retailer sells the merchandise, hopefully for a profit. The difference between what the retailer received from customers (sales) and the cost of the merchandise is the gross profits. The expenses of operating the store represent the business's operating expenses. So deducting the operating expenses from gross profits gives the operating profits. If the retailer borrowed money from a bank, he or she would have to pay interest expense. Subtracting any interest expense from operating profits gives profits before taxes. The retailer then pays income taxes on those taxable profits. The remaining earnings are the company's net profits, which are the profits that are left for the owners. (See Exhibit 10-1 for a graphical representation of the process.)

2. Construct an income statement, using the following information. What are the firm's gross profits, operating profits, and net profits? Which expense is a noncash expense?

Sales		$400,000
Cost of goods sold		160,000
Gross profits		$240,000
Operating expenses:		
Marketing expenses	$ 70,000	
Administrative expenses	50,000	
Depreciation expense	20,000	← Noncash Expense
Total operating expenses		$140,000
Operating profits		$100,000
Interest expense		10,000
Profits before taxes		$ 90,000
Income tax		20,000
Net profits		$ 70,000

Note: The $5,000 in dividends is not shown as an expense in the income statement but is considered to be a return of the owner's capital. Thus, the net profits of $70,000 less the $5,000 in dividends, or $65,000, will be added to the firm's retained earnings in the balance sheet.

---

the following week or month. The wages are reported in the income statement, but since they have not been paid, they are shown as a liability or accrued wages in the balance sheet.

- *Short-term notes* represent cash amounts borrowed from a bank or other lending source for 12 months or less. Short-term notes are a primary source of financing for most small businesses.

Long-term debt includes loans from banks or other sources that lend money for longer than 12 months. When a firm borrows money for five years to buy equipment, it signs an agreement—a long-term note—promising to repay the money over five years. When a firm borrows money for 30 years to purchase real estate, such as a warehouse or office building, the real estate usually stands as collateral for the long-term loan, which is called a *mortgage*. If the borrower is unable to repay the loan, the lender can take the real estate in settlement.

accounts payable (trade credit)
Outstanding credit payable to suppliers.

accrued expenses
Short-term liabilities that have been incurred but not paid.

short-term notes
Cash amounts borrowed from a bank or other lending sources that must be repaid within a short period of time.

long-term debt
Loans from banks or other sources with repayment terms of more than 12 months.

mortgage
A long-term loan from a creditor for which real estate is pledged as collateral.

ownership equity
Owners' investments in a company plus profits retained in the firm.

retained earnings
Profits less withdrawals (dividends) over the life of a business.

EQUITY *Ownership equity* is money that the owners invest in a business. The amount of ownership equity in a business is equal to (1) the total amount of the owners' investments in the business plus (2) the cumulative amount of profits that have been retained in the business since the beginning of the business; that is, profits not paid out as dividends. The second item is called *retained earnings,* because these profits have been reinvested in the business instead of being distributed to the owners. Thus, the basic formula for ownership equity is as follows:

$$\begin{matrix} & & & \overbrace{\qquad\qquad\qquad\qquad\qquad}^{\text{Earnings retained within the business}} \\ \text{Ownership equity} & = & \text{Owners' investment} & + & \text{Cumulative profits} & - & \text{Cumulative dividends paid to owners} \end{matrix}$$

Exhibit 10-4 presents balance sheets for Gilbert & Associates for December 31, 2008, and December 31, 2009, along with the dollar changes in the balance sheets from 2008 to 2009. By referring to the columns representing the two balance sheets, we can see the financial position of the firm at the beginning *and* at the end of 2009.

The 2008 and 2009 balance sheets for Gilbert & Associates show that the firm began 2009 (ended 2008) with $800,000 in total assets and ended 2009 with total assets of $920,000. We see how much has been invested in current assets (cash, accounts receivable, and inventory) and in fixed assets. We also observe how much debt and equity were used to finance the assets. Note also that about half of the equity came from investments made by the owners (common stock), and the other half came from reinvesting profits in the business (retained earnings). Referring back to the income statement in Exhibit 10-2, note that the

10-4 Balance Sheets for Gilbert & Associates Leasing, Inc., for December 31, 2008 and 2009

	2008	2009	Changes
Assets			
Current assets:			
Cash	$ 45,000	$ 50,000	$ 5,000
Accounts receivable	75,000	80,000	5,000
Inventory	180,000	220,000	40,000
Total current assets	$300,000	$350,000	$ 50,000
Fixed assets:			
Gross fixed assets	$860,000	$960,000	$100,000
Accumulated depreciation	(360,000)	(390,000)	(30,000)
Net fixed assets	$500,000	$570,000	$ 70,000
TOTAL ASSETS	$800,000	$920,000	$120,000
Debt (Liabilities) and Equity			
Current liabilities:			
Accounts payable	$ 15,000	$ 20,000	$ 5,000
Short-term notes	60,000	80,000	20,000
Total current liabilities (debt)	$ 75,000	$100,000	$ 25,000
Long-term debt	150,000	200,000	50,000
Total debt	$225,000	$300,000	$ 75,000
Common stockholder's equity (ownership) equity)			
Common stock	$300,000	$300,000	$ 0
Retained earnings	275,000	320,000	45,000
Total common stockholder's equity	$575,000	$620,000	$ 45,000
TOTAL DEBT AND EQUITY	$800,000	$920,000	$120,000

EXHIBIT

$45,000 increase in retained earnings, shown in the Changes column in Exhibit 10-4, is the firm's net profits for the year ($60,000) less the dividends ($15,000) paid to the owners.

In summary, financing for a business is derived from two sources: debt and ownership equity. Debt is money borrowed from financial institutions, suppliers, and other lenders. Ownership equity represents the owners' investment in the company, either through cash invested in the firm or through profits retained in the business (shown as retained earnings on the balance sheet).

Viewing the Income Statement and Balance Sheet Together

Thus far, we have discussed the income statement and the balance sheet as separate reports. But they actually complement each other to give an overall picture of the firm's financial situation. Because the balance sheet is a snapshot of a firm's financial condition at a point in time and the income statement reports results over a given period, both are required to determine a firm's financial position.

3. Explain how viewing the income statement and balance sheets together gives a more complete picture of a firm's financial position.

Exhibit 10-5 shows how the income statement and the balance sheet fit together. To understand how a firm performed during 2009, you must know the firm's financial position at the beginning of 2009 (balance sheet on December 31, 2008), its financial performance during the year (income statement for 2009), and its financial position at the end of the year (balance sheet on December 31, 2009). As you will see, all three statements are needed to measure Gilbert & Associates' cash flows for 2009.

10-5 The Fit of the Income Statement and Balance Sheet

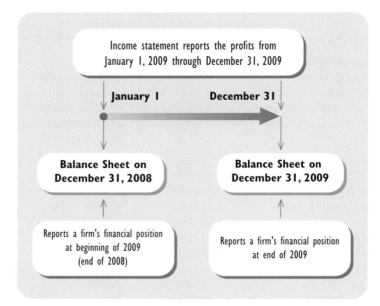

Income statement reports the profits from January 1, 2009 through December 31, 2009

January 1   December 31

Balance Sheet on December 31, 2008

Balance Sheet on December 31, 2009

Reports a firm's financial position at beginning of 2009 (end of 2008)

Reports a firm's financial position at end of 2009

How Did You Do?

Understanding the Balance Sheet?

On page 271, you were asked four questions. Your answers should be similar to those provided below.

1. Give an example of accounts receivable.

   Accounts receivable represent money owed by a customer to a company for goods or services that have already been received by the customer but not yet paid for. For example, an auto repair shop may purchase parts for $200 from a parts supplier and be given 30 days to pay for the parts. At the time of the transaction, the supplier records the $200 sale and the same amount in accounts receivable. When the repair shop pays the $200, the accounts receivable are decreased and cash increases by $200.

2. What relationship would you expect between inventory and accounts payable?

   Accounts payable are the amounts owed a supplier for inventory that was purchased on credit. When a business purchases inventory on credit, inventory increases along with a corresponding increase in accounts payable.

3. What is the difference between common stock and retained earnings?

   Both common stock and retained earnings represent an owner's equity in a firm. Common stock is cash that has been invested in a firm by its owners. Retained earnings are the amount of profits that have been reinvested in a business as opposed to distributing the profits in the form of dividends.

4. Based on the financial data provided on page 271, your balance sheet should read as follows:

Assets

Cash	$ 10,000
Accounts receivable	50,000
Inventory	70,000
Total current assets	$130,000
Gross fixed assets	$ 75,000
Accumulated depreciation	(20,000)
Net fixed assets	$ 55,000
Other assets	15,000
TOTAL ASSETS	$200,000

Debt and Equity

Accounts payable	$ 40,000
Short-term notes	20,000
Total current debt	$ 60,000
Long-term note	5,000
Mortgage	20,000
Total long-term debt	$ 25,000
Total debt	$ 85,000
Common stock	$100,000
Retained earnings	15,000
Total ownership equity	$115,000
TOTAL DEBT AND EQUITY	$200,000

The Cash Flow Statement

4. Use the income statement and balance sheets to compute a company's cash flows.

An entrepreneur once told us how intimidated she felt when her accountant presented the firm's monthly financial reports and how difficult she found it to understand cash flows. Our advice was to get a new accountant—one who would explain the statements carefully—and also to spend the time necessary to gain a solid understanding of the financial statements and the firm's cash flows.

Effectively managing cash flows is critical—and we do mean *critical*—for small business owners. Cash flow problems are a constant concern of most entrepreneurs. For this reason, the small firm owner must understand the sources and uses of the firm's cash. A *cash flow statement* is a financial report that shows the sources of a firm's cash and its uses of the cash. In other words, it answers the questions "Where did the cash come from?" and "Where did the cash go?"

cash flow statement
A financial report showing a firm's sources of cash as well as its uses of cash.

Profits versus Cash Flows

Entrepreneurs need to be aware that the profits shown on a company's income statement are not the same as its cash flows. Do you remember when Cameron (one of the Lemonade Girls) noticed that the girls' profits were not the same as the increase in cash? That simple example plays out every day in the lives of entrepreneurs. In the words of author Jan Norman, "Even profitable companies can go broke. That's a difficult truth for start-up business owners to swallow. But the sooner you learn that when you're out of cash, you're out of business, the better your chances for survival will be."[3]

An income statement is not a measure of cash flows because it is calculated on an *accrual* basis rather than a *cash* basis. This is an important point to understand. In *accrual-basis accounting,* profits are recorded when earned—whether or not the profits have been received in cash—and expenses are recorded when they are incurred—even if money has not actually been paid out. In *cash-basis accounting,* profits are reported when cash is received and expenses are recorded when they are paid.

For a number of reasons, profits based on an accrual accounting system will differ from the firm's cash flows. These reasons include the following:

accrual-basis accounting
An accounting method of recording profits when they are earned, whether or not the profits have been received in cash; additional expenses are recorded when they are incurred, even if payment has not been made.

cash-basis accounting
An accounting method of recording profits when cash is received and recording expenses when they are paid.

1. Sales reported in an income statement include both *cash* sales and *credit* sales. Thus, total sales do not correspond to the actual cash collected.

2. Some inventory purchases are financed by credit, so inventory purchases do not exactly equal cash spent for inventory.

3. The depreciation expense shown in the income statement is a noncash expense. It reflects the costs associated with using an asset that benefits the firm's operations over a period of more than one year, such as a piece of equipment used over five years.

So, the question becomes "How do we compute a firm's cash flows?"

Measuring a Firm's Cash Flows

It's time to return to our young entrepreneurs, Ashley and Cameron, and their lemonade stand. To develop a report that explained the cash flows from their lemonade business, you could simply list all the cash inflows and outflows and see what happened to their cash balance. Here is what it would look like:

Ashley and Cameron's initial investment	$ 10
Loan from their mom	40
Purchased inventory	(40)
Cash collected from the first Saturday's sales	30
Collection of accounts receivable	30
Cash collected from the second Saturday's sales	100
Salaries expense	(25)
Ending cash	$145

So they began with a $10 investment in the business, and ended with $145 in cash, before repaying their mom the $40 she loaned them and contributing $100 toward the Wii purchase. This works quite well in the world of lemonade stands. But the report would become overwhelming in a business of any significant size, where thousands of transactions are recorded in the financial statements each year. Also, there's a better approach to learning what activities contribute to a firm's cash flows. We can explain the cash inflows and outflows of a business by looking at three activities:

1. *Generating cash flows from day-to-day business operations.* It is informative to know how much cash is being generated in the normal course of operating a business on a daily basis, beginning with purchasing inventory on credit, selling on credit, paying for the inventory, and finally collecting on the sales made on credit.

2. *Investing in fixed assets.* When the company purchases fixed assets (like equipment and buildings) to grow the business, there will be significant cash outflows.

3. *Financing the business.* Cash inflows and outflows occur from borrowing or repaying debt, paying dividends, and from issuing stock (equity) or repurchasing stock from the owners.

If we know the cash flows from the activities listed above, we can easily explain a firm's total cash flows. To explain how this is done, we use Gilbert & Associates' income statement (Exhibit 10-2) and balance sheets (Exhibit 10-4).

CASH FLOWS FROM DAY-TO-DAY BUSINESS OPERATIONS

Here we want to convert the company's income statement from an *accrual* basis to a *cash* basis. This conversion can be accomplished in two steps: (1) by adding back depreciation to net profits, since depreciation is not a cash expense, and (2) subtracting any uncollected sales (increase in accounts receivable) and payments for inventory (increases in inventory less increases in accounts payable).

The reason we add back depreciation should be clear. The changes in accounts receivable, inventory, and accounts payable may be less intuitive. Two comments might be helpful for your understanding:

1. A firm's sales either are cash sales or credit sales. If accounts receivable increase, that means customers did not pay for everything they purchased. Thus, any increase in accounts receivable, as in Gilbert & Associates' case, needs to be subtracted from total sales to determine the cash that has been collected from customers. Remember the Lemonade Girls: On their first day, they sold $60 in lemonade, but they only collected $30; the remainder was accounted for by an increase in accounts receivable.

2. The other activity occurring in the daily course of business is purchasing inventory. An increase in inventory shows that inventory was purchased, but if accounts payable (credit extended by a supplier) increase, then we may conclude that the firm did not pay for all of the inventory purchased. Thus, the net payment for inventory is equal to the increase in inventory less what has not yet been paid for (increase in accounts payable).

Referring back to Gilbert & Associates' income statement (Exhibit 10-2) and balance sheets (Exhibit 10-4), we can perform the conversion from accrual basis to cash basis as follows:

Net profits	$60,000	
Plus depreciation	30,000	
Profits before depreciation		$90,000
Less increase in accounts receivable (uncollected sales)		($ 5,000)
Less payments for inventory consisting of:		
Increase in inventory	(40,000)	
Less increase in accounts payable (inventory purchased on credit)	5,000	
Payments for inventory		($ 35,000)
Cash flows from operations		$ 50,000

INVESTING IN FIXED ASSETS

When a company purchases fixed assets, such as equipment or buildings, these expenditures are shown as an increase in *gross* fixed assets in the balance sheet. For instance, Gilbert & Associates spent $100,000 on new plant and equipment in 2009, based on the change in gross fixed assets from $860,000 to $960,000, as shown in their balance sheets (Exhibit 10-4).

FINANCING A BUSINESS

Financing a business involves (1) paying dividends to the owners; (2) increasing or decreasing short-term and long-term debt, which means borrowing more money (an increase in debt) or paying off debt (a decrease in debt); and (3) selling shares of stock (source of cash) or repurchasing stock (use of cash).

We know from Gilbert & Associates' income statement (Exhibit 10-2) that $15,000 in dividends was paid to the owners. Then from its balance sheets (Exhibit 10-4), we see that short-term debt increased $20,000 and long-term debt increased $50,000, both sources of cash flow. Thus, in net, Gilbert & Associates raised $55,000 in financing cash flows:

Cash inflows from borrowing money	
Increase in short-term notes	$ 20,000
Increase in long-term debt	50,000
Less dividends paid to owners	(15,000)
Financing cash flows	$ 55,000

10-6 Cash Flow Statement for Gilbert & Associates Leasing, Inc., for the Year Ending December 31, 2009

Operating activities:		
Net profits	$60,000	
Plus depreciation	30,000	
Profits before depreciation		$90,000
Less increase in accounts receivable (uncollected sales)		($5,000)
Less payments for inventory consisting of:		
Increase in inventories	(40,000)	
Less increase in accounts payable (inventory purchased on credit)	5,000	
Payments for inventory		($35,000)
Cash flows from operations		$50,000
Investment activities:		
Less increase in gross fixed assets		($100,000)
Financing activities:		
Increase in short-term notes	20,000	
Increase in long-term debt	50,000	
Less dividends paid to owners	(15,000)	
Financing cash flows		$55,000
Increase in cash		$5,000

To summarize, Gilbert & Associates generated $50,000 in cash flows from operations; invested $100,000 in plant and equipment, and received $55,000 from financing activities, for a net increase in cash of $5,000. This can be verified from the balance sheets (see Exhibit 10-4), which show that the firm's cash increased by $5,000 during 2009 (from $45,000 to $50,000). The complete statement of cash flows is provided in Exhibit 10-6.

Evaluating a Firm's Financial Performance

Once a firm's owner understands the content of the accounting statements, she or he wants to know how management decisions impact the financial situation of a business. An entrepreneur's decisions play out primarily in four ways when it comes to finances:

5. Analyze the financial statements using ratios to see more clearly how decisions are affecting a firm's financial performance.

1. *The firm's ability to pay its debt as it comes due.* In other words, does the company have the capacity to meet its short-term (one year or less) debt commitments?

2. *The company's profitability from assets.* Is the business providing a good rate of return on its assets? There is no more important question when it comes to determining if a business is strong economically.

3. *The amount of debt the business is using.* Using debt increases a firm's risk, but may also increase the expected rate of return on the owners' equity investment.

4. *The rate of return earned by the owners on their equity investment.* All decisions ultimately affect the rate of return earned by the owners on their equity investment in the business.

Exhibit 10-7 provides a list of financial ratios as they relate to the four issues listed above. The name of each ratio is given, along with how it is computed. We illustrate the ratios by using the 2009 financial data for Gilbert & Associates, as presented in Exhibit 10-2 (income statement) and Exhibit 10-4 (balance sheets). Finally, the last column shows an industry average for each ratio, which comes from financial publications, such as Robert Morris & Associates. Let's look at the ratios as they apply to Gilbert & Associates.

Gilbert & Associates' Liquidity (Ability to Pay Its Debt)

A business—or a person, for that matter—that has enough money to pay off any debt owed is described as being *liquid*. The liquidity of a business depends on the availability of cash to meet maturing debt obligations. The *current ratio* is traditionally used to measure a company's liquidity. This ratio compares a firm's *current assets* to its *current liabilities*, as follows:

$$\text{Current ratio} = \frac{\text{Current assets}}{\text{Current liabilities}}$$

liquidity
The degree to which a firm has working capital available to meet maturing debt obligations.

current ratio
A measure of a company's relative liquidity, determined by dividing current assets by current liabilities.

Financial Ratios	Gilbert & Associates	Industry Norm
1. Ability to pay debt as it comes due		
Current ratio = $\dfrac{\text{Current assets}}{\text{Current liabilities}}$	$\dfrac{\$350{,}000}{\$100{,}000} = 3.50$	2.7
2. Company's profitability on its assets		
Return on assets = $\dfrac{\text{Operating profits}}{\text{Total assets}}$	$\dfrac{\$100{,}000}{\$920{,}000} = 10.87\%$	13.2%
Operating profit margin = $\dfrac{\text{Operating profits}}{\text{Sales}}$	$\dfrac{\$100{,}000}{\$850{,}000} = 11.76\%$	11.0%
Total asset turnover = $\dfrac{\text{Sales}}{\text{Total assets}}$	$\dfrac{\$850{,}000}{\$920{,}000} = 0.92$	1.2
3. The amount of debt the company uses		
Debt ratio = $\dfrac{\text{Total debt}}{\text{Total assets}}$	$\dfrac{\$300{,}000}{\$920{,}000} = 32.60\%$	40%
4. Rate of return earned by the owners on their equity investment		
Return on equity = $\dfrac{\text{Net profits}}{\text{Owners' equity}}$	$\dfrac{\$60{,}000}{\$620{,}000} = 9.68\%$	12.5%

You can see in Exhibit 10-7 that Gilbert & Associates' current ratio is 3.5, compared to an industry average of 2.7. In other words, the firm has $3.50 in current assets for every $1 of short-term debt, compared to an industry average of $2.70 of current assets for every $1 in short-term debt. Thus, based on the current ratio, Gilbert & Associates is more liquid than the average firm in the industry.

Gilbert & Associates' Profitability on Its Assets

A vitally important question to a firm's owners is whether a company's operating profits are sufficient relative to the total amount of assets invested in the company.

Exhibit 10-8 provides a graphical representation of the drivers of a firm's return on assets. As shown in the exhibit, a firm's assets are invested for the express purpose of producing operating profits. A comparison of operating profits to total assets reveals the rate of return that is being earned on the entire firm's capital. For Gilbert & Associates, we compute the *return on assets* as follows:

return on assets
A measure of a firm's profitability relative to the amount of assets invested in the company, determined by dividing operating profits by total assets.

$$\text{Return on assets} = \frac{\text{Operating profits}}{\text{Total assets}}$$

The firm's return on assets of 10.87 percent is less than the industry norm of 13.2 percent, indicating that Gilbert & Associates is generating less operating income on each dollar of assets than its competitors. That is not good!

To gain more understanding about why Gilbert & Associates is not doing as well in generating profits on the firm's assets, you can separate the return on assets into two components: (1) the operating profit margin and (2) the total asset turnover. The equation for the return on assets can be restated as follows:

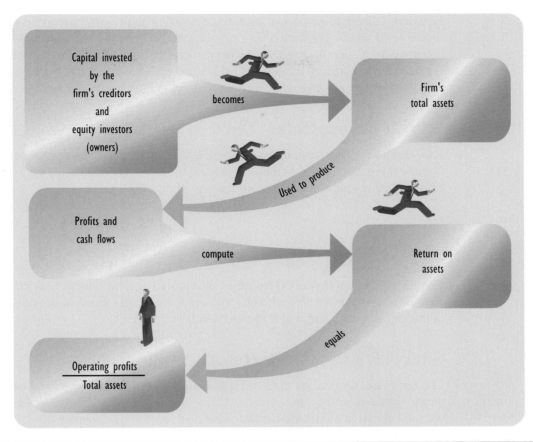

$$\text{Return on assets} = \underbrace{\frac{\text{Operating profits}}{\text{Total assets}}}_{} = \underbrace{\frac{\text{Operating profits}}{\text{Sales}}}_{\substack{\text{Operating} \\ \text{Profit Margin}}} \times \underbrace{\frac{\text{Sales}}{\text{Total assets}}}_{\substack{\text{Total Asset} \\ \text{Turnover}}}$$

The first component of the expanded equation, the *operating profit margin* (operating profits ÷ sales), shows how well a firm is controlling its cost of goods sold and operating expenses relative to a dollar of sales. The second component of a firm's return on assets, the *total asset turnover* (sales ÷ total assets), indicates how efficiently management is using the firm's assets to generate sales.

The operating profit margin and total asset turnover for Gilbert & Associates, along with industry averages, are presented in Exhibit 10-7. You can also show how they relate to Gilbert & Associates' return on assets, as well as the industry:

		Operating Profit Margin		Total Asset Turnover		Return on Assets
Return on assets$_{\text{Gilbert}}$	=	11.76%	×	0.92	=	10.87%
Return on assets$_{\text{Industry}}$	=	11.00%	×	1.20	=	13.20%

operating profit margin
A measure of how well a firm is controlling its costs of goods sold and operating expenses relative to sales, determined by dividing operating profits by sales.

total asset turnover
A measure of how efficiently a firm is using its assets to generate sales, calculated by dividing sales by total assets.

Based on the operating profit margin, Gilbert & Associates is competitive when it comes to managing its income statement—that is, in keeping costs and expenses low relative to sales. However, Gilbert & Associates' total asset turnover shows why the firm is not earning a good return on its assets. The firm is not using its assets efficiently. The company's problem is that it generates $0.92 in sales per dollar of assets, while the competition produces $1.20 in sales from every dollar in assets. Management needs to assess what is causing the problem, looking carefully at how they are managing accounts receivable, inventory, and fixed assets.

Gilbert & Associates' Debt

How much debt, relative to the total assets, is used to finance a business is extremely important. For one thing, the more debt a business uses, the more risk it is taking because the debt has to be repaid no matter how much profit the firm earns; it is a fixed cost.

debt ratio
A measure of what percentage of a firm's assets are financed by debt, determined by dividing total debt by total assets.

The *debt ratio* tells us what percentage of the firm's assets is financed by debt and is computed as follows:

$$\text{Debt ratio} = \frac{\text{Total debt}}{\text{Total assets}}$$

Exhibit 10-7 shows that in 2009 Gilbert & Associates' debt ratio is 32.6 percent, compared to an industry norm of 40 percent. Thus, Gilbert & Associates uses less debt than the average firm in the industry, meaning that it has less risk.

Gilbert & Associates' Return on Equity

The last financial issue we consider is the rate of return the owners are receiving on their equity investment, or the *return on equity*. The return on equity is the net profits divided by the total common equity shown in the balance sheet. The return on equity for the owners of Gilbert & Associates is computed as follows:

return on equity
A measure of the rate of return owners of a firm receive on their equity investment, calculated by dividing net profits by common equity.

$$\text{Return on equity} = \frac{\text{Net profits}}{\text{Owners' equity}} = \frac{\$60,000}{\$620,000} = 0.0968, \text{ or } 9.68\%$$

The industry average for return on equity is 12.5 percent. Thus, it appears that the owners of Gilbert & Associates are not receiving a return on their investment equivalent to that of owners of comparable businesses. Why not? To answer this question, you have to understand the following:

1. A firm with a high (low) return on *assets* will have a high (low) return on *equity*.
2. As a firm's debt ratio increases, return on equity will increase if the return on assets is greater than the interest rate paid on any debt, but return on equity will decrease if the return on assets is less than the interest rate.

In the case of Gilbert & Associates, the firm has a lower return on *equity* in part because it has a lower return on *assets*. It also uses less debt than the average firm in the industry, causing its return on equity to be lower than that of other firms. However, using less debt does reduce the firm's risk.

Our analysis of financial statements is now complete. Hopefully, you are now better prepared to know what financial statements can tell you about a business—knowledge that can be found in no other way than by interpreting the numbers.

In this chapter, we focused on understanding financial statements related to a firm's historical financial performance. We were essentially looking backwards to see how a business performed in a previous time period. In the next chapter, we will continue to work with financial statements, but this time they will be forward-looking. In writing a business plan, you need to show convincingly how your plans will play out in terms of the firm's financial future; you are now ready to prepare the financial plan.

1. Describe the purpose and content of an income statement.

- An income statement is, in its most basic form, represented by the equation:

  Sales (revenue) − Expenses = Profits (income)

- An income statement answers the question "How profitable is the business?" by looking at five broad areas of business activity: (1) sales, (2) cost of producing or acquiring goods or services, (3) operating expenses, (4) interest expense, and (5) taxable profits.

2. Explain the purpose and content of a balance sheet.

- A balance sheet provides a snapshot of a firm's financial position at a specific point in time. It shows the amount of assets the firm owns, the amount of outstanding debt, and the amount of ownership equity.

- In its most simple form, the balance sheet is represented by the formula:

  Total assets = Debt + Ownership equity

- Debt includes the money provided by creditors

- Equity is the owners' investment in the business, both in terms of actual cash invested and earnings that have been retained in the business instead of distributing to the owners.

3. Explain how viewing the income statement and balance sheets together gives a more complete picture of a firm's financial position.

- Because the balance sheet offers a snapshot of a firm's financial condition at a point in time and the income statement reports a firm's performance over a period of time, both are needed to fully evaluate a firm's financial position.

- Three financial reports are needed to evaluate a firm's performance over a given time period: a beginning balance sheet, an ending balance sheet, and an income statement which spans the time period between the two balance sheets.

4. Use the income statement and balance sheets to compute a company's cash flows.

- A cash flow statement shows the sources of a firm's cash as well as its uses of cash.

- A cash flow statement is comprised of three sections (1) cash flows from daily operations (operating activities), (2) cash flows related to the investment in fixed assets (investing activities), and (3) cash flows related to financing the firm (financing activities)

- Cash flows from operations is calculated by taking the net profit of the firm, adding back the depreciation expense and subtracting any uncollected sales and payments for inventory.

- Investments in fixed assets are recorded in the statement of cash flows as a change in gross fixed assets to reflect cash flows which result from the purchase or sale of depreciable assets.

- Financing a business involves (1) paying dividends to owners, (2) any change in short- and long-term debt held by a firm, and (3) any selling or repurchasing of stock.

5. Analyze the financial statements using ratios to see more clearly how decisions affect a firm's financial performance.

- Financial ratios help examine a firm's (1) ability to pay debt as it comes due, (2) profitability from assets, (3) use of debt, and (4) owners' rate of return.

- A firm's ability to pay debt as it comes due is most often evaluated by looking at a firm's current ratio.

- A company's profitability on assets is measured by calculating a company's return on assets as affected by its operating profit margin and the total asset turnover.

- The debt ratio, total debt divided by total assets, is used to evaluate the total amount of debt used by the company to finance its assets.

- The rate of return earned by the owners on their equity investment, the return on equity, is equal to net profits divided by owner's equity.

- The return on equity is driven by a firm's return on assets and its debt ratio.

Key Terms

financial statements
(accounting statements) p. 260

income statement (profit
and loss statement) p. 263

cost of goods sold p. 263

gross profit p. 263

operating expenses p. 263

operating profits p. 264

interest expense p. 264

profits before taxes (taxable
profits) p. 264

net profits p. 264

depreciation expense p. 264

balance sheet p. 267

current assets p. 268

accounts receivable p. 268

inventory p. 268

fixed assets p. 268

depreciable assets p. 268

gross fixed assets p. 268

accumulated depreciation p. 268

net fixed assets p. 268

other assets p. 268

debt p. 268

current debt (short-term
liabilities) p. 268

accounts payable (trade
credit) p. 269

accrued expenses p. 269

short-term notes p. 269

long-term debt p. 269

mortgage p. 269

ownership equity p. 270

retained earnings p. 270

cash flow statement p. 273

accrual-basis accounting p. 274

cash-basis accounting p. 274

liquidity p. 277

current ratio p. 277

return on assets p. 278

operating profit margin p. 279

total asset turnover p. 279

debt ratio p. 280

return on equity p. 280

Discussion Questions

1. Explain the purposes of the income statement and balance sheets.
2. What determines a company's profitability?
3. Distinguish among (a) gross profit, (b) operating profits, and (c) net profits.
4. The balance sheet reports information on a firm's (1) assets, (2) debt, and (3) equity. What is included in each of these reported categories?
5. How are ownership equity and debt different?
6. Distinguish between common stock and retained earnings.
7. What is the relationship between an income statement and a balance sheet?
8. Why aren't a firm's cash flows equal to its profits?
9. Describe the three major components of a cash flow statement.
10. What questions do financial ratios help answer about a firm's financial performance?

You Make the Call

SITUATION 1

The Donahoo Furniture Sales Company was formed on December 31, 2008, with $1,000,000 in equity plus $500,000 in long-term debt. On January 1, 2009, all of the firm's capital was held in cash. The following transactions occurred during January 2009.

- January 2: Donahoo purchased $1,000,000 worth of furniture for resale. It paid $500,000 in cash and financed the balance using trade credit that required payment in 60 days.
- January 3: Donahoo sold $250,000 worth of furniture that it had paid $200,000 to acquire. The entire sale was on credit terms of net 90 days.
- January 15: Donahoo purchased more furniture for $200,000. This time, it used trade credit for the entire amount of the purchase, with credit terms of net 60 days.

- January 31: Donahoo sold $500,000 worth of furniture, for which it had paid $400,000. The furniture was sold for 10 percent cash down, with the remainder payable in 90 days. In addition, the firm paid a cash dividend of $100,000 to its stockholders and paid off $250,000 of its long-term debt.

Question 1 What did Donahoo's balance sheet look like at the outset of the firm's life?

Question 2 What did the firm's balance sheet look like after each transaction?

Question 3 Ignoring taxes, determine how much income Donahoo earned during January. Prepare an income statement for the month. Recognize an interest expense of 1 percent for the month (12 percent annually) on the $500,000 long-term debt, which has not been paid but is owed.

Question 4 What was Donahoo's cash flow for the month of January?

SITUATION 2

At the beginning of 2009, Mary Abrahams purchased a small business, the Turpen Company, whose income statement and balance sheets are shown below.

Income Statement for the Turpen Company for 2009

Sales revenue		$175,000
Cost of goods sold		105,000
Gross profit		$ 70,000
Operating expenses:		
Depreciation	$ 5,000	
Administrative expenses	20,000	
Selling expenses	26,000	
Total operating expenses		$ 51,000
Operating profits		$ 19,000
Interest expense		3,000
Profits before taxes		$ 16,000
Taxes		8,000
Net profits		$ 8,000

Balance Sheets for the Turpen Company for 2008 and 2009

	2008	2009
Assets		
Current assets:		
Cash	$ 8,000	$ 10,000
Accounts receivable	15,000	20,000
Inventories	22,000	25,000
Total current assets	$45,000	$ 55,000
Fixed assets:		
Gross fixed assets	$50,000	$ 55,000
Accumulated depreciation	(15,000)	(20,000)
Net fixed assets	$35,000	$ 35,000
Other assets	12,000	10,000
TOTAL ASSETS	$92,000	$100,000

	2008	2009
Debt (Liabilities) and Equity		
Current debt:		
Accounts payable	$10,000	$ 12,000
Accruals	7,000	8,000
Short-term notes	5,000	5,000
Total current debt	$22,000	$ 25,000
Long-term debt	15,000	15,000
Total debt	$37,000	$ 40,000
Equity	$55,000	$ 60,000
TOTAL DEBT AND EQUITY	$92,000	$100,000

The firm has been profitable, but Abrahams has been disappointed by the lack of cash flows. She had hoped to have about $10,000 a year available for personal living expenses. However, there never seems to be much cash available for purposes other than business needs. Abrahams has asked you to examine the financial statements and explain why, although they show profits, she does not have any discretionary cash for personal needs. She observed, "I thought that I could take the profits and add depreciation to find out how much cash I was generating. However, that doesn't seem to be the case. What's happening?"

Question 1 Given the information provided by the financial statements, what would you tell Abrahams? (As part of your answer, calculate the firm's cash flows.)

Question 2 How would you describe the cash flow pattern for the Turpen Company?

SITUATION 3

Davis Rogers & Associates, Inc., designs, manufactures, and distributes furniture. It was founded in 1999 by Kate Davis and Lydia Rogers, two former college roommates. The company has experienced significant growth, with sales approaching $58 million in 2009.

The firm's products are in the medium- to low-price range and are constructed of aluminum, light steel, and plastic. The products made by the Children's Furniture Division include playpens, strollers, high chairs, walkers, dressing and feeding tables, and portable cribs. The Outdoor Furniture Division makes two lines of chairs, tables, and chaises: one in aluminum and the other in steel. The company's offices and largest warehouse are located in Dallas, Texas, along with two manufacturing plants in China. Finished goods are shipped to a network of 18 warehouses and six showrooms throughout the United States, by means of a fleet of 25 company-owned trucks. Approximately 40 percent of sales are to large distributors such as Sears, Walmart, J.C. Penney, Montgomery Ward, and other national chains. The rest are made to about 400 customers, including regional chain stores and retailers specializing in outdoor or children's furniture.

The financial statements for the company and industry norms are provided below.

Question 1: How would you evaluate the company's liquidity?

Question 2: Assess the company's historical performance at generating operating profits.

Question 3: Describe how the business is financed.

Question 4: Do Davis and Rogers receive a good return on their investment in the business?

Davis Rogers & Asso., Inc. Balance Sheets (in $000s) For years ending 2008 and 2009

	2008	2009
ASSETS		
Current assets		
Cash	$31	$437
Trade accounts receivable	7,930	8,771
Other receivables	48	85
Inventories	8,310	9,356
Prepaid expenses and deposits	277	288
Other current assets	211	211
Total current assets	$16,807	$19,148

Fixed assets

Building and machinery	$12,448	$14,903
Plant, property, and equip under capital leases	2,634	2,135
Less: Accumulated depreciation	7,645	8,754
Net fixed assets	$ 7,437	$ 8,284
Other noncurrent assets	23	2
TOTAL ASSETS	$24,267	$27,434

LIABILITIES AND EQUITY

Current liabilities		
Notes payable to bank	$ 1,250	$ 1,500
Current portion-long-term debt	618	650
Short-term leases	332	234
Accounts payable	3,550	4,267
Taxes payable	312	210
Accrued expenses	1,791	1,768
Dividend payable	50	0
Total current liabilities	$ 7,903	$ 8,629
Noncurrent liabilities		
Long-term debt	$ 5,648	$ 6,967
Capital lease obligations	1,256	1,036
Deferred taxes	324	511
Total noncurrent liabilities	$ 7,228	$ 8,514
Stockholders' equity		
Common stock:	$ 712	$ 783
Additional paid-in capital	996	1,298
Retained earnings	7,428	8,210
Total stockholders' equity	$ 9,136	$10,291
TOTAL DEBT & EQUITY	$24,267	$27,434

Davis Rogers & Asso., Inc.
Income Statements and Reconciliation's of Retained
For years ending 2008 and 2009

	2008	2009
Net sales	$54,138	$57,823
Cost of goods sold	37,761	41,049
Gross profit	$16,377	$16,774
Selling and general and administrative expenses	13,611	13,906
Operating profits	$ 2,766	$ 2,868
Interest expense	963	1,071
Interest income	(11)	(20)
Profits before tax	$ 1,814	$ 1,817
Income taxes	770	754
Net profits	$ 1,044	$ 1,063

RECONCILIATIONS OF
RETAINED EARNINGS

Beginning retained earnings	$ 6,596	$ 7,428
Net profits	1,044	1,063
Dividends	−212	−281
Ending retained earnings	$ 7,428	$ 8,210

Davis Rogers & Asso., Inc.
Statement of Cash Flows (in $000s)
For years ending 2008 and 2009

	2008	2009
Cash flows from operating activities		
Net profits	$ 1,044	$ 1,063
Adjustments to reconcile net income to net cash provided by operating activities		
Depreciation	1,129	1,314
Changes in:		
Accounts receivable	(928)	(841)
Inventories	(1,144)	(1,046)
Prepaid expenses	(38)	(11)
Accounts payables	137	717
Accrual expenses	153	(23)
Taxes payable	22	85
Total adjustments	$ (669)	$ 195
Net cash provided by operations	$ 375	$ 1,258
Cash flows from investing activities:		
Capital expenditures	$(1,769)	$(2,161)
Proceeds from sale of (payments for) short-term investments	45	−37
Proceeds from sale of long-term investments	1	21
Net cash used in investing	(1,723)	(2,177)
Cash flows from financing activities		
Short-term loans	$ 1,250	$ 250
Payments on long-term debt	−901	−451
Proceeds from long-term debt and capital leases	676	1,484
Capital (less noncash)	155	373
Cash dividends paid	−162	−331
Net cash provided by/used in financing	$ 1,018	$ 1,325
Net change in cash and equivalents	$ (330)	$ 406
Plus: Cash and equivalents at beginning of year	361	31
Cash and equivalents at end of year	$ 31	$ 437

Industry norms:

Current ratio	2.2
Return on assets	12.6%
Operating profit margin	6.3%
Total asset turnover	2.00
Debt ratio	40.0%
Return on common equity	15.0%

1. Interview an owner of a small firm about the financial statements she or he uses. Ask the owner how important financial data are to her or his decision making.

2. Acquire a small firm's financial statements. Review the statements and describe the firm's financial position. Find out if the owner agrees with your conclusions.

3. Dun & Bradstreet and Robert Morris Associates compile financial information about many companies. They provide, among other information, income statements and balance sheets for an average firm in an industry.

Go to a library and look up, or search online for, financial information on two industries of your choice, and compute the following data for each industry:

a. The percentages of assets in (1) current assets and (2) fixed assets (plant and equipment)

b. The percentages of financing from debt financing and ownership equity

c. The gross profits sold and the operating profits as percentages of sales

Small Business & Entrepreneurship Resource Center

The Small Business and Entrepreneurship Resource Center offers complete small business management resources through a comprehensive database that covers all major areas of starting, operating, and maintaining a business from financing, management, marketing, accounting, taxes, and more. Use the access code that came with your new book to access the site and perform the exercises in each chapter.

1. In the text Johnny Stites, CEO of J&S Construction, mentions that "The construction industry is one of the riskiest industries you can enter, second only to the restaurant industry. For years, we would bid a job based on our best understanding of the costs that would be incurred. Then we would have to wait to the completion of the job to see if we made or lost

money—not exactly an ideal situation to be in. Today, we have the ability to know how we are doing in terms of profits and costs on a daily basis. Not having accurate and timely accounting information would be deadly. We simply could not exist in such a competitive industry, and certainly not profitably, without understanding where we are financially." The article "Looking Beyond the Bottom Line" talks about the multistep income statement, so that much more can be understood about the business. Describe the multistep income statement, and the trended P&L. How can these be used to help a business become more aware of trends and issues?

Sources: Looking beyond the bottom line. (Business). Leslie Shiner. *The Journal of Light Construction* 23 (9) (June 2005): p. 43(4).

Video Case 10

UNDERSTANDING FINANCIAL STATEMENTS, PART 1 & PART 2 (P. 643)

This case explains the value of understanding financial statements to the small business owner and the importance of their proper interpretation in order to understand and project the firm's financial position.

ALTERNATIVE CASES FOR CHAPTER 10

Case 4, Mo's Chowder, p. 630

Case 11, Missouri Solvent, p. 646

Case 22, Pearson Air Conditioning & Service, p. 669

chapter 11

Forecasting Financial Requirements

In the SPOTLIGHT
Planning for Growth
http://www.builtny.com

Managing rapid growth can become an entrepreneur's worst nightmare. Unhappy customers and employees, a lack of cash, and the inability to fill orders can overwhelm a small business owner.

Entrepreneurs rarely prepare for the challenges that growth brings. "They're too busy working in the business to work on the business," observes Jeff DeGraff, professor at the Ross School of Business at the University of Michigan. But taking the time to plan for growth, especially when it's unexpected, can keep your business on track.

In 2003, Carter Weiss, Aaron Lown, and John Roscoe Swartz started BuiltNY, a supplier of innovative wine totes and other accessories. In the first six months, the company had sales of $600,000 and even turned a profit, which is rare for most startups. By 2006, sales were $13 million; in 2007, the company expected $20 million in sales. Managing this kind of growth is extremely difficult and can be a downfall for many companies.

Weiss says that they followed three rules: "Go sell it, make it, and figure out how to pay for it." Sounds simple, but Weiss warns, "it is not. You have to match expectations with sufficient financing, so we decided not to maximize sales, nor to focus solely on long-term profits. Instead, we traded some of both to have some short-term profits, too, which allowed us to attract bank financing. As a profitable firm with bank financing, we could then approach venture capitalists for expansion financing on better terms."

Weiss continues, "You have to decide what you want from the business and then know what it will take financially to make it happen. And above all, make sure you never run out of cash."

Planning for growth, which may be part of the original business plan or done at a later date, is essential if you want to keep your entrepreneurial dream alive.

Source: Lena Basha, "Growth Gone Wild," *MyBusiness*, February–March 2007, pp. 36–41; and personal interview with Carter Weiss, July 11, 2007.

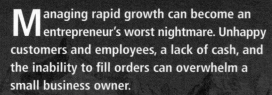

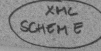

LOOKING AHEAD AFTER STUDYING THIS CHAPTER, YOU SHOULD BE ABLE TO...

1. Describe the purpose and need for financial forecasting.
2. Develop a pro forma income statement to forecast a new venture's profitability.
3. Determine a company's asset and financing requirements based on a pro forma balance sheet.
4. Forecast a firm's cash flows.
5. Give suggestions for effective financial forecasting.

A *good idea may or may not be a good investment opportunity.* As we discussed in Chapter 3, a good investment opportunity requires a product or service that meets a definite customer need and creates a sustainable competitive advantage. To be attractive, an opportunity must generate strong profits relative to the required amount of investment. Therefore, projections of a venture's profits, its asset and financing requirements, and its cash flows are essential in determining whether a venture is economically viable.

The Purpose and Need for Financial Forecasting

In Chapter 10, we followed the Lemonade Girls to see the accounting implications of what was happening in their venture. In that very simple world, there was really no need to plan for the future. Everything just worked out okay. But that is not the case when starting and operating a business with any complexity. In the real world, you need to forecast, as best you can, the financial outcomes that could result from your decisions. You also may have to make financial forecasts if you need financing from lenders and investors who want to know how they will be paid back. In other words, you need to prepare *pro forma financial statements.*

1. Describe the purpose and need for financial forecasting.

The necessity of financial forecasting is described quite aptly by small business consultant Paul A. Broni:

> It doesn't matter whether you're applying for your first bank loan or your fifth, or whether you're seeking venture capital or debt financing. Sooner or later, you'll have to prepare a set of financial projections. Lenders will look for a strong likelihood of repayment; investors will calculate what they think is the value of your company.[1]

The purpose of *pro forma financial statements* is to answer three questions:

1. How profitable can you expect the firm to be, given the projected sales levels and the expected sales–expense relationships?
2. How much and what type of financing (debt or equity) will be needed to finance a firm's assets?
3. Will the firm have adequate cash flows? If so, how will they be used? If not, where will the additional cash come from?

pro forma financial statements Statements that project a firm's financial performance and condition.

Preparing historical financial statements, such as income statements, balance sheets, and cash flow statements, is not a difficult task; however, *projecting* the financials for a business presents a real challenge, especially for a startup, where things seldom go as planned. But it can be done, as explained by Rhonda Abrams, a business plan consultant:

> One of the biggest challenges for a new company doing a business plan is figuring out the financial statements. If you have an existing business, you have a pretty good sense of how much things will cost, how much staff you'll need, and the sales you're likely to make. But when you're just starting out, these things seem a complete mystery.
>
> They're not. At least not entirely. Every decision you make when planning your business has a number attached: If you choose to exhibit at a trade show, there's a cost associated with that; if you choose to locate your business in one town versus another, there's a cost associated with that.

How do you do this homework? The best place to start is by speaking with others in your industry, attending trade shows, and contacting your industry association. Another excellent source is the RMA [Risk Management Association] Annual Statement Studies, which look at actual financial statements of companies in certain industries.[2]

An entrepreneur should always be asking, "What could go wrong, and if it does happen, what will I do?" For instance, you want to plan how to respond if sales are significantly lower or higher than projected. A firm can get into trouble not only when sales are inadequate, but also when the firm is experiencing high growth in sales. James Wong, the co-founder and CEO of Avidian Technologies, should know: His firm grew at 400 percent a year in both 2004 and 2005. To keep up with the expansion, he vigilantly watches cash flows and bottom-line profits. "I've learned that profitability takes conscious effort," he says. "If you just keep growing for growth's sake, you won't be nearly as profitable." Wong never ships a product until payment is received and never lets net profits fall below 15 percent of sales. Consequently, the firm has grown with no significant debt and no outside investors—a feat seldom accomplished by entrepreneurs whose firms are growing rapidly.[3]

When seeking financing, an entrepreneur must be able to give informed answers about the firm's needs. It is vital that she or he be able to answer questions regarding the amount of money needed, the purposes for which it will be used, and when and how the lender or creditor will be paid back. Only careful financial planning can provide answers to these questions.

Let's take a look at the process for projecting a firm's profitability, asset and financing requirements, and cash flows.

How I see it: Winston Wolfe on Knowing Where You Stand

Knowing where you are sounds a bit silly, but when it comes to the first few years of a new business, it is very important, and many times it is neglected.

First of all, I believe it is important for a new business to produce a profit and loss statement every month. If the business involves distribution, this would include a physical inventory. Don't fool yourself by carrying unsalable inventory at cost. The same applies to other assets that may have decreased in value.

Know where you are in your market. Have you found your niche? Are your products or services being offered where they are most viable?

Take the time to find out where you stand in your relationship with your customers, your vendors, and your employees. The biggest challenge for an entrepreneur is being effective in solving problems in these areas. But if you don't know about a problem, you can't solve it.

Take the time to know where you are. If you don't know where you are, you can't know where you're going.

Forecasting Profitability

Profits reward an owner for investing in a company and constitute a primary source of financing for future growth. Therefore, it is critical for an entrepreneur to understand the factors that drive net profits. The graphic presentation of an income statement shown in Exhibit 10-1 on p. 264 highlights these important factors, which are listed below:

1. *Amount of sales.* The dollar amount of sales equals the price of the product or service times the number of units sold or the amount of service rendered.

2. *Cost of goods sold.* Cost of goods sold is the cost of producing or purchasing the firm's products or services. These costs can be either *fixed* (those that do not vary with a change in sales volume) or *variable* (those that change proportionally with sales).

3. *Operating expenses.* These expenses relate to marketing and distributing the product, general and administrative expenses, and depreciation expenses. Like cost of goods sold, operating expenses can be fixed or variable in nature.

4. *Interest expense.* An entrepreneur who borrows money agrees to pay interest on the loan principal. For example, a loan of $25,000 for a full year at a 12 percent interest rate results in an interest expense of $3,000 for the year ($0.12 \times \$25,000$).

5. *Taxes.* A firm's income taxes are figured as a percentage of taxable income (profits before taxes).

A hypothetical example demonstrates how to estimate a new venture's profits.[4] David Allen is planning to start a new business called D&R Products, Inc., which will do wood trim work for luxury homes. A newly developed lathe will allow the firm to be responsive to varying design specifications in a very economical manner. Based on a study of potential market demand and expected costs-to-sales relationships, Allen has made the following estimates for the first 2 years of operations:

1. *Amount of sales.* Allen expects to complete 20 jobs the first year at an average price of $12,500 per job, with total sales for the first year projected to be $250,000, ($12,500 × 20 = $250,000) and total sales for the second year projected at 32 jobs, ($12,500 × 32 = $400,000).

2. *Cost of goods sold.* The fixed cost of goods sold (including production costs and employee salaries) is expected to amount to $100,000 per year, while the variable costs of production will be around 20 percent of dollar sales.

3. *Operating expenses.* The firm's fixed operating expenses (marketing expenses, general and administrative expenses) are estimated at $46,000 per year. In addition, depreciation will be $4,000 annually. The variable operating expenses will be approximately 30 percent of dollar sales.

4. *Interest expense.* Based on the anticipated amount of money to be borrowed and the corresponding interest rate, Allen expects interest expense to be $8,000 in the first year, increasing to $12,000 in the second year.

5. *Taxes.* Income taxes will be 25 percent of profits before taxes (taxable profits).

Given the above estimates, we can forecast D&R Products' net profits as shown in the pro forma statement in Exhibit 11-1. We first enter our assumptions in an Excel spreadsheet (rows 1–10). Then, in rows 13–28, we see the 2 years of pro forma income statements (columns B and C) and the equations used to compute the numbers (columns D and E).

11-1 Pro Forma Income Statements for D&R Products, Inc.

	A	B	C	D	E
1	INCOME STATEMENT ASSUMPTIONS				
2	Year 1 projected units of sales	20			
3	Year 2 projected units of sales	32			
4	Selling price	$ 12,500			
5	Fixed cost of goods sold	$100,000			
6	Fixed operating expenses	$ 46,000		Equations based on assumptions	
7	Depreciation expense	$ 4,000			
8	Variable cost of goods sold	20%			
9	Variable operating expenses	30%			
10	Income tax rate	25%			
11				Equations for	
12		Year 1	Year 2	Year 1	Year 2
13	Sales	$250,000	$400,000	= B2 * B4	= B3 * B4
14	Cost of goods sold				
15	Fixed cost of goods sold	$100,000	$100,000	= B5	= B5
16	Variable cost of goods sold (20% of sales)	$ 50,000	$ 80,000	= B8 * B13	= B8 * C13
17	Total cost of goods sold	$150,000	$180,000	= B15 + B16	= C15 + C16
18	Gross profits	$100,000	$220,000	= B13 − B17	= C13 − C17
19	Operating expenses				
20	Fixed operating expenses	$ 46,000	$ 46,000	= B6	= B6
21	Depreciation expense	$ 4,000	$ 4,000	= B7	= B7
22	Variable operating expenses (30% of sales)	$ 75,000	$120,000	= B13 * B9	= C13 * B9
23	Total operating expenses	$125,000	$170,000	= B20 + B21 + B22	= C20 + C21 + C22
24	Operating profits	($ 25,000)	$ 50,000	= B18 − B23	= C18 − C23
25	Interest expense	$ 8,000	$ 12,000	Given	Given
26	Profits before taxes	($ 33,000)	$ 38,000	= B24 − B25	= C24 − C25
27	Taxes (25% of earnings before taxes)	0	$ 9,500	0	= C26 * B10
28	Net profits	($ 33,000)	$ 28,500	= B26 − B27	= C26 − C27

The computations in Exhibit 11-1 indicate that D&R Products will have a $33,000 loss in its first year, followed by a positive net profit of $28,500 in its second year. A startup typically experiences losses for a period of time, frequently as long as 2 or 3 years.[5] In a real-world situation, an entrepreneur should project the profits of a new company at least 3 years into the future (or 5 years into the future if it can be done with some degree of confidence).

We now shift our attention from forecasting profits to estimating asset and financing requirements.

Forecasting Asset and Financing Requirements

3. Determine a company's asset and financing requirements based on a pro forma balance sheet.

The amount and types of assets required for a new venture will vary, depending on the nature of the business. High-technology businesses—such as computer manufacturers, designers of semiconductor chips, and pharmaceutical companies—often require millions of dollars in investment. Most service businesses, on the other hand, require minimal initial capital. For example, IRM Corporation, a Dallas, Texas–based information technology firm serving the food and beverage industry, has little in the way of assets. The firm leases its office space and has no inventory. Its only asset of any significance is accounts receivable.

Most firms of any size need both working capital (cash, accounts receivable, inventory, etc.) and fixed assets (equipment and buildings). For instance, a food store requires operating cash, inventory, and possibly limited accounts receivable. In addition, the owner will have to acquire cash registers, shopping carts, shelving, office equipment, and a building. The need to invest in assets results in a corresponding need for financing.

Working capital is a financial term frequently used in the business world. A banker might tell you, "I see that your working capital is $40,000, which appears low to me," or something very similar. *Working capital* refers to current assets, namely cash, accounts receivable, and inventory that are required in the day-to-day operations of the business. *It has nothing to do with plant and equipment.* If the term *net working capital* is used, it means the current assets less current liabilities. Net working capital is a measure of a company's liquidity—that is, its ability to pay on any debt commitment as it comes due.

In many small firms, owners have a tendency to underestimate the amount of capital the business requires. Consequently, the financing they get may be inadequate. Without the money to invest in assets, they try to do without anything that is not absolutely essential and try to spend less money on essential items. When Dan Cassidy started Baha's Fajita Bar, a restaurant aimed at serving college students, his goal was to raise $100,000 in capital; however, he opened the restaurant when he had raised only $70,000. As it turned out, Cassidy did not have enough money to operate the business successfully. In six months, he ran out of cash and had to close the bar. The problem became critical when students went home for Spring Break and were slow to eat at restaurants in the week following their return to school. Cassidy's unfortunate experience shows just how risky it can be for a small business to ignore the potential for unexpected challenges and underestimate its capital needs.

While being undercapitalized is rarely, if ever, a good decision, the goal of the entrepreneur should be to "minimize and control," rather than "maximize and own," resources. To the greatest extent possible, the entrepreneur should use other people's resources—for instance, leasing equipment rather than buying, negotiating with suppliers to provide inventory "just in time" to minimize tied-up investment, and arranging to collect money owed the firm before having to pay its bills. This is called *bootstrapping*, and it's the most common way entrepreneurs accomplish more with less. When Cecilia Levine, a member of our "Go-To Team," the owner of MFI International, a manufacturing firm, had the opportunity to get a contract to make clothing for a *Fortune* 500 company, she became a master of bootstrapping.

> I never expected the fast growth and demand that my services would have. To finance the growth, debt financing would have been helpful, but it was not an option. The definition of credit in the dictionary reads, "The ability of a customer to obtain goods or services before payment, based on the trust that payment is going to be made in the future." What it does not say is that for a banker, trust means having collateral, and without collateral you don't get credit. But I still had children to feed and the desire to succeed so I looked for another form of financing—bootstrapping.

working capital
Current assets, accounts receivable, and inventory required in day-to-day operations.

net working capital
Current assets less current liabilities.

bootstrapping
Minimizing a firm's investments.

LIVING THE DREAM:

entrepreneurial experiences

Surviving a Financial Crisis

The financial crisis that mushroomed in 2008 brought with it tremendous uncertainty for large and small firms alike. In a 2009 survey, Inc.com asked its readers, mostly entrepreneurs, "What is the hardest part of owning a business right now?" As shown in the graph below, the leading problem cited was difficulty in forecasting accurately. In summarizing the findings, the author of the study, Kasey Wehrum, commented, "They would settle for just a clearer sense of what lies ahead. Planning a budget, managing inventory, and knowing when to hire and fire employees are never easy, but a dysfunctional economy has now made forecasting all but impossible.

Wehrum also interviewed several entrepreneurs, who provided their own perspectives on planning in a period of tremendous uncertainty: Rick Israel, co-founder of Complete Office, a Seattle supplier of office products, had this to say:

> No one knows how bad the economy is going to get. We just knew it would be harder than in prior years. We budgeted for slight growth but factored in the probability that our business would go backward 10 to 12 percent. The idea is to gear up our sales force and go out there and take more market share.

No one said it would be easy

Inc.com recently asked readers: What is the hardest part of owning a business right now? Here's how you responded:

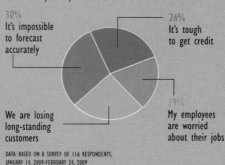

30%
It's impossible to forecast accurately

26%
It's tough to get credit

25%
We are losing long-standing customers

19%
My employees are worried about their jobs

DATA: BASED ON A SURVEY OF 116 RESPONDENTS, JANUARY 14, 2009–FEBRUARY 24, 2009

According to Bryan Zaslow, CEO of JBCStyle, a New York City firm that provides staffing for the fashion and retail industries,

> My accounting team and I are sitting here dumbfounded trying to properly budget. Typically, we prepare our budget in the beginning of the year based on last year's numbers. Maybe we'd revisit it halfway through the year. But 2009 is really about revisiting our budget monthly.
>
> Planning for the worst is the most logical course of action. However, I think that negativity has to stay within the executive team. Too much of it puts everyone in a funk. So, my partner and I try to push the positives, like our strong beginning-of-the-year numbers. We try to keep the sleepless nights to ourselves.

Dennis Brown, CEO of Logistic Dynamics, an Amherst, New York, logistics coordinator, said,

> In the past, business may have been good or bad, but it was much easier to project what your sales, your revenue, your margins, your overhead were going to be. We could predict the business we would do, because our customers normally have a good feel for their projections. But now, they've got clients pushing back orders and canceling contracts, so they don't know what to expect. That trickles down to us. The more vague our customers are with their projections, the more difficult it is for us to make our projections.
>
> We've tightened our credit terms to our customers. We know this year, somebody significant is going to file bankruptcy on us. Statistically, it's going to happen. Therefore, our forecasts have to be more conservative, because we need to be able to subsidize that kick in the pants we know we are going to get. It may be only $30,000, but it may be $300,000. That would hurt bad. We're hoping it's $30,000.

> I had a major customer who believed in me, and who had the equipment I needed. He sold me the equipment and then would reduce his weekly payment of my invoices by an amount to cover the cost of the equipment. Also, the customer paid me each Friday for what we produced and shipped that week. Everyone who worked for me understood that if we didn't perform and finish the needed production for the week, we didn't get paid by our customer. When I received the payment from the customer, I was then able to pay my employees. We were a team, and we understood the meaning of cash flow. Therefore, we performed.[6]

Working with a limited amount of working capital makes forecasting all the more important because you have less room for error. Moreover, the uncertainties surrounding an entirely new venture make estimating asset and financing requirements difficult. Even for an established business, forecasts are never perfect. There are always surprises—you can count on it.

To gather needed information, an entrepreneur may use a double-barreled approach to project asset and financing requirements by searching for relevant information from a variety of sources. Robert Morris Associates, Dun & Bradstreet, banks, trade associations, and similar organizations compile financial information for a variety of industries. Along with the public data, common sense and educated guesswork should also be used. Continually ask yourself, "Does this make economic sense, and what could go wrong?"

The determination of how much financing will be needed should also take into consideration the owner's personal financial situation, especially if no other income is available to make ends meet. Whether or not the owner's personal living expenses during the initial period of operation are part of the business's capitalization, they must be considered in the financial plan. Inadequate provision for personal expenses will inevitably lead to a diversion of business assets and a departure from the plan. Therefore, failing to incorporate these expenses into the financial plan as a cash outflow raises a red flag to any prospective investor.

In fact, a real danger exists that an entrepreneur will neglect personal finances later as well. As a firm grows, an increasing percentage of the owner's net worth is tied up in the firm. For many entrepreneurs, well over half of their net wealth is invested in their businesses. Even more do not plan adequately for their long-term personal financial health. Former SBA director Hector Barreto explains it well:

> Small-business people don't know what they don't know when it comes to financial planning. They're busy building the business, and they don't start asking questions until a need or problem comes up. Entrepreneurs are doing a disservice to their businesses when they ignore even the most basic financial planning. The process isn't as time-consuming or as expensive as you might think."[7]

The key to effectively forecasting financing requirements is first to understand the relationship between a firm's projected sales and its assets. A firm's sales are the primary force driving future asset needs. Exhibit 11-2 depicts this relationship, which can be expressed simply as

EXHIBIT

Increase in Sales

└─Results in─→

Increase in
Asset Requirements

└─Results in─→

Increase in
Financing Requirements

follows: *The greater a firm's sales, the greater the asset requirements will be and, in turn, the greater the need for financing.*

Determining Asset Requirements

Since asset needs tend to increase as sales increase, a firm's asset requirements are often estimated as a percentage of sales. Therefore, if future sales have been projected, a ratio of assets to sales can be used to estimate asset requirements. Suppose, for example, that a firm's sales are expected to be $1 million. If assets in the firm's particular industry tend to run about 50 percent of sales, the firm's asset requirements would be estimated to be $0.50 \times \$1{,}000{,}000$, or $500,000.

Although the assets-to-sales relationship varies over time and with individual businesses, it tends to be relatively constant within an industry. For example, assets as a percentage of sales average 20 percent for grocery stores, compared with 65 percent for oil and gas companies. This method of estimating asset requirements is called the *percentage-of-sales technique*. It can also be used to project figures for individual assets, such as accounts receivable and inventory.

percentage-of-sales technique
A method of forecasting asset investments and financing requirements.

To illustrate the percentage-of-sales technique, let's return to D&R Products, Inc., where we will estimate the firm's asset requirements for the first two years, given the company's sales projections. In Exhibit 11-1, the firm's pro forma income statements, sales were forecasted to be $250,000 and $400,000 in years 1 and 2, respectively. After considerable investigation of the opportunity, Allen estimated the firm's current asset requirements (cash, accounts receivable, and inventory) as a percentage of sales:

Assets	Percentage of Sales
Cash	4%
Accounts receivable	10%
Inventory	25%

Allen will need equipment, at a cost of $10,000. Also, he has found a building suitable for a manufacturing facility for $40,000. Combined, these two items total $50,000 and will be reflected in a balance sheet as *gross fixed assets*.

Net fixed assets is equal to gross fixed assets less accumulated depreciation. Since the depreciation expense reported in the income statement (Exhibit 11-1) was $4,000 per year, then the accumulated depreciation will be $4,000 in year 1, increasing (accumulating) to $8,000 the next year. Given the anticipated sales and the assets-to-sales relationships, Allen is able to forecast the asset requirements for his venture as follows: If sales are $250,000 in year 1 and $400,000 in year 2, then Allen estimates that:

Assets	Assumptions	Year 1	Year 2
Cash	4% of sales	$ 10,000	$ 16,000
Accounts receivable	10% of sales	25,000	40,000
Inventory	25% of sales	62,500	100,000
Total current assets		$ 97,500	$156,000
Gross fixed assets	Equipment and building costs	$ 50,000	$ 50,000
Accumulated depreciation	$4,000 annually	(4,000)	(8,000)
Net fixed assets		$ 46,000	$ 42,000
TOTAL ASSETS		$143,500	$198,000

Thus, Allen expects to need $143,500 in assets by the end of the first year and $198,000 by the conclusion of the second year. Keep in mind that these results will only be as good as his assumptions; therefore, it is always wise to create several scenarios based on different assumptions to think about what you would do under various circumstances.

So Allen understands the asset portion of the balance sheet. Now he needs to consider how the assets will be financed.

Determining Financing Requirements

There must be a corresponding dollar of financing for every dollar of assets. Stated another way, debt plus equity must equal total assets. To forecast a company's financing needs effectively, an entrepreneur must understand certain basic principles that govern the financing of firms, which can be stated as follows:

1. The more assets a firm needs, the greater the firm's financial requirements. Thus, a firm experiencing rapid sales growth requires more assets and, consequently, faces greater pressure to find financing—and that pressure can be unbearable if not managed carefully.

2. A firm should finance its growth in such a way as to maintain adequate liquidity. *Liquidity* measures the degree to which a firm has current assets available to meet maturing short-term debt. The need for adequate liquidity in small firms deserves special emphasis. As already mentioned, a common weakness in small business financing is the tendency to maintain a disproportionately small investment in liquid assets, or what was defined earlier as *net working capital*. An even more conventional measure of liquidity is the *current ratio*, which compares a firm's current assets to its current liabilities on a relative basis.

$$\text{Current ratio} = \frac{\text{Current assets}}{\text{Current liabilities}}$$

To ensure payment of short-term debts as they come due, an entrepreneur should, as a general rule, maintain a current ratio of at least 2—that is, have current assets equal to two times the amount of current liabilities—or have a good reason for not doing so.

3. The amount of total debt that can be used in financing a business is limited by the amount of funds provided by the owners. A bank will not provide all the financing for a firm; owners must put some of their own money into the venture to prove their commitment to it. A business plan should specify that at least half of the firm's financing will come from equity (including the owners') and the rest will come from debt. In other words, management should limit the firm's *debt ratio,* which expresses debt as a percentage of total assets.

$$\text{Debt ratio} = \frac{\text{Total debt}}{\text{Total assets}}$$

4. Some types of short-term debt—specifically, *accounts payable* and *accrued expenses*—maintain a relatively constant relationship with sales; that is, they rise or fall as a firm's sales increase or decrease. Such *spontaneous debt financing* grows as a natural consequence of increases in the firm's sales. For instance, a rise in sales requires more inventory, causing accounts payable to increase when a firm purchases inventory on

liquidity
The degree to which a firm has working capital available to meet maturing debt obligations.

current ratio
A measure of a company's relative liquidity, determined by dividing current assets by current liabilities.

debt ratio
A measure of the fraction of a firm's assets that are financed by debt, determined by dividing total debt by total assets.

spontaneous debt financing
Short-term debts, such as accounts payable, that automatically increase in proportion to a firm's sales.

credit. If sales increase by $1, accounts payable might increase by $.15 or, in other words, by 15 percent of sales. Because of the scale involved, this type of financing is significant for most smaller companies. The rest of debt financing must come from loans by banks and other lending sources.

5. Equity ownership in a business comes from two sources: (1) investments the owners make in the business, such as when a firm issues common stock, and (2) profits that are retained within the company rather than being distributed to the owners, or what we have referred to as *retained earnings*. For the typical small firm, retained earnings are the primary source of equity capital for financing growth. (Be careful not to think of retained earnings as a big cash resource. As already noted, a firm may have significant profits but no cash to reinvest.)

The essence of the foregoing principles can be captured in the following equation:

$$\begin{matrix} \text{Total asset} \\ \text{requirements} \end{matrix} = \begin{matrix} \text{Total sources} \\ \text{of financing} \end{matrix} = \begin{matrix} \text{Spontaneous} \\ \text{debt financing} \end{matrix} + \begin{matrix} \text{Loans from} \\ \text{banks, etc.} \end{matrix} + \begin{matrix} \text{Owner's} \\ \text{investment} \end{matrix} + \begin{matrix} \text{Retained} \\ \text{earnings} \end{matrix}$$

The entrepreneur who thoroughly understands these relationships should be able to accurately forecast her or his firm's financial requirements.

Recall that Allen projected asset requirements of $143,500 and $198,000 for years 1 and 2, respectively. He next made estimates of the financing requirements based on the following facts and assumptions:

1. Allen negotiated with a supplier to receive 30 days' credit on inventory purchases, which means that accounts payable will average about 8 percent of sales.[8]

2. Allen also estimates that accrued expenses will amount to about 4% of sales.

3. Allen plans to invest $110,000 of his personal savings to provide the needed startup equity for the business. He will receive common stock in return for his investment.

4. The bank has agreed to provide a short-term line of credit of $25,000 to D&R Products, which means that the firm can borrow up to $25,000 as the need arises.

5. The bank has also agreed to help finance the purchase of a building for manufacturing and warehousing the firm's product. Of the $40,000 needed to purchase the building, the bank will lend the firm $30,000, with the building serving as collateral for the loan. The loan will be repaid over 10 years in equal principal payments of $3,000 plus interest on the remaining note balance each year.

6. As part of the loan agreement, the bank has imposed two restrictions: (1) The firm's current ratio (current assets ÷ current liabilities) must remain at 2.0 or above, and (2) no more than 50 percent of the firm's financing may come from debt, either short-term or long-term (that is, total debt should be no more than 50 percent of total assets). Failure to comply with either of these conditions will cause the bank loan to come due immediately.

With this information, Allen can now estimate the initial sources of financing for D&R Products. If sales are $250,000 in year 1 and $400,000 in year 2, then Allen estimates that

Sources of Financing	Assumptions	Year 1	Year 2
Accounts payable	8% of sales	$ 20,000	$ 32,000
Accrued expenses	4% of sales	$ 10,000	$ 16,000
Mortgage	$30,000 – $3,000 annual payments	$ 27,000	$ 24,000
Common stock	Founder's investment	$110,000	$110,000

Any remaining financing, up to $25,000, can come from the bank line of credit. If the line of credit is inadequate to meet the firm's needs, Allen will have to put more equity into the business.

Based on the information above, Allen can now develop pro forma balance sheets for D&R Products, Inc. Exhibit 11-3 shows the assumptions made, the equations underlying the numbers, and the actual balance sheets, as developed in an Excel spreadsheet.

EXHIBIT

	A	B	C	D	E
1	BALANCE SHEET ASUMPTIONS				
2	Year 1 projected sales	$ 250,000			
3	Year 2 projected sales	$ 400,000			
4	Cash/sales	4%			
5	Accounts receivables/sales	10%			
6	Inventories/sales	25%			
7	Accounts payable/sales	8%			
8	Accrued expenses/sales	4%			
9	Cost of equipment	$ 10,000			
10	Building cost	$ 40,000			
11					Equations for:
12	**Assets**			Year 1	Year 2
13	Cash	$ 10,000	$ 16,000	=B2*B4	=B3*B4
14	Accounts receivables	25,000	40,000	=B2*B5	=B3*B5
15	Inventories	62,500	100,000	=B2*B6	=B3*B6
16	Total current assets	$ 97,500	$ 156,000	=B13+B14+B15	=C13+C14+C15
17	Gross fixed assets	$ 50,000	$ 50,000	Given	Given
18	Accumulated depreciation	(4,000)	(8,000)	Given	Given
19	Net fixed assets	$ 46,000	$ 42,000	=B17+B18	=C17+C18
20	Total assets	$ 143,500	$ 198,000	=B16+B19	=C16+C19
21					
22	**Debt and Equity**				
23	Accounts payable	$ 20,000	$ 32,000	=B2*B7	=B3*B7
24	Accrued Expenses	$ 10,000	$ 16,000	=B2*B8	=B3*B8
25	Short-term line of credit	9,500	20,500	Required financing	Required financing
26	Total current liabilities	$ 39,500	$ 68,500	=B23+B24+B25	=C23+C24+C25
27	Mortgage	27,000	24,000	Original loan of $35,000 − annual payment $3,500	Year 1 balance of $31,500 − annual payment $3,500
28	Total debt	$ 66,500	$ 92,500	=B26+B27	=C26+C27
29	Equity				
30	Common stock	$ 110,000	$ 110,000	Given	Given
31	Retained earnings	(33,000)	(4,500)	Year 1 loss	Year 1 loss + year 2 profit
32	Total equity	$ 77,000	$ 105,500	=B30+B31	=C30+C31
33	Total debt and equity	$ 143,500	$ 198,000	=B28+B32	=C28+C32
34					
35	Current ratio	$ 2.47	$ 2.28	=B16/B26	=C16/C26
36	Debt ratio	46%	47%	=B28/B20	=C28/C20

Several points about the projected balance sheets presented in Exhibit 11-3 need to be clarified:

1. Total assets and total sources of financing (debt and equity) must always balance. Note that D&R Products' asset requirements of $143,500 for the first year and $198,000 for the second year are the same as the firm's debt and equity totals.

2. To bring sources of financing into balance with total assets, D&R Products will need to borrow on the company's $25,000 short-term line of credit. By the end of the first year, $9,500 of the line of credit is needed to bring the total debt and equity to $143,500. In the second year, line-of-credit borrowing will increase to $20,500 to complete the $198,000 total financing needed.

3. Based on Allen's projections, the firm should be able to satisfy the bank's loan restrictions, maintaining both a current ratio of 2.0 or more and a debt ratio of less than 50 percent. The computations are as follows:

Ratio	Computation	Year 1	Year 2
Current ratio $= \dfrac{\text{Current assets}}{\text{Current liabiliies}}$		$\dfrac{\$97,500}{\$39,500} = 2.47$	$\dfrac{\$156,000}{\$68,500} = 2.28$
Debt ratio $= \dfrac{\text{Total debt}}{\text{Total assets}}$		$\dfrac{\$66,500}{\$143,500} = 0.46 = 46\%$	$\dfrac{\$92,500}{\$198,000} = 0.47 = 47\%$

We have now completed the process for forecasting a company's profitability and its asset and financing needs, as reflected in the income statement and balance sheet, respectively. We will now consider the third and final key financing issue: projecting cash flows.

Forecasting Cash Flows

4. Forecast a firm's cash flows.

As we have mentioned numerous times, profits and cash flows are not the same thing. A business can have positive profits and be running out of cash—or it can incur losses, as shown in the income statement, and have positive cash flows. The income statement simply does not give the small business owner the information he or she needs to know about the firm's cash flows. Forecasting cash flows is *critical* for the small business owner: If the business runs out of money, the consequences can be devastating.

Projecting a company's cash flows can be accomplished in one of two ways. First, we can use the information from the pro forma income statement and balance sheets to develop a pro forma statement of cash flows, just as we did in Chapter 10 to gain an historical view. Second, we can prepare a cash budget, which is no more than a listing of expected cash inflows and outflows.

In forecasting cash flows, an owner must consider the time period used for projections. In a statement of cash flows that covers an entire year, everything may look great on paper, but the firm could very well run out of cash at certain periods in that year. This scenario is particularly true for a business whose sales are seasonal. For instance, a wholesale sunglass company orders inventory in the spring, but most of its sales occur in the summer. Furthermore, the company will extend credit to its customers and not be paid until the end of the summer. If we look at the company's cash flows on an annual basis, all may be well. But during the spring and early summer, there will be large investments in accounts receivable and inventory, putting extreme pressure on the firm's cash flows. In this instance, the owner would want to forecast cash flows on a monthly basis—maybe even on a weekly basis.

In the next two sections, we use D&R Products, Inc., to illustrate how to forecast cash flows. We first prepare pro forma statements of annual cash flows. Then we illustrate how to prepare a monthly cash budget.

LIVING THE DREAM:

entrepreneurial experiences

The Problem with Unplanned Growth

This is a true story, although the names and places have been changed. Everything ended up OK, but the entrepreneur had to endure a lot of unnecessary stress—all of which could easily have been prevented by just a minimum of business planning.

The story takes place in a midsize university town on the West Coast. The main players are Leslie and Terry, co-owners of a consulting business offering computer and network services mostly to local businesses.

At the beginning of this story, Leslie and Terry had a small but comfortable office a few blocks off Main Street, near the university, and a comfortable business, averaging about $20,000 in sales per month with a few steady clients and few seasonal variations in sales. Then came the big, wonderful new opportunity—a contract with a large and fast-growing company to install new Internet facilities in offices on its corporate campus, only 10 miles up the freeway. This was a $200,000 contract that had to be acted on quickly, and it opened up an important new relationship with a potential business-changing client. It was also cause for great celebration. Leslie and Terry

© Rick Graves /Stone/Getty Image

and their spouses marked the occasion with a fancy dinner at the best restaurant in the area.

Both partners quickly got started fulfilling the contract, delivering the network, connecting the systems, and making good on their promises. To be sure the new relationship would turn into a permanent increase in business, they took on five contractor consultants to deal with the needs of installation, training, and the general increase in business demands.

Within two months, it seemed clear to both partners that they had made the leap. Systems were being installed, the clients were happy, and they were on the road to doubling their business volume in a very short period of time. Leslie and Terry decided they could celebrate more, so they both went to a local car dealership and leased new Mercedes sedans.

But then things started going downhill. Though sales and profits were way up, jobs were done and invoicing was underway, Leslie and Terry had no money. Their contractors—good people who Leslie and Terry wanted to keep—needed to be paid, but there was no money. They rushed to their local bank, waving reports of increased sales and profits, but banks need time. The business suffered the classic problems of unplanned growth. Just as the accounting reports looked brightest, the coffers were empty. People were barely done celebrating, but suddenly they were looking at the disaster of unpaid bills and, much worse, unpaid people.

What happened? The company experienced unplanned cash flow problems. The new, larger client had a slow process for paying bills, so the jump in sales didn't mean an immediate jump in cash in the bank. Leslie and Terry were more concerned about delivering good service than delivering necessary paperwork, so their own invoicing process was slow. They were owed about $85,000, but they couldn't go straight to their new clients to get the money—they had already authorized payment and sent the requests to the company's finance department for processing. The people in the finance department were slow to respond and not particularly concerned about paying vendors quickly; their job was to pay slowly, just not so slowly as to get a bad credit rating.

Leslie and Terry had a bad case of "receivables starvation." The money that was owed to them was already showing as sales and profits, but it was not in the bank.

In this case, fortunately, the two partners had enough home equity to get a quick loan and pay their contractors. The business was saved and grew, but not without a great deal of stress and strain, and even second mortgages. The story's ending might have been much different if the owners did not have access to cash from personal assets. This could easily have doomed the company.

The worst moment is worth remembering. One of the partners' spouses was particularly eloquent about the irony of taking on a new mortgage while driving that "[profanity omitted] Mercedes."

The moral of the story: Always have a good cash flow plan. Think ahead about the impact of a sudden rush of new business. Go to the bank early, as soon as you know about new business, and start processing a credit line on receivables. And never lease a Mercedes until you're sure you won't have to take out a new mortgage a few weeks later.

Source: Tim Berry, "The Problem with Unplanned Growth," entrepreneur.com, http://www.entrepreneur.com/startingabusiness/businessplans/businessplancoachtimberry/article172648.html, accessed March 25, 2009.

Pro Forma Statement of Cash Flows

Earlier, we prepared a pro forma income statement and balance sheets for D&R Products, Inc. We can now use that information to prepare a pro forma statement of cash flows. However, instead of dealing with historical numbers, as we did in Chapter 10, we are now working with projections.

The pro forma cash flow statements for D&R Products are presented in Exhibit 11-4.[9] There are three key numbers that you should pay particular attention to in the exhibit: cash flows from operations, cash flows related to the firm's investments in plant and equipment, and cash flows from financing activities (these numbers are shown in boxes in Exhibit 11-4). Looking at these numbers, we see that:

1. In the first year, the business is expected to have negative cash flows from operations of $86,500 and will be investing $50,000 in the building and equipment. To cover these negative cash flows, Allen expects to raise $146,500 in financing from his personal investment of $110,000, $9,500 on the line of credit from the bank, and $27,000 from the mortgage on the building after making the annual $3,000 payment on the principal.[10] The firm would then end the year with $10,000 in cash.

2. In the second year, the firm will be close to erasing the negative cash flows from operations, reducing it to a negative $2,000. (Notice that while the business is expected to have negative cash flows from operations, Allen anticipates having positive profits of $28,500. As we have repeatedly said, *cash flows and profits are not the same thing*.) Moreover, there are no plans to invest in fixed assets in the second year. Thus, given his underlying assumptions, Allen would need to increase the line of credit (short-term debt) from the bank from $9,500 in year 1 to $20,500 in year 2, for an increase of $11,000, and pay $3,000 on the mortgage. The net result will be a $6,000 increase in cash, for total cash of $16,000.

Allen now has a good estimate of the cash flows for the year as a whole and an idea of what contributes to the cash inflows and outflows. But there is also a need to track the firm's cash flows for a shorter time period, usually on a monthly basis.

11-4 Pro Forma Cash Flow Statements for D&R Products, Inc.

		Year 1	Year 2	Sources of Information
Operating activities:				
Net profits		($ 33,000)	$28,500	Pro forma
Depreciation		4,000	4,000	income
Increase in accounts receivable (cash outflow)		(25,000)	(15,000)	statement
Increase in inventory (cash outflow)	($62,500)		($37,500)	
Increase in accounts payable and				
accrued expenses (cash inflow)	30,000		18,000	
Cash payments for inventory (cash outflow)		($ 32,500)	($19,500)	
Cash flows from operations		**($ 86,500)**	**($ 2,000)**	Changes in pro-
Investment in fixed assets:				jected balance
Increase in gross fixed assets (cash outflow)		**($ 50,000)**	**$ 0**	sheets from found-
				ing of business
Financing activities:				to year 1 and from
Increase in short-term line of credit		$ 9,500	$ 11,000	year 1 to year 2
Increase (decrease) in mortgage		27,000	(3,000)	
Increase in stock		110,000	$ 0	
Cash flows from financing		**$146,500**	**$8,000**	
Increase (decrease) in cash		$ 10,000	$ 6,000	
Beginning cash		$0	$10,000	
Ending cash (as shown in the balance sheets)		**$10,000**	**$16,000**	

The Cash Budget

The *cash budget* is one of the primary tools that a small business owner can use to manage cash flows. The budget is concerned specifically with dollars received and paid out. *No single planning document is more important in the life of a small company, either for avoiding cash flow problems when cash runs short or for anticipating short-term investment opportunities if excess cash becomes available.*

To help you understand the process of preparing a cash budget, let's continue with the example of D&R Products, Inc. In the previous section, we prepared a pro forma statement of cash flows for the year. But Allen realizes that he also needs to have a sense of the timing of the cash flows throughout the year, so he has decided to prepare a monthly cash budget for the first year of operations. We will look at the first three months of the cash budget to understand how it was prepared. While he predicts that the firm will have $250,000 in annual sales in the first year, his sales projections for the first three months are as follows:

January	$ 4,000
February	6,000
March	9,000

In addition, the following assumptions will be made:

1. Of the firm's sales dollars, 40 percent are collected the month of the sale, 30 percent one month after the sale, and the remaining 30 percent two months after the sale.

2. Inventory will be purchased one month in advance of the expected sale and will be paid for in the month in which it is sold.

3. Inventory purchases will equal 60 percent of projected sales for the next month's sales.

4. The firm will spend $3,000 each month for advertising.

cash budget
A listing of cash receipts and cash disbursements usually for a relative short time period, such as weekly or monthly.

5. Salaries and utilities for the first three months are estimated as follows:

	Salaries	Utilities
January	$5,000	$150
February	6,000	$200
March	6,000	$200

6. Allen will be investing $110,000 in the business from his personal savings.

7. The firm will be investing $10,000 for needed equipment and $40,000 for the purchase of a building, for a total investment of $50,000. However, the bank has agreed to finance $30,000 of the building purchase price in the form of a mortgage.

Based on this information, Allen has prepared a monthly cash budget for the three-month period ending March 31. Exhibit 11-5 shows the results of his computations, which involve the following steps:

Step 1. Determine the amount of collections each month, based on the projected collection patterns.

Step 2. Estimate the amount and timing of the following cash disbursements:

    a. Inventory purchases and payments. The amount of the purchases is shown in the boxed area at the top of the table. Payments on inventory will be made one month later.

    b. Advertising, wages and salaries, and utilities.

Step 3. Calculate the *cash flow from operations*, which equals the cash receipts (collections from sales) less cash disbursements.

EXHIBIT 11-5 Three-Month Cash Budget for D&R Products, Inc., for January–March

Assumptions:
Anticipated sales collections:
In the month of sale	40%
1 month later	30%
2 months later	30%

	December	January	February	March
Monthly sales	$ 0	$4,000	$6,000	$9,000
Inventory purchases on credit	$2,400	$3,600	$5,400	$7,800

		December	January	February	March
Monthly sales		$0	*$4,000	$6,000	$9,000
Cash receipts					
Step 1:	Collection of sales				
	In month of sale		$1,600	$2,400	$3,600
	1 month later			1,200	1,800
	2 months later				1,200
	Total cash receipts		$1,600	$3,600	$6,600
Step 2:	**Cash disbursements**				
Step 2a:	Payments on inventory purchases		$2,400	$3,600	$5,400
	Advertising		3,000	3,000	3,000
Step 2b:	Wages and salaries		5,000	6,000	6,000
	Utilities		150	200	200
	Total cash disbursements		$10,550	$12,800	$14,600
Step 3:	Cash flows from operations		($8,950)	($9,200)	($8,000)
Step 4:	Allen's personal investment		110,000		
Step 5:	Purchase of equipment and building		(50,000)		
Step 6:	Mortgage (loan from the bank to buy the building)		30,000		
Step 7:	Beginning cash balance		0	81,050	71,850
Step 8:	Ending cash balance		$81,050	$71,850	$63,850

*For example, January sales of $4,000 are collected as follows: (40%) $1,600 in January, (30%) $1,200 in February, (30%) $1,200 in March.

Step 4. Recognize the $110,000 investment in the business by Allen.

Step 5. Note the $50,000 investment in the building and equipment.

Step 6. Show the $30,000 loan from the bank to help pay for the building.

Step 7. Determine the beginning-of-month cash balance (ending cash balance from the prior month).

Step 8. Compute the end-of-month cash balance.

Based on the cash budget, Allen now has a sense of what to expect for the first three months of operations, which could not be seen from the annual pro forma statement of cash flows presented in Exhibit 11-4. He can clearly see that he will be "burning" somewhere between $8,000 and $9,200 of cash per month for the first three months of operations. Given that he will have almost $64,000 in cash remaining at the end of March, he would run out of cash in about seven or eight months if the cash flows from operations continue to be negative $8,000 or $9,000 each month. At that time, he will have to start borrowing on the bank line of credit.

One final thought about the cash budget. Once it has been prepared, an entrepreneur has to decide how to use it. Entrepreneurship is about seeking opportunities, and there is a real danger that a cash budget may lead to inflexibility. A strict cost-containment strategy in order to "make the budget" can discourage managers from being creative and shifting their approach when it makes sense to do so. And inflexible budgets can lead to a "use it or lose it" mentality, where managers spend remaining budgeted money at year's end so that allocations will not be cut the following year. Such a mind-set negatively impacts the entrepreneurial process. Jeremy Hope, a former venture capitalist, describes the risk of becoming too focused on a budget: "I'm not opposed to a budget as a finance statement, but to the way it's used as an almost fixed performance contract on which employees have to deliver. The pressure to deliver on budgets drives a lot of irrational, stupid, and crazy behavior you see within businesses."[11]

Allowing the management team and employees to become focused on the budget instead of opportunities is counterproductive and should be avoided.

Use Good Judgment When Forecasting

5. Give suggestions for effective financial forecasting.

The forecasting process requires an entrepreneur to exercise good judgment in planning, particularly when the planning is providing the basis for raising capital. The overall approach to forecasting is straightforward—entrepreneurs make assumptions and, based on these assumptions, determine financing requirements. But entrepreneurs may be tempted to overstate their expectations in order to acquire much-needed financing. So how do you get it right? Here are some practical suggestions about making financial forecasts.[12]

1. *Develop realistic sales projections.* Entrepreneurs often think they can accomplish more than they actually are able to, especially when it comes to forecasting future sales. When graphed, their sales projections for a new venture often resemble a hockey stick—the sales numbers are flat or rise slightly at first (like the blade of a hockey stick) and then soar upward like a hockey stick's handle. Such projections are always suspect—only the most astonishing changes in a business or market can justify such a sudden, rocketlike performance.

2. *Build projections from clear assumptions about marketing and pricing plans.* Don't be vague, and don't guess. Spell out the kinds of marketing you plan to do—for example, state specifically how many customers you expect to attract. Paul A. Broni offers this advice:

"When putting together your income statement, revenues should show more than just the projected sales figure for each year. You should also show how many units you plan to sell, as well as the mix of revenue (assuming that you have more than one product or service). If you have a service business, you may also want to show how many customers or clients you will have each year. Investors will look at that number to determine whether it's realistic for you to sell to that many customers. For example, if your plan is to go from 12 customers in the first year to 36 customers in the second, can the sales team you've built accomplish that goal? What about marketing and advertising? Does your budget account for the money you'll need to spend to support such an effort?[13]"

3. *Do not use unrealistic profit margins.* Projections are immediately suspect if profit margins (profits ÷ sales) or expenses are significantly higher or lower than the average figures reported by firms in the industry with similar revenues and numbers of employees. In general, a new business should not expect to exceed the industry average in profit margins. Entrepreneurs frequently assume that as their company grows it will achieve economies of scale, and gross and operating profit margins will improve. In fact, as the business grows and increases its fixed costs, its operating profit margins are likely to suffer in the short run. If you insist in your projections that the economies can be achieved quickly, you will need to explain your position.

4. *Don't limit your projections to an income statement.* Entrepreneurs frequently resist providing a projected balance sheet and cash flow statement. They feel comfortable projecting sales and profits but do not like having to commit to assumptions about the sources and uses of capital needed to grow the business. Investors, however, want to see those assumptions in print, and they are particularly interested in the firm's cash flows—and you should be as well.

5. *Provide monthly data for the upcoming year and annual data for succeeding years.* Many entrepreneurs prepare projections using only monthly data or only annual data for an entire 3- or 5-year period. Given the difficulty in forecasting accurately beyond a year, monthly data for the later years are not particularly believable. From year two on, annual projections are adequate.

6. *Avoid providing too much financial information.* Computer spreadsheets are extremely valuable in making projections and showing how different assumptions affect the firm's financials. But do not be tempted to overuse this tool. Instead, limit your projections to two scenarios: the most likely scenario (base case) and the break-even scenario. The base case should show what you realistically expect the business to do; the break-even case should show what level of sales is required to break even.

7. *Be certain that the numbers reconcile—and not by simply plugging in a figure.* All too often, entrepreneurs plug a figure into equity to make things work out. While everyone makes mistakes, that's one you want to avoid because it can result in a loss of credibility.

8. *Follow the plan.* After you have prepared the pro forma financial statements, check them against actual results at least once a month, and modify your projections as needed.

These suggestions, if followed, will help you avoid the old problem of over-promising and under-delivering. Given the nature of starting a business, entrepreneurs at times simply have to have faith that they will be able to deliver on what they promise, even though it may not be clear exactly how this will be accomplished. Risk is part of the equation, and often things will not go as planned. But integrity requires you to honor your commitments, and that cannot be done if you have made unrealistic projections about what you can accomplish.

The information on financial planning provided in this chapter and in Chapter 10 will serve as a foundation for the examination of an entrepreneur's search for specific sources of financing in Chapter 12.

LOOKING BACK

1. Describe the purpose and need for financial forecasting.

- The purpose of pro forma financial statements is to determine (1) future profitability based on projected sales levels, (2) how much and what type of financing will be needed, and (3) whether the firm will have adequate cash flows.

- Accurate financial forecasting is important not only for ensuring that a firm has the resources it needs to grow, but also for managing growth.

2. Develop a pro forma income statement to forecast a new venture's profitability.

- It is important for an entrepreneur to understand the drivers of a firm's profits, not only in a general sense but in the specific ways each factor applies to a unique firm.

- A firm's net profit is dependent on (1) amount of sales, (2) cost of goods sold, (3) operating expenses, (4) interest expense, and (5) taxes.

- In a real-world situation, an entrepreneur should project the profits of a company for at least three years into the future.

3. Determine a company's asset and financing requirements based on a pro forma balance sheet.

- The amount and type of assets required for a venture will vary according to the nature of the business; however, all firms will need to understand how much working capital and fixed assets will be required.

- An entrepreneur should try to bootstrap as many resources as possible in order to minimize a firm's investment while simultaneously ensuring adequate resources.

- Funding for a new venture should cover its asset requirements and also the personal living expenses of the owner.

- A direct relationship exists between sales growth and asset needs: as sales increase, more assets are required. For every dollar of assets needed, there must be a corresponding dollar of financing.

- A firm's financing is determined by considering its (1) asset requirements, (2) need to maintain liquidity, (3) debt ratio, (4) sources of spontaneous debt financing, and (5) equity ownership, as expressed in the following equation:

Total asset requirements = Total sources of financing = Spontaneous debt financing + Loans from banks, etc. + Owner's investment + Retained earnings

4. Forecast a firm's cash flows.

- Forecasting cash flows can be accomplished in one of two ways; (1) prepare a pro forma statement of cash flows, or (2) develop a cash budget. Ideally, an entrepreneur should do both.

- A firm's cash flows involve three activities: operations, investments, and financing.

- A cash budget is concerned specifically with dollars received and paid out.

- A budget should provide boundaries but should not limit creativity and flexibility; entrepreneurship is all about seizing opportunity.

5. Give suggestions for effective financial forecasting.

- Develop realistic sales projections and build projections from clear assumptions about marketing and pricing plans.

- Do not use unrealistic profit margins; in general, new businesses do not exceed industry average profit margins in their first years.

- Do not limit your projections to an income statement; go a step further and provide a balance sheet and cash flow statement.

- Provide monthly data for the upcoming year and annual data for succeeding years.

- Avoid providing too much financial information, and limit projections to two scenarios: the base case and the break-even scenario.

- Be certain that the numbers reconcile.

- Follow the plan, and measure how actual performance compares with forecasted performance so that modifications to future forecasts may be more accurate.

Key Terms

pro forma financial
   statements p. 287

working capital p. 291

net working capital p. 291

bootstrapping p. 291

percentage-of-sales
   technique p. 294

liquidity p. 295

current ratio p. 295

debt ratio p. 295

spontaneous debt
   financing p. 295

cash budget p. 301

Discussion Questions

1. What determines a company's profitability?

2. Discuss how asset and financing requirements might differ among a retail business, a service company, and an information system–based venture.

3. Why is it important to consider an entrepreneur's personal finances when conducting the short- and long-term financial forecasts of a firm?

4. Describe the process for estimating the amount of assets required for a new venture.

5. What are some of the basic principles that govern the financing of a firm? Why are they important?

6. How are a startup's financing requirements estimated?

7. Describe two ways for projecting a venture's cash flows, and discuss when each is appropriate to use.

8. When forecasting cash flows, why is it important to consider the time period covered by the forecast? What issues should the entrepreneur consider when doing financial forecasts?

9. Why is it important for an entrepreneur not only to create a cash budget but also to decide how it will be used within the firm?

10. Choose three of the practical suggestions for making financial forecasts. Discuss the importance of the suggestions and the potential consequences of ignoring these suggestions.

You Make the Call

SITUATION 1

D&R Products, Inc., used as an example in this chapter, is an actual firm (although some of the facts were changed to maintain confidentiality). David Allen bought the firm from its founding owners and moved its operations to his home-town. Although he has estimated the firm's asset needs and financing requirements, he cannot be certain that these projections will be realized. The figures merely represent the most likely case. Allen also made some projections that he considers to be the worst-case and best-case sales and profit figures. If things do not go well, the firm might have sales of only $200,000 in its first year. However, if the potential of the business is realized, Allen believes that sales could be as high as $325,000. If he needs any additional financing beyond the existing line of credit, he could conceivably borrow another $5,000 in short-term debt from the bank by pledging some personal investments. Any additional financing would need to come from Allen himself, thereby increasing his equity stake in the business.

Source: Personal conversation with David Allen. (The entrepreneur's name and financial numbers are hypothetical.)

Question If all of D&R Products' other relationships hold, how will Allen's worst-case and best-case projections affect the income statement and balance sheet in the first year?

SITUATION 2

Adrian Fudge of the Fudge Corporation wants you to forecast the firm's financing needs over the fourth quarter (October through December). He has made the following observations relative to planned cash receipts and disbursements:

- Interest on a $75,000 bank note (principal due next March) at an 8 percent annual rate is payable in December for the three-month period just ended.
- The firm follows a policy of paying no cash dividends.
- Actual historical and future predicted sales are as follows:

Historical Sales
August $150,000
September 175,000

Predicted Sales
October $200,000
November 220,000
December 180,000
January 200,000

- The firm has a monthly rental expense of $5,000.
- Wages and salaries for the coming months are estimated at $25,000 per month.

- Of the firm's sales, 25 percent is collected in the month of the sale, 35 percent one month after the sale, and the remaining 40 percent two months after the sale.
- Merchandise is purchased one month before the sales month and is paid for in the month it is sold. Purchases equal 75 percent of sales.
- Tax prepayments are made quarterly, with a prepayment of $10,000 in October based on earnings for the quarter ended September 30.
- Utility costs for the firm average 3 percent of sales and are paid in the month they are incurred.
- Depreciation expense is $20,000 annually.

Question 1 Prepare a monthly cash budget for the three-month period ending in December.

Question 2 If the firm's beginning cash balance for the budget period is $7,000, and this is its desired minimum balance, determine when and how much the firm will need to borrow during the budget period. The firm has a $50,000 line of credit with its bank, with interest (10 percent annual rate) paid monthly. For example, interest on a loan taken out at the end of September would be paid at the end of October and every month thereafter as long as the loan was outstanding.

SITUATION 3

New York City–based Plum Organics was two weeks away from a production run of its organic kids' meals when the phone rang. On the other line was the company's organic cheese supplier.

"They said, 'We're out of organic parmesan cheese because there's a shortage of organic milk,'" recalls Plum Organics' founder, Gigi Lee Chang. The supplier said it expected a shipment of organic milk to arrive soon and that it could probably meet 3-year-old Plum Organics' production deadline. Chang was skeptical. She called another supplier, but because its organic parmesan wasn't fully aged, Chang, 41, feared it would change the taste of the product.

Chang weighed her options: She could either rely on her primary supplier to come through, or use the parmesan the secondary supplier had to offer.

Source: Chris Penttila, "Risky Business," *Entrepreneur*, November 2008, http://www.entrepreneur.com/magazine/entrepreneur/2008/november/197996.html, accessed April 9, 2009.

Question 1 What would you do, if you were Chang? Support your decision.

Question 2 Is there anything Chang should do in the future to avoid, or at least anticipate, such a situation?

Question 3 What lesson should Chang learn from this situation?

Experiential Exercises

1. Dun & Bradstreet and Robert Morris Associates compile financial information about many companies. They provide, among other information, the income statement and balance sheets for an average firm in an industry. Go to a library and look up, or search online for, financial information on firms in two industries of your choice. Compute the following data for each industry:

   a. The percentages of assets in (1) current assets and (2) fixed assets (plant and equipment)

   b. The percentages of financing from (1) spontaneous debt financing and (2) retained earnings

   c. The cost of goods sold and the operating expenses as percentages of sales

   d. The total assets as a percentage of sales

   Given your findings, how would you summarize the differences between the two industries?

2. Obtain the business plan of a firm that is 3 to 5 years old. Compare the techniques used in the plan to forecast the firm's profits and financing requirements with those presented in this chapter. If actual data are available, compare the financial forecasts with the eventual outcome. What accounts for the differences?

3. Identify a small business in your community that has recently expanded. Interview the owner of the firm about the evaluation methods he or she used before committing to the expansion.

Small Business & Entrepreneurship Resource Center

The *Small Business and Entrepreneurship Resource Center* offers complete small business management resources through a comprehensive database that covers all major areas of starting, operating, and maintaining a business from financing, management, marketing, accounting, taxes, and more. Use the access code that came with your new book to access the site and perform the exercises in each chapter.

1. The text explains that bootstrapping is the most common way that entrepreneurs accomplish more with less. To the extent possible, the entrepreneur should use other people's resources—for instance, lease

rather than buy, negotiate with suppliers to provide inventory "just in time" to minimize the investment in inventories, and arrange to collect money owed the firm before having to pay the firm's bills. Discuss briefly the 10 proven bootstrapping techniques and strategies that every entrepreneur should know.

Source: The art and science of bootstrapping. Raising Capital. The Kiplinger Washington Editors, Inc.. Annual 2000. p81(13).

Case 11

MISSOURI SOLVENTS, P. 646

Missouri Solvents is a regional distributor of liquid and dry chemicals, headquartered in St. Louis. The company has been serving the St. Louis market for 10 years and has a reputation as a reliable supplier of industrial chemicals.

ALTERNATIVE CASES FOR CHAPTER 11

Case 10A, Understanding Financial Statements, Part 1, p. 643

Case 4, Mo's Chowder, p. 630

Case 22, Pearson's, p. 669

 The Business Plan: Laying the Foundation

As part of laying the foundation to prepare your own business plan, you will need to develop the following:

1. Historical financial statements (if applicable) and 5 years of pro forma financial statements, including balance sheets, income statements, and statements of cash flows.

2. Monthly cash budgets for the first year and quarterly cash budgets for the second year.

3. Profit and cash flow break-even analysis. (See Chapter 16 for an explanation of break-even analysis.)

4. Financial resources required now and in the future, with details on the intended use of funds being requested.

5. Underlying assumptions for all pro forma statements.

6. Current and planned investments by the owners and other investors.

A Firm's Sources of Financing

Saharai Sand Duffle, J.W. Hulme Co.

In the SPOTLIGHT
J.W. Hulme Co.
http://www.jwhulmeco.com

When Chuck Bidwell and Jennifer Guarino took over J.W. Hulme Co. a few years ago, their plan was to transform the tiny maker of duck-hunting gear and fishing-rod bags into a luxury luggage company. They applied the modern American business playbook: Borrow heavily to grow fast. The strategy worked—until the credit crisis threw out those rules.

Now the two business partners are struggling to pull their company, and their lives, out of a spiral. The pain is rippling through a broad circle of investors, employees, suppliers, and family members. Guarino, 46, says her dream was to build a business "that was not just a job, but was a passion." Instead, she and Bidwell have had to lay off employees, stop paying investors, and renegotiate bills with their suppliers. Still, there's no guarantee the business will survive.

Bidwell and Guarino's aggressive borrowing was "pretty typical of small businesses," says their main lender, Fizal Kassim of Maple Bank in Champlin, Minn. He loaned Hulme more than $550,000 over five years.

Bidwell and Guarino bought Hulme in 2003. By expanding the mailing list tenfold, to 10,000 households, and more than doubling their product line to 250 items, they calculated that within 5 years Hulme could reach revenue of $2 million with positive cash flow.

Hulme got off to a strong start. Sales grew 89%, to $1.4 million by 2006, and the company turned a profit, Bidwell says. But little setbacks can have big consequences when a strategy relies heavily on debt.

At a coffeeshop one evening in April 2007, Hulme's two owners met to talk about their debt. Guarino told Bidwell they should slow their growth. Bidwell says he reminded her that orders from their previous catalog mailings had met or exceeded projections. If they stuck to the plan, he said, they could bring in enough cash to service debts.

Sticking to the plan meant borrowing more money—and fast. Big chunks of cash were needed at certain times to pay for catalogs. Late mailings aimed at Mother's Day, for example, mean missed sales.

Bidwell borrowed about $500,000 from past business associates, friends,

LOOKING AHEAD

THE OPENING SPOTLIGHT TALE OF BORROWING HEAVILY TO BUY A BUSINESS IS A LESSON IN WHAT NOT TO DO. AN OTHERWISE GOOD BUSINESS OPPORTUNITY CAN BE RUINED BY MAKING BAD FINANCING CHOICES. IN THIS CHAPTER, YOU'LL BE GIVEN A FRAMEWORK FOR EVALUATING THE DIFFERENT OPTIONS AVAILABLE FOR FINANCING A SMALL BUSINESS. AFTER STUDYING THIS CHAPTER, YOU SHOULD BE ABLE TO

1. Describe how the nature of a firm affects its financing sources.

2. Evaluate the choice between debt financing and equity financing.

3. Identify the typical sources of financing used at the outset of a new venture.

4. Discuss the basic process for acquiring and structuring a bank loan.

5. Explain how business relationships can be used to finance a small firm.

6. Describe the two types of private equity investors that offer financing to small firms.

7. Distinguish among the different government loan programs available to small companies.

8. Explain when large companies and public stock offerings can be sources of financing.

Chapter 11 addressed two questions: (1) *How much* financing is needed? and (2) *What types* of financing are available? Three basic types of financing were identified:

1. *Spontaneous debt financing,* such as accounts payable, which increases automatically with increases in sales. For instance, as a firm's sales grow, it purchases more inventory and suppliers extend the firm more credit, which increases accounts payable.

2. *External financing,* which comes from outside lenders and investors. Lenders (such as bankers) and investors (such as common stockholders, partners, or sole proprietors) provide equity financing.

3. *Profit retention,* which is provided by the cash flows generated by the business itself, or what we call *cash flows from operations.* That is, rather than distributing cash to the owners in the form of dividends, the money is retained in the business and becomes part of the owners' equity on the balance sheet.

This chapter discusses the first two sources: spontaneous debt financing and external financing. But first we consider *how* a company should be financed. An understanding of this core issue is critical to identifying appropriate sources of financing, especially if you want to avoid the dilemma faced by Bidwell and Guarino.

The Nature of a Firm and Its Financing Sources

Four basic factors determine how a firm is financed: (1) the firm's economic potential, (2) the size and maturity of the company, (3) the nature of its assets, and (4) the personal preferences of the owners with respect to the tradeoffs between debt and equity.

A Firm's Economic Potential

1. Describe how the nature of a firm affects its financing sources.

A firm with potential for high growth and large profits has many more possible sources of financing than does a firm that provides a good lifestyle for the owner but little in the way of attractive returns to investors. Only firms providing rates of return that exceed the investor's required rate of return create value for the investor. In fact, most investors in startup companies limit their investment to firms that offer potentially high returns within a 5- to 10-year period. Clearly, a company that provides a comfortable lifestyle for its owner but insufficient profits to attract outside investors will find its options for alternative sources of financing limited.

entrepreneurial experiences

Adapting to a New World of Finance

In 2008 and early 2009 when we were revising *Small Business Management*, the U.S. economy was experiencing one of the worst financial downturns in decades. A number of large financial institutions were near collapse. Deepening trouble throughout the financial system and the economy led banks to become more cautious about their lending practices, directing loans to only the most creditworthy customers—and, sometimes, not even to them.

In response to the situation, the federal government created the Troubled Asset Relief Program, or TARP, providing more than $200 billion to troubled financial institutions. The money was to be used for making new loans to individuals and businesses. But something went wrong along the way. Banks did not increase their lending in any significant way and, in many cases, decreased lending.

Jeffrey Campbell, owner of Tau Publishing in Phoenix, described the environment facing many entrepreneurs. Campbell observed, "I find it ironic that TARP money was supposed to ease credit. It is only tightening it up. I don't think it is working the way it is supposed to be working."

Campbell said he and his wife had credit scores well above 700, owned two homes that were worth more than what they owed, and paid their credit cards as soon as they got the bill. Yet the limits on his business credit cards were reduced from $15,000 to $8,800, and a line of credit from another bank was eliminated altogether.

With less credit, Campbell said he would not be able to purchase additional book-binding equipment and would have to seek outside vendors to do the job, thereby raising his expenses. "There is really something wrong with this picture," he said.

Another entrepreneur, Patrick Ryan, co-owner of Ryan Brothers Ambulance Service, of Madison, Wisconsin, commented, "They're making us jump through a few more hoops," explaining that his long-time lender asked for more information than normal on his last visit: "Our banker just said, 'We normally don't do all this research, but the bank is performing more due diligence even for the bank's long-standing customers.'"

So what does this all mean to someone wanting to start a new business? It certainly suggests that processes that worked before don't work in a troubled economy. Does it mean that you should wait to start a business? Possibly, but not necessarily. Opportunities frequently arise during tough economic conditions. You may have to do more bootstrapping than in more "normal" times and be more creative in seeking financing. You should also be more careful in financing with debt. As illustrated in the opening spotlight, a banker can always change the terms of a loan, which may place you in an untenable position. Consequently, you need to prepare better—which is *never* a bad thing—and then, if the opportunity still makes sense, go for it!

Source: Observations of the authors; and Sudeep Reddy, Marshall Eckblad, and Dan Fitzpatrick, "Banks Adopt Tighter Terms for Lending, Survey Says," www.wsj.com, February 3, 2009.

www.federalreserve.gov/bankinforeg/tarpinfo.htm

Ryan Brothers Ambulance

Company Size and Maturity

The size and maturity of a company have a direct bearing on the types of financing available. Larger and older firms have access to bank credit that generally is not available to younger and smaller companies. Also, smaller firms rely more on personal loans and credit cards for financing. In the early years of a business, most entrepreneurs bootstrap their financing—that is, they depend on their own initiative to come up with the necessary capital. Only after the business has an established track record will most bankers and other financial institutions be interested in providing financing.

You have probably read about venture capitalists who helped finance such firms as Yahoo!, eBay, and Apple. But even venture capitalists limit how much they will invest in startup companies. Many of these types of investors believe that the additional risk associated with startups is too great relative to the returns they can expect to receive. On average, about three-fourths of a venture capitalist's investments are in later-stage businesses; only a few of them focus heavily on startups. Similarly, bankers demand evidence that the business will be able to repay a loan—and that evidence usually must be based on what the firm has done in the past and not what the owner says it will achieve in the future. So, a firm's life cycle position is a critical factor in raising capital.

Types of Assets

A banker specifically considers two types of assets when evaluating a loan: tangible assets and intangible assets. Tangible assets, which can be seen and touched, include inventory, equipment, and buildings. The cost of these assets appears on the firm's balance sheet, which the banker receives as part of the firm's financial statements. Tangible assets serve as great collateral when a firm is requesting a bank loan. On the other hand, intangible assets, such as goodwill or past investments in research and development, have little value as collateral. As a result, companies with substantial tangible assets have a much easier time borrowing money than do companies with intangible assets.

Owner Preferences for Debt or Equity

The owner of a company faces the question "Should I finance with debt or equity or some mix of the two?" The answer depends, in part, on his or her personal preference. The ultimate choice between debt and equity involves certain tradeoffs, which will be explained in the following section.

Debt or Equity Financing?

Most providers of financial capital specialize in *either* debt *or* equity financing. Furthermore, the choice between debt and equity financing must be made early in a firm's life cycle and may have long-term financial consequences. To make an informed decision, a small business owner needs to recognize and understand the tradeoffs between debt and equity with regard to potential profitability, financial risk, and voting control. The tradeoffs are presented graphically in Exhibit 12-1. Let's consider each of these tradeoffs in turn.

2. Evaluate the choice between debt financing and equity financing.

Potential Profitability

Anyone who owns a business wants it to be profitable. Of course, profits can be measured as a dollar amount, such as $500,000; however, the really important question is how much profit

12-1 Tradeoffs between Debt and Equity

High Equity and Low Debt Financing

EQUITY

DEBT

Results:
Voting Control: Owners must share control with other equity investors who buy the stock or make a large investment.
Financial Risk: Lower
Potential Profitability: Lower potential return on investment for the owners

High Debt and Low Equity Financing

DEBT

EQUITY

Results:
Voting Control: Owners maintain control without having to make a large investment.
Financial Risk: Higher
Potential Profitability: Higher potential return on investment for the owners

the business makes relative to the size of the investment. In other words, the owner is primarily interested in the rate of return on the investment. Making $500,000 in profits may sound great, but not if the owner must invest $50 million to earn it. It would be better to purchase a certificate of deposit that earned, say, 3 percent or even 2 percent; any rate over 1 percent would provide income greater than $500,000.

To see how the choice between debt and equity affects potential profitability, consider the Levine Company, a new firm that's still in the process of raising needed capital.

- The owners have already invested $100,000 of their own money in the new business. To complete the financing, they need another $100,000.

- Levine is considering one of two options for raising the additional $100,000: (1) investors who would provide $100,000 for a 30 percent share of the firm's outstanding stock, or (2) a bank that would lend the money at an interest rate of 8 percent, so the interest expense each year would be $8,000 (0.08 × $100,000).

- The firm's operating profits (earnings before interest and taxes) is expected to be $28,000, determined as follows:

Sales	$150,000
Cost of goods sold	80,000
Gross profit	$ 70,000
Operating expenses	42,000
Operating profits	$ 28,000

- With the additional $100,000 in financing, the firm's total assets would be $200,000 ($100,000 original equity plus $100,000 in additional financing).

- Based on the projected operating profits of $28,000 and total assets of $200,000, the firm expects to earn $0.14 for each $1 of assets invested ($28,000 operating profits ÷ $200,000 total assets). In other words, there will be a 14 percent *return on assets,* which is the rate of return earned on a firm's total assets invested.

return on assets
Rate of return earned on a firm's total assets invested, computed as operating profits divided by total assets.

$$\text{Return on assets} = \frac{\text{Operating profits}}{\text{Total assets}} = \frac{\$28,000}{\$200,00} = 0.14, \text{ or } 14\%$$

If the firm raises the additional $100,000 in equity, its balance sheet will appear as follows:

Total assets	$200,000
Debt	$ 0
Equity (founders and new investors)	200,000
Total debt and equity	$200,000

But if the firm instead borrows $100,000, the balance sheet will look like this:

Total assets	$200,000
Debt (8% interest rate)	$100,000
Equity (founders)	100,000
Total debt and equity	$200,000

If we assume no taxes (just to keep matters simple), we can use the above information to project the firm's net profits when the additional $100,000 is financed by either equity or debt:

	Equity	**Debt**
Operating profits	$28,000	$28,000
Interest expense	0	(8,000) = (0.08 × $100,000)
Net profits	$28,000	$20,000

From these computations, we can see that net profits are greater if the firm finances with equity ($28,000 net profits) than with debt ($20,000 net profits). But the owners would have to invest *twice* as much money ($200,000 rather than $100,000) to avoid the $8,000 interest expense and get the higher net profits.

Should owners always finance with equity to get higher net profits? Not necessarily. The return on the owners' investment, or *return on equity,* is a better measure of performance than the absolute dollar amount of net profits. We measure the owners' return on equity as follows:

return on equity
Rate of return earned on the owners' equity investment, computed as net profits divided by owners' equity investment.

$$\text{Return on equity} = \frac{\text{Net profits}}{\text{Owners' equity investment}}$$

So when the firm uses *all* equity financing, the return on equity is 14 percent, computed as follows:

$$\text{Return on equity} = \frac{\text{Net profits}}{\text{Owners' equity investment}}$$

$$= \frac{\$28,000}{\$200,000} = 0.14, \text{ or } 14\%$$

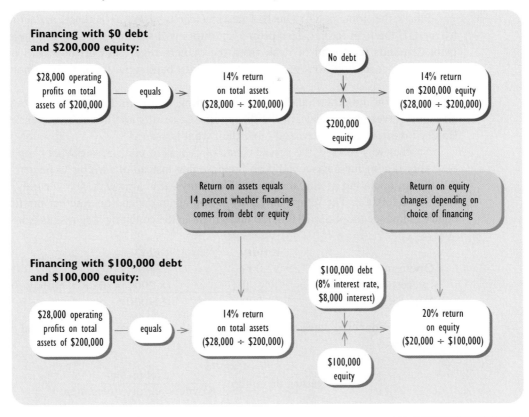

Financing with $0 debt and $200,000 equity:

$28,000 operating profits on total assets of $200,000 — equals → 14% return on total assets ($28,000 ÷ $200,000)

No debt

14% return on $200,000 equity ($28,000 ÷ $200,000)

$200,000 equity

Return on assets equals 14 percent whether financing comes from debt or equity

Return on equity changes depending on choice of financing

Financing with $100,000 debt and $100,000 equity:

$28,000 operating profits on total assets of $200,000 — equals → 14% return on total assets ($28,000 ÷ $200,000)

$100,000 debt (8% interest rate, $8,000 interest)

20% return on equity ($20,000 ÷ $100,000)

$100,000 equity

But if the additional financing comes from debt, leading to interest expense of $8,000 and equity investment of only $100,000, the rate of return on equity is 20 percent, calculated as follows:

$$\text{Return on equity} = \frac{\text{Net profits}}{\text{Owners' equity investment}}$$

$$= \frac{\$20,000}{\$100,000} = 0.20, \text{ or } 20\%$$

Thus, Levine's return on equity is higher if half the firm's financing comes from equity and half from debt. By using only equity, Levine's owners will earn $0.14 for every $1 of equity invested; by using debt, they will earn $0.20 for every $1 of equity invested. So, in terms of a rate of return on their investment, Levine's owners get a better return by borrowing money at 8 percent interest than by using equity financing. That makes sense, because the firm is earning 14 percent on its assets but only paying creditors at an 8 percent rate. Levine's owners benefit from the difference. These relationships are shown in Exhibit 12-2.

As a general rule, *as long as a firm's rate of return on its assets (operating profits ÷ total assets) is greater than the cost of the debt (interest rate), the owners' rate of return on equity will increase as the firm uses more debt.*

Financial Risk

If debt is so beneficial in terms of producing a higher rate of return for the owners, why shouldn't Levine's owners use as much debt as possible—even 100 percent debt—if they can? Then the rate of return on the owners' equity investment would be even higher—unlimited, in fact, if the owners did not have to invest any money.

That's the good news. The bad news: *Debt is risky,* as Bidwell and Guarino painfully learned. If the firm fails to earn profits, creditors will still insist on having their money repaid. Debt demands its pound of flesh from the owners regardless of the firm's performance. In an extreme case, creditors can force a firm into bankruptcy if it fails to honor its financial obligations.

Equity, on the other hand, is less demanding. If a firm does not reach its goal for profits, an equity investor must accept the disappointing results and hope for better results next year. Equity investors cannot demand more than what is earned.

Another way to view the negative side of debt is to contemplate what happens to the return on equity if a business has a bad year. Suppose that instead of earning 14 percent on its assets, or $28,000 in operating profits, the Levine Company earns a mere $2,000, or only 1 percent on its assets of $200,000. The return on equity would again depend on whether the firm used debt or equity to finance the second $100,000 investment in the company. The results would be as follows:

	Equity	**Debt**
Operating profits	$2,000	$2,000
Interest expense	0	(8,000) = (0.08 × $100,000)
Net profits	$2,000	($6,000)

If the added financing came in the form of equity, the return on equity would be a disappointing 1 percent:

$$\text{Return on equity} = \frac{\text{Net profits}}{\text{Owners' equity investment}}$$

$$= \frac{\$2,000}{\$200,000} = 0.01, \text{ or } 1\%$$

But if debt were used, the return on equity would be a painful negative 6 percent:

$$\text{Return on equity} = \frac{\text{Net profits}}{\text{Owners' equity investment}}$$

$$= \frac{-\$6,000}{\$100,000} = -0.06, \text{ or } -6\%$$

If only 1 percent is earned on the assets, the owners would be better off if they financed solely with equity. Thus, debt is a double-edged sword—it cuts both ways. If debt financing is used and things go well, they will go *very* well for the owners; but if things go badly, they will go *very* badly for the owners. In short, debt financing makes business more risky.

Voting Control

The third issue in choosing between debt and equity is the degree of control retained by owners. Raising new capital through equity financing would mean giving up a part of the firm's ownership, and most owners of small firms resist giving up control to outsiders. They do not want to be accountable in any way to minority owners, much less take the chance of possibly losing control of the business.

Out of an aversion to losing control, many small business owners choose to finance with debt rather than with equity. They realize that debt increases risk, but it also permits them to retain full ownership of the firm.

With an understanding of the basic tradeoffs to be considered when choosing between debt and equity, we can now look at specific sources of financing. Where do small business owners go to find the money to finance their companies?

Sources of Financing

3. Identify the typical sources of financing used at the outset of a new venture.

When initially financing a small business, an entrepreneur will typically rely on personal savings and then seek financing from family and friends. If these sources are inadequate, the entrepreneur may then turn to more formal channels of financing, such as banks and outside investors.

Exhibit 12-3 gives an overview of the sources of financing of smaller companies. As indicated, some sources of financing—such as banks, business suppliers, asset-based lenders, and the government—are essentially limited to providing debt financing. Equity financing for most entrepreneurs comes from personal savings and, in rare instances, from selling stock to the public. Other sources—including friends and family, other individual investors, venture capitalists (rarely), and large corporations—may provide either debt or equity financing, depending on the situation. Keep in mind that the use of these and other sources of funds are not limited to a startup's initial financing. Such sources may also be used to finance a firm's day-to-day operations and business expansions.

To gain insight into how startups are financed, consider the responses given by owners of *Inc. Magazine* 500 firms—the 500 fastest-growing privately held firms in the United States—when they were asked about the financing sources they used to start their firms; the results are shown in Exhibit 12-4. Even for these high-growth firms, 70 percent of the startup financing came from the founders' personal savings, with another 10 percent coming from friends and family and 8 percent from bank loans. The remaining sources of financing were relatively insignificant in starting the firms. However, within five years the *Inc. Magazine* 500 entrepreneurs had, on average, raised 17 percent of their financing from private investors and 12 percent from venture capitalists.[1]

In presenting the different sources of financing for smaller companies, we look at (1) sources "close to home"—personal savings, friends and family, and credit cards; (2) bank financing, which becomes a primary financing source as the firm grows; (3) business suppliers

12-3 Sources of Funds

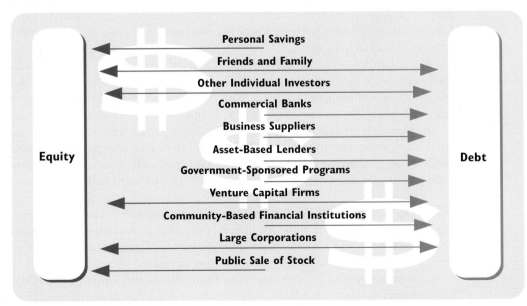

EXHIBIT

Equity / Debt

- Personal Savings
- Friends and Family
- Other Individual Investors
- Commercial Banks
- Business Suppliers
- Asset-Based Lenders
- Government-Sponsored Programs
- Venture Capital Firms
- Community-Based Financial Institutions
- Large Corporations
- Public Sale of Stock

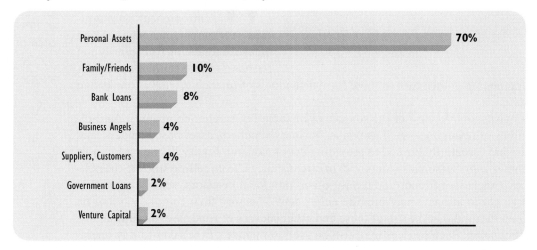

Personal Assets — 70%
Family/Friends — 10%
Bank Loans — 8%
Business Angels — 4%
Suppliers, Customers — 4%
Government Loans — 2%
Venture Capital — 2%

Source: Mike Hofman, "The Big Picture," *Inc. Magazine*, Vol. 25, No. 12 (October 2003), p. 87. Copyright 2003 by Mansueto Ventures LLC. Reproduced with permission of Mansueto Ventures LLC in the format Textbook via Copyright Clearance Center.

and asset-based lenders; (4) private equity investors; (5) the government; and (6) large companies and stock sales.

Sources Close to Home

The search for financial support usually begins close to home. The aspiring entrepreneur basically has three sources of early financing: personal savings, friends and family, and credit cards.

PERSONAL SAVINGS   It is imperative for an entrepreneur to have some personal investment in the business, which typically comes from personal savings. Indeed, personal savings is by far the most common source of equity financing used in starting a new business. With few exceptions, the entrepreneur must provide an equity base. A new business needs equity to allow for a margin of error. In its first few years, a firm can ill afford large fixed outlays for debt repayment. Also, a banker—or anyone else for that matter—is unlikely to loan venture money if the entrepreneur does not have his or her own money at risk, which is sometimes referred to as "having skin in the game."

A problem for many people who want to start a business is that they lack sufficient personal savings for this purpose. It can be very discouraging when the banker asks, "How much will you be investing in the business?" or "What do you have for collateral to secure the bank loan you want?" There is no easy solution to this problem, which is faced by an untold number of entrepreneurs. Nonetheless, many individuals who lack personal savings for a startup have found a way to accomplish their goal of owning their own company. In most cases, it required creativity and some (but not too much) risk taking as well as sometimes finding a partner who could provide the financing or friends and relatives who were willing to help.

FRIENDS AND FAMILY   Personal savings is the *primary* source of financing for most small business startups, with friends and family following in a distant second place. Exhibit 12-5 shows that friends, close family, and other relatives provide almost 80 percent of startup capital from personal sources beyond the entrepreneur's personal savings.

Entrepreneurs who acquire financing from friends and family are putting more than just their financial futures on the line—they're putting important personal relationships in jeopardy, too. "It's the highest risk money you'll ever get," says David Deeds, professor of entrepreneurship

12-5 Sources of Personal Capital for Small Firms

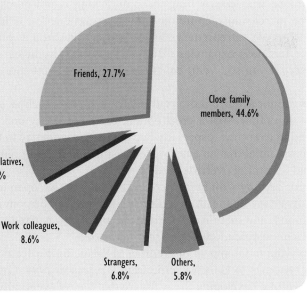

Friends, 27.7%

Close family members, 44.6%

Other relatives, 6.5%

Work colleagues, 8.6%

Strangers, 6.8%

Others, 5.8%

Source: Republished with permission of Dow Jones Inc. from Staff, "Entrepreneurship Monitor 2002," *Wall Street Journal*, August 26, 2003, p. B8; permission conveyed through Copyright Clearance Center, Inc.

at Case Western Reserve University in Cleveland, Ohio. "The venture may succeed or fail, but either way, you still have to go to Thanksgiving dinner."

At times, loans from friends or relatives may be the only available source of new financing. Such loans can often be obtained quickly, as this type of financing is based more on personal relationships than on financial analyses. *But you should accept money from a friend or relative only if that person will not be hurt financially to any significant extent if the entire amount is lost.* In other words, do not borrow money from your brother if he cannot afford the loss, much less from your grandmother's retirement savings.

Friends and relatives who provide business loans sometimes feel that they have the right to offer suggestions concerning the management of the business. And hard business times may strain the relationship. But if relatives and friends are the only available source of financing, the entrepreneur may have no other alternative. To minimize the chance of damaging important personal relationships, the entrepreneur should plan to repay such loans as soon as possible. In addition, any agreements made should be put in writing, as memories tend to become fuzzy over time. It is best to clarify expectations up front, rather than be disappointed or angry later.

Some good advice comes from James Hutcheson, president of Regeneration Partners, a Dallas, Texas–based consulting group that specializes in family-owned businesses:

> Entrepreneurs [should] approach their relatives only after they have secured investments or loans from unbiased outside sources. "Go and get matching funds," he says. "If you need $25,000, then first get $12,500 from others before asking your family for the rest. If you can't do it that way—and if you don't have your own skin in the game— then you need to think twice about why you're asking someone you love to give you money. I believe you should get others to back the idea as well, so a parent or relative doesn't feel as though the money is a gift but rather a worthwhile investment. It puts a higher level of accountability into the entire process."[2]

So, use friends and family very cautiously. Do it if necessary—and carefully and meticulously clarify expectations.

CREDIT CARDS Prior to the financial crisis that started in 2008, unsolicited offers of "free" credit cards arrived in the mail almost daily for many individuals; credit cards were available to almost anyone who was willing to apply. Using credit cards to help finance a small business became increasingly common among entrepreneurs. It has been estimated that approximately half of all entrepreneurs have used credit cards at one time or another to finance a startup or business expansion. But by 2009, the credit card companies were experiencing huge losses. Even so, credit cards remain a significant source of financing for many entrepreneurs.

For someone who cannot acquire more traditional financing, such as a bank loan, credit card financing may be an option—not a great option, but a necessary one. The interest costs can become overwhelming over time, especially because of the tendency to borrow beyond the ability to repay. So it is essential that an entrepreneur using credit card financing be extremely self-disciplined to avoid becoming overextended.

Why use credit cards? Along with being perhaps the only option open to the entrepreneur, credit cards have the advantage of speed. A lender at a bank has to be convinced of the merits of the business opportunity, and that involves extensive preparation. Credit card financing, on the other hand, requires no justification of the use of the money.

Speed was certainly the main appeal of credit card financing for Kelli Greene, who used 10 credit cards plus her savings to launch Pacific Data Designs in 1994. Greene had a day job and spent all of her downtime developing the software that would eventually become the company's hallmark product. "I had no time to talk to a bank, and I didn't want to make the effort of writing a plan," she says. The credit cards, which together accounted for about $50,000 in cash advances, funded Pacific's first 20 months. After that the company generated enough cash flow from its operations to avoid further financing.[3]

Clearly, credit cards provide an important source of financing for many entrepreneurs, particularly early in the game. But the eventual goal is to use credit cards as a method of payment and not as a source of credit. In other words, the sooner you can pay your credit card balance in full each month, the sooner you will be growing a viable business.

Bank Financing

Commercial banks are primary providers of debt capital to *established* firms. Quite simply, they want firms with proven track records and preferably plenty of collateral in the form of hard assets. Bankers are reluctant to loan money to finance losses, R&D expenses, marketing campaigns, and other "soft" assets. Such expenditures should be financed by equity sources. Nevertheless, it is wise to cultivate a relationship with a banker sooner rather than later, and well in advance of making a loan request.

4. Discuss the basic process for acquiring and structuring a bank loan.

TYPES OF LOANS Bankers primarily make business loans in one of three forms: lines of credit, term loans, and mortgages.

LINES OF CREDIT A *line of credit* is an informal agreement or understanding between the borrower and the bank as to the maximum amount of credit the bank will provide the borrower at any one time. Under this type of agreement, the bank has no legal obligation to provide the stated capital. (A similar arrangement that *does* legally commit the bank is a *revolving credit agreement.*) The entrepreneur should arrange for a line of credit in advance of an actual need because banks extend credit only in situations about which they are well informed. Attempts to obtain a loan on a spur-of-the-moment basis are generally ineffective.

line of credit
An informal agreement between a borrower and a bank as to the maximum amount of funds the bank will provide at any one time.

TERM LOANS   Under certain circumstances, banks will loan money on a 5- to 10-year term. Such *term loans* are generally used to finance equipment with a useful life corresponding to the loan's term. Since the economic benefits of investing in such equipment extend beyond a single year, banks can be persuaded to lend on terms that more closely match the cash flows to be received from the investment. For example, if equipment has a useful life of 7 years, it might be possible to repay the money needed to purchase the equipment over, say, 5 years. It would be a mistake for a firm to borrow money for a short term, such as 6 months, when the money is to be used to buy equipment that is expected to last for 7 years. *Failure to match the loan's payment terms with the expected cash inflows from the investment is a frequent cause of financial problems for small firms.* The importance of synchronizing cash inflows with cash outflows when structuring the terms of a loan cannot be overemphasized.

MORTGAGES   Mortgages, which represent a long-term source of debt capital, can be one of two types: chattel mortgages and real estate mortgages. A *chattel mortgage* is a loan for which certain items of inventory or other movable property serve as collateral. The borrower retains title to the inventory but cannot sell it without the banker's consent. A *real estate mortgage* is a loan for which real property, such as land or a building, provides the collateral. Typically, these mortgages extend over 25 or 30 years.

UNDERSTANDING A BANKER'S PERSPECTIVE

To be effective in acquiring a loan, an entrepreneur needs to understand a banker's perspective about making loans. All bankers have two fundamental concerns when they make a loan: (1) how much income the loan will provide the bank, both in interest income and in other forms of income such as fees, and (2) the likelihood that the borrower will default on the loan. A banker is not rewarded adequately to assume large amounts of risk and will, therefore, design loan agreements so as to reduce the risk to the bank.

In making a loan decision, a banker always considers the "five C's of credit": (1) the borrower's *character,* (2) the borrower's *capacity* to repay the loan, (3) the *capital* being invested in the venture by the borrower, (4) the *conditions* of the industry and economy, and (5) the *collateral* available to secure the loan. These issues are readily apparent in the six questions that Jack Griggs, a banker and long-time lender to small businesses, wants answered before he will make a loan:[4]

1. Do the purpose and amount of the loan make sense, both for the bank and for the borrower?
2. Does the borrower have strong character and reasonable ability?
3. Does the loan have a certain primary source of repayment?
4. Does the loan have a certain secondary source of repayment?
5. Can the loan be priced profitably for the customer and for the bank, and are this loan and the relationship good for both the customer and the bank?
6. Can the loan be properly structured and documented?

Obtaining a bank loan requires cultivation of a banker and personal selling. Although a banker's review of a loan request certainly includes analysis of economic and financial considerations, this analysis is best complemented by a personal relationship between the banker and the entrepreneur. This is not to say that a banker would allow personal feelings to override the facts provided by a careful loan analysis. But, after all, a banker's decision as to whether to make a loan is driven in part by the banker's confidence in the entrepreneur as a person and a professional. Intuition and subjective opinion based on past experience often play a role here.

When seeking a loan, an entrepreneur will be required to provide certain information in support of the loan request. Failure to provide such information in an effective manner will almost certainly result in rejection by the banker. Thus, the goal is not merely to present the

revolving credit agreement
A legal commitment by a bank to lend up to a maximum amount.

term loan
Money loaned for a 5- to 10-year term, corresponding to the length of time the investment will bring in profits.

chattel mortgage
A loan for which items of inventory or other movable property serve as collateral.

real estate mortgage
A long-term loan with real property held as collateral.

needed information, but to make an *effective* presentation. Providing inaccurate information or not being able to justify assumptions made in forecasting financial results is sure to make the banker question the entrepreneur's business acumen.

A well-prepared written presentation—something like a shortened version of a business plan—is helpful, if not necessary. Capturing the firm's history and future in writing suggests that the entrepreneur has given thought to where the firm has been and where it is going. As part of the presentation, the banker will want to know early on the answers to the following questions:

- How much money is needed?
- What is the venture going to do with the money?
- When is the money needed?
- When and how will the money be paid back?

An example of a written loan request is provided in Exhibit 12-6. Furthermore, a banker will want, if at all possible, to see the following detailed financial information:

- Three years of the firm's historical financial statements, if available, including balance sheets, income statements, and cash flow statements
- The firm's pro forma financial statements (balance sheets, income statements, and cash flow statements), in which the timing and amounts of the debt repayment are included as part of the forecasts
- Personal financial statements showing the borrower's net worth (net worth = assets − debt) and estimated annual income. A banker simply will not make a loan without knowing the personal financial strength of the borrower. After all, in the world of small business, the owner *is* the business.

12-6 Sample Written Loan Request

EXHIBIT

Date of Request:	December 15, 2009	
Borrower:	Prestige & DeLay, Inc.	
Amount:	$1,000,000	
Use of Proceeds:	Accounts Receivable	$400,000
	Inventory	200,000
	Marketing	100,000
	Officer loans due	175,000
	Salaries	75,000
	Contingencies	50,000
		$1,000,000
Type of Loan	Revolving Line of Credit	
Closing Date	January 3, 2010	
Term	12 months	
Rate	8.5%	
Takedown	$400,000 at closing	
	$300,000 at March 1, 2010	
	$200,000 at June 1, 2010	
	$100,000 on September 1, 2010	
Collateral	70 percent of accounts receivable under 90 days	
	50 percent of current inventory	
Guarantees	Guarantees to be provided by Prestige & DeLay	
Repayment Schedule	Principal and all accrued interest due on anniversary of note	
Source of funds for repayment	a. *Excess* cash from operations (see cash flow)	
	b. Renewable and increase of line if growth is profitable	
	c. Conversion to three-year note	
Contingency source	Sale and leaseback of equipment	

SELECTING A BANKER The wide variety of services provided by banks makes choosing a bank a critical decision. For a typical small firm, the provision of checking-account facilities and the extension of short-term (and possibly long-term) loans are the two most important services of a bank. Normally, loans are negotiated with the same bank in which the firm maintains its checking account. In addition, the firm may use the bank's safe-deposit vault or its services in collecting notes or securing credit information. An experienced banker can also provide management advice, particularly in financial matters, to a new entrepreneur.

The location factor limits the range of possible choices of banks. For convenience in making deposits and conferring about loans and other matters, a bank should be located in the same general vicinity as the firm. All banks are interested in their home communities and, therefore, tend to be sympathetic to the needs of local business firms. Except in very small communities, two or more local banks are usually available, thus permitting some freedom of choice.

Banks' lending policies are not uniform. Some bankers are extremely conservative, while others are more willing to accept some risks. If a small firm's loan application is neither obviously strong nor patently weak, its prospects for approval depend heavily on the bank's approach to small business accounts. Differences in willingness to lend have been clearly established by research studies, as well as by the practical experience of many business borrowers.

NEGOTIATING THE LOAN In negotiating a bank loan, the owner must consider the terms that will accompany the loan. Four key terms are included in all loan agreements: the interest rate, the loan maturity date, the repayment schedule, and the loan covenants.

INTEREST RATE The interest rate charged by banks is usually stated in terms of either the prime rate or the LIBOR. The *prime rate* is the rate of interest charged by banks on loans to their most creditworthy customers. The *LIBOR (London InterBank Offered Rate)* is the interest rate that London-based banks charge other banks in London, which is considerably lower than the prime rate. This rate is published each day in the *Wall Street Journal*.

If a banker quotes a rate of "prime plus 3" and the prime rate is 5 percent, the interest rate for the loan will be 8 percent. If, alternatively, the bank is willing to loan at "LIBOR plus 4" when the LIBOR is at 3 percent, then the loan rate will be 7 percent. Typically, the interest will be lower if the loan rate is tied to the LIBOR than if it is based on the prime rate. The use of the LIBOR as a base rate for determining the interest rate for a business loan developed in the late 1990s, as banks began competing more aggressively for loans.

The interest rate can be a floating rate that varies over the loan's life—that is, as the prime rate or LIBOR changes, the interest rate on the loan changes—or it can be fixed for the duration of the loan. An entrepreneur known to the authors was recently given an option to pay interest on a new loan at LIBOR plus 2, in which case the interest rate would change (float) each month as the LIBOR changed, or a fixed rate of 6 percent. At the time, the LIBOR was 3 percent. So the entrepreneur had the option of paying an interest rate of 5 percent, which could increase if the LIBOR increased, or a constant rate of 6 percent for the duration of the loan.

Although a small firm should always seek a competitive interest rate, concern about the interest rate should not override consideration of the loan's maturity date, its repayment schedule, and any loan covenants.

LOAN MATURITY DATE As already noted, a loan's term should coincide with the use of the money—short-term needs require short-term financing, while long-term needs demand long-term financing. For example, since a line of credit is intended to help a firm with only its short-term needs, it is generally limited to one year. Some banks require that a firm "clean up" a line of credit one month each year. Because such a loan can be outstanding for only 11 months, the borrower can use the money to finance seasonal needs but cannot use it to provide permanent increases in working capital, such as accounts receivable and inventory.

REPAYMENT SCHEDULE With a term loan, the loan is set to be repaid over 5 to 10 years, depending on the type of assets used for collateral. However, the banker may have the option of

prime rate
The interest rate charged by commercial banks on loans to their most creditworthy customers.

LIBOR (London InterBank Offered Rate)
The interest rate charged by London banks on loans to other London banks.

balloon payment
A very large payment
that the borrower may
be required to make
at a specified point
about halfway through
the term over which
the payments were
calculated, repaying the
rest of the loan in full.

imposing a *balloon payment*—a very large payment that the borrower is required to make at a specified point about halfway through the term over which the payments were calculated, repaying the rest of the loan in full. For instance, assume that you borrow $50,000 at an interest rate of 6 percent. If the loan were to be repaid in equal monthly payments over 7 years, the amount of each payment would be $730.[5] However, if the lender has the option of imposing a balloon payment whereby the rest of the loan comes due in full in 3 years rather than 7 years, the lender can reassess the quality of the loan and decide whether to collect the balance or to renew the loan.

LOAN COVENANTS   In addition to setting the interest rate and specifying when and how the loan is to be repaid, a bank normally imposes other restrictions, such as loan covenants, on the borrower. *Loan covenants* require certain activities (positive covenants) and limit other activities (negative covenants) of the borrower to increase the chance that the borrower will be able to repay the loan. Some types of loan covenants a borrower might encounter include the following:

loan covenants
Bank-imposed restric-
tions on a borrower that
enhance the chances of
timely repayment.

1. A bank will usually require that the business provide financial statements on a monthly basis or, at the very least, quarterly.

2. As a way to restrict a firm's management from siphoning cash out of the business, the bank may limit managers' salaries. It also may prohibit any personal loans from the business to the owners.

3. A bank may put limits on various financial ratios to make certain that a firm can handle its loan payments. For example, to ensure sufficient liquidity, the bank may require that the firm's current assets be at least twice its current liabilities (that is, current assets ÷ current liabilities must be equal to or greater than 2). Or the bank might limit the amount of debt the firm can borrow in the future, as measured by the ratio of total debt to the firm's total assets (total debt ÷ total assets).[6]

4. The borrower will normally be required to personally guarantee the firm's loan. A banker wants the right to use both the firm's assets and the owner's personal assets as collateral. If a business is structured as a corporation, the owner and the corporation are separate legal entities and the owner can escape personal liability for the firm's debts—that is, the owner has *limited liability*. However, most banks are not willing to lend money to any small business without the owner's personal guarantee as well. That's what Stephen Satterwhite, founder of Entelligence, a provider of e-business solutions, discovered when he sought financing for the firm. A banker offered to extend a $150,000 line of credit but required that the loan be secured not only by the company's assets but also by the personal assets of Satterwhite and those of an Entelligence investor and board member.[7]

limited
liability
The restriction of an
owner's legal financial
responsibilities to the
amount invested in the
business.

When Bill Bailey, owner of Cherokee Communications, a pay-phone company located in Jacksonville, Texas, borrowed money, the loan was made on certain conditions—conditions that were intended to protect the banker. If Cherokee violated these loan covenants, the loan would become due immediately—or Bailey would have to get the banker's blessing to continue operations without repaying the loan at the time. Some of the loan covenants were as follows:[8]

- Bailey, as the owner, was required to personally guarantee the loan.
- The firm had to provide monthly financial statements to the bank within 30 days of the month's end.
- There were to be no dividend payments to the owners.
- Bailey could not change the fundamental nature of the business.
- Without prior agreement, there could be no additional liens on equipment by other lenders.

- Debt could not exceed a specified amount, nor could it be greater than a specified percentage of the firm's total assets.
- Without prior approval, no assets could be sold and no acquisitions or mergers with other firms could take place.
- The proceeds of the loan could not be used for any other purpose than that designated by the bank.
- There was a limit on the amount of capital expenditures the firm could make.
- Executive compensation could not exceed a specified amount.
- The firm's net worth could not fall below a specified amount.

It is imperative that you pay close attention to the loan covenants being imposed by a banker. Ask for a list of the covenants before the closing date, and make certain that you can live with the terms. If you have an existing company, determine whether you could have complied with the covenants, especially key ratios, if the loan had been in place during the recent past. Then, if necessary, negotiate with your banker and suggest more realistic covenants. Bankers will negotiate, although they may sometimes try to convince you otherwise.

Even firms with straightforward financing needs should bear in mind that a variety of factors determine the cost of a loan, not just the interest rates and the fees a lender charges for reviewing and preparing documents.

Business Suppliers and Asset-Based Lenders

Companies that have business dealings with a new firm are possible sources of funds for financing inventory and equipment. Both wholesalers and equipment manufacturers/suppliers can provide accounts payable (trade credit) or equipment loans and leases.

5. Explain how business relationships can be used to finance a small firm.

ACCOUNTS PAYABLE (TRADE CREDIT)   Credit extended by suppliers is very important to a startup. In fact, trade (or mercantile) credit is the source of short-term funds most widely used by small firms. *Accounts payable (trade credit)* are of short duration—30 days is the customary credit period. Most commonly, this type of credit involves an unsecured, open-book account. The supplier (seller) sends merchandise to the purchasing firm; the buyer then sets up an account payable for the amount of the purchase.

accounts payable (trade credit)
Financing provided by a supplier of inventory to a given company.

The amount of trade credit available to a new company depends on the type of business and the supplier's confidence in the firm. For example, wholesale distributors of sunglasses—a very seasonal product line—often provide trade credit to retailers by granting extended payment terms on sales made at the start of a season. The sunglass retailers, in turn, sell to their customers during the season and make the bulk of their payments to the wholesalers after they have sold and collected the cash for the sunglasses. Thus, the retailer obtains cash from sales before paying the supplier. More often, however, a firm has to pay its suppliers prior to receiving cash from its customers. In fact, this can be a serious problem for many small firms, particularly those that sell to large companies. (This issue will be addressed in a discussion of asset management in Chapter 22.)

EQUIPMENT LOANS AND LEASES   Some small businesses, such as restaurants, use equipment that is purchased on an installment basis through an *equipment loan*. A down payment of 25 to 35 percent is usually required, and the contract period normally runs from

equipment loan
An installment loan from a seller of machinery used by a business.

three to five years. The equipment manufacturer or supplier typically extends credit on the basis of a conditional sales contract (or mortgage) on the equipment. During the loan period, the equipment cannot serve as collateral for another loan.

Instead of borrowing money from suppliers to purchase equipment, an increasing number of small businesses are beginning to lease equipment, especially computers, photocopiers, and fax machines. Leases typically run for 36 to 60 months and cover 100 percent of the cost of the asset being leased, with a fixed rate of interest included in the lease payments. However, manufacturers of computers and industrial machinery, working hand in hand with banks or financing companies, are generally receptive to tailoring lease packages to the particular needs of customers.

It has been estimated that 80 percent of all firms lease some or all of their business equipment. Three reasons are commonly given for the increasing popularity of leasing: (1) the firm's cash remains free for other purposes, (2) available lines of credit (a form of bank loan discussed earlier in this chapter) can be used for other purposes, and (3) leasing provides a hedge against equipment obsolescence.

While leasing is certainly an option to be considered for financing the acquisition of needed equipment, an entrepreneur should not simply assume that leasing is always the right decision. A business owner can make a good choice only after carefully comparing the interest charged on a loan to the implied interest cost of a lease, calculating the tax consequences of leasing versus borrowing, and examining the significance of the obsolescence factor. Also, the owner must be careful about contracting for so much equipment that it becomes difficult to meet installment or lease payments.

asset-based loan
A line of credit secured by working-capital assets.

ASSET-BASED LENDING

As its name implies, an *asset-based loan* is a line of credit secured primarily by assets, such as receivables, inventory, or both. The lender cushions its risk by advancing only a percentage of the value of a firm's assets—generally, 65 to 85 percent against receivables and up to 55 percent against inventory. Also, assets such as equipment (if not leased) and real estate can be used as collateral for an asset-based loan. Asset-based lending is a viable option for young, growing businesses caught in a cash flow bind.

factoring
Obtaining cash by selling accounts receivable to another firm.

Of the several categories of asset-based lending, the most frequently used is factoring. *Factoring* is an option that makes cash available to a business before accounts receivable payments are received from customers. Under this option, a factor (an entity often owned by a bank holding company) purchases the accounts receivable, advancing to the business from 70 to 90 percent of the amount of an invoice. The factor, however, has the option of refusing to advance cash on any invoice considered questionable. The factor charges a servicing fee, usually 2 percent of the value of the receivables, and an interest charge on the money advanced prior to collection of the receivables. The interest charge may range from 2 to 3 percent above the prime rate.

purchase-order financing
Lender advances the amount of the borrower's cost of goods sold for a specific customer order.

Another way to finance working capital is to sell purchase orders. With *purchase-order financing,* the lender advances the amount of the borrower's cost of goods sold for a specific customer order less a fee, typically somewhere between 3 and 8 percent. For instance, if you have a purchase order for $20,000 from a customer and your cost of goods sold for the product being sold is $12,000, the lender will advance the $12,000 less the fee charged. According to Jason Goldberg, vice president of marketing for Westgate Financial, this type of financing "attempts to address the issue of a company growing so rapidly that cash flow can't sustain growth." With a signed purchase order from a credit worthy customer, you can often get financing for almost the entire process provided your gross profit margin (gross profit ÷ sales) is at least 35 percent. Although the fee is not insignificant, it makes sense when the entrepreneur would not otherwise be able to accept an order from a large customer. In times when credit is scarce, says Goldberg, it's an opportunity "to leverage the ability to sell product."[9]

Private Equity Investors

6. Describe the two types of private equity investors that offer financing to small firms.

Over the past decade, private equity markets have been the fastest growing source of financing for entrepreneurial ventures that have potential for becoming significant businesses. For an entrepreneur, these sources fall into two categories: business angels and venture capitalists.

BUSINESS ANGELS *Business angels* are private individuals who invest in early-stage companies.[10] They are the oldest and largest source of early-stage equity capital for entrepreneurs, investing an estimated $19.2 billion in 2008, down from a record of $26 billion in 2007.[11]

business angels
Private individuals who invest in others' entrepreneurial ventures.

The term *angel* originated in the early 1900s, referring to investors on Broadway who made risky investments to support theatrical productions.[12] This type of financing has come to be known as *informal venture capital* because no established marketplace exists in which business angels regularly invest.

The majority of these individuals are self-made millionaires who have substantial business and entrepreneurial experience. Bill Payne, an experienced business angel from Las Vegas, Nevada, and Entrepreneur-in-Residence at the Kauffman Foundation, describes angels in these words:

informal venture capital
Funds provided by wealthy private individuals (business angels) to high-risk ventures.

> Angels invest time and money in startup companies. For most, making money is not the primary motive for investing. These angels have "put away their nuts" for retirement and are investing their "mad money" in entrepreneurs. They do so for a variety of reasons . . . [to] give back to their communities, [to have] the opportunity to work with entrepreneurs, to stay engaged in their retirement years and to work with fellow angels in building enterprises, to name a few. Return on investment is an important metric of their success, but not normally their primary motive for engagement.[13]

Business angels generally make investments that are relatively small—over 80 percent of business angels invest in startup firms with fewer than 20 employees. They invest locally, usually no more than 50 miles from their homes. Some limit their investments to industries in which they have had experience, while others invest in a wide variety of business sectors. For instance, Terry Stevens, a successful entrepreneur turned business angel, has invested in restaurants, a sporting goods firm, a title company, and a specialty advertising firm.

Along with providing needed money, private investors frequently contribute know-how to new businesses. Because many of these individuals invest only in the types of businesses in which they have had experience, they can be very demanding. While they are generally more "friendly" as investors than some venture capitalists, their personal relationship with the entrepreneur has little impact on their decision to invest—unlike friends and family. Thus, the entrepreneur must be careful in structuring the terms of any such investors' involvement.

The traditional way to find informal investors is through contacts with business associates, accountants, and lawyers. Other entrepreneurs are also a primary source of help in identifying prospective investors. In addition, there are now a large number of formal angel networks and angel alliances in all major cities, both in the United States and abroad. Each angel group will have its own process for evaluating the deals. For instance, some angel groups require entrepreneurs who are seeking funding to post their business plan on www.angelsoft.net. The angels then access the website to read the submitted plans. The group screens the plans and selects those entrepreneurs who will be allowed to present to the group. In most cases, individual angels make their own decisions on whether or not to invest, regardless of what the other angels do. If enough angels are interested, a detailed evaluation is undertaken before a final decision is made.[14] Central Texas Angel Network is an example of such a group; it is described on its website as follows:

> The Central Texas Angel Network (CTAN) is a not-for-profit corporation dedicated to providing quality early-stage investment opportunities for accredited Central Texas angel investors, and to assisting, educating and connecting early stage growth companies in Central Texas with information and advisors for the purpose of raising money and assisting in their growth. . . . CTAN will measure its success by the quality of deal flow, amount of dollars invested, number of companies funded and, of course, ROI [return on investment] for members.[15]

Guy Kawasaki, the founder of Garage Technology Ventures, now a venture capitalist in Silicon Valley and author of *The Art of the Start* (a must-read for anyone wanting to start a new business) offers the following suggestions about dealing with business angels:[16]

1. *Make sure the investors are accredited.* Accredited is legalese for "rich enough to never get back a penny." You can get into trouble for selling stock to the proverbial little old lady in Florida, so don't.

2. *Make sure they're sophisticated investors.* Sophisticated angel investors have knowledge and expertise in your industry—they'll have "been there and done that." Sure, you want angels' money, but you also want their expertise.

3. *Don't underestimate them.* The days of angel investors as easy marks are gone forever—if they ever existed. And angels care as much about [how they will get their money back] as venture capitalists do—maybe even more because they're investing their personal, after-tax money.

4. *Understand their motivation.* Angel investors differ from venture capitalists because typically, angel investors have a double bottom line. They've made it, so they want to pay back society by helping the next generation of entrepreneurs. Thus, they're often willing to invest in less proven, riskier deals to help entrepreneurs get to the next stage.

5. *Enable them to live vicariously.* One of the rewards of angel investing is the ability to live vicariously through an entrepreneur's efforts. Angels want to relive the thrills of entrepreneurship, while avoiding the firing line. They enjoy helping you, so seek their guidance frequently.

6. *Make your story comprehensible to the angel's spouse.* The usual membership of an angel's "decision-making committee" consists of one person: a spouse. So, if you've got a "client-server open source OPML carrier class enterprise software" product, you must make it comprehensible to the angel's husband when he asks, "What are we investing $100,000 in?"

7. *Sign up people the angel has heard of.* Angel investors are also motivated by the social aspect of investing with buddies in startups run by bright people who are changing the world. If you get one of these guys or gals, you're likely to attract a whole flock of other angels, too.

8. *Be nice.* Not infrequently, angel investors fall in love with entrepreneurs. The entrepreneurs may remind the investors of their sons or daughters, or even fill the position of the sons or daughters they never had. Venture capitalists will sometimes invest in a schmuck as long as that schmuck is a proven moneymaker. If you're seeking angel capital, then you're probably not a proven moneymaker, so you can't get away with acting like a schmuck. Be nice until you are proven—although I hope that even when you are proven, you'll still be a mensch.

VENTURE CAPITAL FIRMS   In addition to business angels who provide *informal* venture capital, small businesses also may seek out *formal venture capitalists*, groups of individuals who form limited partnerships for the purpose of raising capital from large institutional

formal venture capitalists
Individuals who form limited partnerships for the purpose of raising venture capital from large institutional investors.

LIVING THE DREAM:

entrepreneurial challenges

On the Hunt

Finding investors for your business is all about targeting the right people. Rob Brown doesn't have a rich uncle. So when the 41-year-old co-founder, president and CEO of Healionics Corp. in Redmond, Washington, needed to raise money, he started networking to find wealthy individuals who might invest in his biomaterials company.

An entrepreneur in one of his MBA courses at the University of Washington, Seattle, suggested he try pitching local angel groups. So Brown presented at a meeting for Seattle's Alliance of Angels, an angel group focused on early-stage companies in the Pacific Northwest. A member of the group who is the former CEO of a local biomaterials firm invested in Healionics' initial $200,000 funding round. Later, when Healionics held an invitation-only investor soiree, it attracted another major investor. Healionics was founded last year and already projects 2008 sales of more than $500,000.

As Healionics' success shows, you don't need wealthy friends or family members to find investors for your business. Knox Massey, managing director of Atlanta Technology Angels, says wealthy investors used to be mostly lone-wolf types, but now most belong to at least one individual-investors group. Massey advises researching individual investors and groups to get a sense of the business sectors they like to fund. Be sure to pitch any relevant experience your management team has in your company's sector. Also, have a concise, appealing story, says Joe Rubin, director of FundingPost.com. "Our tag line," says Brown, "is that we are the Gore-Tex of biomaterials."

Source: Carol Tice, "On the Hunt," *Entrepreneur*, March 2008, http://www.entrepreneur.com/magazine/entrepreneur/2008/march/190064.html, accessed April 2, 2009.

http://www.healionics.com

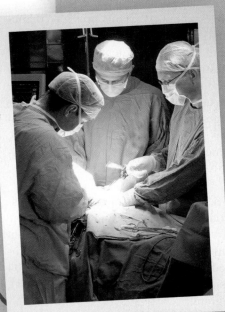

© Brasiliao/shutterstock.com 2009

investors, such as pension plans and university endowments. Within the group, a venture capitalist serves as the general partner, with other investors constituting the limited partners. As limited partners, such investors have the benefit of limited liability.

The venture capitalist raises a predetermined amount of money, called a *fund*. Once the money has been committed by the investors, the venture capitalist screens and evaluates investment opportunities in high-potential startups and existing firms. For example, the Sevin Rosen Funds in Dallas, Texas, raised $600 million for the Sevin Rosen Fund VIII. The money was then used to invest in a portfolio of companies.

For the investment, the venture capitalist receives the right to own a percentage of the entrepreneur's business. Reaching agreement on the exact percentage of ownership often involves considerable negotiation. The primary issues are the firm's expected profits in future years and the venture capitalist's required rate of return. Once an investment has been made, the venture capitalist carefully monitors the company, usually through a representative who serves on the firm's board.

Most often, investments by venture capitalists take the form of preferred stock that can be converted to common stock if the investor so desires. In this way, venture capitalists ensure themselves senior claim over the owners and other equity investors in the event the firm is liquidated, but they can convert to stock and participate in the increased value of the business if it is successful. These investors generally try to limit the length of their investment to between 5 and 7 years, though it is frequently closer to 10 years before they are able to cash out.

Although venture capital as a source of financing receives significant coverage in the business media, *few small companies, especially startups, ever receive this kind of funding*. No more than 1 or 2 percent of the business plans received by any venture capitalist are eventually funded—not exactly an encouraging statistic. Failure to receive funding from a venture capitalist, however, does not indicate that the venture lacks potential. Often, the venture is simply not a good fit for the investor. So, before trying to compete for venture capital financing, an entrepreneur should assess whether the firm and the management team are a good fit for a particular investor.

The Government

Several government programs provide financing to small businesses. Over the past decade, federal and state governments have allocated increasing, but still limited, amounts of money to financing new businesses. Local governments have likewise increased their involvement in providing financial support to startups in their areas. Though funds are available, they are not always easy to acquire. Time and patience on the part of the entrepreneur are required. Let's take a look at some of the more familiar government loan programs offered by various agencies.

7. Distinguish among the different government loan programs available to small companies.

THE SMALL BUSINESS ADMINISTRATION   The federal government has a long history of helping new businesses get started, primarily through the programs and agencies of the Small Business Administration (SBA). For the most part, the SBA does not loan money, but rather serves as a guarantor of loans made by financial institutions. The five primary SBA programs are the 7(a) Loan Guaranty Program, the Certified Development Company (CDC) 504 Loan Program, the 7(m) Microloan Program, small business investment companies (SBICs), and the Small Business Innovative Research (SBIR) Program.

7(a) Loan Guaranty Program
Loan program that helps small companies obtain financing through a guaranty provided by the SBA.

THE 7(A) LOAN GUARANTY PROGRAM   The *7(a) Loan Guaranty Program* serves as the SBA's primary business loan program to help qualified small businesses obtain financing when they might not be eligible for business loans through normal lending channels. Guaranty loans are made by private lenders, usually commercial banks, and may be for as much as $750,000. The SBA guarantees 90 percent of loans not exceeding $155,000. For loans exceeding $155,000, the guaranty percentage is 85 percent. To obtain a guaranty loan, a small business must submit a loan application to a lender, such as a bank. After an initial review, the lender forwards the application to the SBA. Once the loan has been approved by the SBA, the lender disburses the funds. The loan proceeds can be used for working capital, machinery and equipment, furniture and fixtures, land and building, leasehold improvements, and debt refinancing (under special conditions). Loan maturity is up to 10 years for working capital and generally up to 25 years for fixed assets.

Certified Development Company (CDC) 504 Loan Program
SBA loan program that provides long-term financing for small businesses to acquire real estate or machinery and equipment.

THE CERTIFIED DEVELOPMENT COMPANY (CDC) 504 LOAN PROGRAM   The *Certified Development Company (CDC) 504 Loan Program* provides long-term, fixed-rate financing to small businesses to acquire real estate or machinery and equipment for expansion or modernization. The lender in this instance is a certified development company, which is financed by the SBA. The borrower must provide 10 percent of the cost of the property, with the remaining amount coming from a bank and a certified development company funded by the SBA.

THE 7(M) MICROLOAN PROGRAM   The *7(m) Microloan Program* grants short-term loans of up to $35,000 to small businesses and not-for-profit child-care centers for working capital or the purchase of inventory, supplies, furniture, fixtures, and machinery and equipment. The SBA makes or guarantees a loan to an intermediary, which in turn makes the microloan to the applicant. As an added benefit, the lender provides business training and support programs to its microloan borrowers.

SMALL BUSINESS INVESTMENT COMPANIES   *Small business investment companies (SBICs)* are privately owned banks that provide long-term loans and/or equity capital to small businesses. SBICs are licensed and regulated by the SBA, from which they frequently obtain a substantial part of their capital at attractive rates of interest. SBICs invest in businesses with fewer than 500 employees, a net worth of no more than $18 million, and after-tax income not exceeding $6 million during the two most recent years.

THE SMALL BUSINESS INNOVATIVE RESEARCH (SBIR) PROGRAM   The *Small Business Innovative Research (SBIR) program* helps finance small firms that plan to transform laboratory research into marketable products. Eligibility for the program is based less on the potential profitability of a venture than on the likelihood that the firm will provide a product of interest to a particular federal agency.

STATE AND LOCAL GOVERNMENT ASSISTANCE
State and local governments have become more active in financing new businesses. The nature of the financing varies, but each program is generally geared to augment other sources of funding. Several examples of such programs follow:

1. The city government of Des Moines, Iowa, established the Golden Circle Loan Guarantee Fund to guarantee bank loans of up to $250,000 to small companies.
2. The state of Texas will provide up to $500,000 of debt financing in its emerging technologies fund (ETF).
3. Rhode Island offers financing programs tied to job growth.
4. The New Jersey Economic Development Authority makes loans to business owners at the U.S. Treasury rate, significantly lower than interest rates typically charged at banks.
5. The Colorado Housing and Finance Authority makes loans for equipment and real estate with down payments as low as 15 percent and up to 20 years to repay the loan.

Most of these loans are made in conjunction with a bank, which enables the bank to take on riskier loans for entrepreneurs who might not qualify for traditional financing. "And some loans have a lower down payment requirement," explains Donna Holmes, former director of the Penn State Small Business Development Center in University Park. "The bank may do 50 percent, the state program another 40 percent, and the borrower only has to come up with 10 percent; with a straight bank loan, the bank might be looking for 20 percent or 25 percent."[17]

While such government programs may be attractive to an entrepreneur, they are frequently designed to enhance specific industries or to facilitate certain community goals. Consequently, you need to determine that a program is in sync with your specific business objectives.

COMMUNITY-BASED FINANCIAL INSTITUTIONS
Community-based financial institutions are lenders that serve low-income communities and receive funds from federal, state, and private sources. They are increasingly becoming a source of financing for small companies that otherwise would have little or no access to startup funding. Typically, community-based lenders provide capital to businesses that are unable to attract outside investors but do have the potential to make modest profits, serve the community, and create jobs. An example of a community-based financial institution is the Delaware Valley Reinvestment Fund, which provides financing for small companies in Philadelphia's inner-city area.

7(m) Microloan Program
SBA loan program that provides short-term loans of up to $35,000 to small businesses and not-for-profit child-care centers.

small business investment companies (SBICs)
Privately owned banks, regulated by the Small Business Administration, that provide long-term loans and/or equity capital to small businesses.

Small Business Innovative Research (SBIR) program
A government program that helps to finance companies that plan to transform laboratory research into marketable products.

community-based financial institution
A lender that uses funds from federal, state, and private sources to provide financing to small businesses in low-income communities.

Where Else to Look

The sources of financing that have been described thus far represent the primary avenues for obtaining money for small firms. The remaining sources are generally of less importance but should not be ignored by an entrepreneur in search of financing.

8. Explain when large companies and public stock offerings can be sources of financing.

LARGE CORPORATIONS   Large corporations at times make funds available for investment in smaller firms when it is in their self-interest to maintain a close relationship with such a firm. Larger firms are now becoming even more involved in providing financing and technical assistance to smaller businesses. For instance, some large high-tech firms prefer to invest in smaller firms that are conducting research of interest, rather than conduct the research themselves.

Coca-Cola is a good example of a large corporation that invests in smaller firms. The purpose of the investments is to develop technologies that would benefit operations such as bottling and distribution. Coca-Cola also hopes to profit when the companies go public. The program—involving a wholly owned subsidiary called Fizzion—is part of a push to make Coca-Cola more innovative. By involving employees in startups, the company can give managers "a real sense for what it's like to move against deadlines of time and money," says Fizzion CEO Chris Lowe. Although large companies also face those issues, they're "not of the same character or ilk" as in a startup, Lowe says.[18]

STOCK SALES   Another way to obtain capital is by selling stock to outside individual investors through either private placement or public sale. Finding outside stockholders can be difficult when a new firm is not known and has no ready market for its securities, however. In most cases, a business must have a history of profitability before its stock can be sold successfully.

Whether it is best to raise outside equity financing depends on the firm's long-range prospects. If there is opportunity for substantial expansion on a continuing basis and if other sources are inadequate, the owner may logically decide to bring in other owners. Owning part of a larger business may be more profitable than owning all of a smaller business.

private placement
The sale of a firm's capital stock to selected individuals.

PRIVATE PLACEMENT   One way to sell common stock is through A *private placement*, in which the firm's stock is sold to selected individuals—usually the firm's employees, the owner's acquaintances, members of the local community, customers, and suppliers. When a stock sale is restricted to private placement, an entrepreneur can avoid many of the demanding requirements of the securities laws.

initial public offering (IPO)
The issuance of stock that is to be traded in public financial markets.

PUBLIC SALE   When small firms—typically, *larger* small firms—make their stock available to the general public, this is called going public, or making an *initial public offering (IPO)*. The reason often cited for a public sale is the need for additional working capital.

In undertaking a public sale of its stock, a small firm subjects itself to greater governmental regulation, which escalated dramatically following the rash of corporate scandals in publicly owned companies such as Enron, Tyco, and WorldCom. In response to corporate malfeasance in recent years, the U.S. Congress passed legislation, including the Sarbanes-Oxley Act, to monitor public companies more carefully. This has resulted in a significant increase in the cost of being a publicly traded company—especially for small firms. Also, publicly traded firms are required to report their financial results quarterly in 10Q reports and annually in 10K reports to the Securities and Exchange Commission (SEC). The SEC carefully scrutinizes these reports before they can be made available to the public. At times, the SEC requirements can be very burdensome.

Common stock may also be sold to underwriters, which guarantee the sale of securities. Compensation and fees paid to underwriters typically make the sale of securities in this manner expensive. Fees frequently range from 20 to 25 percent of the value of the total stock issue—or even higher. The reason for the high costs is, of course, the elements of uncertainty and risk associated with public offerings of the stock of small, relatively unknown firms.

LIVING THE DREAM:

entrepreneurial experiences

Micro-Business Loans as a Financing Source

When barber Cedric Tillis decided to open His Place Hair Studio in Marietta, Georgia, in 2002, he inquired about getting a loan from a conventional bank but soon realized that he'd need to find other funding sources. "I did a little research on small business loans, but I didn't think I'd be a good candidate. First, my business was a startup, and second, I didn't have any collateral," Tillis says.

Many beginning entrepreneurs face Tillis' situation, but Bob Anderson, a business loan officer with Alternatives Federal Credit Union in Ithaca, New York, says there are other affordable options. "Don't stop at the first rejection or negative reaction, and don't immediately go to credit card financing," he says. "It's worth the time and effort to search out a lender in your community that has a micro-loan business program."

Micro-loans are defined by the Small Business Administration (SBA) as an amount of $35,000 or less, and they often come packaged with business education, something that's crucial for new entrepreneurs. If you know where to find them and what their requirements are, you have a better chance of getting your fair share.

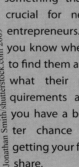

© Jonathan Smith/shutterstock.com 2009

"To find a lender, look at some of the nontraditional, micro-enterprise development organizations," says Leslie Ackerman, director of Alternatives' Business CENTS small business development program. "The Association for Enterprise Opportunity (AEO) is the main nationwide micro-loan support group. You can search their Website (www.microenterpriseworks.org) for AEO members listed by state. Many of these organizations offer business training, too."

"I didn't know there were so many doors open to me when I was starting out," says Tillis. "I felt like I was a man alone in the process." In addition to contacting the AEO, contact your local SBA office (www.sba.gov) to find additional regional resources.

Micro-loans shouldn't be used to cover up fundamental business problems. "Lately, I've seen a trend of a lot of businesses looking for short-term capital because they're feeling pinched in this economy, and the bills are piling up," Ackerman says. "But if you use a loan as a Band-Aid for an ongoing problem, it could turn into a crisis down the road."

Owners can avoid this by making sure they know how to read their financial statements and can anticipate rough times. "No matter where my funding comes from, I know I still have to save money, plan and prepare when managing the shop," Tillis says.

Source: Margarette Burnette, "Alternate Funding Sources: Micro-Loans: What They Are, How to Get Them, www.blackenterprise.com, accessed March 15, 2009.

We have now completed our discussion of what an entrepreneur needs to understand when seeking financing for a company, in terms of a firm's financial statements and forecasts (Chapters 10 and 11) and the different sources of financing typically used by small firms (Chapter 12). We hope that our detailed explanations will help you avoid mistakes commonly made by entrepreneurs when trying to get financing to grow a business.

LOOKING BACK

1. Describe how the nature of a firm affects its financing sources.

- There are four basic factors that determine how a firm is financed: (1) the firm's economic potential, (2) the size and maturity of the company, (3) the nature of the firm's assets, and (4) the personal preferences of the owners as they consider the tradeoffs between debt and equity.

- An entrepreneurial firm that has high growth potential has many more possible sources of financing than does a firm that provides a good lifestyle for the owner but little in the way of attractive returns to investors.

- The size and maturity of a company have a direct bearing on the types of financing that are available.

- Tangible assets serve as great collateral when a business is requesting a bank loan; intangible assets have little value as collateral.

2. Evaluate the choice between debt financing and equity financing.

- Choosing between debt and equity financing involves tradeoffs with regard to potential profitability, financial risk, and voting control.

- Borrowing money rather than issuing common stock (ownership equity) creates the potential for higher rates of return to the owners and allows the owners to retain voting control of the company, but it also exposes the owners to greater financial risk.

- Issuing common stock rather than borrowing money results in lower potential rates of return to the owners and the loss of some voting control, but it does reduce their financial risk.

3. Identify the typical sources of financing used at the outset of a new venture.

- The aspiring entrepreneur basically has three sources of early financing: (1) personal savings, (2) friends and family, and (3) credit cards.

- Personal savings is the primary source of equity financing used in starting a new business; a banker or other lender is unlikely to loan venture money if the entrepreneur does not have his or her own money at risk.

- Loans from friends and family may be the only available source of financing and are often easy and fast to obtain, though such borrowing can place the entrepreneur's most important personal relationships in jeopardy.

- Credit card financing provides easily accessible financing, but with high interest costs that may become overwhelming at times.

- Only if these sources are inadequate will the entrepreneur turn to more formal channels of financing, such as banks and outside investors.

4. Discuss the basic process for acquiring and structuring a bank loan.

- Bankers primarily make business loans in one of three forms: lines of credit, term loans, and mortgages.

- In making a loan decision, a banker always considers the "five C's of credit": (1) the borrower's *character*, (2) the borrower's *capacity* to repay the loan, (3) the *capital* being invested in the venture by the borrower, (4) the *conditions* of the industry and economy, and (5) the *collateral* available to secure the loan.

- Obtaining a bank loan requires cultivating a relationship with a banker and personal selling, including a presentation that addresses (1) how much money is needed, (2) what the venture is going to do with the money, (3) when the money is needed, and (4) when and how the money will be paid back.

- Other detailed financial information might be requested, including three years of the firm's historical financial statements, the firm's pro forma financial statements, and personal financial statements showing the borrower's net worth and estimated annual income.

- An entrepreneur should carefully evaluate available banks before choosing one, basing the decision on factors such as the bank's location, the extent of services provided, and the bank's lending policies.

- In negotiating a bank loan, the owner must consider the accompanying terms, which typically include the interest rate, the loan maturity date, the repayment schedule, and the loan covenants.

5. Explain how business relationships can be used to finance a small firm.

- Business suppliers can offer trade credit (accounts payable), which is the source of short-term funds most widely used by small firms.

- Suppliers also offer equipment loans and leases, which allow small businesses to use equipment purchased on an installment basis.

- Asset-based lending is financing secured by working capital assets, such as accounts receivable and inventory.

6. Describe the two types of private equity investors that offer financing to small firms.

- Business angels are private individuals, generally having moderate to significant business experience, who invest in others' entrepreneurial ventures.

- Formal venture capitalists are groups of individuals who form limited partnerships for the purpose of raising capital from large institutional investors, such as pension plans and university endowments.

- Community-based financial institutions are lenders that use funds from federal, state, and private sources to serve low-income communities and small companies that otherwise would have little or no access to startup funding.

7. *Distinguish among the different government loan programs available to small companies.*

- The federal government helps new businesses get started through the programs and agencies of the Small Business Administration (SBA), which include the 7(a) Loan Guaranty Program, the Certified Development Company (CDC) 504 Loan Program, the 7(m) Microloan Program, small business investment companies (SBICs), and the Small Business Innovative Research (SBIR) Program.

- State and local governments finance new businesses in varying manners, though programs are generally geared to augmenting other sources of funding.

8. *Explain when large companies and public stock offerings can be sources of financing.*

- Large companies may finance smaller businesses when it is in their self-interest to have a close relationship with the smaller company.

- Stock sales, in the form of either private placements or public sales, may provide a few high-potential ventures with equity capital.

Key Terms

return on assets p. 314
return on equity p. 314
line of credit p. 320
revolving credit agreement p. 321
term loan p. 321
chattel mortgage p. 321
real estate mortgage p. 321
prime rate p. 323
LIBOR (London Interbank Offered Rate) p. 323
balloon payment p. 324
loan covenants p. 324

limited liability p. 324
accounts payable (trade credit) p. 325
equipment loan p. 325
asset-based loan p. 326
factoring p. 326
purchase-order financing p. 326
business angels p. 327
informal venture capital p. 327
formal venture capitalists p. 328
7(a) Loan Guaranty Program p. 330

Certified Development Company (CDC) 504 Loan Program p. 330
7(m) Microloan Program p. 331
small business investment companies (SBICs) p. 331
Small Business Innovative Research (SBIR) Program p. 331
community-based financial institution p. 331
private placement p. 332
initial public offering (IPO) p. 332

Discussion Questions

1. How does the nature of a business affect its sources of financing?

2. How is debt different from equity?

3. Explain the three tradeoffs that guide the choice between debt financing and equity financing.

4. Assume that you are starting a business for the first time. What do you believe are the greatest personal obstacles to obtaining funds for the new venture? Why?

5. If you were starting a new business, where would you start looking for capital?

6. Explain how trade credit and equipment loans can provide initial capital funding.

7. a. Describe the different types of loans made by a commercial bank.

   b. What does a banker need to know in order to decide whether to make a loan?

8. Distinguish between informal venture capital and formal venture capital.

9. In what ways does the federal government help with initial financing for small businesses?

10. What advice would you give an entrepreneur who was trying to finance a startup?

SITUATION 1

David Bernstein needs help financing his Lodi, New Jersey–based Access Direct Inc., a six-year-old $3.5 million company. "We're ready to get to the next level," says Bernstein, "but we're not sure which way to go." Access Direct spruces up and then sells used computer equipment for corporations; it is looking for up to $2 million in order to expand. "Venture capitalists, individual investors, or banks," says Bernstein, who owns the company with four partners, "we've thought about them all."

Question 1 What is your impression of Bernstein's perspective on raising capital to "get to the next level"?

Question 2 What advice would you offer Bernstein as to both appropriate and inappropriate sources of financing in his situation?

SITUATION 2

John Dalton is well on his way to starting a new venture—Max, Inc. He has projected a need for $350,000 in initial capital. He plans to invest $150,000 himself and either borrow the additional $200,000 or find a partner who will buy stock in the company. If Dalton borrows the money, the interest rate will be 6 percent. If, on the other hand, another equity investor is found, he expects to have to give up 60 percent of the company's stock. Dalton has forecasted earnings of about 16 percent in operating profits on the firm's total assets.

Question 1 Compare the two financing options in terms of projected return on the owner's equity investment. Ignore any effect from income taxes.

Question 2 What if Dalton is wrong and the company earns only 4 percent in operating profits on total assets?

Question 3 What should Dalton consider in choosing a source of financing?

SITUATION 3

Steve Mack is the president of Griggs Products, a metal stamper based in San Antonio, Texas. Mack has a long-term relationship with his banker. But recently his firm ran into financial difficulty, and the bank is demanding that Mack personally guarantee 100 percent of the company's loans. Mack would prefer not to do so, but isn't sure that he has a choice.

Question 1 Should Mack be surprised by the bank's demand for a personal guarantee? Why or why not?

Question 2 What would you advise Mack to do?

Experiential Exercises

1. Interview a local small business owner to determine how funds were obtained to start the business. Be sure you phrase questions so that they are not overly personal, and do not ask for specific dollar amounts. Write a brief report on your findings.

2. Interview a local banker about lending policies for small business loans. Ask the banker to comment on the importance of a business plan to the bank's decision to loan money to a small business. Write a brief report on your findings.

3. Review recent issues of *Entrepreneur* or *Inc. Magazine,* and report to the class on the financing arrangements of firms featured in these magazines.

4. Interview a stockbroker or investment analyst on his or her views regarding the sale of common stock by a small business. Write a brief report on your findings.

Small Business & Entrepreneurship Resource Center

The *Small Business and Entrepreneurship Resource Center* offers complete small business management resources through a comprehensive database that covers all major areas of starting, operating, and maintaining a business from financing, management, marketing, accounting, taxes, and more. Use the access code that came with your new book to access the site and perform the exercises in each chapter.

1. Managing your debt is a very important aspect of any business. Many small business owners commonly look first at the interest rate for a loan as being most

important. The article "SBA Lending Programs" discusses the "seven truths" of lending. Describe and provide rational for whether the term of the loan (length of the loan or amortization) is more important than the interest rate, especially concerning the impact on cash flow for a business.

2. The text mentions several high-profile angel investors, such as Bill Payne, of the Kauffman Foundation, Terry Stevens, and Guy Kawasaki, the founder of garage.

com. Angel investors can actually be found anywhere, but it does require preparation to successful utilize them as a resource. Describe in detail three things you can do to prepare to use angel investors.

Sources: Advice from on high: finding angel money doesn't have to take a miracle. (2005 ENTREPRENEUR'S Toolkit: FINANCE). Sara Lepro. *Inside Business* 7, 8 (August 2005): pTK7(2).
SBA lending programs': "the seven truths". (INTERNATIONAL FRANCHISE EXPO AND EXHIBITOR GUIDE) (evaluation of Small Business Administration lending programmes). Rick Anderson. *Franchising World* 38, 5 (May 2006): p. 22(3).

Video Case 12

MY OWN MONEY (P. 649)

This case discusses the types of funding used by many entrepreneurs when starting a business; it specifically looks at the use of personal funding and borrowed funding and their use in bootstrap financing.

ALTERNATIVE CASES FOR CHAPTER 12

Case 11, Missouri Solvents, p. 646

The Business Plan: Laying the Foundation

As part of laying the foundation for your own business plan, respond to the following questions regarding the financing of your venture:

1. What is the total financing required to start the business?

2. How much money do you plan to invest in the venture? What is the source of this money?

3. Will you need financing beyond what you personally plan to invest?

4. If additional financing is needed for the startup, how will you raise it? How will the financing be structured—debt or equity? What will the terms be for the investors?

5. According to your pro forma financial statements, will there be a need for additional financing within the first five years of the firm's life? If so, where will it come from?

6. How and when will you arrange for investors to cash out of their investment?

13

Planning for the Harvest

In the SPOTLIGHT
Letting Go Is Never Easy

When Jay Butera told his accountant that he wanted to sell his business, the accountant was not surprised.

"You can sell," my accountant told me, "but I doubt you can walk away for long. Guys like you can't stop. You sell everything, lie on the beach for a year, then get so bored you jump right back in with another business. I see it all the time."

I didn't believe a word of it. I was different. Boredom a problem? Boredom sounded wonderful! "Trust me," I told him. "I can quit anytime."

"Spoken like a true addict," he said.

In the summer of 2003, I sold the company to a group of individual investors and signed papers that would, I thought, change my life. I had no regrets when I walked away. For the first time in decades I felt peace.

Just to be certain that I was really free, after the deal closed I drove 100 miles to the beach, walked to the end of the jetty, and hurled my cell phone into the Atlantic Ocean with a vengeance that twisted my shoulder. It was glorious. I made plans to stay at the shore and do absolutely nothing.

Peace, however, proved fleeting. "Is this all we're doing today?" I began to think. Envy followed, as I thought about new owners running my company. Would they do it better than I had? All this after just a few days in the sand.

Now here's the really sick part: A week later, on a beautiful morning with my wife and kids on the beach, I slipped away, found an Internet café, jumped online for a few hours, and started a new company.

The business plan flowed way too easily, as if my subconscious mind had been developing it all along. Dr. Jekyll was kicking back, but Mr. Hyde was planning the next product launch. I couldn't bring myself to tell my wife what I'd done, but that night she remarked that I looked happier.

So here I stand, at the beginning of the entrepreneurial circle, starting my second lap. I am loving it and cursing it daily. I guess it's just what I do. You can't change who you are just by signing a few documents. And, yes, I did buy another cell phone.

Source: Jay Butera, "Addicted to Startups," *Fortune Small Business*, October 2006, p. 101.

LOOKING AHEAD
AFTER STUDYING THIS CHAPTER, YOU SHOULD BE ABLE TO

1. Explain the importance of having a harvest, or exit, plan.
2. Describe the options available for harvesting.
3. Explain the issues in valuing a firm that is being harvested and deciding on the method of payment.
4. Provide advice on developing an effective harvest plan.

In previous chapters, we have talked about recognizing business opportunities and developing strategies for capturing these opportunities. Such activities represent the cornerstone for everything a company does. But, for entrepreneurs, that's not the end of the story. Experience suggests that an entrepreneur developing a company strategy should think about more than just starting (founding or acquiring) and growing a business; the entrepreneurial process is not complete until the owners and any other investors have exited the venture and captured the value created by the business. This final—but extremely important—phase can be enhanced through an effective harvest, or exit, plan. In other words, the goal is to create value during the entrepreneurial journey by making a difference and then *to finish well!*

The Importance of the Harvest

Most entrepreneurs do not like to think about the harvest, even though few events in the life of an entrepreneur, and of the firm itself, are more significant. Consequently, the decision to harvest is frequently the result of an unexpected event, possibly a crisis, rather than a well-conceived strategy.

1. Explain the importance of having a harvest, or exit, plan.

Harvesting—or *exiting*, as it is frequently called—is the method entrepreneurs and investors use to get out of a business and, ideally, reap the value of their investment in the firm. Many entrepreneurs successfully grow their businesses but fail to develop effective harvest plans. As a result, they are unable to capture the full value of the business they have worked so hard to create.

An entrepreneur needs to understand that harvesting encompasses more than merely selling and leaving a business; it involves capturing value (cash flows), reducing risk, and creating future options—the reason we prefer the term *harvest* over *exit*. In addition, there are personal, nonfinancial considerations for the entrepreneur. An owner may receive a lot of money for the firm but still be disappointed with the harvest if he or she is not prepared for a change in lifestyle. Thus, carefully designing an intentional harvest strategy is as essential to an entrepreneur's personal success as it is to his or her financial success.

The word *success* has different meanings for different people. In this chapter, we offer suggestions for achieving a "successful" harvest. It is a mistake to define success only in terms of the harvest; there should also be success in the entrepreneurial journey. So, throughout the chapter, we encourage you to think about what *success* means to you. Arriving at the end of the journey only to discover that your ladder was leaning against the wrong wall is one of life's tragedies.

The harvest is vitally important to a firm's investors as well as to its founder. Investors who provide high-risk capital—particularly angels and venture capitalists—generally insist on a well-thought-out harvest strategy. They realize that it is easy to put money into a business, but difficult to get it out. As a result, a firm's appeal to investors is driven, in part, by the availability of harvest options. If investors are not convinced that opportunities will exist for harvesting their investment, there will most likely be no investment.

Methods of Harvesting a Business

The four basic ways to harvest an investment in a privately owned company are (1) selling the firm, (2) releasing the firm's cash flows to its owners, (3) offering stock to the public through an initial public offering (IPO), and (4) issuing a private placement of the stock. These options are shown graphically in Exhibit 13-1.

2. Describe the options available for harvesting.

EXHIBIT

13-1 Methods for Harvesting a Business

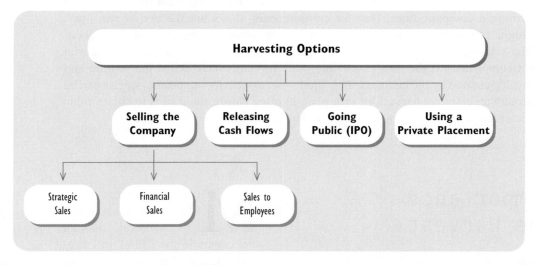

Selling the Firm

In any harvest strategy, the financial questions associated with the sale of a firm include how to value the firm and how to structure the payment for the business. Most frequently, an entrepreneur's motivation for selling a company relates to retirement and estate planning and a desire to diversify her or his portfolio of investments.

Sale transactions can, for all practical purposes, be reduced to three types, based on the motives of the buyers: sales to strategic buyers, sales to financial buyers, and sales to employees. A strategic buyer looks for synergies that can be gained by combining two or more firms, a financial buyer is more often interested in the firm as a stand-alone business, and an employee buyer is primarily concerned about preserving employment and participating in the success of the business. Let's consider each type of transaction in more detail.

SALES TO STRATEGIC BUYERS   Strategic buyers value a business based on the synergies they think they can create by combining the acquired firm with another related business. Since the value of a business to a buyer is derived from both its stand-alone characteristics and its synergies, strategic buyers often will pay a higher price than will financial buyers, who value the business only as a stand-alone entity. Thus, in strategic acquisitions, the critical issue is the degree of strategic fit between the firm to be harvested and the potential buyer's other business interests. If the prospective buyer is a current rival and if the acquisition would provide long-term, sustainable competitive advantages (such as lower cost of production or superior product quality), the buyer may be willing to pay a premium for the company.

SALES TO FINANCIAL BUYERS   Unlike strategic buyers, buyers in financial acquisitions look primarily to a firm's stand-alone, cash-generating potential as its source of value. Often, the value a financial buyer hopes to tap depends on stimulating future sales growth, reducing costs, or both. This fact has an important implication for the owner of the business being purchased. The buyer often will make changes in the firm's operations that translate into greater pressures on the firm's personnel, resulting in layoffs that the current owner might find objectionable. As a result, financial acquisitions are not popular among many small business owners.

How I see it: Scott Salmans on Selling a Business

While you may be an expert at running your business, it is highly unlikely this also makes you an expert at selling a business. I highly recommend finding a reputable partner with the right expertise to assist in selling your business.

It is true that most investment bankers and business brokers don't provide their services for free; but you will more than recoup their fee in the final selling price of the company if they do their job properly. Before selling my company, I received more business sales inquiry letters than any other solicitation from "business brokers" with "partners" interested in buying my business. However, I chose to seek out my own investment banker through a series of interviews of companies referred to me by trusted advisors.

Understand that the fee is negotiable. Don't pay too much cash up front. Also, look for a match with bankers or brokers that specialize in industries and businesses of certain sizes. Be sure to find the right match, or you may end up paying much too much for a service you could have done better without.

In earlier years, the *leveraged buyout (LBO)*, a financial acquisition involving a very high level of debt financing, became synonymous with the *bust-up LBO*, in which the new owners pay the debt down rapidly by selling off the acquired firm's assets. Frequently, acquisitions were financed with $9 in debt for every $1 in equity—thus the name *leveraged* buyout.

For example, Robert Hall, the former owner of Visador Corporation, sold his firm to a financial buyer for $67 million. The buyer financed the purchase as a leveraged buyout, incurring lots of debt to finance the purchase. The firm's total assets and debt and equity (as presented in the balance sheet) before and after the sale were as follows:

	Before the Sale	After the Sale
Total assets	$18,000,000	$67,000,000
Total debt	$5,000,000	$60,000,000
Equity	13,000,000	7,000,000
Total debt and equity	$18,000,000	$67,000,000

Visador's before-sale and after-sale numbers differ in two important respects. First, the total assets (and total debt and equity) increased from $18 million to $67 million. In other words, the founders of Visador had invested just over $18 million in the firm during their years of ownership, up to the point of the acquisition. However, the buyer was willing to pay $67 million for the business, based on future cash flows that were expected to be generated.

Second, before the sale, the assets were financed with 28 percent debt ($5 million total debt ÷ $18 million total assets) compared to 90 percent debt ($60 million total debt ÷ $67 million total assets) after the sale. Consequently, the firm was exposed to significantly more financial risk. If sales decrease, the company may not be able to service its debt. This is typical for bust-up leveraged buyouts.[1]

leveraged buyout (LBO)
A purchase heavily financed with debt, where the future cash flow of the target company is expected to be sufficient to meet debt repayments.

bust-up LBO
A leveraged buyout involving the purchase of a company with the intent of selling off its assets.

build-up LBO
A leveraged buyout
involving the purchase
of a group of similar
companies with the
intent of making the
firms into one larger
company.

More recently, the bust-up LBO has been replaced by the build-up LBO. As the name suggests, the *build-up LBO* involves pulling together a group of smaller firms to create a larger enterprise that might eventually be sold or taken public via an initial public offering.

The process of the build-up LBO begins with the acquisition of a company, which then acquires a number of smaller businesses that in some way complement it. These subsequent acquisitions may expand capacity in related or completely different businesses. The newly formed combination is operated privately for five years or so in order to establish a successful track record, and then it is sold or taken public. These acquisitions continue to rely heavily on debt financing, but to a lesser extent than bust-up LBOs.

During the 1990s and continuing well into the 2000s, build-up LBOs occurred in a number of industries where smaller companies frequently operate, such as funeral services and automobile dealerships. Sometimes, the selling firm's own management initiates an LBO to buy the business from the entrepreneur—in which case the arrangement is referred to as a *management buyout (MBO)*. An MBO can contribute significantly to a firm's operating performance by increasing management's focus and intensity. Thus, an MBO is a potentially viable means of transferring ownership from the founder to the management team. In many entrepreneurial businesses, managers have a strong incentive to become owners but lack the financial capacity to acquire the firm. An MBO can solve this problem through the use of debt financing, which is often underwritten in part by the selling entrepreneur.

management
buyout (MBO)
A leveraged buyout
in which the firm's top
managers become
significant shareholders
in the acquired firm.

employee stock
ownership plan
(ESOP)
A method by which a
firm is sold either in
part or in total to its
employees.

leveraged ESOP
An employee stock
ownership plan that is
financed with borrowed
money.

SALES TO EMPLOYEES   Established by Congress in 1974, *employee stock ownership plans (ESOPs)* have gradually been embraced by more than 10,000 companies. Once established, an ESOP uses employees' retirement contributions to buy company stock from the owner and holds it in trust; over time, the stock is distributed to employees' retirement plans. In a *leveraged ESOP*, the stock is purchased with borrowed money. For ESOPs to work, businesses need to be profitable and have good cash flows; otherwise, they will be unable to make the necessary payments to the ESOP trust.

It is common for an owner to start an ESOP by selling only a portion of the company. But even if the owner sells all of his or her stock, he or she can still retain control of the business. And an ESOP creates significant tax advantages for the seller. For instance, if the entrepreneur sells at least 30 percent of the company, capital gains taxes can be deferred, in some cases indefinitely. For example, the owner-managers of BFW Construction Company in Temple, Texas, created an ESOP. Then in 2003, they sold their business and rolled over the money from the shares into a 401(K) retirement plan. As a result, they have not paid taxes from the time the shares were put into an ESOP and will not have to do so until they are required to begin distributing the money, when they are 70½ years old. Bob Browder, one of the owners, commented that at least 40 percent of the increase in value they have created has been the result of tax savings attributable to having an ESOP.[2]

A reason frequently given for selling to employees is to create an incentive for them to work harder—by giving them a piece of the profits. However, employee ownership is not a panacea. Although advocates maintain that employee ownership improves motivation, leading to greater effort and reduced waste, the value of increased employee effort resulting from improved motivation varies significantly from firm to firm. Selling all or part of a firm to employees works only if the company's employees have an owner's mentality—that is, they do not think in "9-to-5" terms. An ESOP may provide a way for the owner to sell the business, but if the employees lack the required mind-set, it will not serve the business well in the future.

To illustrate the need for employee education if an ESOP is to be effective, consider the experience of Van Meter Industrial, Inc. Mick Slinger, the chief financial officer, thought his company's employee stock program was a great perk. But at a company meeting a few years ago, an employee stood up and said he didn't care at all about the stock fund, asking, "Why don't you just give me a couple hundred bucks for beer and cigarettes?" It was a wake-up call for Slinger. Many employees at the 100 percent employee-owned company, which is based in Cedar Rapids, Iowa, "didn't know what stock was, didn't know what an [employee] owner was," he recalls. "I made the mistake of thinking that everyone thinks like me." So the company created an employee committee to raise awareness of stock ownership and to get workers thinking about what each of them as owners can do to raise the price of company stock—and how it affects their own net worth. Today, employees are much more engaged in the program, and the firm's management believes it has made a significant contribution to increasing its stock price and lowering employee turnover. But it required a lot of effort to make the plan work as desired.[3]

The approaches that have been described in this section for selling a company represent the primary ways entrepreneurs exit their businesses. But the opportunity to sell a business can be affected by market conditions. For instance, in 2009 you could not talk about selling a business without recognizing the effects of the recession. On one hand, there were not as many buyers. But on the other, entrepreneurs who were considering an exit appeared to be holding back until the recession abated in the hope of receiving a better price for the business, so there were not as many companies on the market. As a result, the demand for and supply of businesses seemed more in balance than anyone might have expected. Michael Handelsman, general manager of BizBuySell, an online marketplace that lists companies for sale, offered these tips for selling a business in a difficult economy:[4]

- *Clean up the books.* Pay off small debts if you can, and make sure your records are ready for buyers' review.
- *Keep revenue strong.* Continue marketing and bringing in customers to show buyers that your business is still flourishing.
- *Consider your sector and market.* The downturn isn't the same in every city or every industry. Research businesses sold in your sector or town to see if now is a good time to sell.

While Handelsman offers good advice, these tips are relevant at any time—recession or no recession—and even when you are not interested in selling.

The recession also affected the availability of financing to buy companies. Banks became reluctant to loan money to entrepreneurs who wanted to buy a business. As a result, *seller financing*, in which the seller gives a loan to the buyer for part of the purchase price of the business, became more prevalent. For instance, an entrepreneur who purchased a business for $3.5 million paid $2.7 million in cash, and the seller took a note for the remaining $800,000, which was to be paid off over the next seven years. The $2.7 million in cash came from a bank loan of $2 million and $700,000 from the buyer's personal money. The loan from the seller was subordinated to the bank loan, so that if the buyer missed a payment to the bank, she could not make any payments to the seller until the bank loan was current.

seller financing Financing in which the seller accepts a note from a buyer in lieu of cash in partial payment for a business.

Releasing the Firm's Cash Flows

A second harvest strategy involves the orderly withdrawal of the owners' investment in the form of the firm's cash flows. The withdrawal process could be immediate if the owners simply sold off the assets of the firm and ceased business operations. However, for a value-creating firm—one that earns attractive rates of return for its investors—this does not make economic sense. The mere fact that a firm is earning high rates of return on its assets indicates that the business is worth more as a going concern than a dead one. Thus, shutting down the company is not an economically rational option. Instead, the owners might simply stop growing the business; by doing so, they increase the cash flows that can be returned to investors.

In a firm's early years, all its cash is usually devoted to growing the business. Thus, the company's cash flow during this period is zero—or, more likely, negative—requiring its owners to seek outside cash to finance its growth. As the firm matures and opportunities to grow the business decline, sizable cash flows frequently become available to its owners. Rather than reinvest all the cash in the business, the owners can begin to withdraw the cash, thus harvesting

entrepreneurial experiences

Sellers Offer Financing to Buyers

After multiple conversations with investment bankers, 37-year-old David Sloan, co-owner of Li'l Guy Foods, a family-owned Mexican-food manufacturing business in Kansas City, Mo., realized "there weren't a whole lot of people wanting to jump into this industry."

Mr. Sloan was looking to sell because the 35-employee company was facing huge financial pressure from the rising costs of commodities like corn and other ingredients, as well as plastic packaging. "We were under an assault on margins," he says—something that made outside investors nervous. Still, the business enjoyed a strong base of small-restaurant customers that paid a premium for its products.

That was enough to attract the attention of one of Li'l Guy Foods' competitors, Tortilla King Inc. of Moundridge, Kan. The larger, more sophisticated company had hedging policies in place that allowed [it] to lock in prices, guarding against commodity-price increases. And since it was already familiar with the industry and the company's customer base in the region, it was willing to take risks that an outside investor might not.

With costs high and consumer spending on

Graca Victoria/shutterstock.com 2009

the wane, Tortilla King President Juan Guardiola saw the acquisition of Li'l Guy Foods as a way to reduce competition and increase market share. "We were fighting in the market, cutting each other's margins," he says, "so it made a lot of sense to merge."

The two companies hammered out a deal and a bank agreed to provide financing. But, as the deal was about to close, the bank backed out—part of the broad pullback in business lending [during 2008]. So, Mr. Sloan's company agreed to finance the purchase, [offering] a five-year repayment term with [an interest] rate of around 8 percent.

Mr. Sloan says he would have preferred to walk away without being so invested in the combined company's future. But he felt it would be too difficult to continue running the small business, so he went along with the new terms. "It wasn't the most ideal transaction for us," he says. "I would have rather had it a lot cleaner."

Mr. Guardiola says he was surprised when the company's longtime bank declined to finance the deal, though he understands that banks are extra vigilant these days about debt. With commodity prices "like a train out of control," he says, the bank was concerned. But Mr. Guardiola is convinced the combined company will have greater clout together than they did separately.

Source: Adapted from Arden Dale and Simona Covel, "Sellers Offer a Financial Hand to Their Buyers," *Wall Street Journal*, November 13, 2008, p. B-1.

http://www.lilguyfoods.com

their investment. If they decide to adopt this approach, only the amount of cash necessary to maintain current markets is retained and reinvested; there is little, if any, effort to grow the present markets or expand into new markets.

Harvesting by slowly withdrawing a firm's cash from the business has two important advantages: The owners can retain control of the business while they harvest their investment, and they do not have to seek out a buyer or incur the expenses associated with consummating a sale. There are disadvantages, however. Reducing reinvestment when the firm faces valuable growth opportunities results in lost value creation and could leave a firm unable to sustain its competitive advantage. The end result may be an unintended reduction in harvestable value, below the potential value of the firm as a long-term going concern. Also, there may be tax disadvantages to an orderly liquidation, compared with other harvest methods. For example, if a corporation distributes cash as dividends, both the company and the stockholders will be taxed on the income—what we call *double taxation*. (However, there is no double taxation for a sole proprietorship, partnership, limited liability company, or S corporation.)

Finally, for the entrepreneur who is simply tired of day-to-day operations, siphoning off the cash flows over time may require too much patience. Unless other people in the firm are qualified to manage it, this strategy may be destined to fail.

double taxation
Taxation of income that occurs twice, first as corporate earnings and then as stockholder dividends.

LIVING THE DREAM:

entrepreneurial experiences

Sale Gives PR Firm the Benefits of Becoming Employee-Owned

Mr. Nikolich was ready to start easing out of Tech Image, the technology public-relations firm he had founded nearly 15 years earlier. He didn't want to sell to a much larger PR company, however, because he was concerned the new owner would slash his work force. And he wanted to stay involved in the business.

When Mr. Nikolich, 50 years old, started to consider exit strategies in 2004, he searched in vain for a business incubator or other organization that would take a strategic interest in his firm, rather than a PR firm just looking for a regional office.

At the same time, he pursued the idea of employee ownership. One day, during a meeting with a client, association-management company SmithBucklin Corp., the conversation turned to ESOPs. The client mentioned that the Chicago company was employee-owned and said the process required huge chunks of time and money spent with accountants and lawyers.

At a follow-up meeting a few weeks later with Henry Givray, SmithBucklin's chairman and chief executive, Mr. Givray

Courtesy of SmithBucklin Corporation

sketched out the costs on a napkin. Then he offered an alternative idea: SmithBucklin, with 750 employees and nearly $90 million in annual revenue, could buy Tech Image.

At first, Mr. Nikolich was torn. He worried about "losing our identity" as part of the much larger company and didn't want to change the firm's business model. He was concerned that if the deal didn't go through, he would have a contentious relationship with a client. And, he didn't want employees to think he was reneging on his promise to not take the money and run.

The deciding factor: SmithBucklin was employee-owned.

When the deal closed, Mr. Nikolich and his partner received both cash and equity in SmithBucklin. Mr. Nikolich can sell his stake and exit the company when he is ready—though that won't be anytime soon, he says.

Mr. Nikolich says owning a chunk of their new company means less of an "us vs. them" mentality because employees know that "everything they do will be reflected back in the price of the ESOP."

Source: Simona Covel, "Small Business Link: Sale Gives PR Firm the Benefits of Becoming Employee-Owned," *Wall Street Journal,* February 7, 2008, p. B6.

http://www.techimage.com

Initial Public Offering (IPO)

initial public offering (IPO)
The first sale of shares of a company's stock to the public.

A third method of harvesting a firm is an initial public offering. As discussed in Chapter 12, an *initial public offering (IPO),* occurs when a private firm sells its shares for the first time to the general public. This requires registering the stock issue with the Securities and Exchange Commission (SEC), and adhering to Blue Sky laws that govern the public offering at a state level. The purpose of these federal and state laws is to ensure adequate disclosure to investors and to prevent fraud. Businesses intending to conduct an IPO must file a detailed registration statement with the SEC, which includes in-depth financial, management, and operational information.

Many entrepreneurs consider the prospect of an initial public offering as the "holy grail" of their career, bringing with it increased prestige with many in business circles. However, since 2001 the option to issue an IPO has been limited dramatically, especially for smaller IPOs. Brad Feld, an investor in early-stage businesses and an entrepreneur for more than 20 years, shares his experiences in these words:

> In the 1990s, the aspiration of every VC-backed company was to go public. Especially in the second half of the decade, the IPO was a magical accomplishment. Once a company went public, it was special and valuable, and the entrepreneur was a rock star.
>
> During this period, every entrepreneur I met talked about his goal of taking his company public as his exit strategy. Every company pitch I saw had a slide titled "Exit Strategy" and had "Go Public" as its headline. The fallback strategy was "Be Acquired."
>
> Going public seemed like a great idea at the time, but by 2002, it was an excruciatingly painful experience. That year, I sat on the board of directors of four public companies. At one point, every company was trading at a price below $1, at risk for delisting, and spending a ridiculous amount of energy discussing its crummy stock price and trying to figure out what to do about it.[5]

As shown in Exhibit 13-2, IPOs of less than $25 million have almost become nonexistent. Hopefully, this trend will be reversed, but as of 2009 the situation for an entrepreneur and any investors wanting to go public was bleak to say the least.

EXHIBIT 13-2 IPOs Raising Less Than $25 Million

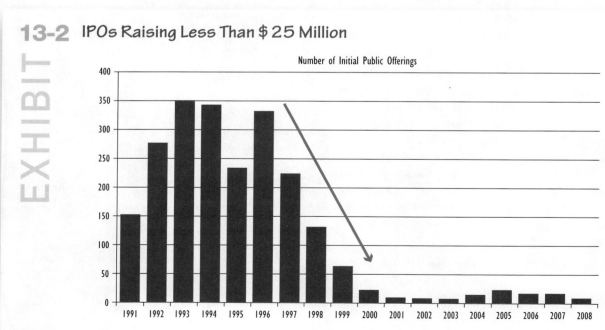

Number of Initial Public Offerings

Source: Dealogic, Capital Markets Advisory Partners, reported in David Weild and Edward Kim, "Why Are IPOs in the ICU?" White Paper, Grant Thornton, LLP, 2008, p. 8.

Beyond the "shutting down" of the IPO market during the first decade of the 21st century, most entrepreneurs do not really understand the process, especially when it comes to how going public relates to the harvest and the actual process by which a firm goes public. We next consider how the process works so that you will have the necessary information if going public once again becomes a viable option.

THE IPO AS A HARVEST STRATEGY   An IPO occurs when a company offers its stock to the general public, rather than limiting its sale to founders, friends and family, and other private investors. The purpose of this process, described below, is to create a ready market for buying and selling the stock. Before the stock is traded publicly, there is no marketplace where the shares can be easily bought and sold, and thus it is difficult to know what the stock is worth.

IPOs have a number of benefits, including the following:[6]

1. An IPO is one way to signal to investors that a firm is a quality business and will likely perform well in the future.

2. A firm whose stock is traded publicly has access to more investors when it needs to raise capital to grow the business.

3. Being publicly traded helps create ongoing interest in the company and its continued development.

4. Publicly traded stock is more attractive to key personnel whose incentive pay includes the firm's stock.

While there are several reasons for going public, the primary reason is to raise capital. In 80 percent of the cases, money raised from selling a firm's stock to the public is used for expansion, paying down debt, and increasing the firm's liquidity (cash). The other 20 percent of initial public offerings result from the entrepreneurs' desire to sell their stock.[7] Thus, in four out of five cases, IPOs are not intended as an *immediate* exit strategy, but rather as a way to raise capital for growth. Eventually, however, entrepreneurs can and frequently do sell their shares as a way to cash out of their companies.

THE IPO PROCESS   The basic steps in the IPO process are as follows:

Step 1.   The firm's owners decide to go public.

Step 2.   If it has not already done so, the company must have its financial statements for the past 3 years audited by a certified public accountant.

Step 3.   An investment banker is selected to guide management in the IPO process.

Step 4.   An S-1 Registration Statement is filed with the Securities Exchange Commission (SEC), which requires about one month to review it.

Step 5.   Management responds to comments by the SEC and issues a Red Herring/Prospectus, describing the firm and the offering.

Step 6.   Management spends the next 10 to 15 days on the road, presenting the firm to potential investors.

Step 7.   On the day before the offering is released to the public, the actual offering price is set. Based on the demand for the offering, the shares are priced to create active trading of the stock.

Step 8.   Months of work come to fruition in a single event—offering the stock to the public and seeing how it is received.

The IPO process may be one of the most exhilarating—but frustrating and exhausting—experiences of an entrepreneur's life. To many, the costs of the IPO process seem exorbitant. Also, owners may find themselves being misunderstood and having little influence on the decisions being made during the process. As a consequence, they are frequently disillusioned with investment bankers and wonder where they lost control of the process.

To understand an IPO, you must consider the shift in power that occurs during the process. When the chain of events begins, the firm's managers are in control. They dictate whether or not to go public and who the investment banker will be. After the prospectus has been prepared and the road show is under way, however, the firm's managers, including the entrepreneur, are no longer the primary decision makers. The investment banker is now in control. Finally, the marketplace, in concert with the investment banker, begins to take over. Ultimately, it is the market that dictates the final outcome.

In addition to being prepared for the shift in control, it is important that the entrepreneur understand the investment banker's motivations in the IPO process. Who is the investment banker's primary customer? Clearly, the issuing firm is compensating the underwriter for its services through the fees paid and participation in the offering. But helping a firm with an IPO usually is not as profitable for the investment banker as are other activities, such as involvement in corporate acquisitions. And the investment banker is also selling the securities to the customers on the other side of the trade. These are the people who will continue to do business with the investment banker in the future. Thus, the investment banker is somewhat conflicted as to who the "customer" is.

An entrepreneur must also consider more than just the initial costs of the IPO; he or she must think hard about the costs of running a publicly traded company. Operating a public firm is far more expensive than operating a private company. A publicly traded company has significant ongoing costs associated with reporting its financial results to investors and to the SEC. These costs were significantly increased in 2001 when, in response to corporate scandals such as those at Enron and WorldCom, the U.S. Congress passed the Sarbanes-Oxley Act. The act places a much greater burden on companies to have good accounting practices and controls that will prevent such egregious offenses by managers. While good came from Sarbanes-Oxley, the costs to a small firm are disproportionate and are no small consideration in the decision as to whether or not to go public.

So, although many entrepreneurs seek to take their firms public through an IPO, this strategy is appropriate for only a limited number of firms. And even for this small group, an IPO is more a means of raising growth capital than an effective harvest strategy.

Private Placement

A fourth method of harvesting is a *private placement* (described in Chapter 12), which is simply money provided by private investors. The private investors can be an individual or group of individuals who act together to invest in companies.

Private equity investors offer two key advantages that public investors do not: immediacy and flexibility. With private equity, an entrepreneur can sell most of her or his stock immediately, an option not available when a company is taken public. Also, private equity investors can be more flexible in structuring their investment to meet the entrepreneur's needs.

Although the situation is complicated by the different needs of each generation, private equity is particularly effective for family-owned businesses that need to transfer ownership to the next generation. In the transfer of ownership between generations, there must be a tradeoff among three important goals: (1) liquidity (cash) for the selling family members, (2) continued financing for company's future growth, and (3) the desire of the buying generation to maintain control of the firm. Thus, the older generation wants to get cash out of the business, while the younger generation wants to retain the cash needed to finance the firm's growth and yet not lose ownership control.

To understand how a private placement might work, consider the following example.[8] Assume that a company could be sold for $20 million through a leveraged buyout (LBO), which would most likely be financed through at least 80 percent debt and 20 percent equity. Many entrepreneurs would find such an arrangement intolerable, even though they would have cashed out. They simply would not want their company subjected to such a high-leverage transaction. Also, with an LBO the family generally loses control of the business.

LIVING THE DREAM:

entrepreneurial challenges

Off-the-Grid IPOs

In some respects, it wasn't such a terrible problem for Martin Lightsey to have: The value of Specialty Blades, Inc., had increased so much since he founded the medical and industrial blade manufacturer in 1985 that some of the company's 11 shareholders, including Lightsey's two daughters, wanted to cash in some of their earnings. In 12 years, the median $42,000 investment in the business, based in Staunton, Virginia, had soared to a value of more than $350,000. The problem was, Lightsey didn't have enough cash to fund the buyouts.

Lightsey briefly toyed with the idea of going public, which would allow his investors to buy and sell shares as they pleased. He called Gordon Smith, a securities lawyer at Richmond law firm McGuire Woods, who told him that the legal and accounting fees related to being a publicly held company would amount to roughly a half million dollars every year, overwhelming for a business booking $6 million in annual sales.

Lightsey asked Smith about a privately held community bank in Staunton that seemed to be trading its shares. Smith explained that the bank was taking advantage of a little-known Securities and Exchange Commission exemption called an intrastate offering, which allowed it to sell stock to Virginia residents without registering with the SEC. It seemed like a perfect solution for

Courtesy of Specialty Blades

Specialty Blades: Lightsey could cash out the company's current investors by selling their stock to a new group of shareholders and avoid the hassle and expense of an IPO. At the same time, he could spread out ownership to a larger, more diverse pool of investors. "The public model is just more stable," Lightsey says.

Lightsey spent the next few months researching intrastate offerings before deciding to take the plunge. Lightsey began working with Bruce Campbell, then executive vice president of Richmond-based brokerage firm Scott & Stringfellow and a Specialty Blades board member who owned several thousand shares of the company. Campbell and some fellow board members estimated a value for the company's stock, based on factors such as cash flow and earnings, and began contacting clients to gauge their interest.

A few months later, Lightsey held a gathering at Specialty Blades' facility for 40 potential investors. Lightsey cautiously launched into his dog-and-pony show, highlighting the company's history and growth strategy. A few weeks later, investors purchased a total of 30,000 shares at $20 per share, which represented 6 percent of the company. All of the shares that were sold belonged to Lightsey's daughters. The offering cost Specialty Blades about $15,000, a small fraction of the price of an IPO. The firm regularly updates the stock price, which was recently $124 per share.

Source: Phaedra Hise, "Off-the-Grid IPOs," *Inc. Magazine*, December 2006, pp. 40–42. Copyright 2006 Mansueto Ventures LLC. Reproduced with permission of Mansueto Ventures LLC in the format Textbook via Copyright Clearance Center.

http://www.specialtyblades.com

As an alternative to an LBO, the retiring generation might sell to private equity investors for $18 million—10 percent less than the LBO price. The seller would receive something less than the $18 million, such as $15 million. But instead of relinquishing all or most of their ownership, the family owners would receive 51 percent of the equity in exchange for the $3 million retained in the company. The remaining $15 million of the purchase price would be financed from two sources: $7 million in debt and $8 million from the private investor, consisting of

EXHIBIT

13-3 Private Placement—An Illustration

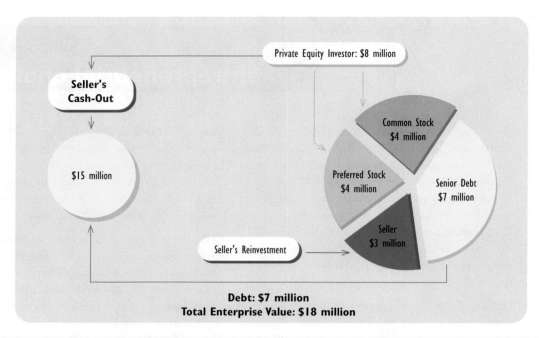

Debt: $7 million
Total Enterprise Value: $18 million

$4 million in preferred stock and $4 million in common stock. The preferred stock would provide an annual dividend, while the common stock would give the new investor 49 percent of the firm's ownership (see Exhibit 13-3).

The differences between the two capital structures are clear. The debt ratio is much lower in the private placement than in the LBO, allowing for a lower interest rate on the debt and permitting the firm's cash flows to be used to grow the firm, rather than pay down debt. This arrangement allows the senior generation of owners to cash out, while the next generation retains control and the cash to grow the firm—a win-win situation. The younger generation also has the potential to realize significant economic gains if the firm performs well after the sale.

Firm Valuation and the Harvest

As a firm moves toward the harvest, two issues are of primary importance: the harvest value (what the firm is worth) and the method of payment.

3. Explain the issues in valuing a firm that is being harvested and deciding on the method of payment.

The Harvest Value

Valuing a company may be necessary on numerous occasions during the life of the business—but it is never more important than at the time of the exit. Owners can harvest only what they have created. Value is created when a firm's return on invested capital is greater than the investors' *opportunity cost of funds,* which is the rate of return that could be earned on an investment of similar risk.

Growing a venture to the point of diminishing returns and then selling it to others who can carry it to the next level is a proven way to create value. How this incremental value is shared between the old and the new owners depends largely on the relative strengths of each party in the negotiations—that is, who wants the deal the most or who has the best negotiating skills.

Business valuation is part science and part art, so there is no precise formula for determining the price of a private company. Rather, the price is determined by a sometimes intricate process of negotiation between buyer and seller. Much is left to the negotiating skills of the respective parties. But one thing is certain: There must be a willing buyer. It doesn't matter what a firm's owner believes the business is worth; it is worth only what someone who has the cash is prepared to pay.

The specific approaches to and methods for valuing a company are described in Appendix B at the end of the book. As described in the appendix, buyers and sellers frequently base the harvest value of a firm on a multiple of earnings. For instance, a company might be valued at five times its earnings. (Entrepreneur Robert Hall sold his firms for a multiple of earnings; his experience provides the basis for the example used in Appendix B.)

opportunity cost of funds
The rate of return that could be earned on another investment of similar risk.

The Method of Payment

The actual value of a firm is only one issue; another is the method of payment. When selling a company, an entrepreneur has three basic choices: sell the firm's assets, sell its stock, or, if the buyer is another company, merge with the buyer (combine the two companies into one firm). The exiting entrepreneur may prefer to sell the firm's stock so that the gain on the sale will be a capital gain, resulting in lower taxes.[9] The buyer, on the other hand, may prefer to purchase the firm's assets rather than buy the company's stock. Buying the assets relieves the buyer of responsibility for any liabilities, known or unknown.

Harvesting owners can be paid in cash or in stock of the acquiring firm, with cash generally being preferred over stock. Entrepreneurs who accept stock in payment are frequently

How I see it: John Stites on Beginning with the End in Mind

When I started my business, I was focused on making money and being successful. I had been taught in business school the fundamentals of being in business. I visited other successful individuals and companies to see what I could replicate in my business to ensure its success. I went right to work and worked hard for 10 years. I did not take the time to sit down and envision what I wanted my business to look like in the future. I did not take the time to set a mission statement and establish that mission in the day-to-day operations of the business. I worked hard, but not smart.

After 10 years of mediocre success, I stepped back and looked at what I was doing and how it was impacting people—people inside my company and people outside my company. What I saw I didn't like. I saw a company finally making money, but not positively influencing lives.

I have determined that if, at the end of my tenure in our family business, I have not inspired individuals to be better spouses, better parents, and better citizens, then I have lost the greatest opportunity to increase the value of the company. A company that doesn't change lives in a positive way and just gives money to employees and provides services to customers is not one to be valued very highly.

disappointed, as they are unable to affect the value of the stock once they have sold the firm. Only an entrepreneur who has great faith in the acquiring firm's stock should accept it in payment, and even then he or she is taking a big chance by not being well diversified. Having such a large investment in only one stock is risky, to say the least.

Developing an Effective Harvest Plan

4. Provide advice on developing an effective harvest plan.

We have discussed why planning for the harvest is important, despite the tendency of many entrepreneurs to ignore it until some crisis or unanticipated event comes along. We have also described the methods for exiting. However, understanding what the options are for harvesting in no way guarantees a successful harvest. More times than not, entrepreneurs who harvest their businesses are disappointed with the process and the outcome. In the sections that follow, we provide suggestions for crafting an effective exit strategy.[10]

Anticipate the Harvest

Entrepreneurs frequently do not appreciate the difficulty of harvesting a company. One investor commented that exiting a business is "like brain surgery—it's done a lot, but there are a lot of things that can go wrong." Harvesting, whether through a sale or a stock offering, takes a lot of time and energy on the part of the firm's management team and can be very distracting from day-to-day affairs. The result is often a loss of managerial focus and momentum, leading to poor performance.

Uncertainties accompanying an impending sale often lower employee morale. The stress can affect the whole organization, as employees become anxious about the prospect of a new owner. Lynn Baker, at Sutter Hill Ventures, offers this advice: "Don't start running the company for the liquidity event. Run the business for the long haul." Jim Porter, at CCI Triad, describes the situation in Silicon Valley in the 1990s, where some owners carried the practice to an extreme:

> Some people don't think in terms of long-term value as much as short-term returns. This carries over into developing an IPO exit strategy. I see a growing number of people who are already planning their next company before they are finished with the first company. They are looking to exit the first one, get the money out and start the second one, get the money out, and pyramid their return. In a hot market, you can do that and get away with it. They are professional company starters.

So, while an entrepreneur should not be caught unaware, there is also the risk of becoming so attentive to "playing the harvest game" that one forgets to keep first things first.

Investors are always concerned about how to exit, and entrepreneurs need to have a similar mind-set. Peter Hermann, general partner at Heritage Partners, a private equity investment group, notes, "People generally stumble into the exit and don't plan for it." However, for Hermann, "The exit strategy begins when the money goes in." Similarly, Gordon Baty, at Zero Stage Capital, Inc., enters each investment with a clear understanding of its investment horizon and harvest plan. In his words, "We plan for an acquisition and hope for an IPO." Jack Kearney, at Dain Rauscher Inc., indicates that an exit strategy should be anticipated in advance, unless "the entrepreneur expects to die in the CEO chair. . . .The worst of all worlds is to realize, for health or other reasons, that you have to sell the company right now." Jim Knister, at the Donnelly Corporation, advises entrepreneurs to start thinking two or three years ahead about how they are going to exit so that they can correctly position their companies.

This type of advice is particularly important when the entrepreneur is planning an IPO. Running a public company requires information disclosures to stockholders that are not required of a privately held firm. Specifically, this means (1) maintaining an accounting process that cleanly separates the business from the entrepreneur's personal life, (2) selecting a strong board of directors that can and will offer valuable business advice, and (3) managing the firm so as to produce a successful track record of performance.

Having a harvest plan in place is also very important because the window of opportunity can open and close quickly. Remember that the opportunity to exit is triggered by the arrival of a willing and able buyer, not just an interested seller. For an IPO, a hot market may offer a very attractive opportunity, and a seller must be ready to move when the opportunity arises.

In summary, an entrepreneur should be sure to anticipate the harvest. In the words of Ed Cherney, an entrepreneur who has sold two companies, "Don't wait to put your package together until something dramatic happens. Begin thinking about the exit strategy and start going through the motions, so that if something major happens, you will have time to think through your options."

Expect Conflict—Emotional and Cultural

Having bought other companies does not prepare entrepreneurs for the sale of their own company. Entrepreneurs who have been involved in the acquisition of other firms are still ill-prepared for the stress associated with selling their own businesses. Jim Porter, who has been involved in a number of acquisitions, says, "It's definitely a lot more fun to buy something than it is to be bought." One very real difference between selling and buying comes from the entrepreneur's personal ties to the business that he or she helped create. A buyer can be quite unemotional and detached, while a seller is likely to be much more concerned about nonfinancial considerations.

For this reason and many others, entrepreneurs frequently do not make good employees. The very qualities that made them successful entrepreneurs can make it difficult for them to work under a new owner. In fact, an entrepreneur who plans to stay with the firm after a sale can become disillusioned quickly and end up leaving prematurely.

Lynn Baker observes, "There is a danger of culture conflict between the acquiring versus the acquired firm's management. The odds are overwhelming that somebody who's been an entrepreneur is not going to be happy in a corporate culture." When Ed Bonneau sold his wholesale sunglass distribution firm, he was retained as a consultant, but the buyer never sought his advice. Bonneau recalled that he "could not imagine that someone could or would buy a company and not operate it. The people who bought the firm had no operations expertise or experience whatsoever and, in fact, didn't care that much about it."

These conflicts occur to varying degrees whenever an entrepreneur remains with the company after the sale. Although the nature of the conflict varies, the intensity of the feelings does not. An entrepreneur who stays with the company should expect culture conflict and be pleasantly surprised if it does not occur.

Get Good Advice

Entrepreneurs learn to operate their businesses through experience gained in repeated day-to-day activities. However, they may engage in a harvest transaction only once in a lifetime. "It's an emotional roller-coaster ride," says Ben Buettell, who frequently represents sellers of small and mid-sized companies.[11] Thus, entrepreneurs have a real need for good advice, both from experienced professionals and from those who have personally been through a harvest. In seeking advice, be aware that the experts who helped you build and grow your business may not be the best ones to use when it's time to sell the company, as they may not have the experience needed in that area. So, choose your advisors carefully.

entrepreneurial experiences

I'll Be Over Here If Anyone Needs Me

Norm Brodsky, a serial entrepreneur and columnist for *Inc. Magazine,* reflects on life after selling his company, CitiStorage.

So you want to know how life changes after you sell a majority interest in your company to an outside investment firm and give up day-to-day management? Let me put it this way: Now I know how Colonel Sanders felt.

OK, maybe that's going a little too far. I'm not a complete figurehead. I still have responsibilities. These days, I work on things like long-term planning, mergers and acquisitions, and putting up new buildings. But my partner Louis Weiner is the president, and he and his managers run the business. Sometimes, it's hard for me to keep from butting in.

The Allied people warned me that the changes would take some getting used to. "The biggest thing for you," they said, "is that we look at everything, and you cannot make on-the-spot decisions anymore. You did a fabulous job building this as an entrepreneurial company, but in order to get to the next level, there has to be more structure. You have to understand that."

So everybody answers to somebody, and here I am,

Evan Kafka

an undisciplined guy all my life, never answering to anybody, except maybe my parents when I was a kid—and even then I was an independent little kid. Now, suddenly, I have to get used to a different way of operating. I have to become a team player.

I have to get used to other changes in my life. For example, I used to have a lot of expenses I could charge to the company—like when I took business associates out to dinner or bought a car to use on company business. I was also in control of my own salary, which I could adjust based on the company's performance. Because of that, we never had to touch the money that Elaine put in our emergency fund, as she called it. Now, whatever I spend comes out of my pocket. Granted, there's enough money in that pocket. I'm certainly not complaining, but that's another psychological adjustment I've had to make.

The biggest problem, however, is that I don't have a clear idea of what I'm doing or where I'm going anymore. My work for CitiStorage doesn't fill all of my time or get my juices flowing the way starting a business does. There's a bit of a hole in my life at the moment, and I don't know yet how I'm going to fill it. So while I loved chasing the rainbow, I have to say that I have mixed feelings about having caught it.

Source: Norm Brodsky, "I'll Be Over Here If Anyone Needs Me," *Inc. Magazine,* Vol. 30, No. 5 (May 2008), pp. 73–74.

Bill Dedmon, at Southwest Securities, advises, "Don't try to do it alone, because it's a demanding process that can distract you from your business." Jack Furst, at HM Capital, a private equity investor, believes that advisors can give entrepreneurs a reality check. He contends that, without independent advice, entrepreneurs frequently fall prey to thinking they want to sell unconditionally, when in fact they really want to sell only if an unrealistically high price is offered.

Professional advice is vital, but entrepreneurs stress the importance of talking to other entrepreneurs who have sold a firm or taken it public. No one can better describe what to expect—both in events and in emotions—than someone who has had the experience. This perspective nicely complements that of the professional advisor.

Perhaps the greatest misconception among entrepreneurs is that an IPO is the end of the line. They often feel that taking their firm public through an IPO means they have "made it." The fact is that going public is but one transition in the life of a firm. Many entrepreneurs are surprised to learn that a public offering is just the beginning, not an end.

An entrepreneur will not be able to cash out for some time after the completion of the IPO. In a sense, investors in the new stock offering have chosen to back the entrepreneur as the driving force behind the company—that is, they have invested in the entrepreneur, not the firm. While the daily stock price quotes will let the management team keep score, the business will have to reach another plateau before the founder can think about placing it in the hands of a new team and going fishing. Ed Bonneau talks of being surprised in this matter:

> The question of an IPO was put to me a number of times over the years. I had some investment bankers come and look at our company to talk about going public; they said, "Yeah, you can go public." Then they asked me why I wanted to go public. I said, "For one thing, I want some money out of the company. I have every dime I've got stuck in here." They responded that I couldn't do that. I asked what they meant. They responded, "Getting money out [is] not the purpose of going public."

Lynn Baker describes the typical entrepreneur's thinking about an IPO as "the *Bride Magazine* syndrome":

> The entrepreneur is like the bride-to-be who becomes fixated on the events of the wedding day without thinking clearly about the years of being married that will follow. Life as head of a public corporation is very different from life at the helm of a private firm. Major investors will be calling every day expecting answers—sometimes with off-the-wall questions.

Under these circumstances, getting good advice is a must.

Understand What Motivates You

For an entrepreneur, harvesting a business that has been an integral part of life for a long period of time can be a very emotional experience. When an entrepreneur has invested a substantial part of his or her working life in growing a business, a real sense of loss may accompany the harvest. Walking away from employees, clients, and one's identity as a small business owner may not be the wonderful ride into the sunset that was expected.

Thus, entrepreneurs should think very carefully about their motives for exiting and what they plan to do after the harvest. Frequently, entrepreneurs have great expectations about what life is going to be like with a lot of liquidity, something many of them have never known. The harvest does provide the long-sought liquidity, but some entrepreneurs find managing money—in contrast to operating their own company—less rewarding than they had expected.

Entrepreneurs may also become disillusioned when they come to understand more fully how their sense of personal identity was intertwined with their business. While Jim Porter understands that a primary purpose of exiting is to make money, watching a number of owners cash out has led him to conclude that the money is not a very satisfying aspect of the event:

> The bottom line is that you need more than money to sustain life and feel worthwhile. I see people who broke everything to make their money. They were willing to sacrifice their wives, their family, and their own sense of values to make money. I remember one person who was flying high, did his IPO, and went straight out and bought a flaming red Ferrari. He raced it down the street, hit a telephone pole, and died the day his IPO money came down. You see these guys . . . go crazy. They went out and bought houses in Hawaii, houses in Tahoe, new cars, and got things they didn't need.

Peter Hermann believes that "seller's remorse" is definitely a major issue for a number of entrepreneurs. His advice is "Search your soul and make a list of what you want to achieve with the exit. Is it dollars, health of the company, your management team or an heir apparent taking over?" The answers to these and similar questions determine to a significant extent whether the exit will prove successful in all dimensions of an entrepreneur's life. There can be conflicting emotions, such as those expressed by Bill Bailey, founder of the Cherokee Corporation:

> There is a period in your life when you get up in age and you begin thinking more about your family. For me, it became important for the first time in my life to have money available to do some long-range personal planning for myself, and for my family. But if there is any one thing to be understood when you are selling a business or anything else, it is the excitement of the journey and the enjoyment for doing what you're doing that matters.

Entrepreneurs are also well advised to be aware of potential problems that may arise after the exit. There are stories about people selling a firm or going public and then losing everything. Ed Cherney says, "It is more difficult to handle success than it is to handle struggling. People forget what got them the success—the work ethic, the commitment to family, whatever characteristics work for an entrepreneur. Once the money starts rolling in, . . . people forget and begin having problems."

And for the entrepreneur who believes that it will be easy to adapt to change after the harvest, even possibly to start another company, William Unger, at the Mayfield Fund, quotes from Machiavelli's *The Prince:* "It should be remembered that nothing is more difficult than to establish a new order of things."

What's Next?

Entrepreneurs by their very nature are purpose-driven people. So, after the exit, an entrepreneur who has been driven to build a profitable business will need something larger than the individual to bring meaning to her or his life. Many entrepreneurs have a sense of gratitude for the benefits they have received from living in a capitalist system. As a result, they want to give back, both with their time and with their money.

Judy Johnston is a great example of an entrepreneur who asked the question "What's next?" For Johnston, it will be a nonprofit venture. She used her life savings of $50,000 to found her first business, PrintPaks, which she sold to Mattel three years later for $26 million. Blue Lake Publishing, Johnston's most recent startup, was founded in 2002—she hopes to sell it in the next five years. Her children's magazine, *Tessie and Tab,* will eventually need a video program, she says, but that's for a successor to figure out. "I know it has to be done, but somebody else needs to own the company when it happens," she says. "There's only so far I can take it, because I'm not motivated by just making more money. I'm not qualified or interested in running a really big company."

Blue Lake will likely be Johnston's last for-profit startup, but not her last startup endeavor. "I want to do something that doesn't involve having to return capital to investors," she says. Nonprofits are still fair game.[12]

The good news is that there is no limit to the number of worthy charitable causes, including universities, churches, and civic organizations. And it may be that, when all is said and done, the call to help others with a new venture may be too strong for an individual with an entrepreneurial mind-set to resist. But whatever you decide to do, do it with passion and let your life benefit others in the process.

1. Explain the importance of having a harvest, or exit, plan.

- Harvesting, or exiting, is the method entrepreneurs and investors use to get out of a business and, ideally, reap the value of their investment in the firm.
- Harvesting is about more than merely selling and leaving a business. It involves capturing value (cash flows), reducing risk, and creating future options.
- A firm's accessibility to investors is driven by the availability of harvest options.

2. Describe the options available for harvesting.

- There are four basic ways to harvest an investment in a privately owned company: (1) selling the firm, (2) releasing the firm's cash flows to its owners, (3) offering stock to the public through an IPO, and (4) issuing a private placement of the stock.
- In a sale to a strategic buyer, the value placed on a business depends on the synergies that the buyer believes can be created.
- Financial buyers look primarily to a firm's stand-alone, cash-generating potential as the source of its value.
- In leveraged buyouts (LBOs), high levels of debt financing are used to acquire firms.
- With bust-up LBOs, the assets of the acquired firm are sold to repay the debt.
- With build-up LBOs, a number of related businesses are acquired to create a larger enterprise, which may eventually be taken public via an initial public offering (IPO).
- A management buyout (MBO) is an LBO in which management is part of the group buying the company.
- In an employee stock ownership plan (ESOP), employees' retirement contributions are used to purchase shares in the company.
- The orderly withdrawal of an owner's investment in the form of the firm's cash flows is one method of harvesting a firm.

- An initial public offering (IPO) is used primarily as a way to raise additional equity capital to finance company growth, and only secondarily as a way to harvest the owner's investment.
- Private placement is a form of outside financing that can allow the original owners to cash out.
- Trying to finance liquidity and growth while retaining control is perhaps the most difficult task facing family firms.

3. Explain the issues in valuing a firm that is being harvested and deciding on the method of payment.

- Value is created when a firm's return on invested capital is greater than the investors' opportunity cost of funds.
- A firm will have greater value in the hands of new owners if the new owners can create more value than the current owners can.
- Often, buyers and sellers base the harvest value of a firm on a multiple of its earnings.
- Cash is generally preferred over stock and other forms of payment by those selling a firm.

4. Provide advice on developing an effective harvest plan.

- Investors are always concerned about exit strategy.
- Entrepreneurs who plan to stay with a business after a sale can become disillusioned quickly and end up leaving prematurely.
- Entrepreneurs frequently do not appreciate the difficulty of selling or exiting a company. Having bought other companies does not prepare entrepreneurs for the sale of their own firm.
- Entrepreneurs have a real need for good advice, both from experienced professionals and from those who have personally been through a harvest.
- Going public is not the end; it's only a transition in the life of a firm.

Key Terms

harvesting (exiting) p. 339
leveraged buyout (LBO) p. 341
bust-up LBO p. 341
build-up LBO p. 342

management buyout (MBO) p. 342
employee stock ownership
  plan (ESOP) p. 342
leveraged ESOP p. 342

seller financing p. 343
double taxation p. 345
initial public offering (IPO) p. 346
opportunity cost of funds p. 351

Discussion Questions

1. Explain what is meant by the term *harvesting*. What is involved in harvesting an investment in a privately held firm?

2. Why should an owner of a company plan for eventually harvesting his or her company?

3. Contrast a sale to a strategic buyer with one to a financial buyer.

4. Explain the term *leveraged buyout*. How is a leveraged buyout different from a management buyout?

5. Distinguish between bust-up LBOs and build-up LBOs.

6. What is the primary purpose of an initial public offering (IPO)? How does an IPO relate to a harvest?

7. Why might an entrepreneur find going public a frustrating process?

8. What determines whether a firm has value to a prospective purchaser?

9. What problems can occur when an entrepreneur sells a firm but continues in the management of the company?

10. How may harvesting a firm affect an entrepreneur's personal identity?

You Make the Call

SITUATION 1

Michael and Melissa Castello founded Casa Bonita. They started with a single fast-food Mexican restaurant in Austin, Texas. At the time, they both worked seven days a week. From that small beginning, they expanded to 84 profitable restaurants located in Texas, Oklahoma, Arkansas, and Colorado. Over the years, other restaurant owners expressed an interest in buying the firm; however, the Castellos were not interested in selling. Then an English firm, Unigate Limited, offered them $32 million for the business and said Michael could remain the firm's CEO. The Castellos were attracted by the idea of having $32 million in liquid assets. They flew to London to close the deal. On the flight home, however, Michael began having doubts about their decision to sell the business. He thought, "We spent 15 years of our lives getting the business where we wanted it, and we've lost it." After their plane landed in New York, they spent the night and then flew back to London the next day. They offered the buyers $1 million to cancel the contract, but Unigate's management declined the offer. The Castellos flew home disappointed.

Question 1 How could the Castellos be disappointed with $32 million?

Question 2 What should the Castellos have done to avoid this situation?

Question 3 What advice would you offer Michael about continuing to work for the business under the new owners?

SITUATION 2

Ed and Barbara Bonneau started their wholesale sunglass distribution firm 30 years ago with $1,000 of their own money and $5,000 borrowed from a country banker in Ed's hometown. The firm grew quickly, selling sunglasses and reading glasses to such companies as Walmart, Eckerd Drugs, and Phar-Mor. In addition, the Bonneaus enjoyed using the company to do good things. For example, they had a company chaplain, who was available when employees were having family problems, such as a death in the family.

Although the company had done well, the market had matured recently and profit margins narrowed significantly. Walmart, for example, was insisting on better terms, which meant significantly lower profits for the Bonneaus. Previously, Ed had set the prices that he needed to make a good return on his investment. Now, the buyers had consolidated, and they had the power. Ed didn't enjoy running the company as much as he had in the past, and he was finding greater pleasure in other activities; for instance, he served on a local hospital board and was actively involved in church activities.

Just as Ed and Barbara began to think about selling the company, they were contacted by a financial buyer, who wanted to use their firm as a platform and then buy up several sunglass companies. After negotiations, the Bonneaus sold their firm for about $20 million. In addition, Ed received a retainer fee for serving as a consultant to the buyer. Also, the Bonneaus' son-in-law, who was part of the company's management team, was named the new chief operating officer.

Question 1 Do you agree with the Bonneaus' decision to sell? Why or why not?

Question 2 Why did the buyers retain Ed as a consultant? (In answering this question, you might consider the quote by Bonneau in the chapter.)

Question 3 Do you see any problem with having the Bonneaus' son-in-law become the new chief operating officer?

SITUATION 3

The question of when to sell your business is seldom easy to answer. An entrepreneur asks just that question:

> I started my telecommunications business when I was 18, and I'm going to be 47 this summer. It's a successful business and provides me with a good living. I love the technology. I love my employees. I love my customers (most of them). Yet each day I feel more and more unfulfilled in what I'm doing. At the risk of sounding arrogant, I feel like a big fish in a little pond, unchallenged and bored. I have a lot of business knowledge that I feel is being wasted here, just doing the same thing year after year. I've tried some side ventures over the years without much success. I've also considered selling the business, but it's too large to be bought by a local competitor—we do about $2.5 million a year—and too small to attract the attention of large companies. Besides, I don't know what I'd do if I did sell it. And will whatever I do next allow me to earn as much money as I'm earning now? More important, will I like it, or will I regret letting go of the one thing I've had all my adult life?

Source: 69-70rodsky, "Street Smarts: Ask Norm," *Inc. Magazine*, July 2008, pp. 69–70

Question 1 Do you agree that the entrepreneur's company is not sellable?

Question 2 Are there any other options for the entrepreneur besides selling his business?

Question 3 What would you recommend the entrepreneur do? Why?

Experiential Exercises

1. Check your local newspaper for a week or so to find a privately held company that has been sold recently. Try to determine the motivation for the sale. Did it have anything to do with the prior owners' desire to cash out of the business? If so, try to find out what happened.

2. Ask a local family business owner about future plans to harvest the business. Has the owner ever been involved in a harvest? If so, ask the owner to describe what happened and how it all worked out, as well as what she or he learned from the experience. If not, ask whether the owner is aware of any company whose owners cashed out. Visit that company owner to inquire about the exit event.

3. Visit a local CPA to learn about his or her involvement in helping entrepreneurs cash out of companies.

4. Search a business magazine to identify a firm that has successfully completed an initial public offering (IPO). See what you can find out about the event on the Internet.

Small Business & Entrepreneurship Resource Center

The *Small Business and Entrepreneurship Resource Center* offers complete small business management resources through a comprehensive database that covers all major areas of starting, operating, and maintaining a business from financing, management, marketing, accounting, taxes, and more. Use the access code that came with your new book to access the site and perform the exercises in each chapter.

1. Specialty Blades, Inc. went public through an off-the-grid IPO with their bank, which saved much of the expense of a traditional IPO process. Profit sharing plans with employees can be a very effective means to increase productivity and an eye toward overall profitability of the firm, but employees must have the correct mind set for it to become an effective strategy. After reading the article "Keeping the cap tight", describe the problem briefly at Specialty Blades, and how the plastic Coke bottle and the idea of the roving bottleneck were an effective way to strengthen productivity and efficiency.

2. Lurita Doan wasn't considered successful at her old job. A computer programmer for a large federal contractor, Doan couldn't help thinking outside the box—and that wasn't a good thing. When she went to her managers with an idea to customize software for their clients, they basically told her to go back to her cubicle and be quiet. Devastated and a little angry, Doan quit her job a few weeks later and started her own company, New Technology Management, Inc., an IT company that specializes in border security and systems integration. The text covers her mentality that success means independence, and that success comes through hard work. Describe how Lurita Doan worked hard to develop a solid reputation, thus earning her major contracts.

Sources: Keeping the cap tight on those bottlenecks. (Brief Article). *Tooling & Production* 65, 10 (Jan 2000): p. 35.

A tradition of success: a legacy of business ownership drives tech security pioneer. (Black Digerati; Lurita Doan).Tamara E. Holmes. *Black Enterprise* 34, 11 (June 2004): p. 75(1).

Case 13

CITISTORAGE, P. 652

The case describes the difficulty an entrepreneur, Norm Brodsky, had in adjusting to life after selling the majority interest in his business. He continued with the business, but was no longer the "decision maker." He was told before the sale that things would change. But even after being warned, he still had trouble adjusting to his new role in the business.

ALTERNATIVE CASES FOR CHAPTER 13

Case 5, W.S. Darley & Co., p. 632

PART 4
Focusing on the Customer: Marketing Growth Strategies

©iStockphoto.com/Tom Hahn

chapters

Building Customer Relationships

In the VIDEO SPOTLIGHT
Rodgers Chevrolet
http://www.rodgerschevrolet.com

The average business keeps only 70 to 90 percent of its customers each year. Even though this may seem like a decent retention rate, keep in mind that it costs around six times as much to acquire a new customer as it does to keep an existing one[1]—and new customers often buy less than existing customers. Long-term customers usually stay with a company because they trust it, and that trust naturally translates to increased sales. Loyal customers tend to buy a company's more expensive products, are less sensitive to price increases, and bring their friends in to do business, too.[2] Experts figure that companies that increase their customer retention by a mere 5 percent per year could see net profits rise by as much as 80 percent.[3] Because keeping customers is so critical, it's essential that a company do it effectively.

The first step in developing a lasting relationship with customers is to put them at the center of the company. Pamela Rodgers understands this: Knowing, serving, and delighting her customers are the foundation of her successful auto dealership, Rodgers Chevrolet. Even though 75 percent of the company's revenue comes from car purchases, service is what sustains the company. Buying a car is exhilarating; having a car repaired is annoying. Rodgers Chevrolet has transformed the unpleasant aspects of car ownership (annual service, repairs, recalls) into a more enjoyable experience through a strong company culture focused on responsiveness, empathy, and reliability. Watch this video spotlight to see how serving the customer can be the lifeblood of this—and any—organization.

Video material provided by Hattie Bryant, Producer of Small Business School, the series on PBS Stations, Worldnet, and the Web at http://www.smallbusinessschool.org.

LOOKING AHEAD

AFTER STUDYING THIS CHAPTER, YOU SHOULD BE ABLE TO...

1. Define customer relationship management (CRM) and explain its importance to a small business.

2. Discuss the significance of providing extraordinary customer service.

3. Illustrate how technology, such as the Internet, can improve customer relationships.

4. Describe techniques used to create a customer profile.

5. Explain how consumers are decision makers and why this is important to understanding customer relationships.

6. Understand certain psychological influences on consumer behavior.

7. Describe certain sociological influences on consumer behavior.

According to Guy Kawasaki, a serial entrepreneur and co-founder of the venture capital firm Garage Technology Ventures, superb customer service starts with having the right attitude toward those who choose to do business with you. If you see customers as troublesome and believe that they always want something for nothing, your mind-set will saturate the company, service will begin to suffer, and business will be lost. That's just the way it works.[4]

When it comes to building customer relationships, some firms do get it right, however, and the response is usually very positive. Dan J. Sanders, CEO of a small chain of supermarkets, highlights the importance of treating customers well in order to build business by describing the experience of a woman who came to one of his company's stores with a serious complaint. She accused the store of selling her a ham that was out-of-date and inedible. The customer was visibly upset and raised her voice as she ranted and raved about having hungry, out-of-town guests at home and no main dish to serve them. The store director apologized but then noticed that the ham had actually come from a competitor down the street. He pointed out the mistake but said, "I know you're upset, so let's go back and find a ham that you like, and we'll get you back home right away—no charge." As they walked to the back of the store to get a replacement, the customer explained that her husband had picked up the ham on the way home from work and she didn't realize that he went to a different store. But within a few minutes, she had a new ham and was on her way home, embarrassed but satisfied with the kindness and sensitivity of the store's management.[5]

No supermarket can stay in business for long if it gives food away for free, but that's not exactly what happened. Sanders clarifies the value of this encounter when it comes to high-quality customer service and firm performance:

> This story is not about a bad ham. Certainly, we have made our share of mistakes. . . . This is about a store director focusing more on the person than on the profits. We gave away a ham, but we earned her business for life. More important, the woman became a champion for [the company]—an extension of the marketing department—telling the story to anyone who would listen.[6]

It pays to develop an attitude of service. This can build solid relationships with customers that will lead to satisfaction for both the customers and the employees who interact with them.[7] This chapter shows you how to create and maintain vital connections with customers that will satisfy your customers, enhance the reputation of your company, and lead to superior company performance.

There is much more to come on this very important topic. Chapter 14 is the first of five chapters comprising Part 4, Focusing on the Customer: Marketing Growth Strategies. Chapters 15 through 18 discuss additional marketing topics essential to growth, based on the vital customer focus that provides the foundation for this chapter.

What Is Customer Relationship Management?

1. Define customer relationship management (CRM) and explain its importance to a small business.

Customer relationship management (CRM) means different things to different firms. To some, it is symbolized by simple smiles or comments such as "thank you" and "come again" communicated by employees to customers who have just made a purchase. For others, CRM embodies a much broader marketing effort, leading to nothing short of complete customization of products and/or services to fit individual customer needs. The goals of a CRM program for most small companies fall somewhere between these two perspectives.

Regardless of the level of a firm's commitment to customer relationship management, the central message of every CRM program is "Cultivate customers for more than a one-time sale." A firm that strongly commits to this idea will appreciate the many benefits a CRM program can offer.

Formally defined, *customer relationship management (CRM)* is a "company-wide business strategy designed to optimize profitability, revenue, and customer satisfaction by focusing on highly defined and precise customer groups."[8] It is a process or method that can be used to learn more about the needs and behaviors of customers with the specific purpose of building stronger relationships with them. In a way, CRM is a mind-set that leads to customer-centric strategies, which put buyers first so that the firm can succeed. CRM involves treating customers the way the entrepreneur would want to be treated if he or she were a customer—the business version of the Golden Rule.[9]

The central theme of CRM isn't new. For decades, entrepreneurs have recognized the importance of treating customers well; "the customer is king" is an old adage. What is new, however, is giving the idea a name and using the latest techniques and innovative technologies to implement customer relationship practices. Modern CRM focuses on (1) customers rather than products; (2) changes in company processes, systems, and culture; and (3) all channels and media involved in the marketing effort, from the Internet to field sales.

The forerunners of many modern CRM techniques were developed in the 1960s by marketers like Sears and various book clubs. They simply stored information about their customers in computers for reasons other than invoicing. Their goal was to learn who their customers were, what they wanted, and what sort of interests they had. Then along came marketers with ideas about the potential benefits of adopting a customer orientation, followed by the rise of the Internet.

It should be noted that CRM, in its purest form, has nothing to do with technology, although Internet technology has definitely been a major force in CRM's development. Just as putting on the latest $300 pair of technologically designed basketball shoes doesn't make the wearer an NBA or WNBA player, buying or developing CRM computer software does not, in itself, lead to higher customer retention. But it can help if it is used properly. (The role of technology in CRM is discussed later in this chapter.) Most importantly, there must be company-wide commitment to the concept if CRM is to be productive.

customer relationship management (CRM) A company-wide business strategy designed to optimize profitability, revenue, and customer satisfaction by focusing on highly defined and precise customer groups.

The Importance of CRM to the Small Firm

As depicted in Exhibit 14-1, a firm's next sale comes from one of two sources—a current customer or a new customer. Obviously, both current and potential customers are valued by a small firm, but sometimes current customers are taken for granted and neglected. While marketing efforts devoted to bringing new customers into the fold are obviously important, keeping existing customers happy should be an even higher priority. A CRM program addresses this emphasis. Some business owners do not seem to recognize this simple truth, however, which is why CRM initiatives can be so different and vary in emphasis. And the trends do not necessarily shake out as you might expect. For example, one interesting study of CRM involvement found that family-owned companies tend to lag behind nonfamily firms when it comes to starting and completing CRM initiatives."[10]

Brian Vellmure, the founder and CEO of Initium Technology, a provider of CRM solutions to small firms, has identified five major economic benefits of maintaining relationships with current customers:[11]

1. Acquisition costs for new customers are high.
2. Long-time customers spend more money than new ones.
3. Happy customers refer their friends and colleagues.
4. Order-processing costs are lower for established customers.
5. Current customers are willing to pay more for products.

14-1 Sources of the Next Sale

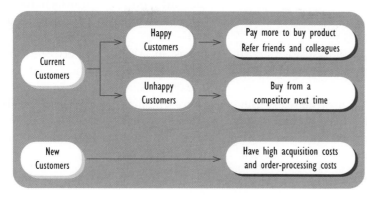

Essential Materials for a CRM Program

When you build something—a house, for example—you follow a plan or blueprint that identifies appropriate materials or component parts. Likewise, assembling a CRM program requires a plan so that the entrepreneur knows what will be required (people, processes, and so on) to establish a successful initiative. In the remainder of this chapter, we consider two of the vital building blocks of any CRM program: (1) outstanding relationships with customers and (2) knowledge of consumer behavior. These components may be constructed with a variety of "materials," as illustrated in Exhibit 14-2. In the sections that follow, we examine those materials we believe to be tremendously important in constructing these two building blocks.

14-2 Essential Materials of a Successful CRM Program

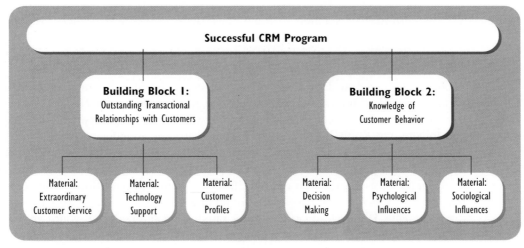

Creating Positive Transactional Relationships through Extraordinary Service

2. Discuss the significance of providing extraordinary customer service.

transactional relationship
An association between a business and a customer that begins (or ends) with a purchase or a business deal.

To be successful in the long run, small companies need to concentrate on building positive transactional relationships with customers (see the first building block in Exhibit 14-2). A *transactional relationship* is an association between a business and a customer that begins (or ends) with a one-time purchase or a business exchange. Clearly, the nature of such relationships can vary greatly. But consumers who have positive interactions with a business are much more likely to become loyal customers, which points to the obvious importance of handling these transactions with great care. Three basic beliefs underlie our emphasis on providing exceptional customer service:

1. Small businesses possess greater potential for providing superior customer service than do large firms.
2. Superior customer service leads to customer satisfaction.
3. Customer satisfaction results in a positive transactional relationship.

As these beliefs suggest, failure to emphasize customer service jeopardizes any effort to attain a positive customer relationship. And the task only gets more challenging as time goes on. "My message to small companies is that big companies are coming after you with better customer service, so you'd better be paying attention," says Edward Reilly, president and CEO of the American Management Association.[12]

There is plenty of room for improvement—for businesses of all sizes. A recent study by CRMGuru.com found that only 22 percent of surveyed customers have experiences with companies that they would describe as "excellent."[13] This creates opportunities for entrepreneurs like Marx Acosta-Rubio, 38, who started his California-based toner cartridge and office supplies company, Onestop, based on what he calls a "customer intimacy model." According to Acosta-Rubio, "Our competitors focus on price and availability, but we discovered a market that craves service." As part of its attentive service efforts, Onestop representatives call clients *before* they run out of supplies, maintaining a sense of personal connection by using the phone rather than expecting clients to place their orders online, which is the norm in the industry. As a result, Onestop generates more than $16 million in annual sales with only 14 salespeople, which means that its sales staff is nearly five times as productive as those working for its major competitors.[14]

Managing Customer Satisfaction

Why is customer satisfaction so important? Because happy customers are loyal customers, and that translates very clearly to company performance. Research conducted by Ruth Bolton, professor of marketing at Arizona State University, has shown that a mere 10 percent increase in customer satisfaction leads to an 8 percent increase in the duration of customer relationships on average, which translates to an 8 percent increase in sales generated over the long term.[15] It certainly pays to think carefully about the company–customer interface!

Bolton's research reports the general (linear) relationship between customer satisfaction and loyalty, but Keith Jezek, a serial entrepreneur and founder of an innovative automobile inventory management service called vAuto.com, has observed that the increase may not track along a straight line (see Exhibit 14-3). In his experience, customer loyalty seems to rise at an increasing rate as satisfaction goes up. In other words, initial efforts to increase satisfaction may not "pack as much punch" as you would like, but there is every reason to continue to make improvements. Higher levels of customer satisfaction can really set your company apart from the competition, with your reward being customers' commitment to doing business with you. Jezek considers the entrepreneur's goal as moving customers from the Zone of Indifference,

Rick Davis on CRM in a Service-Oriented Business

DAVACO is a service-oriented business, so we differentiate our company by the people we employ and the elements that make them more effective and productive at their jobs. Technology plays a very important role in making that happen. By utilizing a proprietary collection of technological components, DAVACO can provide operational efficiencies, increased visibility, and speed to market for a client list that represents the who's who of national retail brands.

For example, we use technology to manage our resources and skill sets internally, so that we can be assured that the right individuals and teams are always assigned to each job.

DAVACO equips its corporate and field employees with mobile technology, like pocket PCs, laptops, cell phones, BlackBerries, and digital cameras, which allows our clients to

receive realtime updates. DAVACO also utilizes client-specific, Web-based portals that provide a centralized location for clients to view their store data, with 24-hour access to information, schedules, and customized reporting.

DAVACO has made it a priority to research, finance, and implement the best technology solutions that provide real business results and efficiencies for everyday operations. The firm's management team has made a conscientious decision to continuously reinvest profits in the company in order to better support our clients—because, in the end, happy clients are what makes our business a success.

where loyalty has not yet been established and customers could easily take their business elsewhere, toward the Zone of Affection, where customer loyalty is stable and profits are higher. He refers to highly committed customers as Apostles, since they have "sold out" to the company and are unlikely to shift to a rival's products. Customer movement in the other direction (toward the Zone of Hostility) is unfavorable and destructive to the business, however, which is why these customers are referred to as Terrorists.[16] All of Jezek's observations underscore the same general point: Improving customer satisfaction creates increased loyalty, which is good for performance.

EXHIBIT 14-3 The Rising Returns of Customer Satisfaction

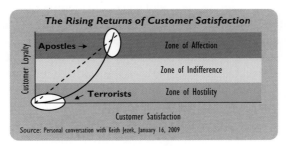

Companies control a number of factors that shape interactions with customers, and some of the more powerful factors can move customers toward increased satisfaction. For example, customers have basic expectations regarding the benefits they should receive from any firm selling the product or service that your company provides. Your offering must meet these most basic expectations to satisfy customers and earn their repeat business. Beyond that, customers anticipate that your business will provide assistance to them at the time they make a purchase and later, if they should encounter problems. And keep in mind that those who buy prestige products, such as a Rolex watch, will expect more intensive assistance.

Truly personal attention is, perhaps, the "gold standard" against which the quality of customer service is judged; customized service never goes out of style. Firms that find a way to provide the best response to the needs of a specific buyer in a given situation are sure to have satisfied and loyal customers—and plenty of them. It follows, however, that personalized service will be an option only for those companies that listen intently to their buyers or clients and thus understand their precise needs.

Small companies are in a unique position to offer truly exceptional service. Because they have fewer customers, they are able to build stronger and closer relationships with those they serve—and hold on to them as customers. The following are some of the more common signposts on the road to extraordinary service:[17]

- *Doing business on a first-name basis.* Small ventures have a big advantage over large corporations like Walmart and McDonalds: They can get to know their customers by name and greet them as friends. Doing so establishes a bond that is powerful and encourages loyalty.

- *Keeping in touch.* Personal interactions are key to building relationships, so face-to-face and phone conversations are much more effective than e-mail messages or mass mailings. Asking for feedback during these interactions is helpful to your business and shows that you are committed to getting customers' approval. It also confirms that you care about more than selling.

- *Finding ways to help.* Helping customers doesn't always lead to an immediate sale, but it can be good for business. Send them articles and information of interest with a kind note attached, remind them of important dates (like birthdays and anniversaries), and so on. The cost to you is minimal, but these acts show you care, and the favor is often returned in the future.

- *Customizing your service to meet customer preferences.* If you remember your customers' personal preferences and adjust your service to meet them, then you have increased the value of what you offer while showing customers that they are important to you.

- *Addressing problems promptly.* When an issue arises, take steps to resolve it quickly, if at all possible. Doing so lets a customer know that he or she is important to you. Contact lost customers to find out why they went elsewhere, and use that information to correct deficiencies.

Denny Fulk, a serial entrepreneur and one of the members of the Go-To Team for this book, emphasizes the importance of building and maintaining customer relationships to business success. Fulk mentions a friend who runs a flourishing Internet-based business and responds regularly to his customers' questions, even if he is traveling outside of the United States. Many of his customers are located in other parts of the world, but he and his staff are committed to responding to all customer phone calls and e-mail within 24 hours. Fulk explains why this emphasis on prompt communication is so important:

If you operate a business, no matter how small or large, customers like to feel there is a person who really cares about their needs. Whether the information shared is by telephone or e-mail, promptness and a personal approach are keys to the customer's having a good feeling about your company. Regardless of whether your business is a startup or a very established company, a customer who receives a prompt, accurate, and understanding response will be very likely to continue doing business with your company.[18]

Guy Kawasaki, the business guru mentioned earlier in this chapter, is a convincing advocate of returning calls and e-mail promptly, following the "24-hour rule" just mentioned. To test Kawasaki's commitment to this principle, an entrepreneur e-mailed him at 10:00 P.M. one evening, and he received a reply in about 10 minutes![19]

In recent years, some small business owners have begun to go beyond simple CRM to emphasize *customer experience management (CEM)*. This approach recognizes that with every interaction, customers learn something about a business that will either strengthen or weaken their satisfaction and desire to return, spend more, and recommend the company to others. Having a positive experience with a business can make all the difference in the world, especially if the products and prices are similar to those of competitors; it actually becomes part of the firm's value equation.

Ensuring pleasant communications with customers is a central focus of CEM initiatives. For example, since no one likes being put on hold during a phone call, entrepreneur and veteran radio talk show host Perry Wright has come up with a way to keep customers entertained while they wait. Known as the On-Hold Guy, Wright has developed software that features one-liners, odd facts, and puns to play for waiting customers. "While I was doing radio, I spent a lot of time on the phone and on hold, listening to sterile, irritating messages," he says. "I thought there had to be a better way, an off-the-wall approach." It turns out that he was right. Automated phone systems can save on costs, but they frustrate callers. According to Wright, 70 percent of business phone callers are put on hold, and nearly 60 percent of these hang up, while 30 percent will not call back . . . ever! Wright's software randomly plays his messages, which can actually put customers in a good mood before they are connected to salespeople. One caller went so far as to say, "Put me back on hold, QUICK; I want to hear the rest."[20] (To hear a sample of the On-Hold Guy's product, go to http://onholdguy.com/ohg/demos.aspx.)

Providing exceptional customer service will give small firms a competitive edge, regardless of the nature of the business, and more tools are available than ever before to make this possible. Once again, keep in mind that it costs far more to replace a customer than to keep one, but small businesses can really shine when it comes to managing this relationship. Because of their close and personal contact with those they serve, small firms are typically better than large firms when it comes to knowing their customers' needs and offering the top-notch and personalized service that keeps customers coming back.

> *customer experience management (CEM)* An approach that recognizes that with every interaction, customers learn something about a company that will affect their desire to do business there in the future.

Evaluating a Firm's Customer Service Health

Establishing an effective customer service program begins with determining the firm's "customer service quotient," which indicates how well the firm is currently serving its customers. Then strategies can be developed to improve the effectiveness of customer service efforts. Exhibit 14-4 lists some popular approaches to creating customer service strategies; it also provides space for evaluating how well a small firm is currently performing in each area and what it can do to improve its customer service.

How good or bad is the quality of customer service among both large and small firms? An overview of research concerning customer service, reported in *USAToday,* described the situation this way:[21]

- *On the phone.* Jon Anaton, director of benchmark research at Purdue University's Center for Customer-Driven Quality, reports that approximately four of every five companies do a poor job of providing customers with the assistance they need.

- *Online.* Companies provide conveniences to customers through their websites, but many still drop the ball when it comes to online interaction. According to Forrester Research,

entrepreneurial challenges

Pampering Customers by Telling Them to Go Away!

Like so many other people, Randall and Leighsa Francis moved to the city of Bend in central Oregon after vacationing there for years and falling in love with the area. They enjoy all that the region has to offer—world-class golf courses, river and mountain activities, and even the city's unique cultural scene. It's no mystery to them that Bend was named one of America's "Top 20 Small Cities" to live in.

But the couple doesn't just *live* in Bend; they have also established a thriving small business there, Bend Real Estate Team, Inc. To set their company apart from the competition, they decided to get (*amazingly*) close to their customers . . . by vacationing with them! For example, they took a local builder and his wife and daughter to Hawaii for a week of tropical adventure. Later, when they sold a house to his cousin, they decided to take his family, too. "It's a great way to say thank you and build strong relationships through a personal touch," says Leighsa. "The investment comes back to you in spades." And then some! The cousin provided four referrals, and the builder has decided to work with Bend Real Estate Team on an exclusive basis. Extraordinary customer service isn't cheap, but it may be time and money well spent.

Sources: Andrea Pope, "Going Places," *Entrepreneur*, Vol. 36, No. 8 (August 2008), p. 68; and "About Us," http://www.bendrealestateteam.com/About_Us.php, accessed January 27, 2009.

http://www.bendrealestateteam.com

©iStockphoto/Sergey Surkov

a technology and market research group, firms fail to answer around 35 percent of their e-mail inquiries within seven days of receiving them, and nearly 25 percent are never answered at all.

- *On hold.* Many companies use Interactive Voice Response (IVR) software, which allows computers to direct callers to the assistance they need; however, Forrester Research found that more than 90 percent of callers don't like these systems.

- *In a rage.* Customer Care Measurement & Consulting, a CRM research company, found that one-third of the customers they surveyed admitted to raising their voices at customer service representatives during the previous year; nearly one in ten say they cursed at the reps in that same one-year period.

- *In response.* PlanetFeedback.com is a website that allows consumers to offer feedback on the products and services they purchase. The site's marketing director estimates that two-thirds of the 800,000 complaints posted to its website over a recent three-year period were prompted by the failure of companies to respond to customers.

As one small business owner observed, "Real service is such a rare commodity out there—it's really a desert of mediocrity."[22] That pretty much says it all.

Although customer service issues may be identified through a formal review process within the small firm, they often surface via customer complaints in the course of normal daily business operations. (Later in this chapter, we will show how complaint activity is part of

EXHIBIT

Which of the following can be used to support your marketing objectives?	For each strategy, comment below on: 1. How well your company is doing. 2. Improvements to pursue further.
Provide an exceptional experience throughout every transaction by ensuring that customers are acknowledged, appreciated, and find it easy to do business with you. Note that this requires you to (1) make a list of the typical chain of contacts between you and your customers—from when they first see your advertisement until you send them a customer survey after the sale and (2) evaluate your company's performance on each contact point.	
Provide sales materials that are clear and easy to understand, including website, marketing materials, retail displays, and sales conversations.	
Respond promptly to customers' requests and concerns by acting with urgency and responsibility in customer inquiries, transactions, and complaints. Have a service recovery plan in place.	
Listen to customers and respond accordingly by soliciting feedback, encouraging interaction, staying engaged throughout transactions, and taking the appropriate action necessary to please the customer.	
Stand behind products/services by providing guarantees and warranties and ensuring customers that you deliver on your promises. Also, create products and deliver services that exceed expectations.	
Treat customers as family members and best friends by valuing them the same way you honor those you care most about.	
Stay in the hearts and minds of customers by not taking customers for granted and finding ways to let them know you hold their best interests.	
Other initiatives? List them here.	

Source: Adapted from "Exceptional Customer Experiences," Ewing Marion Kauffman Foundation, http://www.entrepreneurship.org/uploadedfiles/Documents/Customer_Experiences.pdf, accessed February 3, 2009.

the overall consumer behavior process.) Every firm strives to eliminate customer complaints. When they occur, however, they should be analyzed carefully to uncover possible weaknesses in product quality and/or customer service.

What is the special significance of customer complaints to small businesses? It is that small firms are *potentially* in a much better position to respond to such grievances and, thereby, to achieve greater customer satisfaction. Why? Because most problems are solvable simply by dealing with issues as they arise, thus giving customers more attention and respect. And showing respect is often easier for a small company, because it has fewer employees and can give each of them the authority to act in customers' best interests. In contrast, a large corporation often assigns that responsibility to a single manager, who has limited contact with customers.

This very point is emphasized by John Stites, a member of the Go To Team for this book. In his words, "The advantage that a small firm has over a larger firm in customer relationship management is that the owner of the company is closer to the customers and more likely to get accurate feedback, unfiltered by layers of management." He goes on to explain that most small business owners can't afford to neglect customer relationships, because the owner of a company with only 100 customers will feel the loss of a single customer much more than will the owner of a larger firm with 1,000 customers.[23]

What do consumers do when they are displeased? As Exhibit 14-5 shows, these buyers have several options for dealing with their dissatisfaction, and most of these options threaten repeat sales. Only one—a private complaint to the offending company—is desirable to the business. Because customers have multiple complaint options, quality customer service is critical, both before and after a sale.

Small business owners can also learn about customer service concerns through personal observation and other research techniques. By talking directly to customers or by playing the customer's role anonymously—for example, by making a telephone call to one's own business to see how customers are treated—an entrepreneur can evaluate service quality. Some restaurants and motels invite feedback on customer service by providing comment cards to those they serve.

EXHIBIT

14-5 Consumer Options for Dealing with Product or Service Dissatisfaction

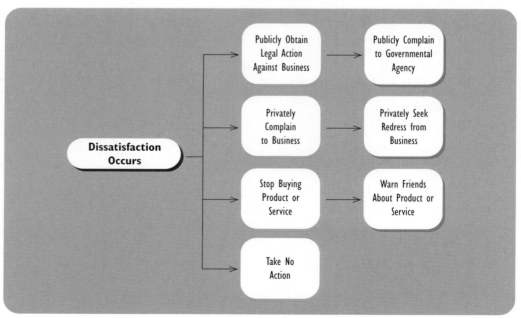

Sometimes a creative twist on standard marketing research methods can improve their effectiveness. This was certainly true for Jason Belkin, owner of Hampton Coffee Company, with two coffee-house locations in New York. Belkin had always used a mystery shopper service (which hires individuals to pose as real customers to evaluate a company's true service performance) to assess customer experiences but decided to turn to comment cards for the information he wanted; he offered a free cup of coffee or tea to customers who fill out a card. Since trying this new approach, Belkin's business has increased, despite competition from new stores opened by Starbucks nearby. He attributes this success partly to the effective use of the information that was collected on the comment cards.[24]

Whatever method is used, evaluating customer service is critical for any business. Reflect on the success that Sewell Village Cadillac had after developing customer service strategies. This car dealership in Dallas, Texas, is famous for its customer service. The owner, Carl Sewell, established the customer service focus a very long time ago, in 1967, when Sewell Village was in third place among three Dallas Cadillac dealers. He realized that most people didn't like doing business with car dealers, so he simply began asking customers what it was that they disliked so much. Three major areas of dissatisfaction were identified—service hours, being without a car during service, and poor or incorrect repairs. By responding to these concerns (for example, by scheduling more service hours), Sewell Village Cadillac improved its customer satisfaction image dramatically. And Sewell continues to sharpen his company's customer service focus by applying the principles he outlined in his very popular book, *Customers for Life*. Successful CRM initiatives require a long-term commitment to customers served and practices that work.

Implementation of some forms of customer service are inexpensive—or even free (for example, customer-contact personnel may just need to be encouraged to smile and greet visitors warmly)—but offering a full program of superior customer service before, during, and after a sale can be a costly undertaking. These costs often can be passed along to the purchaser as part of the price of a product or service, or they can sometimes be recouped separately, based on the amount of service requested (through extended product warranties, for example). It may seem surprising, but many customers are willing to pay a premium price, as long as good service is part of the buying experience.

Using Technology to Support Customer Relationship Management

Long-term transactional relationships with customers are built on good information, and a logical time to gather helpful data is during direct customer contacts, such as when a product is being sold. Customers may be contacted in many ways, including phone calls, letters, faxes, personal interactions, e-mail—even text messages. The ability to enjoy one-on-one contact with customers has always been a competitive advantage for small firms. To make this connection even easier, numerous software packages containing word-processing, spreadsheet, and database tools are also available to assist in supporting customer contacts.

3. Illustrate how technology, such as the Internet, can improve customer relationships.

CRM software programs are designed to help companies gather all customer contact information into a single data management program. Web-based marketers, in particular, are attracted to such technology, because it helps to make their complex job far more manageable. Most online shoppers expect to receive excellent customer service; companies are in a much better position to give it if they adopt e-mail options, live chat, and other platforms for interaction and personal attention. Experts point out that customers typically appreciate the conveniences that are built into many company websites, but they can quickly become frustrated when the experience does not go exactly as planned—which happens far too often.[25]

Deciding which marketing activity should get initial CRM support is not always easy. However, the sales department is a popular place to start, because its personnel nearly always generate the greatest amount of customer contact. CRM emphasizes such sales activities as filling orders promptly and accurately, managing follow-up contacts to ensure customer satisfaction, and providing user-friendly call centers to handle all inquiries, including complaints. It's a complex mix of tasks, but technologies are available to support all of these activities and many others.

Chris McCann, president of 1-800-FLOWERS.COM, seems to be ahead of the competition when it comes to incorporating technology into his business. During the very early days of the Internet, the company already had an online presence; by the late 1990s, it had a full-fledged e-commerce operation. Now McCann is using a CRM software package from SAS Institute, Inc., to build close relationships with customers, and the investment is paying off. In his words, CRM technology "has given me the ability to grow my business, whether the economy has been up or down." Other retailers are being hammered by stiff competition and challenging economic conditions, but the revenues of 1-800-FLOWERS.COM continue to rise, nearly doubling over the last five years.[26]

Using a product called SAS Real-Time Decision Maker, McCann's business can access a range of processes that collect, classify, analyze, and interpret data in order to identify and understand key patterns and relationships that drive the decision to purchase. This allows 1-800-FLOWERS.COM to adjust its approach to the unique needs and habits of each individual customer. For example, when a repeat customer logs on to the firm's website, the first web page will immediately present only those options that match the customer's personal preferences. "If a customer usually buys tulips for his wife, we show him our newest and best tulip selections," says Aaron Cano, the company's vice president for customer knowledge management. With SAS technology to support its customer interactions, Cano points out, "no one else is able to connect customer information with real-time transaction data the way we can." This gives the company a significant competitive advantage.[27]

Having ample support resources for CRM information technology can be a concern for a small firm. This has led some entrepreneurs to outsource certain applications. For example, hosted call centers, which handle e-mail and Web communications for clients, may be more cost effective than comparable in-house centers, a crucial consideration for many cash-strapped small businesses. In addition to cost, a lack of internal expertise is a major justification for using these outside services.

Many companies have decided to control the cost of customer assistance by using alternatives that are cheaper than hiring more sales reps or relying on call center outsourcing. For example, some have adopted automated Web-based self-service systems, sometimes called *customer information management systems*. When a customer service rep handles a single telephone call, text chat, or e-mail, it can cost the company an average of $5 to $7, but self-service inquiries handled on the Internet will cost less than 60 cents per contact. One popular self-service option is to post a list of Frequently Asked Questions (FAQs), and research shows that 40 percent of organizations have these on their websites. But even this simple tool is becoming more sophisticated. A company can now buy smart software that will recognize the questions website visitors are most interested in and place those at the top of the list. Such systems can cut down the cost of serving customers while taking some of the repetition out of tending to their needs.[28]

The list of tools supporting CRM grows longer every day, and they are becoming much more user-friendly as time goes on. For example, the *Wall Street Journal* recently surveyed 30 executives and managers in large and small enterprises that are using Web 2.0 as a source of marketing support tools, and they found that the applications are expanding rapidly. So, what is Web 2.0, anyway? It represents an expanded use of the Internet to support the blogs, wikis, social-networking sites, and other online communities that allow people to build social as well as business connections, to share information, and to collaborate on projects—all online. A growing number of marketers are using Web 2.0 to form relationships with customers, but most companies are behind the curve when it comes to applying the tools provided to build and maintain a business.[29]

Some firms use Web 2.0 applications to promote products or services through blogs and other means of online connection, and this is a good place to start. But the real power comes in the form of building relationships with customers.

> A leading greeting-card and gift company . . . is one of many that have set up an online community—a site where it can talk to consumers and the consumers can talk to each other. The company solicits opinions on various aspects of greeting-card design and on ideas for gifts and their pricing. It also asks the consumers to talk about their lifestyles and even upload photos of themselves, so that it can better understand its market.[30]

Online communities, such as this one, provide a rich source of feedback and ideas for product development, and in a form that is much faster and cheaper to use than the focus groups and surveys that have been a staple of common marketing practice. But perhaps more important, Web 2.0 tools can be used to give customers a sense of connection with the enterprise, an identity that results from their active participation in the company's business. For this, there is no substitute.

But all this talk of technology may lead you to conclude that working with CRM programs is an uninspiring chore for tech-challenged entrepreneurs. Don't be concerned—low-tech solutions can also be effective. Pam Felix started her quick-service Mexican restaurant, California Tortilla, in Bethesda, Maryland, in 1995. Five years later, she launched a company website, with the primary goal of building an e-mail list to improve communication with customers. Since then, she has used the website to communicate the theme of "having fun," and she does this by injecting a touch of lightheartedness into all that she does online. Consider these observations of the highlights of the previous year, which were posted on the site's "Taco Talk" page in January of 2009.[31]

- *Most Exciting Accomplishment.* Breaking the Guinness world record for the largest rock paper scissors contest with 512 contestants. Yee-ha!
- *Least Exciting Accomplishment.* Not breaking the world record for the largest rock paper scissors contest with 512 contestants. Apparently Guinness forgot to tell us that someone else broke the record immediately after we called to find out how many people we'd need to win. What's up with that? ("Did we say 512? It's now 8 bazillion." How hard would that have been?)
- *Most Ill-Advised Phone Call.* The congratulatory phone call I made to the guy who used his Burrito Elito card the second most. Apparently it made him realize he eats here too much and he hasn't been back since. Well that didn't work out how I planned now, did it?
- *Best Trend of 2008.* Winning awards in national publications, including "Best Charitable Promotion," "Most Kid-Friendly Restaurant," and "Best Vegetarian Restaurant."
- *Worst Trend of 2008.* None of these awards came with cash prizes.

"I'm not sure I had any expectations [for the Internet]," says Felix. "But since I put out a goofy, monthly newsletter that most people seem to like, I thought at the very least I could keep conveying that goofy mom-and-pop feel via the Internet." And this has worked well to help her build favorable relationships with customers. "People feel like they have a personal connection with us—and that's something the big chains are never going to have with their customers," Felix believes. The Internet also provides feedback, identifying the restaurant's strengths and weaknesses. Plus, Felix says, "I get a lot of funny/strange e-mails that I get to use in the newsletter. . . . I ran out of things to say about burritos about 6 years ago."[32]

Building Customer Profiles for a CRM Program

customer profile
A collection of information about a customer, including demographic data, attitudes, preferences, and other behavioral characteristics, as defined by CRM goals.

Most entrepreneurs say that the best way to stay in touch with customers and to identify their needs is to talk to them. Such conversations lead to a detailed understanding of each customer and thus offer insights from which to build a *customer profile*, a collection of information about a customer, including demographic data, attitudes, preferences, and other behavioral characteristics, as defined by CRM goals. In a very small business, the customer profiles maintained in the entrepreneur's head often constitute the company's CRM "database." At some point in a company's growth, however, it becomes impossible for the small business owner to continue to develop profiles using this method alone. It is then time to turn to formal, computer-based databases.

Customer profiles are essential to a successful CRM program, as they represent building material for the required knowledge of customers. Customer contact data, from sources such as warranty cards and accounting records, can be used to develop a profile. For Web-based ventures, current information can be collected at the point of contact, as customers order online.

What types of information should be included in a customer profile? Four major categories of information have been identified:[33]

- *Transactions.* A complete purchase history with accompanying details (price paid; SKU, which identifies the product purchased; delivery date).
- *Customer contacts.* Sales calls and service requests, including all customer- and company-initiated contacts.
- *Descriptive information.* Background information used for market segmentation and other data analysis purposes.
- *Responses to marketing stimuli.* Information on whether or not the customer responded to a direct marketing initiative, a sales contact, and/or any other direct contact.

Formal interviews with customers provide another way to gather profile information. These interviews can be in-person, or they can take the form of a questionnaire. Consider, for example, Rejuvenation Lamp and Fixture Company, in Portland, Oregon, which sells reproduction light fixtures mainly through catalogs and its website. Its system for understanding its customers includes a questionnaire.

In every box of lights that is shipped, the company includes a questionnaire with a return stamp. The questionnaire is humorous and fun to fill out. It not only collects information about the purchases, it asks [customers] what products they might want that Rejuvenation doesn't carry. The "how can we help you?" message, combined with the prepaid return and humorous presentation, earns Rejuvenation thousands of responses each month.[34]

Entrepreneur Mac McConnell conducts surveys of walk-in customers at his Artful Framer Gallery in Plantation, Florida. Based on the results of one recent survey, which consisted of a simple one-page questionnaire, he reworked his business to better satisfy customers' desires. The survey showed that quality was first priority for customers and price was last. In response to the feedback, McConnell dropped the low-end line and made higher-priced museum framing his specialty.[35] Making important business decisions based on the results of a one-page survey can be risky, but the changes McConnell made to his company have worked out very well.

Customer profiles primarily reflect demographic variables such as age, gender, and marital status, but they can also include behavioral, psychological, and sociological information. Understanding the aspects of consumer behavior presented in the following sections can help

LIVING THE DREAM:

entrepreneurial challenges

When You Care Enough to Ignore Your Customers

There is an old saying that boldly declares, "The customer is always right." And companies that are committed to listening attentively to their customers are almost always well served by the practice. However, superior customer service sometimes requires a business to *ignore* its patrons' requests and feedback.

GlobalEnglish, a company with a truly global perspective and a leading provider of online language training tools and support services, has learned that customer input can sometimes be way off the mark. The venture's website forthrightly states that its purpose is "to help organizations achieve success by equipping their employees with the business English and communication skills necessary to conduct global business." In line with this vision, Deepak Desai, the firm's CEO, takes customer feedback very seriously . . . he just doesn't always respond to it. From the barrage of comments and complaints that come in, most deserve a response and adjustment—but some do not. The trick is knowing the difference.

GlobalEnglish customers asked for more assistance when writing business documents in English, so the company opened an online writing center with customized sample documents. Others complained about the repetition that is part of the company's language training, which is a natural frustration, but Desai knew that responding to their cries for a change in methods would not serve them well (since repetition is necessary to language learning), so he disregarded these requests. It

©Roger Ressmeyer/Starlight/Corbis

sometimes takes great insight—and courage—to deny a customer's demands.

History is littered with examples of marketers who listened to customers and lived to regret it, such as when the Coca-Cola Co. caved in to customers' preferences and gave them the New Coke they seemed to be asking for, only to see the product fail miserably. *Inc. Magazine* columnist David H. Freedman highlights the many possible marketing landmines that can be set off on the road to highly responsive customer service:

> For starters, you can end up listening to the wrong customers. Online, the loudest and most-oft-heard customers might think very differently from the heart of your customer base. Sometimes a squeaky wheel is simply misaligned and heading in the wrong direction. If Microsoft took its cues from the constant stream of disdain that it attracts from the cranky, iconoclastic message posters who tend to dominate online chatter, the company might have killed its Microsoft software long ago.

Furthermore, the vast herd of potential buyers may push a company to offer a new product that meets their needs wonderfully but is costly to make and out of line with the company's strategic direction. And customers are not in a position to know all that a company can do for them, so allowing them to be the primary driver of new product or service innovation initiatives can be very limiting. It may be difficult to sort out, but ignoring customers' demands can sometimes be the best way to show that you care.

Sources: "A Global Company with a Shared Vision and Purpose," http://www.globalenglish.com/m/about/default.aspx, accessed January 29, 2009; and David H. Freedman, "Ask, and You Shall Be Misled," *Inc., Magazine* Vol. 29, No. 7 (July 2007), pp. 63–64.

http://www.globalenglish.com

entrepreneurs create customer profiles that go beyond demographics. Some entrepreneurs might even want to consider taking a course to broaden their knowledge of consumer behavior concepts. Such courses are commonly offered by local colleges, small business development centers, chambers of commerce, and other educational service providers.

Customers as Decision Makers

5. Explain how consumers are decision makers and why this is important to understanding customer relationships.

If you refer back to Exhibit 14-2 on page 365, you will see that the second primary building block supporting a successful CRM program involves knowledge of customer behavior. The three interrelated "materials" that combine to form that particular building block include the decision-making process, psychological influences, and sociological influences. Offering an expanded view of the first of these materials, Exhibit 14-6 illustrates how consumer decision making flows through four stages:

Stage 1: Problem recognition

Stage 2: Information search and evaluation

Stage 3: The purchase decision

Stage 4: Post-purchase evaluation

We'll use this widely accepted model to examine decision making among small business customers.

Problem Recognition

Problem recognition (stage 1) occurs when a consumer realizes that her or his current state of affairs differs significantly from some ideal state. Some problems are routine conditions of depletion, such as a lack of food when lunchtime arrives. Other problems arise less frequently and may evolve slowly. Recognition of the need to replace the family dining table, for example, may take years to develop.

EXHIBIT 14-6 Simplified Model of Consumer Behavior

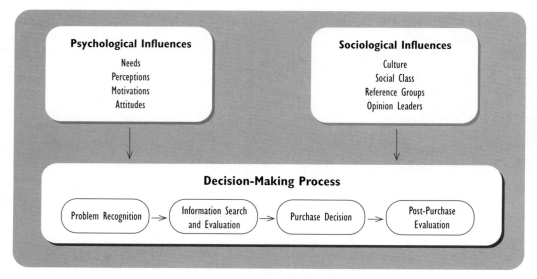

A consumer must recognize a problem before purchase behavior can begin. Thus, the problem-recognition stage cannot be overlooked. Many small firms develop their product strategy as if consumers were in the later stages of the decision-making process, when in reality they have not yet recognized that a problem even exists!

Many factors influence consumers' recognition of a problem—either by changing the actual state of affairs or by affecting the desired state. Here are a few examples:

- A change in financial status (a job promotion with a salary increase)
- A change in household characteristics (the birth of a baby)
- Normal depletion (using up the last tube of toothpaste)
- Product or service performance (breakdown of the DVD player)
- Past decisions (poor repair service on a car)
- The availability of products (introduction of a new product)

An entrepreneur must understand the problem-recognition stage in order to decide on the appropriate marketing strategy to use. In some situations, a small business owner needs to *influence* problem recognition. In other situations, she or he may simply be able to *react* to problems that consumers have identified on their own.

Information Search and Evaluation

The second stage in consumer decision making involves consumers' collection and evaluation of appropriate information from both internal and external sources. The consumer's principal objective is to establish *evaluative criteria*—the features or characteristics of the product or service that the consumer will use to compare brands.

Small business owners should understand which evaluative criteria consumers use to formulate their evoked set. An *evoked set* is a group of brands that a consumer is both aware of and willing to consider as a solution to a purchase problem. Thus, the initial challenge for a new venture is to gain *market awareness* for its product or service. Only then will the brand have the opportunity to become part of consumers' evoked sets.

evaluative criteria
The features or characteristics of a product or service that customers use to compare brands.

evoked set
A group of brands that a consumer is both aware of and willing to consider as a solution to a purchase problem.

Purchase Decision

Once consumers have evaluated brands in their evoked set and made their choice, they must still decide how and where to make the purchase (stage 3). A substantial volume of retail sales now comes from nonstore settings such as catalogs, TV shopping channels, and the Internet. These outlets have created a complex and challenging environment in which to develop marketing strategy. And consumers attribute many different advantages and disadvantages to various shopping outlets, making it difficult for the small firm to devise a single correct strategy. Sometimes, however, simple recognition of these factors can be helpful.

Of course, not every purchase decision is planned prior to entering a store or looking at a mail-order catalog. Studies show that most types of purchases from traditional retail outlets are not planned or intended prior to the customers' entering the store. This fact underscores the tremendous importance of such features as store layout, sales personnel, and point-of-purchase displays.[36]

Post-Purchase Evaluation

The consumer decision-making process does not end with a purchase. Small businesses that desire repeat purchases from customers (and they all should) need to understand post-purchase behavior (stage 4). Exhibit 14-7 illustrates several consumer activities that occur during

EXHIBIT

Post-Purchase
Dissonance
"Did I buy the right one?"

Negative Evaluation
"It doesn't work well."

Consumer
Complaints
"I'm calling the store."

Purchase
"This is the one I want."

Usage
"I found another use for ...."

Product Disposal
"Can I trade this in?"

No Repurchase

Repurchase

Positive Evaluation
"It works great."

cognitive dissonance
The anxiety that occurs when a customer has second thoughts immediately following a purchase.

post-purchase evaluation. Two of these activities—post-purchase dissonance and complaint behavior—are directly related to customer satisfaction.

Post-purchase dissonance is a type of *cognitive dissonance,* a psychological tension that occurs immediately following a purchase decision when consumers have second thoughts as to the wisdom of their purchase. This dissonance can influence how a consumer evaluates a product and his or her ultimate level of satisfaction with it.

Some purchased products are never used, but most are. During and after their use, the product and the purchase process are evaluated. A consumer who is unhappy with the product or process may complain. This is an important opportunity for a business to make things right; a well-handled complaint may prevent the loss of a valuable customer. The outcome of the post-purchase process is a final level of customer satisfaction that affects customer loyalty and the likelihood of repeat purchases and product usage. It can also lead to brand switching and discontinued use of the product.

The best way to preserve customer satisfaction is to deal with issues and complaints as soon as possible and in the most effective way possible. This calls for a well-trained, informed, and cooperative work force. At The Angus Barn in Raleigh, North Carolina, owner Van Eure empowers her employees to ensure customer satisfaction. Diners at the Raleigh landmark do not have to look for a manager when they have a complaint, because Eure encourages employees to use the "twenty-foot rule"—that is, any restaurant employee within 20 feet of a problem, challenge, or opportunity should get involved in making sure that all customers leave completely satisfied. For example, waiters can provide dessert to a diner free of charge or accommodate a customer's needs by altering the seating chart. This rule reflects Eure's belief that employees are better able than managers (who often must juggle many tasks at once) to see all sides of an issue. Because they are so central to the success of the operation, Eure takes very good care of those who work for her, as reflected by the very low turnover rate among her 220 employees. To show her appreciation, Eure hosts an employee banquet each year, where she presents numerous awards. She believes that her approach to resolving customer concerns underlies the high satisfaction quotient of both her customers and her employees.[37]

Understanding Psychological Influences on Customers

A major component of the consumer behavior model, as presented in Exhibit 14-6, is psychological influences. The four psychological influences that have the greatest relevance to small businesses are needs, perceptions, motivations, and attitudes.

6. Understand certain psychological influences on consumer behavior.

Needs

Needs are often described as the starting point for all behavior. Without needs, there would be no behavior. Although consumer needs are innumerable, they can be identified as falling into four categories—physiological, social, psychological, and spiritual.

Consumers' needs are never completely satisfied, thereby ensuring the continued existence of business. One of the more complex characteristics of needs is the way in which they function together in shaping behavior. In other words, various needs operate simultaneously, making it difficult to determine which need is being satisfied by a specific product or service; nevertheless, careful assessment of the needs–behavior connection can be very helpful in developing marketing strategy. But you should keep in mind that purchases of the same product can satisfy different needs. For example, consumers purchase food products in supermarkets to satisfy physiological needs, but they also purchase food in status restaurants to satisfy their social and/or psychological needs. Also, certain foods are demanded by specific market segments to satisfy religious, or spiritual, needs. A needs-based strategy would result in a different marketing approach in each of these situations.

needs
The starting point for all behavior.

Perceptions

A second psychological factor, *perception,* encompasses those individual processes that ultimately give meaning to the stimuli consumers encounter. When this meaning is severely distorted or entirely blocked, consumer perception can cloud a small company's marketing effort and make it ineffective. For example, a retailer may mark its fashion clothing "on sale" to communicate a price reduction from usual levels, but customers' perceptions may be that "these clothes are out of style."

Perception is a two-sided coin—it depends on the characteristics of both the stimulus and the perceiver. Consumers attempt to manage huge quantities of incoming stimuli through *perceptual categorization*, a process by which things that are similar are perceived as belonging together. Therefore, if a small business wishes to position its product alongside an existing brand and have it accepted as comparable, the marketing mix should reflect an awareness of perceptual categorization. For example, comparable quality can be communicated through similar prices or a package design with a color scheme bearing a resemblance to that of an existing brand. These techniques will help a consumer fit the new product into the desired product category.

Small businesses that attach an existing brand name to a new product are relying on perceptual categorization to pre-sell the new product. If, on the other hand, the new product is physically different or is of a different quality, a new brand name should be selected to create a distinctive perceptual categorization in the consumer's mind.

If a consumer has strong brand loyalty to a product, it will be difficult for other brands to penetrate his or her perceptual barriers. That individual is likely to have distorted images of competing brands because of a pre-existing attitude. Consumer perceptions thus present a unique communication challenge.

perception
The individual processes that give meaning to the stimuli confronting consumers.

perceptual categorization
The process of grouping similar things so as to manage huge quantities of incoming stimuli.

Motivations

Unsatisfied needs create tension within an individual. When this tension reaches a certain level, the individual becomes uncomfortable and is motivated to reduce it.

motivations
Forces that organize and give direction to the tension caused by unsatisfied needs.

Everyone is familiar with hunger pains, which are manifestations of the tension created by an unsatisfied physiological need. What directs a person to obtain food so that the hunger pains can be relieved? The answer is motivation. *Motivations* are goal-directed forces that organize and give direction to tension caused by unsatisfied needs. Marketers cannot create needs, but they can offer unique motivations to consumers. If an acceptable reason for purchasing a product or service is provided, it will probably be internalized by the consumer as a motivating force. The key for the marketer is to determine which motivations the consumer will perceive as acceptable in a given situation. The answer is found through an analysis of other consumer behavior variables.

Like physiological needs, the other three classes of needs—social, psychological, and spiritual—can be similarly connected to behavior through motivations. For example, when incomplete satisfaction of a person's social needs is creating tension, a firm may show how its product can fulfill those social needs by providing acceptable motivations to that person. A campus clothing store, for instance, might promote styles that communicate that the college student wearing those clothes has obtained membership in a group such as a fraternity or sorority.

Understanding motivations is not easy. Several motivations may be present in any situation, and they are often subconscious. However, they must be investigated if the marketing effort has any hope of succeeding.

Attitudes

Like the other psychological variables, attitudes cannot be observed, but everyone has them. Do attitudes imply knowledge? Do they imply feelings of good or bad, favorable or unfavorable? Does an attitude have a direct impact on behavior? The answer to each of these questions is a resounding yes. An *attitude* is an enduring opinion, based on a combination of knowledge, feeling, and behavioral tendency.

attitude
An enduring opinion based on knowledge, feeling, and behavioral tendency.

An attitude may act as an obstacle or a driver in bringing a customer to a product. For example, consumers with the belief that a local, family-run grocery store has higher prices than a national supermarket chain may avoid the local store. Armed with an understanding of the structure of a particular attitude, a marketer can approach the consumer more intelligently.

Understanding Sociological Influences on Customers

7. Describe certain sociological influences on consumer behavior.

Sociological influences, as shown in Exhibit 14-6, comprise the last component of the consumer behavior model. Among these influences are culture, social class, reference groups, and opinion leaders. Note that each of these sociological influences represents a different degree of group aggregation: Culture involves large masses of people, social classes and reference groups represent smaller groups of people, and opinion leaders are single individuals who exert influence.

Culture

In marketing, *culture* refers to the behavioral patterns and values that characterize a group of customers in a target market. These patterns and beliefs have a tremendous impact on the purchase and use of products. Marketing managers often overlook the cultural variable because its influences are so subtly embedded within a society. Culture is somewhat like air; you do not think about its function until you have to go without it! International marketers who have experienced more than one culture can readily attest to the impact of cultural influence.

The prescriptive nature of culture should concern the entrepreneur. Cultural norms create a range of product-related acceptable behaviors that influence what consumers buy. However, because culture does change by adapting slowly to new situations, what works well as a marketing strategy today may not work a few years from now.

An investigation of culture within a narrower boundary—defined by age, religious preference, ethnic orientation, or geographical location—is called *subcultural analysis*. Here, too, unique patterns of behavior and social relationships must concern the marketing manager. For example, the needs and motivations of the youth subculture are far different from those of the senior citizen subculture, and certain food preferences are unique to particular ethnic cultures. Small business managers who familiarize themselves with cultures and subcultures are able to create better marketing mixes.

Social Class

Another sociological factor affecting consumer behavior is social class. *Social classes* are divisions within a society having different levels of social prestige. The social class system has important implications for marketing. Different lifestyles correlate with different levels of social prestige, and certain products often become symbols of a type of lifestyle.

For some products such as grocery staples, social class analysis will probably not be very useful. For others—home furnishings, for instance—such analysis may help explain variations in shopping and communication patterns.

Unlike a caste system, a social class system provides for upward mobility. The social status of parents does not permanently fix the social class of their child, a fact you might find encouraging. Occupation is probably the single most important determinant of social class. Other determinants used in social class research include possessions, source(s) of income, and education.

Reference Groups

Technically, social class could be considered a reference group. However, marketers are generally more concerned with small groups such as families, work groups, neighborhood groups, and recreational groups. *Reference groups* are those smaller groups that an individual allows to influence his or her behavior.

The existence of group influence is well established. The challenge to the marketer is to understand why this influence occurs and how it can be used to promote the sale of a product or service. Individuals tend to accept group influence because of the benefits they perceive as resulting from it, and these perceived benefits give influencers various kinds of power. Five widely recognized forms of power—all of which are available to the marketer—are reward, coercive, referent, expert, and legitimate power.

Reward power and coercive power relate to a group's ability to give and to withhold rewards. Rewards may be material or psychological; recognition and praise are typical psychological rewards. A Pampered Chef party is a good example of a marketing technique that takes advantage of reward power and coercive power. The ever-present possibility of pleasing or displeasing the hostess-friend tends to encourage the guests to buy.

Referent power and expert power involve neither rewards nor punishments. They exist because an individual attaches great importance to being like the group or perceives the group as being knowledgeable. Referent power (based on one's admiration or respect for the power holder) influences consumers to conform to a group's behavior and to choose products selected by the group's members. Children are often affected by referent power, so marketers can create a desire for products by using cleverly designed advertisements or packages that appeal to this inclination. And a person perceived as an expert can be an effective spokesperson for a host of products because consumers trust his or her judgment.

Legitimate power involves authority and the approval of what an individual ought to do. We are most familiar with legitimate power at the cultural level, where it is evident in the prescriptive nature of culture, but it can also be used in smaller groups. Social marketing efforts are an attempt to encourage a certain behavior as the right thing to do (for example, wear your seat belt, don't drink and drive).

Opinion Leaders

opinion leader
A group member who plays a key communications role.

According to widely accepted communication principles, consumers receive a significant amount of information through individuals called *opinion leaders*, group members who play a key communications role.

Generally speaking, opinion leaders are knowledgeable, visible, and exposed to the mass media. A small business firm can enhance its own image by identifying with such leaders. For example, a farm-supply dealer may promote its products in an agricultural community by holding demonstrations of these products on the farms of outstanding local farmers, who are the community's opinion leaders. Similarly, department stores may use attractive students as models when showing campus fashions.

When Phil Knight established Nike, Inc., in the early 1970s, he used a marketing strategy that followed what he called the Five Cools Guys Principle. The idea was that if he could get five of the best and most popular athletes on a high school campus to wear his shoes, then others would want to buy the shoes for themselves. The "cool guys" would set the footwear fashion trend. Of course, the strategy can be applied at higher and more visible levels, which is why Nike has paid so much money over the years to get world-class athletes to don the company's product. Nike's tremendously successful marketing efforts are an illustration of the sway and influence of opinion leaders. *Advertising Age* magazine reported that the athletic footwear giant was able to increase its sales by 4 percent during the 2008 fiscal year (despite the global economic slowdown), and its market share reached an all-time high of nearly 50 percent.[38] Though Nike is a huge corporation, small businesses should also think about the power of opinion leaders and the part they can play in attracting and building relationships with potential customers.

After a long and very successful business career, one executive was asked by MBA students to explain the secret to his noteworthy accomplishments. His answer was immediate and firm: "Relationships!" Interpersonal connections are, quite simply, the grease that allows the wheels of commerce to turn efficiently, so it follows that customer relationship management (CRM) will be at the heart of any business that is destined for success.

A satisfied customer is likely to be a repeat customer who will tell others about your company. But establishing an effective CRM program is hard work—it requires a thorough knowledge of the major components of customer satisfaction, the development of customer profiles, wise handling of complaints, and an understanding of the customer decision-making process. Of course, it all starts with maintaining a helpful and positive attitude toward customers, but the more small business owners know about their customers, the better they will be able to meet their needs. Customer satisfaction is truly a key element in small business success.

LOOKING BACK

1. **Define customer relationship management (CRM) and explain its importance to a small business.**

   - Customer relationship management (CRM) is a company-wide strategy that can be used to learn more about the needs and behaviors of customers with the specific purposes of building stronger relationships with them and optimizing profitability.
   - The central message of every CRM program is "Court customers for more than a one-time sale."
   - CRM is primarily a mind-set—the implementation of customer-centric strategies, which put customers first so that the firm can increase profits.
   - A CRM program recognizes the importance of keeping current customers satisfied to ensure their loyalty, given the high costs associated with attracting new customers.
   - Constructing a CRM program requires a plan so that the entrepreneur will know what people, processes, and so on he or she needs.
   - Two vital building blocks of any CRM program are outstanding transactional relationships with customers and knowledge of consumer behavior.

2. **Discuss the significance of providing extraordinary customer service.**

   - To be successful in the long run, small firms must build positive transactional relationships in order to develop and maintain loyal customers.
   - Extraordinary service is one of the factors that small companies are in a unique position to offer.
   - Providing exceptional customer service can give small firms a competitive edge, regardless of the nature of the business.
   - Satisfied customers are loyal customers, which translates to improved company performance.
   - The relationship between customer satisfaction and loyalty is not necessarily linear; customer loyalty seems to increase as satisfaction rises.
   - Truly personal attention is the "gold standard" against which the quality of customer service is judged, and this can be strengthened by doing business on a first-name basis, keeping in touch with customers, findings ways to help them, customizing services offered, and addressing consumer problems promptly.
   - Customer experience management (CEM) recognizes that relationships with customers can be strengthened or weakened depending on the quality of the experience they have with a company.

   - Establishing an effective customer service program begins with determining the firm's "customer service quotient," which indicates how well the firm is currently serving its customers.
   - Excellent customer service is not as common as many people may think.
   - Customer service problems are most often recognized through customer complaints.
   - Small business owners can learn about customer service problems through personal observation and other research techniques.
   - Although many types of customer service cost very little to offer, there are definite costs associated with superior levels of customer service.

3. **Illustrate how technology, such as the Internet, can improve customer relationships.**

   - Long-term transactional relationships are built with information gathered from positive customer contacts.
   - CRM technology helps companies gather all customer contact information into a single data management program.
   - Web-based marketers, in particular, are attracted to CRM technology.
   - CRM focuses on such sales functions as accurate and prompt order filling, follow-up contacts to ensure customer satisfaction, and the use of a user-friendly call center to handle all inquiries, including complaints.
   - Having ample support resources for CRM information technology can be a concern for a small firm, and this concern has led some entrepreneurs to outsource certain applications.
   - The tools to manage CRM are growing in number and are becoming cheaper, more sophisticated, and easier to use.
   - Web 2.0 applications are at the center of many new CRM tools, such as the use of online communities as a means of gathering customer feedback.
   - There are still plenty of low-tech solutions to CRM challenges.

4. **Describe techniques used to create a customer profile.**

   - In a very small business, customer profiles are developed in the entrepreneur's head during conversations with customers.
   - Customer profiles are essential to a successful CRM program, as they represent building material for the required knowledge of customers.

- Four categories of customer profile information are transactions, customer contacts, descriptive information, and responses to marketing stimuli.
- Formal interviews with customers provide another way to gather customer profile information.

5. Explain how consumers are decision makers and why this is important to understanding customer relationships.

- Consumer decision making involves four stages that are closely tied to ultimate customer satisfaction.
- Problem recognition (stage 1) occurs when a consumer realizes that her or his current state of affairs differs significantly from some ideal state.
- Stage 2 in consumer decision making involves consumers' collection and evaluation of appropriate information from both internal and external sources.
- Once consumers have evaluated brands in their evoked set and made their choice, they must still decide how and where to make the purchase (stage 3).
- Post-purchase evaluation (stage 4) may lead to cognitive dissonance and complaint behavior, which can negatively influence customer satisfaction with the product or service.
- The best way to preserve customer satisfaction is to deal with issues and complaints as soon as they come up.

6. Understand certain psychological influences on consumer behavior.

- The four psychological influences that have the greatest relevance to small businesses are needs, perceptions, motivations, and attitudes.

- Needs are often described as the starting point for all behavior.
- Perception encompasses those individual processes that ultimately give meaning to the stimuli confronting consumers.
- Motivations are goal-directed forces that organize and give direction to tension caused by unsatisfied needs.
- An attitude is an enduring opinion, based on a combination of knowledge, feeling, and behavioral tendency.

7. Describe certain sociological influences on consumer behavior.

- Among the sociological influences are culture, social class, reference groups, and opinion leaders.
- In marketing, *culture* refers to the behavioral patterns and values that characterize a group of customers in a target market.
- Social classes are divisions within a society having different levels of social prestige.
- Reference groups are those smaller groups that an individual allows to influence his or her behavior.
- According to widely accepted communication principles, consumers receive a significant amount of information through opinion leaders, group members who play a key communications role.

Key Terms

customer relationship management (CRM) p. 364
transactional relationship p. 366
customer experience management (CEM) p. 369
customer profile p. 376
evaluative criteria p. 379

evoked set p. 379
cognitive dissonance p. 380
needs p. 381
perception p. 381
perceptual categorization p. 381
motivations p. 382

attitude p. 382
culture p. 383
social classes p. 383
reference groups p. 383
opinion leader p. 384

Discussion Questions

1. Define customer relationship management. What is meant by the statement "CRM is a mind-set"?
2. Does CRM put more emphasis on current or potential customers? Why?
3. What are the two essential building blocks of a successful CRM program? What "materials" are used to construct these building blocks?

4. Why is a small business potentially in a better position to achieve customer satisfaction than is a large firm?
5. Discuss how technology can be used to support customer relationship management.
6. What types of information should be part of a customer profile?

7. What techniques or sources of information can be used to develop a customer profile?

8. Briefly describe the four stages of the consumer decision-making process. Why is the first stage so vital to consumer behavior?

9. List the four psychological influences on consumers that were discussed in this chapter. What is their relevance to consumer behavior?

10. List the four sociological influences on consumers that were discussed in this chapter. What is their relevance to consumer behavior?

You Make the Call

SITUATION 1

Jeremy Shepherd is the founder and president of PearlParadise.com, in Los Angeles, California. His jewelry business recognizes the importance of ensuring that customers keep coming back. However, Shepherd is uncertain as to which customer retention techniques he should use to develop a strong foundation for repeat business. PearlParadise.com's website has the software capabilities to support customer interaction.

Question 1 What customer loyalty techniques would you recommend to Shepherd?

Question 2 What information would be appropriate to collect about customers in a database?

Question 3 What specific computer-based communication could be used to achieve Shepherd's goal?

Source: http://www.pearlparadise.com, accessed January 30, 2009.

SITUATION 2

Aspen Funeral Alternatives, a funeral home in Albuquerque, New Mexico, recognizes that families are more cost conscious than ever. As the company's website states, "Outlet malls and discount stores offer convenience and value—why pay more?" The strategy of the owners is to offer lower-priced funeral products with the same personalized, high-quality services, just fewer options. Aspen goes to great lengths to control costs and passes the savings along to its clients. For example, its operating hours are limited to Monday through Friday between 8:00 A.M. and 5:00 P.M. to minimize overtime pay to employees. (Essential staff are still available 24/7.)

Aspen's website says that the company's low-cost service alternatives offer no fancy facilities, no limousines, and no hearses. A general price list, covering Aspen's professional services, use of its facilities, and caskets, is posted on the site.

Question 1 What psychological concepts of consumer behavior are relevant to marketing this service? Be specific.

Question 2 How can the stages of consumer decision making be applied to a person's decision to use a particular funeral home?

Question 3 What types of CRM techniques could be used by this type of business?

Source: http://www.aspenfuneral.com, accessed January 30, 2009.

SITUATION 3

A decade ago, entrepreneur Henry Hobbs was traveling overseas when he first experienced what to him was a new way to own a car. It's called car sharing. Under this concept, a customer wouldn't buy a car outright but could use the vehicle as needed, just as a person would use a timeshare property. The concept isn't new to the United States (competitors already exist), but Hobbs was sure that there would be plenty of demand to support the start of a *new* car-sharing business.

Hobbs hoped to bring the car-sharing concept to large U.S. cities. Based on American Automobile Association data, the average cost of owning or leasing a new car, including insurance, is over $650 a month. He estimated that an average car-sharing member would be willing to pay around $100 a month.

Question 1 What sociological issues may have an impact on the success of this venture?

Question 2 In which consumer decision-making stage do you believe Hobbs's potential customers will be located? Why?

Experiential Exercises

1. For several days, make notes on your own shopping experiences. Summarize what you consider to be the best customer service you receive.

2. Interview a local entrepreneur about her or his company's consumer service efforts. Summarize your findings.

3. Interview a local entrepreneur about what types of customer complaints the business receives. Also ask how he or she deals with different complaints. Report your findings to the class.

4. Consider your most recent meaningful purchase. Compare the decision-making process you used to the four stages of decision making presented in this chapter. Report your conclusions.

Small Business & Entrepreneurship Resource Center

The *Small Business and Entrepreneurship Resource Center* offers complete small business management resources through a comprehensive database that covers all major areas of starting, operating, and maintaining a business from financing, management, marketing, accounting, taxes, and more. Use the access code that came with your new book to access the site and perform the exercises in each chapter.

1. Pam Felix, who started her quick-service Mexican restaurant California Tortilla in Bethesda, Maryland, in 1995, wanted an effective way to increase contacts with customers. The text explains how she started a "goofy" Internet site that would be fun for customers to access. The article "Business Gone Wild" talks about some of Pam's ideas on what can be done at the restaurant

unique and fun, and whether or not you feel this would be a good long-term strategy.

2. The text mentions the Angus Barn in Raleigh, North Carolina. Owner Van Eure, who took over the management of the Raleigh landmark after the death of her father in 1988, empowers employees to handle complaints and ensure customers leave totally satisfied. She implemented a "20 Foot Rule"—any employee within the restaurant who may be within 20 feet of a problem, a challenge, or opportunity should assist in solving that problem. After reading the article, "Kid Control", describe the program for kids. Also discuss how this program may complement or conflict with the "20 Foot Rule."

Source: Business gone wild. (Buzz) (unorthodox marketing) (Brief Article). Gwen Moran. *Entrepreneur* 32,7 (July 2004): p. 69(1).

Kid Control. JOAN LANG. *Restaurant Business* 99.24 (Dec 15, 2000): p. 74.

Video Case 14

RODGERS CHEVROLET (P. 654)

This case illustrates how one entrepreneur utilized customer service management to build a strong customer base, focusing not only on the customer but also on employee satisfaction.

ALTERNATIVE CASE FOR CHAPTER 14

Case 16, Nicole Miller Inc., p. 658

Product and Supply Chain Management

In the VIDEO SPOTLIGHT
Horse.com
http://www.horse.com

Raising horses is an expensive undertaking, and not just for those who race thoroughbreds. A modest estimate of the cost of horse ownership is $6,000 a year, which includes only sheltering, feeding, grooming, and shoeing the animal. Then there are veterinary bills, toys, tack, riding gear for the owner, and so forth. The final expenditures can soar much higher, depending on where you live and how many horses you own. Still, there are over 30 million horse lovers in the United States, who dote on the 11 million horses in the country. Roughly 4 million households spend a combined total of $25 billion on goods and services for their horses!

Scott Mooney, founder of Horse.com (formerly Country Supply), built his company to serve horse lovers. When he was in high school, he started selling horse equipment out of his barn in Ottumwa, Iowa (population 24,998). Despite his local success, Mooney realized that to grow the business, he was going to have to get more exposure for his products.

He decided to transform his firm into a catalog company, which now serves roughly 450,000 customers and generates $17 million in annual revenue.

How was Mooney able to go from selling equine products in Ottumwa to selling equipment, tack, and supplies across the United States? He did it by creating a lean distribution network that keeps costs down, profits healthy, and customers coming back for more. Watch this spotlight to see how an effective distribution strategy can drive success.

Video material provided by Hattie Bryant, Producer of Small Business School, the series on PBS Stations, Worldnet, and the Web at http://www.smallbusinessschool.org.

LOOKING AHEAD

AFTER STUDYING THIS CHAPTER, YOU SHOULD BE ABLE TO...

1. Understand the challenges associated with the growth of a small business.

2. Explain the role of innovation in a company's growth.

3. Identify stages in the product life cycle and the new product development process.

4. Describe the building of a firm's total product.

5. Discuss product strategy and the alternatives available to small businesses.

6. Describe the legal environment affecting product decisions.

7. Explain the importance of supply chain management.

8. Specify the major considerations in structuring a distribution channel.

You have probably heard the words *supply* and *demand* used in discussions about the economy, and with good reason—these are fundamental features of the marketplace that determine how high the prices of goods and services are likely to be. Supply refers to the willingness of businesses to put a certain product or service up for sale; demand represents the interest and ability of buyers to purchase that good or service. If a product is in short supply, its price will almost always rise as demand takes over and motivated buyers scramble to purchase the limited goods available at that time.

Supply and demand also affect the operation of a small business, though in a slightly different way. Robert Kiyosaki, entrepreneur and celebrated author of the *Rich Dad* series of books, explains why these concepts are so important:

> Think of demand as sales and marketing. It's your sales and marketing department's job to create demand by making sure that your customers know and buy what your company has to offer. Meanwhile, supply is represented by manufacturing, warehousing and distribution, aka the supply chain. It's your supply chain's job to be prepared to fulfill the demand created by the sales side.[1]

This simplifies the formula somewhat, but it makes sense and clearly explains the need for balance in these key areas of the company's operations.

In Chapter 14, you learned about demand and the entrepreneur's need to make a strong commitment to customer relationship management (CRM) to ensure that new customers are drawn to the company and connections to current customers are preserved. You also discovered that marketing programs need to reflect consumer behavior concepts if CRM efforts are to sustain the firm's competitive advantage. In this chapter, we discuss the demand side of the equation further, explaining how product innovation can lead to business growth (increased demand), but you will also get a healthy dose of supply-side thinking. That is, we address product and supply chain management decisions, which together have a significant impact on the total bundle of satisfaction targeted to customers. Business growth can be a wonderful thing, but supply–demand balance is critical to enterprise success.

To Grow or Not to Grow

1. Understand the challenges associated with the growth of a small business.

Once a new venture has been launched, the newly created firm settles into day-to-day operations. Its marketing plan reflects current goals as well as any thoughts of expansion or growth, which will impact marketing activities.

Entrepreneurs differ in their desire for growth. Some want to grow rapidly, while others prefer a modest growth rate. Many prefer not to grow at all—maintaining the status quo is challenge enough, and this becomes the driving force behind their marketing decisions. Despite this attitude, growth sometimes happens unexpectedly. The entrepreneur is then forced to concentrate all efforts on meeting demand. Consider what happened to an entrepreneur named Jerry. When he showed a new line of flannel nightgowns to a large chain-store buyer, the buyer immediately ordered 500 of the gowns, with delivery expected in five days! Jerry accepted the order even though he had material on hand for only 50 gowns. He emptied his bank account to purchase the necessary material and frantically begged former college classmates to join him in cutting and sewing the gowns. After several sleepless nights, he fulfilled the order.[2] The lesson: Growing quickly can be a stressful proposition if you are not prepared.

For many small companies, however, growth is an expected and achievable goal. In fact, fast growth is part of the initial plan in some cases. In 2000, after Karen McMasters sold some of her daughter's old baby clothes on eBay, she started going to garage sales to find additional goods to put up for auction. The business continued to expand, and McMasters launched her first online company, a high-end baby products business, in February of 2001. By the end of that year, she had generated $200,000 in sales, and by 2004, her enterprise, BareBabies.com, had grown to become one of the largest online retailers of baby products.[3] But McMasters was far from finished with her quest to increase the size of the business. Company sales exceeded $3.5 million in 2007, and business remains on the rise. McMasters had always wanted to grow her business, but growth did not come without cost. "I haven't had a vacation in years," she reveals. "You try to go away and your business is with you. But it's all a blessing. I wouldn't give it up for the world."[4]

Successful growth seldom occurs on its own. Many factors—including financing—must be considered and managed carefully. When a business experiences rapid growth in sales volume, its income statements will generally reflect growing profits. However, rapid growth in sales and profits may be hazardous to the company's cash flows. A "growth trap" can occur, because growth tends to demand additional cash faster than it can be generated in the form of increased profits.

Inventory, for example, must be expanded as sales volume increases; additional dollars must be spent on merchandise or raw materials to accommodate the higher level of sales. Similarly, accounts receivable must be expanded proportionally to meet the increased sales volume. Obviously, a growing, profitable business can quickly find itself in a financial bind, growing profitably while its bank accounts dwindle.

The growth problem is particularly acute for small companies. Quite simply, increasing sales by 100 percent is easier for a small venture than for a *Fortune* 500 firm, but doubling sales volume makes an enterprise a much different business. This fact, combined with difficulty in obtaining external funding, may have unfavorable effects if cash is not managed carefully. In short, a high-growth firm's need for additional financing may exceed its available resources, even though the venture is profitable. Without additional resources, the company's cash balances may decline sharply, leaving it in an uncertain financial position.

Growth also places huge demands on a small company's personnel and the management style of its owners. When Cody Kramer Imports, a Blauvelt, New York, candy distributor, saw private-label orders triple from the same period the year before, its six-person staff was overwhelmed by the growth. Owners Scott Semel and Reed Chase quickly hired a production supervisor to coordinate shipments, but it "was hard for us to let go for a long, long time—probably to the detriment of the company," explains Semel.[5] High demand for products can stretch a firm's staff too thin and result in burnout, apathy, and poor overall performance.

Despite these and other challenges, the entrepreneurial spirit continues to carry small companies forward in pursuit of growth. Business expansion can occur in many ways. One common path to growth is paved by innovation.

Innovation: A Path to Growth

From a menu of growth options, enterpreneurs generally choose the one they think will lead to the most favorable outcomes, such as superior profitability, increased market share, and improved customer satisfaction. These are some of the "fruits" of competitive advantage, and they all contribute to the value of the venture.

2. Explain the role of innovation in a company's growth.

Competitive Advantage and Innovation

Well-known economist Joseph Schumpeter viewed entrepreneurship as "creative destruction." By this, he meant that making improvements to existing products, manufacturing methods, organizational processes, and other such factors creates new business opportunities—and leads to the destruction of those they replace. In his view, the spirit of innovation permeates any entrepreneurial enterprise.

As indicated in Chapter 1, entrepreneurs often simply see a different and better way of doing things. Studies have shown that small entrepreneurial firms produce twice as many innovations per employee as large firms, and these innovations account for half of all those created and an amazing 95 percent of all *radical* innovations.[6] It could be said that innovation provides the soil in which a startup's competitive advantage can take root and grow, taking on a life of its own. Some of the most widely recognized examples of small firm innovation are soft contact lenses, the zipper, safety razors, overnight national delivery, and air conditioning.

There is a certain glamour associated with innovation, but creating and then perfecting new products or services is often difficult. Clayton M. Christensen, a Harvard business professor and the author of a number of books on innovation, points out that the road to new product development is rarely straight, and potholes are everywhere. According to his statistics, "93% of all innovations that ultimately become successful started off in the wrong direction; the probability that you'll get it right the first time out of the gate is very low."[7] But remember, Christensen is talking about products that are successful in the end and does not take into account tortured attempts to massage life into the 80 percent of all new products that end up failing or performing well below expectations.[8] Nobody said it would be easy.

When innovation is the goal, failure is always a risk. With that fact in mind, we offer a few "rules of thumb" that may help to reduce the risk somewhat:

- *Base innovative efforts on your experience.* Innovative efforts are more likely to succeed when you know something about the product or service technology. This principle led Donna Boone, who swam competitively for her high school, to open the first private warm-water pool facility in the Washington, D.C., area. Today, the business has 1,100 students and 46 instructors.[9]

- *Focus on products or services that have been largely overlooked.* You are more likely to strike "pay dirt" in a vein that has not already been fully mined and in which competitors are few. Inventors and entrepreneurs Ron L. Wilson II and Brian LeGette, co-founders of 180s LLC in Baltimore, Maryland, put a new twist on the familiar earmuff. Their ear warmers fit around the back of the neck and don't mess up the hair. Wilson and LeGette have since moved on to other ventures, but 180s LLC continues to expand its product line and its sales.[10]

- *Be sure there is a market for the product or service you are hoping to create.* This business fundamental is as applicable to innovation in startups as it is to innovation in existing businesses. For example, people who want help losing weight are everywhere. So if William Longley, founder of Scientific Intake in Atlanta, Georgia, can reach the target market for his invention, he should do well. His firm's retainer-like appliance, called the SMART Device, fits into the top of a person's mouth and slows down eating, which translates into less food consumption and weight loss.[11]

- *Pursue innovation that customers will perceive as adding value to their lives.* It is not enough to create a product or service that *you* believe in; people become customers when *they* conclude that your product or service will provide value they cannot find elsewhere. Entrepreneur Sharon Bennett followed this risk-reduction recommendation; her creation is based on concern for the welfare of pets. To give owners a more humane way to control their dogs when tugging on the leash, she developed a front-chest leash, the Easy Walk Harness, which is distributed by her company, Premier Pet Products.[12]

- *Focus on new ideas that will lead to more than one product or service.* Success with an initial product or service is critical, of course, but investment in innovation

LIVING THE DREAM:

Reinventing the Wheel—Entirely!

Innovation can only happen when individuals think about ordinary situations in extraordinary ways, but new ideas are only as important as the problems they solve or the improvements they provide. Californians Eric Sandoz and Ben Werner believe they will pave the way to a new future of driving when they bring their creative hybrid-electric commuter car, the "Dagne," to market. Their company, Revolution Motors, and its experimental vehicle promise to provide solutions to the challenges of modern life, and the car's sleek futuristic design is sure to turn heads.

The Dagne has drifted away from the conventional car concept in many ways: It has a three-wheel design, is computerized to lean perfectly into turns, can go about 600 miles on fully charged batteries and four gallons of fuel, can reach speeds of 120 miles per hour, and can go from 0 to 60 mph in about five seconds. All very cool stuff! But perhaps the most innovative feature of this new vehicle is that it has no foot brake and no steering wheel. These "essentials" have been replaced with a simple joystick, like something out of a video game. "The joystick is more intuitive than the wheel of a regular car," says Werner. That may be true, but making the transition from wheel to stick seems like quite a leap.

Innovation without purpose is unlikely to attract much interest from potential buyers, but the new features on the Dagne just might catch on because they offer distinct, and truly important, advantages—and that can make all the difference. The foot brake is a holdover from the old stagecoach days, which required all the power a driver could muster to slow a heavy coach and the horses pulling it forward. Using the foot also freed up the driver's hands to grip the reins tightly. This issue no longer exists in the age of power brakes.

The car steering wheel has a similar history. The first cars were guided using a tiller-like device similar to what you might find on a boat—it actually looked more like a joystick. But in 1893, a Frenchman named Alfred Vacheron became the first tinkerer to adapt what he called "wheel steering" for use in his race car, which later won several high-profile competitions. He borrowed the idea of a steering wheel from the big sailing ships, and it proved to offer more range of motion than the tiller design that it was destined to replace. But almost all cars today have power-assisted steering . . . and the same old steering wheel.

What are the unique benefits of replacing the steering wheel with a joystick? Because of relatively small and nimble wrist muscles, the hand has a much faster reaction time than the foot (the hand is nearly twice as responsive), which means that it can respond more quickly to traffic. Research shows that improving reaction time by a mere half-second would reduce rear-end collision deaths by 90 percent, and the major cause of death in front-end collisions is the impact of the steering wheel. Despite all of the safety features designed into cars these days—including airbags and collapsible steering columns—many of the 50,000 drivers killed in the United States each year die from being crushed by the steering wheel.

Perhaps the time of the joystick-guided car has come. If the Dagne performs as promised, this new and highly innovative product may have all the staying power it needs to become the new standard in automotive design. And all that time playing video games may finally pay off!

Sources: "Revolution Motors," http://www.revolutionmotors.biz, accessed February 6, 2009; Uncle Saul, "Reinventing the Wheel—A Nonstandard Look at Standards," http://www.infochachkie.com/wheel, accessed February 6, 2009; and Kellie Ragusano, "The Dagne," *The Santa Barbara Independent*, June 12, 2008, http://www.independent.com/news/jun/12/dagne/?print, accessed February 6, 2009.

http://www.revolutionmotors.com

Courtesy of Revolution Motors

packs even more of a punch when it also leads to other innovative products or services. This has been the experience of Markus Moberg and Chad Troutwine, who launched an exam-preparation program called Veritas Prep in 2000. The Malibu, California–based company's core business involves training for those who want to take the GMAT (the entrance exam for graduate business schools), and they now offer courses in 80 cities across 21 countries. But their experience with the GMAT has expanded into online courses and law school admissions consulting, and they recently launched consulting for medical school admissions. What they learned from their initial efforts pointed the way for new business development and reduced the risk of their efforts to grow.[13]

■ *Raise sufficient capital to launch the new product or service.* It is easy to underestimate the cost of bringing an innovation successfully to market. Many small firms run short of cash before they are able to do so. Be prepared to look for new sources of capital along the way, which can be particularly challenging during an economic downturn like the one that started in 2008.[14]

Small companies that are "one-hit wonders" may find that the ride comes to an abrupt and unpleasant ending. While one innovation can provide a launch pad for a new and interesting business, continued innovation is critical to sustaining competitive advantage in the years to follow.

Sustainability and Innovation

How can a company sustain its competitive advantage? Various strategies can help. For example, some entrepreneurs with sophisticated technology obtain patents, and this is often a wise thing to do. Others try to operate "below the radar screen" of competitors, but the effort to avoid attracting attention limits their growth. In some cases, businesses find protection through long-term contracts or alliances with larger and more powerful partners, which can lead to exclusive or protected deals as a distributor, vendor, or user of an important technology.[15] The goal is to expand the competitive muscle of the enterprise while establishing protective features as a safeguard against being swept aside by resource-rich rivals.

sustainable competitive advantage
A value-creating position that is likely to endure over time.

A business can take steps to slow down threats from competitors, but no competitive advantage lasts forever. Research has emphasized the importance of *sustainable competitive advantage,* a value-creating position that is likely to endure over time. To incorporate sustainability into strategy, the entrepreneur should use the unique capabilities of the firm in a way that competitors will find difficult to imitate. Since rivals will discover a way to copy any value-creating strategy sooner or later, it is important to think of new ways to reinvest the "fruits" of performance (financial returns, customer goodwill, etc.) so that the basis of the competitive advantage can be repeatedly renewed over the long run.

Competitive advantage tends to follow a fairly consistent pattern. Building an advantage requires resource commitments that lead to a performance payoff, but returns from that competitive advantage will always diminish over time.

Exhibit 15-1 illustrates the competitive advantage life cycle, which has three stages: develop, deploy, and decline. Simply put, a firm must invest resources to *develop* a competitive advantage, which it can later *deploy* to boost its performance. But that position will eventually *decline* as rival firms build these advantages into their own strategies, new and better technologies emerge, customer preferences change, or other factors come into play.

In order to maintain performance over time, firms must produce a continuous stream of competitive advantages to keep performance from falling off. However, tomorrow's performance can be maintained only if it is supported by today's surplus resources. In other words, a firm must launch a new competitive advantage *before* the current strategy has run its course (see Exhibit 15-2). And that is what many small companies are doing. Entrepreneurs are more likely to maintain their venture's performance if they keep an eye on the

15-1 The Competitive Advantage Life Cycle

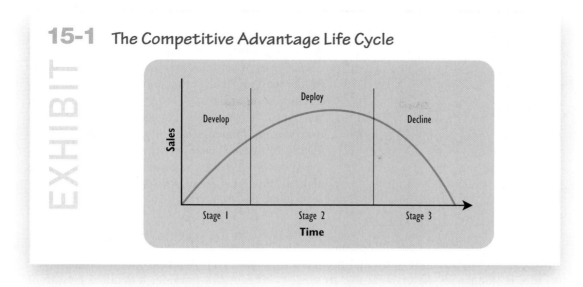

15-2 Sustaining Competitive Advantages

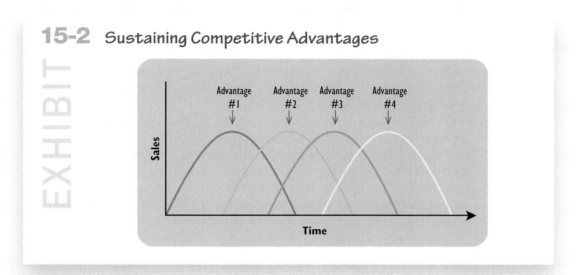

future and continuously improve their product and/or service offerings to meet the rising expectations of customers. In the process, they can sometimes stay at least one step ahead of their competitors.

In October 2001, Dylan Lauren—daughter of well-known designer Ralph Lauren—founded Dylan's Candy Bar, which stocks more than 5,000 varieties of sweet-tooth magic. Starting with its flagship location on the Upper East Side of New York City, the company was "founded upon the principle of elevating a simple candy shop to a world-class destination [that] merges the world of art, popular culture, and fashion with candy." To establish its unique position in the marketplace, the six Dylan's Candy Bar locations feature a café, a private party room, and a candy spa and lifestyle boutique that offers an interesting variety of candy-related gifts. The firm's website, Dylanscandybar.com, was added later to "extend the candy store's sweet adventure online with an unparalleled shopping experience that has something for everyone."[16] And *New York Magazine* reports that the New York City store was just recently expanded by 5,000 square feet to make room for a cocktail bar, a rock-candy aquarium, additional private party rooms, and a "falling-candy staircase."[17] The moral of the story is clear: A marketplace advantage is sustainable only for businesses that are already planning for the future and beating their rivals to the competitive punch.

The Product Life Cycle and New Product Development

Our discussion of growth and innovation illustrates how entrepreneurial firms can be part of the development of new products for the marketplace. At this point, we will focus our discussion more narrowly to answer two additional questions: What creates the need for innovation in a specific business, and how can innovation be managed? We will examine these questions by looking at the product life cycle concept and a four-stage approach to new product development.

3. Identify stages in the product life cycle and the new product development process.

product life cycle
A detailed picture of what happens to a specific product's sales and profits over time.

The Product Life Cycle

An important concept underlying sound product strategy is the product life cycle, which allows us to visualize the sales and profits of a product from the time it is introduced until it is no longer on the market. The *product life cycle* provides a detailed picture of what happens to an *individual* product's or service's sales and profits. (Though its shape is similar to that of the competitive advantage life cycle shown in Exhibit 15-1 on page 395, the two models are very different.) Progressing along the product life cycle (sales) curve in Exhibit 15-3, we can see that the initial stages are characterized by a slow and, ideally, upward movement. The stay at the top is exciting but relatively brief. Then, suddenly, the decline begins, and the downward movement can be rapid. Also, note the shape of the typical profit curve in Exhibit 15-3. The introductory stage is dominated by losses, with profits peaking in the growth stage.

The product life cycle concept is important to the small business owner for three reasons. First, it helps the entrepreneur to understand that promotion, pricing, and distribution policies should all be adjusted to reflect a product's position on the curve. Second, it highlights the importance of revitalizing product lines, whenever possible, before they die. Third, it is a continuing reminder that the natural life cycle of a product follows a trend that resembles the classic normal curve and, therefore, innovation is necessary for a firm's survival. Good business practice entails beginning a new curve before the existing curve of the product life cycle peaks. This parallels the point made earlier about launching a new competitive advantage before the current one has run its course (refer back to Exhibit 15-2).

EXHIBIT 15-3 The Product Life Cycle

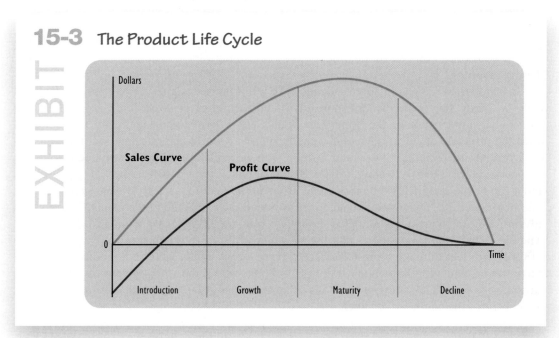

The New Product Development Process

A major responsibility of the entrepreneur is to find, evaluate, and introduce new products. This responsibility requires that the entrepreneur establish a process for developing new products. In big businesses, committees or entire departments are created for that purpose. Even in small firms, however, new product development is best handled through a formalized process.

Entrepreneurs tend to view new product development as a monumental task—and it often is. Many find the four-stage, structured approach—idea accumulation, business analysis, development of the physical product, and product testing—to be the best way to tackle new product development. (Some of these stages will seem similar to those related to the launch of a new venture, as outlined in Chapter 3, but the focus here has shifted to expanding an *existing* business through new product development.)

IDEA ACCUMULATION The first stage of the new product development process—idea accumulation—involves increasing the pool of ideas under consideration. New products start with ideas, and these ideas have varied origins. The many possible sources include the following:

- Sales staff, engineering personnel, or other employees within the firm
- Government-owned patents, which are generally available on a royalty-free basis
- Privately owned patents listed by the U.S. Patent and Trademark Office
- Other small companies that may be available for acquisition or merger
- Competitors' products and their promotional campaigns
- Requests and suggestions from customers (increasingly gathered through online channels such as blogs, online surveys, and other tools)
- Brainstorming
- Marketing research (primary and secondary)

BUSINESS ANALYSIS Business analysis is the second stage in new product development. Every new product idea must be carefully studied in relation to several financial considerations. Costs and revenues are estimated and analyzed with techniques such as break-even analysis. Any idea failing to show that it can be profitable is discarded during the business analysis stage. The following four key factors need to be considered in conducting a business analysis:

1. *The product's relationship to the existing product line.* Some firms intentionally add very different products to their product mix. However, in most cases, any product item or product line added should be consistent with—or somehow related to—the existing product mix. For example, a new product may be designed to fill a gap in a firm's product line or in the range of prices of the products it currently sells. If the product is completely new, it should have at least a family relationship to existing products. Otherwise, the new product may call for drastic and costly changes in manufacturing methods, distribution channels, type of promotion, and/or sales strategy.

2. *Cost of development and introduction.* One problem in adding new products is the cost of their development and introduction. Considerable capital outlays may be necessary, including expenditures for design and development, marketing research to establish sales potential, advertising and sales promotion, patents, and additional equipment. One to three years may pass before profits are realized on the sale of a new product.

3. *Available personnel and facilities.* Obviously, having adequate skilled personnel and adequate production capability is preferable to having to add employees and buy equipment. Thus, introducing new products is typically more appealing if the personnel and the required equipment are already available.

4. *Competition and market acceptance.* Still another factor to be considered in a business analysis is the potential competition facing a proposed product in its target market.

Competition must not be too severe. Some studies, for example, suggest that a new product can be introduced successfully only if 5 percent of the total market can be secured. The ideal solution, of course, is to offer a product that is sufficiently different from existing products or that is in a cost and price bracket where it avoids direct competition.

DEVELOPMENT OF THE PHYSICAL PRODUCT The next stage of new product development entails sketching out the plan for branding, packaging, and other supporting efforts, such as pricing and promotion. An actual prototype (usually a functioning model of the proposed new product) may be needed at this stage. After these components have been evaluated, the new product idea may be judged a misfit and discarded or it may be passed on to the next stage for further consideration.

PRODUCT TESTING The last step in the product development process is product testing, which should determine whether the physical product is acceptable (safe, effective, durable, etc.). While the product can be evaluated in a laboratory setting, a limited test of market reaction should also be conducted.[18]

Building the Total Product

4. Describe the building of a firm's total product.

brand
A verbal and/or symbolic means of identifying a product.

brand image
People's overall perception of a brand.

A major responsibility of marketing is to transform a basic product concept into a total product. Even when an idea for a unique new pen has been developed into physical reality in the form of the basic product, for example, it is still not ready for the marketplace. The total product offering must be more than the materials molded into the shape of the new pen. To be marketable, the basic product must be named, have a package, perhaps have a warranty, and be supported by other product features. Let's examine a few of the components of a total product offering.

Branding

An essential element of a total product offering is a brand. A *brand* is a means of identifying the product—verbally and/or symbolically. Small firms are involved in "branding," whether they realize it or not. An entrepreneur may neither know nor care, but his or her company has a brand identity that features certain components (see Exhibit 15-4). The intangible *brand image* component—people's overall perception of a brand—may be even more important to acceptance of a firm's bundle of satisfaction than the tangible brand mark and brand name elements. For example, prior to 2003, Martha Stewart had arguably one of the strongest brand images in the marketplace. However, her personal legal troubles tarnished the Martha Stewart brand and even resulted in a temporary suspension of her popular home design/cooking show on national television. More recently, though, the Martha Stewart brand has recovered much of its former glory in the marketplace.

Successful entrepreneurs are usually very conscious of their brand as a basic foundation for business; they recognize its power to shape a company's future. Addie Swartz, founder of B*tween Productions (which stands for "between toys and boys"), is convinced that there is room for a cool but wholesome lifestyle brand targeted at the 10 million girls who fall between the ages of 8 and 13. In a youth culture dominated by young actors and singers who regularly check in and out of rehab, there clearly is a need for more wholesome role models. To build a foundation for the company's brand, Swartz decided to start with a series of books about girls like her daughter Aliza and her friends. "I wanted to use the media to empower girls in a positive way," says Swartz. She and her team came up with the composites for the characters in her books and decided the setting would be the real-life town of Brookline, Massachusetts. The characters would be known

15-4 Components of a Brand Identity

Brand Identity

Tangible — Brand Mark

Tangible — Brand Name — Lou's Lures

Intangible — Brand Image

as the Beacon Street Girls. To attract investors, Swartz paired the books with products that appear in the books, including backpacks and pillows. "They wouldn't have invested in a book," says Swartz. "It was about building a brand that can be leveraged aggressively."[19] A positive brand image creates great potential for an entrepreneurial company.

The tangible components of brand identity are brand names and brand marks. A *brand name* is a brand that can be spoken—like the name Dell. A *brand mark* is a brand that *cannot* be verbalized—like the golden arches of McDonald's.

Since a product's brand name is so important to the image of the business and its products, careful attention should be given to the selection of a name. In general, five rules apply in naming a product:

1. *Select a name that is easy to pronounce and remember.* You want customers to remember your product. Help them do so with a name that can be spoken easily—for example, TWO MEN & A TRUCK (a moving service) or Water Water Everywhere (a lawn irrigation business). Before choosing to use your own family name to identify a product, evaluate it carefully to ensure its acceptability.

2. *Choose a descriptive name.* A name that is suggestive of the major benefit of the product can be extremely helpful. As a name for a sign shop, Sign Language correctly suggests a desirable benefit. Blind Doctor is a creative name for a window blind repair business. The Happy Company is a great name for a small firm producing bath toys for young children. However, Rocky Road would be a poor name for a business selling mattresses!

3. *Use a name that is eligible for legal protection.* Be careful to select a name that can be defended successfully. Do not risk litigation by copying someone else's brand name. For example, a new retailer named Wally-Mart would certainly be contested by industry giant, Walmart—even if the new store was actually started by a guy named Wally!

4. *Select a name with promotional possibilities.* Exceedingly long names are not, for example, compatible with good copy design on billboards, where space is at a premium. A competitor of the McDonald's hamburger chain called Bob's has a name that will easily fit on any billboard.

5. *Select a name that can be used on several product lines of a similar nature.* Customer goodwill is often lost when a name doesn't fit a new line. The name Just Brakes is excellent for an auto service shop that repairs brakes—unless the shop plans to expand later into muffler repair and other car repair services.

A brand mark also has tremendous value. The Nike Swoosh and the Chevy badge are marks widely associated with their owners. A small firm's special "signature," or logo, should symbolize

brand name
A brand that can be spoken.

brand mark
A brand that cannot be spoken.

LIVING THE DREAM:

Rapid Prototyping and Blinding Speed

Klock Werks Kustom Cycles is in the business of building one-of-a-kind motorcycles, including choppers and baggers (motorcycles that can carry luggage). The owner, Brian Klock, makes bikes that might better be classified as works of art. His products run with the speed of greased lightning, but Klock can *build* them fast too, thanks to an advanced technology called fused deposition modeling (FDM). This new rapid prototyping process, developed by a company called Stratasys, Inc., can use 3-D computer drawings to produce real thermoplastic end-use parts that "can be sanded, painted, drilled, coated, sealed, and bolted."

Klock's company, based in Mitchell, South Dakota, was recently selected to compete in the popular "Biker Build-Off" challenge, which is featured on the Discovery Channel. His team had 10 days to build a bike, from the ground up, that was then driven to the annual motorcycle rally in Sturgis, South Dakota (an enormous gathering of cyclists), where visitors voted it best of show. Construction of the two-wheeled creation required the team to combine many off-the-shelf parts with several that were created from scratch using rapid prototyping equipment. "Normally, these parts would be produced from injection-molded plastic or machined aluminum," says Jesse Hanssen, the company's mechanical engineer. "But it takes three to four weeks to build parts using either of these methods because they require tooling. Klock Werks had to fabricate all of the components during a five-day filming segment." He also points out that the rapid prototyping process, using durable polycarbonate, shaved the cost of the project by about $15,000.

The equipment manufactures parts by building up material layer upon layer, much as a printer would lay down ink, and to very precise specifications. However, the finished components are extremely functional. After winning the competition at Sturgis, the Klock Werk's team raced the bike at the Bonneville Salt Flats in Utah, where they set a land speed record for baggers at 147 miles per hour. How's that for durability? It's the power of polycarbonate parts.

Sources: "FDM Case Study—Klock Werks Kustom Cycles," http://www.stratasys.com/stratasys.aspx?id=591, accessed February 12, 2009; "Fused Desposition Modeling Technology," http://www.stratasys.com/fused_deposition_modeling_technology.aspx, accessed February 12, 2009; "Biker Build-Off," http://www.pddnet.com/Scripts/ShowPR.asp?RID=21841&CommonCount=0, accessed February 12, 2009; and "Welcome to Klock Werks Kustom Cycles," http://www.kustomcycles.com/about, accessed February 12, 2009.

http://www.kustomcycles.com

Courtesy of Klock Werks Kustom Cycles

positive images of the firm and its products. And if you don't get it right initially, consider a new design. This is what Penny Pritzker did a few years after launching the Parking Spot, an off-airport parking service, in 1998. The original logo on the company's shuttle buses reflected a "ho-hum image" that failed to set it apart from those of its many competitors. Deciding that a much bolder impression was required, the Parking Spot unveiled a new design sporting "black spots of different sizes dancing against a vibrant yellow background."[20] The change was just what the company needed, and it continues to grow. It now operates 17 parking facilities in 9 different cities.[21]

Another example of a successful logo change is provided by the privately held shoe manufacturer White Mountain Footwear, based in Lisbon, New Hampshire. Its black-and-white logo in block lettering was dated, a holdover from its former days as a manufacturer with low-key packaging; it certainly did not represent the fashion-forward image the firm was actually marketing at the time. So a new logo was designed—a stylized W that reflects the letter M, "like a mountain's mirror image in a lake."[22] (You can see the company's logo at http://www.whitemt.com.) According to Elinor Selame, president of BrandEquity International, the branding firm that designed the updated image, "The logo can be your company's hardest-working employee."[23]

Developing an effective logo is very important, but unfortunately this can be an expensive undertaking. The following tips may help you, as a small business owner, to design a logo without breaking the bank:[24]

1. *Be simple.* The best logos are often the simplest. Think of Target, whose red circle with a red dot in the center conveys the essence of affordable, hip practicality. H&R Block uses a green square in association with its name. Simple things are easy to remember and slower to appear dated.

2. *Design for visibility.* Nike paid Carolyn Davidson, a graphic design student, $35 to design the bold red Swoosh that has been the brand's mark since its unveiling at the U.S. Track & Field Olympic Trials in 1972. One of its most positive qualities is the fact that you simply cannot miss it wherever it is displayed.

How I see it: Winston Wolfe on Intellectual Property

I have frequently told my attorney friends that if I were a lawyer, I would be in the field of intellectual property. It is a fascinating subject and can be critical for a new business.

It almost goes without saying that any entrepreneur should be respectful of the patents and trademarks, etc. of others. You should likewise demand that others respect your intellectual property.

If your business is based on a product or process that is unique, pursue a patent as quickly as possible! Keep in mind that protecting intellectual property rights can make or break a business. It is suggested that you work with an attorney whose specialty is intellectual property.

You should strongly consider licensing a brand name if you have a product for which there is an appropriate available name. It can't be emphasized too strongly that the name must be appropriate for the product and the market. Smith and Wesson, for example, is a great brand name for shooting glasses, but not for baby diapers.

Licensing the right name can be magic. It can separate you from the crowd and give you a great sales advantage. It can also allow you greater profit margins, since most consumers are willing to pay more for a brand name they know. Be prepared for scrutiny from the licensor company. Part of being a successful entrepreneur is having a good basic understanding of the laws governing intellectual property and the opportunities that are offered.

3. *Leave it open to interpretation.* The logo should not explain, at a glance, the complete nature of your company. The best logos raise a question and are open to interpretation. One of the reasons the Nike Swoosh is so effective is that it stands as an "empty vessel"—because it has no obvious meaning, Nike can build any image around it that serves the firm's purposes.

4. *Be relentlessly consistent.* Companies with strong graphic identities have built that recognition through years of use. Pick a typeface. Pick a color. Use them over and over again, *on everything.* Eventually, you will be able to establish an identifiable look and feel. That's more valuable than a logo, and much more affordable.

5. *Recognize the importance of logo design.* Logos and colors are often considered "cosmetic," unimportant features of doing business. But most design-driven companies got to be that way through the efforts of highly-placed advocates, such as Steve Jobs at Apple. Design programs work when others know that they are championed by important people.

6. *Get good advice.* You can go pretty far with common sense. But sooner or later, you'll need the services of a professional graphic designer. The website of the American Institute of Graphic Arts (http://www.aiga.org), the largest professional organization for graphic designers, offers useful information about how to find and work with experienced professionals.

7. *Don't expect miracles.* Your company's image is the sum total of many factors. Make sure that your company looks, sounds, and feels smart in every way, every time it goes out in public. That is actually much better than a logo.

trademark
A legal term identifying a firm's exclusive right to use a brand.

service mark
A brand that a company has the exclusive right to use to identify a service.

Trademark and *service mark* are legal terms indicating the exclusive right to use a brand. Once an entrepreneur has found a name or symbol that is unique, easy to remember, and related to the product or service, it is time to run a name or symbol search and then to register the trade name or symbol. The protection of trademarks is discussed later in this chapter.

Packaging

Packaging is another important part of the total product offering. In addition to protecting the basic product, packaging is a significant tool for increasing the value of the total product.

Consider for a moment some of the products you purchase. How many do you buy mainly because of a preference for package design and/or color? The truth is that innovative packaging is often the deciding factor for consumers. If two products are otherwise similar, packaging may create the distinctive impression that makes the sale.

Features like biodegradable packaging materials can certainly distinguish a product from its competition, but the visual impression that packaging creates usually has the greatest appeal to consumers. Discerning entrepreneurs have figured that out. Benjamin and Lisa Nisanoff, founders of a Los Angeles–based bath products manufacturer called Me! Bath, have come up with something more than ordinary bath oil beads—they sell *indulgence* with their Me! Bath Ice Cream and Me! Bath Sherbert. Here's how they make that happen:

> The husband-and-wife team has not only created cute product names, but also has developed distinct packaging shaped like scoops of ice cream. . . . [The couple] discovered their perfect marketing niche while selling bath ice cream at street fairs. Initially they tried to make each unit a perfect sphere, but creating them by hand gave them the look of ice cream scoops. "The idea is [that] the product looks like something you would want to eat," says Benjamin. "It [evokes] all of those sensory experiences.[25]

Keep in mind that the product still performs the same way as others in its category, but the look and design of the packaging are driving consumer interest in this particular brand. And that interest is rising. According to recent reports, Me! Bath Ice Cream, the company's signature product, is "flying off the shelf."[26]

Me! Bath has become one of the fastest growing bath and body companies on the market, helping consumers create a convenient, fun and luxurious spa environment in their own homes.

Though it seems like a straightforward decision, financial constraints often prevent small businesses from pursuing creative packaging strategies that would boost sales. Many entrepreneurs simply can't afford the expensive equipment required for such packaging innovations, but they should not immediately write off the option. They can often work with "contract packagers," who are able to handle such orders at a much lower per-unit cost. [27] It certainly pays to consider what goes on the outside of your product, not just what's in it.

Labeling

Another part of the total product is its label. Labeling serves several important purposes for manufacturers, which apply most labels. One purpose is to display the brand, particularly when branding the basic product would be undesirable. For example, a furniture brand is typically shown on a label and not on the basic product. On some products, brand visibility is highly desirable; Louis Vuitton handbags would probably not sell as well if the name label were only inside the purse.

A label is also an important informative tool for consumers. It often includes information on product care and use and may even provide instructions on how to dispose of the product.

Laws concerning labeling requirements should be reviewed carefully. Government agencies such as the Food and Drug Administration, the Federal Trade Commission, the U.S. Department of Agriculture, and several others issue regulations that must be followed to remain within the law. Very small businesses are exempt from many of these requirements, but it is wise to be innovative with your labeling information. You may even want to consider including information that goes beyond the specified minimum legal requirements, if doing so would give an advantage to your company and the way your products are positioned in the marketplace.

Warranties

A *warranty* is simply a promise, written or unwritten, that a product will do certain things or meet certain standards. All sellers make an implied warranty that the seller's title to the product is good. A merchant seller, who deals in goods of a particular kind, makes the additional implied warranty that those goods are fit for the ordinary purposes for which they are sold. A written

warranty
A promise that a product will perform at a certain level or meet certain standards.

warranty on a product is not always necessary. In fact, many firms operate without written warranties, believing that offering one would likely confuse customers or make them suspicious.

Warranties are important for products that are innovative, comparatively expensive, purchased infrequently, relatively complex to repair, and positioned as high-quality goods. A business should consider the following factors in rating the merits of a proposed warranty policy:

- Cost
- Service capability
- Competitive practices
- Customer perceptions
- Legal implications

Warranties are only one small part of the total product offering. All the factors just discussed come together as guided by a company's product strategy, which we discuss in the next section.

Product Strategy

Product strategy includes decisions about branding, packaging, labeling, and other elements of the core component of the bundle of satisfaction, whether product or service. To be more specific, a *product strategy* describes the manner in which the product component of the marketing mix is used to achieve the objectives of a firm. This involves several supporting features:

5. Discuss product strategy and the alternatives available to small businesses.

product strategy
The way the product component of the marketing mix is used to achieve a firm's objectives.

product item
The lowest common denominator in the product mix—the individual item.

product line
The sum of related individual product items.

product mix
The collection of a firm's total product lines.

product mix consistency
The similarity of product lines in a product mix.

- A *product item,* which is the lowest common denominator in a company's product mix—it refers to an individual item, such as one brand of bar soap.
- A *product line* is the sum of the related individual product items, but the relationship is usually defined generically. So, two brands of bar soap are two product items in one product line.
- A *product mix* is the collection of all product lines within a firm's ownership and control. A firm's product mix might consist of a line of bar soaps and a line of shoe polishes.
- *Product mix consistency* refers to the closeness, or similarity, of the product lines. The more items in a product line, the greater its depth; the more product lines in a product mix, the greater its breadth.

To illustrate how these features can come together, Exhibit 15-5 shows the product lines and product mix of the firm 180s LLC, which was mentioned on page 405.

Product Marketing versus Service Marketing

Traditionally, marketers have used the word *product* as a generic term describing both goods and services. However, whether strategies for marketing goods and those for marketing services are the same is questionable. As shown in Exhibit 15-6, certain characteristics—tangibility, amount of time separating production and consumption, standardization, and perishability— lead to a number of differences between the two strategies. Based on these characteristics, for example, the marketing of a pencil fits the pure goods end of the scale and the marketing of a haircut fits the pure services end. The major implication of this distinction is that *marketing services present unique challenges that are not faced in product strategy development*, a point that deserves to be underscored.

Although we recognize the value of examining the marketing of services as a unique form, we lack space here to describe it separately. Therefore, from this point on in the chapter, a

15-5 Product Lines and Product Mix for 180s LLC

		Ear Warmers	Gloves	Performance Apparel	Booties	Hats	Eyegear
DEPTH OF THE PRODUCT LINES	**Casual & Training**	29 Styles	15 Styles	7 Styles	Powder Bootie Powder Lo Bootie	Ultralite Beanie	Mortise Integral Festo Dovertail
	Sports Apparel	College (74 Teams) NBA (30 Teams) NFL (32 Teams)					
	Work Wear	Basic Fleece Brown Duck High-Viz Reflective	12 Styles			Basic Logo	
	Battle Gear			Combat Desert Jacket			

BREADTH OF PRODUCT MIX (spanning the product columns)

Source: http://www.180s.com, accessed February 20, 2009.

15-6 Services Marketing versus Goods Marketing

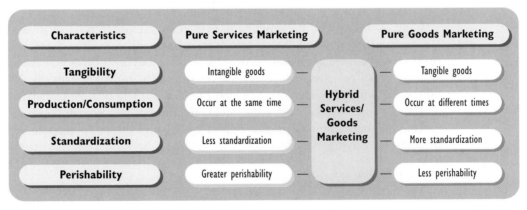

Characteristics	Pure Services Marketing	Hybrid Services/Goods Marketing	Pure Goods Marketing
Tangibility	Intangible goods	—	Tangible goods
Production/Consumption	Occur at the same time	—	Occur at different times
Standardization	Less standardization	—	More standardization
Perishability	Greater perishability	—	Less perishability

product will be considered to include the total bundle of satisfaction offered to customers in an exchange transaction, whether this involves a good, a service, or a combination of the two. In addition to the physical product or core service, a product also includes complementary components, such as its packaging or a warranty (as described in the previous section). The physical product or core service is usually the most important element in the total bundle of satisfaction, but that main feature is sometimes perceived by customers to be similar for a variety of products. In that case, complementary components become the most important features of the product. For example, a particular brand of cake mix may be preferred by consumers not because it is a better mix, but because of the unique toll-free telephone number on the package that can be called for baking hints. Or a certain dry cleaner may be chosen over others because it treats customers with respect, not because it cleans clothes exceptionally well.

product
A total bundle of satisfaction—including a service, a good, or both—offered to consumers in an exchange transaction.

Product Strategy Options

Failure to clearly understand product strategy options will lead to ineffectiveness and conflict in the marketing effort. The major product strategy alternatives of a small business can be condensed into six categories, based on the nature of the firm's product offering and the number of target markets:

1. One product/one market
2. One product/multiple markets
3. Modified product/one market
4. Modified product/multiple markets
5. Multiple products/one market
6. Multiple products/multiple markets

Each alternative represents a distinct strategy, although two or more of these strategies can be attempted at the same time. However, a small company will usually pursue the alternatives in the order listed. Also, keep in mind that once a product strategy has been implemented, sales can be increased through certain additional growth tactics. For example, within any market, a small firm can try to increase sales of an existing product by doing any or all of the following:

- Convince nonusers in the targeted market to become customers
- Persuade current customers to use more of the product
- Alert current customers to new uses for the product

When small businesses add products to their product mix, they generally select related products. But there are, of course, strategies that involve unrelated products. For example, a local dealer selling Italian sewing machines might add a line of microwave ovens, an entirely unrelated product. A product strategy that includes a new product quite different from existing products can be very risky. However, this strategy is occasionally used by small businesses, especially when the new product fits existing distribution and sales systems or requires similar marketing knowledge.

Adding an unrelated product to the product mix to target a new market is an even higher-risk strategy, as a business is attempting to market an unfamiliar product in an unfamiliar market. However, if well planned, this approach can offer significant advantages. One electrical equipment service company recently added a private employment agency. If successful, this product strategy could provide a hedge against volatile shifts in market demand. A business that sells both snow skis and suntan lotion expects that demand will be high in one market or the other at all times, smoothing the sales curve and maintaining a steady cash flow throughout the year. It is tempting to take on new product opportunities—sometimes to the point of becoming overextended—but staying manageably focused is critical.

The Legal Environment

Strategic decisions about growth, innovation, product development, and the total product offering are always made within the guidelines and constraints of the legal environment of the marketplace. Let's examine a few of the laws by which the government protects both the rights of consumers and the marketing assets of companies.

6. Describe the legal environment affecting product decisions.

Consumer Protection

Federal regulations on such subjects as product safety and labeling have important implications for product strategy. For example, to protect the public against unreasonable risk of injury, the federal government enacted the Consumer Product Safety Act of 1972. This act created the Consumer Product Safety Commission to set safety standards for toys and other consumer

EXHIBIT

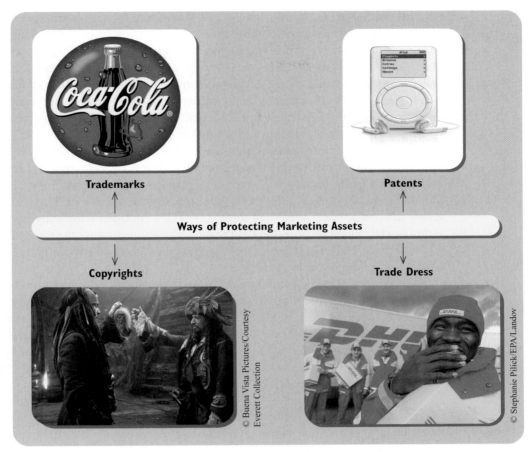

Trademarks

Patents

Ways of Protecting Marketing Assets

Copyrights

Trade Dress

© Buena Vista Pictures/Courtesy
Everett Collection

© Stephanie Pilick/EPA/Landov

products and to ban goods that are exceptionally hazardous, which ultimately increase the cost of doing business.

The Nutrition Labeling and Education Act of 1990 requires every food product covered by the law to have a standard nutrition label, listing the amounts of calories, fat, salt, and nutrients in the product. The law also addresses the accuracy of advertising claims such as "low salt" and "fiber prevents cancer." Though these legal requirements may seem to be a minor burden, some experts estimate that labeling costs can easily run thousands of dollars per product.

Protection Of Marketing Assets

Exhibit 15-7 shows the four primary means firms can use to protect certain marketing assets. The examples shown are representative of trademarks, patents, copyrights, and trade dress.

TRADEMARKS Trademark protection is important to a manufacturer or merchant, because it protects a company's distinctive use of a name, slogan, symbol, picture, logo, or combination of these. In some cases, even a color or scent can be part of a trademark. In essence, trademarks represent the way people identify your business.[28]

Since names that refer to products are often registered trademarks, potential names should be investigated carefully to ensure that they are not already in use. Entrepreneurs can conduct their own trademark searches by using the Trademark Search Library of the U.S. Patent and Trademark Office (USPTO) in Alexandria, Virginia, but this can also be done online by going to http://www.uspto.gov. Entrepreneurs often seek the advice of an attorney for assistance with trademark search and registration, but this may only be necessary if complications arise (for example, if the desired trademark is similar to one that is already registered). Applications for registration can be submitted online at the USPTO website for a fee of between $275 and $325.[29]

Common law recognizes a property right in the ownership of trademarks. However, reliance on common-law rights is not always adequate. For example, Microsoft Corporation, the major supplier of personal computer software, claimed it had common-law rights to the trademark *Windows* because of the enormous industry recognition of the product. Nevertheless, when Microsoft filed a trademark application in 1990 seeking to gain exclusive rights to the name *Windows,* the U.S. Patent and Trademark Office rejected the bid, claiming that the word was a generic term and, therefore, in the public domain.

Registration of trademarks is permitted under the federal Lanham Trademark Act, making protection easier if infringement is encountered. The act was revised in 1989 and now allows trademark rights to begin with merely an "intent to use," along with the filing of an application and payment of fees. Prior to this revision, a firm had to have already used the mark on goods shipped or sold. According to the USPTO, a company's federally registered trademark rights can last indefinitely, as long as the owner "continues to use the mark on or in connection with the goods and/or services in the registration and files all necessary documentation in the USPTO at the appropriate times."[30]

According to the law, a business must *use* a trademark in order to protect it, but it is also important to use it *properly.* Two rules can help with this: First, make every effort to see that the trade name is not carelessly used as a generic name. For example, the Xerox Company never wants people to say that they are "xeroxing" something when they are using one of its competitors' copiers. Second, inform the public that your trademark is exactly that by labeling it with the symbol ™. If the trademark is registered, the symbol ® or the phrase "Registered in the U.S. Patent and Trademark Office" should be used.

PATENTS

A *patent* is the registered, exclusive right of an inventor to make, use, or sell an invention. The two primary types of patents are utility patents and design patents. A *utility patent* covers a new process or protects the function of a product. A *design patent* covers the appearance of a product and everything that is an inseparable part of the product. Utility patents are granted for a period of 20 years, while design patents are effective for 14 years. Patent law also provides for *plant patents*, which cover any distinct, new variety of living plants.

Items that may be patented include machines and products, improvements on machines and products, and original designs. Some small manufacturers have patented items that constitute the major part of their product line. In fact, some now-gigantic firms such as IBM, Polaroid, and Xerox can trace their origins to a patented invention. Small business owners preparing a patent application often retain a patent attorney to act for them, but a patent search can be conducted on the Internet.

Lawsuits concerning patent infringements are costly and should be avoided, if possible. Coming up with the money and legal talent to enforce this legal right is one of the major problems associated with patent protection in small businesses. Monetary damages and injunctions are available, however, if infringement can be proved.

COPYRIGHTS

A *copyright* is the exclusive right of a creator (author, composer, designer, or artist) to reproduce, publish, perform, display, or sell work that is the product of that person's intelligence and skill. Works created on or after January 1, 1978, receive copyright protection for the duration of the creator's life plus 70 years. A "work made for hire" (work created by an employee for an employer) is protected for 95 years from its publication or 120 years from its creation, whichever is shorter. Copyrights are registered in the U.S. Copyright Office of the Library of Congress, whose website (http://www.copyright.gov) provides an extensive supply of useful information about copyrights.

Under the Copyright Act of 1976, copyrightable works are automatically protected from the moment of their creation. However, any work distributed to the public should contain a

---

patent
The registered, exclusive right of an inventor to make, use, or sell an invention.

utility patent
Registered protection for a new process or a product's function.

design patent
Registered protection for the appearance of a product and its inseparable parts.

plant patent
Registered protection for any distinct, new variety of living plant.

copyright
The exclusive right of a creator to reproduce, publish, perform, display, or sell his or her own works.

copyright notice. This notice consists of three elements (all of which can be found on the copyright page in the front of this textbook):

1. The symbol ©
2. The year the work was published
3. The copyright owner's name

The law provides that copyrighted work may not be reproduced by another person without authorization. Even photocopying such work is prohibited, although an individual may copy a limited amount of material for such purposes as research, criticism, comment, and scholarship. A copyright holder can sue a violator for damages.

TRADE DRESS   A small business may also possess a valuable intangible asset called trade dress. *Trade dress* describes those elements of a firm's distinctive operating image not specifically protected under a trademark, patent, or copyright. Trade dress is the "look" that a firm creates to establish its marketing advantage. For example, if the employees of a pizza retailer dress as prison guards and inmates, a "jailhouse" image could become uniquely associated with this business and, over time, become its trade dress. Trade dress can be protected under trademark law if it can be shown "that the average consumer would likely be confused as to product origin if another product were allowed to appear in similar dress."[31] This is only one small part of the intellectual property rights picture, however. A small business needs to take measures to protect its legitimate claims to all such entitlements—that is, trademarks, patents, copyrights, and trade dress.

So far, the focus of this chapter has been on the value of innovation and growth and the importance of effective management of a company's products and services. These are critical considerations; however, a company's offerings are of use only to the extent that consumers have access to them. With this understanding, we now shift our attention to establishing a system that can effectively develop and distribute a company's products and/or services to its customers.

trade dress
Elements of a firm's distinctive image not protected by a trademark, patent, or copyright.

Supply Chain Management

Supply chain management is a system of management that integrates and coordinates the ways in which a firm finds the raw materials and necessary components to produce a product or service, creates the actual product or service, and then delivers it to customers. It also coordinates the flow of payments between entities in the chain of transactions. Recent attention directed toward supply chain management has motivated both large and small firms to create a more competitive, customer-driven supply system. Effective supply chain management can potentially lower the costs of inventory, transportation, warehousing, and packaging, while increasing customer satisfaction.

The Internet and available software are major drivers of recent developments in supply chain management. Years ago, communication between parties in the supply chain was slow or nonexistent. But the Internet, with its simple, universally accepted communication standards, has brought suppliers and customers together in a way never before thought possible.

A comprehensive discussion of supply chain management is beyond the scope of this book. However, we look briefly at the functions of intermediaries, the various distribution channels that make up a supply chain, and the basics of logistics. Entrepreneurs often regard distribution as the least glamorous marketing activity. Nevertheless, an effective distribution system is just as important as a unique package, a clever name, or a creative promotional campaign. Thus,

7. Explain the importance of supply chain management.

supply chain management
A system of management that integrates and coordinates the means by which a firm creates or develops a product or service, delivers it to customers, and is paid for it.

a small business owner should understand the basic principles of distribution, which apply to both domestic and international distribution activities.

In marketing, *distribution* encompasses both the physical movement of products and the establishment of intermediary (middleman) relationships to achieve product movement. The system of relationships established to guide the movement of a product is called the *channel of distribution*; the activities involved in physically moving a product are called *physical distribution (logistics).* Distribution is essential for both tangible and intangible goods. However, since distribution activities are more visible for tangible goods (products), our discussion will focus primarily on products. Most intangible goods (services) are delivered straight to the user—for example, an income tax preparer and a hairdresser both serve their clients directly. Nonetheless, even the distribution of labor can involve channel intermediaries, such as when an employment agency provides a firm with temporary personnel.

Intermediaries

Intermediaries can often perform marketing functions better than the producer of a product can. A producer can perform its own distribution functions—including delivery—if the geographic area of the market is small, customers' needs are specialized, and risk levels are low, as they might be for, say, a doughnut maker. However, intermediaries generally provide more efficient means of distribution if customers are widely dispersed or if special packaging and storage are needed.

Some intermediaries, called *merchant middlemen,* take ownership of the goods they distribute, thereby helping a company to share or shift business risk. Other intermediaries, such as *agents* and *brokers,* do not take title to goods and, therefore, assume less market risk than do merchant middlemen.

Channels of Distribution

A channel of distribution can be either direct or indirect. In a *direct channel,* there are no intermediaries—the product goes directly from producer to user. An *indirect channel* of distribution has one or more intermediaries between producer and user.

Exhibit 15-8 depicts the various options available for structuring a channel of distribution. E-commerce (online merchandising) and mail-order marketing are direct channel systems for distributing consumer goods. Southwest Airlines and EasyJet are examples of companies that use a direct channel to final consumers. Rather than sell their tickets through local travel agents and online travel service distributors like Expedia.com, these two cost-conscious airlines sell flights directly to consumers through their own websites and in-airport ticket counters and self-service kiosks, which reduces their operating costs by 18 to 25 percent.[32]

The systems shown on the right-hand side of Exhibit 15-8 illustrate indirect channels involving one, two, or three levels of intermediaries. As a final consumer, you are naturally familiar with retailers; industrial customers are equally familiar with industrial distributors. Channels with two or three stages of intermediaries are probably the ones most typically used by small firms producing products with geographically large markets. It is important to note that a small firm may use more than one channel of distribution, a practice called *dual distribution.*

Small businesses that successfully employ a single distribution channel may switch to dual distribution if they find that an additional channel will improve overall profitability. This is what Alex Romanov, owner of Chagrin Shoe Leather & Luggage Repair in Woodmere, Ohio, has done. His business saw its sales increase by 25 percent after the U.S. economy slowed in 2008

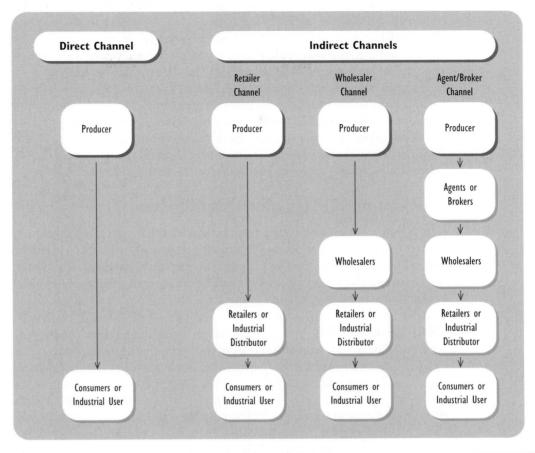

Direct Channel	Indirect Channels		
	Retailer Channel	Wholesaler Channel	Agent/Broker Channel
Producer	Producer	Producer	Producer
			Agents or Brokers
		Wholesalers	Wholesalers
	Retailers or Industrial Distributor	Retailers or Industrial Distributor	Retailers or Industrial Distributor
Consumers or Industrial User	Consumers or Industrial User	Consumers or Industrial User	Consumers or Industrial User

and Americans decided that it would be cheaper and wiser to repair their shoes than to buy new ones. "We fix everything except broken relationships," quips Romanov. His son, Ilya, had decided that he had no interest in being a cobbler like his father, so he launched American Heelers, an online business that receives, by mail, about 100 pairs of repair-needy shoes each week. These shoes are serviced in the elder Romanov's shop and returned to their owners. Establishing this father–son partnership has expanded the business by opening up two fronts for sales: a physical operation that takes orders directly from customers and an e-commerce operation that generates revenue from customers that live in other areas.[33] This is the advantage of dual distribution.

dual distribution A distribution system that involves more than one channel.

A logical starting point in structuring a distribution system is to study systems used by competing businesses. Such an analysis should reveal some practical alternatives, which can then be evaluated. The three main considerations in evaluating a channel of distribution are costs, coverage, and control.

COSTS In many cases, the least expensive channel may be indirect (that is, it has no intermediaries). For example, a firm producing handmade dolls need not purchase trucks and warehouses to distribute its product directly to customers if it costs less to use established intermediaries that already own such facilities. Small companies should look at distribution costs as an investment—spending money in order to make money. They should ask themselves whether the cost of using intermediaries (by selling the product to them at a reduced price) is more or less expensive than distributing the product directly to customers.

COVERAGE Small businesses can often use indirect channels of distribution to increase market coverage. Suppose a small manufacturer's internal sales force can make 10 contacts a week with final users of the venture's product. Creating an indirect channel with 10 industrial distributors, each making 10 contacts a week, could expose the product to 100 final users a week.

CONTROL A direct channel of distribution is sometimes preferable because it provides more control. Some intermediaries may not market a product with care, so an entrepreneur must deliberately select intermediaries that provide the desired support.

A small business that chooses to use intermediaries to market and distribute its product must be sure that the intermediaries understand how the product is best used and why it's better than competitors' offerings. Additionally, if a wholesaler carries competing products, an entrepreneur must be sure that her or his product gets its fair share of marketing efforts. Distributors must know what makes the product special and how best to market it. An intermediary's sloppy marketing efforts and insufficient product knowledge can undermine the success of even the best product.

The Scope of Physical Distribution

In addition to the intermediary relationships that make up a channel, there must also be a system of physical distribution. The main component of physical distribution is transportation. Additional components include storage, materials handling, delivery terms, and inventory management. The following sections briefly examine all of these topics except inventory management, which is discussed in Chapter 21.

TRANSPORTATION The major decision regarding physical transportation of a product is which method to use. Available modes of transportation are traditionally classified as airplanes, railroads, trucks, pipelines, and waterways. Each mode has unique advantages and disadvantages. For example, the train operator CSX Corporation ran radio ads in 2009 that boldly announced, "A gallon of fuel in a CSX train can move one ton of freight 423 miles. Just think what that can do for the environment."[34] The purpose of the ad campaign was twofold: to let potential customers know that the company offers inexpensive transportation services that also minimize environmental impact. But the choice of a specific mode of transportation is usually based on several criteria: relative cost, transit time, reliability, capability, accessibility, and traceability.

Transportation intermediaries are legally classified as common carriers, contract carriers, and private carriers. *Common carriers,* which are available for hire to the general public, and *contract carriers,* which engage in individual contracts with shippers, are subject to regulation by federal and/or state agencies. Transport lines owned by the shippers are called *private carriers.*

common carriers
Transportation intermediaries available for hire to the general public.

contract carriers
Transportation intermediaries that contract with individual shippers.

private carriers
Lines of transport owned by the shippers.

STORAGE Lack of space is a common problem for small businesses. When a channel system uses merchant middlemen or wholesalers, ownership of the goods is transferred, as is responsibility for the storage function. With other options, the small business must plan for its own warehousing. If a firm is too small to own a private warehouse, it can rent space in a public warehouse. If storage requirements are simple and do not involve much special handling equipment, a public warehouse can provide inexpensive storage.

MATERIALS HANDLING Even if it is in the right place at the right time, a damaged product is worth very little. Therefore, a physical distribution system must arrange for suitable materials-handling methods and equipment. Forklifts, as well as special containers and packaging, are part of a materials-handling system.

DELIVERY TERMS A small but important part of a physical distribution system is the delivery terms, specifying which party is responsible for several aspects of the distribution:

- Paying the freight costs
- Selecting the carriers

- Bearing the risk of damage in transit
- Selecting the modes of transport

The simplest delivery terms—and the most advantageous to a small business as the seller—is F.O.B. (free on board) origin, freight collect. This shifts all of the responsibility for freight costs to the buyer. Ownership of the goods and risk of loss also pass to the buyer at the time the goods are shipped.

Logistics companies specialize in transportation and distribution services, providing trucking, packaging, and warehousing services for small and medium-sized companies with limited in-house staff. Many small businesses believe that using these *third-party logistics firms* (sometimes referred to as *3PLs*) is more cost effective than carrying out the same functions on their own. For example, Premier Inc., of Greenwich, Connecticut, uses a firm named APL Logistics to handle packaging and shipping of its health and beauty-aid products. Products produced in plants around the country go to the APL warehouse in Dallas, Texas, and are then shipped to distribution outlets nationwide. More familiar firms offering 3PL services include household names such as FedEx and UPS, both of which offer customized assistance for small businesses that would prefer to focus on their primary operations and leave the transportation and distributions challenges to others.[35]

The business of distribution is always evolving, as new service concepts are developed, perfected, and offered to companies in need of them. This has led to the creation of *fourth-party logistics firms* (or *4PLs*), a term that was coined by global consulting giant, Accenture, which actually holds a trademark on the name. The company defines a 4PL as "an integrator that assembles the resources, capabilities, and technology of its own organization and other organizations to design, build, and run comprehensive supply chain solutions."[36] That's quite a mouthful, but in layman's terms the concept refers to a logistics coordinator that acts something like a "supermanager," a kind of general supervisor that coordinates every aspect of a manufacturer's or distributor's supply chain and acts as the sole point of contact between that company and all of its logistics and information service providers.[37]

The services of a 4PL are usually of interest only to large companies with very complex supply chain combinations, so small businesses rarely need to consider this option. However, less sophisticated logistics providers offer an exceptionally important service to small companies, especially those that need assistance with the physical distribution of their product so that they can concentrate their time and energy on the core activities of their business. While this is only one small part of the supply chain management system, it is obviously a critical function that merits thoughtful planning.

third-party logistics firm (3PL)
A company that provides transportation and distribution services to companies that prefer to focus their efforts on other facets of their business.

fourth-party logistics firm (4PL)
A company that coordinates every aspect of a manufacturer's or distributor's supply chain and acts as the sole point of contact between that company and all of its logistics and information service providers.

Pulling the Pieces Together

This chapter has covered a broad range of issues. It started by explaining that innovation and growth are critical to competitive advantage and small business success. But effective management of a company's products requires attention to both maintaining existing products and developing new ones. Like people, products pass through life cycle stages and face different obstacles at each stage. Therefore, a successful entrepreneur must have a carefully planned product strategy. Thought must also be given to all facets of the physical flow of inputs and outputs. Managing the supply chain requires that you plan how and where you will get the components for your products and how you will deliver the finished products to your customers. Of course, various channels of distribution exist to deliver your product to your customers, but the benefits and drawbacks of each of these must be considered carefully. If these critical tasks are not managed effectively, the performance of the company is almost certain to decline.

LOOKING BACK

1. Understand the challenges associated with the growth of a small business.

- Simply maintaining the status quo is a goal of some entrepreneurs.
- Growing a business too quickly can be stressful for a small firm and its personnel.
- For many small companies, growth is an expected and achievable goal.
- A growth trap may occur when a firm's growth soaks up cash faster than it can be generated.

2. Explain the role of innovation in a company's growth.

- Coming up with and perfecting new products or services is often difficult.
- The risk of failure increases when innovation is the goal.
- The "rules of thumb" that can reduce the risk of innovation include basing innovative efforts on experience, targeting products or services that have been overlooked, ensuring a market for the product or service, emphasizing value creation for customers, pursuing new ideas that will lead to more than one product or service, and raising sufficient capital before launching a new product or service.
- Innovation is a means by which a firm can sustain its competitive advantage.
- The competitive advantage life cycle has three stages: develop, deploy, and decline.
- Companies must produce a continuous stream of competitive advantages to keep their performance from declining over time.

3. Identify stages in the product life cycle and the new product development process.

- The product life cycle portrays a product from introduction through growth and maturity to sales decline.
- The new product development process is a four-stage approach: idea accumulation, business analysis, development of the physical product, and product testing.

4. Describe the building of a firm's total product.

- The brand identity of a firm and/or product has an important intangible image component.
- The name is a critical component of a product; it should be easy to pronounce and remember, descriptive, eligible for legal protection, full of promotional possibilities, and suitable for use on several product lines.
- In order to develop an effective but inexpensive logo, be simple, design for visibility, leave room for interpretation, emphasize consistency, recognize the importance of logo design, get good design advice, and don't expect miracles.
- Packaging is a significant tool for increasing total product value.
- A label is an important informative tool, providing instructions on product use, care, and disposal.
- A warranty can be valuable for achieving customer satisfaction.

5. Discuss product strategy and the alternatives available to small businesses.

- Product strategy describes how a product is used to achieve a firm's goals.
- Marketing services presents unique challenges not faced in product strategy development.
- There are six categories of major product strategy alternatives, which are based on the nature of the firm's product offering and the number of target markets.

6. Describe the legal environment affecting product decisions.

- Federal legislation regarding labeling and product safety was designed to protect consumers.
- The legal system provides protection for a firm's marketing assets through trademarks, patents, copyrights, and trade dress.

7. Explain the importance of supply chain management.

- Effective supply chain management can potentially lower the costs of inventory, transportation, warehousing, and packaging, while increasing customer satisfaction.
- Distribution encompasses both the physical movement of products and the establishment of intermediary relationships to guide the movement of products from producer to user.
- Intermediaries provide an efficient means of distribution if customers are widely dispersed or if special packaging and storage are needed.

8. Specify the major considerations in structuring a distribution channel.

- A distribution channel can be either direct or indirect; many firms successfully employ more than one channel of distribution.
- Costs, coverage, and control are the three main considerations in building a channel of distribution.
- Transportation, storage, materials handling, delivery terms, and inventory management are the main components of a physical distribution system.

Key Terms

sustainable competitive advantage p. 394

product life cycle p. 396

brand p.398

brand image p. 398

brand name p. 399

brand mark p. 399

trademark p. 402

service mark p. 402

warranty p. 403

product strategy p. 404

product item p. 404

product line p. 404

product mix p. 404

product mix consistency p. 404

product p. 405

patent p. 408

utility patent p. 408

design patent p. 408

plant patent p. 408

copyright p. 408

trade dress p. 409

supply chain management p. 409

distribution p. 410

channel of distribution p. 410

physical distribution (logistics) p. 410

merchant middlemen p. 410

agents/brokers p. 410

direct channel p. 410

indirect channel p. 410

dual distribution p. 411

common carriers p. 412

contract carriers p. 412

private carriers p. 412

third-party logistics firm (3PL) p. 413

fourth-party logistics firm (4PL) p. 413

Discussion Questions

1. Discuss some of the limitations on growth in a small firm.

2. Describe the recommendations for reducing risk associated with innovation in a small business.

3. How does an understanding of the product life cycle concept help with product strategy?

4. Discuss briefly each stage of the product development process.

5. Select two product names, and then evaluate each with respect to the five rules for naming a product.

6. What are the six basic product strategy options available to a small company? Which ones are most likely to be used?

7. Identify and briefly describe the three ways to increase sales of an existing product once a product strategy has been implemented.

8. Explain how registration of a small firm's trademark would be helpful in protecting its brand.

9. Why do small businesses need to consider indirect channels of distribution for their products? Why involve intermediaries in distribution at all?

10. Discuss the major considerations in structuring a channel of distribution.

You Make the Call

SITUATION 1

Tomboy Tools are just that—tools for women who want to do their own home improvement and repair projects. Friends Sue Wilson, Mary Tatum, and Janet Rickstrew, all of Denver, Colorado, were concerned that the tools they used for home repair projects were designed for men, not women. So, they started Tomboy Tools, whose goal is to offer "professional grade tools for women, along with the information they need to know on how to use them," says Wilson. What is most interesting is how the products are sold— exclusively at in-home workshops led by Tomboy Tools' independent sales representatives. Instead of Tupperware or cosmetics, guests see basic home repair tools in action and learn simple home repair and improvement techniques. The company's founders chose the in-home approach to market their products because of its proven success with consumers, particularly women.

Sources: "Pink Tools for Women," http://www.tomboytools.com/index.asp, accessed February 20, 2009; and Susan Hirshon, *The Costco Connection*, April 2005, p. 15.

Question 1 What are the advantages and disadvantages of the in-home method of selling Tomboy Tools?

Question 2 What other channels of distribution might Tomboy Tools use?

Question 3 What do you think about the name Tomboy Tools?

SITUATION 2

Who hasn't heard of the energy drink Red Bull? It established a position as the 900-pound gorilla in the growing energy drink market, the best seller in its product category. But Monster energy drink (an entrepreneurial rival that is now bottled by the Coca-Cola Company) has challenged Red Bull and its place at the top. In fact, *Beverage Digest* reports that Monster has gained the edge, selling more volume in 2008 than Red Bull. Monster reaches its core market of males aged 18 to 32 by flooding retailers with giant (16-ounce) cans of its various energy drink offerings, in essence super-sizing the much smaller cans sold by Red Bull. Its aggressive image, striking packaging, and oversized cans have helped Monster expand its position in the growing energy drink market.

Sources: Kenneth Hein, "Monster Goes Small While Amp Goes Big," *Brandweek*, April 14, 2009, http://www.brandweek.com/bw/content_display/news-and-features/packaged-goods/e3i6266a3e7e491921c7fc1807ad26b877b?pn=1, accessed February 20, 2009; and Roben Farzad, "Who's Afraid of the Shorts? Not Monster," *BusinessWeek*, November 28, 2006, p. 40.

Question 1 What is it about Monster's logo that makes it effective? (Hint: What tips does this textbook provide regarding logo design?)

Question 2 How can good packaging help a product?

Question 3 Why is labeling an important part of the packaging for energy drinks like Monster?

SITUATION 3

What does the Internet have to do with making ice cream? Answer: It supports the MooBella ice-cream machine. The MooBella robotic ice-cream manufactory and vending machine can custom-make and sell a cup of fresh, premium ice cream in 45 seconds. The consumer feeds the vending machine from $2.00 to $2.50 per scoop and uses the large LCD touch screen to make his or her choice of up to 12 flavors plus any of five toppings. The computer that makes each cup of ice cream instantly reports via a wireless Internet connection when it needs supplies or maintenance. MooBella will be placing machines in Boston and the surrounding area.

Sources: "Moobella—The Art of Indulgence," http://moobella.com, accessed February 20, 2009; and Peter Lewis, "Cream of the Crop," *Fortune*, March 6, 2006, p. 178.

Question 1 Where would be the best locations for the MooBella ice-cream vending machine?

Question 2 What are the primary advantages and disadvantages of this retailing strategy?

Experiential Exercises

1. Interview the owner or owners of a local manufacturing business to find out how they view innovation in their market. Summarize your findings.

2. Ask some owners of small firms in your area to describe their new product development processes. Report your findings to the class.

3. Visit a local retail store and observe brand names, package designs, labels, and warranties. Choose good and bad examples of each of these product components, and report back to the class.

4. Consider your most recent meaningful purchase. Compare the decision-making process you used to the four stages of the new product development process. Report your conclusions to the class.

5. Interview two different types of local retail merchants (for example, a boutique owner and a manager of a franchise) to determine how the merchandise in their stores is distributed to them. Contrast the channels of distribution used, and write a brief report on your findings.

Small Business & Entrepreneurship Resource Center

The *Small Business and Entrepreneurship Resource Center* offers complete small business management resources through a comprehensive database that covers all major areas of starting, operating, and maintaining a business from financing, management, marketing, accounting, taxes and more. Use the access code that came with your new book to access the site and perform the exercises in each chapter.

1. Maureen Kelly started a company named Tarte because it seemed playful, sassy, and fun—a theme that has permeated every aspect of her company and its product development. After reading the article "Tarte looks smarte" describe the new product introduced as Cheek Stain. Describe how the product and packaging have been designed and how they may or may not appeal to more than one customer segment.

2. Unclaimed Baggage sells luggage that is left at airports. This business has developed a sustainable advantage because of long-term contracts with airports around the world, thus keeping new competitors away. Describe how a small business, located in the foothills of the Appalachian Mountains, used the Internet to expand its marketing footprint to successfully sell products around the world, as well as its physical location. Describe how web sales for Unclaimed Baggage is an ideal method for its unique type of product mix.

Sources: Tarte looks smart with stock cosmetics package.(Brief Article). *Food & Drug Packaging* 65, 5 (May 2001): p. D2. http://find.galegroup.com/sbrc

Lost travel treasures: Unclaimed Baggage Center is a shopper's gold mine.(Buying Power) (Brief Article).Kimberly J. Hamilton-Wright. Black Enterprise 34, 6 (Jan 2004): p. 93(1).

Video Case 15

COUNTRY SUPPLY (P. 656)

This case demonstrates how one innovative entrepreneur recognized the need to expand his customer base in order for his business to grow and describes how he met that need by utilizing available resources to expand his distribution network.

ALTERNATIVE CASES FOR CHAPTER 15

Case 3, Firewire Surfboards, p. 628
Case 7, eHarmony, p. 636
Case 9, Le Travel Store, p. 641

16

Pricing and Credit Decisions

In the VIDEO SPOTLIGHT
Nicole Miller
http://www.nicolemiller.com

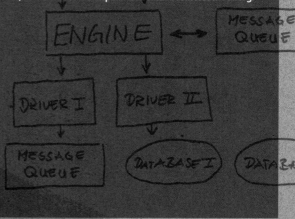

When designer Nicole Miller and business manager Bud Konheim decided to strike out on their own, the company they both worked for gave them its blessing—and three weeks' worth of salaries for each person they had working for them. The only requirement was that Miller and Konheim clear out all existing inventory in their division before leaving the company. Surprisingly, they had no trouble at all: They just notified their existing customers that their division was changing its name to Nicole Miller.

Nicole Miller sells youthful, whimsical designs, primarily in women's wear. While Miller enjoys designing for her customers, Konheim thinks that pricing should contribute to the fun as well. That is, Konheim likes to price Miller's products so that a woman buying a Nicole Miller design will be able to enjoy her

purchase without the gnawing regret that she just spent too much money. However, creating that "I-got-a-great-deal" feeling at a price that will still sustain the business is not easy.

Setting the right price for a product or service is one of the most difficult marketing activities a businessperson in any company will undertake. What makes it all the more challenging for Miller is that she is committed to manufacturing all of her clothing lines domestically, in New York's garment district, even though her competition is going offshore to reduce costs. Watch this spotlight to see how Miller and Konheim are navigating the tough challenges of pricing.

Video material provided by Hattie Bryant, Producer of Small Business School, the series on PBS Stations, Worldnet, and the Web at http://www. smallbusinessschool.org.

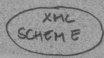

LOOKING AHEAD
AFTER STUDYING THIS CHAPTER, YOU SHOULD BE ABLE TO...

1. Discuss the role of cost and demand factors in setting a price.
2. Apply break-even analysis and markup pricing.
3. Identify specific pricing strategies.
4. Explain the benefits of credit, factors that affect credit extension, and types of credit.
5. Describe the activities involved in managing credit.

Pricing and credit decisions are vital because they influence the relationship between the business and its customers. These decisions also directly affect both revenue and cash flow. Of course, customers dislike price increases and restrictive credit policies; therefore, the entrepreneur needs to set prices and design credit policies as wisely as possible, to avoid the need for frequent changes.

Because a value must be placed on a product or service by the provider before it can be sold, pricing decisions are a critical issue in small business marketing. The *price* of a product or service specifies what the seller requires for giving up ownership or use of that product or service. Often, the seller must extend credit to the buyer in order to make the exchange happen. *Credit* is simply an agreement between buyer and seller that payment for a product or service will be received at some later date. This chapter examines both the pricing decisions and the credit decisions of small firms.

price
A specification of what a seller requires in exchange for transferring ownership or use of a product or service.

credit
An agreement between a buyer and a seller that provides for delayed payment for a product or service.

Setting a Price

In setting a price, the entrepreneur decides on the most appropriate value for the product or service being offered for sale. This task might seem easy, but it isn't. The first pricing lesson is to remember that total sales revenue depends on just two components—sales volume and price—and even a small change in price can drastically influence revenue. Consider the following situations, *assuming no change in demand*:

1. Discuss the role of cost and demand factors in setting a price.

Situation A
Quantity sold × Price per unit = Gross revenue
250,000 × $3.00 = $750,000

Situation B
Quantity sold × Price per unit = Gross revenue
250,000 × $2.80 = $700,000

The price per unit is only $0.20 lower in Situation B than in Situation A. However, the total difference in revenue is $50,000! Clearly, a small business can lose significant revenues if a price is set too low.

Pricing is also important because it indirectly affects sales quantity. Setting a price too high may result in lower quantities sold, reducing total revenue. In the above example, quantity sold was assumed to be independent of price—and it very well may be for such a small change in price. However, a larger increase or decrease might substantially affect the quantity sold. Pricing, therefore, has a dual influence on total sales revenue. It is important *directly* as part of the gross revenue equation and *indirectly* through its impact on demand.

Before beginning a more detailed analysis of pricing, we should note that services are generally more difficult to price than products because of their intangible nature. However, the impact of price on revenue and profits is the same. Because estimating the cost of providing a service and the demand for that service is a more complex process, the following discussions will focus on product pricing.

Cost Determination for Pricing

For a business to be successful, its pricing must cover total cost plus an appropriate profit margin. Pricing, therefore, must be based on an understanding of the nature of costs. As illustrated in Exhibit 16-1, *total cost* includes three components. The first is the cost of goods offered for sale. An appliance retailer, for example, must include in the selling price the cost of the appliance and related freight charges. The second component is the selling cost, which includes

total cost
The sum of cost of goods sold, selling expenses, and overhead costs.

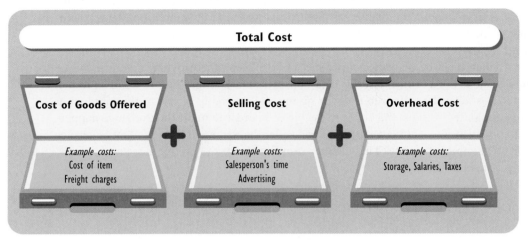

the direct cost of the salesperson's time (salary plus commissions), as well as the cost of other selling activities such as advertising and sales promotion. The third component is the overhead cost applicable to the given product, which includes costs related to warehouse storage, office supplies, utilities, taxes, and employee salaries and wages. *All* of these cost classifications must be incorporated into the pricing process.

variable costs
Costs that vary with the quantity produced or sold.

Costs respond differently as the quantity produced or sold increases or decreases. *Variable costs* are those that increase in total as the quantity of product increases. Material costs and sales commissions are typical variable costs incurred as a product is made and sold. For instance, material costs may be $10 per unit. If the company sells 1,000 units, the variable costs would be $10,000 but would change as the number of units increases or decreases. *Fixed costs* are those that remain constant at different levels of quantity sold. For example, advertising campaign expenditures, factory equipment costs, and salaries of office personnel are fixed costs.

fixed costs
Costs that remain constant as the quantity produced or sold varies.

An understanding of the nature of different kinds of costs can help a seller minimize pricing mistakes. Although fixed and variable costs do not behave in the same way, small businesses often treat them identically. An approach called *average pricing* exemplifies this high-risk practice. With average pricing, you divide the total cost (fixed costs plus variable costs) over a previous period by the quantity sold in that period to arrive at an average cost, which is then used to set the current price. For example, consider the cost structure of a firm selling 25,000 units of a product in 2010 at a sales price of $8.00 each (see Exhibit 16-2). The average unit cost would be $5.00 (that is, $125,000 ÷ 25,000). The $3.00 markup provides a profit at this sales volume (25,000 × $3 = $75,000).

average pricing
An approach in which total cost for a given period is divided by quantity sold in that period to set a price.

However, the impact on profit will be very negative if sales in 2011 reach only 10,000 units and the selling price has been set at the same $3.00 markup, based on the average cost in 2010 (see Exhibit 16-3). At the lower sales volume (10,000 units), the average unit cost increases to $9.50 (that is, $95,000 ÷ 10,000). This increase is, of course, attributable to the need to spread fixed costs over fewer units. *Average pricing overlooks the reality of higher average costs at lower sales levels.*

On rare occasions, pricing at less than total cost can be used as a special short-term strategy. Suppose some fixed costs are ongoing even if part of the production facility is temporarily idle. In this situation, pricing should cover all marginal or incremental costs—that is, those costs incurred specifically to get additional business. In the long run, however, all costs must be covered.

How Customer Demand Affects Pricing

Cost analysis can identify a level below which a price should not be set under normal circumstances. However, it does not show how much the final price might exceed that minimum figure

entrepreneurial experiences

To Cut or Not to Cut

Bundling more services for the same price can be an effective way to be more competitive without cutting deeply into profits.

As the economy slowed in 2008, Siamak Taghaddos and David Hauser, the founders of Grasshopper (formerly GotVMail), began toying with the idea of price cuts. Grasshopper, a Needham, Massachusetts–based company that offers virtual phone systems, had a few competitors, and the founders feared it couldn't gain market share without a price change. But given that their plans started at $9.95 per month, [Taghaddos and Hauser] felt their prices were already low.

The founders surveyed customers and [discovered] that what users wanted were more predictable prices, a simpler set of plans, and more features for their money. It turned out that the average Grasshopper user was frequently exceeding the monthly allotment of minutes in his or her plan. That meant more revenue for Grasshopper, but annoying fees for customers. Customers also balked at paying for extra features such as employee extensions. The founders began reexamining Grasshopper's offerings. "We asked ourselves, 'How generous can we be without losing money?'" says Taghaddos.

In October, the company increased the number of minutes offered. Features that customers used to pay extra for are now included in most plans. Taghaddos and Hauser say the new pricing structure cuts Grasshopper's margins about 10 percent but allows the company to offer an average savings of about 40 percent to its customers. In November, Grasshopper noticed a surge in sign-ups, up 40 percent compared with the previous year—many of them from newly out-of-work professionals starting their own businesses.

Despite shrinking margins, Grasshopper is still profitable, say the founders. "I didn't think we were recession proof," says Taghaddos. "But my intuition always told me that during a down economy, we could do really well."

Source: Ryan McCarthy, "Pricing: How Low Can You Really Go?" *Inc. Magazine* March 2009, pp. 91–92.

http://grasshopper.com

Courtesy of Grasshopper

and still be acceptable to customers. You must consider demand factors before making this determination.

ELASTICITY OF DEMAND   Customer demand for a product is often sensitive to the price level. *Elasticity* is the term used to describe this sensitivity, and the effect of a change in price on the quantity demanded is called *elasticity of demand.* A product is said to have *elastic demand* if an increase in its price *lowers* demand for the product or a decrease in its price *raises* demand. A product is said to have *inelastic demand* if an increase in its price *raises* total revenue or a decrease in its price *lowers* total revenue.

elasticity of demand
The degree to which a change in price affects the quantity demanded.

16-2 Cost Structure of a Hypothetical Firm, 2009

Sales revenue (25,000 units @ $8)		$200,000
Total costs:		
Fixed costs	$75,000	
Variable costs ($2 per unit)	50,000	
		125,000
Gross margin		$ 75,000

$$\text{Average cost} = \frac{\$125,000}{25,000} = \$5$$

16-3 Cost Structure of a Hypothetical Firm, 2010

Sales revenue (10,000 units @ $8)		$80,000
Total costs:		
Fixed costs	$75,000	
Variable costs ($2 per unit)	20,000	
		95,000
Gross margin		($15,000)

$$\text{Average cost} = \frac{\$95,000}{10,000} = \$9.50$$

elastic demand
Demand that changes significantly when there is a change in the price of the product.

inelastic demand
Demand that does not change significantly when there is a change in the price of the product.

In some markets, the demand for products is very elastic. With a lower price, the amount purchased increases sharply, thus providing higher revenue. For example, in the personal computer industry, a decrease in price will frequently produce a more than proportionate increase in quantity sold, resulting in higher total revenues. For products such as salt, however, the demand is highly inelastic. Regardless of price, the quantity purchased will not change significantly, because consumers use a fixed amount of salt.

The concept of elasticity of demand is important because the degree of elasticity sets limits on or provides opportunities for higher pricing. A small firm should seek to distinguish its product or service in such a way that small price increases will incur little resistance from customers and thereby yield increasing total revenue. Entrepreneur Damon Risucci built his Synergy Fitness Club in midtown Manhattan into a successful business despite stiff competition from several chain fitness clubs. For nearly a decade, members paid only $49.99 a month. "We thought our prices had to be low," Risucci recalls. Finally, prompted by falling margins, he raised monthly fees 16 percent; no one complained, and he didn't lose a single member![1] We can conclude from Risucci's experience that demand for his fitness club service is quite inelastic—at least through the price range presented here.

PRICING AND A FIRM'S COMPETITIVE ADVANTAGE Several factors affect the attractiveness of a product or service to customers. One factor is the firm's competitive advantage—a concept discussed in Chapter 3. If consumers perceive the product or service as an important solution to their unsatisfied needs, they are likely to demand more.

Only rarely will competing firms offer identical products and services. In most cases, products differ in some way. Even if two products are physically similar, the accompanying services typically differ. Speed of service, credit terms offered, delivery arrangements, personal attention from a salesperson, and warranties are but a few of the factors that can be used to distinguish one product from another. A unique and attractive combination of goods and services may well justify a higher price.

A pricing tactic that often reflects a competitive advantage is *prestige pricing*—setting a high price to convey an image of high quality or uniqueness. Its influence varies from market to market and product to product. Because higher-income buyers are usually less sensitive to price variations than those with lower incomes, prestige pricing typically works better in high-income markets.

When Anthony Shurman, president of Yosha Enterprises Inc. in Westfield, New Jersey, introduced Momints breathe mints, he set the price high. Shurman explains, "I think when you're launching a new product or starting a new business, there are plenty of examples of businesses going after a target audience and creating a cachet for themselves by pricing a little higher and adopting an elite strategy, where you present yourself as this high-end competitor in the market."[2] Later, when he took Momints nationwide, Shurman dropped the price to be competitive with other brands in the new markets.

prestige pricing
Setting a high price to convey an image of high quality or uniqueness.

Applying a Pricing System

A typical entrepreneur is unprepared to evaluate a pricing system until he or she understands potential costs, revenue, and product demand for the venture. To better comprehend these factors and to determine the acceptability of various prices, the entrepreneur can use break-even analysis. An understanding of markup pricing is also valuable, as it provides the entrepreneur with an awareness of the pricing practices of intermediaries—wholesalers and retailers.

2. Apply break-even analysis and markup pricing.

Break-Even Analysis

Break-even analysis allows the entrepreneur to compare alternative cost and revenue estimates in order to determine the acceptability of each price. A comprehensive break-even analysis has two phases: (1) examining cost–revenue relationships and (2) incorporating sales forecasts into the analysis. Break-even analysis can be presented by means of formulas and graphs.

EXAMINING COST AND REVENUE RELATIONSHIPS The objective of the first phase of break-even analysis is to determine the sales volume level at which the product, at an assumed price, will generate enough revenue to start earning a profit. Exhibit 16-4(a) presents a simple break-even chart reflecting this comparison. *Fixed* costs and expenses, as represented by a horizontal line in the bottom half of the graph, are $300,000. The section for variable costs and expenses is a triangle that slants upward, depicting the direct relationship of variable costs and expenses to output. In this example, variable costs and expenses are $5 per unit. The entire area below the upward-slanting total cost line represents the combination of fixed and variable costs and expenses. The distance between the sales and total cost lines reveals the profit or loss position of the company at any level of sales. The point of intersection of these two lines is called the *break-even point,* because sales revenue equals total costs and expenses at this sales volume. As shown in Exhibit 16-4(a), the break-even point is approximately 43,000 units sold, which means that the break-even point in dollar revenue is $514,000.

break-even point
Sales volume at which total sales revenue equals total costs and expenses.

EXHIBIT

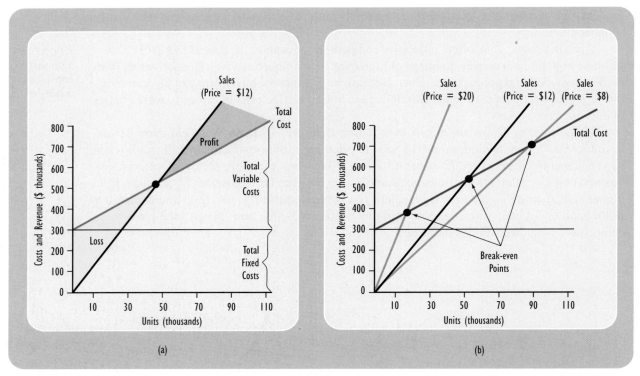

(a)

(b)

While Exhibit 16-4(a) helps us to visualize the break-even concept, we can compute the exact break-even point in unit sales using the following equation:[3]

$$\text{Break-even units sold} = \frac{\text{total fixed costs and expenses}}{\text{selling price} - \text{unit variable costs and expenses}}$$

$$\text{Break-even units sold} = \frac{\$300,000}{\$12 - \$5} = 42,857$$

We can now see that the exact break-even point in units sold is 42,857. And given the $12 sales price, the dollar break-even point is $514,284 ($12 sales price per unit × 42,857 break-even units sold).

This example shows that the break-even point is a function of (1) the firm's fixed operating costs and expenses (numerator), and (2) the unit selling price less the unit variable costs and expenses (denominator). The higher the *fixed* costs, the more units we must sell to break even; and the greater the difference between the unit selling price and the unit *variable* costs and expenses, the fewer units we must sell to break even. The difference between the unit selling price and the unit variable costs and expenses is the *contribution margin*; that is, for each unit sold, a contribution is made toward covering the company's fixed costs.

To evaluate other break-even points, the entrepreneur can plot additional sales lines for other prices on the chart. On the flexible break-even chart shown in Exhibit 16-4(b), the higher price of $20 yields a much more steeply sloped sales line, resulting in a break-even point of 20,000 units and a sales dollar break-even point of $400,000. Similarly, the lower price of $8 produces a flatter revenue line, delaying the break-even point until 100,000 units are sold and we have $800,000 in sales. Additional sales lines could be plotted to evaluate other proposed prices.

Because it shows the profit area growing larger and larger to the right, the break-even chart implies that quantity sold can increase continually. Obviously, *this assumption is unrealistic*

contribution margin
The difference between the unit selling price and the unit variable costs and expenses.

16-5 A Break-Even Graph Adjusted for Estimated Demand

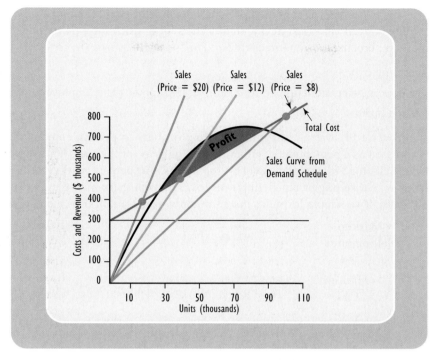

and should be factored in by modifying the break-even analysis with information about the way in which demand is expected to change at different price levels.

INCORPORATING SALES FORECASTS   The indirect impact of price on the quantity that can be sold complicates pricing decisions. Demand for a product typically decreases as price increases. However, in certain cases price may influence demand in the opposite direction, resulting in increased demand for a product at higher prices. Therefore, estimated demand for a product at various prices, as determined through marketing research (even if it is only an informed guess), should be incorporated into the break-even analysis.

An adjusted break-even chart that incorporates estimated demand can be developed by using the initial break-even data from Exhibit 16-4(b) and adding a demand curve, as done in Exhibit 16-5. This graph allows a more realistic profit area to be identified.

We see that the break-even point in Exhibit 16-5 for a unit price of $20 corresponds to a quantity sold that appears impossible to reach at the assumed price (the break-even point does not fall within the demand curve). No customers are willing to pay $20 for any quantity—the demand curve line is always below the $20 sales line. So, at the low price of $8, we would never break even—the more we sell, the greater the loss would be. Only at a price of $12 does the revenue from the demand curve rise above the total cost line. The potential for profit at this price is indicated by the shaded area in the graph.

Markup Pricing

Up to this point, we have made no distinction between pricing by manufacturers and pricing by intermediaries such as wholesalers and retailers, since break-even concepts apply to all small businesses, regardless of their position in the distribution channel. Now, however, we briefly present some of the pricing formulas used by wholesalers and retailers in setting their prices.

markup pricing
Applying a percentage to a product's cost to obtain its selling price.

In the retailing industry, where businesses often carry many different products, *markup pricing* has emerged as a manageable pricing system. With this cost-plus approach to pricing, retailers are able to price hundreds of products much more quickly than they could using individual break-even analyses. In calculating the selling price for a particular item, a retailer adds a markup percentage (sometimes referred to as a *markup rate*) to cover the following:

- Operating expenses
- Subsequent price reductions—for example, markdowns and employee discounts
- Desired profit

It is important to have a clear understanding of markup pricing computations. Markups may be expressed as a percentage of either the *selling price* or the *cost*. For example, if an item costs $6 and sells for $10, the markup of $4 represents a 40 percent markup of the selling price [($4 markup ÷ $10 selling price) × 100] or a 662/3 percent markup of the cost [($4 markup ÷ $6 cost) × 100]. Two simple formulas are commonly used for markup calculations.

$$\frac{\text{Markup}}{\text{Selling price}} \times 100 = \text{Markup expressed as a percentage of selling price}$$

or

$$\frac{\text{Markup}}{\text{Cost}} \times 100 = \text{Markup expressed as a percentage of cost}$$

To convert markup as a percentage of selling price to markup as a percentage of cost, use the following formula:

$$\frac{\text{Markup as a percentage of selling price}}{100\% - \text{Markup as a percentage of selling price}} \times 100 = \text{Markup expressed as a percentage of cost}$$

To convert the other way, use this formula:

$$\frac{\text{Markup as a percentage of cost}}{100\% + \text{Markup as a percentage of cost}} \times 100 = \text{Markup expressed as a percentage of selling price}$$

Selecting a Pricing Strategy

3. Identify specific pricing strategies.

Techniques such as break-even analysis yield a good idea of a feasible price for a specific product. But their seemingly precise nature can be very misleading. Such analyses are only one kind of tool for pricing and should not by themselves determine the final price. *Price determination must also consider market characteristics and the firm's current marketing strategy.* Pricing strategies that reflect these additional considerations include penetration pricing, skimming pricing, follow-the-leader pricing, variable pricing, price lining, and pricing at what the market will bear.[4]

Penetration Pricing

A firm that uses a *penetration pricing strategy* prices a product or service at less than its normal, long-range market price in order to gain more rapid market acceptance or to increase existing market share. This strategy can sometimes discourage new competitors from entering a market niche if they mistakenly view the penetration price as a long-range price. Obviously, a firm that uses this strategy sacrifices some profit margin to achieve market penetration.

Skimming Pricing

A *skimming price strategy* sets prices for products or services at high levels for a limited period of time before reducing prices to lower, more competitive levels. This strategy assumes that certain customers will pay a higher price because they view a product or service as a prestige item. Use of a skimming price is most practical when there is little threat of short-term competition or when startup costs must be recovered rapidly.

Follow-the-Leader Pricing

A *follow-the-leader pricing strategy* uses a particular competitor as a model in setting a price for a product or service. The probable reaction of competitors is a critical factor in determining whether to cut prices below a prevailing level. A small business in competition with larger firms is seldom in a position to consider itself the price leader. If competitors view a small firm's pricing as relatively unimportant, they may not respond to a price differential. On the other hand, some competitors may view a smaller price-cutter as a direct threat and counter with reductions of their own. In such a case, the use of a follow-the-leader pricing strategy accomplishes very little.

penetration pricing strategy
Setting lower than normal prices to hasten market acceptance of a product or service or to increase market share.

skimming price strategy
Setting very high prices for a limited period before reducing them to more competitive levels.

follow-the-leader pricing strategy
Using a particular competitor as a model in setting prices.

Variable Pricing

Some businesses use a *variable pricing strategy* to offer price concessions to certain customers, even though they may advertise a uniform price. Lower prices are offered for various reasons, including a customer's knowledge and bargaining strength. In some fields of business, therefore, firms make two-part pricing decisions: They set a standard list price but offer a range of price concessions to particular buyers—for example, those that purchase large quantities of their product.

Sellers using a type of variable pricing strategy called a *dynamic (personalized) pricing strategy* charge *more* than the standard price after gauging a customer's financial means and desire for the product. The information-gathering capability of the Internet has allowed such retailers as Amazon.com to use dynamic pricing.[5]

Price Lining

A *price lining strategy* establishes distinct price categories at which similar items of retail merchandise are offered for sale. For example, men's suits (of differing quality) might be sold at $250, $450, and $800. The amount of inventory stocked at different quality levels would depend on the income levels and buying desires of a store's customers. A price lining strategy has the advantage of simplifying the selection process for the customer and reducing the necessary minimum inventory.

Pricing at What the Market Will Bear

The strategy of pricing on the basis of what the market will bear can be used only when the seller has little or no competition. Obviously, this strategy will work only for nonstandardized products. For example, a food store might offer egg roll wrappers that its competitors do not carry. Busy consumers who want to fix egg rolls but have neither the time nor the knowledge to prepare the wrappers themselves will buy them at any reasonable price.[6]

Some Final Notes on Pricing Strategies

In some situations, local, state, and federal laws must be considered in setting prices. For example, the Sherman Antitrust Act generally prohibits price fixing. A case in point is a suit brought by Leegin Creative Leather Products of City of Industry, California, against Kay's Kloset, a Dallas, Texas–area retailer, because Kay's repeatedly discounted Leegin's popular Brighton handbags. Leegin lost its case in the Fifth Circuit Court of Appeals and was ordered to pay damages after it stopped shipping handbags to Kay's Kloset. However, the United States Supreme Court reversed the earlier decision and allowed Leegin to set minimum prices for its products being sold by distributors.[7]

When a small business markets a line of products, some of which may compete with each other, pricing decisions must take into account the effects of a single product price on the rest of the line. For example, the introduction of a cheese-flavored chip will likely affect sales of an existing naturally flavored chip. Pricing can become extremely complex in these situations.

Continually adjusting a price to meet changing marketing conditions can be both costly to the seller and confusing to buyers. An alternative approach is to use a system of discounting designed to reflect a variety of needs. For example, a seller may offer a trade discount to a particular buyer (such as a wholesaler) because that buyer performs a certain marketing function for the seller (such as distribution). The stated, or list, price is unchanged, but the seller offers a lower actual price by means of a discount.

Small firms should not treat bad pricing decisions as uncorrectable mistakes. Remember, pricing is not an exact science. *If the initial price appears to be off target, make any necessary adjustments and keep on selling!*

LIVING THE DREAM:

entrepreneurial challenges

e-Business Pricing

Web shoppers may not always be looking for the lowest prices, as they once were. Just like other businesses, online stores are learning that they need to differentiate their businesses from the competition based on factors other than price in order to attract customers.

This is what Jeff Rhoads, president and founder of JR's Sports Collectibles (which created SportStation.com), learned. Rhoads, a graduate of Chapman University, was a restaurant manager for 13 years prior to becoming a retailer of sports collectibles and apparel. "You have to run an e-business like any other business," says Rhoads, whose company had sales of $2.5 million in 2004. "You can't be one-sided with just price."

Today's more sophisticated online shoppers look for customer service, privacy and security, and product selection. Rhoads still keeps a close eye on bigger competitors, knowing that "we have to have a lower price than the goliaths." But his prices have gone up over time, and he offers fewer discounts. Rhoads competes through promotions offering free shipping and handling and a free upgrade from ground to three-day delivery. All these "freebies" cost money, and that impacts pricing.

Sources: http://www.sportstation.com, accessed March 15, 2007; and Melissa Campanelli, "Price Point," *Entrepreneur*, November 20, 2005, pp. 56–58.

http://www.jrsportscollectibles.com

© iStockphoto.com/© Pascal Genest

Offering Credit

In a credit sale, the seller provides goods or services to the buyer in return for the buyer's promise to pay later. The major reason for granting credit is to make sales; credit encourages decisions to buy by providing an incentive for customers, who can buy now but would prefer to pay later. Most firms offering credit actively promote this option to potential customers. An added bonus to the seller is that it provides credit records containing customer information that can be used for sales promotions, such as direct-mail appeals to customers.

4. Explain the benefits of credit, factors that affect credit extension, and types of credit.

Benefits of Credit

If credit buying and selling did not benefit both parties in a transaction, their use would cease. Borrowers obviously enjoy the availability of credit, and small firms, in particular, benefit from being able to buy on credit from their suppliers. Credit provides small firms with working capital, often allowing marginal businesses to continue operations. Additional benefits of credit to customers (borrowers) are as follows:

- The ability to satisfy immediate needs and pay for them later
- Better records of purchases on credit billing statements
- Better service and greater convenience when exchanging purchased items
- Establishment of a credit history

Suppliers, on the other hand, extend credit to customers in order to facilitate increased sales volume and also to earn money on unpaid balances. They expect the increased revenue to more than offset the costs of extending credit, so profits will increase. Other benefits of credit to sellers are as follows:

- Closer association with customers because of implied trust
- Easier selling through telephone- and mail-order systems and over the Internet
- Smoother sales peaks and valleys, since purchasing power is always available
- Easy access to a tool with which to stay competitive

Factors That Affect Selling on Credit

An entrepreneur must decide whether to sell on credit or for cash only. In many cases, credit selling cannot be avoided, as it is standard trade practice in many types of businesses. It is important to note that in today's marketplace credit-selling competitors will almost always outsell a cash-only firm.

Although a seller always hopes to increase profits by allowing credit sales, it is not a risk-free practice. Small firms frequently shift or at least share credit risk by accepting credit cards carried by customers rather than offering their own credit. For example, the operator of a Texaco gasoline station may accept Texaco credit cards and other major credit cards, thereby avoiding the hassles of credit management. The business will pay a fee to the credit card company, but that cost may be less than the expense of managing its own independent credit system, especially when losses from bad debts are factored in. A retailer following this strategy must obtain merchant status with individual credit card companies. This is not an automatic process and can be problematic, particularly for home-based businesses.

Unfortunately, the cost of accepting major credit cards for payment over the Internet has increased. To deal with Internet fraud, small e-retailers turn to third-party firms that specialize in handling Internet credit card payments. These firms provide a degree of fraud protection for the small business. For example, PayPal (http://www.paypal.com) lets firms (and individuals) accept credit card payments. There are no setup costs and no monthly fees. PayPal is compensated with a transaction fee of 2 to 3 percent, plus 30 cents.[8] Other credit card–processing companies include Charge.com, eCommerce Exchange, Merchant Accounts Express, and the Canadian corporation InternetSecure, Inc.

Also, if a small firm makes credit sales online, it is subject to "chargebacks" whenever buyers dispute a transaction. Some credit card companies assess fines and threaten account termination if the number of chargebacks is excessive.

For a variety of reasons, a small business may or may not decide to sell on credit. Four factors related to the entrepreneur's decision to extend credit are the type of business, credit policies of competitors, customers' income levels, and the availability of working capital.

TYPE OF BUSINESS   Retailers of durable goods typically grant credit more freely than do small grocers that sell perishables or small restaurants that serve primarily local customers. Indeed, most consumers find it necessary to buy big-ticket items on an installment basis, and the life span of such a product makes installment selling feasible.

CREDIT POLICIES OF COMPETITORS   Unless a firm offers some compensating advantage, it is expected to be as generous as its competitors in extending credit. Wholesale hardware companies and retail furniture stores are examples of businesses that face stiff competition from credit sellers.

INCOME LEVEL OF CUSTOMERS   The age and income level of a retailer's customers are significant factors in determining its credit policy. For example, a drugstore adjacent to a high school might not extend credit to high school students, who are typically undesirable credit customers because of their lack of both maturity and steady income.

AVAILABILITY OF WORKING CAPITAL   Credit sales increase the amount of working capital needed by the business doing the selling. Open-credit and installment accounts tie up money that may be needed to pay business expenses.

Types of Credit

There are two broad classes of credit: consumer credit and trade credit. *Consumer credit* is granted by retailers to final consumers who purchase for personal or family use. A small business owner can sometimes use his or her personal consumer credit to purchase supplies and equipment for use in the business. *Trade credit* is extended by nonfinancial firms, such as manufacturers and wholesalers, to business firms that are customers. Consumer credit and trade credit differ with respect to types of credit instruments, the paperwork, sources for financing receivables, and terms of sale. Another important distinction is that credit insurance is available only for trade credit.

A study of credit and small business, sponsored by the National Federation of Independent Business, reported extensively on credit use by small firms.[9] The survey found that 45 percent of small business owners feel that their most significant problem in the area of consumer credit is slow or late payment.

CONSUMER CREDIT   The three major kinds of consumer credit accounts are open charge accounts, installment accounts, and revolving charge accounts. Many variations of these credit accounts are also used.

OPEN CHARGE ACCOUNTS   When using an *open charge account*, a customer takes possession of goods (or services) at the time of purchase, with payment due when billed. Stated terms typically call for payment at the end of the month, but it is customary to allow a longer period than that stated. There is no finance charge for this kind of credit if the balance on the account is paid in full at the end of the billing period. Customers are not generally required to make a down payment or to pledge collateral. Small accounts at department stores are good examples of open charge accounts.

INSTALLMENT ACCOUNTS   An *installment account* is a vehicle for long-term consumer credit. A down payment is normally required, and annual finance charges can be 20 percent or more of the purchase price. Payment periods are commonly from 12 to 36 months, although automobile dealers often offer an extended payment period of 60 months or even longer. An installment account is useful for large purchases such as that of a car, washing machine, or television.

REVOLVING CHARGE ACCOUNTS   A *revolving charge account* is a variation of the installment account. A seller grants a customer a line of credit, and charged purchases may not exceed the credit limit. A specified percentage of the outstanding balance must be paid monthly, forcing the customer to budget and limiting the amount of debt that can be carried. Finance charges are computed on the unpaid balance at the end of the month. Although credit cards offer this type of account, they are discussed separately in the next section because of their widespread use.

CREDIT CARDS   Credit cards, frequently referred to as plastic money, have become a major source of retail credit. As just mentioned, credit cards are usually based on a revolving charge account system. Depending on the issuer, we can distinguish three basic types of credit cards: bank credit cards, entertainment credit cards, and retailer credit cards.

consumer credit
Financing granted by retailers to individuals who purchase for personal or family use.

trade credit
Financing provided by a supplier of inventory to a given company.

open charge account
A line of credit that allows the customer to obtain a product at the time of purchase, with payment due when billed.

installment account
A line of credit that requires a down payment, with the balance paid over a specified period of time.

revolving charge account
A line of credit on which the customer may charge purchases at any time, up to a preestablished limit.

BANK CREDIT CARDS   The best known bank credit cards are MasterCard and VISA. Bank credit cards are widely accepted by retailers that want to offer credit but don't provide their own credit cards. Most small business retailers fit into this category. In return for a set fee (usually 2 to 5 percent of the purchase price) paid by the retailer, the bank takes the responsibility for making collections. Some banks charge annual membership fees to their cardholders. Also, cardholders are frequently able to obtain cash up to the credit limit of their card.

ENTERTAINMENT CREDIT CARDS   Well-known examples of entertainment credit cards are American Express and Diner's Club cards. While these cards have traditionally charged an annual fee, American Express now offers the Blue Card, which has no fee for use. Originally used for services, these cards are now widely accepted for sales of merchandise. As with bank credit cards, the collection of charges on an entertainment credit card is the responsibility of the sponsoring agency.

RETAILER CREDIT CARDS   Many companies—for example, department stores, oil companies, and telephone companies—issue their own credit cards specifically for use in their outlets or for purchasing their products or services from other outlets. Customers are usually not charged annual fees or finance charges if their balance is paid each month.

Trade Credit

Firms selling to other businesses may specify terms of sale, such as 2/10, net 30. This means that a 2 percent discount is given by the seller if the buyer pays within 10 days of the invoice date. Failure to take this discount makes the full amount of the invoice due in 30 days. For example, with these terms, a buyer paying for a $100,000 purchase within 10 days of the invoice date would save 2 percent, or $2,000.

Sales terms for trade credit depend on the product sold and the buyer's and the seller's circumstances. The credit period often varies directly with the length of the buyer's inventory turnover period, which obviously depends on the type of product sold. The larger the order and the higher the credit rating of the buyer, the better the sales terms will be, assuming that individual terms are fixed for each buyer. The greater the financial strength and the more adequate and liquid the working capital of the seller, the more generous the seller's sales terms can be. Of course, no business can afford to allow competitors to outdo it in reasonable generosity of sales terms. In many types of businesses, terms are so firmly set by tradition that a unique policy is difficult, if not impossible, for a small firm to implement.

Managing the Credit Process

5. Describe the activities involved in managing credit.

Unfortunately, many small firms pay little attention to their credit management systems until bad debts become a problem. Often, this is too late. Credit management should precede the first credit sale (in the form of a thorough screening process) and then continue throughout the credit cycle.

As mentioned previously, many small firms transfer all or part of the credit function to another party. For example, a small repair shop or retail clothing store that accepts VISA or MasterCard is transferring much of the credit risk; in effect, the fee that the business pays the credit card company covers the credit management process. Nevertheless, a number of small firms want to offer their own credit to their customers and, therefore, need to understand the credit function. Let's take a look at some of the major considerations in developing and operating a comprehensive credit management program for a small business.

Evaluation of Credit Applicants

In most retail stores, the first step in credit investigation is having the customer complete an application form. The information obtained on this form is used as the basis for examining an applicant's creditworthiness. Since the most important factor in determining a customer's credit limit is her or his ability to pay the obligation when it becomes due, it is crucial to evaluate the customer's financial resources, debt position, and income level. The amount of credit requested also requires careful consideration. Drugstore customers usually need only small amounts of credit. On the other hand, business customers of wholesalers and manufacturers typically expect large credit lines. In the special case of installment selling, the amount of credit should not exceed the repossession value of the goods sold. Automobile dealers follow this rule as a general practice.

THE FOUR CREDIT QUESTIONS In evaluating the credit status of applicants, a seller must answer the following questions:

1. Can the buyer pay as promised?
2. Will the buyer pay?
3. If so, when will the buyer pay?
4. If not, can the buyer be forced to pay?

The answers to these questions have to be based in part on the seller's estimate of the buyer's ability and willingness to pay. Such an estimate constitutes a judgment of the buyer's creditworthiness. For credit to be approved the answers to questions 1, 2, and 4 should be "yes" and the answer to question 3 should be "on schedule."

Every applicant is creditworthy to some degree; a decision to grant credit merely recognizes the buyer's credit standing. But the seller must consider the possibility that the buyer will be unable or unwilling to pay. When evaluating an applicant's credit status, therefore, the seller must decide how much risk of nonpayment to assume.

THE TRADITIONAL FIVE C'S OF CREDIT As already explained in Chapter 12, the ability to repay a loan, is frequently evaluated in terms of the five C's of credit: character, capital, capacity, conditions, and collateral. The same is true as an indicator of a firm's ability to repay trade credit and deserves repating:

- *Character* refers to the fundamental integrity and honesty that should underlie all human and business relationships. For business customers, character is embodied in the business policies and ethical practices of the firm. Individual customers who are granted credit must be known to be morally responsible persons.
- *Capital* consists of the cash and other liquid assets owned by the customer. A prospective business customer should have sufficient capital to underwrite planned operations, including an appropriate amount invested by the owner.
- *Capacity* refers to the customer's ability to conserve assets and faithfully and efficiently follow a financial plan. A business customer should utilize its invested capital wisely and capitalize to the fullest extent on business opportunities.
- *Conditions* refer to such factors as business cycles and changes in price levels, which may be either favorable or unfavorable to the payment of debts. For example, economic recession places a burden on both businesses' and consumers' abilities to pay their debts. Other adverse factors that might limit a customer's ability to pay include fires and other natural disasters, strong new competition, and labor problems.
- *Collateral* consists of designated security given as a pledge for fulfillment of an obligation. It is a secondary source for loan repayment in case the borrower's cash flows are insufficient for repaying a loan.

Sources of Credit Information

One of the most important, and most frequently neglected, sources of credit information is a customer's previous credit history. Properly analyzed, credit records show whether a business customer regularly takes cash discounts and, if not, whether the customer's account is typically slow. One small clothing retailer has every applicant reviewed by a Dun & Bradstreet–trained credit manager, who maintains a complete file of D&B credit reports on thousands of customers. Recent financial statements of customers are also on file. These reports, together with the retailer's own credit information, are the basis for decisions on credit sales, with heavy emphasis on the D&B credit reports. Nonretailing firms should similarly investigate credit applicants.

Manufacturers and wholesalers can frequently use a firm's financial statements as an additional source of information. Obtaining maximum value from financial statements requires a careful ratio analysis, which will reveal a firm's working-capital position, profit-making potential, and general financial health (as discussed in Chapter 10).

Pertinent data may also be obtained from outsiders. For example, arrangements may be made with other sellers to exchange credit data. Such credit information exchanges are quite useful for learning about the sales and payment experiences others have had with the seller's own customers or credit applicants.

Another source of credit information for the small firm, particularly about commercial accounts, is the customer's banker. Some bankers willingly supply credit information about their depositors, considering this to be a service that helps those firms or individuals obtain credit in amounts they can successfully handle. Other bankers believe that credit information is confidential and should not be disclosed.

Organizations that may be consulted regarding credit standings are trade-credit agencies and credit bureaus. *Trade-credit agencies* are privately owned and operated organizations that collect credit information on businesses only, not individual consumers. After analyzing and evaluating the data, trade-credit agencies make credit ratings available to client companies for a fee. Dun & Bradstreet, Inc. (http://www.dnb.com/us/), a nationwide, general trade-credit agency, offers a wide array of credit reports, including the Small Business Risk New Account Score and the Payment Analysis Report. Manufacturers and wholesalers are especially interested in Dun & Bradstreet's reference book and credit reports. Available to subscribers only, the reference book covers most U.S. businesses and provides a credit rating, an evaluation of financial strength, and other key credit information on each firm.

Credit bureaus are the most common type of consumer reporting agency. These private companies maintain credit histories on individuals, based on reports from banks, mortgage companies, department stores, and other creditors. These companies make possible the exchange of credit information on persons with previous credit activity. Some credit bureaus do not require a business firm to be a member in order to get a credit report. The fee charged to nonmembers, however, is considerably higher than that charged to members. Most credit bureaus operate on one of the three online data-processing networks: Experian, Equifax, or TransUnion.[10]

trade-credit agencies
Privately owned organizations that collect credit information on businesses.

credit bureaus
Privately owned organizations that summarize a number of firms' credit experiences with particular individuals.

Aging of Accounts Receivable

aging schedule
A categorization of accounts receivable based on the length of time they have been outstanding.

Many small businesses can benefit from an *aging schedule,* which divides accounts receivable into categories based on the length of time they have been outstanding. Typically, some accounts are current and others are past due. Regular use of an aging schedule allows troublesome collection trends to be spotted so that appropriate actions can be taken. With experience, a small firm can estimate the probabilities of collecting accounts of various ages and use them to forecast cash conversion rates.

Exhibit 16-6 presents a hypothetical aging schedule for accounts receivable. According to the schedule, four customers have overdue credit, totaling $200,000. Only customer 005 is

EXHIBIT

Account Status (Days past due)	CUSTOMER ACCOUNT NUMBER					
	001	002	003	004	005	Total
120 days	—	—	$50,000	—	—	$ 50,000
90 days	—	$ 10,000	—	—	—	10,000
60 days	—	—	—	$40,000	—	40,000
30 days	—	20,000	20,000	—	—	40,000
15 days	$50,000	—	10,000	—	—	60,000
Total overdue	$50,000	$ 30,000	$80,000	$40,000	$ 0	$200,000
Not due (beyond discount period)	$30,000	$ 10,000	$ 0	$10,000	$130,000	$180,000
Not due (still in discount period)	$20,000	$100,000	$ 0	$90,000	$220,000	$430,000
Credit rating	A	B	C	A	A	—

current. Customer 003 has the largest amount overdue ($80,000). In fact, the schedule shows that customer 003 is overdue on all charges and has a past record of slow payment (indicated by a credit rating of C). Immediate attention must be given to collecting from this customer. Customer 002 should also be contacted, because, among overdue accounts, this customer has the second largest amount ($110,000) in the "Not due" classification. Customer 005, however, could quickly have the largest amount overdue and should be watched closely.

Customers 001 and 004 require a special kind of analysis. Customer 001 has $10,000 more overdue than customer 004. However, customer 004's overdue credit of $40,000, which is 60 days past due, may well have a serious impact on the $100,000 not yet due ($10,000 in the beyond-discount period plus $90,000 still in the discount period). On the other hand, even though customer 001 has $50,000 of overdue credit, this customer's payment is overdue by only 15 days. Also, customer 001 has only $50,000 not yet due ($30,000 in the beyond-discount period plus $20,000 still in the discount period), compared to the $100,000 not yet due from customer 004. Both customers have an A credit rating. In conclusion, customer 001 is a better potential source of cash. Therefore, collection efforts should be focused on customer 004 rather than on customer 001, who may simply need a reminder of the overdue amount of $50,000.

Billing and Collection Procedures

Timely notification of customers regarding the status of their accounts is one of the most effective methods of keeping credit accounts current. Most credit customers pay their bills on time if the creditor provides them with information verifying their credit balance. Failure on the seller's part to send invoices delays payments.

Overdue credit accounts tie up a seller's working capital, prevent further sales to the slow-paying customer, and lead to losses from bad debts. Even if a slow-paying customer is not lost, relations with this customer are strained for a time at least.

A firm extending credit must have adequate billing records and collection procedures if it expects prompt payments. Also, a personal relationship between seller and customer must not be allowed to tempt the seller into being less than businesslike in extending further credit and collecting overdue amounts. Given the seriousness of the problem, a small firm must decide whether to collect past-due accounts directly or turn the task over to an attorney or a collection agency.

Perhaps the most effective weapon in collecting past-due accounts is reminding the debtors that their credit standing may be impaired. Impairment is certain to happen if the account is turned over to a collection agency. Delinquent customers will typically attempt to avoid damage to their credit standing, particularly when it would be known to the business community. This concern underlies and strengthens the various collection efforts of the seller.

A small firm should deal compassionately with delinquent customers. A collection technique that is too threatening not only may fail to work but also could cause the firm to lose the customer or become subject to legal action.

Many businesses have found that the most effective collection procedure consists of a series of steps, each somewhat more forceful than the preceding one. Historically, the process has started with a gentle written reminder; subsequent steps may include additional letters, telephone calls, registered letters, personal contacts, and referral to a collection agency or attorney. The timing of these steps should be carefully standardized so that each one automatically follows the preceding one in a specified number of days. More recently, some businesses have started to send text messages and e-mails as reminders, especially when the firm has a significant percentage of younger customers.

Various ratios can be used to monitor expenses associated with credit sales. The best known and most widely used expense ratio is the *bad-debt ratio,* which is computed by dividing the amount of bad debts by the total amount of credit sales. The bad-debt ratio reflects the efficiency of credit policies and procedures. A small firm may thus compare the effectiveness of its credit management with that of other firms. A relationship exists among the bad-debt ratio, profitability, and size of the firm. Small profitable retailers have a much higher bad-debt ratio than large profitable retailers do. In general, the bad-debt losses of small firms range from a fraction of 1 percent of net sales to percentages large enough to put them out of business!

bad-debt ratio
The ratio of bad debts to credit sales.

Credit Regulation

The use of credit is regulated by a variety of federal laws, as well as state laws that vary considerably from state to state. Prior to the passage of such legislation, consumers were often confused by credit agreements and were sometimes victims of credit abuse.

By far the most significant piece of credit legislation is the federal Consumer Credit Protection Act, which includes the 1968 Truth-in-Lending Act. Its two primary purposes are to ensure that consumers are informed about the terms of a credit agreement and to require creditors to specify how finance charges are computed. The act requires that a finance charge be stated as an annual percentage rate and that creditors specify their procedures for correcting billing mistakes.

Other federal legislation related to credit management includes the following:

- *The Fair Credit Billing Act* provides protection to credit customers in cases involving incorrect billing. A reasonable time period is allowed for billing errors to be corrected. The act does not cover installment credit.

- *The Fair Credit Reporting Act* gives certain rights to credit applicants regarding reports prepared by credit bureaus. Amendments such as the FACT Act, signed into law in December 2003, have strengthened privacy provisions and defined more clearly the responsibilities and liabilities of businesses that provide information to credit reporting agencies.

- *The Equal Credit Opportunity Act* ensures that all consumers are given an equal chance to obtain credit. For example, a person is not required to reveal his or her sex, race, national origin, or religion to obtain credit.

- *The Fair Debt Collection Practices Act* bans the use of intimidation and deception in collection, requiring debt collectors to treat debtors fairly.

It should be apparent by now that pricing and credit decisions are of prime importance to a small firm because of their direct impact on its financial health. *Ultimately, experience will be the entrepreneur's best teacher*, but we hope that the concepts presented in this chapter will help smooth the trip.

LOOKING BACK

1. Discuss the role of cost and demand factors in setting a price.

- The revenue of a firm is a direct reflection of two components: sales volume and price.
- Price must be sufficient to cover total cost plus some margin of profit.
- A firm should examine elasticity of demand—the relationship of price and quantity demanded—when setting a price.
- A product's competitive advantage is a demand factor in setting price.

2. Apply break-even analysis and markup pricing.

- Analyzing costs and revenue under different price assumptions identifies the break-even point, the quantity sold at which total costs equal total revenue.
- The usefulness of break-even analysis is enhanced by incorporating sales forecasts.
- Markup pricing is a generalized cost-plus system of pricing used by intermediaries with many products.

3. Identify specific pricing strategies.

- Penetration pricing and skimming pricing are short-term strategies used when new products are first introduced into the market.
- Follow-the-leader and variable pricing are special strategies that reflect the nature of the competition's pricing and concessions to customers.
- A price lining strategy simplifies choices for customers by offering a range of several distinct prices.

- State and federal laws must be considered in setting prices, as well as any impact that a price may have on other product line items.

4. Explain the benefits of credit, factors that affect credit extension, and types of credit.

- Credit offers potential benefits to both buyers and sellers.
- Type of business, credit policies of competitors, income level of customers, and availability of adequate working capital affect the decision to extend credit.
- The two broad classes of credit are consumer credit and trade credit.

5. Describe the activities involved in managing credit.

- Evaluating the credit status of applicants begins with the completion of an application form.
- A customer's ability to pay is evaluated through the five C's of credit: character, capital, capacity, conditions, and collateral.
- Pertinent credit data can be obtained from several outside sources, including formal trade-credit agencies such as Dun & Bradstreet.
- An accounts receivable aging schedule can be used to improve the credit collection process.
- A small firm should establish a formal procedure for billing and collecting from charge customers.
- It is important that a small firm follow all relevant credit regulations.

Key Terms

price p. 419
credit p. 419
total cost p. 419
variable costs p. 420
fixed costs p. 420
average pricing p. 420
elasticity of demand p. 421
elastic demand p. 422
inelastic demand p. 422
prestige pricing p. 423

break-even point p. 423
contribution margin p. 424
markup pricing p. 426
penetration pricing strategy p. 427
skimming price strategy p. 427
follow-the-leader pricing strategy p. 427
variable pricing strategy p. 428
dynamic (personalized) pricing strategy p. 428

price lining strategy p. 428
consumer credit p. 431
trade credit p. 431
open charge account p. 431
installment account p. 431
revolving charge account p. 431
trade-credit agencies p. 434
credit bureaus p. 434
aging schedule p. 434
bad-debt ratio p. 436

Discussion Questions

1. Why does average pricing sometimes result in a pricing mistake?

2. Explain the importance of fixed and variable costs to the pricing decision.

3. How does the concept of elasticity of demand relate to prestige pricing? Give an example.

4. If a firm has fixed costs of $100,000 and variable costs per unit of $1, what is the break-even point in units, assuming a selling price of $5 per unit?

5. What is the difference between a penetration pricing strategy and a skimming price strategy? Under what circumstances would each be used?

6. If a small business conducts its break-even analysis properly and finds the break-even volume at a price

of $10 to be 10,000 units, should it price its product at $10? Why or why not?

7. What are the major benefits of credit to buyers? What are its major benefits to sellers?

8. How does an open charge account differ from a revolving charge account?

9. What is meant by the terms 2/10, net 30? Does it pay to take discounts when they are offered?

10. What is the major purpose of aging accounts receivable? At what point in credit management should this activity be performed? Why?

You Make the Call

SITUATION 1

Steve Jones is the 35-year-old owner of a highly competitive small business, which supplies temporary office help. Like most businesspeople, he is always looking for ways to increase profit. However, the nature of his competition makes it very difficult to raise prices for the temps' services, while reducing their wages makes recruiting difficult. Jones has, nevertheless, found an area—bad debts—in which improvement should increase profits. A friend and business consultant met with Jones to advise him on credit management policies. Jones was pleased to get this friend's advice, as bad debts were costing him about 2 percent of sales. Currently, Jones has no system for managing credit.

Question 1 What advice would you give Jones regarding the screening of new credit customers?

Question 2 What action should Jones take to encourage current credit customers to pay their debts? Be specific.

Question 3 Jones has considered eliminating credit sales. What are the possible consequences of this decision?

SITUATION 2

Tom Anderson started his records storage business in the New York metropolitan area. His differentiation strategy was to offer competitive prices while providing state-of-the-art technology, easy access to his warehouse, and, of course, great service.

After opening the business, Anderson learned that most potential customers had already signed long-term storage contracts with competitors. These contracts included a removal fee for each box permanently removed from the storage company's warehouse, making it difficult for customers to consider switching.

Anderson believes that the survival of his company hinges on his view of what the essence of his business is. In other words, is he operating a storage company or a real estate business? He is convinced that he must answer this question before making any decision regarding pricing strategy.

Question 1 What do you think Anderson means when he asks, "Is my business storage or real estate?" Why do you think he feels a need to ask this question prior to developing a pricing strategy?

Question 2 What pricing strategy would be effective in combating the existing contractual relationships between potential customers and competitors?

Question 3 Assuming that business costs would allow Anderson to lower prices, what problems do you see with this approach?

Question 4 Do you believe his business could benefit from offering credit to customers? Why or why not?

SITUATION 3

Paul Bowlin owns and operates a tree removal, pruning, and spraying business in a metropolitan area with a population of approximately 200,000. The business has grown to the point where Bowlin uses one and sometimes two crews, with four or five employees on each crew. Pricing has always been an important tool in gaining business, but Bowlin realizes that there are ways to entice customers other than quoting the lowest price. For example, he provides careful cleanup of branches and leaves, takes out stumps below ground level, and waits until a customer is completely satisfied before taking payment. At the same time, he realizes his bids for tree removal jobs must cover his costs. In this industry, Bowlin faces intense price competition from operators with more sophisticated wood-processing equipment, such as chip grinders. Therefore, he is always open to suggestions about pricing strategy.

Question 1   What would the nature of this industry suggest about the elasticity of demand affecting Bowlin's pricing?

Question 2   What types of costs should Bowlin evaluate when he is determining his break-even point?

Question 3   What pricing strategies could Bowlin adopt to further his long-term success in this market?

Question 4   How can the high quality of Bowlin's work be used to justify somewhat higher price quotes?

Experiential Exercises

1. Interview a small business owner regarding his or her pricing strategy. Try to ascertain whether the strategy being used reflects the total fixed and variable costs of the business. Prepare a report on your findings.

2. Interview a small business owner regarding his or her policies for evaluating credit applicants. Summarize your findings in a report.

3. Interview the credit manager of a retail store about the benefits and drawbacks of extending credit to customers. Report your findings to the class.

4. Ask several small business owners in your community who extend credit to describe the credit management procedures they use to collect bad debts. Report your findings to the class.

Small Business & Entrepreneurship Resource Center

The *Small Business and Entrepreneurship Resource Center* offers complete small business management resources through a comprehensive database that covers all major areas of starting, operating, and maintaining a business from financing, management, marketing, accounting, taxes, and more. Use the access code that came with your new book to access the site and perform the exercises in each chapter.

1. Anthony Shurman, president of Yosha Enterprises Inc. in Westfield, New Jersey, offers a valuable service to customers through its Momints breath mints—eliminating bad breath. When Momints debuted its price was high, but coming up with a pricing strategy was not an easy task. Describe each of the 5 Golden Rules of Pricing, as given by Dilip Soman, marketing professor at the University of Toronto. Is there any Golden Rule that you could/would add to that list?

2. PayPal is an online credit service provider that takes out the risk of handling on-line credit card sales for small e-tailers. According to the article "A battle at the checkout" Rajiv Dutta, PayPal's President says "We have more account holders than American Express, yet the vast majority of e-commerce sites don't offer us." Discuss what might be causing this—why would on-line vendors be reluctant to utilize the PayPal service, and instead use Google's Checkout service?

Sources: Name your price: stumped about what to charge? Setting prices is both an art and a science-and a little bit of guesswork. Here's how to figure it out. (The Plumbush Inn) (Yosha Enterprises Inc.).Geoff Williams. *Entrepreneur* 33, 9 (Sept 2005): p. 108(4).
A battle at the checkout; Online payments. (PayPal vs Google Checkout). *The Economist* (US) 383, 8527 (May 5, 2007): p. 88US.

Video Case 16

NICOLE MILLER INC. (P. 658)

This case illustrates how choosing a price strategy appropriate to a firm's industry can create perceived added value to the product when it is coupled with an effective marketing campaign.

ALTERNATIVE CASES FOR CHAPTER 16

Case 14, Rodgers Chevrolet, p. 654
Case 21, Modern Postcard, p. 667

Promotional Planning

It was his destiny. Shaun Clancy's family owned an award-winning restaurant and bar in Ireland. His father worked in Toots Shor's, perhaps the most famous restaurant and nightclub in New York City in the 1940s and 1950s. So, after working in different clubs, it was only natural for Clancy to run his own place. In 2003, he opened Foley's NY Pub & Restaurant. But did New York really need another restaurant? What would make Foley's stand out?

Something Clancy learned during his days as a bartender was that people like talking about baseball—all year 'round. He wanted Foley's to be an "Irish Bar with a Baseball Attitude." Even the name of the business was chosen with baseball in mind. Arthur "Red" Foley was a famous sportswriter with the *New York Daily News*. Clancy made Foley's the home of the "Irish Baseball Hall of Fame,"

filling the restaurant with memorabilia. But how could Clancy draw people into his restaurant to enjoy the atmosphere he had created?

Clancy focused on attracting celebrities to Foley's, especially current and former baseball players. Perhaps his best sports-related promotion, however, was with NASCAR champion Jimmie Johnson, earning Foley's a write-up in the *New York Daily News*. Clancy's real breakthrough, though, came in 2008. Going into Saint Patrick's Day in March, this Irish-themed pub and restaurant banned the singing of "Danny Boy." Clancy argued that the song was too depressing, and on top of that, it had been written by an Englishman who had never set foot in Ireland!

This ban resulted in Foley's being featured in *The New York Times*, on MSNBC, and on *The Colbert Report*, among others. As a result, Clancy and Foley's are now icons on the New York scene. Call it a simple stunt, if you like, but thinking through inexpensive opportunities for promoting a small business can make all the difference.

Sources: http://www.foleysny.com, accessed March 21, 2009; Geoff Williams, "An Entrepreneur Walks into a Bar . . ." *Entrepreneur*, April 2009, pp. 46–48; and Cahir O'Doherty, "Oh Danny Boy—Shut Up!" *Irish Voice*, http://www.irishabroad.com, accessed March 21, 2009.

LOOKING AHEAD

AFTER STUDYING THIS CHAPTER, YOU SHOULD BE ABLE TO

1. Describe the communication process and the factors determining a promotional mix.
2. Explain methods of determining the appropriate level of promotional expenditures.
3. Describe personal selling activities.
4. Identify advertising options for a small business.
5. Discuss the use of sales promotional tools.

A cliché in the business world is that "nothing happens until somebody sells something." If you are starting your own business, you will not get anywhere unless you have a customer willing to buy your product or service. But how does that customer know that you have something to sell? Does she or he randomly drive by your store and see your sign? Stumble across your website while surfing the Internet? Hear about you from a friend or neighbor? If you want people to buy what you are selling, you need to let them know that you are open for business—and why they should buy from you. The way you get that message across is called *promotion.*

Promotion consists of marketing communications that inform potential consumers about a firm or its product or service and try to persuade them to buy it. Small businesses use promotion in varying degrees; a given firm seldom uses all of the many promotional tools available. In order to simplify our discussion of the promotional process, we group the techniques discussed in this chapter into three traditional categories—personal selling, advertising, and sales promotional tools. And we give special attention to public relations, a strategy that Shaun Clancy used when he obtained so much free publicity for banning "Danny Boy."

A key decision in developing a promotional strategy is determining what you want to get out of it. Are you attracting customers to your store? Do you want them to visit your website? Are you asking them to buy a specific product or service? Or do you just want to plant the name of your business firmly in customers' minds so that they will think of you when they are ready to buy? This first decision will drive what you choose to communicate to prospective customers and the means for getting your message out to them.

Before examining the categories in the promotional process, let's look at the basic process of communication that characterizes promotion. If an entrepreneur understands that promotion is just a special form of communication, she or he will be better able to grasp the entire process.

promotion
Marketing communications that inform and persuade consumers.

The Communication Process in Promotion

Promotion is based on communication. In fact, promotion is wasted unless it effectively communicates a firm's message.

1. Describe the communication process and the factors determining a promotional mix.

Communication is a process with identifiable components. As shown in Exhibit 17-1, every communication involves a source, a message, a channel, and a receiver. Each of us communicates in many ways every day, and these exchanges parallel small business communications. Part (a) in Exhibit 17-1 depicts a personal communication—a daughter away at college who is communicating with her parents. Part (b) depicts a small business communication—a firm communicating with a customer.

As you can see, many similarities exist between the two. The receiver of the daughter's message is her parents. The daughter, the source in this example, uses three different channels for their message: e-mail, a personal visit, and a gift card. The receiver of the message from the XYZ Company is the customer. The XYZ Company uses three message channels: a newspaper, a sales call, and a business gift. The daughter's e-mail and the company's newspaper advertisement both represent nonpersonal forms of communication --there is no face-to-face contact. The daughter's visit to her parents' home and the sales call made by the company's representative are personal forms of communication. Finally, the gift card and the business gift are both special methods of communication. Thus, the promotional efforts of the small firm, like the communication between parents and daughter, can be viewed as encompassing nonpersonal (advertising), personal (personal selling), and special (sales promotion) forms of communication.

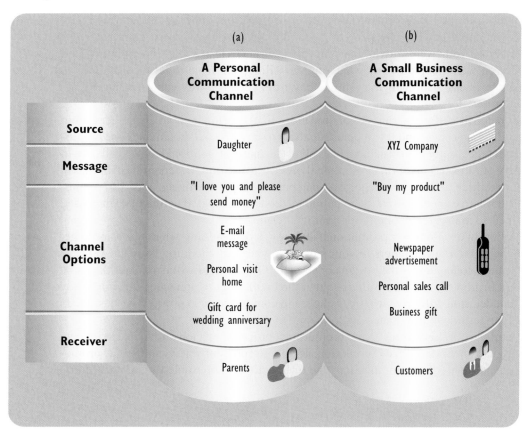

(a) **A Personal Communication Channel** / (b) **A Small Business Communication Channel**

	(a)	(b)
Source	Daughter	XYZ Company
Message	"I love you and please send money"	"Buy my product"
Channel Options	E-mail message / Personal visit home / Gift card for wedding anniversary	Newspaper advertisement / Personal sales call / Business gift
Receiver	Parents	Customers

promotional mix
A blend of nonpersonal, personal, and special forms of communication aimed at a target market.

A term commonly used to describe how a business combines its promotional methods is *promotional mix*. A *promotional mix* is the blend of nonpersonal, personal, and special forms of communication techniques aimed at a target market. The particular combination of the various promotional methods—advertising, personal selling, and sales promotional tools—is determined by many factors. One important factor is the geographical nature of the market to be reached. A widely dispersed market generally requires mass coverage through advertising, in contrast to the more costly individual contacts of personal selling. On the other hand, if the market is local or if the number of customers is relatively small, personal selling may be more feasible.

Another factor is the size of the promotional budget. Small firms may not select certain forms of promotion because the costs are just too high. Television advertising, for example, is generally more expensive than radio advertising.

A third factor that heavily influences the promotional mix is the product's characteristics. If a product is of high unit value, such as a boat or a recreational vehicle, personal selling will be a vital ingredient in the mix. Personal selling is also an effective method for promoting highly technical products, such as a helicopter or a home gym, because a customer normally has limited knowledge about such products. On the other hand, nonpersonal advertising is more effective for a relatively inexpensive item, like chewing gum.

There are, of course, many other considerations to be evaluated when developing a unique promotional mix. When you start your business, you should take a close look at the promotional tactics of successful competitors. They have probably learned, through trial and error, effective methods to communicate with customers. You will probably make some adjustments based on what you see others doing, your budget, your location, and your product/service selection. Over time, you will undoubtedly cut back on particular efforts or seek more funds to support your promotional plan.

Determining the Promotional Budget

Unfortunately, no mathematical formula can answer the question "How much should a small business spend on promotion?" There are, however, four commonsense approaches to budgeting funds for small business promotion:

2. Explain methods of determining the appropriate level of promotional expenditures.

1. Allocating a percentage of sales
2. Deciding how much can be spared
3. Spending as much as the competition does
4. Determining how much is needed for specific results

Allocating a Percentage of Sales

Often, the simplest method of determining how much to budget for promotion is to earmark promotional dollars based on a percentage of sales. A firm's own past experiences should be evaluated to establish a promotion-to-sales ratio. If 2 percent of sales, for example, has historically been spent on promotion with good results, the firm should budget 2 percent of forecasted sales for future promotion. Secondary data on industry averages can also be used for comparison. *Advertising Age* magazine is one of several sources that report what firms are doing with their advertising dollars.

A major shortcoming of this method is an inherent tendency to spend more on promotion when sales are increasing and less when they are declining. If promotion stimulates sales, then reducing promotional spending when sales are down is illogical. Additionally, new firms have no historical sales figures on which to base their promotional budgets.

Deciding How Much Can Be Spared

Another piecemeal approach to promotional budgeting widely used by small firms is to spend whatever is left over when all other activities have been funded. The decision about promotional spending might be made only when a media representative sells an owner on a special deal that the business can afford. Such an approach to promotional spending might present opportunities, but action should be taken only if the deal allows the business to accomplish promotional goals.

Spending as Much as the Competition Does

Sometimes, a small firm builds a promotional budget based on an analysis of competitors' budgets. By duplicating the promotional efforts of close competitors, the business hopes to reach the same customers and will be spending at least as much as the competition. If the competitor is a large business, this method is clearly not feasible; however, it can be used to react to short-run promotional tactics by small competitors. Unfortunately, this approach may result in the copying of competitors' mistakes as well as their successes.

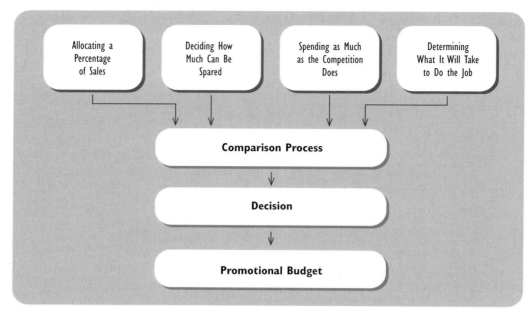

EXHIBIT

17-2 Four-Step Method for Determining a Promotional Budget

Determining How Much Is Needed for Specific Results

The preferred approach to estimating promotional expenditures is to decide what it will take to do the job. This method requires a comprehensive analysis of the market and the firm's goals. If these estimates are reasonably accurate, the entrepreneur can determine the total amount that needs to be spent.

In many cases, the best way for a small business to set promotional expenditures incorporates all four approaches. In other words, compare the four estimated amounts and set the promotional budget at a level that is somewhere between the maximum and minimum amounts (see Exhibit 17-2). After the budget has been determined, the key decision is how dollars will be spent on the various promotional methods. Which methods are chosen depends on a number of factors. We will now examine personal selling, a frequent choice for small firms.

Personal Selling in the Small Firm

3. Describe personal selling activities.

Many products require *personal selling*—a sales presentation delivered in a one-on-one manner. Personal selling includes the activities of both the inside salespeople of retail, wholesale, and service establishments and the outside sales representatives who call on business customers and final consumers. It is important to keep in mind that for a small business, every person in the company may be a salesperson. If a customer walks in, places a phone call, or sends an e-mail, that customer should not have to wait for hours or days to be taken care of by the owner or a certain employee—everyone must be ready to meet the customer's needs. The entrepreneur's responsibility is to make sure that all employees are prepared to do personal selling.

personal selling
A sales presentation delivered in a one-on-one manner.

The Importance of Product Knowledge

Effective selling is built on a foundation of product knowledge. If a salesperson is well acquainted with a product's advantages, uses, and limitations, she or he can educate customers

444   PART 4 * Focusing on the Customer: Marketing Growth Strategies by successfully answering their questions and countering their objections. Most customers expect a salesperson to provide knowledgeable answers, whether the product is a camera, a coat, an automobile, paint, a machine tool, or office equipment. Customers are seldom experts on the products they buy; however, they can immediately sense a salesperson's knowledge or ignorance. Personal selling degenerates into mere order-taking when a salesperson lacks product knowledge.

The Sales Presentation

The heart of personal selling is the sales presentation to a prospective customer. At this crucial point, an order is either secured or lost. A preliminary step leading to an effective sales presentation is *prospecting,* a systematic process of continually looking for new customers. Prospecting also includes consideration of whether a potential customer can be well-served by the company.

prospecting
A systematic process of continually looking for new customers.

USING PROSPECTING TECHNIQUES   One of the most efficient prospecting techniques is obtaining *personal referrals.* Such referrals come from friends, customers, and other businesses. Initial contact with a potential customer is greatly facilitated when the salesperson is able to say, "You were referred to me by. . . ."

Another source of prospects is *impersonal referrals* from media publications, public records, and directories. Newspapers and magazines, particularly trade magazines, often identify prospects by reporting on new companies and new products. Engagement announcements in a newspaper can serve as impersonal referrals for a local bridal shop. Public records of property transactions and building permits can be impersonal referrals for a garbage pick-up service, which might find prospective customers among home buyers or those planning to build houses or apartment buildings.

A high-tech variation of impersonal referrals is taking place on various social websites like Facebook, Twitter, and MySpace, where more and more subscribers are providing reviews of establishments they patronize. For example, a satisfied home buyer registered on LinkedIn might post a recommendation of the real estate agent who helped locate the property and close the sale. The reviews can be positive or negative. Yelp.com now uses automated software to screen postings that could be untrustworthy, such as criticisms about a company that might have been posted by a competitor.[1]

Prospects can also be identified without referrals through *marketer-initiated contacts.* Telephone calls or mail surveys, for example, help locate possible buyers. Finally, inquiries by a potential customer that do not lead to a sale can still create a "hot prospect." Small furniture stores often require their salespeople to fill out a card for each person visiting the store. These *customer-initiated contacts* can then be systematically followed up by telephone calls or by e-mail. Contact information should be updated periodically. Firms with websites can similarly follow up with visitors who have made inquiries online.

PRACTICING THE SALES PRESENTATION   Practicing always improves a salesperson's success rate; after all, "practice makes perfect." Prior to making a sales presentation, a salesperson should give his or her "pitch" in front of a spouse, friend, or mirror. Even better, he or she may want to record the presentation in order to study it later and improve delivery.

The salesperson should think about possible customer objections to the product and prepare to handle them. The best salespeople have done their homework. They have not only practiced their presentations, but they have also studied their prospective customers. Knowing something about your customer's wants and needs will prepare you for most of their likely objections. Most objections can be categorized as relating to (1) price, (2) product, (3) timing, (4) source, (5) service, or (6) need. Although there is no substitute for actual selling experience, salespeople find training helpful in learning how to deal with customers' objections. Successful salespeople develop techniques, such as the ones mentioned on page 447, for responding to customers' objections.[2]

entrepreneurial challenges

The Making of a Great Salesperson

Selena Cuffe built her business working one on one. Selena and her husband, Khary, launched Heritage Link Brands in 2005, after getting their inspiration for the venture at the Soweto Wine Festival in South Africa. There they discovered that few black South African wine producers were represented by international distributors. But it was more than just a gap in the distribution system that excited the Cuffes. They were impressed by the quality of the wines and felt consumers in the United States would be passionate about the products.

Selena quickly discovered that a high-quality product was not sufficient to bring buyers to her door. She found it necessary to make personal contact with restaurants and retailers to introduce them to the wines and assure them that a steady supply could be made available. "As a salesperson, you are up against a lot of no's, a lot of reasons people can't take the product, and you have to convince them," Selena says. "Passion is what creates the ability to meet your customers' needs on the scene and get the sale." The Cuffes also discovered that they had to negotiate with state government officials to meet import and distribution regulations associated with wine. By the end of 2007, they employed eight commission-based salespersons, known as "Brand Ambassadors," and were projecting sales in the range of $1 million.

The Cuffes also discovered that personal selling can target both customers and suppliers. The South African vintners had faced discrimination in the marketplace and were inexperienced in meeting the demands of international trade. Selena had to modify her vocabulary after determining that the corporate jargon she had learned during her Harvard education made it difficult to communicate with the vineyard owners. She now makes trips to South Africa twice a year, where she conducts training sessions for her suppliers to help them improve their business management practices and to introduce them to alliance partners who will help them to succeed.

Heritage Link Brands now sells worldwide through distributors in 40 states as well as on its Internet site. And the Cuffes are reaching beyond their South African suppliers, showcasing wines harvested by African descendents who now reside worldwide.

Sources: http://www.heritagelinkbrands.com, accessed March 22, 2009; Erin Patrice O'Brien, "What Makes a Great Salesperson? Passion for the Product," *Inc. Magazine* February 25, 2009, http://www.inc.com, accessed April 10, 2009; and Leigh Buchanan, "The Believer," *Inc. Magazine* December 2007, http://www.inc.com, accessed March 22, 2009.

http://www.heritagelinkbrands.com

Lim Ching

The first two responses are appropriate when a potential buyer states an objection that is factually untrue; the remaining suggestions can be used when a buyer raises a valid objection.

- *Direct denial.* Deny the prospect's objection and give facts to back up the denial. This is appropriate when a prospect states an objection that is factually incorrect.
- *Indirect denial.* Express concern about the prospect's objection and follow with a denial.
- *Answer objections with the words* feel, felt, *and* found. Don't argue; instead, say, "I understand how you feel. A lot of my customers felt the same way. But when they found out how much they saved by using our product, they were amazed."
- *Take notes.* Write down objections to show the prospect that you are really listening.
- *Compensation method.* Admit to agreeing with the objection and then proceed to show compensating advantages.
- *Pass-up method.* Acknowledge the concern expressed by the prospect and then move on.
- *Find the true objection.* Don't jump to the conclusion that the objection raised was the prospect's primary concern. Ask for more details about the objection so that you can handle it.
- *Follow up and follow through.* If you promised to gather more information, do it and deliver. If you promised you would call back, make that call. Some prospects raise objections just to defer a decision. They think that once you leave, they will not hear from you again. Persistence on your part can pay off.

MAKING THE SALES PRESENTATION   Salespeople must adapt their sales approach to meet customers' needs. A "canned" sales talk will not succeed with most buyers. For example, an individual selling exercise equipment must demonstrate how the products will fill a customer's specific needs. Similarly, a home security system salesperson must understand the special interests of particular customers and speak their language. Every sales objection must be answered explicitly and adequately.

Successful selling involves a number of psychological elements. Personal enthusiasm, friendliness, and persistence are required. Just as an entrepreneur should be passionate about the business he or she is starting, a salesperson should show true passion about what the product or service can do for the customer. For most companies, only about 20 percent of the salespeople bring these elements to the task of selling, but they are responsible for as much as 80 percent of all sales.

Some salespeople have special sales techniques that they use with success. One health products salesperson, for example, found that medical doctors could effectively influence his prospective customers. He left a list of substances that pregnant women should avoid with obstetricians. The list also contained information about his company's products. Needless to say, the patients appreciated the safety information and viewed receiving the list from a physician as the equivalent of a medical endorsement for the health products.[3]

Customer Goodwill and Relationship Selling

A salesperson must look beyond the immediate sale to building customer goodwill and creating satisfied customers who will continue buying from the company in the future. Selling effectiveness is enhanced when a salesperson displays a good appearance, has a pleasant personality, and uses professional etiquette in all contacts with customers. A salesperson can also build goodwill by listening carefully to the customer's point of view. The salesperson should never be so focused on delivering a well-prepared sales presentation that he or she neglects paying attention to what the customer is saying. Courtesy, attention to details, and genuine friendliness will help gain a customer's confidence and acceptance.

Of course, high ethical standards are of primary importance in creating customer goodwill. For repeat business, goodwill can count as much as a good price, good quality, and good service. Personal integrity rules out any misrepresentation of the product and requires confidential treatment of a customer's plans.

Cost Control in Personal Selling

Both efficient and wasteful methods exist for achieving a given volume of sales. For example, routing traveling salespeople economically and making appointments prior to arrival can save time and transportation expenses. The cost of an outside sales call on a customer is likely to be considerable—perhaps hundreds of dollars—so efficient scheduling is crucial. Moreover, a salesperson for a manufacturing firm can contribute to cost economy by pushing certain products, thereby giving the factory a more balanced production run. Similarly, a salesperson can increase profits by emphasizing high-margin products.

Cost considerations are especially important for a new business that may have very limited resources. The entrepreneur must first recognize that she or he is first and foremost a salesperson for the enterprise. Nothing can substitute for the entrepreneur's personal efforts to sell products and services and to represent the image and reputation of the firm. Additionally, in the startup and early growth stages, the business may not have funds to support a full-time sales staff. The most cost-efficient mode of selling may be to use *sales or marketing representatives*. These are individuals who are self-employed or who are employees of a company whose purpose is to represent multiple businesses, spreading the costs of selling products or services across all of these lines. They will not focus on your products alone, as your own employees would, but your company will only have to compensate them as merchandise is actually sold. That does not mean you can simply provide the sales reps with products and then ignore them. Think of them as your partners. Provide them with any sales aids they may need to make their job easier. Keep communication channels open, and let them know that you are committed to making them successful. If they do a good job for you, send a letter to their boss applauding their work.[4]

The Compensation Program for Salespeople

Salespeople are compensated in two ways for their efforts—financially and nonfinancially. A good compensation program allows its participants to work for both forms of reward, while recognizing that a salesperson's goals may be different from those of the entrepreneur. For example, an entrepreneur may be willing to sacrifice income to grow the business or may gain personal satisfaction from introducing an innovative product. The salesperson, on the other hand, expects immediate and appropriate salary or commission compensation in order to pay bills and enjoy a desired quality of life.

NONFINANCIAL COMPENSATION Personal recognition and the satisfaction of reaching a sales quota are examples of nonfinancial rewards that motivate many salespeople. Small retail businesses sometimes post the photograph of the top salesperson of the week or the month for all to see. Engraved plaques are also given as a more permanent record of sales achievements.

Nonfinancial compensation may also relate to personal and career advancement. Rewards for being a desired employee include opportunities for promotion, advanced education and training, and an assurance of job security. Business owners should be aware that effective sales personnel are often competitive. They gain a sense of accomplishment by measuring their achievements against those of their peers.

FINANCIAL COMPENSATION Typically, financial compensation is the more critical factor for salespeople. Two basic plans used for financial compensation are commissions and straight salary. Each plan has specific advantages and limitations for the small firm.

Most small businesses would prefer to use commissions as compensation, because such an approach is simple and directly related to productivity. Usually, a certain percentage of the sales generated by a salesperson represents his or her commission. A commission plan thereby incorporates a strong incentive for sales effort—no sale, no commission! Also, with this type of plan, there is less drain on the firm's cash flow until a sale is made.

The straight salary form of compensation provides salespeople with more income security because their level of compensation is ensured, regardless of sales made. However, working for a straight salary can potentially reduce a salesperson's motivation by providing income despite low performance or no sales at all.

Variations on financial compensation include valuable prizes. While these rewards do not necessarily put money in the pockets of the salespeople, they do have a monetary value. Examples are expense-paid trips for the salesperson and one or more family members, jewelry, premium food products, and many others. One caution: Prizes should not result from contests in which there are winners and losers. You do not want your salespeople to withhold information from each other or otherwise fail to cooperate. Prizes should be based on goals and performance, such that all who excel can win. There is a cost to the firm for the prizes, but that cost should be offset by sales and profits. In addition, a business may be able to negotiate a below-retail price for the prize and thus reward the salesperson for less than a cash payment.

Combining the salary and commission forms of compensation is typically the most attractive plan for most small businesses. It is common practice to structure combination plans so that salary represents the larger part of compensation for a new salesperson. As the salesperson gains experience, the ratio is adjusted to provide more money from commissions and less from salary. And do not put a cap on what a salesperson can earn through commission. Many companies have lost their top producers by limiting incentives. Why would you stop rewarding someone who is making more money for your business?

Advertising Practices for Small Firms

Another significant promotional expenditure for the small firm is advertising. *Advertising* is the impersonal presentation of an idea that is identified with a business sponsor. Ideas in advertising are communicated to consumers through media such as television, radio, magazines, newspapers, billboards, and the Internet.

4. Identify advertising options for a small business.

advertising
The impersonal presentation of a business idea through mass media.

Advertising Objectives

As its primary goal, advertising seeks to sell by informing, persuading, and reminding customers of the availability or superiority of a firm's product or service. To be successful, it must rest on a foundation of positive features such as product quality and efficient service. It is important to remember that advertising can bring no more than temporary success to an otherwise second-rate product. Advertising must always be viewed as a complement to a good product and never as a replacement for a bad product.

The entrepreneur should avoid creating false expectations with advertising, as such expectations are likely to disappoint customers and leave them dissatisfied. Advertising can accentuate a trend in the sale of an item or product line, but it seldom has the power to reverse a trend. It must, consequently, be able to reflect changes in customer needs and preferences.

At times, advertising may seem to be a waste of money. It is expensive and adds little value to the product. But the primary alternative to advertising is personal selling, which is often more expensive and time-consuming.

Jerry Markland/Getty Images for NASCAR

Types of Advertising

The two basic types of advertising are product advertising and institutional advertising. *Product advertising* is designed to make potential customers aware of a particular product or service and create a desire for it. *Institutional advertising,* on the other hand, conveys information about the business itself. It is intended to make the public aware of the company and enhance its image so that its product advertising will be more credible and effective. Allen Weiss, CEO of MarketingProfs.com, tells his clients that the right "tag line" can make a strong impression in customers' minds regarding brand and company. Think "Just Do It" and "Breakfast of Champions"—companies (like Nike) and brands (like Wheaties) leap out at you. But not every tag line works. Some tips for developing a tag line include the following:[5]

- *Focus on benefits.* What does your audience care about?
- *Start from scratch.* You can change your theme with a tag line without having to change the whole brand. If you shift from an emphasis on price to one on service, a new tag line is far cheaper than changing the name of the company.
- *Get help.* Use a professional writer or branding company. If you can't afford one, bounce ideas around in a forum such as the one at Copywriting.com.
- *Test it out.* Ask customers for their reaction to the tag line before you put it on your stationery and business cards. What does it mean to them?

Most small business advertising is of the product type. Small retailers' ads often stress products, such as weekend specials at a supermarket or sportswear sold exclusively in a women's clothing store. It is important to note, however, that the same advertisement can convey both product and institutional themes. Furthermore, a firm may stress its product in newspaper advertisements, for example, while using institutional advertising on websites. Decisions regarding the type of advertising to be used should be based on the nature of the business, industry practice, available media, and the objectives of the firm.

Obtaining Assistance with Advertising

Most small businesses rely on others' expertise to create their promotional messages. Fortunately, there are several sources for this specialized assistance, including advertising agencies, suppliers, trade associations, and advertising media.

Advertising agencies can provide the following services:

- Furnish design, artwork, and copy for specific advertisements and/or commercials
- Evaluate and recommend the advertising media with the greatest "pulling power"

- Evaluate the effectiveness of different advertising appeals
- Advise on sales promotions and merchandise displays
- Conduct market-sampling studies to evaluate product acceptance or determine the sales potential of a specific geographic area
- Furnish mailing lists

Since advertising agencies charge fees for their services, an entrepreneur must be sure that the return from those services will be greater than the fees paid. Quality advertising assistance can best be provided by a competent agency. According to Gary Slack, CEO of Slack Barshinger, a marketing communications company, the small business owner should seek an agency that asks good questions and should contact both current and past clients of the agency for references.[6] Of course, with the high level of computer technology currently available, creating print advertising in-house is becoming increasingly common among small firms.

Other outside sources may assist in formulating and carrying out promotional programs. Suppliers often furnish display aids and even entire advertising programs to their dealers. Trade associations also provide helpful assistance. In addition, the advertising media can provide some of the same services offered by an ad agency.

Frequency of Advertising

Determining how often to advertise is an important and highly complex issue for a small business. Obviously, advertising should be done regularly, and attempts to stimulate interest in a firm's products or services should be part of an ongoing promotional program. Continuity reinforces the presence of the company as the place for customers to buy when they are ready. One-shot advertisements that are not part of a well-planned promotional effort lose much of their effectiveness in a short period. Of course, some noncontinuous advertising may be justified, such as advertising to prepare consumers for acceptance of a new product. Such an approach may also be used to suggest to customers new uses for established products or to promote special sales. Most products and services have some kind of seasonal demand—air conditioners for spring and summer, trendy clothing for going back to school, toys at Christmas—leading to special advertising campaigns associated with seasons or holidays. Deciding on the frequency of advertising involves a host of factors, both objective and subjective, and a wise entrepreneur will seek professional advice.

Robert Kiyosaki, author of *Rich Dad, Poor Dad*, claims that promotion is on a six-week cycle. Do not expect results from an advertising campaign unless you invest in it for six weeks. In his view, you should never stop promoting. This is particularly true during economic downturns. He finds that in those tough times, customers migrate to businesses that fight hard to keep their name visible.[7]

Where to Advertise

Most small firms restrict their advertising, either geographically or by customer type. Advertising media should reach—but not overreach—a firm's present or desired target market. From among the many media available, a small business entrepreneur must choose those that will provide the greatest return for the advertising dollar.

The most appropriate combination of advertising media depends on the type of business and its current circumstances. A real estate sales firm, for example, may rely almost exclusively on classified advertisements in the local newspaper, supplemented by institutional advertising and multi-listing services on the Internet. A transfer-and-storage firm may use a combination of radio, billboard, and Yellow Pages advertising to reach individuals planning to move household furniture. A retailer of home furniture may emphasize television advertisements, while an office furniture company may find participation in trade fairs to be more productive. The selection of media should be based not only on tradition but also on a careful evaluation of the various methods that are available to cover a firm's particular market.

Medium	Advantages	Disadvantages
Newspapers	Geographic selectivity and flexibility; short-term advertiser commitments; news value and immediacy; year-round readership; high individual market coverage; co-op and local tie-in availability; short lead time	Little demographic selectivity; limited color capabilities; low pass-along rate; may be expensive
Magazines	Good reproduction, especially for color; demographic selectivity; regional selectivity; local market selectivity; relatively long advertising life; high pass-along rate	Long-term advertiser commitments; slow audience buildup; limited demonstration capabilities; lack of urgency; long lead time
Radio	Low cost; immediacy of message; can be scheduled on short notice; relatively no seasonal change in audience; highly portable; short-term advertiser commitments; entertainment carryover	No visual treatment; short advertising life of message; high frequency required to generate comprehension and retention; distractions from background sound; commercial clutter
Television	Ability to reach a wide, diverse audience; low cost per thousand; creative opportunities for demonstration; immediacy of messages; entertainment carryover; demographic selectivity with cable stations	Short life of message; some consumer skepticism about claims; high campaign cost; little demographic selectivity with network stations; long-term advertiser commitments; long lead times required for production; commercial clutter
Outdoor Media	Repetition; moderate cost; flexibility; geographic selectivity	Short message; lack of demographic selectivity; high "noise" level distracting audience
Internet	Fastest-growing medium; ability to reach a narrow target audience; relatively short lead time required for creating Web-based advertising; moderate cost	Difficult to measure ad effectiveness and return on investment; ad exposure relies on "click-through" from banner ads; not all consumers have access to the Internet

Entrepreneurs should learn about the strengths and weaknesses of each medium. Exhibit 17-3 summarizes important facts about major advertising media. Study this information carefully, noting the particular advantages and disadvantages of each medium. Special attention is given to Web advertising in the next section because the Internet continues to grow so quickly, almost demanding the presence of even the smallest companies.

Web Advertising

The Internet has provided an entirely new way for small firms to advertise. With color graphics, two-way information exchanges, streaming video, and 24-hour availability, online advertising is challenging traditional media for promotional dollars. Web advertising allows advertisers to reach large numbers of global buyers in a timely manner and with more impact than many alternative forms of advertising. With careful targeting of market segments, costs should be lower as well.

Small businesses have tended to underutilize Web advertising. This is indicated by the fact that 80 percent of advertising expenditures are local, but local ads represent a minority percentage of total advertising on the Internet.[8] In a global survey of marketing executives, however, McKinsey & Company reported that the overwhelming majority of respondents predicted increases in advertising expenditures for every category of digital media—e-mail, video ads, podcasts, and more.[9]

Advertisers of all types have flocked to the Internet, hoping (with good reason) that the information superhighway will be the next great mass medium. Large businesses have found they must have a presence on the Web, and more and more small firms are using Internet technology. The basic methods of Web advertising are (1) banner ads and pop-ups, (2) e-mail, (3) sponsorships and linkages, (4) a corporate website, and (5) blogs.

BANNER ADS AND POP-UPS *Banner ads* are advertisements that appear across a webpage, most often as moving rectangular strips. In contrast, *pop-up ads* burst open on webpages but do not move. When viewers respond by clicking on an ad, they are automatically linked to the site providing the product or sales activity. Both banner and pop-up ads can be placed on search engine sites or on related webpages.

These types of Web advertising are often carried out through an affiliate program. In an affiliate program, a website carries a banner ad or a link for another company in exchange for a commission on any sales generated by the traffic sent to the sponsoring website. Affiliate programs have become quite popular among Web retailers, with one of the most lucrative being eBay's program. One primary reason for the success of eBay's affiliate program is the sheer volume of visitors to its website every day. An eBay affiliate is paid a commission not only on sales generated by the users it sends to eBay, but also on each already-registered eBay user it sends back to eBay and on each bid and qualified Buy it Now transaction.

There is some skepticism about the cost effectiveness of banner ads and pop-ups. One study indicated that online users who click on these ads tend to have lower household incomes and prefer auction, gambling, and career services sites. Experienced advertisers recommend targeting prospective customers through specialty websites and making sure that the ads include offers.[10] One company that has taken targeting to a new level is Fetchback, Inc., whose strategy is "retargeted advertising." If someone visits your website and then moves on to other sites, you can follow that person using Fetchback's technology and one of your ads will appear while he or she is visiting another site. Over a 30-day period, the prospect may see as many as five of your ads, each offering an incentive to return to your site. Fetchback charges you for the click-throughs, so the more efficient you are at enticing browsers to return, the cheaper the service will be for your company.[11]

Price comparison pop-ups are an effective way to lure surfers from competitors' websites. Here's how they work: When a shopper who is browsing in an online store clicks on a specific product, comparison shopping software generates a pop-up ad that features links to other vendors selling the same item at a lower price. This software works much the same way as a bargain-hunting website like Shopping.com, but it offers competitive prices wherever consumers shop on the Web.

DIRECT E-MAIL PROMOTION *E-mail promotion,* in which electronic mail is used to deliver a firm's message, provides a low-cost way to pinpoint customers and achieve response rates higher than those for banner ads. However, as more and more businesses use e-mail for this purpose, customer inboxes are becoming cluttered. And users are reluctant to open some e-mail messages, fearing they may contain computer viruses. Mark Brownlow, editor of *Email Marketing Reports*, says that your e-mail strategy should have a purpose. You should be encouraging immediate action, such as a purchase, or you should be building a long-term relationship by sharing information, such as through a newsletter.[12]

According to a recent McKinsey & Company survey, e-mail is the most frequently used mode of digital advertising, ahead of display ads, branded sponsorships, podcasts, and other practices. But the survey also reports that measurement tools for assessing the effectiveness of digital advertising have not kept up with technological advances.[13]

Two obstacles to e-mail promotion have arisen, as the volume of unsolicited e-mails (better known as *spam*) has turned many customers against this type of advertising. First, Congress passed the Can-Spam Act of 2003, which took effect on January 1, 2004, and established standards regarding the use of commercial e-mail enforceable by the Federal Trade Commission (FTC).[14] Second, anti-spam software, which sometimes also blocks legitimate e-mails, became

banner ads
Advertisements that appear across a Web page, most often as moving rectangular strips.

pop-up ads
Advertisements that burst open on computer screens.

e-mail promotion
Advertising delivered by means of electronic mail.

popular. Before sending a promotional message by e-mail, marketers should consider testing their message by putting it through a preview tool. MailWasher Free and SpamWeed are examples of software packages that permit previews. Previewing allows you to see advertisements that may be delivered as e-mails without customers' having to download them to their computers.

SPONSORSHIPS AND LINKAGES   In *Web sponsorship*, a firm pays to be part of another organization's webpage. When the webpage includes a click-on link to the paying firm's site, a *linkage* has been established. Research shows that a significant number of online purchases originate from online links. Blog2Print, for example, provides services to bloggers and lets its target market know what it has to offer on sites where bloggers might go for information. The company is a sponsor on CNNMoney.com, which can also be accessed through *Business 2.0* magazine. When someone conducts a search for "blog" on that site, Blog2Print appears as a sponsor, promoting its ability to help create blog books.[15] Unfortunately for many firms that choose to advertise through Web sponsorship, blocking software from such companies as Webwasher can be used to prevent ads from appearing on a viewer's webpage.[16]

CORPORATE WEBSITES   The fourth form of Web advertising involves a more serious commitment by a small firm—launching a corporate website. Numerous decisions must be made prior to launching a site. Three critical startup tasks are related to the likely promotional success of a corporate website: (1) creating and registering a site name, (2) building a user-friendly site, and (3) promoting the site.

CREATING AND REGISTERING A SITE NAME   The Domain Name System (DNS) allows users to find their way around the Internet. Selecting the best domain name for a corporate website is an important promotional decision, and contrary to general opinion, plenty of website names remain available. Domain names can have up to 63 characters preceding the domain designation. Popular domain designations are .com, .net, .biz, and .org.[17]

Since a domain name gives a small business its online identity, it's desirable to select a descriptive and appealing name. Obviously, some of the shorter, more creative names have already been taken. But, like real estate, website names can be bought and sold. In 2009, the name Toys.com sold at a bankruptcy auction for $5,100,000. Most go for far less than that, typically under $10,000.[18]

Once a desired name has been selected, it should be checked for availability and then registered. The Internet Corporation for Assigned Names and Numbers (ICANN) is a nonprofit corporation currently overseeing the global Internet. ICANN, however, does not register names; this must be done through a domain registration firm. InterNIC, a registered service mark of the U.S. Department of Commerce, provides an Accredited Registrar Directory that lists ICANN-accredited domain registrars, such as NameSecure. Several domain registrars allow a search of the Internet to see if a proposed name is already taken. One authority recommends registering your own name and that of your children in order to take control of your identities.[19]

BUILDING A USER-FRIENDLY WEBSITE   First impressions are important, and high-quality Web design gives a small e-commerce business the opportunity to make a good first impression on each visitor. The technical aspects of developing a website are beyond the scope of this chapter. But, fortunately, many technical specialists are available to help design and build a site. An expert, for example, may recommend that you include a webcam if live views into your office, warehouse, or factory might spark interest from current and prospective customers. In such cases, this would be a very low cost way of making customers feel intimately connected to your company. An added benefit is that the webcam would show the inside of your firm at all hours, giving you extra security.[20] Our purpose here, however, is simply to provide some useful ideas about website design. Exhibit 17-4 offers six design tips for e-commerce websites.

There are many reasons why websites fail to retain customers. One of the most frequent problems is slow downloading. Online shoppers are a fickle bunch, and the slightest inconvenience sends them away. If your business is conducting a considerable amount of online

Web sponsorship
A type of advertising in which a firm pays another organization for the right to be part of that organization's webpage.

linkage
A type of advertising agreement in which one firm pays another to include a click-on link on its site.

17-4 Website Design Tips

Tip 1: Know Your Purpose
What do you want the website to accomplish? Do you want customers to come to your store? Do you want an immediate purchase? Are you building a network of contacts that may turn into clients?

Tip 2: Think Like Your Customer
What are your customers looking for? Can you make life simpler and easier for them? Are you relieving their pain? Can they find what they need, pay for it, and move on?

Tip 3: Make It Easy to Navigate
Will customers understand the first thing they see? What tools will enable them to move through the site? Should you offer a sitemap or even an internal search engine?

Tip 4: Reduce the Load Time
Can customers find the most popular items in the quickest time? Do you really need a "Wow" factor, full of graphics and animation that may take extra time to load?

And how many pages do your customers have to click through before they can do business with you?

Tip 5: Avoid Surprises
Web design offers opportunities for great creativity, but do you want potential customers visiting your site to be surprised or to buy something? How can you make your site immediately understandable and usable? Are you making it easy for customers to get what they want and move on?

Tip 6: Document Everything
Do you have a model that allows the website to be reviewed, changed, and improved? Did you use a graphic organizer, or *storyboard*, to design individual pages, giving you a record of the purpose, title, and description of each page? How have you structured and categorized the information in your website so that you can access what you need to ensure that the site reflects your business as it changes and grows?

Sources: Gary Klingsheim, "How to Create an Attractive, User Friendly Website," March 20, 2009, http://www.webdesign.org, accessed April 11, 2009; and http://www.usability.gov, accessed June 30, 2009.

business, a slow website translates into lost sales revenue. Lost revenue can be direct—missed sales if you're selling online—or indirect—loss of customer confidence if you're providing Web-based solutions to clients. The more important a website is to your business, the less you can afford to have it perform slowly or, worse, experience downtime.[21]

Believe it or not, studies show that first-time visitors to your website spend as little as 10 seconds there before deciding whether or not to stay. Web entrepreneurs cannot afford to squander any of these precious seconds with slow downloads. Whenever possible, reduce the number and size of files on your webpages. The more files a page contains and the larger they are, the longer it will take to load.[22] Software programs can show you the "bounce rate" of your website, that is, the percentage of visitors who leave your site without looking at more than one page. These programs can help you to know whether your site is slow—or, perhaps, boring.[23]

Websites also will fail if they do not satisfy visitors' information needs. Frequently, this is because designers look inward to the business for Web design ideas, rather than outward to customer needs. Some experts recommend that firms integrate social networking into their websites from the beginning. When Debbie Wexler launched her online jewelry company, Whiteflash.com, she made contact and developed relationships with prospective customers in chat rooms and fashion and gossip blogs. This strategy not only promoted her name, but it also helped her learn about her customers.[24] Several programs are available to help you with social networking, and they do not require you to be an experienced programmer. Google Friend Connect, Ning, Wetpaint, and Yuku all offer a variety of tools for interacting with your visitors.[25]

PROMOTING THE WEBSITE How do customers learn about a website? You have to tell them—and there are many ways to do this. A Web address can be promoted both to existing customers and to prospects by including the URL on print promotions, business cards, letterhead, and packaging. Special direct mail and radio campaigns can also be designed for this purpose. Additionally, a website can be promoted by placing banner advertisements on other websites, where a quick click will send users to the advertised site. The advantage of banner advertisements is that they are placed in front of thousands of visitors to other websites. Payment for banner advertising is usually based on the number of people who actually click on the banner.

Many companies find additional digital means to interest others in their websites. Trunkt, a firm that represents creative designers and artists, places videos on YouTube showing its clients' unique items.[26] Another company that uses YouTube is a lot less exotic: Crack Team USA is a concrete repair business that promoted its brand through a spoof of the television show *The Sopranos*. Its management team was surprised and gratified to get hundreds of viewers.[27]

Probably the most direct approach to website promotion is making sure that the site is listed on Internet search engines. Search engines allow users to find websites based on keywords included in the site's pages. If a popular search engine does not list a firm's website, many potential visitors will undoubtedly miss it. Registering a site with a search engine is free.

Search engine optimization (SEO) is the process of increasing the volume and quality of traffic to a particular website. The sooner your small business is presented in search engine results (i.e., the higher it ranks), the more visitors it will attract. An important goal is to make your website as search engine–friendly as possible.

Obviously, your website should include keywords that someone looking for that particular subject might use. Many businesses try to get to the top of a search engine's results by designing their websites to match a particular search engine's ranking index. If they don't, business can be hurt. Catherine Seda, author of *Search Engine Advertising*, recommends links as a tactic for increasing traffic to your site. She explains that by submitting a comment or article to a blog or other site relevant to your content, you will be linked to that site. Be sure to use the most important keyword phrase that will bring viewers to that link.[28]

Keep in mind, too, that there are many specialized search engines. Everyone thinks immediately of Google and Yahoo!, but your company might benefit from being registered with an engine such as Spook.com, which focuses exclusively on people searches.[29] A description of options for submitting a website to search engines appears in Exhibit 17-5.

17-5 Options for Getting Your Website Listed in Search Engines

EXHIBIT

1. Use a Free Submission Service
Basically, free submission services offer to submit your website to hundreds of the top search engines at no cost. Be aware, however, that every search engine has a different "rule book" that it uses to decide where your website will rank. As a result, you may not get a top-ranking position for your business.

2. Use a Low-Cost, Automated Submission Service
Low-cost, automated submission services offer to submit your website to as many as 900+ search engines for a minimal fee (usually between $40 and $80). Much like the free submission services, automated submission services automatically submit the same set of information to all of the search engines. Once again, your website is being submitted to multiple search engines without being optimized to meet their individual requirements.

3. Do It Yourself by Manually Submitting Your Website to Individual Search Engines
This is one of the best ways to submit your website to the search engines. Visit each search engine separately, and manually submit the information for each webpage you wish to have listed. On the downside, submitting your

website this way can be very time consuming and labor intensive. Although there are no professionals to help you, many websites and blogs offer step-by-step instructions for individual registration.

4. Use a Professional Search Engine Consultant
Search engine consultants will educate you and work with you to maximize your site's exposure in each search engine. They know all of the latest tricks and techniques for securing a top spot and will show you exactly what you need to do to optimize your website for the best possible ranking.

5. Use Submission Software
Most of the software out there does exactly what the free and low-cost automated submission services do—it submits the same set of information to all of the search engines. So, your site is never optimized, and you are not likely to secure the top ranking you want.

6. Pay for Inclusion
Many search engine companies charge fees for websites to be included in their search indexes. This is a revenue generator for the search engine company, but it also is a filter for more trivial website submissions.

Sources: Adapted from the Internet Marketing Center's website. http://www.marketingtips.com/newsletters/search-engines/search-engine-strategies.html, accessed July 13, 2007; and Joe Burns, "So, You Want to Register Your Pages, Huh?" http://www.htmlgoodies.com, accessed April 11, 2009.

BLOGS The word *blog* is a contraction of the term *weblog*. *Blogs* are websites in which an individual can maintain a personal online journal, post comments and reflections (and many other types of materials, such as photos), and may provide hyperlinks.[30] Blogs are interactive, allowing readers to leave comments. Many business owners have set up blogs related to their company and its products; this can be done for free on WordPress.com or Blogger.com. An owner can then comment on other blogs that may have related topics, each time including links back to his or her company blog. Some entrepreneurs even invite guest bloggers to comment on their business and products or services.[31]

Sally Falkow, president of Internet marketing and public relations company Expansion Plus, encourages her clients to create blogs for their businesses. She tells them to start with research—learning about and reading blogs—then to practice before launching by posting content on other people's blogs. Next, they should engage by delivering information that has value to people who may become customers. Finally, Falkow wants her clients to refresh their blogs by entering new content several times a week.[32] Co-preneurs Rhonda and Lee Walmsley, owners of FastbackStack, a company selling classic Mustang parts, selected eBay as the host for their blog (http://blogs.ebay.com/fastbackstack), where they enter facts and restoration tips for Mustangs. Interacting on the blog has helped the Walmsleys learn more about what their customers want.[33]

Companies that ignore blogging do so at their own peril. According to a 2008 study by BlogHer and Compass Partners, 36 million women blog every week. More than half surveyed reported that blogs influence their purchasing decisions.[34] And it is important to recognize that blogs can work in both positive and negative ways. Entrepreneurs need to be aware if someone—perhaps a competitor, an unhappy customer, or a disgruntled former employee—may be making derogatory comments about their business on these websites.

blog
an interactive website in which an individual can maintain a personal online journal, post comments and reflections, and provide hyperlinks.

Sales Promotional Tools

Sales promotion serves as an inducement to buy a certain product while typically offering value to prospective customers. Generally, *sales promotion* includes any promotional technique, other than personal selling or advertising, that stimulates the purchase of a particular good or service.

Sales promotion should seldom comprise all the promotional efforts of a small business. For best results, it typically is used in combination with personal selling and advertising. Popular sales promotional tools include specialties, contests, premiums, trade show exhibits, point-of-purchase displays, free merchandise, publicity, sampling, and coupons. Denise Dorman, founder of marketing communications company WriteBrain Media, encourages her clients to establish loyalty programs. She recommends giving a gift to new members and then letting them know about members-only opportunities, such as shopping previews, sales, industry previews, discounts, and other incentives.[35]

We briefly examine three of the most widely used promotional tools: specialties, trade show exhibits, and publicity.

5. Discuss the use of sales promotional tools.

sales promotion
An inclusive term for any promotional techniques other than personal selling and advertising that stimulate the purchase of a particular good or service.

Specialties

The most widely used specialty item is a calendar. Other popular specialty items are pens, key chains, coffee mugs, and shirts. Almost anything can be used as a specialty promotion, as long as each item is imprinted with the firm's name or other identifying slogan.

The distinguishing characteristics of specialties are their enduring nature and tangible value. Specialties are referred to as the "lasting medium." As functional products, they are worth something to recipients. Specialties can be used to promote a product directly or to create goodwill for a firm; they are excellent reminders of a firm's existence.

Finally, specialties are personal. They are distributed directly to the customer in a personal way, they can be used personally, and they have a personal message. A small business needs to retain its unique image, and entrepreneurs often use specialties to achieve this objective. More information on specialties is available on the website of Promotional Products Association International at http://www.ppa.org.

Trade Show Exhibits

Advertising often cannot substitute for trial experiences with a product, and a customer's place of business is not always the best environment for product demonstrations. Trade show exhibits allow potential customers to get hands-on experience with a product.

Trade show exhibits are of particular value to manufacturers. The greatest benefit of these exhibits is the potential cost savings over personal selling. Trade show groups claim that the cost of an exhibit is less than one-fourth the cost of sales calls, and many small manufacturers agree that exhibits are more cost-effective than advertising. One website devoted to marketing tactics lists the following helpful tips regarding trade shows:[36]

- *Check out the trade show's history.* Does the show regularly attract large crowds? Will the show be adequately promoted to your potential customers?

- *Prepare a professional-looking display.* You do not need to have the biggest, flashiest booth on the trade show floor to attract attendees. But signs, photographs of your products, and other business-related elements used in the display should appear to be professionally prepared.

- *Have a sufficient quantity of literature on hand.* Have plenty of professionally prepared brochures or other handouts to distribute, and have them prepared well in advance of the show.

- *Make sure you have a good product.* If your product doesn't work or doesn't work properly, you'll lose more customers than you'll ever gain.

- *Do pre-show promotion.* To get the most traffic at your booth, send out mailings prior to the show, inviting your customers and prospects to stop by your booth. Insert announcements in bills you send out, on your webpage, and in ads you run near the show date.

- *Have a giveaway or gimmick.* The giveaway or gimmick doesn't have to be big or elaborate. Samples of your product given away at intervals during the show are ideal. Novelty items such as key chains, pencils, and pads of paper with your company name and product name are good, too.

- *Train booth personnel.* Choose your booth staff carefully, and be sure they know how to deal with the public, especially prospective customers.

- *Follow up!* Have a plan in place for following up on leads as soon as you get home from the show.

One company found trade shows to be the path to international markets. Brothers Reid and JC Smoot designed 3-in-1 pet toys, which serve as a plush toy, a soft pillow, and a "comfy" blanket. Their idea came from watching their younger siblings pack all three items into cars. The Smoots introduced their products at the Toy Fair 2007 trade show. One hundred stores, including FAO Schwartz, placed orders, and they now enjoy international distribution.[37]

Publicity

publicity
Information about a firm and its products or services that appears as a news item, usually free of charge.

Of particular importance to small firms is *publicity,* which provides visibility for a business at little or no cost. Publicity can be used to promote both a product and a firm's image; it is a

LIVING THE DREAM:

Experiential Marketing

If you have an interesting story, let the media tell it for you. William P. Angrick III and Jaime Mateus-Tigue found ways to do that. They launched Liquidity Services, Inc., in 1999 as an online auction marketplace for wholesale, surplus, and salvage assets. According to the company's website, Liquidity Services enables "our corporate and government sellers to enhance their financial returns from the sale of excess assets by providing a liquid marketplace and integrated value-added services, including sales and marketing, logistics and transaction settlement." But just what does this mean, and why should anyone care?

Apparently a lot of people care about what this business is doing. By the time Liquidity Services was five years old, the company had been ranked by several business publications as one of the fastest growing businesses in the United States. And several newspapers, both print and online, were anxious to tell their story. Television and radio followed suit. The company and its leaders were profiled in a variety of media, including Fox News, National Public Radio, Reuters, *Washington Business Journal*, and Telemundo. Journalists reported on the role Liquidity Services was playing through its subsidiary, Government Liquidation, in handling the sales of surplus equipment for the Pentagon. Through its govliquidation.com auction site, Government Liquidation is able to enjoy sales and profits and provide cost savings to the purchasers of the products while helping government agencies recoup funds from surplus and scrap materials.

In frequent interviews in 2008 and 2009, the executives at Liquidity Services explained the importance of the surplus equipment market in recessionary periods. In an interview with GlobeSt.com, CEO Angrick described the positive impact of his company: "It's healthy for the economy because it puts the assets in the hands of small business and entrepreneurs that can get a positive return on capital from using those items, and gets capital back in the hands of these companies to redeploy to healthier parts of their business. This over time will allow them to grow again, hire people, and bring value to the consumer."

2006 Nasdaq Photo Services

Sources: http://www.liquidityservicesinc.com, accessed March 27, 2009; http://www.govliquidation.com, accessed March 27, 2009; http://www.govdeals.com, accessed March 27, 2009; http://www.foxnews.com/story/0,2933,265696,00.html, accessed March 27, 2009; and http://www.globest.com/news/1367_1367/insider/177462-1.html, accessed March 27, 2009.

http://www.liquidityservicesinc.com

vital part of public relations for the small business. A good publicity program requires regular contacts with the news media.

Although publicity is not always free, the return on a relatively small investment can be substantial. When a bank opened a neighborhood branch, employees gave out plants to homes and other businesses, getting both publicity and word-of-mouth advertising from local residents. Similarly, a bagel shop gave out free bagels during its first morning in business and also was featured in the media because it had an all-tuba band whose bells (horn openings) were covered by photos of bagels.[38]

Other examples of publicity efforts that entail some expense include underwriting school yearbooks and sponsoring youth athletic programs. While the benefits are difficult to measure, publicity is nevertheless important to a small business and should be used at every opportunity.

A high-tech spin on publicity can be found in the phenomenon of social shopping websites. A social shopping website results from the merging of a search engine, such as Google, with a social networking element, such as Twitter. Although the power of Google can't be contested, Google can't tell shoppers what is cool or what their friends or other consumers recommend. But social shopping websites like StyleFeeder, Kaboodle, WhatsBuzzing, and ThisNext do just that. A search on a typical search engine yields the most prominent brands and retailers on its first few pages. A similar search on a social shopping site displays a wider array of smaller and arguably "cooler" brands. It also includes the recommendations of the site's most fashion-conscious and influential users. Marketing on such sites must be done carefully, as they are geared toward consumers, not marketers. A forward-thinking entrepreneur, however, can post his or her own favorite products on such sites and potentially influence other users' buying decisions.

When to Use Sales Promotion

A small firm can use sales promotion to accomplish various objectives. For example, small manufacturers can use it to stimulate channel members—retailers and wholesalers—to market their product. Wholesalers can use sales promotion to induce retailers to buy inventories earlier than they normally would, and retailers, with similar promotional tools, may be able to persuade customers to make a purchase.

Consider Scott Androff and Bruce Hilsen, co-founders of Twin Star Industries in Bloomington, Minnesota. After introducing Atmos-Klear Odor Eliminator, a nontoxic biodegradable spray that gets rid of odors, they needed a low-cost promotional approach. Androff decided to use publicity. His strategy was to send a news release to magazines and newspapers, followed up by a phone call to the editors. The company also demonstrated the product at trade shows. Prior to using these two promotional tactics, sales had been slow, but they've now picked up considerably.[39]

At its core, successful promotion is all about effective communication. The source (a small business) must send out its message in such a way that intended recipients (in the target market) receive it, understand it, and are moved to respond to it. But this is no simple exercise. Many decisions must be made along the way—decisions regarding the size of the promotional budget, the promotional mix, the nature and placement of advertising, the identification of high-potential prospects, participation in trade shows, and the list goes on. You will, no doubt, make promotional errors along the way. But practice makes perfect. Learn from your mistakes, and move on. Don't give up.... Success awaits you!

1. Describe the communication process and the factors determining a promotional mix.

- Every communication involves a source, a message, a channel, and a receiver.
- A promotional mix is a blend of nonpersonal, personal, and special forms of communication techniques.
- A promotional mix is influenced primarily by three important factors: the geographical nature of the market, the size of the promotional budget, and the product's characteristics.

2. Explain methods of determining the appropriate level of promotional expenditures.

- Earmarking promotional dollars based on a percentage of sales is a simple method for determining expenditures.
- Spending only what can be spared is a widely used approach to promotional budgeting.
- Spending as much as the competition does is a way to react to short-run promotional tactics of competitors.
- The preferred approach to determining promotional expenditures is to decide what it will take to do the job, while factoring in elements used in the other methods.

3. Describe personal selling activities.

- A sales presentation is a process involving prospecting, practicing the presentation, and then making the presentation.
- Selling effectiveness is enhanced when a salesperson displays a good appearance, has a pleasant personality, and uses professional etiquette in all contacts with customers.

- For repeat business, goodwill can count as much as a good price, good quality, and good service.
- Salespeople are compensated for their efforts in two ways—financially and nonfinancially.
- The two basic plans for financial compensation are commissions and straight salary, but the most attractive plan for a small firm combines the two.

4. Identify advertising options for a small business.

- Common advertising media include television, radio, magazines, newspapers, billboards, and the Internet.
- Product advertising is designed to promote a product or service, while institutional advertising conveys information about the business itself.
- Sources for assistance with advertising include advertising agencies, suppliers, trade associations, and advertising media.
- A small firm must decide how often to advertise, where to advertise, and what the message will be.
- A firm's Web advertising generally takes the form of banner ads and pop-ups, e-mail campaigns, sponsorships and linkages, a corporate website, and blogs.

5. Discuss the use of sales promotional tools.

- Sales promotion includes all promotional techniques other than personal selling and advertising.
- Typically, sales promotional tools are used along with advertising and personal selling.
- Three widely used sales promotional tools are specialties, trade show exhibits, and publicity.

Key Terms

promotion p. 441
promotional mix p. 442
personal selling p. 444
prospecting p. 445
advertising p. 449

product advertising p. 450
institutional advertising p. 450
banner ads p. 453
pop-up ads p. 453
e-mail promotion p. 453

Web sponsorship p. 454
linkage p. 454
blog p. 457
sales promotion p. 457
publicity p. 458

Discussion Questions

1. Describe the parallel relationship that exists between a small business communication and a personal communication.

2. Discuss the advantages and disadvantages of each approach to budgeting funds for promotion.

3. Outline a system of prospecting that could be used by a small camera store. Incorporate all the techniques presented in this chapter.

4. Why are a salesperson's techniques for handling objections so important to a successful sales presentation?

5. Assume you have the opportunity to "sell" your course instructor on the idea of eliminating final examinations. Make a list of the objections you expect to hear from your instructor, and describe how you will handle each objection, using some of the techniques listed on page 447.

6. What are some nonfinancial rewards that could be offered to salespeople?

7. What are the advantages and disadvantages of compensating salespeople by salary? By commissions? What do you think is an acceptable compromise?

8. What are some approaches to advertising on the Web?

9. Discuss some recommendations for designing an effective website.

10. How do specialties differ from trade show exhibits and publicity? Be specific.

You Make the Call

SITUATION 1

The driving force behind Cannon Arp's new business was several bad experiences with his car—two speeding tickets and four minor fender-benders. Consequently, his insurance rates more than doubled, which resulted in Arp's idea to design and sell a bumper sticker that read "To Report Bad Driving, Call My Parents at . . . ." With a $200 investment, Arp printed 15,000 of the stickers, which contain space to write in the appropriate telephone number. He is now planning a promotion to support his strategy of distribution through auto parts stores.

Question 1 What role, if any, should personal selling have in Arp's total promotional plan?

Question 2 Arp is considering advertising in magazines. What do you think about this medium for promoting his product?

Question 3 Of what value might publicity be for selling Arp's stickers? Be specific.

SITUATION 2

Cheree Moore owns and operates a small business that supplies delicatessens with bulk containers of ready-made salads. When served in salad bars, the salads appear to have been freshly prepared from scratch at the delicatessen. Moore wants additional promotional exposure for her products and is considering using her fleet of trucks as rolling billboards. If the strategy is successful, she may even attempt to lease space on other trucks. Moore is concerned about the cost-effectiveness of the idea and whether the public will even notice the advertisements. She also wonders whether the image of her salad products might be hurt by this advertising medium.

Question 1 What suggestions can you offer that would help Moore make this decision?

Question 2 How could Moore go about determining the cost-effectiveness of this strategy?

Question 3 What additional factors should Moore evaluate before advertising on trucks?

SITUATION 3

The founder of Panchero's Mexican Grill, Rodney Anderson, felt the company ought to be involved in social networking, but he and his management team weren't sure how to do it. Along came 22-year-old Joel Johnson, looking for a job and very comfortable with Web surfing. Now an employee of Panchero's, Johnson spends most of his day on Twitter, Facebook, and other networking sites. He visits chat rooms regularly, looking for people who are talking about burritos or about where they might go to eat. He then recommends Panchero's. Johnson also works with Panchero's franchisees, teaching them how to get visitors to their websites to become in-restaurant guests and then to post comments about their experiences. From watching Johnson at work, Anderson has learned that social networking is not something you can push. He says, "You have to let it have a life of its own."

Sources: Nancy Weingartner, "Citizen Marketing: Playing Catch-up with Technology Advances," *Franchise Times*, April 2009, pp. 61–62; and http://www.pancheros.com, accessed April 1, 2009.

Question 1 There is more than a 10-year age difference between members of Panchero's top management team and Joel Johnson. Do you think that difference could have contributed to Johnson's effectiveness in social networking? Why or why not?

Question 2 Is it ethical for Johnson to be recommending the restaurant chain where he works? Why or why not?

Question 3 Have you ever posted any comments on a website about a business that you have visited? Do you check for customer comments before you shop at a particular business?

Experiential Exercises

1. Interview the owners of one or more small businesses to determine how they develop their promotional budget. Classify the owners' methods into one or more of the four approaches described in this chapter. Report your findings to the class.

2. Plan a sales presentation. With a classmate role-playing a potential buyer, make the presentation in class. Ask the other students to critique your technique.

3. Locate a small business website and evaluate its promotional effectiveness.

4. Interview a media representative about advertising options for small businesses. Summarize your findings for the class.

Small Business & Entrepreneurship Resource Center

The *Small Business and Entrepreneurship Resource Center* offers complete small business management resources through a comprehensive database that covers all major areas of starting, operating, and maintaining a business from financing, management, marketing, accounting, taxes, and more. Use the access code that came with your new book to access the site and perform the exercises in each chapter.

1. Shoebuy.com began its Web-based sales operation with the concept of free shipping in mind. Studies show that offering free shipping encourages customers to fill their shopping carts more than they would otherwise. Describe why Shoebuy.com is able to provide free shipping cost effectively. Also describe when it may not be recommended that a company offer free shipping.

2. The Bear Naked line of granola and breakfast products is heavily promoted through the use of in-store free samples. This strategy has worked well for the company and helped it to secure its first major store accounts. However, sampling is not always an appropriate strategy. Describe when sampling may not be an appropriate strategy. Also describe how a company can make sampling more effective.

Sources: Shipping out: if you can afford to join the fray, offering online customers free shipping may help you compete. (Net Profits). Melissa Campanelli. *Entrepreneur* 31, 6 (June 2003): p. 42(2).

Get out, hand out: in-store sampling attracts new consumers. (LAUNCH OF THE MONTH) (Kelly Flatley and Brendan Synnott launch Bear Naked granola). Kent Steinriede. Stagnito's *New Products Magazine* 7, 5 (May 2007): p. 32(2).

Video Case 17

GLIDDEN POINT OYSTER COMPANY, A.G.A. CORREA & SON, HARDY BOAT CRUISES, MAINE GOLD (P. 660)

This case looks at four distinct businesses and their individual promotional techniques, offering suggestions and clear examples of how to market goods and services to customers outside a business's immediate customer base.

ALTERNATIVE CASES FOR CHAPTER 17

Case 1, Nau, p. 623
Case 21, Modern Postcard, p. 667

chapter 18

Global Opportunities for Small Business

In the SPOTLIGHT
New York Chocolatier Finds
a Sweet Spot Far from Home
http://www.chocolatebarnyc.com

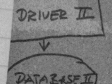

When Allison Nelson opened her first Chocolate Bar in 2002, she had visions of some day expanding into big and prestigious markets like Chicago, Miami, and Los Angeles. Little did she know that her first locations outside of New York City (where she owns and operates three stores today) would be on the other side of the globe—in exotic Middle Eastern cities like Dubai and Qatar. Small U.S. companies often do not venture abroad until they have saturated the U.S. market and need more room to grow, but the shaky domestic economy and the steadily growing consumer class in some overseas markets are changing the formula for success. Nelson is hoping to be at the front of that trend. Despite having only 25 employees and around $2 million in annual sales revenue, she now has an ambitious plan to open 30 new international stores over a 10-year period.

When the concept of expanding to the Middle East was first mentioned, Nelson wasted no time rejecting the idea. "My first mental image was the [Iraq] war," she says. "I haven't opened a store in Los Angeles. How am I going to open [one] clear across the globe?" But then she studied the market and realized that Middle Eastern consumers have become very globalized through travels abroad, satellite TV, and the Internet, and many are attracted to the cachet of American and European brands of chocolate. The original suggestion to expand there was starting to look like a stroke of genius!

But then questions of strategy came to mind. Should she open her own stores in the region? Organize the business as a franchisor and locate potential franchisees in promising overseas markets? License products to international partners and let them determine what to sell and how to sell it? Adapt products to local tastes, or just offer those already developed that may have potential in new markets? How would she even get started?

Nelson connected with a Middle Eastern business operator who was willing to talk chocolate. After nine months of negotiations, Nelson struck a licensing deal with her new partner in the United Arab Emirates and has

LOOKING AHEAD — AFTER STUDYING THIS CHAPTER, YOU SHOULD BE ABLE TO...

1. Describe the potential of small firms as global enterprises.
2. Identify the basic forces prompting small firms to engage in global expansion.
3. Understand and compare strategy options for global businesses.
4. Explain the challenges that global enterprises face.
5. Recognize the sources of assistance available to support international business efforts.

since worked out a contract with a second company to expand into South Asia. But the arrangements call for substantial product adaptations. Because Middle Easterners eat a lot of chocolate when celebrating engagements, births, and other special occasions, Nelson had to create big platters for gift giving. Dark chocolate is popular in the United States and Europe, but buyers in Dubai want more milk and white chocolate in their products. To tap into the attraction of figs and dates in the region, Nelson had to add chocolate-dipped versions of these fruits to the menu.

And the way these products are delivered had to change as well. Many Arabs don't like sitting next to strangers, so the facilities had to be redesigned to allow greater privacy—and to create dining areas with secluded sections where women could sit and men wouldn't see them. Nelson even had to adjust the way she operates when traveling to the region. For example, a simple meeting with a supplier can easily last four hours—nothing like the fast pace of business life in New York City—and most vendors are not listed online, so Google searches have to be replaced with the painstaking process of calling around town in search of assistance.

Allison Nelson's enterprise is small, but she has proved that you don't have to be a large corporation to go global. With a little vision and a lot of hard work, you can go global, too.

Sources: Simona Covel, "New York Eatery Looks for the Sweet Spot Overseas," *Wall Street Journal,* September 4, 2008, http://www.online.wsj.com/article/SB122047376978596329.html, accessed February 19, 2009; Chris Shott, "Death by Chocolate," *The New York Observer*, April 8, 2008, http://www.observer.com/2008/death-chocolate, accessed February 27, 2009; and "Who We Are," http://www.chocolatebarnyc.com/about, accessed February 27, 2009.

Entrepreneurship provides the basic energy that drives the modern market economy, as new businesses around the world spur competition and economic growth. And while differences in the number of existing companies in various countries are stark, the rate of new business creation is consistent and strong. Research has shown that approximately 8.35 percent of all registered businesses around the globe are recent startups.[1] Regardless of their nationality, entrepreneurs who smell opportunity are rushing to seize it—no matter where in the world they have to go to find it.

There was a time when national economies were isolated by trade and investment barriers, differences in language and culture, distinctive business practices, and various government regulations. However, these dissimilarities are fading over time as market preferences converge, trade barriers fall, and national economies integrate to form a global economic system. This process is the essence of *globalization.* Though the trend toward convergence has been developing for some time, the pace is quickening, creating global opportunities that did not exist even a few years ago. And with the astounding rate of economic growth in countries such as China and India, it would be unwise to ignore overseas opportunities.

This may sound all well and good, but becoming a global entrepreneur may seem beyond your reach. After all, the world is a very big place! And as you read in the pages that follow about the challenges of international business and the many decisions that are involved in expanding abroad, you may become even more convinced that this option is not for you. This is a normal reaction. But the opportunities are tremendously rewarding, and available resources can help you overcome any obstacles that may stand in your way. In the last part of the chapter, you will read about numerous forms of assistance that can help you achieve your global ambitions. And as you will see, many small businesses have already shown that it can be done—you can do it, too!

globalization
The expansion of international business, encouraged by converging market preferences, falling trade barriers, and the integration of national economies.

Small Businesses as Global Enterprises

1. Describe the potential of small firms as global enterprises.

born-global firms
Small companies launched with cross-border business activities in mind.

The potential of a global business is clear, but does that potential extend to small companies?[2] Research has shown that recent startups and even the smallest of businesses are internationalizing at an increasing rate. In fact, small companies in virtually all major trading countries are increasingly being launched with cross-border business activities in mind.[3] The arrangements in these companies, often called *born-global firms*,[4] sometimes can get more than a little crazy. You may be familiar with a company called Skype, which was acquired by eBay in 2005; here is its born-global startup story:

> [Niklas] Zennstrom, who is Swedish, and his partner Janus Friis, a Dane, launched their Internet telephony company Skype in Luxembourg, with sales offices in London. But they outsourced product development to Estonia, the same fertile womb that had earlier gestated their music-sharing system, Kazaa.[5]

You may be thinking, "That's fine in this case—Skype is a big company." That's true today, but in 2003 the company was just a startup, and it was clearly an international business right from the beginning. Many new ventures, as well as established small businesses, are being swept up in the wave of globalization.

As global communication systems become more efficient and trade agreements pry open national markets to foreign competition, entrepreneurs are focusing more and more on international opportunities. Networking options are expanding through various forms of creative partnerships, allowing small firms to find new ways to enter the global economy and novel pathways for international growth. Entrepreneurs may decide to go global to expand their opportunities, or they may be forced to enter foreign markets in order to compete with firms in their industry that have already done so. There is no doubt that these developments, and so many others, help to explain how companies have been able to accelerate the pace of their international involvement.[6] But the research is clear: *Size does not necessarily limit a firm's international activity—small companies can build upon their unique resources to become global competitors.*[7]

In some cases, the global option is practically unavoidable. For example, when Howard Pedolsky, a Bethesda, Maryland–based entrepreneur, began to market his innovative and eco-friendly refrigeration technology a few years back, he found that European supermarkets were far more interested in it than were their American counterparts. It turned out that their attraction was the result of the strict standards of European regulators, so Pedolsky realized that he would need to focus on developing a customer base in Europe first. "Our first customer ended up being a French company," he says. "The European environment was just much stronger in our direction, and [supermarkets there] tend to spend more money on our products."[8]

But motivations for global startup vary. Joseph Blumenfeld founded the global public relations firm Tradewind Strategies because of his vast experience in corporate marketing overseas. "And that's really where the market is," says the Natick, Massachusetts–based entrepreneur, "because there's so much competition in the United States."[9] As a signal of the importance of international markets to this startup, the company's website features mailing addresses both in the United States and in Beijing, China.[10]

The fact that many firms are going global does not mean that it is *easy* for small companies; the challenges small businesses face in international markets are considerable. First, a small business owner must decide whether the company is up to the task. To help entrepreneurs assess the impact of going global on their small business, the U.S. Department of Commerce publishes *A Basic Guide to Exporting*. This handbook outlines important questions

EXHIBIT

Management Objectives	• What are the company's reasons for going global?
	• How committed is top management to going global?
	• How quickly does management expect its international operations to pay off?
Management Experience and Resources	• What in-house international expertise does the firm have (international sales experience, language skills, etc.)?
	• Who will be responsible for the company's international operations?
	• How much senior management time should be allocated to the company's global efforts?
	• What organizational structure is required to ensure success abroad?
Production Capacity	• How is the present capacity being used?
	• Will international sales hurt domestic sales?
	• What will be the cost of additional production at home and abroad?
	• What product designs and packaging options are required for international markets?
Financial Capacity	• How much capital can be committed to international production and marketing?
	• How are the initial expenses of going global to be covered?
	• What other financial demands might compete with plans to internationalize?
	• By what date must the global effort pay for itself?

Source: Adapted from U.S. Department of Commerce, *A Basic Guide to Exporting: The Official Government Resource for Small and Medium-Sized Businesses*, cited in John B. Cullen and K. Praveen Parboteeah, *Multinational Management: A Strategic Approach*, 4th ed. (Cincinnati, OH: Thomson South-Western, 2008), p. 208.

entrepreneurs should consider when assessing their readiness for the challenges of global business (see Exhibit 18-1).

Once small business owners decide to expand internationally, they should study the cultural, political, and economic forces in foreign markets to figure out how best to adapt their business practices as well as their product or service to local circumstances or make other adjustments that are necessary to ensure smooth market entry. For example, doing business in the Middle East can require significant changes in what many small business owners would consider to be "standard business procedures."

> In Saudi Arabia, the workweek begins on Saturday and ends on Wednesday, appointments are generally scheduled around five daily prayer times, and many businesses are closed in the afternoon. Most real business is conducted face to face, with far less reliance on documents and contracts than is typical in the Western world; therefore, the time it takes to do business is relative.[11]

And that's just the beginning! When you add to this the fact that collecting or paying interest is forbidden in Islamic states—along with a host of other fundamental differences—it becomes clear that navigating the unique hurdles of an international market, like Saudi Arabia, can be a serious challenge.

The Forces Driving Global Businesses

2. Identify the basic forces prompting small firms to engage in global expansion.

Given the difficulty of international business, why would any entrepreneur want to get involved? Among the reasons small firms have for going global are some that have motivated international trade for centuries. Marco Polo traveled to China in 1271 to explore the trading of Western goods for exotic Oriental silks and spices, which would then be sold in Europe. Clearly, the motivation to take domestic goods to foreign markets and bring foreign goods to domestic markets is as relevant today as it was in Marco Polo's day. Consider the clothing designer who sells Western wear in Tokyo or the independent rug dealer who scours the markets of Turkey to locate low-cost sources of high-quality products to sell.

Complementing these traditional reasons for going global are motivations that epitomize the core of entrepreneurial drive. Leigh Buchanan describes the impulse to go global as follows:

> **Because it's what entrepreneurs do**. To wax deductive: Globalization is risky. Entrepreneurs embrace risk. Therefore entrepreneurs embrace globalization. Of course there's risk and then there's risk, with the latter including such potential spoilers as an unfamiliar language, an alien business landscape, and political volatility. Still, the chance to try new things in new places is like a jumper cable to the entrepreneurial engine. [Small company owners] describe running their international efforts as the most exciting aspect of doing business, not just for themselves but for their employees as well.[12]

In other words, many entrepreneurs are looking to do more than simply expand a profitable market when they get involved in international business. And they also recognize that their enterprises are no longer insulated from global challengers; they must consider the dynamics of the new competitive environment.[13] In some cases, the rival on the other side of the street may be a minor threat compared to an online competitor on the other side of the globe!

One way to adjust to these emerging realities is through innovation. In many industries, innovation is essential to competitiveness; small businesses that invest heavily in research and development often can outperform their large competitors. But as R&D costs rise, they seldom can be recovered from domestic sales alone. Increasing sales in international markets may be the only viable way to recover a firm's investment. In some cases, this may require identifying dynamic markets that are beginning to open around the world and then locating in or near those markets.[14]

The basic forces behind global expansion can be divided into four general categories: expanding markets, gaining access to resources, cutting costs, and capitalizing on special features of location (see Exhibit 18-2). Within each category fall some tried and true motivations, as well as some new angles that have emerged with the global economy. We discuss each of these four categories in the sections that follow.

Expanding the Market

More than 95 percent of the world's population lives outside the United States. It follows that globalization greatly increases the size of an American firm's potential market. A recent study of small companies found that their primary interest in internationalization was accessing new markets and growing their business, as opposed to seeking resources abroad, gaining access to technologies, avoiding regulatory pressures at home, etc.[15]

COUNTRIES TARGETED Because the primary motivation for going global is to develop market opportunities outside the home country, the focus of globalization strategies tends to be on those countries with the greatest commercial potential. In the past, these were the developed countries (those with high levels of widely distributed wealth). Today, companies are paying

LIVING THE DREAM:

Surf's Up, but Sales Are Down

Pete Dooley began making surfboards in the Cocoa Beach, Florida, area in 1972 and then decided to build a business on this rare skill (referred to as "shaping" by industry insiders). His love for the sport and passion for creating the boards led to the creation of a company, Natural Art. The enterprise did so well that Dooley expanded the operation into a 6,000-square-foot factory and hired 12 people to work for the company. "We doubled our business every year until [the recession in] 1991," says Dooley, who is now in his late fifties. To adjust, he had to lay off his employees and downsize the business, but he kept making boards and a good living—that is, until around five years ago when globalization started to sweep over the industry like a giant tsunami. What, specifically, is the challenge? Cheap imports from China.

©iStockphoto.com/Ian McDonnell

"The Chinese can land a board here for what it costs us to glass one," says Dooley, referring to the process of laying down layers of resin to form the durable coating that protects the foam core inside. "I visited one of their factories and I was impressed. There were 25 shaping rooms and 500 employees. People [in the United States]

have to work two jobs to support themselves [making surfboards] now." Reluctantly, Dooley and his wife are shutting down their surf shop on one of Florida's most famous beachside highways, though they plan to continue selling custom-made surfboards from their website.

But what is happening to Dooley is not an isolated situation—mass-produced surfboards are putting many shapers out of business. Some are fighting the trend, arguing that the pressure is unfair and definitely unwanted. Others blame the big established surf companies who taught Chinese competitors the craft, or the popular surf magazines that hyped overseas alternatives beyond their true value. And, of course, some shapers in the United States were turning out shoddy quality, so customer loyalty ebbed like a receding wave. Many buyers simply don't care where their boards come from, but they care very much about price. Regardless of the analysis, the reality of globalization cannot be denied— even in a limited industry like surfboard construction. Ultimately, no business is immune to the threat of international competition.

Sources: Mike Williams, "Chinese Imports, Bad Economy Swamp Surfboard Shapers," Cox News Service, **http://www.coxwashington.com/news/content/reporters/stories/2008/04/13/SURFBOARD_WOES13_COX.html,** accessed March 5, 2009; "Chinese Surfboard Takeover," **http://www.magicseaweed.com/community/viewtopic.php?f=13&t=13280,** accessed March 5, 2009; and **http://www.naturalart.com, accessed March 5, 2009.**

http://www.naturalart.com

---

greater attention to emerging markets, where income and buying power are growing rapidly. In 2001, the bank holding company Goldman Sachs came up with the term *BRICs* to refer to the fast-growing economies of *B*razil, *R*ussia, *I*ndia, and *C*hina (see Exhibit 18-3). Based on their rapid development, Goldman Sachs projects that by 2050 the BRIC economies, taken together, could very well eclipse the combined economies of what are currently the richest countries of the world.[16] While this vision may not roll out as predicted, the markets of the BRICs have definitely captured the interest of many entrepreneurs, and that is not likely to change.

Because of their immense populations and potential market demand, China and India have attracted the greatest attention from international firms. Combined, these two nations account for an astounding 40 percent of the world's six billion inhabitants, thus providing fertile ground

18-2 Basic Forces Driving Global Enterprises

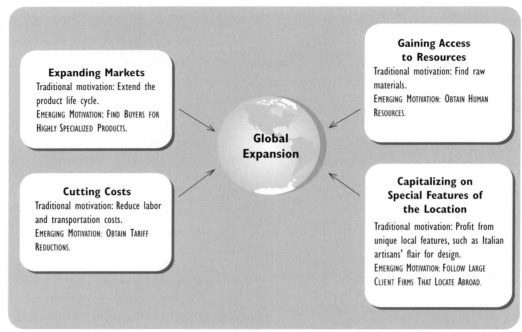

Expanding Markets
Traditional motivation: Extend the product life cycle.
EMERGING MOTIVATION: FIND BUYERS FOR HIGHLY SPECIALIZED PRODUCTS.

Gaining Access to Resources
Traditional motivation: Find raw materials.
EMERGING MOTIVATION: OBTAIN HUMAN RESOURCES.

Global Expansion

Cutting Costs
Traditional motivation: Reduce labor and transportation costs.
EMERGING MOTIVATION: OBTAIN TARIFF REDUCTIONS.

Capitalizing on Special Features of the Location
Traditional motivation: Profit from unique local features, such as Italian artisans' flair for design.
EMERGING MOTIVATION: FOLLOW LARGE CLIENT FIRMS THAT LOCATE ABROAD.

18-3 BRIC Markets

Country	2005 Population (in millions)	2005 Wealth (GNI per capita)	2006–2007 Economic Growth (GDP growth, %)
Brazil	191.6	5,910	5
Russia	141.6	7,560	8
India	1,123.3	950	9
China	1,320.0	2,360	12
World	**6,612.0**	**7,950**	**4**

Source: Adapted from The World Bank Group, "World Development Indicators, 2007," http://ddp-ext.worldbank.org/ext/DDPQQ/member.do?method=getMembers&userid=1&queryId=135, accessed March 4, 2009.

for international expansion. And small companies are among the countless competitors that are battling for position in these emerging markets. That's why a small public relations firm like Tradewind Strategies (discussed earlier) maintains a second office in China.[17]

PRODUCTS PROMOTED In the mid-1960s, international business authority Raymond Vernon observed that firms tend to introduce new products in the United States first and then sell them in less-advanced countries later, as demand in the home market declines.[18] In other words, they use international expansion to extend a product's life cycle.

Although this approach is effective under some circumstances, it has become less viable as customer preferences, income levels, and delivery systems have become more similar and product life cycles have contracted. Consider the following observations, based on the experience of two small business practitioners:

> The time lags between U.S. and foreign adoption have . . . disappeared. Today it is essential to roll out new products in several countries almost simultaneously. . . . No longer does the small company have the luxury of using cash flow from domestic sales to support the building of international marketing a few years later. The ever-shortening product cycle virtually dooms such a strategy. Terrific. Now, in addition to getting the product to work, setting up your new team, getting some U.S. customers, and finding money, you now have to worry about selling in six or eight additional countries, most of whom don't even speak English![19]

Products that sell at home are now more likely to be introduced very quickly abroad, with little or no adaptation in many cases. The role of television programs, movies, print media, and the Internet in shaping cultural tastes throughout the world has eased the entry of small businesses into international markets. American interests have long held a starring role in the cultural arena, inspiring widespread purchases of products such as blue jeans and fast food and generating international interest in U.S. sports and celebrities. By informing consumers about the lifestyles of others, globalization is leading the world toward common consumer preferences.

In addition to the trendy products associated with popular culture, another type of product well suited to international markets is the highly specialized product. As technology makes possible increasingly sophisticated goods, this allows markets to demand more differentiated products that satisfy their unique needs and interests. Because a highly differentiated (and often more expensive) product is targeted to a very narrow range of consumers in the home market, a company may need to search for markets abroad that have the same unique demand. This is often the only way to increase sales enough to recover the higher product development costs involved in the creation and manufacture of a very specialized product. Small companies that aspire to grow rapidly often follow focused business strategies with limited domestic market potential. For them, efforts to exploit the competitive advantage of specialized products across several international markets may be even more important than for their large corporate counterparts.[20]

Martin Goodwin sells a highly specialized product in international markets. He started IT Retail in Riverside, California, in 1993 after growing tired of running a supermarket retailing operation with limited software solutions. No available software could monitor inventories, price products, issue purchase orders, and handle other basic functions as part of one integrated solution, so he decided to create his own. He came up with the system design and hired Microsoft Consulting to build the solution. Then, he brought in his own team of developers to finish the software and make it ready for other retailers.[21]

Once the product was offered for sale, it became apparent that market interest in the United States for this focused product was healthy but limited, leaving IT Retail with scant opportunity to recover development costs. To overcome this constraint, Goodwin decided to go global, and business has really taken off. Using strategic partnerships, IT Retail has managed to sell over 44,000 licenses in 20 nations—amazing growth for such a small company! And the expansion continues. On the company's website, Goodwin remarks, "This is only the start. Retail is the best and most complete grocery supermarket package available today, and grocery retailers are beginning to find out about us. Sales activity is exploding!" With offices in Europe, South America, Central America, and India, the company can attest to the importance of going global to exploit a competitive advantage.[22]

MAKING THE MOST OF EXPERIENCE No matter which countries are targeted or products promoted, international expansion has the potential to provide benefits beyond the standard per-unit profits on additional items sold. As a venture expands and volume grows, it usually can find ways to work smarter or to generate efficiencies. Analysts first observed such *experience curve efficiencies* in the aircraft manufacturing industry. They noticed that each time a manufacturer doubled its total output, the production cost per aircraft dropped by 20 percent. In other words, per-unit costs declined by 20 percent when the firm manufactured four units instead of two, declined again by 20 percent when the firm made eight units instead of four, and so on.

What can explain this gain in efficiency? Most credit the outcome to learning effects and economies of scale. *Learning effects* occur when the insight an employee gains from experience leads to improved work performance. Learning effects can also take place at the level of the firm if the experiences of individual employees are shared, leading to improved practices and production routines across the organization. These gains from learning are greatest during the startup period and gradually decline over time. Efficiencies from *economies of scale,* on the other hand, continue to rise as the business grows and volume increases, because these savings derive from spreading investment costs across more units of output and acquiring more specialized (and thus more efficient) plants, equipment, and employees.

Small firms can accelerate the gains from experience curve efficiencies by emphasizing international expansion, assuming they can manage the growth. Prior to the 1990s, startups were encouraged to consider international expansion only after they had established a solid position in their domestic market. Times have changed.[23] Recent studies have shown that starting with a global presence or globalizing early in a company's life leads to increased performance, especially sales growth. And for high-potential ventures, sales growth is usually considered one of the most important dimensions of performance. The benefits of learning effects and economies of scale are especially apparent in startups based on complex technologies. The possibility of achieving experience curve efficiencies through accelerated globalization of emerging technologies is likely to stimulate the interest of startups and small companies in international business.

Gaining Access to Resources

Just as fortune seekers abandoned their comfortable lives in the eastern United States to flock to California following the discovery of gold at Sutter's Mill in 1848, small firms today leave the United States to gain access to essential raw materials and other factors of production. For example, the oil fields of Kuwait are tended not just by employees of the global oil giants, but also by hundreds of support personnel who work for small companies that have contracted to assist their large clients. These small players choose to locate operations in Kuwait (or Mexico, Nigeria, Saudi Arabia, etc.) for one simple reason: That's where the oil is! The same principle holds for manufacturers that require scarce inputs. For example, many aluminum producers have relocated to Iceland to tap the country's abundant and inexpensive hydroelectric and geothermal energy.[24]

Though small firms have traditionally pursued international ventures to obtain raw materials, increasingly the focus of their search is skilled labor. For example, a small software development company in Chicago found it necessary to locate programming operations in Russia to get access to the people it needed to do routine computer programming. Despite the fact that installation of a telephone can take several months and crime bosses sometimes pay visits to demand protection money, the entrepreneur was lured to Russia by its talented but low-priced human capital, a necessary resource that he found to be in short supply in the United States.[25]

Of course, American businesses of all sizes have increasingly been accessing foreign labor through contracts with independent providers (an arrangement called *international outsourcing*) or by relocating their stateside operations abroad (sometimes referred to as *offshoring*). These initiatives have been especially popular in countries such as India and China, where relatively high-skilled labor is low in cost.[26]

Many small businesses are getting into the game of international outsourcing. In fact, some of the most creative examples of this practice have been spawned by entrepreneurial companies. Dorothy Clay Sims is a Florida attorney who often has to cross-examine medical experts. But she is also the creator of MD in a Box, a startup that specializes in providing access to highly qualified doctors who can serve as expert witnesses in legal proceedings. The creative twist in Sims's new venture is that her experts offer their insights by long distance—*from India*! Here's how it works: An attorney in the United States can depose the opposing counsel's medical expert while a doctor in India listens in via Skype. The Indian doctor sends instant messages with suggested responses for the attorney, who can then refute the doctor being cross-examined, using correct medical terms in the process. Such expert advice typically costs $500 to $1,000 per hour in the United States, but Sims has hired a stable of Indian medical experts who receive $20 to $35 an hour for their services. Indian doctors typically earn around $11,000 a year in their practices, so they are pleased with the extra income. MD in a Box charges $75 an hour ($200 per hour if the case is won), leaving Sims with a hefty profit.[27] But, in the end, everyone comes out ahead—except for the losing attorney and his or her client, that is.

The business concept developed by Sims may be far from ordinary, but in a way it fits the common outsourcing pattern precisely. Most entrepreneurs who choose to outsource internationally, or relocate offshore, are seeking two things that are always important to the success of small companies: access to talented employees and/or reduced costs. MD in a Box just happens to address both needs.

This section has focused on the resource access side of the equation; now let's look more closely at cost-cutting initiatives.

Cutting Costs

Sometimes firms go global to reduce the costs of doing business. Among the costs that firms have traditionally reduced by venturing abroad are those related to raw materials, labor, and manufacturing overhead.

Kirkham Motorsports is headquartered in Provo, Utah, where a handful of employees complete the final assembly of the company's high-performance Cobra automobiles. To be cost-competitive, however, the firm relocated the labor-intensive production of aluminum car bodies and frames to a former Soviet advanced fighter jet factory near Warsaw, Poland. The facility there employs three generations of craftsmen who ply their advanced metal-fabrication skills to turn out these automotive works of art.[28] Perhaps Cobra buyers will savor the notion that their lightning-fast cars were constructed in a facility that once produced jet aircraft that continue to command respect all over the world.

Although Kirkham went global to control labor costs, the critical factor is not always labor. For example, transportation costs would likely be the controlling factor for a small business that sells cement products used in construction (concrete columns, bridge girders, decorative statues). These goods are extremely heavy but do not command a premium price. Since the cost of overseas transportation could exceed the price of the product, international sales would make sense only if the firm were to locate production in-country and near customers.

The advantages of globalization in reducing labor and transportation costs have long been recognized. However, the emerging global economy has brought a new means of lowering costs through relocation. In recent years, a number of countries have formed regional free trade areas, within which commerce has been facilitated by reducing tariffs, simplifying commercial regulations, or even—in the case of the European Union—adopting a common currency. These cost-cutting measures can be a powerful inducement to small firms to move into the prescribed area. After the enactment of the North American Free Trade Agreement, for instance, a number of Japanese firms located manufacturing facilities in Mexico to reap the advantage of reduced tariffs on trade within that region.

How I see it: Cecilia Levine on Global Quality Control

My first experience in competing against China occurred when I was making backpacks for a U.S. corporation. My customer ordered half of its seasonal sales from me and the other half from China.

The price for the Chinese bags was much lower than what I was able to do, but the bags from China were not of the same quality that I could offer. My bags were made with 14 oz. denim, while the Chinese bags were made with 10 oz. denim. Consequently, the Chinese bags were not as durable, nor did they hold their shape as well. Also, the Chinese bags were several inches smaller. Since I had worked with my customer's research and development group to develop the backpacks, I understood the product quality that the customer was looking for, from the weight of the material to the exact measurements of the bag. To realize a quality product, you have to maintain quality control people in the country where you are working. Otherwise, your product will be unacceptable to your customers.

We have facilities in the United States for small production and in Mexico for medium-sized production, which provide for fast turnaround time, almost as if you were in the U.S. We then use China for products that are already mature and have our own field quality control people check for quality. It's also important to remind customers who may be comparing a product from Mexico with one from China that they need to take into consideration the extra administrative staff in China as part of their cost.

Capitalizing on Special Features of Location

Some of the benefits of location are simply the result of unique features of a local environment. For example, Italian artisans have long been well known for their flair for design, and Japanese technicians have shown an ability to harness optical technologies for application in cameras, copiers, and other related products. Small companies that depend on a particular strength may find that it makes sense to locate in a region that provides fertile ground for that type of innovation.

In some cases, there is no way to be authentic apart from being local. Josh Pollock's only claim to insight into the food service industry used to be that he grew up eating Western food. So what's this 33-year-old American doing in China? He's started a restaurant, a business born of true opportunity. Pollock, along with his Japanese wife and two of their American friends, found that the Western food in China was absolutely dreadful, but locals were still eating it up. So, in 2004 the team cobbled together $40,000 in investment money and started a new company: Kunming Salvador's Food and Beverage Co., Ltd. This allowed them to open a coffee house in Kunming (a city of more than 4 million inhabitants in Yunnan province) and offer Western products—including ice cream, bagels and cream cheese, and salsa—to local customers.[29]

The way forward has not always been easy, and the team has had much to learn. For example, early on they ran into a bureaucratic brick wall, which required the outsiders to turn to a practice that is common in China—that is, they had to build their *guanxi*, or personal connections, to get the government approvals they needed. The move proved to be very helpful, so Pollack and his partners have further honed their relational skills as well as picking up other local practices that work to the advantage of the company. Though still young, the enterprise has been wonderfully successful, which has led to yet another business opportunity: consulting with local or international companies that want to establish a successful enterprise in China. Here is Pollack's pitch:

> Business in China is latent with unexpected obstacles. Let us help you avoid the labyrinth of government bureaucracy and help save you time and money. We guarantee we can successfully navigate the changing China business arena to accommodate your company or business needs.[30]

If it sounds like he is speaking from experience, you can be sure that is exactly what he is doing. For $125 an hour, the Salvador team will show you the ropes of doing business in China, a service that is legitimate only as a result of being in-country and based on first-hand experience.

Sometimes the appeal of regional free trade areas lies partly in locational features unrelated to cost. As the countries in Europe talked about coming together to form the European Union, many non-European executives worried that a "Fortress Europe" mentality would arise. That is, they assumed that increased trade among European countries would discourage trade with other nations. In response, many businesses, large and small, located physical facilities in Europe to guarantee future access to that market. In hindsight, they have concluded that the EU has not seriously hindered trade with firms outside of Europe; nonetheless, firms have taken similar measures to ensure market access in other trade areas.

Finally, a recent trend among small businesses is to follow large client firms to their new locations. As major corporations locate their operations abroad, their small suppliers find it necessary to go global with the client firms to ensure the continuation of important sourcing contracts. The small business owner may have no personal desire to expand internationally, but dependence on a major customer relocating abroad might leave the owner with no alternative. Researchers conducting a study of the international expansion of small businesses put it this way:

> Our on-site interviews with small firm owners have [shown that following client firms] is a key issue that is overlooked by most research. Many firms end up overseas not because of some strategy or long-term plan. Instead, they are forced there to keep a business presence with a current client. In some cases, small firms have no choice in the matter. A larger firm determines to move to a particular overseas location and the smaller supplier is simply expected to follow.[31]

Ford Motor Corporation is convinced that taking its suppliers overseas ensures quality, reduces startup costs, and helps meet local-content restrictions. So when it decided to open a new plant in Europe, it offered a multi-year contract to Loranger Manufacturing Corporation, a small automobile parts manufacturer based in Warren, Pennsylvania. But there was a catch: The contract required Loranger to locate near the new plant. Since Ford was its primary customer, the small supplier accepted the offer and in 1993 opened its Hungarian facility to manufacture plastic parts for Ford. Within a decade, Loranger had 150 employees there and was generating nearly $10 million a year in sales.[32]

Traditional and emerging motivations for small businesses to go global are numerous, but the ultimate incentive is this: If you fail to seize an international market opportunity, someone else will. Under these conditions, the best defense is a good offense. Establishing a position outside of the domestic setting may preempt rivals from exploiting those opportunities and using them against you in the future.

Strategy Options for Global Firms

Once an entrepreneur has decided to go global, the next step is to plan a strategy that matches the potential of the firm. For most small businesses, the first step toward globalization is a decision to export a product to other countries or to import goods from abroad to sell in the domestic market. These initial efforts are often followed by more sophisticated non-export strategies, such as licensing, franchising, forming strategic alliances with international partners, or even locating facilities abroad (see Exhibit 18-4). Each of these options is described further below.

3. Understand and compare strategy options for global businesses.

Exporting

Exporting involves the sale of products produced in the home country to customers in another country. The U.S. Small Business Administration (SBA) recently announced that small firms represent more than 97 percent of American exporters, contributing nearly 29 percent of the value of exported goods.[33] In some cases, this activity is a reflection of the reality of international competition. That is, American companies are steadily moving toward overseas markets because they recognize that foreign-owned companies are already competing against them in the U.S. market. The SBA describes conditions in today's global marketplace as follows:

exporting
Selling products produced in the home country to customers in another country.

> The division between domestic and international markets is becoming increasingly blurred. In a world of over 6 billion people, global communication networks, next-day airfreight deliveries worldwide and CNN, it no longer makes sense to limit your company's sales to the local or even to the national market. Your business cannot ignore these international realities if you intend to maintain your market share and keep pace with your competitors.[34]

EXHIBIT 18-4 Strategy Options for Global Enterprises

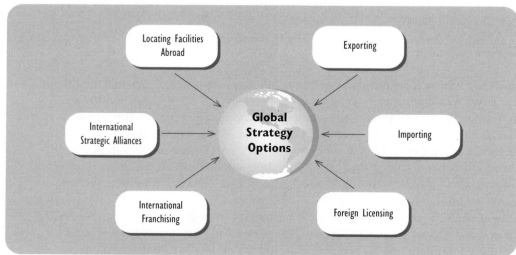

As the SBA statistics reveal, entrepreneurs are taking note and accepting the challenge. In fact, exporting is one of the most popular international strategies among small businesses because it provides a low-cost way to expand into the international arena. Taking this approach, small export companies can market and distribute their products in other countries without incurring the expense of supporting costly operations in those markets. If the financial benefits from international sales more than offset shipping costs and tariffs, exporting is a favorable option.

The Internet has fueled vigorous growth in export activity. Small firms now see the Web as a powerful tool for increasing their international visibility, allowing them to connect with customers who were previously beyond their reach. Entertainment Earth is an Internet retailer, based in Los Angeles, California, that specializes in action figures, gifts, and other collectibles. Aaron and Jason Labowitz and a friend started the company in 1995, operating out of a garage in the San Fernando Valley. It wasn't long before they decided to expand their reach by selling over the Internet. They describe their motivations on the company's website:

> We admit to being selfish when we started this business. We wanted to find a simple way to personally buy all of the new action figures and toys at reasonable prices without wasting our time [driving around to shop]. Our solution was right in front of us—and it was similar to the big-box warehouse store model coupled with the old fashion mail order business placed on a website.[35]

To date, Entertainment Earth has sold collectibles to hundreds of thousands of clients all around the world. When asked about its customer profile, Jason Labowitz responded, "We're essentially marketing to people just like us—the adult collector of these items. That was kind of hard to explain to the manufacturers, since they were unprepared to see them as anything but toys, really. They had no idea that adults wanted their stuff . . . [but] we don't market to children at all." The company employs 25 people (plus warehouse staff), offers more than 7,000 items for sale, and generates around $14 million in annual revenues.[36] It appears that Entertainment Earth knows its globe-spanning market well, which allows it to offer high-quality service that has earned the company extremely high marks from e-commerce rating services.

But you don't have to go it alone, as Entertainment Earth did. Just ask Jeff Nipert, owner of CarAlarmsEtc. He tries to give customers peace of mind where auto theft is concerned. His Bonney Lake, Washington, venture specializes in mobile electronics—specifically, car alarms, keyless entry units, remote starters, and other related accessories. Though Nipert's company is just a small operation, the world is his sales floor. How did he manage to go global? In a word, eBay. The online marketplace giant can help the tiniest of businesses connect with customers anywhere in the world, and getting started takes about as much time as it would to apply for a passport! And consider this: Of those who buy products on eBay, half live outside the United States—and that half of the business is growing twice as fast as the U.S. segment! Nipert concluded, "I felt if it wasn't costing me a dime extra for the [worldwide] exposure, I would be a fool not to take advantage of it."[37] After learning so much from his global experiences on eBay, Nipert is taking a more independent direction these days, but you could easily follow in his footsteps. To find out more about support services offered to eBay sellers, check out the firm's publication *How to Sell Internationally*.

Of course, exporting can be very challenging. Suddenly, you have to worry about communicating in a language other than English, translating payments into other currencies, and setting up international shipping. Products may have to be modified to meet government standards or the unique interests of buyers abroad, poor government connections may very well put your company at a great disadvantage in negotiations, and unfavorable exchange rates can make it difficult or even impossible to offer products at competitive prices and still make a profit. In some countries, the government may not allow a company to enter its market unless it is willing to reveal the specifics of its core technologies, which are often the bedrock of its competitive advantage.[38] Nobody said it would be easy.

Nonetheless, small companies are proving that export success is within reach. For example, a recent study revealed that the value of goods shipped to China alone (a challenging market to crack) by small and medium-sized American manufacturers increased by 281 percent to $9.3 billion over a five-year span of time, and 49 percent of these exporters had fewer than 20 employees.[39] What's the secret? These companies did their homework and figured out what products would sell (for example, what products local companies could not yet make for themselves), got close to the market and developed personal connections with influential decision makers, and got assistance wherever they could find it. A good place to start in your search for customers abroad is the U.S. Department of Commerce's Commercial Service website (http://export.gov). Or, get in touch with the foreign embassy community (http://embassy.org), select a country where you want to do business, and e-mail the country specialist for assistance. You may be surprised at the leads this can generate. Finally, you can check with officials from your state to see if they provide assistance; many do. An Internet search on "[insert name of your state here] foreign trade office" should lead you where you need to go.

Importing

importing
Selling goods produced in another country to buyers in the home country.

The flip side of exporting is *importing,* which involves selling goods from abroad in the firm's home market. When a small company finds a product overseas that has market potential at home or identifies a product that would sell at home but cannot find a domestic producer that can offer the product at a competitive price, an import strategy may be the best solution.

If you are traveling abroad and notice attractive products that are not available back home or are very inexpensively priced, you may have stumbled on an unexpected business opportunity. An alternative strategy is to link up with vendors at international trade shows, which can open the door to opportunity. This is exactly what Holly Pennington did with her venture, Compass Trading Co. Using imported products found at such shows, she sells fashion accessories through her eight shops located in central Texas. Because of the depth of its merchandise, the company can accommodate both classic styles that create a professional look and cutting-edge designs featured in current fashion magazines—and many styles in between. Best of all, its products sell for a fraction of the prices charged for similar goods at high-end retailers. And customers like what they are getting—so much so that this small company has been opening a new store each year.[40]

Regardless of the import strategy used, the most important factor for success is finding a good product vendor. This sounds easy enough to do, especially in this era of Internet-enabled matching services, online communication tools (from e-mail to videoconferencing), and flexible and affordable travel. But finding and managing international suppliers can be difficult. Thad Hooker learned this the hard way in 2001 when he and his wife, Lisa, bought a high-end furniture store in Fort Lauderdale, Florida, called Spirit of Asia. Their experiences were similar to those of many small company owners who choose to work with international suppliers to build a business. "I decided to source from Southeast Asia, but I had to find out everything myself," Hooker says. "It felt like a crapshoot."

Before venturing abroad, Hooker studied his options thoroughly, comparing possible sourcing countries. Then he did some on-the-ground research, visiting the country he targeted and looking for clues that would lead him to the best sourcing partners available. Of course, a lucky break or two also helped. "On [his] initial trip to Chiang Mai, a city in northern Thailand, Hooker caught a ride with a local taxi driver who was interested in art and antiques. Hooker signed the man up, gave him a digital camera, and now employs the former driver as a furniture scout on the ground."[41]

Today the shop in Fort Lauderdale is profitable, and the Hookers are thinking about opening new locations to leverage their overseas sourcing power. In fact, the couple recently has gone national by launching a website that will allow them to sell furniture and accessories across the United States.[42]

LIVING THE DREAM:

entrepreneurial challenges

Importing Products Can Get Downright Dirty

Steven Friedman may have hit pay dirt—literally! He is the founder of Holy Land Earth, which imports 16-ounce bags of soil from Israel for use at groundbreakings, burials, and other ceremonial events. The company's website explains the unique appeal of its product:

> Throughout history, the Holy Land of Israel has been held in reverence by many of the world's religions. Indeed, to most people, the very ground on which the nation is built is deemed holy. And for the first time in recorded history, Holy Land Earth brings a small piece of Israel directly to you.

Somewhat the same as verifying that a food product is Kosher, each parcel of Holy Land Earth is certified to be genuine by Rabbi Velvel Brevda, the director of the Council of Geula, a neighborhood in the center of Jerusalem. He oversees soil collection and processing so that Holy Land Earth's customers can be assured that the product they receive is genuine.

At $39.95 per bag (and free shipping on orders over $100), the price may seem dirt cheap to most interested buyers, but that doesn't mean that the company has not had obstacles to overcome. When Friedman first came up with the idea for his business, his research revealed that others had considered the concept but took a pass. But why? Friedman learned that import operations can be very difficult to set up, especially if they involve organic matter. The problem is that soil products cannot be imported without the permission of the U.S. Department of Agriculture, which requires getting them treated, tested, and formally approved. The new venture would have to bear these costs on top of normal business expenses—obtaining soil, shipping it, packaging it, storing it, marketing it, and delivering it to buyers. These demands had discouraged other entrepreneurs, but Friedman worked with scientists to come up with a soil-cleaning process that satisfies U.S. import regulations, giving his startup a competitive advantage if others should try to enter the same market space.

So now Holy Land Earth is up and running, and Friedman is considering ways to expand the market and potential of his young company. For example, he is thinking about marketing his soil product to Christian Evangelicals, and his website suggests a number of other applications, which include using the soil to feed potted plants, to promote good luck, or even to save as a keepsake. The future looks promising, but for now Friedman can take pleasure in knowing that his import operation is finally off the ground . . . in more ways than one.

Sources: "About Holy Land Earth," http://www.holylandearth.com/about.asp, accessed March 5, 2009; Norm Brodsky, "You Do What?" *Inc. Magazine*, Vol. 30, No. 2 (February 2008), pp. 59–60; and "10 Minutes With . . . Steven Friedman," Religion News Service, May 23, 2007, http://www.religionnews.com/index.php?/tenminutes/10_minutes_with_steven_friedman/, accessed March 5, 2009.

http://www.holylandearth.com

© Holy Land Earth LLC/Steven Friedman

It's worth repeating that global sourcing presents its share of hassles, so don't expect this to be an easy option. However, it holds tremendous potential, especially if you follow a few simple guidelines:

- Learn as much as you can about the culture and business practices of the country from which you will be sourcing to avoid making deal-breaking mistakes.
- Do your research and be sure to select a source that is not a competitor or a company that hopes to learn from your operations so as to compete against you in the future.

- Protect your intellectual property so that your suppliers cannot easily take it from you. Some entrepreneurs require their sourcing partners to sign nondisclosure agreements so that they cannot patent the item in the country where the sourcing takes place.

- Don't rush the process of forming a relationship with a sourcing partner. You need time to ask difficult questions about important factors such as quality standards and capabilities, manufacturing flexibility, and time to order fulfillment.

- Work out transportation logistics ahead of time. A good freight forwarder can assist you with the mechanics of shipping, as well as help you with the confusing jumble of required documents. To get a sense of the process, review the rules and regulations on the U.S. Customs and Border Protection website at http://cbp.gov and read the SBA notes on importing at http://www.smallbusinessnotes.com/international/importing.html.

At times, the process may seem so complicated that you may wonder if small companies should even be attempting to source from abroad, but take heart—*others have done it, and so can you!*

Foreign Licensing

Importing and exporting are the most popular international strategies among small firms,[43] but there are also other options. Because of limited resources, many small firms are hesitant to go global. One way to deal with this constraint is to follow a licensing strategy. *Foreign licensing* allows a company in another country to purchase the rights to manufacture and sell a firm's products in overseas markets. The firm buying these rights is called the *licensee.* The licensee makes payments to the *licensor,* or the firm selling those rights, normally in the form of *royalties,* which is a fee paid for each unit produced.

International licensing has its drawbacks. The licensee makes all the production and marketing decisions, and the licensor must share returns from sales with the licensee. However, foreign licensing is the least expensive way to go global, since the licensee bears all the costs and risks related to setting up a foreign operation.[44]

Recall that IT Retail (described on page 471) uses a foreign licensing strategy, and it has sold more than 44,000 licenses in 20 countries around the globe. The small company could never have achieved such rapid expansion if it had to set up its own offices abroad, learn the culture and tax laws, and establish a market position in each country in which it did business. Licensing agreements with major computer hardware manufacturers covering the markets in regions such as South and Central American have paid off. IT Retail may not have a marketing team, a direct sales staff, or even venture capital, but the company makes money every time a licensee sells its product to a foreign retailer.[45] This is the beauty of foreign licensing.

Small companies tend to think of products when they explore international licensing options, but licensing intangible assets such as proprietary technologies, copyrights, and trademarks may offer even greater potential returns. Just as Disney licenses its famous Mickey Mouse character to manufacturers around the world, a small retailer called Peace Frogs has used licensing to introduce its copyrighted designs in Spain. As Peace Frogs' founder and president, Catesby Jones, explains, "We export our Peace Frogs T-shirts directly to Japan, but in Spain per capita income is lower, competition from domestic producers is stronger, and tariffs are high, so we licensed a Barcelona-based company the rights to manufacture our product."[46] From this agreement, Peace Frogs has been able to generate additional revenue with almost no added expense.

Foreign licensing can also be used to protect against *counterfeit activity,* or the unauthorized use of intellectual property. Licensing rights to a firm in a foreign market

foreign licensing
Allowing a company in another country to purchase the rights to manufacture and sell a company's products in international markets.

licensee
The company buying licensing rights.

licensor
The company selling licensing rights.

royalties
Fees paid by the licensee to the licensor for each unit produced under a licensing contract.

counterfeit activity
The unauthorized use of intellectual property.

provides a local champion, which can help to ensure that other firms do not use protected assets in an inappropriate way.

International Franchising

International franchising is a variation on the licensing theme. As outlined in Chapter 4, the franchisor offers a standard package of products, systems, and management services to the franchisee, which provides capital, market insight, and hands-on management. Though international franchising was not widely used before the 1970s, today it is the fastest growing market-entry strategy of U.S. firms, with Canada as the dominant market (followed by Japan and the United Kingdom, in that order). This approach is especially popular with U.S. restaurant chains that want to establish a global presence. McDonald's, for example, has raised its famous golden arches in more than 121 countries around the world. But international franchising is useful to small companies as well.

Danny Benususan is the owner of Blue Note, a premier jazz club in Manhattan that opened its doors in 1981. Considered one of the top venues in the world for jazz and other forms of music, this club has attracted the attention of international businesspeople who have established franchises abroad. The Tokyo location was opened in 1988, followed by clubs in Osaka, Fukuoka, and Nagoya, Japan. The first European club, in Milan, Italy, was added to the Blue Note family in March of 2003. As a result of these international extensions, the club has successfully established itself as the world's only franchised or licensed jazz club network.[47] Blue Note has proved that there is more than one way for a small business to globalize.

international franchising
Selling a standard package of products, systems, and management services to a company in another country.

International Strategic Alliances

Moving beyond licensing and franchising, some small businesses have expanded globally by joining forces with large corporations in cooperative efforts. An *international strategic alliance* allows firms to share risks and pool resources as they enter a new market, matching the local partner's understanding of the target market (culture, legal system, competitive conditions, etc.) with the technology or product knowledge of its alliance counterpart. One of the advantages of this strategy is that both partners take comfort in knowing that neither is "going it alone."[48]

There are many different ways in which strategic alliances can be used by small companies to gain advantage internationally. Tony Raimondo is CEO of Behlen Mfg. Co., a Columbus, Nebraska–based maker of agricultural grain bins, drying systems, and metal-frame buildings. At one time, the company exported products to China, but Raimondo suspended shipments when he found out that Chinese copycats were making the same products, using local advantages such as cheaper labor to undercut Behlen on cost and sell at much lower prices. For a time, it looked as if the company would no longer be able to tap into this huge market, the largest on earth! But then Raimondo hit on the idea of forming a 50/50 joint venture (a form of alliance in which two companies share equal ownership in a separate business) in Beijing. "In order for us to sustain market share," says Raimondo, "we had to be on the inside." Making product within China made it possible for Behlen to capitalize on the same advantages that Chinese factories had, and that has made all the difference. Behlen's success in China has spread to other international business initiatives. The company now does about 10 percent of its business overseas.[49]

international strategic alliance
A combination of efforts and/or assets of companies in different countries for the sake of pooling resources and sharing the risks of an enterprise.

Locating Facilities Abroad

A small business with advanced global aspirations may choose to establish a foreign presence of its own in strategic markets, especially if the firm has already developed an international customer base. Most small companies start by locating a production facility or sales office overseas, often as a way to reduce the cost of operations. Amanda Knauer, 28, wanted to start a business, but she concluded that launching a new venture in the United States was too expensive. On the advice of a friend, she set her sights on Argentina. After doing some research, she went to Buenos Aires in late 2004. A few months later, she was running her own business, Qara Argentina, a luxury leather goods manufacturer. "I came to Argentina looking for my opportunity," she says. "The beauty of the leather inspired me, and I saw it as an entryway into this world [of business ownership]." It hasn't been easy. Knauer has had to pick up the local Spanish dialect and learn about a new set of laws and business practices, but the work is paying off—and fast! The company had more than $1 million in sales before the end of its first year in business.[50]

Opening an overseas sales office can be a very effective strategy, but small business owners should wait until sales in the local market are great enough to justify the move. An overseas office is costly to establish, staff, manage, and finance; thus, this alternative is beyond the reach of most small companies. Furthermore, the anticipated advantages of overseas offices are sometimes difficult to achieve. Often U.S. firms locate their first international sales office in Canada, but some small companies are finding it profitable to open an office that provides access to the European region (the English-speaking United Kingdom and Ireland are popular locations). Still others have selected Asia, because of its economic dynamism and fast-growing consumer demand.

cross-border acquisition
The purchase by a business in one country of a company located in another country.

greenfield venture
A wholly owned subsidiary formed from scratch in another country.

Some small firms have grand ambitions that go beyond locating a production facility or sales office overseas. For example, they may purchase a foreign business from another firm through what is known as a *cross-border acquisition,* or even start a *greenfield venture* by forming from scratch a new wholly owned subsidiary in another country. Either option is likely to be fraught with difficulties.

Emerald Packaging, Inc., which offers flexible packaging services for food products, is run by Kevin Kelly, whose family has owned the company for many years. Interested in expansion, Kelly attempted to put together two acquisition deals only to see them fall through. Ready to try again, he looked over the terms of yet another contract—a factory in Tijuana, Mexico. The facility had the right equipment and was being offered at a fair price, but international acquisitions can be tricky (especially in Mexico), and it wasn't long before Kelly learned the deal was in trouble. Machines in disrepair, sagging sales, and potential liability for the company's difficult-to-verify debts all raised red flags. And the fact that the seller was now requesting far more money than Kelly was willing to pay didn't help. Kelly describes his experience with the owner of the factory as follows:

> Both of us had our confidence rattled by small surprises. During the late summer the [factory owner] decided, without notifying us, to stop taking new orders—essentially announcing to customers that he was closing his doors. I had counted on his $5 million in annual sales to help make the deal work. On my side, I was so distracted by the day-to-day demands of running my family's business that I often went weeks without talks with him. Those communication issues doomed the deal.[51]

Entrepreneurs often find that foreign acquisitions are extremely difficult to pull off. An international acquisition program can be important to a small company's growth plan, but given the number of ways a good deal can run aground, it certainly calls for an extra dose of caution and care in the handling.

Go-it-alone strategies are complex and costly. They offer maximum control over foreign operations and eliminate the need to share generated revenues, but they also force companies to bear the entire risk of the undertaking. If the new subsidiary is a greenfield venture, the firm may have much to learn about running an enterprise in a foreign country, managing host-country nationals, and developing an effective marketing strategy. The commercial potential of a wholly owned international subsidiary may be great, but the hassles of managing it can be even greater. This option is not for the faint of heart.

Challenges to Global Businesses

4. Explain the challenges that global enterprises face.

Small businesses face challenges; *global* small businesses face far greater challenges. How well can a small firm do in the global marketplace? The success of enterprising entrepreneurs in international markets proves that small firms can do better than survive—they can thrive! However, success requires careful preparation. Small business owners must recognize the unique complications facing global firms and adjust their plans accordingly. Specifically, they need to pay attention to political risks, economic risks, and managerial limitations.

Political Risk

The potential for a country's political forces to negatively affect the performance of business enterprises operating within its borders is referred to as *political risk.* Often, this risk is related to the instability of a nation's government, which can create difficulties for outside companies. Potential problems range from threats as trivial as new regulations restricting the content of television advertising to risks of a government takeover of private assets. Political developments can threaten access to an export market, require a firm to reveal trade secrets, or even demand that work be completed in-country. Exhibit 18-5 highlights variations in political risk across nations, based on the "Country Risk Rankings" published in *Euromoney* magazine. Countries are color-coded to indicate their riskiness—green represents "go," or safe, countries; yellow, "proceed with caution" countries; and red, "stop and think very carefully" countries. Firms hoping to do business in "red" countries should make appropriate adjustments.

political risk
The potential for political forces in a country to negatively affect the performance of businesses operating within its borders.

18-5 Country Risk Rankings Map

EXHIBIT

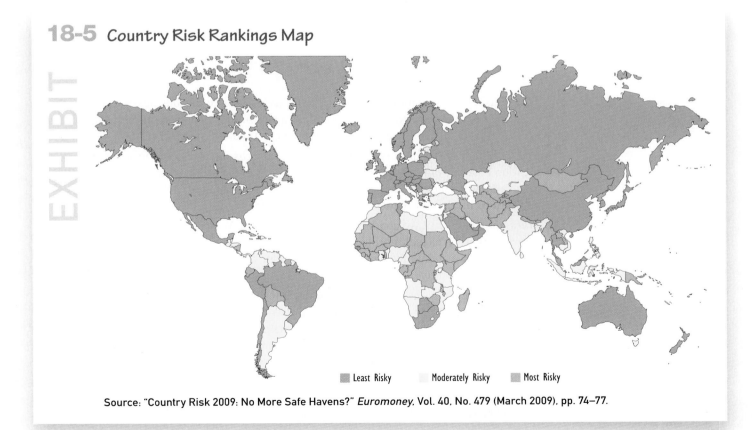

Least Risky   Moderately Risky   Most Risky

Source: "Country Risk 2009: No More Safe Havens?" *Euromoney*, Vol. 40, No. 479 (March 2009), pp. 74–77.

Economic Risk

economic risk
The probability that a government will mismanage its economy in ways that hinder the performance of firms operating there.

Economic risk is the probability that a government will mismanage its economy and affect the business environment in ways that hinder the performance of firms operating there. Economic risk and political risk are therefore related.[52] Two of the most serious problems resulting from economic mismanagement are inflation and fluctuations in exchange rates. While a discussion of these factors is beyond the scope of this book, it is important to recognize that inflation reduces the value of a country's currency on the foreign exchange market, thereby decreasing the value of cash flows that the foreign firm receives from its operations in the local market.

exchange rate
The value of one country's currency relative to that of another country.

Exchange rates represent the value of one country's currency relative to that of another country—for example, the number of Mexican pesos that can be purchased with one U.S. dollar. Sudden or unexpected changes in these rates can be a serious problem for small international businesses, whether they export to that market or have a local presence there.

Mary Ellen Mooney of California-based Mooney Farms kept an eye on the European market, as well as that of Mexico. She recognized the potential of exporting her sun-dried tomato products to France and came close to striking a deal with a local distributor a few years ago, but the negotiations fell through when the value of the dollar rose sharply relative to European currencies.[53] To understand her dilemma, suppose the French distributor was willing to pay 5 euros for a package of sun-dried tomatoes. If the dollar and the euro were exchanged one to one, Mooney could convert the 5 euros to $5.00. If $4.50 covered costs of production, transportation, insurance, and so on, then Mooney would earn a $.50 profit ($5.00 − $4.50) per unit. But when the dollar *increased* in value relative to the local currency, the situation changed drastically. Assume the exchange rate changed to $0.80 per euro. Then units selling for 5 euros would yield only $4.00 each (5 × $0.80), which would result in a $0.50 loss on every sale.

Mooney's experience illustrates how a good deal can quickly fall apart if exchange rates take a turn for the worse. This risk is especially serious for small companies that are just getting established in international markets. To protect against exchange rate shifts, such firms should take measures such as stating contracts in U.S. dollars or using other financial strategies that minimize this risk.

Managerial Limitations

Conducting business internationally will never be as easy as doing business at home—it is likely to stretch managerial skills and resources to the limit. Global commerce complicates every task and raises difficult questions related to every function of the firm.

- *Product Planning.* Will the product/service satisfy customer tastes? Does the foreign location have the employees we need to manufacture the products we plan to offer? Do available workers have the skills required for our operations? Will government restrictions hinder our planned product introductions?

- *Marketing.* How will we conduct marketing research? Who should be included in the target market? What sales projections are reasonable in the international market? What price should we charge for our product? How can we deal with counterfeit products manufactured locally?

- *Finance.* Can we maintain cash flow for our international operations? How will we manage currency exchange rate fluctuations? Will government policy impact capital transfers? Will local law allow us to send home profits from the foreign market? Does the host country government maintain sufficient foreign currency reserves to allow us to take profits out of the country? Will barter or other forms of countertrade be necessary to do business?

- *Management.* Will the management approaches used at home work in the international setting? How can we identify the people best suited for overseas positions with our company? How much should we pay our local employees? How should we work with labor unions in foreign locations? How can we overcome language, culture, and communication barriers? Can we develop a trusting relationship with foreign employees? What should we do when ethical standards are different in the host nation? Given that the Foreign Corrupt Practices Act prohibits U.S. firms from engaging in corrupt behaviors, how can we compete when our foreign rivals offer bribes to obtain preferential treatment?

- *Accounting.* What will it take to integrate accounting systems across global operations? How do we account for currency conversions that are continually changing? Can we harmonize accounting rules that vary from country to country? Does our accounting system capture the information necessary for international trading?

- *Legal Issues.* What are the IRS reporting requirements for international firms? How can we be sure that we are paying appropriate taxes in the home and host environments? What is required to comply with local government regulations? Will host country trade restrictions, including tariffs and nontariff barriers, hinder our export program? Do we have patent protections to shield our key technologies?

As you can see, international business decisions are complicated, which explains why many small firm owners choose to focus solely on their home market. However, the motivations to go global are sound, and others have already proved that it can be done. You can do it too, if you plan carefully and take advantage of the resources available to help you achieve your global aspirations.

Assistance for Global Enterprises

Help is available to small companies with international interests—you need only open your eyes to find it. Once you decide to enter the global marketplace, you will be amazed at how many resources there are to help you.

5. Recognize the sources of assistance available to support international business efforts.

Analyzing Markets and Planning Strategy

Among the many activities required to prepare a small firm for the challenges of going global, two are especially fundamental to success abroad: finding international markets that fit the company's unique potentials and putting together a game plan for entry into the markets targeted.

A small business should begin its research of foreign markets and entry strategy options by exhausting secondary sources of information. The U.S. government offers a number of publications on how to identify and tap into global market opportunities. The Small Business Administration stands ready to help small companies expand abroad. The international programs and services of the SBA are delivered through U.S. Export Assistance Centers (USEACs).

One excellent source of information about global business for small companies is *Breaking into the Trade Game: A Small Business Guide to Exporting.* This SBA publication, which is available online, provides an overview of export strategy that is useful for new and experienced exporters. The nuts-and-bolts handbook is designed to guide small firms through the complexities of going global, with chapters focused specifically on identifying markets, choosing an entry strategy, managing transactions, financing trade, arranging transportation, and forming strategic alliances.

Though not focused on small businesses alone, a website maintained by the International Trade Administration of the U.S. Department of Commerce (http://trade.gov) supplies helpful insights about international expansion. Publications such as *World Trade* magazine (http://www.worldtrademag.com) can also be useful, providing timely, in-depth analyses of world trade markets and business issues. Beyond these resources, state and private organizations are excellent sources of trade information, trade leads, and company databases. One such source, TradePort (http://www.tradeport.org), offers information online to promote international trade with California-based companies.

Talking with someone who has lived in or even just visited a potential foreign market can be a valuable way to learn about it. For example, conversations with international students at a local university can be very helpful. However, the best way to study a foreign market is to visit the country personally. A representative of a small firm can do this either as an individual or as a member of a group that is organized for the purpose of exploring new international business possibilities.

Connecting with International Customers

A small company cannot sell abroad unless it connects with customers in targeted international markets. But numerous resources are available to help you connect.

TRADE LEADS   Trade leads are essential in identifying potential customers in target markets. Accessed most often via the Internet, they offer an inexpensive way to establish vital links with buyers and suppliers in target markets. One good online source of trade leads is provided by the Center for International Business Education and Research at Michigan State University at http://globaledge.msu.edu/resourcedesk/_tradeLeads.asp. This website offers a wealth of international business resources, including leads that can direct a company to valuable partners in most of the world's markets. The website of the Federation of International Trade Associations (http://www.fita.org) will also help you to identify trade leads; in addition, it provides news, announced events, and links to over 8,000 trade-related websites.

TRADE MISSIONS   Joining a trade mission is another excellent way to evaluate a foreign market and link up with overseas customers. A *trade mission* is a planned visit to a potential international market, designed to introduce U.S. firms to prospective foreign buyers and to establish strategic alliances. These missions usually involve groups of 5 to 10 business executives and are set up to promote international sales. Members of the group typically pay their own expenses and share in the operating costs of the mission. Foreign governments sometimes sponsor trade missions in order to promote business links with U.S. firms.

TRADE INTERMEDIARIES   Perhaps the easiest way to break into international markets is to use a *trade intermediary,* which is an agency that distributes products to international customers on a contract basis. These agencies tap their established web of contacts, as well as their local cultural and market expertise. In short, an intermediary can manage the entire export end of a business, taking care of everything except filling the orders—and the results can be outstanding. American Cedar, Inc., located in Hot Springs, Arkansas, is a producer of cedar wood products. With the assistance of a trade intermediary, American Cedar generated 30 percent of its sales from exporting. Company president Julian McKinney reports, "We displayed our products at a trade show, and an export management company found us. They helped alleviate the hassles of exporting directly. Our products are now being distributed throughout the European Community from a distribution point in France."[54] An export management company is only one of the many types of trade intermediaries. Exhibit 18-6 describes the trade intermediaries that can best provide the assistance small businesses need.

Financing

Arranging financing is perhaps the biggest barrier to international expansion. The more information small firms have about direct and indirect sources of financing, the more favorably they

---

trade mission
A trip organized to help small business owners meet with potential buyers abroad and learn about doing business there.

trade intermediary
An agency that distributes a company's products on a contract basis to customers in another country.

Confirming Houses	If a foreign firm is interested in purchasing U.S. products, it may retain the services of a confirming house (sometimes called a *buying agent*). These finders "shop" for the lowest possible price for items requested and are paid a commission for their services. In some cases, foreign government agencies or quasi-governmental firms may serve this purpose.
Export Management Companies	An export management company (EMC) acts as the export department for one or several producers of goods or services. It solicits and transacts business in the names of the producers it represents or in its own name, in exchange for a commission, salary, or retainer plus commission. Some EMCs provide immediate payment for the producer's products by either arranging financing or directly purchasing products for resale. The best EMCs know their products and the markets they serve very well and usually have well-established networks of foreign distributors already in place. This immediate access to foreign markets is one of the principal reasons for using an EMC.
Export Trading Companies	An export trading company (ETC) facilitates the export of U.S. goods and services. Like an EMC, this type of intermediary can either act as the export department for producers or take title to the product and export for its own account. Some ETCs are set up and operated by producers. These can be organized along multiple- or single-industry lines and can also represent producers of competing products.
Export Agents, Merchants, or Remarketers	Export agents, merchants, or remarketers purchase products directly from the manufacturer, packing and marking the products according to their own specifications. They then sell these products overseas in their own names through their contacts and assume all risks for accounts. In transactions with these intermediaries, a firm gives up control over the marketing and promotion of its product. This can hinder future sales abroad if the product is underpriced or incorrectly positioned in the market or if after-sales service is neglected.
Piggyback Marketers	Piggyback marketers are manufacturers or service firms that distribute a second firm's product or service. This is commonly seen when a U.S. company has a contract with an overseas buyer to provide a wide range of products or services.

Source: U.S. Department of Commerce, *A Basic Guide to Exporting* (Washington, DC: Department of Commerce and Unz & Co., Inc.), http://www.unzco.com/basicguide/c4.html#indirect, accessed March 12, 2009.

tend to view foreign markets. Sources of this information include private banks and the Small Business Administration.

PRIVATE BANKS Commercial banks typically have a loan officer who is responsible for handling foreign transactions. Large banks may have an entire international department. Exporters use banks to issue commercial letters of credit and to perform other financial activities associated with exporting.

A *letter of credit* is an agreement to honor a draft or other demand for payment when specified conditions are met. It helps to assure a seller of prompt payment. A letter of credit may

letter of credit
An agreement issued by a bank to honor a draft or other demand for payment when specified conditions are met.

be revocable or irrevocable. An irrevocable letter of credit cannot be changed unless both the buyer and the seller agree to the change. The process of establishing a letter of credit is quite involved and can be very confusing; however, banks and other financial institutions that offer this service will have expert staff who can explain how these documents work and will walk you through the process.

A guarantee from a reputable bank that the exporter will indeed be paid is critical to a small business that has stretched its resources to the limit just to enter the global game and thus cannot afford an uncollected payment. But what if the small business is on the import end of the exchange? How will its interests be protected? The letter of credit provides security for the receiving firm as well, because the exporter does not receive payment from the bank until it has released the title, or proof of ownership, of the delivered goods. Once the product has been shipped and the title transferred, the exporter receives a document called a *bill of lading* to confirm this. This document must be received before the bank will pay on the letter of credit. In brief, the letter of credit ensures that the exporter will receive payment only when the goods are delivered in-country, and it also guarantees that the exporter will be paid.

bill of lading
A document indicating that a product has been shipped and the title to that product has been transferred.

SMALL BUSINESS ADMINISTRATION The Small Business Administration (SBA) serves small U.S. firms primarily through its regional, district, and branch offices. Small businesses that are either already exporting or interested in doing so can receive valuable information from the SBA through conferences and seminars, instructional publications, and export counseling. An extended list of the financial assistance programs offered by the SBA to small firms is posted on the agency's website at http://www.sba.gov/services/financialassistance/index.html.

It is clear that a growing number of small firms are choosing to participate in international business. The reasons for this expansion include both time-honored motivations and those emerging in the new competitive landscape. To achieve their global aspirations, most small businesses follow an export strategy; however, this is not the only alternative. Small companies can also implement international strategies that involve licensing, franchising, developing strategic alliances, or establishing a presence in foreign markets. In any case, firms that enter the global arena are certain to run up against serious challenges that purely domestic firms do not have to face. This is the nature of the terrain, but assistance is available in abundance from a number of private and public agencies. With a little help and a lot of hard work, your company can succeed in the global marketplace.

LOOKING BACK

1. Describe the potential of small firms as global enterprises.

- Recent startups and even the smallest of businesses are internationalizing at an increasing rate.
- Small companies called born-global firms are increasingly being launched with cross-border business activities in mind.

- Before going global, it is important for a small business owner to determine whether her or his company is up to the task.
- Small business owners who decide to go global must study the political, cultural, and economic forces in the foreign markets to figure out how best to adapt products and ensure smooth entry.

2. Identify the basic forces prompting small firms to engage in global expansion.

- The basic forces behind global expansion are expanding markets, gaining access to resources, cutting costs, and capitalizing on special location features.

- Since more than 95 percent of the world's population lives outside the United States, globalization greatly expands the size of a firm's potential market.

- The fast-growing markets of the BRIC countries (Brazil, Russia, India, and China) are attracting small firms that wish to tap their enormous market potential.

- Small businesses with a highly differentiated product may need an international market in order to increase sales enough to recover product development costs.

- Going global can accelerate gains from experience curve efficiencies (resulting from learning effects and economies of scale), especially for startups based on complex technologies.

- Sometimes small businesses go global to gain access to resources, including raw materials and skilled labor.

- Another reason small firms enter foreign markets is to cut their costs in such areas as labor, transportation, or tariffs.

- Small businesses may want to capitalize on special features of an international location: exploiting the unique features of a local environment, taking advantage of favorable government policies, establishing a presence within an emerging trade area, or following a large client firm.

3. Understand and compare strategy options for global businesses.

- Exporting, an international strategy commonly used by small firms, can be facilitated by using the Internet to increase firms' international visibility.

- Importing involves selling goods from abroad in the home market; it should be used when products manufactured abroad have market potential at home.

- Non-export strategies include foreign licensing, international franchising, international strategic alliances, and locating facilities abroad.

- Although they can be more complex than export strategies, some non-export strategies (especially licensing) are actually the safest options for the small global business.

4. Explain the challenges that global enterprises face.

- Political risk is the potential for a country's political forces to negatively affect the performance of small businesses operating there. Political risk varies greatly across nations.

- Economic risk is the probability that a government will mismanage its economy and affect the business environment in ways that hinder the performance of firms operating there (most notably through inflation and fluctuations in exchange rates).

- Globalization raises numerous concerns related to every function of the firm, thus stretching managerial skills and resources to the limit.

5. Recognize the sources of assistance available to support international business efforts.

- Numerous public and private organizations provide assistance to small businesses in analyzing markets and planning a strategy.

- Small businesses can connect with international customers by reviewing sources of trade leads, joining trade missions, or using the services of trade intermediaries.

- For assistance in financing its entry into a foreign market, a small firm can turn to private banks (which can issue letters of credit) and programs initiated by the Small Business Administration.

Key Terms

globalization p. 465
born-global firms p. 466
experience curve efficiencies p. 472
learning effects p. 472
economies of scale p. 472
international outsourcing p. 472
offshoring p. 472
exporting p. 476
importing p. 478

foreign licensing p. 480
licensee p. 480
licensor p. 480
royalties p. 480
counterfeit activity p. 480
international franchising p. 481
international strategic alliance p. 481
cross-border acquisition p. 482
greenfield venture p. 482

political risk p. 483
economic risk p. 484
exchange rate p. 484
trade mission p. 486
trade intermediary p. 486
letter of credit p. 487
bill of lading p. 488

Discussion Questions

1. What is a "born-global" enterprise? What factors are encouraging the increase in the number of these companies?

2. Discuss the importance of a careful cultural analysis to a small firm that wishes to enter an international market.

3. Do you believe that small companies should engage in international business? Why or why not?

4. Identify the four basic forces driving small businesses to enter the global business arena. Which do you think is the most influential in the globalization of small firms?

5. Give examples of some emerging motivations persuading small business owners to go global. Are any of these motivations likely to remain powerful forces 10 years from now? Twenty years from now?

6. Why is exporting such a popular global strategy among small businesses? Do you think this should be the case?

7. What impact has the Internet had on the globalization of small firms? How do you think small companies will use the Internet for business in the future?

8. What non-export strategies can small businesses adopt? In view of the unique needs and capabilities of small firms, what are the advantages and disadvantages of each of these strategies?

9. What are the three main challenges small businesses face when they go global? What strategies can a small company use to deal with each of these challenges?

10. What forms of assistance are available to small global firms? Which is likely to be of greatest benefit to small companies? Why?

You Make the Call

SITUATION 1

Luis Aburto recognized the advantages of outsourcing development work when he decided to start Scio Consulting International LLC, an information technology company. But he still has a question: Where in the world (literally) should he go for the talent he needs? He has considered linking up with a service provider in Bangalore, India, because the wages are very low, the pool of well-trained employees is deep, and technical skills are strongly emphasized in the university system. But India is a long way from the company's home office in San Jose, California, which means greater travel costs and dealing with the hassle of working between times zones that are nearly opposite one another. Also, the cultural gap would be significant, even though most educated workers in India speak English.

Aburto has also been in touch with an operation in Morelia, Mexico. His contacts there tell him that the skilled workers he needs are available, the cultural gap is limited, turnover is very low, and technical staff will not need special visas to travel between Mexico and project sites in the United States. However, wages are significantly higher than in Bangalore, university graduates in Mexico receive little practical training, and the law makes it very difficult to fire staff once you hire them.

The clock is ticking. Aburto needs to line up employees for three big contracts he is currently negotiating, and his potential clients all want to get their projects started within a month or so of a final decision. If he even gets two of the three deals to pan out, he will have much more work than his staff in the United States can handle. He will need additional employees—he's just not certain where to go for outsourcing support.

Sources: Adapted from Gail Dutton, "Outsource Closer to Home," *Entrepreneur*, Vol. 36, No. 10 (October 2008), p. 22; and Philip J. Fersht, "Claims of Death Greatly Exaggerated," Forbes.com, March 5, 2008, http://www.forbes.com/2008/03/05/mitra-india-outsourcing-tech-enter-cx_pf_0305outsource_print.html, accessed March 12, 2009.

Question 1 What additional information would be helpful to Aburto as he ponders this decision?

Question 2 What additional advantages and disadvantages can you think of that Aburto should consider when choosing between offshoring this work to India and "near-shoring" it to Mexico?

Question 3 Which location would you choose—India or Mexico? Be sure to build a strong case for your final decision.

SITUATION 2

Bill Moss and several other small business owners joined a trade mission to China to explore market opportunities there. The group learned that China has a population of 1.3 billion and is the third-fastest-growing export market for small and medium-sized U.S. firms. Average annual income for rural workers in China is approximately $690 per person; typical urban annual income is about $2,290, with an average of $3,962 a year in the more prosperous city of Shanghai and $3,822 in the capital, Beijing. In any given year, the Chinese software market grows by 30 percent and the number of Internet users quadruples. Furthermore, the demand for management consulting services is increasing, especially information technology consulting. Members of the group were surprised by the number of people who had cell phones and regularly surfed the Internet, especially in large urban centers. On the downside, they found that counterfeit goods (from clothing and leather goods to software and CDs) were readily available at a fraction of the cost of legitimate merchandise and that local merchants expressed an interest in doing business only with vendors with whom they had established relationships.

Sources: Data from BBC News, "China Rural-Urban Wage Gap Widens," January 16, 2009, http://news.bbc.co.uk/2/hi/asia-pacific/7833779.stm, accessed March 12, 2009; China Financial News Headlines, "China Disposable Income," November 9, 2008, http://www.cnguy.com/financial/news/2008/11/09/1312/china-disposable-income-shanghai-disposable-income-and-other-countries.html, accessed March 12, 2009; and "China Software Market Forecast to 2012," http://www.bharatbook.com/Market-Research-Reports/China-Software-Market-Forecast-to-2012.html, accessed March 12, 2009.

Question 1 What types of businesses would prosper in China? Why?

Question 2 What are the challenges and risks associated with doing business in China?

Question 3 What steps should Moss take to address these challenges and risks in order to increase his chance of success in the market?

SITUATION 3

Dr. Juldiz Afgazar, a native of the Republic of Kazakhstan, had been invited to spend a semester in the United States as a visiting scholar in entrepreneurial finance. Kazakhstan gained its independence from the former Soviet Union in 1991, and only after that were laws passed allowing citizens to own private businesses. Dr. Afgazar wanted to learn more about the free market economy of the United States to determine whether such a system could be implemented in Kazakhstan.

Prior to this visit to the United States, Dr. Afgazar had not traveled extensively outside her country. Although she enjoyed many aspects of U.S. culture, she was particularly impressed by the seemingly unlimited quantity and variety of goods and foods that were readily available. After a visit to a local restaurant's pizza buffet, she became an avid fan of American-style pizza! Dr. Afgazar found the crisp yeast crust, spicy tomato sauce, melted mozzarella cheese, and assortment of toppings to be a delicious combination. Pizza was an entirely new type of food for her, since it was not available in Kazakhstan. A true entrepreneur, Dr. Afgazar began to wonder if a pizza restaurant could be successful in her country.

Source: Developed by Elisabeth J. Teal of Northern Georgia College and State University, Dahlonega, Georgia, and Aigul N. Toxanova of Kokshetau Higher College of Management and Business, Kazakhstan.

Question 1 What obstacles would an entrepreneur have to overcome to establish a pizza restaurant in a country with a developing market-based economy, such as Kazakhstan?

Question 2 Is Dr. Afgazar's idea of developing a pizza restaurant in Kazakhstan ahead of its time? That is, do you think the economy of Kazakhstan is sufficiently developed to support a pizza restaurant?

Question 3 What methods could an entrepreneur use to evaluate the likelihood of success of a pizza restaurant in Kazakhstan?

Experiential Exercises

1. Conduct phone interviews with 10 local small business owners to see if they engage in international business. Discuss their reasons for going global or for choosing to do business only domestically.

2. Contact a local banker to discuss the bank's involvement with small firms participating in international business. Report your findings to the class.

3. Review recent issues of *Entrepreneur, Inc. Magazine,* and other small business publications, and be prepared to discuss articles related to international business.

4. Do a Web search to find an article about a small business that first expanded internationally using an entry strategy other than exporting. From what you understand of the company's situation, suggest guidelines that could lead a firm to go global with non-export strategies.

5. Consult secondary sources to develop a political/economic risk profile for a given country. Select a small company and explain what it would have to do to manage these risks if it were to enter the market of the country profiled.

6. Speak with the owner of a small international company. Which sources of assistance did that entrepreneur use when launching the global initiative? Which sources did the entrepreneur find most helpful? Which did the entrepreneur find least helpful?

Small Business & Entrepreneurship Resource Center

The Small Business and Entrepreneurship Resource Center offers complete small business management resources through a comprehensive database that covers all major areas of starting, operating, and maintaining a business from financing, management, marketing, accounting, taxes, and more. Use the access code that came with your new book to access the site and perform the exercises in each chapter.

1. One variation on the import theme is an international sourcing strategy, which is essentially an effort to connect with overseas suppliers that can provide the products or services a company needs to operate successfully. This sounds easy enough to do, especially in this era of Internet-enabled matching services, online communication tools (from email to videoconferencing), and flexible and affordable travel options. However, finding and managing international suppliers can be challenging. Thad Hooker learned this the hard way when he and his wife, Lisa, bought a Florida-based high-end furniture company called Spirit of Asia in 2001. After reading the article "On foreign soil," describe a few crucial keys to success when finding a supplier overseas.

2. In franchising, the franchisor offers a standard package of products, systems, and management services to the franchisee, which provides capital, market insight, and hands-on management. Though international franchising was not widely used before the 1970s, today it is the fastest-growing market entry strategy of U.S. firms. Describe the U.S. Commercial Services' Global Franchising Team's "Webinars" and how they might assist a domestic franchise to expand internationally. Also describe the U.S. Commercial Service and the major services they provide.

Sources: On foreign soil: arm yourself with the information and advice you need for sourcing your product overseas so your efforts don't get lost in translation. Joshua Kurlantzick. *Entrepreneur* 33, 6 (June 2005); p. 88(5).

U.S. Commercial Service offers tools to explore new franchise markets: a key ingredient to enable a franchise concept's international growth lies in a business ability to cultivate the right information. (fw focus: international development). Mona Musa. *Franchising World* 38, 7 (July 2006); p. 65(2).

Case 18

SMARTER.COM, (P. 662)

This case describes the experiences of an entrepreneur who has hired and must work with engineers and other staff for back-office operations in China that he has set up to support his Web-based business.

ALTERNATIVE CASES FOR CHAPTER 18

Case 12, My Own Money, p. 649

PART 5

Managing Growth in the Small Business

Professional Management in the Entrepreneurial Firm

In the VIDEO SPOTLIGHT
Goshow Architects
http://www.goshow.com

Creating a high-performance company takes leadership. When Nancy and Eric Goshow founded their architecture firm in their living room, they probably weren't thinking as much about leadership as about the survival of their enterprise. Over time, though, as their firm grew, they needed to consider how to build and lead a team capable of developing and managing the large projects required to sustain the company in the long run.

The key to building that team has been collaboration. Eric Goshow likens the process to creating a harmonious choir with a perfect blend of male and female voices. The Goshows look for people with different yet complementary strengths so that the company can go after a broad spectrum of work. And the formula has been successful. Not only has the firm been responsible for numerous residential projects, it has also worked on the renovations of U.S. post offices throughout New York City and has landed contracts with the Port Authority of New York, the U.S. Departments of Energy and Labor, and the New York City School Construction Authority.

Watch this video spotlight to see how the Goshows have shored up weaknesses, overcome constraints, and used solid planning to build their management team, develop their business, and ensure long-term success.

Video material provided by Hattie Bryant, Producer of Small Business School, the series on PBS Stations, Worldnet, and the Web at http://www.smallbusinessschool.org.

LOOKING AHEAD
AFTER STUDYING THIS CHAPTER, YOU SHOULD BE ABLE TO

1. Discuss the entrepreneur's leadership role.
2. Explain the distinctive features of small business management.
3. Identify the managerial tasks of entrepreneurs.
4. Describe the problem of time pressure and suggest solutions.
5. Explain the various types of outside management assistance.

In his play *The Tempest,* Shakespeare gave the now-famous line "What's past is prologue. . . ."[1] to a character named Antonio who is intent on persuading the brother of the king of Naples to murder his monarch sibling and take the crown for himself. Antonio is saying that what happened in the past has put his friend in the present-day position of being able to take a very bold step (and committing murder surely qualifies as a bold step!). When you think about it, the past is *always* prologue—it always sets the stage for what lies ahead, shaping the direction of that which follows.

In a similar way, a startup leaves its imprint on the established company it will later become—even though the two are very different. But a startup's needs are unique, so adjustments will be necessary sooner or later. Unless you plan to remain a tiny one-person business forever, leadership and management problems are sure to come your way. When that time arrives, you must find ways to integrate the efforts of employees and give new direction to the business. This is absolutely necessary if production employees, salespeople, support service staff, and other personnel are to work together effectively. Even long-established businesses need vigorous leadership if they are to avoid stagnation or failure. This chapter examines the leadership challenges facing entrepreneurs and the managerial activities required as firms mature and grow.

Entrepreneurial Leadership

1. Discuss the entrepreneur's leadership role.

Leadership roles differ greatly, depending on the size of the business and its stage of development. For example, an enterprise that is just getting started will face problems and uncertainties unlike those of a family firm that has been functioning well over several generations. We must begin, therefore, with the recognition that leadership cannot be reduced to simple rules or processes that fit all situations.

What Is Leadership?

The question is simple, but the answer is not. Here is the response of one business leader, Richard Barton, former president and CEO of Expedia, Inc., to the question "How do you define leadership?"

> Leadership to me means leaning forward, looking ahead, trying to improve, being fired up about what you're doing and being able to communicate that, verbally and nonverbally, to those around you.[2]

Briefly stated, leadership involves pointing the way and getting others to follow willingly. It is far more focused on the destination than on the details of getting there. An entrepreneur must convey his or her vision of the firm's future to all other participants in the business so that they can contribute most effectively to the accomplishment of the mission. Although leaders must also engage in many, more routine processes, particularly as the company grows, the first task of the entrepreneur is to create and communicate a vision for the company.

Leadership Qualities of Founders

The entrepreneur is the trailblazer who enlists others, both team members and outsiders, to work with him or her in a creative endeavor. Others may then buy into this vision for the venture as they join their efforts with those of the entrepreneur.

In a totally new venture, the leader faces major uncertainties and unknowns. Therefore, individuals who are launching promising startups, or startups having the prospect of attaining significant size or profitability, need to have certain qualities. One of the most important would be tolerance for ambiguity, that condition of foggy vagueness that is almost always present when launching a new business. But because of the uncertainty involved in starting a new business, entrepreneurs must also be adaptable, able to adjust to unforeseen problems and opportunities. One small business expert expressed this in poetic terms: "Anyone can be an entrepreneur, who wants to experience the deep, dark canyons of uncertainty and ambiguity, and . . . walk the breathtaking highlands of success."[3] Being able to tolerate and adjust to circumstances as they unfold are two basic qualities that can be useful in many business settings, but they are never more important than in the startup situation.

What Makes a Leader Effective?

Many people assume that a business leader must have a flashy, highly charismatic, "I'm-in-charge" personality to be effective, but this is not the norm and it is not required. In fact, charisma has little to do with it, and it's not so much about wanting to *be* in charge as it is having the ability to *take* charge and inspire others to follow your lead. This is exactly the point made by Judith Cone, vice president of emerging strategies at the Kauffman Foundation, where she leads new program opportunities to advance innovation and entrepreneurship:

> A leader is able to explain a vision in a compelling way that motivates people to follow or to become a part of that vision. [Leaders] are solid, smart, they have integrity, people respect them, and people want to follow them because of the [high] quality person they are.[4]

Leaders exhibit a resolve and a determination to do whatever is needed to lead their companies to success. It seems clear that effective leadership is based not on a larger-than-life personality but, instead, on a focus on reaching business goals.

In most small firms, leadership of the business is personalized. The owner-manager is not a faceless unknown, but an individual whom employees see and relate to in the course of their normal work schedules. This situation is entirely different from that of large corporations, where most employees never see the chief executive. If the employer-employee relationship is good, employees in small enterprises develop strong feelings of personal loyalty to their employer.

In a large corporation, the values of top-level executives must be filtered through many layers of management before they reach those who produce and sell the products. As a result, the influence of those at the top tends to be diluted by the process. In contrast, personnel in a small company receive the leader's messages directly. This face-to-face contact facilitates their understanding of the leader's vision as well as her or his stand on integrity, customer service, and other important issues. In the end, this infused sense of purpose, high standards, and achievement can actually create a competitive advantage for the small business over its corporate rivals.

Leadership Styles

Leaders use many different styles of leadership, and these styles may be described in various ways. Specific leadership styles may be better suited to certain situations, but most leaders choose from a variety of approaches as they deal with different issues. Daniel Goleman and his colleagues have described six distinct leadership styles. In their study of nearly 4,000 managers, they found that effective leaders shift fluidly and often between the first four styles listed below, and they make very limited but skillful use of the last two styles.[5]

1. *Visionary leaders* mobilize people toward a shared vision.
2. *Coaching leaders* develop people, establishing a relationship and trust.
3. *Affiliative leaders* promote emotional bonds and organizational harmony.

4. *Democratic leaders* build consensus through participation.

5. *Pacesetting leaders* set challenging and exciting standards and expect excellence.

6. *Commanding leaders* demand immediate compliance.

An entrepreneur may use different styles at different times as she or he attempts to draw the best out of the organization and its employees. Though it should be used sparingly, commanding leadership might be necessary and expected in a genuine emergency situation, for example, but it would not be appropriate in most settings.

For most entrepreneurial firms, leadership that recognizes and values individual worth is strongly recommended. Several decades ago, many managers were hard-nosed autocrats, giving orders and showing little concern for those who worked under them. Over the years, this style of leadership has given way to a more sensitive and effective variety that emphasizes respect for all members of the organization and shows an appreciation both for their work and for their potential. Employees usually find this kind of direction far more motivating.

Danny Meyer owns five of New York's best and most popular restaurants, so he has had his share of successes. But it has not always been easy. Meyer recalls a time, in his twenties, when his managers and waiters were continually testing him and pushing him to the limit. Responding to advice from a highly respected and successful mentor, Meyer came up with his own unique management approach. In fact, he has a name for it: *constant, gentle pressure.* Problems are going to arise, conspiring to throw everything out of balance, but Meyer is committed to moving things "back to center," where they should be. That's the "constant" feature of his approach. But he'll never respond in a way that robs his employees of their dignity. That's why he calls it "gentle." He also insists on excellent performance, overseeing the details of every table and even moving an out-of-place saltshaker to its proper place. That's where the "pressure" comes in. It's not easy, but it's a management style that works.[6]

In many cases, progressive managers seek some degree of employee participation in decisions that affect personnel and work processes. Often the focus is on important features of the business, such as shaping the mission of the firm or establishing everyday workplace practices. Managers may carry this leadership approach to a level called *empowerment.* The manager who uses empowerment goes beyond solicitation of employees' opinions and ideas by increasing their authority to act on their own and to make decisions about the processes they're involved with. Glenn Ross, an expert on dealing with customers, points out how small business owners can use employee empowerment to help resolve customer complaints.

empowerment
Giving employees authority to make decisions or take actions on their own.

> As the immortal philosopher, Barney Fife [from "The Andy Griffith Show"], used to say, "Nip it! You've got to nip it in the bud!" Stop the complaint before it escalates into something major. The best way to do that is to see that your employees understand your vision, policies, and procedures as they relate to customer service. Empowering your employees also shows them that you trust them to do the right thing. This in turn has a positive impact on employee morale. The higher the employee morale, the better service they will provide to your customers. It's that "Circle of Life" thing.[7]

Ross goes on to point out that empowering frontline staff to take care of customers in this way offers additional benefits, such as freeing up time for the owners and managers to take care of other pressing business challenges.

Some companies actually carry employee participation a step further by creating self-managed *work teams.* Each work team is assigned a given task or operation; its members manage that task or operation without direct supervision and assume responsibility for the results. When work teams function properly, the number of supervisors needed decreases sharply. While this approach may not be appropriate for some small businesses, it certainly provides a powerful model for the management of many ventures.

work teams
Groups of employees with freedom to function without close supervision.

Leaders Shape the Culture of the Organization

Over time, an organization tends to take on a life of its own. As indicated in Chapter 2, an organizational culture begins to emerge in every small business, establishing a tone that helps employees understand what the company stands for and how to go about their work. You could think of organizational culture as the factor that determines the "feel" of a business. It tends to be the "silent teacher" that sets the tone for employee conduct, even when managers are not present.

A company's culture does not emerge overnight; it unfolds over the lifetime of the business and usually reflects the character and style of the founder. (You may recall that we discussed the founder's imprint on organizational culture in the family business in Chapter 5.) Because of its power to shape how business is conducted, the culture of the organization should not be left to chance. If a founder is honest in his or her dealings, supportive of employees, and quick to communicate, he or she will likely set a standard that others will follow. An entrepreneur can create an innovative cultural environment by setting aside his or her ego and opening up to the ideas of others, supporting experimentation through the elimination of unnecessary penalties for failure, and looking for and tapping into the unique gifts of all employees. Like empowerment, creating an organizational culture that fosters innovation tends to draw employees into the work of the company and often provides a boost to commitment and employee morale.[8]

The above-mentioned actions are largely symbolic, focusing attention on the thrust of the business and its purpose. However, deliberate physical design efforts can also influence the culture, shaping the way people in the organization interact and what they achieve together. Joe Anthony owns New York City–based Vital Marketing, a company that brings in around $20 million a year doing multicultural and youth marketing. Anthony and his management team have taken very intentional steps to set the tone of business and generate specific results. In Anthony's words, "We group our project teams together . . . [and] create these bullpens so people will always be able to turn around and troubleshoot."[9]

Jonathan Vehar, senior partner of New & Improved, an innovation training and development company in Evanston, Illinois, offers more office design suggestions. For example, he notes that creativity can be spurred by sprinkling all work spaces with visually stimulating features like idea-inspiring artwork, video monitors, and well-positioned windows that open up the view. It is also possible to encourage communication, for example, by positioning work spaces far away from bathroom facilities, which naturally creates occasions for employees to run into one another and start idea-generating conversations.[10] These relatively simple adjustments in physical space can have a profound effect on the mind-set employees assume at work.

Another important lever for shaping culture is to hire new employees based on their attitude, style, and fit with the personality of the company. Tony Hsieh is only in his mid-30s, but he has built Zappos.com into a billion-dollar company in less than a decade. His Las Vegas–based online shoe retailer now also sells apparel, bags, housewares, electronics, and cookware, but standing at its core is a strong and carefully crafted culture. It's a little quirky—values such as "embrace and drive change" and "create fun and a little weirdness" top the list—but it's hard to argue with the company's approach, given its success. During the interview process, potential new employees are screened for their fit with the Zappos.com culture, and even highly qualified prospects are rejected if there is no match. As Hsieh puts it, "The most important thing is that there's a culture you believe in and are willing to hire and fire based upon [it]."[11] To put it another way, organizational culture is serious business; it can easily make or break a company.

It should be clear by now that, in large part, business management is a mental sport, and those who have the right frame of mind are most likely to win. Therefore, every leader should strive to incorporate a positive, "can-do" attitude into the organizational culture. You can work on your own attitude and inspire others to follow your lead. Attitude often is everything— whether an event is mentally framed as a setback or a positive life experience is entirely up to

LIVING THE DREAM:

entrepreneurial challenges

Nice Guys Finish Last . . . or So the Saying Goes

The Kaplan Thaler Group (KTG) competes in the savagely competitive world of advertising, but you wouldn't guess it by the attitude of its founder. Linda Kaplan Thaler launched the agency in 1997, and it has expanded from a single account and limited revenues to annual billings of around $1 billion. And KTG has advertising smash hits to its credit, such as the Aflac duck campaign. Kaplan clearly knows what she is doing. But if you ask this CEO and chief creative officer for the secret to her success, she will offer a simple but surprising formula: It pays to be nice and to cultivate a culture of niceness in your enterprise. Kaplan believes this so strongly that she and her company's president, Robin Koval, put it in writing when they coauthored the national bestseller *The Power of Nice: How to Conquer the Business World with Kindness*. The message resonates powerfully with readers.

The corporate world glorifies a dog-eat-dog mentality, but KTG has found that a spirit of warmth, friendliness, and collaboration generates more favorable results. For example, the agency featured Donald Trump's wife, Melania, in an Aflac commercial, and they gave Mrs. Trump her own trailer and made sure she was looked after and comfortable—in a word, they were polite and respectful to her, just as they are to all talent involved in advertising shoots. Months later, Kaplan was asked to be a judge on Trump's television show "The Apprentice." Just before the segment was shot, she introduced herself to Trump, mentioning that her agency had used Melania in an Aflac commercial. He clearly remembered his wife's experience and said, "You were so nice to my wife. Watch how I return the favor." In the segment, he described KTG as "one of the hottest ad agencies in the country" (free promotion on network television!) and went out of his way to include Kaplan in on-camera discussions. This is just one of countless examples the authors relate in their book to show how niceness pays off.

Being nice is not the same as playing the part of a doormat. Nice people can still be strong and assertive. According to Kaplan and Koval, nice people "address problems, motivate teams, and win high-profile accounts. They just do so with a positive and memorable style." In other words, they get results! And research has shown that nice people have stronger relationships, make more money, have better health, and spend less time in court. This is probably not a surprise to you. Deep down inside, most people know that being nice leads to a much more satisfying life.

Loyal customers, high-quality employees, and strategic partners are all attracted to companies that have that special "niceness" factor. But this is about much more than just doing well in business. Kaplan and Koval say, "You have to treat everyone you meet as if they are the most important person in the world—because they are. If not to you, then to someone; and if not today, then perhaps tomorrow."

Sources: "About Us," http://www.kaplanthaler.com, accessed March 31, 2009; http://www.thepowerofsmallbook.com/index.php/home/pon, accessed March 31, 2009; "The Power of Nice," http://www.randomhouse .com/doubleday/catalog/display.pperl?isbn=9780385518925&view= excerpt, accessed April 1, 2009; Carol Tice, "Play Nice," *Entrepreneur*, Vol. 35, No. 9 (September 2007), p. 24.

http://www.kaplanthaler.com

Thomas J. Gibbons/Getty Images

you. If all the parking spaces close to the store are full, taking one farther away can be seen as a chance to get some exercise. A new competitor can present a fresh reminder of why it is so important to serve your customers to the best of your ability. And a lost sale can show you how to improve your product or adjust your presentation so that many more sales can be generated in the future. Develop a positive mind-set, and let it shape the culture of those you have hired to work alongside you.

Distinctive Characteristics of Small Firm Management

As one entrepreneur commented, "Unless you thrive on chaos, a small company can be tough." Small firm operations are not always chaotic, of course, but small business owners face challenges that differ greatly from those of corporate executives. Furthermore, small companies experience changes in their leadership and management processes as they move from startup to the point where they employ a full staff of *professional managers,* trained in the use of systematic, analytical methods.

2. Explain the distinctive features of small business management.

professional manager
A manager who uses systematic, analytical methods of management.

Professional-Level Management

There is, of course, much variation in the way businesses and other organizations are managed. Between the extremes of very unskilled and highly professional types of management lies a continuum. At the less professional end of this range are entrepreneurs and other managers who rely largely on past experience, rules of thumb, and personal whims in giving direction to their businesses. In most cases, their ideas of motivation are based on the way they were treated in earlier business experiences or family relationships.

Other entrepreneurs and managers display much more professionalism. They are analytical and systematic in dealing with management problems and issues. Because they emphasize getting the facts and working out logical solutions, their approach is sometimes described as scientific in nature. The challenge for small firm leaders is to develop as much professionalism as possible, while still retaining the entrepreneurial spirit of the enterprise.

Limitations of Founders as Managers

Founders of new firms are not always good organization members. As discussed in Chapter 1, they are creative, innovative, risk-taking individuals who have the courage to strike out on their own. Indeed, they are often propelled into entrepreneurship by precipitating events, sometimes involving their difficulty in fitting into conventional organizational roles. But even very capable entrepreneurs may fail to appreciate the need for good management practices as the business grows.

Though he believes the problem may sometimes be overstated, Adam Hanft, CEO of Hanft Unlimited Inc., a New York City–based consulting, advertising, and publishing firm, points out that many experts believe it is very difficult (often impossible) for entrepreneurs to make the transition from founder to professional manager.

> If I had a dime for every time I have heard it, I could start another business: Entrepreneurs are passionate people, great at building companies, but only to a certain level. As their enterprises reach maturity, these impatient, impetuous founders need to be replaced by "professional" managers. . . . In [venture capital] land they even have a name for the problem: founderitis.[12]

Some entrepreneurs recognize the problem early on and make adjustments. Sara Blakely, founder of women's shapewear trendsetter SPANX and a true "business dynamo," reports that building a team to run her company was one of her greatest challenges. Before becoming an entrepreneur, Blakely had no formal business training or managerial experience, but starting a new venture meant taking on the responsibility of her employees and their livelihoods. She soon felt very overwhelmed, but then she realized, "It's OK if you're not good at this; hire someone who is." So she hired a CEO ("one of the smartest business decisions I ever made") and gave up control of tasks that did not align with her natural skills so that she could focus on those that play to her strengths. Today, job responsibilities at the company have been dramatically reconfigured. Blakely is the public "face of SPANX," an evangelist for the company and its products, but she continues to work on product development and marketing ideas as well. This has turned out to be a much more comfortable and practical arrangement for her. As Blakely puts it, "The person who starts a company from the ground up is not always the best person to grow it. I think this is the most important lesson an entrepreneur can learn."[13]

Although many entrepreneurs are professional in their approach to management and many corporate managers are entrepreneurial in that they are truly innovative and are willing to take risks, a founder's less-than-professional management style can act as a drag on business growth. Ideally, the founder should be able to add a measure of professional management without sacrificing the entrepreneurial spirit and basic values that have given the business a successful start.

To be sure, some small business owners also excel as leaders of the large corporations into which their new ventures have grown. Examples abound of "startup artists" who have made the transition to highly accomplished professional managers, including Steve Jobs (Apple Computer), Mary Kay Ash (Mary Kay Cosmetics), Fred DeLuca (SUBWAY Restaurants), and Sam Walton (Walmart Stores). They have proved that it can be done. Perhaps you will do the same in your own business!

Managerial Weakness in Small Firms

Although some large corporations experience poor management, small enterprises seem particularly vulnerable to this weakness. Many small firms are marginal or unprofitable businesses, struggling to survive from day to day. At best, they earn only a meager living for their owners. They operate, but to say that they are managed would be an exaggeration.

It is common to hear about businesses that become successful, are praised for their problem-solving wizardry, and start to take on high-prestige customers. But it is precisely at that point when many companies start to lose their business grip. When these ventures were small, with perhaps a few dozen employees in the shop and a handful of projects in the pipeline, they were able to perform quite well. But when they expanded beyond some comfortable point, problems began to mount. Suppliers started to gripe about late payments, customers became unhappy because of delayed deliveries and shoddy workmanship, employee morale began to drift. This can easily be the beginning of the end, and bankruptcy is all too often the final outcome. In the post-mortem, it becomes clear that the cause of failure in many cases was a lack of professional management. The good news, however, is that poor management is neither universal nor inevitable.

Constraints That Hamper Management

Managers of small firms, particularly new and growing companies, are constrained by conditions that do not trouble the average corporate executive—they must face the grim reality of small bank accounts and limited staff. A small firm often lacks the money for slick sales brochures, and it cannot afford much in the way of marketing research. The shortage of cash also makes it difficult to employ an adequate number of clerical employees. Such limitations are painfully apparent to large-firm managers who move into management positions in small firms.

A former CEO of a telecommunications company described some of the drastic differences between her experiences managing in a *Fortune* 500 firm and in a startup. In a startup situation,

> Money doesn't come from any single source. There's no single boss to whom you make your case. In fact, the money to build the business comes from several external sources—each with slightly different agendas. . . . [T]here's no guarantee that you can survive even if you hit your milestones. In other words, there's no room for error. . . .
>
> [U]nless you also realize that you have to become a one-person version of your Fortune 500's chief financial officer, investor-relations and PR staffs, and fund-raising machine, you will be ill-prepared for the mission.[14]

Small firms typically lack adequate specialized professional staff. Most small business managers are generalists. Lacking the support of experienced specialists in such areas as marketing research, financial analysis, advertising, and human resource management, the manager of a small firm must make decisions in these areas without the expertise that is available in a larger business. This limitation may be partially overcome by using outside management assistance. But coping with a shortage of internal professional talent is part of the reality of managing an entrepreneurial company.

Firm Growth and Managerial Practices

As a newly formed business becomes established and grows, its organizational structure and pattern of management change. To some extent, management in any organization must adapt to growth and change. However, the changes involved in the early growth stages of a new business are much more extensive than those that occur with the growth of a relatively mature business.

A number of experts have proposed models related to the growth stages of business firms.[15] These models typically describe four or five stages of growth and identify various management issues related to each stage. Exhibit 19-1 shows four stages of organizational growth characteristic of many small businesses. As firms progress from Stage 1 to Stage 4, they add layers of management and increase the formality of operations. Though some firms skip the first stage or two by starting as larger businesses, thousands of small firms make their way through each of the stages pictured in Exhibit 19-1.

EXHIBIT

19-1 Organizational Stages of Small Business Growth

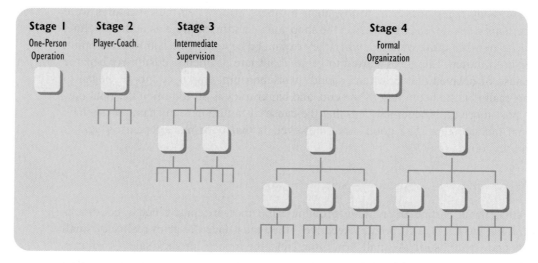

Stage 1
One-Person Operation

Stage 2
Player-Coach

Stage 3
Intermediate Supervision

Stage 4
Formal Organization

In Stage 1, the firm is simply a one-person operation. Some firms begin with a larger organization, but the one-person startup is by no means rare. Many businesses remain one-person operations indefinitely. In Stage 2, the entrepreneur becomes a player-coach, which implies continuing active participation in the operations of the business. In addition to performing the basic work—whether making the product, selling it, writing checks, keeping records, or other activities—the entrepreneur must also coordinate the efforts of others.

A major milestone is reached in Stage 3, when an intermediate level of supervision is added. In many ways, this is a turning point for a small firm, because the entrepreneur must rise above direct, hands-on management and work through an intervening layer of management. Stage 4, the stage of formal organization, involves more than increased size and multi-layered organization. The formalization of management entails adoption of written policies, preparation of plans and budgets, standardization of personnel practices, computerization of records, preparation of organizational charts and job descriptions, scheduling of training conferences, institution of control procedures, and so on. While some formal managerial practices may be adopted prior to Stage 4, the steps shown in Exhibit 19-1 outline a typical pattern of development for successful firms. Flexibility and informality may be helpful when a firm is first started, but the firm's growth requires greater formality in planning and control. Tension often develops as the traditional easygoing patterns of management become dysfunctional. Great managerial skill is required of the entrepreneur in order to preserve a "family" atmosphere while introducing professional management.

As a venture moves from Stage 1 to Stage 4, the pattern of entrepreneurial activities changes. The entrepreneur becomes less of a doer and more of a leader and manager. Managers who have strong doing skills often have weak managing skills, and this is understandable. Most entrepreneurs build businesses on their specialized capabilities; for example, they may know software development inside and out, have a knack for raising money, or possess enviable selling skills. But when it comes to tasks like assessing talent in others, they often come up short. That is simply not their strong suit, and this limitation can be a serious problem.

As a firm grows, the entrepreneur needs to fill key positions with individuals who have the capacity to perform well as managers. Can the best salesperson or most skilled technician be advanced to a higher level? Sometimes, but not always.

> Erika Mangrum was a year into her business and was feeling pressured to promote a star employee to general manager. "She wanted more responsibility and more pay," says Mangrum, co-founder and president of Iatria Day Spas and Health Center, a 40-employee company in Raleigh, North Carolina. Mangrum felt a deep sense of loyalty to this employee, who had been with the company from the start, so she went ahead with the promotion. However, it wasn't long before Mangrum realized she was promoting doom and gloom.[16]

The new manager's rudeness and inability to manage conflict created customer complaints and tension among employees. The manager left 14 months after the promotion. And unfortunately, the business also lost key employees in the turmoil.[17]

Sometimes the personal talent or brilliance of the entrepreneur can enable a business to survive while business skills are being acquired. Consider Ronald and Rony Delice, Haitian-born twin brothers, who are igniting fashion runways and men's clothing with their edgy designs. After earning degrees from New York's acclaimed Fashion Institute of Technology, Ronald and Rony worked as custom tailors and designers. They soon started their own business and won awards for their designs, and by 2003 their company already was generating nearly half a million dollars in annual revenue. However, the business side of their venture presented their biggest challenges. The twins found that keeping the books, paying bills, and preparing a business plan were much harder than designing clothing. As Ronald explained it, "We're more artists than businesspeople." Overcoming that challenge meant bringing in qualified people.[18]

Small firms that hesitate to move through the various organizational stages and acquire the necessary professional management often limit their rate of growth. On the other hand, a small business may attempt to grow too quickly. If an entrepreneur's primary strength lies in product development or selling, for example, a quick move into Stage 4 may saddle the entrepreneur with managerial duties and deprive the organization of her or his valuable talents.

Entrepreneurs play different roles in starting businesses than they play in operating firms as the businesses become more fully developed. And the personal qualities involved in starting ventures differ from the qualities required to manage over the long haul. This helps explain why so few new ventures actually become established businesses with staying power. Growing a business requires maturation and adaptation on the part of the entrepreneur.

Managerial Responsibilities of Entrepreneurs

So far, our discussion of the management process has been very general. Now it is time to look more closely at how entrepreneurs organize and direct a company's operations.

3. Identify the managerial tasks of entrepreneurs.

Planning Activities

Beyond creating an initial business plan to guide the *launch* of a new venture (the focus of Chapter 6), most entrepreneurs also plan for the ongoing operation of their enterprises. However, the amount of planning they complete is typically less than ideal. And what little planning they do tends to be haphazard and focused on specific, immediate issues—for example, how much inventory to purchase, whether to buy a new piece of equipment, and other such questions. Circumstances affect the degree to which formal planning is needed, but most businesses can function more profitably by increasing the amount of planning done by managers and making it more systematic.

Planning pays off in many ways. First, the process of thinking through the issues confronting a firm and developing a plan to deal with those issues can improve productivity. Second, planning provides a focus for a firm: Managerial decisions over the course of the year can be guided by the annual plan, and employees can work consistently toward the same goal. Third, evidence of planning increases credibility with bankers, suppliers, and other outsiders.

TYPES OF PLANS A firm's basic path to the future is spelled out in a document called a *long-range plan,* or *strategic plan.* As noted in Chapter 3, strategy decisions concern such issues as identifying niche markets and establishing features that differentiate a firm from its competitors. But planning is important even in established businesses, in order to ensure that changes in the business environment can be addressed as they occur.

Short-range plans are action plans designed to deal with activities in production, marketing, and other areas over a period of one year or less. An important part of a short-range operating plan is the *budget,* a document that expresses future plans in monetary terms. A budget is usually prepared each year (one year in advance), with a breakdown of figures for each month or quarter. (Budgeting is explained more fully in Chapter 22.)

PLANNING TIME Small business managers all too often succumb to what is sometimes called the "tyranny of the urgent." In other words, they can easily become distracted by pressing problems. Ryan Gibson, a young entrepreneur in central Texas, commented to one of the authors, "As my enterprise gets larger, there is increased pressure to fight the everyday fires of business when I need to be thinking about how to move my company forward."[19] This makes it easy to ignore or postpone planning to free up time and energy to concentrate on more urgent issues in such areas as

long-range plan (strategic plan)
A firm's overall plan for the future.

short-range plan
A plan that governs a firm's operations for one year or less.

budget
A document that expresses future plans in monetary terms.

production and sales. And, just as quarterbacks focusing on a receiver may be blindsided by blitzing linebackers, managers who have neglected to plan may be bowled over by competitors.

Creating an Organizational Structure

While an entrepreneur may give direction through personal leadership, she or he must also define the relationships among the firm's activities and among the individuals on the firm's payroll. Without some kind of organizational structure, operations eventually become chaotic and morale suffers.

THE UNPLANNED STRUCTURE In small companies, the organizational structure tends to evolve with little conscious planning. Certain employees begin performing particular functions when the company is new and retain those functions as it matures.

This natural evolution is not all bad. Generally, a strong element of practicality characterizes these types of organizational arrangements. The structure is forged through the experience of working and growing, rather than being derived from a textbook or another firm's organizational chart. Unplanned structures are seldom perfect, however, and growth typically creates a need for organizational change. Periodically, therefore, the entrepreneur should examine structural relationships and make adjustments as needed for effective teamwork.

THE CHAIN OF COMMAND A *chain of command* implies superior-subordinate relationships with a downward flow of instructions, but it involves much more. It is also a channel for two-way communication. As a practical matter, strict adherence to the chain of command is not advisable. An organization in which the primary channel of communication is rigid will be bureaucratic and inefficient. At the same time, frequent and flagrant disregard of the chain of command quickly undermines the position of the bypassed manager.

In a *line organization,* each person has one supervisor to whom he or she reports and looks for instructions. All employees are directly engaged in the firm's work, producing, selling, or performing office or financial duties. Most very small firms—for example, those with fewer than 10 employees—use this form of organization.

A *line-and-staff organization* is similar to a line organization in that each person reports to a single supervisor. However, a line-and-staff structure also has staff specialists who perform specific services or act as management advisors in particular areas (see Exhibit 19-2).

chain of command
The official, vertical channel of communication in an organization.

line organization
A simple organizational structure in which each person reports to one supervisor.

line-and-staff organization
An organizational structure that includes staff specialists who assist management.

EXHIBIT 19-2 Line-and-Staff Organization

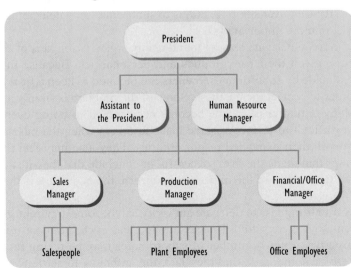

Staff specialists may include a human resource manager, a production control technician, a quality control expert, and an assistant to the president. The line-and-staff organization is widely used in small businesses.

span of control
The number of subordinates supervised by one manager.

SPAN OF CONTROL   The *span of control* is the number of employees who are supervised by a manager. Although some authorities have stated that six to eight people are all that one individual can supervise effectively, the optimal span of control is actually a variable that depends on a number of factors. Among these factors are the nature of the work and the manager's knowledge, energy, personality, and abilities. In addition, if the abilities of subordinates are better than average, the span of control may be broadened accordingly.

As a very small firm grows and adds employees, the entrepreneur's span of control is extended. The entrepreneur often has a tendency to stretch the span too far—to supervise not only the first five or six employees hired, but also the new employees added as time goes on. Eventually, a point is reached at which the attempted span of control exceeds the entrepreneur's reach, demanding more time and effort than she or he can devote to the business. It is at this point that the entrepreneur must establish intermediate levels of supervision and dedicate more time to management, moving beyond the role of player-coach.

Understanding Informal Groups

The types of organizational structures just discussed address the formal relationships among members of an organization. However, all organizations also have informal groups composed of people with something in common, such as a particular job, hobby, carpool, or affiliation with a civic association.

Although informal groups are not created by management, managers should observe them and evaluate their effect on the functioning of the total organization. An informal group, for example, may foster an attitude of working hard until the very end of the work day or doing just the opposite, perhaps easing up and coasting for the last half-hour. These tendencies are almost always directed by informal leaders, who naturally emerge and influence employee behavior in a significant way. Ordinarily, no serious conflict arises between informal groups and the formal organization, but a wise manager understands the potentially positive contribution of informal groups and knows that informal leadership is sure to develop.

Delegating Authority

delegation of authority
Granting to subordinates the right to act or make decisions.

Through *delegation of authority*, a manager grants to subordinates the right to act or to make decisions. Turning over some functions to subordinates by delegating authority frees the superior to perform more important tasks.

Although failure to delegate may be found in any organization, it is often a special problem for entrepreneurs, given their backgrounds and personalities. Because they frequently must pay for mistakes made by subordinates, owners are inclined to keep a firm hold on the reins of leadership in order to protect the business. Some of the problem is simply a matter of habit and momentum. Many entrepreneurs have become accustomed to doing everything themselves, which makes it difficult to turn over some tasks to others when the business grows and they truly need help with their expanded responsibilities. They also may feel the need to continue doing those things that made the firm successful or conclude that they just do them better than their employees. Regardless of the underlying concern, the end result is the same: insufficient delegation.

Inability or unwillingness to delegate authority can become apparent in a number of ways. For example, employees may find it necessary to clear even the most minor decisions with the boss. At any given time, a number of subordinates may be trying to get the attention of the owner to resolve some issue that they lack the authority to settle. This keeps the owner exceptionally busy—rushing from assisting a salesperson to helping iron out a production bottleneck to setting up a new filing system. Entrepreneurs often work long hours, and those who have difficulty delegating compound the problem, imposing on themselves even longer work hours.

When Russ Lewis operated a small bakery in Vermont with his wife, Linda, he faced this problem at a very basic level. He personally baked between 2,000 to 3,500 loaves of bread each day, and the pace drained away all of Russ's energy, along with his love for baking. The bakery supplied restaurants and cafés with great bread and provided the owners with the highest income they ever had, but it also dominated their lives. Six days a week, Russ would get up very early to arrive at the bakery at 1:00 in the morning and bake for 13 hours straight. In the summer, when Vermont would swell with tourists, Russ had to start his workday two or three hours earlier! He would often say, "I'm so tired of being tired." The truth is, he was so tired that he wasn't even able to change the habits that made him so tired. The couple could have taken the business to a higher level, but Russ could not bring himself to give up his duties or his control, saying, "I enjoy baking, but I like to handle everything myself." By refusing to delegate, Russ Lewis became a victim of his own success.[20]

As one small business writer has observed, "By delegating authority, entrepreneurs unleash the same force in their subordinates that makes them so productive: the thrill of being in charge."[21] This is not to say that delegation is a cure-all for management challenges; in fact, turning over duties can easily lead to its own problems as a result of a subordinate's carelessness or other failure. But this can be minimized, if the handover is managed well. We offer the following suggestions to ease the transition:

- Accept the fact that you will not be able to make all of the decisions anymore. If you don't, you will blunt the venture's potential to grow and develop.

- Prepare yourself emotionally for the loss of control that small business owners feel when they first start to delegate. This is completely natural.

- Manage carefully the process of finding, selecting, hiring, and retaining employees who are trustworthy enough to handle greater responsibility. In other words, keep an eye on the future when you hire new staff.

- Delegation involves significant adjustment, so be sure to move forward one step at a time. Start by delegating those functions that you are most comfortable giving up. Even then, continue to provide reasonable oversight to smooth the transition and to ensure the quality of the work.

- Plan to invest the time needed to coach those who are taking over new responsibilities so that they can master required skills. The first thing to do is to write job descriptions to help minimize confusion.

- Make delegation meaningful. Focus on results and give subordinates the flexibility to carry out assignments. To realize the benefits of delegation, you must build leadership in subordinates, who can then take on more advanced and complex tasks.

Controlling Operations

Despite good planning, organizations never function perfectly. As a result, managers must monitor operations to discover deviations from plans and to ensure that the firm is functioning as intended. Managerial activities that check on performance and correct it when necessary are part of managerial control; they serve to keep the business on course.

The control process begins with the establishment of standards, which are set through planning and goal setting. (This is evidence of the connection between planning and control.) Planners translate goals into norms (standards) by making them measurable. A goal to increase market share, for example, may be expressed as a projected dollar increase in sales volume for the coming year. Such an annual target may, in turn, be broken down into quarterly target standards so that corrective action can be taken early if performance begins to fall below the projected amount.

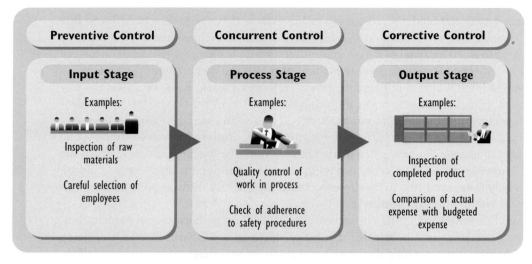

EXHIBIT

Preventive Control

Input Stage

Examples:

Inspection of raw materials

Careful selection of employees

Concurrent Control

Process Stage

Examples:

Quality control of work in process

Check of adherence to safety procedures

Corrective Control

Output Stage

Examples:

Inspection of completed product

Comparison of actual expense with budgeted expense

As Exhibit 19-3 shows, performance measurement occurs at various stages of the control process. Performance may be measured at the input stage (perhaps to determine the quality of materials purchased), during the process stage (perhaps to determine if the product being manufactured meets quality standards), and/or at the output stage (perhaps to check the quality of a completed product).

Corrective action is required when performance deviates significantly from the standard in an unfavorable direction. To prevent the problem from recurring, such action must be followed by an analysis of the cause of the deviation. If the percentage of defective products increases, for example, a manager must determine whether this is caused by substandard raw materials, untrained workers, equipment failure, or some other factor. For a problem to be effectively controlled, corrective action must identify and deal with the true cause.

Communicating

Another key to a healthy organization is effective communication—that is, getting managers and employees to talk with one another and openly share problems and ideas. To some extent, the management hierarchy must be set aside so that personnel at all levels can speak freely with those higher up. The result is two-way communication—a far cry from the old-fashioned idea that managers give orders and employees simply carry them out. The need for good communication has been eloquently expressed as follows: "It's a no-brainer—you've got to talk, email, and kibitz with employees. The speed with which information moves through a company is critical to how well the mechanism works. Information is the oil that turns the gears."[22]

To communicate effectively, managers must tell employees where they stand, how the business is doing, and what the firm's plans are for the future. While negative feedback may be necessary at times, giving positive feedback to employees is the primary tool for establishing good human relations. Perhaps the most fundamental concept managers need to keep in mind is that employees are people, not machines. They can quickly detect insincerity but respond to honest efforts to treat them as mature, responsible individuals. In short, an atmosphere of trust and respect contributes greatly to good communication.

LIVING THE DREAM:

entrepreneurial challenges

Dude, Where's My Ability to Communicate?

In a way, businesses are like families: People work together (in part, because they have to), but they also have plenty of disagreements along the way. Because of intergenerational differences in values, attitudes, and style, miscommunication and conflict are unavoidable, and managing this sometimes wild mix of mind-sets and workplace habits can be a great challenge.

Most companies today have employees from three generations: Baby Boomers (born between 1946 and 1964), Generation X (born between 1965 and 1980), and Generation Y (born between 1981 and 2000). Because these generations were exposed in their early years to different technologies, forms of entertainment, cultural practices, and other factors, they each have adopted their own ways of doing things, which often clash in the workplace. David Galbenski, the 39-year-old founder and CEO of a company called Lumen Legal has seen this firsthand among his 25 staff members, of whom 35 percent are Boomers, 40 percent are Gen Xers, and 25 percent are Gen Yers. The "critical" practice in question? Whether to use e-mail or Instant Messaging (IM) to communicate with one another.

[In 2008] there was a communication breakdown. The company's twenty-something Gen Yers kept trying to IM their Gen X and baby boomer co-workers, who weren't always logging on to IM. It was becoming a source of irritation at the Royal Oak, Michigan, attorney outsourcing firm. . . . For the company's twenty-somethings, "there's this frustration, like, 'Well, I was going to try to IM you, but you're not logged on— and why aren't you logged on?'"

Jim Arbogast/Digital Vision/Getty Images

To solve the problem, the $10 million company set up its computers so that they would automatically log into IM when turned on, and Lumen is also thinking about laying down new "rules" so that all employees know when it's best to use e-mail or IM.

Welcome to the new world of workplace behavior and communication. It is becoming clear that the generations differ significantly in their attitude toward and level of comfort with technology, demands for raises and time off, problem-solving approaches, and social networking styles, just to name a few of the many issues that often flare up. This can lead to problems that are not always easy to anticipate. For example, Gen Yers grew up using virtual communication tools, so they have spent less time socializing face to face. As a result, they have less experience reading nonverbal cues in face-to-face or even voice-to-voice communication, leading Boomers to charge that they lack important interpersonal skills, such as knowing how to show respect toward leaders and regard for others.

Boomers, on the other hand, have not exactly welcomed technology with open arms, learning what they must know to get by and leaving the "technological heavy lifting" to others—mostly younger workers. This creates its own set of frustrations. All three generations have much to learn, including how to appreciate one another and the special insights and capabilities that each group brings to the enterprise. Bringing some resolution to generational communication differences isn't going to be easy, but it is nonetheless very important in a business world that grows increasingly competitive.

Sources: Karen Auby, "A Boomer's Guide to Communicating with Gen X and Gen Y," http://www.businessweek.com/magazine/content/08_34/b4097063805619.htm, accessed April 2, 2009; Chris Penttila, "Talking about My Generation," *Entrepreneur*, Vol. 37, No. 3 (March 2009), pp. 53–55; Ruth Sherman, "Gen Y v. Boomers: Generational Differences in Communication," *Fast Company*, February 7, 2008, http://www.fastcompany.com/node/659409/print, accessed April 2, 2009; and "Lumen Legal—About Us," http://www.lumenlegal.com/about/index.htm, accessed April 3, 2009. http://www.lumenlegal.com

Many practical tools and techniques can be used to stimulate two-way communication between managers and employees. Here are some that may work for you and your enterprise:

- Periodic performance review sessions to discuss employees' ideas, questions, complaints, and job expectations
- Bulletin boards (physical or electronic) to keep employees informed about developments affecting them and/or the company
- Blogs (user-generated websites where entries are made in journal style) for internal communication, especially in companies that have open organizational cultures and truly want transparent dialogue[23]
- Suggestion boxes to solicit employees' ideas
- Wikis (websites that allows visitors to add, remove, edit, and change content) set up to bring issues to the surface and draw feedback from employees
- Formal staff meetings to discuss problems and matters of general concern
- Breakfast or lunch with employees to socialize and just talk

These methods and others can be used to supplement the most basic of all channels for communication—the day-to-day interaction between each employee and his or her supervisor.

So far, the focus has been on interpersonal communication, but entrepreneurs must also make presentations to groups of people, from pitching product ideas at trade shows to selling bankers on the need for funding to offering keynote speeches at community events. And the need for public speaking skills is sure to increase as the company grows and develops. The fear of public speaking is one of the most common phobias (ranking even above the fear of dying!), and an inability to communicate in public can hold back the progress of the business. The good news is that, through practice, you can keep your stage fright under control (if that is a problem) and you can certainly improve your delivery. Exhibit 19-4 provides some tips that will help you develop confidence in your speaking and be more interesting as a presenter.

Negotiating

When operating a business, entrepreneurs and managers must personally interact with other individuals much of the time. Some contacts involve outsiders, such as suppliers, customers, bankers, realtors, and business service providers. Typically, the interests of the parties are in conflict, to some degree at least. A supplier, for example, wants to sell a product or service for the highest possible price, and the buyer wants to purchase it for the lowest possible price. To have a successful business, a manager must be able to reach agreements that both meet the firm's requirements and contribute to good relationships over time.

Even within the business, personal relationships pit different perspectives and personal interests against one another. Subordinates, for example, frequently desire changes in their work assignments or feel that they are worth more to the company than their salary levels indicate. Managers in different departments may compete for services offered by a maintenance department or a computer services unit.

negotiation
A two-way communication process used to resolve differences in interests, desires, or demands.

The process of developing workable solutions through discussions or interactions is called *negotiation.* We are all negotiators in our daily lives, both inside and outside our family relationships. Conflicting interests, desires, and demands require that we reconcile, or negotiate, differences in order to live together peacefully.

Many people consider negotiation to be a win–lose game; that is, one party must win, and the other must lose. There is a problem, however, with this concept of negotiation. If parties feel that they have lost, they may go away with thoughts of getting even in subsequent negotiations. Clearly, such feelings do not contribute to good long-term relationships. In contrast, other negotiators advocate a win–win strategy. A win–win negotiator tries to find a solution that will satisfy at least the basic interests of both parties.

EXHIBIT

1. **Do your homework.** You need to know the purpose of the presentation and to whom you will be presenting. If you can find out in advance who will be attending your presentation, you will be able to adapt your comments to their needs and concerns.

2. **Know your material "spot on."** The better you know what you plan to talk about, the more you can concentrate on the delivery. And being prepared inspires confidence.

3. **Be interactive.** It's easy for listeners to be lulled into disinterest when they are not engaged. Find ways to get the audience involved in what you have to say. And don't, for example, read from your notes for extended periods of time—doing so will ensure that the communication goes in only one direction, and your audience will know it immediately.

4. **Make vivid mental connections in the minds of listeners.** Telling stories helps here, but so can other tools and techniques. For example, use props to focus attention, or employ a metaphor throughout the presentation to draw listeners back to a central theme. Humor is entertaining and can provide comic relief, but it can also be used to make a point unforgettable.

5. **Emphasize relevance.** Your listeners are busy people, so be sure to deliver information that they will find useful and worth their time.

6. **Be dynamic, but be yourself.** Let your listeners know that you are passionate about the topic by the way you invest yourself in the presentation. It is much easier for an audience to remain engaged when the presenter is energetic and uses voice, gestures, movement, and facial expressions to show it. Maintaining eye contact communicates that you want to connect with each individual in the room, which is motivating. However, if your level of energy and your use of your voice and body are less than authentic, listeners will quickly pick up on that and may write off the talk as insincere.

7. **Use PowerPoint with care.** Text-laden slides can produce the same effect as sleeping pills. If a picture paints a thousand words, then adding pictures and graphics can certainly help the audience access the ideas you want to convey (as long as they are not flashy to the point of distraction). Limit the text on each slide, and do not read from the slides you are showing. Try to imagine how you would respond to the slides if you were not particularly interested in the topic, and then make adjustments based on what you conclude.

8. **Dress appropriately.** Though your audience may be wearing more casual clothing, it is safest to dress in business-professional attire. Avoid distracting clothing (like a tie that draws attention away from what you have to say), and check to be sure your collar is straight, your blouse or shirt is tucked in, and everything else is in order before standing up to speak.

9. **Avoid food and drink that make speaking difficult for you.** Caffeinated drinks and sugary foods can make you jittery, which will only add to your nervousness. If you find that you need to clear your throat often after consuming certain foods or beverages, avoid them before speaking engagements.

10. **Practice, practice, practice.** The more presentations you give, the more you will feel confident while giving them. And one of the best ways to conquer stage fright is to spend time speaking in front of others. Recognize that your discomfort with public speaking is likely to fade with experience on the podium.

Sources: Adapted from Naomi Rockler-Gladen, "Fear of Public Speaking," January 12, 2007, http://collegeuniversity .suite101.com/article.cfm/fear_of_public_speaking, accessed March 15, 2007; "Presentation Tips for Public Speaking," A Research Guide for Students, http://www.aresearchguide.com/3tips.html, accessed March 15, 2007; and Kimberly L. McCall, "All That Jazz," *Entrepreneur*, Vol. 34, No. 1 (March 2006), p. 36.

Implementing a win–win strategy in relationships involves thinking about one's own interests and also exploring the interests of the other party. After clarifying the interests of the involved parties and their needs, the negotiator can explore various alternatives to identify their overall fit, looking for a solution that will produce a plan that is workable for all. There are situations in which a win–win solution is impossible, but a positive solution should be pursued whenever possible. And, of course, a foundation for successful negotiation is created by developing strong relationships between the negotiating parties, which can facilitate cooperation.[24]

Personal Time Management

4. Describe the problem of time pressure and suggest solutions.

A typical entrepreneur spends much of the working day on the front lines—meeting customers, solving problems, listening to employee complaints, talking with suppliers, and the like. She or he tackles such problems with the assistance of only a small staff. As a result, the owner-manager's energies and activities are diffused, and time becomes a scarce resource. This highlights the importance of what is called time management. But as author and personal achievement expert Barry Farber points out, "When you think about time management, realize that you don't really manage time—you manage activities."[25] It's an interesting way to think about one of the challenges you are sure to face.

The Problem of Time Pressure

The hours worked by most new business owners are particularly long. Many owner-managers in small firms work from 60 to 80 hours per week. A frequent and unfortunate result of such a schedule is inefficient work performance, especially when the entrepreneur has not made the necessary effort to set priorities in life and work. Owner-managers may be too busy to see sales representatives who could supply market information on new products and processes, too busy to read technical or trade literature that would tell them what others are doing and what improvements might be adapted to their own use, too busy to listen carefully to employees' opinions and grievances, and too busy to give employees the instructions they need to do their jobs correctly.

Getting away for a vacation seems impossible for some small business owners. In extremely small firms, owners may find it necessary to close the business during their absence. Even in somewhat larger businesses, owners may fear that the firm will not function properly if they are not there. Unfortunately, keeping one's nose to the grindstone in this way may cost an entrepreneur dearly in terms of personal health, family relationships, and effectiveness in business leadership.

Time Savers for Busy Managers

Part of the solution to the problem of time pressure is application of the managerial approaches discussed in the preceding section. For example, when possible, the manager should assign duties to subordinates who can work without close supervision. For such delegation to work, though, a manager must first select and train qualified employees.

The greatest time saver is the effective use of time. Little will be achieved if an individual flits from one task to another and back again. Use of modern technology, including cell phones, e-mail, and the Internet, can be very helpful in allowing a manager to make the most of his or her time. (A note of caution is in order: Because these tools can become a distraction, they need to be used wisely. For example, checking and responding at length to incoming e-mail messages throughout the day can distract from the tasks at hand and should be minimized.)

The first step in time management should be to analyze how much time is normally spent on various activities. Relying on general impressions is not only unprofessional but also unscientific and likely to involve error. For a period of several days or (preferably) weeks, the manager should record the amounts of time spent on various activities during the day. An analysis of these figures will reveal a pattern, indicating which projects and tasks consume the most time and which activities are responsible for wasted time. It will also reveal chronic time wasting due to excessive socializing, work on trivial matters, coffee breaks, and so on.

If your habits are typical, you will probably find that the workplace "time-wasters" in your life are similar to those that surfaced in a survey of employees. These included time lost from telephone interruptions, drop-in visitors, ineffective delegation, losing things in desk clutter, procrastination, and frequent or lengthy meetings.[26] Knowing the distractions that others find to be time-wasters may help you to pinpoint those that are creating a problem for you. Only after recognizing these distractions can you take steps to deal with them.

After eliminating practices that waste time, a manager can carefully plan his or her use of available time. A planned approach to a day's or week's work is much more effective than a haphazard do-whatever-comes-up-first style. This is true even for small firm managers whose schedules are continually interrupted in unanticipated ways.

Many time management specialists recommend the use of a daily written plan of work activities, often called a "to-do" list. A survey of 2,000 executives from mostly small companies found that around 95 percent of them keep a list of things to do. Those executives may have 6 to 20 items on their list at any given time, though fewer than 1 percent of them complete all listed tasks on a daily basis.[27] Many entrepreneurs use Microsoft Outlook or a day planner to create and manage these lists, but others use PDAs, note cards, or even sticky notes. Regardless of the medium selected, the method you use should highlight priorities among listed items. By classifying duties as first-, second-, or third-level priorities, you can identify and focus attention on the most crucial tasks.

There are countless guides to time management, and they offer many valuable tips: Get a good time management system and use it, try to make meetings more efficient, unsubscribe from magazines and catalogues you never read, create a file folder for active projects, keep your desk and office organized, use deadlines to promote focus, manage e-mail effectively, and so on. However, the one bit of advice that seems to show up on just about every list of suggestions is to set aside time to work undisturbed.[28] As the pace of business and the flow of information pick up speed and new technologies and media channels increasingly compete for your attention, preserving time for focused work on important projects becomes more and more difficult—but it is critical that you do so. The health and future of your company may very well depend on it!

In the final analysis, effective time management requires firmly established priorities and self-discipline. An individual may begin with good intentions but lapse into habitually attending to whatever he or she finds to do at the moment. Procrastination is a frequent thief of time—many managers delay unpleasant and difficult tasks, retreating to trivial and less threatening activities with the rationalization that they are getting those duties out of the way in order to be able to concentrate better on the more important tasks.

Outside Management Assistance

Because entrepreneurs tend to be better doers than they are managers, they should consider the use of outside management assistance. Such support can supplement the manager's personal knowledge and the expertise of the few staff specialists on the company's payroll.

5. Explain the various types of outside management assistance.

The Need for Outside Assistance

Entrepreneurs often lack opportunities to share ideas with peers, given the small staff in most new enterprises. Consequently, they may experience a sense of loneliness. Some entrepreneurs reduce their feelings of isolation by joining groups such as the Entrepreneurs' Organization and the Young Presidents' Organization,[29] which allow them to meet with peers from other firms and share problems and experiences.

By obtaining help from peer groups and other sources of outside managerial assistance, entrepreneurs can overcome some of their managerial deficiencies and ease their sense of loneliness. Outsiders can bring a detached, often objective point of view and new ideas. They may also possess knowledge of methods, approaches, and solutions beyond the experience of a particular entrepreneur.

Sources of Management Assistance

Entrepreneurs seeking management assistance can turn to any number of sources, including business incubators, SBA programs, and management consultants. Other approaches the entrepreneur can take to obtain management help include consulting public and university libraries, attending evening classes at local colleges, and considering the suggestions of informed friends and customers.

BUSINESS INCUBATORS   As discussed in Chapter 9, a business incubator is an organization that offers both space and managerial and clerical services to new businesses. According to the National Business Incubation Association, there are now more than 1,100 incubators in the United States and about 7,000 worldwide.[30] Around 94 percent of the incubators in North America are operated as nonprofit organizations, many of which involve the participation of government agencies or universities; however, some (around 4 percent) have been launched as private endeavors.[31] The primary motivation for establishing incubators has been a desire to encourage entrepreneurship and thereby contribute to economic development.

Often, individuals who wish to start businesses lack relevant knowledge and appropriate experience. In many cases, they need practical guidance in marketing, record keeping, management practices, business plan preparation, and other forms of operating expertise. A more complete list of the services typically available in an incubator is shown in Exhibit 19-5.

EXHIBIT 19-5 Services Provided by Business Incubators to New Firms

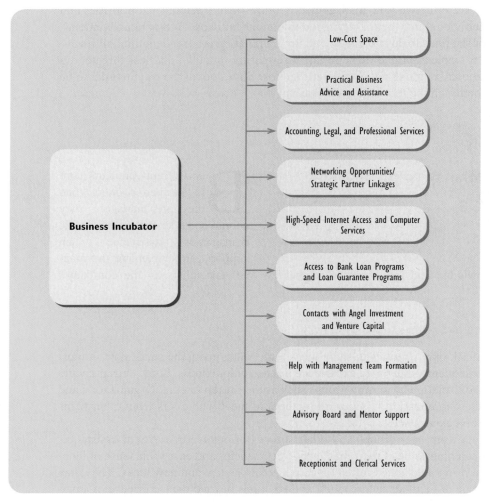

Business Incubator

- Low-Cost Space
- Practical Business Advice and Assistance
- Accounting, Legal, and Professional Services
- Networking Opportunities/ Strategic Partner Linkages
- High-Speed Internet Access and Computer Services
- Access to Bank Loan Programs and Loan Guarantee Programs
- Contacts with Angel Investment and Venture Capital
- Help with Management Team Formation
- Advisory Board and Mentor Support
- Receptionist and Clerical Services

An incubator provides a supportive atmosphere for a business during the early months of its existence, when it is most fragile and vulnerable to external dangers and internal errors. If the incubator works as it should, the fledgling business gains strength quickly and soon leaves the incubator setting. Most incubators "graduate" startups within a certain time period (typically, three years) or when the company achieves certain performance milestones. Generally, startups are not released "into the wild" until they can withstand the competition they will encounter in the marketplace.

Today, some incubators in the United States are reinventing themselves as "virtual incubators"—that is, they no longer require client companies to set up shop at a single location. Instead, they focus on connecting a greater number of entrepreneurs with the high-quality experts and mentors they need. This model is less expensive to operate, so the cost savings can be passed on to the entrepreneurs. When Christie Stone, co-founder of Tico Beans Coffee, a coffee distributor in New Orleans, was just getting started, she needed help executing her business plan. However, relocating to an incubator was out of the question—she wanted an office near a warehouse where her beans could be stored. She eventually joined a virtual incubator called The Idea Village, without having to move. The team of lawyers, accountants, and salespeople assigned to the company helped her get off to a very solid start, at very little cost. Tico Beans received around $30,000 worth of legal and consulting services for only $3,000 from lawyers and accountants who saw that providing assistance was a way to build their networks.[32] Everyone walked away happy!

EDUCATIONAL INSTITUTIONS

Many colleges and universities have student consulting teams willing to assist small businesses. These teams of upper-class and graduate students, under the direction of a faculty member, work with owners of small ventures in analyzing and devising solutions to their business problems.

The program has mutual benefits: It provides students with a practical view of business management and supplies small firms with answers to their problems. The students who participate are typically combined in teams that provide a diversity of academic backgrounds. An individual team, for example, may include students specializing in management, marketing, accounting, and finance.

Some colleges and universities offer training directly to aspiring small business owners. For example, nearly 300,000 entrepreneurs have gone through a business development program called FastTrac, which is available in all 50 U.S. states and select countries around the world. This curriculum was developed by the Ewing Marion Kauffman Foundation and is offered through more than 300 alliance partners, including colleges and universities, chambers of commerce, business development centers, consulting firms, and many other organizations.[33] FastTrac is a practical, hands-on program designed to show entrepreneurs how to hone the practical skills they will need to launch, manage, and grow a successful business. Participants don't just learn about business—they *live it* by working on their own business ideas.[34]

SERVICE CORPS OF RETIRED EXECUTIVES (SCORE)

By contacting any SBA field office, small business managers can obtain free management advice from a group called the *Service Corps of Retired Executives*, or *SCORE*.[35] SCORE is an organization of retired business executives who serve as consultants to small business managers. Functioning under the sponsorship of the SBA, SCORE provides an opportunity for retired executives to contribute to the business community and, in the process, help small business managers solve their problems. The relationship is thus mutually beneficial.

Judson Lovering, an entrepreneur who operated a specialty bakery in New England, wished to improve his business. A SCORE business counselor, who had formerly owned a small business, helped him capitalize on the bakery's most popular products and eliminate low-profit offerings. This required Lovering to decline some specialty orders that had made the business a "personal bakery" without adequate profit margins. Following the counselor's advice, Lovering has been able to grow his business.[36]

Service Corps of Retired Executives (SCORE)
An SBA-sponsored group of retired executives who give free advice to small businesses.

**small business
development
centers (SBDCs)**
University-affiliated
centers offering
consulting, education,
and other support to
small businesses.

SMALL BUSINESS DEVELOPMENT CENTERS (SBDCs)   Patterned after the Agricultural Extension Service, *small business development centers (SBDCs)* are affiliated with colleges or universities as a part of the SBA's overall program of assistance to small business. SBDCs provide direct consultation, continuing education, research assistance, and export services. One of their special priorities is to lend support to minority-owned firms. The staff typically includes faculty members, SCORE counselors, professional staff, and graduate student assistants.

MANAGEMENT CONSULTANTS   Management consultants serve small businesses as well as large corporations. Types of consultants range from large global firms to one- and two-person operations. Small firm managers, however, are often reluctant to use outside advisors, for a host of reasons. For example, some believe that they can solve problems themselves, that an outsider could never truly understand the business, or that bringing in an outside advisor would simply cost too much. But some small businesses need analysis by consultants and find that the enterprise can easily recover the cost of such services in the revenue resulting from improved performance. Results definitely vary.

For small companies that decide to pursue this option, the owner and the consultant should reach an understanding on the nature of the assistance to be provided before it begins. This can help to ensure satisfaction for both the provider and the client. Any consulting fees should be specified, and the particulars of the agreement should be put in writing. Fees are often quoted on a per-day basis and can easily range from $500 to $5,000, or more. Although the cost may seem high, it must be evaluated in terms of the expertise that it buys.

Directories are available to help entrepreneurs find the right management consultant. One such directory is published by the Institute of Management Consultants USA (http://www .imcusa.org). The code of ethics to which institute members subscribe is an indication of their desire to foster professionalism in their work.

networking
The process of
developing and
engaging in mutually
beneficial relationships.

ENTREPRENEURIAL NETWORKS   Entrepreneurs can also gain management assistance from peers through *networking,* the process of developing and engaging in mutually beneficial informal relationships. When business owners meet, they discover a commonality of interests that leads to an exchange of ideas and experiences. The settings for such meetings may be trade associations, civic clubs, fraternal organizations, or any other situation that brings businesspeople into contact with one another. Of course, the personal network of an entrepreneur is not limited to other entrepreneurs, but those individuals may be the most significant part of his or her business network.

Business networking opportunities often come from unexpected settings. For example, in 2004 Ryan Bonifacino used connections from his university fraternity to launch a special event and corporate photography company. Today, his New York City–based business has a new name, Bozmedia, and has expanded to offer digital media services, brand management, and Internet marketing and advertising. "Our main investor was actually one of our sponsors for a fraternity philanthropic event," says the 25-year-old entrepreneur. "He loved the plan, the fraternity, and our energy." Bonifacino's relationship with his fraternity was a huge help. His first gigs were at Greek events, where he was able to connect with thousands of people. Bonifacino graduated in 2005 and led Bozmedia to sales of around $460,000 in 2006, but that was just the start. He has pulled together a strong nine-person management team, which should lead the company into a very bright future.[37] So, just hanging out can really pay off!

Harnessing a personal network can provide a tremendous boost to the launch of a new business. For example, fellow garden club members could serve as a focus group to assess startup ideas or as a PR team to spread news of your new landscaping and water pond business across town. Alumni connections from your college days may lead you to professionals who can take care of your legal, banking, or other needs. They may even become loyal and effective business partners, if the fit is right.

OTHER BUSINESS AND PROFESSIONAL SERVICES   A variety of business and professional groups provide management assistance. In many cases, such assistance is part of the business relationship. Sources of management advice include bankers, certified public accountants, attorneys, insurance agents, suppliers, trade associations, and chambers of commerce.

It takes initiative to draw on the management assistance available from such groups. For example, rather than limiting his or her business relationship with a certified public accountant (CPA) to audits and financial statements, an owner-manager must think to ask the CPA to advise on a much broader range of subjects.

A good accountant can not only offer advice on tax matters, but also recommend an appropriate severance package when it comes time to fire someone. If you are thinking about opening a new branch, an accountant can tell you if your cash flow will support it. Considering the launch of an additional business? An accountant's insight will help you determine whether the margins will be adequate. Accountants can help you make informed assessments of your insurance needs, the impact of taking on a big account (as well as the downside of losing it), and the bottom-line effects of cutting expenses.

As you can see from these examples, potential management assistance often comes disguised as service from professionals and firms encountered in the normal course of business activity. By taking advantage of such opportunities, an entrepreneur can strengthen a small firm's management and improve its operations with little, if any, additional cost. But that doesn't mean it will be easy. Leading and overseeing the work of an entrepreneurial firm requires professionalism, which can be developed only through great effort and attention to management details. Reaching this state is a challenge, but the insights in this chapter can help guide you toward the competencies you will need.

LOOKING BACK

1. Discuss the entrepreneur's leadership role.

- Entrepreneurs must establish and communicate a vision of the firm's future.
- Founding entrepreneurs need a tolerance for ambiguity and a capacity for adaptation.
- Entrepreneurs need resolve to make the business succeed more than they need a flashy personality.
- An entrepreneur exerts strong personal influence in a small firm.
- Progressive managers use various leadership styles, incorporating participative management, empowerment, and even self-managed work teams.
- Entrepreneurs should deliberately shape the organizational culture, which can greatly influence how business is conducted in the company and how the company performs.

2. Explain the distinctive features of small business management.

- Many founders tend to be more action-oriented and less analytical than professional managers.

- A founder's less-than-professional management style can adversely affect business growth.
- Small companies are particularly vulnerable to managerial inefficiency, and even failure.
- Small firm managers face special financial and personnel constraints.
- As a new business grows, it adds layers of supervision and increases formality of management.
- A firm's growth requires the entrepreneur to become more of a manager and less of a doer.

3. Identify the managerial tasks of entrepreneurs.

- Both long-range planning and short-range planning are required, but they are often postponed or neglected.
- Managers must create an organizational structure to provide for orderly direction of operations.
- Informal groups within the organization can be encouraged to make a beneficial contribution to the firm.
- Managers who delegate authority successfully can devote more time to more important duties.

- Managers exercise control by monitoring operations in order to detect and correct deviations from plans.

- Effective two-way communication is important in building a healthy organization.

- Entrepreneurs will need to develop their group presentation skills to meet the demands of being the leader of a growing business.

- Managers must be able to negotiate with both insiders and outsiders.

4. Describe the problem of time pressure and suggest solutions.

- Time pressure creates inefficiencies in the management of a small firm because the entrepreneur's energies are diffused.

- A manager can reduce time pressure through such practices as eliminating wasteful activities and planning work carefully, using such tools as a "to-do" list.

- The greatest time saver is the effective use of time, which requires self-discipline.

5. Explain the various types of outside management assistance.

- Outside management assistance can be used to remedy staff limitations and reduce an entrepreneur's sense of isolation, among other things.

- Business incubators provide guidance as well as space for beginning businesses.

- Three government- and/or university-sponsored sources of assistance are educational institutions, the Service Corps of Retired Executives (SCORE), and small business development centers (SBDCs).

- Management assistance may be obtained by engaging management consultants and by networking with other entrepreneurs.

- Professionals such as bankers and CPAs can also provide valuable management assistance.

Key Terms

empowerment p. 497

work teams p. 497

professional manager p. 500

long-range plan (strategic plan) p. 504

short-range plan p. 504

budget p. 504

chain of command p. 505

line organization p. 505

line-and-staff organization p. 505

span of control p. 506

delegation of authority p. 506

negotiation p. 510

Service Corps of Retired Executives (SCORE) p. 515

small business development centers (SBDCs) p. 516

networking p. 516

Discussion Questions

1. Would most employees of small firms welcome or resist a leadership approach that sought their ideas and involved them in meetings to let them know what was going on? Why might some employees resist such an approach?

2. Is the quality of management likely to be relatively uniform in all types of small businesses? If not, what might account for differences?

3. What are the four stages of small business growth outlined in this chapter? How do management requirements change as the firm moves through these stages?

4. Some professional football coaches have written game plans that they consult from time to time during games. If coaches need formal plans, does it follow that small business owners also need them as they engage in their particular type of competition? Why or why not?

5. What type of small firm might effectively use a line organization? When might it be necessary to change the firm's structure? To what type of structure? Why?

6. Explain the relationship between planning and control in a small business. Give an example.

7. There is a saying that goes "What you do speaks so loudly I can't hear what you say." What does this mean, and how does it apply to communication in small firms?

8. What practices can a small business manager use to conserve time?

9. What are some advantages and possible drawbacks for a startup retail firm of locating in a business incubator?

10. Are student consulting teams of greater benefit to the client firm or to the students involved?

You Make the Call

SITUATION 1

John Smithers learned all about leadership in the military, and he is hoping to apply those skills to running John's Deals on Wheels, his small automobile leasing company. One interesting feature of life in the armed services is that considerable responsibilities are delegated to young men and women who have very little work experience. Smithers was only 27 when he was assigned duties as a purchasing manager at Kandahar Airport, Afghanistan, in 2003. As a young marine, he was directly responsible for nearly $50 million in purchasing contracts, which forced him to grow up—really fast!

To parallel his military experience, Smithers and his small management team have decided to use various methods to delegate decision making to employees at the operating level in his company. New employees are trained thoroughly after they are first hired, but supervisors will not monitor their work closely once they have learned their duties. Management is willing to jump in and help if truly needed, but they purposely leave workers alone when they take on their assigned duties. Managers will not look over employees' shoulders to be sure that they are doing their jobs as assigned, and they certainly do not monitor the work just to try to catch someone making a mistake. Smithers's managerial philosophy is that people work best when they sense that their superiors trust their abilities and their business integrity.

Smithers and his team sometimes leave for day-long meetings and allow the employees to run the business by themselves. Job assignments are defined rather loosely, but management expects employees to assume responsibility and to take necessary action whenever they see that something needs to be done. To reinforce the message of trust, employees who ask for direction are sometimes simply told to solve the problem in whatever way they think best.

Question 1 Is such a loosely organized firm likely to be as effective as a firm that defines jobs more precisely and monitors performance more closely? What are the advantages and the limitations of the managerial style described above?

Question 2 How might such managerial methods affect morale?

Question 3 Would you like to work for this company? Why or why not?

SITUATION 2

A few years after successfully launching a new outdoor advertising business, Sean Richeson found himself spending 16-hour days running from one appointment to another, negotiating with customers, drumming up new business, signing checks, and checking up as much as possible on his six employees. The founder realized that his own strength was in selling, but general managerial responsibilities were very time consuming and interfered with his sales efforts. Richeson even slept in the office two nights a week just to try to keep up with his work.

Despite his diligence, however, Richeson knew that his employees weren't organized and that many problems needed to be addressed. For example, he lacked the time to set personnel policies or to draw up specific job descriptions for his six employees. Just last week, he had been warned that one employee would sometimes take advantage of the lax supervision and skip work. Invoices often were sent to customers late, and delivery schedules were not always kept. Fortunately, the business was profitable in spite of the numerous problems.

Question 1 Is Richeson's problem one of time management or general managerial ability? Would it be feasible to engage a management consultant to help solve the firm's problems?

Question 2 If Richeson asked you to recommend some type of outside management assistance, would you recommend a SCORE counselor, a student consulting team, a CPA firm, a management consultant, or some other type of assistance? Why?

Question 3 If you were asked to improve this company's management system, what steps would you would take first? What would be your initial goal?

SITUATION 3

After a slow start in a spare bedroom in her home, Sarah Sullivan's media sales business was flourishing. Even though it had been only three and a half years since she launched the company, Sullivan was beginning to wonder if she had the necessary talent to ensure its continued success. The business had grown to 100 employees after two years, and now it was approaching 200 employees. When the business was small, Sullivan could figure out solutions to problems on a case-by-case basis, but now the problems were becoming increasingly complicated.

Question 1 What kinds of practices or procedures will Sullivan need to adopt to enable the business to continue to operate successfully?

Question 2 What resources might Sullivan use to get good feedback to help her assess her competence and understand the issues her growing business is facing?

1. Interview a management consultant, SCORE member, university director of student consulting teams, or representative of a CPA firm to discuss small business management weaknesses and the willingness or reluctance of small firms to use consultants. Prepare a report on your findings.

2. Diagram the organizational relationships in a small business of your choice. Report on any organizational problems that are apparent to you or that are recognized by the manager or others in the firm.

3. Prepare a report on your personal observations of leadership and delegation of authority by a supervisor in an organization where you have been an employee or volunteer. Include references to the type(s) of leadership exercised and the adequacy of authority delegation (if any), clarity of instructions, and any problems involved.

4. Select an unstructured time block of one to four hours in your schedule—that is, hours that are not regularly devoted to class attendance, sleeping, and so on. Carefully record your use of that time period for several days. Prepare a report summarizing your use of the time and outlining a plan to use it more effectively.

Small Business & Entrepreneurship Resource Center

The *Small Business and Entrepreneurship Resource Center* offers complete small business management resources through a comprehensive database that covers all major areas of starting, operating, and maintaining a business from financing, management, marketing, accounting, taxes, and more. Use the access code that came with your new book to access the site and perform the exercises in each chapter.

1. Elise and Rick Wetzel founded Pasadena, California-based iSold It, LLC, a franchisor of drop-off stores for those who want someone to sell items on eBay for them. Within a year, the wild growth of the company led the husband and wife team to conclude that the business was more than they could handle. Rick Wetzel realized that "You have to set your ego aside . . . and say, 'This is too big for me; we need a stronger team.'" The Wetzels were able to find an experienced manager and brought him on as CEO in 2004, and now the company is running at top speed. The owners realized that professional management was crucial to growth. The article "Selling Point" discusses a franchisee's perspective on hiring the right talent. Describe the perspective of franchisee, Kenny Byrne, about the types of employees they need to hire and the skills required to grow.

2. The text states that the quality of delegation can also be determined just by the way entrepreneurs think about it. For example, Stephen R. Covey describes a preferred method as "stewardship" delegation. Stewardship delegation focuses on results and allows the individual receiving an assignment some latitude in carrying it out. Only stewardship delegation provides the benefits of delegation to both parties. The article "Stephen R. Covey: The Seven Habits" discusses Covey's seven habits of highly effective people. Briefly describe each of the seven habits.

Sources: Selling point: bidding on the success of eBay auction assistance pays off. (Brief Article). April Y. Pennington. *Entrepreneur* 33, 11 (Nov 2005): p. 117(1).
Stephen R. Covey: The Seven Habits of Highly Effective People. (Book review). *Thinkers*. Chartered Management Institute. March 2003. p. NA.

Case 19

DIAMOND WIPES INTERNATIONAL, P. 664

This case points out how the growth of a business requires leadership and managerial adjustments, with a focus on the entrepreneur's need to hire capable personnel and delegate responsibilities to be able to manage the many new challenges that arise when a firm expands.

ALTERNATIVE CASES FOR CHAPTER 19

Case 8, D'Artagnan, p. 638

chapter 20

Managing Human Resources

In the SPOTLIGHT
Some People Ask Too Many
(Bad) Questions

If interviewing is an important part of the human resource management function, you wouldn't know it by the carelessness with which the process is all too often handled. One anonymous employee mentions some less-than-positive personal experiences as an interviewee and then describes a few of the negative impressions of the hiring company that were created as a result.

First, there are the seemingly small things. When I come in for an interview and a company doesn't validate my parking, it usually indicates to me that it's not very financially stable. When they don't offer me a drink or a bathroom break during a lengthy interview or series of interviews, I get the impression that they don't care or provide for their employees. If my interviewer is late to interview me and seems to be looking at my résumé for the first time, it's a clue that the company is somewhat hectic and unorganized. And if the interviewer isn't enthused about the company mission or work responsibilities, then how can I be?

A big red flag is if an interview it too easy. This is usually a sign that the company doesn't have a high standard for its employees—that almost anyone walking in off the street could get a job—and that my coworkers wouldn't be able to teach me anything that I didn't already know.

On the opposite end of the spectrum, brutal interviews also make a bad impression. I've had one too many situations where interviewers seemed out to prove that they were smarter than me. They appeared to take pleasure in stumping me with questions that I'm pretty sure I wouldn't need to know to be successful at my job. It's also a big turnoff realizing I would have to work with these competitive egomaniacs.

For many capable individuals, the job interview will be their first significant contact with the company. If the experience goes poorly or the interaction leaves a negative impression, the chance of hiring a high-quality employee goes down. But perhaps even more harmful would be the negative word of

LOOKING AHEAD

AFTER STUDYING THIS CHAPTER, YOU SHOULD BE ABLE TO...

1. Explain the importance of employee recruitment and list some sources that can be useful in finding suitable applicants.

2. Identify the steps to take in evaluating job applicants.

3. Describe the roles of training and development for both managerial and nonmanagerial employees in a small business.

4. Explain the various types of compensation plans, including the use of incentive plans.

5. Discuss the human resource issues of co-employment, legal protection, labor unions, and the formalizing of employer–employee relationships.

Small businesses have various types of resources. Money in the bank, for example, is a *financial* resource, and a unique patent may be a *technological* resource. But employees represent a venture's *human* resources and are perhaps the most vital of all to its operations. To build a competitive business, you need to think carefully about how to find and hire the best people available and then consider how to hold on to them. Honest, competent, motivated employees are the lifeblood of the small business, so it is critical for entrepreneurs to manage them competently and efficiently.

Many of the human resource management (HRM) practices used by giant corporations like Walmart and General Motors will not work for small businesses. However, these businesses can, and should, use personnel management methods that are suitable for smaller firms. Sadly, many small companies follow what is, at best, a haphazard HRM program, choosing to "shoot from the hip" on personnel management decisions, only to miss their employment targets entirely in many cases. Research has shown that, compared to large corporations, small businesses are much less likely to use professional HRM practices related to recruitment, training, performance assessment, and other processes.[1] This regrettable state of affairs may be the result of a lack of knowledge; we hope to prevent it from hampering your business. The goal of this chapter is to present HRM practices that work best for entrepreneurial companies.

Recruiting Personnel

Recruitment brings applicants to a business; the goal is to obtain a pool of applicants large enough to contain a number of talented prospects. In a subsequent stage of the selection process, management decides which applicants are "keepers."

1. Explain the importance of employee recruitment and list some sources that can be useful in finding suitable applicants.

The Need for Quality Employees

There is no substitute for high-quality employees—in most cases, the more capable and motivated, the better. Joel Spolsky, founder and CEO of a software development company in New York City, describes the remarkable impact that excellent employees can have on a business:

> I keep hearing people say that they only hire the top 1 percent of job seekers. At my company, Fog Creek Software, I want to hire the top 1 percent, too. We're doubling in size each year, and we're always in the market for great software developers. In our field, the top 1 percent of the workforce can easily be 10 times as productive as the average developer. The best developers invent new products, figure out shortcuts that save months of work, and, when there are no shortcuts, plow through coding tasks like a monster truck at a tea party.[2]

Having the right people "on board" can provide an enormous boost to the overall performance of the company. And it's about more than the individual contribution of each high-potential employee. The presence of one capable and motivated worker tends to raise expectations of all the others, and interactions between two or more high-impact employees will often lead to outcomes that are significantly greater than the sum of their already excellent individual contributions.

Recruitment and selection of employees establish a foundation for a firm's ongoing human relationships. In a sense, the quality of a firm's employees determines its potential. A solid, effective organization can be built only with a talented, ambitious workforce. And since payroll is one of the largest expense categories for most businesses, wise employment decisions can have a direct impact on the company's bottom line. By recruiting the best personnel possible, an entrepreneurial firm can improve its return on each payroll dollar.

Most successful companies have moved ahead of their competition because they recognize that employees *are* the business, and vice versa. There is no getting around this, especially for entrepreneurial firms that are expanding. "You cannot separate the need to grow from the number of people you will need to hire," observes Matthew Guthridge, an associate principle at global management consulting firm McKinsey & Co. "And that at the very basic level is the essence of what [an employment] strategy should be about."[3] Hiring and holding on to the right people can easily make or break a small business.

The Lure of Entrepreneurial Firms

Competing for well-qualified business talent requires small firms to identify their distinctive advantages, especially when recruiting outstanding prospects for managerial and professional positions. Fortunately, there are many good reasons to work for an entrepreneurial business. This is especially true of growing enterprises led by individuals or teams with a compelling vision of a desirable and attainable future. It is exciting to work for a company that is going somewhere!

Chris Resto, Ian Ybarra, and Ramit Sethi, coauthors of the book *Recruit or Die*, have concluded that entrepreneurs can compete with ace recruiters such as Microsoft, McKinsey & Co., and Goldman Sachs when it comes to attracting and hiring promising employees. The secret is coming up with a strategy that will convince the best and brightest to join a small company. Offering competitive salaries helps (more on that later in the chapter), but many recruits are even more interested in opportunities for high-level achievement, job variety, interesting experiences, personal recognition, and the potential to do work that they believe is important.[4] Many small businesses are in an excellent position to offer such attractive opportunities to prospective employees.

Because of their small size and limited staff, new managers in entrepreneurial companies are closer to the CEO (often the founder), which can lead to quicker action. It also provides opportunities to make decisions and to obtain the general, high-level management or professional experience that achievement-oriented hires find attractive. Rather than toiling in obscure, low-level, specialized positions in a large firm while "paying their dues" and working their way up the corporate ladder, capable newcomers can quickly move into positions of responsibility in a well-managed small business. In such jobs, they get a front-row seat for interesting experiences and can see the fruits of their labor and know that they are making a difference in the success of the company.

Small firms can also structure the work environment to offer professional, managerial, and technical personnel greater job variety and freedom than they would normally have in a larger business. In this type of environment, individual contributions can be recognized rather than hidden under numerous layers of bureaucracy. In addition, compensation packages can be structured to create powerful incentives for outstanding performance.

To be sure, there are drawbacks to working for a small company—for example, managerial blunders are harder to absorb and thus tend to be obvious to everyone, support systems from legal or human resource staff may not be readily available, and limited employee benefits can lead to high levels of turnover and constant changes in personnel.[5] But many small employers offer to offset these disadvantages with appealing tradeoffs, such as flexible work scheduling, job-sharing arrangements, less travel, and other potential advantages. All things considered, this can be shaped into a very attractive employment opportunity.

Many former employees of large corporations who now work for small firms prefer their new life in the entrepreneurial world. Here are the comments of some who have made the transition and like where they are today:[6]

- "There's less bureaucracy," says Jeff Macdonald, when comparing his work at Acorda Therapeutics, a small biotech company, with life in a big pharmaceutical firm. "Decisions are made without having to go through a number of layers of approval."
- Patrick Crane once worked for a large Internet company but now is with fast-growing LinkedIn Corp. "At Yahoo I shook [the CEO's] hand twice and had maybe five conversations with him in four years," he reports. "Now I meet with our CEO several times a day."
- Scott Ruthfield finds his work at WhitePages.com to be more fulfilling than his previous managerial position with Amazon.com: "Everybody plays a core role, so if you do a good job, you are directly contributing to the way the business is going to succeed."
- The sense of contribution is also important to Dean Medley, senior vice president of recruiting at Medical Methods Inc., a Florida-based staffing firm with 50 employees. "When you land a new account, it's a huge deal."

These comments represent some of the "selling points" that small companies can use to attract employees who are likely to be moving toward a career in a large corporation. With a little thought and some careful positioning, entrepreneurs can actually win the competitive challenge to lure the best talent available.

Sources of Employees

To recruit effectively, the small business manager must know where and how to find qualified applicants. Sources are numerous, and it is impossible to generalize about the best source in view of the differences in companies' personnel needs and the quality of the sources from one locality to another. The following discussion describes some sources of employees most popular among small firms.

WALK-INS   A firm may receive unsolicited applications from individuals who walk into the place of business to seek employment. Walk-ins are an inexpensive source of personnel, particularly for hourly work, but the quality of applicants varies. If qualified applicants cannot be hired immediately, their applications should be kept on file for future reference. In the interest of good community relations, all applicants should be treated courteously, whether or not they are offered jobs.

HELP-WANTED ADVERTISING   Hanging a "Help Wanted" sign in the window is one traditional form of recruiting used by some small firms, mostly retailers and fast-food restaurants. A similar but more aggressive form of recruiting consists of advertising in the classifieds section of local newspapers. For some technical, professional, and managerial positions, firms may advertise in trade and professional journals. Although the effectiveness of help-wanted advertising has been questioned by some, many small businesses recruit in this way.

SCHOOLS   Secondary schools, career schools, colleges, and universities are desirable sources of personnel for certain positions, particularly those requiring no specific work experience. Some secondary schools and colleges have internship programs that enable students to gain practical experience in firms, which can be very helpful. Applicants from career schools often have useful educational backgrounds to offer a small business. Colleges and universities can supply candidates for positions in management and in various technical and professional fields. In addition, many college students can work as part-time employees.

To achieve its goal of delighting its customers by providing superior construction services, Kay Construction uses a team approach, which wouldn't be possible without high-quality staff. The principals of the company, Lorraine Kay and Steve Walsh, believe that it is necessary to support the local education system to "build a reservoir of appropriately trained and motivated employees." So they work with nearby colleges to fine-tune courses offered to project management, engineering, and architecture students. By hiring some of the students as interns, the company gets inexpensive part-time help for the present and the inside track on offering them full-time positions after they graduate. This approach has worked very well for the company.[7]

PUBLIC EMPLOYMENT OFFICES   At no cost to small businesses, employment offices in each state offer information on applicants who are actively seeking employment and administer the state's unemployment insurance program. These offices, located in all major cities, are for the most part a useful source of clerical workers, unskilled laborers, production workers, and technicians. They do not actively recruit but only counsel and assist those who come in. Although public employment offices can be a source of good employees, the individuals they work with are, for the most part, untrained or only marginally qualified. Nonetheless, the role of such agencies is likely to become more important as time goes on, especially where the employment needs of small businesses are concerned.[8]

PRIVATE EMPLOYMENT AGENCIES   Numerous private firms offer their services as employment agencies. In some cases, employers receive these services without cost because the applicants pay a fee to the agency; however, more often, the hiring firms are responsible for the agency fee. Private employment agencies tend to specialize in people with specific skills, such as accountants, computer operators, and managers.

TEMPORARY HELP AGENCIES   The temporary help industry, which is growing rapidly, supplies employees (or temps)—such as word processors, clerks, accountants, engineers, nurses, and sales clerks—for short periods of time. By using an agency such as Kelly Services or Manpower Inc., small firms can deal with seasonal fluctuations and absences caused by vacation or illness. For example, a temporary replacement might be obtained to fill the position of an employee who is taking leave following the birth of a child—a type of family leave mandated by law for some employees. In addition, the use of temporary employees provides management with an introduction to individuals whose performance may justify an offer of permanent employment. Staffing with temporary employees is less practical when extensive training is required or continuity is important.

INTERNET RECRUITING Recruiters are increasingly seeking applicants via the Internet. A variety of websites, such as CareerBuilder.com, Monster.com, and Yahoo! HotJobs, allow applicants to submit their résumés online and permit potential employers to search those

LIVING THE DREAM:

entrepreneurial challenges

All A-Twitter about Recruiting

Jason Throckmorton is co-founder of LaunchSquad, a small San Francisco public relations company with a staff of 35. One day, while searching Twitter for comments about his client, he came across an interesting post from a University of Oregon student. Searching other online sources, he found a blog from the same student, commenting on the future of the PR industry. Throckmorton concluded very quickly that this was exactly the kind of employee they needed at his firm, so he contacted her. She came in for a visit and today is part of the LaunchSquad team.

Throckmorton isn't the only entrepreneur who is using Internet tools like social networks and blogs to recruit employees. Ben Swartz, co-founder and president of Marcel Media, an interactive marketing consulting venture in Chicago, estimates that he has snagged three-fourths of his 21-person staff using Web 2.0 tools. He is especially pleased with the tremendous depth of insight about job candidates that he gets by using LinkedIn and Facebook.

In a typical résumé, you might get a line on interests. On LinkedIn, you can find out who they associate with. On Facebook, you might find some groups and associations and even pictures. It gives us more dimensions than a static résumé can offer.

Such tools are allowing employers to completely reshape the recruiting landscape and find exactly the right employees for the jobs they seek to fill—at a much lower cost (in many cases, no cost at all).

Using online tools for recruitment is especially important for companies that hope to reach younger employees, 89 percent of whom spend time on the Internet every day. These job seekers are not likely to glance at the help-wanted ads in a newspaper, so catching their attention may very well require online outreach. Besides, any company that refuses to use Web 2.0 tools for recruitment risks being seen as behind the times, not exactly the kind of impression that draws in the forward-thinking prospects that most businesses need. Given their broad reach and low cost, these emerging technologies continue to open up new possibilities for small companies to compete with large corporations for the best hires available. It certainly pays to give them a try.

Sources: Mark Henricks, "How Entrepreneurs Are Using Social Networking, Blogging, and Other Internet Tools to Hire the Best Employees," *Entrepreneur*, Vol. 37, No. 2 (February 2009), pp. 55–57; Derek Gagne, "New Tools to Find Prime Job Candidates," *Fast Company*, March 3, 2009, http://www.fastcompany.com/blog/derek-gagne/talent-edge/new-tools-find-prime-job-candidates, accessed May 5, 2009. http://www.launchsquad.com

Photo Courtesy of Launch Squad

résumés for qualified applicants. And as the Internet becomes more popular as a source of applicants, many firms are posting job openings on their own websites.

Using the Internet for recruiting is convenient, but it carries some risks. Scott Wheeler founded a diesel engine repair company in Chesapeake, Virginia. Within five years, the business had doubled in size, reaching $10 million in sales and 44 employees. Wheeler was having trouble finding qualified mechanics to add to the rowdy mix of ex-French Foreign Legionnaires, bikers "with tattoos you wouldn't believe," and others who worked on engines for the company. So when an online service told him that it had 93 résumés for "generator technicians," Wheeler couldn't resist signing up. Unfortunately, the results were disappointing—very few of the candidates were even close to qualified. Wheeler's advice? "Don't give them your credit card number based on what they tell you. Make them send some sample résumés first."[9]

EMPLOYEE REFERRALS Recommendations of suitable candidates from good employees may provide excellent prospects. Ordinarily, employees will hesitate to recommend applicants unless they believe in their ability to do the job. Also, the family and friends of current workers can be among the best and most loyal employees available, because these individuals are well known and trusted. Many small business owners say that this source accounts for more new hires than any other. A few employers go so far as to offer financial rewards for employee referrals that result in the hiring of new employees.

Scott Glatstein is often looking to hire skilled management consultants for Imperatives, his $2.5 million Minnetonka, Minnesota, consulting company, but he has not had much luck finding them using standard recruiting tools. "It's hard to advertise for independent consultants," says Glatstein. Not that he hasn't tried! After using a variety of recruitment approaches, including Internet advertising, he has found that only one yields the results he is looking for: recommendations from his 40 current employees. Glatstein estimates that he has hired eight people in a recent six-month period, all of them through employee referrals. He didn't have to run a single ad to get the people he needed! Using referrals saves money (costing around 70 percent less than advertising or employment agencies) and reduces turnover, but perhaps the most important advantage is that these new hires become productive in less time and tend to have superior skills. Gladstein pays $300 for each referral hired. But if $300 would be a budget-buster for your company, adjust the figure down, or use a different incentive; you may very well end up with the same result.[10]

Hiring based on referrals is really just a way of tapping into the personal networks of employees. However, network recruiting becomes more important as the responsibilities associated with the position increase. Networking can be an indispensable tool when filling leadership positions in a small business, providing the best connections to individuals who have the background, skills, and integrity that are essential to a position of great responsibility in the company.

EXECUTIVE SEARCH FIRMS When filling key positions, small companies sometimes turn to executive search firms, often called *headhunters,* to locate qualified candidates. The key positions for which such firms seek applicants are those paying a minimum of $50,000 to $70,000 per year. The cost to the employer may run from 30 to 40 percent of the first year's salary. Because of the high cost, use of headhunters may seem unreasonable for small, entrepreneurial firms. At times, however, the need for a manager who can help a firm "move to the next level" justifies the use of an executive search firm. A headhunter is usually better able than the small business to conduct a wide-ranging search for individuals who possess the right combination of talents for the available position.

headhunter
A search firm that locates qualified candidates for executive positions.

Diversity in the Workforce

Over time, the composition of the workforce has changed with respect to race, ethnicity, gender, and age. The U.S. Department of Labor projects that the trend will continue, with much of the change attributed to an increase in the number of Hispanic workers. It offers the following statistics:

> The U.S. workforce will become more diverse by 2016. White, non-Hispanic persons will continue to make up a decreasing share of the labor force, falling from 69.1 percent in 2006 to 64.6 percent in 2016. [The proportion of Hispanics in the labor force will grow] from 13.7 percent to 16.4 percent. Asians are projected to account for an increasing share of the labor force by 2016, growing from 4.4 to 5.3 percent. Blacks will also increase their share of the labor force, growing from 11.4 percent to 12.3 percent.[11]

workforce diversity
Differences among employees on such dimensions as gender, age, ethnicity, and race.

The balance is shifting rapidly toward greater *workforce diversity,* not only because of increased participation of racial minorities but also because of higher proportions of women and older workers entering the labor force. As a result, the challenge for human resource management is to adapt to a more diverse pool of potential employees. To remain fully competitive, business owners need to step up recruitment of women and minorities and be open to innovative ways to access the available pool of applicants. In many cases, hiring more workers from diverse groups can help a company maintain good relations with an increasingly heterogeneous client or customer base.[12]

More small businesses are tapping immigrants as a source of workers. In fact, small companies are more likely to employ immigrants than are larger firms. Approximately 17 percent of small company workers are immigrants (citizens and noncitizens), which works out to nearly one out of every five employees. Of the almost 20 million immigrants employed in the United States, around two-thirds work for small companies—about 3.3 million of these in companies with fewer than 10 employees.[13] We strongly discourage entrepreneurs from hiring illegal or undocumented workers and suggest that they consult the U.S. Department of Labor website for information on certifying foreign workers and other applicable laws.[14] However, it is important to cast the employment net as broadly as possible to find the best people available. By developing an awareness of the potential of various parts of the talent pool, small firms can improve the effectiveness of their recruitment methods.

Adapting to diversity is important not only because the workforce is becoming more diverse, but also because diversity in itself can be a good thing, through the innovation it introduces to the workplace and the positive effect it has on problem solving. Researchers at Northwestern University studied the value of diversity by asking 50 groups of subjects to solve a murder mystery. Groups that included individuals from different social backgrounds were more likely to solve the case; homogeneous groups were both more often wrong and more confident that they were right.[15] Venture capitalists are very much aware of this phenomenon and thus are less likely to invest in a company when the management team more closely resembles the results of a cloning experiment than a group of individuals who bring unique perspectives to bear on business challenges. Evidence suggests that various forms of diversity (based on gender and ethnicity, as well as more subtle forms of variation related to personality, sensibility, work style, and the like) are beneficial, especially when innovation is important to a firm's competitiveness.

Job Descriptions

A small business manager should analyze the activities or work to be performed to determine the number and types of jobs to be filled. Knowing the job requirements permits more intelligent selection of applicants for specific positions.

job description
An outline, or summary, of the work to be performed for a particular position.

Certainly, an owner-manager should not select personnel simply to fit rigid specifications of education, experience, or personal background. Rather, he or she must concentrate on the overall ability of an individual to fill a particular position in the business. Making this determination requires an outline, or summary, of the work to be performed, which is often referred to as a *job description.*

Duties listed in a job description should not be defined too narrowly. It is important that such descriptions minimize overlap but also avoid creating a "that's not my job" mentality. Technical competence is as necessary in small firms as it is in large businesses, but versatility and flexibility may be even more important. Engineers may occasionally need to make sales calls, and marketing people may need to pinch-hit in production.

In the process of examining a job, an analyst should list the knowledge, skills, abilities, and other characteristics that an individual must have to perform the job. This statement of requirements is called a *job specification* and may be a part of the job description. A job specification for the position of stock clerk, for example, might state that the individual must be able to lift 50 pounds and have completed 10 to 12 years of schooling.

Job descriptions are very important human resource management tools, but only if they are taken seriously. There are sound legal reasons for developing great—not just good—job descriptions.[16] For example, if you do not specify important aspects of the job and how it is to be done *in detail,* the Americans with Disabilities Act presumes that an employee can go about the actual job duties in any way he or she wants to, regardless of company policy or what you think is the best and proper way of doing them. Also, the precise wording of a job description will determine whether an employee in that job is eligible for overtime pay, according to the guidelines established by the U.S. Department of Labor.[17] Getting the job description right can avert serious legal hassles, saving you money and giving you one less worry when you go to bed at night!

While job descriptions are primarily an aid in personnel recruitment, they also have other practical uses. For example, they can bring focus to the work of employees, provide direction in training, and supply a framework to guide performance reviews.

Evaluating Prospects and Selecting Employees

Recruitment activities identify prospects for employment. Additional steps are needed to evaluate these candidates and to extend job offers. To reduce the risk of taking an uninformed gamble on applicants of unknown quality, an employer can follow the steps below.

2. Identify the steps to take in evaluating job applicants.

Step 1: Using Application Forms

By using an application form, an employer can collect enough information to determine whether a prospect is minimally qualified and provide a basis for further evaluation. Typically, an application asks for the applicant's name, address, Social Security number, educational history, employment history, and references.

Although an application form need not be lengthy or elaborate, it must be carefully written to avoid legal complications. In general, a prospective employer cannot seek information about sex, race, religion, color, national origin, age, or disabilities. The information requested should be focused on helping the employer make a better job-related assessment. For example, an employer is permitted to ask whether an applicant has graduated from high school. However, a question regarding the year the applicant graduated would be considered inappropriate, because the answer would reveal the applicant's age.

Step 2: Interviewing the Applicant

An interview permits the employer to get some idea of the applicant's appearance, job knowledge, intelligence, and personality. Any of these factors may be significant to the job to be filled.

Although the interview can be a useful step in the selection process, it should not be the only step. Some managers have the mistaken idea that they are infallible judges of human character and can choose good employees on the basis of interviews alone. Even when conducted with care, an interview can lead to false impressions. Applicants who interview well have a talent for quick responses and smooth talk, but this skill set may not be helpful when it comes to managing people and technology. The interview may reveal little about how well they work under pressure or, when part of a team, what motivates them, and other important issues. In fact, research has shown that the typical job interview (unstructured and unfocused) is of limited value in predicting success on the job.[18]

In light of a growing concern regarding the value of interviews as they are typically used, many companies have adopted new methods that are variations on the interview theme. For example, some companies have found *behavioral interviews* to be much more predictive of a candidate's potential for success on the job. Jeffrey Pfeffer, a highly regarded management expert at Stanford University's Graduate School of Business, describes this form of interviewing as "asking people not so much about accomplishments but how they might react to hypothetical situations, how they spend their free time, and how they embody core values."[19] Though it can be a taxing process that may come across to the applicant as a barrage of challenging questions, the behavioral interview is designed to get a sense of the applicant's past performance and likely responses in future situations. The nature of the method makes bluffing difficult, and the focus on facts rather than feelings leads to a more accurate impression of what a person is *capable* of doing as well as what he or she is *likely* to do on the job.

Many companies have decided that behavioral interviews are the way to go, but this requires them to select a set of questions that will uncover the insights they need to make an informed hiring decision. To give you a sense of how such an interview can be structured, here is a sample of the kinds of questions that are often asked:[20]

- Give me a specific example of a time when you used good judgment and logic when solving a problem.
- Tell me about a time when you set a goal and were able to achieve it.
- Can you recall a time when you had to conform to a company policy with which you did not agree? How did you handle that situation?
- How do you typically deal with workplace conflict? Describe an experience that required you to make such an adjustment.
- Give me an example of a time when your integrity was tested and yet prevailed in a workplace situation.

As you can see from these questions, the focus is on patterns of performance and behaviors in past situations similar to situations that are likely to come up in the job for which the applicant is being considered. Designing this emphasis into the interview process will lead to more effective hiring decisions.

Regardless of the interview method you choose, remember that serious legal consequences can result from a poorly conceived process. Just as in application forms, it is very important to avoid asking questions that conflict with the law. Some companies believe that applicants should be interviewed by two or more individuals in order to provide a witness to all interactions and to minimize bias and errors in judgment, but this is not always possible—and it certainly makes the process more expensive. In any case, careful process planning up front can prevent serious trouble in the future from discrimination lawsuits and poor employee selection.

Time spent in interviews, as well as in other phases of the selection process, can save the company time and money in the long run. In today's litigious society, firing an employee can be quite difficult and expensive. A dismissed employee may bring suit even when an employer had justifiable reasons for the dismissal.[21]

behavioral interview
An interview approach that assesses the suitability of job candidates based on how they would respond to hypothetical situations.

It's important to remember that employment interviewing is actually a two-way process. The applicant is evaluating the employer while the employer is evaluating the applicant. In order for the applicant to make an informed decision, she or he needs a clear idea of what the job entails and an opportunity to ask questions.

Step 3: Checking References and Other Background Information

Careful checking with former employers, school authorities, and other references can help an employer avoid hiring mistakes. Suppose, for example, that you hired an appliance technician who later burglarized a customer's home. If you failed to check the applicant's background and she had a criminal record, your decision might be considered a negligent hiring decision. Trying to prevent such scenarios from arising is becoming more important as time goes on, since the number of negligent hiring lawsuits is on the rise.

It is becoming increasingly difficult to obtain more than the basic facts about a person's background from previous employers because of the potential for lawsuits brought by disappointed applicants. Although reference checks on a prior employment record do not constitute infringements on privacy, third parties are often reluctant to divulge negative information, and this limits the practical usefulness of reference checking.

At the same time, gathering information online about an applicant's financial, criminal, and employment history has never been easier. While some employers conduct their own background checks by accessing databases that are readily available, most outsource this function to one of hundreds of vendors that specialize in performing this service. A number of companies advertise that they will provide *free* background checks over the Internet. This certainly sounds appealing. But, given the importance of the task, we suggest that you check with the National Association of Professional Background Screeners (http://napbs.com) before selecting a company for this purpose.

A few final cautions on background checks are in order. First, you should keep in mind that if a prospective employer requests a credit report to establish an applicant's employment eligibility, the Fair Credit Reporting Act requires that the applicant be notified in writing that such a report is being requested. But this is good practice, in general, when it comes to background checks. Most experts suggest that you require applicants to sign a written consent (detailing how and what you plan to check) before you conduct a check, to ensure legal compliance and to give the applicant the opportunity to withdraw from further consideration. If an applicant refuses to sign the consent form, it is legal for the company to decide against hiring him or her based on that refusal.[22]

Getting access to data is critical to making an informed hiring decision; however, you may be legally prevented from using some of the insights revealed to reject an applicant. One small business expert points out some of the things you can and cannot use: "Anything recent and relevant to job duties can legally be taken into account, but even a past felony conviction may be considered irrelevant if it was more than seven years ago."[23]

Finally, some entrepreneurs question the accuracy of the information that surfaces from criminal background checks. George Zimmer, founder of the fast-growing clothing store Men's Warehouse, has declared that no employee or interviewee at his company will ever undergo such a check. "I don't trust the U.S. justice system to get it right," he boldly declares. "I'd rather make my own decisions, and I believe in giving people a second chance." Conventional wisdom suggests that such a policy would lead to "petty larceny on a grand scale," but this has not been Zimmer's experience. The company loses only about 0.4 percent of its revenues to theft, well below the national average of 1.5 percent lost by big retailers.[24] But while Zimmer's trusting attitude seems to create a bounty of goodwill, it may leave the company open to greater legal liability if an employee is accused of criminal conduct toward a customer or other workers. These tradeoffs need to be weighed carefully.

George Zimmer, shown here with Leonard Nimoy, is the founder of the fast-growing clothing store Men's Warehouse. He has declared that no employee or interviewee at his company will ever undergo a criminal background check.

Step 4: Testing the Applicant

Many kinds of jobs lend themselves to performance testing. For example, an applicant for a secretarial or clerical position may be given a standardized keyboarding or word-processing test. With a little ingenuity, employers can develop practical tests that are clearly related to the job in question, and these can provide extremely useful insights for selection decisions.

In 2001, Marvis Nichols took over Computer Friends, Inc., a Pittsburgh, Pennsylvania, business that provides information-technology services for small companies. When the recession made it difficult to find new business, she decided to hire a sales representative. She was impressed with one prospect, a woman experienced in selling technical services. But to be sure the candidate was right for the job, Nichols retained her for a one-time project—a networking event that was intended to produce sales leads. Nichols then took the prospective sales manager with her to follow-up meetings. This trial period showed Nichols that her initial impression of the prospective hire was totally wrong. Aghast at the prospect's bizarre combination of aggression and confusion, Nichols says, "At the end of the day, I felt it was a disaster." [25] If Nichols had hired the sales representative before those meetings, she would never have known about her jarring demeanor. A practical test averted a hiring disaster!

Psychological examinations may also be used by small businesses, but the results can be misleading because of difficulty in interpreting the tests or adapting them to a particular business. In addition, the U.S. Supreme Court has upheld the Equal Employment Opportunity Commission's requirement that any test used in making employment decisions must be job-related.

validity
The extent to which a test assesses true job performance ability.

reliability
The consistency of a test in measuring job performance ability.

To be useful, tests of any kind must meet the criteria of *validity* and *reliability*. For a test to be valid, its results must correspond well with job performance; that is, the applicants with the best test scores must generally be the best employees. For a test to be reliable, it must provide consistent results when used at different times or by various individuals.

Step 5: Requiring Physical Examinations

A primary purpose of physical examinations is to evaluate the ability of applicants to meet the physical demands of specific jobs. However, care must be taken to avoid discriminating against those who are physically disabled. The Americans with Disabilities Act requires companies with 15 or more employees to make "reasonable" adaptations to facilitate the employment of such individuals.

Although some small businesses require medical examinations before hiring an applicant, in most cases the company must first have offered that individual a job.[26] As part of the physical examination process, the law permits drug screening of applicants. The National Federation of Independent Business conducted a poll of small businesses and found that 35 percent check a potential employee's background for drug and/or alcohol abuse, though very few actually require drug testing. Only 8 percent had asked one or more employees to take a drug and/or alcohol test in the previous three years, and most of those were random tests or requirements for a new hire.[27]

As you can see, a sound program for evaluating and selecting employees involves a number of "moving pieces," but many small companies pull all of the pieces together very skillfully. For example, Rick Davis (a member of the Go-To Team for this book) describes how he and the staff at his retail services company, DAVACO Inc., pull out all the stops in order to ensure the quality of the hiring process.

> Recruiting the best people is the single most important thing DAVACO can do. Not only do I make every effort to meet all employees before they are hired, but our human resources team also takes every measure to assure that we've recruited and selected the top candidate for every position to maximize their, and the company's, success. We incorporate practices into our recruiting efforts based on position, including telephone screening, face-to-face interviews, background checks, credit checks, drug screening, personality and behavior testing, skills assessment, and motor vehicle record checks.[28]

In addition to emphasizing industry expertise, the company also believes that strength of character is just as important as skills, if not more so. Skills can be taught, but Davis recognizes that ethics, loyalty, and high standards are inherent qualities that are difficult to pass on in a business setting. Therefore, the hiring process must take all of this into account.[29]

Training and Developing Employees

Once an employee has been recruited and added to the payroll, the process of training and development must begin. The purpose of this process is to transform a new recruit into a well-trained and effective technician, salesperson, manager, or other employee.

3. Describe the roles of training and development for both managerial and nonmanagerial employees in a small business.

Basic Components of Training and Development

Though the terms are often combined, a training and development program can be separated into its two basic components. *Employee training* refers to planned efforts to help workers master the knowledge, skills, and behaviors that they need to perform the duties for which they were hired. In contrast, *management development* is more focused on preparing employees for future roles in business and emphasizes the formal education, job experiences, relationship formation, and assessment necessary to reach long-term career goals and fulfill managerial potential. While the two components are different, they are obviously related.

Most positions require at least some training. If an employer fails to provide such instruction, a new employee must learn by trial and error, which usually leads to a waste of time, materials, and money—and sometimes alienates customers. At the same time, training to improve basic capabilities should not be limited to new hires; the performance of existing employees can often be improved through additional training. Due to constant changes in products, technology, policies, and procedures in the world of business, continual training often is necessary to update knowledge and skills—in firms of all sizes. Only with such training can employees meet the changing demands being placed on them.

Both employers and employees have a stake in the advancement of qualified personnel to higher level positions. Preparation for advancement usually involves developmental efforts, which typically are quite different than the support needed to sharpen skills for current duties. Because most able employees are particularly concerned about their personal development and advancement, a small business can profit from careful attention to this phase of the personnel program. Opportunities to grow and move up in an organization not only improve the morale of current employees but also serve as an inducement for potential applicants.[30]

Orientation for New Personnel

The training and development process often begins with an individual's first two or three days on the job. It is at this point that the new employee tends to feel lost and confused, confronted with a new physical layout, a different job title, unknown fellow employees, a different type of supervision, changed hours or work schedule, and/or a unique set of personnel policies and procedures. Any events that conflict with the newcomer's expectations are interpreted in light of his or her previous work experience, and these interpretations can either foster a strong commitment to the new employer or lead to feelings of alienation.

Recognizing the new employee's sensitivity at this point, the employer can contribute to a positive outcome through proper orientation. Taking steps to help the newcomer adjust will minimize her or his uneasiness in the new setting.

Some phases of the orientation can be accomplished by informal methods. For example, a software company in San Mateo, California, uses bagels and muffins as a means of introducing newcomers to the rest of the staff. On the first morning of work for a new employee, a tray of breakfast food is strategically placed near her or his desk. An e-mail invites everyone to come by and get acquainted.

Other phases of the orientation must be structured or formalized. In addition to explaining specific job duties, supervisors should outline the firm's policies and procedures in as much detail as possible. A clear explanation of performance expectations and the way in which an employee's work will be evaluated should be included in the discussion. The new employee should be encouraged to ask questions, and time should be taken to provide careful answers. Since new employees are faced with an information overload at first, a follow-up orientation after a week or two is suggested.

One way to support the orientation process is by providing new hires with a written description of company practices and procedures, which is often referred to as an employee handbook. The handbook may include an expression of company philosophy—an overall view of what the company considers important, such as standards of excellence or quality considerations. This document typically covers such topics as recruitment, selection, training, and compensation, as well as more immediately practical information about work hours, paydays, breaks, lunch hours, absences, holidays, overtime policy, employee benefits, and so on. Such policies should be written carefully and clearly to avoid misunderstandings. Also, bear in mind that an employee handbook is considered part of the employment contract in some states.

Training to Improve Quality

Employee training is an integral part of comprehensive quality management programs. Although quality management is concerned with machines, materials, and measurements, it also focuses on human performance.

Training programs can be designed to promote high-quality workmanship. The connection between effective quality management programs and employee training has been supported by at least one study of small manufacturing firms.[31]

Christian Kar, operator of Espresso Connection, an 11-store chain of drive-through coffee bars in Everett, Washington, found he was losing customers at the same time he was advertising for new ones. In an effort to keep the customers he already had, he beefed up employee training. New hires now spend a week learning how to use the equipment and prepare drinks. Later, they undergo another 40 hours of on-the-job training at a store. By improving customer service, the business almost doubled daily store revenues and increased per-store profits by 50 percent.[32]

To a considerable extent, training for quality performance is part of the ongoing supervisory role of all managers. In addition, special classes and seminars can be used to teach employees about the importance of quality control and ways in which to produce high-quality work.

Training of Nonmanagerial Employees

If a company has job descriptions or job specifications, these may be used to identify abilities or skills required for particular jobs. To a large extent, such requirements determine the appropriate type of training.

Phenix and Phenix, Inc., a small literary publicity firm based in Austin, Texas, encourages sharing of learning among its employees.[33] Anyone attending a "learning situation"—which might be anything from a breakfast meeting to a several-day seminar—is expected to write up a summary and present it at a staff meeting or distribute it to coworkers.

For all classes of employees, more training is accomplished on the job than through any other method. However, on-the-job training may be haphazard unless it follows a sound method of teaching. One program designed to make on-the-job training effective is known as *Job Instruction Training.* The steps in this program, shown in Exhibit 20-1, are intended to help supervisors become more effective in training employees.

Job Instruction Training
A systematic step-by-step method for on-the-job training of nonmanagerial employees.

From Training to Implementation

Regardless of the level of the position involved, the goal of a training program is to teach employees new knowledge, skills, and behaviors that will lead, in turn, to improved job performance. But this requires more than just learning—training must also be put to use. However, research indicates that only 10 to 40 percent of the training provided to employees each year is ever actually applied on the job. In other words, the lion's share of the tens of billions of dollars that organizations spend on training each year is simply wasted.[34] Small companies must get more "bang for the buck" from training efforts to justify the investment.

The barriers to the implementation of training in the workplace are many, but much of this is rooted in human nature. For starters, training suggests that change is necessary, but many people find that change provokes anxiety, so they often fall back on more familiar methods. Old habits and routines are hard to break, and workplace pressures or time demands can easily lead employees to turn to tried-and-true approaches.[35] As sometimes happens when trying to learn about improved software, it may be easier to go back to the old software program (which always worked in the past) than to take the time to master an updated version offering new features that could improve performance and efficiency over the long run.

So what is a small business to do? If you want to get a better return on training and development spending, you must create a workplace environment that encourages people to use that training once they're back on the job. That can be accomplished by emphasizing the following training and development program features, adapted from suggestions made by Harry J. Martin, a management and labor relations professor:[36]

- *Put it on paper.* People are more likely to do what they write down, so employees should develop a personal action plan for implementing the training they receive. One manufacturing company requires its training participants to spell out what they will

EXHIBIT 20-1 Steps in Job Instruction Training

PREPARE EMPLOYEES

- Put employees at ease.
- Place them in appropriate jobs.
- Find out what they know.
- Get them interested in learning.

PRESENT THE OPERATIONS

- Tell, show, and illustrate the task.
- Stress key points.
- Instruct clearly and completely.

TRY OUT PERFORMANCE

- Have employees perform the task.
- Have them tell, show, and explain.
- Ask employees questions and correct any errors.

FOLLOW UP

- Check on employees frequently.
- Tell them how to obtain help.
- Encourage questions.

do to apply the concepts they have learned and when. They also are asked to describe the results they expect, how they will be measured, and when they expect to see them. Finally, they must identify the assistance needed to implement their plan.

■ *Measure results.* Employees will be more likely to put training to use if they know their performance will be assessed in light of the new concepts learned. Companies can do this by measuring skills addressed in the training or by assessing productivity improvements of work groups.

- *Get peers to help.* Of all the features listed here, Martin's research found that peer support had the greatest impact on the effective translation of training to workplace application. When trainees get together to discuss the use of training concepts, they are more inspired to give them a try.

- *Involve supportive superiors.* Management involvement increases the odds that trainees will use what they learn. When supervisors meet with trainees, they can communicate expectations, promote focus on concepts, provide encouragement, and eliminate obstacles that can block success.

- *Provide access to experts.* Companies can assist their employees with their action plans by helping to fill in gaps in their understanding. Lingering questions can be answered by providing access to reference materials, additional information on training topics, and experts within the company or from outside sources. Research shows that employees who have follow-up meetings with instructors are more likely to apply their training.

In the end, training is of value only when it is actually used on the job. And those companies that make sure their employees apply the concepts they learn to their work are likely to outperform their competitors. In fact, the worst of all scenarios would be for an enterprise to bear the expense of an extensive training program but fail to enjoy any of the fruits of that investment. That venture is much more likely to fail in a competitive marketplace.

Development of Managerial and Professional Employees

A small business has a particularly strong need to develop managerial and professional employees. Whether the firm has only a few key positions or many, it must ensure that the individuals who hold these positions perform effectively. Such employees should be developed to the point where they can adequately carry out the responsibilities assigned to them. Ideally, other staff members should be trained as potential replacements in case key individuals retire or leave for other reasons. Although an entrepreneur often postpones grooming a personal replacement, this step is crucial in ensuring a smooth transition in the firm's management.

Establishing a management development program requires serious consideration of the following factors:

- *The need for development.* What vacancies are expected? Who needs to be developed? What type of training and how much training are needed to meet the demands of the job description?

- *A plan for development.* How can the individuals be developed? Do they currently have enough responsibility to permit them to learn? Can they be assigned additional duties? Should they be given temporary assignments in other areas—for example, should they be shifted from production to sales? Would additional schooling be beneficial?

- *A timetable for development.* When should the development process begin? How much can be accomplished in the next six months or one year?

- *Employee counseling.* Do the individuals understand their need for development? Are they aware of their prospects within the firm? Has an understanding been reached as to the nature of the development program planned? Have the employees been consulted regularly about progress in their work and the problems confronting them? Have they been given the benefit of the owner's experience and insights without having decisions made for them?

Management development strategies often work wonderfully, but they do have their limits. For example, in many situations the best development strategy is to be careful not to promote an employee beyond the position he or she is best suited to perform. Mike Faith, founder, CEO, and president of the online retailer Headsets.com, found this out the hard way.

One of my longest-standing employees—in fact my only employee in the early days— is a good example [of promoting a person beyond success]. With us now for about ten years, this guy is a genius. Really. He can see the big picture and take an idea and make it work. Because he was so good at what he did, we wanted to get him into middle management. So we moved him into a management position, and it was a disaster. My A player quickly became a B player; management became a millstone around his neck. Recognizing our mistake, we moved him out of management. Now he takes on a variety of projects and is back to being a genius.[37]

From this experience, Faith learned that an A player in one position can end up being a B player in another, but he remains steadfast in his belief that everyone has the ability to be an A player if they are placed in the right job.[38]

Compensation and Incentives for Employees

Compensation is important to all employees, and small firms must acknowledge the role of the paycheck in attracting and motivating personnel. In addition, small firms can offer several nonfinancial incentives that appeal to both managerial and nonmanagerial employees.

4. Explain the various types of compensation plans, including the use of incentive plans.

Wage and Salary Levels

In general, small firms must be roughly competitive in wage and salary levels in order to attract well-qualified personnel. Payments to employees either are based on increments of time—such as an hour, a day, or a month—or vary with the output of the employees. Compensation based on time is most appropriate for jobs in which performance is not easily measured. Time-based compensation is also easier to understand and used more widely than incentive systems that are based on specific dimensions of employee performance.

Small businesses often struggle to pay their lowest-level employees even the minimum wage required by law. However, some employers choose to improve the lives of their employees and express their support by paying wages that exceed that legal minimum. For example, In-N-Out Burger has grown quickly over the years by following a few simple practices from the beginning, including caring for its employees by paying above-minimum wages. That is why the company's website says, "We start all our new Associates at a minimum of $10.00 an hour for one simple reason . . . you are important to us. And our commitment to a higher starting wage is just one of the ways in which we show it."[39] In cases such as this, businesses often benefit along with the employees. Many see an improvement in recruiting and retention, particularly in hard-to-fill positions. These businesses may also enjoy an improved public image with customers and the community. In other words, they can earn a respectable return on their investment—and on more than one front!

Financial Incentives

Incentive plans are designed to motivate employees to increase their productivity. Incentive wages may constitute an employee's entire earnings or merely supplement regular wages or salary. The commission system for salespeople is one type of incentive compensation (see Chapter 17 for an expanded discussion of this topic). In manufacturing, employees are sometimes paid according to the number of units they produce, a practice called *piecework*. Although most incentive plans apply to employees as individuals, they may also involve the use of group incentives and team awards.

piecework
Financial incentive based on pay according to number of units produced.

General bonus or profit-sharing plans are especially important for managers and other key personnel, although they may also include lower-level employees. These plans provide employees with a "piece of the action" and may or may not involve assignment of shares of stock. Many profit-sharing plans simply entail distribution of a specified share of all profits or profits in excess of a target amount. Profit sharing serves more directly as a work-related incentive in small companies than in large corporations, because the connection between individual performance and success can be more easily appreciated in a small business.

Performance-based compensation plans must be designed carefully if they are to work successfully. Such plans should be devised with the aid of a consultant and/or an accountant's insight. Some keys to developing effective bonus plans are the following:

- *Set attainable goals.* Performance-based compensation plans work best when workers believe they can meet the targets. Tying pay to broad, companywide results leaves workers feeling frustrated and helpless. Complex financial measures or jargon-heavy benchmarks should be avoided—employees are motivated only by goals that they understand.

- *Include employees in planning.* Employees should have a voice in developing performance measures and changes to work systems. Incentive plans should be phased in gradually so that employees have a chance to get used to them.

- *Keep updating goals.* Performance-based plans must be continually adjusted to meet the changing needs of workers and customers. The life expectancy of such a plan may be no more than three or four years.

Stock Incentives

In young entrepreneurial ventures, stock options are sometimes used to attract and hold key personnel. The option holders get the opportunity to share in the growing—perhaps even skyrocketing—value of the company's stock. If the business prospers sufficiently, such personnel can become millionaires.

But stock ownership need not be reserved only for executives or key personnel. Some small firms have created employee stock ownership plans (ESOPs), which give employees a share of ownership in the business.[40] These plans may be structured in a variety of ways. For example, a share of annual profits may be designated for the purchase of company stock, which is then placed in a trust for employees. When coupled with a commitment to employee participation in business operations, ESOPs can motivate employees, resulting in improvements in productivity.

ESOPs also provide a way for owners to cash out and withdraw from a business without selling the firm to outsiders. (See Chapter 13 for a discussion of this topic.)

Employee Benefits

Employee benefits include payments by the employer for such items as Social Security, vacation time, holidays, health insurance, and retirement compensation. All told, these benefits are expensive; their cost to many firms is equal to 40 percent or more of salary and wage payments. Furthermore, increases in the cost of some benefits have slowed in recent years, but their escalation continues to outpace the rate of inflation in the economy overall. In general, small companies are less generous than large firms when it comes to providing benefits for employees. Even so, the cost of such benefits is a substantial part of total labor costs for these businesses.

employee benefits
Supplements to compensation, such as health care insurance and life insurance programs, designed to be attractive and beneficial to employees and to maintain their commitment to the firm.

Though employee benefits are expensive, a small firm cannot ignore them if it is to compete effectively for good workers. A limited but growing number of small businesses now use flexible benefit programs (or cafeteria plans), which allow employees to select the types of benefits they wish to receive. All employees receive a core level of coverage, such as basic health insurance, and then are allowed to choose how an employer-specified amount is to be divided among additional options—for example, dependent care assistance, group term life insurance, and additional health insurance.[41]

For small companies that wish to avoid the detailed paperwork associated with administering cafeteria plans, outside help is available. Many small firms—some with fewer than 25 employees—turn over the administration of their flexible benefit plans to outside consulting, payroll accounting, or insurance companies that provide such services for a monthly fee.

Providing a full range of employee benefits may be prohibitively expensive for many small businesses. A number of firms, however, have devised relatively affordable but meaningful "perks" that are customized to their particular situation but still signal appreciation for workers. Buying pizza for everyone on Fridays and giving employees a paid day off for their birthday are just two examples. These small benefits make employment more attractive for employees and are motivating because they are often thoughtful and sometimes even personalized. With a little creativity, these perks can be used to build morale, promote loyalty, and encourage healthy behavior.

John Roberson owns a small Nashville, Tennessee–based experiential marketing company, and he is very committed to growing his business. But he also cares about his employees and their physical and emotional health, and he has ways of persuading them to get involved in programs that support wellness. Tailoring rewards to his employees' specific interests, he has given away a guitar, yoga lessons, time with a personal trainer, paid time off to build orphanages in Central America—even a pair of cowboy boots! This has been good for both the workers and the company. Says Roberson, "We attract employees who see we are about more than just profits."[42]

Special Issues in Human Resource Management

So far, this chapter has dealt with the recruitment, selection, training, and compensation of employees. Several related issues—co-employment agreements, legal protection of employees, labor unions, formalizing employer–employee relationships, and the need for a human resource manager—are the focus of this final section.

5. Discuss the human resource issues of co-employment, legal protection, labor unions, and the formalizing of employer–employee relationships.

Co-Employment Agreements

Entrepreneurs can choose to outsource part of the burden of managing employees through an arrangement known as *co-employment,* an option that has become a common alternative to direct hiring. Today, an estimated 700 co-employment companies, also known as *professional employer organizations (PEOs),* operate in all 50 states and assist small businesses with their human resource management needs. For a fee of 2 to 6 percent of payroll, a PEO writes paychecks, takes care of payroll taxes, and files reports required by government agencies. Although small companies using this service avoid a certain amount of paperwork, they do not escape the tasks of recruitment and selection. In most cases, the entrepreneur or the venture's management still determines who works, who gets promoted, and who gets time off.

Many employees like the co-employment arrangement. It may allow small employers to provide better benefit packages, since PEOs generally cover hundreds or thousands of employees and thus qualify for better rates. Of course, the small business must bear the cost of insurance and other benefits obtained through a co-employment partner, in addition to paying a basic service fee. However, this may be the only way the company can afford to offer the benefits necessary to attract and keep high-quality employees. The fact that the PEO also assumes the burden of managing payroll and other administrative processes makes this arrangement even more attractive.

When a company decides to use the services of a PEO, both parties share legal obligations as a result. That is, the law holds both companies responsible for payment of payroll taxes and workers' compensation insurance and compliance with government regulations—the client company cannot simply offload these obligations to the PEO and forget about its responsibilities to staff. This highlights the importance of selecting a PEO carefully to ensure that you are dealing with a responsible firm. When you are choosing a PEO, we recommend that you follow the guidelines offered by the National Association of Professional Employer Organizations (www.napeo.org) to be sure you are linking up with a service provider that is honest, dependable, and right for your company.

Using a PEO can also change the application of government regulations to small businesses. Very small ventures are often excluded from specific rules. For example, companies with fewer than 15 employees are exempt from the Americans with Disabilities Act. However, when these employees officially become part of a large PEO, the small company using the co-employed workers becomes subject to this law. It always pays to treat your employees with care and respect, of course, but taking on added legal obligations by working with a PEO can actually make managing a small company much more complicated.

Legal Protection of Employees

Employees are afforded protection by a number of federal and state laws.[43] One of the most far-reaching statutes is the *Civil Rights Act,* originally enacted in 1964, and its amendments. This law, which applies to any employer of 15 or more people, prohibits discrimination on the basis of race, color, religion, sex, or national origin. Other laws extend similar protection to the aged and handicapped. Any employment condition is covered, including hiring, firing, promotion, transfer, and compensation.

The Civil Rights Act includes protection against sexual harassment, an issue that must be addressed by small businesses as well as large corporations. Education and prompt response to complaints are the best tools for avoiding sexual harassment and the possibility of liability claims. The following practical action steps have been expressly recommended for small companies:[44]

1. Establish clear policies and procedures regarding sexual harassment in the workplace.
2. Require employees to report incidents of harassment to management immediately.
3. Investigate any and all complaints of sexual harassment fairly and thoroughly.
4. Take appropriate action against violators and maintain claimant confidentiality.
5. If a lawsuit is likely to be filed, contact an attorney.

Employees' health and safety are protected by the *Occupational Safety and Health Act* of 1970. This law, which applies to business firms of any size involved in interstate commerce, created the Occupational Safety and Health Administration (OSHA) to establish and enforce necessary safety and health standards.

Compensation of employees is regulated by the minimum wage and overtime provisions of the *Fair Labor Standards Act (FLSA),* as well as by other federal and state laws. The FLSA applies to employers involved in interstate commerce and having two or more employees; it sets the minimum wage (which is periodically increased by Congress) and specifies time-and-a-half pay for nonsupervisory employees who work more than 40 hours per week.

The *Family and Medical Leave Act* was passed and signed into law in February 1993. The law requires firms with 50 or more employees to allow workers as much as 12 weeks of unpaid leave for childbirth, the adoption of a child, or other specified family needs.[45] The worker must have been employed by the firm for 12 months and have worked at least 1,250 hours. Furthermore, the employer must continue health care coverage during the leave and guarantee that the employee can return to the same job or one that is comparable.[46]

co-employment
Outsourcing part of the burden of managing personnel to an organization that handles paperwork and administers benefits for those employees.

professional employer organization (PEO)
A company that sets up co-employment agreements, assisting businesses with the administrative demands of keeping employees on their payrolls.

Civil Rights Act
Legislation prohibiting discrimination based on race, color, religion, sex, or national origin.

Occupational Safety and Health Act
Legislation that regulates the safety of workplaces and work practices.

Fair Labor Standards Act (FLSA)
Federal law that establishes a minimum wage and provides for overtime pay.

Family and Medical Leave Act
Legislation that assures employees of unpaid leave for childbirth or other family needs.

Labor Unions

As a general rule, entrepreneurs prefer to operate independently and to avoid using union labor. Indeed, most small businesses are not unionized. To some extent, this results from the predominance of small business in services, where unionization is less common than in manufacturing. Also, unions typically focus their attention on large corporations.

Though uncommon, labor unions are not unknown in small firms. Many types of small businesses—building and electrical contractors, for example—negotiate labor contracts and employ unionized personnel. The need to work with a union formalizes and, to some extent, complicates the relationship between a small company and its employees.

If employees wish to bargain collectively—that is, to be represented in negotiations by a union—the law requires the employer to participate in such bargaining. The demand for labor union representation may arise from employees' dissatisfaction with their pay, work environment, or employment relationships. By following constructive human resource policies, a small company can minimize the likelihood of labor organization or improve the relationship between management and union.

Formalizing Employer–Employee Relationships

As explained earlier in this chapter, the management systems of small companies are typically less formal than those of larger firms. A degree of informality can be a virtue in small organizations. As personnel are added, however, the benefits of informality decline and its costs increase. Large numbers of employees cannot be managed effectively without some system for regulating employer–employee relationships. This situation can be best understood in terms of a family relationship. House rules are generally unnecessary when only two people are living in the home. But when several children are added to the mix, Mom and Dad soon start sounding like a government regulatory agency.

Growth, then, produces pressure to formalize personnel policies and procedures. Determining how much formality to introduce and how soon involves judgment. Some employee issues should be formalized from the very beginning; on the other hand, excessive regulation can become paralyzing.

Procedures relating to management of personnel may also be standardized. One way to do this is to establish a performance assessment system that follows a set timetable for reviews—often on an annual basis. Effective performance review programs typically bear certain hallmarks. For example, they are guided by clearly established benchmarks that are based on goals that are SMART—that is, *S*pecific, *M*easurable, *A*chievable, *R*ealistic, and *T*ime-bound. They also tend to follow a well-planned process that emphasizes continual communication between managers and employees and ongoing performance tracking. Effective annual review meetings require sufficient time (from 40 minutes to an hour) and your undivided attention, and they should begin with positive feedback before summarizing objective judgments of attitudes and behaviors in need of improvement. Used correctly, employee reviews can be a powerful tool for building a small business.[47]

The Need for a Human Resource Manager

A firm with only a few employees cannot afford a full-time specialist to deal with personnel problems. Some of the more involved human resource techniques used in large corporations may be far too complicated for small businesses. As a small company grows in size, however, its personnel problems will increase in both number and complexity.

The point at which it becomes logical to hire a human resource manager cannot be precisely specified. In view of the increased overhead cost, the owner-manager of a growing business must decide whether circumstances make it profitable to employ a personnel specialist. Hiring a part-time human resource manager—a retired personnel manager, for example—is a possible first step in some instances.

Conditions such as the following favor the appointment of a human resource manager in a small business:

- There are a substantial number of employees (100 or more is suggested as a guideline).
- Employees are represented by a union.
- The labor turnover rate is high.
- The need for skilled or professional personnel creates problems in recruitment or selection.
- Supervisors or operative employees require considerable training.
- Employee morale is unsatisfactory.
- Competition for personnel is keen.

Until a human resource manager is hired, however, the owner-manager typically functions in that capacity. His or her decisions regarding employee selection and compensation, as well as other personnel issues, will have a direct impact on the operating success of the firm.

As this chapter points out, the human resource management function is simple in concept, but it can be challenging to put into practice. From recruitment to prospect evaluation and selection to training and development programs to the administration of compensation and benefit plans—there is so much to do! And if that weren't enough to keep track of, these activities must be conducted within the constraints of some very specific laws. While this may seem overwhelming, keep in mind that working with the people who join your enterprise is likely to be the most fulfilling feature of being in business. If they are managed carefully and motivated to do their best, capable employees can take your business to new heights. There is no limit to what can be done with the right people in the right enterprise with the right care and handling. You will see that for yourself soon enough.

LOOKING BACK

1. Explain the importance of employee recruitment and list some sources that can be useful in finding suitable applicants.

- Recruitment of good employees can boost the overall performance of a small business.
- Small companies can attract applicants by stressing unique work features and opportunities.
- Recruitment sources include walk-ins, help-wanted advertising, schools, public and private employment agencies, temporary help agencies, the Internet, employee referrals, and executive search firms.
- The increasing diversity of the workforce requires a broadening of the scope of recruitment, but the varied perspectives of a diverse workforce can offer advantages, such as improved decision making.
- Job descriptions outline the duties of the job; job specifications identify the knowledge, skills, abilities, and other characteristics applicants need to have to do the job effectively.

2. Identify the steps to take in evaluating job applicants.

- In the first step, application forms help the employer obtain preliminary information from applicants. (Employers must avoid questions about sex, race, religion, color, national origin, age, and disabilities.)
- Additional evaluation steps are interviewing the applicant (with behavioral interviews offering the best insights),

checking references and other background information, and testing the applicant.

- The final evaluation step is often a physical examination, which may include drug screening.

3. Describe the roles of training and development for both managerial and nonmanagerial employees in a small business.

- Effective employee training enables workers to perform their current jobs effectively; management development prepares them for career advancement.

- An orientation program helps introduce new employees to the firm and its work environment.

- Training is an integral component of a comprehensive quality management program.

- Training is more likely to be put to use if it is written down, measured, structured for peer support, encouraged by management, and supplemented with ongoing advice from experts.

- A management development program should be guided by an understanding of the need for development, a plan for development, and a timetable for development. It should also provide appropriate employee counseling.

4. Explain the various types of compensation plans, including the use of incentive plans.

- Small companies must be roughly competitive in salary and wage levels.

- Payments to employees either are based on increments of time or vary with employee output.

- Incentive systems relate compensation to various measures of performance.

- Employee stock ownership plans enable employees to own a share of the business.

- Employee benefit costs are often equal to 40 percent or more of payroll costs.

5. Discuss the human resource issues of co-employment, legal protection, labor unions, and the formalizing of employer–employee relationships.

- Small businesses can reduce paperwork by transferring personnel to the payroll of a professional employer organization, but legal obligations remain.

- All small businesses with 15 or more employees must observe laws that prohibit discrimination, protect employee health and safety, establish a minimum wage, and provide for family and medical leave.

- Some small businesses must work with labor unions.

- As small firms grow, they must adopt more formal human resource management methods.

- Employment of a human resource manager becomes necessary at some point as a company continues to add employees.

Key Terms

headhunter p. 527
workforce diversity p. 528
job description p. 528
job specification p. 529
behavioral interview p. 530
validity p. 532
reliability p. 532

employee training p. 533
management development p. 533
Job Instruction Training p. 535
piecework p. 539
employee benefits p. 539
co-employment p. 540
professional employer organization (PEO) p. 540

Civil Rights Act p. 541
Occupational Safety and Health Act p. 541
Fair Labor Standards Act (FLSA) p. 541
Family and Medical Leave Act p. 541

Discussion Questions

1. Why is it so important to have high-quality employees?

2. What factor or factors would make you cautious about going to work for a small business? Could these reasons for hesitation be overcome? How?

3. In what ways is the workforce becoming more diverse, and how do these changes affect recruitment by small companies?

4. Based on what you know from this chapter or your own experience as an interviewee, what do you think are the most serious weaknesses in the interviewing process? How could these be remedied?

5. What are the positive and negative features of background checks? How important are these checks to the selection of high-quality employees?

6. What steps and/or topics would you recommend for inclusion in the orientation program of a printing firm with 65 employees?

7. What problems are involved in using incentive plans in a small company? How would the nature of the work affect management's decision concerning the use of such a plan?

8. Is the use of an employee stock ownership plan desirable in a small business? What might lessen such a plan's effectiveness in motivating employees?

9. How does a professional employer organization differ from a temporary help agency? What are the greatest benefits of co-employment?

10. Explain the impact of the Civil Rights Act and the Fair Labor Standards Act on human resource management.

You Make the Call

SITUATION 1

The following is an account of one employee's introduction to a new job:

> It was my first job out of high school. After receiving a physical exam and a pamphlet on benefits, I was told by the manager about the dangers involved in the job. But it was the old-timers who explained what was really expected of me.
>
> The company's management never told me about the work environment or the unspoken rules. The old-timers let me know when I could take breaks and which supervisors to avoid. They told me how much work I was supposed to do and which supervisor to see if I had a problem.

Question 1 To what extent should a small firm use "old-timers" to help introduce new employees to the workplace? Is it inevitable that newcomers will look to old-timers to find out how things really work?

Question 2 How would you rate this firm's orientation effort? What are its strengths and weaknesses?

Question 3 Assume that this firm has fewer than 75 employees and no human resource manager. Could it possibly provide more extensive orientation than that described here? How? What low-cost improvements, if any, would you recommend?

SITUATION 2

When the economy declines and sales begin to fall off, entrepreneurs often have to make difficult decisions regarding their employees. This was the challenge facing James Tilton, founder of Tilton Construction Services, a light construction firm in Riverside, California. Since the launch of his business in 1997, he has used the fact that his company has never fired anyone as a tool to attract and retain workers, but he is up against the wall now and something has to give. By early 2008, the recession and the freefall of the real estate market had started to put financial pressure on his company. Now it is clear that he cannot continue to keep all of his 17 full-time employees busy, and there is no way he can continue to make payroll. But nearly half of his loyal workers have been

with him for several years, and he feels a sense of responsibility to them and their families. What should he do?

Tilton has decided that he would like to make some adjustments that would allow him to avoid a layoff, if possible. He estimates that he could reduce total payroll by 6 percent ($50,000 a year) just by tightening up his workers' schedules and avoiding overtime pay. That would certainly help. But it might be simpler and seem more fair if everyone just took a 10 percent cut in pay, including himself. If he doesn't make some kind of adjustment, Tilton figures that he will have to terminate at least four, and perhaps as many as six workers, depending on how bad the recession gets. But there must be other options. Tilton struggles with his dilemma as he tries to go to sleep, but he realizes that he won't get much rest until he can solve this problem.

Question 1 What other options can you think of for Tilton's company? Can you come up with better alternatives than the ones Tilton has considered so far?

Question 2 Do you think there is any possibility that Tilton will be able to avoid laying off at least a few of his workers? If you were one of the company's best workers, what would you recommend that Tilton do?

Question 3 What impact will this decision have on the training and development that Tilton has invested in his employees? How important is this factor to the decision he will have to make?

SITUATION 3

When Peter Mathis learned that a former employee had filed a complaint alleging that Ready Delivery, his Albuquerque-based freight hauling business, had fired her because of her race, it seemed like the right time to rethink his company's human resource management methods. The complaint was eventually dismissed, but that didn't stop Mathis from worrying about the possibility that other employee problems might arise in the future. And with 12 workers already on the payroll, he was finding that the paperwork associated with payroll preparation, government regulation, tax reporting, and other human resource management matters was beginning to consume too much of his time at the office.

A professional employer organization (PEO) approached him about taking over much of Ready Delivery's human resource management work. It would cost the company 3 percent of payroll, but the PEO could also offer additional benefits and services (at additional cost, of course) that might help the company in other ways, too. For example, joining the PEO would give Mathis's employees access to better health and dental care plans that would actually be less expensive than those the company currently offered. It could also provide affordable group life insurance benefits, making the switch even more attractive. Mathis realized that partnering with the PEO could reduce his flexibility in selecting benefit options, but he was nonetheless giving serious consideration to accepting the offer.

Question 1 How can Mathis be sure that the PEO is reputable and that his company and employees will receive real value for the money?

Question 2 How might contracting with the PEO affect employee relationships at Ready Delivery? Is there any chance that his employees' loyalty might be transferred to their new "employer"?

Question 3 What steps should Mathis take before entering into an agreement with the PEO?

Experiential Exercises

1. Interview the director of the placement office for your college or university. Ask about the extent to which small companies use the office's services, and obtain the director's recommendations for improving college recruiting by small firms. Prepare a one-page summary of your findings.

2. Examine and evaluate the help-wanted section of a local newspaper. Summarize your conclusions and formulate some generalizations about small business advertising for personnel.

3. With another student, form an interviewer–interviewee team. Take turns posing as job applicants for a selected type of job vacancy. Critique each other's performance, using the interviewing principles outlined in this chapter.

4. With another student, take turns playing the roles of trainer and trainee. The student-trainer should select a simple task and teach it to the student-trainee, using the Job Instruction Training method outlined in Exhibit 20-1. Jointly critique the teaching performance after each turn.

Small Business & Entrepreneurship Resource Center

The *Small Business and Entrepreneurship Resource Center* offers complete small business management resources through a comprehensive database that covers all major areas of starting, operating, and maintaining a business from financing, management, marketing, accounting, taxes, and more. Use the access code that came with your new book to access the site and perform the exercises in each chapter.

1. Mike Faith, founder, CEO, and President of the online retailer, Headsets.com, has learned to be careful not to promote employees beyond the position they are best suited to perform, as mentioned in the text. The article "Headsets.com happy with its growth spurt" talks about how the company has taken measures to ensure that all employees are focused in the same direction. Describe what Headsets.com has done to ensure this, and discuss how effective (or not) you feel this type of approach may be.

Sources: Headsets.com Happy with Its Growth Spurt. (Headsets.com). *Catalog Age* 21, 3 (March 1, 2004): p. NA.

Case 20

SALARY ENVY, P. 666
One of the most important features of a company's human resource management program involves its compensation practices, and this case highlights some of the complications that can surface when various inadequate compensation policies are adopted.

ALTERNATIVE CASES FOR CHAPTER 20

Courtesy of Modern Postcard

In the VIDEO SPOTLIGHT
Modern Postcard
http://www.modernpostcard.com

Modern Postcard prides itself on being able to turn around a customer's order in two days. That means designing the postcard, printing it, and mailing it out to the addresses on the customer's mailing list. On the surface, it sounds quite simple, but these postcards are anything but. They showcase beautiful color photography and elegant, powerful design. And when you consider that the company produces 100 million postcards a year for some 150,000 customers, producing such a high-quality product in just two days is quite a feat.

The founder of Modern Postcard, Steve Hoffman, started with real-estate brochures—full-color, glossy ones with Architectural Digest–style photography. The costs of producing the upscale brochures were quite high, so Hoffman, in an effort to make something that people could afford, began thinking about postcards. Even though his colleagues had serious reservations about producing postcards, which they perceived as "cheap," Hoffman persisted, because he realized that providing an affordable, high-quality product would be the best way to build his business.

So how does Modern Postcard continue to produce beautifully designed postcards of superior quality in such quantities for so many customers—and for one-sixth the cost of a full-color glossy brochure? The answer lies in its operations. This video spotlight will show you how manufacturing, service, and technology can work together to create an operations process that satisfies many customers, day in and day out.

Video material provided by Hattie Bryant, Producer of Small Business School, the series on PBS Stations, World-net, and the Web at http://www.smallbusinessschool.org.

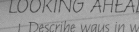

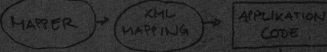

LOOKING AHEAD
AFTER STUDYING THIS CHAPTER, YOU SHOULD BE ABLE TO . . .

1. Describe ways in which operations can enhance a small company's competitiveness.

2. Discuss the nature of the operations process for both products and services.

3. Identify ways to control inventory and minimize inventory costs.

4. Recognize the contributions of operations management to product and service quality.

5. Explain the importance of purchasing and the nature of key purchasing policies.

6. Describe lean production and synchronous management and their importance to operations management in small firms.

W hen you hear the word *operations,* you might imagine special agents taking on foreign spies or risking life and limb in some super-secret government assignment. These images provide a useful place to begin our discussion, but in this chapter we apply the principles of operations in a distinct way—to the small business.

Many of the concepts presented in this chapter were pioneered and perfected by large corporations. However, this does not mean that they have no place in the world of small business. Most of them do. In some cases, the concepts can be applied directly; in others, they must be adapted before they can meet the needs of small companies. So, some illustrations of the ideas presented in this chapter will come from the experiences of large corporations, but we always offer the concepts with consideration for how they can be applied to small businesses.

Entrepreneurs who pay attention to their operations and work to make them better find that their companies are more fit to stand up to the escalating pressures of the competitive marketplace—including those coming from the Microsofts and Walmarts of the world. Besides, understanding and adopting the best practices established by industry giants may give your small company a pattern to follow as it grows to become a market leader of the future! Whether they are used in a manufacturing business or a service-based company, these principles can provide profit power. Let us show you how.

Competing with Operations

operations
The processes used to create and deliver a good or service.

operations management
The planning and control of a conversion process that includes turning inputs into outputs that customers desire.

I n very simple terms, *operations* refers to the processes used to create and deliver a good or service. By now, it should be clear that companies vary considerably in how they compete for customers, and the planning and management of operations almost always play a major role in this. You may be familiar with high-profile examples such as Walgreens' emphasis on convenient locations, Walmart's highly efficient supply chain and distribution capabilities, McDonald's speed of service, and Apple's superior design efforts—these are truly world-class players. In the end, however, the formula for gaining competitive strength is surprisingly similar for all firms. That is, companies gain power to the degree that they excel in satisfying customer needs and wants more *precisely* and/or *efficiently* than their competitors.

To be successful, a company's operations must involve all of the activities required to create value for customers and earn their dollars. A bakery, for example, purchases ingredients, combines and bakes them, and makes baked products available to customers at some appropriate location. For a service business like a hair salon, the activities include the purchase of supplies and shampooing, haircutting, and other tasks and processes involved in serving its clients. It's difficult to imagine how a bakery could offer its product if it refuses to operate ovens, or how a hair salon could serve its customers without actually cutting hair. (Outsourcing these activities presents one impractical, but highly unlikely scenario for this.) In the end, *all* necessary activities must be handled in some form or fashion if the company's operations are to function.

Operations management refers to the planning and control of a conversion process that includes bringing together inputs (such as raw materials, equipment, and labor) and turning them into outputs (products and services) that customers want. An operations process is required whether a firm produces a tangible product, such as clothing or sandwiches, or an intangible service, such as dry cleaning or operating a movie theater. Examples include the production process in apparel manufacturing, the process of putting together a sandwich in a deli, the cleaning process in dry cleaning, and the process of producing a play for a community theater.

Operations are at the heart of any business; indeed, they are the reason for its very existence. It should come as no surprise, then, that their design and effectiveness can determine the success of an enterprise. The following questions can help you to identify operations factors that will impact firm performance and to recognize adjustments that need to be made:

- How much flexibility is required to satisfy your customers over time?

- What is customer demand today? What is the demand trend for the future? Are existing facilities and equipment adequate to keep up with current and future demand?

- What options are available for satisfying your customers? For example, should you set up in-house fabrication, outsource production, or enter a joint venture for manufacturing?

- What skills or capabilities set your firm apart from its competitors? How can you best take advantage of these distinctive features in the market?

- Does the competitive environment require certain capabilities that your enterprise lacks?

The focus of this chapter is on examining ways a business can function economically and profitably, providing a high-quality product and/or service that keeps customers coming back for more. But even more significantly, we discuss how operations management is an important means of building competitive strength in the marketplace. For this, there is no substitute!

The Operations Process

2. Discuss the nature of the operations process for both products and services.

Goods-oriented and service-oriented operations are similar in that they change inputs into outputs. Inputs can include money, raw materials, labor, equipment, information, and energy—all of which are combined in varying proportions, depending on the nature of the finished product or service. Outputs are the products and/or services that a business provides to its customers. Thus, the operations process may be described as a conversion process. As Exhibit 21-1 shows, the operations process converts inputs of various kinds into products, such as baked goods, or services, such as dry cleaning. A printing plant, for example, uses inputs such as paper, ink, the work of employees, printing presses, and electric power to produce printed material. Car wash facilities and motor freight firms, which are service businesses, also use operating systems to transform inputs into car-cleaning and freight-transporting services.

Managing Operations in a Service Business

The operations of firms providing services differ from those of firms producing products in a number of ways. One of the most obvious is the intangible nature of services—that is, the fact that you cannot easily see or measure them. As pointed out earlier, managers of businesses such as auto repair shops and hotels face special challenges in assuring and controlling the quality of their services, given the difficulty inherent in measuring and controlling intangibles.

Another distinctive feature of most service businesses is the extensive personal interaction of employees with customers. In a physical fitness facility, for example, the customer is directly involved in the process and relates personally to trainers and other service personnel. In a beauty salon, the customer is a participant in the various processes of hair styling. This naturally allows for customer input and feedback into creation and delivery processes. In addition, services are created and delivered on demand. That is, a haircut cannot be entered into finished goods inventory.

Some service businesses have taken unique steps to understand the service provider–customer connection. Companies like Southwest Airlines, for example, want their managers to get close enough to customers to see what they have to say about various facets of the operation. To that end, they are sent into the field periodically to fill customer contact positions, which allows them to return to their normal responsibilities with much greater insight into the strengths and weaknesses of services offered. Research into employee–customer relations has shown that greater closeness with customers enables employees to understand and report customer sentiment more accurately.

For a service business, the critical importance of its relationship with customers carries implications for managing personnel. For example, those making hiring decisions must consider whether an open position requires relating to the firm's clientele and select individuals capable of relating to others for that position. Employee training must emphasize the skills needed to serve customers well and encourage employees to find ways to improve customer satisfaction. Employee relationships with customers can create unique problems in scheduling work, as we discuss later in this chapter.

The adoption of various technologies has enabled customers of many businesses to provide more of their own services. Self-service gasoline stations permit customers to pay at the pump, and many telephone systems allow customers to obtain information without speaking to a salesperson or other personnel. The extent to which such systems are satisfactory from a customer's point of view depends on whether they are more convenient

LIVING THE DREAM:

entrepreneurial challenges

Making the Most of Motown

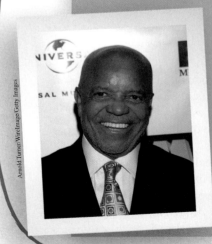

Berry Gordy started Motown Records in 1959 in Detroit, Michigan, using a family loan of $800. By 1964, Motown had become the largest and most successful independent record label in the United States. It had an amazing "Top 40" hit ratio of 75 percent! How did Gordy achieve such amazing results? By creating an assembly-line production process for making music and closely managing quality.

Gordy paid low-wages to high school students to write songs or to sing and dance for him. (Many of the performers were amateurs, living in Detroit's housing projects.) To manage impressions, he required his artists to go to etiquette training. He also controlled everything about their image, including their style, costumes, and choreography. But the payoff from his production approach was truly remarkable! He signed artists who later became huge successes, like Smokey Robinson, Diana Ross, The Four Tops, The Commodores, Stevie Wonder, and The Jackson Five.

Although the hits continued into the 70s and 80s, Motown was up against an onslaught of competition, so Gordy decided to sell Motown Records in 1988 for a cool $61 million. But along the way, he proved that sound operations management principles can be applied with effect to just about any industry, including the music business.

Sources: "Berry Gordy," Entrepreneur.com, http://www.entrepreneur.com/growyourbusiness/radicalsandvisionaries/article197634.html, accessed July 3, 2009; and Dave Zuchowski, "Rock Hall Exhibit Honors Motown," CNHI News Service, http://blogs.cnhins.com/node/1482, accessed July 3, 2009.

http://motown.com

21-1 The Operations Processes (Input → Processes → Output)

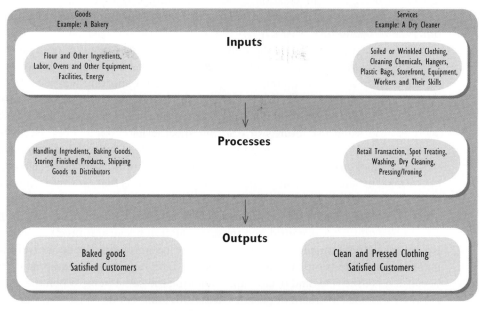

Goods
Example: A Bakery

Services
Example: A Dry Cleaner

Inputs

Flour and Other Ingredients, Labor, Ovens and Other Equipment, Facilities, Energy

Soiled or Wrinkled Clothing, Cleaning Chemicals, Hangers, Plastic Bags, Storefront, Equipment, Workers and Their Skills

Processes

Handling Ingredients, Baking Goods, Storing Finished Products, Shipping Goods to Distributors

Retail Transaction, Spot Treating, Washing, Dry Cleaning, Pressing/Ironing

Outputs

Baked goods
Satisfied Customers

Clean and Pressed Clothing
Satisfied Customers

than traditional systems and whether they function efficiently and accurately in meeting customer needs.

In some cases, technology can provide dramatically better service than the traditional model. Compare traditional brick-and-mortar bookstores to their online counterparts. Customers and their feedback are fundamental and critical to the value of online sites. When browsing the Amazon.com website, for example, the shopper is provided with customer-driven information such as the following:[1]

- Frequently Bought Together
- Customers Who Bought This Item Also Bought
- What Do Customers Ultimately Buy after Viewing This Item?
- Customer Reviews
- Customer Discussions

The insights provided by these options can help visitors find products that interest them, which leads to increased customer satisfaction.

Types of Manufacturing Operations

Manufacturing operations can take many forms, depending on the degree to which they are repetitive. For example, a master craftsman furniture maker who makes customized pieces follows a very different process than do workers at an automobile manufacturer who assemble hundreds of cars on a production line each day. The former deals with great variety and must maintain flexible operations, whereas the latter follow a set routine that allows them to build cars at a very low per-unit cost compared to a garage mechanic who tries to build a single automobile in a shop at home. Most manufacturing operations can be classified as one of three types—job shops, project manufacturing, and repetitive manufacturing.

job shop
A manufacturing operation in which short production runs are used to produce small quantities of unique items.

project manufacturing
Operations used to create unique but similar products.

repetitive manufacturing
Operations designed for long production runs of high-volume products.

continuous manufacturing
A form of repetitive manufacturing with output that more closely resembles a stream of product than individual goods.

flexible manufacturing systems
Operations that usually involve computer-controlled equipment that can turn out products in smaller or more flexible quantities.

Job shops are designed for short production runs. Skill sets are grouped, and work moves in batches from location to location. Only a few products are produced before the general-purpose machines are shifted to a different production setup. Machine shops represent this type of operation.

When most people think about manufacturing, they often picture a factory operation, but this is not always the case. *Project manufacturing* is used to create unique but similar products, such as site-built homes and grandstands for sporting facilities. In some cases, these operations may not even seem to belong to the manufacturing family. Creative work, such as composing music or painting portraits, can fall into this category, as may professional work, such as processing tax returns or drafting specific legal documents. Because each project is unique, this type of operation has to be highly flexible to meet the requirements of the job and the demands of customers. However, because of the similarity involved, a company can achieve operational efficiencies by using manufacturing methods that, in some ways, resemble those of repetitive manufacturing, which is described next.

Firms that produce one or relatively few standardized products use *repetitive manufacturing.* This is considered mass production because it involves long production runs. Repetitive manufacturing is associated with the assembly-line production of high-volume products, such as televisions and apparel items. Highly specialized equipment can be employed, because it is used over and over again in making the same item. When the output created more closely resembles a stream of product than individual goods (such as water from a purification plant or power generated by a hydroelectric dam), this form of repetitive manufacturing is sometimes referred to as *continuous manufacturing.*

Most businesses do not implement a pure version of any of these process types, but rather mix and match in order to gain the benefits of each. For instance, home builders will frequently blend job shop operations (building several houses using specialized subcontractors for plumbing, painting, and electrical work) with project manufacturing features (being unique, individualized, and customized). To meet the increasing market demands for unique products that are low in price, many companies are turning to *flexible manufacturing systems,* which usually involve computer-controlled equipment that can turn out a variety of products in smaller or more flexible quantities. In other words, machine automation, while expensive, can help cut manufacturing costs while giving customers exactly what they want.

Capacity Considerations

A small company's capacity to serve or produce goods or services is a critical factor. It puts a ceiling on the firm's ability to meet demand and match competitors, but it may also determine startup costs and usually represents a long-term commitment.

To illustrate how this works, lawn mower manufacturers have to accommodate seasonal demand. Customers want to buy lawn mowers in the spring and summer, but their orders drop to nearly zero in the fall and winter. Usually, manufacturers set their capacity to meet the average level of this demand, produce year round, and store up excess product as inventory to satisfy orders when they come in. However, service companies cannot hold inventory, so a provider such as Starbucks must have the capacity to meet peak demand throughout the day.

Capacity for the lawn mower manufacturer is determined by factory space, machinery, workers, and other such factors. Although capacity at Starbucks is similarly determined by store space, equipment, and workers, adjusting capacity to meet market changes may look very different for these two firms.

Planning and Scheduling

In manufacturing, production planning and scheduling procedures are designed to achieve the orderly, sequential flow of products through a plant at a rate matching deliveries to customers.

In order to reach this objective, it is essential to avoid production disruptions and to utilize machines and personnel efficiently. Simple, informal control procedures are often used in small plants. If a procedure is straightforward and the output is small, a manager can keep things moving smoothly with a minimum of paperwork. However, any manufacturing venture that experiences growth will eventually have to establish formal procedures to ensure production efficiency.

Because service firms are closely tied to their customers, they are limited in their ability to produce services and hold them in inventory for customers. An automobile repair shop must wait until a car arrives before starting its operations, and a beauty shop cannot function until a customer is available. A retail store can perform some of its services, such as transporting and storing inventory, but it, too, must wait until the customer arrives to perform other services.

Part of the scheduling task for service firms relates to planning employees' working hours. Restaurants, for example, schedule the work of servers to coincide with variations in customer traffic. In a similar way, stores and medical clinics increase their staff to handle the crush of customers or patients during periods of peak demand. Other strategies of service firms focus on scheduling customers. Appointment systems are used by many automobile repair centers and beauty shops. Service firms such as dry cleaners and plumbers take requests for service and delay delivery until the work can be scheduled. Still other firms, including banks and movie theaters, maintain a fixed schedule of services and tolerate some idle capacity. Some businesses attempt to spread out customer demand by offering incentives for customers to use services during off-peak hours—examples of this would include early-bird dinner specials at restaurants and lower-price tickets for the afternoon showing of a movie.

To smooth out and delay investment in additional capacity, companies are turning increasingly to *demand management strategies*. These strategies are used to stimulate customer demand when it is normally low and are limited only by the entrepreneur's imagination. For example, Six Flags theme parks have implemented the Flash Pass rider reservation system. The Flash Pass is a pager that holds your place in line so that you can be waiting for a popular ride while enjoying other activities in the park. When it is time for you to ride, the pager indicates that you have 10 minutes to get to the ride to claim your spot. Of course, Six Flags charges an extra fee for this privilege, but the net result is both a smoothing and a prioritization of demand. Those customers willing to pay more get more value from their time in the park.[2]

demand management strategies Strategies used to stimulate customer demand when it is normally low.

Inventory Management and Operations

You have probably gathered from the previous section that inventory management is an important concept. It may not be glamorous, but it can make the difference between success and failure for a small firm. When examined sensibly, inventory management can help an entrepreneur understand the vital balance between two competing pressures in the business. The company may need *more* inventory to satisfy customers (meeting customer demand and providing high-quality service), but it will want to maintain *less* inventory to keep the company's balance sheet healthy (see Exhibit 21-2). Small businesses are often highly customer-focused; however, many also are constantly strapped for cash, so the often-substantial cost of inventory and its storage pushes the business to try to carry less of it. Inventory management is particularly important in small retail or wholesale companies, because inventory typically represents a major financial investment by these businesses.

3. Identify ways to control inventory and minimize inventory costs.

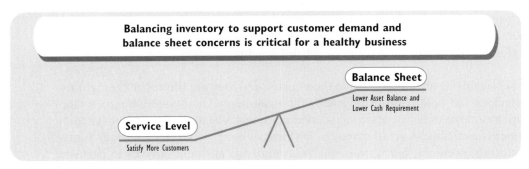

Balancing inventory to support customer demand and balance sheet concerns is critical for a healthy business

Balance Sheet
Lower Asset Balance and
Lower Cash Requirement

Service Level
Satisfy More Customers

Objectives of Inventory Management

The reasons for carrying inventory are numerous. Perhaps a "kitchen pantry" analogy will help you to see why this is the case. Why do you keep more Cheerios (or whichever cereal you prefer) in the pantry than you need today?

- To eat (to meet customer demand)
- To avoid going to the grocery store for each meal (to be less dependent on the source)
- To have breakfast supplies for guests to eat (to protect against stockouts)
- To benefit from price discounts (to gain from sales or quantity-based cost reductions)
- To buy before prices go up (to protect against price increases)

The point of this exercise is to show that you probably keep extra Cheerios around for a number of reasons. You may have thought that it was just a matter of having something to eat for breakfast, but that is likely to be only one of your objectives for keeping the pantry well stocked with cereal and your "kitchen operation" working.

Ensuring continuous operations is particularly important in manufacturing, because delays caused by lack of materials or parts can be costly. Furthermore, sales can be maximized by completing production in a timely manner and by stocking an appropriate assortment of merchandise for distribution to wholesale establishments and retail stores. Protecting inventory from theft, misplacement, and deterioration and optimizing investments likewise contribute to operational efficiency and business profits.

You may conclude that carrying more stock is the key to maintaining high-quality service. Inventory management may be crucial, but it is not a cure-all. Daniel Corsten, vice director of the Kuehne-Institute for Logistics at the University of St. Gallen in Switzerland, reports that one study showed that when it comes to stockouts, "72% of the root causes could be found in the store"—that is, from problems such as incorrect forecasting, lost or misplaced inventory, poor shelving or storage systems, and inadequate stock measurement.[3] Having more inventory on hand would increase costs, but it would not solve these other fundamental problems.

Inventory Cost Control

economic order quantity
The quantity to purchase in order to minimize total inventory costs.

Maintaining optimal inventory—the level that minimizes stockouts and eliminates excess inventory—saves money and contributes to operating profits. Traditional methods of determining ideal inventory levels may be sufficient for your business. One such method is calculating the *economic order quantity,* a relatively simple index that determines the purchase quantity of an item (some of which will be carried in inventory) that minimizes total inventory costs.[4]

Preferring more advanced methods, many small businesses have turned to *statistical inventory control*, which characterizes the variability of supply and demand using a targeted service level. This method allows you to determine statistically the appropriate amount of inventory to carry, and it is easier to use than you might imagine. In fact, the tools required for this computation are built into many inexpensive, off-the-shelf accounting systems, such as Microsoft Dynamics or SAP's Business One Software.

If a firm could order merchandise or raw materials and carry inventory with no expenses other than the cost of the items, there would be little concern about order quantity at any given time. However, this is not the case. Inventory comes with many other related costs, and these are easy to overlook. At a minimum, you should consider the following:

- Storage (land and buildings required, as well as shelving and organization systems)
- Theft, weathering, spoilage, and obsolescence
- Cost of capital (the cost of tying up cash in inventory that could be better used elsewhere)
- Transaction costs (costs from ordering, receiving, inspecting, transporting, and distributing inventory)
- Insurance and security
- Disposal costs (when inventory ultimately cannot be sold)

Your business may have to bear these costs and others. While some of them are fixed, others will rise and fall based on the quantity of inventory held. Optimizing these costs can be a complex challenge.

ABC INVENTORY CLASSIFICATION Some inventory items are more valuable or more critical to a firm's operations than others. Stated another way, some items have a greater effect on the costs and profits of a business. As a general rule, managers will be most attentive to those inventory items requiring the largest investment. Managing inventory, according to its priority, can help boost a company's performance.

One approach to inventory analysis, the *ABC method*, classifies items into three categories based on *dollar velocity* (purchase price × annual quantity consumed). The purpose of the ABC method is to focus managerial attention on the most important items. The number of categories could easily be expanded to four or more, if that seemed more appropriate for a particular firm.

In category A are a few high-value inventory items that account for the largest percentage of total dollars or are otherwise critical in the production process and, therefore, deserve close control. These might be monitored using an inventory system that keeps a running record of receipts, withdrawals, and balances of each item. In this way, a company can avoid an unnecessarily heavy investment in costly inventory items.

Category B items are less costly but deserve moderate managerial attention because they still make up a significant share of the firm's total inventory investment. Category C contains low-cost or noncritical items, such as paper clips in an office or nuts and bolts in a repair shop. The carrying costs of such items are not large enough to justify close control. These items might simply be checked periodically to ensure that a sufficient supply is available.

JUST-IN-TIME INVENTORY SYSTEMS The *just-in-time inventory system* is designed to cut inventory carrying costs by making or buying what is needed *just as it is needed*. First popularized by the Japanese, the just-in-time approach has led to cost reductions in many countries. New items are received, presumably, just as the last item of that type from existing inventory is placed into service. The just-in-time concept rests mostly on a few basic principles, but chief among these is the emphasis on the *pull* of inventory over the *push* of the same. That is, inventory items are to be made or bought in response to demand (pull), rather than based on what is planned or anticipated (push). This focus prevents the buildup of unnecessary inventory, which would defeat the advantages of the just-in-time approach.

Many large firms have adopted some form of the just-in-time system for inventory management, but small businesses can also benefit from its use. It's important to note that adoption of this approach requires careful coordination with suppliers. Supplier locations, production schedules, and transportation schedules must be carefully considered, as they all affect a firm's ability to obtain materials quickly and in a predictable manner—a necessary condition for using this approach. The just-in-time method also requires a production system to be more flexible, with short setup and turnaround times.

The benefits of just-in-time management go beyond reducing in-house inventory and creating a healthier balance sheet. Quality problems become more evident, and sooner, which reduces waste. Storage space, insurance costs, and revolving credit are freed up for other purposes. Finally, the ultimate objective and outcome of this method is a smooth and balanced system that responds nimbly to market demand.

The just-in-time inventory system has been used by businesses of all sizes, and with good results. You may be familiar with McAlister's, a franchised chain of well over 200 deli restaurants, which was started in 1989 by Don Newcomb. Since McAlister's is a franchise, the operation of each store is carefully dictated by the corporate handbook. Its prescribed approach specifies that each restaurant is to set up four sandwich-making workstations or production cells and to use as many of these as needed based on the hour of the day and the flow of customers. Each station has a single operator who receives sandwich orders in batches. So, if a party of eight comes in, one workstation would prepare sandwiches for all eight diners.

A McAlister's restaurant in central Texas is one of the higher volume outlets, and it earned its franchisor's permission to experiment with the production system by making two changes. First, to accommodate the high volume, the four cells were changed to two assembly lines with specialized workers. Only one of the lines is used most of the time, but it is operated by four to six workers. The second modification, and one that is consistent with the spirit of the just-in-time approach, is that the batch size has been changed to *one sandwich,* regardless of the order size. That is, even when the two assembly lines are operating, the sandwiches in a large order will be split, based on available capacity. The result has been reduced order lead time and variability, fewer mistakes, and higher efficiency. Because this new arrangement is working so well, the local owner is happy with the change, and so is the franchisor.[5]

Inventory Record-Keeping Systems

The larger the company, the greater the need for record keeping, but even a very small business needs a system for keeping tabs on its inventory. Because manufacturers are concerned with three broad categories of inventory (raw materials and supplies, work in process, and finished goods), their inventory records are more complex than those of wholesalers and retailers. Small firms should emphasize simplicity in their control methods. Too much control can be as wasteful as it is unnecessary.

In most small businesses, inventory records are computerized. Many different software programs are available for this purpose. The owner or manager, in consultation with the company's accounting advisors, can select the software best suited for the particular needs of the business.

Inventory checks can be carried out in different ways. A *physical inventory system* depends on an actual count of items on hand. The counting is done in physical units such as pieces, gallons, or boxes. By using this method, a firm can create an accurate record of its inventory level at a given point in time. Some businesses have an annual shutdown to count everything—a complete physical inventory. Others use *cycle counting,* scheduling different segments of the inventory for counting at different times during the year. This simplifies the inventorying process and makes it less of an ordeal for the business as a whole.

physical inventory system
A method that provides for periodic counting of items in inventory.

cycle counting
A system of counting different segments of the physical inventory at different times during the year.

A *perpetual inventory system* provides an ongoing, current record of inventory items. It does not require a physical count. However, a physical count of inventory should be made periodically to ensure the accuracy of the system and to make adjustments for such factors as loss or theft.

The simplest method is called a *two-bin inventory system.* For each item in inventory, the business sets up two containers, each holding enough to cover lead time. When one is emptied, it is replaced with the second and a new container is ordered. You may already be managing sugar at home using this approach. You use sugar out of one bag, but you keep a second bag in the pantry. When the first is empty, you open the second and buy a new one at the grocery store. As a result, your "sweet tooth" is always covered.

perpetual inventory system
A method for keeping a running record of inventory.

two-bin inventory system
A method of inventory control based on use of two containers for each item in inventory: one to meet current demand and the other to meet future demand.

Operations Management and Quality

Quality is *much* more than a nice theme for a slogan. Owners of successful small firms realize that quality management is serious business and that a strong commitment to the achievement of quality goals is essential. So, how is quality related to operations? Quality can be achieved only to the extent that operations lead to the outcomes that customers want. Following this logic, companies that fail to produce quality in their operations will not have the buyers they need to stay in business for long.

4. Recognize the contributions of operations management to product and service quality.

Quality as a Competitive Tool

Quality may be defined as the characteristics of a product or service that determine its ability to satisfy stated and implied needs. Quality obviously has many dimensions. For example, a restaurant's customers base their perceptions of its quality on the taste of the food, the attractiveness of the décor, the friendliness and promptness of servers, the cleanliness of silverware, the appropriateness of background music, and many other factors. The operations process establishes a level of quality as a product is being produced or as a service is being provided. Although costs and other considerations cannot be ignored, quality must remain a primary focus of a firm's operations.

International competition is increasingly turning on quality differences. Automobile manufacturers, for example, now place much greater emphasis on quality in their attempts to compete effectively with foreign producers. However, it is not solely big firms that need to make quality a major concern: the operations process of a small business also deserves careful scrutiny. Many small companies have been slow to give adequate consideration to producing high-quality goods and services. In examining the operations process, therefore, small business managers must direct special attention to achieving superior product or service quality.

The American Society for Quality (ASQ) has been the leading quality improvement organization in the United States for more than 50 years and has introduced many quality improvement methods throughout the world. Among these is an approach known as *total quality management (TQM),* an aggressive effort by a firm to achieve superior quality. Total quality management is an all-encompassing, quality-focused management approach that is characterized by the following features:

quality
The features of a product or service that enable it to satisfy customers' needs.

total quality management (TQM)
An all-encompassing management approach to providing high-quality products and services.

- It is ***customer driven***: Customer needs and wants are the core drivers.
- It emphasizes ***organizational commitment***: Management leads, but the entire organization participates.
- It focuses on a ***culture of continuous improvement.***

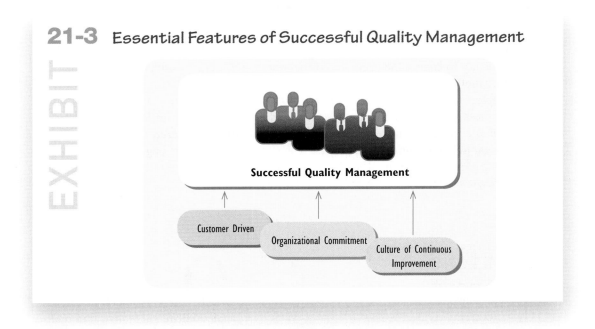

21-3 Essential Features of Successful Quality Management

Successful Quality Management

Customer Driven

Organizational Commitment

Culture of Continuous Improvement

Many businesses merely give lip service to achieving excellent quality standards; others have introduced quality programs that have failed. The most successful quality management efforts incorporate the three features just mentioned, which are highlighted in Exhibit 21-3.

The Customer Focus of Quality Management

A firm's quality management efforts should begin with a focus on the customers who purchase its products or services. Without such a focus, the quest for quality easily degenerates into an aimless search for some abstract, elusive ideal. To get started in the right direction, the entrepreneur should ask the following question: "What products and services will be provided to customers?"

Quality is ultimately determined by the extent to which a product or service satisfies customers' needs and expectations. Customers have expectations regarding the quality of products (durability and attractiveness, for example) and services (such as speed and accuracy). A customer is concerned with *product* quality when purchasing a camera or a loaf of bread; a customer's primary concern is *service* quality when having an automobile repaired or a suit tailor-made. Frequently, a customer expects some combination of product *and* service quality—when buying a flatscreen TV, a purchaser may be concerned with the performance of the model selected, knowledge and courtesy of the salesperson, credit terms offered, and warranty coverage.

At times, it can be easy to misread what customers want, but what they desire is usually very simple. For example, a car owner who takes his automobile to a repair shop hopes to receive competent service (that is, a successful repair), to get a reasonable explanation of what had to be done, and to be treated with respect. Similarly, a hotel patron anticipates being provided with a clean room, having reasonable security, and being treated like a guest. Such uncomplicated expectations open up an avenue of opportunity. Exceeding these basic expectations can leave a lasting, favorable impression on customers, which often results in repeat business and free promotion through positive word of mouth. As a bonus, a genuine concern for customer needs and satisfaction can be a powerful force that energizes the total quality management effort of a company.

RETAIL IS DETAIL Perhaps you've heard of the anonymous quote "Retail is detail." This means that operating details can make or break a business, especially in an industry such as food service. In 1971, Richard Melman founded R. J. Grunt's, a low-priced burger joint. After a few successful years, Melman began to turn his attention to launching other kinds of restaurants, and R. J. Grunt's started to lose its luster. Cost-conscious managers cut back on some of the ingredients and became less meticulous in food preparation. Eventually, the eatery began to lose money.

In 2002, Melman turned R. J. Grunt's over to his son, who already had experience managing one of Melman's other successful restaurants. Together, father and son found problems—the milkshakes weren't as good as they used to be, and neither were the hamburgers and fries. The Melmans began improving ingredients, recipes, and menus. Grilling instructions were posted

and enforced. They bought new equipment. And, eventually, the Melman team's hard work paid off. They were able to rescue the burger hot spot, leading R. J. Grunt's back to its best month in nine years. The business was saved by carefully attending to the details of its basic operations and correcting the weaknesses that were dragging down the system.[6]

CUSTOMER FEEDBACK Listening attentively to customers' opinions can provide information about their level of satisfaction. Employees having direct contact with customers can serve as the eyes and ears of the business in evaluating existing quality levels and customer needs. Unfortunately, many managers are oblivious to the often subtle feedback from customers. Preoccupied with operating details, managers may not listen carefully to, let alone solicit, customers' opinions. Employees having direct contact with customers—such as servers in a restaurant—are seldom trained or encouraged to obtain information about customers' quality expectations. Careful management and training of servers could make them more alert to consumers' tastes and attitudes and provide a mechanism for reporting these reactions to management.

Experts now recommend that firms work hard to involve and empower customers in efforts to improve quality. The marketing research methods of observation, interviews, and customer surveys, as described in Chapter 7, can be used to investigate customers' views regarding quality. Some businesses, for example, provide comment cards for their customers to use in evaluating service or product quality.

Another approach to gathering customer-based information is to "mine" company sales data, statistically analyzing it in search of useful "nuggets of insight" on customer behavior. To learn a lesson or two from an operations superstar, consider Walmart and its response to the tragedy surrounding Hurricane Katrina. Because it has carefully studied its own sales data, Walmart is well aware of customer buying patterns preceding storms. Before a serious weather event strikes, customers stock up on the expected: water, flashlights, and generators. But in the aftermath of such a storm, customers buy yard and home cleanup items such as mops and trash bags. Some items that are commonly purchased are less predictable, such as strawberry Pop-Tarts (a quirk in buying behavior). By recognizing past trends and adjusting operations to match them (including having an ample supply of Pop-Tarts available after a storm), Walmart can help those most in need and make a profit by serving their known, and perhaps unknown, needs with great precision.

But Walmart is a huge corporation, so how does this relate to small enterprises? Most business management software programs now include "business intelligence" modules that can help even the smallest of companies discover customer buying patterns so they can respond accordingly.[7] Data mining techniques can provide powerful insights to guide small business operations; this approach should not be overlooked.

"The Basic Seven" Quality Tools

Another important element in effective quality management consists of the various tools, techniques, and procedures needed to ensure high-quality products and services. Once the focus is shifted to the customer and the entire organization is committed to continuous improvement, operating methods become critical concerns. Kaoru Ishikawa, a professor of engineering at Tokyo University and the father of "quality circles," contends that 95 percent of a typical company's quality problems can be solved by using the following seven tools (sometimes called "The Basic Seven"):[8]

1. A *cause-and-effect diagram* (or *Ishikawa chart* or *fishbone chart*) identifies potential causes for an effect or problem while sorting them into categories.

2. A *check sheet* provides a structured, prepared form for collecting and analyzing data.

3. A *control chart* transforms data into graphs that can be used to determine if a process errs in some predictable, and correctable, way.

4. A *histogram* is the most commonly used graph for showing how often each different value in a set of data occurs.

5. A *Pareto chart* presents bar graphs that reveal which causes are significant, separating the "vital few" from the "useful many."

6. A *scatter diagram* graphs pairs of different sets of variables, allowing a search for quality relationships or patterns.

7. A *flow chart* (or *run chart*) represents visually the series of steps required to complete an operation.

This list may seem overwhelming, but do not despair. Most of these tools are straightforward and require almost no training, except for control charts, which are discussed in more detail later in this section. And you can learn more about how to use all seven of these tools through online resources.

Quality Assurance Using Inspection versus Poka-Yoke

inspection
The examination of a part or a product to determine whether it meets quality standards.

Management's traditional method of maintaining product quality has been *inspection*, which consists of examining a part or a product to determine whether or not it is acceptable. An inspector often uses gauges to evaluate important quality variables. For effective quality control, the inspector must be honest, objective, and capable of resisting pressure from shop personnel to pass borderline cases.

Although the inspection process is usually discussed with reference to product quality, comparable steps can be taken to evaluate service quality. Follow-up calls to customers of an auto repair shop, for example, might be used to measure the quality of the firm's repair services. Customers can be asked whether recent repairs were performed in a timely and satisfactory manner.

The problem with inspection is that it occurs after the fact—that is, after faulty goods or inadequate services have been created or offered for sale. At that point, considerable resources have already been consumed in a company's operations, but with nothing of quality to show for it. This can result in unnecessary costs. In fact, this can lead to both internal costs (those related to repair, inspection, prevention, and training) and external costs (those related to the loss of reputation or repeat customers). Knowing this inspired quality guru Philip Crosby to declare, "Quality is free!" In other words, the *savings* associated with getting quality right more than offset the *cost* of a total quality management program.

Poka-Yoke
A proactive approach to quality management that seeks to mistake-proof a firm's operations, thus avoiding problems and waste before they can occur.

Quality inspection processes are helpful, but *Poka-Yoke* (an actual concept, despite its strange name) is a more proactive approach that seeks to mistake-proof a firm's operations. For example, a microwave oven may be designed so that it will not work with the door open, thereby preventing radiation leakage. Fryers at many fast food restaurants now raise the product out of the hot grease using a timed machine, rather than relying on a vigilant employee and an audible alarm. This innovation prevents food waste (from over- or under-cooked foods) and removes an opportunity for grease-burn injuries.

Statistical Methods of Quality Control

The use of statistical methods and control charts often can make controlling product and service quality easier, less expensive, and more effective. Because some knowledge of quantitative methods is necessary to develop a quality control method using statistical analysis, a properly qualified employee should be available to lead this part of the process. The savings made possible by use of an efficient statistical method usually will more than justify the cost of setting it up and managing it.

Acceptance sampling involves taking random samples of products and measuring them against predetermined standards. Suppose that a small business receives a shipment of 10,000 parts from a supplier. Rather than evaluate all 10,000 parts, the purchaser might check the acceptability of a small sample of parts and then accept or reject the entire order based on the results. The smaller the sample, the greater the risk of either accepting a defective lot or rejecting a good lot due to what is called *sampling error.* A larger sample reduces this risk but increases the cost of inspection. A well-designed plan strikes a balance, simultaneously avoiding excessive inspection costs and minimizing the risk of accepting a bad lot or rejecting a good lot.

acceptance sampling
The use of a random, representative portion of products to determine the acceptability of an entire lot.

The use of statistical analysis makes it possible to establish tolerance limits that allow for inherent variation due to chance. When measurements fall outside these tolerance limits, however, the quality controller knows that a problem exists and must search for the cause. A control chart graphically shows the limits for the process being controlled. As current data are entered, it is possible to tell whether a process is under control or out of control (random or nonrandom). Control charts may be used for either variable or attribute inspections.

Attributes are product or service parameters that can be counted as being either present or absent. A light bulb either lights or doesn't light; similarly, a water hose either leaks or doesn't leak. *Variables* are measured parameters that fall on a continuum, such as weight. If a box of candy is to be sold as containing a minimum of one pound of candy, an inspector may judge the product acceptable if its weight falls within the range of 16 ounces to 16.5 ounces.

attributes
Product or service parameters that can be counted as being present or absent.

variables
Measured parameters that fall on a continuum, such as weight or length.

A problem might be caused by variations in raw materials, machine wear, or changes in employees' work practices. Consider, for example, a candy maker that is producing one-pound boxes of chocolates. Though the weight may vary slightly, each box must weigh at least 16 ounces. A study of the operations process has determined that the actual target weight must be 16.5 ounces, to allow for normal variation between 16 and 17 ounces. During the production process, a set of boxes is weighed every 15 or 20 minutes. If the average weight of a box falls outside the tolerance limits—below 16 or above 17 ounces—the quality controller must immediately try to find the problem and correct it.

Continuing improvements in computer-based technology have advanced the use of statistical control processes in small enterprises. In fact, many off-the-shelf enterprise resource planning systems (computer software systems that coordinate all major facets of a firm's operations) for smaller businesses now include statistical quality control tools.

International Certification for Quality Management

A firm can obtain international recognition of its quality management program by meeting a series of standards, known as *ISO 9000,* developed by the International Organization for Standardization (ISO) in Geneva, Switzerland. The certification process requires full documentation of a firm's quality management procedures, as well as an audit to ensure that the firm is operating in accordance with those procedures. In other words, the firm must show that it does what it says it does.

ISO 9000
The standards governing international certification of a firm's quality management procedures.

ISO 9000 certification is particularly valuable for small firms, because they usually lack a global image as producers of high-quality products. Buyers in other countries, especially in

Europe, view this certification as an indicator of supplier reliability. Some large U.S. corporations, such as the major automobile makers, require their domestic suppliers to conform to these standards. Small firms, therefore, may need ISO 9000 certification either to sell more easily in international markets or to meet the demands of their domestic customers.

Environmental concerns and a focus on social responsibility have created new opportunities and challenges for entrepreneurs. Although no general certifications have been offered, the International Organization for Standardization also offers an ISO 14001 certification. This certification reflects how efficiently companies have set up and improved their operations processes in order to control the impact of vehicle and smokestack emissions, noise, and other fallout on air, water, and soil.

Quality Management in Service Businesses

As discussed earlier, maintaining and improving quality are no less important for service businesses than for manufacturers. In fact, many firms offer a combination of tangible products and intangible services and effectively manage quality in both areas.

According to the American Customer Satisfaction Index (published by the University of Michigan), customer satisfaction with service businesses overall has been higher in recent years,[9] but there is still plenty of room for improvement. For example, some large corporations gear the quality of the services they provide to the profitability of the customer—with better customers getting better service—and this can easily lead to dissatisfaction. But poor service from larger businesses (automated telephone answering systems that do not allow callers to speak to a live representative, long lines, reluctance to respond to customer problems, and so forth) opens the door for small service-oriented companies. Although some services are too costly to be used as powerful competitive weapons, providing high-quality service may sometimes involve nothing more than simple attention to detail.

Gathering relevant and useful measurements can be problematic when assessing the quality of a service. It is easier to measure the length of a piece of wood than the quality of motel accommodations. As noted earlier, however, methods can be devised for measuring the quality of services. For example, a motel manager might maintain a record of the number of problems with travelers' reservations, complaints about the cleanliness of rooms, and so on. Frequently, the "easy to measure" becomes the only measure. It is critical that you choose measures carefully to find parameters most relevant to a customer's perspective on quality.

For many types of service firms, quality control constitutes management's most important responsibility. All that such firms sell is service, and their success depends on customers' perceptions of the quality of that service.

Purchasing Policies and Practices

Although its role varies with the type of business, purchasing constitutes a key part of operations management for most small businesses. Through purchasing, firms obtain materials, merchandise, equipment, and services to meet production and marketing goals. For example, manufacturing firms buy raw materials, merchandising firms purchase goods to be sold, and all types of firms obtain supplies.

5. Explain the importance of purchasing and the nature of key purchasing policies.

The Importance of Purchasing

The quality of a finished product depends on the quality of the raw materials used. If a product must be made with great precision and close tolerances, the manufacturer must acquire high-quality materials and component parts. Then, if the maker uses a well-managed production process, excellent products will result. Similarly, the acquisition of high-quality merchandise makes a retailer's sales to customers easier and reduces the number of necessary markdowns and merchandise returns.

Purchasing also contributes to profitable operations by ensuring that goods are delivered when they are needed. Failure to receive materials, parts, or equipment on schedule can cause costly interruptions in production operations. In a retail business, failure to receive merchandise on schedule may mean a loss of sales and, possibly, a permanent loss of customers who were disappointed.

Another aspect of effective purchasing is securing the best possible price. Cost savings go directly to the bottom line, so purchasing practices that seek out the best prices can have a major impact on the financial health of a business.

Note, however, that the importance of the purchasing function varies according to the type of business. In a small, labor-intensive service business—such as an accounting firm—purchases of supplies are responsible for a very small part of the total operating costs. Such businesses are more concerned with labor costs than with the cost of supplies or other materials that they may require in their operations process.

MAKE OR BUY?   Many firms face *make-or-buy decisions*. Such choices are especially important for small manufacturing companies that have the option of making or buying component parts for products they produce. A less obvious make-or-buy choice exists with respect to certain services—for example, purchasing janitorial or car rental services versus providing for those needs internally. Some reasons for making component parts, rather than buying them, follow:

- More complete utilization of plant capacity permits more economical production.
- Supplies are assured, with fewer delays caused by design changes or difficulties with outside suppliers.
- A secret design may be protected.
- Expenses are reduced by an amount equivalent to transportation costs and the outside supplier's selling expense and profit.
- Closer coordination and control of the total production process may facilitate operations scheduling and control.
- Products produced may be of higher quality than those available from outside suppliers.

Some reasons for buying component parts, rather than making them, follow:

- An outside supplier's part may be cheaper because of the supplier's concentration on production of the part.
- Additional space, equipment, personnel skills, and working capital are not needed.
- Less diversified managerial experience and skills are required.
- Greater flexibility is provided, especially in the manufacture of a seasonal item.
- In-plant operations can concentrate on the firm's specialty—finished products and services.
- The risk of equipment obsolescence is transferred to outsiders.

The decision to make or buy should be based on long-run cost and profit optimization, because it may be expensive to reverse. Underlying cost differences need to be analyzed carefully; small savings from either buying or making may greatly affect profit margins.

OUTSOURCING   Buying products or services from other business firms is known as *outsourcing*. As mentioned earlier, firms can sometimes save money by buying from outside suppliers specializing in a particular type of work, especially services such as accounting, payroll, janitorial, and equipment repair services. The expertise of these outside suppliers may enable them to provide better-quality services by virtue of their specialization.

make or buy decisions
A choice small manufacturing companies must make when they have the option of making or buying component parts for products they produce.

outsourcing
Purchasing products or services that are outside the firm's area of specialization.

Under Armour Finds Outsourcing Is "No Sweat"

Under Armour is an amazing success story, and one with a surprisingly recent startup history. The company creates and sells sports apparel designed to regulate body temperature while enhancing comfort and mobility. It was founded in 1996 on a simple idea. Kevin Plank, a University of Maryland football player, was tired of wearing wet cotton T-shirts under his football pads, so he made undershirts out of a material that provided compression as well as the ability to wick moisture away from the skin. The concept has become tremendously popular with serious athletes and weekend warriors everywhere. After just over a decade of operations, sales reached $725 million, and the firm employed 2,200 people. Over the last five years, Under Armour has had a 44 percent compounded growth rate.

Like most clothing and apparel makers, the firm's production is almost completely outsourced to Asia, Mexico, Central and South America. Only a few of its specialty products are manufactured in Baltimore, Maryland.

The special fabric comes from unaffiliated suppliers, resulting in finished goods' lead times ranging from 90 to 120 days. Forecasting demand, another critical element of operations management, is made more complex due to the company's rapid growth rate, expansion into new product categories and distribution, and the advancement of systems and processes to meet these changing needs. The combination of overseas outsourcing, variable demand, and long lead times has resulted in a large finished goods inventory of $187 million, but with only $6,000 in work-in-process inventory.

The company is now using a dual manufacturing arrangement where the same goods are being manufactured with multiple manufacturing partners in order to mitigate the risk of supply chain disruption, while others are produced in the United States to be more responsive to demand. This allows the firm to balance sensitivity to customer demand with inventory carrying costs.

Currently, all U.S. distribution begins in Maryland. Another change Under Armour has implemented is regional warehousing and distribution to retailers from three strategic locations: California and Florida (third-party providers), and Maryland. One new method of distribution is direct shipment to customers, which is efficient for lead time and cost savings considerations. The goal, then, of these methods is to increase responsiveness while reducing distribution lead times and transportation costs. Will such a strategy work? Only time will tell.

Sources: "Under Armour," http://www.underarmour.com, accessed May 15, 2009; conversation with Alexandra Pettit, Director of Investor Relations, Under Armour Inc., July 30, 2009.

http://www.underarmour.com

Michael Fabus/Getty Images

When fashion stylist Natalie Chanin designed and hand-sewed a one-of-a-kind garment from a recycled T-shirt, she realized she had a product that would sell. But Chanin was unable to find a manufacturer in New York able to do the extensive handwork required to adorn and embroider the shirts with everything from flowers to roosters. The similarity of the work process to quilting inspired her to think of the quilting circles back in her native Alabama. After locating a group of women in Alabama who could provide the skilled handwork necessary to produce the uniquely decorated shirts, she outsourced the basic production process. Even though it's made from recycled T-shirts, Chanin's unique, high-fashion product is sold at prices as high as $2,000 in stores in the United States, Europe, and Asia. The shirts are featured in such stores as Barney's in New York, Brown's in London, and Maxfield's in Los Angeles. Thanks to outsourcing, the product is created by a contemporary version of the old-fashioned quilting circle.

Outsourcing can take many forms. Chapter 20 explained the practice of co-employment, through which a small company can transfer its employees to a professional employer organization, which then leases them back to the firm. In that case, the small business is outsourcing the payroll preparation process.

COOPS AND THE INTERNET

Some small companies find that they can increase their buying power if they join *cooperative purchasing organizations* (often just called *coops*). In this type of arrangement, several smaller businesses combine their demand for products and services with the goal of negotiating, as a group, for lower prices and better service from suppliers. Coops usually focus on a specific industry to maximize the benefits to participating businesses, and they can be very effective.

Coops have been around for a long time, but newer alternatives are quickly emerging. Increasingly, small companies are turning to the Internet as a powerful purchasing venue. Many tasks that once required telephone calls or out-of-office time can now be accomplished simply and quickly on the Web.

In the past, small businesses had scant buying power and very limited access to resources and information, which put them at a serious disadvantage relative to their large competitors. That has all changed, thanks (mostly) to the Internet. Today's connected small business owners can line up hundreds of suppliers, large and small, to bid for their business—with just a few mouse clicks. They can also outsource all sorts of tasks, from business planning and product design to sales presentations and warranty service. Technology has opened the door to a world of outsourcing alternatives that was unimaginable just a few decades ago.

cooperative purchasing organization (coop)
An arrangement whereby small businesses combine demand for products or services in order to negotiate as a group with suppliers.

DIVERSIFICATION OF SUPPLY

Small businesses often must decide whether or not it is better to use more than one supplier when purchasing a given item. The somewhat frustrating answer is "It all depends." For example, a business would rarely need more than one supplier when buying a few rolls of tape. However, several suppliers might be involved when a firm is buying a component part to be used in hundreds of products.

A small company might prefer to concentrate purchases with one supplier for any of the following reasons:

- A particular supplier may be superior in its product quality.
- Larger orders may qualify for quantity discounts.
- Orders may be so small that it is impractical to divide them among several suppliers.
- The purchasing firm may, as a good customer, qualify for prompt treatment of rush orders and receive management advice, market information, and flexible financial terms in times of crisis.

Also, a venture may be linked to a specific supplier by the very nature of its business—if it is a franchisee, for instance. Typically, the franchise contract requires purchasing from the franchisor.

The following reasons favor diversifying rather than concentrating sources of supply:

- Shopping among suppliers allows a firm to locate the best source in terms of price, quality, and service.
- A supplier, knowing that competitors are getting some of its business, may provide better prices and service.
- Diversifying supply sources provides insurance against interruptions caused by strikes, fires, or similar problems with sole suppliers.

Some companies compromise by following a purchasing policy of concentrating enough purchases with a single supplier to justify special treatment and, at the same time, diversifying purchases sufficiently to maintain alternative sources of supply. The point is that a small business can adopt any of a number of alternative approaches in order to diversify its sourcing strategy.

Measuring Supplier Performance

Supply Chain Operations Reference (SCOR) model
A list of critical factors that provides a helpful starting place when assessing a supplier's performance.

When working with suppliers, what measures of their performance matter most? The Supply Chain Council has an answer to that question. It has developed the *Supply Chain Operations Reference (SCOR) model,* a list of critical factors that provides a helpful starting place when assessing a supplier's performance. Five attributes stand out above all others.[10]

- *Reliability:* Does the supplier provide what you need and fill orders accurately?
- *Responsiveness*: Does the supplier deliver inputs when they are needed?
- *Flexibility:* Does the supplier respond quickly to changes in your order?
- *Cost:* Does the supplier help you control your cost of goods sold, your total supply chain management costs, and your warranty/returns costs?
- *Asset efficiency:* Does the supplier help you improve efficiencies by shortening the cash cycle, inventory holding time, and demand on assets?

These attributes can also prove helpful when first selecting a supplier. Since they are commonly used performance measures, some suppliers have data to show potential new customers how they stack up (along with references to verify their claims). Just remember that an outstanding rating on a measure that is not important to your business does not provide an advantage—in fact, it can be a form of waste.

When choosing a supplier, the services it offers should also be considered. The extension of credit by suppliers provides a major portion of the working capital of many small businesses. Some suppliers also plan sales promotions, provide merchandising aids, and offer management advice.

Small companies sometimes find that their greatest challenges in business come from working with large-firm suppliers. When Ross O. Youngs finds something that doesn't work as well as it should, the inventor in him just has a way of coming out. For example, he never did like hard plastic jewel cases for CDs, so he combined a piece of soft plastic with a piece of fabric to create the Safety-sleeve, a product that serves the same purpose—only better. To turn this product idea into a startup, Youngs launched Univenture Media Packaging. Within a few months, he had $1,200 in orders. The next month, that number jumped to $12,000. But no product had been delivered to customers. The supplier, a large manufacturer, kept pushing the small order aside. And when the manufacturer finally delivered, the quality of the product was pathetic. Every single sleeve had to be cleaned individually.[11]

Of course, Youngs fixed the problem as soon as he could, but his experience shows just how important it is to choose suppliers carefully. If a supplier fails to deliver what you need when you need it and with the quality you require, the entire operation breaks down—as does your business.[12]

Building Good Relationships with Suppliers

Good relationships with suppliers are essential for firms of any size, but they are particularly important for small businesses. The small company is only one among dozens, hundreds, or perhaps thousands buying from that supplier. And the small company's purchases are often very limited in volume and, therefore, of little concern to the supplier.

To implement a policy of fair play and to cultivate good relations with suppliers, a small business should try to observe the following purchasing practices:

- Pay bills promptly.
- Give sales representatives a timely and courteous hearing.
- Minimize abrupt cancellation of orders merely to gain a temporary advantage.
- Avoid attempts to browbeat a supplier into special concessions or unusual discounts.
- Cooperate with the supplier by making suggestions for product improvements and/or cost reductions, whenever possible.

- Provide courteous, reasonable explanations when rejecting bids, and make fair adjustments in the case of disputes.

Some large corporations, such as UPS, Dell, FedEx, and Office Depot, have made special efforts to reach out to small business purchasers. By offering various kinds of assistance, such suppliers can strengthen small companies, which then continue as customers. Of course, it still makes sense to shop around, but low prices can sometimes be misleading. If a low bid looks too good to be true, perhaps that's because it is. Low bids often exclude crucial items. Nonetheless, building strong relationships with the right large suppliers can clearly help small businesses become more competitive.

Forming Strategic Alliances

Some small firms have found it advantageous to develop strategic alliances with suppliers. This form of partnering enables the buying and selling firms to work much more closely together than is customary in a simple contractual arrangement.

The strategic alliance option can be a good one, but the choice of partner can quickly determine whether the arrangement succeeds or fails—so choose carefully! Laurel Delaney is a successful entrepreneur, author, and educator with more than 20 years of experience in business. During that time, she guided her small businesses into strategic alliances with global powerhouses like Mitsui & Co., Ltd., the Japanese trading company. From those experiences, Delaney gained some important insights on selecting a strategic alliance partner. For example, she learned to begin her search by looking at companies with which she already had a relationship, such as a faithful supplier or distributor or a trading company that was struggling to keep up with demand. And she learned to look for partners that offered the right fit, were trustworthy, and had track records of true performance.[13] If a strategic alliance is well planned and executed, everyone involved comes out ahead.

Some potential alliance partners design their business especially to help small firms. After graduating from Columbia University, Michael Prete went to work for a major investment bank in New York City. But he soon tired of the corporate life and decided to redirect his time and energy to one of his true passions—motorcycles. He started a company called Gotham Cycles. As a Platinum Power Seller on eBay, the business sells parts for Ducati, Aprilia, MV Agusta, and other Italian motorcycles. After only a year or so in his new business, he was already bringing in $30,000 a month in income. Not bad for a guy who insists on working alone. But the fact is, he doesn't exactly work alone. He has eBay as his one and only employee. Of course, the online auction site isn't exactly an employee—it's more like an army of employees (more than 16,000 strong, in fact) that can help an online company with many of its needs. Prete knows he never could have accomplished what he did all by himself; making use of eBay's rich stable of resources to automate his operation allowed him to concentrate on building his company.[14]

A powerful partner for a small business, eBay offers sophisticated tools that can help with shipping, handling e-mail messages and feedback for buyers, and managing listings. It can even help you decide which tools are right for your business (see http://pages.ebay.com/sell/tool recommendations.html). As Prete has observed, "These tools have enabled me to continue to work alone while allowing my business to expand."[15]

Forecasting Supply Needs

How much cash is needed for the next quarter? How much inventory will be carried to support the next season? Forecasting can help with understanding where the business is going and the level of resources—from personnel to capital funding—that will be required. Forecasting techniques can be as simple as projecting what will happen based on what happened last year, last week, or an average of several previous periods. Some businesses may require higher accuracy and thus need a more complex model for forecasting.

Associative forecasting takes a variety of driving variables into account when determining expected sales. The amount of sales expected at a local ice cream parlor, for example, is a product of many underlying predictors, such as the day of the week or season of the year, weather (rain versus shine, hot versus cool), local events (such as sporting events or movie premieres), and promotions (which could include sales or coupons). Each of these has a different impact on expected sales. Using tools such as regression, we can determine the impact of each variable on attendance in the past and then use that association to predict future attendance.

Using Information Systems

In recent years, small firms have greatly improved operational efficiency by using computers, new software, and Internet links with suppliers and customers. Tedious, paper-based processes for tracking orders, work in process, and inventory have been replaced by simplified and accelerated computer-based processes.

Forrester Research has shown that accounts payable electronic invoicing and processing can cut the cost of an invoice process from $20 to $5. For a company that processes thousands of invoices per month, this savings can have a substantial impact on costs. The software can be purchased off the shelf, so changing how things are done and training personnel on a new system may actually be more challenging than the installation of new software.[16]

Management information systems are continually being reinvented and improved. Microsoft alone spends billions of dollars to build software that will automate practically every aspect of a small company's business (such as order processing and inventory management) and create a base layer of technology upon which smaller software makers can build applications. This software is also designed to work for a variety of businesses, from retail to distribution and manufacturing.[17] The information systems options available to small companies just keep getting better, more powerful, and less expensive.

Lean Production and Synchronous Management

A revolution is sweeping over operations management practices, changing the way business is done in many firms. With a focus on eliminating waste, lean production and synchronous management have made their mark on both large and small companies.

6. Describe lean production and synchronous management and their importance to operations management in small firms.

lean production
An approach that emphasizes efficiency through elimination of waste.

Lean Production

Companies are widely adopting principles of lean production, an influential model that is fundamentally reshaping the way operations are planned and managed. *Lean production* is more than a simple set of practices—it is a guiding philosophy and management approach that emphasizes efficiency through the elimination of all forms of waste in a company's operations.

The ideas at the center of lean production certainly are not new. In fact, the seeds of the concept were sown more than a century ago by Henry Ford, a leading visionary for the automobile industry and an outspoken opponent of manufacturing inefficiency. Later, Shoichiro Toyoda, former president of Toyota Motors, built on Ford's concepts and focused on the need to eliminate waste, in all of its many forms, from his production system. He defined waste as "anything in excess of the minimum amounts of materials, parts, equipment, facilities, labor, and time that are essential to produce and deliver the desired product and service to the customer."[18] In other words, the goal of lean production is to use the minimum amount of resources to satisfy the greatest customer wants and needs.

The lean production mind-set that has been integrated into the operations of most major corporations, including the Toyota Production System (TPS), makes the elimination of waste a top priority. Consider the following:

- *Defects* are costly because they have to be repaired or scrapped.
- *Overproduction* must be stored and may never be sold.
- *Transportation* can be minimized by locating close to suppliers and customers.
- *Waiting* can be wasteful because resources are idle.
- *Inventory* in excess of the minimum required is unproductive and costly.
- *Motion,* whether by product, people, or machinery, can be wasteful.
- *Processing* itself is wasteful if it is not productive.

As companies of all sizes around the world have subscribed to the principles of lean production, the supply chain (introduced in Chapter 15) has become susceptible to disruption, and this can be a problem. Toyota, for example, keeps only two hours of inventory in their assembly plants, so there is little margin for error on the supply side of the equation. However, this incredibly low amount of inventory also leads to a variety of benefits, ranging from capital efficiency to a smooth production process.

Synchronous Management

Going a step beyond lean production, *synchronous management* views the assets and activities of an organization as interdependent and suggests that they be managed in a way that optimizes the performance of the entire company. This approach presumes that the goal of the organization, and the definition of performance that flows from it, is known and influences all decision making. It requires an understanding of how a shift in one area of operations can affect the rest of the organization—that is, it provides insight regarding interrelationships between assets, changes in activities, and achievement of the firm's goal.

Although these ideas are not original, they are finally being understood and implemented, in many cases for the first time. More than 75 years ago, Henry Ford concluded that the key to manufacturing efficiency lies in a synchronized flow of materials and products into, through, and out of the plant in concert with market demand. Stated another way, companies that understand crucial interactions between the firm's assets and activities are likely to produce the greatest profits.[19]

Identifying bottlenecks is imperative to making synchronous management work. A *bottleneck* is any point in an operations system where limited capacity reduces the production capability of an entire chain of activities so that it cannot satisfy market demand for products or services. For example, a bottleneck would be created by a machine that could not operate fast enough to keep up with the rest of the equipment on an assembly line. In a more complex production system, it is possible to have more than one bottleneck (that is, more than one resource whose capacity is lower than the market demand for what is being produced). In this case, the most restrictive of the bottlenecks is called a *constraint.* Since the constraint determines the capacity of the entire system, it is imperative to synchronize all other organizational activities with it.

Finding the bottlenecks in an organization can be a challenging exercise. But once a constraint is found, what can be done to address it? The three basic options shown in Exhibit 21-4 provide common ways to deal with bottlenecks and constraints.

For resources that do not contribute to a bottleneck or constraint in a production line or service firm, it is far less important to make investments to improve their functioning and increase their efficiency. These parts of the system do not have any trouble keeping up with the flow of operations. That is, if a non-bottleneck resource goes down momentarily, the productive capacity of the overall system will not suffer. However, any loss of throughput at a bottleneck or constraint translates to lower production for the entire line or organization. It follows that

synchronous management
An approach that recognizes the interdependence of assets and activities and manages them to optimize the entire firm's performance.

bottleneck
Any point in the operations process where limited capacity reduces the production capability of an entire chain of activities.

constraint
The most restrictive of bottlenecks, determining the capacity of the entire system.

21-4 Common Methods for Addressing Bottlenecks and Constraints

Add Capacity	• Expand resources. • Subdivide the work. • Outsource production to a company with more capacity.
Increase Efficiency	• Arrange schedules so that the resource takes no breaks (for example, have employees take breaks during setup, teardown, or maintenance activities). • Schedule maintenance on nights, weekends, and holidays rather than during productive time. • Increase productivity through training, upgraded tools, or automation.
Filter Production	• Inspect quality prior to a constraint. • Allow only work that achieves firm goals and contributes to performance (that is, a finished goods inventory would be unnecessary).

these points in an operations system deserve special attention, for the sake of the company and its performance.

Hopefully, it is apparent to you by now that operations management is very important to the functioning and performance of all kinds of businesses, whether large or small. Best practices typically are perfected in large corporations, but the principles and approaches they refine can usually be adapted to the management of smaller enterprises, at least at some level—and it is important to try to do just that. In a competitive marketplace, efficient and effective operations are necessary to survival. And where this is not the case, these practices can still add to customer benefits, firm performance, and the satisfaction of the venture's owners. Practices such as managing inventory wisely, treating suppliers well, and ensuring the quality of products made or services offered protect and enhance the reputation of the company, which helps everyone. Reaching these grand heights will be impossible unless you follow sound operations management practices. The commitment of time and energy required to reach excellence certainly pays off over the long run.

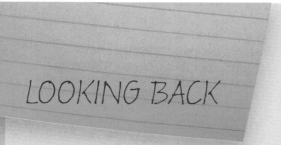

LOOKING BACK

1. *Describe ways in which operations can enhance a small company's competitiveness.*

- The term *operations* refers to the processes used to create and deliver a good or service.
- Companies gain power to the degree that they excel in satisfying customer needs and wants more precisely and efficiently than their competitors.
- To be successful, a company's operations must involve all of the activities required to create value for customers and earn their dollars.

2. *Discuss the nature of the operations process for both products and services.*

- Goods-oriented and service-oriented operations are similar in that they change inputs into outputs.
- Managers of service businesses face special challenges in assuring and controlling quality, given the difficulty inherent in measuring and controlling intangibles.
- In service businesses, employees interact extensively with customers.

- The adoption of various technologies has enabled customers of many businesses to provide more of their own services.
- Manufacturing operations can be classified as one of three types—job shops, project manufacturing, and repetitive manufacturing.
- A small company's capacity to serve or produce goods or services is a critical factor.
- Planning and scheduling procedures are designed to achieve the orderly sequential flow of products through a plant at a rate matching deliveries to customers.
- Demand strategies are used to stimulate customer demand when it is normally low.

3. Identify ways to control inventory and minimize inventory costs.

- Inventory management can help an entrepreneur understand the vital balance between two competing pressures in the business—increasing inventory to satisfy customer demand and reducing inventory to maintain a healthy balance sheet.
- When examined sensibly, inventory management can help an entrepreneur understand the vital balance between two competing pressures in the business. The company may need *more* inventory to satisfy customers (meeting customer demand and providing high-quality service), but it will want to maintain *less* inventory to keep the company's balance sheet healthy.
- One method of determining ideal inventory levels is economic order quantity, an index that determines the purchase quantity of an item that minimizes total inventory costs.
- Another method is statistical inventory control, which characterizes the variability of supply and demand using a targeted service level.
- The ABC method classifies items into three categories based on dollar velocity.
- Just-in-time inventory systems are designed to cut inventory carrying costs by making or buying what is needed just as it is needed.
- Types of inventory record-keeping systems are physical inventory systems, perpetual inventory systems, and two-bin inventory systems.

4. Recognize the contributions of operations management to product and service quality.

- *Quality* can be defined as the characteristics of a product or service that determine its ability to satisfy customers' stated and implied needs.
- Total quality management is an all-encompassing, quality-focused management approach that is customer driven, emphasizes organizational commitment, and focuses on a culture of continuous improvement.

- A firm's quality management efforts should begin with a focus on meeting the expectations of customers who purchase its products or services.
- Paying careful attention to the details of a firm's operations and correcting any weaknesses, as well as listening to customer feedback, helps ensure that customers get the quality they expect.
- One useful approach to gathering customer-based information is to "mine" company sales data to learn more about customer behavior.
- An important element in effective quality management consists of the various tools, techniques, and procedures needed to ensure high-quality products and services.
- Product quality can be maintained by inspection or by using the Poka-Yoke approach, which seeks to mistake-proof a firm's operations.
- Acceptance sampling is one statistical method of quality control.
- ISO 9000 certification requires full documentation of a firm's quality management procedures and is particularly valuable for small firms.

5. Explain the importance of purchasing and the nature of key purchasing policies.

- The quality of a finished product depends on the quality of the raw materials used.
- Purchasing also contributes to profitable operations by ensuring that goods are delivered when they are needed.
- Purchasing practices that seek out the best prices can have major impact on the financial health of a business.
- The decision to make or buy should be based on long-run cost and profit optimization, because it may be expensive to reverse.
- Firms can sometimes save money by outsourcing to suppliers specializing in a particular type of work.
- Cooperative purchasing organizations help smaller firms negotiate as a group for lower prices and better service from suppliers.
- The Internet provides small business owners with connections to hundreds of suppliers.
- Diversifying purchases from suppliers can help a small business maintain alternative sources of supply.
- Developing strategic alliances, forecasting supply needs, and using information systems are other purchasing policies used by small companies.

6. Describe lean production and synchronous management and their importance to operations management in small firms.

- Lean production emphasizes efficiency through the elimination of all forms of waste in a company's operations.

- Maintaining a low amount of inventory leads to a variety of benefits, ranging from capital efficiency to a smooth production process.
- Synchronous management views the assets and activities of an organization as interdependent and suggests that they be managed in a way that optimizes the performance of the entire company.
- Understanding how a shift in one area of operations can affect the rest of the organization underlies synchronous management and is likely to produce the greatest profits.
- Bottlenecks and constraints must be managed carefully because these determine the capacity of the entire production system.

Key Terms

operations p. 548
operations management p. 548
job shop p. 552
project manufacturing p. 552
repetitive manufacturing p. 552
continuous manufacturing p. 552
flexible manufacturing systems p. 552
demand management strategies p. 553
economic order quantity p. 554
statistical inventory control p. 555
ABC method p. 555

just-in-time inventory system p. 555
physical inventory system p. 556
cycle counting p. 556
perpetual inventory system p. 557
two-bin inventory system p. 557
quality p. 557
total quality management (TQM) p. 557
inspection p. 560
Poka-Yoke p. 560
acceptance sampling p. 561
attributes p. 561
variables p. 561

ISO 9000 p. 561
make or buy decisions p. 563
outsourcing p. 563
cooperative purchasing organization (coop) p. 565
Supply Chain Operations Reference (SCOR) model p. 566
associative forecasting p. 568
lean production p. 568
synchronous management p. 569
bottleneck p. 569
constraint p. 569

Discussion Questions

1. How important is managing operations to the competitiveness of a small business? Why is this the case?

2. What are some distinctive features of the operations process in service firms?

3. Customer demand for services is generally not uniform during a day, week, or other period of time. What strategies can be used by service businesses to better match the company's capacity to perform services to customers' demand for those services?

4. What are the major features of the just-in-time inventory system? Is it applicable to small companies? Be prepared to defend your answer.

5. Why is the customer focus of quality management so important in a small firm? What can be done to ensure that the quality of a small venture's products or services remains high?

6. How important is effective purchasing to a small business? Can the owner-manager of a small firm safely delegate purchasing authority to a subordinate? Explain.

7. Under what conditions should a small manufacturer either make component parts or buy them from others?

8. What are the relative merits of inspection approaches and Poka-Yoke to quality assurance in a small company?

9. What steps can a company take to build good relationships with suppliers? Can you think of any ethical issues that should be taken into account when deciding how to interact with suppliers?

10. Explain the meaning of the terms *lean production* and *synchronous management*. How are these relevant to operations in a small company?

SITUATION 1

Christina Poole owns two pizza restaurants in a city with a population of 150,000 and is studying her company's operations to be sure they are functioning as efficiently as possible. About 70 percent of the venture's sales represent dine-in business, and 30 percent come from deliveries. Poole has always attempted to produce a good-quality product and minimize the waiting time of customers both on- and off-premises.

Poole recently read a magazine article suggesting that quality is now generally abundant and that quality differences between businesses are narrowing. The writer advocated placing emphasis on saving time for customers rather than producing a high-quality product. Poole is contemplating the implications of this article for her pizza business. Realizing that her attention should be focused, she wonders whether to concentrate primary managerial emphasis on delivery time.

Question 1 Is the writer of the article correct in believing that quality levels now are generally higher and that quality differences among businesses are minimal?

Question 2 What are the benefits and drawbacks of placing the firm's primary emphasis on minimizing customer waiting time?

Question 3 If you were advising the owner, what would you recommend?

Question 4 Would your answers to the previous questions be different if Poole sold a $6 pizza? What if it were a $40 pizza?

SITUATION 2

Derek Dilworth, owner of a small manufacturing firm, is trying to deal with the firm's thin working capital situation by carefully managing payments to major suppliers. These suppliers extend credit for 30 days, and customers are expected to pay within that time period. However, the suppliers do not automatically refuse subsequent orders when a payment is a few days late. Dilworth's strategy is to delay payment of most invoices for 10 to 15 days beyond the due date. Although he is not meeting the "letter of the law" in his agreement, he believes that the suppliers will go along with him rather than risk losing future sales. This practice enables Dilworth's firm to operate with sufficient inventory, avoid costly interruptions in production, and reduce the likelihood of an overdraft at the bank.

Question 1 What are the ethical issues raised by Dilworth's payment practices?

Question 2 What impact, if any, might these practices have on the firm's supplier relationships? How serious would this impact be?

Question 3 What changes in company culture, employee behavior, or relationships with other business partners may result from Dilworth's practices?

SITUATION 3

Tyler Smithson owns Joe on the Run, a small chain of three coffee shops, all of which are facing a challenge that is common to most service businesses: They have to deal with highly variable demand, with two or three very busy times each day. If a waiting line develops, we can assume that a constraint exists somewhere in the product or service delivery. Typical workstations behind the counter include the barista station (where specialty hot drinks are made), the drive-thru station, and the cashier station. Because the goal of the company is to satisfy the most customers possible (and increase resulting profits), a constraint at one of these workstations must be addressed quickly.

Question 1 What can be done to improve capacity?

Question 2 What can be done to improve efficiency?

Question 3 What can be done to improve the filtering process?

Question 4 What could be done at a store level to improve the performance of the business?

1. Outline the operations process involved in your present educational program. Be sure to identify inputs, processes, and outputs.

2. Outline, in as much detail as possible, your customary practices in studying for a specific course. Evaluate the methods you use and specify changes that might improve your productivity.

3. Using the ABC inventory analysis method, classify some of your personal possessions into the three categories. Include at least two items in each category.

4. Interview the manager of a bookstore about the type of inventory control system used in the store. Write a report in which you explain the methods used to avoid buildup of excessive inventory.

The *Small Business and Entrepreneurship Resource Center* offers complete small business management resources through a comprehensive database that covers all major areas of starting, operating, and maintaining a business from financing, management, marketing, accounting, taxes, and more. Use the access code that came with your new book to access the site and perform the exercises in each chapter.

1. Founded in 1948 as a single tiny drive-through in a Los Angeles suburb, the In-N-Out Burger chain business has maintained the original menu of burgers, fries, sodas, and ice cream shakes—no chicken, no salads, no desserts, and no toys for the kids . . . just great quality! In-N-Out has always been a family-owned firm, and it operates by a very simple business philosophy: "Give customers the freshest, highest quality foods you can buy and provide them with friendly service in a sparkling clean environment." The formula is obviously working, but the company has come to a crossroads. The company's future became uncertain when co-founder Esther Snyder died in August 2006. The Snyder family has historically avoided the media, choosing to keep the operations of In-N-Out to themselves. However, Lynsi Martinez, the 24-year-old heir to the company, has indicated that she wants to increase growth, potentially going public with stock options and franchising opportunities. Describe the slow-growth and minimal change model that co-founder Harry Snyder advocated since the inception of the firm. Also discuss how this strategy has been instrumental in creating a cadre of devoted fans (patrons).

Sources: Using childhood memory elicitation to gain insights into a brand at a crossroads; the In-N-Out burger situation (analysis of restaurant management)(In-N-Out Burgers). Kathryn A. Braun-Latour, and Michael S. Latour. *Cornell Hotel & Restaurant Administration Quarterly* 48,3 (August 2007): p. 246(28).

Video Case 21

MODERN POSTCARD (P. 667)
This case focuses on the use of new technology and advances in operations management that can lead to higher quality and greater efficiency, which allows a company to respond better to customer needs and market trends.

ALTERNATIVE CASES FOR CHAPTER 21
Case 18, Smarter.com, p. 662

Case 19, Diamond Wipes International, p. 664

Case 23, Protecting Intellectual Property, p. 672

Managing the Firm's Assets

In the SPOTLIGHT
Pacific Writing Instruments
http://www.penagain.com

Colin Roche and Bobby Ronsse, who in 2001 founded Pacifica, California–based Pacific Writing Instruments, have truly enjoyed their entrepreneurial ride. The source of their happiness? Their company's ergonomic pen, the Pen Again, is now carried in more than 2,000 stores, including Walmart, Office Depot, Publix, and FedEx Office. In other words, they have arrived.

But on their way, they found that business growth can be a double-edged sword. "Before our product got into the big stores, we weren't selling as many pens, but business was steadier, the fluctuations weren't as big and the dollar amounts were certainly a lot smaller," Ronsse says. "If we needed $10,000, we could find it pretty easily from our own savings, a bank loan, or a business line of credit. But when you're selling 100,000 pens, and you have to pay your factory $50,000 before you get paid for those pens, then your sources for solving cash-flow problems are a lot more limited."

The key, Ronsse says, is to be prepared, lining up and weighing your options way before feeling any cash squeeze.

"There's always a way to get the money," he says. "It just depends on how much you want to give up. Money's not free, so you

either have to pay interest or give up equity in your company to investors."

Besides having investors by their side from day one, Ronsse and Roche worked out pay-when-paid arrangements with some of their sub-suppliers, including the factory that makes the pens. "It's a best-case scenario, but it's not something you can count on," Ronsse says. The deal was approved because the company had built its reputation by paying on time and providing the factory with a steady stream of business.

As a backup, they also looked into factoring, or accounts receivable funding. In this scenario, Pacific Writing Instruments would sell a purchase order at a discount to a third-party lender (the factor), who would then be paid by the store that ordered the pens. This process would let their company pay for up-front costs associated with the big order—but it would

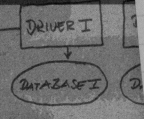

LOOKING AHEAD   AFTER STUDYING THIS CHAPTER, YOU SHOULD BE ABLE TO

1. Describe the working-capital cycle of a small business.

2. Identify the important issues in managing a firm's cash flows.

3. Explain the key issues in managing accounts receivable, inventory, and accounts payable.

4. Calculate and interpret a company's cash conversion period.

5. Discuss the techniques commonly used in making capital budgeting decisions.

6. Describe the capital budgeting practices of small firms.

also reduce profits from the sale. It wasn't an ideal situation, but it could have saved a business that was experiencing a cash-flow crunch.

"You can be a super-successful company, have a great product distributed all over the place, be profitable, and still go out of business because of cash flow, " Ronsse says. "You have to have quick access to capital. Nothing else matters if you can't pay your bills. "

In 2009, Pacific Writing Instruments merged with Baumgartens, an office products supplier based in Atlanta, Georgia, in order to take advantage of the added marketing, creative, and distribution skills as well as the reach that the company could offer to a fledgling business like Pacific Writing Instruments. "Most large retailers and wholesalers do not want to deal with a single product company" says Clive Roux, CMO of Baumgartens. "Instead, they are all trying to consolidate suppliers and product lines. The merger made sense because now we have complementary offers that make us more relevant to our customers."

Sources: Lana Basha, "Handle the Headaches," *MyBusiness*, June-July 2007, pp. 26–29; and http://www.mybusinessmag .com/fullstory.php3?sid51589, accessed January 23, 2009.

When a firm grows as Pacific Writing Instruments did, the entrepreneur's dream can become a nightmare. The nightmare results in part from problems with managing the firm's assets during high-growth periods, in terms of both working capital and long-term investments, such as those for computer systems, equipment, and buildings. In this chapter, we look at what is involved in effectively managing a company's assets.

The Working-Capital Cycle

1. Describe the working-capital cycle of a small business.

working-capital management
The management of current assets and current liabilities.

working-capital cycle
The daily flow of resources through a firm's working-capital accounts.

Ask the owner of a small business about financial management and you will likely hear about the joys and tribulations of managing cash, accounts receivable, inventory, and accounts payable. *Working-capital management*—managing short-term assets (current assets) and short-term sources of financing (current liabilities)—is extremely important to most small companies.[1] In fact, there may be no financial discipline that is more important, and yet more misunderstood. Good business opportunities can be irreparably damaged by ineffective management of a firm's short-term assets and liabilities.

A firm's *working-capital cycle* is the flow of resources through the company's accounts as part of its day-to-day operations. As shown in Exhibit 22-1, the steps in a firm's working-capital cycle are as follows:

Step 1: Purchase or produce inventory for sale, which increases inventories on hand and increases accounts payable if the inventory is purchased on credit.

Step 2: a. Sell the inventory for cash, which increases cash, or

b. Sell the inventory on credit, which increases accounts receivable.

Step 3: a. Pay the accounts payable, which decreases accounts payable and decreases cash.

b. Pay operating expenses and taxes, which decreases cash.

Step 4: Collect the accounts receivable when due, which decreases accounts receivable and increases cash.

Step 5: Begin the cycle again.

22-1 Working-Capital Cycle

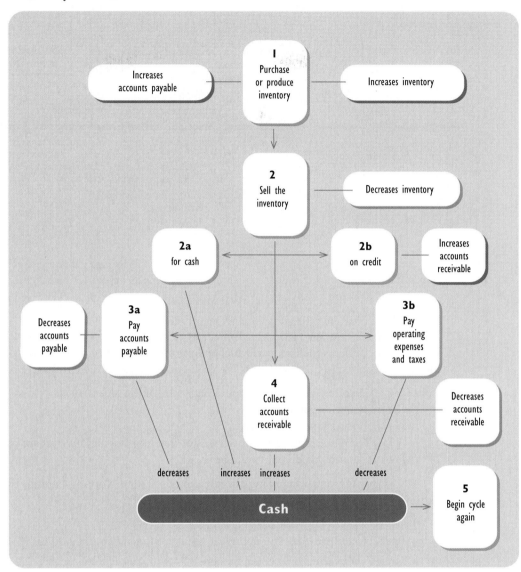

Depending on the industry, the working-capital cycle may be long or short. For example, it is only a few days in a restaurant business; it is longer, most likely months, in a computer hardware business. Whatever the industry, however, management should be working continuously to shorten the cycle.

The Timing and Size of Working-Capital Investments

It is imperative that owners of small companies understand the working-capital cycle, in terms of both the timing of investments and the size of the investment required (for example, the amounts necessary to maintain inventory and accounts receivable). The owners' failure to understand these relationships underlies many of the financial problems of small companies. Too many entrepreneurs wait until a problem with working capital develops.

22-2 Working-Capital Time Line

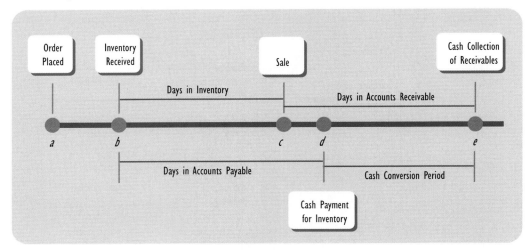

Exhibit 22-2 shows the chronological sequence of a hypothetical working-capital cycle. The time line reflects the order in which events unfold, starting with purchasing inventory and ending with collecting accounts receivable. The key dates in the exhibit are as follows:

Day a. Inventory is ordered in anticipation of future sales.
Day b. Inventory is received.
Day c. Inventory is sold on credit.
Day d. Accounts payable for purchases of inventory come due and are paid.
Day e. Accounts receivable are collected.

The investing and financing implications of the working-capital cycle reflected in Exhibit 22-2 are as follows:

- Money is invested in inventory from day *b* to day *c*.
- The supplier provides financing for the inventory from day *b* to day *d*.
- Money is invested in accounts receivable from day *c* to day *e*.
- Financing of the firm's investment in accounts receivable must be provided from day *d* to day *e*. This time span, called the *cash conversion period,* represents the number of days required to complete the working-capital cycle, which ends with the conversion of accounts receivable into cash. During this period, the firm no longer has the benefit of supplier financing (accounts payable). The longer this period lasts, the greater the potential cash flow problems for the firm.

cash conversion period
The time required to convert paid-for inventory and accounts receivable into cash.

Examples of Working-Capital Management

Exhibit 22-3 offers two examples of working-capital management by firms with contrasting working-capital cycles: Pokey, Inc., and Quick Turn Company. On August 15, both firms order inventory that they receive on August 31, but the similarity ends there.

Pokey, Inc., must pay its supplier for the inventory on September 30, before eventually reselling it on October 15. It collects from its customers on November 30. As you can see, Pokey, Inc., must pay for the inventory two months prior to collecting from its customers. Its cash conversion period—the time required to convert the paid-for inventory and accounts

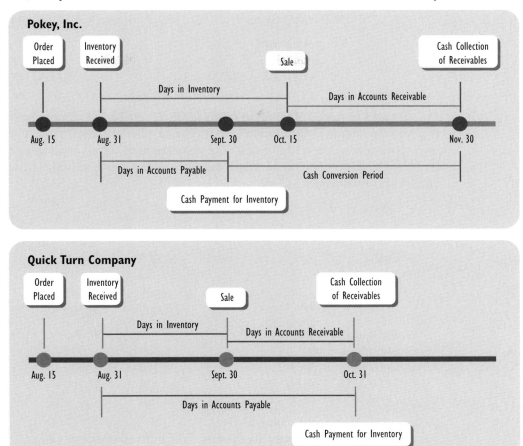

receivable into cash—is 60 days. The firm's managers must find a way to finance this investment in inventory and accounts receivable, or else they will experience cash flow problems. Furthermore, although increased sales should produce higher profits, they will compound the cash flow problem because the company will have to finance the investment in inventory until the accounts receivable are collected 60 days later.

Now consider Quick Turn Company's working-capital cycle, shown in the bottom portion of Exhibit 22-3. Compared to Pokey, Quick Turn Company has an enviable working-capital position. By the time Quick Turn must pay for its inventory purchases (October 31), it has sold its product (September 30) and collected from its customers (October 31). Thus, there is no cash conversion period because the supplier is essentially financing Quick Turn's working-capital needs.

To gain an even better understanding of the working-capital cycle, let's see what happens to Pokey's balance sheet and income statement. To do so, we will need more information about the firm's activities. A month-by-month listing of its activities and their effects on its balance sheet follow. Pay close attention to the firm's working capital, especially its cash balances.

July: Pokey, Inc., is a new company, having started operations in July with $1,000, financed by $300 in long-term debt and $700 in common stock. At the outset, the owner purchased $600 worth of fixed assets, leaving the remaining $400 in cash. At this point, the balance sheet would appear as follows:

	$ 400
Cash	$ 400
Fixed assets	600
TOTAL ASSETS	$1,000
Long-term debt	$ 300
Common stock	700
TOTAL DEBT AND EQUITY	$1,000

August: On August 15, the firm's managers ordered $500 worth of inventory, which was received on August 31 (see Exhibit 22-3). The supplier allowed Pokey 30 days from the time the inventory was received to pay for the purchase; thus, inventory and accounts payable both increased by $500 when the inventory was received. As a result of these transactions, the balance sheet would appear as follows:

	July	August	Changes: July to August
Cash	$ 400	$ 400	
Inventory	0	500	+$500
Fixed assets	600	600	
TOTAL ASSETS	$1,000	$1,500	
Accounts payable	$ 0	$ 500	+$500
Long-term debt	300	300	
Common stock	700	700	
TOTAL DEBT AND EQUITY	$1,000	$1,500	

So far, so good—no cash problems yet.

September: On September 30, the firm paid for the inventory; both cash and accounts payable decreased by $500, shown as follows.

	July	August	September	Changes: August to September
Cash	$ 400	$ 400	($ 100)	−$500
Inventory	0	500	500	
Fixed assets	600	600	600	
TOTAL ASSETS	$1,000	$1,500	$1,000	
Accounts payable	$ 0	$ 500	$ 0	−$500
Long-term debt	300	300	300	
Common stock	700	700	700	
TOTAL DEBT AND EQUITY	$1,000	$1,500	$1,000	

Now Pokey, Inc., has a cash flow problem in the form of a cash deficit of $100.

October: October was a busy month for Pokey. On October 15, merchandise was sold on credit for $900; sales (in the income statement) and accounts receivable increased by that amount. The firm incurred operating expenses (selling and administrative expenses) in the amount of $250, to be paid in early November; thus, operating expenses (in the income statement) and accrued operating expenses (current liabilities in the balance sheet) increased by

$250. (An additional $25 in accrued expenses resulted from accruing taxes that will be owed on the firm's earnings.) Finally, in October, the firm's accountants recorded $50 in depreciation expense (to be reported in the income statement), resulting in accumulated depreciation on the balance sheet of $50.

The results are as follows:

	July	August	September	October	Changes: September to October
Cash	$ 400	$ 400	($ 100)	($ 100)	
Accounts receivable	0	0	0	900	+$900
Inventory	0	500	500	0	−500
Gross fixed assets	600	600	600	600	
Accumulated depreciation	0	0	0	(50)	−50
TOTAL ASSETS	$1,000	$1,500	$1,000	$1,350	
Accounts payable	$ 0	$ 500	$ 0	$ 0	
Accrued operating expenses	0	0	0	250	+$250
Income tax payable	0	0	0	25	+25
Long-term debt	300	300	300	300	
Common stock	700	700	700	700	
Retained earnings	0	0	0	75	+75
TOTAL DEBT AND EQUITY	$1,000	$1,500	$1,000	$1,350	

The October balance sheet shows all the activities just described, but there is one more change in the balance sheet: It now shows $75 in retained earnings, which had been $0 in the prior balance sheets. As you will see shortly, this amount represents the firm's income. Note also that Pokey, Inc., continues to be overdrawn by $100 on its cash. None of the events in October affected the firm's cash balance. All the transactions were the result of accruals recorded by the firm's accountant, offsetting entries to the income statement. The relationship between the balance sheet and the income statement is as follows:

Change in the Balance Sheet		Effect on the Income Statement
Increase in accounts receivable of $900	→	Sales of $900
Decrease in inventory of $500	→	Cost of goods sold of $500
Increase in accrued operating expenses of $250	→	Operating expenses of $250
Increase in accumulated depreciation of $50	→	Depreciation expense of $50
Increase in accrued taxes of $25	→	Tax expense of $25

November: In November, the accrued expenses were paid, which resulted in a $250 decrease in cash along with an equal decrease in accrued expenses. At the end of November, the accounts receivable were collected, yielding a $900 increase in cash and a $900 decrease in accounts receivable. Thus, net cash increased by $650. The final series of balance sheets is as follows:

	July	August	September	October	November	Changes: October to November
Cash	$ 400	$ 400	($ 100)	($ 100)	$ 550	+$650
Accounts receivable	0	0	0	900	0	−900
Inventory	0	500	500	0	0	
Gross fixed assets	600	600	600	600	600	
Accumulated depreciation	0	0	0	(50)	(50)	
TOTAL ASSETS	$1,000	$1,500	$1,000	$1,350	$1,100	
Accounts payable	$ 0	$ 500	$ 0	$ 0	$ 0	
Accrued operating expenses	0	0	0	250	0	−$250
Income tax payable	0	0	0	25	25	
Long-term debt	300	300	300	300	300	
Common stock	700	700	700	700	700	
Retained earnings	0	0	0	75	75	
TOTAL DEBT AND EQUITY	$1,000	$1,500	$1,000	$1,350	$1,100	

As a result of the firm's activities, Pokey, Inc., reported $75 in profits for the period. The income statement for the period ending November 30 is as follows:

Sales revenue		$900
Cost of goods sold		500
Gross profits		$400
Operating expenses:		
Cash expense	$250	
Depreciation expense	50	
Total operating expenses		$300
Operating profits		$ 100
Income tax (25%)		25
Net profits		$ 75

The $75 in profits is reflected as retained earnings on the balance sheet to make the numbers match.

The somewhat contrived example of Pokey, Inc., illustrates an important point that deserves repeating: An owner of a small firm must understand the working-capital cycle of his or her firm. Although the business was profitable, Pokey ran out of cash in September and October (–$100) and didn't recover until November, when the accounts receivable were collected. This 60-day cash conversion period represents a critical time when the firm must find another source of financing if it is to survive. Moreover, when sales are ongoing throughout the year, the problem can be an unending one, unless financing is found to support the firm's sales. Also, as much as possible, a firm should arrange for earlier payment by customers (preferably in advance) and negotiate longer payment schedules with suppliers (preferably over several months).

An understanding of the working-capital cycle provides a basis for examining the primary components of working-capital management: cash flows, accounts receivable, inventory, and accounts payable.

Managing Cash Flows

2. Identify the important issues in managing a firm's cash flows.

At numerous points throughout our study of small businesses, we have emphasized the importance of effective cash flow management. As you will frequently hear, CASH IS KING! From our discussion of Pokey, Inc., and Quick Turn Company in the previous section, it should also be clear that the core of working-capital management is monitoring cash flows. Cash is continually moving through a business. It flows in as customers pay for products or services, and it flows out as payments are made to other businesses and individuals who provide products and services to the firm, such as employees and suppliers. The typically uneven nature of cash inflows and outflows makes it imperative that they be properly understood and managed. Keith Lowe, an experienced entrepreneur and co-founder of the Alabama Information Technology Association, expresses it this way:

> If there's one thing that will make or break your company, especially when it's small, it's cash flow. A banker once told me that of the many companies he saw go out of business, the majority of them were profitable—they just got in a cash crunch, and that forced them to close. If you pay close attention to your cash flow and think about it every single day, you'll have an edge over almost all your competitors, and you will keep growing while other companies fall by the wayside. The amount of attention you pay to cash flow can literally mean the difference between life and death for your company.[2]

A firm's net cash flow may be determined quite simply by examining its bank account. Monthly cash deposits less checks written during the same period equal a firm's net cash flow. If deposits for a month add up to $100,000 and checks total $80,000, the firm has a net positive cash flow of $20,000. The cash balance at the end of the month is $20,000 higher than it was at the beginning of the month.

Exhibit 22-4 graphically represents the flow of cash through a business. It includes not only the cash flows that arise as part of the firm's working-capital cycle (shown in Exhibit 22-1) but

22-4 Flow of Cash through a Business

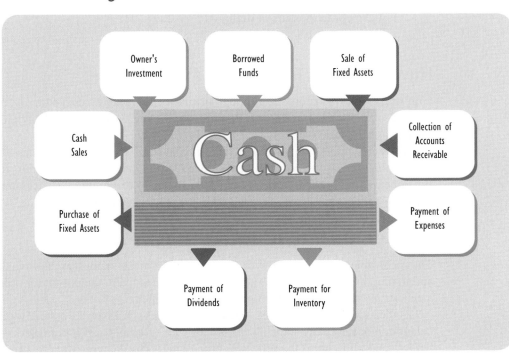

other cash flows as well, such as those from purchasing fixed assets and issuing stock. More specifically, cash sales, collection of accounts receivable, payment of expenses, and payment for inventory reflect the inflows and outflows of cash that relate to the working-capital cycle, while the other items in Exhibit 22-4 represent other, longer-term cash flows.

As has been emphasized on several occasions, calculating cash flow requires that we distinguish between sales revenue and cash receipts—they are seldom the same. Revenue is recorded at the time a sale is made but does not affect cash flow at that time unless the sale is a cash sale. Cash receipts, on the other hand, are recorded when money actually flows into the firm, often a month or two after the sale. Similarly, it is necessary to distinguish between expenses and disbursements. Expenses occur when materials, labor, or other items are used. Payments (disbursements) for these expense items may be made later, when checks are issued. Depreciation, while shown as an expense, is not a cash outflow.

Given the difference between cash flows and profits, it is absolutely essential that the entrepreneur develop a cash budget to anticipate when cash will enter and leave the business. (The cash budget was explained in Chapter 11 when we described financial forecasting.)

Managing Accounts Receivable

3. Explain the key issues in managing accounts receivable, inventory, and accounts payable.

Chapter 16 discussed the extension of credit by small firms and the managing and collecting of accounts receivable. This section considers the impact of credit decisions on working capital and particularly on cash flows. The most important factor in managing cash well within a small firm is the ability to collect accounts receivable quickly.

Managing a firm's accounts receivable becomes particularly critical during a recession when customers are having difficulty paying bills. For example, as we moved into the 2008 economic downturn, a survey of 751 businesses with fewer than 10 employees found that[3]

■ Small businesses average $1,500 in overdue payments from customers each month.

■ Forty-two percent of small business owners say that "getting paid quickly" is a key issue keeping them up at night.

■ Nearly 40 percent of small business owners have invoices that exceed 30 days.

How Accounts Receivable Affect Cash

Granting credit to customers, although primarily a marketing decision, directly affects a firm's cash account. By selling on credit and thus allowing customers to delay payment, the selling firm delays the inflow of cash.

The total amount of customers' credit balances is carried on the balance sheet as accounts receivable—one of the firm's current assets. Of all noncash assets, accounts receivable are closest to becoming cash. Sometimes called *near cash,* or *receivables,* accounts receivable typically are collected and become cash within 30 to 60 days following a sale.

The Life Cycle of Accounts Receivable

The receivables cycle begins with a credit sale. In most businesses, an invoice is then prepared and mailed to the purchaser. When the invoice is received, the purchaser processes it, prepares a check, and mails the check in payment to the seller.

Under ideal circumstances, each of these steps is taken in a timely manner. Obviously, delays can occur at any stage of this process. For example, a shipping clerk may batch invoices before sending them to the office for processing, thus delaying the preparation and mailing of invoices to customers. Such a practice will also delay the receipt of customers' money and its

LIVING THE DREAM:

entrepreneurial experiences

Kindness Can Collect

Small companies are largely dependent on their cash flows. But if they push their slow payers too hard, they risk losing customers. Hiring collection attorneys is also expensive, and if late payers are pushed into bankruptcy, their small-business creditors may find themselves empty-handed, waiting at the end of a long queue.

"The last thing you want to do is get in an adversarial position with your great clients; they're your lifeline," says Charles Doyle, managing director at Business Capital, a San Francisco company that helps businesses restructure their debts.

[In fall 2008], more than half of the customers of United Companies Inc., a Houston-based handler of plastic resin, were more than 30 days past due on their bills. The company's bank had slashed its credit line 20%, to $2.4 million. United Companies was paying its own bills late, because of the cash-flow crunch.

Marc Levine, chief executive of the company, which has 350 employees and $40 million in revenue, began personally calling customers who were more than 30 days past due. He says he explained that he needed to be paid because his business was suffering, too.

"I made sure I told them how much we loved them," he says, "but in order to do a fine job in serving them, I needed them to accelerate payment and return my cash flow to where it was in summer '08 and prior."

Mr. Levine says his personal approach worked, and many of the customers paid up after his call. He adds that he also stopped shipping for some small, financially weak customers until they began paying within 30 days. And he made some cost cuts, including laying off about 50 employees.

Source: Simona Covel and Kelly K. Spors, "To Help Collect the Bills, Firms Try the Soft Touch, *Wall Street Journal*, January 27, 2009, p. B1.

http://www.uniteddc.com

© iStockphoto.com/Aldo Murillo

deposit in the bank—money that is then used to pay bills. In other words, receivables may be past due because of problems in a company's organization, where information is not getting transferred on a timely basis among salespeople, operations departments, and accounting staff. The result: delayed payments from customers and larger investments in accounts receivable.

Credit management policies, practices, and procedures affect the life cycle of receivables and the flow of cash from them. It is important for small business owners, when establishing credit policies, to consider cash flow requirements as well as the need to stimulate sales. A key goal of every business should be to minimize the average time it takes customers to pay their bills. By streamlining administrative procedures, a firm can facilitate the task of sending out bills, thereby generating cash more quickly.

To know how long, on average, it is taking to collect accounts receivable, we can compute the *days sales outstanding*, also called the *average collection period*, by dividing a firm's accounts receivable by daily credit sales, as follows:

$$\text{Days sales outstanding} = \frac{\text{Accounts receivable}}{\text{Annual credit sales} \div 365 \text{ days}}$$

days sales outstanding (average collection period)
The number of days, on average, that a firm is extending credit to its customers.

Consider the following information about two businesses, Fast Company and Slow Company:

	Fast Co.	**Slow Co.**
Total sales	$1,000,000	$1,000,000
Credit sales	700,000	700,000
Average credit sales per day	1,918	1,918
Accounts receivable	48,000	63,300

These two companies are very similar in that they both have $1 million in annual sales, including $700,000 in credit sales. Thus, on average, they both have average daily credit sales of $1,918 ($700,000 total credit sales ÷ 365 days). However, there is an important difference between the two firms. Fast Company only has $48,000 invested in accounts receivable, while Slow Company has $63,300 in accounts receivable. Why the difference? It is simple: Fast Company collects its credit sales every 25 days on average, while Slow Company takes 33 days to collect its accounts receivable, computed as follows:

Fast Company:

$$\text{Days sales outstanding} = \frac{\text{Accounts receivable}}{\text{Annual credit sales} \div 365 \text{ days}} = \frac{\$48,000}{\$700,000 \div 365} = 25 \text{ days}$$

Slow Company:

$$\text{Days sales outstanding} = \frac{\text{Accounts receivable}}{\text{Annual credit sales} \div 365 \text{ days}} = \frac{\$63,300}{\$700,000 \div 365} = 33 \text{ days}$$

In other words, Slow Company takes longer to convert its accounts receivable into cash. It could very well have a cash flow problem if it does not have the ability to finance the greater investment in accounts receivable. This illustration, while hypothetical, is a real problem for many small businesses. Michelle Dunn, who owns M.A.D. Collection Agency, says, "One thing business owners always tell me is that they never thought about [the difficulties in collecting their receivables] when they started their own business."[4]

For Ann LaWall, president of Ann LaWall and Company, chasing customers over delinquent payments to her New York–based consulting business was a burden that distracted her from managing the growth of her company.[5] Worse, she feared the dreaded collection calls would jeopardize professional and personal relationships she cherished. "I got tired of telling people I am not their banker," says LaWall. "Sometimes you are dealing with friends or people you run into at the golf course, and you don't want to be hunting them down for money."

By delegating and implementing preemptive measures, LaWall's stress over collections has disappeared. She says that some of the approaches cost her a little revenue, but she insists that they've been worth the expense. "It saves you huge headaches in the long run," she says. To lower the stress involved, LaWall suggests the following:[6]

- Hire someone else to handle collections one day per week.
- Accept credit cards.
- Sell the receivables to a third party.
- Where possible, require prepayment.
- For a service business, write a detailed work plan and payment schedule and have it signed by the customer.

When dealing with large corporations, small companies are especially vulnerable to problems caused by slow collections. Some large firms have a practice of taking 60 or 90 days to pay an invoice, regardless of the credit terms stated in the invoice. Many a small company has had to file bankruptcy because it could not get a large customer to pay according to the terms of the sale. Susana Ortiz, president of Caroline's Desserts in Redmond, Washington, was surprised to find as many large retail customers were paying late as small ones during the 2008 economic slowdown. "If you're small," she says, "big companies think they can wait to pay you."[7]

The following credit management practices can also have a positive effect on a firm's cash flows:

- Minimize the time between shipping, invoicing, and sending notices on billings.

- Review previous credit experiences to determine impediments to cash flows, such as continued extension of credit to slow-paying or delinquent customers.

- Provide incentives for prompt payment by granting cash discounts or charging interest on delinquent accounts.

- Age accounts receivable on a monthly or even a weekly basis to identify quickly any delinquent accounts.

- Use the most effective methods for collecting overdue accounts. For example, prompt phone calls to customers with overdue accounts can improve collections considerably.

- Use a *lock box*—a post office box for receiving remittances. If the firm's bank maintains the lock box to which customers send their payments, it can empty the box frequently and immediately deposit any checks received into the company's account.

lock box
A post office box for receiving remittances from customers.

Accounts Receivable Financing

Some small businesses speed up the cash flow from accounts receivable by borrowing against them. By financing receivables, these firms can often secure the use of their money 30 to 60 days earlier than would be possible otherwise. Although this practice was once concentrated largely in the apparel industry, it has expanded to many other types of small businesses, such as manufacturers, food processors, distributors, home building suppliers, and temporary employment agencies. Such financing is provided by commercial finance companies and by some banks.

Two types of accounts receivable financing are available. The first type uses a firm's *pledged accounts receivable* as collateral for a loan. Payments received from customers are forwarded to the lending institution to pay off the loan. In the second type of financing, a business sells its accounts receivable to a finance company, a practice known as *factoring* (discussed in Chapter 12). The finance company thereby assumes the bad-debt risk associated with the receivables it buys.

pledged accounts receivable
Accounts receivable used as collateral for a loan.

The obvious advantage of accounts receivable financing is the immediate cash flow it provides for firms that have limited working capital. As a secondary benefit, the volume of borrowing can be quickly expanded proportionally in order to match a firm's growth in sales and accounts receivable.

A drawback to this type of financing is its high cost. Rates typically run several points above the prime interest rate, and factors charge a fee to compensate them for their credit investigation activities and for the risk that customers may default in payment. Another weakness of accounts receivable financing is that pledging receivables may limit a firm's ability to borrow from a bank by removing a prime asset from its available collateral.

Managing Inventory

Inventory is a "necessary evil" in the financial management system. It is "necessary" because supply and demand cannot be managed to coincide precisely with day-to-day operations; it is an "evil" because it ties up funds that are not actively productive.

Reducing Inventory to Free Cash

Inventory is a bigger problem for some small businesses than for others. The inventory of many service companies, for example, consists of only a few supplies. A manufacturer, on the other hand, has several types of inventory: raw materials, work in process, and finished goods. Retailers and wholesalers—especially those with high inventory turnover rates, such as firms in grocery distribution—are continually involved in solving inventory management problems.

Chapter 21 discussed several ideas related to purchasing and inventory management that are designed to minimize inventory-carrying costs and processing costs. The emphasis in this section is on practices that will minimize average inventory levels, thereby releasing funds for other uses. The correct minimum level of inventory is the level needed to maintain desired production schedules and/or a certain level of customer service. A concerted effort to manage inventory can trim excess inventory and pay handsome dividends.

Monitoring Inventory

One of the first steps in managing inventory is to discover what's in inventory and how long it's been there. Too often, items are purchased, warehoused, and essentially forgotten. A yearly inventory for accounting purposes is inadequate for proper inventory control. Items that are slow movers may sit in a retailer's inventory beyond the time when they should have been marked down for quick sale.

Computers can provide assistance in inventory identification and control. Although a physical inventory may still be required, its use will only serve to supplement the computerized system.

days in inventory
The number of days, on average, that a company is holding inventory.

A commonly used statistic for monitoring inventory is *days in inventory,* which is the number of days, on average, that a business is holding its inventory. Similar in concept to days sales outstanding, described earlier, it is computed as follows:

$$\text{Days in inventory} = \frac{\text{Inventory}}{\text{Cost of goods sold} \div 365 \text{ days}}$$

Returning to Fast Company and Slow Company, recall that both firms had $1 million in annual sales. Let's assume that they also had the same cost of goods sold of $600,000. So, they both sold their products for $1 million, and it cost them $600,000 to produce the products that were sold. If we restate the annual cost of goods sold to a daily cost of goods sold, we find it to be $1,644 ($600,000 cost of goods sold ÷ 365 days) for both companies. But while they sold the same amount of product at identical cost, Fast Company carries only $46,000 in inventory, compared to Slow Company, which maintains inventory of $57,500. This information is summarized as follows:

	Fast Co.	Slow Co.
Total sales	$1,000,000	$1,000,000
Cost of goods sold	600,000	600,000
Daily cost of goods sold	1,644	1,644
Inventory	46,000	57,500

Why would Slow Company have more inventory than Fast Company, given that they both have the same amount of sales? The answer is that Slow Company takes longer to sell its inventory. Fast Company, on average, carries inventory for 28 days, compared to 35 days for Slow Company, calculated as follows:

Fast Company:

$$\text{Days in inventory} = \frac{\text{Inventory}}{\text{Cost of goods sold} \div 365} = \frac{\$46,000}{\$600,000 \div 365 \text{ days}} = 28 \text{ days}$$

Slow Company:

$$\text{Days in inventory} = \frac{\text{Inventory}}{\text{Cost of goods sold} \div 365} = \frac{\$57,500}{\$600,000 \div 365 \text{ days}} = 35 \text{ days}$$

In other words, Slow Company's slow rate of moving its inventory can lead to cash flow problems if it does not have the ability to finance the larger inventory.

Controlling Stockpiles

Small business managers tend to overbuy inventory for several reasons. First, an entrepreneur's enthusiasm may lead him or her to forecast greater demand than is realistic. Second, the personalization of the business–customer relationship may motivate a manager to stock everything customers want. Third, a price-conscious manager may be overly susceptible to a vendor's appeal to "buy now, because prices are going up."

Managers must exercise restraint when stockpiling. Improperly managed and uncontrolled stockpiling may greatly increase inventory-carrying costs and place a heavy drain on the funds of a small business.

Managing Accounts Payable

Cash flow management and accounts payable management are intertwined. As long as a payable is outstanding, the buying firm can keep cash equal to that amount in its own checking account. When payment is made, however, that firm's cash account is reduced accordingly. Thus, all else being the same, an entrepreneur would want to delay payment as long as possible without damaging the firm's reputation by failing to live up to his agreements.

Although payables are legal obligations, they can be paid at various times or even renegotiated in some cases. Therefore, financial management of accounts payable hinges on negotiation and timing.

Negotiation

Any business is subject to emergency situations and may find it necessary to ask creditors to postpone payment on its payable obligations. Usually, creditors will cooperate in working out a solution because it's in their best interest for a client firm to succeed.

Timing

"Buy now, pay later" is the motto of many entrepreneurs. By buying on credit, a small business is using creditors' funds to supply short-term cash needs. The longer creditors' funds can be borrowed, the better. Payment, therefore, should be delayed as long as acceptable under the agreement. As we did with accounts receivable and inventory, we can compute *days in payables,* which tells us how many days a company is taking to pay its accounts payable. We compute it as follows:[8]

$$\text{Days in payables} = \frac{\text{Accounts payables}}{\text{Cost of goods sold} \div 365 \text{ days}}$$

days in payables
The number of days, on average, that a business takes to pay its accounts payable.

Using the information we have already provided for Fast Company and Slow Company and knowing that they have $65,800 and $49,300 in accounts payable, respectively, we can compute the days in payables for each firm as follows:

Timetable (days after invoice date)	Settlement Costs for a $20,000 Purchase
Days 1 through 10	$19,400
Days 11 through 30	$20,000
Day 31 and thereafter	$20,000 + possible late penalty 1 deterioration in credit rating

Fast Company:

$$\text{Days in payables} = \frac{\text{Accounts payables}}{\text{Cost of goods sold} \div 365 \text{ days}} = \frac{\$65,800}{\$600,000 \div 365 \text{ days}} = 40 \text{ days}$$

Slow Company:

$$\text{Days in payables} = \frac{\text{Accounts payables}}{\text{Cost of goods sold} \div 365 \text{ days}} = \frac{\$49,300}{\$600,000 \div 365 \text{ days}} = 30 \text{ days}$$

Typically, accounts payable (trade credit) involve payment terms that include a cash discount. With trade-discount terms, paying later may be inappropriate. For example, terms of 3/10, net 30 offer a 3 percent potential discount. Exhibit 22-5 shows the possible settlement costs over the credit period of 30 days. Note that for a $20,000 purchase, a settlement of only $19,400 is required if payment is made within the first 10 days ($20,000 less the 3 percent discount of $600). Between day 11 and day 30, the full settlement of $20,000 is required. After 30 days, the settlement cost may exceed the original amount, as late-payment fees are added.

The timing question then becomes "Should the account be paid on day 10 or day 30?" There is little reason to pay $19,400 on days 1 through 9, when the same amount will settle the account on day 10. Likewise, if payment is to be made after day 10, it makes sense to wait until day 30 to pay the $20,000.

By paying on the last day of the discount period, the buyer saves the amount of the discount offered. The other alternative of paying on day 30 allows the buyer to use the seller's money for an additional 20 days by forgoing the discount. As Exhibit 22-5 shows, the buyer can use the seller's $19,400 for 20 days at a cost of $600. The percentage annual interest rate can be calculated as follows:

$$\text{Percentage annual interest rate} = \frac{\text{Days in year}}{\text{Net period} - \text{Cash discount period}} \times \frac{\text{Cash discount \%}}{100\% - \text{Cash discount \%}}$$

$$= \frac{365}{30 - 10} \times \frac{3\%}{100\% - 3\%}$$

$$= 18.25 \times 0.030928$$

$$= 0.564, \text{ or } 56.4\%$$

By failing to take a discount, a business typically pays a high rate for use of a supplier's money—56.4 percent per year in this case. Payment on day 10 appears to be the most logical choice. Recall, however, that payment also affects cash flows. If funds are extremely short, a small firm may have to wait to pay until the last possible day in order to avoid an overdraft at the bank.

Cash Conversion Period Revisited

4. Calculate and interpret a company's cash conversion period.

Earlier in the chapter, we presented the working-capital cycle, explaining that the cash conversion period should be a key concern for any small business. As you will recall, the cash conversion period is the time span during which the firm's investment in accounts receivable and inventory must be financed or, more simply, the time required to convert paid-for inventory and accounts receivable to cash. To reinforce this concept, we can use the information we have for Fast Company and Slow Company to compute these two firms' cash conversion periods:

Cash conversion period = Days in inventory + Days sales outstanding – Days in accounts payables

	Fast Co.	**Slow Co.**
Days in inventory	28	35
Days sales outstanding	25	33
Days in inventories and receivables	53	68
Less days in payables	(40)	(30)
Cash conversion period	13	38

So, from the time that inventory is purchased until it is sold on credit and the accounts receivable have been collected, it is 53 days for Fast Company and 68 days for Slow Company. But both firms are granted trade credit from their suppliers. Fast Company has negotiated credit terms of 40 days before having to pay for its purchases, compared to Slow Company's 30 days. Essentially, Fast Company's suppliers have granted it a loan for 40 days, while Slow Company has a loan for only 30 days.

We see that Fast Company will need to finance 13 days with working capital, while Slow Company will have to finance 38 days. Thus, as both firms grow, Slow Company will have much more pressure on its cash flows than will Fast Company.

We now turn from management of a firm's working capital to management of its long-term assets—equipment and plant—or what is called *capital budgeting*.

Capital Budgeting

capital budgeting analysis
An analytical method that helps managers make decisions about long-term investments.

Capital budgeting analysis helps managers make decisions about long-term investments. In order to develop a new product line, for example, a firm needs to expand its manufacturing capabilities and to buy the inventory required to make the product. That is, it makes investments today with an expectation of receiving profits or cash flows in the future, possibly over 5 or 10 years.

Some capital budgeting decisions that might be made by a small firm include the following:

- Develop and introduce a new product that shows promise but requires additional study and improvement.
- Replace a firm's delivery trucks with newer models.
- Expand sales activity into a new territory.
- Construct a new building.
- Hire several additional salespersons to intensify selling in the existing market.

In a study by the National Federation of Independent Business, small business owners were asked, "In terms of dollars, what was the purpose of the largest investments made in your business over the last 12 months?" Their responses were as follows:[9]

Replacement and maintenance	45.6%
Extension of existing product or service lines	21.2
Expansion into new business areas	22.9
Safety or environmental improvement	3.5
No response	6.7

Thus, nearly half of all long-term capital investments by small companies are made for replacement and maintenance; when we add in the extension of existing product lines, we can account for two-thirds of all dollars invested by small owners. Nearly one-fourth of all dollars are invested in new product lines and businesses.

Although an in-depth discussion of capital budgeting is beyond the scope of this textbook, in the following sections we discuss techniques used in making capital budgeting decisions and the capital budgeting practices of small companies.

Capital Budgeting Techniques

5. Discuss the techniques commonly used in making capital budgeting decisions.

The three major techniques for making capital budgeting decisions are (1) the accounting return on investment technique, (2) the payback period technique, and (3) the discounted cash flow technique, using either net present value or internal rate of return. They all attempt to answer the same basic question: Do the future benefits from an investment exceed the cost of making the investment? However, each technique addresses this general question by focusing on a different specific question. The specific question each addresses can be stated as follows:

1. *Accounting return on investment.* How many dollars in average profits are generated per dollar of average investment?

2. *Payback period.* How long will it take to recover the original investment outlay?

3. *Discounted cash flows.* How does the present value of future benefits from the investment compare to the investment outlay?

Three simple rules are used in judging the merits of an investment. Although they may seem trite, the rules state in simple terms the best thinking about the attractiveness of an investment.

1. The investor prefers more cash rather than less cash.

2. The investor prefers cash sooner rather than later.

3. The investor prefers less risk rather than more risk.

With these criteria in mind, let's now look at each of the three capital budgeting techniques in detail.

accounting return on investment technique
A capital budgeting technique that evaluates a capital expenditure based on the expected average annual after-tax profits relative to the average book value of an investment.

ACCOUNTING RETURN ON INVESTMENT   A small business invests to earn profits. The *accounting return on investment technique* compares the average annual after-tax profits a firm expects to receive with the average book value of the investment.

Average annual profits can be estimated by adding the after-tax profits expected over the life of the project and then dividing that amount by the number of years the project is expected to last. The average book value of an investment is equivalent to the average of the initial outlay and the estimated final projected salvage value. In making an accept–reject decision, the owner compares the calculated return to a minimum acceptable return, which is usually determined based on past experience.

To examine the use of the accounting return on investment technique, assume that you are contemplating buying a piece of equipment for $10,000 and depreciating it over four years to a book value of zero (it will have no salvage value). Further assume that you expect the investment to generate after-tax profits each year as follows:

Year	After-Tax Profits
1	$1,000
2	2,000
3	2,500
4	3,000

The accounting return on the proposed investment is calculated as follows:

$$\text{Accounting return on investment} = \frac{\text{Average annual after-tax profits}}{\text{Average book value of the investment}}$$

$$\text{Accounting return on investment} = \frac{\left(\dfrac{\$1,000 + \$2,000 + \$2,500 + \$3,000}{4}\right)}{\left(\dfrac{\$10,000 - \$0}{2}\right)}$$

$$= \frac{\$2,125}{\$5,000} = 0.425, \text{ or } 42.5\%$$

For most people, a 42.5 percent profit rate would seem outstanding. Assuming the calculated accounting return on investment of 42.5 percent exceeds your minimum acceptable return, you will accept the project. If not, you will reject the investment— provided, of course, that you have confidence in the technique.

Although the accounting return on investment is easy to calculate, it has two major shortcomings. First, it is based on accounting profits rather than actual cash flows received. An investor should be more interested in the future cash produced by the investment than in the reported profits. Second, this technique ignores the time value of money. Thus, although popular, the accounting return on investment technique fails to satisfy any of the three rules concerning an investor's preference for receiving more cash sooner with less risk.

PAYBACK PERIOD The *payback period technique,* as the name suggests, measures how long it will take to recover the initial cash outlay of an investment. It deals with cash flows as opposed to accounting profits. The merits of a project are judged on whether the initial investment outlay can be recovered in less time than some maximum acceptable payback period. For example, an owner may not want to invest in any project that will require more than five years to recoup the original investment.

To illustrate the payback method, let's assume that an entrepreneur is considering an investment in equipment with an expected life of 10 years. The investment outlay will be $15,000, with the cost of the equipment depreciated on a straight-line basis, at $1,500 per year. If the owner makes the investment, the annual after-tax profits have been estimated to be as follows:

payback period technique
A capital budgeting technique that measures the amount of time it will take to recover the cash outlay of an investment.

Years	After-Tax Profits
1–2	$1,000
3–6	2,000
7–10	2,500

To determine the after-tax cash flows from the investment, the owner merely adds back the depreciation of $1,500 each year to the profit. The reason for adding the depreciation to the profit is that it was deducted when the profits were calculated (as an accounting entry), even though it was not a cash outflow. The results, then, are as follows:

Years	After-Tax Cash Flows
1–2	$2,500
3–6	3,500
7–10	4,000

By the end of the second year, the owner will have recovered $5,000 of the investment outlay ($2,500 per year). By the end of the fourth year, another $7,000, or $12,000 in total, will have been recouped. The additional $3,000 can be recovered in the fifth year, when $3,500 is expected. Thus, it will take 4.86 years [4 years + ($3,000 ÷ $3,500)] to recover the investment. Since the maximum acceptable payback is less than five years, the owner will accept the investment.

Many managers and owners of companies use the payback period technique in evaluating investment decisions. Although it uses cash flows, rather than accounting profits, the payback period technique has two significant weaknesses. First, it does not consider the time value of money (cash is preferred sooner rather than later). Second, it fails to consider the cash flows received after the payback period (more cash is preferred, rather than less).

DISCOUNTED CASH FLOWS Managers can avoid the deficiencies of the accounting return on investment and payback period techniques by using discounted cash flow analysis. Discounted cash flow techniques take into consideration the fact that cash received today is more valuable than cash received one year from now (called the *time value of money*). For example, interest can be earned on cash that is available for immediate investment; this is not true for cash to be received at some future date.

discounted cash flow (DCF) techniques
Capital budgeting techniques that compare the present value of future cash flows with the cost of the initial investment.

Discounted cash flow (DCF) techniques compare the present value of future cash flows with the investment outlay. Such an analysis may take either of two forms: net present value or internal rate of return.

net present value (NPV)
The present value of expected future cash flows less the initial investment outlay.

The *net present value (NPV)* method estimates the current value of the cash that will flow into the firm from the project in the future and deducts the amount of the initial outlay. To find the present value of expected future cash flows, we discount them back to the present at the firm's cost of capital, where the cost of capital is equal to the investors' required rate of return. If the net present value of the investment is positive (that is, if the present value of future cash flows discounted at the rate of return required to satisfy the firm's investors exceeds the initial outlay), the project is acceptable.

internal rate of return (IRR)
The rate of return a firm expects to earn on a project.

The *internal rate of return (IRR)* method estimates the rate of return that can be expected from a contemplated investment. To calculate the IRR, you must find the discount rate that gets the present value of all future cash inflows just equal to the cost of the project, which is also the rate that gives you a zero net present value. For the investment outlay to be attractive, the internal rate of return must exceed the firm's cost of capital—the rate of return required to satisfy the firm's investors.

Discounted cash flow techniques can generally be trusted to provide a more reliable basis for decisions than can the accounting return on investment or the payback period technique.

Capital Budgeting Analysis in Small Firms

6. Describe the capital budgeting practices of small firms.

Historically, few small business owners have relied on any type of quantitative analysis in making capital budgeting decisions. The decision to buy new equipment or expand facilities has been based more on intuition and instinct than on economic analysis. And those who do conduct some kind of quantitative analysis rarely use discounted cash flow techniques, neither net present value nor internal rate of return.

In the study cited earlier, the National Federation of Independent Business asked entrepreneurs to indicate the method(s) they used in analyzing capital investments. The results were encouraging:[10]

Gut feel	25.3%
Payback period technique	18.7
Accounting return on investment technique	13.6
Discounted cash flow techniques	11.9
Combination	10.5
Other	6.1
No response	4.5
Not applicable—no major investments	2.6

Interestingly, 55 percent of the small business owners indicated that they use some form of quantitative measure (payback period, accounting return on investment, discounted cash flow techniques, or some combination) to assess a capital investment; only 25 percent of the respondents said that they use their intuition (gut feel). Furthermore, 67 percent of the company owners said that they make some effort to project future cash flows.

We could conclude that the small business owners surveyed were not very sophisticated about using theoretically sound financial methods, given that only 12 percent said they use discounted cash flow analyses. However, the cause of their limited use of DCF tools probably has more to do with the nature of the small business itself than with the owners' unwillingness to learn. Several more important reasons might explain these findings, including the following:

- For many owners of small firms, the business is an extension of their lives—that is, business events affect them personally. The same is true in reverse: What happens to the owners personally affects their decisions about the firm. The firm and its owners are inseparable. We cannot fully understand decisions made about a company without being aware of the personal events in the owners' lives. Consequently, nonfinancial variables may play a significant part in owners' decisions. For example, the desire to be viewed as a respected part of the community may be more important to an owner than the present value of a business decision.

© iStockphoto.com/Harris Shiffman

- The undercapitalization and liquidity problems of a small business can directly affect the decision-making process, and survival often becomes the top priority. Long-term planning, therefore, is not viewed by the owners as a high priority in the total scheme of things.

- The greater uncertainty of cash flows within small firms makes long-term forecasting and planning seem unappealing and even a waste of time. The owners simply have no confidence in their ability to predict cash flows beyond two or three years. Thus, calculating the cash flows for the entire life of a project is viewed as a futile effort.

- The value of a closely held firm is less easily observed than that of a publicly held firm whose securities are actively traded in the marketplace. Therefore, the owner of a small firm may consider the market-value rule of maximizing net present values irrelevant. Estimating the cost of capital is also much more difficult for a small company than for a large firm.

- The smaller size of a small firm's projects may make net present value computations less feasible in a practical sense. The time and expense required to analyze a capital investment are generally the same, whether the project is large or small. Therefore, it is relatively more costly for a small firm to conduct such a study.

- Management talent within a small firm is a scarce resource. Also, the owner-manager frequently has a technical background, as opposed to a business or finance orientation. The perspective of owners is influenced greatly by their backgrounds.

The foregoing characteristics of a small business and its owner have a significant effect on the decision-making process within the firm. The result is often a short-term mind-set, caused partly by necessity and partly by choice. However, the owner of a small firm should make every effort to use discounted cash flow techniques and to be certain that contemplated investments will, in fact, provide returns that exceed the firm's cost of capital.

LOOKING BACK

1. Describe the working-capital cycle of a small business.

- The working-capital cycle begins with the purchase of inventory and ends with the collection of accounts receivable.
- The cash conversion period is critical because it is the time period during which cash flow problems can arise.

2. Identify the important issues in managing a firm's cash flows.

- A firm's cash flows consist of cash flowing into a business (through sales revenue, borrowing, and so on) and cash flowing out of the business (through purchases, operating expenses, and so on).

- Calculating cash flows requires that a small business owner distinguish between sales revenue and cash receipts.

- It is also necessary to distinguish between expenses and disbursements.

- To anticipate when cash will enter and leave a business, an entrepreneur *must* develop a cash budget.

3. Explain the key issues in managing accounts receivable, inventory, and accounts payable.

- Granting credit to customers, primarily a marketing decision, directly affects a firm's cash account.

- A firm can improve its cash flows by speeding up collections from customers, minimizing inventory, and delaying payments to suppliers.

- Days sales outstanding measures how many days, on average, a firm is extending credit to its customers.

- Some small businesses speed up the cash flows from receivables by borrowing against them.

- A concerted effort to manage inventory can trim excess inventory and free cash for other uses.

- Days in inventory calculates the number of days, on average, that a company is carrying inventory.

- Improperly managed and uncontrolled stockpiling may greatly increase inventory-carrying costs and place a heavy drain on the funds of a small business.

- Accounts payable, a primary source of financing for small firms, directly affect a firm's cash flow situation.

- Financial management of accounts payable hinges on negotiation and timing.

- Days in payables measures how long a business is taking to pay its suppliers.

4. Calculate and interpret a company's cash conversion period.

- The cash conversion period is the time span during which a firm's investment in accounts receivable and inventory must be financed.

- A cash conversion period equals days in inventory plus days sales outstanding minus days in payables.

5. Discuss the techniques commonly used in making capital budgeting decisions.

- Capital budgeting techniques attempt to determine whether future benefits from an investment will exceed the initial outlay.

- Capital budgeting techniques include the accounting return on investment, the payback period, and the discounted cash flow techniques.

- The accounting return on investment technique has two significant shortcomings: It is based on accounting profits rather than actual cash flows received, and it ignores the time value of money.

- The payback period technique also has two major weaknesses: It ignores the time value of money, and it doesn't consider cash flows received after the payback period.

- The discounted cash flow techniques—net present value and internal rate of return—provide the best accept–reject decision criteria in capital budgeting analysis.

6. Describe the capital budgeting practices of small firms.

- Few small firms use any type of discounted cash flow technique. However, the majority of small companies do use some type of formal analysis.

- The very nature of small firms may explain, to some degree, why they seldom use the conceptually richer techniques for evaluating long-term investments.

Key Terms

working-capital management p. 576
working-capital cycle p. 576
cash conversion period p. 578
days sales outstanding (average collection period) p. 585
lock box p. 587

pledged accounts receivable p. 587
days in inventory p. 588
days in payables p. 589
capital budgeting analysis p. 591
accounting return on investment technique p. 592
payback period technique p. 593

discounted cash flow (DCF) techniques p. 594
net present value (NPV) p. 594
internal rate of return (IRR) p. 594

Discussion Questions

1. List the events in the working-capital cycle that directly affect cash and those that do not. What determines the length of a firm's cash conversion period?

2. What are some examples of cash receipts that are not sales revenue? Explain how expenses and cash disbursements during a month may be different.

3. How may a seller speed up the collection of accounts receivable? Give examples that may apply to various stages in the life cycle of receivables.

4. Suppose that a small firm could successfully shift to a just-in-time inventory system—an arrangement in which inventory is received just as it is needed. How would this affect the firm's working-capital management?

5. How do working-capital management and capital budgeting differ?

6. Compare the different techniques that can be used in capital budgeting analysis.

7. What does net present value measure?

8. Define internal rate of return.

9. a. Find the accounting return on investment for a project that costs $10,000, will have no salvage value, and has expected annual after-tax profits each year of $1,000.

   b. Determine the payback period for a capital investment that costs $40,000 and has the following after-tax profits. (The projected outlay of $40,000 will be depreciated on a straight-line basis over 7 years to a zero salvage value.)

Year	After-Tax Profits
1	$4,000
2	5,000
3	6,000
4	6,500
5	6,500
6	6,000
7	5,000

10. Why would owners of small businesses not be inclined to use the net present value or internal rate of return measurements?

You Make the Call

SITUATION 1

A small company specializing in the sale and installation of swimming pools was profitable but devoted very little attention to management of its working capital. It had, for example, never prepared or used a cash budget.

To be sure that money was available for payments as needed, the firm kept a minimum of $25,000 in a checking account. At times, this account grew larger; it totaled $43,000 on one occasion. The owner felt that this approach to cash management worked well for the small company because it eliminated all of the paperwork associated with cash budgeting. Moreover, it enabled the firm to pay its bills in a timely manner.

Question 1 What are the advantages and weaknesses of the minimum-cash-balance practice?

Question 2 There is a saying "If it ain't broke, don't fix it." In view of the firm's present success in paying bills promptly, should it be encouraged to use a cash budget? Be prepared to support your answer.

SITUATION 2

Ruston Manufacturing Company is a small firm selling entirely on a credit basis. It has experienced successful operation and earned modest profits.

Sales are made on the basis of net payment in 30 days. Collections from customers run approximately 70 percent in 30 days, 20 percent in 60 days, 7 percent in 90 days, and 3 percent bad debts.

The owner has considered the possibility of offering a cash discount for early payment. However, the practice seems costly and possibly unnecessary. As the owner puts it, "Why should I bribe customers to pay what they legally owe?"

Question 1 Is offering a cash discount the equivalent of a bribe?

Question 2 How would a cash discount policy relate to bad debts?

Question 3 What cash discount policy, if any, would you recommend?

Question 4 What other approaches might be used to improve cash flows from receivables?

SITUATION 3

Below are the financial statements of two general contractors. The two companies are primarily commercial builders, as opposed to residential builders. They typically bid for the opportunity to build such facilities as office buildings, hospitals, and university buildings. As the general contractor, they use subcontractors who undertake most of the actual work.

Balance Sheet	BRC, Inc.		Arch Construction	
Assets				
Current assets:				
Cash	$ 1,199,921	4.1%*	$ 2,826,328	10.2%*
Short-term investments	14,704,137	50.4%	16,239,811	58.7%
Accounts receivable	12,460,468	42.7%	7,307,234	26.4%
Other current assets	21,482	0.1%	34,067	0.1%
Total current assets	$ 28,386,008	97.2%	$26,407,440	95.5%
Property and equipment	807,592	2.8%	1,252,408	4.5%
TOTAL ASSETS	$ 29,193,600	100.0%	$ 27,659,848	100.0%
Debt (Liabilities) and Equity				
Current liabilities:				
Short-term notes	$ 72,322	0.2%*	$ 79,564	0.3%*
Accounts payable	19,975,233	68.4%	14,898,131	53.9%
Accrued liabilities	899,472	3.1%	2,068,695	7.5%
Total current liabilities	$ 20,947,027	71.8%	$ 17,046,390	61.7%
Long-term debt	1,862,265	6.4%	1,782,700	6.4%
Total debt	$ 22,809,292	78.1%	$ 18,829,090	68.1%
Stockholders' equity:				
Common stock	$ 4,254	0.0%	$ 4,254	0.0%
Paid in capital	768,281	2.6%	768,281	2.8%
Retained earnings	5,611,773	19.2%	8,058,223	29.1%
Total stockholders' equity	$ 6,384,308	21.9%	$ 8,830,758	31.9%
TOTAL DEBT AND EQUITY	$ 29,193,600	100.0%	$ 27,659,848	100.0%
INCOME STATEMENT				
Construction revenues	$ 90,070,000	100.0%*	$72,822,725	100.0%*
Cost of goods sold	86,889,570	96.5%	68,090,781	93.5%
Gross profits	$ 3,180,430	3.5%	$ 4,731,944	6.5%
Interest income	941,631	1.0%	1,308,801	1.8%
Total revenues	$ 4,122,061	4.6%	$ 6,040,745	8.3%
Operating expenses	1,665,711	1.8%	2,033,400	2.8%
Interest expense	226,367	0.3%	172,158	0.2%
Other expense	79,630	0.1%	123,737	0.2%
Total expenses	$ 1,971,708	2.2%	$ 2,329,295	3.2%
Net profits	$ 2,150,353	2.4%	$ 3,711,450	5.1%

*All percentages have been rounded.

Note: While the financial information provided is real in this situation, the names of the companies have been changed to maintain confidentiality.

Question 1 Based on the information in the balance sheets, what do you notice about the nature of the general contracting business in terms of their working capital? How are the two companies alike, and how do they differ?

Questions 2 Talk to a general contractor to have her explain what the financial statements tell us about this type of business.

Question 3 Compute the cash conversion period for each company. Interpret your findings.

Small Business & Entrepreneurship Resource Center

The *Small Business and Entrepreneurship Resource Center* offers complete small business management resources through a comprehensive database that covers all major areas of starting, operating, and maintaining a business from financing, management, marketing, accounting, taxes, and more. Use the access code that came with your new book to access the site and perform the exercises in each chapter.

1. Cash flow is vital to the continuing operation of any small business, and poor cash flow forces approximately 40% of new businesses to shut down each year. Brian Hamilton, senior analyst at ProfitCents, and two small business owners offer eight tips for improving your cash flow in the article "Let It Flow." Describe each of the eight tips for improving small business cash flow.

2. When seeking financing, a yes or no answer can make or break any small business. There are alternatives when credit problems hamper a company's ability to secure working capital. The article "Getting to the Cash Flow" discusses the Doucettes, and their franchise called Liquid Capital of Northeast Ohio. Discuss the types of clients and services that are provided by Liquid Capital and how they may benefit a small business.

Sources: Let it flow; smart ways to manage your cash. Marcia Layton Turner. *Black Enterprise* 36, 10 (May 2006): p. 50(1).

Getting the cash to flow: finding alternative financing sources can mean the difference between a growing or stagnant business. (Entrepreneur's TOOLKIT: Finance). Kyle Swenson. *Inside Business* 9, 8 (August 2007): p. 65(3).

Case 22

PEARSON, P. 669

This case looks at the financial performance of a small air conditioning and heating services company, with emphasis on its working-capital policies.

ALTERNATIVE CASES FOR CHAPTER 22

Case 11, Missouri Solvents, p. 646

chapter

23

Managing Risk in the Small Business

In the SPOTLIGHT
Leidenheimer Baking Company
http://www.leidenheimer.com

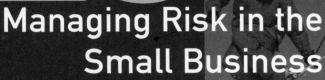

Sandy Whann is the fourth generation of Leidenheimer men to run [the Leidenheimer Baking Company], which was founded in 1896 in the city of New Orleans by Sandy's great-grandfather, George Leidenheimer of Germany. The bakery produces French bread made famous by traditional local dishes like the muffaletta and po boy sandwiches that originated in the heart of the French Quarter. As a lifetime citizen of New Orleans, Sandy has experienced many evacuations and has become adept at hurricane planning through the years.

When the hurricane alert [for Katrina] was issued on Saturday, August 27, 2006, this veteran immediately put his family emergency plan into effect as his wife and two children prepared to leave the city. Sandy remained near the plant to keep a close eye on his 110-year-old company and keep production working at a minimal capacity. With his family out of the city, Sandy uncharacteristically decided to shut the bakery down, secure its exterior, gas lines and doors and encouraged his employees to prepare their own homes and loved ones for the storm and potential evacuation. Both Sandy and the Leidenheimer management team keep home phone numbers and emergency evacuation contact information for all employees.

After most of his employees had left, only Sandy, his plant manager, and chief engineer, all of whom play key roles in the business's preparedness plan, remained in New Orleans. Once Sandy and the others had completed their assigned duties in the emergency shutdown, they left as well.

While driving to meet with his family in Baton Rouge, Sandy was struck by the unusualness of the event. "Things were very different this time around," said Sandy. "But in the gridlock I still made the most of the little time we had before the storm hit. Having an emergency preparedness plan helps you focus your priorities and helps you know what you need to be doing with the limited time you

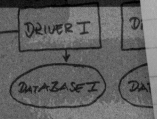

LOOKING AHEAD   AFTER STUDYING THIS CHAPTER, YOU SHOULD BE ABLE TO . . .

1. Define business risk and explain its two dimensions.
2. Identify the basic types of pure risk.
3. Describe the steps in the risk management process and explain how risk management can be used in small companies.
4. Explain the basic principles used in evaluating an insurance program.
5. Identify the common types of business insurance coverage.

have in any situation." En route, Sandy checked with his insurance provider, accountants, legal consultant, and spoke with customers via cell phone to keep them abreast of the situation and the effect of his shutdown on their supply of baked goods.

Sandy's business evacuation kit played a large part in his success. Sandy's kit included: financial and payroll records, utility contact information, updated phone lists for his customers and employees, back-up files and software, as well as computer hard drives. Well before the evacuation Sandy placed the kit in a mobile waterproof/fireproof case that could be taken with him at a moment's notice. As part of Sandy's written plan, he set-up a satellite office for the Leidenheimer Baking Company in Baton Rouge where he made contact with his bank, forwarded phone lines, and was receiving forwarded mail within two days after the evacuation.

Two days later, on August 29th, Sandy breathed a sigh of relief that his family and his company had escaped a major disaster. Sandy was able to return to his plant within a week of the storm hitting. When he returned, he was met with widespread damage, but without the flooding he had expected. In the facility, thousands of pounds of melted yeast and other ingredients had been sitting wet without refrigeration. The roof had severe damage, there was no power, no usable water, and no one was permitted back into the city except the National Guard. The plant was 120 degrees of foul smells emanating from every square inch.

Despite caring deeply for his business, the most important thing to Sandy was his employees and he felt fortunate that all of the company's employees were safe. "The rebuilding process included a handful of things," said Sandy. "Number one is the employees. . . . It is important to listen to the needs of employees," Sandy expresses.

In summing up his experience, Sandy said, "Katrina was severe enough to teach even us experienced hurricane survivors a few new things about our emergency planning." Since Hurricane Katrina, Sandy has revised his business emergency plan and gained a more extensive understanding of the importance of preparation.

Source: "Sandy Whann Case Study, http://www.ready .gov/business/_downloads/sandywhann.pdf, accessed April 30, 2009.

We live in a world of uncertainty, so how we see risk is vitally important in almost all dimensions of life. Risk must certainly be considered in making any business decisions. As sixth-century Greek poet and statesman Solon wrote,

> There is risk in everything that one does, and no one knows where he will make his landfall when his enterprise is at its beginning. One man, trying to act effectively, fails to foresee something and falls into great and grim ruination, but to another man, one who is acting ineffectively, a god gives good fortune in everything and escapes from his folly.[1]

While Solon gave more credit than we would to Zeus for the outcomes of ventures, his insight reminds us that little is new in this world—least of all, the need to acknowledge and compensate as best we can for the risks we encounter.

Risk means different things to different people. For a student, risk might be represented by the possibility of failing an exam. For a coal miner, risk might be represented by the chance of an explosion in the mine. For a retired person, risk could mean the likelihood of not being able to live comfortably on his or her limited income. Of course, an entrepreneur's risk takes the form of the chance that a new venture will fail.

As Benjamin Franklin once said, "In this life nothing is certain except death and taxes." Entrepreneurs might extend this adage to include small business risks. Chapter 1 noted the moderate risk-taking propensities of entrepreneurs and their desire to exert some control over the risky situations in which they find themselves by seeking to minimize business risks as much as possible. This chapter outlines how this can be done. Our study of this important topic begins with a definition of risk.

What Is Business Risk?

Simply stated, *risk* is the "possibility of suffering harm or loss."[2] *Business risk,* then, is the possibility of losses associated with the assets and earnings potential of a firm. Here, the term *assets* includes not only inventory and equipment, but also such factors as the firm's employees, its customers, and its reputation.

1. Define business risk and explain its two dimensions.

business risk
The possibility of losses associated with the assets and earnings potential of a firm.

The nature of business risk can be observed from two perspectives: market risk and pure risk. *Market risk* is the uncertainty associated with an investment decision. An entrepreneur who invests in a new business hopes for a gain, but realizes that the eventual outcome may be a loss. Only after identifying the investment opportunity, developing strategies, and committing resources will she or he find out whether the final result is a gain or a loss.

market risk
The uncertainty associated with an investment decision.

Pure risk describes a situation where only loss or no loss can occur—there is no potential gain. Owning property, for instance, creates the possibility of loss due to fire or severe weather; the only outcomes are loss or no loss. As a general rule, only pure risk is insurable. That is, insurance is not intended to protect investors from market risks, where the chances of both gain and loss exist.

pure risk
The uncertainty associated with a situation where only loss or no loss can occur.

Basic Types of Pure Risk

The pure risks that any business faces can be put into the following categories: property, liability, and personnel. Let's take a look at these risks, which are related to the physical, legal, and human aspects of a business.

2. Identify the basic types of pure risk.

Property Risks

In the course of establishing a business, an owner acquires property that will be necessary to provide the goods and services of the company. If this property is damaged or destroyed, the business sustains a loss. In addition, the temporary loss of use of the property can add to the negative financial impact on the business. Several characteristics of business property and the risks associated with it are worthy of attention.

There are two general types of property—real property and personal property. *Real property* consists of land and anything physically attached to land, such as buildings. Some business owners purchase land and buildings, while others choose to lease necessary real property. It is important to note, however, that some leases make the lessee responsible for any damage or loss to the leased premises. *Personal property* can be defined simply as any property other than real property. Personal property includes machinery, equipment (such as computers), furniture, fixtures, stock, and vehicles. While the location of real property is fixed, personal property can be moved from place to place. Among the risks to the personal property of the small firm are the security threats to its computers posed by hackers and spyware, for example. (See Exhibit 23-1.)

real property
Land and anything physically attached to the land, such as buildings.

personal property
Any property other than real property, including machinery, equipment, furniture, fixtures, stock, and vehicles.

EXHIBIT

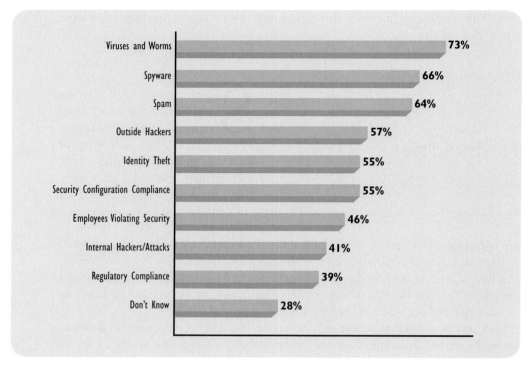

Viruses and Worms	73%
Spyware	66%
Spam	64%
Outside Hackers	57%
Identity Theft	55%
Security Configuration Compliance	55%
Employees Violating Security	46%
Internal Hackers/Attacks	41%
Regulatory Compliance	39%
Don't Know	28%

replacement value of property
The cost of replacing personal property and rebuilding real property at today's prices.

Property can be valued in several ways. The *replacement value of property* is the cost of replacing personal property and rebuilding real property at today's prices. For example, a building that was constructed 10 years ago at a cost of $1 million may have a current replacement value of $1,400,000 because of the rising costs of materials and labor. The *actual cash value (ACV)* of property is very different from its replacement value, as this insurance term refers to the depreciated value of property. Assuming a rate of depreciation of 3 percent per year for the same 10-year-old building, we would find the building to have an estimated actual cash value of $980,000 (that is, $1,400,000 − (0.03 × 10 × $1,400,000). By common practice, most commercial property insurance policies provide replacement value coverage as opposed to actual cash value coverage.

actual cash value (ACV)
An insurance term that refers to the depreciated value of a property.

Property insurance also takes into account two primary features: perils (the cause) and losses (the effect).

peril
A cause of loss, either through natural events or through the actions of people.

PERILS   A *peril* is defined as a cause of loss. Some perils are naturally occurring events, such as windstorms, floods, earthquakes, and lightning. The location of property may increase the likelihood of its loss from certain perils—for example, coastal properties are more susceptible to wind damage and flooding, and properties near fault lines are more prone to damage from earthquakes.

Not all perils, however, are natural events; some are related to the actions of people. Perils such as robbery and employee dishonesty involve criminal acts performed by people against business owners. The rapid growth of e-commerce has led to new forms of dishonest acts, such as hacking, denial of access, and improper use of confidential information.

direct loss
A loss in which physical damage to property reduces its value to the property owner.

LOSSES   Usually, when you think of property loss, you envision a *direct loss,* in which physical damage to property reduces its value to the property owner. The direct loss of property as a result of windstorm, fire, or explosion is obvious to everyone and has the potential to significantly hinder any business.

A less obvious type of property loss is an *indirect loss,* which arises from an inability to carry on normal operations due to a direct loss. For example, if a delivery truck is damaged in an accident, the resulting loss of use can impair the ability of a business to get its goods to customers. The indirect loss component of this event may cause a reduction in revenue or an increase in expense (from having to outsource the delivery function), either of which will have an adverse impact on business income.

It should be pointed out that business income can also be reduced by events or conditions that are not related to direct losses. For example, a strike by UPS employees several years ago created serious logistical problems for many of its business customers, which were unable to receive goods from suppliers or deliver goods to customers. The financial impact of such a labor action may be just as real to a business as physical damage to property, but the insurance protection available for indirect losses applies only when *direct* damage events trigger the loss of use. This issue is discussed in more detail later in the chapter.

indirect loss
A loss arising from inability to carry on normal operations due to a direct loss of property.

Liability Risks

A growing business risk today is the legal liability that may arise from various business activities. A society creates laws to govern interactions among its members. Individual rights and freedoms are protected by these laws. If a business or any of its agents violates these protected rights, the business can be held accountable for any resulting loss or damage to the affected party. Legal liability may arise from statutory liability, contractual liability, or tort liability.

STATUTORY LIABILITY   Some laws impose a statutory obligation on a business. For example, each state has enacted *workers' compensation legislation* that in most cases requires employers to provide certain benefits to employees when they are injured in a work-related incident. This means that fault is not an issue; an employer is responsible for work-related injuries without regard to fault. While the benefits differ slightly from state to state, most workers' compensation statutes require employers to provide the following benefits to employees injured at work: coverage of medical expenses, compensation for lost wages, payment of rehabilitation expenses, and death benefits for employees' families.

workers' compensation legislation
Laws that obligate the employer to pay employees for injury or illness related to employment, regardless of fault.

EXHIBIT

23-2 Risk-Taking Begins Early

"WE'RE STARTING FIRST-AID TRAINING, DAD. I NEED $150,000 FOR MALPRACTICE INSURANCE."

© Harley I. Schwadron

This statutory liability is potentially significant for any business. The attacks on the World Trade Center provided a stark example of the magnitude of this liability, especially for companies whose employees worked in a concentrated area. Marsh, Inc., one of the leading insurance brokers in the world, lost over 300 employees in the 9/11 disaster, creating an enormous financial obligation on the part of the employer to the families of the victims. Most businesses protect themselves from this type of financial loss through the purchase of workers' compensation insurance. Some large employers choose to self-insure (that is, they set aside part of their earnings to offset any potential future losses), but most purchase extra insurance protection to guard against catastrophic events such as the 9/11 tragedy.

CONTRACTUAL LIABILITY Businesses often enter into contracts with other parties. These contracts could involve a lease of premises, a sales contract with a customer, an agreement with an outsourcing firm, or a contract with a construction company. One common denominator among most of these contracts is the inclusion of some sort of indemnification clause. As businesses sign contracts containing indemnification clauses, they need to be well aware of the potential legal liabilities they may be assuming by virtue of the language used. Simply put, an *indemnification clause* requires one party (the indemnitor) to assume the financial consequences of another party's legal liabilities (the indemnitee). In other words, the indemnitor agrees to "pay on behalf" of the indemnitee the legal liabilities of the indemnitee.

> **indemnification clause**
> A contractual clause that requires one party to assume the financial consequences of another party's legal liabilities.

The idea behind the contractual transfer of liability is to shift the responsibility to the party with the most control over the risk exposure. Consider, for example, a general contractor, who signs an agreement to construct a new building on a piece of land for an owner. Should someone be injured during the building process, it is highly unlikely that the injury would be a result of the negligence of the property owner. In all likelihood, the negligent party—the party causing or contributing to the accident—would be the general contractor or perhaps a subcontractor hired by the general contractor. Therefore, it is quite common and most appropriate for the general contractor to agree to indemnify the owner for any liability arising from the construction work.

In many cases, insurance covers the potential legal liabilities that a business may assume as a result of an indemnification clause in a contract. But good communication between a business owner and his or her insurance agent or broker is essential. In a review of contracts that contain indemnification clauses, the insurance agent or broker should be able to point out the main limitations or shortcomings of an insurance policy as they pertain to the firm's assuming the legal liabilities of another party.

> **torts**
> Wrongful acts or omissions for which an injured party can take legal action against the wrongdoer for monetary damages.

TORT LIABILITY Civil wrongs include breach of contract and torts. *Torts* are wrongful acts or omissions for which an injured party can take legal action against the wrongdoer to seek monetary damages. Tort actions commonly include an allegation of negligence, but four elements must be present for someone to be found guilty of a negligent act:

1. *Existence of a legal duty between the parties.* For example, a restaurant owner has a legal duty to provide patrons with food and drink that are fit for consumption. Likewise, an employee making a delivery for an employer has a duty to operate a vehicle safely on public roads.

2. *Failure to provide the appropriate standard of care.* The standard of care normally used is the *reasonable (prudent person) standard,* based on what a reasonable or prudent person would have done under similar circumstances. This standard of care may be elevated, however, if a "professional" is involved. In professional liability actions, the standard of care is determined by the established standards of the profession. For example, a negligence action against a CPA would use the standards of the accounting profession as the benchmark. Expert witnesses are often used to help establish the standard and determine what clients can reasonably expect.

> **reasonable (prudent person) standard**
> The typical standard of care, based on what a reasonable or prudent person would have done under similar circumstances.

3. *Presence of injury or damages.* Negligence may exist, but if no injury or damage is sustained by the claimant, tort liability does not exist. Two types of damages may be awarded in a tort action: compensatory and punitive damages.

- *Compensatory damages* are intended to make the claimant whole—that is, to compensate the claimant for any injuries or damage arising from the negligent action. Compensatory damages can be economic or noneconomic in nature. *Economic damages* relate to economic loss, such as medical expenses, loss of income, or the cost of property replacement/restoration. Economic damages are relatively easy to quantify. *Noneconomic damages* cover such losses as pain and suffering, mental anguish, and loss of physical abilities. In comparison to economic damages, noneconomic damages are difficult to express in financial terms. Civil courts usually have a hard time setting these awards, but many of today's substantial awards include a large amount for noneconomic damages.

- *Punitive damages* are a form of punishment that goes beyond any compensatory damages. Punitive damages have a dual purpose. First, they punish wrongdoers in instances where there is gross negligence or a callous disregard for the interests of others. Second, punitive damages are intended to have a deterrent effect, sending a message to society that such conduct will not be tolerated. Whether or not an insurance policy will pay for the punitive damages awarded against a business is determined by the state in which the lawsuit is filed. As a matter of public policy, some states will allow insurance companies to pay for punitive damages, while other states will not.

4. *Evidence that the negligent act is the proximate cause of the loss.* There must be proof that the negligence actually caused the damages sustained. There may be negligence and there may be damages, but if no link can be established between the two, there is no tort liability.

Tort liability can arise from a number of business activities. Some of the more significant sources of tort liability follow:

- *Premises liability.* People may sustain injuries while on a business's premises. Retailers have significant premises liability exposure because they have many customers entering stores to purchase goods. Some other businesses, however, have little in the way of premises liability exposure. A consulting firm or a Web-design company would not typically have clients visit its business location; therefore, its premises liability exposure would be minimal.

- *Operations liability.* People may also sustain injuries as a result of a company's operations that take place away from its premises. Contractors have significant operations liability exposure because they are performing work at various job sites, and such work could easily result in injury to another person. At the same time, some businesses (such as retailers) have little in the way of operations liability exposure; their exposure is limited to their store's premises.

- *Professional liability.* Any business providing professional services to the public is potentially subject to professional liability claims. Recognizing this exposure is important, since separate liability insurance is necessary to properly protect a business from professional liability claims.

- *Employers' liability.* As previously mentioned, employers have a statutory obligation to pay certain benefits to employees injured in the course of employment. At the same time, it is possible that an employer may be sued by an altogether different party as a result of an injury to an employee. Perhaps the employee's injury in the workplace was caused by a faulty piece of equipment manufactured by another firm; the employee may sue the manufacturer of that faulty product. The manufacturer may then take action against the employer, alleging that the employer failed to maintain the equipment, which consequently caused injury to the employee.

compensatory damages
Economic or noneconomic damages intended to make the claimant whole, by indemnifying the claimant for any injuries or damage arising from the negligent action.

economic damages
Compensatory damages that relate to economic loss, such as medical expense, loss of income, or the cost of property replacement/restoration.

noneconomic damages
Compensatory damages for such losses as pain and suffering, mental anguish, and loss of physical abilities.

punitive damages
A form of punishment that goes beyond compensatory damages, intending to punish wrongdoers for gross negligence or a callous disregard for the interests of others and to have a deterrent effect.

proximate cause
A negligent act that is the clear cause of damages sustained.

manufacturing defect
A defect resulting from a problem that occurs during the manufacturing process causing the product to subsequently not be made according to specifications.

design defect
A defect resulting from a dangerous design, even though the product was made according to specifications.

marketing defect
A defect resulting from failure to convey to the user that hazards are associated with a product or to provide adequate instructions on safe product use.

- *Automobile liability.* A business that uses vehicles for various purposes has automobile liability exposure. Even a company that does not own or lease vehicles has potential liability if employees use their personal vehicles for business purposes.

- *Product liability.* The products manufactured or sold by a business can be a source of legal liability. For example, someone who was injured while using a product may claim that the product was defective. She or he may allege that there was either a manufacturing defect, a design defect, or a marketing defect. A *manufacturing defect* exists when something actually goes wrong during the manufacturing process and the product is not made according to the manufacturer's specifications. A *design defect* exists when the product is made in accordance with the manufacturer's specifications but the product is still unreasonably dangerous as designed. As an example, perhaps there is a rotating blade inside a piece of equipment that is not properly covered by a shield. Someone could be injured by the rotating blade and claim a design defect since there was no protective shield covering the blade. Finally, a *marketing defect* exists when the manufacturer has failed to convey to the user of the product a fair indication of the hazards associated with the product or has given inadequate instructions as to how to use the product safely.

- *Completed operations liability.* The completed operations or completed work of a business can be a source of legal liability. Take as an example a general contractor that has constructed a new building for another party. Following the construction of the building, someone could be standing on a balcony of the building and leaning against a rail that gives way, thus causing the person to fall and sustain bodily injury. This would generally result in a lawsuit against the general contractor.

- *Directors and officers liability.* An increasing concern among businesses today is the threat of lawsuits against the directors and officers of a company. The exposure is greater for publicly owned organizations, but it also exists for privately owned firms and nonprofit organizations. Specific areas of exposure for directors and officers include lawsuits with allegations of financial mismanagement, conflicts of interest, actions taken beyond the authority granted in bylaws, and wrongful acts that pertain to employment practices. Wrongful employment practices may include discrimination, sexual harassment, or wrongful termination.

Personnel Risks

personnel risks
Risks that directly affect individual employees but may have an indirect impact on a business as well.

Personnel risks are risks that directly affect individual employees but may have an indirect impact on a business as well. The primary risks in this category include premature death, poor health, and insufficient retirement income.

PREMATURE DEATH   The risk associated with death is not if, but when. We all expect to die; however, there is a risk that we may die early in life. This risk poses a potential financial problem for both the family of the person and his or her employer. Individuals deal with this risk by maintaining a healthy lifestyle and purchasing life insurance to protect family members who rely on their income.

Employers can be quite adversely impacted by the untimely death of an employee if that employee cannot be easily replaced. And what if a partner or owner of the business dies? Normally, such an event triggers a buyout of the interest of the deceased owner. Life insurance is often used to fund these buyout provisions.

POOR HEALTH   A more likely occurrence than death of an employee is poor health. The severity of poor health varies, ranging from a mild disorder to a more serious, disabling malady. And as with premature death, the consequences of this event may affect an employer as well as family members.

The financial consequences of poor health have two dimensions. First are medical expenses, which can range from the cost of a doctor's visit to catastrophic expenses related to surgeries and hospitalization. Second are consequences of the inability to work. Disability most often is a temporary condition, but it can be lengthy or even permanent. A worker's permanent disability can have the same financial impact on her or his family as death.

Employers often provide some form of health insurance as a benefit of employment. In some instances, the cost of the health insurance is shared by the employer and the employee; in most instances, however, the bulk of the cost is absorbed by the employer. In addition to the health insurance costs, the fact that the employer is without the services of the employee for some time period may add to the adverse financial impact on the business.

INSUFFICIENT RETIREMENT INCOME The final category of personnel risk involves the possibility of outliving one's wealth. The goal in dealing with this risk is to defer income and accumulate sufficient wealth to provide a satisfactory level of income during the nonworking years.

There are three primary sources of retirement income: Social Security, employer-funded retirement programs, and personal savings. Social Security provides a retirement income benefit, although for most retirees this benefit is not sufficient to meet expected consumption during retirement. To supplement this income, most workers have a retirement program associated with their employment. In the past, these programs were primarily funded by employers as a form of deferred compensation. While employer-funded pension plans still exist, it is more common today to encounter employee-funded retirement plans, where the employee can elect to defer current income for retirement. Usually, these plans are partially funded by employers as an incentive for employees to participate. Finally, individual savings can be used to accumulate wealth for retirement. All of these sources should be carefully considered in the retirement income planning process.

Risk Management

Risk management consists of all efforts to preserve the assets and earning power of a business. Since risk management has grown out of insurance management, the two terms are often used interchangeably. However, risk management has a much broader meaning, covering both insurable and uninsurable risks and including non-insurance approaches to reducing all types of risk. Risk management involves more than trying to obtain the most insurance for each dollar spent; it is concerned with finding the best way possible to reduce the cost of dealing with risk. Insurance is only one of several approaches to minimizing the pure risks a firm is sure to encounter.

3. Describe the steps in the risk management process and explain how risk management can be used in small companies.

risk management
Ways of coping with risk that are designed to preserve the assets and earning power of a firm.

The Process of Risk Management

Five steps are required to develop and implement a risk management program.

Step 1: *Identify and understand risks.* It is essential that a business owner be aware of the risks the firm faces. To reduce the chance of overlooking important risks, a business should adopt a systematic approach to identifying risks. Useful identification methods include insurance policy checklists, questionnaires, analysis of financial statements, and careful analysis of a firm's operations, customers, and facilities. Exhibit 23-3 depicts just a few of the risks that a small company may encounter.

EXHIBIT

23-3 Risks on the Road to Success

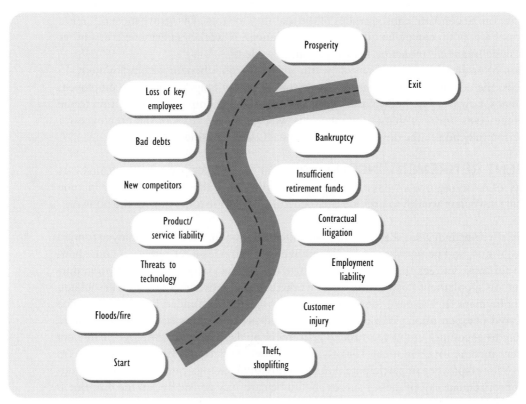

Step 2:   *Evaluate risks.* Once the various risks have been identified, they must be evaluated in terms of the potential size of each loss and the probability that it will occur. At a minimum, risks should be classified into three groups: critical (losses that could result in bankruptcy), extremely important (losses that would require investment of additional capital to continue operations), and moderately important (losses that can be covered with current income or existing assets).

Step 3:   *Select methods to manage risk.* The two approaches used in dealing with risk are risk control and risk financing, both of which will be discussed later in this chapter.

Step 4:   *Implement the decision.* Once the decision has been made to use a particular technique or techniques to manage a firm's risks, this decision must be followed by action, such as purchasing insurance and setting aside dedicated funds to cope with any risks that have been retained. Failure to act—or even simple procrastination— could be fatal.

Step 5:   *Review and evaluate.* Review and evaluation of the chosen risk management technique are essential because conditions change—new risks arise and old ones disappear. Also, reviewing earlier decisions to use specific methods may identify mistakes made previously.

Risk Management and the Small Business

Regardless of the nature of a business, risk management is a serious issue for small companies, as well as large corporations. Too often, small businesses pay insufficient attention to analyzing potential risk. "Small companies often spend more time planning their company picnics than for an event that could put them out of business," says Katherine Heaviside, a partner in Epoch 5, a Huntington, New York, public relations firm that specializes in crisis communication.[3] To avoid being put out of business by an unexpected development, the small business owner must take an active role in managing the risks of her or his firm.

Risk management in a small business differs from that in a large firm. In a large firm, the responsibilities of risk management are frequently assigned to a specialized staff manager. It is more difficult for a small company to cope with risk management since its risk manager is usually the owner and the owner wears so many hats. For this reason, the small business owner needs to rely more heavily on his or her insurance agent for advice. Furthermore, risk management is not something that requires immediate attention—until something happens. A prudent small business owner will take the time to identify the different types of risks faced by the firm and find ways to cope with them, through either risk control or risk financing.

RISK CONTROL

Risk control involves minimizing loss through prevention, avoidance, and/or reduction. *Loss prevention,* as the name implies, focuses on preventing losses from ever happening. For example, a business with a machine shop or manufacturing process may require all employees to wear safety glasses so as to prevent foreign particles from injuring their eyes. *Loss avoidance* is achieved by choosing not to engage in a particular hazardous activity. For instance, the liability exposure associated with operating a large truck on an interstate highway for the purposes of delivering a company's products to the marketplace is quite severe. An accident caused by a large truck on the highway can result in serious bodily injury and/or property damage. Therefore, to avoid this liability exposure, a business may choose to hire a common carrier to deliver its products to the marketplace. This eliminates the exposure altogether. *Loss reduction* addresses the potential frequency, severity, or unpredictability of loss, thereby lessening the impact of the loss on the business. Crisis planning is a form of loss reduction in that it provides a template to follow in the case of a catastrophic loss. Installing automatic sprinkler systems in a building is another good example of a loss reduction strategy. If a fire occurs in a building with an automatic sprinkler system, the sprinklers will be activated, minimizing the amount of fire damage to the building.

RISK FINANCING

Risk financing focuses on making funds available for losses that cannot be eliminated by risk control; it involves transferring the risk or retaining the risk. *Risk transfer* is accomplished largely through buying insurance but can also be achieved by making other contractual arrangements that transfer the risk to others. As described earlier, indemnification clauses provide a means by which risk can be transferred from one party to another.

Risk retention entails financing all or part of a loss from a company's cash flows. Assuming a firm's balance sheet is strong enough, the owner may choose to carry a high deductible applicable to property losses (perhaps a $25,000 deductible instead of a $5,000 deductible). For example, in the event of fire damage to a company's building, the business owner would pay the first $5,000 to $25,000 out of his or her pocket. The higher the deductible, the lower the insurance premium paid to the property insurance carrier. As another example, a business owner may choose to have a high deductible for a liability-type insurance claim. Again, in exchange for the higher deductible, the business owner is given a discounted liability insurance premium. Another form of risk retention is *self-insurance.* However, self-insurance is usually only appropriate for larger companies. Under self-insurance programs, a part of the organization's earnings is earmarked for a contingency fund against possible future losses.

Some small businesses have successfully relied on *partially self-funded programs* as they pertain to medical coverage for employees. Partially self-funded programs allow the business to self-fund a "portion" of the medical coverage for its employees (also referred to as health insurance benefits). For most small businesses, this self-funded portion is limited to between $30,000 and $80,000 per employee, depending on the number of employees and the firm's financial strength. This limitation per employee is more commonly referred to as a

---

risk control
Minimizing potential losses by preventing, avoiding, or reducing risk.

loss prevention
Keeping a loss from happening.

loss avoidance
Avoiding loss by choosing not to engage in hazardous activities.

loss reduction
Lessening the frequency, severity, or unpredictability of losses.

risk financing
Making funds available to cover losses that could not be eliminated by risk control.

risk transfer
Buying insurance or making contractual arrangements with others in order to transfer risk.

risk retention
Financing loss intentionally, through a firm's cash flows.

self-insurance
Designating part of a firm's earnings as a cushion against possible future losses.

partially self-funded program
Designating part of a firm's earnings to fund a portion of employee medical coverage.

entrepreneurial experiences

Crisis Averted

In November 2006, while Nichole Yarbrough, owner of Shepherd, Texas–based Shepherd Auto Sales, and her husband were at a car auction, thieves broke into her truck and stole her purse, which contained credit cards, checks, $5,000 in cash, and more than 40 car titles—ownership papers for all of the used cars on her lot. The theft could have put Yarbrough out of business permanently. But it didn't. Thanks to a lot of old-fashioned legwork and a little gumption, she replaced every lost title, and within two months, her lot was running at 100 percent again.

Yarbrough's story is a perfect example of how a single act can change the course of your business. . . . [U]nless you plan ahead and take every precaution, your business and livelihood can be completely destroyed [often] through no fault of your own.

"I think the biggest mistake people make is not planning for command and control after a disaster," says Leo A. Wrobel, author of *Business Resumption Planning* (CRC Press, 2008) and owner of Dallas-based b4Ci Inc, a business continuity firm. "Companies don't plan for the worst, and they don't plan on what they'll need to come back from the worst." The worst, Wrobel says, can come in many forms, including natural disasters, fires, floods, embezzlement, theft, lawsuits or even something as simple as an extended loss of telephone, Internet or electric services. In every case, unless you've got a Plan B, you've got a problem.

Shepherd Auto Sales' Yarbrough wasted no time putting her Plan B into place. She's tightened security both on and off her car lot, installing cameras and locking her office door, especially if she's alone. She also makes copies of every form and title that come into her office—and stores them separately from the originals. "They go into a locked place so I have a copy of everything if something bad happens," she says.

Source: http://www.nfib.com/tabid/56/Default.aspx?cmsid=46220&v=1A, accessed May 8, 2009.

Courtesy of Custom Air Photo Inc.

---

specific stop loss limit
A firm's per-employee limit on self-funding for medical claims.

specific stop loss limit. After the specific stop loss limit has been met on any particular claim, the health insurance company takes over the claim and pays the remaining portion.

In April 2009, an employer in Waco, Texas, compared the costs of a traditional health insurance plan (also referred to as a fully insured medical plan) and a partially self-funded program. This particular employer had 93 employees. The fully insured plan would have cost the organization approximately $1,220,000 in premiums for a 12-month period. The partially self-funded medical plan had cost the employer a total of only $950,000 the previous year. So it appeared to be in the employer's best interest to maintain a partially self-funded program in anticipation of again saving approximately $270,000. Clearly, some risks are associated with a partially self-funded plan, since an employer never knows ahead of time how many employees might actually reach their specific stop loss limit. For this reason, these plans also have what is referred to as an *aggregate stop loss limit,* so as to provide a cap on expenses for the year should a number of employees reach the specific stop loss limit.

aggregate stop loss limit
A comprehensive limit on annual expenses should a number of employees reach the specific stop loss limit.

		Probability of Loss	
		Low Frequency	**High Frequency**
Amount of Loss	**High Severity**	• Loss prevention • Loss reduction	• Loss prevention • Loss reduction
	Low Severity	• Loss avoidance • Loss prevention • Loss reduction • Risk retention	• Risk retention

Note: To find a listing of the risk management tools appropriate for dealing with a potential loss, see the box corresponding to the severity and frequency of the potential loss.

It should be understood that partially self-funded programs are not suitable for every small business. As a rule of thumb, a business should have a net worth of at least $1 million and 80 or more employees to be considered a good candidate for a partially self-funded program.

In choosing the appropriate method for managing risk, the small business owner should consider the size of each potential loss, its probability of occurrence, and what resources would be available to cover the loss if it did occur. Exhibit 23-4 shows the appropriate risk management techniques for potential losses of different probabilities (low frequency and high frequency) and loss amounts (low severity and high severity).

Basic Principles of a Sound Insurance Program

What kinds of risks can be covered by insurance? What types of coverage should be purchased? How much coverage is adequate? Unfortunately, there are no clear-cut answers to these questions.

4. Explain the basic principles used in evaluating an insurance program.

A reputable insurance agent can provide valuable assistance to a small company in evaluating risks and designing proper protection plans, but an entrepreneur should become as knowledgeable as possible about what types of insurance are available. Three basic principles should be followed in evaluating an insurance program:

1. Identify business risks that can be insured.
2. Secure insurance coverage for all major potential losses.
3. Consider the feasibility and affordability of insuring smaller potential losses.

IDENTIFY BUSINESS RISKS THAT CAN BE INSURED   A small business must first obtain the insurance coverage that is either required by law or by contract with another party. This generally includes workers' compensation insurance and automobile liability insurance. A reputable insurance agent with expertise in providing business insurance coverage will be an important resource in identifying business risks that can be insured, while also establishing the premium costs for insuring such risks. As a part of this process, business owners should take the necessary time to determine the replacement cost of their buildings and personal property, including all furniture, fixtures, equipment, inventory, and supplies.

Denny Fulk on Managing Risk

The area of risk management as it relates to the purchase of insurance has been well covered in the text. It is a particularly challenging issue for the newer, smaller startup. My personal perspective is that you should not place your family, your employees, or others involved with you at risk by not purchasing the proper insurance. Plan for it, budget for the most essential coverage, and buy it. Income protection for your dependents in case of death or disability is a top priority. All lending institutions require the pledge of security or guarantee to repay business debt or personal borrowing, so purchasing your own insurance to cover the amount of the debt is a better alternative than purchasing the lender's "credit life" insurance.

My business partner and I agreed that purchasing whole life insurance rather than term insurance for buy-sell insurance and real estate and equipment debt provided sound protection for our young families. It proved to be an excellent investment decision for the years we operated as a regular corporation. Having the premiums paid as a business expense of the corporation resulted in each of us being charged a certain percentage of that amount as additional personal income, but this was still an advantageous situation. The resulting cash values of the policies after 32 years were a very significant asset. Over the long term, the returns realized from a quality, dividend-paying, fixed premium, whole life insurance policy from a reputable company will far outweigh the benefits of buying a term policy (with annual premiums increased for age and current health conditions). Attempting to invest any amount of premium saved from the purchase of term insurance in something that will provide a greater return is difficult, at best. Your top priority should be to focus on your company's business objectives rather than gamble with guaranteed protection for your family.

After selling the corporation, along with investing in stocks and mutual funds, I invested a significant portion of the resulting funds in a single payment annuity policy. This policy provides a selection of well-diversified mutual funds that, in the event of my death, guarantee the market value of the investments at that time but no less than the amount I originally invested. We also maintained disability policies on both partners until the sale of the company.

SECURE COVERAGE FOR ALL MAJOR POTENTIAL LOSSES   Small businesses must avoid incurring major uninsured losses that have the capacity to threaten the very existence of the business. For example, it would be exceedingly difficult to overcome the total destruction of a building or facility caused by a significant fire or windstorm event. For this reason, a business owner should make certain that insurance covers the full replacement value of the firm's buildings and personal property. In an effort to save a relatively small amount of premium dollars, some small business owners elect to insure their property for a value somewhat less than the full replacement value, which is unmistakably a bad decision.

Equally devastating might be a $1 million liability judgment against the business as a result of an automobile accident or someone's slipping on the premises or being injured by the firm's products. It is imperative for the longevity of the business that these major potential loss exposures be properly insured.

CONSIDER THE FEASIBILITY AND AFFORDABILITY OF INSURING SMALLER POTENTIAL LOSSES   Smaller potential losses do not pose the same threat to businesses as major potential losses do. Thus, a business owner will need to weigh the feasibility and affordability of absorbing smaller potential losses. Of course, what determines whether a potential loss is "small" or "large" varies by each small business, depending on the strength of its financial position. The types of claims that arise from employment practices include employee lawsuits alleging wrongful termination, sexual harassment, and discrimination in the workplace. For the most part, the dollar value of such claims ranges from $50,000 to $150,000, with insurance premiums ranging from $2,500 to $7,500. Therefore, the entrepreneur must decide if the potential loss would be best handled through self-insurance or through payment of annual premiums. The company's ability to absorb such a loss determines what the small business owner should do. In this case, there is no single right answer.

Common Types of Business Insurance

In this section, we examine the basic insurance policies used by many small companies. These policies fall under one of two categories: property and casualty insurance and life and health insurance.

5. Identify the common types of business insurance coverage.

Property and Casualty Insurance

Property and casualty insurance includes property insurance, commercial general liability insurance, automobile insurance, workers' compensation insurance, and crime insurance.

PROPERTY INSURANCE A property insurance policy is used by a business owner to insure buildings and personal property owned by the business, as well as buildings not owned by the business but for which the business owner, as lessee, has a responsibility to insure. As previously mentioned, property can be insured for either its replacement value or actual cash value.

When purchasing property insurance, a business owner must also determine which "perils" will be covered by the policy. With the *named-peril approach,* the specific perils covered by the policy are identified. Covered perils generally include damage caused by fire, smoke, lightning, explosion, windstorm, hail, aircraft, vehicles, riot, vandalism, sprinkler leakage, sinkhole collapse, and volcanic action. With this approach, any damage caused by a peril not named in the policy is simply not covered. Examples of claims not covered by the named-peril approach include damage caused by frozen pipes within the building, falling objects, the weight of snow, and theft.

In contrast to the named-peril approach, a business owner can select property insurance using the *all-risk approach.* This approach provides the broadest protection available to business owners. With the all-risk approach, all direct damage to property is covered except damage caused by perils specifically excluded. In other words, if it's not excluded, it's covered. Exclusions typically include damage caused by flood, earthquake, fungus or mold, normal wear and tear, and loss caused by the dishonest acts of employees.

An important provision found within the property insurance policy is the *coinsurance clause.* A coinsurance clause requires the business owner to insure the company's building and personal property for at least 80 percent of what it would cost to replace the building and the personal property. If at the time of a claim, the building and personal property are insured for less than 80 percent of their replacement cost, then the business owner is assessed a penalty by the insurance company and, in essence, becomes a co-insurer.

As an example, assume that the replacement cost of a building is $1 million. The insured is therefore required to carry insurance equal to $800,000 (0.80 × $1,000,000) in order to avoid a co-insurance penalty. If the business owner insures the property for only $600,000, he or she then becomes a co-insurer, even in the case of a partial claim. Because the actual insurance is only 75 percent ($600,000 ÷ $800,000) of what it should have been, the insured is penalized

named-peril approach
Identifying, in an insurance policy, the specific perils covered.

all-risk approach
Stating, in an insurance policy, that all direct damages to property are covered except those caused by perils specifically excluded.

coinsurance clause
A clause found within the property insurance policy that requires the business owner to have insurance that will cover a certain percentage (usually 80 percent) of what it would cost to rebuild the building or replace the personal property.

25 percent in the event of a claim. So, should the building experience partial fire and smoke damage in the amount of $100,000, the insurance company will pay only $75,000, even though the amount of insurance on the policy clearly exceeds the amount of the claim. The remaining $25,000 must be paid by the business owner in his or her role as co-insurer. Therefore, it is important for a business owner to insure a building and personal property for an amount that exceeds at least 80 percent of its replacement value. Of course, in the event of a catastrophic type of loss, the business owner will be better served by insuring the building and personal property for 100 percent of what it would cost to replace. Indeed, the limits of property insurance should be carefully considered by all business owners.

business interruption insurance
Coverage that reimburses a business for the loss of anticipated income following the interruption of business operations.

One type of optional coverage that can be added to the property insurance policy is *business interruption insurance*. As previously noted, the financial loss associated with a property loss is not limited to direct damage to the property. There may be an indirect loss associated with the "loss of use" of the damaged property. Business interruption insurance provides coverage for the loss of income following the interruption of business operations. Without such income, it would be difficult for a business to continue paying for ongoing expenses, such as payroll expenses. This coverage also provides reimbursement for income that would have been earned by the business had no damage occurred. Business interruption insurance may also cover "extra expenses" that may be incurred following an insured loss. For example, following major fire damage to a building, a business owner may have to secure a temporary location elsewhere in order to continue business operations. Otherwise, the business would stand to lose all of its customers. Business interruption insurance is a critical element of coverage for a business owner's survival following a significant property loss event. Unfortunately, many business owners fail to appreciate the importance of this coverage and consequently fail to add this protection to their property insurance policy.

commercial general liability (CGL) insurance
Coverage for general liability loss exposure, including premises liability, operations liability, product liability, and completed operations liability.

COMMERCIAL GENERAL LIABILITY INSURANCE A *commercial general liability (CGL) insurance* policy is the cornerstone liability policy for small businesses. A CGL policy protects against premises liability, operations liability, product liability, and completed operations liability. Simply put, we live in a litigious society, and small businesses are easy targets for liability lawsuits. A CGL policy provides frontline protection against claims arising from any accident that results either in bodily injury or in property damage and is not otherwise excluded by the policy. It does not cover automobile liability, professional liability, or employer liability, all of which require a separate policy for adequate protection.

A CGL policy also provides for both medical payments coverage and protection against personal and advertising injury liability. The medical expenses of someone who is injured on the company's premises or as a result of its operations are reimbursed through medical payments coverage. The unique feature of this coverage is that it does not require any fault on the part of the business. This "no fault" coverage is intended to build goodwill and prevent someone from then suing the business for negligence. Personal and advertising injury liability protection covers lawsuits alleging intentional torts, such as libel or slander (injury to a person's reputation within the community), false arrest, or malicious prosecution.

automobile insurance
Coverage designed to protect against liability and physical damage to a vehicle resulting from insured perils such as collision, theft, vandalism, hail, and flood.

AUTOMOBILE INSURANCE An *automobile insurance* policy is designed to provide liability protection as well as physical damage coverage as a result of such insured perils as collision, theft, vandalism, hail, and flood. The risk of physical damage to vehicles is much less than the risk of a large liability lawsuit following an at-fault accident. Small business owners may choose to self-insure against the lesser exposure from physical damage but should *not* self-insure when it comes to liability exposure.

workers' compensation insurance
Coverage that provides benefits to employees for medical expenses, loss of wages, and rehabilitation expenses, as well as death benefits for employees' families.

WORKERS' COMPENSATION INSURANCE *Workers' compensation insurance* provides employee benefits in compliance with states' statutes. Generally speaking, these benefits to employees include coverage for medical expenses, loss of wages, and rehabilitation expenses, as well as death benefits for employees' families. The policy also protects the business owner from various types of liability lawsuits that may arise following an injury to or death of an employee.

CRIME INSURANCE While there are different types of crime insurance policies that the small business owner may want to consider, first and foremost is coverage against employee dishonesty. Small businesses are generally very trusting of their employees and would not knowingly have someone working within the organization if they thought that person was dishonest. Unfortunately, not every employee is honest. This fact, combined with the weak financial controls often found in a small business, offers a perfect opportunity for a dishonest employee to embezzle large sums of money. The potential for loss can easily be covered by a *crime insurance* policy at a nominal cost. Premiums vary according to the size of the small business, running from a few hundred dollars up to $2,000 for a $500,000 policy. Because it is possible for an embezzlement scheme to continue for a number of years, significant crime insurance coverage should be obtained.

crime insurance
Coverage against employee dishonesty.

PACKAGE POLICIES Property insurance and commercial general liability insurance can generally be obtained together under a single insurance policy, called a *business owners policy (BOP)*. However, construction-type businesses, manufacturers, financial institutions, or any other businesses with annual revenues in excess of $10 million will frequently not qualify for a BOP. The advantages of a BOP include (a) a lower premium than would otherwise be required to purchase all coverages separately, (b) the automatic inclusion of business interruption insurance, and (c) automatic replacement value protection, as opposed to actual cash value protection.

For businesses that do not qualify for a BOP, property insurance and commercial general liability insurance can be combined together in a *package policy*. The advantages of a package policy include (a) a lower premium than would otherwise be required to purchase all coverages separately, (b) the ease of adding other coverages more economically, (c) the inclusion of business interruption insurance, and (d) the inclusion of crime insurance.

business owners policy (BOP)
A business version of a homeowner's policy, designed to meet the property and general liability insurance needs of some small business owners.

package policy
A policy for small businesses that do not qualify for a BOP that combines property insurance and commercial general liability insurance.

Life and Health Insurance

Three types of insurance provide coverage for employees within a business: health insurance, key-person life insurance, and disability insurance.

HEALTH INSURANCE Also commonly referred to as medical insurance, *health insurance* is one of the most basic and yet valuable benefits that a small business can offer its employees. Provided on a group basis for all employees, typical health insurance policies offer coverage for medical care at hospitals, doctors' offices, and rehabilitation facilities. Outpatient services and prescription drugs are also generally covered by the policies.

Often, coverage is offered to employees only through a specific group of health care providers, or "network." Types of health insurance plans that fall into this category include *health maintenance organizations (HMOs)* and *preferred provider organizations (PPOs)*. An HMO is a managed-care network that provides health insurance that is generally less expensive than a PPO, but it limits employees' choices of medical care providers more than a PPO does. However, with a PPO, employees still must stay within a network of providers or face higher out-of-pocket expenses in the event of a claim.

Out-of-pocket expenses that employees must pay themselves, regardless of the type of health insurance plan provided by the employer, generally include

- A deductible, or "co-pay," at the doctor's office for each office visit; usually between $20 and $40.
- A deductible at the pharmacy for each prescription drug purchased; usually between $10 and $50.

health insurance
Coverage for medical care at hospitals, doctors' offices, and rehabilitation facilities, that usually includes outpatient services and prescription drugs.

health maintenance organization (HMO)
A managed-care network that provides health insurance that is generally less expensive than that of a PPO but limits employees' choices of medical care providers more than a PPO does.

entrepreneurial experiences

Providing Health Care for Your Employees Can Be Frustrating—and Costly

In 2003, Tonya Jones and four of her employees learned they were being dropped from the insurance plan they had been on since the early '80s. Jones knew that finding a new plan would mean paying more, but didn't realize just how much she'd be expected to pay—the first policy she researched would have cost her $700 a month per employee for a total of $3,500.

"The rent for my office is $2,000 a month," explains Jones, who owns Mark IV Enterprises, a Nashville, Tenn.–based construction company. "And they wanted almost double that for health insurance? It's as if all we're working for is health insurance, and that's ridiculous."

©iStockphoto.com/Richard Gerstner

After four years of looking for new coverage and experiencing what she calls "a really rocky roller coaster," she finally found a plan that she could afford. The plan, a PPO, is not as flexible as Jones had hoped, but it was the only plan her company could afford. "I'm just glad it's over," Jones says.

When they lost coverage in 2003, several employees were immediately able to find alternate coverage, either through their spouses plans or on their own (for which Mark IV reimbursed up to $280 a month). But for four years, Jones and two of her employees were uninsured.

"It was a scary place," she said. "I tried to take care of myself, but you never know what could happen. As for my employees, I believe that part of my role is to help them manage their responsibilities for themselves, and not being able to provide health care for everyone really hurts."

Source: Lana Basha, "Handle the Headaches," *MyBusiness,* June–July 2007, pp. 26–29, http://www.mybusinessmag.com/fullstory.php3?sid=1589, accessed April 28, 2009.

---

preferred provider organization (PPO)
A managed-care network that provides health insurance that is generally more expensive than an HMO but offers a broader choice of medical providers.

key-person life insurance
Coverage that provides benefits to a firm upon the death of the firm's key personnel.

- A deductible at the hospital for each hospital admission; usually between $1,000 and $3,000.
- A percentage of the total cost of the health care provided by a hospital; usually between 20 and 30 percent, up to a maximum out-of-pocket cost to the employee of between $3,000 and $5,000.

KEY-PERSON LIFE INSURANCE By carrying *key-person life insurance*, a small business can protect itself against the death of key personnel. Such insurance may be written on an individual or group basis. It is purchased by a firm, with the firm as the sole beneficiary.

Most small business advisors suggest term insurance for key-person life insurance policies, primarily because of lower premiums. How much key-person life insurance to buy is more difficult to decide. Face values of such policies usually begin around $100,000 and may go as high as several million dollars.

DISABILITY INSURANCE One risk that small businesses often do not consider is loss due to the disability of a partner or other key employee of the company. Statistics, however, show that the odds of a person being disabled are much higher than most people think. For example, the Social Security Administration cites studies showing that a 20-year-old worker has a 30 percent chance of being temporarily disabled before retirement age.[4]

The most common type of *disability insurance* provides for the payment of a portion (typically two-thirds) of the disabled person's normal monthly income for a period of time after the disability occurs. However, it protects only the disabled person and not the business. Alternatively, partners can purchase disability buyout insurance. This type of disability insurance protects both partners by guaranteeing that the healthy partner will have enough cash to buy out the disabled partner without draining capital from the business.

Also available is disability insurance that replaces lost revenue because of the disability of a key employee. For example, if a firm's top salesperson, who brings in $5,000 a month, becomes disabled, this coverage will provide up to 125 percent of replacement income for a year or more. This gives the firm time to recruit and train someone else.

Another type of disability insurance is designed to cover fixed overhead expenses, such as rent, utilities, employee salaries, and general office expenses, while an owner or other key employee recuperates. This type of insurance is especially well suited for a sole proprietorship, since the firm would have no income if the owner were unable to work.

There is no question that risk is a part of life, but how you manage it will affect the success of your small business. That's why an understanding of business risks, the basic principles of a sound insurance program, and the various types of business insurance is so important. It can help you deal with many of the uncertainties that you will surely encounter. In fact, you can bet on it . . . but gambling can be risky, too.

disability insurance
Coverage that provides benefits upon the disability of a firm's partner or other key employee.

LOOKING BACK

1. Define business risk and explain its two dimensions.

- Business risk is the possibility of losses associated with the assets and earnings potential of a firm.
- Business risks can be classified into two broad categories: market risk and pure risk.
- Market risk is the uncertainty associated with an investment decision.
- Pure risk exists in a situation where only loss or no loss can occur—there is no potential gain.
- In general, only pure risk is insurable.

2. Identify the basic types of pure risk.

- Pure risks that face any business fall into three groups: property risks, liability risks, and personnel risks.
- Property risks involve potential damage to or loss of real property (e.g., land and buildings) and personal property (e.g., equipment).
- For insurance purposes, property may be valued based on its replacement value or its actual cash value (ACV).
- A peril is defined as a cause of loss, either from naturally occurring events or from the actions of people.

- Property losses are categorized as direct losses, arising from obvious physical damage, or indirect losses, which result from inability to carry on normal operations because of a direct loss to property.
- Liability risks arise from statutory liability, contractual liability, or tort liability.
- Personnel risks, such as premature death, poor health, and insufficient retirement income, directly affect individuals but may indirectly impact the business as well.

3. Describe the steps in the risk management process and explain how risk management can be used in small companies.

- Risk management is concerned with protection of the assets and the earning power of a business against loss.
- The risk management process involves identifying and understanding risks, evaluating the potential severity of risks, selecting methods to manage risk, implementing the decision, and evaluating and reviewing the chosen risk management technique.
- The two ways to manage business risks are risk control and risk financing.

- Risk control is designed to minimize loss through prevention, avoidance, or reduction of risk.
- Risk financing involves transferring the risk to someone else or retaining the risk within the firm.

4. Explain the basic principles used in evaluating an insurance program.

- Three basic principles should be followed in evaluating an insurance program: (1) Identify business risks that can be insured, (2) secure coverage for all major potential losses, and (3) consider the feasibility and affordability of insuring smaller potential losses.
- A firm must first secure risk coverage required by law or by contract. An example of this is workers' compensation insurance.
- Property insurance must cover the full replacement value of a firm's buildings and personal property.
- A company should determine for itself what distinguishes a "smaller" potential loss from a "major" potential loss and then decide if it makes sense to insure against smaller potential losses.

5. Identify the common types of business insurance coverage.

- A property insurance policy is used by a business owner to insure both buildings and personal property owned or leased by the business.

- A decision must be made by the business owner as to whether to insure the firm's property using a named-peril approach or an all-risk approach.
- Business interruption insurance should be given careful consideration as an optional coverage that can be added to the property insurance policy.
- A commercial general liability insurance policy is the cornerstone liability policy for small businesses and protects against premises liability, operations liability, product liability, and completed operations liability.
- An automobile insurance policy is designed to provide liability protection for the business owner arising from the use of vehicles for business purposes as well as physical damage coverage on owned vehicles.
- Workers' compensation insurance provides employee benefits in compliance with states' statutes.
- A small business owner must accept the fact that he or she is vulnerable to the possibility of employee dishonesty and therefore purchase the appropriate crime insurance coverage.
- A small business owner should consider the advantages of purchasing either a business owners policy or a package policy as a way to consolidate coverage at less cost and with broader protection.
- The three types of life and health insurance that provide protection for employees within a business are health insurance, key-person life insurance, and disability insurance.

Key Terms

business risk p. 603
market risk p. 603
pure risk p. 603
real property p. 603
personal property p. 603
replacement value of property p. 604
actual cash value (ACV) p. 604
peril p. 604
direct loss p. 604
indirect loss p. 605
workers' compensation legislation p. 605
indemnification clause p. 606
torts p. 606
reasonable (prudent person) standard p. 606
compensatory damages p. 607
economic damages p. 607
noneconomic damages p. 607

punitive damages p. 607
proximate cause p. 607
manufacturing defect p. 608
design defect p. 608
marketing defect p. 608
personnel risks p. 608
risk management p. 609
risk control p. 611
loss prevention p. 611
loss avoidance p. 611
loss reduction p. 611
risk financing p. 611
risk transfer p. 611
risk retention p. 611
self-insurance p. 611
partially self-funded program p. 611
specific stop loss limit p. 612
aggregate stop loss limit p. 612

named-peril approach p. 615
all-risk approach p. 615
coinsurance clause p. 615
business interruption insurance p. 616
commercial general liability (CGL) insurance p. 616
automobile insurance p. 616
workers' compensation insurance p. 616
crime insurance p. 617
business owners policy (BOP) p. 617
package policy p. 617
health insurance p. 617
health maintenance organization (HMO) p. 617
preferred provider organization (PPO) p. 618
key-person life insurance p. 618
disability insurance p. 619

Discussion Questions

1. Define business risk, and then distinguish between pure risk and market risk.

2. What are the different types of risk that a business may encounter?

3. What are the basic ways to manage risk in a business?

4. Describe the different sources of legal liability.

5. Why would a business owner want to insure against "smaller potential losses"?

6. What are the common types of property and casualty insurance?

7. What are some of the key provisions that should be considered when purchasing property insurance?

8. What are the common types of life and health insurance?

9. Describe a business owners policy. List the advantages of this type of policy, and tell what types of insurance coverage are available with a BOP.

10. What is the purpose of a coinsurance clause, and how does it work?

You Make the Call

SITUATION 1

The Amigo Company manufactures motorized wheelchairs in its Bridgeport, Michigan, plant, under the supervision of Alden Thieme. Alden is the brother of the firm's founder, Allen Thieme. The company has 100 employees and does $10 million in sales a year. Like many other firms, Amigo is faced with increased liability insurance costs. Although Alden is contemplating dropping all coverage, he realizes that the users of the firm's product are individuals who have already suffered physical and emotional pain. Therefore, if an accident occurred and resulted in a liability suit, a jury might be strongly tempted to favor the plaintiff. In fact, the company is currently facing litigation. A woman in an Amigo wheelchair was killed by a car on the street. Because the driver of the car had no insurance, Amigo was sued.

Question 1 Do you agree that the type of customer to whom the Amigo Company sells should influence its decision regarding insurance?

Question 2 In what way, if any, should the outcome of the current litigation affect Amigo's decision about renewing its insurance coverage?

Question 3 What options does Amigo have if it drops all insurance coverage? What is your recommendation?

SITUATION 2

Pansy Ellen Essman is a 48-year-old grandmother who is chairperson of a company that does $5 million in sales each year. Her company, Pansy Ellen Products, Inc., based in Atlanta, Georgia, grew out of a product idea that Essman had as she was bathing her squealing, squirming grand-daughter in the bathroom tub. Her idea was to produce a sponge pillow that would cradle a child in the tub, thus freeing the caretaker's hands to clean the baby. From this initial product, the company expanded its product line to include nursery lamps, baby food organizers, strollers, and hook-on baby seats. Essman has seemingly managed her product mix risk well. However, she is concerned that other sources of business risk may have been ignored or slighted.

Question 1 What types of business risk do you think Essman might have overlooked? Be specific.

Question 2 Would risk retention be a good strategy for this company? Why or why not?

Question 3 What kinds of insurance coverage should this type of company carry?

SITUATION 3

H. Abbe International, owned by Herb Abbe, is a travel agency and freight forwarder located in downtown Minneapolis. When the building that housed the firm's offices suffered damage as a result of arson, the firm was forced to relocate its 2 computers and 11 employees. Moving into the offices of a client, Abbe worked from this temporary location for a month before returning to his regular offices. The disruption cost him about $70,000 in lost business and moving expenses. In addition, he had to lay off four employees.

Question 1 What are the major types of risk faced by a firm such as H. Abbe International? What kind of insurance will cover these risks?

Question 2 What kind of insurance would have helped Abbe cope with the loss resulting from arson? In purchasing this kind of insurance, what questions must be answered about the amount and terms?

Question 3 Would you have recommended that Abbe purchase insurance that would have covered the losses in this case?

Experiential Exercises

1. Log on to *Entrepreneur* magazine's website at http://www.entrepreneur.com and find two articles on new small business startups. Select one new firm that is marketing a product and another that is selling a service. Compare their situations relative to business risks. Report on your analysis to the class.

2. Contact a local small business owner and obtain his or her permission to conduct a risk analysis of the business. Report to the class on the business's situation in regard to risk and what preventive or protective actions you would suggest.

3. Arrange to interview the owner or one of the agents of a local insurance agency. Determine in the interview the various types of coverage the agency offers for small businesses. Write a report on your findings.

Small Business & Entrepreneurship Resource Center

The *Small Business and Entrepreneurship Resource Center* offers complete small business management resources through a comprehensive database that covers all major areas of starting, operating, and maintaining a business from financing, management, marketing, accounting, taxes, and more. Use the access code that came with your new book to access the site and perform the exercises in each chapter.

1. Sambazon, based in San Clemente California, has survived the market risk of large beverage companies following it into the market with a drink using a Brazilian berry called acai. Risk management, in this case, has much to do with the product development process. Describe the three key steps of product development to formulate a winning new beverage, while reducing risk.

2. Health insurance and retirement programs are two fringe benefits that are important to many employees of small businesses. After reading the article "Benefits at risk" describe the current state of insurance and retirement programs for most small businesses. Also describe how many small businesses are dealing with this situation.

Sources: Hit it out of the ballpark: formulating a hit product. (HOW TO: R&D). Heather Landi. *Beverage World* 126, 6 (June 15, 2007): p. 104(3).

Benefits at risk? (Future Focus) (health insurance and retirement benefits in small business). Jennifer Schramm. *HRMagazine* 52, 2 (Feb 2007): p. 152(1).

Video Case 23

PROTECTING INTELLECTUAL PROPERTY (P. 672)

This case explores the definition of intellectual property, its importance to the small firm, and its history.

ALTERNATIVE CASES FOR CHAPTER 23
Case 8, D'Artagnan, p. 638

Nau

> Passion and Creativity Led to a High-Growth Startup That Had to Start Again

In 2005, several individuals with experience in the outdoor clothing industry met at Portland's Urban Grinds coffee shop to sketch out their new retailing concept. Their idea was to combine the eco-friendly and mountain-climbing chic of Patagonia with the fashion-forward urban cool of, say, Prada. Not only would their clothes be practical on the trail, but they would look sleek and hip in the city as well. The firm, to be named Nau (pronounced *now*), would design its own fabrics with new sorts of eco-friendly materials. Even Nau's retail outlets—the business plan called for 150 of them—would be constructed from recycled wood and plastic. The team also decided to donate 5 percent of sales to worthy nonprofit organizations that buyers would choose. The clothes would be pricey, but shoppers would feel good knowing that by buying a $40 T-shirt or a $350 jacket, they would also be supporting a charitable cause.

Chris Van Dyke would be the firm's CEO and Ian Yolles would become its marketing chief. Formerly, Van Dyke and Yolles had worked as marketing executives at Patagonia and Nike, respectively. Mark Galbraith, recently a top Patagonia designer, would be the lead designer for Nau.

The founders' timing was impeccable, or so it appeared. The green movement was in full swing, and a booming economy was giving rise to a sort of mass philanthropic movement. But Nau also had its eye on running a successful business. Stores would be about half the size of typical specialty apparel stores, with tiny inventories, representing a huge cost savings. To make these small stores work, Nau would offer shoppers a 10 percent discount at the register in exchange for Nau's shipping clothes from its warehouse directly to their homes. Customers went wild when the first stores opened in March 2007 in Portland, Oregon; Chicago, Illinois; and Boulder, Colorado.

The founders intended for Nau to be more than merely another clothing company—they wanted to *make meaning* (mentioned in Chapter 1 as one possible reason for starting a business):

We're a small group of people committed to [using] the power of business as a force for change . . . seeking to balance the triple bottom line: people, planet, and profit. We believe that doing good and doing good business are one and the same. We only deserve to exist if our products and our practices are capable of contributing to positive, lasting, and substantive change. Our goal: To demonstrate the highest levels of citizenship in everything we do: product creation, production, labor practices, the way we treat each other, environmental practices, and philanthropy. We believe that companies have a broader responsibility than simply generating profit. That's one reason we're blending profitability and philanthropy, what we believe is the new measure of success.

As an example of Nau's uniqueness, company bylaws prohibited any Nau executive from earning more than 12 times what the lowest-paid U.S. worker earned.

In planning for a successful venture, Nau's management believed that a key factor would be its design philosophy:

We believe great design has enormous power and we're trying to use it to change the world, one sustainable fabric at a time. Our design philosophy is built on the balance of three criteria: beauty, performance, and sustainability. Far from mutually exclusive, the integration of these concepts defines a new standard for apparel. Many people make exceptional clothing that embraces one of those criteria. A select few manage to combine two of the three, at the most exacting levels. As far as we know, no one has made a dedicated effort to integrate all three with unflagging commitment to each.

The Nau team wasted no time ramping up. Among its moves: investing in an IT infrastructure powerful enough to handle $250 million in annual revenue and striking deals with fabric makers in the United States, Hong Kong, and elsewhere in Asia. By 2007, Nau had opened five stores in Portland, Bellevue, Chicago, Boulder, and Los Angeles and had started construction

Sources: http://www.nau.com/about-us/business-unusual/our-goals .html; http://www.inc.com/magazine/20081101/contributors.html; and http://www.entrepreneur.com/localnews/1630478.html, accessed June 1, 2009.

on another four stores. To finance the company's growth, the management raised an amazing $35 million from private investors.

While the company was experiencing phenomenal growth, troubles soon began surfacing. On May 2, 2008, with little, if any, warning, a statement on the company's website announced that the company would be shut down. The announcement read, "Goodbye for Nau," blaming a "highly risk-averse" capital market for the shutdown. "We simply could not raise the necessary funds to continue to move forward," the statement read. "We believe this is not so much a reflection of the viability of our business, but the result of an unfortunate confluence of events." All the stores were closed, and the firm's 95 employees were dismissed.

Nau's leadership had assumed that additional financing would be available for future growth. Then the credit crunch hit. With no recourse to bank financing, the team implored its biggest investors for additional funding. But the investors who had been so generous just a few months earlier were no longer interested in investing more money in the business. "Everyone on the board understood we had gotten in too far to turn around and pare this thing down," says Gomez, then board chairman of Nau. The money was gone. The board voted to close down Nau's stores and suspend all business.

Nau's management was stunned. The day after the closure, Yolles and Galbraith contemplated life after Nau and felt a deep emptiness. "We had poured everything into this," says Yolles. "I just could not believe it would end—and end so quickly." Galbraith looked over his designs and wondered how well they would have sold. "We had only one season to get traction," he says. "If we had just gotten one more season, then we would have been OK."

After the board put Nau into liquidation, Van Dyke organized a buyout effort to acquire the Nau brand and its website. His plan was to relaunch Nau. Yolles and Galbraith, like Van Dyke, also remained committed to seeing the Nau brand and what it represented continue. "We recognized there was incredible value in the product and in the brand," says Yolles.

In addition to Van Dyke's efforts, Yolles and Galbraith set out to find a buyer who would keep the business going. They first went about preserving business relationships. "We called up factories," says Galbraith. "They agreed to hang on for a period of time to see if something could get resurrected." To attract a buyer, they decided they would need to overhaul Nau's business plan, which they realized had been too idealistic and too ambitious. Rather than attempt to ramp up a huge number of stores, they decided that Nau should grow slowly and organically. They also blamed themselves for how they had run the company. They could have gotten into wholesaling. The website could have been stronger. Perhaps they had overextended themselves by offering too many styles. No aspect of the business was left unexamined.

After dozens of inquiries, Yolles and Galbraith got the attention of Gordon Seabury, the CEO of Horny Toad, a large casual-clothing line in Santa Barbara, California. They felt Horny Toad's outdoorsy image could be a good fit for Nau. And they liked linking the Nau brand to the back-office support and infrastructure of a successful apparel maker.

Seabury's initial reaction was lukewarm: "I still wasn't clear about how we could help." But on a visit to Nau's headquarters, Seabury liked what he saw. He offered to purchase Nau, trumping Van Dyke's bid and several other bids. Seabury also agreed to hire Yolles and Galbraith, who would continue in their same positions.

Currently, Nau's line shares Horny Toad's distribution network and is being sold in such stores as Uncle Dan's in Chicago and Paragon in New York.

QUESTIONS

1. What were Nau's founders' primary motivations for founding Nau?

2. What kind of entrepreneurial venture is Nau?

3. How do you feel about management's decision to give a percentage of the firm's sales to charity? Describe the pros and cons of such a decision.

4. Nau's owners think of their clothing line as part Patagonia (http://www.patagonia.com) and part Prada (http://www.prada.com). Review the websites of these two companies. What do you believe Nau's owners saw in Patagonia and Prada that was relevant to their idea for a startup?

5. Describe Nau's competitive advantage.

6. What characteristics of successful entrepreneurs do the founders embody?

7. What mistakes do you believe Nau's management made in executing their strategy?

8. Do you believe it was a wise decision for Nau to partner with Horny Toad? Why or why not?

ACTIVITIES

1. Now that you are familiar with Nau and its history, do some research to determine the latest status of the firm.

2. Go to Nau's website (http://www.nau.com) to find stores that sell its clothing near your location. If you find one, visit the store and interview the manager about Nau's products.

3. Try to set up an interview with one of Nau's founders. The firm's general phone number is 877-454-5628. Draft a set of interview questions that address issues you learned about in Chapter 1. Here are several examples to get you started:

   - When did you get the idea for the business?
   - Why did you want to start this business?
   - What made you take the plunge into entrepreneurship?
   - What obstacles did you encounter while starting the business?
   - What are Nau's competitive advantages?

Many other questions are also possible. Write a brief summary of what you learned during the interview.

Joseph's Lite Cookies

> Integrity Creates a Strong Foundation for Growth

Recall from the video spotlight that opened Chapter 2 that Joseph Semprevivo, a diabetic and founder of Joseph's Lite Cookies, began his entrepreneurial career at the age of 12, when he created and sold gourmet sugar-free ice cream in his family's restaurant. Three years later, when his parents perfected their recipe for a sugar-free cookie for him, Semprevivo decided to expand his business and offer the cookie to diabetics around the country.

From its humble beginnings in 1986, Joseph's Lite Cookies has grown into a business that generates annual sales of over $100 million, producing over 9 billion cookies a year. Although the financial success of the business is impressive, money is not the whole story. What puts Semprevivo's business into the spotlight is the way he runs it—as a team effort, with honesty, integrity, and a commitment to his employees. For instance, when someone joins the Joseph's Lite Cookies team, Semprevivo promises, "You start with me, you can end with me. You can work with me the rest of your life until you retire."

Semprevivo's upbringing strongly influences how he runs his business, which currently employs 26 team members at its New Mexico plant, 12 team members in its Florida offices, and about 1,000 independent sales representatives nationwide. He took to heart the advice of his father, who said, "Son, always ask yourself right before you go to bed, did you give 100 percent that day? And if your answer is ever no, when you wake up the next morning, you give it 100 percent that day." Semprevivo lives out that advice every day, and he decided to make it possible for each of his team members to do the same.

As you read in Chapter 2, an employee may fail in his or her ethical obligation to do "an honest day's work" by loafing on the job or working too slowly. But Semprevivo has found that with the guarantee of a lifetime job, his team members are happy to give 100 percent effort. He has also built in other incentives for employees to give their all, including profit sharing and matching 401(k) contributions. The company matches each dollar a team member contributes to his

or her 401(k) retirement savings account with $2.19—more than any other company on record. Because team members know they will continue to share in the company's success, they have a stake in building Joseph's Lite Cookies into an efficient and profitable operation. As Semprevivo states at the end of the video, "Believe in your team members, give them great benefits, and empower them, and you know what? They'll perform."

Before you answer the questions and work the activities, you will need to watch the video case on Joseph's Lite Cookies. You may also want to review the video spotlight that introduced Chapter 2.

QUESTIONS

1. Based on what you saw in the videos, describe how Semprevivo reveals his underlying values and applies them to building a strong business.

2. Referring to the video and the text, describe the components of a business that constitute a "framework for integrity." Explain how the framework for integrity on which Joseph's Lite Cookies is built may contribute to the company's position in a competitive environment.

3. Review what you learned in Chapter 1 about building an entrepreneurial team and the advantages of doing so. Explain how this relates to the video segment in which Semprevivo says an employee will perform well if *empowered*.

ACTIVITIES

1. Large corporations often have documents outlining ethical guidelines for their employees. Kellogg's, the world's leading producer of cereal and a leading producer of cookies and convenience foods, is one such corporation. At the company's website, http://www .kelloggcompany.com, you will find Kellogg's corporate social responsibility statement and a long list of what it terms "K Values"—written very much like a mission statement. Draft a

Video material provided by Hattie Bryant, Producer of Small Business School, the series on PBS Stations, Worldnet, and the Web at http://www.smallbusinessschool.org.

SmallBusinessSchool
the Series on PBS stations and the Web

Sources: http://www.josephslitecookies.com; April Y. Pennington, "Making Their Mark," Entrepreneur.com, February 15, 2006; http://www.stevieawards.com; and http://www.kelloggcompany.com.

mission/values statement for Joseph's Lite Cookies that reflects what you saw in the videos. (At the time this book was published, there was no such document posted on the Joseph's Lite Cookies website.) Share your work with your classmates or study group partners.

2. Now practice writing a mission/values statement for your own business enterprise. Even if you don't currently have a business concept or plan, you can still organize your thoughts about the values that will guide your future business ventures. How detailed should you be? Dow Chemical's Code of Business Conduct is 35 pages; Nordstrom's fits on a 3 × 5 index card.

3. Once you have written down your own underlying values, consider ways in which you will act on them. You may find the following list of questions a good starting point for thinking about how your business will reflect your personal values:

- Will your business give to charities? If so, how will you select the organizations and groups that will receive donations?
- Will you be involved in the community? If so, how? If not, why not?
- How will you find employees? For example, will your recruitment efforts take into account the disabled, those with low income, minorities, and others in underrepresented groups?
- How will you manage your company's waste? If it costs more to recycle, will you still do so?
- Will you reward employees for their community involvement with non-profit organizations or civic groups? Will you encourage your employees to become active in their community?
- How will you determine pay levels?
- What kinds of benefits will you offer?
- Where will you locate?

Firewire Surfboards

> Positioning a Startup to Compete against Competitors

San Diego–based Firewire Surfboards has blazed a bold new trail in surfing, but it's not clear yet if core enthusiasts will follow. The company was launched in 2005 by co-owner and CEO, Mark Price, who partnered with friends to create wave-riding magic for anyone who wants to "hang ten" with weekend waterdogs or the best of surfers.

Firewire boards are far lighter, stronger, and more flexible than the polyurethane foam–based competition. Although Firewire uses unorthodox and high-tech materials such as bamboo and carbon, the real advances are in the factory, where, over the last two years, Firewire has developed a high-capacity computer-aided process that includes environmentally friendly lamination. The result is a featherweight product that suggests new ways of riding waves. "When Firewire came on the scene, it was a disruptive technology," says Price, a former surfing pro. "It represented a real threat to the entrenched surfboard manufacturing interests."

In fact, the biggest hurdle for Firewire is the past: Surfers prefer their gear old school—custom-shaped to order. Firewire's products come in off-the-rack sizes, but that too is about to change: This fall, the company is introducing its first custom board line.

The made-to-order products will cost a little more than the company's standard $600 sticks, which already come in more than 90 models, from longboard cruisers to shortboard scalpels. Price, 48, notes that an off-the-rack board from Channel Islands (a competitor to Firewire), which he calls the industry's "gold standard," costs $650. The difference, he says, is performance, with Firewire offering flex and maneuverability never seen before. He likens the Firewire board to a racecar you can drive on the street. "You're buying a Formula 1 surfboard here," he says, "and I think that's an important distinction vs. the competition."

This may all sound larger-than-life, but Firewire's capabilities were on display when teen surfing sensation Dusty Payne was awarded $50,000 this spring for winning the Kustom Air Strike best-aerial contest. Payne shot off a wave, spun 360 degrees in the air and landed with nary a hair out of place. The jaw-dropping, skateboarding-style trick, caught on video on the North Shore of Oahu, could shake surfing the way Tony Hawk's two-and-a-half-rotation "900" helped to launch ESPN's X Games into popular culture 10 years ago.

Indeed, Price says, competitive surfing was once about carving the surface of a wave; now the sport is heading "above the lip"—in the air—where skate-style moves are becoming de rigueur for a new generation of riders.

Timing has been on Firewire's side. In 2005, the company's first year in business, a Laguna Niguel, California, concern called Clark Foam, which supplied as much as 90 percent of surfboard-makers' core materials (chemically toxic "foam blanks") shut its doors. Owner Gordon "Grubby" Clark was wary of environmental regulations that he said would invite crippling lawsuits. The loss set off a mad scramble for new sources of foam and new ways of making boards. Surftech, a Santa Cruz, Calif.–based company that peddles Asian-made, plastic-like epoxy boards for beginners, took flight. Firewire is aiming its manufactured boards at daily surfers, a fickle bunch who even Price says "can be very myopic at times." It's another challenge.

"Hardcore surfers, who surf weekly or more, ride boards made for them specifically," says Steve Pezman, publisher of *Surfer's Journal*. "When the performance outweighs the advantages of the custom shape, the manufactured surfboard has a chance to make deep inroads."

Matt Biolos, co-founder and head designer for San Clemente, Calif.–based Lost Surfboards, liked Firewire's products enough to order 250 of them when they debuted. He was denied. Firewire wanted to establish its own name, instead of supplying outside brands. Last year, however, Biolos finally struck a deal to have Firewire make a run of Lost-branded and -designed Firewires. Biolos is a believer, but he says it's hard to get other surfers to convert. "As long as we remain steadfastly spoiled with our ability to order custom surfboards, Firewire will always come in second," says the 40-year-old.

Firewire has a 10,000-foot warehouse in San Diego, but it makes virtually all of its boards in a factory it opened in Thailand in 2007. Price says developing the step-by-step board-making process from months of trial and error was Firewire's most challenging feat. "It was unbelievably torturous, stressful, and expensive," he says.

Source: Dennis Romero, "Surfing's Next Safari," *Entrepreneur*, Vol. 37, No. 7 (July 2009), pp. 24–27.

Its latest line of sticks, Rapidfire, has a core of basic, beer-cooler-type foam. Carbon rods are inlaid at the bottom for flex; the top is lined with gorgeous finished bamboo for strength and stiffness. Vacuum bags are used to bind the inner materials before they're glassed in epoxy.

Price says the process and materials mean his boards are "50 times less toxic and emit 2 percent of the volatile organic compounds found in a traditional polyurethane surfboard."

After riding a Firewire design, marketing manager Chuy Reyna quit his job of 14 years to join the company in 2007. "It's rare to have that much difference in a product," he says. "This marketplace has been saturated with a level playing field of boards. This is so overdue."

The gear has its share of converts, to be sure. The company signed Taj Burrow as its signature rider in 2007, and he rode his Firewire to a No. 2 world ranking that year. And Biolos notes that seasoned professional Shea Lopez has ridden a Lost-branded model and raved about it. "You could buy one and say it's the best board you've ever ridden," Biolos says.

Long Beach Surf Shop on Long Island, N.Y., caters to core city surfers for whom 43-degree water in spring is like a walk in Central Park. The store carries Firewire boards proudly. The gear-maker, says shop owner Luke Hamlet, "is using technology to benefit surfers rather than its own costs."

At the factory in San Diego, boards are lined up like soldiers in marching formation. Price shows off a board that's been sliced into pieces. It's elegant and organized—its stacked materials beckoning like a piece of high-tech layer cake. Performance art rarely comes from a factory, but here it does.

"Materials have always led the advances in surfboards," says Pezman. "If they get into lighter, stronger, more flexible dynamics that make the performance more desirable over hand-shaped boards, then those older boards will be toast."

He says that when foam boards finally took over surfing, it happened in 12 months. "That was 1959." It was the year of *Gidget*. It was the year that Hobie Alter, using Clark's original foam, launched a brand dynasty by churning out easy-to-ride, easy-to-carry longboards. It was 10 years after the invention of the modern surfboard.

QUESTIONS

1. Identify and describe Firewire Surfboard's major competitors. How are these rivals positioned in the marketplace?

2. Put yourself in the role of Firewire's entrepreneurial team at the time of the company's founding. What should they have anticipated in the way of competitor reaction and the response of prospective customers?

3. What is Firewire's core competence? Is it sustainable?

4. Complete a SWOT analysis for the company. Does this analysis reveal any promising future opportunities for Firewire? Will pursuit of those opportunities lead to competitive response by current or potential rivals?

5. What broad-based strategy is Firewire following? Is this the best way to position the company? Why or why not?

6. Given the company's recent shift in strategy, what do you think its major challenges will be?

7. What recommendations would you make to Mark Price, Firewire's CEO, as he thinks about the company and its future?

Mo's Chowder

> An Entrepreneur from Within

Many people find the idea of running a restaurant appealing but lose their motivation at the prospect of creating a business plan, finding investors, navigating legal issues, and juggling the other complexities associated with new startups. For those disheartened by the prospect of such risky undertakings, buying an existing restaurant often seems like a simpler and safer alternative. Still, buying a restaurant is not for the fainthearted. According to a study conducted by H.G. Parsa, a professor in the hospitality program at Ohio State University, 25 percent of restaurants close or change ownership within their first year in business. Over three years, the number rises to 60 percent, a figure that is comparable to cross-industry failure rates cited by the Small Business Administration.

One avenue that might increase your chance of success, as well as your comfort level, is to buy a business in an industry you've worked in for a long time. Better yet, buy the actual business you've worked in for a long time, as Cindy McEntee did.

McEntee is the current owner of Mo's Chowder, a diner chain along the Pacific Northwest coast. McEntee's grandmother, Mohava Neimi, or "Mo," started a neighborhood diner in Newport, Oregon, to support her two growing boys during World War II. Mo chose the diner business because she loved to feed—and socialize with—her neighbors. For years, Mo's Chowder operated as a simple diner, where McEntee grew up working as a dishwasher, waitress, and cook. The evolution of Mo's into the business that would become an Oregon landmark didn't begin until the day McEntee asked her grandmother how much she paid for clams.

Mo confessed that she had no idea. She had been content to use whatever was in the cash register at the end of the day to buy supplies for the next day's menu.

Because McEntee had worked in so many areas of the business, she was starting to see ways to improve the diner's operations. She installed accounting software and food preparation equipment to save time and money. Eventually, Mo and McEntee made plans for McEntee to formally buy the business from her grandmother over time. Mo changed the legal form of the business from a sole proprietorship to a corporation, and McEntee began buying stock in the company through payroll deductions.

Eventually, McEntee was able to buy more locations along the coast with some investment partners. Now a culinary tourist attraction, Mo's has more than 200 employees and $3.5 million in annual revenues, with six store locations and new distribution channels for its chowder. And the company recently won the Oregon Governor's Community Service Award for Restaurants and the National Restaurant Neighbor Award, given out by the National Restaurant Association.

To learn more about what it takes to buy an existing business, watch the video case for Chapter 4 and then answer the questions and work the activities below.

QUESTIONS

1. Which of the advantages of buying an existing business, as explained in the textbook, did McEntee enjoy when she bought her grandmother's diner? Explain.

2. How could an entrepreneur who does not have a stake in an existing family business re-create for himself or herself the advantages McEntee enjoyed?

3. What five features of family firms offer unique advantages? Which of these features did Mo's Chowder possess?

Video material provided by Hattie Bryant, Producer of Small Business School, the series on PBS Stations, Worldnet, and the Web at http://www.smallbusinessschool.org.

Sources: http://www.moschowder.com; Kerry Miller, "The Restaurant-Failure Myth," *BusinessWeek* (Small Business Edition), April 16, 2007, http://www.businessweek.com/smallbiz/content/apr2007/sb20070416_ 296932.htm; http://www.score.org/template_gallery.html; http://www. sba.gov/sbdc; and http://www.startupjournal.com.

ACTIVITIES

Imagine that you have just inherited $500,000 in business capital from an elderly relative who admired your entrepreneurial spirit. The only stipulation in the will is this: You must use the money to buy and run one of the small businesses for sale locally. Also, before the money will be released to you, you must submit a preliminary business plan to the trustees of the estate (your instructor). Finally, you must start the process of buying an existing business immediately or else the inheritance will pass to another likely entrepreneur in the family! How will you start?

1. Local businesses are often advertised for sale in the classifieds of the local paper. You can also find many listings by looking on the *Wall Street Journal*'s online center for entrepreneurs at http://www.startupjournal.com or by conducting a Web search using the key terms "business for sale." Do some preliminary research to see what's available that interests you and select one of those businesses to use in this activity.

2. Once you have identified a company that interests you, find the template "Business Plan for an Established Business" on the SCORE website, at http://www.score. org/template_gallery.html. Fill out page 5, the General Company Description, with all the information that you can gather on your target purchase.

3. When your plan is complete, make sure that you have covered everything by checking your plan against the recommendations of the Small Business Administration at http://www.sba.gov/smallbusinessplanner/start/ buyabusiness/index.html.

W.S. Darley & Co.
> Sustaining Family Connections

On the firm's website, the leaders of W.S. Darley & Co. proudly declare, "We remain a family owned and operated business committed to customer service and our employees." The current CEO, Bill Darley, was seven years old when his father, company founder W.S. Darley, died. Bill's mother might have sold the business then; instead, she selected a nonfamily member to manage the company until Bill was ready to take charge. In 1960, the year he turned 31, Bill Darley accepted responsibility for the family business.

W.S. Darley & Co. provides products and services for fire-fighting and emergency services. The company was founded in 1908 and sold its first fire truck in the 1920s for $690. Today, the company offers thousands of products on a global basis. In recent years, it has sold systems, pumps, and truck bodies and engaged in design services for customers in Australia, Brazil, Indonesia, Saudi Arabia, New Zealand, and many other countries. Most recently, it began investing heavily in the development of water purification and conservation products.

PLANNING FOR SUCCESSION

When Bill Darley was in his 50s, he underwent emergency triple bypass surgery. He treated the experience as a wake-up call for the company. How would W.S. Darley & Co. survive if he died? He recognized that it was time for a succession plan. Bill, his brother Reg, and his sister Pat felt there were at least three candidates in the third generation ready to step into senior management positions: Bill's sons Peter and Paul and Reg's son, Jeff. Each of the three candidates was given the assignment of designing a business plan describing what he would do if he were named president of the company.

Time passed, and it became obvious that Bill could not make the necessary choice. Each candidate seemed to Bill to be essential to the company. He did not want to lose one by showing a preference for another. Finally, he called on the three candidates to decide on a course of action. Should there be a co-presidency? Should they rotate the job among themselves? Or should they pick a single president? All parties recognized the sensitivity of their working relationships and the potential for

a wrong step to not only damage the business, but also literally tear the family apart.

More than two years passed before the brothers and their cousin reached agreement. Paul would serve as president and chief operating officer, while Peter and Jeff would each hold the title of executive vice president and chief operating officer. Although many family businesses look to the first-born son for generational transition, Paul was, in fact, the sixth of Bill's seven children, his fifth son, and the youngest of the three executive committee members being groomed for a leadership role.

BRINGING FAMILY AND BUSINESS TOGETHER

The three COOs worked closely to develop a succession plan to help the company progress and keep other family members informed. Some specific steps that this executive committee took to strengthen the family and business relationship included

- Recruiting independent board members. An example is Steven Rogers, Gund Professor of Entrepreneurship at Northwestern University, who describes the board's responsibilities as looking "at what's in the best interest of the company combined with what's in the best interest of the family. It's not just black and white—there's gray."

- Developing a family constitution and participation plan. These initiatives anticipate disagreements among family members. The family constitution mandates relying on outside professional help in cases of serious disagreements. The participation plan contains the qualifications family members must have before being considered for employment in the firm.

- Creating a family council. The W.S. Darley & Co. family members meet once every other year as a council, usually at a location away from company headquarters. The family constitution was created in council meetings, which also serve to introduce the business to fourth-generation family members. The council is led by a family member who is not part of the COO group.

Sources: Margaret Steen, "Planning a Smooth Succession," *Family Business*, Vol. 20, No. 3 (Summer 2009), pp. 41–44; http://www.darley.com, accessed June 21, 2009.

No one believes that the company has achieved perfection. In fact, focusing on the succession plan distracted the management team from business basics; the company even lost money in the process. Some family members felt the selection process was something of a black box, mysteriously handled by the three COOs. Board meetings are sometimes characterized by serious disagreements.

A major goal of the leaders of W.S. Darley & Co. is to generate sufficient growth to create career paths for members of the fourth generation who want to join the company. According to Paul Darley, "We've really billed ourselves as 'the family business.' That translates into trust, great service, longevity—that's not easily replicable by our competitors."

QUESTIONS

1. Why do you think Bill Darley delegated the selection of his successor to the executive committee? What were some advantages and disadvantages to having the third generation develop their own succession plan?

2. What do you think might have happened to the company if the candidates had decided to rotate the president's job among themselves? What are some of the positives and negatives you would expect as outcomes of such a leadership strategy?

3. How might serious disagreements at the office affect the feelings family members have for each other off the job? What kind of professional outside help would you recommend that the family use for handling serious disagreements?

4. In addition to a procedure for resolving disagreements, what else do you think the family members should have in their constitution? Why?

5. If you were a member of the fourth generation of this family, what would you expect to learn about the company at family council meetings?

Benjapon's
> Raising Capital for a Thai Restaurant

Benjapon Jivasantikarn is planning to start Benjapon's, a Thai restaurant, after graduating from Babson College. To raise the needed capital, Jivasantikarn has prepared a business plan. The executive summary is provided below.

BENJAPON'S EXECUTIVE SUMMARY
The Opportunity

1. Thai food is one of the fastest growing food trends in the U.S. and is rapidly moving into the mainstream.[1]

2. Americans are leading a busier lifestyle and thus rely more on meals outside the home. Restaurants account for 46% of total food dollars spent,[2] up from 44.6% in 1990 and 26.3% in 1960.[3] By 2010, 53% of food dollars will be spent on away-from-home sources.[4]

3. Americans are demanding better quality food and are willing to pay for that quality. As a result, fast food establishments have recently added premium items to their menu. For example, Arby's has a line of "Market Fresh" items;[5] Carl's Jr. offers "The Six-Dollar Burger."[6]

The fast casual segment emerged to meet the demands for better-quality foods at a slightly higher price than that of fast food. Despite the immense popularity of Asian food, and Thai food in particular, the fast casual segment is dominated by cafés/bakeries (Panera Bread, Au Bon Pain) and Mexican (Chipotle Grill, Baja Fresh, Qdoba). In recent years, however, Asian fast casual players have begun to emerge in various regions in the U.S. Such players include Mama Fu's, Nothing but Noodles, and Pei Wei Asian Diner, but are still considered regional players.

Therefore, customers are limited in choices:

- Thai food patrons are currently limited to full-service restaurant options, requiring more time and money than fast food or fast casual options.

- Busy consumers are currently limited to hamburgers, sandwiches, pizzas, and Mexican food, when it comes to fast-served options.

The Company

- *Benjapon's* is a fast casual restaurant serving fresh Thai food, fast, at affordable prices, in a fun and friendly atmosphere. We will open our first location in February 2006, with future plans to grow through franchising.

- The restaurant will be counter-order and table-service with an average ticket price of $8.50. Store hours are from 11 AM to 10 PM, seven days a week. We expect 40% of our business to come from take-out orders.

- Our target customers are urban, 18–35-year-old college students and young working professionals.

- The size of the restaurant will be approximately 1,500 square feet with 50 seats. The first location will be selected from one of the bustling neighborhood squares in the city of Somerville or Cambridge, Massachusetts, due to proximity to the target market.

The Growth Plan

Our plan is to grow via franchising after opening two company-owned stores. We plan to first saturate the Greater Boston Area, and then move toward national expansion via Area Development Agreements. According to our calculations, the city of Boston can support three to five stores, while the Greater Boston Area can support twenty stores.

1. Packaged Facts, Marketresearch.com, 2003.
2. "Restaurant Industry Report," The Freedonia Group, Inc., 2003.
3. "Restaurant Industry Report," Standard and Poor's, 2003.
4. National Restaurant Association.
5. Arby's website: www.arbys.com.
6. Carl's Jr. website: www.carlsjr.com.

The Team

Management Team
Benjapon Jivasantikarn, Founder and Owner—Six years of experience in finance and business incentives at KPMG, a Big Four professional services firm. MBA,

Magna Cum Laude, from Babson College. Douglass Foundation Graduate Business Plan Competition Finalist. Sorensen Award for Entrepreneurial and Academic Excellence.

Zack Noonprasith, General Manager—Six years experience in financial services. Five years experience in restaurant management.

Supranee Siriaphanot, Chef—Over 15 years experience as Thai restaurant owner and chef in the U.S.

Board of Advisors

Rick Hagelstein—Lifelong successful entrepreneur. Founder and CEO of The Minor Group, a marketing, manufacturing, food, property, and hotel development company in Thailand and Asia Pacific. The Minor Food Group is the Thai franchisee of Burger King, Swensen's, Dairy Queen, and Sizzler, and a franchisor of The Pizza Company, which owns 75% of the pizza market in Thailand.

Steve Sabre—Co-founder of Jiffy Lube International and expert in entrepreneurship and franchising.

Hull Martin—Former venture capitalist in the restaurant industry and current advisor to start-up ventures.

The Financials

We estimate an initial required investment of $550,000. The following are our summary financials for a five-year forecast period.

QUESTIONS

1. Is Benjapon's executive summary more of a synopsis or a narrative?

2. If you were an investor, would the executive summary spark your interest in the opportunity? In other words, would you continue reading the business plan for more details?

3. What do you like about this executive summary? What do you dislike?

4. Would you suggest that Jivasantikarn make any changes or additions to the executive summary? If so, what do you suggest?

	Year 1	Year 2	Year 3	Year 4	Year 5
Summary Financials ($)					
# Company-Owned Stores	1	1	2	2	2
# Franchises Sold	—	—	—	3	13
# Franchises in Operations	—	—	—	—	3
Revenue	691,200	881,280	1,977,590	2,293,859	2,874,559
Gross Profit	451,080	601,749	1,380,195	1,623,578	2,122,505
Operating Profit	(110,145)	74,104	129,202	363,687	525,670
Operating Profit Before Depreciation	(72,526)	111,723	204,440	430,592	592,575
Net profits	(138,145)	48,904	81,602	196,068	296,922
Cash	109,784	168,277	561,526	751,112	989,152
Total Equity	(28,179)	20,725	302,327	498,395	795,317
Total Debt	350,000	315,000	595,000	525,000	385,000
Profitability					
Gross Profit/Sales	65.3%	68.3%	69.8%	70.8%	73.8%
Operating Profit/Sales	−15.9%	8.4%	6.5%	15.9%	18.3%
Operating Profit Before Depreciation/Sales	−10.5%	12.7%	10.3%	18.8%	20.6%
Returns					
Return on Assets	−37.1%	12.2%	8.0%	16.8%	21.8%
Return on Equity	490.2%	236.0%	27.0%	39.3%	37.3%
Return on Capital (LT Debt + Equity)	−42.9%	14.6%	9.1%	19.2%	25.2%

Source: Provided by Benjapon Jivasantikarn.

eHarmony

> In the Market for Marriage

You read in Chapter 7 of your textbook that successfully applying the marketing concept to a small business is a two-stage process: (1) identifying the needs of the consumer and (2) satisfying those needs. Dr. Neil Clark Warren, eHarmony's founder and a clinical psychologist for 35 years, believed that his decades of marriage counseling and research could be applied to satisfy a need. Warren explained, "Forty-three percent of all people over 18 in this country are single . . . Most of them have never been around a single really good marriage, but do they want it? Oh my gosh . . . they are so pulling for a good marriage for themselves."

Warren was convinced that the current divorce rate is so high because many couples are ill-matched from the beginning. Compatibility, he argued, is the key to a strong, long-term relationship. Eventually, Warren and his son-in-law, Greg Forgatch, launched a series of seminars based on the principles of his best-selling book, *Finding the Love of Your Life*. By 2000, the team had transitioned their work to the Web and established the first online relationship service—eHarmony.com.

In the video, Forgatch says that finding a mate for life is something that most of us really desire, but that determining how to go about finding the perfect mate is perhaps "one of the largest unmet consumer needs" out there today. Indeed, by 2003, as many as 55 million Americans had visited dating sites on the Internet and were spending more than $300 million on Internet dating services. These numbers proved that people were using the Internet to find dates, but eHarmony was interested in creating more than just another dating service, so the team set out to come up with a means by which people could be screened for compatibility. Warren's team developed an extensive online questionnaire that screens for "29 dimensions of compatibility" and patented the resulting Compatibility Matching System™. The team also targeted a particular market segment—single, serious relationship

seekers, especially women. And unlike the myriad Internet dating services at the time, eHarmony did not allow subscribers to search its database of people. Matches and subsequent invitations to meet occur in a very careful manner, and registered users are given the power to decide if, when, and how they want to share a photograph of themselves.

Online analysts determined that many women are put off by dating services that seem to be based on looks or are poorly screened. eHarmony responded by building into its system an exhaustive questionnaire that casual daters would probably not take the time to fill out. eHarmony then uses the results of the questionnaire to determine a respondent's number of previous marriages, assess psychological health (e.g., depression), and identify other characteristics the company deems too challenging to result in relationship success. eHarmony rejects up to 20 percent of its respondents because they do not meet the criteria for participating in a successful, long-term relationship. Though the policy might seem a bit harsh, it must be working: More than 6,000 marriages are credited to eHarmony so far, and the site has more than six million registered users and 10,000 to 15,000 new users each day.

eHarmony was not an overnight success, however. During its first couple of years, Warren almost gave up. He suggested they refund the money to registered eHarmony users, because they just didn't have enough people in their database to build compatible matches. Forgatch persisted, however, and after spending upward of $10 million on radio advertising and $40 million on television ads, eHarmony began to reach millions of prospective clients. Today, eHarmony is worth approximately $165 million.

Before answering the questions and working the activities, re-read Chapter 7 in your textbook and watch the video on eHarmony.

Video material provided by Hattie Bryant, Producer of Small Business School, the series on PBS Stations, Worldnet, and the Web at http://www.smallbusinessschool.org.

SmallBusinessSchool ▣
the Series on PBS stations and the Web

Sources: http://www.eharmony.com; Neil Clark Warren and Ken Abraham; "Falling in Love for All the Right Reasons: How to Find Your Soul Mate," 2005; and http://www.startup-review.com/blog/eharmony-case-study-offline-advertising-the-key-to-scale.php.

QUESTIONS

1. Describe eHarmony in terms of its bundle of satisfaction.

2. How does eHarmony define its market segment? What strategy or strategies does eHarmony use to target one particular segment?

3. Referring to the video, describe the four parts of eHarmony's winning ad campaign. In what way(s) do you think the ad campaign reveals components of the company's marketing plan?

ACTIVITIES

What entrepreneurs create for a specific market often finds unexpected success with a completely different target market. For example, after becoming discouraged trying to fix broken marriages (his initial target market), Dr. Neil Clark Warren shifted his focus to single people who wanted to find the right person to marry in the first place (his new target market) and found great success.

For this activity, break into groups of three to four students.

1. Working as a team, identify a problem in the university system that presents an opportunity for an entrepreneur—that is, a problem that can be solved by a new product or service. For instance, a common problem in universities is night security; a business opportunity might be a volunteer escort service. Once you have identified the problem, describe the product or service that could solve the problem.

2. Identify a specific target market for your product or service. You may think that college students represent a single target market, but if you think less broadly, you will see that the group "college students" is composed of many subsets of students: international students, returning students, commuting students, part-time and full-time students, and work-study students, as well as segments identified by college attended, major field of study, social group, and so on. Using the discussion of segmentation variables from the chapter, describe your target market segment in great detail. Why did you choose this group?

3. Continue to develop your marketing plan by identifying competitors (present or future), assessing the external business environment, and outlining your distribution, pricing, and promotion plans.

4. Present your plan to the class. Consider creating visual materials to make your presentation more engaging.

D'Artagnan

> The Troubled Partnership
of Ariane Daguin and George Faison

Ariane Daguin was a 20-year-old student from a family of Gascon chefs when she met George Faison, a Texan with a taste for French food. It was 1979, and they were students at Columbia University. They sealed their friendship over rowdy outings to New York City bistros, where they and their friends would pool funds to split a bottle of good wine. That is how their story begins.

When Daguin joined a charcuterie[1] company, she suggested that Faison, who had just completed his MBA, run the operations, which he agreed to do. In 1985, a New York farm announced it would start raising ducks for foie gras. Although foie gras—fattened goose or duck liver—had never been produced in or imported fresh to the United States, Daguin had grown up on the stuff in Gascony, and she and Faison believed Americans would devour it. When the charcuterie owners disagreed, Daguin and Faison decided to start their own foie gras distributorship in New Jersey. They were in their twenties and full of energy, and they named it D'Artagnan, after Alexandre Dumas's musketeer—all for one and one for all.

Daguin and Faison began the business by distributing foie gras and other local farm-raised delicacies to chefs. Soon they were selling prepared products to retailers, too. Their partnership was strong: She knew the food and could talk chefspeak (her father had a renowned restaurant in France), and he ran the business side. And their timing, it turned out, was sublime. Young and influential chefs, trained in the latest techniques, were arriving in New York, and they started signing on with D'Artagnan.

By 1986, the company had sales of $2 million. Those were the golden times, those honeymoon months of late nights and tough work and driving a clanking delivery truck around town. That was when they worked in the same office and propped each other up and argued each other down. It was going to be forever—but there are no guarantees with partnerships, many of which fail to stand the test of time. (For the sake of discussion here, the term *partners* refers to co-owners of a business, whether it's a legal partnership, a limited liability company, or a corporation—in any case, they are people with roughly the same stake in the business.)

In the early years of D'Artagnan, Faison and Daguin, underpaid and subsisting on sample products, took a tag-team approach. When one was begging farms to produce free-range poultry, the other was frantically sorting 12 young chickens for this hotel and 16 rabbits for that restaurant and jumping in the truck to make deliveries at dawn. "There was not one day when one of us did not tell the other, 'I'm quitting,' and the other one would say, 'One more day, okay? Just show up tomorrow morning,'" says Daguin. "[Still,] it was an incredibly good feeling. We felt part of a group of people who were changing the food world." And as chefs learned about the new products D'Artagnan could provide, it almost seemed that business was doubling on a daily basis. As a chef at one exclusive New York restaurant pointed out, "Now we take them for granted, but [D'Artagnan] was one of the first to familiarize American consumers with these products at a very high level of quality."

Delivering that quality required crisis management on the back end. Suppliers were sprinkled all over the country, products would expire if they were in transit too long, and chefs wanted extraordinary quality extraordinarily quickly. Faison and Daguin were together so much that arguments erupted frequently, but they had no choice but to solve them immediately. When resentment lingered, "we would go somewhere else and say, 'Okay. When you did this, I really didn't agree. So I did this because I was [angry],'" says Daguin. Perhaps because they're both straightforward and tough—and they're evenly matched physically at six feet tall—the head-on approach seemed to work.

Their first big argument came after Daguin had a daughter in June of 1988. A single mother, Daguin brought little Alix to the office to care for her, but tending to the baby's needs distracted her from the work at hand. After a couple of months, Faison, visibly upset, sat her down and said he felt she wasn't pulling her weight—and that he should draw more salary for a while. Though disturbed by Faison's attitude, Daguin realized that he had a point. She hadn't been working the way she had been before. She agreed to let him take more salary for the next six months. After that, her daughter could be placed in the care of a nanny.

---

[1]Charcuterie refers to a branch of cooking that is devoted to prepared meat products, including bacon, ham, sausage, terrines, galantines, pâtés, and confit.

Source: Adapted from Stephanie Clifford, "Until Death, or Some Other Sticky Problem, Do Us Part," *Inc. Magazine*, Vol. 28, No. 11 (November 2006), pp. 104–111.

Until 1993, Daguin and Faison were still running the business as informally as they had at the start. Though they had set up the company as a corporation when they launched it, they hadn't established clear roles, which meant they were stepping on each other's toes. Advisors suggested dividing the business into two groups, which they did—Daguin took sales and marketing, and Faison took finance and operations. For the first time, it was obvious who was responsible for what. But it also meant that the partners were now separated physically and some employees were now dealing with only one of the partners. It also meant that Daguin and Faison no longer communicated regularly, which allowed problems to fester.

Around the same time, D'Artagnan's lawyer wisely suggested the parties sign a buy-sell agreement. Buy-sell agreements dictate what happens to a partner's ownership shares if he or she leaves the business. In the form Daguin and Faison chose, if a partner died, the survivor would be offered his or her shares at a determined price. "Initially," Faison says, "the idea was to make sure that if one of us got hit by a truck, we wouldn't have any succession problems." At the same time, Daguin and Faison took out life insurance on each other, so that if one died, the insurance payment would fund the survivor's share purchase. They also included what's known as a shotgun clause. If things go south between partners, the shotgun clause provides a fair price for one partner to buy out the other and a lawsuit-free way for the business to survive. For Daguin and Faison, this would become key.

By 1999, D'Artagnan was continuing to grow, but a Centers for Disease Control and Prevention investigation found that several D'Artagnan items from a single factory tested positive for listeria, a dangerous bacteria. Together, Faison and Daguin handled the problem aggressively and responsibly, but many retailers were angry. And even if they weren't, they needed someone to supply products, and it was five months before D'Artagnan was selling those products again. For the first time, the company lost money—a lot of it.

Hoping to rebuild the company's reputation, Daguin decided that opening a restaurant in New York City (a longtime dream of hers) would help. The company tended to get good press only when it launched new products, she told Faison, and this shifted too much attention to product development. Opening a new restaurant would address that issue and also further establish D'Artagnan's brand among consumers. When Daguin was able to line up outside investors, Faison thought it was an excellent idea—as did reviewers. The *New York Times* awarded D'Artagnan The Rotisserie two stars in July 2001, saying it "has so much personality, it can sell it by the pound."

But seven weeks later, it was September 11. New York's economy plummeted. And a year and a half after that, France opposed the Iraq war and French restaurants were spurned. While Faison spent his days in Newark, where D'Artagnan is headquartered, Daguin was now at the restaurant most afternoons and evenings. They both had had to invest more money than they'd expected, and they began to argue about the venture. Faison believed Daguin had pitched it as a side project, and now he found himself going on sales calls for the main business in her place, since she was at the restaurant all day. "She asked me for help with running the restaurant, and I told her, absolutely not, I had a job," Faison says. Daguin, for her part, thought that while he'd supported the restaurant initially, Faison was now showing up for a meal there twice a year. "We were in this together," she says now. "Why wasn't he in there more?" At the same time, she loved running the restaurant, and "in some ways, if he had been there, maybe we would have fought about things unnecessarily." But the business never came back, and they agreed to close the restaurant at the beginning of 2004.

By that time, though, Faison had come to believe that D'Artagnan's problems extended beyond the restaurant. Disagreements started to erupt between Daguin and Faison over matters such as incentive systems for company employees, minimum order sizes, and the number of delivery routes that should be run. In November 2004, a competitor offered to buy D'Artagnan, but the partners rejected the offer, and Daguin assumed the talk of selling was over. "After that, he didn't talk about it anymore. I should have smelled something, but I didn't. I really didn't," she says.

In reality, Faison was warming to the notion of selling. "I did not tell her," he says, "because I felt there was really no respect for the directions we had previously discussed. At that point, it was moot." The problems he'd outlined—which he thought Daguin had pledged to fix—remained, and Faison was convinced that the business should be more profitable. But, as one D'Artagnan executive observed, "[That] wasn't going to happen with the two of them running the business at odds with each other."

The rift spread to the employees. When chefs rejected items, Faison's truck drivers wouldn't alert Daguin's salespeople about the issue. Or a salesperson, deciding warehouse workers were disregarding her specs, would pluck a rack of lamb from the shelves herself. Faison used to ask to sit in on Daguin's operations meetings, but she stopped going, finding his temper too unpredictable and the meetings pointless. "The company was splitting in two, and nothing was getting done," she says. Employees could see the problems growing. "There was a dividing line," says Kris Kelleher, who, as purchasing director, would sit in on meetings with Daguin and Faison and marvel at the consistently different directions they sought. "Sometimes I wondered why it was one company." Something had to give.

On June 16, 2005, Faison walked into Daguin's office and handed her a certified letter. She read it, then stared at him, flabbergasted. He was exercising the shotgun clause and offering to buy the company for several million dollars. By the rules they'd agreed to, she had two choices: She had 30 days to sell her shares or buy his shares at the price he'd offered, with another 30 days to raise the money. There could be no negotiating. "It was—wow. I never saw this coming," she says. "And then it was all kinds of feelings: How dare he? How could he do that?" But Faison believed Daguin had stopped listening to him and was wrong about the direction of the company. He felt he was at a dead end.

Daguin retreated to a friend's beach house to consider her options. She thought about taking the money and opening a seaside restaurant. But when her now 17-year-old daughter mentioned that she might like to join D'Artagnan someday, Daguin decided, "All right. Let's go fight." She cold-called banks, which wanted a stake in the company, until a friend helped arrange a loan at a French bank. It required higher interest payments and a personal guaranty, but it didn't want shares of D'Artagnan. With that loan and personal savings, Daguin matched Faison's price. She presented her counterproposal to the surprised Faison, and the deal closed a month later. It was a very frosty finish to their 26-year relationship, and the two have barely spoken since the dissolution of their partnership. "We talked with two voices before, and it's not good for [the company's] well-being," Daguin said. "Now we're going to talk with one voice."

And that is how their story ends. As for Faison, he now has a nice check and is considering his next move;

his noncompete expired in August of 2006. "I learned that my identity is not what I do for work," he says, "and if I hadn't had the opportunity to reflect on that, I might never have gotten that gift."

QUESTIONS

1. How would you describe the entrepreneurial team of Daguin and Faison? Was it ever a balanced team? What did each member bring to the business? Can you see gaps in their skills and capabilities that should have been covered in some way?

2. What does this case reveal about the critical factors that can determine the success or failure of a business that is led by more than a single entrepreneur? What was "the beginning of the end" for Daguin and Faison's working relationship?

3. What form of organization did Daguin and Faison choose for D'Artagnan? Assess the advantages and disadvantages of the major organizational forms mentioned in Chapter 8 and decide which one would have been the best choice for D'Artagnan.

4. Would a formal board of directors have made a difference in the relationship between Daguin and Faison and the operation of D'Artagnan? Draw up a profile of an ideal board for the company.

Le Travel Store

> Moving with the Times

From the casual beachfront store to the glitzy urban shopping mall to the big-box retail model (selling more for less), Bill and Joan Keller have successfully adapted the location of their travel business, Le Travel Store, to match the expectations of their customers. Even as the location changed and the business evolved, however, the Kellers have continued to indulge their original passion for independent travel.

The Kellers started Le Travel Store in 1976 in a beachfront store near San Diego. They used $3,000 in wedding presents to rent a storefront, from which they sold charter flights, rail passes, travel books, and other items for the budget-conscious international traveler. In their first year, while Joan continued to work full-time at a bank, the couple set themselves the goal of selling 300 flights to Europe; they managed to sell 328, and the business survived. Thirty years later, Le Travel Store is in its third location.

The Kellers' decisions to change location were, in part, prompted by changes in their target market. The first customers of Le Travel Store were students, who would pull up to the store in beat-up Volkswagen bugs and vans. Over time, Bill began to notice those same customers pulling up in Volvo sedans or station wagons. These customers now had less time but more money to spend. They were taking shorter trips and staying in better hotels. The customers no longer needed—or wanted—budget travel materials (think *Europe on $20 a Day*). The Kellers decided to adapt to this changing business model and move off the beachfront property

into a new development, Horton Plaza shopping center, which was part of the city's revitalization plan for the San Diego downtown area.

As exciting as the Horton Plaza location was, Joan calculated that the Kellers had paid a million dollars in rent over the 10-year term of the lease. For that kind of money, they could own a building. With an SBA loan, they purchased a 10,000-square-foot building in a historic district that soon became energized with retail ventures. Having realized the potential for growth and revenue in the new setting, the Kellers now invest their profits back into the building. Joan calls the excitement surrounding the re-growth of historic city centers as ideal places for business "the wave of the future."

Before answering the questions and working the activities, re-read Chapter 9 in your textbook and watch the video on Le Travel Store.

QUESTIONS

1. Review the five key factors in selecting a good business location. Which of those factors guided the Kellers' choice for the site of the original Le Travel Store? Explain.

2. Referring to the video, determine which factor or combination of factors the Kellers seem most excited about in their newest location. Recall how the text describes the importance of a building's "image." Describe how each of the Kellers' locations reflects the evolution of their business plan.

Video material provided by Hattie Bryant, Producer of Small Business School, the series on PBS Stations, Worldnet, and the Web at http://www.smallbusinessschool.org.

SmallBusinessSchool
the Series on PBS stations and the Web

Sources: http://www.letravelstore.com; and Karen Spaeder, "How to Find the Best Location," Entrepreneur.com, accessed June 5, 2007.

ACTIVITY

Many successful entrepreneurs got their start working out of their garage, basement, or home office. But part of what made those entrepreneurs successful was their ability to visualize and plan for growth. In essence, the company had to grow up and move away from home.

Imagine your start-up business is ready to move out of the house. (Give your business idea some shape—for example, consider what you're going to sell.) Review local or regional newspapers or real estate websites for business properties for sale. Choose two properties and analyze the advantages and disadvantages of buying each for your startup venture. Then make your final selection.

- What were the three most important criteria you used when deciding where to locate your company? Why?

- What were the three least important criteria you used? Why?

- Write a brief paragraph about the advantages and disadvantages each location offers your business and why you ultimately selected the location you did.

Understanding Financial Statements, Part 1

> Measure Your Growth in Real Numbers

As an entrepreneur, you won't know whether your business venture is economically feasible without a good understanding of financial statements. That's because your financial statements allow you to forecast your business venture's profits, its asset and financing requirements, and its cash flow—all critical elements in determining the profitability of your business.

In the video segment, you'll meet Jim Schell, business owner, author, and small business advisor. He says that if you ask an entrepreneur "How's business?" he or she invariably says, "Sales are up." He never hears the response "I made a return on sales of 10 percent." Schell's goal as an advisor is to get small business owners to measure their results in real numbers, and to know those numbers, the small business owner must know the company's financials.

After years of observing and consulting, Schell realized that the majority of small business owners do not understand how to properly use their financial statements to manage and grow their business. He says the typical small business owner thinks that his or her greatest opportunities for improvement are in the day-to-day management of the business, such as dealing with employees or marketing the product or service. Few, if any, will mention learning how to use financial statements. Bankers, CPAs, and business consultants have a different perspective: they all agree that the small business owner's number one opportunity to improve day-to-day management is to learn how to better utilize the information in the company's financial statements. Having a certain level of financial literacy allows an entrepreneur to spot potential problems in the company and work more intelligently with his or her financial advisors.

Does having money in your checking account mean your business is profitable? Do you have a clear understanding of the difference between profit and cash? Which financial statement allows you to keep an eye on the financial trends of your business? You learn in this video segment that Schell wrote a book, entitled *Understanding Your Financial Statements,* to help small business owners. In the book, Schell starts with the basics: selecting a CPA, working with your banker, using your balance sheet to determine your business's solvency, using your profit and loss statement to manage your business's direction, understanding the concept of cash flow, and so on. The exercises below are designed to help you start thinking about, and practicing, the basics of finance.

Before answering the questions and working the activities, watch the video entitled "Understanding Financial Statements, Part 1."

QUESTIONS

1. In the video, what three things does Schell say the small business owner must do to make a positive impact on his or her company's profitability? Why does Schell think that understanding the relationship among those three things is so important? How does gross margin differ from gross profit?

2. What does Schell advise Nani to do to improve her company's gross margin? Given what you learned in the text about the four variables on which net income is dependent, do you think that advice is sound? Explain.

3. What are the three parts of a financial statement? How does each part serve as a snapshot of your business in time? Create a diagram of a basic balance sheet, using the explanation and example Schell gives in the video.

Video material provided by Hattie Bryant, Producer of Small Business School, the series on PBS Stations, Worldnet, and the Web at http://www.smallbusinessschool.org.

 **SmallBusinessSchool**
the Series on PBS stations and the Web

Sources: Jim Schell, "Understanding Your Financial Statements," *Visuality,* 2002, http://www.opp-knocks.org/Order_Our_Book, accessed June 12, 2007; Pam Newman, "Financial Fundamentals," April 10, 2006, Entrepreneur.com, accessed June 13, 2007; and Financial Ratio Worksheets, http://www.inc.com/tools/2000/10/20612.html, accessed June 13, 2007.

ACTIVITIES

1. Imagine that you are the finance person in your small business but, unfortunately, you don't have any accounting experience. Since you are expected to fill the role of the company's accountant, you need to purchase some accounting software. An online retailer lists the following accounting software as its top-rated sellers: MYOB Premier Accounting Small Business Suite 2007, QuickBooks Simple Start 2007, Microsoft Office Accounting Express, Timeslips 2007, and Microsoft Office Accounting 2007. Which software will you choose and why? Be prepared to share your decision with the class.

2. You've just watched the video segment and are determined to start watching your company's financial trends. You decide to build a spreadsheet to help monitor changes between the most recent month's findings and the previous month's results, which will let you set monthly goals. You know the spreadsheet will also help you write your annual business plan and make strategies for the future. You can find an excellent two-page spreadsheet for download on *Inc. Magazine's* website at http://www.inc.com/tools/2000/10/20612.html (free with registration at inc.com), or you can build your own spreadsheet with examples found in Chapter 10. Print out the spreadsheet, with the real or imaginary name of your company as its title.

3. Most business advisors insist that an entrepreneur acquire at least basic financial skills before starting a business. As your business grows, you may need someone, such as a CPA, with the qualifications to advise you on your business finances and to prepare your income and payroll tax returns. Visit the website of the American Institute of Certified Public Accountants to learn more about CPAs and accounting regulations (http://www. aicpa. org/MediaCenter/FAQs.htm#aicpa_answer12). Summarize the answers to the following questions in a one-page report.

   a. What are the requirements for becoming a CPA?

   b. What is the FASB?

   c. What are GAAP, and who determines them?

Understanding Financial Statements, Part 2

> Create a Key Indicator Report

A common problem area for many business managers is a lack of understanding of financial statements. As you learned in Chapter 10, the three major financial statements include the income statement, the balance sheet, and the cash flow statement. These three financial statements provide the structure for your planning efforts. If used properly, they act as a budgeting tool, an early warning system, a problem identifier, and a solution generator. You'll learn in this video segment that keeping track of your business's finances should be a priority for you as business owner, but it also should be the job of everyone who works with you and for you.

The best way to make that possible is to encourage everyone in your company to read, understand, and act on your monthly financial statements. Jim Schell, business consultant and the author of the book *Understanding Your Financial Statements,* says that successful business owners share their financial information with partners and employees—giving everyone accountability through what he calls "key indicators" in the company's financial statements.

Once they are made partially responsible for tracking and interpreting the firm's key indicators, a company's employees, advisors, bankers, and advocates are often inspired with ideas on how to save money and focus attention on emerging business trends and directions. Likewise, you, as the business owner and manager, will be better positioned to plan profitable strategies, make better business decisions, and set reasonable objectives for the future. In the video, Jim Schell says, "When a business owner gets to the point where his favorite day is the day his financials come out—or even better than that, his favorite day of the month is the day he can push the button on his software and out will kick a preliminary income statement—then you know you've arrived at the point where financial statements are meaningful to you. When you know that, you get it—that it's all about numbers."

Before answering the questions and working the activities, watch the video case for Chapter 23, entitled Understanding Financial Statements, Part 2.

QUESTIONS

1. Based on what you learned in the video, tell where in a company's financial statements you would find each of the 11 key indicators suggested by Jim Schell. What is the purpose of a key indicator report?

2. What are the four questions you learned in Chapter 23 that can be used to evaluate a firm's financial performance? How are these questions best answered? What relationship do you see between the answers to the questions and the key indicators you defined above?

3. What is an internal control system? How do you think a company can implement effective internal controls and also include employees and partners in the management of the company's financials?

Video material provided by Hattie Bryant, Producer of Small Business School, the series on PBS Stations, Worldnet, and the Web at http://www.smallbusinessschool.org.

Small**BusinessSchool** ▣
the Series on PBS stations and the Web

Sources: http://www.microsoft.com/smallbusiness/hub.mspx, accessed June 15, 2007; Karen Berman and Joseph Knight "Unlock The Secret to a Better Banking Relationship with These 4 Strategies," Business Literacy Institute; and Pam Newman, "The Ins and Outs of Cash Flow Statements," http://www.entrepreneur.com/money/moneymanagement/financialmanagementcolumnist-pamnewman/article178302.html.

Missouri Solvents

> Financial Forecasting

Missouri Solvents is a regional distributor of liquid and dry chemicals, headquartered in St. Louis. The company has been serving the St. Louis market for 10 years and has a reputation as a reliable supplier of industrial chemicals.

CHEMICAL DISTRIBUTION

A chemical distributor is a wholesaler. Operations may vary, but a typical distributor purchases chemicals in large quantities (in bulk, by railcar load or truckload) from a number of manufacturers. Bulk chemicals are stored in "tank farms," a number of tanks located in an area surrounded by dikes, while packaged chemicals are stored in a warehouse. Other distributor activities include blending, repackaging, and shipping in smaller quantities (for example, tote tanks, 55-gallon drums, and other smaller package sizes) to meet the needs of a variety of industrial users. In addition to the tank farm and warehouse, a distributor needs access to specialized delivery equipment (specialized truck transports and tank railcars) to meet the handling requirements of different chemicals. A distributor adds value by supplying its customers with the chemicals they need, in the quantities they desire, when they need them. This requires maintaining a sizable inventory and operating efficiently. Distributors usually operate on very thin profit margins.

THE SITUATION

Missouri Solvents is 10 years old, and sales and profits have continued to grow rapidly. The growth in sales has required the acquisition of additional fixed assets (warehouse expansion and material handling machinery and equipment) and current assets (accounts receivable and inventory). While the company ended last year with a healthy cash balance, on several occasions during the year it was necessary to obtain short-term bank loans to keep the company operating. Financing the additional assets has also been a challenge and placed a strain on the firm's ability to raise capital. Over the past three years, the company's debt ratio has increased from 51 percent to 57 percent.

To anticipate cash flows throughout the year, Ron Wilson, the founder and CEO of Missouri Solvents, has prepared a monthly cash budget for 2009. Assumptions are focused on the timing of cash inflow (collection of receivables) and cash outflow (payment of vendors,

operating expenses, capital expenditures, financing charges, tax payments, etc.). The cash budget indicated that the company would need additional cash (additional financing) during the second quarter (April, May, and June) of approximately $2,000,000.

Wilson is also concerned about the company's increasing use of debt financing. As a result, he is reluctant to increase the firm's bank borrowing, even for a short period of time. The other alternatives he considered were

1. *Reducing inventory levels.* Wilson thought this might be possible, given that the firm had an ongoing program to systematically review inventory levels of all items and levels were slowly being reduced.

2. *Attempting to collect accounts receivable faster.* Missouri Solvents' selling terms are net 30. Thus, it might be possible to increase credit standards and collection efforts, but this could not be accomplished without some resistance from the sales staff. The sales force already feels that they are losing sales because of a conservative approach to granting credit and an overly aggressive collection effort.

3. *Postponing capital expenditures scheduled for the first half of the year to the second half.* Wilson feels this is possible, but it would require reworking the entire financial plan because the projected benefits of the capital expenditures for the first half of the year were included in the sales forecast for the last six months of the year.

4. *Slowing down the repayment of the bank debt.* Wilson thought that delayed payments to the bank could be arranged, but he was reluctant to approach the bank. Doing so could cause the bank to be concerned about the firm's ability to manage its cash.

5. *Slowing payments to vendors (accounts payable).* During the first two years of operation, the company was not always able to pay its vendors according to terms. The paying of an invoice after the due date resulted in some vendors threatening to stop extending credit to Missouri Solvents. This never happened, but the lack of vendor credit would have caused substantial problems. Since that period, a

concerted effort has been made to avoid late payments to vendors. However, Wilson thinks that slowing vendor payments for a few months is possible, and that vendors would likely not notice a change in Missouri Solvents' payment pattern.

Income statements and balance sheets for Missouri Solvents (historical and projected) are provided in Exhibit C11-1. Selected industry average financial ratios are provided in Exhibit C11-2.

C11-1

EXHIBIT

Appendix 1

Missouri Solvents
Income Statement ($000)

For the Year Ended December 31, 2009	2007	2008	2009	Projected 2010	Industry Average 2009
Sales revenue	$ 67,700,000	$ 79,200,000	$ 89,200,000	$ 99,200,000	$ 100,000,000
Loss: Cost of goods sold	59,400,000	70,100,000	79,100,000	87,700,000	87,000,000
Gross profits	$ 8,300,000	$ 9,100,000	$ 10,100,000	$ 11,500,000	$ 13,000,000
Less: Operating expenses					
Selling expense	3,100,000	3,280,000	3,480,000	3,880,000	3,500,000
General and administrative expenses	1,700,000	1,825,000	2,025,000	2,325,000	2,400,000
Depreciation expense	1,150,000	1,550,000	1,750,000	2,050,000	2,000,000
Total operating expense	$ 5,950,000	$ 6,655,000	$ 7,255,000	$ 8,255,000	$ 7,900,000
Operating profits	$ 2,350,000	$ 2,445,000	$ 2,845,000	$ 3,245,000	$ 5,100,000
Less: Interest expense	855,000	895,000	925,000	1,025,000	700,000
Net profits before taxes	$ 1,495,000	$ 1,550,000	$ 1,920,000	$ 2,220,000	$ 4,400,000
Less: Taxes (rate = 40%)	598,000	620,000	768,000	888,000	1,760,000
Net profits after taxes	$ 897,000	$ 930,000	$ 1,152,000	$ 1,332,000	$ 2,640,000
Dividends	100,000	100,000	100,000	100,000	400,000

Balance Sheet ($000)
As of December 31, 2009

Assets	2007	2008	2009	Projected 2010	Industry Average 2009
Current assets					
Cash	$ 220,000	$ 215,000	$ 265,000	$ 190,000	$ 400,000
Accounts receivable	7,555,000	8,575,000	9,615,000	10,275,000	12,000,000
Inventories	8,825,000	9,982,000	11,082,000	10,992,000	12,000,000
Total current assets	$ 16,600,000	$ 18,772,000	$ 20,962,000	$ 21,457,000	$ 24,400,000
Gross fixed assets	32,650,000	34,800,000	40,100,000	47,800,000	35,000,000
Less: Accumulated depreciation	18,375,000	19,925,000	21,675,000	23,725,000	18,000,000
Net fixed assets	$ 14,275,000	$ 14,875,000	$ 18,425,000	$ 24,075,000	$ 17,000,000
Total assets	$ 30,875,000	$ 33,647,000	$ 39,387,000	$ 45,532,000	$ 41,400,000

(continues)

EXHIBIT

Liabilities and Stockholders' Equity	2007	2008	2009	Projected 2010	Industry Average 2009
Current liabilities					
Accounts payable	$ 5,130,000	$ 6,100,000	$ 6,500,000	$ 6,500,000	$ 8,500,000
Notes payable	2,210,000	2,270,000	2,870,000	2,070,000	2,700,000
Accruals	560,000	412,000	470,000	666,000	700,000
Total current liabilities	$ 7,900,000	$ 8,782,000	$ 9,840,000	$ 9,236,000	$ 11,900,000
Long-term debts	7,875,000	8,935,000	12,565,000	18,082,000	9,000,000
Total liabilities	$ 15,775,000	$ 17,717,000	$ 22,405,000	$ 27,318,000	$ 20,900,000
Stockholders' equity					
Common stock (at par)	7,200,000	7,200,000	7,200,000	7,200,000	8,500,000
Retained earnings	$ 7,900,000	8,730,000	9,782,000	11,014,000	12,000,000
Total stockholders' equity	$ 15,100,000	$ 15,930,000	$ 16,982,000	$ 18,214,000	$ 20,500,000
Total liabilities and stockholders' equity	$ 30,875,000	$ 33,647,000	$ 39,387,000	$ 45,532,000	$ 41,400,000

C11-2

EXHIBIT

Ratio	Industry Average 2009
Current ratio[1]	2.05
Inventory turnover (times)[2]	8.33
Accounts receivable turnover[3]	8.45
Fixed (net) asset turnover (times)[4]	5.88
Total asset turnover (times)[5]	2.42
Accounts payable turnover[6]	10.39
Debt ratio[7]	50.48%
Gross profit margin[8]	13.00%
Operating profit margin[9]	5.10%
Return on assets[10]	6.38%
Return on equity[11]	12.88%

QUESTIONS

1. Prepare a statement of cash flows for the 2010 projections, which will require you to use the projected 2010 income statement and the changes from 2009 to the projected 2010 balance sheet.

2. Prepare a report evaluating the alternatives and recommending a course of action. Use ratio analysis to support your evaluations and recommendation.

3. Would your recommendation change if the projected cash shortfall was for six or nine months rather than three months?

4. Is it ethical to delay payments to vendors beyond the agreed-on terms?

[1] Current assets/current liabilities
[2] Cost of goods sold/inventory
[3] Sales/accounts receivable
[4] Sales/net fixed assets
[5] Sales/total assets
[6] Cost of goods sold/accounts payable
[7] Total debt/total assets
[8] Gross profits/sales
[9] Operating profits/sales
[10] Operating profits/total assets
[11] Net profits/stockholder's equity

Source: Adapted from David A. Kunz and Rebecca Summary, "Missouri Solvent: Managing Cash Flows," *2008 Proceedings of the International Academy for Case Studies,* Vol. 15, No. 1, Allied Academies International Conference, pp. 25–30.

My Own Money

> Finding Sources for Funding

Entrepreneurs often want to the know the answer to the question "Where do I find money to start or grow my business?" Initially, most depend on their own money—personal assets, earnings retained from their business, or a creative mix of the two types of personal funding. This kind of self-funding, or internal financing, is commonly called MOM, or "My Own Money." In this video segment, you'll learn that one entrepreneur sold his home and invested almost every dime from the sale back into his business, sharply cutting his living expenses. Another entrepreneur quit his job, sold his home, and lived in the Australian outback in order to take the photos that would become his sole asset. When he's asked how he started his business, he says he just "knocked on doors" until he found a buyer. A pair of entrepreneurs closed out their profit-sharing plans to invest in their start-up venture. These entrepreneurs relied heavily on investments they had made earlier in life: equity from their home and savings. Others started with even less: One entrepreneur started with nothing more than the proceeds from an insurance policy, and another worked the night shift for 10 years while running his startup during the day.

As you read in Chapters 10 and 11, bootstrap financing is a resourceful way to come up with the capital to finance a startup. Bootstrap financing is one of the most popular forms of self-financing, or using MOM. In bootstrap financing, the entrepreneur must utilize all of the company's resources to free the capital needed to meet operational needs or expand the business. By managing his or her finances better, the entrepreneur can finance the growth of the startup with its current earnings and assets, eliminating—or at least delaying—the need to go after outside sources of funding. Types of bootstrap financing mentioned in the text include trade credit and factoring.

Trade credit, or accounts payable, involves getting your supplier to extend credit to you, interest free, for 30, 60, or even 90 days. Usually a supplier won't extend

credit to a new account until it proves reliable, but entrepreneurs with sound financial plans can sometimes talk suppliers into extending credit on their first orders to allow them to launch their business. Factoring is a type of asset-based loan in which you sell your accounts receivable to a buyer to raise capital. A "factor," such as a commercial finance company, buys your accounts receivable at a discount rate and becomes the creditor and collector of the receivables. Numerous other options that can be considered bootstrap financing include operating your business from home, accepting credit card payments, drop-shipping products, obtaining advance deposits and retainers from your customers, licensing your invention for royalties, aggressively controlling costs, bartering, getting extended terms from suppliers, establishing strict credit and collection policies and procedures, renting or leasing equipment instead of buying, buying used equipment instead of new, selling off excess inventory and equipment, and obtaining free publicity instead of paying for advertising.

If an entrepreneur decides to widen the net beyond using MOM, he or she may tap into OPM, or "Other People's Money." Entrepreneurs featured in this video borrowed money from parents, secured financing from a business for sale by owner, and found an established business owner who was willing to cosign on a loan from a bank. One entrepreneur was frustrated that he couldn't secure a loan because he didn't have enough experience in the type of business he wanted to launch. Eventually, he and his partner started to work with an attorney who, as it turned out, served as a board member at a bank and was willing to put in a good word for them with the bank. Financing with OPM seems to work best when entrepreneurs have the support of someone who knows them, has the means to provide financial support, and is convinced of the worth of the business plan.

Before answering the questions and working the activities, re-read Chapter 11 and watch the video entitled "My Own Money."

Video material provided by Hattie Bryant, Producer of Small Business School, the series on PBS Stations, Worldnet, and the Web at http://www.smallbusinessschool.org.

Sources: Michael S. Malone, "John Doerr's Startup Manual," February 1997; and Garage Technology Ventures, "Writing a Compelling Executive Summary," http://www.garage.com/resources/writingexecsum.shtml.

QUESTIONS

1. Why would an entrepreneur choose MOM over OPM, and vice versa?

2. What is bootstrap financing, and why is it popular with entrepreneurs?

3. Why do you think investors expect an entrepreneur to have some "skin in the game"? What kinds of sacrifices did the featured entrepreneurs make to fund their business ventures?

4. What evidence of networking did you see in the video segment? How were those networks established? How did networking and other relationships benefit the entrepreneurs?

ACTIVITIES

1. Arrange for an interview with the owner of a start-up business in your community. Ask the following questions, and share your results with the class.

   ■ How did you decide to start [business name], and how did you get funding to get it off the ground?

   ■ How does [business name] make money, and where do you see your growth coming from in the future?

   ■ What is the most important thing you've learned in the course of developing [business name]?

   ■ What advice would you give to other entrepreneurs who want to start their own company?

   ■ What are your thoughts on the following quote by John Doerr, a venture capitalist? *If you focus on success, you won't get there. If you focus on contribution and customer value, then you can win.*

2. Imagine you're just stepping into an elevator in the hotel that is hosting a seminar you're attending: "Funding for Continued Growth: Investors Meet One on One with Entrepreneurs." The venture capitalist whom you really, really wanted to talk to about your business venture gets in at the same time. You have about 20 seconds to make a good impression. "Thank goodness for Jay," you think. Jay, a friend who runs an animal training center, always begins business introductions by saying, "Hi, I'm Jay Doe. I help pet owners raise likeable pets. I work with people who want

to avoid letting bad behaviors come between them and their friends, but don't know where to start. As a result of working with me, my clients say they enjoy their pets so much more." Jay encouraged you to plan out a 15-second introduction of yourself and your company before coming to the event. You take a semi-deep breath and start, "Hello, my name is . . . .

Write a creative elevator speech of your own to share with the class. To get started, follow the three steps below. A template has also been provided.

Step 1. Get someone's attention. Say who you are and what you can do for others (not what you do). Get the person to think, "How do you do that?"

Step 2. Tell the person about your deliverables. Explain what your product or service provides.

Step 3. Explain the benefits of your product or service.

"I'm the [occupation/line of work you're in] who [grab their attention—think up a "hook" for your line of work]. I specialize in [action verb followed by your deliverables] for the [target market]. I help [audience types] [benefits]."

3. Jay also encouraged you to have a business plan ready; yours is 30 pages. The venture capitalist you just met in the elevator gave you her business card, but she asked you to send over only your executive summary. She's going to review it and then call to arrange a time to meet and discuss how she can help you grow your business. It's a good thing you have an executive summary that is clear, concise, and compelling; you really want to make a good first impression and sell your business idea.

Search the Internet for two examples of executive summaries (use the keywords "example executive summary" to get started). Print them out, and then evaluate them on the criteria listed below. Rate each executive summary from 1 to 5 on each criterion, with 1 indicating that the summary does not incorporate that key component and 5 indicating that it contains a stellar example of that key component. Where applicable, label the portion of the executive summary with the letter of the guideline it meets.

THE EXECUTIVE SUMMARY FOR [BUSINESS NAME]

_____a. leads with a compelling statement about why the company is qualified to offer a unique solution to a big problem/opportunity.

_____b. makes it clear that a problem or opportunity exists and how it plans to solve or exploit that problem or opportunity.

_____c. clarifies what it has or what it does to solve or exploit the problem or opportunity.

_____d. describes its market: the number of people or companies, dollars available, the growth rate, what drives its market segment.

_____e. states its competitive advantage (unique benefits and advantages).

_____f. specifies what levels it will reach in three to five years: how much revenue will be generated and how it will be evaluated (customers, units, margin, etc.).

_____g. presents a uniquely qualified and winning team or management.

_____h. outlines a believable financial projection summary.

_____i. states the amount of funding expected.

CitiStorage

> How Life Changes after the Harvest

Norm Brodsky, a serial entrepreneur, describes how he felt after selling the majority ownership in his company:

> Let me put it this way: Now I know how Colonel Sanders felt. OK, maybe that's going a little too far. I'm not a complete figurehead. I still have responsibilities.... But my partner Louis Weiner is the president, and he and his managers run the business. Sometimes, it's hard for me to keep from butting in. I'm talking about simple things, like going through the mail. I used to do it fairly often. It would give me a good feel for the business. Not that I sorted the mail or opened all the letters; I just flipped through them quickly. Occasionally, one would catch my attention, and I'd think, Hmm, what's this all about? I'd also learn things about our customers—how much business they were doing with us, how fast they paid their bills. It's easy to lose track of that stuff as a company grows. Going through the mail helped keep me up to date, and it became a habit.

Brodsky recalls a moment when he heard the announcement over the public address system that the mail had arrived and quickly got up to check on it. "Where are you going?" Weiner asked. "I'm going for the mail," he responded. "You shouldn't be doing that," Weiner said. "That's my job now." And he was right. Brodsky was not even an employee anymore, let alone the boss. Once the deal with Allied Capital closed, Brodsky no longer had a job at CitiStorage. He still had an office and was still getting paid, but the money was a consulting fee, not a salary. Six months after he sold his share of the business, Brodsky still had not fully made the adjustment.

While the organizational culture is much the same at CitiStorage, the decision-making process is very different. For example, Brodsky now works as part of a team to purchase new accounts.

> Before, I would ... do a little checking and make a decision. I didn't need anyone's permission. If I didn't have the money to do the deal,

I'd borrow it from a bank, using the contract as collateral. Now I don't have to worry about financing, but I can't make the decision on my own, which is strange to me.

The Allied Capital management team warned Brodsky that the changes would take some getting used to. "The biggest thing for you," they advised, "is that we look at everything, and you cannot make on-the-spot decisions anymore. You did a fabulous job building this as an entrepreneurial company, but in order to get to the next level, there has to be more structure. You have to understand that."

Brodsky agrees that the changes were necessary for CitiStorage to make the transition to a much larger, professionally managed business.

> Indeed, those are precisely the changes that I refused to make in my first company, Perfect Courier, 20 years ago. Back then, I was also buying companies and doing private equity deals, but I had no structure, didn't ask anyone for advice, reported to no one, and wound up in Chapter 11.

As much as he hated to admit it at the time, employees had very limited opportunities to advance as long as he remained the majority owner. There was a danger that they would find their work less and less challenging, maybe even boring, as time went along.

> I began to see a few signs of this in the past couple of years, and it concerned me, but what could I do? I really didn't want to put in the time and effort required to build a huge company, and I knew from experience that I wasn't any good at it. At my stage in life, moreover, it didn't pay for me to take additional risk with my equity, and aggressive growth always involves risk. Now, with Allied Capital, we'll be taking calculated risks with the goal of getting much, much bigger in four to six years. That will open up opportunities for people throughout the organization. Some will thrive in the new environment....

Before the sale, Brodsky described himself as the benevolent dictator of CitiStorage. Now, there's a board of directors—of which he's not a member, by choice.

> I ha[d] to become a team player, which meant adapting to Allied's methods. Allied's people don't make snap decisions. They have standards. They look at formulas and ratios. They go into a level of detail that feels excruciating to a nondetail person like me. They have to do it because they need the approval of a committee to get the money for buying a company or building a new warehouse. We never had a committee. Our decision-making process was simple: Order a couple of corned beef sandwiches, and hash it out over lunch.
>
> Don't get me wrong. We were prudent. If we were buying a business, we checked out the customers, the contracts, the receivables, and so on. But we didn't go to anywhere near the lengths that Allied Capital goes. When Allied was buying our company, for example, it hired a big consulting firm to call our customers and find out how happy they were with our service. The firm produced a report of a couple hundred pages, and it was very interesting. We learned about some improvements we could make. The report cost Allied Capital many thousands of dollars. I would never have done such a survey, let alone spent that much money on it.
>
> But money doesn't play the same role for Allied's people that it played for us. They have it, we didn't, and that makes all the difference. If we were buying land to put up a new warehouse, financing was the first thing we thought about. For Allied Capital, it's the last. Its people want to look at the returns. They want to take into account what might happen with our other buildings. They want to think about renting instead of buying and building. They want to consider how big the warehouse really needs to be. For me, the process can get a little tedious, but I understand why they do it their way. Maybe I make one mistake in a hundred, and they make one mistake in a thousand. That's how you have to do things in a large, public company, when you're taking risks with other people's money.

Brodsky has experienced other changes as well:

> I used to have a lot of expenses I could charge to the company—like when I took business associates out to dinner or bought a car to use on company business. I was also in control of my own salary, which I could adjust based on the company's performance. Because of that, we never had to touch the money ... in our emergency fund ... Now, whatever I spend comes out of my pocket. Granted, there's enough money in that pocket. I'm certainly not complaining, but that's another psychological adjustment I've had to make.

Clearly, Brodsky has had to deal with a number of changes, both personally and professionally, but he has felt the greatest effect of the harvest on a very personal level:

> I don't have a clear idea of what I'm doing or where I'm going anymore. My work for CitiStorage doesn't fill all of my time or get my juices flowing the way starting a business does. There's a bit of a hole in my life at the moment, and I don't know yet how I'm going to fill it. So while I loved chasing the rainbow, I have to say that I have mixed feelings about having caught it.

QUESTIONS

1. What method of harvesting his business did Brodsky choose? Describe the other methods of harvesting a business that were discussed in Chapter 13.

2. What advice would you have given Brodsky before he sold his business?

3. What suggestions would you give him for the future?

4. Interview an entrepreneur who has sold his or her business. Compare his or her experience with Brodsky's experience.

Source: Norm Brodsky, "I'll Be Over Here if Anyone Needs Me," *Inc. Magazine,* May 2008, pp. 73–74.

Rodgers Chevrolet
> Keep Your Customers

Recall from the video spotlight for this chapter that an average business keeps only 70 to 90 percent of its customers each year and that it costs nearly five times as much to acquire a new customer as to keep an existing one. Statistics on the auto industry further indicate that if an auto dealer can hold on to an additional 5 percent of its customers each year—increasing its retention rate from 90 to 95 percent, for example—then total lifetime profits from a typical customer will rise, on average, by 81 percent.

The president of Rodgers Chevrolet, one of the nation's first woman-owned car dealerships, knows about customer retention. Pamela Rodgers considers service to be her company's backbone. She says, "This is where our customer stability is going to be . . . providing good service to our customers. That will keep customers coming back, and the referral business coming back."

Rodgers also attributes her business success to employee satisfaction. In a recent interview, she said, "[The] client is the reason we come to work every day, [and in order] for your clients to be happy, you have to have satisfied employees." That is, she considers the employees of Rodgers Chevrolet to be her "customers" as well. She must be doing something right. In 1996, when Rodgers moved in, the dealership was selling 40 cars per month. Today, that figure has grown to more than 200, with annual sales averaging around $75 million.

How can you build customer and employee satisfaction into your business plan? One way to do so is by learning to listen. That is, to meet or exceed customer needs, the business owner must really listen to what the customer is saying. Your customer should feel listened to, valued, and important to you and your company. One study indicates that 68 percent of customers leave a business relationship because of a "perceived attitude of indifference" from the business. At Rodgers Chevrolet, Rodgers makes certain the company's service advisors speak to each and every customer. To be successful, she says, "It's important that they know their stuff . . . that they're trained properly, that they have good communication skills and good customer relation skills."

Before working the activities, re-read Chapter 13 and watch the video on Rodgers Chevrolet. You may also want to review the simplified model of consumer behavior in Chapter 13. The three interrelated aspects of the model include the consumer's decision-making process, psychological influences, and sociological influences.

ACTIVITY

Imagine that you are the customer service manager at Rodgers Chevrolet. You have begun sorting customer comments into groups based on the type of vehicle owned. After reviewing a couple of years of feedback, you discover that Corvette owners do not feel they are being served as well as their friends who own foreign sports cars. Many comments mention the service level of the Lexus brand and indicate that customers may be considering changing to a Lexus SC just to get the whiteglove service. You would like to develop a way

Video material provided by Hattie Bryant, Producer of Small Business School, the series on PBS Stations, Worldnet, and the Web at http://www.smallbusinessschool.org.

SmallBusinessSchool ■
the Series on PBS stations and the Web

Sources: http://www.rodgerschevrolet.com; G. Brewer, "The Ultimate Guide to Winning Customers: The Customer Stops Here," *Sales and Marketing Management*, March 1998, p.150; C.B. Furlong, "12 Rules for Customer Retention," *Bank Marketing*, January 5, 1993; Frederick F. Reichheld and Thomas Teal, *The Loyalty Effect: The Hidden Force Behind Growth, Profits, and Lasting Value* (Cambridge: Harvard Business School Press, 2001); and Robert L. Desatnick and Denis H. Detzel, *Managing to Keep the Customer: How to Achieve and Maintain Superior Customer Service Throughout the Organization* (San Francisco: Jossey Bass Business and Management Series, 1993).

to serve your high-end clients better (the base price of a Corvette is $45,000, compared to $10,000 for a Chevy Aveo).

- Identify the elements of consumer behavior affecting your situation.
- Outline the criteria that car owners use to evaluate service to their vehicles. Do those criteria change as the vehicle sticker price rises? How?

- What new service offering could you provide to Corvette owners to entice them to continue to drive a Corvette and use Rodgers Chevrolet for service?
- Create an ad campaign or marketing program (a multimedia piece, poster, or brochure) that promotes your new service features and takes into account the elements influencing the behavior of your target market.

Country Supply

> An Effective Distribution Strategy

Scott Mooney built his business for customers like himself. He wanted supplies for his horse, he wanted the very best price, and he wanted those supplies right away. Mooney started out selling horse tack to people in his small Iowa town, but he knew the town offered a limited customer base. For his business to grow, he needed to reach customers outside his geographic area. That meant sending out a catalog.

Catalogs are an important contributor to retail sales in the United States. In 2006, U.S. catalog purchases topped $160 billion, a figure which represents a compound annual growth rate of about 6 percent over a five-year period. Consumers accounted for a whopping $96 billion of that total.

Establishing a successful catalog, however, takes a tremendous amount of work. Unlike traditional retail, where customers visit a store to make a purchase, the catalog channel requires the additional expenses of printing and mailing the catalog and packing and shipping the products. Costs need to be lower in other areas of the business to offset the increased expenses. So Mooney sought out lowcost suppliers who offered products he knew would sell. He found a friend of the family to print the catalog for him for free until he made some money.

Printing a catalog and stocking a warehouse are useless without a mailing list of potential customers. To build his list, Mooney scoured newspapers, magazines, and phone books for names and addresses of people involved with horses; he then made mailing labels on the local library's copy machine. He scrounged packing boxes from his local supermarket to ship his supplies.

The first headquarters of Country Supply was a small barn on his parents' property, where Mooney stored and managed his inventory. He shipped orders as soon as he could, to be certain his new mail-order customers would have their purchases within a few days.

Mooney was a typical entrepreneur in that he recognized an opportunity and took some risks to build a business around that opportunity. He was atypical in that he was only 14 years old when he started his venture. Mooney started very small, appealed to a customer base of like-minded people, shoved all his profits into growing that business, and did all of the work himself. Country Supply provides a stellar example of a very lean supply chain management system.

Before you answer the questions and work the activities, watch the video on Country Supply. You may also want to review the video spotlight that introduced Chapter 14.

QUESTIONS

1. Based on what you saw in the videos, describe Country Supply's initial channel of distribution. Why do you think customers continue to choose Country Supply as an intermediary?

2. How did Mooney differentiate his distribution system so as to be successful in satisfying customer needs? How do you think that helped Mooney sustain his competitive advantage? What else do you see in the video that shows how Mooney strives to sustain competitive advantage?

Video material provided by Hattie Bryant, Producer of Small Business School, the series on PBS Stations, Worldnet, and the Web at http://www.smallbusinessschool.org.

SmallBusinessSchool
the Series on PBS stations and the Web

Sources: http://www.countrysupply.com; and http://retailindustry .about.com/library/bl/q2/bl_dma060401a.htm.

ACTIVITIES

1. In the video, you learned that Scott Mooney decided at a young age to sell horse supplies because those were the products he needed himself and horses were something he found endlessly interesting. What did you find endlessly interesting at the age of 14? Go back in time and have your 14-year-old self build a business around one of your hobbies or interests. Write an outline describing which product you'd like to sell, who your customers would be, what channels you would use, etc. Share your ideas with your classmates.

2. In the video, Mooney does not mention the Internet as one of his distribution channels. Country Supply does operate a website, however. Visit http://www.countrysupply.com and write down any examples of competitive advantage you find on the site. Then search using the keywords "horse tack" or "horse supplies" on Google or Yahoo! Visit the websites of some of Country Supply's competitors, and compare their Internet presence to that of Country Supply. What evidence of competitive advantage did you find on their sites?

Nicole Miller Inc.

> The Challenges of Pricing

Bud Konheim, chief executive officer of Nicole Miller Inc., is a fourth-generation apparel producer in New York. He's been in the clothing industry for 52 years, so he's seen many changes. One unpleasant change was the United States' loss of its competitive advantage of cost-efficient production to Asia. The shift so unnerved him that he made a commitment that took him in a different direction. When most fashion houses were outsourcing the production of their clothing overseas, Konheim brought all of his company's production back to the United States.

With that decision made, Konheim turned his focus to building a business around design, instead of demographics. When Konheim and Miller decided to start their own business, after working together for years in the industry, Konheim told Miller that she should design what she herself would wear. "You make stuff that you really love to wear, and I'll find a crowd in the United States that shares your aesthetic," he said.

Focusing on design generally results in higher-priced clothing. For Konheim, however, the pricing strategy has to be "part of the fun" of shopping. So the Nicole Miller team decided to design a women's clothing line that was youthful and fun—Miller's specialty—but wasn't priced so high that women would consider the cost and worry about regretting the purchase. That is, a woman shopping for a Nicole Miller design shouldn't look at the price tag and say, "This is uncomfortable for me; it's not fun." The price and quality must be in line with the customer's expectations.

Jerry Bernstein is a renowned pricing strategy expert whose advice to entrepreneurs confirms Konheim's pricing strategy. Bernstein, founder of Price Improvement Team in St. Louis, encourages entrepreneurs to find out how their customers "perceive, use, and apply" their product—in other words, how they "value" the product. He also urges business owners to determine what they are doing right with their profitable customers. Research helps an entrepreneur determine the value of a product or service to the marketplace. That value should be communicated in every sales and marketing promotion, and in every conversation with customers. In fact, Bernstein reveals, the price selected for the product is one of the most powerful means by which the entrepreneur communicates the value of the product.

Before answering the questions and working the activities, watch the video on Nicole Miller. Watch for the various types of pricing decisions you learned about in Chapter 15.

QUESTIONS

1. Which pricing strategy (or strategies) has Bud Konheim used to build the Nicole Miller design house? Be specific, citing examples you saw in the video clip. What evidence do you see that Konheim is using pricing to build a competitive advantage?

2. Why do you think Konheim says that price strategy has to be "part of the fun"? Do you agree or disagree with his selling philosophy? Explain.

Video material provided by Hattie Bryant, Producer of Small Business School, the series on PBS Stations, Worldnet, and the Web at http://www.smallbusinessschool.org.

SmallBusinessSchool
the Series on PBS stations and the Web

Sources: http://www.nicolemiller.com; http://www.licensing .org/ intro/Introduction.cfm; Evan Clark, "The 'Sorcerer's Apprentice," *WWD*, March 20, 2007, p. 18S; and "The Secrets to Price-Setting: Price Is the Most Important Factor in Determining Profit Yet Countless Businesses Fail to Get Their Pricing Strategy Right," *Business Week Online*, November 6, 2006.

ACTIVITIES

1. Nicole Miller's core clothing collection is strong and remains a priority, but lately Miller has broadened her design portfolio. Use the Internet to research Nicole Miller's product lines. Write a brief analysis of Miller's new products' relationship to the existing product line. In your analysis, try to anticipate the implications of the new products on manufacturing methods, distribution channels, type of promotion, and/or manner of personal selling. How do you think Konheim determines pricing for the new product?

2. Nearly half of Nicole Miller Inc.'s $130 million in annual revenue comes from licensing Miller's designs to 15 different firms that make handbags, travel accessories, socks, and more. Visit the International Licensing Industry Merchandisers' Association website at http://www.licensing.org/intro/Introduction.cfm. Summarize the characteristics of licensing and the advantages to the licensor. What is the difference between licensing one's products and franchising?

Glidden Point Oyster Company, A.G.A. Correa & Son, Hardy Boat Cruises, Maine Gold

> Promotion from a Distance

At first glance, the four companies featured in the video for this chapter seem to have little in common outside of the fact that they're all located in Maine. What can a small business that harvests oysters possibly have in common with one that offers birding cruises? What connects a business that designs nautical jewelry to one that produces maple syrup? Once you watch the video and become a little more familiar with the products each company offers, you'll realize the connection—each offers a top-quality, unique product that draws customers from a distance.

Barbara Scully takes a great deal of pride in offering the best oysters to be had anywhere. She and her husband started harvesting their oysters, by hand, in 1987. Every part of the process is demanding—even the constant water-quality monitoring they must do to assure their oysters are grown in pristine waters. The care the Glidden Point Oyster team puts into its product results in an oyster of exceptional quality, which means Scully can target a customer who can afford to buy the best. Glidden Point Oyster Company does direct mailing and has an Internet site, but Scully credits her marketing success to customer service (not easy to come by in the seafood industry) and her reputation for offering the highest-quality oyster available.

When Tony Correa was a young man, he started designing jewelry with a nautical theme, based on his love for sailing and marine hardware. Today, Correa and his son, Andy, sell the jewelry in a highly successful direct-mail catalog business. Andy Correa says the catalog they send out is beautiful, with copy that makes the customer feel confident about ordering a piece of jewelry he or she can only see in a picture. But Tony argues that their marketing success is as likely the result

of their purchase of very specific mailing lists from a list broker. The jewelers mail their catalog only to a targeted group of people—customers who have a recent history of purchasing through mail order.

Hardy Boat Cruises also engages in distance marketing. Al and Stacie Crocetti started their nature cruise and ferry business with just an idea and a boat. Today, they are winners of a Gulf of Maine Visionary Award, for sustaining both their business and their community while preserving the health of the marine environment. Part of the company's promotion strategy involves mailing out brochures to names on mailing lists from birding groups. The Crocettis also rely a great deal on word-of-mouth advertising, hoping that a cruise on the Hardy Boat will be such a great experience that tourists will tell other tourists and townspeople, who in turn will recommend the cruises to even more people. Stacie is most excited, however, by the ever-expanding reach of the Web, saying that it is the number one advertising tool they couldn't do without. Type a keyword such as "Maine puffins" or "Monhegan Island" into a search on the Web and the Hardy Boat website will be in the search engine's list.

Further inland are Perry Gates and Deborah Meehan, owners of Maine Gold, a maple-product gift business. Gates and Meehan had been tapping maple trees for 30 years and knew where all the sweetest trees were located when they came across a maple syrup contest sponsored by Maine's Department of Agriculture. After winning first prize in the contest for five years running, the couple decided to try to build a business out of their talent. Today, they have about 13,000 people on their mailing list and have never bought a name or a list. Maine Gold just keeps growing, as tourists buy their products from the retail store and then send for the mail-order brochure or buy products through the

Video material provided by Hattie Bryant, Producer of Small Business School, the series on PBS Stations, Worldnet, and the Web at http://www.smallbusinessschool.org.

Sources: http://www.oysterfarm.com; http://www.agacorrea.com; http:// www.hardyboat.com; http://www.mainegold.com; and http:// www. gulfofmaine.org/mediaroom/documents/2006Visionaryawards .pdf.

company's website. Those initial customers then turn their friends and relatives into customers by sending gifts of sweet maple syrup products to them. Gates and Meehan agree that their business success is built on relationships, including the connections between the customer and the Maine Gold staff and the customer and the person who is receiving their gift.

Before answering the questions and working the activities, watch the video on Glidden Point Oysters, Correa jewelers, Hardy Boat Cruises, and Maine Gold. Watch for the various types of promotion you learned about in Chapter 16.

QUESTIONS

1. Which promotional techniques has each of the companies used to build its business? Be specific. Once you have a list of ways in which they promote their business, organize the promotional techniques on your list into the categories discussed in the chapter (personal selling, advertising, and sales promotion).

2. The objectives of advertising are to inform, persuade, and remind consumers about the existence or superiority of a firm's product or service. Which function best describes the goal of each company's advertising? Explain why you think as you do. What type of advertising does each company create—product, institutional, or something else altogether?

ACTIVITIES

1. Stacie Crocetti of Hardy Boat Cruises considers her website to be one of her best promotional activities. Visit http://www.hardyboat.com and write down the types of promotional strategies being used on the site. Then search using keywords "Maine puffin" or "Maine boat tours" on Google or Yahoo! Visit the websites of some of the competitors, and compare their Internet presence to that of Hardy Boat Cruises.

2. Imagine that you have recently been hired by Correa jewelers as a marketing manager. You are familiar with the company's current website, and you would like to improve it. Before you present your ideas to the company owners, however, you decide to mock up some four-color (i.e., full-color) website plans to show them. Create a full-page webpage that communicates a message consistent with the company's business philosophy but utilizes a more user-friendly or more appealing format. (See the company's website at http://www.agacorrea.com.) Use call-outs to describe the various sections on the page and explain how the elements you have chosen convey your intended message. Share your ideas with your classmates.

Smarter.com

> The Challenges of Doing Business in China

It was Harry Tsao's first month doing business in China, and he had just made a serious blunder. Eager to get started, Tsao had hurriedly hired 10 engineers and editors for the Shanghai back office of Smarter.com, his e-commerce start-up based in Monrovia, California. Then he learned about China's exorbitant payroll taxes. According to Chinese law, his fledgling company would have to shoulder another 40 percent in expenses—$26,000—that wasn't exactly in the budget. "I had no choice," says Tsao, 36. "I had to take on those costs."

That was back in 2003, when Tsao and co-founder Talmadge O'Neill were launching their English-language comparison-shopping website. They knew that China's inexpensive labor could make the difference between reaping profits and shutting down. But Tsao quickly learned that cost-cutting comes at a price. Business owners expanding into China face legal hurdles, security issues, and a foreign workplace culture. Foreign executives often trip over government bureaucracy, fail to understand the culture, underestimate the local staff as well as the competition, or like Tsao, simply don't do their homework.

Tsao and O'Neill founded Smarter.com's parent, MeziMedia, in 2001. Their first website, CouponMountain.com, quickly attracted thousands of visitors looking for deals on everyday products. But the two men had bigger ideas and began laying the groundwork for Smarter.com, which would provide pricing information and reviews on hundreds of thousands of items—from musical instruments to electronics—sold by thousands of online retailers. In the past, MeziMedia had outsourced engineering tasks to the Ukraine. But this new project was beyond the capabilities of its employees there. So Tsao started hunting for a place with whip-smart, yet cheap, programmers.

China was a natural choice. Tsao's parents hailed from Shanghai and the family lived in Taipei for 16 years before emigrating to the United States in 1996. Tsao is fluent in Mandarin and Shanghaiese, the dialect spoken in China's largest city, and thought he knew how to navigate Eastern business culture. So while O'Neill managed the business in California, Tsao set up shop in China.

Source: Michelle Tsai, "Shanghai Surprises: The Perils of Opening an Office in China," *Inc. Magazine*, Vol. 29, No. 3 (March 2007), pp. 47–48.

In many ways, the basic formula—go to China, save money—hit the mark. Chinese employees were a bargain, costing an average of $750 to $1,000 a month—a good $4,000 less than their U.S. counterparts. But recruiting and staff development proved to be a challenge. Tsao was shocked by the resumés that came across his desk. Almost all of them showed applicants flying through four to six jobs in just two years, reflecting the national mentality of *Qi lu zhao ma*, or "Ride a mule as you seek a horse." Turnover was high, and Tsao was constantly training new employees as staff took flight for posts at bigger companies. Surprisingly, the turnover worked to Tsao's advantage. That first crop of overpaid employees? They all left within months.

Tsao realized an American approach to talent management would not work in Shanghai. He started giving each employee a meal subsidy of about $26 a month, enough for a lavish lunch every day. He hired a staff trainer, who coaches the employees on everything from e-mail correspondence to sticking to timelines and making presentations. Each department also has a quarterly fun budget for managers to spend on staff skiing trips and karaoke outings—perks that MeziMedia doesn't offer in the U.S. but which are the norm for quality companies in China.

Meanwhile, Tsao discovered he needed to preach the entrepreneurial spirit. His workers, while adept at identifying problems and potential answers, wouldn't take initiative or make decisions on their own. Some even brought their mothers to job interviews. Shanghai, he realized, was no Silicon Valley. At first, Tsao ended staff meetings with a call for questions, but his workers almost never volunteered. These days, he picks on them one by one. "Then you get a lot of opinions," he says, "though you really have to pull it out of them." He tried to cultivate innovation with bonus incentives but discovered what worked best was publicly praising employees in group e-mails and in front of management. Tsao has found that solutions do emerge, but slowly, and only after a lot of trial and error.

Despite the obvious advantages of "setting up shop" in China, Tsao's experiences clearly show that plenty of potential perils await those with the drive to cut costs and the nerve to move operations there. Success will come only to those with the patience to wade through the challenges and a commitment to learning and adopting a very different way of doing business.

QUESTIONS

1. What is the primary force that motivated Tsao and his partner to internationalize? Did they make a good decision when they relocated their software development operations to China? What other countries should have been considered? Why?

2. What global strategy option did Tsao and O'Neill select for their move to China? Did they choose the right strategy?

3. Do you think Tsao's adjusting his management style will make a difference in the performance of his new workforce in China? What do you think he did right? What do you think he did wrong? What recommendations do you have for Tsao that would help him improve the performance of the Shanghai office?

4. Given the details of this case and other key facts that you know about China, assess the opportunities for U.S. firms in China. What features of the country should be particularly attractive to small businesses that are seeking to expand internationally?

5. What challenges to doing business in China did Tsao experience? List any issues that may present distinct problems for other small U.S. firms that may want do business there.

Diamond Wipes International, Inc.

> Adjusting for Expansion

Entrepreneurs are often reluctant to delegate tasks to others, even when they are stretched to the limit and really have no spare time to give to the duties that they so desperately need to turn over to associates. But when the reality of expanding sales and workplace demands grow out of control, the wise entrepreneur will analyze the situation and realize that it is time to delegate tasks to capable subordinates. Unfortunately, the handoff often does not go smoothly, and adjustments have to be made—some of them painful. This is how the transition went for Eve Yen, founder of Diamond Wipes International, when her company had to deal with the pains of rapid growth. Yen tells the story in her own words.

When I founded Diamond Wipes International, hot hand towels were a new phenomenon in American restaurants. I had moved to the U.S. from Taiwan because I wanted my daughter to get a good education, but I saw a business opportunity in the largely untapped market for disposable moist napkins. In 1995 I put together a production process, hired a secretary and brought in two machine operators who manufactured about 4,000 wrapped towels a day.

The company has grown rapidly. Today our 100 employees operate 40 production lines that churn out 3 million units daily. Our offerings have also grown: We now make private-label and branded wipes that are premoistened with sunblock, makeup remover or disinfectant for use in the cosmetics, health-care and janitorial industries.

The changes have been exciting but also nerve-racking. Between 2002 and 2003 sales increased 82%, to $9 million. By 2006, I had started to worry that the company might not be able to cope with more expansion. Our small sales team was overworked, interdepartmental communication was poor, and I had no way to monitor every worker's daily performance. Meanwhile, our inventory system was inefficient; paperwork was often duplicated, and some parts of the system were too dependent on manual processes, which led to costly mistakes.

One time the sales and art departments created a new custom package design for a client. Somehow that information never reached the warehouse, where employees kept ordering the old packaging. That error cost us 200 cases of wipes—and the goodwill of the client, whose delivery was severely delayed. Similar incidents happened two or three times a year, costing us about $100,000 annually.

I decided to take action. In late 2006 I hired a general manager and told him that his mission was to turn the company into a well-oiled machine. I asked him to coordinate the work of all departments, to make sure they communicated with one another and to report to me on their performance.

That was just the beginning. Within a few months I had hired three new department managers and four office assistants. In February 2007 I installed a new computer system and put the entire staff through multiple training sessions to learn how to use it. As if that weren't enough to deal with, I also redesigned the packaging for my La Fresh brand.

It was a chaotic year. My ideas were good but poorly implemented. No one had time to train the department heads—they had to learn on the job. And the office assistants had been hired hastily because I needed more staff to answer the phones. But their tasks also included inputting orders, which required attention to detail. Three of them, it turned out, were not up to the job, and I had to let them go.

My general manager was less effective than I'd hoped. He was a good guy, but he had trouble enforcing deadlines. As a result, I didn't get the reports or see the numbers I expected from him. Sometimes I felt as if I didn't know what was going on. Eventually I let him go, too.

That year was costly, both in stress and in dollars (all the hiring and firing probably set us back about $150,000). But it helped me view things differently. With hindsight, I could see that the general manager's failures reflected some of my own. I realized that it wasn't enough to be the entrepreneurial, creative force behind my company. If I didn't learn how to manage my own organization, it would fail.

I stepped in and took back control. I did some research and decided which key numbers I wanted to see from each department every day, such as the defect rate. Those are the figures we now use to understand each department's daily performance. We routinely make adjustments to improve them.

Over the past two years, I've trained myself to be a decent general manager. I'm still planning to hire someone for the job, but at least now I know exactly what to ask of him or her. I've also learned to prioritize my to-do list. We may need more of everything, but more of everything at once is not a good idea.

Here's the irony: After we jumped through all those hoops to prepare the company for growth, our 2008 sales were flat at $15 million, largely because the price of raw materials skyrocketed unexpectedly and then the economy tanked.

This year, however, I'm aiming to increase sales by 15%. I think my firm and I are ready for it. Growing without chaos is difficult, but we're building the systems that will keep us on track.

QUESTIONS

1. Based on what you've just read, how would you rate the leadership skills of Eve Yen? In what ways does she fit the profile of the typical business founder? In what ways is she different? How would you describe her leadership style?

2. Do you think Yen has the capacity to make the transition from founder to general manager of a now-sizable company?

3. How would you rate Yen's delegation skills? Was her timing appropriate for the handoff of responsibilities to a general manager? Was she too quick to take back delegated responsibilities? Is she too quick to terminate employees?

4. What outside sources of management assistance might help Diamond Wipes International reach its full potential?

Source: Eve Yen, "Delegate Smart," excerpted from *Fortune Small Business,* Vol. 19, No. 3 (April 2009), http://money.cnn.com/2009/04/14/smallbusiness/delegate_smart.fsb/index.htm, accessed July 8, 2009.

Salary Envy

> Compensation Practices and Employee Commitment

As you learned in Chapter 20, a small company's employees can easily make or break the business. That's why it is so important to recruit, select, and train workers well. But perhaps no feature of a firm's human resource management program can spoil morale and drag down employee performance faster than flawed compensation practices. That's why the observations of "Employee X," reported below, are so important to consider.

I make enough money to live a relatively comfortable life. I don't need the finer things to make me happy. So why is it that I often find myself obsessing over my salary? Why am I dying to know how much money my co-workers make? I'd like to think it has less to do with my greediness and more to do with my sense of fairness.

At each job I've quit, my salary has left me feeling cheated to some extent. In my first job out of college, I made a little more than $30,000 and was thrilled about my steady income. I loved my job: the people, the laid-back atmosphere, the work I was doing. However, my excitement quickly began to fade after checking a salary comparison website. I realized that workers in my position and location were making twice as much as I was. And apparently I wasn't the only one being underpaid, as other disgruntled employees "joked" about how little our company paid. Soon, a couple of co-workers left the company and reported back that they were earning tens of thousands of dollars more to do the same work. I knew then that as comfortable as I was at that job, I really was getting played for a fool.

So I was determined to get a good salary bump with my next job. After the recruiter assured me that raises were common and the stock options were going to be worth a lot, I accepted an offer that was only slightly higher than my previous salary. Still, I couldn't help but feel bitter from Day One. It only got worse as rumors spread that newer hires were getting paid a lot more than the veterans. I reached my breaking point when I learned that a co-worker

I trained and supervised (and was honestly not a great employee) was making about $20,000 more than me.

At my current job, I finally get paid what I feel is fair compensation. Others get paid more than I do, but it doesn't bother me because they actually deserve it. Even in this tight job market of layoffs, pay cuts and raise freezes, employees still seek fairness. Employers should not give huge salaries to some and low salaries to others without justification. With all the available information out there—whether it's office rumors, friends in the industry or websites disclosing salary information—if employees are grossly underpaid, they'll find out. And if they feel slighted, it won't be long before they look somewhere else for some fairness.

QUESTIONS

1. Employee X felt cheated in previous jobs, but was his or her attitude justified? After all, the hiring companies made offers that he or she willingly accepted and considered fair (at least at first). Is there anything unethical about the compensation practices followed by these employers?

2. What should be the goal of a compensation program? What are the likely outcomes of offering inadequate pay to employees?

3. Critique the compensation practices of the first employer mentioned. The salary offered was obviously limited. Did the company offer any offsetting benefits? If so, did these justify the limited pay?

4. Critique the compensation practices of the second employer mentioned. The salary offered was much higher, but Employee X was still very dissatisfied. What was the problem? Should the company fix the problem? If so, how?

5. Critique the compensation practices of the last employer mentioned. The salary offered varies from employee to employee, and Employee X seems to accept this. But, as a general practice, do you think it is ever wise to offer different levels of salary to different employees who have similar jobs in the firm?

Source: Employee X, "Salary Envy," *Entrepreneur*, Vol. 37, No. 6 (June 2009), p. 58.

Modern Postcard

> Leveraging the Quality Process

Operations management is an important means of building any firm's competitive strength in the marketplace. You learned in Chapter 20 that quality concerns drive operations management. You also read that, to remain competitive, a firm should continually try to improve its productivity. At one time, productivity and quality were viewed as potentially conflicting. However, if a firm is able to consistently produce at a superior quality level, the company saves the high costs of scrap and rework. One expert says, "If you can consistently do your work faster, cheaper, and better than the other guy, then you get to wipe the floor with him—without any accounting tricks. Relentless operational innovation is the only way to establish a lasting advantage." Our featured entrepreneur for this video segment combined his passion for high-quality work and his technical savvy to create an efficient organization that gave him a definite competitive advantage during an economic slump and beyond.

Like many entrepreneurs, Steve Hoffman found a profitable niche market that allowed him to turn a passion into a business. In 1976, he started offering his services as a photographer to realtors who wanted to showcase their high-end real estate properties in glossy, photo-filled brochures. Eventually, Hoffman purchased printing equipment to expand his business and develop entire brochures for his clients. Then, in 1993, a business downturn affected his core market. Demand for luxury real estate dropped, and real estate agents were less interested in spending money on glossy brochures to advertise their listed properties. Hoffman and his team had to reposition the company and its product to be more affordable. Being resourceful, Hoffman used his technological know-how to make a product that the rest of the team thought of as cheap—the postcard—into something affordable and beautiful. The resulting company, Modern Postcard, is now the industry leader in postcard products and mailing solutions.

Hoffman was one of the first in his industry to embrace technology as the means to gain advantage over his competitors. In 1993, before many companies had even implemented company-wide e-mail systems, Hoffman employed a completely digital work flow, using automated systems before anyone else in the industry. The resulting efficiencies allowed Hoffman to price his products much lower than those of competitors who still had not made the conversion to digital processes. By integrating technology throughout the organization and bringing in house functions that other companies were outsourcing, Modern Postcard grew faster and better than its competitors.

Today, Modern Postcard prints more than 1 billion postcards per year and serves over 250,000 clients from 40 unique industries. But Hoffman is still not satisfied with his system. He is constantly planning ways to keep his processes efficient—as he says, to "serve better, faster, less expensively, [and] be able to pay out larger bonuses."

Before answering the questions and working the activities, watch the video on Modern Postcard.

QUESTIONS

1. What kind of manufacturing operation is Modern Postcard?

2. In the video, Hoffman mentions using a process called the theory of constraints (ToC). What is the theory of constraints, and how does it relate to total quality management (TQM), the managerial approach you learned about in Chapter 20? Do you agree with Hoffman that constraints are the "weakest link in a chain"? Explain.

3. When Hoffman decided to branch out into printing postcards, he found that the product quality was inconsistent. How did he solve the quality-control issue?

Video material provided by Hattie Bryant, Producer of Small Business School, the series on PBS Stations, Worldnet, and the Web at http://www.smallbusinessschool.org.

SmallBusinessSchool
the Series on PBS stations and the Web

Sources: http://www.modernpostcard.com; http://www.asq.org/; Jessica Long, "Entrepreneurs Learn How to Win at All Stages of the Game: Startups and Entrenched Businesses Overcome Barriers to Beat the Odds," *San Diego Business Journal*, January 22, 2007, p. 23; and Michael Hammer, "Forward to Basics," *Fast Company*, November 2002, p. 38.

ACTIVITIES

1. Total quality management (TQM) is based on having all members of an organization participate in the overall improvement of the processes, products, and services, as well as the culture in which they work. Methods for implementing TQM can be found in the teachings of Philip B. Crosby, W. Edwards Deming, Armand V. Feigenbaum, Kaoru Ishikawa, and Joseph M. Juran. Look on the Web or in the business section of the library to find works by these leaders in the field. In one paragraph or so, summarize the contribution that each man made to TQM. Be certain to include, attribute, and explain the following terms or concepts in your written report: the "hidden" plant, "the vital few and the trivial many," the System of Profound Knowledge, DIRTFT, and quality circles.

2. a. Imagine that you are the purchasing manager for a company that buys postcards to announce additions to its product line. Your factories are in New England, Missouri, and Montana, and you have been a customer of Modern Postcard for years. Your boss recently talked to you about diversifying your supplier base for postcards. You, however, prefer to concentrate your purchases with one supplier. Use the Internet to research at least three other postcard manufacturers and find out what they offer. Write a memo to your boss listing the reasons why you are against diversifying. Include specifics about the competition, where possible.

   b. Imagine that you are now the boss in the scenario. Write a memo to your purchasing manager about why you think diversifying your supplier base is important. Compare Modern Postcard to at least two other companies.

Pearson Air Conditioning & Service

> Managing a Firm's Working Capital

Brothers Scott and Bob Pearson, father and son, are the owners of Pearson Air Conditioning & Service, based in Dallas, Texas. Scott serves as president, and Bob as general manager. The firm sells General Electric, Carrier, and York air-conditioning and heating systems to both commercial and residential customers and services these and other types of systems. Although the business has operated successfully since the Pearsons purchased it in 2002, it continues to experience working-capital problems.

PEARSON'S FINANCIAL PERFORMANCE

The firm has been profitable under the Pearsons' ownership. In fact, profits for 2009 were the highest for any year to date. Exhibit C22-1 shows the income statement for the year ending December 31, 2009.

The balance sheet as of December 31, 2009, is presented in Exhibit C22-2. Note that the firm's total debt now exceeds the owners' equity. However, $10,737 of the firm's liabilities was a long-term note payable to a stockholder. This note was issued at the time the Pearsons purchased the business, with payments going to the former owner.

PEARSON'S CASH BALANCE

The Pearson Air Conditioning & Service currently has a cash balance in excess of $28,000. The owners have a policy of maintaining a minimum cash balance of $15,000, which allows them to "sleep well at night." Recently, Bob has thought that they would still be able to "breathe comfortably" as long as they kept a minimum balance of $10,000.

PEARSON'S ACCOUNTS RECEIVABLE

The accounts receivable at the end of 2009 were $56,753, but at times during the year, receivables could be twice this amount. These accounts receivable were not aged, so the firm had no specific knowledge of the number of overdue accounts. However, the firm had never experienced any significant loss from bad debts. The accounts receivable were thought, therefore, to be good accounts of a relatively recent nature.

Customers were given 30 days from the date of the invoice to pay the net amount. No cash discounts were offered. If payment was not received during the first 30 days, a second statement was mailed to the customer and monthly carrying charges of 1/10 of 1 percent were added.

On small residential jobs, the firm tried to collect from customers when the work was completed. When a service representative finished repairing an air-conditioning system, for example, he or she presented a bill to the customer and attempted to obtain payment at that time. However, this was not always possible. On major items, such as unit changeouts—which often ran as high as $2,500—billing was almost always necessary.

On new construction projects, the firm sometimes received partial payments prior to completion, which helped to minimize the amount tied up in receivables.

C22-1 Pearson Air Conditioning & Service Income Statement for the Year Ending December 31, 2009

Sales revenue	$727,679
Cost of goods sold	466,562
Gross profit	$261,117
Selling, general, and administrative expenses (including officers' salaries)	189,031
Profits before tax	$ 72,086
Income tax	17,546
Net profits	$ 54,540

Balance Sheet for Pearson Air Conditioning & Service for December 31, 2009

EXHIBIT

Assets

Current assets:

Cash	$ 28,789
Accounts receivable	56,753
Inventory	89,562
Prepaid expenses	4,415
Total current assets	$179,519
Loans to stockholders	41,832
Autos, trucks, and equipment, at cost, less accumulated depreciation of $36,841	24,985
Other assets	16,500
Total Assets	$262,836

Debt (Liabilities) and Equity

Current debt:

Current maturities of long-term notes payable*	$ 26,403
Accounts payable	38,585
Accrued payroll taxes	2,173
Income tax payable	13,818
Other accrued expenses	4,001
Total current debt	$ 84,980
Long-term notes payable*	51,231
Total stockholders' equity	126,625
Total Debt and Equity	$262,836

*Current and long-term portions of notes payable:

	Current	Long-Term	Total
• 10% note payable, secured by pickup, due in monthly installments of $200, including interest	$ 1,827	$ 1,367	$ 3,194
• 10% note payable, secured by equipment, due in monthly installments of $180, including interest	584	0	584
• 6% note payable, secured by inventory and equipment, due in monthly installments of $678, including interest	6,392	39,127	45,519
• 9% note payable to stockholder	0	10,737	10,737
• 12% note payable to bank in 30 days	17,600	0	17,600
	$26,403	$51,231	$77,634

PEARSON'S INVENTORY

Inventory accounted for a substantial portion of the firm's working capital. It consisted of the various heating and air-conditioning units, parts, and supplies used in the business.

The Pearsons had no guidelines or industry standards to use in evaluating their overall inventory levels. They believed that there *might* be some excessive inventory, but, in the absence of a standard, this was basically an opinion. When pressed to estimate the amount that might be eliminated by careful control, Scott pegged it at 15 percent.

The firm used an annual physical inventory that coincided with the end of its fiscal year. Since the inventory level was known for only one time in the year, the income statement could be prepared only on an annual basis. There was no way of knowing how much of the inventory had been used at other points and, thus, no way to calculate profits. As a result, the Pearsons lacked quarterly or monthly income statements to assist them in managing the business.

Scott and Bob had been considering changing from a physical inventory to a perpetual inventory system, which would enable them to know the inventory levels of all items at all times. An inventory total could easily be computed for use in preparing statements. Shifting to a perpetual inventory system would require that they purchase new computer software. However, the cost of such a system would not constitute a major barrier. A greater expense would be involved in the maintenance of the system—entering all incoming materials and all withdrawals. The Pearsons estimated that this task would necessitate the work of one person on a half-time or three-fourths-time basis.

PEARSON'S NOTE PAYABLE TO THE BANK

Bank borrowing was the most costly form of credit. The firm paid the going rate, slightly above prime, and owed $17,600 on a 90-day renewable note. Usually, some of the principal was paid when the note was renewed. The total borrowing could probably be increased if necessary. There was no obvious pressure from the bank to reduce borrowing to zero. The amount borrowed during the year typically ranged from $10,000 to $25,000.

The Pearsons had never explored the limits the bank might impose on borrowing, and there was no clearly specified line of credit. When additional funds were required, Scott simply dropped by the bank, spoke with a bank officer (who also happened to be a friend), and signed a note for the appropriate amount.

PEARSON'S ACCOUNTS PAYABLE

A significant amount of Pearson's working capital came from its trade accounts payable. Although accounts payable at the end of 2009 were $38,585, payables varied over time and might be double this amount at another point in the year. Pearson obtained from various dealers such supplies as expansion valves, copper tubing, sheet metal, electrical wire, and electrical conduit. Some suppliers offered a discount for cash (2/10, net 30), but Bob felt that establishing credit was more important than saving a few dollars by taking a cash discount. By giving up the cash discount, the firm obtained the use of the money for 30 days. Although the Pearsons could stretch the payment dates to 45 or even 60 days before being "put on C.O.D.," they found it unpleasant to delay payment more than 45 days because suppliers would begin calling and applying pressure for payment.

Their major suppliers (Carrier, General Electric, and York) used different terms of payment. Some large products could be obtained from Carrier on an arrangement known as "floor planning," meaning that the manufacturer would ship the products without requiring immediate payment. The Pearsons made payment only when the product was sold. If still unsold after 90 days, the product had to be returned or paid for. (It was shipped back on a company truck, so no expense was incurred in returning unsold items.) On items that were not floor-planned but were purchased from Carrier, Pearson paid the net amount by the 10th of the month or was charged 18 percent interest on late payments.

Shipments from General Electric required payment at the bank soon after receipt of the products. If cash was not available at the time, further borrowing from the bank became necessary.

Purchases from York required net payment without discount within 30 days. However, if payment was not made within 30 days, interest at 18 percent per annum was added.

CAN GOOD PROFITS BECOME BETTER?

Although Pearson Air Conditioning & Service had earned a good profit in 2009, the Pearsons wondered whether they were realizing the *greatest possible* profit. The slowdown in the construction industry during 2009 was currently affecting their business. They wanted to be sure they were meeting the challenging times as prudently as possible.

QUESTIONS

1. Evaluate the overall performance and financial structure of Pearson Air Conditioning & Service.

2. What are the strengths and weaknesses in this firm's management of accounts receivable and inventory?

3. Should the firm reduce or expand the amount of its bank borrowing?

4. Evaluate Pearson's management of accounts payable.

5. Calculate Pearson's cash conversion period. Interpret your computation.

6. How could Pearson Air Conditioning & Service improve its working-capital situation?

Protecting Intellectual Property
> How Innovators Can Manage Risk

Peter Drucker, the legendary management consultant, said an entrepreneur is a business leader who creates something new, something different—someone who changes or transmutes values. Entrepreneurs are innovators. This video segment focuses on the protection of innovation. Specifically, the topic under discussion is the protection of intellectual property— innovations in the world of "intangible creativity." You read in Chapter 11 that there are two types of business assets: tangible (such as inventories, equipment, and buildings) and intangible (such as goodwill, patents, copyrights, and investment in research). Intellectual property (IP) is becoming a very valuable intangible asset.

In the past, protecting against risks to IP was difficult. Until very recently, neither accountants nor bankers recognized intangible assets in financial statements or for insurance purposes. In 1997, one business journalist wrote, "How ironic that accounting is the last vestige of those who believe that things are assets and that ideas are expendable." Another journalist wrote in 1999 that the intangible assets of high-tech companies "walk out the door every night." In the video segment, you will learn that about 35 percent of software installed on PCs worldwide is pirated. How can a company protect itself against the theft of its intangible assets? Just what is the definition of loss?

Intangibles are not lost to tangible threats, such as storms, floods, or fire. The risk to intangible assets comes from intangible forces, such as increased competition, new technology, and changes in employment and overall economic conditions. Losses that threaten the value of IP include loss of royalty earnings, invalidations, unenforceability, infringement, and loss of ownership. Arriving at the value of intangible assets has been, so far, an unreliable process. However, there is little doubt today that innovative ideas and IP have value and innovators must protect against their loss.

All businesses are vulnerable to IP theft, but small businesses are at a particular disadvantage because litigation insurance is expensive. Nevertheless, such insurance is necessary to protect a company that is trying to enforce an IP claim against a competitor or defending itself against an allegation of IP infringement. Some banks have begun accepting intangible assets as collateral, based on appraisals. New accounting standards recognize certain intangible assets, such as trademarks, Internet domain names, customer lists, advertising contracts, patented and unpatented technologies, and secret formulas.

Copyright law protects authors of original works, including literary, dramatic, musical, artistic, audiovisual, and architectural works. One of the most significant developments in copyright law in the past 20 years was the Supreme Court's ruling in *Metro-Goldwyn-Mayer Studios v. Grokster,* which protects copyright and innovation. In that online music distribution case, the Court ruled that those who offer products and services in a way that encourages others to engage in copyright infringement can be held liable for that infringement. Such a high-profile case helped raise public awareness that unauthorized file sharing of copyrighted works is illegal.

Putting the law into place also led to increasing competition for legitimate online music services—something many people in the music and movie industries were desperately hoping for. Under the *Grokster* decision, legitimate services can obtain some relief from unfair competition by unlawful services that offer copyrighted works for free. Mark Litvack, a lawyer featured in the video segment who once worked for the Motion Picture Association, said that when the framers of the U.S. Constitution included copyright protections, they understood that "to encourage people to create intellectual property, you have to protect that property." Or, as Abraham Lincoln once said, you have to add "the fuel of interest to the fire of genius."

Watch the video for Chapter 21, and then answer the questions and work the activities below.

Video material provided by Hattie Bryant, Producer of Small Business School, the series on PBS Stations, Worldnet, and the Web at http://www.smallbusinessschool.org.

Small**BusinessSchool** ◾
the Series on PBS stations and the Web

Sources: http://www.ladas.com/Patents/USPatentHistory.html; http://www.uspto.gov/web/offices/dcom/olia/aipa/index.htm; Jon Dudas "A Copyright Refresher," U.S. Patent and Trademark Office, http://www.uspto.gov/web/offices/dcom/olia/copyright/ copyrightrefresher.htm; and http://www.quickmba.com/strategy/ porter.shtml, accessed June 15, 2007.

QUESTIONS

1. What do you think Mark Litvack meant when he said that the writers of the U.S. Constitution understood that "to encourage people to create intellectual property, you have to protect that property"? Before recent laws and standards were put into place to protect IP, how do you think innovators protected their innovations and the profit they could make from them? What changed that made innovators seek new laws and standards?

2. What is risk control? Based on the video, describe how businesses and individuals implement risk control in the music and video industries.

3. What is the difference between tangible and intangible assets? What are the risks to a company's intangible assets?

ACTIVITIES

1. Using the Internet or your local library as your source, choose one of the following topics to summarize in a brief written report. Include examples of products or services that are protected.
   a. The constitutional basis for federal patent and copyright systems
   b. American Inventor's Protection Act of 1999
   c. First Inventor Defense of 1999
   d. Copyright law

2. Shown below is a graphical representation of Porter's Five Forces, a tool that is normally used to measure the competitive intensity of a marketplace. For this exercise, you'll use the tool to measure risk. In a group of three to four students, brainstorm the factors that contribute to business risk in the software, video gaming, music, or movie industry. Once you've filled out the risk portion of the graphic, write a summary statement explaining how the industry can protect its intellectual property. (You may also write a summary of how it does protect its intellectual property if you're familiar with the particular industry you're covering.) Be prepared to share your results with the rest of the class.

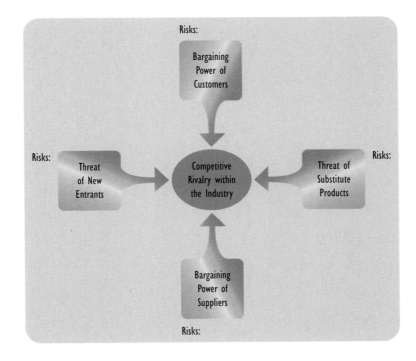

Atayne leverages innovative technologies to create high performing athletic gear that is safe for people and the planet.

Atayne, LLC
Membership Prospectus
January 2009

Primary Contact
Jeremy Litchfield
+1.207.232.9536
jeremy@atayne.com

PERFORMANCE WITH A POINT OF VIEW

Executive Summary

> Atayne, LLC has a simple vision: inspire positive environmental and social change through the power of sports and active lifestyles.
>
> We deliver a powerful message for fellow members of the eco-active community: you do not have to sacrifice your environmental and social values for performance.

Management Team
Jeremy Litchfield
Chief Pacesetter/President

Rebecca Darr
VP/International Development

Lara Dittoe
VP/Product Development

Michael Hall
VP/Community Development

Parker Karnan
VP/Strategy & Development

Kathleen Lendvay
VP/Operations

Board of Advisors
Charlie Jones
President and Founder
Brand Intersection Group

Brad Nierenberg
President/CEO
RedPeg Marketing

James F. Kenefick
Chairman and Co-founder
Better World Telecom

Ray and Cathy Pugsley
Brendan and Margie Shapiro
Potomac River Running Stores

Legal Representation
Gordon Kushner & Dennis Lambert

Financing Plan
Round I - $350k (Dec 2008, $135k raised to date)

Round II - $650k (June 2009)

Round III - $2MM (Jan 2010)

Business and Company Overview

Atayne is a newly launched company established in May 2007 to fill a void in the sporting goods market: performance and lifestyle apparel, footwear, accessories, and equipment that are sensitive on the environment and safe for the people that make and use them. Atayne employs a fundamentally different approach than the traditional industry model in developing its line of products: guided by Cradle-to-Cradle™ design philosophy, Atayne uses "trash" (worn garments, factory scraps, plastic bottles, etc.) as the primary input materials for its products.

The Product Line

Atayne will fulfill the needs of the eco-active community as they pursue their athletic and life goals. Atayne's initial product offerings, performance and lifestyle apparel, are being developed from cutting edge recycled textiles and materials. Current materials include recycled polyester, Cocona (activated carbon derived from coconut shells), and Chitosan (derived from snow crab shells). Atayne will continually evolve its fabric and material composition with advancements in the sustainable textile industry.

The primary benefits of the line are technical performance, environmental sensitivity, and human safety. From a performance standpoint, recycled polyester provides the moisture management properties of virgin polyester, while the embedded, activated carbon particles from Cocona enhance moisture transfer, provide odor control, and offer SPF 50 UV protection.

On the environmental side, Atayne's products have a dramatically lower environmental impact than the industry norm. By using recycled polyester, production energy savings are estimated at over 75% as well as reductions in CO_2 emissions of over 70% when compared to virgin polyester manufacturing processes. Additionally, in its first six years, Atayne will avert the use of over 270,000 gallons of petroleum, the equivalent of removing 650+ cars from the road, and prevent nearly 540,000 pounds of waste from entering landfills—doing its part to help address climate change and pollution.

From a human safety standpoint, Atayne is designing products following a strict restricted substance list that will prevent the use of commonly used yet harmful materials and chemicals such as PVC, phthalates, heavy metals, antimony, and Azo dyes. Many of these are known carcinogens and contaminate ground water during production and laundering. Additionally, there are concerns about the absorption of these chemicals into the body of wearers, especially when their pores are wide open during exercise.

Atayne launched sales in late August 2008, with a product line that included a men's and a women's performance top. In 2009, Atayne will introduce an expanded line that includes performance and active lifestyle tops, bottoms, layering pieces, and outer wear, establishing the groundwork for a full line of apparel, footwear, accessories, and equipment. All products will be priced on par with or at a premium to other high-quality performance brands like Under Armour, Nike, Adidas, Brooks, and New Balance.

THE MARKET

The opportunity for a sustainable performance sporting goods brand is readily apparent due to the convergence of two significant market-driving trends: the green movement and the increasing number of people aspiring to live more active lifestyles. Driving the convergence of these trends is a group of consumers who are ambitious and achievement-oriented, and strive for high performance in everything they do—from their career and athletic pursuits to their commitment to environmental and social causes.

This group of consumers, which Atayne calls the Game Changers, demand high quality products that are aligned with their values—compromises are rarely tolerated. However, the current market offerings of performance and lifestyle apparel, footwear, and accessories are forcing them to compromise, choosing between their environmental and social values and product performance. This market gap represents a highly profitable business opportunity. Based upon average Game Changer spending of US$90.13 per year on active apparel and the current base of 13.7MM[1] Game Changers, the estimated US market potential is over US$1.2bn. Conservatively, growth of the market over the next 5 years is expected to follow a similar pattern as traditional performance products, outperforming that of the sports apparel industry by a factor of two, if not more.

REVENUE MODEL

Initially, sales will come through four primary channels: direct web sales, direct event sales, wholesale through specialty retailers, and custom performance tops sales. Revenues will grow from over US$30k in 2008 to over US$11.1MM by 2013. In the first year of operation it is expected that 99% of sales will be direct to consumer (website and events). Wholesale revenues will start to gain traction in 2010 growing to approximately 30% of total sales by 2013, with the remaining 70% of sales to come from events, web, and custom sales. Gross margins will level off around 65% by 2013, a figure that is higher than the industry average due to Atayne's primarily direct sales model.

Table 1: Six-Year Financial Summary

(all dollars in MM USD)	2008	2009	2010	2011	2012	2013
Units Sold (thousands)	.82	8.6	17.9	61.9	156.9	330.8
Revenues	$0.03	$0.30	$0.60	$2.24	$5.49	$11.13
Gross Margin	43%	57%	60%	64%	66%	67%
EBIT	($0.08)	($0.36)	($0.87)	($0.21)	$1.35	$3.68
Cum. Cash Flow	$0.06	$0.47	$1.43	$0.94	$1.30	$2.93

---

[1] The 13.7MM Game Changer figure was obtained from Simmons Market Research Bureau's National Consumer Survey

Table of Contents

Product Description and Development

Atayne's initial product development strategy focuses on performance and lifestyle apparel for eco-active consumers in North America. Products will be made from environmentally sensitive and people-safe materials and technologies using the most socially and environmentally responsible manufacturing processes.

Atayne launched sales in late August 2008, with its men's and women's short sleeve (SS) performance tops at a retail price of US$38. The company has completed design and development of its Spring 2009 line, set to launch in April 2009. The line will include two men's and women's bottoms, two men's and women's tops, and a men's and women's top for customization programs (races, non-profits, fundraising, etc.).

All products will be priced on par with or at a premium to other high quality performance brands like Under Armour, Nike, Adidas, Brooks, and New Balance.

Figure 1: Atayne's POV (Point of View) Performance Tops

Men's   Women's

Throughout the remainder of 2009, Atayne will develop and launch an additional 7 items for the line. These items will include:

- Women's Jog Bra (Summer '09)
- Men's & Women's LS Top (Fall '09)
- Men's & Women's Pants (Fall '09)
- Men's & Women's Jacket (Fall '09)

Atayne differentiates its line from the sea of sameness in the performance and lifestyle apparel category in four ways:

- **Quality and Performance:** While staying true to environmental and human safety values, Atayne will not compromise the quality or the performance of its products. Only the highest quality materials will be used and the best manufacturing partners selected to make Atayne products. As the unsolicited consumer feedback reveals in Figure 3 at the end of this section, the first product offering is already exceeding consumer expectations.

- **Environmental Sensitivity and Product Safety:** Atayne will use strict guidelines to ensure its products and the production of them is safe for people and the planet. Atayne will adopt the highly respected bluesign international standard for product safety. The goal is to have all products meet the bluesign standard by the end of 2010.

- **Design Point of View**
  - □ Atayne's products will be designed to fulfill its vision of inspiring positive change. Pieces in the line (as shown with the tops above) will be emblazoned with Point of View (POV) statements that express the values of the brand and the people who wear it.
  - □ Products will be designed for multi-functionality across the many activities (running, biking, hiking, yoga, Pilates, fast packing, etc.) of the eco-active lifestyle.

Figure 2: Atayne's Spring 2009 Collection

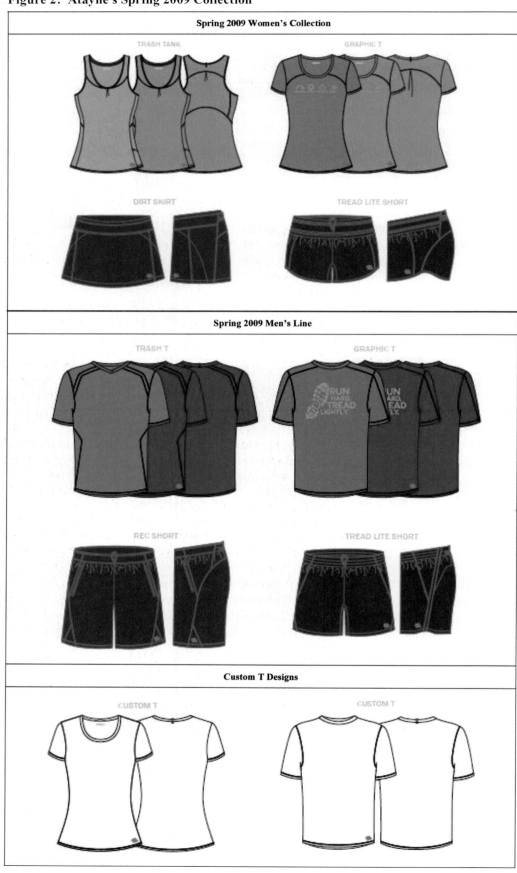

- [] Product enhancements will be integrated to encourage consumer behavior change in regard to usage and care. For example, "dry loops" will encourage customers to rinse their apparel after use and hang to dry. This will help to reduce unnecessary laundering, decreasing energy and water usage by Atayne customers.
- **Localized Manufacturing:** Atayne is dedicated to developing a localized production model—manufacture products where they are going to be primarily sold. The purpose of this is not only to support the local economy, but also avoid unnecessary emissions and energy use by moving materials across the globe. Since most of Atayne's current sales are in North America, the company has established its initial production here. As the company grows and volume warrants, Atayne will establish manufacturing partners in international markets for sales in those markets.

Table 2: Spring 2009 Product Line and Pricing Summary

Item	Est. Standard Cost	Est. Wholesale Price	Est. Retail Price
Men's Trash Tee	$13.00	$19.00	$38.00
Women's Trash Tank	$13.00	$38.00	$38.00
Men's Graphic Tee	$13.00	$19.00	$38.00
Women's Graphic Tee	$13.00	$19.00	$38.00
Men's Tread Light Short	$20.00	$22.50	$45.00
Women's Tread Light Short	$20.00	$22.50	$45.00
Men's REC Short	$20.00	$22.50	$45.00
Women's Dirt Skirt	$20.00	$22.50	$45.00
Unisex Custom Tee	$11.00	N/A	$15.00

Atayne is finalizing the selection of its production partners for its Spring 2009 line and beyond. As previously mentioned, the goal is to develop a supply chain that is consolidated in the region were the bulk of sales occur. Atayne will likely source its woven fabrics in Asia in the short term but aims to source fabric in North America as soon as Atayne can meet the minimum quantities required of North American textile vendors. Below is the current short list of potential fabric and manufacturing partners.

Fabric

- United Knitting (Cleveland, TN)—United Knitting is a world leader in the production of performance stretch fabrics. Since their inception in 1984, they have focused their vertical resources in developing technologically innovative fabric systems. Today, United Knitting continues to produce high performance technical fabrics for leading brands in high profile markets including the Outdoor, Fitness, Team Sports, Military, Workwear and Protective Markets. United Knitting is a member of the Green Steps Program. Green Steps is a voluntary program that highlights changes that companies in the outdoor and sporting industry can take to reduce their negative impact on the environment. United Knitting is the preferred partner for knit fabrics for use in tops and linings in bottoms.
- Everest Textile (Taiwan)—Until an appropriate domestic partner is identified, Everest Textile is the preferred supplier of woven fabrics for use in shorts and active skirts. Founded in 1988, Everest manufactures filament and staple textiles combining high technology with fashion. Everest develops various products including multi-functional membranes, fabrics for whole markets (sports & outdoor, city & casual), multi-functional synthetic leather, high performance industrial fabric, home textile, and green fabrics complying with Everest Sustainability Model including PLA, Organic Cotton, and Recycled Polyester. Everest is a major textile supplier to companies such as Nike, Adidas, Puma, Patagonia, The North Face, and Columbia. Everest recently became a partner of bluesign®.

Manufacturing

Atayne is evaluating two manufacturing partners with production capabilities in North America that meet the company's environmental and social requirements. Selection of a partner will be finalized in December 2008. The two final candidates are AN'K Apparel Source Inc. (Vancouver, BC Canada) and AJ Wear Inc. (Scarborough, ON Canada).

Market Analysis and Potential

The opportunity for a sustainable performance sports brand becomes readily apparent when one examines the convergence of two significant market-driving trends: the green movement and the increasing number of people aspiring to live more active lifestyles.

The green movement is one of the most significant trends in the US marketplace today. In 2007, Americans witnessed the movement transform from environmental dialogue into environmental action. One of the biggest indicator s of this action was a change in consumer spending as millions began actively seeking more environmentally friendly products and services. A 2007 survey by Information Resources, Inc (IRI) showed that approximately 50% of US consumers consider at least one sustainability factor when selecting a consumer good.[2] Another survey by global consulting firm Accenture showed that consumers are willing to pay more for these products and services, on average 11% more.[3]

---

[2] "Consumers Consider Sustainability when Picking CPG Brand," *Marketing Vox*. 11 January 2008. http://www.marketingvox.com/archives/2008/01/11/consumers-consider-sustainability-when-picking-cpgbrands/?camp=newsletter&src=mv&type=textlink.

[3] "Two-Thirds of People Will Pay Premium For Green Products," *Environmental Leader*. 9 January 2008. http://www.environmentalleader.com/2007/10/18/two-thirds-of-people-will-pay-premium-for-green-products/.

The movement does not appear to be waning anytime soon. Publications from *Vanity Fair* to *Runners World* have permanently integrated green issues into their calendar. Other media companies such as Discovery Communications (Planet Green) have established permanent franchises dedicated to environmental issues. More importantly, consumers are pledging their commitment. Even in an economic downturn, 70% of consumers say they will stay loyal to a brand if it supports important causes.[4] One industry that has more recently started to respond to the green movement is fashion. The presence of sustainable apparel and fabrics has seen considerable growth over the past several years, and this trend is expected to intensify. Global sales of organic cotton alone are expected to reach US$6.8 billion in 2010 up from $245MM in 2001.[5] The main driver of this explosive growth is consumer demand. 18% of US consumers reported an interest in sustainable fashion products in 2006, up from just 6% in 2004. This increase precedes the upsurge of mainstream interest in all things green that occurred in 2007.[6]

Figure 4: The Growth of Organic Cotton

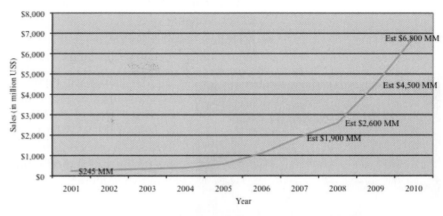

As conscientious consumers demand more environmentally friendly products and apparel options, the obesity epidemic has people aspiring to live more active and healthy lifestyles. One of the biggest indicators of this trend is people getting off their couch and tying on a pair of running shoes. Running is one of the fastest growing fitness activities in the US, seeing a 9.5% increase in participation from 2005 to 2006.[7] Additionally, the top 100 US running events in 2006 saw nearly 2MM people compete, a participation number that has nearly doubled since 1996.[8] As people are trying to become more active, they are also trying to dress the part. Consumers are grabbing performance sportswear off the shelves, resulting in the category far outpacing the growth of overall apparel and sportswear sales.[9]

In recent years, a consumer group that Atayne calls the Game Changers, has started to drive the convergence of these trends.[10] A subset of the Cultural Creatives, the segment driving the growth of Lifestyles of Health and Sustainability (LOHAS), the Game Changers are an ambitious and achievement oriented group who strive for high performance in everything they do from their career and athletic pursuits to their commitment to environmental and social causes. The Game Changers demand high quality products that are aligned with their values—compromises are rarely tolerated. However, the current market offerings of performance and lifestyle apparel are forcing the Game Changers to compromise, choosing between their environmental and social values and performance. Existing alternatives include:

■ A product thought to be more environmentally friendly that athletes avoid due to poor performance during athletic pursuits (organic cotton from various brands)

[4] "The Second Annual Edelman Good Purpose Study." *Good Purpose*. 1 December 2008. http://www.goodpurpose community.com/study.html.

[5] Marquardt, Sandra. "Global Organic Cotton Apparel and Home Products Market Tops $1 Billion in 2006." *Press Release News Wire*. 21 Oct 2007.

[6] "Green Sleeves: Eco-Friendly Incentive Clothing." *Economic Times*. 14 May 2007: 4.

[7] Lampa, Ryan. "Road Running Information Center Trends and Demographic," *Running USA*. 19 October 2007. http://www.runningusa.org/cgi/trends.pl.

[8] Ibid.

[9] Albergotti, Reed. "Smells Like Team Spirit," 2007. *The Wall Street Journal*. Accessed 13 January 2008 at. http://online.wsj.com/article/SB119888106821856441.html.

[10] The Game Changers are a custom consumer segment developed and modeled by Jeremy Litchfield and Charlie Jones through a series of ethnographic and quantitative consumer studies through their work for numerous clients of RedPeg Marketing Inc.

- A product designed for performance but using environmentally harmful and unsustainable materials in planet and people-harmful processes (e.g., Nike and Under Armour)
- A product designed for the outdoor lifestyle, performance, and planet, but not for highly athletic pursuits (Patagonia and GoLite)

This market gap represents a lucrative business opportunity. Based on average Game Changer spending of $90.13[11] per year on athletic apparel and the current base of 13.7MM Game Changers, the estimated US market potential is over US$1.2bn. Conservatively, growth of the market over the next 5 years is expected to follow a similar pattern as traditional performance apparel growth, outperforming that of the sports apparel industry by a factor of two or more.[12]

The initial launch of Atayne tops indicates the target market has been eagerly awaiting a product to fill this void. In less than 15 weeks, Atayne has sold over 550 tops and distributed another 180+ to influential athletes and media in the running community. In addition to the highly favorable feedback previously shared, consumers are paying a premium price for Atayne tops ($38 for 1, $70 for 2) at expos in the face of heavily discounted products by leading brands such as Nike, Brooks, Adidas, and New Balance. Consumers are making this purchase from a relatively unknown brand during this time of economic uncertainty.

Additionally, Atayne has started to receive highly favorable recognition from magazines, newspapers, and bloggers in the running community. In the December 2008 issue of *Trail Runner* magazine, Atayne's POV top was featured as one of five items in the Green Gear Review. This is on top of coverage in *The Times Record, The Portland Press Herald,* and several prominent blogs such as I Run Far, Eco-Runner, Trail Monster Running, and Run to Win.

Business & Revenue Strategy

From an operational standpoint, Atayne's goal is to transform the current business approach in the product manufacturing industry from cradle-to-grave to cradle-to-cradle. The current model is energy and water intensive and is reliant upon virgin, non-renewable materials that enter through the production process ("cradle"), move across the supply chain to the end consumer, and ultimately find a home in a "grave," a landfill or incinerator. This approach creates a transactional revenue model that promotes conspicuous consumption in order to be successful.

Atayne will design and operate under a more intelligent and sustainable (both environmentally and economically) model than what currently exists. Atayne's goal is to transform the traditional, linear model of the industry into a closed loop system, thereby reducing the amount of energy, water, nonrenewable, and non-recycled materials used in production as well as diminishing post industrial and consumer waste and providing incentives for responsible consumption.

The Atayne Model will operate on two levels: the traditional, forward supply chain and a progressive, reverse supply chain.

FORWARD SUPPLY CHAIN   At a high-level, Atayne's forward supply chain will work much as it does in the traditional manufacturing industry. However, the materials that enter the production phase will be recycled or renewable and will not contain harmful chemicals or materials.

---

[11] Simmons Market Research Bureau, National Consumer Survey, Spring 2007 Adult Full Year.
[12]"Taking the Lead in Performance Apparel," 2006. *Just-Style*. Accessed 16 January 2008 at http://www.just-style.com/article.aspx?ID=95066.

Figure 5: Atayne Revenues by Channel

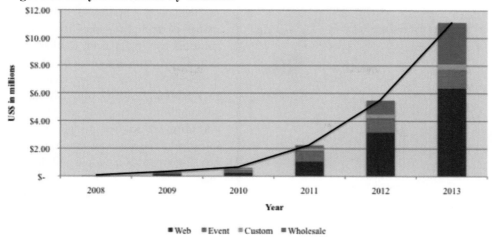

■Web ■Event ▧Custom ■Wholesale

REVERSE SUPPLY CHAIN   The reverse supply chain of the model is something that is relatively nonexistent in the product manufacturing industry but an emerging trend. Partnering with retailers and TerraCycle[13], Atayne will establish the infrastructure to take back unwanted products to be recycled into new ones. To encourage the return of products, Atayne will give consumers a credit in exchange for used materials that can be recycled. Additionally, Atayne will work with race directors to collect plastic bottles from events to recycle into polyester. The infrastructure for this program is currently being developed and will roll out in phases over the course of 2009 and 2010.

Based upon this model, revenues will be generated through four channels:

- Direct sales through the Atayne website
- Direct sales through events (race expos and lifestyle events)
- Wholesale through specialty retailers (running, cycling, multisport, outdoor, lifestyle)
- Direct sales through a custom shirt program (races, fundraisers, co-branded apparel)

Under this distribution strategy, revenues will grow from over US$30,000 in 2008 (4 months of sales) to over US$11.1MM by 2013. In the first year of operation, it is expected that 99% of sales will be direct to consumer (website and events). Wholesale revenues will start to gain traction in 2010 growing to approximately 30% of total sales by 2013, with the remaining 70% of sales coming from events, the web, and custom top sales. It is estimated that gross margins will level off around 65% by 2013, a figure that is higher than the industry average due to Atayne's primarily direct sales model.

Competition and Competitive Strategy

The Competitive Landscape

Competition in the performance apparel category is best segmented using two variables: product function and product sustainability. On the product function side, sports apparel is

---

[13]Terracycle is a company that is dedicated to eliminating waste. The company recently launched take-back programs with Clif Bar and Target.

Figure 6: Performance Apparel Competitive Landscape Map

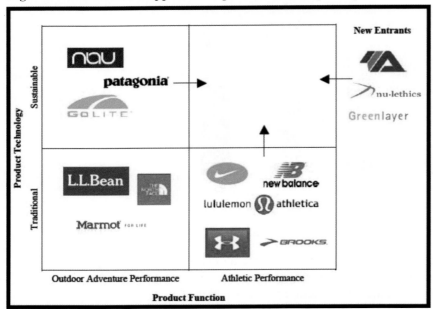

most often designed for athletic or outdoor performance. Apparel for athletic performance is created for specific sports such as running, cycling, soccer, football, and basketball. Apparel for outdoor performance is designed for activities such as hiking, rock climbing, skiing, and fishing. Product sustainability deals with an organization's commitment to designing and developing products in a way that minimizes its negative impact on people and the environment.

Combining these variables creates a landscape with four competitive quadrants. On the lower end of the sustainability scale there are many well-known and established companies offering performance apparel for both outdoor and athletic pursuits. Moving up the sustainability scale reveals there are also several companies offering outdoor performance products using more environmentally sensitive and people safe materials and processes. However, no one has fully addressed the intersection of athletic performance and sustainability. As initial consumer response to Atayne has shown, the market is ready and waiting.

The athletic performance + highly sustainable quadrant is unlikely to remain wide open for much longer. Entrants are likely to come from three sources:

1. Traditional athletic performance companies such as Nike, Brooks, and New Balance are starting to experiment with some of the sustainable product technologies, and they are likely to enter the space once these technologies become more commercialized. Nike has already set a goal of having their entire apparel line meet certain environmental criteria by 2012.

2. Outdoor performance companies already using sustainable product technologies are poised to enter the space using their knowledge. The companies most likely to make this move are Patagonia and Golite.

3. The opportunity is attracting new entrants in addition to Atayne. Two organizations to watch in particular are Nulethics and Greenlayer, both of which are marketing a line of environmentally sensitive sportswear.

Atayne will likely face the biggest competitive threats from Nike, Patagonia, and Greenlayer. However, the management team at Atayne believes they have the right mix of authenticity, focus, and go-to-market strategy to become the leader in this space.

Nike presents a formidable threat. Despite the strength of their brand and their seemingly limitless resources, Nike lacks an important tool in capturing the leadership position: authenticity. While Nike has become synonymous with getting out there and playing hard (Just Do It), they will be hard pressed to define "Just Do It with Meaning." Nike will successfully sell products in the athletic performance/sustainable category; however, they will never own the category.

While Patagonia does have the necessary authenticity, they lack the required focus. Historically, Patagonia has had a limited line of trail running apparel; however, recently they have started to retreat from the sport. Instead, the company is placing its focus on water sports such as surfing. Patagonia estimates that in the next five years over 50% of its sales will come from water sports, shifting considerably from the mountain sports that have come to define their brand.

Finally, while Greenlayer may have authenticity and focus, they lack the appropriate go-to-market strategy to capture Atayne's target consumers, the Game Changers. The Game

Changers require that brands engage them on a personal level. Greenlayer has opted for the traditional wholesale model, putting at least two layers between them and their end users. This will make it exceedingly difficult for them to develop the deep relationship that the Game Changers seek.

Competitive Advantages

Atayne has four primary competitive advantages that will help to position it as the leader in this emerging space.

First, Atayne will enter the market with a clean slate. This will enable Atayne to develop the authenticity to capture and define this new space. Industry giants will be able to develop products or sub lines in this segment; however, it is unlikely they will ever be able to define it. Under Armour proved how powerful this advantage can be when they took the performance apparel industry by storm starting in the mid 90s. Even today, despite the fact their sales are dwarfed by companies like Nike and Adidas, Under Armour clearly defines the category.

Second, Atayne is finalizing relationships with well-established, complementary brands that will give Atayne credibility with its core consumer. Atayne is developing relationships with TerraCycle for the development of its product take-back program and with Clif Bar for its 2009 event schedule. Not only will Atayne's association with these companies lend a tremendous amount of credibility in the socially responsible brand space, it opens up significant opportunities with non-traditional lifestyle retailers such as Whole Foods.

Third, Atayne has built a management team with the skills and backgrounds to achieve success. Parker Karnan is one of the most respected running industry leaders and brings well-established relationships with specialty retailers across the country. Additionally, the product development team (Lara Dittoe and Libby Vance) brings a tremendous amount of experience from leading companies such as Brooks, Lululemon, Prana, Sugoi, and Nordstrom. The remaining team complements their industry experience with strong backgrounds in consumer goods, marketing, sales, operations, socially responsible business, retail, international business, and entrepreneurship.

Finally, Atayne's operational structure provides the company two major benefits. First, by implementing a reverse supply chain with the take-back program, the company's core operations will be based on a model that enhances the Game Changers' preference for Atayne. The model shows consumers true dedication to sustainability, moving beyond the all too frequent green washing[14] in the marketplace. The "all talk, no walk" mentality of greenwashing has destroyed many companies' hopes of leveraging the green movement. The model also builds Atayne's operations around the future of the textile and apparel industry, enabling the company to operate seamlessly as others are forced to change. Textile and apparel industry events across the world are abuzz with sustainability and the impending government regulations. A recent event in New York City on greening the sports industry had considerable discussion of regulations that will require companies to take more responsibility for their products after their usable life. Many experts expect required take back and recycling programs similar to what the electronics industry is starting to face.

Growth Strategy

To achieve the aggressive growth that Atayne is targeting over the next five years, the company will focus on five primary areas:

- Apparel Line Expansion
- Atayne.com Sales Growth

14A.k.a. stretching of the truth of a company's environmental friendliness

Table 3: Growth Strategy Summary

	2008	2009	2010	2011	2012	2013
Est. Revenues (MM USD)	$0.03	$0.30	$0.60	$2.24	$5.49	$11.13
Est. Units Sold (thousands)	.82	8.6	17.9	61.9	156.9	330.8
# SKUs	3	15	30	50	75	100
# of Retailers	0	15	30	100	400	600
# of Events	1	20	30	40	50	60
International Markets	0	0	0	1	3	5

- Wholesale Distribution Expansion
- Event Sales Growth
- International Expansion

Apparel Line Expansion

In late August 2008, Atayne launched sales of its shortsleeve top. This will be followed by the launch of its long-sleeve top in December. Over the next five years, Atayne will continue to add items offering consumers a full line of performance and lifestyle apparel.

In the Spring of 2009, Atayne will expand its line to include two men's and women's tops and two men's and women's bottoms. In the Fall, Atayne will introduce cold weather gear including pants, jackets, and a re-designed long-sleeve top. Additionally in 2009, the company will launch its custom top program specifically targeting green races and non-profit organizations. (A pilot program is already underway with a school in Virginia Beach, VA.)

Over the next five years, Atayne will continue to add more styles, as well as items designed for specific activities such as cycling and triathlon. Once its apparel business is well established around 2012, Atayne will pursue opportunities to extend the brand to include other athletic gear such as equipment and footwear.

Atayne.com Sales Growth

As Atayne grows and expands distribution channels, the company will focus on retaining 50 to 60% of total sales direct-to-consumer through the company website. To facilitate these sales, Atayne will support aggressive PR and online marketing programs, such as loyalty and referral programs and digital communities (e.g., Facebook).

Wholesale Distribution Expansion

In 2009, Atayne will start to pursue distribution with key retailers in priority geographic markets. Atayne will focus on specialty retail (running, cycling, multi-sport, and outdoor), lifestyle retail (Whole Foods and sustainable living retailers), and Internet/Catalog (Athleta, Title IX, Backcountry.com). The goal for 2009 is to be in 15 retail locations. Atayne has already secured distribution in 5 of these locations.

Event Sales Growth

From late August-early December 2008, Atayne will have sold product at 8 events (Health & Fitness Expos and Green Lifestyle Events) primarily on the East Coast of the US. The company will continue to expand its direct sales through events over the next five years. To create a more scalable event model, Atayne is finalizing an agreement with Clif Bar on a partnership for 15 to 20 events in 2009. This will not only provide the benefit of reducing overall event costs, but also associate Atayne will a highly respected and complementary company.

International Expansion

Starting in 2011, Atayne will look to pursue sales in key international markets with the goal of establishing sales in five international markets by 2013. International efforts will focus on

Figure 7: Key Milestones through Q2 2009

	Nov 08	Dec 08	Jan 09	Feb 09	Mar 09	Apr 09	May 09	Jun 09
Finalize Spring 2009 Designs	■							
Secure remaining $215k of Round 1 Financing		■						
Order Fabrics for 2009 Spring Line		■						
Begin Production of 2009 Spring Line			■					
Delivery of 2009 Spring Line					■			
Launch 2009 Line at Boston Marathon						■		
Secure Round 2 Financing ($650k)								■

developed countries with cities that have a high concentration of Game Changers. Examples of these markets include London, Tokyo, and Sydney.

Key Milestones

In the short term, there are several milestones that Atayne must hit to stay on track and lay the foundation for the above growth plan. Figure 7 shows the major milestones through the second quarter of 2009.

Financial Plan

The initial financial goal of Atayne is to manage rapid growth while bringing the company to profitability in its 4th year of sales. Atayne estimates it will generate sales of US$11.12MM by 2013 leading to pre-tax profits of US$3.68MM. As described in the previous section, the organization will achieve this growth through apparel line expansion, Atayne.com sales growth, wholesale distribution expansion, event sales growth, and international expansion. In the first 15 weeks of sales, the company is approaching $20,000 in revenues. Revenues (from 4 months of sales) in 2008 should exceed $30k.

Anticipated start-up cash needs (first 30 months) are approximately $2.0MM. The primary usage of funds includes Working Capital, Employee Compensation, Sales & Marketing, and Product Manufacturing. To meet these cash needs and facilitate future growth, Atayne will raise funds in three rounds. In Rounds I and II, Atayne will raise a total of $1.0MM from friends/family and angel investors using convertible bridge financing. The money will initially be issued to Atayne as debt and will convert to equity at a 20% discount once the company has raised a minimum of $2.0MM in Round III.

Round I funds ($350k) must be raised by the end of December 2008. To date, Atayne has secured $135k and is currently working to close the remaining $215k through individual investments ranging

Table 4: Six-Year Financial Summary

(dollars in MM USD)	2008	2009	2010	2011	2012	2013
Units Sold (thousands)	.82	8.6	17.9	61.9	156.9	330.8
Revenues	$0.03	$0.30	$0.60	$2.24	$5.49	$11.13
Gross Margin	43%	57%	60%	64%	66%	67%
EBIT	($0.08)	($0.36)	($0.87)	($0.21)	$1.35	$3.68
Cum. Cash Flow	$0.06	$0.47	$1.43	$0.94	$1.30	$2.93

Table 5: Estimated Start-Up Cash Needs

Item	Cash Need
Working Capital	$500,000
Employee Compensation	$480,000
Sales & Marketing	$420,000
Product Manufacturing	$270,000
Product Design & Dev	$85,000
Business Expenses	$85,000
Legal & Accounting	$80,000
Travel	$60,000
Shipping & Logistics	$20,000
Total	**$2,000,000**

Table 6: Three Round Investment Schedule

	Date	Amount
Round I	December 2008	$350,000
Round II	June 2009	$650,000
Round III	January 2010	$2,000,000
	Total	**$3,000,000**

from $10k to $50k. If the amount is not secured by this time, the principal owner will continue to run the organization by self-funding. However, without a cash infusion, Atayne will need to delay the launch of the Spring 2009 line until that funding is secured.

An additional $650k and $2MM will be sought in Rounds II and III. These funds must be raised by June 2009 and January 2010 respectively. The primary usage of these funds will be for product line and distribution expansion. Both angel and institutional investors will be targeted for this round. To date, the principal owner has invested over $160,000 ($25,000 in cash and $135,000 in deferred wages) in the development of Atayne.

After five full years of operation, Atayne will create a liquidity event enabling its early stage investors to cash out and realize a healthy return. Atayne will look to follow the paths of companies such as Stonyfield Farms, Tom's of Maine, and Honest Tea[15] by securing a strategic investment from a larger company that will not only provide funds for growth, but also existing supply chain and distribution infrastructure to help support the company's growth. With this deal, Atayne will strive to retain a majority of the voting rights for the core ownership group.

Based upon the growth projections and the investment terms, the five-year return on Round I and II investments is estimated to be between 600 and 690%.

Risk Assessment and Contingency Strategies

As with any new start-up, Atayne faces several strategic, operational, and financial risks that will challenge the organization during its launch and growth. Below is an assessment of some of these risks and the steps the company will take to minimize them.

Strategic Risks

The primary strategic risks that Atayne faces are from entrenched competitors and consumer inertia. As the green movement becomes more ingrained in mainstream brands, the current leaders in the performance apparel category will likely move into the emerging sustainable space. As detailed in the Competition and Competitive Strategy section, competition is likely to enter from three primary areas: existing individual performance brands, outdoor performance brands with green processes in place, and new entrants. In evaluating this landscape, Atayne believes the companies that present the biggest risk are Nike and Patagonia.

Nike is the most powerful force in the sports apparel and footwear industry and has the ability to define the entire industry because they control over 60% of the market.[16] At the same time, Nike has become one of the leaders in efforts to design and produce more sustainable products. Nike is the second largest purchaser of organic cotton in the world[17], has a line of environmentally sensitive products—Nike Considered, and is a leading player in the Outdoor Industry Association Eco Working Group. Patagonia has been the long time leader in designing and producing environmentally sensitive performance apparel. Their focus has always been on outdoor apparel but they do a small trail running apparel line.

[15] For background on this deal, see *Fast Company's* July 25, 2008 blog: http://www.fastcompany.com/blog/saabira-chaudhuri/itinerantmind/coca-cola-and-honest-tea-plot-thickens.

[16] Information obtained via SportScanInfo. 2008.

[17] "Global Organic Cotton Market Tops US$1 Billion," 2007. *Ecotextile News*. Accessed 7 February 2008 at http://www.ecotextile.com/archive_news_details.php?id=691.

Both Nike and Patagonia are well positioned to turn their focus on producing sustainable apparel for individual performance sports and be a major competitive threat to Atayne. To address this risk, Atayne has focused on building a model that is not just about selling "greener" performance apparel. Atayne has a vision of transforming the entire textile and apparel industry with eco-effective design and production, as well as responsible consumption. Atayne has created a unique value proposition that will enable it to define the emerging sustainable space in the market for performance and lifestyle sports apparel—ecoconscious athletes no longer have to compromise their environmental and social values for performance. This is a similar strategy that Under Armour leveraged in their ascent to become the $600MM company they are today.

The other primary strategic risk that Atayne faces is consumer inertia. The Atayne model requires consumers to make two major shifts. First, they must believe that a more sustainable option performs equally well as traditional options, and they must make the move away from the brands to which they are already loyal.

To reduce the risk of consumer inertia, Atayne will focus its efforts on a niche target market that is most likely to adopt Atayne. Initial marketing efforts will focus on engaging the Game Changers, a group of consumers segmented around values, behaviors, and attitudes (the most significant indicators of brand and product selection). The Game Changers possess the characteristics that make them highly likely to adopt Atayne. This makes the company's way of doing business an easy sell and a comfortable adjustment for the Game Changers.

Operational Risks

Atayne is designing a business model very different than the industry norm combining a forward supply chain using environmentally sensitive and people safe manufacturing processes and materials and a reverse supply chain that brings used products back into the production process.

The main operational risk facing Atayne is its ability to seamlessly implement and integrate all elements of its model. To develop this model, the organization will not only need to find partners across the supply chain with the right capabilities, but also get the individual partners to work together for the collective good—advancing industry norms.

There are two primary ways Atayne will address this risk. First, the company will select partners with a similar vision and passion for changing the current linear model of the industry. The current and potential partners are listed in the Product Description and Development section.

Second, Atayne will create a more substantial relationship with its partners. One way the company will look to do this is through vendor equity. By combining a partner's vision to create change, with a financial interest beyond payment for services, Atayne will develop a collection of partners who are fully dedicated to the success of developing a new model for the industry.

Another operational risk that Atayne faces is supply of input materials. Atayne's product line is based on materials that are not conventional in the apparel industry. Materials such as recycled polyester are not fully commercialized and this could lead to materials acquisition issues, especially if suppliers give priority to more established organizations. By developing the company's business model around more substantial relationships, Atayne will put itself in the position to reduce the possibility of this problem.

Finally, Atayne faces the more general organizational and management risks that accompany a new startup, including recruiting and retaining key staff while managing aggressive growth. To minimize this risk, Atayne will develop an organizational structure and culture that is designed to empower individuals. Atayne will empower employees through decentralized decision making and by providing an equity interest in the organization. This will help to align all individuals to the best interests of the company and provide all employees the opportunity to have a true impact on Atayne's success as well as reap the financial rewards.

Financial Risks

The primary financial risks that Atayne faces are the recession in the US and exposure to foreign exchange fluctuations.

The US economy has officially fallen into a recession, and this could have a negative impact on the organization in two ways.

First, it could make it more difficult to acquire the funds necessary to grow the company. It is likely investors will be much more conservative with their funds and may be less willing to take a risk on a start-up in the uncertain economic environment. To address this risk, Atayne is currently developing some non-traditional investment options. One of these includes the opportunity to spread an investment out over monthly payments. This may attract investors who are nervous about parting with a large sum of cash but capable of making an investment from their personal monthly cash flow.

Second, consumers are also likely to tighten their wallets. If consumers stall their spending, it will be much more difficult for a start-up to handle than an established company with relatively better access to commercial financing. This is a tough risk to address because there are many factors at play that Atayne does not have control over. However, Atayne does not think a recession would affect it as much as it may other companies. The primary reason for this is that the core target has a considerable amount of disposable income, and they are unlikely to need to drastically change their spending patterns. Additionally, history has shown that in times of hard economic times people move away from lavish consumerism and toward quality, "feel good" brands and products. Atayne offers consumers something they can be proud of in these tough economic times.

The other financial risk facing Atayne comes from its exposure to foreign exchange fluctuations. Atayne will be manufacturing in Canada and if the Canadian dollar rises in value against the US dollar (as it did this past summer), cost of goods will rise, leading to lower gross margins and lower profits/higher losses. To hedge against this risk, Atayne will be seeking quotes from Canadian based companies in US dollars (with payment made in US dollars).

Management Team and Advisors

At this time, Atayne has one full-time staff member, President and Founder Jeremy Litchfield, who has been dedicated full-time to the building of Atayne since August 2007. In addition to Jeremy, Atayne has developed a core team who conduct work on various initiatives to support the building of the company. Many of these people will be joining the company on a full time basis, once funding warrants.

JEREMY LITCHFIELD • CHIEF PACESETTER/PRESIDENT, ATAYNE, LLC   Jeremy is a life long environmentalist and athlete, playing basketball in college and running 5 marathons in the past two years, including a recent Boston qualifying time at the Maine Marathon. His professional experience has centered on the consumer experience and growing brands through non-traditional channels. From 2004–2007 Jeremy served as the Director of Brand Strategy and Consumer Insights at RedPeg Marketing. Prior to RedPeg, Jeremy was Operations Manager at Pierce Promotions. His brand strategy experience cuts across a variety of categories and includes large and small brands such as Gillette Venus, Dove, Pepperidge Farm, Diet Pepsi, Drambuie, Zyrtec, and The I Do Foundation. Jeremy received a BA in Biology from Bowdoin College and an MBA from American University.

REBECCA DARR • VICE PRESIDENT/INTERNATIONAL DEVELOPMENT, ATAYNE, LLC   As an independent management consultant, Rebecca helps clients in North America and Asia with sustainability strategy development, operations effectiveness, and change management. Clients come from multiple industries and have included a global apparel manufacturer. Rebecca was part of the first global corporate responsibility team at Deloitte Touche Tohmatsu from 2004–2006 and was a management consultant with Deloitte from 1996–2004. Rebecca has a BA from Rice University, an MBA from the University of Michigan, and a post-graduate certificate in cross-sector partnerships from Cambridge University, England. Rebecca has lived, worked in or visited 34 countries on 6 continents and speaks a smattering of Mandarin, Cantonese, Japanese, French, Spanish, Hindi, and Tamil.

LARA DITTOE • VICE PRESIDENT/PRODUCT DEVELOPMENT, ATAYNE, LLC Lara has 20+ years in the sports apparel arena. She has a keen eye for market trends and is able to transform that vision into leading product. Lara was a founding member and V.P. of Merchandising for Athleta, a women's sports lifestyle company, which was recently purchased by Gap Inc. for US$150MM. Additionally, she was a Product Line Manager for 3 years at Brooks Sports. Working on both the women's and men's lines, she consistently produced 20 to 40% yearly growth. Her experience also includes retail management, sales representation, and retail buying. Lara has a BA from the University of Washington and currently lives in the Seattle area with her husband and two children.

MICHAEL HALL • VICE PRESIDENT/MARKETING AND COMMUNITY BUILDING, ATAYNE, LLC Michael was a three-sport athlete in college, playing hockey, baseball, and football. Professionally, Mike has spent 9 years in the Consumer Packaged Goods (CPG) industry with roles spanning sales strategy and execution, trade promotion management, national account sales, customer development, and sales finance. He has worked for large CPG firms including M&M/Mars and Church & Dwight and more recently the smaller, entrepreneurial company Dr. Fresh, Inc. Mike received his BA from Bowdoin College and an MBA from Northeastern University.

PARKER KARNAN • VICE PRESIDENT/STRATEGY AND DEVELOPMENT Parker is a 15+ year veteran of the sporting goods industry having spent most of his career at Brooks Sports, Inc. Parker was the Vice President of Apparel Sales where he led US sales efforts for 4 divisions of the $150MM company. Prior to heading up Apparel Sales, Parker directed the apparel brand's reposition from parity to premium over a 3 year period, increasing the annual margin by 1300 basis points, thereby establishing the business as a profitable unit of Brooks. After leaving Brooks, Parker founded Karnan Associates, a consultancy that works closely with presidents and owners of businesses to help them achieve their business vision and goals. Parker holds an undergraduate degree from Dartmouth and a graduate degree from the University of San Francisco.

KATHLEEN LENDVAY • VICE PRESIDENT/OPERATIONS, ATAYNE, LLC Kathleen brings drive, clarity, and relentless focus on execution to help achieve Atayne's vision. Kathleen has 12 years of consulting and product management experience working with start-ups and Fortune 100 companies in a variety of industries. She has provided interim leadership to execute strategic initiatives such as product launches, alliance development, vendor management, and process design. To find her, follow the sound of the the voice asking "how, why, when, who, and how much?" Kathleen has a BA from Rice University and currently lives with her husband, son, and golden retriever in Seattle.

LIBBY VANCE • PRODUCT DEVELOPMENT CONSULTANT, ATAYNE, LLC Libby is a product expert with a passion for organic and sustainable apparel. In senior apparel positions at Brooks Sports, Sugoi, and Lululemon Athletica, Libby has helped lead positive changes in the apparel industry toward a more sustainable future. Her current work as an independent consultant is focused on private brand development and creation of the women's athletic brand Zella for Nordstrom. Libby lives in Vancouver, BC (home of the 2010 Winter Olympics), with her husband Mark and their dog Rusty.

WAYNE HENNINGER • PR CONSULTANT   Independent publicist Wayne Henninger has over 16 years of public relations, marketing, and feature writing experience. As co-founder of WAVE PR and Sports, Wayne was responsible for overseeing, promoting, and generating business for the entire firm. He coordinated publicity campaigns for athletes and sports entities including the Senior Olympics, Major League Lacrosse, the Baltimore Marathon, Sports & Entertainment Direct, the Hail Redskins book, and BikeDC. Earlier in his career, Wayne was a member of the Detroit Pistons public relations department and a freelance writer for *ESPN—The Magazine*.

In addition to the current team, Atayne has formed a **Board of Advisors** with a wealth of experience in the management of new, growing, and mature businesses across a variety of industries. The current Board of Advisors includes:

CHARLIE JONES • PRESIDENT AND FOUNDER, BRAND INTERSECTION GROUP, LLC   Charlie's 20-year career includes brand work in the advertising, direct marketing, public relations, interactive, sports marketing, grassroots promotions, social marketing, cause related marketing, and entertainment fields. He has worked on brands such as Pepperidge Farm, Jockey, GEICO, McDonald's, Spalding, Major League Baseball, The Virginia Lottery, and Sprint. Charlie recently launched the branding consultancy Brand Intersection Group. Charlie was formerly CMO of RedPeg Marketing, CMO of Arnold Worldwide, and President of Earle Palmer Brown. Charlie is a current marketing faculty member at Georgetown's McDonough School of Business.

JAMES F. KENEFICK • CHAIRMAN, BETTERWORLD TELECOM, LLC • MANAGING DIRECTOR, WEX PARTNERS   Jim is a seasoned entrepreneur with 20+ years of experience as a CEO/operator in the high tech, nutrition, and telecommunications industries. As CEO/Co-founder of 3 companies he led growth from zero to US$15MM, $30MM, and $70MM, all within 10 years. He founded an executive coaching and strategic management consulting firm called Working Excellence in 2006 to support CEOs, corporate boards, and executive management teams. In 2007, he co-founded Working Excellence Capital Partners to advise on corporate development and to provide capital, networking, strategic, and legal advisory services.

BRAD NIERENBERG • PRESIDENT/CEO, REDPEG MARKETING, INC.   In just over a decade, Brad Nierenberg has built RedPeg Marketing into a 50-person marketing powerhouse with clients such as Anheuser-Busch, the National Guard, GEICO, Bacardi and the State of Texas. Brad's leadership skills and marketing insight has positioned RedPeg as a highly-respected, award winning agency with accolades including a yearly Top 25 ranking in *Promo Magazine's* Promo 100, a consistent position in Inc. Magazine's Inc. 500, multiple Ex Awards from *Event Marketer* magazine and a Best Place to Work honor from *Washingtonian magazine*. In 2004, *Fortune Small Business* and Winning Workplaces named Brad as a Best Boss, one of 15 recipients chosen from a pool of US executives.

POTOMAC RIVER RUNNING OWNERSHIP GROUP   Ray and Cathy Pugsley and Brendan and Margie Shapiro are the owners of Potomac River Running, a group of five specialty-running stores in the Washington, DC metropolitan area. The Running Network consistently ranks Potomac River Running in the top 50 running stores in the US. In addition to their stores, the group runs a popular running club that successfully melds the functions of organizing, scheduling, coaching, and selling in one seamless process. All four owners competed in track and field in high school and college. Margie now competes on the international Triathlon Union professional circuit, and she is a USA Triathlon National Team Member.

Appendices

Appendix 1: Pro-Forma Income Statement

	2008	2009	2010	2011	2012	2013
Revenues						
Direct Revenues	$ 36,000	$ 277,000	$ 554,000	$ 2,036,000	$ 4,492,000	$ 8,127,000
Wholesale Revenues	$ -	$ 20,000	$ 50,000	$ 200,000	$ 1,000,000	$ 3,000,000
Total Revenues	**$ 36,000**	**$ 297,000**	**$ 604,000**	**$ 2,236,000**	**$ 5,492,000**	**$ 11,127,000**
COGS	$ 20,455	$ 127,021	$ 243,457	$ 802,240	$ 1,893,418	$ 3,713,376
Gross Profit (Loss)	**$ 15,545**	**$ 169,979**	**$ 360,543**	**$ 1,433,760**	**$ 3,598,582**	**$ 7,413,624**
Operating Expenses						
Employee Compensation	$ 7,107	$ 169,000	$ 613,600	$ 890,500	$ 1,251,593	$ 2,276,556
Sales & Marketing	$ 54,553	$ 175,000	$ 380,000	$ 410,000	$ 512,500	$ 748,750
Product Design & Dev	$ 15,000	$ 40,000	$ 60,000	$ 90,000	$ 108,000	$ 129,600
Shipping & Logistics	$ 3,200	$ 8,613	$ 17,928	$ 61,885	$ 156,863	$ 330,825
Office, Admin, & Comm	$ 5,200	$ 50,000	$ 60,000	$ 72,000	$ 79,200	$ 87,120
Travel	$ 7,000	$ 35,000	$ 42,000	$ 50,400	$ 55,440	$ 60,984
Legal & Accounting Fees	$ 4,047	$ 50,000	$ 60,000	$ 72,000	$ 86,400	$ 103,680
Total Operating Expenses	**$ 96,107**	**$ 527,613**	**$ 1,233,528**	**$ 1,646,785**	**$ 2,249,996**	**$ 3,737,515**
Operating Profit (Loss)	**$ (80,561)**	**$ (357,634)**	**$ (872,986)**	**$ (213,024)**	**$ 1,348,586**	**$ 3,676,108**
Tax Expense	$ -	$ -	$ -	$ -	$ 539,434	$ 1,470,443
Net Profit (Loss)	**$ (80,561)**	**$ (357,634)**	**$ (872,986)**	**$ (213,024)**	**$ 809,152**	**$ 2,205,665**

Appendix 2: Pro-Forma Statement of Cash Flow

	2008	2009	2010	2011	2012	2013
Operating Activities						
Sources of Cash						
Cash from Services	$ -	$ -	$ -	$ -	$ -	$ -
Cash from Products	$ 30,242	$ 297,000	$ 604,000	$ 2,236,000	$ 5,492,000	$ 11,127,000
Uses of Cash						
Cash Paid for Inventory	$ 91,419	$ 147,886	$ 412,424	$ 1,075,034	$ 2,348,408	$ 4,285,032
Cash Paid for Employees	$ 7,107	$ 169,000	$ 613,600	$ 890,500	$ 1,251,593	$ 2,276,556
Cash Paid for SG & A	$ 89,000	$ 358,613	$ 619,928	$ 756,285	$ 998,403	$ 1,460,959
Taxes Paid	$ -	$ -	$ -	$ -	$ 539,434	$ 1,470,443
Net Cash from Operating Activities	$ (157,284)	$ (378,498)	$ (1,041,953)	$ (485,819)	$ 354,162	$ 1,634,009
Investing Activities						
Sources of Cash						
Sale of Assets	$ -	$ -	$ -	$ -	$ -	$ -
Uses of Cash						
Purchase of Property and Equipment	$ -	$ -	$ -	$ -	$ -	$ -
Net Cash from Investing Activities	$ -	$ -	$ -	$ -	$ -	$ -
Financing Activities						
Sources of Cash						
Proceeds from New Borrowings	$ 201,763	$ 790,000	$ -	$ -	$ -	$ -
Proceeds from Sale of Equity	$ -	$ -	$ 2,000,000	$ -	$ -	$ -
Owner Capital Contributions	$ -	$ -	$ -	$ -	$ -	$ -
Uses of Cash						
Repayment of Loans	$ -	$ -	$ -	$ -	$ -	$ -
Dividends/Distributions	$ -	$ -	$ -	$ -	$ -	$ -
Net Cash from Financing Activities	$ 201,763	$ 790,000	$ 2,000,000	$ -	$ -	$ -
Change in Cash and Cash Equivalents	**$ 44,479**	**$ 411,502**	**$ 958,047**	**$ (485,819)**	**$ 354,162**	**$ 1,634,009**
Cumulative Cash Flow	**$ 60,119**	**$ 471,621**	**$ 1,429,668**	**$ 943,850**	**$ 1,298,012**	**$ 2,932,021**

Valuing a Business

At certain times, an entrepreneur may need to determine the value of her or his business. Despite the subjective nature of assigning value to a privately held company—that is, a firm whose stock is not traded publicly—and especially a *small* privately owned firm, there are times when the value must be estimated.

The Need to Compute Firm Value

A variety of specific situations may call for a firm valuation, including the following:

1. An entrepreneur decides to buy a business, rather than starting one from scratch. He or she needs to know the answers to two questions, which may seem the same but are not: "How much is the business worth to me?" and "What should I pay for it?"

2. An owner has decided to make an employee stock ownership plan (ESOP) part of the firm's retirement program (see Chapter 12). The stock has to be valued each year so that the appropriate number of shares can be contributed to the employees' retirement plan.

3. A firm is raising money from outside investors. The firm's value must be determined to establish the percentage of ownership the new investors will receive in the company (see Chapter 11).

4. One partner wants to buy out another partner or the interest of a deceased partner. The value of the business must be set so that a price can be agreed on.

5. An owner wants to exit (harvest) the business. Knowing the value of the company is essential if the business is to be sold or transferred to family members (see Chapter 12).

These are the most common reasons for valuing a business. Note that they are, for the most part, driven by external influences and exceptional circumstances. But it is a good idea to value a business on an ongoing basis—at least once a year. As a firm grows and becomes more profitable, the owner needs to know if the business is also increasing in value. In some situations, a profitable business may lose value over time. Therefore, being aware of its value is important in the management of a business. Knowing your firm's value provides critical insight into how the firm is performing, what options it has, and how it can improve long-term.

Valuation Methods

firm value (enterprise value)
The value of the entire business, regardless of how it is financed.

equity value (owner's value)
The value of the firm less the debt owed by the firm.

In valuing firms, it is important to distinguish between *firm value* and *owner value. Firm value, or enterprise value,* is the value of the entire business, regardless of how it is financed. It reflects the value of the underlying assets of the business. *Equity value,* or *owner's value,* on the other hand, is the total value of the firm less the amount of debt owed by the firm. That is,

$$\text{Firm value} - \text{Outstanding debt} = \text{Equity value}$$

Some approaches to determining firm value focus on the first quantity on the left side of the equation—estimating the value of the firm as an entity. The question is "Given the firm's assets and its ability to produce profits from these assets, what is the firm worth?" The equity value is then found by subtracting the outstanding debt from the total firm value.

Other approaches involve determining the value of the outstanding debt and the equity value separately. In those cases, firm value is found by summing the amount of outstanding debt and the equity value. While both processes produce similar results, we recommend finding the firm value and then subtracting the outstanding debt in order to determine the equity, or owner's, value.

There are three basic methods for valuing a business: (1) asset-based valuation, (2) valuation based on comparables, and (3) cash flow-based valuation. Each of these methods can be used as a stand-alone measure of firm value, but more often they are used in combination.

ASSET-BASED VALUATION

An *asset-based valuation* assumes that the value of a firm can be determined by examining the value of the underlying assets of the business (the left-hand side of the balance sheet). Three variations of this approach use (1) the modified book value of assets, (2) the replacement value of assets, and (3) the liquidation value of assets.

The *modified book value method* starts with the numbers shown on a company's balance sheet. These amounts are adjusted to reflect any obvious differences between the historical cost of each asset (as given on the balance sheet) and its current market value. For instance, the market value of a firm's plant and equipment may be totally different from its depreciated historical cost or book value. The same may be true for real estate. The *replacement value method* entails estimating the cost to replace each of the firm's assets. And the *liquidation value method* involves estimating the amount of money that would be received if the firm ended its operations and liquidated its assets.

Asset-based valuation is of limited worth in valuing a business. The historical costs shown on the balance sheet may be very different from the current value of the assets. The three variations to some extent adjust for this weakness, but their estimate of value has a weak foundation, as all asset-based techniques fail to recognize the firm as an ongoing business. However, the liquidation value method yields an estimate of the value that could be realized if the assets of the business were all sold separately, which is sometimes helpful information.

VALUATION BASED ON COMPARABLES

A *valuation based on comparables* looks at the actual market prices of recently sold firms similar to the one being valued—either publicly traded firms (market comparables) or private firms that have been sold (transaction comparables). "Similar" means that the two firms are in the same industry and are alike in such characteristics as growth potential, risk, profit margins, assets-to-sales relationships, and levels of debt financing.

For instance, you might start by finding several recently sold companies with growth prospects and levels of risk comparable to those of the firm being valued. For each of these firms, you calculate the *earnings multiple*, or *value-to-earnings ratio*,[1]

$$\text{Earnings multiple} = \frac{\text{Value}}{\text{Earnings}}$$

Earnings may be one of the following:

1. *Earnings before interest, taxes, depreciation, and amortization, frequently referred* to as *EBITDA*
2. Earnings before interest and taxes (EBIT), which is also a firm's operating income
3. Net income

Of these three options, earnings before interest, taxes, depreciation, and amortization is the most popular.

asset-based valuation Determination of the value of a business by estimating the value of its assets.

modified book value method Determination of the value of a business by adjusting book value to reflect obvious differences between the historical cost and the current market value of the assets.

replacement value method Determination of the value of a business by estimating the cost of replacing the firm's assets.

liquidation value method Determination of the value of a business by estimating the money that would be available if the firm were to liquidate its assets.

valuation based on comparables Determination of the value of a business by considering the actual market prices of firms that are similar to the firm being valued.

earnings multiple A ratio determined by dividing a firm's value by its annual earnings; also called *value-to-earnings ratio*.

earnings before interest, taxes, depreciation, and amortization (EBITDA) A firm's profits after subtracting cost of goods sold and cash operating expenses, but before subtracting depreciation and amortization, interest expense, and taxes.

Then, assuming that the company being valued should have an earnings multiple comparable to those of similar firms, you apply the calculated ratio to estimate the company's value. That is, you apply the multiple in the following equation:

Value = Earnings of company being valued × Earnings multiple of comparable firms

Potential buyers of one novelty manufacturer and importer in Missouri offered 4.9 times the firm's annual EBITDA of $45,000. That is, the buyer was willing to pay $220,500 for the firm (EBITDA of $45,000 × 4.9 = $220,500).[2]

The market-comparable valuation method is not as easy to use as it might seem. First, finding other firms that are comparable in every way to the firm being valued is often difficult. It is not enough simply to find a firm in the same industry, although that might provide a rough approximation. As already noted, the ideal comparable firm is one that is in the same industry, is a similar type of business, and has a similar growth rate, financial structure, asset turnover ratio (sales ÷ total assets), and profit margin (profits ÷ sales). Fortunately, considerable information is published about firm sales. For instance, a publication called *Mergerstat* reports the prices of all such sales announced in the public media. Also, some accounting firms can provide information about the selling prices of comparable businesses.

normalized earnings
Earnings that have been adjusted for unusual items, such as fire damage, and leakages, such as an excessive salary for the owner.

Second, ideally *normalized earnings* should be used in this computation. Normalizing earnings involves adjusting for any unusual items, such as a one-time loss on the sale of real estate or as the consequence of a fire. In addition, normalizing earnings involves adding back any "leakages" that are occurring in the firm's income. For instance, if the owners have been paying themselves a salary above what it would take to find a similarly qualified manager, the excess should be deducted in ascertaining the firm's normalized earnings.

A variation on valuation based on comparables is simply to assign an appropriate earnings multiple. There are two fundamental drivers of a firm's earnings multiple—risk and growth. The two are related as follows:

1. The more (less) risky the business, the lower (higher) the appropriate earnings multiple and, as a consequence, the lower (higher) the firm's value.

2. The higher (lower) the projected growth rate in future earnings, the higher (lower) the appropriate earnings multiple and, therefore, the higher (lower) the firm's value.

These relationships are presented graphically in Exhibit B-1.

As already noted, earnings multiples vary with the nature of the firm. (In practice, of course, earnings multiples are also affected by conventional wisdom and the perspective and

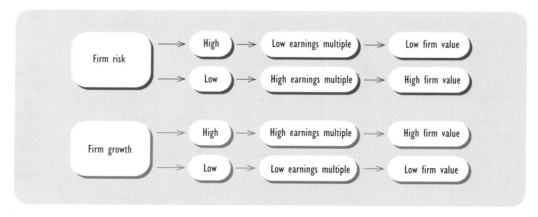

EXHIBIT B-1 Risk and Growth: Key Factors Affecting the Earnings Multiple and Firm Value

experience of the person performing the valuation.) Following are some examples of multiples based on the type of firm:

Type of Firm	Earnings Multiple
Small, well-established firm, vulnerable to recession	7
Small firm requiring average executive ability but operating in a highly competitive environment	4
Firm that depends on the special, often unusual, skill of one individual or a small group of managers	2

Earnings multiples also vary by industry, as shown by the following average multiples in different industries:[3]

Industry	Earnings Multiple
Manufacturing	5.5 to 8.5
High-tech	6.0 to 12.0
Health-care services	5.0 to 9.0
Retail	4.5 to 7.5
Public relations, advertising, media	3.0 to 6.5
Restaurant	4.0 to 8.0

Consider a real-life example. When Robert Hall, former owner of Visador Corporation, was considering selling his firm, he received an offer based on a multiple of five times the firm's operating income plus depreciation expense.[4] The offer was presented to Hall in the following format:[5]

Company's operating income plus depreciation expense	$ 3,300,000
Earnings multiple	× 5
Firm value	$16,500,000

To determine what Hall would receive for his ownership of the business, we subtract the $750,000 of debt owed by the firm, to get $15,750,000.

Hall rejected the offer of $15.75 million but made a counter-offer of $20 million for his ownership. Hall's counter-offer was accepted, which suggests that the buyer wanted the firm more than he let on initially.

The appropriateness of using earnings to value a firm is the subject of ongoing debate. Some contend that markets value a firm based on future cash flows, not reported earnings. Moreover, they argue, there are simply too many ways (within generally accepted accounting principles) to influence a firm's reported earnings, leading to material differences in valuation estimates when there is no difference in the intrinsic value of the firm. For these individuals, a firm's value is the present value of the firm's projected future cash flows.

CASH FLOW-BASED VALUATION

Although not popular among smaller companies, *cash flow-based valuation,* in which a company is valued based on the amount and timing of its future cash flows, makes a lot of sense. Valuations based on earnings, although used more often, present a conceptual problem. From an investor's or owner's perspective, the value of a firm should be based on future cash flows, not reported earnings—especially not reported earnings for just a single year.

Measuring the value of a firm's future cash flows for a cash flow-based valuation is a three-step process:

Step 1. Project the firm's expected future cash flows.

Step 2. Estimate the investors' and owners' required rate of return on their investment in the business.

Step 3. Using the required rate of return as the discount rate, calculate the present value of the firm's expected future cash flows, which equals the value of the firm.

cash flow-based valuation
Determination of the value of a business by estimating the amount and timing of its future cash flows.

The cash flow-based approach is the most complicated of the three valuation methods discussed here; an in-depth explanation is well beyond the scope of this book. But it has one distinct advantage: A cash flow-based evaluation requires that *explicit* assumptions be made about the firm's future growth rates, its profit margins (profits to sales), how efficiently it is managing its assets (sales relative to the amount of the assets), and the appropriate discount rate (required rate of return). In contrast, a valuation based on comparables only *implicitly* considers the relationship between the multiple being used and the factors that should determine the multiple. Thus, using cash flow-based valuation requires the estimator to examine more carefully *why* the firm has value.

end notes

CHAPTER 1

1. Global Entrepreneurship Monitor.

2. Reynolds and Curtin, *op. cit.*

3. For an extensive report of the role of small businesses in the U.S. economy, see "The Small Business Economy: A Report to the President," United States Government Printing Office, Washington, D.C., 2009, http://www.sba.gov/advo/research/sb_econ2008.pdf, accessed February 28, 2009.

4. Mark Hendricks, "Oh Hire Ground," *Entrepreneur Magazine*, February 2008, p. 19

5. Simona Covel, "Slump Batters Small Business, Threatening Owners' Dreams," *WSJ Online*, http://online.wsj.com/article/SB123025114273834377.html?mod=djemSB, accessed September 30, 2008.

6. John J. Fernandes, "Management and Entrepreneurship Education: Looking over the Horizon," speech given at the 2006 United States Association of Small Business and Entrepreneurship/Small Business Institute Conference, Tucson, Arizona, January 15, 2006.

7. Patricia B. Gray, "Business Class," *Fortune*, April 17, 2006, http://money.cnn.com/magazines/fortune/fortune_archive/2006/04/17/8374351/index.htm, accessed Octoer 6, 2008.

8. The description of Table Occasions is based on an interview with Chia Stewart, one of the firm's founders, in September 2008.

9. This description of Bert and John Jacobs, the founders of Life Is Good, is based on an interview by Leigh Buchman in "Life Lessons," *Inc. Magazine*, October 2006, p. 86.

10. Sara Wilson, "A Business Comes into Fruition," *Entrepreneur Magazine*, http://www.entrepreneur.com/worklife/successstories/youngmillionaires/article196572.html, accessed September 15, 2008.

11. Lena Basha, "The Entrepreneurial Gene," *MyBusiness*, December/January 2007, p. 15.

12. For a discussion on "making meaning," see Guy Kawasaki, *The Art of the Start* (The Woodlands, TX: Portfolio, 2004), pp. 4–6.

13. Avivia Yael, "The Get Ahead Guide: Erin McKenna Makes the Best Cupcakes in New York City," *Inc. Magazine*, July 2008, p. 89.

14. Thomas J. Stanley and William D. Danko, *The Millionaire Next Door* (New York: Simon & Schuster, 1996), p. 227.

15. Gangaram Singh and Alex De-Noble, "Early Retirees as the Next Generation of Entrepreneurs," *Entrepreneurship Theory and Practice*, Vol. 27, No. 3 (Spring 2003), pp. 218–220.

16. Ram Charan, "Stop Whining, Start Thinking," *Business Week*, August 24, 2008, p. 58.

17. Michelle Conlin, editor, "How to Get a Life and Do Your Job," *Business Week*, August 14, 2008, pp. 37–38.

18. Personal conversation with Rick Davis, October 15, 2008.

19. William J. Dennis, Jr., "Success, Satisfaction and Growth," *NFIB National Small Business Poll* (Washington: National Federation of Independent Business, 2001), p. 1.

20. A 2004 NFIB Research Foundation.

21. Lena Basha, "Like a Good Neighbor," *MyBusiness*, December/January 2008, p. 28.

22. *Ibid.*

23. Norman R. Smith, *The Entrepreneur and His Firm: The Relationship between Type of Man and Type of Company* (East Lansing: Bureau of Business and Economic Research, Michigan State University, 1967). See also Norman R. Smith and John B. Miner, "Type of Entrepreneur, Type of Firm, and Managerial Motivation: Implications for Organizational Life Cycle Theory," *Strategic Management Journal*, Vol. 4, No. 4 (October–December 1983), pp. 325–340; Carolyn Y. Woo, Arnold C. Cooper, and William C. Dunkelberg, "The Development and Interpretation of Entrepreneurial Typologies," *Journal of Business Venturing*, Vol. 6, No. 2 (March 1991), pp. 93–114.

24. Sara Wilson, "Leading Ladies," *Entrepreneur Magazine*, November 2008, p. 66.

25. It was with great sadness that we learned of the death of Jeff Timmons in 2008. He truly made a difference in this world. There is simply no way to measure the contribution he made to entrepreneurship education and in helping his students and others start and operate successful businesses. His passion for what he taught was truly contagious. Even more important, he was good to other people. You were always encouraged when you spent time with him. He will be missed by many.

26. Jeffry A. Timmons and Stephen Spinelli, *New Venture Creation: Entrepreneurship for the 21st Century* (New York: McGraw-Hill/Irwin, 2009), p. 367.

27. Thomas L. Friedman, *The World Is Flat* (Waterville, ME: Thorndike Press, 2005).

28. Chris Pentilla, "All Shook Up," *Entrepreneur*, December 2005, pp. 112–113.

29. Amar Bhide, *The Venturesome Economy* (Princeton, NJ: Princeton University Press, 2008).

30. Chris Penttila, "Keeping Fresh," *Entrepreneur*, Vol. 33, No. 4 (April 2005), p. 86.

31. Pete Engardio, with Michael Arndt and Dean Foust, "The Future of Offshoring," *Business Week*, January 30, 2006, p. 46.

32. Sarah Wilson, "Learning from the Best," *Entrepreneur*, March 2006, p. 62.

33. Cited in Gary M. Stern, "Young Entrepreneurs Make Their Mark," *Nation's Business*, Vol. 84, No. 8 (August 1996), pp. 49–51.

34. Personal conversation with Tyler Self, October 29, 2008. Also, for a great reference on the importance of experience in being successful, see Malcom Gladwell, *Outliers: The Story of Success* (New York: Little, Brown, 2009).

35. Tamera Erikson, "Don't Treat Them Like Baby Boomers," *Business Week*, August 14, 2008, p. 64.

36. This description of the Millennials comes from Donna Fenn, "Cool, Determined & Under 30," *Inc. Magazine*, October 2008, p. 97.

37. *Ibid.*

38. http://www.womenhomebusiness,com/success/glenfiddich.htm, accessed February 8, 2006.

39. J. B. Rotter, "Generalized Expectancies for Internal versus External Control of Reinforcement," *Psychological Monographs*, 1966. A more recent review is given in Robert H. Brockhaus, Sr., and Pamela S. Horwitz, "The Psychology of the Entrepreneur," in Donald L. Sexton and Raymond W. Smilor (eds.), *The Art and Science of Entrepreneurship* (Cambridge, MA: Ballinger, 1986), pp. 25–48.

40. Timmons and Spinelli, *op. cit.*, pp. 46–54.

41. This quote comes from an interview of Scott Cook by John Koten, as reported in "Everything Will Change," *Inc. Magazine*, September 2007, http://www.inc.com/magazine/20070901/everything-will-change.html, accessed September 2008.

CHAPTER 2

1. "In the Game of Business, Playing Fair Can Actually Lead to Greater Profits,"

Knowledge at Wharton, March 13, 2008, http://knowledge.wharton.upenn.edu/article.cfm;jsessionid=9a30d49231903b653224?articleid=1916, accessed September 4, 2008.

2. Karl Eller, *Integrity Is All You've Got: And Seven Other Lessons of an Entrepreneurial Life* (New York: McGraw-Hill, 2005), p. 89.

3. Leslie E. Palich, Justin G. Longenecker, Carlos W. Moore, and J. William Petty, "Integrity and Small Business: A Framework and Empirical Analysis," Proceedings of the 49th World Conference of the International Council for Small Business, Johannesburg, South Africa, June 2004.

4. Laura L. Nash, *Good Intentions Aside: A Manager's Guide to Resolving Ethical Problems* (Boston: Harvard Business School Press, 1993), p. 61.

5. *Milton Friedman, Capitalism and Freedom* (Chicago: University of Chicago Press, 1963), p. 133.

6. Jana Matthews and Jeff Dennis, *Lessons from the Edge: Survival Skills for Starting and Growing a Company* (Oxford: Oxford University Press, 2003), pp. 119–123.

7. Hattie Bryant, Producer of Small Business School, the series on PBS Stations, Worldnet, and the Web at http://smallbusinessschool.org.

8. Jodie Carter, "Rolling in Dough," *Entrepreneur*, Vol. 31, No. 6 (June 2003), p. 106; and personal conversation with Mike Jacobs, October 6, 2006.

9. David Dorsey, "Happiness Pays," *Inc. Magazine* Vol. 26, No. 2 (February 2004), pp. 88–94.

10. Palich et al., *op. cit.*

11. Nathan Bennett, "Munchausen at Work," *Harvard Business Review*, Vol. 85, No. 11 (November 2007), pp. 24–27.

12. "Employee Theft: Legal Aspects—Estimates of Cost," http://law.jrank.org/pages/1084/Employee-Theft-Legal-Aspects-Estimates-cost.html, accessed September 4, 2008.

13. "Employee Theft," http://www.criminal-law-lawyer-source.com/terms/employee-theft.html, accessed September 4, 2008.

14. "Executive Team," http://www.salesforce.com/company/leadership/executive-team, accessed September 21, 2008.

15. Chris Penttila, "Got Skills?" *Entrepreneur*, Vol. 34, No. 9 (September 2006), pp. 100–101; and personal conversation with David Shapiro, February 13, 2007.

16. Raymund Flandez, "Small Companies Put Charity into Their Business Plan," *The Wall Street Journal* (November 20, 2007), p. B3.

17. The popular business press provides numerous examples to support this position, but we recognize that the evidence from academic studies on the subject is mixed. For an excellent review of this research, see Michael L. Barnett, "Stake-holder Influence Capacity and the Variability of Financial Returns to Corporate Social Responsibility," *Academy of Management Review*, Vol. 32, No. 3 (July 2007), pp. 794–816.

18. "2004 Cone Corporate Citizenship Study Results," http://www.causemarketingforum.com/page.asp?ID=330, accessed November 12, 2008.

19. William J. Dennis, Jr., "Contributions to Community," National Federation of Independent Business, quarterly research report, Vol 4, No. 6 (2004).

20. Eric Knopf, "One Step at a Time," in Michael McMyne and Nicole Amare (eds.), *Beyond the Lemonade Stand: 14 Undergraduate Entrepreneurs Tell Their Stories of Ethics in Business* (St. Louis, MO: St. Louis University, 2004), pp. 47–48.

21. Martin Vaughn, "IRS Too Easy on Payroll Taxes, Study Finds," *The Wall Street Journal* (July 29, 2008), p. A8.

22. Paulette Thomas, "Virtual Business Plans Require Human Touch," *The Wall Street Journal* (August 2, 2005), p. B2.

23. Nadine Heintz, "For Rolling up Her Sleeves," *Inc. Magazine* (April 2004), pp. 128–129.

24. Justin G. Longenecker, Joseph A. McKinney, and Carlos W. Moore, "Egoism and Independence: Entrepreneurial Ethics," *Organizational Dynamics*, Vol. 16, No. 3 (Winter 1988), pp. 64–72.

25. These differences were significant at the .05 level.

26. Karl Eller, *op. cit.*, p. 90.

27. As cited in Jeffrey L. Siglin, "Do It Right," *MBA Jungle* (November 2001), p. 69.

28. David H. Freedman, "Worried That Employees Are Wasting Time on the Web? Here's Why You Shouldn't Crack Down," *Inc. Magazine*, Vol. 28, No. 8 (August 2006), pp. 77–78.

29. American Management Association, "2005 Electronic Monitoring & Surveillance Survey: Many Companies Monitoring, Recording, Video-taping—and Firing—Employees" (May 18, 2005), http://www.amanet.org/press/amanews/ems05.htm, accessed November 12, 2008.

30. "Handbagged," *Economist* (June 19, 2008), http://www.economist.com/business/Printer/Friendly.cfm?story_id=11580287, accessed July 10, 2008.

31. Brad Stone, "Court Clears eBay in Suit over Sale of Counterfeit Goods," *The New York Times* (July 15, 2008), http://www.nytimes.com/2008/07/15/technology/15ebay.html?_r=1&pagewanted=print&oref=slogin, accessed September 10, 2008.

32. "Fake Gucci, Vuitton Bags Seized in Italy," CNNMoney.com (September 25, 2006), http://money.cnn. com/2006/09/25/news/international/ counterfeit_bags.reut/index.htm? postversion=2006092518, accessed October 2, 2006.

33. A study by Justin G. Longenecker, Joseph A. McKinney, and Carlos W. Moore ("Religious Intensity, Evangelical Christianity, and Business Ethics: An Empirical Study," *Journal of Business Ethics,* Vol. 55, No. 2 [2004], pp. 373–386) provides evidence to support this position. The authors examined data from 1,234 business leaders responding to a national survey. They asked study participants to evaluate the ethical quality of responses described in a series of vignettes (from "never acceptable" to "always acceptable") and also to identify which of the following five broad categories best described their religious faith: Catholic, Protestant, Jewish, other religions, no religion. Study results found no difference between these general groups. However, respondents who indicated that religious interests were of high or moderate importance to them demonstrated a higher level of ethical judgment than did others in the study, as did those who considered their beliefs to be consistent with the basic tenets of Evangelical Christianity. These findings suggest that religious values play a part in ethical decision making, though *general* religious categorizations do not seem to have this same impact.

34. Kent Jennings Brockwell, "10 Questions: Jeff Ukrop," Richmond.com (August 27, 2007), http://www.richmond.com/local-life/120, accessed September 12, 2008; "Ukrop's," NationMaster.com, http://www.nationmaster.com/encyclopedia/Ukrop's-Super-Market, accessed September 12, 2008.

35. Nicholas G. Moore, "Ethics: The Way to Do Business," http://www.bentley.edu/cbe/events/lecture_sears_moore.cfm, accessed September 12, 2008.

36. Excerpt from an interview with J. C. Huizenga in "Virtuous Business and Educational Practice," *Religion & Liberty* (a publication of the Acton Institute for the Study of Religion and Liberty), Vol. 12, No. 2 (September–October 2002), p. 1.

37. Kenneth H. Blanchard and Norman Vincent Peale, *The Power of Ethical Management* (New York: Harper-Collins, 1989).

38. J. Michael Alford, "Finding Competitive Advantage in Managing Workplace Ethics," paper presented at the 2005 meeting of the United States Association for Small Business and Entrepreneurship, Indian Wells, California, January 13–16, 2005.

39. More specific insights and guidance for writing a code of conduct can be found at the following website: http://www.ethics.org/resources/common-code-provisions.asp, accessed September 21, 2008.

40. "Resource Toolkit: The PLUS Decision Making Model," Ethics Resource Center, http://www.ethics.org/resources/decision-making-process.asp, accessed September 12, 2008.

41. "Guiding Principles," http://www.rotary.org/en/AboutUs/RotaryInternational/GuidingPrinciples/Pages/ridefault.aspx, accessed September 21, 2008.

42. Brian K. Burton and Michael Goldsby ("The Golden Rule and Business Ethics: An Examination," *Journal of Business Ethics,* Vol. 56, No. 3 [2005], pp. 371–383) offer an extended discussion of the history, meaning, and problems of the Golden Rule. They document the appearance of this general principle in the writings of several major world religions and philosophers and provide examples of companies that have used the Golden Rule explicitly as a guide for decision making (e.g., JCPenney and Lincoln Electric Co.). The influence of the Golden Rule is so pervasive that Burton and Goldsby conclude that it "seems to be one of the few candidates for a universally acceptable moral principle."

43. Kant actually offered a critique of the Golden Rule, but only as a footnote to his discussion of the categorical imperative. In his opinion, the categorical imperative is a superior concept for a number of reasons, all of which are related to his expanded view of the imperative (see Immanuel Kant, *Grounding for the Metaphysics of Morals, with a Supposed Right to Lie Because of Philanthropic Concerns,* 3rd ed., trans. J. W. Ellington [Indianapolis: Hackett Publishing, 1993]).

44. This definition is offered in James Austin, Howard Stevenson, and Jane Wei-Skillern, "Social and Commercial Entrepreneurship: Same, Different, or Both?" *Entrepreneurship Theory & Practice,* Vol. 30, No. 1 (2006), pp. 1–22. However, the authors recognize that definitions of the term vary from an emphasis on nonprofit enterprises to corporate philanthropy and many other activities. Indeed, in their article, Austin, Stevenson, and Wei-Skillern identify key differences between social and commercial entrepreneurship. Using Sahlman's analytical framework (W. A. Sahlman, "Some Thoughts on Business Plans," in W. A. Sahlman, H. Stevenson, M. J. Roberts, and A. V. Bhide (eds.), *The Entrepreneurial Venture* [Boston: Harvard Business School Press, 1996], pp. 138–176), the authors compare the two forms of entrepreneurship across four factors: the *people,* the *context,* the *deal,* and the *opportunity.* They highlight substantial differences across all four factors. For example, commercial entrepreneurs tend to focus on breakthrough opportunities where new needs are emerging, whereas social entrepreneurs are concerned with opportunities centered on basic, longstanding needs that can be served more effectively with innovative approaches. However, they also conclude there are notable similarities. Taken together, the authors' observations suggest that the concept of social entrepreneurship, though becoming less ambiguous, is still not

defined to the satisfaction of many entrepreneurship researchers.

45. Paul Sloan, "Doughing the Right Thing," *Business 2.0,* Vol. 7, No. 7 (August 2006), p. 82.

46. Elaine Pofeldt, "Beyond the Bottom Line," *Fortune,* Vol. 150, No. 13 (December 27, 2004), p. 170[H].

47. "Tanzania—Hero Rats," http://www.pbs.org/frontlineworld/stories/tanzania605/video_index.html, accessed September 19, 2008.

48. "Greening Your Business: A Primer for Smaller Companies," http://www.greenbiz.com/resources/resource/greening-your-business-a-primer-smaller-companies, accessed September 22, 2008.

49. http://www.epa.gov/epaoswer/hazwaste/sqg/sqghand.htm?cm_sp=ExternalLink-_-Federal-_-EPA, accessed September 12, 2008.

50. See David Worrell, "Keen on Green," *Entrepreneur,* Vol. 34, No. 9 (September 2006), pp. 67–71, for a helpful summary of trends related to "green" technologies and the investments they have attracted.

51. http://www.bigbellysolar.com, accessed September 15, 2008.

52. Marc Gunter, "Tree Huggers, Soy Lovers, and Profits," *Fortune,* Vol. 147, No. 12 (June 23, 2003), pp. 99–104.

CHAPTER 3

1. Clay Shirky, "The (Baysian) Advantage of Youth," http://many.corante.com/archives/2007/05/19/the_bayesian_advantage_of_youth.php, accessed January 13, 2009.

2. To read more about an interesting framework that integrates three forms of the search process (deliberate search, industry insight guided search, and alertness to opportunities), see Robert A. Baron, "Opportunity Recognition as Pattern Recognition: How Entrepreneurs 'Connect the Dots' to Identify New Business Opportunities," *Academy of Management Perspectives,* Vol. 20, No. 1 (February 2006), pp. 104–119.

3. Israel M. Kirzner, *Competition and Entrepreneurship* (Chicago: University of Chicago Press, 1973), p. 74.

4. Andrew C. Corbett and Jeffery S. McMullen built upon Kirzner's concept of entrepreneurial alertness by introducing the practice of "mindfulness" to the opportunity recognition discussion. They describe the differences between the two perspectives as follows: "Unlike entrepreneurial alertness, mindfulness can be developed. This potential for development allows entrepreneurial alertness to be transformed from a trait that someone either does or does not have to a skill that can be learned." For more on the concept and practice of mindfulness, see Andrew C. Corbett and

Jeffery S. McMullen, "Perceiving and Shaping New Venture Opportunities Through Mindful Practice," in Andrew Zacharakis and Stephen Spinelli, Jr. (eds.), *Entrepreneurship: The Engine of Growth* (Westport, CT: Praeger Perspectives, 2007), pp. 43–64.

5. For an in-depth discussion of the concept and the essence of the mind-set of the entrepreneur, see Jeffery S. McMullen and Dean A. Shepherd, "Entrepreneurial Action and the Role of Uncertainty in the Theory of the Entrepreneur," *Academy of Management Review,* Vol. 31, No. 1 (2006), pp. 132–152.

6. We should point out that the process of opportunity recognition is not entirely cognitive (driven by thoughts); in fact, affect (feelings and emotions) can also play a very important role. For an interesting analysis of the interplay of affect and cognitive processes, see Robert A. Baron, "The Role of Affect in the Entrepreneurial Process," *Academy of Management Review,* Vol. 33, No. 2 (2008), pp. 328–340.

7. Quoted in April Y. Pennington, "Copy That: In Business, Imitation Is More Than a Form of Flattery," *Entrepreneur,* Vol. 34, No. 3 (March 2006), p. 22.

8. Lee Gimpel, "Idea Mining," *Entrepreneur,* Vol. 34, No. 12 (December 2006), p. 70.

9. Sara Wilson, "A Step Ahead," *Entrepreneur,* Vol. 36, No. 11 (November 2008), p. 41.

10. Jada Cash, "Cure Couture," *Entrepreneur,* Vol. 34, No. 12 (December 2006), p. 128.

11. Gerry E. Hills and R. P. Singh, "Opportunity Recognition," in W. B. Gartner, K. G. Shaver, and P. D. Reynolds (eds.), *Handbook of Entrepreneurial Dynamics: The Process of Business Creation* (Thousand Oaks, CA: Sage Publications, 2004), Table 24.4, p. 268.

12. "About Cabana Life," http://www.cabanalife.com/about.php, accessed January 13, 2009; Nichole L. Torres, "Transform a Negative Experience into a Positive Business Idea," *Entrepreneur,* Vol. 35, No. 12 (December 2007), pp. 108–109.

13. http://www.bestkiteboarding.com/09-Company, accessed January 13, 2009; Lindsay Holloway, "To the Extreme," *Entrepreneur,* Vol. 36, No. 3 (March 2008), p. 21.

14. http://www.totelemonde.com/aboutus.html, accessed November 13, 2008.

15. For an expanded discussion of this framework, see Peter F. Drucker, *Innovation and Entrepreneurship: Practice and Principles* (New York: HarperCollins, 2006), pp. 30–129.

16. *Ibid.,* p. 30.

17. To learn more about the application of creativity to the process of business idea generation, see Dimo Dimov, "Idea Generation from a Creativity Perspective," in Andrew Zacharakis and Stephen Spinelli, Jr. (eds.), *Entrepreneurship: The Engine of Growth* (Westport, CT: Praeger Perspectives, 2007), pp. 19–41.

18. "A Revolutionary Concept," http://www .aimiesdinnerandmovie.com/about.asp, accessed January 13, 2009.

19. Lauren Etter, "The Joys of Juggling," *Wall Street Journal*, January 30, 2006, p. R9.

20. "About Us," http://www.leasetrader.com/ car/lease/info/agreement/about_us.aspx, accessed January 13, 2009; James Park, "New Lease on Life," *Entrepreneur*, Vol. 35, No. 5 (May 2007), p. 116.

21. Chris Pentila, "Hit or Miss," *Entrepreneur*, Vol. 32, No. 6 (June 2004), pp.108–113.

22. *Ibid.*

23. Nichole L. Torres, "New and Improved," *Entrepreneur*, Vol. 33, No. 5 (May 2005), p. 96.

24. "Adventure Bachelor Party," http:// adventurebachelorparty.com, accessed January 13, 2009; Amanda Pennington, "Creature Comforts," *Entrepreneur*, Vol. 34, No. 7 (July 2006), pp. 120–122.

25. "Overview," http://www.obecure.com/ apage/9748.php, accessed January 13, 2009; Loolwa Khazzoom, "Beating Obesity with an Old Drug," *Business 2.0*, Vol. 8, No. 7 (August 2007), p. 28.

26. Kristin Ohlson, "Save Water, Save Money," *Entrepreneur*, Vol. 36, No. 10 (October 2008), p. 20.

27. "RFID Is a Winner in the Sports Arena," RFID Journal, http://www.rfidjournal.com/ article/articleview/4028/5/474, accessed January 13, 2009; Siri Schubert, "A Duffer's Dream," *Business 2.0*, Vol. 7, No. 10 (November 2006), p. 56.

28. Tony Manning, *Making Sense of Strategy* (New York: American Management Association, 2002), p. 17.

29. As something of a parallel to the outside-in and inside-out options, Dimo Dimov ("From Opportunity Insight to Opportunity Intention: The Importance of Person-Situation Learning Match," *Entrepreneurship Theory and Practice*, Vol. 31, No. 4 [July 2007], p. 566) mentions two very different opportunity insight–inducing situations. In *demand-driven* situations, the entrepreneur is aware of customer needs but does not know of any products that could meet those needs. Dimov uses the example of Phil Knight and Bill Bowerman, co-founders of Nike, who came up with the first long-distance running shoe. They had known for some time that runners needed shoes that were lighter, promoted lateral stability, and could better cushion impact, but it wasn't until later that they discovered they could create a new sole by pouring latex onto a household waffle iron. *Supply-driven* situations are just the opposite. Here, awareness of an emerging product exists, but the entrepreneur is not aware of customer needs that could be satisfied by it. This is closer to the experience of Roy Jacuzzi, who used his inventive knowledge of pump systems to come up with the first whirlpool bath. Only later did he discover a market for his product.

30. Much of the research on this subject is based on firms of all sizes, not just small businesses; however, there is no reason to rule out entirely the applicability of this research to entrepreneurial companies. Some studies present strong evidence that context is important (Suresh Kotha and Anil Nair, "Strategy and Environment as Determinants of Performance: Evidence from the Japanese Machine Tool Industry," *Strategic Management Journal*, Vol. 16, No. 7 [1995], pp. 497–518; A. M. McGahan and Michael E. Porter, "How Much Does Industry Matter, Really?" *Strategic Management Journal*, Vol. 18, Summer Special Issue [1997], pp. 15–30; R. Schmalensee, "Do Markets Differ Much?" *American Economic Review*, Vol. 75, No. 3 [1985], pp. 341–351), whereas others show that context is important but not as great a driver of firm performance as such internal factors as a company's resources (Gabriel Hawawini, Venkat Subramanian, and Paul Verdin, "Is Performance Driven by Industry- or Firm-Specific Factors? A New Look at the Evidence," *Strategic Management Journal*, Vol. 24, No. 1 [2003], pp. 1–16; Mona Makhija, "Comparing the Resource-Based and Market-Based Views of the Firm: Empirical Evidence from Czech Privatization," *Strategic Management Journal*, Vol. 24, No. 3 [2003], pp. 433–451). Thomas J. Douglas and Joel A. Ryman ("Understanding Competitive Advantage in the General Hospital Industry: Evaluating Strategic Competencies," *Strategic Management Journal*, Vol. 24, No. 2 [2003], pp. 333–347) interpret the results of their study to suggest that both external context and internal factors are important to the formation of competitive advantage, a conclusion that is consistent with evidence from studies of small and medium-sized enterprises, such as those conducted by Bo Eriksen and Thorbjorn Knudsen ("Industry and Firm Level Interaction: Implications for Profitability," *Journal of Business Research*, Vol. 56, No. 3 [2003], pp. 191–199), Stewart Thornhill ("Knowledge, Innovation and Firm Performance in High- and Low-Technology Regimes," *Journal of Business Venturing*, Vol. 21, No. 5 [2006], pp. 687–703), and Clement K. Wang and Bee Lian Ang ("Determinants of Venture Performance in Singapore," *Journal of Small Business Management*, Vol. 42, No. 4 [2004], pp. 347–363).

31. Kevin J. Delaney, "Searching for Clients from Above," *Wall Street Journal*, July 31, 2007, p. B1; Logan Kugler, 69 "Targeting the Eye in the Sky," *Business 2.0*, Vol. 7, No. 3 (April 2006), p. 26.

32. Rich Karlgard, "Schumpeter on Speed," *Forbes*, Vol. 178, No. 3 (August 14, 2006), p. 35.

33. Delaney, *op. cit.*

34. Krysten Crawford, "The Big Opportunity," *Business 2.0*, Vol. 7, No. 5 (June 2006), pp. 95–99.

35. Michael Porter, *Competitive Advantage* (New York: Free Press, 1985), pp. 7–29.

36. William A. Sahlman, "How to Write a Great Business Plan," *Harvard Business Review*, Vol. 75, No. 4 (July–August 1997), pp. 103–104.

37. Robert Levine, "The Kopy Kat Kids," CNNMoney.com ,October 2, 2007, http:// money.cnn.com/2007/10/02/technology/ kopy_kat_kids.biz2/index.htm, accessed January 13, 2009.

38. Gary Hamel, "Strategy as Revolution," *Harvard Business Review*, Vol. 74, No. 4 (July–August 1996), p. 80.

39. For an interesting discussion of this case and others where relaxing assumptions that guide business behavior has made a significant difference in entrepreneurial efforts of businesses around the world, see C. K. Prahalad, *The Fortune at the Bottom of the Pyramid: Eradicating Poverty Through Profits* (Upper Saddle River, NJ: Wharton School Publishing, 2005).

40. http://www.starbucks.com, accessed January 13, 2009.

41. "Heartwood Studios," http://www.hwd3d .com, accessed January 13, 2009; Nichole L. Torres, "Biz U: Industrial Evolution," *Entrepreneur*, Vol. 35, No. 11 (November 2007), pp. 142–143.

42. It should be pointed out that a recent study of small businesses conducted by the National Federation of Independent Business found that 34.4 percent of all small businesses surveyed said that competing on price is a very significant feature of their strategy, which is consistent with an emphasis on controlling costs (specifically, 51 percent said that keeping overhead to a minimum is a very significant feature of their strategy). However, it is also important to note that providing better service and offering the highest quality possible were significantly important to even more firms (83.4 percent and 86.3 percent, respectively), which indicates that differentiation strategies are even more important to small businesses. See William J. Dennis, Jr. (ed.), "Competition," *National Small Business Poll*, Vol. 3, No. 8 (2003).

43. "Spirit Airlines – About Us," http://www .spiritair.com/AboutUs.aspx, accessed June 7, 2009.

44. Scott McCartney, "The Next Airline Fee: Buying Tickets?" *Wall Street Journal* (March 3, 2009), http://online.wsj.com/ article/SB123604492886515417.html, accessed June 7, 2009.

45. "Radio Tag: We Put You All over the Radio," http://www.getradiotag.com, accessed January 13, 2009; Sara Wilson, "Maximizing Air Time," *Entrepreneur*, Vol. 36, No. 11 (November 2008), p. 71.

46. Philip Kotler, *Marketing Insights from A to Z* (New York: John Wiley & Sons, 2003), p. 65.

47. "Welcome!" http://www.personalized bottlewater.com/aboutus.asp, accessed January 13, 2009.

48. Brian O'Reilly, "A Small Firm That Sells Custom-Labeled H2O Looks to Pump Online Sales," *Fortune Small Business*, Vol. 17, No. 1 (February 26, 2007).

49. "Spin—Portfolio," http://www.spin-la.com/ port_ac_cobra.html, accessed January 13, 2009.

50. Laura Tiffany, "Road to Success," *Entrepreneur*, Vol. 36, No. 11 (November 2008), pp. 88–97.

51. *Ibid.*

52. "COBB Tuning—History," http://www .cobbtuning.com/info/?id=2953, accessed January 13, 2009.

53. Tiffany, *op. cit.*

54. Marc J. Dollinger, *Entrepreneurship: Strategies and Resources* (Lombard, IL: Marsh Publications, 2008), p. 144.

55. Porter, *op. cit.*, p. 5.

56. Quoted in Mark Henricks, "What Not to Do," *Entrepreneur*, Vol. 32, No. 2 (February 2004), pp. 84–90.

57. John W. Mullins, *The New Business Road Test* (London: Financial Times Prentice Hall, 2006), pp. 3–4.

58. *Ibid.*, p. 10.

CHAPTER 4

1. http://www.referenceforbusiness.com, accessed March 2, 2009.

2. http://www.theukfranchisedirectory.net, accessed March 2, 2009.

3. Roger D. Blair and Franchine Lafontaine, *The Economics of Franchising* (Cambridge: Cambridge University Press, 2005).

4. Hilary Strahota, "Benjamin Franklin: Father of Franchising? *Franchising World*, September 2007.

5. http://www.franchise.org/industrysecondary, accessed December 29, 2008.

6. International Franchise Association, *Membership Handbook* (2007), p. 4.

7. Nichole L. Torres, "Staying Power," http:// www.entrepreneur.com/magazine/2006/ january, accessed January 17, 2009.

8. http://www.subway.com/subwayroot/ legalDisclaimer, accessed January 17, 2009.

9. http://www.franchise.org/Veteran-Franchise, accessed January 19, 2009.

10. Dennis L. Monroe, "Teamwork," *Franchise Times*, Vol. 14, No. 9 (October, 2008), p. 90.

11. http://www.franchiseregistry.com/ partnership.asp, accessed March 3, 2009.

12. "Legal Briefs," *Franchise Time*, Vol. 14, No. 7 (August, 2008), p. 51.

13. *Ibid.*

14. *Inc. Magazine* Staff, "How to Buy a Business," www.inc.com/magazine, accessed March 5, 2009.

15. http://www.astutediligence.com, January 12, 2007.

16. *Ibid.*

CHAPTER 5

1. Frank Hoy and Pramodita Sharma, *The Entrepreneurial Family Business* (Upper Saddle River, NJ: Pearson Prentice Hall, 2010).

2. James Olan Hutcheson, "In with the Old; Out with the Older," *Family Business*, http:// www.familybusinessmagazine.com/ worldsoldest.html, accessed September 27, 2008.

3. "The World's 250 Largest Family Businesses," *Family Business*, www.familybusiness magazine.com/topglobal.html, accessed September 27, 2008.

4. http://www.amserv.com/familystatistics .html, accessed September 28, 2008.

5. J. H. Chua, J. J. Chrisman, & P. Sharma, "Defining the Family Business by Behavior," *Entrepreneurship Theory & Practice*, Vol. 23, No. 4, pp. 19–39.

6. Alternatively, the European Group of Owner-Managed and Family Enterprises classifies a firm, of any size, as a family enterprise, if (1) the majority of votes is in possession of the natural person(s) who established the firm, or in possession of the natural person(s) who has/have acquired the share capital of the firm, or in the possession of their spouses, parents, child, or children's direct heirs; (2) at least one representative of the family or kin is involved in the management or administration of the firm; or (3) the person(s) who established or acquired the firm or their families or descendents possess 25 percent of the right to vote mandated by their share capital.

7. Lowell J. Spirer, *The Human Factor in Starting Your Own Business* (Blue Bell, PA: Lowell J. Spirer, n.d.), e-book.

8. Daniel L. McConaughy, "Family CEOs vs. Non-Family CEOs in the Family-Controlled Firm: An Examination of the Level and Sensitivity of Pay to Performance," *Family Business Review*, Vol. 13, No. 2 (June 2000), pp. 121–131; and Simon Bartholomeusz and George A. Tanewski, "The Relationship Between Family Firms and Corporate Governance," *Journal of Small Business Management*, Vol. 44, No. 2 (April 2006), pp. 245–267.

9. http://www.scjohnson.com/family/, accessed September 28, 2008.

10. David G. Sirmon and Michael A. Hitt, "Managing Resources: Linking Unique Resources, Management, and Wealth Creation in Family Firms," *Entrepreneurship Theory and Practice*, Vol. 27, No. 4 (Summer 2003), pp. 341–344. These findings are consistent with the results of other recent research—see, for example, Ronald C. Anderson and David M. Reeb, "Founding-Family Ownership and Firm Performance: Evidence from the S&P 500," *Journal of Finance*, Vol. 58, No. 3 (June 2003), pp. 1301–1328.

11. John L. Ward, "New Research on Family Business Culture," proceedings of the Fifth Annual Kellogg Family Business Invitational Conference, Evanston, IL, May 16–17, 2006, pp. 51–65.

12. W. Gibb Dyer and David A. Whetten, "Family Firms and Social Responsibility: Preliminary Evidence from the S&P 500," *Entrepreneurship Theory and Practice*, Vol. 30, No. 6 (November 2006), pp. 785–802.

13. Patricia Olsen, "At the Helm," *Family Business*, Vol. 18, No. 4 (Autumn 2007), p. 12.

14. A description of these bases of commitment and an extensive discussion of the theory and analysis that back up these conclusions can be found in Pramodita Sharma and P. Gregory Irving, "Four Bases of Family Business Successor Commitment: Antecedents and Consequences," *Entrepreneurship Theory and Practice*, Vol. 29, No. 1 (January 2005), pp. 13–33. Our discussion of these commitment bases and the quotes we use are sourced from this article.

15. *Ibid.*, pp. 25–26.

16. Bill Glavin, Joe Astrachan, and Judy Green, *2007 American Family Business Survey* (Springfield, MA: Massachusetts Mutual Life Insurance Company, 2007).

17. Quoted in Jeff D. Opdyke, "Readers' Views on Family, Feuds and Quality of Life," CareerJournal.com, April 26, 2005, http://www.careerjournal.com/myc/ workfamily/20050426-opdyke.html, accessed December 13, 2006.

18. Pia Chatterjee, "Making Beautiful Startups Together," *Business 2.0*, September 2007, pp. 42–44.

19. Krissah Williams, "We Do: Copreneurs Simultaneously Build Happy Marriages and Thriving Enterprises," *Black Enterprise*, February 2008.

20. "Ask Inc.," *Inc. Magazine*, March 2007, pp. 81–82.

21. Sue Birley, "Attitudes of Owner-Managers' Children Toward Family and Business Issues," *Entrepreneurship Theory and Practice*, Vol. 26, No. 3 (Summer 2002), pp. 5–19.

22. Stephanie Clifford, "Splitting Heirs," *Inc. Magazine*, August 2007, pp. 103–110.

23. *Family Business*, "Ask the Experts: A Sibling Rivalry Festers After a Chairman's Death," Vol. 18, No. 4 (Autumn 2007), pp. 8, 10, 14.

24. John L. Ward, "Family Humor," proceedings of the Fifth Annual Kellogg Family Business Invitational Conference, Evanston, IL, May 16–17, 2006, p. 45.

25. *Ibid.*

26. Darren Dahl, "Was Firing Him Too Drastic?" *Inc. Magazine,* Vol. 28, No. 10 (October 2006), pp. 51–54.

27. John L. Ward, quoted in Margaret Steen, "The Decision Tree of Family Business," *Stanford Business,* August 2006, http://www .gsb.stanford.edu/news/bmag/ sbsm0608/ feature_familybiz.html, accessed December 22, 2006.

28. Joe Astrachan, Andrew Keyt, Suzanne Lane, and Dan Yarmalouk, "Non-Family CEO's in the Family Business: Connecting Family Values to Business Success," proceedings of the Family Business Network World Conference, Helsinki, Finland, 2002.

29. Steven White, quoted in Kenneth Meeks, "Family Business," *Black Enterprise,* Vol. 34, No. 1 (August 2003), p. 91.

30. Matthew Fogel, "A More Perfect Business," *Inc. Magazine,* Vol. 25, No. 8 (August 2003), p. 44.

31. Daniela Montemerlo, "Regulating Relations Between Family, Ownership and Company: The Role and Variety of Formal Agreements—Some Italian Experiences," proceedings of the Family Business Network Academic Research Forum, London, 2000.

32. *Ibid.*

33. John L. Ward, "Family Humor," proceedings of the Fifth Annual Kellogg Family Business Invitational Conference, Evanston, IL, May 16–17, 2006, p. 46.

34. *Ibid.*, p. 47.

35. Adam Bluestein, "The Success Gene," *Inc. Magazine,* April 2008, pp. 83–94.

36. For an extended discussion of various aspects of mentoring in the family firm, see Barbara Spector (ed.), *The Family Business Mentoring Handbook* (Philadelphia: Family Business Publishing Co., 2004). Only one of many resources on mentoring, this edited volume provides articles outlining a number of proven mentoring strategies, as well as case examples of family companies that have used these approaches to achieve effective succession transitions. The book addresses processes and strategies as they apply specifically to family businesses.

37. This topic is explored in depth in Johan Lambrecht, "Multigenerational Transition in Family Businesses: A New Explanatory Model," *Family Business Review,* Vol. 18, No. 4 (2005), pp. 267–282. We base our model of succession in this chapter primarily on the work of Lambrecht.

38. Austin Ramirez, quoted in Margaret Steen, "The Decision Tree of Family Business," *Stanford Business,* August 2006, http://www .gsb.stanford.edu/news/bmag/sbsm0608/ feature_familybiz.html, accessed December 22, 2006.

CHAPTER 6

1. The MIT Enterprise Forum (http://web.mit .edu/entforum) sponsors sessions across the United States in which aspiring entrepreneurs present business plans to panels of venture capitalists, bankers, marketing specialists, and other experts.

2. David E. Gumpert, *How to Really Create a Successful Business Plan,* 4th ed. (Needham, MA: Lauson Publishing Co., 2003), p. 10.

3. Several of these studies include Stephen C. Perry, "The Relationship Between Written Business Plans and the Failure of Small Business in the U.S.," *Journal of Small Business Management,* Vol. 39, No. 2 (2001), pp. 201–208; Frederic Delmar and Scott Shane, "Does Business Planning Facilitate the Development of New Ventures?" *Strategic Management Journal,* December 2003, pp. 1165–1185; Scott Shane and Frederick Delmar, "Planning for the Market: Business Planning Before Marketing and the Continuation of Organizing Efforts," *Journal of Business Venturing,* Vol. 19 (2004), pp. 767–785; Tomas Karlsson and Benson Honig, "Business Planning Practices in New Ventures: An Institutional Perspective," presented at the Babson Entrepreneurship Research Conference, April 2007; and Julian E. Lange et al., "Pre-Startup Formal Business Plans and Post-Startup Performance: A Study of 116 New Ventures," forthcoming in *Venture Capital Journal.*

4. Thomas Stemberg, "What You Need to Succeed," *Inc. Magazine,* Vol. 29, No. 1 (January 2007), pp. 75–77.

5. Kelly Spors, "Do Start-Ups Really Need Formal Business Plans?" *Wall Street Journal,* January 9, 2007, p. B9.

6. Amar Bhide, *The Origin and Evolution of New Businesses* (New York: Oxford University Press, 2000), p. 53.

7. Stephen Lawrence and Frank Moyes, "Writing a Successful Business Plan," http:// leeds-faculty.colorado.edu/ moyes/html/ resources.htm, accessed December 15, 2008.

8. Bhide, *op. cit.,* p. 70.

9. "Conversations with Ewing Marion Kauffman," Ewing Marion Kauffman Foundation, March 2004.

10. Peter Drucker, quoted in Brian Tracy, "7 Secrets to Success," *Entrepreneur,* Vol. 35, No. 2 (February 2007), pp. 96–103.

11. Gumpert, *op. cit.,* pp. 30–34.

12. An alternative framework for a feasibility analysis to what is presented in Chapter 3 is provided by Frank Moyes, a professor at the University of Colorado, at his website http://leeds-faculty.colorado.edu/moyes/ html/documents/FeasibilityPlan2007, accessed December 15, 2008.

13. Portions of the content in this section draw on Jeffry A. Timmons, Andrew Zacharakis, and Stephen Spinelli, *Business Plans That Work* (New York: McGraw-Hill, 2004).

14. Rhonda M. Abrams, *The Successful Business Plan: Secrets and Strategies,* 2nd ed. (Grants Pass, OR: Oasis Press, 2003).

15. http://www.inc.com/articles/1999/ 10/14877.html, accessed January 17, 2009.

16. Personal conversation with Rudy Garza, November 18, 2008.

17. http://www.powerhomebiz.com/vol3/ badbplan.htm, accessed November 9, 2006; http://www.bpiplans.com/Articles.htm, accessed December 9, 2008; and Robert A. Baron and Scott A. Shane, *Entrepreneurship: A Process Perspective,* 2nd ed. (Cincinnati: Thomson South-Western, 2008), p. 220.

18. Mark Stevens, "Seven Steps to a Well-Prepared Business Plan," *Executive Female,* Vol. 18, No. 2 (March 1995), p. 30.

19. Jeffrey Bussgang "Think Like a VC, Act like an Entrepreneur, *BusinessWeek,* http:// www.businessweek.com/magazine/ content/08_34/b4097042749532.htm? chan=magazine+channel_special+report, accessed September 2, 2008.

20. Kenneth Blanchard, Don Hotson, and Ethan Willis, *The One-Minute Entrepreneur* (New York: Doubleday, 2008).

21. Personal conversation with Tim Smith, September 2008.

22. For additional information on business plans, visit http://www.cengage.com/ management/ longenecker.

23. Jill Andresky Fraser, "Who Can Help Out with a Business Plan?" *Inc. Magazine,* Vol. 21, No. 8 (June 1999), pp. 115–117.

24. http://www.entrepreneur.com/startinga business/businessplans/article38314.html,

CHAPTER 7

1. http://www.lakepowell.com, accessed February 21, 2009; http://knowledge.wpcarey .asu.edu, accessed February 21, 2009.

2. From the business plan of Calico Computer Consulting, http://www.bplans.com, accessed February 22, 2009.

3. From the business plan of Borrow My Tools, http://www.bplans.com, accessed February 22, 2009.

4. Personal conversation with Todd Stoner of Disciplined Investors, December 2006.

5. From the Private Placement Memorandum for Spira Footwear, *Inc. Magazine,* June 2007.

6. Carl McDaniel and Roger Gates, *Marketing Research,* 8th ed. (New York: John Wiley & Sons, 2009).

7. http://blog.dirtbag.com, accessed March 13, 2009.

8. McDaniel and Gates, *op. cit.,* pp. 94–95.

9. Isabella Trebond, "On Target," *Entrepreneur,* August 2004.

10. Michael Porter, *Competitive Advantage* (New York: Free Press, 1985), p. 5.

CHAPTER 8

1. Michael Fitzgerald, "Turning Vendors into Partners," *Inc. Magazine*, Vol. 27, No. 8 (August 2005), p. 95.

2. The exact percentage of solo startups is hard to pin down. Recent analyses of startups based on data from the Panel Study of Entrepreneurial Dynamics have determined that nearly one-half of all new ventures are launched by individuals [see "Teaming with Entrepreneurs: A Look at the Research of Howard Aldrich," in *Understanding Entrepreneurship: A Research Policy Report* (Kansas City, MO: Ewing Marion Kauffman Foundation, 2005), p. 40; and Paul D. Reynolds, Nancy M. Carter, William B. Gartner, Patricia G. Greene, and Larry W. Cox, *The Entrepreneur Next Door: Characteristics of Individuals Starting Companies in America* (Kansas City, MO: Ewing Marion Kauffman Foundation, 2002), p. 5]. A study of small businesses conducted by the National Federation of Independent Business found that more than 58 percent of the companies in the study sample were owned by a single individual [see "Business Structure," in William J. Dennis (ed.), *National Small Business Poll*, Vol. 4, No. 7 (Washington, DC: National Federation of Small Business, 2004), p. 10]. One recent review of studies on the topic puts the number of solo startups closer to one-third of new ventures [see Gaylen N. Chandler, "New Venture Teams," in Andrew Zacharakis and Stephen Spinelli, Jr. (eds.), *Entrepreneurship: The Engine of Growth* (Westport, CT: Praeger Perspectives, 2007), pp. 75–76]. Regardless of the percentage accepted, it is clear that many firms are started by individual entrepreneurs.

3. Chandler, *op. cit.* It also bears noting that, in many cases, one or more members of high-performing entrepreneurial teams have had prior experience with business startups. This pattern is evident in studies by Michael D. Ensley, Allison W. Pearson, and Allen C. Amason, "Understanding the Dynamics of New Venture Top Management Teams: Cohesion, Conflict, and New Venture Performance," *Journal of Business Venturing*, Vol. 17, No. 4 (July 2002), pp. 365–366; and Elizabeth J. Teal and Charles W. Hofer, "Key Attributes of the Founding Entrepreneurial Team of Rapidly Growing New Ventures," *Journal of Private Equity*, Vol. 4, No. 2 (Spring 2001), pp. 19–31.

4. This point is emphasized in Daniel P. Forbes, Patricia S. Borchert, Mary E. Zelmer-Bruhn, and Harry J. Sapienza, "Entrepreneurial Team Formation: An Exploration of New Member Addition," *Entrepreneurship Theory and Practice*, Vol. 30, No. 2 (March 2006), p. 226.

5. The field has evolved toward a view that sees management team members as those with financial ownership and significant decision-making responsibilities in the venture (see Chandler, *op. cit.*). Other definitions are more restrictive and emphasize factors such as being a part of the founding of the venture [see Iris Vanaelst, Bart Clarysse, Mike Wright, Andy Lockett, Nathalie Moray, and Rosette S'Jegers, "Entrepreneurial Team Development in Academic Spinouts: An Examination of Team Heterogeneity," *Entrepreneurial Theory and Practice*, Vol. 30, No. 2 (March 2006), p. 251]. At the other end of the spectrum, some entrepreneurs consider all employees and advisors to be a part of the team. Because our discussion is focused on those who hold important leadership positions in the small business but may not share ownership in the firm, we use the broader term *management team* rather than *entrepreneurial team* to reflect this more general view.

6. For an interesting study of the addition of members to the management team, see Daniel P. Forbes, Patricia S. Borchert, Mary E. Zellmer-Bruhn, and Harry J. Sapienza, "Entrepreneurial Team Formation: An Exploration of New Member Addition," *Entrepreneurship Theory and Practice*, Vol. 30, No. 2 (March 2006), pp. 225–248.

7. This may explain why research using Panel Study of Entrepreneurial Dynamics data found that around three-fourths of *solo* entrepreneurs were starting service firms (49 percent) or retail businesses (26 percent). These types of startups tend to be less complicated than technology-based firms or manufacturing businesses, so a single founder is more likely to have the knowledge and experience necessary to get the business going. A more complex startup may well require the combined expertise and insight of a *team* of entrepreneurs. For a closer look at the data, see *Expected Costs of Startup Ventures*, a consulting report prepared for the SBA's Office of Advocacy by Blade Consulting Corporation, Vienna, VA, November 2003.

8. It should be noted that research has not always supported the view that functional balance leads to improved venture performance. Some studies have found that functional heterogeneity is correlated with small firm growth, while others offer no evidence to indicate a relationship with team performance (see Chandler, *op. cit.*).

9. Andy Lockett, Deniz Ucbasaran, and John Butler, "Opening Up the Investor-Investee Dyad: Syndicates, Teams, and Networks," *Entrepreneurship Theory and Practice*, Vol. 30, No. 2 (March 2006), p. 119.

10. Chandler, *op. cit.*, p. 71.

11. Howard E. Aldrich and Nancy M. Carter, "Social Networks," in William B. Gartner, Kelly G. Shaver, Nancy M. Carter, and Paul D. Reynolds (eds.), *Handbook of Entrepreneurial Dynamics: The Process of Business Creation* (Thousand Oaks, CA: Sage, 2004), p. 331.

12. Lauren Tara LaCapra, "Social Networking Can Be a Friend Indeed," July 28, 2008, http://www.thestreet.com/story/10430499/3/social-networking-can-be-a-friend-indeed.html, accessed January 13, 2009.

13. Robert B. Cialdini, *Influence: Science and Practice* (Needham Heights: MA: Allyn & Bacon, 2009).

14. This percentage from the Internal Revenue Service includes enterprises organized as limited liability companies (an organizational form that is introduced later in the chapter), but you should note that other sources indicate the number of startups formed as LLCs is quite small.

15. The figures offered here are based on Internal Revenue Service projections of returns for the 2009 tax year. These numbers differ from those reported elsewhere, however, and this deserves some explanation. For example, some may choose to use PSED data, but Paul D. Reynolds, ["Nature of Business Start-ups," in William B. Gartner, Kelly G. Shaver, Nancy M. Carter and Paul D. Reynolds (eds.), *Handbook of Entrepreneurial Dynamics: The Process of Business Creation* (Thousand Oaks, CA: Sage, 2004), p. 250] points out that 52.7 percent of nascent entrepreneurs intend to operate as sole proprietorships, whereas actual tax filings put the figure at 71.9 percent. While we cannot rule out the possibility that this is a result of the PSED sampling frame, it would be reasonable to conclude that many entrepreneurial hopefuls fully anticipate incorporating or forming a partnership, but they end up moving toward the least complicated form, the sole proprietorship, when the more pressing challenges of starting and running a business take priority. On the other hand, a recent survey of small businesses from the NFIB reveals that only 20.9 percent are organized as sole proprietorships, which is far more at variance with IRS data [see "Business Structure," in William J. Dennis, Jr. (ed.), *NFIB National Small Business Poll*, Vol. 4, No. 7 (Washington, DC: NFIB Research Foundation, 2004), p. 8]. The sampling frame was drawn from the files of the Dun & Bradstreet Corporation, which may represent more mature businesses, many of which started as proprietorships but changed to more sophisticated organizational forms as a shield against liability or for other reasons. We use IRS figures here because they are based on the population of all companies submitting returns and represent the most recent data available.

16. Liability insurance and other forms of protection are discussed further in Chapter 23. However, there are many forms of liability protection, and a full discussion of these goes beyond the scope of this text. Experts and specific sources of information should be consulted when making these decisions.

17. Fred S. Steingold, *Legal Guide for Starting and Running a Small Business* (Berkeley, CA: Nolo Press, 2008).

18. Karen Cheney, "Meet Your Match," http://www.quicken.com/cms/viewers/article/small_business/ 55318, accessed January 29, 2007.

19. Karen Cheney, "The Perfect Partnership Plan," http://www. quicken.com/cms/viewers/article/small_business/55340, accessed January 29, 2007.

20. Steingold, *op. cit.*

21. Ira Nottonson, *Forming a Partnership: And Making It Work* (Irvine, CA: Entrepreneur Press, 2007), pp. 6–7.

22. Nichole L. Torres, "Left in the Lurch?" *Entrepreneur,* Vol. 34, No. 5 (May 2006), p. 108.

23. John Seely Brown, quoted by Stephen J. Dubner, "How Can We Measure Innovation? A Freakonomics Quorum," April 25, 2008, http://freakonomics.blogs.nytimes.com/2008/04/25/how-can-we-measure-innovation-a-freakonomics-quorum/, accessed January 13, 2009.

24. Internal Revenue Service, "Table 1A. Calendar Year Projections of Individual Returns by Major Processing Categories for the United States," http://www.irs.gov/pub/irs-soi/d6187.pdf (data for sole proprietorships), accessed January 13, 2009; Internal Revenue Service, "Table 1. Fiscal Year Projections of the Number of Returns to be filed with the IRS," http://www.irs.gov/pub/irs-soi/d6292.pdf (data for partnerships, regular corporations, and S corporations); accessed January 13, 2009.

25. Chris Harrison, "Form Is Everything," http://www.welcomebiz.com/Guest/index.php?deptID=4&articleID=49, accessed December 5, 2008.

26. "Piercing the Corporate Veil," http://www.residual-rewards.com/piercingthecorporateveil.html, accessed March 6, 2009.

27. Rieva Lesonsky, *Start Your Own Business: The Only Start-Up Book You'll Ever Need* (Irvine, CA: Entrepreneur Press, 2007).

28. For tax years beginning after 2004, the law increased the maximum number of shareholders permitted in an S corporation from 75 to 100. (Note that husband and wife count as one stockholder.)

29. The rules have been modified in recent years to allow more types of trusts to hold Subchapter S stock.

30. As stated, S corporations can own other business entities but cannot be owned by C corporations, other S corporations, many trusts, limited liability companies, or partnerships. For more information on the subject, see "Small Business Answer Handbook," *Entrepreneur,* Vol. 34, No. 10 (October 2006), pp. 41–46.

31. Kelly Spors, "Small Talk," *Wall Street Journal,* September 9, 2006, p. B8.

32. For a description of the tax advantages of the limited liability company, see Steingold, *op. cit.*

33. Nichole L. Torres, "Lofty Ideals," *Entrepreneur,* Vol. 34, No. 6 (June 2006), pp. 150–151.

34. "Strategic Alliances," in William J. Dennis, Jr. (ed.), *National Small Business Poll,* Vol. 4, No. 4 (Washington, DC: NFIB Research Foundation, 2004), pp. 1–8.

35. *Ibid.,* p. 4.

36. Chris Penttila, "Dream Teams," *Entrepreneur,* Vol. 36, No. 6 (June 2008), p. 76.

37. "Strategic Alliances," *op. cit.,* pp. 9–14.

38. Michael Fitzgerald, "Turning Vendors into Partners," *Inc. Magazine,* Vol. 27, No. 8 (August 2005), pp. 95–100.

39. Chris Penttila, "All Together Now," *Entrepreneur,* Vol. 35, No. 8 (August 2007), pp. 92–93; "Company History," http://www.topics-ent.com/company_history.php, accessed January 13, 2009.

40. *Ibid.*

41. Mark Hendricks, "License to Thrive: How You Can Profit from Big Companies' Tech Ideas," *Entrepreneur,* Vol. 33, No. 10 (October 2005), p. 22.

42. "Strategic Alliances," *op. cit.,* p. 7.

43. Jeffrey Shuman, Janice Twombly, and David Rottenberg, *Everyone Is a Customer: A Proven Method for Measuring the Value of Every Relationship in the Era of Collaborative Business* (Chicago: Dearborn Trade Publishing, 2002).

44. National Association of Corporate Directors, *Effective Entrepreneurial Boards: Findings from the 2001–2002 Entrepreneurial Boards Survey* (Washington, DC: National Association of Corporate Directors, 2002), p. 3.

45. National Association of Corporate Directors, *op. cit.,* p. 17.

46. "Boards for Beginners," *Inc. Magazine,* Vol. 27, No. 2 (February 2005), p. 44.

CHAPTER 9

1. Eric Schlosser, *Fast Food Nation: The Dark Side of the All-American Meal* (New York: Harper Perennial, 2002), p. 66.

2. Del Jones, "California Proves Too Costly for Departing Businesses," *USAToday,* October 2, 2003, p. 1B.

3. Jacquelyn Lynn, "Location Is Key," *Entrepreneur,* Vol. 36, No. 11 (November 2008), p. 26.

4. Adapted from J. D. Ryan and Gail P. Hiduke, *Small Business—An Entrepreneur's Business Plan,* 8th ed. (Cincinnati: South–Western Cengage, 2009), pp. 148–150.

5. http://www.lids.com, accessed December 17, 2008.

6. Ryan Chittum, "A New Mantra: Location, Location, Technology," *Startup Journal,* WSJ.com, accessed July 21, 2005.

7. "COBBTuning—History," http://www.cobbtuning.com/info/?id=2953, accessed January 13, 2009.

8. According to the 2009 State Business Tax Climate Index, published by the Tax Foundation (http://www.taxfoundation.org/files/bp58.pdf, accessed January 13, 2009), Wyoming tops the rankings of best state business tax climates, followed by South Dakota, Nevada, Alaska, Florida, Montana, Texas, New Hampshire, Oregon, and Delaware, ordered here by their respective rankings.

9. "Wyoming Department of Revenue," http://revenue.state.wy.us, accessed January 13, 2009.

10. Jacquelyn Lynn, "Tax Relief," *Entrepreneur,* Vol. 36, No. 7 (July 2008), p. 24.

11. Jacquelyn Lynn, "What's It Worth," *Entrepreneur,* Vol. 36, No. 3 (March 2008), p. 32.

12. "Oregon Business—Enterprise Zones," http://www.oregon4biz.com/enterthezones, accessed December 18, 2008.

13. Rieva Lesonsky, *Start Your Own Business: The Only Start-Up Book You'll Ever Need* (Irvine, CA: Entrepreneur Press, 2007).

14. Lynn, *op. cit.* Research shows that this is certainly true for small businesses that are in high-technology manufacturing. According to a recent study, the availability of technical labor was the most important factor in the location decisions of this group of firms. [See Craig S. Galbraith, Carlos L. Rodriguez, and Alex F. DeNoble, "SME Competitive Strategy and Location Behavior: An Exploratory Study of High-Technology Manufacturing," *Journal of Small Business Management,* Vol. 46, No. 2 (April 2008), pp. 183–202.]

15. National Federation of Independent Businesses, "411 Small Business Facts," http://www.411sbfacts.com/sbpoll-tables-res.php?POLLID=0048&QID=0000 0001378&KT_back=1, accessed January 13, 2009.

16. "The Dyson Story," http://www.dyson.com/about/story, accessed January 13, 2009; Zareer Masani, "Not So Doomed," *New Statesman,* March 5, 2007, http://www.newstatesman.com/writers/zareer_masani, accessed December 22, 2008; Joshua Levine, "Carpet Diem," Forbes.com, October 14, 2002, http://www.forbes.com/forbes/2002/1014/206.html, accessed January 13, 2009; "Dyson Plant Shuts Up Shop," http://news.bbc.co.uk/2/hi/uk_news/england/2282809.stm, accessed January 13, 2009.

17. Cecilia Goodnow, "New Designs and Technology Take Treehouses to a Higher Level for Adults," *Seattle Post-Intelligencer,* August 23, 2007, http://seattlepi.nwsource.com/lifestyle/328618_treehouse23.html, accessed January 13, 2009.

18. "2005 Outstanding Incubator Graduate Award Winners," http://www.nbia.org/awards_showcase/2005/graduate.php, accessed January 13, 2009.

19. Gwendolyn Bounds, "My Office Is Your Office: Small Firms Share Space," *Wall Street Journal*, March 18, 2008, p. B4.

20. Jacquelyn Lynn, "Room to Grow," *Entrepreneur*, Vol. 36, No. 6 (June 2008), p. 26; Jacquelyn Lynn, "And the Winners Are . . . ," *Entrepreneur*, Vol. 35, No. 12 (December 2007), p. 28.

21. National Federation of Independent Businesses, "411 Small Business Facts," http://smallbusiness.findlaw.com/business-operations/commercial-real-estate/commercial-real-estate-lease-purchase.html, accessed December 22, 2008.

22. Richard Breeden, "Small Businesses Favor Buying over Leasing," *Wall Street Journal*, February 24, 2004, p. B11.

23. Emily Maltby, "Dressing Up a Sub," *Fortune Small Business*, Vol. 17, No. 9 (November 2007), p. 62.

24. *Ibid.*

25. See Candida G. Brush, Linda F. Edleman, and Tatiana S. Manolova, "The Effects of Initial Location, Aspirations, and Resources on Likelihood of First Sale in Nascent Firms," *Journal of Small Business Management*, Vol. 46, No. 2 (April 2008), pp. 159–182. The researchers note that this may be the result of freed-up resources that can be focused on the product/service or the capabilities of the business, or it may result from home-based businesses being able to organize their schedules more quickly. It should also be pointed out, however, that the study found that home-based businesses do not always enjoy advantages related to aspirations and resource formation.

26. Nichole L. Torres and April Y. Pennington, "Home Court Advantage," *Entrepreneur's Start-Ups,* May 2005.

27. Broderick Perkins, "Realize the Dream of a Home-Based Business," http://www.startupjournal.com, accessed April 9, 2004.

28. Susan Smith Hendrickson, "Balancing Work and Family," http://www.allbusiness.com/specialty-businesses/home-based-business-work-life-balance/1170-1.html, accessed January 13, 2009.

29. Torres and Pennington, *op. cit.*

30. Michael J. McDermott, "Avoid Zoning Pitfalls When Working from Home," http://www.busop1.com/pitfall.html, accessed January 13, 2009.

31. For the details of supporting research, see David A. Johnson, Michael Wade, and Ron McClean, "Does eBusiness Matter to SMEs? A Comparison of the Financial Impacts of Internet Business Solutions on European and North American SMEs," *Journal of Small Business Management*, Vol. 45, No. 3 (July 2007), pp. 354–361. The findings were based on a study of nearly 1,700 small and medium-size companies in five nations in North America and Europe, which revealed that the performance benefits from Internet business solutions were greater for American and Canadian companies than for their European counterparts. The researchers also concluded that the benefits from customer-facing applications (like e-commerce) were greater than supplier-facing alternatives (such as sales force automation and supply chain management).

32. Sara Wilson, "Global Scents," *Entrepreneur,* Vol. 35, No. 12 (December 2007), p. 164.

33. See Prashanth Nagendra Bharadway and Ramesh G. Soni, "E-Commerce Usage and Perceptions of E-Commerce Issues Among Small Firms: Results and Implications from an Empirical Study," *Journal of Small Business Management*, Vol. 45, No. 4 (October 2007), pp. 501–521.

34. http://www.witiger.com/ecommerce/benefits-limitations.htm, accessed January 13, 2009.

35. Raymund Flandez, "Help Wanted—and Found," *Wall Street Journal,* October 13, 2008, http://online.wsj.com/article/SB122347721312915407.html?mod=googlenews_wsj, accessed January 5, 2009.

36. http://www.odesk.com, accessed January 5, 2009.

37. Flandez, *op. cit.*

38. "About Us," http://www.kosher.com/help/about-us.html, accessed January 13, 2009; Melissa Campanelli, "Taking Off," *Entrepreneur*, Vol. 34, No. 5 (May 2006), pp. 42–43.

39. Shelly Banjo, "Wholesalers Set Up Shop Online to Tap Customers," *Wall Street Journal,* September 18, 2008, p. B9.

40. "eBay Marketplace Fast Facts," http://pages.ebay.in/community/aboutebay/news/infastfacts.html, accessed January 5, 2009.

41. http://www.premium.hoovers.com, accessed December 20, 2006.

42. "Goodbye and Thanks from eBay Express," http://pages.ebay.com/express, accessed January 5, 2009.

43. "eBay Stores FAQ," http://pages.ebay.com/storefronts/faq.html#what, accessed January 6, 2009.

44. Kelly K. Spors, "New Services Help Bloggers Bring in Ad Revenue," *Wall Street Journal*, January 15, 2008, p. B6.

45. Personal communication with Adam Weinroth, August 6, 2007; http://www.easyjournal.com/about.html, accessed January 6, 2009.

46. "Our Products," http://www.q3i.com/products.php, accessed January 6, 2009.

47. Nichole L. Torres, "Weekenders," *Entrepreneur*, Vol. 33, No. 8 (August 2005), p. 80; personal conversation with Chad Ronnebaum, February 7, 2007.

48. "Q3 Innovations LLC," http://www.q3i.com/aboutus.php, accessed January 6, 2009.

CHAPTER 10

1. Norm Brodsky, "Secrets of a $110 Million Man," *Inc. Magazine*, October 2008, p. 77.

2. Philip Campbell, "Are You Really Focused on Profits?" http://www. inc.com/resources/finance/ articles/20080601/campbell.html, accessed February 26, 2007. *Inc. Magazine*, June 2008. Copyright 2008 by Mansueto Ventures LLC. Reproduced with permission of Mansueto Ventures LLC in the Format Textbook via Copyright Clearance Center.

3. Jan Norman, "You're Making Sales, but Are You Making Money?"http://www.entrepreneur.com/ article/0,4621,228680,00.html, March 2004, accessed October 14, 2006.

CHAPTER 11

1. Paul A. Broni, "Persuasive Projections," *Inc. Magazine,* Vol. 22, No. 4 (April 2000), p. 38.

2. Rhonda Abrams, "How Can I Make Financial Projections in My Business Plan When I Have No Solid Numbers?" Inc.com, September 2000, http://www.inc.com/articles/2000/09/20226.html, accessed February 15, 2009.

3. David Worrell, "A Penchant for Profits," *Entrepreneur,* Vol. 33, No. 8 (August 2005), pp. 53–57.

4. This example is based on an actual situation; however, the name of the founder has been changed, as have some of the numbers.

5. Investors also look to financial projections to determine the sales level necessary for the firm to break even. A firm's break-even point, while important from a financial perspective, is also important for pricing its products or services. The issue of pricing is discussed in Chapter 16.

6. Personal communication with Cecilia Levine, November 28, 2008.

7. Scott Bernard Nelson, "Fee Agents," *Entrepreneur,* January 2003, p. 63.

8. This percentage can be found by dividing the number of days of credit the supplier is offering (30 days, in this case) by the 365 days in a year (30/365 = 8.2%).

9. If you need to review the process for creating a statement of cash flows, return to the discussion of cash flows in Chapter 10.

10. Note that the changes in the balance sheet for year 1 are actually the year-end balances, since the business did not exist in the prior year.

11. Suzanne McGee, "Breaking Free from Budgets," *Inc. Magazine,* October 2003, p. 73.

12. Information in this section was taken from Linda Elkins, "Real Numbers Don't Deceive,"

Nation's Business, Vol. 85, No. 3 (March 1997), pp. 51–52; Broni, op. cit., pp. 183–184.

13. Broni, op. cit.

CHAPTER 12

1. Mike Hofman, "The Big Picture," Inc. Magazine, Vol. 25, No. 12 (October 2003), p. 87.

2. Ilan Mochari, "The Numbers Game," Inc. Magazine, Vol. 24, No. 12 (October 2002), pp. 65–66.

3. Ibid., p. 64.

4. Personal conversation with Jack Griggs, Fall 2006.

5. To compute the $730 monthly payment, we can use a financial calculator or a computer spreadsheet.

PV (present value)	= 50,000 (current loan)
N (number of payments)	= 84 (7 years × 12 months = 84)
I/yr (interest rate/month)	= 0.5% (6% interest rate per year ÷ 12 months = 0.005 = 0.5%)
FV (future value)	= 0 (in 7 years)
Then solve for PMT (payment)	= $730.43

6. As discussed in Chapters 10 and 11, the ratio of current assets to current liabilities is called the current ratio; the ratio of total debt to total assets is called the debt ratio.

7. Mochari, op. cit, p. 64.

8. Personal interview with Bill Bailey, former owner of Cherokee Communications, Spring 2005.

9. C. J. Prince, "New Money," Entrepreneur, March 2008, http://www.entrepreneur .com/magazine/entrepreneur/2008/ march/190066.html, accessed October 2, 2008.

10. For an excellent source on business angels, see Frances M. Amatucci and Jeffrey E. Sohl, "Business Angels: Investment Processes, Outcomes, and Current Trends," in Andrew Zacharakis and Stephen Spinelli, Jr. (eds.), Entrepreneurship: The Engine of Growth (Westport, CT: Praeger, 2007), pp. 87–107.

11. Jeffry Sohl, "The Angel Investor Market In 2008: A Down Year in Investment Dollars but Not in Deals," Center for Venture Research, March 30, 2009.

12. Julian Lange, Benoit Leleux, and Bernard Surlemont, "Angel Network for the 21st Century," Journal of Private Equity, Spring 2003, p. 18.

13. William H. Payne, "Joining Angel Organizations—A Win-Win Opportunity," unpublished notes.

14. For a description of how angel networks function, see Aja Carmichael, "The Money Game: In Search of an Angel," Wall Street Journal, January 30, 2006, p. R4.

15. http://www.centexangels.org, accessed January 10, 2007.

16. Guy Kawasaki, "Garnering Angels," Entrepreneur, January 2008, http://www .entrepreneur.com/magazine/entrepreneur/ 2008/january/187614.html, accessed October 2, 2008, p. 38.

17. C. J. Prince, "Alternate Financing Routes," Entrepreneur, March 2007, pp. 66–68.

18. Jim Hopkins, "Corporate Giants Bankroll Start-Ups," USA Today, March 29, 2001, p. 1B.

CHAPTER 13

1. Personal interview with Robert Hall, former CEO of Visador Corporation, August 18, 2007.

2. Personal conversation with Bob Browder, former CEO, BFW Construction Company, February 1, 2009.

3. Simona Covel, "How to Get Workers to Think and Act Like Owners," Wall Street Journal, February 7, 2008, p. B-1.

4. Carol Tice, "Is It Time to Sell?, Entrepreneur, January 2009, http://www.entrepreneur .com/magazine/entrepreneur/2009/ january/199016.html, accessed February 5, 2009.

5. Brad Feld, "What's Your Exit Strategy?" Entrepreneur, May 2009, p. 30.

6. S. T. Certo, "Influencing Initial Public Offering Investors with Prestige: Signaling with Board Structure," Academy of Management Review, Vol. 28, No. 3 (2003), pp. 432–447.

7. Woojin Kim and Michael S. Wiesbach, "Do Firms Go Public to Raise Capital?" presented at the annual Financial Management Association Meeting, October 14, 2005.

8. The source for this example is Heritage Partners, a Boston venture capital firm, which obtained a registered trademark for a process it calls the Private IPO®.

9. Richard D. Dorf and Thomas H. Byers, Technology Ventures: From Idea to Enterprise (New York: McGraw-Hill, 2005), p. 120.

10. The unattributed quotes in this part of the chapter are taken from personal interviews conducted as part of a research study on harvesting, sponsored by the Financial Executive Research Foundation and cited in J. William Petty, John D. Martin, and John Kensinger, Harvesting the Value of a Privately Held Company (Morristown, NJ: Financial Executive Research Foundation, 1999). To acquire a copy of the book, write the Financial Executive Research Foundation, Inc., P.O. Box 1938, Morristown, NJ 07962-1938, or call 973-898-4600.

11. Jeff Bailey, "Selling the Firm—and Letting Go of the Dream," Wall Street Journal, December 10, 2002, p. B6.

12. Jennifer Wang, "Confessions of Serial Entrepreneurs," Entrepreneur, January 8, 2009, http://www.entrepreneur.com/ startingabusiness/successstories/

article199436.html, accessed April 18, 2009.

CHAPTER 14

1. "Getting More from Existing Customers," http://www.startupnation.com/ articles/1387/1/grow-business-existing-customers.asp, accessed January 14, 2009.

2. Knowledge@W.P.Carey, "The Neglected Moneymaker: Customer Retention," April 25, 2007, http://knowledge.wpcarey.asu.edu/ article.cfm?articleid=1408#, accessed January 14, 2009.

3. Frederick Reichheld, The Loyalty Effect: The Hidden Force Behind Growth, Profits, and Lasting Value (Boston: Harvard Business School Press, 2008).

4. Guy Kawasaki, "At Their Service," Entrepreneur, Vol. 35, No. 8 (August 2007), p. 24.

5. Dan J. Sanders, Built to Serve: How to Drive the Bottom Line with People-First Practices (New York: McGraw-Hill, 2008), p. 163–164.

6. Ibid., pp. 164–165.

7. A recent study indicates that increased levels of customer satisfaction leads the employees who serve them to feel better about their employers (see Xueming Luo and Christian Homburg, "Neglected Outcomes of Customer Satisfaction," Journal of Marketing, Vol. 71, No. 2 [April 2007], pp. 133–149). Satisfied employees tend to produce increased customer satisfaction, especially when they have direct contact with customers. Furthermore, this research shows that higher levels of customer satisfaction are linked to a firm being able to hire better employee and managerial talent. Reasoning from evidence in this study and others shows that customer satisfaction is beneficial to firm performance for a number of reasons, some of them a result of direct influences and others of indirect benefits that often are not even taken into consideration.

8. Charles W. Lamb, Joseph F. Hair, and Carl McDaniel, Marketing, 10th ed. (Cincinnati: South-Western Cengage Learning, 2010), p. 632.

9. Interestingly enough, research has shown that the entrepreneur–customer relationship is actually a reciprocal one (see Dirk De Clercq and Deva Rangarajan, "The Role of Perceived Relational Support in Entrepreneur-Customer Dyads," Entrepreneurship Theory & Practice, Vol. 32, No. 4 [2008], pp. 659–683). In other words, most customers recognize that the way an entrepreneurial company treats them has an impact on their level of satisfaction with and commitment to the venture; but De Clercq and Rangarajan also found that the customer's reputation and the reliability of their exchanges with the company influence the entrepreneur's satisfaction with

and commitment to that customer. In other words, one builds upon the other.

10. Marjorie J. Cooper, Nancy Upton, and Samuel Seaman, "Customer Relationship Management: A Comparative Analysis of Family and Nonfamily Business Practices," *Journal of Small Business Management,* Vol. 43, No. 3 (July 2005), pp. 242–256.

11. Brian Vellmure, "Let's Start with Customer Retention," http://www.initiumtech.com/newsletter_120602.htm, September 4, 2004.

12. Amy Barrett, "True Believers," http://www.businessweek.com/magazine/content/06_52/b4015401.htm?chan=smallbiz_smallbiz+index+page_sales+and+marketing, accessed January 15, 2009.

13. "CRM: You (Should) Love Your Customers, Now Work to Keep Them," http://www.startupnation.com/articles/1533/1/crm-software-strategy.asp, accessed January 16, 2009.

14. Lindsay Holloway, "Marx Acosta-Rubio," *Entrepreneur,* Vol. 36, No. 9 (September 2008), pp. 66–67.

15. Knowledge@W.P.Carey, *op. cit.*

16. Personal conversation with Keith Jezek, January 16, 2009.

17. Some of these suggestions were adapted from the following article: Lesley Spencer Pyle, "Keep Your Customers from Straying," June 12, 2008, http://www.entrepreneur.com/article/printthis/194784.html, accessed January 16, 2009.

18. Personal communication with Denny Fulk, May 7, 2007.

19. Uncle Saul, "Personal Pitch," http://www.infochachkie.com/personal-pitch, accessed January 16, 2009.

20. Bill Hudgins, "Hold Please," *MyBusiness,* April/May 2005, p. 50; http://www.onholdguy.com, accessed August 3, 2009.

21. Bruce Horovitz, "Whatever Happened to Customer Service?" *USAToday,* September 26, 2003, pp. 1A–2A.

22. Pattie Simone, "A Marketing Tool That's Obvious, Overlooked and Cheap," Entrepreneur.com, October 27, 2008, http://www.entrepreneur.com/article/printthis/198194.html, accessed January 14, 2009.

23. Personal communication with John Stites, October 23, 2007.

24. Heather Larson, "Coffee Talk," *MyBusiness,* October–November 2006, p. 12; "Our Locations," http://www.hamptoncoffeecompany.com/Hampton_Coffee_Company_Our_Locations.html, accessed February 2, 2009.

25. Dionne Searcey, "For Better or Worse," *Wall Street Journal,* October 30, 2006, p. R5.

26. "SAS® Helps 1-800FLOWERS.COM Grow Deep Roots with Customers," http://www.sas.com/success/1800flowers.html, accessed January 23, 2009.

27. *Ibid.*

28. Darren Dahl, "What Seems to Be the Problem? Self Service Gets a Tune-Up," *Inc. Magazine,* Vol. 30, No. 2 (February 2008), pp. 43–44.

29. Salvatore Parise, Patricia J. Guinan, and Bruce D. Weinberg, "The Secrets of Marketing in a Web 2.0 World," *Wall Street Journal,* December 15, 2008, p. R4.

30. *Ibid.*

31. "Taco Talk," No. 162, http://www.californiatortilla.com, accessed January 23, 2009.

32. Sharon Fling, "California Tortilla Customers Love Taco Talk," http://www.geolocal.com/public/79.cfm?sd=45, accessed January 23, 2009.

33. Russell S. Wimer, "Customer Relationship Management: A Framework, Research Directions, and the Future," http://groups.haas.berkeley.edu/fcsuit/PDF-papers/CRM%20paper.pdf, accessed January 23, 2009.

34. "Get to Know Your Customers with a Customer Profile," http://www.edwardlowe.org/index.elf?page=sserc&storyid=0035&function=story, accessed January 26, 2009.

35. *Ibid.*

36. See, for example, Del I. Hawkings, David L. Mothersbaugh, and Roger J. Best, *Consumer Behavior: Building Marketing Strategy,* 10th ed. (New York: McGraw-Hill Irwin, 2007), Chapter 17.

37. Laurie Zuckerman, "Picture Perfect," *MyBusiness,* April–May 2005, p. 12; http://www.angusbarn.com, accessed January 26, 2009.

38. Jeremy, Mullman, "Nike: What Slowdown? Swoosh Rides Games to New High," *Advertising Age,* October 17, 2008, http://adage.com/print?article_id=131755, accessed January 27, 2009.

CHAPTER 15

1. Robert Kiyosaki, "Even Steven," *Entrepreneur,* Vol. 36, No. 8 (August 2008), p. 36.

2. Debra Kahn Schofield, "Grow Your Business Slowly: A Cautionary Tale," http://www.gmarketing.com/articles/read/76/Grow_Your_Business_Slowly:_A_Cautionary_Tale.html, accessed February 4, 2009.

3. "BareBabies," http://www.carstock.com.ua/Dictionary/BareBabies, accessed February 4, 2009.

4. "Karen McMasters—BareBabies.com," http://br.video.yahoo.com/watch/1581802/5350194, accessed February 4, 2009.

5. Julie Fields, "Caught in a Candy Crunch," http://www.businessweek.com/smallbiz/content/oct2000/sb20001027_096.htm, accessed February 5, 2009.

6. Jeffry A. Timmons and Stephen Spinelli, *New Venture Creation: Entrepreneurship for the 21st Century* (Boston: McGraw-Hill/Irwin, 2009), p. 18.

7. Reported in an interview with Martha E. Mangelsdorf, "Hard Times Can Drive Innovation," *Wall Street Journal,* December 15, 2008, p. R2.

8. Neale Martin, "How Habits Undermine Marketing," *Financial Times,* July 1, 2008, http://www.ftpress.com/articles/article.aspx?p=1223844, accessed February 5, 2009.

9. "About Potomac Swim School," http://www.potomacswimschool.com/New%20Gallery/New%20Gallery.htm, accessed February 9, 2009; Kara Clark, "Loudoun's Entrepreneurs: With Risk Comes Reward," *Leesburg Today,* January 13, 2009; Donna Boone, "Entrepreneurial Growth: Think Regional, Act Local," http://www.entrepreneurship.org/Resources/Detail/Default.aspx?id=11334, accessed February 9, 2009.

10. http://www.180s.com, accessed February 9, 2009; "180s L.L.C.," http://www.fundinguniverse.com/company-histories/180s-LLC-Company-History.html2, accessed February 9, 2009.

11. "Science and Research," http://www.scientificintake.com, accessed February 10, 2009; "Scientific Intake," http://www.onemedplace.com/database/list/cid/11013, accessed February 10, 2009.

12. "About Premier," http://www.premier.com/View.aspx?page=about/premier, accessed February 10, 2009; "Innovators," August 3, 2005, http://www.richmond.com/print.aspx?articleId=4018, accessed February 10, 2009.

13. Dennis Romero, "Master Minds," *Entrepreneur,* Vol. 37, No. 3 (March 2009), pp. 20–25.

14. "VC Cash Crunch May Impact Innovation," http://www.us-tech.com/RelId/702033/ISvars/default/VC_Cash_Crunch_May_I.htm, accessed February 11, 2009.

15. Anne Field, "Creating a Sustainable Competitive Advantage for Your Small Business," http://devsun.startupnation.com/articles/1522/1/competitive-advantage-small-business.asp, accessed February 20, 2009.

16. "Dylan's Candy Bar," http://www.dylanscandybar.com/custserv/customerservicemain.jsp?cid=1, accessed February 11, 2009.

17. Daniel Maurer, "Scream for Free Ice Cream," *New York Magazine,* November 12, 2008, http://nymag.com/daily/food/2008/11/scream_for_free_ice_cream.html, accessed February 11, 2009.

18. Brian Tracy, "Test Marketing Your New Product or Service," http://www.1000ventures.com/business_guide/marketing_test_bybt.html, accessed February 11, 2009.

19. "Beacon Street Girls Overview," http://www.tradevibes.com/company/profile/beacon-street-girls, accessed February 13, 2009; Nadine Heintz, "Hands On Case

Study," *Inc. Magazine,* Vol. 27, No. 3 (March 2005), pp. 44–46.

20. "The Parking Spot," http://www.theparkingspot.com, accessed February 12, 2009; Elizabeth J. Goodgold, "Dot Your Eyes," *Entrepreneur,* February 2002, http://findarticles.com/p/articles/mi_m0DTI/is_2_30/ai_83663520, accessed February 23, 2009.

21. "The Parking Spot—Location Directory," http://www.theparkingspot.com/Facilities/LocationDirectory.aspx, accessed February 12, 2009.

22. "Logo Design, *op. cit.*

23. *Ibid.*

24. Adapted from Gwen Moran, "Best and Worst Marketing Ideas. . . Ever," *Entrepreneur,* Vol. 37, No. 1 (January 2009), p. 48 and "Logo Design – Not Just a Pretty Typeface," http://www.logomojo.com/logotype.html, accessed February 13, 2009.

25. Nichole L. Torres, "Package Deal," *Entrepreneur,* Vol. 35, No. 10 (October 2007), p. 114.

26. *Ibid.*

27. Laura Tiffany, "What Whole Package," *Entrepreneur,* Vol. 36, No. 2 (February 2008), p. 24.

28. Rieva Lesonsky, "In the Know," *Entrepreneur,* Vol. 35, No. 6 (June 2007), pp. 96–101.

29. Kelly Spors, "Small Talk," *Wall Street Journal,* July 15, 2008, p. B6.

30. "All About Trademarks," http://www.uspto.gov/smallbusiness/trademarks/faq.html, accessed February 18, 2009.

31. "Trade Dress," http://www.nolo.com/definition.cfm/Term/B8808518-8553-483A-932DD2E4BC63E155/alpha/T/, accessed February 18, 2009.

32. Fare Scanners and 'Compare Fare' Sites," http://www.airkiosk.com/ttt_item_2.php?item=2, accessed February 25, 2009.

33. Sarah E. Needleman, "In a Sole Revival, the Recession Gives Beleaguered Cobblers New Traction," *Wall Street Journal,* February 2, 2009, pp. A1, A13.

34. "How Tomorrow Moves—Radio Ad: One Gallon," http://www.csx.com/?fuseaction=about.tomorrow_moves, accessed February 19, 2009.

35. "FedEx Service Enhancements Pay Off," *Shippers Today,* http://info.hktdc.com/shippers/vol26_3/vol26_3_aircargo05.htm, accessed February 25, 2009; "UPS—3PL," http://www.ups-scs.com/support/3pl.html, accessed February 25, 2009.

36. "Toolbox for IT," http://supplychain.ittoolbox.com/documents/what-is-4pl-17878, accessed February 25, 2009.

37. Kurt C. Hoffman, "Just What Is a 4PL Anyway?" http://www.supplychainbrain.com/archives/8.00.4pl.htm?adcode75, accessed February 25, 2009.

CHAPTER 16

1. Nadine Heintz, "Flexing Your Pricing Muscles," *Inc. Magazine,* Vol. 26, No. 2 (February 2004), pp. 25–26.

2. Geoff Williams, "Name Your Price," *Entrepreneur,* September 2005, pp. 108–112.

3. To measure a company's break-even point, we can use an equation that is an adaptation of the income statement. We know that operating profits are measured as follows:

Total dollar sales − cost of goods sold − operating expenses = operating profits

Using the above equation, we simply want to find the number of units sold and the corresponding dollar sales where *operating profits* are equal to 0. In other words, we want to calculate the sales level where

Total dollars sales − cost of goods sold − operating expenses = 0

If we reclassify the costs and expenses into fixed and variables costs and expenses, we have

Total dollar sales − total variable costs and expenses − total fixed costs and expenses = 0

Also, since a firm's total dollar sales equals selling price per unit × number of units sold, and variable costs and expenses equal variable costs and expenses per unit × number of units sold, then the break-even equation may be restated as

(selling price − units sold) − (unit variable costs and expenses − units sold) − total fixed costs and expenses = 0

Solving for the numbers of units sold that produce an operating profit of 0, we have

break-even units sold = total fixed costs and expenses/selling price − unit variable costs and expenses

4. For an excellent discussion of price setting, see Charles W. Lamb, Jr., Joseph H. Hair, Jr., and Carl McDaniel, *Marketing,* 9th ed. (Cincinnati: South-Western, 2008), Chapter 18.

5. http://www.technewsworld.com/story/31271.html, accessed March 16, 2007.

6. John A. Boyd, "Market-Driven Pricing Strategies," Iowa Small Business Development Centers, http://www.iabusnet.org, accessed March 15, 2009.

7. For more details, see Sarah Goldstein, "Who Gets to Say When the Price Is Right?" *Inc. Magazine,* March 2007, p. 24; Leegin Creative Leather Products, Inc., v. PSKS, Inc. *Magazine, DBA Kay's Kloset,* on writ certiorari to the United States Court of Appeals, No. 06–480, June 28, 2007.

8. "Online Payment Processing," *Inc. Magazine,* June 2006, p. 86.

9. Jonathan A. Scott, William C. Dunkelberg, and William J. Dennis, Jr., *Credit, Banks and Small Business—The New Century* (Washington, DC: NFIB Research Foundation, 2003).

10. For a detailed look at a Equifax credit report, see https://www.econsumer.equifax. com/consumer/sitepage.ehtml?forward=cs_cpo.

CHAPTER 17

1. Rachel Metz, "Social Network Faces Transparency Questions," The Associated Press, http://www.google.com/hostednews/ap/article, accessed March 22, 2009.

2. Barton A. Weitz, Stephen B. Castleberry, and John F. Tanner, Jr., *Selling: Building Partnerships* (New York: McGraw-Hill/Irwin, 2007), Chapter 11; Rieva Lesonsky, "Wind in Your Sales," *Entrepreneur,* June 2007, pp. 102–105; Barry Farber, "Good Connections," *Entrepreneur,* January 2009, p. 60.

3. Gwen Moran, "Better Business: Get Ready," *Entrepreneur,* October 2007, p. 24; http://www.babyganics.com, accessed, March 29, 2009.

4. Romanus Wolter, "Success Coach: Sales on Your Side," *Entrepreneur,* October 2008, pp. 138–139.

5. Gwen Moran, "Take Your Tag Line from Drab to Fab," *Entrepreneur,* March 2009, p. 26; http://www.marketingprofs.com, accessed March 28, 2009.

6. Gary Slack, "How to Hire an Ad Agency," *Entrepreneur,* June 2007, p. 71; http://www.slackbarshinger.com, accessed March 28, 2009.

7. Robert Kiyosaki, "Rich Returns: Go Big or Go Home," *Entrepreneur,* November 2008, p. 34.

8. Chris Morrison, "Interactive Ads Save Newspapers," *Business 2.0,* Vol. 8, No. 8 (September 2007), p. 26.

9. Jacques Bughin, Christoph Erbenich, and Amy Shenkan, "How Companies Are Marketing Online," http://www.mckinseyquarterly.com/Marketing, accessed March 31, 2009.

10. Gwen Moran, "Clicks: Natural Born Clickers," *Entrepreneur,* September 2008, p. 79.

11. Susanna Hamner, "Cyberstalking Your Customers," *Business 2.0,* September 2007, pp. 24–25; http://www.fetchback.com, accessed March 31, 2009.

12. Leigh Buchanan, Max Chafkin, and Ryan McCarthy, "On Messages," *Inc. Magazine,* February 2008, p. 78; Steve Strauss, "Ask an Expert: Don't Overlook the Value of E-mail Marketing," http://www.usatoday.com/money/smallbusiness/columnist/strauss/2009-3-30-email.marketing_N.htm?loc=interstitialskip, accessed April 1, 2009.

13. http://www.mckinseyquarterly.com, accessed March 29, 2009.

14. http://www.ftc.gov/spam, accessed March 27, 2009.

15. http://blog2print/sharedbook.com, accessed April 14, 2009; http://money.cnn.com/magazine/business2/, accessed April 14, 2009.

16. http://www.securecomputing.com, accessed April 11, 2009.

17. For more details regarding domain name rules, see http://www.register.com/domain-rules.cgi.

18. http://www.dnjournal.com/ytd.-sales-charts.htmi, accessed March 31, 2009.

19. Carol Tice, "What's in a Name?" *Entrepreneur*, August 2007, p. 21.

20. Lindsay Holloway, "Webcams Gone Creative," *Entrepreneur*, April 2009, p. 32.

21. Chris Kivelhan, "Improve Your Website's Performance," *Entrepreneur,* May 3, 2006, http://www.entrepreneur.com/ebusiness/operations/article159400.html, accessed July 30, 2007.

22. Corey Rudl, "4 Fatal Website Design Mistakes," http://www.entrepreneur.com, accessed January 29, 2007.

23. Leigh Buchanan, Max Chafkin, and Ryan McCarthy, "How to Jazz up Your Site," *Inc. Magazine*, February 2008, p. 76.

24. Heather Clancy, "Web Sight: Social Marketing," *Entrepreneur*, November 2008, p. 44; http://www.whiteflash.com, accessed March 29, 2009.

25. Amanda C. Kooser, "Make Your New Site Social," *Entrepreneur*, February 2009, p. 120.

26. Heather Clancy, "Web Sight: Do You See What I See?" *Entrepreneur*, October 2007, p. 58.

27. Gwendolyn Bounds, "Cracking the YouTube Market Even If Your Product Is Boring," *Wall Street Journal*, October 30, 2007, p. B9.

28. Catherine Seda, "How to SEO like a Pro," *Entrepreneur*, June 2007, p. 69; http://wwwsedacommunication.com, accessed March 31, 2009.

29. Amanda C. Kooser, "Net Profits: Start a Search Engine," *Entrepreneur*, October 2008, pp. 132–133.

30. http://www.merriam-webster.com/dictionary/blog, accessed April 14, 2009.

31. Gwen Moran, "Get Noticed," *Entrepreneur*, October 2008, p. 58.

32. Gwen Moran, "Keep Them Posted," *Entrepreneur*, October 2007, p. 39.

33. Janelle Elms, "In the Fast Lane," *Entrepreneur*, June 2007, pp. 122–123; http://fastbackstack.com, accessed March 29, 2009.

34. Kim T. Gordon, "Marketing: Reaching Multitaskers," *Entrepreneur*, October 2008, p. 86.

35. Moran, "Get Noticed," *op. cit.*.

36. Adapted from Janet Attard, "Trade Show Dos and Don'ts," http://www.businessknowhow.com/tips/tradesho.htm, accessed April 11, 2009.

37. Gail Dutton, "Global: Mass Appeal," *Entrepreneur*, November 2008, p. 78.

38. Laura Tiffany, "Generate Buzz About Your Business," *Entrepreneur*, February 2009, p. 26.

39. Don Debelak, "Make Your Mark," *Entrepreneur,* May 2004, p. 146; http://www.maryellenproducts.com, accessed February 5, 2007.

CHAPTER 18

1. See Leora Klapper, Raphael Amit, Mauro F. Guillen, and Juan Manuel Quesada, "Entrepreneurship and Firm Formation Across Countries," http://knowledge.wharton.upenn.edu/papers/1345.pdf, accessed March 2, 2009.

2. Statistics have already answered this question. Data published by the International Trade Administration indicate that small and medium-sized enterprises (SMEs) account for 97 percent of all U.S. exporters and that these firms represent 29 percent of all U.S. goods exported. These findings show that SMEs are already actively involved in international trade. The data reflect only export activity, so the numbers would be even more striking if other forms of globalization were included in the report. For an extensive analysis of the ITA study, see Leslie E. Palich and D. Ray Bagby, "Trade Trends in Transatlantica: A Profile of SMEs in the United States and Europe," in Lester Lloyd-Reason and LeighSears (eds.), *Trading Places—SMEs in the Global Economy: A Critical Research Handbook* (Cheltenham, UK: Edward Elgar Publishing, 2007).

3. Michael V. Copeland ["The Mighty Micro-Multinational," *Business 2.0*, Vol. 7, No. 6 (July 2006), pp. 107–114] points out just how fast the number of startups with global ambitions is growing. He cites UN data to indicate that the number of startups that are global from day one doubled between 1990 and 2006, from 30,000 to 60,000. Many of these are technology-focused companies, but the phenomenon certainly extends to non-tech companies as well. But, in many cases, the emphasis is not on starting a business in the United States and selling product abroad; rather, it is on establishing operations wherever in the world it makes sense to do so. In other words, it could be a way to draw on the talents of highly trained employees or to locate near abundant resources or low-cost labor to enhance the value proposition of the new venture.

4. Terms other than *born global* are sometimes used to refer to this category of firms and others that are similar to them; other labels include *born international firms, global startups, international new ventures,* and *instant exporters*. See Pat H. Dickson, "Going Global," in Andrew Zacharakis and Stephen Spinelli, Jr. (eds.), *Entrepreneurship: The Engine of Growth* (Westport, CT: Praeger Perspectives, 2007), pp. 155–161; Gary A. Knight and S. Tamar Cavusgil, "Innovation, Organizational Capabilities, and the Born-Global Firm," *Journal of International Business Studies*, Vol. 35, No. 2 (March 2004), pp. 124–141; Svante Andersson, "Internationalization in Different Industrial Contexts," *Journal of Business Venturing*, Vol. 19, No. 6 (2004), p. 856; and Erkko Autio, Harry J. Sapienza, and James G. Almeida, "Effects of Age at Entry, Knowledge Intensity, and Imitability on International Growth," *Academy of Management Journal*, Vol. 43, No. 5 (October 2000), pp. 909–924.

5. Leigh Buchanan, "The Thinking Man's Outsourcing," *Inc. Magazine,* Vol. 28, No. 5 (May 2006), pp. 31–33.

6. For an important theoretical analysis on this, see John A. Matthews and Ivo Zander, "The International Entrepreneurial Dynamics of Accelerated Internationalisation," *Journal of International Business Studies*, Vol. 38, No. 3 (May 2007), pp. 387–403.

7. Buchanan, *op. cit.*

8. The Sloan Brothers, "Taking Your Startup to a Foreign Market," http://www.startupnation.com/articles/1471/1/startupforeign-market.asp, accessed March 2, 2009; "Eco-Fridge Revolutionizes Food Transport," http://www.ebrd.com/new/stories/2006/060911.htm, accessed March 2, 2009.

9. *Ibid*.

10. "Tradewind Strategies—Contact," http://www.tradewindstrategies.com/tradewind_contact.html, accessed March 2, 2009.

11. Shelby Scarborough, "A Whole New World," *Entrepreneur*, Vol. 36, No. 6 (June 2008), p. 21.

12. Leigh Buchanan, "Gone Global," *Inc. Magazine*, Vol. 29, No. 4 (April 2007), pp. 88–91.

13. This point is made in Stephanie A. Fernhaber, Patricia P. McDougall, and Benjamin M. Oviatt, "Exploring the Role of Industry Structure in New Venture Internationalization," *Entrepreneurship Theory and Practice*, Vol. 31, No. 4 (July 2007), pp. 517–542. However, these authors provide an analysis that shows how major fields of research (including industrial economics, international business, and entrepreneurship) can shed light on the role that industry structure plays in new ventures' inclination to internationalize. For example, they conclude that variables such as industry growth, knowledge intensity, local industry internationalization, an industry's general level of global integration, and venture capital involvement will encourage the internationalization of new ventures. Factors such as the general level of industry maturity are believed to moderate the relationships predicted.

14. Svante Andersson, "Internationalization in Different Industrial Contexts," *Journal*

of Business Venturing, Vol. 19, No. 6 (2004), pp. 851–875; "Don't Laugh at Gilded Butterflies," Economist, Vol. 371, No. 8372 (April 22, 2004), pp. 71–73; Oliver Burgel, Andreas Fier, Georg Licht, and Gordon C. Murray, "The Effect of Internationalization on Rate of Growth of High-Tech Start-Ups—Evidence for UK and Germany," in Paul D. Reynolds et al. (eds.), Frontiers for Entrepreneurship Research, proceedings of the 20th Annual Entrepreneurship Research Conference, Babson College, June 2002.

15. This study focused on the expansion of U.S. firms into Europe. It is possible that the primary motivation for involvement in other parts of the world is different. For example, it could very well be that most U.S. small companies doing business in Asia are seeking to access low-cost component sources or to relocate business processes via outsourcing. For an extended discussion of the particular study cited, see Edmund Prater and Soumen Ghosh, "Current Operational Practices of U.S. Small and Medium-Sized Enterprises in Europe," Journal of Small Business Management, Vol. 43, No. 2 (April 2005), pp. 155–169.

16. Dominic Wilson and Roopa Purushothaman, "Dreaming with BRICs: The Path to 2050," GS Global Economics paper, http://www2.goldmansachs.com/ideas/brics/book/99-dreaming.pdf, accessed March 4, 2009; Economist.com, "Another BRIC in the Wall," April 21, 2008, http://www.economist.com/finance/displaystory.cfm?story_id=11075147, accessed March 4, 2009.

17. "Tradewind Strategies," op. cit.

18. Raymond Vernon, "International Investment and International Trade in the Product Cycle," Quarterly Journal of Economics, Vol. 80, No. 2 (May 1966), pp. 190–207.

19. Gordon B. Baty and Michael S. Blake, Entrepreneurship: Back to Basics (Washington, DC: Beard Books, 2003), p. 166.

20. Palich and Bagby, op. cit., pp. 64–65.

21. "Company Background," http://www.itretail.com/about/company.php, accessed March 4, 2009.

22. Ibid.; "IT RETAIL Announces Integrated Support for BlackHawk Gift Cards and the Integration of MTXEPS' ServerEPS Electronic Payment Engine," http://www.itretail.com/news/PressRelease.php?id=59, accessed March 4, 2009.

23. This is not to suggest that small businesses no longer follow the pattern of establishing themselves first in the domestic market before stepping out into international opportunities. Pat H. Dickson (op. cit.) refers to firms in this category as gradual globals and mentions that this pattern of expansion is consistent with the well-developed and still influential Uppsala Internationalization Model. The Uppsala school suggests that firms internationalize slowly and incrementally, perhaps taking years to

gain the knowledge, skills, and resources necessary to expand into international markets. Stepping out is likely to begin with low-commitment strategies first (such as sourcing abroad or exporting) and then move into more resource-intensive options (such as forming a joint venture with an overseas partner and then moving in time to establish a wholly owned international subsidiary). The logic extends to selection of markets as well, suggesting that companies first seek to enter countries that are similar and easy to penetrate. They will expand into markets that are more and more dissimilar as they develop the capabilities to move in that direction and find that they have tapped out the potential of the markets they are currently in. Though we now have evidence that many startups internationalize early on (the born-global phenomenon), many other entrepreneurs choose the gradual-global option instead.

24. Palich and Bagby, op. cit., p. 66.

25. In the United States, this problem has been exacerbated by problems related to the War on Terror. In an attempt to prevent dangerous individuals from entering the country, the U.S. government has tightened visa and work permit restrictions, which has made it more difficult for companies to bring in the foreign talent they need. To make the situation worse, many international students from countries like China and India train in the best universities in the United States and then return home, hoping to use their skills to get in on the ground floor of opportunities that are emerging in their rapidly developing home countries.

26. The Boston Consulting Group/Knowledge@ Wharton, "China and the New Rules for Global Business," http://knowledge.wharton.upenn.edu/papers/download/BCG-KW specialreport-final.pdf, accessed March 11, 2009.

27. Francine Russo, "Doc in a Box," Business 2.0, Vol. 8, No. 5 (June 2007).

28. "Kirkham Motorsports History," http://www.kirkhammotorsports.com/about/index.html, accessed March 8, 2009.

29. "Salvador's Coffee House," http://www.salvadors.cn, accessed March 8, 2009; Christopher J. Horton, "Ex-Coloradans See Hope in Sister City," Denver Post, http://www.salvadors.cn/Denver%20Post%20article.htm, accessed April 24, 2009; Paul Sloan "East Meets—and Eats—West," Business 2.0, Vol. 6, No. 7 (August 2006), p. 76.

30. "Salvador's Investment and Business Opportunities," http://www.salvadors.cn/investmentopp.htm, accessed March 8, 2009.

31. Prater and Ghosh, op. cit., p. 161.

32. Jan Stojaspal, "Back in the Driver's Seat," http://www.time.com/time/europe/

specials/ff/trip6/hungarybuses.html, accessed March 8, 2009; Palich and Bagby, op. cit.

33. SBA Office of Advocacy, "Small Business Frequently Asked Questions," http://www.sba.gov/advo/stats/sbfaq.pdf, accessed March 8, 2009.

34. SBA, "Small Business Guide to Exporting: Making the Export Decision," http://www.sba.gov/idc/groups/public/documents/sba_program_office/oit_bitg4th_chpt1.pdf, accessed March 8, 2009.

35. "About Entertainment Earth," http://www.entertainmentearth.com/help/aboutee.asp, accessed March 11, 2009.

36. "EntertainmentEarth.com," http://www.secretstotheirsuccess.com/industry-categories/7-giftsmemorabilia/149-entertainment-earth.html, accessed March 11, 2009.

37. Janelle Elms, "Go Global," Entrepreneur, Vol. 34, No. 9 (September 2006), pp. 130–131.

38. For an informative discussion of this issue as it applies specifically to export approval for shipments to China, see Ted C. Fishman, "America's Most Innovative Industries Are Being Robbed Every Day on the Floors of Chinese Factories," Inc. Magazine, Vol. 28, No. 6 (June 2006), pp. 98–102.

39. Ian Mount, "Right Back at You," Fortune Small Business, Vol. 16, No. 2 (March 2006), p. 18.

40. "Compass Trading Co.—About Us," http://www.compasstradingco.com/pages/about_us.html, accessed March 11, 2009; Personal conversation with store management, February 8, 2008.

41. Joshua Kurlantzick, "On Foreign Soil," Entrepreneur, Vol. 33, No. 6 (June 2005), pp. 88–92.

42. Ibid.

43. A study of small and medium-sized enterprises (SMEs) in the European Union revealed that international sourcing is used far more than exporting strategies. While 16 percent of firms in the study used exporting alone, 49 percent engaged in foreign sourcing alone. Twenty-seven percent had both foreign suppliers and exports. These findings may not generalize beyond European firms, given their unique setting within the region, but they certainly highlight the importance of these two international strategies for SMEs. For more details, see the 2003 Observatory of European SMEs: 2003/4 Internationalization of SMEs, which can be accessed at http://ec.europa.eu/enterprise/enterprise_policy/analysis/observatory_en.htm.

44. Michael A. Hitt, R. Duane Ireland, and Robert E. Hoskisson, Strategic Management: Competitiveness and Globalization (Cincinnati, OH: Thomson South-Western, 2007), p. 246.

45. "Company Background," http://www.itretail.com/about/company.php, accessed March 11, 2009.

46. U.S. Small Business Administration, *Breaking into the Trade Game: A Small Business Guide to Exporting,* http://www.sba.gov/aboutsba/sbaprograms/internationaltrade/exportlibrary/sbge/OIT_SB_GUIDE_EXPORT_INDEX.html, accessed March 11, 2009.

47. http://www.bluenote.net/ franchise/index.shtml, accessed March 11, 2009.

48. Space is limited here, but there is much more to know about strategic alliances and small business. For example, Dickson (*op. cit.,* pp. 162–163) reviews research showing that features of national culture can shape the formation of alliances and the use of equity ties. This source will lead interested readers to other important studies on the topic.

49. Elizabeth Wasserman, "Happy Birthday, WTO?" *Inc. Magazine,* Vol. 27, No. 1 (January 2005), pp. 21–23.

50. Karen E. Klein, "An American in South America's Paris," *BusinessWeek,* June 15, 2006, http://www.businessweek.com/smallbiz/content/jun2006/sb20060615_849958.htm?chan=smallbiz_spr_bestplaces, accessed March 11, 2009; Nichole L. Torres, "Change of Scenery," *Entrepreneur,* Vol. 34, No. 8 (August 2006), p. 90.

51. Kevin Kelly, "Mexican Standoff," *Fortune Small Business,* Vol. 16, No. 2 (March 2006), p. 29.

52. Some forms of risk are not within the control of a country's government, but these may have very serious effects on business performance and thus should be factored into business startup and expansion decisions. One emerging example involves what some researchers are calling *environmental risk,* which suggests that climate change risks vary across global regions and should be a recognized decision-making factor [see Peter Romilly, "Business and Climate Change Risk: A Regional Time Series Analysis," *Journal of International Business Studies,* Vol. 38, No. 3 (May 2007), pp. 474–480]. However, the state and quality of climate change science is still hotly debated, so its predictive value in business decision making is still open to question.

53. http://www.mooneyfarms.com/about_us.htm, accessed June 7, 2004.

54. "Chapter 3—Foreign Market Entry," http://www.foreign-trade.com/reference/trad8.htm, accessed March 11, 2009.

CHAPTER 19

1. William Shakespeare, *The Tempest,* Act 2, Scene 1.

2. Julie H. Case, "The Art of Leadership," *U.W.* [University of Washington] *Business,* Spring 2003, p. 17.

3. Deepa D. Singh, "Entrepreneur—Crashing Fear/Cashing Fortitude," http://www.indianmba.com/Faculty_Column/FC362/fc362.html, accessed March 17, 2009.

4. As quoted in Brent Bowers, *The 8 Patterns of Highly Effective Entrepreneurs* (New York: Currency Doubleday, 2006), p. 61.

5. Daniel Goleman, Richard E. Boyatzis, and Annie McKee, *Primal Leadership: Learning to Lead with Emotional Intelligence* (Cambridge, MA: Harvard Business School Press).

6. Danny Meyer, "The Saltshaker Theory," *Inc. Magazine,* Vol. 28, No. 10 (October 2006), pp. 69–70; http://www.unionsquarecafe.com/aboutusc.html, accessed April 16, 2009; http://www.cbsnews.com/stories/2003/03/03/sunday/main542606.shtml, accessed April 6, 2009.

7. Glenn Ross, "Employee Empowerment Contributes to the Customer Service Experience," http://www.allbusiness.com/sales/customer-service/3876268-1.html, accessed April 6, 2009.

8. For more on this topic, see Nichole Torres, "Thinking Bigger," *Entrepreneur,* Vol. 34, No. 8 (August 2006), p. 53.

9. Nichole Torres, "Setting the Mood," *Entrepreneur,* Vol. 34, No. 8 (August 2006), p. 52.

10. *Ibid.*

11. Sara Wilson, "Build a Billion Dollar Business," *Entrepreneur,* Vol. 37, No. 3 (March 2009), pp. 45–47.

12. Adam Hanft, "Save the Founder," *Inc. Magazine,* Vol. 27, No. 10 (October 2005), p. 156.

13. Personal communication with Sara Blakely, May 3, 2007.

14. Gwen Edwards, "Going from *Fortune* 500 to Startup," March 5, 2007, http://www.businessweek.com/print/smallbiz/content/mar2007/sb20070305_965709.htm, accessed April 6, 2009.

15. The model we offer in this chapter could be viewed as a relatively smooth curve with no disruptions or downward trends. Our focus is mostly on the managerial challenges that go along with each of these stages of growth, and it would seem to be implicit that these are always manageable. However, we recognize that very few entrepreneurial firms develop along such a straightforward path, and the smooth sailing will often be upset by moments of crisis along the way, and perhaps even failure. Edward P. Marram, entrepreneur and professor at Babson College, offers more creative stage names and notes more specifically the perils that companies face at different points in their growth and development. His model includes the following five stages: Wonder, Blunder, Thunder, Plunder, and Asunder. As reported by Jeffry A. Timmons and Stephen Spinelli (*New Venture Creation: Entrepreneurship for the 21st Century* [Boston: McGraw-Hill Irwin, 2009], p. 556), "Wonder is the period that is filled with uncertainty about survival. Blunder is a growth stage when many firms stumble and fail. The Thunder stage occurs when growth is robust and the entrepreneur has built a solid management team. Cash flow is robust during Plunder, but in Asunder the firm needs to renew or will decline." This model obviously runs relatively parallel to what we present in this section of the chapter, but the emphasized dynamics are clearly somewhat different.

16. Chris Penttila, "Can You Manage?" *Entrepreneur,* Vol. 31, No. 7 (July 2003), pp. 74–75.

17. *Ibid.*

18. Demetria Lucas, "Twin Tailors," *Black Enterprise,* Vol. 33, No. 9 (April 2003), p. 47.

19. Conversation with Ryan Gibson, Waco, Texas, April 13, 2009.

20. *Startup Journal,* "The Long-Term Perils of Being a Control Freak," http://www.managementsite.com/currentevents/167/The-Long-Term-Perils-of-Being-a-Control-Freak.aspx, accessed March 26, 2009.

21. Brent Bowers, *The 8 Patterns of Highly Effective Entrepreneurs* (New York: Currency Doubleday, 2006), p. 67.

22. Rodes Fishburne, "More Survival Advice: Communicate," http://www.forbes.com/asap/2000/0403/120.html, accessed March 27, 2009.

23. The use of blogs for the expression of personal opinions online has been increasing rapidly, but applications to the business setting are expanding even faster. For example, blogs can be employed as a public relations tool or a channel to address customer complaints or to pass along product or service insights.

24. Numerous resources provide excellent background on the principles and skills of negotiation. One popular book on the subject, a national bestseller, is by Roger Fisher, William Ury, and Bruce Patton: *Getting to Yes: Negotiating Agreement Without Giving In* (New York: Random House, 2003). This book emphasizes several very important concepts, including bargaining for mutual gains, separating people from the problem and positions from interests, and agreeing on objective criteria for evaluating outcomes. With its readable style and practical orientation, this book—and others like it—would be very useful reading for any small business owner.

25. Barry Farber, "Putting Ideas into Action," *Entrepreneur,* Vol. 37, No. 2 (February 2009), p. 62.

26. Erika Kotite, "Focus, People!" *Entrepreneur,* Vol. 34, No. 9 (September 2006), p. 34.

27. As reported in Mark Henricks, "Just 'To-Do' It," *Entrepreneur,* Vol. 32, No. 8 (August 2004), p. 71.

28. Suggestions were adapted from the following articles: *Inc. Magazine,* "Ask *Inc.*," Vol. 30, No. 1 (January 2008), p. 60; Emma Johnson, "A Stress-Free Guide to Time Management," *MyBusiness,* October–November 2005, pp. 29–33; Lisa Kanarek, "Clean Sweep," *Entrepreneur,* Vol. 34, No. 6 (June 2006), pp. 43–44; Chris Penttila, "Rush Hour," *Entrepreneur,* Vol. 36, No. 8 (August 2008), p. 74; Chris Penttila, "Time Out," *Entrepreneur,* Vol. 35, No. 4 (April 2007), pp. 71–73; Jeffrey Pfeffer, "Why Deadlines Matter," *Business 2.0,* Vol. 8, No. 5 (June 2007), p. 54; Nichole L. Torres, "In Good Time," *Entrepreneur,* Vol. 33, No. 12 (December 2005), p. 38; Romanus Wolter, "A Clean Sweep," *Entrepreneur,* Vol. 32, No. 7 (July 2004), pp. 108–109; Romanus Wolter, "Easy Does It," *Entrepreneur,* Vol. 33, No. 10 (October 2005), pp. 122–123.

29. Visit the Entrepreneurs' Organization website at http://www.eonetwork.org and the Young Presidents' Organization at http://www.ypo.org for more information.

30. "Business Incubation FAQ," http://www.nbia.org/resource_center/bus_inc_facts/index.php, accessed March 20, 2009.

31. *Ibid.*

32. Darren Dahl, "Percolating Profits," *Inc. Magazine,* Vol. 27, No. 2 (February 2005), pp. 38–40.

33. "FastTrac," http://www.fasttrac.org, accessed March 31, 2009.

34. Interested in signing up? Visit the organization's website at http://www.fasttrac.org to learn more about the program.

35. For more information about SCORE, visit the organization's website at http://www.score.org.

36. "The Baker's Peel," http://www.score.org/success_bakers_peel.html, accessed March 30, 2009.

37. "Bozmedia," http://www.bozmedia.com/about.html, accessed March 31, 2009; Nichole L. Torres, "Family Ties," *Entrepreneur,* Vol. 34, No. 10 (September 2006), pp. 132–133; personal communication with Ryan Bonifacino, May 2, 2007.

CHAPTER 20

1. For an extended discussion of small business and HRM practices, especially as applied to family firms, see Jan M. P. de Kok, Lorraine M. Uhlaner, and A. Roy Thurik, "Professional HRM Practices in Family Owned-Managed Enterprises," *Journal of Small Business Management,* Vol. 44, No. 3 (May 2006), pp. 441–460.

2. Joel Spolsky, "There's a Better Way to Find and Hire the Very Best Employees," *Inc. Magazine,* Vol. 29, No. 5 (May 2007), pp. 81–82.

3. Chris Penttila, "Talent Scout," entrepreneur.com, July 2008, http://www. entrepreneur.com/magazine/entrepreneur/2008/july/194508.html, accessed June 30, 2009.

4. Chris Resto, Ian Ybarra, and Ramit Sethi, *Recruit or Die: How Any Business Can Beat the Big Guys in the War for Young Talent* (New York: Penguin Group, 2008).

5. For findings of an informative study of the relationship between employee benefits and turnover in large versus small businesses, see John B. Hope and Patrick C. Mackin (SBA Office of Advocacy), "The Relationship Between Employee Turnover and Employee Compensation in Small Business," *Small Business Research Summary,* Report No. 308, July 2007, http://www.sba.gov/advo/research/rs308.pdf, accessed May 15, 2009.

6. Sarah E. Needleman, "Small Firms Offer More Responsibility, Credit," *Wall Street Journal,* March 4, 2008, p. B6.

7. "Our Goal," http://www.kayconstruction.com, accessed April 23, 2009; Mark Henricks, "Search Party," *Entrepreneur,* Vol. 35, No. 2 (February 2007), p. 83.

8. To get an idea of the kinds of services that public employment offices can provide, visit the website of Workforce Solutions of El Paso, Texas, which operates under the oversight of the Upper Rio Grande Workforce Development Board. Its programs are outlined at http://www.urgjobs.com/index.php?option=com_frontpage&Itemid=1, accessed on May 15, 2009.

9. Henricks, *op. cit.*

10. "Imperatives," http://www.imperativesllc.com, accessed April 23, 2009; Mark Henricks, "You Know Who?" *Entrepreneur,* Vol. 35, No. 5 (May 2007), pp. 89–90.

11. "Tomorrow's Jobs," http://stats.bls.gov/oco/oco2003.htm, accessed April 27, 2009.

12. Mark Henricks, "In the Mix," *Entrepreneur,* Vol. 35, No. 10 (October 2007), p. 109.

13. Bruce D. Phillips, "The Future Small Business Workforce," paper presented at the national meeting of the United States Association for Small Business and Entrepreneurship, Indian Wells, CA, January 2005.

14. See "Foreign Labor Certification," http://www.foreignlaborcert.doleta.gov, accessed May 13, 2009.

15. As reported in Dee Gill, "Dealing with Diversity," *Inc. Magazine,* Vol. 27, No. 11 (November 2005), p. 38.

16. Chris Kelleher, "Writing Great Job Descriptions," http://www.entrepreneur.com/humanresources/hiring/article70642.html, accessed May 6, 2009.

17. For more detail on overtime regulations as they may apply to small businesses, visit the U.S. Department of Labor's website at http://www.dol.gov/esa/regs/compliance/whd/fairpay/main.htm, accessed April 23, 2009.

18. For more on this and other features of the hiring process, see Stephanie Clifford, "The Science of Hiring," *Inc. Magazine,* Vol. 28, No. 8 (August 2006), pp. 90–98. The article reports that the correlation between interview-based assessments and actual performance is a mere 0.20, which is not very encouraging. However, the author offers many insights that could be used to improve the hiring process.

19. Jeffrey Pfeffer, "Why Resumes Are Just One Piece of the Puzzle," *Business 2.0,* Vol. 6, No. 11 (December 2005), p. 106.

20. For more behavioral interview questions that could be adapted to a specific company's needs, see "Sample Behavioral Interview Questions," http://www.quintcareers.com/sample_behavioral.html, accessed April 23, 2009.

21. Recent studies indicate that around 25 percent of small businesses find it necessary to fire employees each year ("First, Fire Your Assistant. Then, Ax All the Sales Guys," *Inc. Magazine,* Vol. 29, No. 7, (July 2007), p. 26; William J. Dennis, Jr., "Unemployment Compensation," National Federation of Independent Business, quarterly research report, Vol. 7, No. 1, (2007). When a small business has to fire an employee, it always runs the risk of being sued for wrongful termination. However, released employees are much less likely to file a lawsuit if they conclude that their employer has been fair throughout the process and has provided ample opportunity for them to improve their work performance before termination.

22. Beth Gaudio, "Tell Me About Yourself," *MyBusiness,* October–November 2006, p. 14.

23. Mark Henricks, "Check That Temp," *Entrepreneur,* Vol. 34, No. 4 (April 2006), pp. 91–92.

24. Susanna Hamner, "Give People a Second Chance," *Business 2.0,* Vol. 8, No. 4 (May 2007), p. 67.

25. Paulette Thomas, "Case Study: Not Sure of a New Hire? Put Her to a Road Test," *Wall Street Journal,* January 7, 2003, p. B-7.

26. As with many governmental regulations that affect small businesses, this applies only to those companies that have at least 15 employees. In this case, crossing the 15-employee threshold means that the company is subject to federal laws against disability discrimination.

27. William J. Dennis, Jr. (ed.), "Alcohol, Drugs, Violence and Obesity in the Workplace," *NFIB National Small Business Poll,* Vol. 4, No. 3 (2004), pp. 7–8.

28. Communication with Rick Davis, August 21, 2007.

29. *Ibid.*

30. For a substantive study of reported training practices of small businesses, see William J. Dennis Jr. (ed.), "Training Employees," *NFIB National Small Business Poll,* Vol. 5, No. 1 (2005), pp. 1–39.

31. Gaylen N. Chandler and Glenn M. McEvoy, "Human Resource Management, TQM, and Firm Performance in 62 Small and

Medium-Size Enterprises," *Entrepreneurship Theory and Practice,* Vol. 25, No. 1 (Fall 2000), pp. 43–57.

32. Emily Barker, "Hi-Test Education," http://www.inc.com/magazine/20010701/22888.html, accessed April 27, 2009.

33. "Welcome to Bookpros," http://www.bookpros.com, accessed May 6, 2009; "NFIB—Small Business Toolbox," http://74.125.47.132/search?q=cache:9ZD8hbPZrY0J:www.nfib.com/object/2991858.html+phenix+and+phenix+%22learning+situation%22&cd=1&hl=en&ct=clnk&gl=us, accessed May 6, 2009.

34. Harry J. Martin, "The Key to Effective Training Isn't Necessarily What Happens in the Classroom. It's What You Do Afterward," *Wall Street Journal,* December 15, 2008, p. R-11.

35. *Ibid.*

36. These recommendations were adapted from suggestions presented in Martin, *op. cit.*

37. Mike Faith, "A Systems Approach to Hiring the Right People," http://www.entrepreneurship.org/Resources/Detail/Default.aspx?id=10574, accessed April 27, 2009; http://www.headsets.com, accessed April 27, 2009.

38. Faith, *op. cit.*

39. "In-N-Out Burger—Great Benefits," http://www.in-n-out.com/employment_restaurant.asp, accessed May 1, 2009.

40. Get more information about ESOPs from the website of the National Center for Employee Ownership at http://www.nceo.org.

41. For more information on guidelines for cafeteria plans for businesses, see the relevant IRS website at http://www.irs.gov/publications/p15b/ar02.html#en_US_publink1000101745, accessed April 30, 2009.

42. Karen E. Spaeder, "All Well and Good," *Entrepreneur,* Vol. 36, No. 11 (November 2008). p. 24.

43. For more detailed information on laws protecting employees, see the website of the U.S. Department of Labor, http://www.dol.gov/opa/aboutdol/lawsprog.htm, accessed May 6, 2009.

44. Beth Gaudio, "Stay Out of Court," *MyBusiness,* October–November 2005, p. 46.

45. In 2008, the 12-week leave was expanded to 26 weeks in a 12-month period for any individual who needs time to care for a member of the U.S. military who has a serious injury or illness.

46. For more information on the provisions of the Family and Medical Leave Act, consult the following website: http://www.dol.gov/esa/whd/regs/compliance/whdfs28.pdf, accessed May 4, 2009.

47. For more insights on effective performance review processes, see "How to Conduct Annual Employee Reviews," *Inc. Guidebook,* Vol. 1, No. 9 (December 2008), Special supplement.

CHAPTER 21

1. Found by browsing the following website: http://www.amazon.com, accessed May 15, 2009.

2. "The Flash Pass," http://www.sixflags.com/overTexas/tickets/flashpass.aspx, accessed May 15, 2009.

3. Knowledge at Wharton, "Delving into the Mystery of Customer Satisfaction: A Toyota for the Retail Market?" August 10, 2005, http://knowledge.wharton.upenn.edu/article.cfm?articleid=1255, accessed May 15, 2009.

4. The economic order quantity is the lowest point on the total costs curve, which coincides with the intersection of the carrying costs and ordering costs curves for a firm. In cases in which sufficient information on costs is available, this point can be calculated with some precision. Even when the economic order quantity cannot be calculated precisely, however, a firm's goal must be to minimize both ordering costs and carrying costs. Most operations management textbooks offer formulas and calculations for determining the economic order quantity. One exceptionally good resource for this and many other operations management computations is Wallace J. Hopp and Mark L. Spearman, *Factory Physics,* 3rd ed. (Boston: Irwin McGraw-Hill, 2007), pp. 49–53.

5. "McAlister's Corporation," http://www.answers.com/topic/mcalister-s-corporation, accessed May 15, 2009; "McAlister's Deli," http://www.mcalistersdeli.com/, accessed May 15, 2009.

6. Jeff Bailey, "A Restaurant's Turnaround Is All in the Details," *Wall Street Journal,* May 20, 2003, p. B-3; http://www.leye.com/company/history.htm, accessed April 20, 2007.

7. http://money.cnn.com/magazines/fortune/fortune_archive/2005/10/03/8356743/index.htm, accessed June 1, 2009; http://www.nytimes.com/2004/11/14/business/yourmoney/14wal.html, accessed June 1, 2009.

8. http://src.alionscience.com/pdf/QualityTools.pdf, accessed June 2, 2009; http://www.asq.org/learn-about-quality/seven-basic-quality-tools/overview/overview.html, accessed June 2, 2009.

9. "Customer Spending Growth Likely to Remain Strong as Customer Satisfaction Hits an All-Time High," *ASCI News,* February 20, 2007, http://www.theasci.org/index?option=com_content&task=view&id=165&Itemid+161, accessed April 24, 2007.

10. http://www.scpiteam.com/SCOR%20Metrics.htm, accessed May 25, 2009; http://www.scelimited.com/sitebuildercontent/sitebuilderfiles/howdoesscormeasureup.pdf, accessed May 25, 2009.

11. Nadine Heintz, "Ross O. Youngs: The Fix It Man," *Inc. Magazine, 500 Special,* Vol. 25, No. 12 (Fall 2004), pp. 28, 30.

12. *Ibid.*; http://www.univenture.com/company/history.html, accessed April 22, 2007.

13. Laurel Delaney, "Howdy Partner," *Entrepreneur,* Vol. 35, No. 4 (April 2007), p. 87.

14. Janelle Elms, "Automatic Transition," *Entrepreneur,* Vol. 35, No. 2 (February 2007), p. 118; http://www.gotham-cycles.com, accessed April 20, 2007.

15. *Ibid.*

16. http://www.google.com/finance; Duncan Jones, "Best Practices: Invoice-To-Pay Process Automation," November 19, 2008, Forrester Research.

17. http://www.microsoft.com/dynamics/default.mspx, accessed May 20, 2009.

18. "Connecting the Dots: Aligning Lean Operational and Financial Metrics," http://www.sme.org/cgi-bin/get-newsletter.pl?LEAN&20070810&4&, accessed June 26, 2009

19. Henry Ford first discussed these ideas in his seminal book from 1926, *Today and Tomorrow* more recently published in 1988 by Productivity Press.

CHAPTER 22

1. Accruals are not considered in terms of managing working capital. Accrued expenses, although shown on financial statements as a short-term liability, primarily result from the accountant's effort to match revenues and expenses. There is little that can be done to "manage" accruals.

2. Keith Lowe, "Managing Your Cash Flow," *Entrepreneur,* December 3, 2001, http://www.entrepreneur.com/article/0,4621,295043,00.html, accessed.

3. Simona Covel and Kelly K. Spors, "To Help Collect the Bills, Firms Try the Soft Touch," *Wall Street Journal,* January 27, 2009, p. B1.

4. Paulette Thomas, "Why Debt Collection Is So Essential for Startups," *Wall Street Journal Online,* September 25, 2005, http://www.startupjournal.com/runbusiness/billcollect/20050920-thomas.html, accessed August 21, 2007.

5. Lana Basha, "Handle the Headaches," *MyBusiness,* June–July 2007, pp. 26–29, http://www.mybusinessmag.com/fullstory.php3?sid=1589, accessed April 30, 2009.

6. *Ibid.*

7. Covel and Spors, *op. cit.,* p. B6.

8. To be more accurate, the equation should use the amount of purchases a company has made from suppliers; however, we use cost of goods sold as an approximation

because it is available in the income statement and purchases are not.

9. William J. Dennis, Jr. (ed.), *The National Small Business Poll: Reinvesting in the Business,* Vol. 3, No. 3 (2003), NFIB Research Foundation, p. 13.

10. *Ibid.,* p. 11.

CHAPTER 23

1. Translated by Arthur W. H. Adkins from the Greek text of Solon's poem "Prosperity, Justice and the Hazards of Life," in M. L. West (ed.), *Iambi et Elegi Gracci ante Alexandrum Canttati,* Vol. 2 (Oxford: Clarendon Press, 1972).

2. "Risk," http://www.thefreedictionary.com/ risk, accessed March 26, 2007.

3. Daniel Tynan, "In Case of Emergency," *Entrepreneur,* Vol. 3, No. 4 (April 2003), p. 60.

4. Social Security Administration, as cited in Randy Myers, "The Fine Art of Self-Protection," *CFO,* July 1, 2006, http://www .cfo.com, accessed July 27, 2007.

APPENDIX B

1. Other multiples, besides value to earnings, that are used in valuing a firm include value to sales, value to equity book value, and value to cash flows, just to mention a few.

2. http://www.buysellbiz.com/Mid%20 west%20fsbos.htm, February 4, 2004.

3. Justin Martin, "What's Your Business Worth—Really?" http:// money.cnn.com/magazines/fsb/fsb_ archive/2006/09/01/8384898/index.htm, accessed August 28, 2007.

4. Depreciation expense was added back to operating income, since it is a non-cash expense. The resulting number is equal to the firm's cash flow from operations.

5. The numbers in this example have been changed, but they still represent the valuation process.

A

24/7 e-tailing Electronic retailing providing round-the-clock access to products and services.

7(a) Loan Guaranty Program Loan program that helps small companies obtain financing through a guaranty provided by the SBA.

7(m) Microloan Program SBA loan program that provides short-term loans of up to $35,000 to small businesses and not-for-profit child-care centers.

ABC method A system of classifying items in inventory by relative value.

Acceptance sampling The use of a random, representative portion of products to determine the acceptability of an entire lot.

Accounting return on investment technique A capital budgeting technique that evaluates a capital expenditure based on the expected average annual after-tax profits relative to the average book value of an investment.

Accounts payable (trade credit) Financing provided by a supplier of inventory to a given company.

Accounts receivable The amount of credit extended to customers that is currently outstanding.

Accrual-basis accounting An accounting method of recording profits when they are earned, whether or not the profits have been received in cash; additional expenses are recorded when they are incurred, even if payment has not been made.

Accrued expenses Short-term liabilities that have been incurred but not paid.

Accumulated depreciation Total depreciation expense taken over the asset's life.

Actual cash value (ACV) An insurance term that refers to the depreciated value of a property.

Actual product/service The basic physical product/service that delivers those benefits.

Advertising The impersonal presentation of a business idea through mass media.

Advisory council A group that functions like a board of directors but acts only in an advisory capacity.

Agents/brokers Intermediaries that do not take ownership of the goods they distribute.

Aggregate stop loss limit A comprehensive limit on annual expenses should a number of employees reach the specific stop loss limit.

Aging schedule A categorization of accounts receivable based on the length of time they have been outstanding.

All-risk approach Stating, in an insurance policy, that all direct damages to property are covered except those caused by perils specifically excluded.

Area developers Individuals or firms that obtain the legal right to open several franchised outlets in a given area.

Artisan entrepreneur A person with primarily technical skills and little business knowledge who starts a business.

Asset-based loan A line of credit secured by working-capital assets.

Associative forecasting Forecasting that considers a variety of variables to determine expected sales.

Attitude An enduring opinion based on knowledge, feeling, and behavioral tendency.

Attractive small firm A small firm that provides substantial profits to its owner.

Attributes Product or service parameters that can be counted as being present or absent.

Auction sites Web-based businesses offering participants the ability to list products for consumer bidding.

Augmented product/service The basic product/service plus any extra or unsolicited benefits to the consumer that may prompt a purchase.

Automobile insurance Coverage designed to protect against liability and physical damage to a vehicle resulting from insured perils such as collision, theft, vandalism, hail, and flood.

Average pricing An approach in which total cost for a given period is divided by quantity sold in that period to set a price.

B

Bad-debt ratio The ratio of bad debts to credit sales.

Balance sheet A financial report showing a firm's assets, liabilities, and ownership equity at a specific point in time.

Balloon payment A very large payment that the borrower may be required to make at a specified point about halfway through the term over which the payments were calculated, repaying the rest of the loan in full.

Banner ads Advertisements that appear across a Web page, most often as moving rectangular strips.

Behavioral interview An interview approach that assesses the suitability of job candidates based on how they would respond to hypothetical situations.

Benefit variables Specific characteristics that distinguish market segments according to the benefits sought by customers.

Bill of lading A document indicating that a product has been shipped and the title to that product has been transferred.

Blog An interactive website in which an individual can maintain a personal online journal, post comments and reflections, and provide hyperlink.

Board of directors The governing body of a corporation, elected by the stockholders.

Bootstrapping Doing more with less in terms of resources invested in a business, and where possible controlling the resources without owning them.

Born-global firms Small companies launched with cross-border business activities in mind.

Bottleneck Any point in the operations process where limited capacity reduces the production capability of an entire chain of activities.

Brand A verbal and/or symbolic means of identifying a product.

Brand image People's overall perception of a brand.

Brand mark A brand that cannot be spoken.

Brand name A brand that can be spoken.

Breakdown process (chain-ratio method) A forecasting method that begins with a larger-scope variable and works down to the sales forecast.

Break-even point Sales volume at which total sales revenue equals total costs and expenses.

Brick-and-mortar store The traditional physical store from which businesses have historically operated.

Budget A document that expresses future plans in monetary terms.

Build-up LBO A leveraged buyout involving the purchase of a group of similar companies with the intent of making the firms into one larger company.

Buildup process A forecasting method in which all potential buyers in the various submarkets are identified and then the estimated demand is added up.

Business angels Private individuals who invest in others' entrepreneurial ventures.

Business format franchising A franchise arrangement whereby the franchisee obtains an entire marketing and management system geared to entrepreneurs.

Business incubator A facility that provides shared space, services, and management assistance to new businesses.

Business interruption insurance Coverage that reimburses a business for the loss of anticipated income following the interruption of business operations.

Business model A group of shared characteristics, behaviors, and goals that a firm follows in a particular business situation.

Business owners policy (BOP) A business version of a homeowner's policy, designed to meet the property and general liability insurance needs of some small business owners.

Business plan A document that presents the basic idea for the venture and includes descriptions of where you are now, where you want to go, and how you intend to get there.

Business risk The possibility of losses associated with the assets and earnings potential of a firm.

Business-to-business (B2B) model A business model based on selling to business customers electronically.

Business-to-consumer (B2C) model A business model based on selling to final customers electronically.

Bust-up LBO A leveraged buyout involving the purchase of a company with the intent of selling off its assets.

C

C corporation An ordinary corporation, taxed by the federal government as a separate legal entity.

Capabilities The integration of various organizational resources that are deployed together to the firm's advantage.

Capital budgeting analysis An analytical method that helps managers make decisions about long-term investments.

Cash budget A listing of cash receipts and cash disbursements usually for a relative short time period, such as weekly or monthly.

Cash conversion period The time required to convert paid-for inventory and accounts receivable into cash.

Cash flow statement A financial report showing a firm's sources of cash as well as its uses of cash.

Cash-basis accounting An accounting method of recording profits when cash is received and recording expenses when they are paid.

Certified Development Company (CDC) 504 Loan Program SBA loan program that provides long-term financing for small businesses to acquire real estate or machinery and equipment.

Chain of command The official, vertical channel of communication in an organization.

Channel of distribution The system of relationships established to guide the movement of a product.

Chattel mortgage A loan for which items of inventory or other movable property serve as collateral.

Churning Actions by franchisors to void the contracts of franchisees in order to sell the franchise to someone else and collect an additional fee.

Civil Rights Act Legislation prohibiting discrimination based on race, color, religion, sex, or national origin.

Co-branding Bringing two franchise brands together under one roof.

Code of ethics Official standards of employee behavior formulated by a firm.

Co-employment Outsourcing part of the burden of managing personnel to an organization that handles paperwork and administers benefits for those employees.

Cognitive dissonance The anxiety that occurs when a customer has second thoughts immediately following a purchase.

Coinsurance clause A clause found within the property insurance policy that requires the business owner to have insurance that will cover a certain percentage (usually 80 percent) of what it would cost to rebuild the building or replace the personal property.

Commercial general liability (CGL) insurance Coverage for general liability loss exposure, including premises liability, operations liability, product liability, and completed operations liability.

Common carriers Transportation intermediaries available for hire to the general public.

Community-based financial institution A lender that uses funds from federal, state, and private sources to provide financing to small businesses in low-income communities.

Compensatory damages Economic or noneconomic damages intended to make the claimant whole, by indemnifying the claimant for any injuries or damage arising from the negligent action.

Competitive advantage A benefit that exists when a firm has a product or service that is seen by its target market as better than those of competitors.

Competitive environment The environment that focuses on the strength, position, and likely moves and countermoves of competitors in an industry.

Comprehensive plan A full business plan that provides an in-depth analysis of the critical factors that will determine a firm's success or failure, along with all the underlying assumptions.

Constraint The most restrictive of bottlenecks, determining the capacity of the entire system.

Consumer credit Financing granted by retailers to individuals who purchase for personal or family use.

Content-based model A business model in which the website provides access but not the ability to buy or sell products and services.

Continuous manufacturing A form of repetitive manufacturing with output that more closely resembles a stream of product than individual goods.

Contract carriers Transportation intermediaries that contract with individual shippers.

Contribution margin The difference between the unit selling price and the unit variable costs and expenses.

Cooperative purchasing organization (coop) An arrangement whereby small businesses combine demand for products or services in order to negotiate as a group with suppliers.

Co-preneurs Husband and wife teams who own and manage businesses.

Copyright The exclusive right of a creator to reproduce, publish, perform, display, or sell his or her own works.

Core competencies Those capabilities that provide a firm with a competitive edge and reflect its personality.

Core product/service The fundamental benefit or solution sought by customers.

Corporate charter A document that establishes a corporation's existence.

Corporation A business organization that exists as a legal entity and provides limited liability to its owners.

Cost of goods sold The cost of producing or acquiring goods or services to be sold by a firm.

Cost-based commitment Commitment based on the belief that the opportunity for gain from joining a business is too great to pass up.

Cost-based strategy A plan of action that requires a firm to be the lowest-cost producer within its market.

Counterfeit activity The unauthorized use of intellectual property.

Credit An agreement between a buyer and a seller that provides for delayed payment for a product or service.

Credit bureaus Privately owned organizations that summarize a number of firms' credit experiences with particular individuals.

Crime insurance Coverage against employee dishonesty.

Critical risks A section of the business plan that identifies the potential risks that may be encountered by an investor.

Cross-border acquisition The purchase by a business in one country of a company located in another country.

Culture Behavioral patterns and values that characterize a group of consumers in a target market.

Current assets Assets that can be converted into cash within a company's operating cycle.

Current debt (short-term liabilities) Borrowed money that must be repaid within 12 months.

Current ratio A measure of a company's relative liquidity, determined by dividing current assets by current liabilities.

Customer experience management (CEM) An approach that recognizes that with every interaction, customers learn something about a company that will affect their desire to do business there in the future.

Customer profile A collection of information about a customer, including demographic data, attitudes, preferences, and other behavioral characteristics, as defined by CRM goals.

Customer relationship management (CRM) A company-wide business strategy designed to optimize profitability, revenue, and customer satisfaction by focusing on highly defined and precise customer groups.

Cycle counting A system of counting different segments of the physical inventory at different times during the year.

D

Days in inventory The number of days, on average, that a company is holding inventory.

Days in payables The number of days, on average, that a business takes to pay its accounts payable.

Days sales outstanding (average collection period) The number of days, on average, that a firm is extending credit to its customers.

Debt Business financing provided by creditors.

Debt ratio A measure of what percentage of a firm's assets are financed by debt, determined by dividing total debt by total assets.

Delegation of authority Granting to subordinates the right to act or make decisions.

Demand management strategies Strategies used to stimulate customer demand when it is normally low.

Demographic variables Specific characteristics that describe customers and their purchasing power.

Depreciable assets Assets whose value declines, or depreciates, over time.

Depreciation expense The cost of a firm's building and equipment, allocated over their useful life.

Design defect A defect resulting from a dangerous design, even though the product was made according to specifications.

Design patent Registered protection for the appearance of a product and its inseparable parts.

Desire-based commitment Commitment based on a belief in the purpose of a business and a desire to contribute to it.

Differentiation-based strategy A plan of action designed to provide a product or service with unique attributes that are valued by consumers.

Direct channel A distribution system without intermediaries.

Direct forecasting A forecasting method in which sales is the estimated variable.

Direct loss A loss in which physical damage to property reduces its value to the property owner.

Disability insurance Coverage that provides benefits upon the disability of a firm's partner or other key employee.

Disclosure document A detailed statement provided to a prospective franchisee, containing such information as the franchisor's finances, experience, size, and involvement in litigation.

Discounted cash flow (DCF) techniques Capital budgeting techniques that compare the present value of future cash flows with the cost of the initial investment.

Disintermediation A situation where a wholesaler in a B2B operation chooses to bypass the "middleman" and sell its product or service directly to the final consumer.

Distribution Physically moving products and establishing intermediary relationships to support such movement.

Double taxation Taxation of income that occurs twice, first as corporate earnings and then as stockholder dividends.

Dual distribution A distribution system that involves more than one channel.

Due diligence The exercise of reasonable care in the evaluation of a business opportunity.

Dynamic (personalized) pricing strategy Charging more than the standard price when the customer's profile suggests that the higher price will be accepted.

E

E-commerce The paperless exchange of business information via the Internet.

Economic damages Compensatory damages that relate to economic loss, such as medical expense, loss of income, or the cost of property replacement/restoration.

Economic order quantity The quantity to purchase in order to minimize total inventory costs.

Economic risk The probability that a government will mismanage its economy in ways that hinder the performance of firms operating there.

Economies of scale Efficiencies that result from expansion of production.

Elastic demand Demand that changes significantly when there is a change in the price of the product.

Elasticity of demand The degree to which a change in price affects the quantity demanded.

Electronic Customer Relationship Marketing (eCRM) An electronically based system that emphasizes customer relationships.

E-mail promotion Advertising delivered by means of electronic mail.

Employee benefits Supplements to compensation, such as health care insurance and life insurance programs, designed to be attractive and beneficial to employees and to maintain their commitment to the firm.

Employee stock ownership plan (ESOP) A method by which a firm is sold either in part or in total to its employees.

Employee training Planned efforts to help workers master the knowledge, skills, and behaviors they need to perform their duties.

Empowerment Giving employees authority to make decisions or take actions on their own.

Encroachment The franchisor's selling of another franchise location within the market area of an existing franchisee.

Enterprise zones State-designated areas that are established to bring jobs to economically deprived regions through regulatory and tax incentives.

Entrepreneur A person who is relentlessly focused on an opportunity, either in a new or existing business, to create value both for the customer and the owner. The entrepreneur assumes both the risk and reward for his or her effort.

Entrepreneurial alertness Readiness to act on existing, but unnoticed, business opportunities.

Entrepreneurial legacy Material assets and intangible qualities passed on to both heirs and society.

Entrepreneurial opportunity An economically attractive and timely opportunity that creates value for interested buyers or end users.

Entrepreneurial team Two or more people who work together as entrepreneurs on one endeavor.

Environmentalism The effort to protect and preserve the environment.

Equipment loan An installment loan from a seller of machinery used by a business.

Ethical imperialism The belief that the ethical standards of one's own country can be applied universally.

Ethical issues Questions of right and wrong.

Ethical relativism The belief that ethical standards are subject to local interpretation.

Evaluative criteria The features or characteristics of a product or service that customers use to compare brands.

Evoked set A group of brands that a consumer is both aware of and willing to consider as a solution to a purchase problem.

Exchange rate The value of one country's currency relative to that of another country.

Executive summary A section of the business plan that conveys a clear and concise overall picture of the proposed venture.

Experience curve efficiencies Per-unit savings gained from the repeated production of the same good.

Exporting Selling products produced in the home country to customers in another country.

External locus of control A belief that one's life is controlled more by luck or fate than by one's own efforts.

F

Factoring Obtaining cash by selling accounts receivable to another firm.

Fair Labor Standards Act (FLSA) Federal law that establishes a minimum wage and provides for overtime pay.

Family and Medical Leave Act Legislation that assures employees of unpaid leave for childbirth or other family needs.

Family A group of people bound by a shared history and a commitment to share a future together, while supporting the development and well-being of individual members.

Family business An organization in which *either* the individuals who established or acquired the firm, *or* their descendants, significantly influence the strategic decisions and life course of the firm.

Family business constitution A statement of principles intended to guide a family firm through times of crisis and change.

Family council An organized group of family members who gather periodically to discuss family-related business issues.

Family protocol An extension of the constitution incorporating additional agreements.

Family retreat A gathering of family members, usually at a remote location, to discuss family business matters.

Fatal flaw A circumstance or development that alone could render a new business unsuccessful [SPSI].

Feasibility analysis A preliminary assessment of a business idea that gauges whether or not the venture envisioned is likely to succeed.

Financial plan A section of the business plan that projects the company's financial position based on well-substantiated assumptions and explains how the figures have been determined.

Financial statements (accounting statements) Reports of a firm's financial performance and resources, including an income statement, a balance sheet, and a cash flow statement.

Fixed assets Relatively permanent assets intended for use in the business, such as plant and equipment.

Fixed costs Costs that remain constant as the quantity produced or sold varies.

Flexible manufacturing systems Operations that usually involve computer-controlled equipment that can turn out products in smaller or more flexible quantities.

Focus strategy A plan of action that isolates an enterprise from competitors and other market forces by targeting a restricted market segment.

Follow-the-leader pricing strategy Using a particular competitor as a model in setting prices.

Foreign licensing Allowing a company in another country to purchase the rights to manufacture and sell a company's products in international markets.

Formal venture capitalists Individuals who form limited partnerships for the purpose of raising venture capital from large institutional investors.

Founder An entrepreneur who brings a new firm into existence.

Fourth-party logistics firm (4PL) A company that coordinates every aspect of a manufacturer's or distributor's supply chain and acts as the sole point of contact between that company and all of its logistics and information service providers.

Franchise The privileges conveyed in a franchise contract.

Franchise contract The legal agreement between franchisor and franchisee.

Franchise Disclosure Document (FDD) A document that provides the accepted format for satisfying the franchise disclosure requirements of the FTC.

Franchise Rule A rule that prescribes that the franchisor must disclose certain information to prospective franchisees.

Franchisee An entrepreneur whose power is limited by a contractual relationship with a franchising organization.

Franchising A marketing system involving a legal agreement, whereby the franchisee conducts business according to terms specified by the franchisor.

Franchisor The party in a franchise contract that specifies the methods to be followed and the terms to be met by the other party.

G

General environment The broad environment, encompassing factors that influence most businesses in a society.

General partner A partner in a limited partnership who has unlimited personal liability.

General-purpose equipment Machines that serve many functions in the production process.

Globalization The expansion of international business, encouraged by converging market preferences, falling trade barriers, and the integration of national economies.

Greenfield venture A wholly owned subsidiary formed from scratch in another country.

Gross fixed assets Original cost of depreciable assets before any depreciation expense has been taken.

Gross profit Sales less the cost of goods sold.

H

Harvesting (exiting) The process used by entrepreneurs and investors to reap the value of a business when they leave it.

Headhunter A search firm that locates qualified candidates for executive positions.

Health insurance Coverage for medical care at hospitals, doctors' offices and rehabilitation facilities that usually includes outpatient services and prescription drugs.

Health maintenance organization (HMO) A managed-care network that provides health insurance that is generally less expensive than that of a PPO but limits employees' choices of medical care providers more than a PPO does.

High-potential venture (gazelle) A small firm that has great prospects for growth.

Home-based business A business that maintains its primary facility in the residence of its owner.

I

Importing Selling goods produced in another country to buyers in the home country.

Income statement (profit and loss statement) A financial report showing the profit or loss from a firm's operations over a given period of time.

Indemnification clause A contractual clause that requires one party to assume the financial consequences of another party's legal liabilities.

Indirect channel A distribution system with one or more intermediaries.

Indirect forecasting A forecasting method in which variables related to sales are used to project future sales.

Indirect loss A loss arising from inability to carry on normal operations due to a direct loss of property.

Industry environment The combined forces that directly impact a given firm and its competitors.

Inelastic demand Demand that does not change significantly when there is a change in the price of the product.

Informal venture capital Funds provided by wealthy private individuals (business angels) to high-risk ventures.

Information-based model A business model in which the website provides information about a business, its products, and other related matters but doesn't charge for its use.

Initial public offering (IPO) The issuance of stock that is to be traded in public financial markets.

Inspection The examination of a part or a product to determine whether it meets quality standards.

Installment account A line of credit that requires a down payment, with the balance paid over a specified period of time.

Institutional advertising The presentation of information about a particular firm, designed to enhance the firm's image.

Intangible resources Those organizational resources that are invisible and difficult to assess.

Integrity An uncompromising adherence to the lofty values, beliefs, and principles that an individual claims to hold.

Intellectual property Original intellectual creations, including inventions, literary creations, and works of art, that are protected by patents or copyrights.

Interest expense The cost of borrowed money.

Internal locus of control A belief that one's success depends on one's own efforts.

Internal rate of return (IRR) The rate of return a firm expects to earn on a project.

International franchising Selling a standard package of products, systems, and management services to a company in another country.

International outsourcing A strategy that involves accessing foreign labor through contracts with independent providers.

International strategic alliance A combination of efforts and/or assets of companies in different countries for the sake of pooling resources and sharing the risks of an enterprise.

Inventory A firm's raw materials and products held in anticipation of eventual sale.

ISO 9000 The standards governing international certification of a firm's quality management procedures.

J

Job description An outline, or summary, of the work to be performed for a particular position.

Job Instruction Training A systematic step-by-step method for on-the-job training of nonmanagerial employees.

Job shop A manufacturing operation in which short production runs are used to produce small quantities of unique items.

Job specification A list of skills and abilities needed to perform a specific job.

Joint and several liability The liability of each partner resulting from any one partner's ability to legally bind the other partners.

just-in-time inventory system A method of reducing inventory levels to an absolute minimum.

K

Key-person life insurance Coverage that provides benefits to a firm upon the death of the firm's key personnel.

L

Lean production An approach that emphasizes efficiency through elimination of waste.

Learning effects Insights, gained from experience, that lead to improved work performance.

Legal entity A business organization that is recognized by the law as having a separate legal existence.

Letter of credit An agreement issued by a bank to honor a draft or other demand for payment when specified conditions are met.

Leveraged buyout (LBO) A purchase heavily financed with debt, where the future cash flow of the target company is expected to be sufficient to meet debt repayments.

Leveraged ESOP An employee stock ownership plan that is financed with borrowed money.

LIBOR (London InterBank Offered Rate) The interest rate charged by London banks on loans to other London banks.

Licensee The company buying licensing rights.

Licensor The company selling licensing rights.

Lifestyle business A microbusiness that permits the owner to follow a desired pattern of living.

Limited liability The restriction of an owner's legal financial responsibilities to the amount invested in the business.

Limited liability company A form of organization in which owners have limited liability but pay personal income taxes on business profits.

Limited partner A partner in a limited partnership who is not active in its management and has limited personal liability.

Limited partnership A partnership with at least one general partner and one or more limited partners.

Line of credit An informal agreement between a borrower and a bank as to the maximum amount of funds the bank will provide at any one time.

Line organization A simple organizational structure in which each person reports to one supervisor.

Line-and-staff organization An organizational structure that includes staff specialists who assist management.

Linkage A type of advertising agreement in which one firm pays another to include a click-on link on its site.

Liquidity The degree to which a firm has working capital available to meet maturing debt obligations.

Loan covenants Bank-imposed restrictions on a borrower that enhance the chances of timely repayment.

Lock box A post office box for receiving remittances from customers.

Long-range plan (strategic plan) A firm's overall plan for the future.

Long-term debt Loans from banks or other sources with repayment terms of more than 12 months.

Loss avoidance Avoiding loss by choosing not to engage in hazardous activities.

Loss prevention Keeping a loss from happening.

Loss reduction Lessening the frequency, severity, or unpredictability of losses.

M

Make or buy decisions A choice small manufacturing companies must make when they have the option of making or buying component parts for products they produce.

Management buyout (MBO) A leveraged buyout in which the firm's top managers become significant shareholders in the acquired firm.

Management development Preparation of employees for career advancement through education, job experiences, network development, and performance assessment.

Management team A section of the business plan that describes a new firm's organizational structure and the backgrounds of its key players.

Management team Managers and other key persons who give a company its general direction.

Manufacturing defect A defect resulting from a problem that occurs during the manufacturing process causing the product to subsequently not be made according to specifications.

Market A group of customers or potential customers who have purchasing power and unsatisfied needs.

Market analysis The process of locating and describing potential customers.

Market risk The uncertainty associated with an investment decision.

Market segmentation The division of a market into several smaller groups with similar needs.

Marketing defect A defect resulting from failure to convey to the user that hazards are associated with a product or to provide adequate instructions on safe product use.

Marketing mix The combination of product, pricing, promotion, and distribution activities.

Marketing plan A section of the business plan that describes the user benefits of the product or service and the type of market that exists.

Marketing research The gathering, processing, interpreting, and reporting of market information.

Markup pricing Applying a percentage to a product's cost to obtain its selling price.

Master licensee An independent firm or individual acting as a sales agent with the responsibility of finding new franchisees within a specified territory.

Matchmakers Specialized brokers that bring together buyers and sellers of businesses.

Mentor A knowledgeable person who can offer guidance from their experience in a given field.

Merchant middlemen Intermediaries that take ownership of the goods they distribute.

Microbusiness A small firm that provides minimal profits to its owner.

Mini-plan A short form of a business plan that presents only the most important issues and projections for the business.

Mortgage A long-term loan from a creditor for which real estate is pledged as collateral.

Motivations Forces that organize and give direction to the tension caused by unsatisfied needs.

Multi-brand franchising The operation of several franchise organizations within a single corporate structure.

Multiple-unit ownership Ownership by a single franchisee of more than one franchise from the same company.

Multisegment strategy A strategy that recognizes different preferences of individual market segments and develops a unique marketing mix for each.

N

Named-peril approach Identifying, in an insurance policy, the specific perils covered.

Need-based commitment Commitment based on an individual's self-doubt and belief that he or she lacks career options outside the current business.

Needs The starting point for all behavior.

Negotiation A two-way communication process used to resolve differences in interests, desires, or demands.

Net fixed assets Gross fixed assets less accumulated depreciation.

Net present value (NPV) The present value of expected future cash flows less the initial investment outlay.

Net profits Income that may be distributed to the owners or reinvested in the company.

Net working capital Current assets less current liabilities.

Networking The process of developing and engaging in mutually beneficial relationships.

Niche market A market segment identified by an identifiable but narrow range of product or service interests.

Noneconomic damages Compensatory damages for such losses as pain and suffering, mental anguish, and loss of physical abilities.

Nonprofit corporation A form of corporation for enterprises established to serve civic, educational, charitable, or religious purposes but not for generation of profits.

O

Obligation-based commitment Commitment that results from a sense of duty or expectation.

Occupational Safety and Health Act Legislation that regulates the safety of workplaces and work practices.

Offering A section of the business plan that indicates to an investor how much money is needed and when, and how the money will be used.

Offshoring A strategy that involves relocating operations abroad.

Open charge account A line of credit that allows the customer to obtain a product at the time of purchase, with payment due when billed.

Operating expenses Costs related to marketing and selling a firm's product or service, general and administrative expenses, and depreciation.

Operating profit margin A measure of how well a firm is controlling its costs of goods sold and operating expenses relative to sales, determined by dividing operating profits by sales.

Operating profits Earnings or profits after operating expenses but before interest and taxes are paid.

Operations The processes used to create and deliver a good or service.

Operations and development plan A section of the business plan that offers information on how a product will be produced or a service provided, including descriptions of the new firm's facilities, labor, raw materials, and processing requirements.

Operations management The planning and control of a conversion process that includes turning inputs into outputs that customers desire.

Opinion leader A group member who plays a key communications role.

Opportunistic entrepreneur A person with both sophisticated managerial skills and technical knowledge who starts a business.

Opportunity cost of funds The rate of return that could be earned on another investment of similar risk.

Opportunity recognition Identification of potential new products or services that may lead to promising businesses.

Organizational culture Patterns of behaviors and beliefs that characterize a particular firm.

Organizational test Verification of whether a nonprofit organization is staying true to its stated purpose.

Other assets Assets other than current assets and fixed assets, such as patents, copyrights, and goodwill.

Outsourcing Purchasing products or services that are outside the firm's area of specialization.

Ownership equity Owners' investments in a company plus profits retained in the firm.

P

Package policy A policy for small businesses that do not qualify for a BOP that combines property insurance and commercial general liability insurance.

Partially self-funded program Designating part of a firm's earnings to fund a portion of employee medical coverage.

Partnership A legal entity formed by two or more co-owners to carry on a business for profit.

Partnership agreement A document that states explicitly the rights and duties of partners.

Patent The registered, exclusive right of an inventor to make, use, or sell an invention.

Payback period technique A capital budgeting technique that measures the amount of time it will take to recover the cash outlay of an investment.

Penetration pricing strategy Setting lower than normal prices to hasten market acceptance of a product or service or to increase market share.

Percentage-of-sales technique A method of forecasting asset investments and financing requirements.

Perception The individual processes that give meaning to the stimuli confronting consumers.

Perceptual categorization The process of grouping similar things so as to manage huge quantities of incoming stimuli.

Peril A cause of loss, either through natural events or through the actions of people.

Perpetual inventory system A method for keeping a running record of inventory.

Personal property Any property other than real property, including machinery, equipment, furniture, fixtures, stock, and vehicles.

Personal selling A sales presentation delivered in a one-on-one manner.

Personnel risks Risks that directly affect individual employees but may have an indirect impact on a business as well.

Physical distribution (logistics) The activities of distribution involved in the physical relocation of products.

Physical inventory system A method that provides for periodic counting of items in inventory.

Piecework Financial incentive based on pay according to number of units produced.

Piercing the corporate veil A situation in which the courts conclude that incorporation has been used to perpetuate a fraud, skirt a law, or commit some wrongful act, and thus remove liability protections from the corporate entity.

Piggyback franchising The operation of a retail franchise within the physical facilities of a host store.

Plant patent Registered protection for any distinct, new variety of living plant.

Pledged accounts receivable Accounts receivable used as collateral for a loan.

Poka-Yoke A proactive approach to quality management that seeks to mistake-proof a firm's operations, thus avoiding problems and waste before they can occur.

Political risk The potential for political forces in a country to negatively affect the performance of businesses operating within its borders.

Pop-up ads Advertisements that burst open on computer screens.

Pre-emptive right The right of stockholders to buy new shares of stock before they are offered to the public.

Preferred provider organization (PPO) A managed-care network that provides health insurance that is generally more expensive than an HMO but offers a broader choice of medical providers.

Prestige pricing Setting a high price to convey an image of high quality or uniqueness.

Price A specification of what a seller requires in exchange for transferring ownership or use of a product or service.

Price lining strategy Setting a range of several distinct merchandise price levels.

Primary data New market information that is gathered by the firm conducting the research.

Prime rate The interest rate charged by commercial banks on loans to their most creditworthy customers.

Private carriers Lines of transport owned by the shippers.

Private placement The sale of a firm's capital stock to selected individuals.

Pro forma financial statements Statements that project a firm's financial performance and condition.

Pro forma statements Projections of a company's financial statements for up to five years, including balance sheets, income statements, and statements of cash flows, as well as cash budgets.

Product A total bundle of satisfaction—including a service, a good, or both—offered to consumers in an exchange transaction.

Product advertising The presentation of a business idea designed to make potential customers aware of a specific product or service and create a desire for it.

Product and trade name franchising A franchise agreement granting the right to use a widely recognized product or name.

Product item The lowest common denominator in the product mix—the individual item.

Product life cycle A detailed picture of what happens to a specific product's sales and profits over time.

Product line The sum of related individual product items.

Product mix The collection of a firm's total product lines.

Product mix consistency The similarity of product lines in a product mix.

Product strategy The way the product component of the marketing mix is used to achieve a firm's objectives.

Product/service plan A section of the business plan that describes the product and/or service to be provided and explains its merits.

Professional corporation A form of corporation that shields owners from liability and is set up for individuals in certain professional practices.

Professional employer organization (PEO) A company that sets up co-employment agreements, assisting businesses with the administrative demands of keeping employees on their payrolls.

Professional manager A manager who uses systematic, analytical methods of management.

Profits before taxes (taxable profits) Earnings after operating expenses and interest expenses but before taxes.

Project manufacturing Operations used to create unique but similar products.

Promotion Marketing communications that inform and persuade consumers.

Promotional mix A blend of nonpersonal, personal, and special forms of communication aimed at a target market.

Prospecting A systematic process of continually looking for new customers.

Prospectus (offering memorandum) A document that contains all the information necessary to satisfy federal and state requirements for warning potential investors about the possible risks of the investment.

Proximate cause A negligent act that is the clear cause of damages sustained.

Publicity Information about a firm and its products or services that appears as a news item, usually free of charge.

Punitive damages A form of punishment that goes beyond compensatory damages, intending to punish wrongdoers for gross negligence or a callous disregard for the interests of others and to have a deterrent effect.

Purchase-order financing Lender advances the amount of the borrower's cost of goods sold for a specific customer order.

Pure risk The uncertainty associated with a situation where only loss or no loss can occur.

Q

Quality The features of a product or service that enable it to satisfy customers' needs.

R

Real estate mortgage A long-term loan with real property held as collateral.

Real property Land and anything physically attached to the land, such as buildings.

Reasonable (prudent person) standard The typical standard of care, based on what a reasonable or prudent person would have done under similar circumstances.

Reciprocation A powerful social rule based on an obligation to repay in kind what another has done for or provided to us.

Reference groups Groups that an individual allows to influence his or her behavior.

Refugee A person who becomes an entrepreneur to escape an undesirable situation.

Reliability The consistency of a test in measuring job performance ability.

Reluctant entrepreneur A person who becomes an entrepreneur as a result of some severe hardship.

Repetitive manufacturing Operations designed for long production runs of high-volume products.

Replacement value of property The cost of replacing personal property and rebuilding real property at today's prices.

Resources The basic inputs that a firm uses to conduct its business.

Retained earnings Profits less withdrawals (dividends) over the life of a business.

Return on assets A measure of a firm's profitability relative to the amount of assets invested in the company, determined by dividing operating profits by total assets.

Revolving charge account A line of credit on which the customer may charge purchases at any time, up to a preestablished limit.

Revolving credit agreement A legal commitment by a bank to lend up to a maximum amount.

Risk control Minimizing potential losses by preventing, avoiding, or reducing risk.

Risk financing Making funds available to cover losses that could not be eliminated by risk control.

Risk management Ways of coping with risk that are designed to preserve the assets and earning power of a firm.

Risk retention Financing loss intentionally, through a firm's cash flows.

Risk transfer Buying insurance or making contractual arrangements with others in order to transfer risk.

Royalties Fees paid by the licensee to the licensor for each unit produced under a licensing contract.

S

S corporation (Subchapter S corporation) A type of corporation that offers limited liability to its owners but is taxed by the federal government as a partnership.

Sales forecast A prediction of how much of a product or service will be purchased within a market during a specified time period.

Sales promotion An inclusive term for any promotional techniques other than personal selling and advertising that stimulate the purchase of a particular good or service.

Secondary data Market information that has been previously compiled.

Segmentation variables The parameters used to distinguish one form of market behavior from another.

Self-insurance Designating part of a firm's earnings as a cushion against possible future losses.

Seller financing Financing in which the seller accepts a note from a buyer in lieu of cash in partial payment for a business.

Serendipity A gift for making desirable discoveries by accident.

Service Corps of Retired Executives (SCORE) An SBA-sponsored group of retired executives who give free advice to small businesses.

Service mark A brand that a company has the exclusive right to use to identify a service.

Short-range plan A plan that governs a firm's operations for one year or less.

Short-term notes Cash amounts borrowed from a bank or other lending sources that must be repaid within a short period of time.

Single-segment strategy A strategy that recognizes the existence of several distinct market segments but focuses on only the most profitable segment.

Skimming price strategy Setting very high prices for a limited period before reducing them to more competitive levels.

Small business A business that is small compared to large companies in an industry, is geographically localized, is financed by only a few individuals, and has a small management team.

Small business development centers (SBDCs) University-affiliated centers offering consulting, education, and other support to small businesses.

Small Business Innovative Research (SBIR) program A government program that helps to finance companies that plan to transform laboratory research into marketable products.

Small business investment companies (SBICs) Privately owned banks, regulated by the Small Business Administration, that provide long-term loans and/or equity capital to small businesses.

Small business marketing Business activities that direct the creation, development, and delivery of a bundle of satisfaction from the creator to the targeted user and that satisfy the targeted user.

Social capital The advantage created by an individual's connections in a social network.

Social classes Divisions within a society having different levels of social prestige.

Social entrepreneurship Entrepreneurial activity whose goal is to find innovative solutions to social needs, problems, and opportunities.

Social network An interconnected system comprising relationships with other people.

Social responsibilities A company's ethical obligations to the community.

Sole proprietorship A business owned by one person, who bears unlimited liability for the enterprise.

Span of control The number of subordinates supervised by one manager.

Special-purpose equipment Machines designed to serve specialized functions in the production process.

Specific stop loss limit A firm's per-employee limit on self-funding for medical claims.

Spontaneous debt financing Short-term debts, such as accounts payable, that automatically increase in proportion to a firm's sales.

Stages in succession Phases in the process of transferring leadership of family business from parent to child.

Stakeholders Individuals who either can affect or are affected by the performance of the company.

Startups New business ventures started "from scratch."

Statistical inventory control A method that uses a targeted service level, allowing statistical determination of the appropriate amount of inventory to carry.

Stock certificate A document specifying the number of shares owned by a stockholder.

Strategic alliance An organizational relationship that links two or more independent business entities in a common endeavor.

Strategic decision A decision regarding the direction a firm will take in relating to its customers and competitors.

Strategy A plan of action that coordinates the resources and commitments of an organization to achieve superior performance.

Supply chain management A system of management that integrates and coordinates the means by which a firm creates or develops a product or service, delivers it to customers, and is paid for it.

Supply Chain Operations Reference (SCOR) model A list of critical factors that provides a helpful starting place when assessing a supplier's performance.

Sustainable competitive advantage A value-creating position that is likely to endure over time.

SWOT analysis A type of assessment that provides a concise overview of a firm's strategic situation.

Synchronous management An approach that recognizes the interdependence of assets and activities and manages them to optimize the entire firm's performance.

T

Tangible resources Those organizational resources that are visible and easy to measure.

Term loan Money loaned for a 5- to 10-year term, corresponding to the length of time the investment will bring in profits.

Third-party logistics firm (3PL) A company that provides transportation and distribution services to companies that prefer to focus their efforts on other facets of their business.

Torts Wrongful acts or omissions for which an injured party can take legal action against the wrongdoer for monetary damages.

Total asset turnover A measure of how efficiently a firm is using its assets to generate sales, calculated by dividing sales by total assets.

Total cost The sum of cost of goods sold, selling expenses, and overhead costs.

Total quality management (TQM) An all-encompassing management approach to providing high-quality products and services.

Trade credit Financing provided by a supplier of inventory to a given company.

Trade dress Elements of a firm's distinctive image not protected by a trademark, patent, or copyright.

Trade intermediary An agency that distributes a company's products on a contract basis to customers in another country.

Trade mission A trip organized to help small business owners meet with potential buyers abroad and learn about doing business there.

Trade-credit agencies Privately owned organizations that collect credit information on businesses.

Trademark A legal term identifying a firm's exclusive right to use a brand.

Transactional relationship An association between a business and a customer that begins (or ends) with a purchase or a business deal.

Transaction-based model A business model in which the website provides a mechanism for buying or selling products or services.

Transfer of ownership Passing ownership of a family business to the next generation.

Two-bin inventory system A method of inventory control based on use of two containers for each item in inventory: one to meet current demand and the other to meet future demand.

Type A ideas Startup ideas centered around providing customers with an existing product not available in their market.

Type B ideas Startup ideas, involving new technology, centered around providing customers with a new product.

Type C ideas Startup ideas centered around providing customers with an improved product.

U

Underlying values Unarticulated ethical beliefs that provide a foundation for ethical behavior in a firm.

Unlimited liability Liability on the part of an owner that extends beyond the owner's investment in the business.

Unsegmented strategy (mass marketing) A strategy that defines the total market as the target market.

Utility patent Registered protection for a new process or a product's function.

V

Validity The extent to which a test assesses true job performance ability.

Variable costs Costs that vary with the quantity produced or sold.

Variable pricing strategy Setting more than one price for a good or service in order to offer price concessions to certain customers.

Variables Measured parameters that fall on a continuum, such as weight or length.

W

Warranty A promise that a product will perform at a certain level or meet certain standards.

Web sponsorship A type of advertising in which a firm pays another organization for the right to be part of that organization's webpage.

Work teams Groups of employees with freedom to function without close supervision.

Workers' compensation insurance Coverage that provides benefits to employees for medical expenses, loss of wages, and rehabilitation expenses, as well as death benefits for employees' families.

Workers' compensation legislation Laws that obligate the employer to pay employees for injury or illness related to employment, regardless of fault.

Workforce diversity Differences among employees on such dimensions as gender, age, ethnicity, and race.

Working capital Current assets, accounts receivable, and inventory required in day-to-day operations.

Working-capital cycle The daily flow of resources through a firm's working-capital accounts.

Working-capital management The management of current assets and current liabilities.

Z

Zoning ordinances Local laws regulating land use.